5.95

BUSINESS

JOB HUNT

GOING TO
WORK

GOING TO
WORK

LISA BIRNBACH

Villard Books
New York
1988

For Steven

Grateful acknowledgment is made to Alfred A. Knopf, Inc. for permission to reprint an excerpt from the poem "To be of use" from *Circles on the Water* by Marge Piercy. Copyright © 1969, 1971, 1973 by Marge Piercy. Reprinted by permission of Alfred A. Knopf, Inc.

Library of Congress Cataloging-in-Publication Data
Birnbach, Lisa.
Going to work.
1. Job hunting. I. Title.
HF5382.7.B56   1988   650.1′4   87-40573
ISBN 0-394-75874-9 (pbk.)

Manufactured in the United States of America
9   8   7   6   5   4   3   2
First Edition

MAPS DESIGNED BY ERIC ELIAS

BOOK DESIGN BY JESSICA SHATAN

This page is a special thank-you to Annette Geldzahler. There is no way to measure her significant contributions to *Going to Work*—including the title—but her writing, her hard work, her bagel breakfasts, and her good humor have been invaluable to me.

The people I love best
jump into work head first
without dallying in the shallows
and swim off with sure strokes almost out of sight.
They seem to become natives of that element,
the black sleek heads of seals
bouncing like half-submerged balls.

—"To be of use," Marge Piercy

"Lisa, do your homework!"

—Mr. and Mrs. Birnbach, 1962–1978

FOREWORD BY TOM PETERS

Extraordinary! There is no other way to describe Lisa Birnbach's new book. Comprehensive —yes. But unique breadth and sensitivity, too. It will be a joy for those whom she principally wishes to reach, typically somewhat disoriented, naive (but appropriately skeptical) job seekers. But, as I see it, the book will be at least as valuable to practicing businesspersons in small and large firms, and even to academic researchers.

Birnbach doesn't shilly-shally around. After the briefest introduction, she gets down to describing life at work, in big manufacturers and small law firms and consultancies, some fifty enterprises in all. The organization is by city, starting with Atlanta and, eleven cities later, ending with Washington, D.C. For each firm, she leads off with a short and exceptionally well-researched history (in every instance I, who am purportedly well briefed, learned something here—even about firms I had thought I knew cold). Next up are the outfit's bread-and-butter characteristics. Who is hired? How much are they paid? When can they expect a raise? A promotion? What are the benefits, formal and informal? And so on. Again, Birnbach's special combination of sobriety and humor brings even these details to life.

But the heart of the matter comes next: What does it feel like to work here? I was, and remain, an admirer of *The 100 Best Companies to Work for in America;* once again, it passed my acid test—I learned a lot from it, even about familiar cases. But I was a lover, not just an admirer, of Studs Terkel's *Working.* For Terkel, a matchless reporter, was able to draw the most extraordinary descriptions of life at work from real people in diverse settings. Well, if Ms. Birnbach hasn't topped Terkel, she has surely given him a run for his money.

Lisa's stories of people who work in the organizations catalogued here are exceptionally rich. Despite the fact she entered a firm only after an official invitation to do so, she has unfailingly gotten people to open up. She is not, as her somewhat controversial earlier books clearly indicate, "owned" by anyone—and she demonstrates it once again, though this time in much tougher, more closed corporate settings (any number of very conservative firms are represented on the list).

So the people stories are the straight poop, as we called it when I was in the Navy. And it's all topped off with the by-products of brilliantly trained eyes that record what it's really like to hang out in one of these workplaces.

Specifics? She starts, for example, with Delta Airlines, a company I have profiled in numerous books, television shows, and columns. But she puts my earlier insights to shame. The details about Delta are followed by well over a half-dozen fully developed sketches of employees, senior and junior, which provide a flavor of their life on the job, including colorful (and helpful) details on how they made it, what constraints they have to live with, and so on.

I commend this product to those who are supposed to read it, the by and large uninitiated. You'll marvel at the usefulness, flair, and fun that resides between these covers. But I wish especially to recommend the book to practicing managers, top, middle, or bottom, and aspiring entrepreneurs as well. You will learn from the hundreds of stories about the feel, pleasures, and frustrations of the workplace at superior companies of all shapes and sizes. With the greatest of ease, you will be able to dredge up a hundred practical tips, as well as a guide to the philosophies that have led others to excel and sustain at creating challenging—and productive—workplaces.

There's yet another level of usefulness. America's economy is taking a licking, in almost every nook and cranny. Much of our problem stems from firms that have become sluggish and dispirited—and then noncompetitive. At the core, the issue is a demoralized and wildly underutilized, work force—blue and gold collar alike. Ms. Birnbach provides fifty breaths of very fresh air in that respect. Here are a host of role models that, despite their occasional warts (unerringly pointed out in these pages), provide a useful road map to improved American competitiveness.

Dip in and enjoy!

ACKNOWLEDGMENTS

This book would never have been completed without the encouragement and help of the following people: Esther Newberg, Peter Gethers, Marc Jaffe, Janis Donnaud, Maks Birnbach, Gershon Kekst, Baba Paul, John Gerlach, Tony Wainwright, Debbie Kaplan, Mark Attanasio, Tommy Schwartz, Jon Banton, Jonathan Birnbach, Norman Birnbach, Peter Felcher, Rick Pappas, Linda Laager, Thomas Wynbrandt, Nathaniel de Rothschild, Larry Levy, Mark Levy, Michael Schwartz, Adam Klein, Walter Anderson, Stanley Buchthal, Dan Schrier, Tom Tisch, Janis Hirsch, Jon Potter, Richard Greenberg and Paula Silver, Henry Grossman, Arthur Bowen, Mary Beth Wainwright, Cindy Gelb, Anne Barkelew, Laurie Burrows Grad, Richard Fischoff, Patricia Zohn, Deverah Kettner, Seth Jaffe, Jim and Penny Risen, Jo Schuman and her best friends, Carol Levy, John Marshall, Julianna Hallowell, Jamie Gangel, Sharon Williams, Kathy Dalle-Molle, Rebecca Chase Williams, Pam and Lewis Lee, Steve Nothman, Nancy McTague, Laura Godfrey, Heather Lehr, Kathy Pohl, Carol McCutchen, Naomi Osnos, Sally Berk, Janet Fifer, Lynn Anderson, Wendy Bass, David Goodman, Mark Mondry, and the public relations staffs of the fifty companies, who had enough to do without our incessant inquiries.

I am grateful to the following individuals for their time and candor: Saul Steinberg, Leonard Stern, Herbert A. Allen, Grant Tinker, Stu Erwin, Leonard Lauder, Bob Pittman, Marty Ransohoff, Sally Frame, Bernie Brillstein, Tony Wainwright, Allen Neuharth, Fred Joseph, Bill Smithburg, Ginnie and Gerry Johansen, Roger Staubach, Robert Greenberg, Rance, Keith, and Mrs. Gertrude Crain, George Katz, Doug Tompkins, Michael Garin, David Salzman, and Dick Robertson, Duane Kullberg, Kenneth Macke, Tom Monaghan, Donald Petersen, Jay Chiat, Jeffrey Breslow, Howard Morrison, and Rouben Terzian, Marvin Sloves, Robert Zimmer, Jack Connors, Bill Bain, Gene Kohn, Tom Freston, Bradley Hale, Chuck Sloan, Robert Stock, Mike Wright, Bill McGowan, and Tom Peters.

Thanks again to Leonard Lauder and Bob Nielsen, for allowing me to become part of "Team Prescriptives" at Bloomingdale's for a week in June 1986, and to the Ford News Bureau for allowing me to drive on the test track.

My love to my pals: Rose Gasner, Bonni Kogen, and Nancy Stock, who called every day to cheer me on.

CONTENTS

AN INTRODUCTION

I don't have a job. That doesn't mean I don't work hard or wish for a longer lunch hour. Having been self-employed for the last eight years, my view of the working world out there was, well, inadequate . . . vague. What I knew was mostly secondhand from listening to friends and relatives recount their tales and trials. Occasionally I got to see them on their own turf. This usually meant meeting them in the lobby of their office building and then having lunch.

But upon visiting fifty of America's most interesting (to me) companies, I saw a different topography, populated with people who seem to have a variety of reasons for being there, not the least of which were gleaning dignity from what they do, and loyalty.

We are now experiencing a phase in which we define ourselves through our companies, industries, and jobs. Consider this! Some of the iconoclasts who eschewed labels fifteen and twenty years ago are now identified—by choice—with their offices. They are borrowing from and taking comfort in the largesse of those offices' reputations.

How can business be the bad guy today? We are tracking down excellence from within and without. We're embarrassed if we don't have concerned management styles.

Perhaps because I hadn't experienced it, I wanted to find out how and where the identification process began. I wanted to know why workers allowed their companies to make major life decisions for them. I wanted to learn if their loyalty were reciprocated by the organizations that demanded it of them. I wanted to figure out why my friends worked so damn hard. And I wanted to write a book for those of us who are excluded by the standard business press.

I see myself as a tourist on the 1980s version of the Grand Tour. I am a visitor at the most vital sources of creativity, social change, and culture. While not quite walking in Daisy Miller's updated shoes (the purpose, after all, has not been to find a husband), I am still a young (okay, not *that* young) female outsider, trying firsthand to learn the rules of this world.

This is a very personal journey. I did not come armed with a background in business, an MBA, or an ax to grind. I asked people at these corporations and partnerships *how they felt*, a question, it seems, they had rarely if ever been asked. I asked them what they did, what a typical day was like, if they were scared of their bosses, and if they used the products or services they promoted. Often their responses were guarded, and very frequently we were chaperoned by a member of their company's public relations staff. I tried hard to make them feel I was one of them. I wore conservative suits and dresses, but I drew the line at wearing pinstripes and bow ties. I communicated by letter and phone, distributed my business card promiscuously, and spoke in reserved tones. That strategy seemed to work, as did familiarizing myself with the language of the corner office.

Businesspeople have a language of their own. Furthermore, each company has its own vocabulary, seemingly impossible to pick up in a day or two. This dialect is in part a way for employees to feel privileged, inside, and therefore a way to keep outsiders ignorant. While I made an effort to understand the appropriate jargon everywhere, I cannot say I ever became fluent. Again, ever the tourist.

Every company's approach to participating in this book was different. And revealing. Some companies were enthusiastic about my proposal during my initial phone call. Talking to them, in particular The Tom Peters Group, Leo Burnett, Chiat/Day, The Levy Organization, Ginnie Johansen Designs, Plum Productions, Wachtell, Lipton, Rosen & Katz, Crain Communications, Marvin Glass & Associates, R/Greenberg Associates, and Domino's Pizza was a pleasure. Others needed only a letter to decide yes: Rainier Bancorporation, Covington & Burling, Prescriptives, the Southland Corporation, Ford, Drexel Burnham Lambert, Kohn Pedersen Fox Associates, MTV, and General Mills. Still others required extensive conversations reassuring them that they would not regret this. Some needed personal meetings to determine the safety of this project for their public relations.

Many companies declined. Their reasons included "It will take too many people hours to set up," "If we say yes to you, we'll have to say yes to everyone," "Your book about college was too controversial," "We've had too much publicity this year," and the ever popular "We're not interested." Procter & Gamble needed to read the manuscript before they could reach a decision. As much as I would have loved to visit P&G, I could not comply. My contact at J. C. Penney's was shockingly rude. A lawyer for McDonald's threatened me after the company had agreed to participate. Those are the breaks.

I salute all the companies here, companies that took me at my word. They prove one doesn't have to be stereotyped by one's previous work.

Lisa Birnbach
New York City
May 1988

AN EVOLUTION

Why write a book about American business when it is undergoing its most dramatic period of change? Let me explain the evolution of the project. In September 1984 my guide to college life was published, and I was on the road promoting it. I had spent the previous three years visiting almost three hundred colleges and universities, feeling like the world's oldest undergraduate. Reporters asked, "What's next for Lisa Birnbach?" Although I was thinking, "A shower, a vacation, a new pair of high heels," they were thinking about new books. It made sense for me to move on with my readers. I didn't want to go to graduate or professional schools. I wanted to spend time with adults. I thought I'd go on a reconnaissance mission to the real world.

I wrote a proposal for a book to be entitled *Welcome to the Real World*. I thought it would be a semi-tongue-in-cheek guided tour through a number of companies around the country, focusing on burning issues like their Muzak and cafeteria fare. In talking with various members of America's business community, I saw that this was taking a short-term view, if not one that was downright insulting. As I was no expert in this area, I relied on these advisers, each of whom tried to reshape my project. "Why don't you focus on *Fortune* 500 companies only?" "It sounds promising, but you should only write about CEOs." "It's a good idea, Lisa, but you should concentrate on financial services only."

To make a long story short, these suggestions were all valuable, but they shook my determination ever to write about business, a world which by now mystified, overwhelmed, and scared me. I didn't want to narrow my focus as much as my sources urged me to do. I was as interested in smaller, more maverick companies as I was in huge, well-established ones. I wanted to visit law firms. (If for no other reason except to satisfy my curiosity about what life is like in major private firms, the spawning grounds for corporate executives.) I wanted to understand the differences between private and public organizations, as well as family-run businesses. Finally, as a native New Yorker who is sensitive about overemphasizing her hometown, I wanted to visit a number of American cities to see if corporate life is influenced by region.

Frankly, by this point I had spent the better part of a year getting the outline in order. There were many times I wanted to cancel the book altogether and find a topic that was more manageable. As I was muddling my way through business publications, periodicals, and books, I was certain I was in way over my head; these organizations were constantly changing. How could I ever permeate them, understand them, and stay up to date? But too much time and effort had already gone into the project for me to give up.

I had to begin interviewing and spending time in the world I had undertaken to examine. So, in fact, the act of working on this book determined what it became. The more time I spent with workers, the more serious became my approach. And my interests became surer: Why do you work here? What is it about this company that keeps you here and has earned your loyalty? Could you ever contemplate changing employers? Changing careers? Is your life what you expected it to be?

This is not a book of theories. I tried to let the people I met speak for their companies as well as for themselves. I wanted to hear stories. This is a book about Americans and their jobs.

I would never consider this book "scholarly," but I would place it squarely in the middle ground between informational and anecdotal.

When you work for yourself, you can't help but wonder whether you're missing something out there, in the real world, if you will. (The act of working is different when it entails walking into the adjoining bedroom.) By interviewing approximately a thousand people at positions ranging from CEO to entry-level clerks, I enjoyed the routine, the structure, and the pleasure of going to work vicariously.

Unless I was acquainted with senior executives or partners of a firm, I dealt through the public relations officers. These people organized my visits and preselected the employees I met. Often my interviews were chaperoned by PR folks. They didn't inhibit me from asking what I was there to ask, but they could have represented a warning from management to present a positive picture of the organization. Obviously, this book is no seamy underside of corporate life gathered from disgruntled employees (most people were quite gruntled, it turns out), and I did not eavesdrop or spy in washrooms or parking lots. Interestingly, no one called me after my visits to tell me what they might have felt uncomfortable about revealing during our on-premises talks. I wasn't looking for "dirt," and I didn't find any. In other words, this book takes a favorable point of view. For lack of a better word, we're friends—the business community and I—and while we were all on our best behavior, we did agree to trust one another.

The book is divided into chapters according to city. Why? Why not? To group company profiles by industry, number of employees, or revenues would suggest a tacit comparison among them. No company is compared to another one in this book. That could not be further from my goals. And I'm hoping that with the exception of Seattle, which has only the Rainier Bancorporation to represent it, when you read about each city's companies, you'll get a sense of what working in that city feels like. In my opinion, going to work in Minneapolis offers a different life from that of Chicago. (Incidentally, I took the liberty of calling Silicon Valley a city. For our purposes, its culture is significantly different from that of San Francisco, and otherwise we'd only have had eleven cities.)

Certainly *Going to Work* could have been organized in a half dozen other ways. But since this book is personal, this is my own approach. I have attempted to codify the urban life of the employer and the employee.

There are no big answers here. What's right for you may not be right for me. (In fact, I'm certain of it; otherwise I'd try to work for most of the companies I visited.) This is not an advice or self-help book. I can offer you no secrets to job satisfaction other than what it takes for you to become a useful contributor to society. I'm convinced that many people have no idea what they're getting themselves into when they start with a new company. Chances are, if they liked the people they met during the interview process, the salary offered was reasonable, and there was a chance to have something interesting (or less pressured or not boring or responsible, etc.) to do, they leaped in.

If you're interested in big business but don't feel quite comfortable reading the business pages, I hope *Going to Work* will fill some of the gaps.

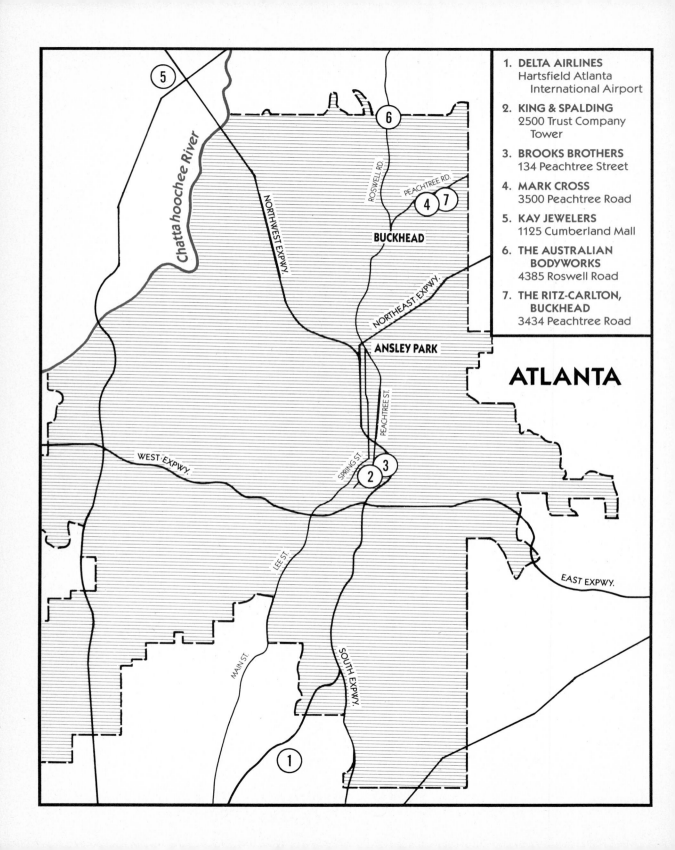

1. **DELTA AIRLINES**
   Hartsfield Atlanta
   International Airport
2. **KING & SPALDING**
   2500 Trust Company
   Tower
3. **BROOKS BROTHERS**
   134 Peachtree Street
4. **MARK CROSS**
   3500 Peachtree Road
5. **KAY JEWELERS**
   1125 Cumberland Mall
6. **THE AUSTRALIAN
   BODYWORKS**
   4385 Roswell Road
7. **THE RITZ-CARLTON,
   BUCKHEAD**
   3434 Peachtree Road

ATLANTA

Chattahoochee River

BUCKHEAD

ANSLEY PARK

NORTHWEST EXPWY.

NORTHEAST EXPWY.

ROSWELL RD.

PEACHTREE RD.

PEACHTREE ST.

WEST EXPWY.

SPRING ST.

LEE ST.

MAIN ST.

SOUTH EXPWY.

EAST EXPWY.

ATLANTA

ATLANTA

ooking for the soul of Atlanta, one could get waylaid, in the city's gigantic Hartsfield International Airport. "You are now entering the transportation mall," an unseen female voice intones in a wacky futuristic notion of comfort. They say you have to go through this airport if you want to get to heaven, and you might as well believe them.

Finding the Atlanta you've read about is an elusive matter. It seems to be a city of contradictions, embodying that which is thought of as "southern" while aiming hard at being progressive.

One Atlanta is filled with ex-civil rights workers, still politically involved, a liberal enclave in the state. (That Jimmy Carter ever got elected governor is almost as remarkable as his winning the presidential election in 1976. His long history of tolerance must have rendered him politically unsuitable to some Georgians. Only five years ago a senior at the University of Georgia told me he didn't mind going to classes with black students, but he didn't think his sister should have to.)

Black Atlanta is large, cohesive, and politically intact. It is still unified by the memory of

Martin Luther King, and his legacy is visible at Morehouse College, the excellent men's school he attended.

Atlantans are commuters. The downtown is not a primary residential neighborhood, so the forward thinking are forced to live in the suburbs. But they love their drive! It is frequently pointed out that it is possible to live beautifully in a house with land within a short drive of downtown. (Traffic can reach toxic proportions, though.)

Corporate Atlanta leaves the office for the day and doesn't take it home. Perhaps a tad more laid back than executives in other cities, professional men and women can transform themselves into their other identities—fathers and mothers—with ease. Maybe it's that pleasant commute home that enables them to decompress so efficiently. Young, childless couples act very grown-up and have adult dinner parties. They hold their liquor very well.

Atlanta's Junior League chapter is one of the largest in the country, often causing emergency droughts of blond hair-streaking chemicals in the other forty-nine states.

The following lists (and all similar lists throughout the book) represents the services and resources used by people on the way up the corporate ladder, by their nonworking spouses, and by those who've already made it. The information has been gathered from sources close to the author, all of whom are valued for their good taste. The word "yuppie" will not appear elsewhere in this book, and this list does not just represent that small (though acquisitive) segment of the population. Wherever possible, we have tried to narrow down specific attributes, e.g., "*Nicest* Neighborhood with Decent Public Schools" or "*Best* Health Club for Meeting Potential Mates." Sometimes a category will simply be denoted "best." This means that a group of discerning people has been unanimous in its praise. These lists attempt to reflect the way people live in particular cities, although the categories are ours, not theirs.

BEST NEIGHBORHOODS WITH DECENT PUBLIC SCHOOLS: People move to North Fulton and Cobb Counties for the public schools. Atlanta's "magnet" schools—selective public schools are good—like the International School and the Northside School of Performing Arts.

NICEST NEIGHBORHOODS (BUT YOU'LL PROBABLY HAVE TO SEND YOUR KIDS TO PRIVATE SCHOOL): "If you can afford them—Buckhead, Morningside, and Ansley Park" are VERY desirable neighborhoods in town. Midtown and Inman Park are pricey areas being reclaimed by the yuppies. Cascade Heights in the southwest part of the city is a charming neighborhood home to Atlanta's large black middle class population.

BEST PLACE TO LIVE IF YOU'RE AN ASPIRING ARTIST OR YOU WANT TO LIVE NEAR PEOPLE WHO ONLY WEAR BLACK: Virginia Highland. ("A combination of charming small bungalows with a street life.") Also, Little Five Points, sort of an ex-hippie neighborhood in Inman Park.

BEST NEIGHBORHOOD WITH TAKE-OUT FOOD AND SINGLE PEOPLE WHO ARE ALSO REPUBLICANS: Midtown

MOST OVERPRICED COMMUNITIES FOR SUMMER HOMES: Sea Island—"millionaire city"

BEST PRIVATE SCHOOLS: Westminster School, Lovett School, Woodward Academy (used to be a military school), and some Catholic schools (Mavis; St. Pius)

BEST PUBLIC SCHOOLS: Atlanta magnet schools

BEST ALTERNATIVE SCHOOLS: The Padaeia School ("Used to be a school without walls. We suspect they have walls now.") Also the Galloway School.

ARCHITECT WHO HAS MOST INFLUENCED THE CITY'S SKYLINE: John Portman

MOST POPULAR RESIDENTIAL ARCHITECT: "For years—Neal Reid. Whenever a 'Neal Reid house' comes on the market . . . beautiful mansions."

SOCIALLY INCLINED REALTOR: Sotheby's, Harry Norman Realtors

DECORATORS WHO WOULD DECORATE HOMES PURCHASED THROUGH THAT REALTOR: Dottie Travis

MOST PROMINENT ART DEALER: Fay Gold of Fay Gold Gallery ("She brings New York art to Atlanta and promotes Southern artists.")

TRENDY GALLERY FOR PEOPLE WHO WEAR ALL BLACK AND HAVE A LOT OF MONEY: Nexus Contemporary Gallery

MOST EXCLUSIVE GOLF CLUB: The Peachtree Golf Club, The Ansley Golf Club

BEST PUBLIC GOLF FACILITY: The Bobby Jones Golf Course

MOST EXPENSIVE HEALTH CLUB: Australian Body Works—"best aerobics"; Downtown Athletic Club—"politicians and power brokers pump iron, and make deals in the steam room."

BEST HEALTH CLUB FOR MEETING POTENTIAL MATES: The Sporting Club—"They advertise their restaurant and bar."

BEST HOTEL FOR BUSINESS TRIPS: The Ritz-Carlton hotels—downtown and in Buckhead

RESTAURANT KNOWN FOR BEST CUISINE: Pano's & Paul's; Nikolai's Roof; The Dining Room at the Ritz-Carlton Buckhead

BEST RESTAURANTS FOR PEOPLE WHO WEAR BLACK: Any of the "Peasants" restaurants: "Trendy—can't get a bad meal there; after-theater crowd."

BEST RESTAURANT FOR AN INEXPENSIVE DATE: Mick's: an art deco, sophisticated soda shop

BEST SPORTS BAR: Stooge's: people watch games there

BEST DARK BAR: Johnny's Hideaway—packed every night; for the over-forty or fifty crowd; big band music and dancing too.

BEST GIMMICKY BAR: Sports Rock Bar

BEST BAR TO IMPRESS A CLIENT: Oak Room at the Ritz-Carlton Buckhead; with its hunting prints, it looks like the lawyers' (who go there) offices.

MOST EXCLUSIVE CITY CLUB: Piedmont Driving Club ("Money won't get you in, only bloodlines") Capital City Club

FANCIEST WINE STORE WHENCE CEOS PROBABLY STOCK THEIR OWN CELLARS: Herman's; Pearson's

GOURMET STORE GUARANTEED NOT TO RUN OUT OF GOAT CHEESE OR SUN-DRIED TOMATOES: Proof of the Pudding

NICEST MOM-AND-POP GROCERY STORE: A slew of Korean markets

LARGEST DRUGSTORE WITH MOST REMARKABLE SELECTION: The chains

HIGH-SOCIETY PARTY PLANNER: Timmy Silvers; Dan Carrithers

POWER BARBER: Jabaley's Barber Shop ("Everyone talks politics"); Don Shaw

NEW WAVE HAIRSTYLIST: Giorgio Ponce de Leon ("always just back from Milan")

JUNIOR LEAGUE BEAUTY PARLOR: Who's Who

PLACE WHERE LADIES WHO LUNCH ARE LIKELY TO HAVE TEA AFTER A HARD DAY OF SHOP-PING, VOLUNTEER WORK, AND TENNIS: The Swan Coach House (part of the Atlanta Historical Society) and the Ritz-Carlton-Buckhead.

BEST STORE FOR EXECUTIVE WOMEN: Saks, Neiman's, Alcott & Andrews

BEST STORE FOR EXECUTIVE MEN: Saks, Rich's, Brooks Brothers, Britches

BEST STORES FOR DRESS-UP CLOTHES: The department stores

BEST SHOPPING RESOURCE FOR PEOPLE WHO WEAR ONLY BLACK CLOTHES: Little boutiques

DEBUTANTE BALL: The Atlanta Debutante Ball (for members of The Piedmont Driving Club); The Phoenix Society—for everyone else.

BUSIEST SOCIAL SEASON OF THE YEAR FOR THOSE WHO CARE ABOUT SUCH THINGS: Fall to spring

PARTICULAR SOCIAL HIGHLIGHT: Piedmont's big ball; Festival of Trees (Christmas time)

MOST RELIABLE FLORIST: Marvin's Gardens

MOST EXOTIC FLORIST: Marvin's Gardens

TOP JEWELER FOR RESETTING MOTHER'S EMERALDS: Maier & Berkle, Skippy Musket

MOST COMPLETE BRIDAL REGISTRY: Rich's and Macy's—computerized

FAVORITE FOREIGN CAR DEALER: RBM (Mercedes-Benz)

MOST PROMINENT PHYSICIAN: Dr. Charlie Harrison (physician for the Atlanta Falcons)

BEST SEAMSTRESS OR TAILOR FOR ALTERATIONS: A-1 Alterations

POPULAR FACIAL SALON: Judith Sands, Seydel

POWER TOOLS

MEN'S POWER DRESSING

BROOKS BROTHERS
134 Peachtree Street, N.W.
Atlanta, GA 30303
(404) 577-4040

BEST-SELLING EXECUTIVE SUIT: Two-button (slimmer cut), tropical weight, charcoal gray, 100 percent wool, $360

POWER SHIRT: Oxford cloth button-down white, 100 percent cotton, $40

POWER TIE: Reptie (striped); burgundy, navy, and white, 100 percent silk, $25

POWER ACCESSORIES

MARK CROSS
3500 Peachtree Road, NE
Atlanta, GA 30326
(404) 237-2417

BRIEFCASES AND ATTACHÉS (Italian calfskin): $425–$975.

WALLETS (Italian calfskin, pigskin, ostrich, etc.): $75–$400.

LEATHER-BOUND BOOKS (hand-bound in buffalo skin—address books, scrap books, series of great books including the works of Shakespeare, a book on wines, an atlas, and *The Book of Executive Manners* [$175]: $160–$400.

POWER WATCHES

KAY JEWELLERS
1125 Cumberland Mall
Atlanta, GA 30339
(404) 435-7537

BEST SELLER AMONG EXECUTIVE MEN: Longines 1000, $595; fourteen-karat gold bracelet with a black dial, no day, no date, very thin, "real nice" mesh bracelet. "The most popular watch for executive men, and most popular style."

BEST SELLER AMONG EXECUTIVE WOMEN: Paul Brigette, $595; fourteen-karat gold. "Most popular with the ladies is a braided bracelet, tricolor gold, white, yellow, and rose gold, one fifth of a carat total weight in diamonds in it," no calendar.

"Eighty percent of all watches sell to women. Most [executive] men buy watches for themselves. For women, more watches are bought for them as gifts.
"Most executive men have two watches, and most executive women have at least two—in fact, most probably have more than men."

POWER CARS

RBM OF ATLANTA
360 Pharr Road
Atlanta, GA 30305
(404) 261-3171

RBM of Atlanta is a Mercedes-Benz dealership that has been in existence for over twenty years. We talked with Larry Mustard, who has worked there for seventeen years.

AMONG EXECS BUYING CARS FOR THEMSELVES, WHAT IS THE RATIO OF MEN TO WOMEN?
"On registrations alone, it's eighty percent male to twenty percent female. Those numbers would probably hold true among executives. Our sales haven't shown anything different."

WHAT IS THE MOST POPULAR MODEL OF MERCEDES, AMONG EXECUTIVES?

"Mercedes Benz 300E is our best-seller because we import more of those than any other model. It's a four-door sedan. Other models popular among executives are the 300 SEL, the 420 SEL, and the 560 SEL, which are all bigger, limousine type vehicles."

WHAT ARE THE MOST POPULAR "EXECUTIVE COLORS"?

"Conservative colors like silver, black pearl, anthracite gray, black [different than black pearl], white, white-ivory, and smoked silver (like beige metallic)." RBM offers twenty-four different colors.

WHAT KINDS OF EXTRAS DO EXECUTIVES CHOOSE?

"Telephones. Most cars come with a lot of equipment, so they don't add anything there. The 300 series has everything standard except leather seats, reading lamps in the rear, heated seats, and orthopedic seats. The SELs have all the same features except that leather seats are standard and rear reading lamps are standard. Most of them seem to like the way the car comes. They don't go for gadgetry, just good basic engineering."

WHAT PERCENTAGE OF YOUR EXECUTIVE CLIENTS GET CAR PHONES?

In the big S series cars, 65 percent to 70 percent. "In the last couple of years, it seems to be quite a phenomenon. We don't install them here, but phone companies sell a lot of telephones."

AVERAGE COST FOR THE "EXECUTIVE MODELS":

300E, $37,000 base; 300 SEL, $53,300; 420 SEL, $59,000; 560 SEL, about $70,000 ("The bigger models sell both to individuals and companies. For the last two or three years, the business write-off is the same whether it's purchased in the individual's name or the company's name."

HAS THERE BEEN A SLUMP IN BUSINESS SINCE BLACK MONDAY?

No. In fact, "October was one of our best months here. It was the second or third best month of a twelve-month period. November was down, but December is very strong."

WHO ARE SOME OF YOUR NOTABLE CLIENTELE:

"We have probably eight or ten thousand. I wouldn't be in a position to mention names without their permission."

EXECUTIVE FITNESS

THE AUSTRALIAN BODY WORKS
4385 Roswell Road
Atlanta, GA 30342
(404) 255-2217

Unlike its full-service sister clubs in other Atlanta neighborhoods, the Australian Body Works in Buckhead focuses primarily on aerobics, which make up a full 70 percent of its fitness activities. Not surprisingly, women make up the bulk of its membership, although recently its male membership has been growing—it's now 60 percent women and 40 percent men—as have its facilities, which now boast racquetball courts and a swimming pool. We spoke to Tina Eddy-Pulley about the club's executive clientele.

DO WOMEN EXECUTIVES DO MUCH NETWORKING AT THE CLUB?

"Networking is encouraged and we've initiated a new corporate program. Women probably network most in the locker rooms. Many are in service fields, such as cosmetics, clothing, et cetera. We allow members to leave business cards and brochures at the desk. We also have bulletin boards, where they can post information about sample sales, et cetera."

IF YOU HAD TO GENERALIZE, WHAT WOULD YOU SAY WERE THE FITNESS GOALS OF YOUR EXECUTIVE CLIENTS?

"Executives need to reduce stress, and need a release to break the routine of work. People are now more educated in health and fitness."

WHY DO EXECUTIVES CHOOSE YOUR CLUB OVER OTHERS IN THE AREA?

"We're a service-oriented club and we strive for quality, certified instructors. And, we offer a safe, effective, and consistent exercise program."

FEES: The Australian Body Works' fees are comparatively low. The club charges an average initiation fee of $100 plus $29–$35 per month in dues.

DELTA
AIRLINES, INC.

HISTORY & OPERATIONS

The history of Delta Airlines is inextricably linked with that of the boll weevil, a pernicious insect which in the early 1900s immigrated over the Mexican border in swarms and devastated thousands of acres of cotton crops in the South. A laboratory was set up in Louisiana to create ways of destroying the bugs, and among the scientists working there was one C. E. Woolman, an agricultural engineer and aviation enthusiast. The scientists invented a pesticide that Woolman determined would be most effective when sprayed from the air. Toward this end, a little company called Huff Daland Dusters was established in 1925, with Woolman as its vice-president and field manager. When the boll weevil threat was finally contained in 1928, Woolman arranged to purchase Huff Daland's equipment and changed the name of the company to Delta, after the Mississippi River delta region in which it was located. In 1929 the company bought three six-passenger planes and inaugurated a passenger service to supplement the crop-dusting business, a division the airline continued operating until Woolman's death in 1966.

Four months after Delta initiated its passenger service, the stock market collapsed. Nonetheless, and despite competition from far wealthier and larger rivals, Delta persevered. A significant step in the company's growth was the launch in 1934 of an airmail and air cargo service, which today generates around $250 million in annual revenues. In 1941 the company established its headquarters in Atlanta.

Delta, which has maintained a reputation for being fiscally conservative, expanded slowly over the years, mostly from within. But three mergers have contributed significantly to the airline's growth. In 1953 Delta merged with Chicago and Southern Air Lines, adding major north-south routes, including the Caribbean. In 1972 the company merged with Northeast Airlines, extending Delta's service into New England, Canada, Bermuda, and the Bahamas. And on April 1, 1987, Delta merged with Los Angeles–based Western Airlines, adding forty new cities to its routes in the West, where it formerly had only a limited presence.

Delta is now ranked as the third or fourth largest among all U.S. airlines, depending upon who's doing the ranking and the criteria by which they're ranked. But Delta takes greater pride in the fact that for the past thirteen years, the company consistently has garnered fewer passenger complaints than any other carrier, according to records maintained by the Department of Transportation. The airline currently services more than 150 cities in Canada, the Caribbean, Bermuda, England, Germany, and recently Japan. Delta has 2,180 flights per day and, since the Western merger, accommodates about 60 million passengers each year.

The company is structured around six main divisions: Marketing, Technical Operations (maintenance), Finance, Personnel, Operations (passenger service area), and Legal (Delta also has an executive division, which includes Chairman of the Board and CEO Robert W. Allen, who succeeded David C. Garrett when he retired in June 1987, and President and COO-chief operative officer Hollis L. Harris. All told, Delta employs a full-time staff of more than 51,000 people. And the airline, which—with the Western merger—is now generating in the neighborhood of $15 billion in yearly revenues, has been profitable for every year in its recent history except one—fiscal 1983, when the entire airline industry was suffering from the repercussions of deregulation. Despite a spate of airborne mishaps in the late summer of 1987, the company's record, both financially and in terms of employee satisfaction, is unparalleled by any other major airline, according to outside, independent sources.

(Information provided by Richard E. Jones, company spokesperson.)

REVENUES: More than $4.5 billion in 1986. With the Western merger, 1987 revenues were $5.3 billion.

EARNINGS: $263.7 million in 1987. (This figure includes the expenses of Delta's merger with Western.)

INITIAL PUBLIC OFFERING: Public since inception.

NUMBER OF SHAREHOLDERS: 29,988.

OFFICES: Delta maintains offices in every city it serves, plus others—more than 153 worldwide.

NUMBER OF EMPLOYEES: More than 51,000, counting those who came with the Western merger. (Delta voluntarily extended jobs to all nonofficer, full-time, permanent Western employees.) Since Delta's administration is located in Atlanta, there are very few corporate offices outside the city. "There are no heavy regional offices. If people demonstrate their expertise in another city, they are recruited to Atlanta and promoted through the ranks to become a corporate officer. You don't get to be a corporate officer by starting off and staying in Atlanta. You need to be pretty well rounded and have a broad experience in the airline."

RECRUITMENT: Delta has never found it necessary to go out and recruit. It has over 250,000 applications on file at all times at Atlanta headquarters, with 2,000–2,500 new ones pouring in each day (applications are kept on file for six months). And that's just in Atlanta—applications come in to Delta offices all over the country.

NUMBER OF NEW HIRES PER YEAR: On average, 2,200 in all classes and all specialties.

TYPES OF JOBS AVAILABLE: In addition to pilots, flight attendants, and reservationists, Delta hires people to work in technical operations—shops in which avionics repairs are made, wheel shops, brake shops, cleaning shops, sheet metal shops, handling and distributing the multitude of parts that have to be available for the day-to-day maintenance of the fleet of 365 planes. People work at cleaning the planes, filing flight plans, computer programming, data processing, marketing, sales, and training. There is a weather department as well as a communications system (air-to-ground, air-to-air, ground-to-ground), and on and on.

RANGE OF STARTING SALARIES: The company will not disclose figures. "It's a variable based on the job function at the company. Delta's wages are equal to or better than industry standards."

POLICY FOR RAISES: No fixed policy or review period. Raises are determined on the basis of merit.

TRAINING PROGRAMS: Vary depending upon position for which a person is hired. As far as training for an individual job assignment, there is some classwork and on-the-job training programs with the supervisory staff. Reservationists have specific training programs. Flight attendants go through a four-week training program, and pilots—who already have licenses and federal authority to operate airplanes—go through a six-week program to learn Delta's systems and techniques.

BENEFITS: Health and accident insurance, which includes major medical and major dental; a retirement program, including survivor benefits; a savings plan program, under which the company puts in matching funds in proportion to what the employee puts in, up to 4 percent of annual salary; life insurance; tuition reimbursement, as long as the subject matter of the class will benefit an employee's career at Delta. Reimbursement for classes is contingent on an employee's grade, and the company will give 75 percent for an A and nothing for anything below a C.

ADDITIONAL PERKS: All employees, their spouses, and dependent children are entitled to free flight privileges on Delta, depending on available space (meaning that employees fly standby and their priority for space is based on their seniority and the type of pass they're flying on). Flight privileges start after an employee's first six months with the company and increase on an incremental scale with every year of work. Upon their tenth anniversary at Delta, employees receive an annual pass that entitles them to unlimited domestic free trips (again, depending upon available space) and two transocean trips per year.

VACATION: Starts off with two weeks after one year of work and goes up to seven weeks after thirty years.

BONUSES: Company does not give bonuses.

AVERAGE WORKDAY: Most employees work eight-hour shifts. Pilots and flight attendants work an average of eighty hours per month, which is calculated only for the time their planes are away from the gate and does not include time spent waiting in airports and staying away overnight. The company operates twenty-four hours per day, 365 days per year.

DRESS CODE: Delta has strict standards, which differ according to whether an employee has contact with the public. *For men:* no facial hair other than a "neatly trimmed mustache," no hair below the collar, shirt and tie at all times for executives. *For women:* "appropriate attire," the meaning of which is cause for an ongoing debate. Women can now wear slacks, but that is a relatively recent development. In other words, the dress code is extremely conservative.

NUMBER OF CITIES ON DELTA'S ROUTES: The airline now services 153 destinations from Munich to Tokyo, from Alaska to Puerto Rico, from Montreal to Mexico.

NUMBER OF PASSENGERS PER YEAR: 41,062,000 in 1986. For 1987, with the Western merger, the number was in excess of 58 million.

MOST POPULAR MENU: Of the special-order meals, of which there are fifty (e.g., low-sodium, vegetarian, kosher, etc.), the fruit plate is most popular.

NUMBER OF DELTA FLIGHTS PER DAY: 2,180.

HEADQUARTERS: Delta's headquarters are made up of five buildings, three of which were built after 1980, at the Hartsfield Atlanta International Airport. "They have been referred to as 'Spartan.' "

CHARITABLE CONTRIBUTIONS: Company will not disclose.

INTERESTED APPLICANTS CAN SEND RÉSUMÉS TO:
Employment Office
P.O. Box 20530
Delta Airlines, Inc.
Hartsfield Atlanta International Airport
Atlanta, GA 30320
(404) 765-2600

E veryone who works at Delta Airlines knows someone who had to apply three or four or seven times before he or she was hired. Known as a beneficent sugar daddy, it seems that anyone who grew up near Atlanta, aviation nut or not, has considered pursuing a job here.

No matter what you've read, Atlanta is not a big city. Everything is called Peachtree, and two companies dominate the Peachtree City (although Ted Turner's empire threatens to join them from time to time): Coca-Cola and Delta. Oh hell, let's give Atlanta to Coke, since Delta's out by the airport. Atlanta is obviously not a one- or two-industry town. But guaranteed, even if you work in a boutique over in Phipps Plaza (way out on Peachtree in Buckhead), you know someone at Delta.

A leader of the "promote from within" corporate philosophy and one of its strictest adherents, Delta offers only four entry-level jobs: ramp agent, flight attendant, clerk-typist, and customer service support agent—the person who services the planes on the ground. There are few exceptions. (Lawyers do get to start off in the legal department.) Employees do not admit to being thwarted by Delta's hiring policies. They love learning Delta culture as they rise in the organization. They are happy, and they travel a lot. (If you have trouble locating a Deltan, chances are he or she is using some time off to go to Hawaii.)

And if you don't believe me, tune into a Delta commercial on TV. Those aren't actors telling you how happy they are to work for Delta; those are employees, who mean it when they tell you that serving you makes them smile.

A station break. Rudy Wilson, of the huge smile, is the "Redcoat Agent" (customer and crisis manager) you may have caught on your tube. While he doesn't look nearly old enough, he's been with Delta since 1969, when he started in air cargo handling. He settles back to reminisce about his path to Delta. (This is not in the commercial.):

"I can remember being in the fourth grade and we had to write about a state. I chose Hawaii, and then I wanted to visit Hawaii. There was not much money at the time, and I knew I would need to be associated with an airline to do that. I can remember sitting at the desk, thinking all about it. I'd never been on a plane. I went to Hawaii for the first time in 1971." It lived up to his expectations.

Rudy expected to work for Delta for about six months and then go to college. His goal was law school and a career as a country lawyer, helping the underprivileged in his home county. But he married young, and with his new family obligations, he thought he'd stay at Delta a little longer. "I needed to figure out whether Delta was compatible with me and if it would be the company I'd want to devote my life to. I remember during orientation in 1969, they talked about the 'family structure' of the company. I thought they were snowing me. What major corporation can really be a family?

"Next, I wanted to see how the company was going to invest its profits—if I were going to retire from this company. I wanted to see how the senior management lived. I remember coming off the B shift at two P.M. I was still nineteen years old, but I saw my life following a pattern. I took a stroll toward the general offices. I walked up and down hallways and peeked in."

To his delight, he saw signs of humility. "I looked to see the plush carpeting, the fancy mahogany desks. I didn't want to see that, and I didn't. That really made my spirit soar. I saw green speckled tile floors, airplane pictures on the wall. Plain metal desks, like school. Everything was very plain. That impressed me. I was impressed that management, which needed ten haywagons to load cargo, only ordered five. Even though I had to do the loading, I was impressed by the conservativeness of the company. I wanted to make sure Delta would be around a long time."

Rudy might be more thoughtful than many Delta employees, or maybe he's just invested his memories with a bit more tenderness, but he is absolutely typical in his hopes for a company that is much bigger than the sum of its parts. "Many times I get out here when everything is falling apart around me," he says, "and I love being in the airport with people. I am eager to do my work because I love it, and I want to put on my uniform. I need to feel the company has good, fair, workable guidelines. That's more important to me than the dollar."

Rudy's had many jobs in his nineteen years at Delta. He's gone from handling baggage to handling the touchiest of customer problems. So far, being a Redcoat Agent is his favorite job, although he has his eye on a new one a bit down the runway. "I've had it on my mind for a year," he admits. "I'm told it's in the department of properties. It's purchasing planes," he says shyly. "I want to do real strong negotiating. It would take me away {from home} two or three days a week, but I wouldn't mind."

How does one change jobs at Delta? "When you want to move, you must let it be known.

You have to straighten out shortcomings and be ready. You have to talk to your immediate supervisor with your feet on the ground." Wilson has already had about six jobs so far, and he plans to talk to someone in properties to see if that's the job he really wants. He'll fill out a form and channel it properly, and "If there's a job opening, I'd hope they'd interview me and feel I'm the right man for the job."

Although Delta numbers its total employees at more than 51,000, there is just one employment office, as it is called, made up of eight personnel representatives. These eight propagators of Delta culture are located in Atlanta and interview everyone considered an interesting candidate. They do not recruit. "We don't have to," says one of the eight. "Monday we received 1,926 applications. Yesterday we got eight hundred," he says on an ordinary Wednesday. "We usually receive five hundred applications for flight attendants *per day*." Of this unfathomable number, the employment office will invite twenty-five to thirty per day to Atlanta. (Delta will pay for round-trip airfare for any invited candidate from the closest Delta city. If an overnight stay is required, hotel and meals are the responsibility of the interviewee.) At one time it was estimated that five women per day, or a hundred per month, were offered flight attendant jobs. (That statistic is now officially unofficial.) The word at Delta is that between 60 and 70 percent of its flight attendants (now a coed position), are college graduates. They are hired to fit into the airline's schedule of training classes, of which there are about six a year. "If we have a class of 165 flight attendants, we expect 165 to graduate."

Deborah Lowery began her still new (seven-year) stint at Delta as a flight attendant. Her previous job was as the associate director of financial aid at the Georgia Institute of Technology. I know what you're thinking, and I asked her the same question. After two and a half years in financial aid, she had moved so quickly, there was nowhere else to turn. In order to get a director's job, she'd have had to move to a smaller institution (with a student population of fewer than nine thousand students), which would have almost certainly meant less money (to distribute and for her salary). "A good friend who was a flight attendant at Delta influenced me," she explains. "I got to see her lifestyle. I wanted an ease from those pressures. I wanted to travel.

"This is a great job. The time off is incredible. The pay—to stay in San Diego for thirty hours and be paid—is great. I like people. I make them feel good for a few hours." Deborah is aware that to most customers, she *is* Delta. But her representation ends when they deplane. "I'm not responsible for the long term." She admits to feeling occasional stress, but nothing like the stress she felt denying money to qualified students. "It's the kind I can leave behind."

It is important to remember that anyone who starts at Delta, regardless of the age at which they begin their Delta career, regardless of education, regardless of present salary, has few job choices. What might seem a career regression to outsiders seems fair to insiders.

A promotion will be determined by one's department, but the (I'm tempted to add "all-powerful") employment office is responsible for the fates of many employees already ensconced in Delta's secure environment. Possibly the most important aspect of its role is in maintaining a consistency throughout Delta. The office runs the job bid system, whereby management-approved openings are posted on every Delta bulletin board with job titles, salaries, locations, and descriptions. Anyone in the company who's interested in one of them must inform the Atlanta employment office within a week of the job posting, and his or her files will be reviewed. Approximately two to three hundred people may apply for one job, and 10 percent of them will usually be interviewed for the position. A member of this elite office says that this system proves a certain democracy on Delta's part. "We allow people to figure out where their interests lie. We don't tell them. We've had lawyers go into marketing."

Bob Miller signed on in Chicago, never a Delta hub. He was recruited from the Humboldt Institute, an aviation school in Minneapolis. He applied to Humboldt after seeing an advertisement for it in the back of *Good Housekeeping* magazine. "I selected Delta because of the company's good track record. I was hired to load luggage." He moved to Columbus, Ohio, with another carrier, since there was no job at Delta for him there, but a year later, he got rehired in Columbus. Now he works in Atlanta.

What does he like about Delta? "The opportunities. They never close the door." He's in ramp service now, "downstairs, because I don't have enough seniority to work days." Otherwise, he'd prefer being a ticket agent . . . upstairs. His workday starts at 7:15 A.M. "I've been down here for four years. But I can see the light at the end of the tunnel. You can't have total burnout at Delta because you can move around. Supervisors tell you they're trying to help you advance. Nothing's black and white. It's gray. We're nonunion." (In fact, the only employees who are organized—and that by choice—are some pilots and some flight dispatchers.)

Bob's wife is a flight attendant. With Delta Airlines. They met at work. "We travel for fun," he says of everyone's favorite perk. "We've been to Hawaii eleven times." The Millers don't socialize too much with other Delta couples. "At 3:45, when I leave," he says, "I put it behind me." When he meets people outside the airport who ask him what he does for a living, "I tell them I change pillowcases." Would Bob prefer to do something else? "I've never been tempted to leave. I've never seen anything better."

It would be too easy, when meeting Delta employees en masse and discovering there's no grind behind their smiles, to suggest there is a cult of Deltoids, people who've sold their souls to the big birds hovering over the Dixie skies. People don't fall into jobs here; they must actively seek them and prove they have the right mettle to fit in. The fit, the pleasure in serving customers, and the honor they feel in doing that well seem universal. Indeed, in 1982 satisfied employees chipped in to raise $30 million to buy their company a gift, its first Boeing 767, called the *Spirit of Delta* as permanent, tangible proof of their high regard.

Yet ask about fit, who will be happy here, and who will succeed here, and no one has an answer. It's not possible that no one has given this a thought; it's probable that self-selection works best here at Hartsfield International Airport, first home of the "fishbowl scuba diver." (Only frequent travelers will understand this last reference.) One manager, in response to the question "Who is hired?" says, "Someone who's reasonably intelligent, with a good appearance, reasonably articulate." If this sounds casually stated, it is. One gets the feeling that this corporate profile was created on the spot, although not irresponsibly. "Many positions require a degree from a four-year college. We do background checks on most candidates. We prefer some previous job experience." For a company that feels it's one big happy family, it's hard to believe that the cohesion isn't more willful. Oh, just a second; someone is experiencing a realization: "Delta expects a high degree of moral conduct, on and off work. Anything else could end in the termination of your job."

Russ Heil, the vice-president of personnel, explains why people are happy at Delta. "There are some deliberate things we do which help create a positive attitude. Number one: Look at employees as family, and their families as our extended family. Number two: Our principles are based on what's right to protect members of the family. Number three: Strict promotion-from-within policy. You could probably count on one hand the number of times we went out and hired from the outside in twenty years. And only when we needed a special skill. Number four: No furloughs. No layoffs. In 1973 the oil embargo tested us. After a rapid hiring spurt, we had a lot of people and nothing for them to do. We reassigned people from various functions. At the height of the crisis, five hundred flight attendants were reassigned to reservations, clerical . . . two hundred new pilots were sent to ramp, loading, engineering. We gave leaves to pilots for military duty.

"Not one person lost a paycheck because of the crisis. It's not a written policy. The company doesn't necessarily guarantee forever. There's no mission statement." Policy books exist, but they provide stuff like how many sick days you get, not philosophy.

Heil adds another component: "We have a longstanding open-door program. Anyone with a problem who can't resolve it through the normal chain of command can go see anyone without worrying about it reflecting badly on them." And, contrary to industry practice, senior managers are not encouraged to take early retirement.

While policy statements have a certain coldness to them, it should be pointed out that the average length of service of a Delta officer is twenty-six years. That's a long time. Delta's management stands for the "right" things, cares about its employees, and obviously is able to demonstrate that concern to its satisfied constituency. That the tenets are expressed with all the warmth of Morse code may be irrelevant. This is a business that works. Many airline industry observers will tell you without hesitation that Delta is the best-run airline in the country. That point cannot be understated. And the payoff is great. Meeting employees of five, ten, even fifteen years, one often hears, "I'm a newcomer." No one who's been imbued in Delta culture ever thinks of Delta not being the locus of his or her entire career. Delta's ex-CEO, Dave Garrett, started out in phone reservations in 1946, when that was an entry-level job. Today, a spokesman confirms that reservations is highly coveted by junior employees.

What have we learned so far? Delta takes no chances. It wants to be the best American airline. And although this goal seems to have been reached, "We knew we had to get bigger in order to assume Delta's place in history." In its quest to match its size to its reputation, on December 16, 1986, Delta closed a deal to purchase Western Airlines, based in Los Angeles, and make it a wholly owned subsidiary. Western was an unbelievably compatible match, since the two had very little overlap in their routes as well as what had been determined a close cultural fit. April 1, 1987, was the day Western ceased to exist in name, except perhaps as a fond memory. The acquisition increased Delta's size by a cool 25 percent in terms of employees, passengers, flights, and revenues.

Delta's last major merger had occurred in 1972, with the purchase of Northeast Airlines, headquartered in Boston. "They were highly unionized," a manager relates, "and we weren't. Yet there were no problems." Based on this experience, "We thought we could predict the outcome of the merger with Western." Eight hundred families relocated to Atlanta in 1973. A mechanic who moved (and still misses the Celtics, Red Sox, and Bruins) considers himself lucky. "The company is interested in me as an individual. No one is twisting my arm to say this. I don't feel I'm part of a gigantic company. I feel I'm listened to. It's really a family."

"It shows up at the death of an employee. They all show up at the funeral—they don't have to. If I were sick, people would call me at home. If I needed time off, they'd give it to me." Unlike what happens in biological families, he will have to retire in a few years. He's starting to make plans. "I would like to fly to every station flown by Delta. I'd start with the first page of the air schedule book."

If you grow up in Georgia, no one has to sell you on the virtues of Delta. One young accountant, a native of the Peach State, recalls that while she was growing up, several of her parents' friends worked for the airline. It seems their travel benefits were widely discussed and envied. "I had a friend who got to go to Hawaii for her high school graduation," she remembers. "I thought that sounded good."

Once she enrolled at the University of Georgia, she learned that Delta was considered a good employer. Now, with less than a decade of tenure on her résumé, she regards the prestige associated with the company a bona fide job perk. "You can cash checks anywhere" with a Delta employee identification card. "I enjoy being proud of where I work. So many thousands of people get rejected."

Maria's story provides some sound advice. She applied to Delta three times. She never felt she was not qualified; she felt she couldn't beat the numbers. "I finally got in as a temp. It *is* a way to get into the company if you can't get past the application process. You can't mind the lower pay and no benefits," she cautions. But, she advises Delta hopefuls, "Be persistent. It was tough, but very worth it." She started as a fill-in secretary but was able to make her desire to work in accounts payable known. "I started out at the bottom, *and* I had a college degree."

In addition to perks of recognition and prestige, she's developed friendships at work and a sense of independence. "Each person has a job to do. There's no standing over anyone's shoulder." Plus, of course, the lure of free air travel. "Every couple of months we fly somewhere. I notice my husband and I have stayed home for two months. It's time to take a trip."

Our next-to-last endorsement comes from Linda, a reservations sales agent with ten years at Delta to her credit. Linda had been married for many years to a Delta pilot. After their divorce she realized she had been spoiled by all his benefits. She got her job after raising her family, and she exudes her love of the company by wearing a uniform (optional for phone work) and a button featuring the logos of Delta and Western claiming, "The Best Get Better," along with a wide smile and her exclamations. "I love my work! It's my turn to have a good time!" Linda says it's better to be a Delta employee than a Delta spouse, but it should be pointed out that her ex-husband is still flying for the company. "He's a good pilot!"

Finally, a testimony from Wilma, a marketing representative. Wilma loves her work, which would explain her happy fifteen-year stint—so far. Of the necessity to start in an entry-level position regardless of professional or educational background, she says, "Even if I were starting now, I would not consider it a step backward." Her job entails selling Delta and its services to travel agents, corporate travel specialists, and companies. "I like selling Delta because it's an easy and fantastic product to sell. I can't believe how many hours I work. The paperwork is overwhelming. I take it home. I work weekends. I work every single night." But the rewards compensate for the hours. "The best part of my job is making an unhappy Delta passenger happy again."

KING & SPALDING

KING & SPALDING

HISTORY & OPERATIONS

King & Spalding, one of Atlanta's oldest continuously operating law firms and considered by many to be its most prestigious, was founded by Alexander Campbell King and Jack Johnson Spalding in 1885, twenty years after the end of the Civil War. Both of the founding partners, neither of whom came from Atlanta (King was from South Carolina and Spalding was from Kentucky) were twenty-eight years old when they started the firm. Despite a surfeit of lawyers in the country at the time and a dearth of clients (by 1882 the ratio of attorneys to potential clients was 1 to 270—including children), the firm gained a reputation for excellence and prospered.

King, who had a photographic memory and an insatiable thirst for knowledge, became known as the scholar of the partnership, while Spalding made a name for himself as a formidable businessman. Both men were excellent lawyers as well as active and respected members of their community. Toward the end of his life, King left the firm to serve as solicitor general of the United States in the Wilson Administration, and he later served as a judge on the United States Circuit Court of Appeals for the Fifth Circuit, also under President Wilson.

Afterward he returned briefly to the firm but left due to ill health and died in 1926. Spalding retired from the firm in 1929 and remained active in politics into his eighties. He died in 1938 at the age of 82. Upon Spalding's retirement, his son Hughes Spalding took over the leadership of the firm.

As the firm gained and lost partners over the years, its name went through several changes. In 1962 it was again named King & Spalding. When Hughes Spalding joined the firm in 1918, it had consisted of the original two partners and one additional lawyer. When he died in 1969 at the age of 82, that number had grown to forty-six. In 1979, at the behest of Coca-Cola, one of the firm's major clients since 1930, King & Spalding opened an office in Washington to handle Coke's dealings with the Food and Drug Administration. That office now houses twenty-two lawyers and eight paralegals and handles work for a number of other corporate clients.

Since the days of its founding partners, King & Spalding has encouraged its lawyers to become active in the political life of their communities and country, although the firm does have a policy prohibiting partners from actively seeking public office while still practicing law. When Jimmy Carter became president in 1976, he appointed several of the firm's lawyers to prominent positions in his administration. Partner Jack Watson was appointed head of Carter's transition team, and partner Griffin Bell was named attorney general. Another partner, Charles Kirbo, served as one of Carter's closest advisers throughout the President's term. In keeping with the same political tradition, former Georgia Governor George Busbee joined King & Spalding as a partner in 1983.

Today King & Spalding has 214 lawyers, with eighty-eight partners and 126 associates. It takes 7 years to become a partner. The firm, which was restructured into specialized departments in the early 1960s, practices a broad spectrum of general law, with a heavy emphasis on corporate law. The individual practice areas and number of lawyers in each are: tax, 13; trusts and estates, 6; real estate, 21; commercial, 14; public finance, 10; international, 6; corporate finance, 44; commercial litigation 47; products liability litigation, 6; labor, ERISA, and employment, 10; patent, trademark, antitrust counseling, environmental, food and drug, 17; health care, 13; and miscellaneous (2). Among the firm's corporate clients are The Coca-Cola Corporation, E. F. Hutton & Company, Inc., Arthur Andersen & Co., General Motors Corporation, SunTrust Banks, Inc., Arthur Lanier Business Products, Bell South Corporation, and Life of Georgia Insurance Company.

In 1985 the firm celebrated its hundredth anniversary. In the same year it replaced its long-standing five-person management committee with a seven-person policy committee headed by Managing Partner Bradley Hale.

(Information provided by Linda G. Arnold and Emy Brown, firm spokespersons.)

REVENUES: Firm will not disclose.

EARNINGS: Firm will not disclose.

OFFICES: Headquarters in Atlanta plus an additional office in Washington, D.C., which houses twenty-two full-time lawyers.

NUMBER OF EMPLOYEES: 500–520 with 88 partners, 126 associates, 54 paralegals, and a support staff that fluctuates between 230 and 250.

NUMBER OF WOMEN AND MINORITY ASSOCIATES: 41 women, 2 of whom are black, and 1 black male associate as of March, 1988.

NUMBER OF WOMEN AND MINORITY PARTNERS: Four women (three in Atlanta and one in Washington, D.C.) and one black partner in Atlanta as of March 1988.

RECRUITMENT: The firm recruits from thirty to forty law schools across the country, including those at the University of Alabama, Case Western Reserve University, Columbia University, Duke University, Emory University, University of Florida, Florida State University, George Washington University, University of Georgia, Harvard University, Mercer University, University of Michigan, New York University, University of North Carolina, Northwestern University, University of South Carolina, University of Texas, Vanderbilt University, University of Virginia, and Yale University. Forty-two percent of the new associates come from outside of the Southeast.

NUMBER OF NEW HIRES PER YEAR: The firm hires between twenty and thirty new associates per year and has hired an average of eighty-five new nonlawyers for each of the past three years.

RANGE OF STARTING SALARIES: The starting salary for associates in 1987 was $46,000 in Atlanta and $50,000 in Washington, D.C. The 1988 summer associates were paid $900 per week in Atlanta and $1,000 per week in Washington, D.C. The firm will not disclose the starting salaries for its support staff.

POLICY FOR RAISES: "We would prefer not to address that. Each group is handled differently. It varies between associates and support staff."

SUMMER ASSOCIATE PROGRAM: In 1987 the firm hired thirty-nine summer associates, most of whom had completed their second year of law school. Summer associates rotate through several areas of the firm's practice and are urged to work with as many lawyers as possible. Each summer associate is assigned an adviser to help ensure that the experience is professionally rewarding and enjoyable. The firm requires summer associates to spend at least six weeks at its offices and encourages longer stays. Over the last few years, more than 90 percent of the summer associates have been invited to join the firm as associates.

BENEFITS: The firm provides group life insurance, hospitalization and medical insurance (with an HMO option), dental insurance, disability insurance, and maternity leave. All the above are available to lawyers and support staff, though the amounts of coverage and eligibility requirements may be different. Associates' professional fees and dues and continuing legal education and expenses are paid by the firm. All employees are eligible for participation in the firm's profit-sharing plan.

VACATION: Varies from group to group. "We don't want to answer that."

BONUSES: King & Spalding does not have a bonus system.

ANNUAL PARTY: The firm generally hosts two parties during the year, one of which is usually held during the Christmas–New Year holiday season. At its centennial in 1985, King & Spalding hosted three parties: one for all lawyers and professional alumni, one for various officials and representatives of the Coca-Cola Company and the Trust Company of Georgia, and one for the descendants of the founding members of the firm.

AVERAGE WORKDAY: "Information not available."

DRESS CODE: Conservative professional.

HEADQUARTERS: King & Spalding occupies eight floors in the Trust Company Tower in the middle of downtown Atlanta and two floors in the adjacent Hurt Building, a restored landmark building. The firm plans to move in 1991 to a brand-new building (as yet unbuilt), also in downtown Atlanta, where it will lease enough space so that all the Atlanta personnel can be grouped together.

CHARITABLE CONTRIBUTIONS: The firm will not disclose amounts. It is represented on at least seventy-five local charitable and civic boards.

INTERESTED APPLICANTS CAN SEND RÉSUMÉS TO:
(For associate and summer associate programs:)
Ms. Linda G. Arnold
Recruiting Director

(For Paralegals:)
Ms. Kitty E. Russel
Paralegal Coordinator

(For nonlegal staff positions:)
Ms. Gearline P. Eley
Director of Personnel

King & Spalding
2500 Trust Company Tower
Atlanta, GA 30303
(404) 572-4600

People in the know were awfully surprised that King & Spalding agreed to participate in this book. By many accounts one of the most conservatively run law firms in the country, it has endured a long spate of negative publicity due to a lawsuit initiated in 1979 by a female associate who was denied partnership. Based in Atlanta, with an additional satellite office in Washington, D.C., King & Spalding is the firm that best embodies the dignity of the old South, and it represents some of the most coveted blue chip clients in Georgia.

If you are searching for a prestigious firm with high-powered connections in Atlanta, look no further. King & Spalding has an impressive roster of attorneys: ex-judges, legislators, governors, and a former U.S. attorney general. While the offices do resemble an exclusive men's club, women are not scarce, except perhaps on the partner level.

King & Spalding is top of the line. It is the long shot law students add to their applications in a gesture of bravado. Just getting an interview at King & Spalding is considered something of an event, one of those experiences, like applying to Harvard, that one does "just to see." To be chosen is a supreme ego boost, one that's hard to decline.

King & Spalding *feels* southern, if that is possible, at least to this northerner. The soft drawl prevails, along with a gentlemanly demeanor. The corridors are quiet, the furnishings elegant. While it is not mandatory that a new associate be a product of a southern law school, JD degrees from Duke, Vanderbilt, Emory, and the University of Georgia are common.

Atlantans—especially transplanted ones—constantly extol the quality of life offered by their city. The commute, the fine suburbs, the weather, and the people are all cited as part of the rationale for living here. Which could induce a young lawyer to consider working at King & Spalding in lieu of say, a Washington or New York firm. One young associate says he accepted his job offer "after a weekend in Atlanta playing basketball and going to a Hawks game. I enjoyed the people here and thought the economics of King and Spalding and Atlanta would be better. My thought was, if I'm going to be in Atlanta, I might as well try King and Spalding. And going to a big firm with a large commercial practice would maximize my opportunities."

A partner assesses the firm this way: "It's an anomaly, the backdrop of traditional southern gestalt with that of a growing, aggressive national firm. The tension's good and should be evoked." As the most cosmopolitan city in the South, Atlanta is still engaged in a tug-of-war between worldly sophistication and old-time values. "A certain level of discretion is required here. For example, living together would be less frowned upon than it was ten years ago. It's no longer a career stopper."

Another lawyer talks about Atlanta as the capital of the Sunbelt, where home buying is easy. "The bloom is on. We compete against other Atlanta firms, but not hard. [When we lose,] most times we lose cases to [firms in] other big cities." The most emphatic of the city's endorsements comes from partner Ralph Levy, a native of Larchmont, New York, one of Manhattan's bedroom suburbs. After three and a half years in the Navy, posted in the South, this University of Pennsylvania Law School graduate felt more at home below the Mason-Dixon line than above. "I concluded that with the exception of some zeros at the end of checks, Atlanta was as sophisticated as New York, Chicago, or San Francisco."

I know you're thinking, "Enough of Atlanta, already." I can't quite leave it alone. The practice of law, though not restricted to the clients and concerns of one's home turf, is a fairly accurate reflection of the culture and habits of one's location. When you pause further to consider that many lawyers applied to and attended law school with a "What-the-hell-I-might-as-well-have-a-law-degree-at-least-I-can-delay-any-real-life-decisions-for-three-years" attitude, young lawyers who may be convincing themselves of their compatibility with the law must also take the city into equal consideration with the nature of the particular practice. Add to that mix the fact that when partnership is the collective and individual goal, you're talking about a long-term investment. Except for the top 10 percent of students at the revolving list of Top Ten law schools, third-year students are not assured of getting a job in the city of their choice, let alone at their favorite firm. They simply apply and hope.

Doc Schneider was a sixth-year litigation associate when we met. He graduated from a Long Island high school in 1972 and enlisted in the Navy in 1973. After a year in hospital training in Vietnam, he was sent to the U.S. Naval Academy Preparatory School "for good athletes with low SATs. It was to raise them high enough to get into Annapolis. It was a country club with English, physics, calculus, lacrosse, and a full salary [of six hundred dollars per month]." At the Naval Academy in Annapolis, which he entered in 1975, he was an English major. "My goal was to write novels and screenplays, and teach. (It still is.) I changed my major in the last quarter of college. I switched to prelaw. I didn't know you didn't have to have that to get into law school."

Schneider, already married, "saw a guy from Mercer Law School [a nearby Baptist university]. The application was only ten dollars, as opposed to fifty or sixty dollars for other schools, which was hard to come by. I got a letter offering me a three-year merit scholarship. I got to keep my whole G.I. Bill. School was free. Mercer had just bought a beautiful building, and I loved it."

King & Spalding recruited Doc on campus. Atlanta was the big city, a bit daunting for most students at rural Mercer. As a new father with financial constraints, he started work at King & Spalding two days after his last law school exam. "I like the practice I have here because the firm attracts interesting business. People are bright and for the most part have a sense of humor. There is a general sense of excellence, which makes working here challenging. We're better lawyers. It's fun and tedious, and both mentally and physically exhausting."

Schneider puts in long days, from 8:30 A.M. to 2:30 A.M. "at least once a week." But not just to be seen. "The way you get noticed is not to campaign, but to do fine work. The partnership is based on self-interest; you want to keep good people here." A partner concurs. "All our people work very hard. They have a commitment to their work and to their clients. They're not here till midnight [just] because that's how we do our work."

Like most large law firms, King & Spalding operates on a modified caste system. Associates toil not only to satisfy the needs of their clients and their supervisors but to break through the barrier separating them from partnership. It is difficult not to be obsessed with one's chances of making partner. Yet associates here maintain that it is not on their minds all the time.

A fourth-year associate claims that "making partner is a subject people don't bring up. Making partner is compatible with the pursuit of excellence." During your first three years, you are reviewed by the partners in your department. Your first firmwide review comes in your fourth year, when you are rated on a scale from one to ten. It is now that you are informed whether you are (a) "on track"; (b) "need work"; (c) "not on track"; or (d) "no contact"—if a partner really doesn't have a sense of who you are or the quality of your work. "There's a reasonable amount of satisfaction with the process," another associate says. "There might be a little more advance warning or a printed form for associates."

The statistics for 1988 indicate that King & Spalding is made up of 88 partners and 126 associates. Eighty-four of the partners are men; one of them is black. The partnership track is ordinarily seven years long. It is said that there are few surprises by the end of this apprentice-ship, and young lawyers are given gentle expressions of hope or redirection as they close in on judgment day. "We're changing," an enthusiastic white male associate says. "We're getting people here we would never have had five years ago: women, minorities, and people from outside Atlanta. We have been forced to adapt."

One fifth-year associate says, "Now that I'm drawing nearer, I think about it more. I trust the judgment of these people. They are my friends. We've done good work together."

Another fifth-year man says, "People joke about making partner. We have a huge possibility of screwing things up. I spent my first couple of years just worried that I'd screw things up. (I did, a little.) Until I hear otherwise, I'll assume I'll make it. I see what young partners do. Your life gets easier, you make a lot of money, and you're still a lawyer and a worrier. For my other friends, it turned out to be the greatest thing that happened to them. I've always got my eyes open. I'm not looking to leave, but I'm young."

But he has legitimate reasons to enjoy his position now. He touts the firm's early bestowal of responsibility. "It's amazing. I know the general counsel of Coca-Cola, and he knows me by name. When I say my name on the phone, followed by 'King and Spalding,' it's the greatest, when dealing with smaller firms. It's scary. It's amazing how many clients come here to get business clout. Our reputation is tied with the [older generation of the] community. It means a lot to the firm. Our legal work is as good as anywhere else in town, but maybe, due to our history, more effective.

"Your reputation is all you have as a lawyer. We're a service business." One partner admits that the firm is still learning how to make new associates "feel a part of King and Spalding. It's all people. The effective management of people *is* the law practice. Our departments got too big, so they all got chunked into teams. Identification with the team unit helps young people feel a part of this place, but frankly, I doubt team loyalty will ever supersede King and Spalding loyalty."

This team talk is not a blithe repetition of the vogueish management style heard from Silicon Valley to Wall Street. King & Spalding actually hired the management consulting firm of McKinsey & Company to reorganize the governance of the firm. "It's too soon to tell, and we have no empirical proof," a supporter begins, "but the team strategy's a good start. The leaders of our firm *really* want it. Hiring McKinsey was a radical move for a law firm. The conceptual framework represents the partners' collective vision and direction. It provides a constitution. A lot is symbolic."

Working as an attorney in a large firm means being driven in a way that working for a small firm doesn't. It is by nature a competitive situation. "We try not to engender competition among lawyers," a partner says. "We promise to try to assess your work fairly and objectively." Relenting, he admits, "We are team players in a solitarily competitive environment. Obviously, they can't all be partners."

Some of the more introspective lawyers worry about the future of those who seek careers in the law and how that will affect King & Spalding. "Vietnam [-era] kids were service-oriented. The last generation was struggling. They took their careers, marriages, and kids seriously. Thank God women became equals. Now [young people] are quite willing to subordinate their personal lives to their public lives. They are delaying marriage and children. Money is motivation for them. It's proof. It enables them to keep score. It says, 'I've succeeded.' I hope it's not what brings them to the law.

"To be a lawyer you've got to take some risks. Lots of advice isn't black and white, and you're hired by clients for your judgment." When a new client solicits King & Spalding's counsel, he is submitted to a conflicts check. Then he "must be okayed by a small committee. In the course of a week, maybe twenty new business matters come in. And we do turn most of them down."

One associate laments, "I'll never be a decision maker." Read one of the many articles published everywhere from *The New York Times* to in-flight magazines about lawyers who've jumped ship to become investment bankers. (Or anything else.) The reason most frequently cited for their change of heart is a frustration with being an adviser, not a doer. (Then there is the issue of how much more money their colleagues at investment banks are earning on deals on which they collaborate.) This is certainly endemic to the profession, and not at all peculiar to King & Spalding. "We're highly paid scriveners. Eighty percent of the time it's the bad deals you hear about. You never hear about how things work out."

On a day-to-day basis, after an orientation period, life at King & Spalding should not be intimidating. One enters the firm with one's class, i.e., other associates who graduated from law school the previous spring. Chances are that most first-year associates spent the summer prior to their last year of law school as summer associates and got an inside line on what being a lawyer at King & Spalding *means*. (The typical summer after law school is spent in studying for, taking, and passing the bar exam, followed by a vacation or at least a long nap before responsibility sets in. The class usually enters around Labor Day.)

Chilton Varner, a Smith College graduate and King & Spalding's seventy-second lawyer and second female partner, was married and had a daughter before she matriculated to law school. Her husband was a lawyer at another Atlanta firm. In her beautifully decorated office —it could be a den in an elegant house—she reminisced about her selection of King & Spalding and the firm's selection of her. "In law school I had different ideas about what I wanted to do. I didn't want a large firm. I didn't think I'd fit in. I interviewed with King and Spalding for the experience, to make contacts, and because it's generally agreed to be the best firm in Atlanta. I had a great day. I liked the people a lot. I was surprised to get an offer. They didn't have any reason to take the leap of faith with an older woman and mother. But they did."

But that doesn't explain why she has stayed on. "I was unusual in that if I had wanted to walk away from the firm, there would have been no problem. I had financial freedom and a family. I liked what I did here a lot. I got good work and was surrounded by good folks. The firm was very good to me. I looked forward to coming in every day—and I still do—and I wanted to be good. So you obviously decide to be a partner. It did not consume me. Some days it never crossed my mind. I assumed unless the sky fell down, I would make partner. I was more worried about being accepted in the beginning than I was worried about being made partner. I was benefited by the fact that there weren't other women here. I couldn't fade into the woodwork.

"Your class all knows each other and are going through the same things at the same time. We're all in it together. There's not a lot of territoriality. People are helpful and bail each other out." When Chilton was under consideration for partnership, her class had dwindled to four. "All of us were in litigation. Yet, we were all supportive, and we all were made partners. They are my dearest friends."

Sipping tea from a porcelain cup, she says, "It never bothered me particularly to be around so few women. It was not part of what affects the quality of life at King and Spalding." One senses that Ms. Varner is frequently asked this. "We're hiring good women. They do have an equal chance at making partner. The firm is where you'd expect it to be with women. The numbers are increasing. It didn't bother me that there wasn't a group of women above me." Voicing a lighthearted gripe, she adds, "Sometimes I get sick of hearing all bass voices."

Varner says she works with "a collegial group of people. My partners are concerned when I have family problems. They rally remarkably around me." She'll never forget how helpful they were when her mother was suffering from her terminal illness. It is these kinds of memories that create loyalty and permanent goodwill toward one's organization. "These are my dear friends. I don't want to get away from these people during leisure time. We have real affection toward one another."

As a woman with King & Spalding on her business cards, Chilton Varner feels that "people take me seriously. It feels good to be part of the top firm."

Lest one imagine that King & Spalding is a bastion of polite southern Democrats and nonreactionary Republicans, a few lawyers hail the "passion for public works and the streak of liberality" that touch the firm. King & Spalding was involved in civil rights. And pro bono work is encouraged.

At lunch with two senior partners—Bradley Hale, the firm's seventeenth lawyer and its first managing partner, and George Busbee, former governor of Georgia—the ideologies of King & Spalding are discussed, along with the virtues of shad roe, the Commerce Club luncheon specialty. I am told that the Hildebrand Company, long-range planning consultants to law firms, were "surprised by the openness in partners and the lack of emphasis on money." Busbee reports that "as fast as we're growing—which is fast—we're trying to reinforce the culture before we lose it."

And the culture? "Not dog eat dog. All clients belong to the firm. There is no stealing of other lawyers' clients. Propriety isn't priggish. Our lawyers all have a sense of security. They gained admission and proved themselves. Associates who don't make it become part of the Alumni Club and get placement help. We keep the environment personal; birthdays and births are celebrated. Self-starters don't like a bureaucratic matrix over them. They do better when left alone. We take advantage of our history."

In an effort to coalesce a growing body of increasingly heterogeneous people, Hale has created "Breakfast with Bradley." He is concentrating on lessening the gap between associates and senior partners. An associate praises Hale's enterprise. "Bradley is very approachable, sincere. I could go talk to Bradley any time. He's helped communications with associates. Before he was made managing partner, there used to be a policy-making committee, and decisions were made by compromise."

One thing Hale has recognized is the aforementioned tendency for young lawyers to throw themselves into their work to the abandonment of their personal lives. "We have to get involved in lowering billable hours. I've budgeted fewer hours," he says at lunch. "Institutionally, we're saying it's not healthy to work as hard as they do. We think it's important for our people to get involved in civic and philanthropic activities—for lots of reasons, including self-interest." Plus there's promoting "our legacy"—a history of good works. Ask around Atlanta, and you'll hear that "it's difficult to find a board in town without King & Spalding people on it. The firm acts as a clearinghouse for community activities."

Alternate Fridays see a big firmwide meeting "with jokes," and on the fourth Friday of each month, an outside speaker is brought in to entertain or inform the lawyers of King & Spalding. "People are witty and laugh. We try not to take ourselves too seriously." Both Hale and Busbee acknowledge that King & Spalding is regarded as conservative. This is how they deal with that reputation. "We're known as blue bloods. We're not so sure it's hurt us. We don't walk around perceiving we're stuffy."

One rather progressive lawyer urges his colleagues to mingle in the halls, talk law, and learn from each other and by osmosis. In fact, the socializing and friendly fraternity that is King & Spalding makes the environment look especially appealing to newcomers and creates an oral history of these times. "It's important for us to bump into each other and mix in each other's daily lives. That's how culture is transmitted."

The kinds of attorneys who are attracted to King & Spalding are exactly the kinds who would not be offended by charges of "stuffy" when the firm's name is invoked. "Conservative" and "stodgy" are matters of perception, anyway, and the trade-off is a sense of security—that no matter what, this office will be open for business next week, next year, and five years from now. (Consider the fact that these lawyers remember exactly how many people were hired before them!) "Externally our persona is stiff. People walk around with suit jackets on and can't walk in the halls carrying their coffee cups. But people who work here say, 'I don't know where that [reputation] comes from. How did it get this way? I think it's relaxed.' " If there is a notion of stodge, one attorney traces it to three factors. One is that a significant number of lawyers belong to the Piedmont Driving Club, a conservative all-men's club that publicly prohibits Jews, minorities, and women (other than widows of members) from being members. (During the Carter presidency, there was a great deal of pressure on former and future King & Spalding partner Griffin Bell, then the U.S. attorney general, to renounce his membership. Second is the firm's long relationship with Coca-Cola. Third is its long relationship with the Trust Bank of Atlanta.

In recruiting, which is termed by one partner "an art, not a science," King & Spalding looks at two things. "One is the academic performance in the broad sense—not just grades— and two is the ability of applicants to present themselves well to the client. Good judgment. We see the cream of the crop in this office, at half-hour interviews. We interview at thirty to forty schools, to broaden our pool of applicants." The goal is forty hires per year; the top suppliers are southern law schools. "Harvard people don't come here. Southerners are maligned [there]."

This recruiter recalls one interview with a female law student. "I can't imagine a woman coming here and not asking about the [discrimination] case. How stupid! They don't want to ask and risk offending us. But such a red flag was raised! In general, you notice how nervous applicants are in the beginning."

Vis-à-vis the case: Betsy Hishon, the plaintiff, was the first woman ever to come up for partnership. Other associates who were under consideration the same year were also turned down. "I don't think anyone here has trouble looking at themselves in the mirror," says a lawyer whose vote was counted in that decision. (Hishon is now a partner at O'Callaghan, Saunders & Stumm in Atlanta.)

Larry Thompson opens our appointment with a dry "I'm in the minority here." Thompson is King & Spalding's lone black partner. A lifelong "soloist," Thompson has pioneered integration almost everywhere he's been: at school, in industry, and here. After graduation from Culver-Stockton College, a small church-related liberal arts school in Missouri, his home state, he received a master's in sociology and industrial relations from Michigan State, then spent almost two years at the Ford Motor Company. From there he enrolled at the University of Michigan Law School. Armed with his degree, he became an in-house lawyer at the Monsanto Corporation.

"Monsanto hired King and Spalding to do work on Astroturf. I though that in order to get to become the general counsel of Monsanto, I'd have to go to a good private firm." He arrived at King & Spalding in 1977, a member of the class of 1977. Larry had to pass the Georgia Bar, "a negative." He was allotted a pay credit for his years of practice but nevertheless took a pay cut. As he had an interest in politics, Thompson, a Republican, who says, "this firm has a high Democratic profile," worked in his free time for Matt Mattingly, the first Republican senator to win a statewide election since Reconstruction.

In 1982 Thompson became the attorney general for Georgia. "I took another pay cut. I left at an inopportune time, after five and a half years here. Things were going well, but I'd never prosecuted before or worked for the federal government before. I was encouraged by Judge [Griffin] Bell to take the position. In 1979, when Judge Bell returned to the firm [from Washington], he gave a speech to the associates, urging us to do pro bono or public service: 'Society has been good to us and our clients,' " he remembers.

Larry began discussing his return to the firm a year before it actually happened. Although not the first black associate at King & Spalding, he was made the first black partner in 1986. "I realize every morning when I shave that I'm black. You're conscious of who and what you are. I hope my career, knock wood, helps others.

"I was the only American black at Culver-Stockton my freshman year. There were only two blacks in my graduate program at MSU. Out of 360 students per class at Michigan Law School, there were less than twenty in my entering class. I was the first black ever in Monsanto's law department, and that was in a city with many black lawyers. So King and Spalding wasn't entirely unusual." Neither of Thompson's parents graduated from high school. His father was a railroad laborer. "I feel compatible with the people here. I'm convinced that from a political point of view, I'm probably the most conservative."

Ralph Levy, the ex-New Yorker, chose King & Spalding solely on the basis of a great day of interviews there. "I felt the most comfortable at King & Spalding, and that was frankly what I based my decision on. Also, the reputation." Coming to this (for lack of a better term) WASPy firm was "a choice I had to make, but it was not an issue I even had to grapple with." He was not the first Jew hired, and it did not merit a moment's hesitation. "My considerations were, one, Atlanta, and two, a large corporate firm. King and Spalding never gave me a reason to doubt. It presented to me damn near the same challenges as Wall Street. I was more concerned about Atlanta's growth spurt than King and Spalding's. I didn't know if I were arriving too late. At the time, I would never have imagined that after twelve years here there would be almost two hundred lawyers."

Levy, the firm's current chairman of the hiring committee, says, "We shouldn't grow at a rate that will jeopardize our culture. Things we took for granted have to be worked on now. We have to assimilate new groups of lawyers. I want new lawyers to learn King and Spalding as I did.

"People who come here are people who, all their lives, have been at the top of wherever they were. They are competitive, aggressive overachievers. There's inevitable competition with others. We do not pay salary or bonus on work; you're in lockstep with your classmates, to reduce competition within peer groups. There is no quota system for partner.

"King and Spalding isn't King and Spalding because of me. I was handed a goodwill, a reputation, a desirable bill of goods, a piece of the institution I had no part in building. Now I feel a very keen responsibility not to mess up. That's the best thing I can do. The people coming behind me are my future."

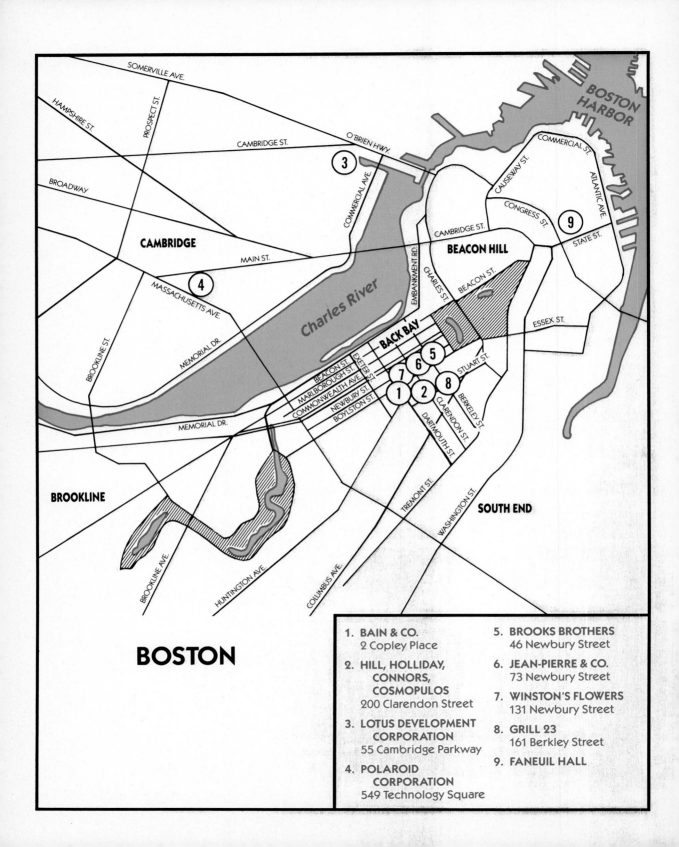

BOSTON

1. **BAIN & CO.**
   2 Copley Place

2. **HILL, HOLLIDAY, CONNORS, COSMOPULOS**
   200 Clarendon Street

3. **LOTUS DEVELOPMENT CORPORATION**
   55 Cambridge Parkway

4. **POLAROID CORPORATION**
   549 Technology Square

5. **BROOKS BROTHERS**
   46 Newbury Street

6. **JEAN-PIERRE & CO.**
   73 Newbury Street

7. **WINSTON'S FLOWERS**
   131 Newbury Street

8. **GRILL 23**
   161 Berkley Street

9. **FANEUIL HALL**

BOSTON

BOSTON

Boston's business community seems to be an outgrowth of its vast academic community. Many people end up in the metropolitan Boston area for college—there are at least forty among which to choose—and stay, thinking cities don't get better than this. And they're right, as long as warm weather isn't a goal. Boston, Cambridge, and the area encompassed by Route 128 (the only legitimate holder of the title "the Silicon Valley of the _____" —fill in the region) are pleasant, offer a high (though somewhat expensive) quality of life, are civilized, and are *very* New England. Four real seasons. Good foliage. The Charles River (which people use and enjoy). More bookstores than anywhere else in America, including Guam. And (I mention this reluctantly) Harvard.

Reluctantly, because Harvard does not need the plug. Reluctantly, because there are other fine undergraduate and graduate insititutions in this city. Which came first, Boston or Harvard? Tough to say, but Boston has become the center of management consulting, a field that seems to have been spawned by *the* business school itself. Think tanks and firms that engage in such arcane fields as biogenetic engineering are not uncommon, and there is an abundance of high-technology companies. (Boston/Cambridge has MIT to thank for some of this activity.) People have jobs that are difficult to explain to laypeople. Of course, they toil in law, retailing, medicine (the Harvard hospitals are considered among the finest in the world), publishing— the whole gamut.

To born-and-bred Bostonians, there is no better possible place in which to live or raise a family. Boston's suburbs are very close to the city's downtown, and the further townships not only reek with history—i.e., Lexington and Concord—but feel very much like the "country." Woods, fields, lakes, hills. Prep schools.

The New World's first and oldest continuing academy, the Boston Latin School, was founded in 1635. It is now a public school. In general, most public schools in the area are rungs above the national norm. The great majority of high school seniors end up going to college.

Cambridge, Boston's sister city, is a real city. Aside from the dauntingly monolithic presence of Harvard, it's a bit more bookish, artsy, and precious than Massachusetts' capital city. People attend poetry readings and drink white wine. They are good, studious cooks. One can get pizza in Cambridge with healthy zucchini and cauliflower instead of the more nefarious nitrites found as toppings elsewhere.

BEST NEIGHBORHOOD WITH DECENT PUBLIC SCHOOLS: Brookline (a suburb)

NICEST NEIGHBORHOODS (BUT YOU'LL PROBABLY HAVE TO SEND YOUR KIDS TO PRIVATE SCHOOL): Back Bay, Beacon Hill

BEST PLACES TO LIVE IF YOU'RE AN ASPIRING ARTIST OR YOU WANT TO LIVE NEAR PEOPLE WHO WEAR ONLY BLACK: Fort Point Channel, South End

BEST NEIGHBORHOOD WITH TAKE-OUT FOOD AND SINGLE PEOPLE WHO ARE ALSO REPUBLI-CANS: Back Bay

MOST OVERPRICED COMMUNITIES FOR SUMMER HOMES: Martha's Vineyard, Nantucket

BEST PUBLIC SCHOOL: Boston Latin School

BEST PRIVATE SCHOOLS: Buckingham, Browne & Nichols; Winsor School (for girls)

BEST ALTERNATIVE SCHOOL: Commonwealth School

ARCHITECT WHO HAS MOST INFLUENCED THE CITY'S SKYLINE: I. M. Pei

MOST POPULAR RESIDENTIAL ARCHITECT: Graham Gund

SOCIALLY INCLINED REALTORS: Landvest; Sotheby's, Itzkan & Marchiel

DECORATORS WHO WOULD DECORATE HOMES PURCHASED THROUGH THOSE REALTORS: William Hodgins, Richard Fitzgerald

DEALERS IN THE FINEST, MOST VALUABLE ART: Vose Galleries, Barbara Krakow

TRENDY GALLERIES FOR PEOPLE WHO WEAR ALL BLACK AND HAVE A LOT OF MONEY: Stux Gallery, Mario Diacono

MOST EXCLUSIVE GOLF CLUB: The Country Club (Brookline)

BEST PUBLIC GOLF FACILITY: Stow Acres (Stow)

MOST EXPENSIVE HEALTH CLUB: Might be the University Club

BEST HEALTH CLUB FOR MEETING POTENTIAL MATES: Back Bay Racket Club

BEST HOTEL FOR BUSINESS TRIPS: Meridien

BEST HOTEL FOR TRYSTS: Out of town (you do not want to have a tryst in Boston)

RESTAURANTS KNOWN FOR BEST CUISINE: Jasper, L'Espalier

BEST RESTAURANTS FOR PEOPLE WHO WEAR BLACK: Commonwealth Grill, St. Cloud

BEST RESTAURANT FOR AN INEXPENSIVE DATE: The Commonwealth Grill (Blue Plate Special)

NOISIEST RESTAURANTS (INTIMACY IMPOSSIBLE): Grille 23, Friday's

BEST SPORTS BAR: Daisy Buchanan

BEST GIMMICKY BAR: Friday's

BEST BARS TO IMPRESS A CLIENT: Ritz Bar, the bar at the Meridien

MOST EXCLUSIVE CITY CLUBS: Chilton Club (women only), Somerset Club (men only)

FANCIEST WINE STORE WHENCE CEOS PROBABLY STOCK THEIR OWN CELLARS: Wine Cellar of Silene

GOURMET STORE GUARANTEED NOT TO RUN OUT OF GOAT CHEESE OR SUN-DRIED TOMATOES: Bildner's

NICEST MOM-AND-POP GROCERY STORE: Deluca's Market

LARGEST DRUGSTORE WITH MOST REMARKABLE SELECTION: Guild's

CORPORATE PARTY PLANNER: Annie B's Catering

HIGH-SOCIETY PARTY PLANNER: Marilyn Riseman

POWER HAIR SALON: Jean Pierre & Co.

NEW WAVE HAIRSTYLIST: Frank Xavier, Diego at the Loft

JUNIOR LEAGUE BEAUTY PARLOR: Michel Kazan

PLACES WHERE LADIES WHO LUNCH ARE LIKELY TO HAVE TEA AFTER A HARD DAY OF SHOPPING, VOLUNTEER WORK, AND TENNIS: Ritz, Four Seasons, Women's Educational and Industrial Union

BEST STORES FOR EXECUTIVE WOMEN: Rae Brewer, Amalia

BEST STORES FOR EXECUTIVE MEN: Louis, Robert Todd

BEST STORES FOR DRESS-UP CLOTHES: Suzanne (for women), Charles Sumner (for women), Sara Fredericks (for women), Serenella (for women), Louis (for men)

BEST SHOPPING RESOURCE FOR PEOPLE WHO WEAR ONLY BLACK CLOTHES: Alan Bilzerian

MOST RELIABLE FLORIST: Winston's

MOST EXOTIC FLORIST: Winston's

TOP JEWELER FOR RESETTING MOTHER'S EMERALDS: Firestone and Parsons

MOST COMPLETE BRIDAL REGISTRIES: Bloomingdale's, Shreve Crump and Low

PROMINENT PHYSICIANS: Dr. Morton Buckley (cardiologist), Dr. Gerald Austin, Lahey Clinic, Dr. Henry Mankin (orthopedics), Dr. Charles Trey (gastroenterologist)

PROMINENT PLASTIC SURGEON WITH EQUALLY PROMINENT CLIENTELE: Dr. John Constable

BEST SEAMSTRESS OR TAILOR FOR ALTERATIONS: Jerry's

POPULAR FACIAL SALON: Elizabeth Grady

MOST EXPENSIVE GARAGE: Brimmer Street Garage

BEST INNOVATIVE JEWELRY: Body Sculpture

POWER TOOLS

POWER LUNCHES

THE HARVEST
44 Brottel Street
Cambridge, MA 02138
(617) 492-1115

Although the restaurant's menu changes every month, these are some typical executive lunch items:

Seafood enchilada, $9.50
Smoked salmon with saffron linguine with dill vinaigrette, $9.50
Veal medallions with fresh melted mozzarella, marinated tomatoes and basil (sandwich), $8.00
Watercress and daikon with clementines and hazel nuts (salad), $5.25
White chocolate kalhua mousse, $4.50
Chocolate hazelnut angel food cake, $4.00

PROMINENT CLIENTELE: Derek Bok (president of Harvard University), Robert Parker (writer, *Spenser* novels), and "a lot of architects and professors from MIT and Harvard."

GRILL 23, Boston
161 Berkley Street
Boston, MA 02116
(617) 542-2255

APPETIZERS:
Cajun shrimp, $8.25
Oysters on the half shell, $6.25

MAIN COURSES:
Caesar salad, $5.50
23 burger (bacon and cheese most popular toppings), $7.50

Cajun chicken sandwich, $7.75
Grilled swordfish, $13.50
Shrimp and scallion omelette, $6.50
New York sirloin, $15.00

DESSERTS:
Cheesecake, $3.75
Brownie à la mode, $4.50
Fresh berries, $9.00

PROMINENT CLIENTELE:
Richard Simmons, Joyce Kuhalik (local Channel 5 News), Liz Walker (local Channel 4 News), Roz Gorin (one of the owners of the restaurant, also runs Gorin Associates—"one of most prominent people in Boston"), Natalie and Chet Curtis (Channel 5 News), Danny DeVito and Rhea Perlman, Robert Urich, Robert Parker, Jane Fonda (came in once)

POWER WATCHES

BAILEY, BANKS & BIDDLE
232 Newbury Street
Boston, MA 02116
(617) 262-7854

BEST SELLER AMONG EXECUTIVE MEN: Men's two-tone Rolex, $2,860; bracelet watch with day and date calendar, eighteen-karat gold and stainless steel. Dials in different colors, including champagne, white, and blue

BEST SELLER AMONG EXECUTIVE WOMEN: Women's two-tone Rolex, $2,480; exactly the same as the men's watch, only in women's dial size

"Most [executive] men buy watches for themselves. They say, 'I'm looking for a men's two-tone Rolex,' then I show them the different-colored dials and they say, 'Put it on my American Express.' Women generally buy for themselves, too, and they also generally have an American Express. They buy the Rolex for a status symbol if they're in business. Christmastime is the only time they get them for gifts."

POWER HAIR

JEAN-PIERRE & COMPANY
73 Newbury Street
Boston, MA 02116
(617) 262-4660

Jean-Pierre is located on Newbury Street in the heart of Boston's commercial district. According to proprietor Jean-Pierre Sanchez, men make up 30 percent of his clientele and of those, 100 percent are executives. (Of the remaining female 70 percent, only some are executives.) When asked how his executive clients differed from the nonexecutives, Jean Pierre offered: "Executives do tend to be very punctual clients. I have not noticed any problems with executive clients, one only notices when there is a problem. But men are, of course, less patient in general than women.

ON TRENDS IN EXECUTIVE HAIR: "Most [executives] change their hairstyles about twice a year. They are willing to do this if the hairdresser takes the time to explain the new style and how it will work for them. They want something that works and something easy. The style will depend on the quality of their hair, their face shape, et cetera. Men tend to be more traditional —a part and a short cut—but that is changing, especially with young executives, anyone under forty-five. The new male executive wants a more avant-garde look, not like in the past. Now they are more willing to go with the style of the season—if it's a longer hair length, then they are more eager to try that than before. Executive women in suits very much still want to look feminine."

ON PERMS: "Perms are very popular. But perms are different today, now you have a variety— root perm, half perm—there are many ways to perm. It will make the hairstyle look softer, and women equate softness with curl and fluff. Some women can pull off a straight, short look, but most want something that is soft, and a curl provides that."

ON COLORING: "Very few women look gorgeous with gray hair unless they are beautiful and have the right complexion. I like the 'young gray' on some, with that steel-gray look on a young face. But mostly, we dye a woman's hair. If they have a small percentage of gray hair, then maybe we just highlight the hair. If there is fifty percent or more gray, then we use a permanent, semipermanent, a tint, stains, etc.—it depends on their lifestyle. For men, I suggest a two-tone, more natural look, and we'll cover the gray with just a tint."

ON BALDING: "Many, many [men with toupees] look as though they have a basket woven on their heads. It is most important, whatever course you take, to have a good haircut. A great haircut can make an implant work better. We change the part, we look at the direction and the weight of the hair. It is the haircut that is important."

ON FACIAL HAIR: "There are no beards. Some men keep moustaches, but they take care of these themselves."

ON NETWORKING IN THE SALON: "Our salon creates a very relaxed, intimate feeling. Clients do not have to network, they can talk about anything, there is no pressure here."

PROMINENT CLIENTS: "We do two of the Boston Celtics, some from the Red Sox, Jean Stapleton, Liv Ullmann (when she is in town), and Ethel Kennedy was in last week."

FEES:
Haircut, including set and blow-dry, $20–$40
Permanent, $50
Hair coloring/highlighting, $60

MOTTO: "Whatever the client wants—no problem!"

FLORIST

WINSTON'S FLOWERS
131 Newbury Street
Boston, MA 02116
(617) 536-6861

Executives make up 90 percent of Winston's Flowers' clientele. According to Mr. Winston, "It's unbelievable! My business has changed dramatically in the past few years. I guess people find I have fair prices and good quality and service, so my business has dramatically increased by word of mouth—the best kind of advertising. It's unbelievable because we are located in the Back Bay area, not the downtown area, so I guess people like what we do." Winston's has fifteen employees plus seven or eight truckers. The shop does a lot of corporate business, delivering flowers to seventy-five to a hundred offices every Monday morning. "We start at 5.00 A.M." The average cost for an arrangement is $40–$70, "depending on the occasion."

WHAT DIFFERENCES DO YOU NOTICE BETWEEN YOUR EXECUTIVE AND NONEXECUTIVE CLIENTS?

"The executives spend more money than the average person, and many businesses send flowers to one another these days. Of course, executives still send flowers to their wives, husbands, girlfriends, or boyfriends, too."

DO EXECUTIVE WOMEN SEND FLOWERS TO MEN, OR IS IT MAINLY MEN SENDING FLOWERS TO WOMEN?

"We send flowers from both men to women and women to men. Men love to get flowers, too, you know. It's such a great gesture to send flowers—there can never be a wrong occasion."

WHAT ARE YOUR MOST POPULAR FLOWERS?

"Generally arrangements, unless they are sending roses, then we usually send cut flowers. Red roses are the most popular—very romantic." When asked about pink or peach or yellow roses, he responded, "We find them so much more romantic and soft." But "the red is for serious courting!"

WHO ARE SOME OF YOUR PROMINENT CLIENTS?

Mr. Winston would not mention names, but he did say that his clientele included "doctors, lawyers, politicians, and real estate moguls."

BAIN &
COMPANY, INC.

Bain & Company, Inc.

HISTORY & OPERATIONS

William W. Bain founded Bain & Company, one of the foremost management consulting firms in the world, shortly after embarking on a career in business. After graduating from Vanderbilt University, where he majored in history and economics, Bain went to work as a fundraiser for his alma mater, a job which paid only a minimal salary (reported in *Fortune* as $19,000 per year). When Vanderbilt considered starting a business school, Bain sought the advice of fellow alumnus Bruce Henderson, the founder of the Boston Consulting Group (BCG), a leading management consulting firm. Instead, Henderson offered him a job, and Bain, with no prior experience, went to work as a management consultant. That was in 1967. By 1973 Bain was earning $150,000 as a group vice-president and was ready to move out on his own.

That year, Bain started Bain & Company with Patrick Graham, a colleague from the Boston Consulting Group, and several other BCGers. He built up business for the firm by devising strategies that were unique in management consulting. (Bain's innovative methods have since come to be known as "relationship consulting.") Bill Bain felt that in order to best improve a company's fortunes, he would have to have a thorough understanding of the competition, as well as access to proprietary information. In order to secure such access, he guaranteed potential clients that his firm would not work for any other company in their field, either domestically or internationally. In exchange for that exclusivity, Bain asked for a long-term commitment from his clients. In addition, he stipulated that his firm be allowed to work in direct partnership with the chief executive officers of its client companies.

Bain & Company has grown steadily since its inception, primarily on the basis of its reputation for achieving remarkable success. Though the firm will not disclose the names of its clients, it claims to add at least five to ten times the cost of its services to the profitability to those companies. Since the firm was started in Boston with fewer than a dozen professionals in 1973, Bain has expanded its presence to San Francisco, London, Munich, Paris, and Tokyo and now has a staff of almost nine professionals.

Recruitment and training are among the most important of the company's functions and the means by which it stays at the forefront of its field. Though Bain has traditionally relied on recruiting MBAs from the top of their classes at the top business schools in the United States and abroad, the salaries they command are so high that the firm has begun recruiting increasing numbers of promising college graduates, who become associate consultants. (Until about four years ago they were known as research associates.) ACs begin their careers at Bain with a rigorous two-week in-house training program, and they can expect to be promoted to consultants—on a par with MBA consultants—within several years without ever attending business school.

In 1983 Bain & Company started Bain Venture Capital, a venture capital and leveraged buyout firm that is a separate legal entity from the firm proper. The rationale behind starting the offshoot firm was that Bain consultants should apply the same strategies they use to improve the growth of client companies to companies in which the partners have an ownership stake. To date, Bain Venture Capital—which has nine professionals—has acquired or founded about twenty companies: GS ROOFING PRODUCTS COMPANY, a manufacturer of roofing materials based in Irving, Texas; NAPPE-BABCOCK, a manufacturer of vinyl products (including replacement cushions and accessories for outdoor furniture and food and beverage coolers and cases) based in Richmond, Virginia; CALUMET COACH COMPANY, a manufacturer of mobile CAT-scan systems based in Calumet City, Illinois; HOLSON COMPANY, the largest manufacturer and distributor of photo albums in the United States, based in Wilton, Connecticut; SANBORN ASSOCIATES, a designer, manufacturer, and marketer of high-speed centrifugal fluid recycling systems for use primarily in metal-working plants, based in Wrentham, Massachusetts; KEY AIRLINES, an air charter carrier based in Salt Lake City; OMNI/MEDIVISION, THE EYE COOPERATIVE (formerly three separate companies), an operator of ambulatory surgical centers dedicated to eye care, a manager of ophthalmic clinics, and a distributor of ophthalmic surgical products throughout the United States, based in Boston; STAPLES, a chain of retail discount office supply stores based in Newton, Massachusetts; BABBAGES, a retailer of software for home computers (with forty-eight stores in eight markets at the end of 1987) based in Dallas; WYNDMERE CAPITAL MANAGEMENT, a manager of institutional pension fund money based in Hartford, Connecticut; COMMERCIAL MORTGAGE COMPANY OF AMERICA, a financial firm that acquires commercial mortgages from lending institutions, packages them, and sells financial instruments to the secondary market, based in Boston; DOMAIN, a group of home furnishing stores based in Norwood, Massachusetts; BRIGHT HORIZONS, a network of high-quality child care centers located at worksites, based in Cambridge, Massachusetts; PRESIDENTIAL AIRLINES (operates under the name Continental Express), a carrier closely associated with Continental Airlines, based in Washington, D.C.; BURNES OF BOSTON, a manufacturer and retailer of picture frames based in Newton Center, Massachusetts; and SPORTS AUTHORITY, a discount sporting goods store based in Fort Lauderdale, Florida. Among those for which financial assessments have been made, all but one have increased the value of the original investment.

Today, Bain & Company houses roughly 1,400 employees with more than 800 professionals and approximately 70 officers. The company's revenues have grown at an average of 50 percent per year since its founding, to more than $150 million in 1986 and almost $200 million in 1987, with 30 percent from consulting for overseas clients, which has become the fastest-growing part of the firm's business. Bain's highly confidential list of clients—more than fifty—includes Guinness, Baxter-Travenol Laboratories, Chrysler Motors, Dunn & Bradstreet, Owens Illinois, and Sterling Drugs. (The above clients were made public in an article in *Fortune* magazine of April 27, 1987.)

Professionals work in case teams, and up until the vice-presidential level they tend to move around among assignments. (Vice-presidents generally stay with one client longer). New members of the consulting staff are typically exposed to three or four different cases in their first year. The majority of professionals work for two clients at a time, although some officers work for only one at a time. Professionals are transferred to the firm's offices overseas either by their own request or in accordance with the needs of the firm.

Bain & Company, which has been called "the KGB of consulting," is known for what remains unknown about the firm. Upon being hired, all employees are required to sign nondisclosure forms. Different forms are used at different levels of the company, but disclosure at all levels includes names of clients, financial information about Bain, financial information about clients, any description of client work from which clients could be identified, and certain data about Bain such as the number of employees in different offices. According to Bain's in-house publication, *The Bain Arrow*, "We do not disclose the names of clients—even when a client relationship has become more or less public knowledge. We do not discuss in public our specific work for a client in a way that would even suggest the client's identity. Any competitive information developed for a client belongs to the client—it is proprietary and secret. We will also keep confidential any information about our firm which we consider proprietary and which, if disclosed, could result in competitive disadvantage. In general, this includes such facts as our revenues, our fees, the exact number and location of clients, our profitability, the number of employees in our offices, the exact number of new hires, exact figures in our compensation and the mix of staff."

(Information provided by Clint Collins, company spokesperson.)

REVENUES: More than $150 million in 1986. 1987 revenues approached $200 million.

EARNINGS: Firm will not disclose.

OFFICES: Headquarters in Boston and additional offices in San Francisco, London, Munich, Paris, and Tokyo.

NUMBER OF EMPLOYEES: Nearly 1,400 worldwide, with more than nearly 900 professionals, and between 400 and 500 support staff. (Firm will not release numbers for associate consultants and consultants). Bain Venture Capital employs 14 people.

AVERAGE AGE OF EMPLOYEES: About thirty-two, not counting associate consultants. The average age of associate consultants is probably around twenty-three or twenty-four.

TURNOVER: No specific figures, but the firm claims that turnover among professional staff is close to half the normal rate for professional service firms.

RECRUITMENT: *Consultants—Domestic:* Brigham Young University, University of Chicago, Columbia University, Dartmouth College, Harvard University, Massachusetts Institute of Technology, New York University, Northwestern University, Stanford University, Wharton School of Finance at the University of Pennsylvania, Yale University. *International:* Imede, Inseat, London Business School. *Associate Consultants:* Amherst College, Brown University, Brigham Young University, Bucknell University, University of California at Berkeley and Davis, University of Chicago, Claremont McKenna College, Columbia University, Georgetown University, Harvard University, Massachusetts Institute of Technology, Notre Dame University, Oberlin College, Princeton University, Rice University, Stanford University, Trinity College (Connecticut), Tufts University, University of Virginia, Wellesley College, Wesleyan University, Wharton School of Finance, Williams College, Yale University. *International:* University of Bristol, Cambridge University, University of Durham, University of Essex, Imperial University, University of Liverpool, London School of Economics, University of Manchester, University of Nuremburg, Oxford University, University of Tokyo, University of Warwick.

NUMBER OF NEW HIRES PER YEAR: Over two hundred people for the consultancy staff.

RANGE OF STARTING SALARIES: Base starting salary for consultants is in the mid-$60,000 range. For associate consultants, it's in the mid-$30,000 range.

POLICY FOR RAISES: Professionals are reviewed twice a year, and raises are awarded once a year on the basis of merit.

TRAINING PROGRAMS: All new associate consultants go through the Associate Consultant Training program. The program is an intense two weeks and brings together associates from around the world. Additional programs include the Management Training Vehicle (MTV) for managers and formal training for consultants, vice-presidents, and support staff.

BENEFITS: Comprehensive medical and dental insurance; noncontributory life insurance (three times salary, with contributory insurance as an option); employee stock ownership plan; deferred compensation (amounts to a profit-sharing plan, but is not strictly profit sharing); tuition reimbursement (which varies according to an employee's individual situation); long-term disability insurance; ninety-day salary compensation plan (short-term disability); and accident insurance while traveling for the company.

VACATION: Three weeks after the first year, four weeks at the officer level or after ten years, five weeks after fifteen years or after three years as a vice-president, plus nine and a half regular paid holidays per year.

ADDITIONAL PERKS: The firm has an officer sabbatical program through which officers can elect to take a yearlong sabbatical after a certain number of years with the firm.

BONUSES: Everyone on the consultancy staff is on a base salary plus bonus compensation. Bonuses are based on company performance plus merit, although most people get approximately the same bonuses as others at their level. Support staff is not eligible for bonuses.

ANNUAL PARTY: Every Bain office has an annual summer party for employees and their spouses and friends. The party is relatively informal. (In 1987 the Boston office planned one with a Hawaiian theme. 1988 was Bain's fifteenth anniversary. The theme, "What Were You Doing 15 Years Ago?" was carried out in seventies dress and music. In addition, the Boston office hosts an informal Christmas party for employees. The policy at other offices varies. The Munich office, for example, hosts an annual ski weekend.

DRESS CODE: Standard professional. "Men in suits and ties, women in suits or dresses."

AVERAGE WORKDAY: Hours for the support staff are 8:30 A.M. to 5:30 P.M. "The consulting staff generally puts in longer hours than that."

SOCIAL ATMOSPHERE: "A good bit of socializing after office hours, particularly among younger employees. I would say there's a pretty congenial atmosphere at the firm."

HEADQUARTERS: Bain leases four floors in a building in the Back Bay section of Boston, in a large, modern, shopping, hotel, and office building complex called Copley Place.

CHARITABLE CONTRIBUTIONS: Firm will not disclose amounts. Major areas of giving are education and pro bono work in health care.

INTERESTED APPLICANTS CAN SEND RÉSUMÉS TO:
Recruiting
Bain & Company, Inc.
2 Copley Place
Boston, MA 02116
(617) 572-2000

If you've heard of Bain & Company, chances are you've heard it's a secretive place. Well, it is, and that's why it's noteworthy that the firm has decided to go public via this book. Bain is a leading management consulting firm that conducts its business quite differently from the industry norm: rather than accumulating many clients within certain industries, Bain will not accept more than one client per; how else, the firm feels, can one win in the marketplace? How else does one avoid conflicts of interest? In return, Bain and its clients (who shall remain nameless by virtue of company policy) endeavor to embark on long-term relationships, another anomaly.

Based in Boston, the consulting business's mecca, Bain is a confederation of some of the hardest-working people I have ever met. Does your client (who shall remain nameless) need to talk to you? Is he based in another city? You'll fly to see him at a moment's notice, won't you? (Come, come—your bag is probably packed just in case.) Bainies are well groomed, well spoken, highly motivated, and nice. If you were to write a collective biography of its professionals, you would include an undergraduate degree from a prestigious college (preferably Ivy League or Brigham Young—more on that in a moment) and an MBA from Harvard (or Stanford, or Wharton, or Columbia, or Brigham Young, but mostly Harvard). Bain hires more than a few graduates of BYU for several reasons: The success of earlier BYU alumni portends well for future graduates (who are now recruited), it has a well-regarded business school, and it offers upstanding citizens as well. They fit fine at Bain.

Primarily a grabber of MBAs, the firm is making a concerted effort to expand its undergraduate recruitment and bypass the graduate business degree. John Rutherford, a native New Zealander and the partner responsible for hiring and training, explains, "Most consulting firms hire 'experts.' Our kind of consulting requires more thorough analysis, so we tend to hire people who are just smart, but green. We generally hire MBAs, but BAs have been impressive, and now we hire more of them, maybe sixty percent. We used to encourage them to leave for business school. We all went to business school." These days, a job offer from Bain is one of the plummier opportunities a college senior can receive. Period. "We used to hire nice folks from nice schools," John continues. "Now we hire the top people from top schools." And thus the *crème de la* competitive school *crème* who do not wish to matriculate immediately to Harvard Business School come here. ("Some leave to go to business school, return, and get tuition reimbursement.") And they're thrilled. And they know they'll have to work like crazy. They've been abundantly warned.

Management consulting is a relatively new field. Although a service long offered by the large public accounting firms, as a distinct industry it started to hit its stride in the seventies. Its leaders have been McKinsey & Company and the Boston Consulting Group. Darrell Rigby, a vice-president at Bain, joined the company officially in 1978 after graduation from Harvard Business School. (He had worked at Bain the previous summer.) Also a graduate of Brigham Young, he says, "When I joined this company, people thought it was too risky." (At the time, Bain was only five years old.) "I chose Bain because I enjoyed my interviews [here] the most. And I thought the people would be fun. Consulting was my first choice. You get exposure to a wide variety of industries." Today recruiting is one of Rigby's responsibilities.

"Recruiting isn't an evaluative testing process," he explains. "It's a 'fit' process." He has three criteria uppermost in his mind during an interview, in this order: "One, do I see evidence that this is a good team player?" For the applicants who have not had team (sports) experience, Darrel gauges "teamability" thus: "I put them in a group of three and see how they behave. We'll talk about the Boston Celtics, anything. How do they relate to other people? Two, do I see the intellectual capability to solve tough analytic problems?" Ultimately, he is looking for "people who know how to set a goal for themselves, and no matter what stands between themselves and the goal, they surmount it. I'm looking for people who don't make excuses for why they almost did it. Work is very demanding, and you must be self-directing. There's no road map. You must determine your next three or four steps. Three—this is the hardest to assess—can this person grow to be a peer of the most important CEOs in the world?" You see, the thing about Bain is that its people permeate their client companies from the top down. A consulting engagement means working with the CEO as well as with lower-level managers. A working relationship with Bain is like taking an antibiotic; people work from the inside at all levels when the virus hits, and afterward, too, to ensure efficacy.

The process begins at Associate Consultant Training, held two weeks every October for new associate consultants from all the company's offices. A hundred of them from London, San Francisco, Tokyo, Paris, Munich, and Boston gather at different conference centers in the Boston area. In 1987 AC training was held on Cape Cod; in 1986 it was conducted at the Sheraton Tara in Danvers, Massachusetts, in rooms that were divested of their televisions and other worldly distractions before the ACs' arrival. (In 1988, however, the TVs were reinstated, Bain risking the extra expense of ACs' watching the pay movie channel.) [Author's note: I resist the temptation to refer to ACs as "students," although that is their role.] For two weeks, under the leadership of "trainers"—Bainies just a few years senior to them—the ACs go through a punishing regimen that begins with breakfast with one's case team at 7:00 A.M.

through a punishing regimen that begins with breakfast with one's case team at 7:00 A.M. and ends long after dinner, with homework. (My last experience traveling with a group this young was during spring break in Florida—they were mostly interested in drinking, sunning, and coming home alive; *these* kids are carrying their HP-12C calculators and talking about their companies' strategies! There is no boister, no revelry. It's work all day and evening, and it's serious.)

ACs are divided into case groups for the entire duration. At seminars patterned after the Harvard Business School case system, Bainies discuss solutions for ailing businesses. In group exercises, they make slides—3M acetates for overhead projectors—of graphs and pies and other graphic theses. Teams get a lot of feedback, both from their own trainers and from rotating trainers. The value of the slides is emphasized throughout. (When the ACs' slides are reviewed, they are critiqued for their neatness and design, as well as for their clarity of content. By the end of the program, people will have created umpteen slide masterpieces.)

The trainers at AC Training have never trained before (to keep the experience fresh). They do, however, spend two days being trained to train. Bain is large enough at this point for no one to have to be a trainer twice. This is preferable: "It's too draining, too much time. If you give it your all once, you can't always perform as well." Nick Prettejohn of Bain London is saddled with the title and responsibility of head trainer. At twenty-six, he seems a seasoned leader. He also seems tired by the evening of the tenth (second-to-last) night. "You use the same skill managing a case team as you do managing training." His preparation included meeting with Bain partners in Boston every three weeks for the previous five months, as well as the training he received when he was an AC. "People get wrapped up in helping other people. They feel a personal responsibility as role models." While there is help and support from management, the trainers run their own program. They are all under the age of thirty. "Trainees are all self-motivated and desperate to learn. Trainers are inundated with requests to do more. There's a real letdown at the end."

One of the first things to make a strong impression [on me] was how this program almost erases the cultural differences among the various offices and locations around the world. Aside from the spread of the shirt collar and the diverse accents, it is one world, one culture. Each group is made up of people from the different offices speaking the same language, using the same jargon, sharing front page business concerns, be that the front page of *The Boston Globe, The San Francisco Examiner, The Times* (London), *Le Monde, Asahi Shimbun* (Tokyo), or *Süddeutsche Zeitung* (Munich). Nick, who studied PPE—philosophy, politics, and economics, a notoriously demanding and prestigious program at Oxford, and was president of the famed Oxford (Debating) Union, reveals his surprise at the similarities among Bainies around the world. "I am struck when I meet trainers from Boston—we do the same job." Furthermore, he met his American wife during AC Training in 1985, when he was an associate. (His wedding took place a mere six weeks prior to the 1986 session.) His wife left Bain, moved to England, and is now enrolled in graduate school. "The most pronounced difference is that on the Monday following this boot camp, the Americans must report to work, but the Europeans get the day off."

Why is this fortnight so grueling? Nick maintains, "The first time out, that's what we wanted to do." He admits there is an us-them mentality at first. "Trainers are viewed as Bain management, and the trainees feel themselves to be the labor union. We graded people and wanted them to realize it wasn't a holiday. That wasn't necessary. If we give them a free hour, they want more work. They want more value for their time. Each day, associates fill out forms evaluating what they've done." Anyway, Nick dislikes the term grueling. "It's *intense.* Emotionally. They have to become a team under these circumstances. They begin to understand the purpose of working in a team. People who dread this—both trainers and trainees—become the most avid fans." It is likely that most consultants will be trainers at some point in their young lives." They are notified about their participation six months ahead of time. "It's an honor, but really a mixed blessing."

We are discussing a Harvard case study on a company we'll call "Winnebago." There are about thirty people in this room, called "Camelot IV." (At the Tara Sheraton, bellmen dress like Beefeaters, and conference rooms have that royal touch.) The twenty men and nine women are dressed in business suits, required during the day. It's 8:45 A.M., and even though the associates worked late—no *Late Night with David Letterman* for this gang—they are attentive and professional. They are seated in a large square with their names printed on cards before them, and the class, one of four following the exact same curriculum, is conducted by a trainer from the Boston office. I notice that I am not noticed, which I appreciate (I did do the reading in advance, just in case) and the process is not one of intimidation, but rather one of collaboration.

It is evident that everyone here has done his or her homework. Everyone is prepared to make a presentation. True, when Patrick is called on, everyone else sighs with relief. An associate calculates, "There's a one-in-eighteen chance of being called on." The presenter's hands are trembling, but his voice and comments reflect assurance. Most of the guys are wearing red ties, some speak with German and British accents . . . still a surprise. I spy a note-passing maneuver, but that, too, seems conscientious and mostly about the content of the class. When on participant asks, "Did we think right?" he is rejoined by general laughter. "Winnebago" soon becomes "we." Aha! This is the genesis of the strong identification with the client for which Bain is famous. The lead presenter is applauded and presented with a toy recreational vehicle as a reward.

At the Tara Sheraton, the goofing around is minimal—no, virtually nonexistent—save for that of the Bain senior management, who appear not to take themselves too seriously. At the banquet luncheon that noon, we are greeted at our tables with tiny plastic dinosaurs. This is a clue, though to what we do not know. The buffet is followed by speeches introducing the Integrative Exercise, the last rite of AC Training. Amid great drama, our new "Master Trainer" makes his way into the room. He is a life-sized (well, human-sized) dinosaur. "No more Mr. Nice Guy," Nick intones. "Integrative Exercise Rex is a breaker of spirit." Whereupon the Master Trainer shows his deadpan comedic training film. It spoofs boot camp to the tune of the *M*A*S*H* theme music. The footage is spectacular. It shows actual senior management in camouflage, disembarking from helicopters and engaged in guerrilla warfare. The associates are overwhelmed. Their faces register, "I can't believe these people are so cool!" Ralph Willard, one of Bill Bain's original partners and the head of Bain-Europe, is seen battling the dinosaur, Integrative Exercise Rex. He says, "I love the smell of napalm in the morning," quoting *Apocalypse Now*. The next scene shows a collapsed Willard. He's lost the battle. Does this man have any dignity? Does anyone?

While the ACs are working on matters far too esoteric and difficult for my poor illogical no-math-since-eleventh-grade mind to comprehend, I get to screen some of Bain's videos, which are some of the most effective recruiting propaganda I've ever seen in my life. It's a shame, since Bain & Company wears the mantle of privacy, that applicants won't get to see them. I'll try to reveal as much as I can, however.

In *The Right Stuff,* which deals with life before Bain, consultants talk about their passions outside the office. One fellow was a creator of and performer in a rock musical slated to open at New York's Public Theater. One professional worked in a literacy project in South Africa. One was a pizza delivery entrepreneur as a student at Oxford. One woman with an MBA was the foreman of a heavy machinery factory before joining Bain. Another woman, an American living in Hamburg, became the manager of a country-and-western band there. There was a triathlete. And an Israeli woman, who graduated first in her class at Harvard Business School, having arrived without a command of the English language.

If this tape is any indication, there is less homogeneity at Bain than can be detected by the naked eye. Sure, at the office people look more or less alike, but their expressions of what they have done and what they do contain no buzzwords. They are not programmed. While a bit of brainwashing probably occurs during training and during the early period of being a zealous newcomer, by and large these folks are themselves and not some figment of what Bainies must be.

In the first place, to be a Bainie, you must survive six to ten interviews (presuming your academic record justifies them).

The associates' tenure is about three years, although many depart after two. Three-year veterans become consultants-in-training, then consultants. It takes an average of three more years to become manager, and two to three more after that to become a vice-president. No one knows how long it takes to get from AC to VP, since the program hasn't been in place long enough. "The definition of having made it at this firm is to become a vice-president." Arriving MBAs can make vice-president in about five years. "It's a very important goal for people. We don't have an 'up-or-out' policy as other consulting firms do, but it sort of happens anyway. If your classmates move up and you don't, your ego wouldn't allow you to stay. You were always in the top of the class through school."

Bain used to be a partnership. Professionals of the rank of vice-president think of themselves as partners and use the term more frequently than they do "VP." "We feel that way about each other." At the top of the totem pole is a group of eight people (not counting Bill Bain, who, as president and chairman, participates in senior management meetings) designated "Directors." It's a new title, a special honor; part of management. Directors are a tad older than everyone else, with an average of just over forty years.

As far as attrition is concerned, "People do not leave to work for a client directly. It's discouraged. Our success with clients is due to their feeling that we're independent and objective. Clients used to frequently offer Bainies jobs, but it's not in either party's interest. If I worked for the client, I wouldn't be able to effect so much change," a vice-president explains. "Also, we get paid a lot here. And there's a breadth of opportunity here. When people leave, by and large they go into start-up and entrepreneurial situations." It is conceivable that Bainies would be interested in having more hands-on control than is afforded them in the role of consultant. "Most of the things we recommend *do* get implemented. But if I'd rather be a doer than an adviser, I'd much rather it be my own," he says. "If you want to work for big business, Bain is where you want to work."

Bain's mission statement seems to have been memorized by the ACs prior to their training. It focuses on three points: "The Bain vision of the most productive client relationship and *single-minded dedication* to achieving it with each client; The Bain community of *extraordinary teams;* The Bain approach to *creating value,* based on a sharp competitive and customer focus, the most effective analytic techniques, and our process for collaboration with the client." (Italics mine.) Throughout the training program, associates use the three criteria in their analyses of companies. And Bill Bain talks about single-minded dedication in the videotape made expressly for trainees. He cites the mandate of "being needed by important clients, and by 'important,' I mean any of our clients." "We're so used to having them with us," a client says on camera, "we sometimes forget who's us and who's them. Bain hates our competition more than we do."

This outward competitiveness is supposedly not a reflection of Bain's internal culture. "It's competitive to get a job at Bain, but we try to direct peoples' innate competitiveness to our clients. There used to be stars at Bain, although the emphasis was on the team," John Rutherford, now a director, says. "People who try to separate themselves don't go over too well." He draws a comparison between the outstanding consultant and Larry Bird, forward of the most favorite of Bain's institutionalized pleasures: the Boston Celtics. (Bill Bain has two autographed basketballs—one by Red Auerbach and another by Auerbach and the team—in places of honor in his otherwise sedate office.) "He's not out for himself. We used to promote or raise people with special talent, but it was creating a bit of competition. We promote within one's class. Competition among consultants is actively discouraged." It engenders a sense of betrayal to the organization.

New associates are placed into case teams before training and returned whence they came immediately following their two-week immersion, "for perhaps a year. Plus they're added to another team. You're pretty transferable after a year. If you want, you can switch to other clients. The first couple of years you're not an industry expert but a good analyzer and problem solver. At a senior level, you stay with your client—you have a great stake in them, they need continuity, and you are a close personal adviser." Employees sit in "neighborhoods" or "bays" —alcoves of ten to fifteen people who may or may not be working for the same client. Bainies have dubbed their work stations "Upper Back Bay," "Bay-Jing," "Marvin Bay," "Bombay," "The Bay of Pigs," and "Montego Bay," which hosted a beach party in November 1987. Glass is the stuff many walls are made of; they are the construction material equivalent of the first-name-only culture that prevails.

To a chief executive officer, the act of hiring a consultant—like seeking psychiatric counseling—can be (mis)interpreted as an act of weakness. "Clients are sometimes macho in their attitude that they think they should know how to solve or manage for themselves. They hire lawyers because they recognize that they are not lawyers." To assuage the resistant CEO's fears, Bain will never reveal the identity of its clients, and "we strongly encourage the company to take credit for Bain's strategies." Again, that's *team* thinking. Value added. CEOs must "take ownership" of the ideas and strategies Bain recommends in order to champion them within their own teams. "All it takes is the chief executive to hire us, not the company." However, if Bain were to interact only with the uppermost levels of their clients' companies, there would be resentment at the lower tiers of company management, not to mention spotty reinforcement of the new policies. "The best thing about a service company is to get the client to feel ownership." Admittedly, "it's hard to give away your ideas sometimes."

Bain has become the comfortable terminus of the careers of many motivated young people who possibly never pictured themselves in the midst of big business. Mark Nunnelly (his real name) is a graduate of Centre College of Kentucky, where he studied liberal arts. In the back of his mind, he imagined being a teacher somewhere along the road. He moved to Washington, D.C., to work as a legislative aide on Capitol Hill, then on to Procter & Gamble in Cincinnati. There Mark faced the question of continuing his education through either law or business school. "I felt business made yeses happen. In terms of making an impact, business was it. My long-term interest is in the public sector; money is less important." And away it was to Harvard Business School.

He spent his in-between summer at Bain, returning after graduation the following spring because "I decided Bain was the best fit." Soon afterward, Nunnelly began to travel on business. "I worked for three clients for one and a half years, then I commuted between Boston and Tokyo for two months. I moved there for six months." Mark was not told he *had* to relocate. "If I had turned down the move to Tokyo, there would have been no risk. I risked more by leaving my current boss to try a new project." When he returned to the States, he commuted to London. "I've been in four of Bain's six offices regularly. The Bain culture is

intact in Boston, London, and Paris. It's different in Japan; they hate their competitors and
love their teams, but there's less openness of personality."

One of Mark's favorite aspects of his job is "watching clients go from hating me to thanking
me."

I sit in a hotel room adjoining the trainers' lounge and office screening videotapes, somewhat
oblivious to the hubbub next door. While *The Bain Community at First Glance* is playing,
four Bainies come into the room to watch the man-on-the-street-style interviews, as familiar
as a favorite *Honeymooners* rerun. If they know all the lines, they do not recite them in sync to
the tape.

R alph Willard is one of the founders of Bain. He's just flown into Danvers from London,
to which he has just moved. In addition to running Bain's international business ("thirty
percent of our business"), he is the man in charge of human resources and one of three vice-
chairmen. His Burberry barely doffed, he's ready to chat. Born in Kansas, Willard matriculated at Stanford (class of '65) and worked for a few years before entering . . . yes . . . the
Harvard Business School. It was there he was turned on to the notion of consulting. "There
was reinforcement during business school that consulting was intellectually rigorous, like
Harvard. It seemed like what I always knew I could do." He spent his summer between his
first and second years at McKinsey and, though offered a permanent job there, chose the
Boston Consulting Group, "which seemed more exciting.

"Bill [Bain] was my boss at BCG." When Bain left the firm to start his own, Willard came
soon after. "I joined a few hours after he left BCG. It wasn't a hard decision to make. It took
two minutes."

The beginning of the new consulting firm was more than a rejection of the values and
practices of their previous employer. Bain, Willard, et al. had succeeded at BCG, but they
clearly had ideas about what they would not do: "Not work for competitor companies. That's
why Bill left BCG. Head-to-head competitors needed information; there were leaks, no integrity. We finally said, 'Screw it.' " There was no formal codification of bylaws and policies, at
first, but they represented "the personal beliefs of a small number of people. We were
interested in solving problems, helping people, and the rush you get in helping people. The
key was making it something we wanted to do ourselves for a long time, not to develop it like
a [temporary] consulting exercise. The negative was having to constantly sell yourself to new
business. We were the most successful guys at BCG, so it was more than a hunch. This culture
wasn't intuitive or antirational; the way we were succeeding was anticultural where we were
[at BCG]."

No one in the pilot group ever imagined that this fledgling company in this fledgling
industry would ever be so big or so prosperous. Today Bain is the second largest consulting
firm specializing in strategy, domestically and internationally; "number two in Europe, but
it's close, number three in Germany, and the leader in the market in France." Willard
continues, "Success has its own momentum. It doesn't make us cocky, it makes us scared. I

am anxious that we live up to ourselves. I get a little scared myself. I can't coast. I'm forty-five years old, I made my forture, I came off the farm, and I can't relax. I think of our obligation. We're winning. We have time to determine how we can be the best company."

New business typically finds Bain, not the other way around. Word of mouth, often coming from CEOs who are on the boards of directors of client companies, is the firm's most powerful tool. The fact of the matter is that according to a Price Waterhouse audit commissioned by *Fortune* magazine, "the stock market value of all Bain's U.S. clients has increased 319% since 1980, compared with 141% for the Dow-Jones industrial average and 67% for an index of stocks in industries in which Bain has clients" (*Fortune,* April 27, 1987, p. 99). [Author's note: Prior to "Black Monday," October 19, 1987.]

The client relationship is initially nurtured in a gratis consultation lasting approximately three months, "for a quick-hit solution. We pitch our approach and the long-term relationship. If the business is continued, there are no retroactive charges." Bain wants to start off with a measure of goodwill.

I t is almost time for each group to make its final presentation. Integrative Exercise has reared its ugly head this Friday afternoon, and teamwork is definitely in action. "My" case team has mastered the art of delegation, and everyone is handling the aspects of the problem he or she can do best. {I offer to call out for pizza.} When the exercise gets the best of me, I investigate the facilities.

The Bainies have succeeded in turning a normal (albeit Anglicized) convention-ready hotel into the prototypical "smart nerd dorm"—the kind where people knock on each other's doors to keep the noise down because they're studying. (They go so far as to decorate the doors to their rooms the way they probably did in college.) One difference is that even after two weeks of finalslike pressure, the Bainies are attractive. They manage to look fresh because their white, blue, and striped shirts are laundered for them. In fact, in between classes, students —ACs, I mean—pick up their dry cleaning from large racks. How they can distinguish their button-down shirts from one another is yet another dimension of the Bain mystique.

In addition to the travel and lodging costs and the billable hours of the associates and trainers, who are unavailable for two weeks, this is a huge production. There are six full-time staff people on call twenty-four hours a day. (One AC from Munich needed an emergency appendectomy.) Bain has brought in fifty computers, several photocopy machines, overhead projectors up the wazoo, file cabinets, shelving, VCRs, video cameras, tables, lights, papers, supplies, toy dinosaurs—no wonder each year the company spends well over a million dollars on training.

Except for the Saturday and half of the Sunday in the middle of the program, there is almost no free time. (There are two fifteen-minute breaks each day. All told, in twelve days there's a total of nineteen hours and fifteen minutes off, if you're counting.) People literally don't go outside at all. Still, it doesn't look like sex occurs here. And even though trainers get their own rooms (trainees must share doubles), they say that sex is less likely for them than it is for the ACs. (Anyway, many of the trainers are married.)

As my team makes its final presentation, their attentiveness belies their exhaustion. As if on the hot seat, they work hard to impress a partner who's just driven up from Boston. We are told we did "a very, very good" job. (I am proud.) We never did find out the significance of the toy dinosaurs.

Finally, the ACs are released from their business decorum, responsibilities, and attire in order to change for the cocktail party and graduation banquet. Finally, in casual garb, they do look their ages: twenty-one and twenty-two.

It honestly feels like graduation, with the partners appearing like professors, deans, and trustees at the final celebration. Here is the rambunctious playful side that's been missing. Here are funny wearable party favors—masks, fake teeth, wax lips, and furry beards—which everyone applies between sips of their drinks. (It's Halloween. Whether they give out masks every year at AC Training, I do not know.) There's so much hugging and screaming and impromptu speechifying, it's as if the associates had gone through a profound transformation within the half hour between Integrative Exercise and the party.

The highlight of this frivolity is a performance by the legendary Bain Band. Made up of consultants and staff people (who shall remain nameless), these men and women perform— more than competently—Top Forty hits with Bainified lyrics. "Jesus is Just All Right with Me" becomes "Working at Bain's All Right with Me." I can't tell whether this band is truly sensational or whether I'm just having a great time. I already feel nostalgic for the two days I've been sequestered. They *are* musically sophisticated, and as the lyrics are provided on a movie screen, people try to sing along. "Secret Agent Man" becomes "Frequent Flyer Man," "The Boogie-Woogie Bugle Boy of Company C" comes alive as "The Biggie Wiggie CEO of Company B," "Fame" not surprisingly translates into "Bain!" "Strangers in the Night" finds its soul as "ACs in the Night," and, for the sheer singability of it, the hit of the evening is Bain's—actually manager Kevin Rollins'—version of the Eagles' song "Lyin' Eyes":

MISSIN' SLIDES

CHORUS:

I can't find those missin' slides,
Like to know where they reside.
If they don't turn up it's my hide,
I just can't seem to find those missin' slides.

Got a preez on Monday, it's a big one,
Givin' this one to the CEO.
Late Friday night my ACs check production,
They get me the last slides and home I go.

Saturday arrives, I wake up slowly,
I'll put the slides in order and review.
But as I check them one by one I panic,
I find that I am missin' quite a few.

CHORUS

My life passes before me like a vision,
The blood drains from my face and so I sit,
Then leaping up I race back to the office,
If I don't find them I'll be in deep . . . trouble.

I ransack desks of case team and production,
And make some phone calls but nobody's home.
A phone mail APB could be the answer,
But they've gone to the Cape and I'm alone.

It's amazing what we'll do when we get desperate,
If my house was burglarized I'd have a chance.
But calmer thoughts prevail, I call my manager,
And launch into a world-class song and dance.

But he sees through all the smoke and seems undaunted,
I'm amazed how calm he is amidst the mess,
With perspicacious wisdom and keen insight,
He says the missin' slides are sitting on his desk.

Now I've found those missin' slides,
And my anxious heartbeat will subside.
He's adding value to this side,
My manager has got my missin' slides.

BILL BAIN DID NOT ATTEND THE HARVARD BUSINESS SCHOOL

Nor any other business school, for that matter. This has never stood in his way as a superb strategic thinker or manager. A seemingly mild-mannered Tennesseean, he is serving lunch in his large, elegantly appointed blue office. He transferred to Vanderbilt University as a junior after spending two years at East Tennessee State. After bouts of engineering and prelaw, he majored in history. As a student, Bain worked part time for a steel reinforcements start-up company. A Woodrow Wilson Fellowship allowed him a year of graduate work at Vanderbilt in 1959. "I thought I'd get my Ph.D.," he says. "After a year of collecting three-by-five cards on an obscure subject, I didn't want to write a thesis." He worked at the steel company full time until December 1960, when he joined the Vanderbilt Development Office.

"I got interested in business then, through the trustees of the school. They were *major* CEOs and national business leaders. I got heavy exposure to that world—at a senior level—as a naive kid. It was very exciting. We started a serious fund-raising effort from scratch. Relative to my friends in Nashville, I was doing very well, professionally and financially. I never felt that I was deprived. I didn't feel an urgency to get out of it." By 1967, "I did hit a point where it became repetitive." In talks with trustees of the university, Bain "realized there was another world out there."

Of all the movers and shakers accessible to Bain, the one with the strongest influence was Bruce Henderson, then the head of the consulting division at think tank Arthur D. Little. Bain called on his fellow alumnus to raise money for a new business school at their alma mater. "He took me into his confidence at our first meeting and told me he'd be starting Boston Consulting Group. He had a unique way of talking about business that made sense to me and was different from the way anyone else spoke. He felt a real fit between us. He saw me as his protégé." Bill Bain moved to Boston in 1967, taking his wife, son, and a pay cut (plus the higher cost of living in Boston). "I took a pay cut with each of my three jobs."

The adjustment to New England was traumatic. "I moved from a nice house in a nice neighborhood to a third- or fourth-floor walk-up apartment. It was bitter cold. There was no Dr. Pepper here. My mother would have to mail cases of it." Not to mention the loss of the familiar academic community. "Everyone was focusing on things I didn't know, which was a lot. But there was a lot I knew about CEOs. I wasn't awed."

A lot of Bill's early observations were based on his understanding of human nature. "Getting a client to try something new is the biggest hurdle to get over. You've got to get a client to feel comfortable with you. Basically, they like a drink before dinner, to go to a football or basketball game. They like things presented in a way that doesn't condescend to or challenge them. A lot of people are comforted by a higher authority."

Bain found that in his individual relationships with his clients, he was on his own, running his own business. He and codefector Pat Graham "drifted apart internally from the rest. It began to be awkward. Pat and I had between forty and fifty percent of the revenue with very few clients. We were evolving into a separate group with separate philosophies." Furthermore, "there is a spectrum of people who want to work for others, and those who want to work for themselves." Bill Bain realized he belonged to the latter group.

"I never got to the point of saying, 'Oh, my God, I can't take it anymore.' When you're almost desperate, it gets dangerous; you make mistakes. We tried not to leave on bad terms with BCG, but it happened anyway. There was no lawsuit. We didn't do anything different from what Bruce Henderson did when he left Arthur D. Little. We were even more care- ful than we had to be. We could've told our clients [in advance]. We didn't." As it turns out, Henderson and Bain "have completely restored our relationship. He's teaching at Van- derbilt's Business School," for which Bain first approached Henderson. They've come full circle.

For a guy who uses the pronoun "we" so much and talks about teams so much, it is surprising that he would consent to the firm's being his namesake. "When we started the company, I didn't intend to call it 'Bain and Company.' Once we got started, we had to get a name for the incorporation. At first we just listed the names of all five founders. Then we went away from names of people altogether. Each time we found that someone [already] owned the name. I told three guys to spend an afternoon choosing a name. Days into our being a company, it never occurred to me to name the company after me. Now, after fifteen years with my name, I have a sense of the future."

In the early days, Bain recalls, "we were all pretty cocky and confident and thought individually somehow, we'd all be successful. We didn't know it would be this vehicle. We all knew if this didn't work out, we'd all have an easy time getting other jobs. In our opinion, we were each the people at BCG that we respected the most." Bain draws a parallel between the founding of his company and an Andy Hardy movie: haphazard, modest, and with an optimistic sense of possibility.

"There's an annual rumor," he says, "that we're going to sell the company. Of course, we're approached by prospective buyers." Bain has no idea what he'd do if he sold the company or simply left it. "Even a lot of money would be a bad exchange, as far as I'm concerned." Bain & Company's revenues neared $200 million in 1987. "When I get much older," the fifty-one- year-old says, "I think of delegating more, not dream of being the secretary of the treasury." On the other hand, Bain is the front man, the top cat, with responsibilities that preclude his spending much time as an actual management consultant.

"I miss the actual consulting. I try to do it vicariously. I keep up to date. It's like reading the sports pages." The assurance that Bill Bain will be on the case is no longer a contingency for winning a client. "A number of new clients I haven't met until after they've been working with us. I always tell them my father started the company."

I ask Bain about the essence of the "fit" that consultants at his company mention so often. "I imagine I can feel a sense of 'Bainness.' I'm not good at articulating it, as odd as that may seem. I'm too close to it." When he meets groups of new employees, he's "content to have totally social conversations, not business. I'm interested in seeing which one'll notice people who are out of it and try to draw them into conversation. It's better than monopolizing. [I can tell from] the way people treat a waiter at a lunch. I like to see people who are bright and quick, articulate—but they might not strike you that way at first. People who can see the full picture, and don't have tunnel vision."

"If we can do the appropriate training, we'd just as soon ACs stayed here to become consultants. Someone without an MBA can still be a superior consultant. I didn't have an MBA. If they go to get one, we'll still be interested in them."

Another day, another case. A media case team convenes in a conference room for our meeting. Vice-president Royce Yudkoff is the team leader. Present are Bob, David, Julie, Patty, Ron, Ben, Daniel, and Mika. They went to MIT, Harvard, Duke, Providence College, Brigham Young, Dartmouth, Georgia Tech, and Yale—in that order. Bob is working part time during his second year at HBS. He's not positive that he'll continue his career at Bain as a consultant when he gets his degree. David thought he was headed for a journalism career as an undergraduate at Harvard. "April of my senior year I looked for a job. I heard that Bain was cool. Almost at once I wanted to work here. The secrecy was appealing." Patty heard of Bain when a friend came for an interview. Ron, a chemical engineer and self-proclaimed member of "the Mormon Mafia," says, "After too many plant tours, I decided to come here." Ben says he just knew he "wanted *business*." Daniel came to Bain during his business school summer and was "impressed by the people I met. They were fun and smart." Royce owned two radio stations in Maine not long after his graduation from Dartmouth. One of his myriad duties was selling airtime. "I had a moment of epiphany at a shoe store where I was waiting to sell spots." He sold his stations, joined the Citibank training program, and arrived at Harvard in 1978. "I had never heard of consulting. I got a job solicitation from BCG. I took a summer job there and liked the intellectual environment. I didn't want to work there, and I joined Bain part time during my last year of school."

A sampling of the associates reveals that Ron, Ben, and Mika are going to Harvard in the fall, while David is entering Harvard's joint business-law program. Patty is staying, and Julie is waiting to decide.

This room is filled with people who basically could choose their field (if not their employer) when looking for jobs. And they pretty much chose Bain instead of investment banking. The feeling on campus these days is that consulting and investment banking (before Black Monday; since, investment banking has begun to pall) offer the best buck and the biggest hit of prestige. "Money: if it were the only motivator, I'd be in investment banking. Money can't buy you happiness, but it can buy you a car to look for it," a new associate says.

Their experience is still in that early, reflective stage. "Your first few assignments are well defined. You are hand-held the first month, but you have lots of responsibility." Heads nod at this one, with murmurs of "I can't believe they're letting me have responsibility." You wonder how clients cotton to their youth. Early client calls are made with senior members of the team, "which is less threatening to the client. We get the client to think of us as experts." Generally the "clients' first question is 'How long have you been at Bain?' " One client urged a female associate to date his son.

The amounts of work facing a new Bainie are perhaps less staggering than expected. Ron says his hours are the same as he was required to put in as a student. "I worked the same hours

—fifty per week, but I worked harder in school than here, with senior projects, part-time jobs, et cetera." Everyone agrees that the eighty-hour weeks are rare, "but the most exciting. You don't work eighty hours on a dull project. Seventy-five percent of the time, my hours are my own choice." Another associate volunteers, "Partners work as hard. They put their lives on hold and work hard, travel. They set an example." Not only do they feel the blood of Bain coursing through their veins, but associates feel a tremendous allegiance to their case teams. "You don't mind spending your Sunday afternoons here."

Furthermore, there is no sense of having to alert your colleagues to the work and value you have added to an assignment. "Individual contributions are clear. Your manager knows exactly what you're doing. You work on discrete parts by yourself. You can't hide." The loyalty to the client also makes Bainies feel the need to give so much of themselves. "I don't think twice about my sense of duty," someone offers. "The clients are virtually our employers."

Who would not fit into this high-powered environment? "Loners. A rocket scientist may not work well with clients. Noncreative people. People who can't learn quickly." What attributes will make life at Bain comfortable? "A good sense of humor is necessary, especially when traveling with people. Someone who is versatile. The job rewards people who are ambitious and aggressive, who think creatively and are self-starters."

While Yudkoff is almost a decade older than the associates in his case team, he maintains he's "not a grown-up. Bain has affected my life in ways I'd never have thought of. People skills: I find I get along with many kinds of people. Bain's made me more analytical than I'd been. I'm a little impatient with service people, now that I'm a service person."

Joining Bain does not put the finishing touch on one's career. "A lot of people see this as a way of learning about lots of industries. They're no closer to figuring out what they want to be. They're generalists and never do the same thing twice. Through self-discovery, they become Bainies. There's a sense you're doing something useful: You're saving and creating jobs and helping to make the economy healthy. There's a sense of altruism here," an AC adds. "I don't feel I've sold out."

Bill Achtmeyer came to Bain in 1977 with a degree from Princeton's Woodrow Wilson School. There were forty employees at the company, and he was offered the then-incredible salary of $11,000. "I was overwhelmed by the amount. Reluctantly, I returned to [Amos Tuck] business school." While finishing up, Achtmeyer was tapped to be the assistant to the CEO of an auto parts supplier. When his boss got fired ten months later, Bill Bain called to renew the invitation to work as a consultant. In 1982 Bill Achtmeyer showed up for work at a firm that was now three hundred strong. "The people who were here when I left were still here when I returned."

He describes his working community by saying, "For a closed environment, it's surprisingly open within. You can't tell anyone who you work for [which clients, he means]. It's embarrassing at cocktail parties. People need to talk about themselves and what they're doing." Because all employees of Bain & Company must sign a nondisclosure statement upon arrival, "it does allow for me to not talk about work at home. I have to develop other interests."

Bill concedes that he's opted for a life "that will never mean a forty-hour work week," but he's able to leave it behind at the end of the day in order to focus on his family.

We talk about the public's murky comprehension of the consulting business. "People are very skeptical about what the hell they're getting themselves into. Clients do come from bad experiences with other consultants. But they see us work hard. We say we'll stick around. Our most effective clients are on top of what they do and know what we can do. It's not like the CEO can't do it. He has no time. An outside organization can do the job as well.

"No matter what way you cut it, at the end of the day at Bain, you're still giving advice—less so here than with other firms with shorter-term relationships." Bill likes the combination of being an adviser and having major responsibility. "Most people work for two clients. There has to be a natural allegiance to one or another on a typical day. It balances itself out, and if it doesn't, you or they make a change. We've stopped a number of relationships with clients that weren't going anywhere." The telltale sign? "No one was having fun anymore.

"The company hasn't gotten carried away with itself. We don't rest on our laurels. If we did, I might leave. If something's wrong, we all address it. Nobody here's ever had the experience of running a company this size or larger. People should be humble."

Orit Gadiesh is the striking Israeli woman who appeared in *The Right Stuff* videotape. Tall, attractive, dramatic, and with no perceptible accent to her English, she came to the States in 1976 while working on her doctorate in psychology, to attend the Harvard Business School. Although advised against it, Orit wanted to get her doctorate in business administration [a four-year degree called a DBA] in order to return to Israel to teach. To this day, she is the only Israeli woman ever to have attended the Harvard Business School.

Her English was, by her own admission, poor. "At first, it took me four hours to read seven pages [of text]. With a dictionary." She had no business vocabulary in her native tongue. "I can't speak business in Hebrew. It doesn't come naturally to me, and I never had to try to do it in Hebrew." But Gadiesh became her class's Baker Scholar, graduating first in the program. After her first two years (with an MBA), "I identified the companies I wanted to work for. I wanted to work in New York or Europe. It came down to where I wanted to live versus Bain. It shocked me that I chose Bain because of Boston. I've always felt like a New Yorker.

"I liked the company, I liked the way they described their strategy, and I liked every single person I met. Bill Bain is one of the most impressive people I ever met." Orit is not coy. "I never played the game. When I decided to work here, I didn't think it would be for the short term." Within a year of her arrival, Gadiesh discovered she would require fourteen months of medical treatment. "I hadn't yet done anything for the company. Bill Bain said, 'We want you and see you as an investment.' All he had were my grades at business school. I will never forget that."

Orit is high-powered. Unlike many women with similar accomplishments, she is satisfied with what she does and where she does it. "You don't do this kind of job if you don't want to. I'm a grown-up. There's no other place I'd ever want to work."

Gadiesh is not the first person at Bain to point out that the success and youth of Bain & Company have not made for arrogance. "Because of Bill Bain. [The corporate personality] is not arrogant. It starts from the top. And you want people with you who are like you." She says it's difficult to assess a person's fit objectively. "It's a gut feeling. Because you've been working in teams, you know how to size people up."

Being a woman, an executive vice-president, and a client head (running the relationship with a client, which requires a longer stay on a piece of business than another consultant assigned to it) has not made life more difficult for Orit. "A guy I'm working with [at my client's] has been told by his CEO that I'm coming in. It's scary to him. And *I'm* giving *them* advice." She does nothing to mask her femininity. Wearing a bright red sweater, she says, "I used to design my own clothes. I had my suits made, only in black and white. They were formal, and I added my own touches. There's already a distance between you and your clients. So I try to compromise between [what they expect] and my sense of style. I couldn't find anything I liked. I couldn't have a role model. I *was* the role model."

The portrait of Bain & Company that Gadiesh and others describe is warm and tolerant, challenging and fun. There seems no end to the devotion they have toward their clients. "People here are sometimes more committed than the people in the client company." Everyone gets feedback at every level. "I gave a speech yesterday, and ten people stopped me to tell me how much they enjoyed it. People are just that way. It's a pleasure to tell someone they've done a good job."

HILL, HOLLIDAY, CONNORS, COSMOPULOS, INC.

HILL, HOLLIDAY

HISTORY & OPERATIONS

Hill, Holliday, Connors, Cosmopulos, Inc., the largest advertising agency in New England, was founded in 1968 in Boston by four former executives at the Boston office of the New York–based agency Batten, Barton, Durstine & Osborn (BBD&O). Each of the founding partners specialized in a different aspect of advertising: George "Jay" Hill came in as the copywriter, Stavros Cosmopulos was the art director, Alan Holliday handled marketing, and Jack Connors, at twenty-five the youngest of the bunch, was in charge of selling ads, maintaining client contact, and bringing in new business. Each contributed $1,500, and they set up shop in such tight quarters that their desks faced one another's.

The partners, who started the agency without a single client, struggled to make a go of it. Alan Holliday, figuring it wasn't worth the effort, dropped out after six months. Hill, Holliday's first assignment—for $350—came from a local food broker named Bill Klein, who hired the firm to compose a trade ad. When they handed him the result of their creative efforts —a photograph of a woman's face with the headline "Let's Hear It for Bill Klein, the Food Broker" and a comic-strip balloon emanating from the woman's mouth that read "Burp"—

Klein balked and wouldn't agree to run the advertisement until Hill, Holliday attached its name to it.

Klein's reaction, dubbed the "gulp factor," became Hill, Holliday's early barometer of efficacy. If a client gulped upon first being presented with a campaign, it meant the agency was on target. Another of their early ads, for a local ice cream parlor chain called Brigham's, read "Worship this sundae at Brigham's," and a campaign for the state of Maine, which played on the abbreviation of the state's name, featured lines such as "Lover come back to Me.," "You, Me. and the Kids," and "There will never be another Me." At the time, compared to the local competition—which was for the most part turning out bland, formula advertising— Hill, Holliday's efforts were considered to be "breakthrough."

Though the agency slowly built up a reputation as a "hot creative" shop, its early success was relatively modest. One factor holding it back was its failure to develop a sophisticated research department, an omission potential clients considered to be a liability. Cosmopulos, who headed the creative side and maintained a clear division between the creative and business ends, felt that too much research cramped creative style. Connors, who had done much to build up the business side and wanted to do even more, disagreed. Tensions came to a head in 1978, when Connors and Hill asked for Cosmopulos's resignation and bought out his share of the agency.

Hill, Holliday's big break came in 1975, when it secured the Wang Laboratories account. Wang, which was virtually unknown outside of the high-tech field at the time, had previously devoted its small advertising budget to computer journals. When Hill, Holliday got the account, Connors promised Wang's founder, Dr. An Wang, that if he spent $1 million on a television campaign, the agency would double the company's name recognition. Wang agreed, and Wang Laboratories became the first computer company besides IBM ever to advertise on national television. The campaign originally aired in 1977 during the Super Bowl pregame show, with the final commercial slated for the same time the following year. Fortuitously for Wang (and Hill, Holliday), the 1978 pregame show ran late, and when people all over the country turned on their sets to see the Super Bowl kickoff, they saw the Wang commercial instead. The campaign *tripled* Wang's name recognition, and Wang subsequently devoted millions of dollars to mass market advertising.

Connors and Hill used the money generated from the Wang account to build up the agency. They raised salaries far above the standard for Boston, brought in more account executives, and hired a first-rate research and marketing team. When Wang began expanding into international markets, Hill, Holliday opened offices abroad. The agency's billings, which hovered around $15 million at the time the 1978 Super Bowl commercial aired, have doubled in every two-year period since then.

As the New England economy boomed, Hill, Holliday took on more and more new accounts and eventually became the largest agency in the region. In 1983 it opened a New York office, which was an immediate success. (Billings for the New York office increased from $4 million in 1984 to an estimated $46 million in 1987.) HHCC's most visible and highly touted campaign in recent years was for John Hancock Financial Services, which hired the agency's Boston team in 1985. The $20 million campaign, which has been called "cinema vérité" in style, depicts real-life family scenarios of people in various stages of their lives who need financial advice. The actors look and sound like real people with real problems, and their names and financial statistics are flashed across the screen. (For legal purposes, Hill, Holliday actually used the names of people from the agency in these case studies.) The campaign, which has been called the "*1984* of 1986" (a reference to Chiat/Day's much-talked-about commercial for Apple computers [see page 288]), was praised throughout the industry and won the Grand Prix "Best of Show" award at the International Advertising Film Festival in Cannes (the most prestigious industry award in the world). Hill, Holliday was named as *Advertising Age*'s 1985–86 "Agency of the Year."

Today, Hill, Holliday employs about five hundred people in its offices in Boston, New York, London, and Hong Kong. In 1987 Hill, Holliday was ranked as the twenty-ninth largest agency in the United States in terms of worldwide gross income. The entire agency's roster of 129 clients include Wang Laboratories, John Hancock Financial Services, NYNEX Corporation (Business Information Systems Company), Spalding Sports Worldwide, Gillette Company's PaperMate, Personal Care, and Safety Razor divisions, Southland Corporation's 7-Eleven Stores, Polaroid (Business and Professional Products), L. L. Bean, Revlon, Royal Crown Cola, *The Boston Globe,* and Hyatt Hotels.

Hill, Holliday is divided into five departments: Advertising, which is subdivided into Creative, Account Service, and Media; Marketing Research, which includes an information resources center with almost two hundred different data bases; Public Relations; Design; and Direct Marketing. Each account is assigned a team made up of people from Marketing Research, Creative, Media, and These Services—that works on campaigns from the initial research to the final placement of advertisements. These teams, which consist of an average of seven people, are guided by senior-level executives from the Creative Department.

(Information provided by Liz Packer, agency spokesperson.)

1987 *ADVERTISING AGE* RANKING: Twenty-ninth largest U.S. agency in terms of worldwide gross income.

REVENUES: Worldwide billings of $289.6 million in 1987.

GROSS INCOME: Worldwide, $43.4 million in 1987.

OFFICES: Headquarters in Boston and additional offices in New York, London, and Hong Kong.

EMPLOYEES: About 500, with approximately 380 in the United States and about 110 abroad.

AVERAGE AGE OF EMPLOYEES: Twenty-five to thirty.

TURNOVER: 37 percent in fiscal year 1987.

RECRUITMENT: Although Hill, Holliday is not actively recruiting on college campuses at present, it has recruited in the past and intends to do so again. Through a program called "Opportunities in Boston," in which a number of Boston agencies participate, Hill, Holliday actively recruits minorities for all kinds of positions. The human resources department goes to job fairs, which are attended by recent college graduates, and looks for candidates there. For secretarial positions, the agency recruits from Katharine Gibbs. In addition, the agency has a college internship program.

NUMBER OF NEW HIRES PER YEAR: One hundred, on average.

RANGE OF STARTING SALARIES: Assistant account executives, $18,000–$20,000; secretaries, $13,000–$18,000.

POLICY FOR RAISES: Employees receive raises annually, based on evaluations from their supervisors.

TRAINING PROGRAMS: "Word processing training for new employees, if desired. The agency also has an account service training seminar, and most entry-level jobs have personal on-the-job training."

BENEFITS: Six or seven options for health insurance (the agency assumes half of the premium for the first eighteen months of full-time employment; after eighteen months, it pays the entire premium), dental (the agency assumes half the premium), life insurance (begins three months after full-time employment), long-term disability insurance, short-term disability insurance (eight weeks' full pay, applies also to maternity leave), and profit sharing.

VACATION: Ten days per year—prorated monthly—plus two extra days in 1987; after five years at the agency, employees get fifteen days. Employees also get thirteen regular paid holidays each year.

ADDITIONAL PERKS: The Boston office has two exercise facilities with Nautilus, free weights, bicycles, showers, etc. The agency operates a near-site day care center, HHCC Day Care, Inc. Fees for the center are set on a sliding scale based on an employee's salary, and are partially subsidized by the agency. The center has capacity for thirty-six children, and twenty-six are currently enrolled. Hill, Holliday also has what it calls a "support staff bonus." Support staff openings are posted at the agency, and any employee who refers someone for one of these positions receives a $250 bonus one month after that person starts work. In addition, all employees are entitled to a corporate rate, deducted from their paychecks, for passes on Boston public transportation.

BONUSES: "Bonuses are awarded based on merit and performance." The agency would not disclose who is eligible.

ANNUAL PARTY: Hill, Holliday hosts annual company parties at Christmas and in May for the agency's anniversary. The Christmas party is generally held at a hotel (in 1987 it was at the Hyatt Regency Hotel) for employees and their spouses or guests. Hors d'oeuvres are served, there's an open bar, and there is dancing to a live band. The party, which is dressy though not black tie, usually starts about 7:00 P.M. and lasts until 1:00 or 2:00 A.M. On the morning of the agency's anniversary, there's a breakfast meeting at a Boston hotel for New York and Boston employees, with formal presentations. Agency partners give speeches concerning the state of the agency and its plans for the next year and show some of the best work done over the past year and the awards they've garnered. The people responsible for the work are recognized. After breakfast, employees return to the office, change into play clothes and travel an hour or so to Crane's Castle, a restored castle in Ipswich. Lunch is served, and everyone stays there for the full day. (In 1987 they held the "Hill, Holliday Olympics" there.) Presentations are made for the "rookie and rookette of the year"—the man and woman with the "most spirit" who have been at the agency for less than a year—for whom employees have voted a month earlier. There's a disc jockey and dancing, and employees generally stay until 7:00 or 8:00 P.M. Afterward, a lot of people go out in Boston.

DRESS CODE: No stated dress code. "Most employees dress in a stylishly professional manner —a style that reflects personality and taste."

AVERAGE WORKDAY: Official hours are 8:30 A.M. to 5:30 P.M. "However, most people are here at 7:30 or 8:00 A.M. and some stay until 9:00 or 10:00 P.M." The average is probably 8:00 A.M. to 6:00 P.M.

SOCIAL ATMOSPHERE: "Most employees seem to truly enjoy each other's company—socially and professionally. As a tight-knit agency in a tight-knit advertising community such as Boston, it is often impossible *not* to socialize with co-workers—a plus to Hill, Holliday's open and lively working environment."

HEADQUARTERS: The agency's headquarters are housed on roughly three floors of the John Hancock Tower in Boston. (Hill, Holliday shares two floors with other companies.) In New York, the agency occupies two floors of the "Lipstick building" in midtown.

CHARITABLE CONTRIBUTIONS: Hill, Holliday gave $155,000 in direct donations in fiscal 1987. The agency contributed to approximately fifty organizations, most of them in the Boston area, in service, cultural, educational, and health-related fields. "With time and services, HHCC Community Relations has estimated a yearly donation of $1 million serving over seventy clients."

INTERESTED APPLICANTS CAN SEND RÉSUMÉS TO:
Hill, Holliday, Connors, Cosmopulos, Inc.
200 Clarendon Street
John Hancock Tower
Boston, MA 02116
(617) 437-1600

Hill, Holliday, Connors, Cosmopulos, the Boston advertising agency, is also a New York agency worth reckoning. It is also an international agency with offices in London and Hong Kong. Named "Agency of the Year" by *Advertising Age* in 1985, Hill, Holliday added oomph to the theory that you don't have to be headquartered in New York to be good, hip, and national. Very much in the cinematic tradition of how we imagine advertising, it seems to attract the attractive, young, and enthusiastic. Life at Hill, Holliday seems no more or less real than a movie about advertising. "We always suffered from self-delusion," a senior executive says. "We always saw ourselves as a big, national agency, but that only happened in the last five years."

The Boston offices, in the John Hancock Tower on Copley Square, are bright and active, yet (though I think its denizens will disagree with this) somehow not too frantic. They occupy three floors, one primarily devoted to account work, the others to creative and media services.

Jack Connors, the chairman of the entire operation, is surrounded by green. His office is large and green: upholstery, walls, Perrier bottles. The floor looks more like a golf green than anything else, and his cocoon flatters his ruddy complexion and whitening hair. He's exhausted. He and his team have just pitched Reebok, and it was a herculean effort. What's more, he's pessimistic about his agency's chances at winning the account. (Ultimately, the shoe company gave its business to Chiat/Day [see p. 287.]) Connors is a curious mixture of irreverent cynic and a company man. He'll say things like "This is not a business of brain surgeons," but he'll prominently display client Dr. An Wang's autobiography, *Lessons from the Doctor,* on his coffee table. He'll self-deprecatingly confess to "cheap courage," citing a quotation by F. Scott Fitzgerald, yet talk forcefully about strategic thinking. The one thing he makes clear is that he does not take himself seriously. Which must be assimilated, even unconsciously, by his employees.

A local boy and graduate of Boston College (both of which hold him in good stead with local businesses), Connors's first real job was selling Campbell's Soup. He then joined the new Boston office of BBD&O in 1965, on the account side. New England businesses were not impressed with local talent; they felt if they were going to spend money on advertising, they might as well go to the fulcrum of the industry, New York. "New York was the Florence of advertising," says Connors. "It was where the masters were." After a period of disenchantment, he started a new agency in partnership with some co-workers at BBD&O. "We were not buddies. We didn't snap towels at each other in the locker room. We respected each other. We started on our own because we wanted something better for ourselves—as most entrepreneurs feel."

Also consistent with most entrepreneurs was the risk the partners took. They opened their doors before they had the promise of clients, with each man chipping in $1,500. Today's Hill, Holliday, Connors, Cosmopulos—minus Holliday and Cosmopulos—now employs about five hundred people and has billings of $289.6 million. It was the thirty-eighth largest advertising agency in this country at the time of my visit in 1987. (It has since moved to twenty-ninth.) As far as success stories go, it is not an unusual one, but it is satisfying to its progenitors.

Connors says there's a common denominator linking his clients, which include John Hancock Mutual Life Insurance (Boston), Revlon (New York), Jordan Marsh (Boston), Wang Computer (Boston), Hyatt Hotels Corporation (Chicago), R. C. Cola (Chicago), the Boston Museum of Fine Arts, and Gillette (Boston). "They each believe they're not at the top of the game and maybe Hill, Holliday will help them get there." He characterizes the group that will lead them as "very eclectic. A deluxe pizza. There's a lot of cheese and tomato in advertising, but this has anchovies, pepperoni, mushrooms. And not just mushrooms"— Connors takes the metaphor to a new extreme—"but shiitake mushrooms. We have old, young, gay, and straight."

The potpourri will not be home for just anyone. Connors is looking for "the fire in the belly; spirit and enthusiasm. We get so up and so down—a full range of emotion. We harness our people's energy. We want some of the best people. Not all [of them]. This is a sort of pick-up game."

It sounds like a casual approach to corporate life. Hill, Holliday has no employee manual. "We don't have a five-year plan. If we work for *The Boston Globe,* we want to beat the piss out of *The Boston Herald.*" For all the competitive talk, however, Connors also takes the high road. "We're in a business that's advertising, but really we're in the business of change. We like to think we deal with change better than the average competitor. We try to convince clients of that." Connors has often been quoted as saying his agency is in the business of building relationships, which is astute for a service industry. Before anyone actually knew how potent and rich a market the Route 128 high-tech companies would become, he created a relationship with Wang Computer, tripling its name recognition with that one well-timed pre–Super Bowl television commercial. It also put HHCC on the map as a national agency.

Hill, Holliday's work is known as "hot creative." It will take chances on the air and in print. Connors eschews a strictly bottom-line approach. "Numbers never had a bearing; it was quality. That's our 'search for excellence.' We don't try to make it fun; we try to create this environment." It's a place filled with people who are, by and large, happy. They feel they work for a winner.

Management installed a day care center in the bottom floor of a church across the street from the Hancock Tower. "It's like Happyville over there. Other organizations wanted to join it. We didn't create it to make people happy, but so we can get wonderful people to stay here."

Judy Penny is a young art director. She came to Hill, Holliday in 1982, after attending the

Art Institute of Boston. A former painter, "I never thought about the existence of advertising." When she got there, it felt right. "I loved it immediately. Hill, Holliday was already considered hot," she says over a desk filled with markers, color separations, and layouts. "I knew I wanted to stay in Boston, and I loved the advertising here.

"It's interesting to see how I've grown. I work with a lot of writers." She pulls out a large print ad for the Museum of Fine Arts. "I'm thrilled with it." A commercial she designed for the Massachusetts State Lottery predates the renaissance of the Richie Valens hit "La Bamba." To the golden oldie, an ordinary-looking fellow simply jumps up and down. "I love that commercial," she smiles. "It's one of my favorites."

It is rumored that it is harder to get ads approved internally at Hill, Holiday than it is by clients. "I think we have a really good system," Penny says of the creative standard bearing. "There's good pressure. You present work to the creative directors." If they give their blessing, the creatives who actually make the ads get to present them to the clients. "We like to present our own work. We can get really excited." Working for an agency that's considered to be creative-driven can sometimes make for a creative elite that shuns collaboration with the account group. "We try not to make account people feel like 'them.' My best relationship is with the account executive on my team." However, "we don't rely on account executives to judge creative." Occasionally, there might be conflicts between what the client has ordered and what the creatives perceive as their integrity, but Penny is confident that compromises can occur without too much pain on either side.

In answer to the question "What do you imagine yourself doing other than advertising?"— so many creatives at so many agencies say they're just biding their time until they sell their movie script, shoot their video, move to Hollywood, etc.—Judy says, "I have Plan B through Z all the time, but at the moment, not instead of advertising. I do projects on the side." One wall of her office is dedicated to her monumental shopping bag collection, and she pulls out her invention, "The HHCC Art Director's layout pad," which is, in fact a sketchpad made up of cocktail-sized napkins.

David McPherson is an account supervisor on John Hancock. A business major at Colorado State University, he saw that it would be tough establishing himself in other cities without an MBA. "I didn't know what I wanted to do, but I figured that exposure to so many different kinds of companies would be a great apprenticeship. One year into it, advertising felt good. You get to analyze, find solutions, direct creatives. The first balloon that gets popped is that advertising is glamorous." Yeah, where did that come from? "It's work." A veteran of two other Boston agencies, he claims that one of Hill, Holliday's salient characteristics is that creative work must be appreciated.

"I was always very visual. When I came home from the movies at an early age, I'd describe the movie to my parents from beginning to end." Nevertheless, Creative isn't solely responsible for the agency's success. Maybe Creative gets too much damn credit. "The strategy on the [mega-award-winning] Hancock series came from up here, not down there. We said we need to talk about consumers, not the towers, not the signature, not how big we are."

After working closely with one client, doesn't he ever feel a tug between loyalty to the client and loyalty to the agency? David answers, "I feel absolutely closer to the agency than to the client. It's not loyalty as much as what works. I work for an agency, and I want to sell the agency's product. Make no mistake about that. There are a lot of spineless account people out there," he sneers.

After almost five years, McPherson can picture himself at Hill, Holliday for the rest of the decade. "I'm *not* interested in starting my own company. I don't know where I'd go. There's a frustration that builds when you realize you're smarter than you're allowed to be. I'd like to be a movie director."

When Kevin Power was asked to open HHCC's Hong Kong office, he was given two weeks' notice. He was gone for two and a half years and spent another year and a half in Sydney, Australia. Although an account supervisor, Power enjoys working for a creative-driven shop more than working for an agency motored by account people. "The last agency I worked at was account-driven. It was too much. I prefer it here. I understand creative people, and they now appreciate what we do: keeping clients away from them, if nothing else. The team is for real."

But what is the quintessence of the Boston office? To find out, we attended (okay, took) a power lunch with some of Hill, Holliday's most trusted soldiers. Here is one woman's story.

Eleven years ago, Felice Kincannon started in the accounting department. After more than a year had gone by, "I told Jack Connors I didn't like my job and I wanted something better. He gave me an IOU for a better job. I didn't know what I wanted; just something more interesting." He meant it; today she is HHCC's senior vice-president/director of media sales.

Felice, Ann Finucane, the senior vice-president/group account director, and Carol Corcoran, the new vice-president/director of human resources and a friend of Ann's from Elizabeth Seton High School in New York, elaborate on their agency's culture. Those who will best fit in, they posit, are "fairly independent types who don't need structure." This does not obviate the need for "pats on the back," they add. (Everyone around the table was impressed by the "Unsung Hero" award. In 1986 Jack Connors gave four people tickets to the Super Bowl, plus an all-expenses-paid VIP trip to L.A. "They were people who probably didn't know Connors knew who they were.") "There's no specific career path. You stay late," not in order to be seen, "but as an opportunity to do good work. You're generally recognized for good work. Versatility is important. You have to cover a range" of clients, industries, and personalities.

Fast forward on the air shuttle to New York and Philip Johnson's new "Lipstick Building" on Third Avenue, home of Hill, Holliday's New York office. Chris Miller is late for our appointment. But that's okay; she's the person who opened HHCC's New York presence in 1983 after ten years in politics, two years at Harvard Business School ("for a midcareer mechanism"), and five years at Doyle, Dane, Bernbach. She says, "There are myths about advertising. They don't attribute brains to people in it."

The good news, though, is that people drawn to this field have "very high 'get-it' factors; they're very alive, current, interesting, and interested. There's a sense of humor in the business. It's both creative and a service. It's fast-paced." Certainly, in its heyday, Doyle, Dane was the epitome of what was good about advertising. It wasn't easy for Miller to leave, but she had the opportunity of making a mark on the new agency. "DDB and Hill, Holliday have the same characteristics: a good creative product, smart and funny people, good marketers, and compulsives."

One of her better moves was hiring Mal MacDougall as the president and creative director of HHCC New York. "We decided if we tried, we'd go first class. He said it'd take three to five years" to establish themselves. Obviously, they beat their projections. "The Boston office helped" in the early pitches, but Chris declares, "We do not have a 'branch' mentality. We're Hill, Holliday. When this office grew, we had to call on them for help less. We still report to them. To grow significantly, we had to move away. We can grow hugely here. Boston's a small town; we're multinational." Most people don't move back and forth between the two cities. "We're homegrown. A lot of people in Boston wouldn't find a move to New York City as attractive." Miller points out that Hill, Holliday and Chiat/Day "are the only two out-of-town agencies that have succeeded in New York."

Within four years her office has swollen to about seventy employees and a real identity. It feels like a New York agency. The pace is faster; things seem a tad more urgent than they do in Boston. Not that it's been easy. Chris resorts to "a middle-of-the-night notepad. We may generate some stress ourselves. We seek it out. There's a point at which you can leave for home at a reasonable hour, but I try not to obsess. I consider that an achievement." On the subject of agency versus client, Miller takes the latter's side. "If you believe in the campaign and that it'll help the client's business, you try [to sell it]. But the person who pays the bills gets to decide. You can work it out if you want a long-term relationship."

Having come from a large agency, she finds a smaller one presents its own set of concerns. "It's full throttle. We ask people to stretch to their full capacity. Not everyone wants to be entrepreneurial, but to make a difference in a smaller agency is very satisfying to advertising professionals."

The distinguished, witty, and urbane Mal MacDougall is the man who gave the world "It takes two hands to handle a Whopper," Diet Coke's "Just for the taste of it," "Come to think of it, I'll have a Heineken," "Nothing unimportant ever happens at the Plaza," and many other slogans he refuses to divulge. In accepting his position at Hill, Holliday, MacDougall did the unthinkable times two: As a founder and creative director of Boston's HBM—Humphrey Browning MacDougall—he used to compete head to head against HHCC. (He usually won.) Then he made a huge leap of fortune and recognition when he was made the president of giant Sullivan, Stauffer, Colwell & Bayleff (SSC&B), then the tenth largest agency in the country, and a New York agency at that. And then he moved to little Hill, Holliday. "I left a $300 million agency for a $2 million agency." One guesses that few would have made the same move.

"It wasn't too hard a decision to make. At SSC&B I was sitting in meetings, discussing the fall of the yen. I wasn't doing advertising; I was going to meetings. I missed the fun— building the company, hands-on, writing ads myself. The larger the place, the harder it was to maintain."

He joined a year after Chris opened HHCC's doors in the city and after a few years resigned his creative director title. A graduate of Harvard College in the "mid-fifties," Mal says he "feels a crisis of young people. The agency business is in desperate trouble. Advertising used to be the most exciting, fun, high-paying business. It can offer a hell of a lot more than any business, any time. It's the only field you can enter out of college and find yourself working on ten or twelve businesses simultaneously. There's such variety!" He despairs that the new graduates who should be gravitating toward his industry are heading into financial services. Just for big bucks.

"A talented person who wants to exist as an individual can make more money in five years than a stupid banker. You work your ass off. You understand your business is to make your clients's business, not just advertising." Why else did advertising once aggressively recruit MBAs? MacDougall says, "We went through a stage in the seventies trying to be respectable. Creatives went back into their cells, and the leaders became deal makers."

Yet one of the reasons Mal adores advertising is "because it takes such a big chunk of [the client's] budget, you meet the high end of business. You never get bored. The second reason I love it: You can see your creative work on television, you can hear it on radio, you can see it in magazines. Constantly. People talk about what you do all the time. That's ego gratification."

MacDougall is pleased that in this day and age of merger fever, "this agency will resist the temptation to sell out. This agency will do good work we'll be proud of. And we'll sell product. The agency will grow—we can't plan on growth or set a target. We're one of the last independent agencies. I hope we can hold off and not sell and not buy. [Either of those options] would change our character. It's too big a risk. It's fun to be the feisty upstart."

He offers the heart of advertising: "We don't create trends. We respond to them. And we identify them. That's why young people are so valuable—to identify trends. How people want to dress, feel. The tempo of life." Advertising is sort of a young person's business, since they are themselves frequently the targets with disposable cash. "Fundamentally, you're addressing a hostile audience. Advertisements are interruptions. The point is not to entertain, it's to inform."

And who is right to carry out this mandate? "We won't hire anybody who won't be liked by everyone here. (Obviously, he or she also has to be talented.) We have to have fun together. I can tell in five minutes if they're nice. Are they enthusiastic about the work they're showing me, even if it's lousy? I'm looking for the spark of originality. Nine out of ten prove they can do dull advertising or repeat what's been done," Mal says. "I want surprises."

Some of the young people he's met in the last few years "seemed embarrassed to be selling. I can't stand when people hide their product. The good advertisers know they're *selling* products. If you feel you're a creative person selling out, A, you'll fail, and B, you'll be miserable. It's sad there are so many like this. The best funny stuff in the United States (like the Federal Express campaign) is very hard sell. It's great salesmanship, not showmanship. My biggest thrill is beating our rivals' products. That's ego-gratifying. When Diet Coke—which I introduced {at SSC&B]—became the largest-selling diet drink, that was the happiest day for me in advertising.

"I don't think this is a tasteless business. It requires imagination and creativity. Advertising is getting more intelligent. We're not writing ads for twelve-year-old mentalities. We assume our people [the audience] are relatively intelligent and tough customers. It's an honest business. We don't lie because it doesn't work." Before Mal leaves for the day a colleague mentions that MacDougall has published some novels. In February 1987 I asked Mal about his plans for the future. "I have never known what I'll be doing tomorrow," he says, "but I know it'll be turmoil." (In fact, in September 1987, he left Hill, Holliday to become vice-chairman of Jordan, McGrath, Case & Taylor, the thirty-fourth largest advertising agency in the country according to *Advertising Age*'s 1987 listing.)

LOTUS
DEVELOPMENT
CORPORATION

HISTORY & OPERATIONS

Mitchell D. Kapor, Lotus's founder, attended Yale University during the 1960s and drifted through most of the seventies. During his postcollege years he was variously a rock disc jockey, a Transcendental Meditation instructor, a stand-up comic, and a counselor in the psychiatric unit of a suburban hospital. When the first Apple personal computers were introduced, Kapor, who had studied computer science in college, figured out that there was money to be made in programming and eventually went to work for VisiCorp, a small software company. A hack who knew only the simplest computer language, his strength was in designing programs which were "user friendly." When in 1982 VisiCorp rejected his idea for a new program for businesspeople which would integrate spreadsheet, graphics, and data base functions on one disc, Kapor left to start his own company.

Such was the birth of 1-2-3, the biggest hit in the history of business software, and of Lotus Development Corporation, which, until recently, was the largest software manufacturer in the business. (Microsoft has since surpassed them.) In a single year, Lotus went from revenues of zero to $53 million and from fifty to three hundred employees. And despite minor setbacks, business continued to boom.

Though Lotus has diversified into many areas of business software, it hasn't yet developed a program to match the success of 1-2-3, which has topped the Softsell best-seller list (an industry standard) since April 1983. Symphony, an expanded version of 1-2-3 that includes word processing functions, is Lotus's second largest seller and, if it were an independent company, would rank fourth in the software industry. Other Lotus products include, among others, Jazz, a program identical to Symphony but designed for the Apple Macintosh (both 1-2-3 and Symphony were designed primarily for IBM PCs), Lotus One Source, a program contained on compact discs which provides regularly updated information about stocks and bonds, Lotus Manuscript, a powerful word processing program, Lotus Metro, a desktop management program, Lotus HAL, a companion to 1-2-3 that responds to English-language phrases to express 1-2-3 commands, designed specifically for scientists and engineers. Lotus is now developing new programs to accommodate recent advances in computer hardware, as well as ones that will incorporate new discoveries in artificial intelligence. The company's most recent products include Graphwriter II (a graphics program for automated charting of 1-2-3 and Symphony spreadsheet data); two add-ins to 1-2-3 called Lotus Speedup and Lotus Learn; 1-2-3 Deleting Business Productivity software, which combines spreadsheet, graphics, and database; the 1-2-3 Small Business Kit, which assists business owners and managers in identifying ways to improve their day-to-day operations; and Lotus Selects, a catalogue that offers over seventy-five products developed by third-party software developers for Lotus.

In 1985 Lotus set out to expand from without and restructure from within. Toward this end, it has since acquired six companies: Software Arts, Inc.; Dataspeed, Inc.; GNP Development Corporation; ISYS Corporation; InfoCenter Software, Inc.; and Graphic Communications, Inc. The company now has subsidiaries in the United Kingdom, France, West Germany, Italy, Sweden, Japan, and Australia and has manufacturing facilities in Cambridge (Massachusetts), Ireland, and Puerto Rico. Lotus maintains twenty-five sales offices around the world—eighteen in North America and seven overseas—and its products are marketed in sixty-five countries in nine different languages.

In July 1986 Mitch Kapor stepped down as Lotus's chairman to pursue outside interests. (In November 1987, he announced the formation of ON Technology, a new software company, located near Lotus's headquarters in Cambridge.) He handed over the reins to Jim Manzi, who joined Lotus as director of marketing. Manzi had come from McKinsey & Company, where he was a management consultant working on the Lotus account, in 1983. Manzi rose rapidly through the Lotus ranks to become president and CEO in 1984 and took over most of the company's administrative duties before Kapor's resignation.

In April 1987 Lotus made a surprise announcement that it had entered into a ten-year agreement with IBM to design software for its largest computers, starting with a version of 1-2-3 for IBM's System/370 mainframes. The agreement makes Lotus the first major personal computer software company to develop software for computers of that size. Manzi also announced that the company now plans to diversify into every major segment of the software industry. In 1987, Lotus's CEO was the highest paid executive in the *Fortune* 500.

(Information provided by Aggie Nteta, firm spokesperson.)

REVENUES: $395.6 million in sales in 1987.

NET INCOME: $72 million in 1987.

INITIAL PUBLIC OFFERING: October 6, 1983.

NUMBER OF SHAREHOLDERS: 4,714 shareholders own Lotus stock in their own names.

OFFICES: In addition to its Cambridge headquarters, Lotus has twenty-five sales offices—in New York, Philadelphia, Boston, Toronto, San Francisco, Seattle, Los Angeles, Newport Beach (California), Dallas, Houston, St. Louis, Chicago, Minneapolis, Detroit, Cleveland, Pittsburgh, Atlanta, Washington, D.C., the United Kingdom, Japan, Sweden, France, West Germany, and Australia; factories in Puerto Rico and Ireland, and labs in Windsor, England, and Tokyo.

NUMBER OF EMPLOYEES: 1,800 worldwide.

AVERAGE AGE OF EMPLOYEES: Thirty-one.

TURNOVER: No exact figures available, but low. Most of the people who started out with the company have remained.

RECRUITMENT: There is a program, but it's still in its infancy. Although the company has recruiting officers, they don't yet visit college campuses.

NUMBER OF NEW HIRES PER YEAR: More than two hundred.

RANGE OF STARTING SALARIES: "Competitive."

POLICY FOR RAISES: "Employees are given annual performance reviews which are applied against merit increases."

TRAINING PROGRAMS: Though some departments, such as sales, conduct sophisticated training programs, most new Lotus employees are not required to undergo specific training for their jobs.

BENEFITS: Generous and comprehensive. The company offers major medical and dental coverage, including psychiatric, as well as a stock purchase plan and programs for investment and profit sharing. The employee assistance program at Lotus is so exhaustive, it could be considered a perk in itself. Each employee receives a diskette listing specialties, specialists, and fees for all kinds of medical and psychological counseling all over the metropolitan Boston area. Obviously, the service is confidential. The company provides tuition reimbursement for any courses relevant to an employee's job, and "relevant" is loosely defined. The company has a referral service for day care and future plans include its own child care facility in an additional building that will be built across the street from Cambridge headquarters.

ADDITIONAL PERKS: Minimal athletic facilities (which they plan to expand when they add their new building) and an agreement with a health club near headquarters, where Lotus employees get a membership discount. Employees are also entitled to discounts on computer hardware.

VACATION: All employees, regardless of when they started working for Lotus, receive, in addition to regular paid holidays, fifteen days off per year—five sick days, five personal days, and five vacation days—which they're entitled to take at their discretion.

BONUSES: Given out at Christmas; all employees are eligible, according to merit.

ANNUAL PARTIES: Lotus hosts an annual holiday party for employees and spouses or their guests in December. The party is formal—not quite black tie, but fairly close—and the location changes from year to year. (In 1987 it was held in a ship terminal.) The company also hosts a children's party, based on different themes, for the employees' offspring. (In 1987 the theme was "international." Some of the kids dressed in foreign costumes, and the entertainment followed suit.) The company holds a casual afternoon summer party out of doors each year, with refreshments and a DJ, for all employees. In addition, individual departments hold their own parties, and Lotus hosts receptions for product launches (which are more for the press and vendors than for employees).

AVERAGE WORKDAY: 9:00 A.M. to 5:00 P.M., though there is some flextime and some departments have shifts that start earlier or go later. Lunch is technically an hour, but flexible. Some employees work late evenings and on weekends for particular projects, but there is no cultural imperative to put in long hours.

DRESS CODE: Relaxed. Employees wear everything from jeans to three-piece suits.

SOCIAL ATMOSPHERE: Congenial. Employees do socialize after working hours.

LANGUAGES INTO WHICH PROGRAMS HAVE BEEN TRANSLATED: German, Dutch, Swedish, Italian, Japanese, Spanish, French, and Portuguese.

HEADQUARTERS: Lotus leases a nine-story building with 240,000 square feet of office space, overlooking the Charles River in Cambridge.

CHARITABLE CONTRIBUTIONS: Just over $1 million in cash and software donations (including administrative expenses) in 1987. Lotus contributes cash to Boston-area organizations that work in the areas of improved race relations and computer-related skills transfer. The company also makes software donations to various organizations across the country. Internationally, Lotus contributes through its manufacturing facility in Dublin to charitable organizations in the United Kingdom, Ireland, France, and Germany.

INTERESTED APPLICANTS CAN SEND RÉSUMÉS TO:
Lotus Development Corporation
Human Resources Department
55 Cambridge Park Way
Cambridge, MA 02142
(617) 577-8500

Lotus Development Corporation has become, perhaps illogically, the logical corporate home for many people who imagined no corporation would be able to contain or sustain them. It may not be perfect harmony or bliss, but many of its young staff express a sense of elation in being able to find a real job in a real company in the real world that is interesting.

Lotus is a six-year-old computer software manufacturer, the brainchild of Mitch Kapor, a graduate of Yale who worked at a wide variety of offbeat jobs before discovering computer software. As is the case with many brave new entrepreneurs, his personality and philosophy inform the sensibility of the company, even though he has now departed from the chairman's office.

While applicants aren't screened for their ideological quirks or brand of humanism, somehow Kapor's organization has attracted a thorough mix of liberal artists; look elsewhere for computer nerds.

One senior manager, a veteran of four years—"which makes me a venerated dowager"—claims all she was looking for was a job in downtown Boston with a good dental plan. "I said, 'I hate computers and weird people.' I didn't know anything about the company, and I threw caution to the winds." The speaker holds undergraduate and graduate degrees in music (performance) and claims that when she was considering her job offer from Lotus, her parents warned her against working at this small new organization of a hundred people. (Today there are 1,800 employees.)

She says her experience has been positive. "I still get the 'warm fuzzies' here. I feel I've gotten my MBA without going to school." Certainly there's been no pressure for her to join the ranks of the officially annointed MBAs.

Her experience is not unique. Many Lotus employees had violently negative reactions to the words "computer," "high tech," and "software" before they discovered Lotus, which is more to them than a software manufacturer. "We're a company first, but we all know something about software," a manager declares.

Working at Lotus is a way of grabbing the high-tech world by its throat without being inundated by techie bullies. According to one employee, whose path to Lotus was paved in journalism, "You get the sense of being on the leading edge of everything. This is where the world is heading, and I wanted to be an insider." She doesn't wear a calculator suspended from her belt. Even normal people get wrapped up in Lotus's mission and culture.

"The expression 'corporate culture' is used a lot. That's a good sign," I'm told. "It means we're treated well as employees." An ex-management consultant enthuses that working at Lotus has provided him with "the best job I could imagine at the leading company in my favorite industry without leaving Boston." A former partner at Bain & Company (see p. 40) he explained his decision to emigrate to Lotus: "I had two world-class opportunities of a lifetime facing me: To continue being vice-president and partner with people I loved working with—half of my study group at Harvard Business School—or the chance to fundamentally shape an agenda in the industry I care very much about."

No one takes a casual approach to working here. The work done at Lotus is important. People care about what they do and the values of the organization. This is so key to the life at Lotus that it bears repeating. People do *care* about the values of this organization.

"This is a meaningful thing to do," says one of the ex-journalists (there are several, including current CEO Jim Manzi) based here. "This is the final resting place for the seventies idealist."

The life of the software designers probably best embodies the Lotus ambience and most closely resembles life in the early days of the company. (At the very least, it presents a microcosm of the way outsiders would like to idealize it.) The data base system/scientific programming people are located in a separate building across the street from the minimalist yet funky (check out the posters on the walls) headquarters on the banks of the Charles River in Cambridge. This building is a comfortable mixture of brick walls, carpeting, and bright enamel—more like intelligently renovated apartments than offices. People here are smart, aggressively so. Their day begins later than most—around 9:30 in the morning. "The first one in in the morning makes the coffee. Strong. We drink African coffee from the Coffee Connection. We're big on Kenyan."

"Is there a difference between here and the other building?" a designer asks rhetorically. "We hope so. It's quieter—there's no ambient noise. We walk around barefoot. It's bohemian and hedonistic." What goes on in this building requires the cooperation of everyone here. It's the honors dorm, where "the best ideas are created in the halls. We don't have *meetings*," they say, eschewing the routine of businesspeople. "We have a dynamic life of the mind here. The environment feels right. We eat sushi. We drink single malt scotch. And wine." (This is said only somewhat facetiously.) "We take pleasure in each other. People down the hall help you out. They psych you up. We have heated debates, like philosophy students."

This may sound too good to be true. While residents of this building acknowledge that being here is like the best of what college can be, the stakes are much, much higher than just a few accumulated papers written in a week of all-nighters. Obviously, this is big business. Furthermore, as Lotus has aged, its people have aged, and the exigencies of maintaining a home life have taken over. "You can get most people to bust ass, not see their wives and husbands, and be driven for one project. But it's hard to get psyched up again." Although a year had passed—at the time of my visit—since the introduction of Jazz, the best-selling adaptation of Lotus's best-selling Symphony created specifically for the Macintosh computer, the people who designed it remembered the intensity, the all-nighters, and the deadlines vividly.

"I still believe in Jazz and am emotionally involved and interested, but I'm not putting myself under the same pressure," says a married member of the team. "There was a certain macho aspect to the project," he admits, a certain peer pressure to spend long hours and weekends and devote oneself to the development of a great product, "but no one's impressed by martyrdom. We're result-oriented."

Above all, there's a pride in and identification with the products. The Jazz designers' names are forever inscribed on every piece of software they produce. You might not call that a perk, but it is a reward for a herculean effort.

"You must be self-disciplined and motivated to fit in. Doing great software takes a lot of work." Anyone interested in working here is given problems to solve during their interview. "We're not interested in 'right' answers; we like to watch people think. We like to see their reasoning."

Lotus is not a scary place. On the contrary, it seems rather inviting, as only an employer of multitudinously diverse talents could be. Regardless of their function, employees tend to be tremendously well spoken, another manifestation of the strong proprietary feelings often expressed. "People assume everyone feels the same way."

High on many people's lists of what makes Lotus terrific is the existence of the Philanthropy Committee. Made up of twelve people from different parts of the company, its credo is "Fortune is worth sharing." There is an in-house charity called LotusAid, which helps the hungry in Boston and contributes to the fight against AIDS. "I don't know if big companies would do that," a manager says. "We all have causes."

A former professional musician now ensconced in the Engineering and Scientific Products Division (ESPD) says, "The mythology of Lotus is true. I'm proud of any company that'll make their first employee the human resources director." Indeed, Lotus spends a lot of time trying to make good lives for its people. This includes fun. A former prep school classics teacher agrees. "Lotus gives you a ready-made social life that can be fantastic." You work with your peers—bright and (for the most part) young people with high social awareness. Official and unofficial activities are fostered by the company. "Last summer at a party, we agreed not to speak of the place we all had in common," a senior product manager remembers. "There was a five-dollar penalty [if you talked about work]."

Sometimes all the closeness may seem overwhelming. One woman recalls, "In the beginning, I was real tied in with Lotus people socially, and even dated a few guys. No more. It is very intense while you're here. I don't want it when I leave."

As a pioneer in a developing industry, the senior management of Lotus took extraordinary steps to ensure they could change and grow as demanded. "When we started, there were no rules in the microcomputer industry." Even before "the company *was* Lotus, we created a structure, with job descriptions, pay plans, et cetera." Employees' needs were considered from the beginning. Growth was deliberate. There have been periods of understaffing and overstaffing. "We don't always have time to hire, so people often carry other people's jobs." But your career at Lotus is a function of what you want to do and how you want to grow. "They allow you to craft your own career," employees say. "This is the best place for matching the needs of a person to the needs of the company."

Talk of growth and change in the industry and company is constant. It is impossible not to be almost obsessed with the strides made in just six years. "A fast-growing company isn't easy on its people," one of the first employees reasons. One of the toughest issues is dealing with new bosses as your responsibilities change. Issues of status and ego seem to emerge. "One friend has had ten bosses in three years. It's tiring to have to keep proving yourself over and over again," a sympathetic colleague says. "Someone might be hired to be your boss."

One of the victims of the rapid expansion has been communication. People who worked at early Lotus complain they no longer know everyone they see in the hall. "As the company's gotten bigger, we can accomplish more over a case of beer than in a meeting." Meetings used to accommodate the rare ability to rely on consensus to make major decisions. "Staff meetings used to be forums for decisions. The company was even named at one. At this point, they are dog-and-pony acts." Held at the nearby Sonesta Hotel, between 70 and 80 percent of all those in Cambridge attend. But forums they're not. They are described as "one way—microphone devices for communication."

Large-scale events just exaggerate the feeling that there is an ever increasing pool of new people who will never truly know what the real Lotus was like. Like many other pioneering companies, Lotus had one spirit in its first private years and another in its larger public incarnation. The tide turned with the shipping of 1-2-3, the single most popular spreadsheet software, still the core of the business. People who were around in the beginning have a definite pride in having been there in the good old informal, uncertain days. They fought the good fight together and, like military veterans, have little patience for those who arrived after the armistice. Furthermore, the first forty employees—the total Lotus work force before 1-2-3—"were the only ones with potential to earn lots of money." (Lotus's initial public offering was October 6, 1983. Happily for the original forty, Wall Street, in the words of one analyst, "went nuts.")

Old Lotus was comprised of the risk takers, who really believed in their product. "People worked tremendously long hours. There was so much to be done. You arrived between seven-thirty and eight in the morning and *snuck* out at eight P.M." Earlybird employees saw themselves as entrepreneurs. They describe new Lotus as "more fast-track types who want prestige. A certain yuppie aspect. *Very* Cambridge."

Old Lotus versus new Lotus. Old is personified by Mitch, the guru to many. New is embodied by CEO Jim Manzi (often termed "ruthless"), who was lured by Kapor from McKinsey. Where Mitch could wax rhapsodic, Manzi waxes numeric. His imprint is in making Lotus a grown-up marketing-driven company. His strengths are alleged to be bottom-line strengths; his people reflect that.

Old Lotus-ites often refer to the "blue suits" who've invaded their comfortable modern offices. (They're the marketing alumni of "Big Blue"—IBM.) "We will now hire the traditional applicant," an engineer explains. "Someone who went to college, has an MBA, and had two jobs. They must appreciate the early employees here. We'll never outgrow our founders."

"Sometimes I feel stressed out," one early hire confesses, "and I'll go to a staff meeting and look around, and I'll think, 'these aren't my people.' " He's old Lotus.

Do not misinterpret the sniping of old Lotus. There is no color war, no tripping of enemies in the corridors—no enemies, for that matter. Always, the "old-timers" feel a sense of pride, nay perhaps a sense of self-righteousness that newcomers can't even approach. They are pleased with themselves for having caught on early, even though they may only have lucked out— and sometimes they lord that over the next generation.

The new generation often envies the seniority of its forebears. Like the younger siblings of radicals on missions, they wish to borrow the romance of the rebellion. How ironic, then, that the appeal of the hard times has given birth to a more respectable class of employees!

Lotus's reputation has lured people to a company that in some respects no longer exists. As one designer explains, "At first [it] was very opulent—lots of parties, a lot of money, and we bought as much equipment as was manageable. Then, there was the awful realization that our resources were finite." Lotus is still considered "a cool place to work," but the party is over. "It's not just an adventure," in the final analysis, "it's a job."

One of the tasks facing Lotus is integrating the world outside Cambridge with that within. With manufacturing plants in Puerto Rico and Ireland, research and development facilities in Windsor (England) and Tokyo, and sales offices in Munich and Paris, Lotus hires local talent, people who've never worked in Cambridge. "Our culture *is* Cambridge. We want people outside the city to feel a part of Lotus, but we're painfully aware they'll never totally bridge the gap." Again, it was determined early on in the life of the company that it would be far more intelligent to staff these off-site facilities with natives than to import a ruling class from the States. This certainly fosters a positive regard by Lotus's foreign cultures, as Lotus can provide jobs and revenue, but it adds to the sense of loss felt by the home office that today's company is less within its grasp than ever before.

Add to this the previously mentioned gripe that "for better or worse, most of our salespeople are from IBM." While it is acknowledged that IBM's sales training is superb, it is feared that these employees will perhaps manifest IBM style while touting the Lotus message. Because they spend most of their time out in the field, whether in Dayton or in Deauville, chances are they'll have more difficulty in getting to know Lotus. It is extremely revealing that understanding the personality of the company is so important a concern to everyone here. It is certainly a rare corporate attribute.

Keeping culture and those "warm fuzzies" intact is a high priority at Lotus, and so we segue to the extravagantly staffed employee relations office. Lotus provides ample opportunity for employees to air grievances, both personal and professional, with guaranteed confidentiality. One vehicle is the suggestion box, which is painted purple. Suggestions are called "grapes," and they are given and received in earnest.

All employees are entitled to a software diskette to be used in conjunction with Symphony —another best-selling software program—of a painstakingly researched list of referrals of all kinds in the greater Boston area. If your problem is alcohol and you live on the North Shore, punch that up on your computer and you will find a list of local counselors, Alcoholics Anonymous meetings, social workers, and detox centers, with addresses, phone numbers, prices, and so on. If your problem is domestic abuse, the same wealth of information exists. (Lotus's medical coverage is also generous: For example, each employee is entitled to $1,250 toward mental health expenses, as is each of his or her dependents.) When employees simply wish to talk with someone in the human relations function, that, too, can be conducted with secrecy. (If, for example, you can only have this talk Tuesday at 10:00 P.M., that's when you will be called by a member of this staff.)

Interestingly, 90 percent of the problems handled by this office are work-related. Again, we are reminded that working in a fast-paced place such as Lotus is "stresssful and hard, especially now that employees are starting to raise families. It requires an adjustment." Furthermore, there is the struggle to keep up with the peer pressure that asks co-workers to put in long hours. "Frankly, some people take the 'cult' too seriously." As the microcomputer industry enters adulthood, so, too, does Lotus. This is a generation of people who prepared themselves for professional success at the expense, perhaps, of marriage and raising a family. No one warned them that these dual needs could collide. That isn't to say everyone is young. Jim Manzi has said he wants to bring more "gray hair" into the company. "There's something to be said for young people who'll bust their asses, but older people do fit in."

Career feedback is available all the time. No one should be surprised during his or her annual performance reviews, although approximately 30 percent of the employees write responses or rebuttals. (Three of the twenty-three people in employee relations handle face-to-face problem resolution.)

The payoff is huge. While Lotus's turnover rate is no better or worse than industry averages, those who intuit a continuing role for themselves plan to stay on. "Lotus is a company of superlatives. We're able to define ourselves. The supportive atmosphere allows me to do a good job." Lotus is still a place where you can bike to work, although if you drive a BMW, your car will not be conspicuous in the parking lot. Lotus embraces blue jeans and blue suits, liberals and conservatives (at least some, maybe). People don't contemplate leaving for other jobs at other companies, software or otherwise. Lotus's employees claim they would only leave to start their own companies. Working for a star entrepreneurial company can spoil a person.

"I have to ask myself why I spend so much time here," a "strictly liberal arts" graduate-turned-marketing-person says. "I have a lot of confidence in the senior management. I have confidence in our products. I like my view. The coffee's free. And we're still a family. We like each other. And my ideas will be taken seriously."

POLAROID CORPORATION

Polaroid

HISTORY & OPERATIONS

The technology that ultimately led to Polaroid instant photographs was developed by Edwin Land, a Harvard science student who was studying light polarization during the 1920s. In 1932 Land announced that he had invented a means of producing a synthetic light-polarizing material that would enable scientists to investigate the phenomenon more cheaply and outside the laboratory, to which such studies had formerly been confined. Realizing that his discovery would lead to a new applied science with commercial applications, Land left Harvard and formed Land-Wheelwright Laboratories.

In 1933, Land incorporated the laboratory, which manufactured light polarizers—which block reflected glare and improve visual acuity—and obtained a patent on his product, one of the 533 patents he holds, second in number only to Thomas Edison. Eastman Kodak purchased the polarizers for the manufacture of photographic filters, and the American Optical Company bought them for the manufacture of Polaroid Day glasses. In 1937 Land founded the Polaroid Corporation (other name under consideration for the company: Epibolipol) to acquire Land-Wheelwright Laboratories and to further both technical and commercial developments in the field of light polarization. In establishing Polaroid, Land wanted to create a working environment in which talented technical people could exchange ideas and invent products. This goal was as important to him as developing the new company into a profit center, and his pro-employee philosophy was evident in the company's generous policies (e.g., any employee who worked for the company for at least ten years was guaranteed lifetime employment).

Between 1937 and 1941, the Polaroid Corporation introduced a series of products that employed polarizing materials, including variable density windows for trains, glare-free desk lamps, and glass-testing equipment. The company also produced a new type of three-dimensional photograph called the Vectrograph, which was viewed through Polaroid polarizing glasses. Polaroid's annual revenues increased from $142,000 in 1937 to $1 million in 1941.

During World War II, Polaroid produced products to aid in the war effort, and by the end of the war, the company had 1,250 employees and annual revenues of $16 million. In 1947 Polaroid announced it had invented a revolutionary new camera that produced finished photographs—in sepia tones—within one minute after taking the picture. The new cameras were an immediate hit, and Polaroid sold $5 million worth of them the first year they went on sale. Utilizing the same technology, Polaroid subsequently introduced a copy maker, an oscilloscope camera and film back, a piece of hardware to adapt professional cameras to accept Polaroid instant films. In 1951 Polaroid introduced instant film for radiography, the first of a continuing series of Polaroid instant X-ray products.

Land continued to develop and refine the new technology and products for commercial, scientific, medical, and industrial use. In 1959 and 1960 Polaroid extended its operations abroad by establishing subsidiary companies in West Germany, Canada, and Japan. In 1963, after fifteen years of development, Polaroid introduced the first instant color film, and by 1970 the company's annual revenues had reached $500 million.

By 1972 Polaroid had fully refined the instant camera and introduced the SX-70, which was lightweight and completely automatic and produced photographs that developed in front of the user's eyes. The fixed-focus OneStep Land camera, which the company launched in 1977, was, for four years, the best-selling camera in the United States, and Polaroid's annual sales exceeded $1 billion the first year it was introduced. In the same year, the company launched an instant home movie system, Polavision, which was mediocre in quality and flopped, costing the company between $600 and $700 million. In 1978 Polaroid's earnings peaked with the sale of 9.4 million cameras. That year, Kodak entered the instant photography market with its first instant camera and film. Polaroid immediately filed a patent infringement suit, which was finally settled in Polaroid's favor in 1986. Kodak, which by then had won 25 percent of the instant photography market, was forced to cease production of all instant photography products, as well as to recall all those it had already produced. Though an amount has not yet been determined, Kodak may have to pay Polaroid as much as $1 billion in damages.

Since the late 1970s, with the introduction of inexpensive and easy-to-use 35 mm cameras —which produce photographs cheaper than and superior in quality to Polaroids—instant pictures have lost some of their allure for amateur photographers, and Polaroid has felt the effects. Though Polaroid is still a lucrative operation, it has yet to regain the profit margin it had in the sixties and seventies. Dr. Land resigned as Polaroid's director and chairman of the board in 1982 and was replaced by William J. McCune, who joined Polaroid as an MIT graduate in 1939 and has served as CEO since 1980. Under McCune's leadership, Polaroid has begun diversifying into a number of different areas, including the manufacture of videocassettes and floppy disks for computers, both highly competitive fields. McCune has also striven to expand Polaroid's nonconsumer business—all products not sold to amateur photographers—which has increased considerably under his reign.

INNER CITY, INC.

Polaroid, long known for its progressive philosophy, operates Inner City, Inc., a wholly owned subsidiary that functions as a real-world training program for disadvantaged people. Inner City, Inc., trains people who lack the skills and experience to hold a job in the basics of working in an industrial environment. The Inner City, Inc., staff teaches trainees everything from personal grooming to remedial English and math—anything they need to enable them to become effective employees. Then trainees get a chance to do real work. Polaroid and outside companies contract with Inner City, Inc., for almost any kind of work they need to farm out. For example, when Polaroid decided to test market triple packs of film in limited quantities, rather than designing an expensive new machine, they contracted with Inner City, Inc., to hand pack the boxes.

The Inner City, Inc., program is geared primarily to young adults, and the average age of trainees is around twenty-five. The length of a trainee's stay in the program varies dramatically, depending on an individual's skills and progress. Inner City, Inc., is not a charitable enterprise but a legitimate profit-making business. Virtually 100 percent of all trainees are eventually placed in real working environments.

In 1986 Polaroid introduced the Spectra camera, its first major new product since Polavision in 1978. The Spectra, which was launched with a $30 million advertising campaign aimed at upscale consumers, retails for around $200 and produces instant photographs that are reputedly equal in quality to 35 mm film. Thus far, sales have been very good. In 1986 Polaroid's earnings roughly tripled, and the company attributes much of this increase to sales of the Spectra.

Today, Polaroid employs around 13,500 full-time, permanent employees, with about 9,800 working in the United States and more than 3,600 overseas. Approximately 40 percent of the company's sales are abroad, and the two primary foreign markets are Japan and Germany. Sixty percent of the company's sales are to the amateur instant photography market, with the rest coming mostly from nonconsumer products in the medical, technical, and professional fields.

(Information provided by Harry Johnson and Meg Crowley, company spokespersons.)

REVENUES: Worldwide sales were $1.76 billion in 1987.

NET EARNINGS: $116.1 million, or $1.88 per share, in 1987.

INITIAL PUBLIC OFFERING: Polaroid has been public since Edwin Land founded it in 1937.

NUMBER OF SHARES OUTSTANDING: Over 61 million.

OFFICES: Headquarters in Cambridge (Massachusetts) and about five different Massachusetts locations. The company also has distribution and service centers in the following locations: Atlanta, Cleveland, Dallas, El Segundo (California), Oakbrook (Illinois), Paramus (New Jersey), and Santa Ana (California). All manufacturing in the United States is done in eastern Massachusetts.

FOREIGN SUBSIDIARIES: Polaroid has foreign subsidiaries in Australia, Austria, Belgium, Brazil, Canada, Denmark, France, Germany, Hong Kong, Ireland, Italy, Japan, Mexico, the Netherlands, New Zealand, Norway, Panama, Puerto Rico, Singapore, Spain, Sweden, Switzerland, and the United Kingdom. Roughly 40 percent of sales are in foreign markets, and the primary markets outside the United States are Japan and Germany.

NUMBER OF EMPLOYEES: 13,421: 9,776 full-time permanent employees in the United States, and 3,645 overseas. The company employs an additional five-hundred temporary workers in the United States.

AVERAGE AGE OF EMPLOYEES: 42.9.

TURNOVER: 2.9 percent; 2.5 percent of hourly employees and 3.6 percent of salaried employees. ("Under 5 percent is considered very low.")

RECRUITMENT: Polaroid recruits actively at thirty-four schools, among them thirteen traditionally black colleges.

NUMBER OF NEW HIRES PER YEAR: From 1978 to 1985 Polaroid reduced the number of its employees from roughly 20,000 to roughly 13,000. In 1986 the company hired 185 salaried and 42 hourly employees, and in 1987 it hired 300 salaried and 124 hourly employees.

RANGE OF STARTING SALARIES: Between $25,000 and $32,000 for bachelor's and/or master's degree holders. "We aim always to be nationally competitive."

POLICY FOR RAISES: Raises are awarded by a recently adopted process called pay for performance. Under the program, Polaroid divisions are allocated a limited budget from which to award promotions and merit increases. The purpose of the plan is to link salaried employees' compensation as closely as possible to their job performance and to avoid overspending, a problem that plagued Polaroid during its years of automatic generous raises (part of Dr. Land's legacy of progressive, pro-employee policies).

TRAINING PROGRAMS: Technically, each department is responsible for the training of its employees, and a great deal of decentralized training goes on. In addition there is a large companywide training department that has extensive entry-level training for a whole host of particular jobs. Polaroid also has an extensive basic skills program—English as a second language, adult basic education, and so on—which is available to all employees at no cost.

BENEFITS: Generous and comprehensive. *Nonretirement benefits:* choice of medical and dental plans (company pays 80 percent of both for employees and their families); life insurance is optional and paid for by the employee for coverage of up to two and a half times base pay; two disability and insurance programs: short-term, which guarantees 100 percent of base pay for up to one year and is paid entirely by the company, and long-term (more than a year), which is 65 percent of base pay up to the age of sixty-five (company pays 75 percent); tuition reimbursement for any course or degree program that is job-related (company pays 100 percent and "job-related" is very generously defined); paid maternity leave and day care subsidies.

(Polaroid pioneered a voucher system for child care. The employee chooses any type of day care, and the company pays a portion of the cost on a sliding scale—the more money an employee makes, the less Polaroid pays). *Retirement benefits:* a pension plan, paid by the company; a profit-sharing plan (a portion of company profits goes into the plan, and employees get their share upon either retirement or resignation from the company); stock plan (which accumulates until an employee either retires or resigns); a pretax savings plan and a posttax savings plan; and a first-dollar, cash bonus plan (when the company makes a profit, a certain percentage is set aside as an employee cash bonus pool, which every year is divided among employees to be held for retirement. The amount a given employee receives increases with tenure).

ADDITIONAL PERKS: An employee store in which company products are discounted.

VACATION: Two weeks, with one additional day each year for the next ten years. After ten years, employees get four weeks. Also, there is a seniority vacation bonus. Every fifth year, employees receive either an extra week's pay or an extra week's vacation.

BONUSES: Everyone below senior management level who has worked for Polaroid for more than six months gets an automatic bonus determined by a formula based on seniority, pay grade, and the company's performance. Senior managers' bonuses are based on performance.

ANNUAL PARTY: No companywide annual party, though individual work groups often host Christmas parties or other annual events at their own discretion. The company is much too large to hold an all-company event.

AVERAGE WORKDAY: Corporate employees work from 9:00 A.M. to 5:00 P.M. or longer, depending on the project and time of year. "We're not clock watchers, by and large." Manufacturing employees work in one of three eight-hour shifts around the clock.

DRESS CODE: No stated code. "You only have to walk through here three minutes to know that. We're petty laid back." Employees can wear anything they want, within certain broad limits. Women don't wear shorts, for instance, but a lot of them do wear jeans. In corporate headquarters you see slacks but not jeans. Many men do wear jackets and ties, but research and engineering people don't. "No real pressure."

SOCIAL ATMOSPHERE: Depends on the division. Some are highly social, while in others there is essentially no fraternization after working hours. "It's very localized."

HEADQUARTERS: "Corporate headquarters is located in leased facilities at Technology Square in Cambridge, Massachusetts. At this location are Corporate Administration, Marketing, Finance, Patent Research and Engineering headquarters. The well-landscaped square has cafeteria, banking, and travel services located on the premises."

CHARITABLE CONTRIBUTIONS: Polaroid has its own foundation, which distributed $2.1 million in cash contributions in 1987. The primary areas of donations are educational, cultural, and community. Of the total, $328,282 was given in matching gifts. The foundation matches an employee's donation to the charity of his or her choice, two to one, up to $500.

INTERESTED APPLICANTS CAN SEND RÉSUMÉS TO:
Polaroid Corporation
Personnel Department
549 Technology Square
Cambridge, MA 02139
(617) 577-2000

The thing about Polaroid is that the name has become eponymous, like Kleenex, or Xerox, or Frigidaire. We've all heard about its products and probably owned one at one time or another or, at the very least, been photographed by a Polaroid camera and given the result. (If you've seen one of the never-ending string of commercials for the Craft-Matic bed, you know that if you agree to submit to a personal sales pitch for the bed, you get a certificate redeemable for one free Polaroid camera.) (And according to an executive of Polaroid International in Great Britain, "Polaroid" is synonymous with "sunglasses," a major portion of the company's business overseas.)

The Polaroid Corporation is not as well known as its familiar products, but it, too, enjoys a certain recognition among noncorporate consumers. Based in Cambridge, Massachusetts, it has enjoyed the reputation of being a pioneer in an *interesting* technology. The American style of instant gratification is so . . . Polaroidian. In addition, faint recollections of the company's goodness nip at our collective subconscious.

Edwin Land, known as "Dr. Land" even before he amassed his honorary doctorates from institutions like Harvard (the college he attended without completing his undergraduate degree), Yale, MIT, Columbia, Williams, Carnegie Institute of Technology (which became Carnegie-Mellon), Brandeis, and so on, was the founder of Polaroid, a name coined based on his work in light polarization. He cared a great deal about creating an environment that would be nourishing to the inventor. While the corporation experienced lean times in the early 1980s, it is again prospering in this last half of the decade and reappropriating its claim of being a good place to work.

Many on Polaroid's work force were educated as engineers. Marie Smyth holds her bachelor's degree in electrical engineering from SUNY at Stony Brook, class of 1978, "during a boom for engineers. You could pick and choose what you'd do." Her path to Polaroid was directed by a desire to live in Boston and get her master's degree at night, which she did at Northeastern University. Having studied optics, specifically holography, "I sent my résumé to Steven Benton, the inventor of white light holography, who worked at Polaroid." Her first job at the company was in the consumer product area, as a designer on "a new camera in the Sonar line that was canceled. But our work was incorporated into a later model."

At Polaroid, one has to learn to work in teams. Marie reflects that being a capable engineer does not necessarily imply being a good cooperator. "We bring new people in slowly and work interdependently. I was always the kind of person who liked to build something and see it work. When you design a small part of something, you get to see it as a complete system."

Smyth confesses that "grown-up life is tough. Sometimes it's like having more than I can handle. I'm in by seven-thirty. Ninety percent of the time, I work through lunch." She usually can leave before 5:00 P.M., though, and has rarely worked a sixty-hour week. "My boss says, 'We're not paying you for the hours, but for the work you do.' " Marie used to work in an office with a fellow she liked. Now they're married and work two floors apart. Polaroid marriages "are quite common. Unless it poses a problem, Polaroid is lenient about it. [My husband and I] arrive together when we can, which makes a nicer commute. We don't usually see each other here, and we don't usually eat [lunch] together."

In order to keep their jobs in their proper perspectives, the Smyths try not to discuss work at home. "It's an unspoken rule. I don't really know what my husband does, but we understand each other's environment. We will not talk technical details at all." Many of their friends are fellow Polaroidians. "Half of our department [Product Electronics] is under forty. I feel sorry for people who are young and single in an older, married group." She characterizes her group's culture as "pleasant, fairly light, even though we work under a fairly remarkable set of circumstances. We never scream; we get along."

The corporate conscience is also quite appealing to Smyth, although it was certainly not the major reason she sought employment at Polaroid. "I didn't know enough about the points of views of companies when I was interviewing. I wanted benefits that included a hundred percent tuition reimbursement, and I didn't want to do any kind of military work." Polaroid normally offers working mothers an eight-week paid maternity leave. "The few women I know who had children came right back to full-time work."

Marie, who is childless (as of this interview), admits she had considered leaving the company every couple of years, but it's nothing she would act upon anymore. "Every two years I'd get the bug to leave. Headhunters would call, but I always decided to stay. I'd voice my grievances and stay. Now I have too many years here, and I don't want to disrupt my life. I feel people will listen to complaints. You can get things done. And at ten years, you become vested."

The company she joined is not exactly the same place where she works today. Smyth joined a work force of 21,000 that is now a corporation of 14,000 (although the word on the street is that Polaroid will grow again). She joined a corporation built on film for the consumer market that is becoming more important as a supplier of technology to the professional and medical communities. Even between 1978 and 1985, when Polaroid reduced its existing work force by some 7,000 employees, the electronics division, in which Marie works, was hiring. She participates in the recruiting process.

Smyth finds that "applicants respond differently to male and female interviewers. None of the women is shy. They had to survive four years of school [as members of a minority in their fields]. Those percentages don't change when you go to work."

Sometimes relying on her "gut feeling" during interviews, she says, "After five minutes with someone, I know. There are rarely borderline cases. We're looking for fairly outgoing, articulate, social beings. We're not hiring nerdy engineers. We're a changing environment, and new people have to be able to interface with other groups." Obviously, the applicants Marie sees must be able to satisfy certain academic requirements, providing an adequate transcript and answering technical questions orally or in a written test. "I look at how they approach the answer as much as getting the right answer. We tend not to hire people with narrow interests. Our people go all over the place."

Lloyd Taylor is a research scientist at Polaroid, sort of an emeritus figure with thirty years of tenure to his credit, a chemist by training. On the subject of fitting in at the company, he says, "I'm barely compatible with Polaroid. If you're a creative person, you have a ferocious need for independence." [Author's note: At this point, I like to remember Dr. Taylor lighting his pipe. I think he did. If he didn't, it would certainly become the tweedy gentleman.] "If you cave in and become a bureaucrat, it's all over." Somehow Taylor got roped into certain administrative duties. "I'm a senior company officer. I'm considered a maverick, although I've never asked anyone. I have the sense of people's eyes rolling when I speak."

His office has the cluttered look of a professor who refuses to take his sabbatical. In addition to all the books and papers, his blackboards have the markings of calculations-in-progress. His twenty-five-year rocking chair (from Polaroid, not MIT, his alma mater) enhances the academic decor. A calendar squashed into a bookcase indicates the date is Wednesday, January 24, 1979. (Today is May 21, 1986.) Taylor calls Polaroid "one of the more creative places around. We're doing a lot of nice work in our little lab. It's fun watching my young people doing so well. It's really neat."

Dr. Taylor is proud of the work he has done during his quarter century plus. He has approximately seventy-five patents to his credit. "They're in your name, but you assign them to Polaroid for a dollar. That's the way you do it." You don't moan over the possible revenues you've signed away. That's not what it means to work in a creative corporation. "The company gives you freedom and pays you well. I don't think they owe you more.

"Anytime you invent something that solves a problem, you're proud. Or you drive past the factory on Route 128, and you know they're making your chemical. It's a thrill." Taylor enjoyed a special "kick" when he invented "special polymers that solved problems of the SX-70," the instant color camera that turned Mariette Hartley and James Garner into the all-American couple. "Those compounds didn't exist before."

Working with Edwin Land was "really spectacular. You did what he wanted, and you did what you wanted. Land was something else. It was easy for him to exercise his vision [as the president, CEO, and director of research]. Dr. Land wore all hats. So when he was in charge, it was all harmonious. When I arrived here, Land said, 'Ten to fifteen percent of your time is your own.' I still hold them to it. It was part of why I came here. Part of my compensation. The problems were so vast you had the opportunity of doing all kinds of chemistry." Tolerance of mistakes was another Land policy. "Dr. Land was on a failure kick in the sixties. He'd say, 'Do many experiments until you get it right.' We try to encourage and not laugh at people. It's a very important attitude. One of the worst problems now is that people are afraid to fail.

"Sometimes you invent something twenty years ahead of its time, and you don't have the other stuff needed to use with it. A patent only endures seventeen years, and there are no renewals. You could invent something great and not make a cent until nineteen years later, when people figure out what it's used for." Personal wealth is not the goal. It seems that posterity is also a weak incentive, as at best, you are only inventing an interdependent piece of the product at large. "The purpose is to teach. The inventions give you the right, and then they enter the public domain."

What comes through Taylor's words is that working at Polaroid is a privilege for the creative. "I dream all the time. If I didn't have that, I couldn't come to the office. You can't fake that.

"I was always interested in taking pictures, and instant photography was a dream. I still don't think we're there. We need the perfect all-temperature photograph. It's a good excuse to do chemistry. You can still find little Polaroids all over the place." Taylor's lab is working on a faster, clearer direct thermal color transparency. "It's our 'Post-It Note' [see p. 392]. The fun part is, 'How big will this be?' We need some squeaky wheels around here."

Pennye Williams is a financial analyst at Polaroid, a 1983 graduate of Howard University, and the only college recruit who came to Cambridge that year. The two-year financial program that lured her here consists of three eight-month assignments in different areas, to get an overview of the manufacturer. "The program is structured to figure out where you and they want you to go. I didn't really have a choice since I was alone in the program. The steering committee gave me advice on what would be best for my career. I had good exposure and visibility in the company."

Her stint as financial analyst is her first posttraining assignment. Compensation and seniority are conferred through a system of grades. An entry-level job direct from college is a grade four. Pennye's training guaranteed her a grade six. Being a six doesn't signify an exact salary, just a range. "People don't talk about [the money]. Salaries overlap with grades." There are ten grades at Polaroid, but that doesn't quite take care of the most senior personnel, who are ungraded.

Pennye's adjustment to Polaroid has not been as trying as her adjustment to the North. "Professionally, it's not tough. Socially, it's not easy. People are colder up here than they are in the South. Being a black young professional is harder." Being a young black professional woman is lonely. "I tend to become a workaholic. If there's only an empty apartment to return to—I might as well stay in the office." At an age at which many of her friends are getting married, Williams can say, "I don't regret my ambitiousness. If I had stayed at home, I'd envy career women."

Marian Stanley has not had to sacrifice having a family since she's been with Polaroid. "They allowed me time off. I've had four children. I stayed because the grip was loose." Also, the twenty-one-year veteran says, "Usually, if you worked part time, you'd get terrible stuff to do. They gave me significant work part time. I advanced. That's not done in the corporate world. Polaroid has some unorthodox managers." Today she is the manager of new business planning and development.

A former schoolteacher, Marian was attracted to the company initially as a way to be around adults. But the heart of Polaroid, integrating human values and, yes, the occasional oddball, was what made it irresistible. "Polaroid allows eccentricity. It's absorbed the Cambridge environment. It's a highly ethical company where you don't have to worry: A lot of engineers come here who don't want to work in defense. It's clean. You can have a good work life. Your company is earnestly trying to be a force for social good." An example she cites was Polaroid's nominal involvement in South Africa in 1971. "We were very involved in social change. We don't want to be a part of any system whose beliefs we don't believe in. We turned down [offers to establish ourselves in] two South American countries . . . for good money. Land surrounded himself with people of good ethical sense. Twenty-five years ago, we had one of the first community relations offices." Polaroid is known locally as a good guy, even by those who are not employed by the corporation. "I'm always amazed by how many people seem to know so much about us."

A cause for some concern, though far from troubling, is the paucity of women in senior management. Certainly the fields from which Polaroid has gleaned its work force have not been populated by many women. "The board is white, male, and technical . . . as it was years ago. They feel they've made tremendous leaps and are men of goodwill. We [women] are getting closer and closer to the door of the club, and we believe it'll open. The company's been through a lot of social change. They've loaded middle management with blacks and women, and [senior] management does have class. Technical guys may not have been raised and trained with women, but they are very rational." Admittedly, when Marian arrived in 1967, most women at Polaroid were there for short periods of time, putting their husbands through MIT or Harvard and not looking for senior status.

The consensus here is that though women haven't advanced to the rank of vice-president, titles are not terribly important. "Everyone's on a first-name basis, even the president. Only some Ph.D.s like to be called 'Doctor.' " (Lloyd Taylor is not one of them.)

As we've seen, Polaroid is a good place for the nonscientist to work. For him, personal satisfaction will be derived from sales, marketing, and, according to vice-president Joe McLaughlin, "a chance to stretch yourself. A chance to think big." After working in sales at Procter & Gamble and Johnson & Johnson, McLaughlin came to Cambridge, "feeling it could be my career company." He had "almost" felt that way about one of his previous employers, but at Polaroid, "there was no struggle to make changes.

"Throughout this time [thirty years], I've seen the same personality, with some distortion. Polaroid's values have been transmitted through its people. There isn't anyone in the company I wouldn't want as a neighbor." Another benefit of working here is the nature of the products themselves. A camera is a neutral, happy product. "We sell a product that adds a dimension to your life. Being able to share a memory with a picture. Recording the moment is now part of the moment." The proliferation of one-hour photo stores "has dramatized the need for fast pictures. The Spectra," McLaughlin says paternally of the new camera that is reversing Polaroid's flat prospects, "will help make better photographers. You get a hundred percent of what you see in the viewfinder for your composition. The film quality is better. You can do more with it, with an ease of use." Whereupon he whips out an envelope of pictures he took on a recent trip to Bermuda. It's as if the colors, trees, water, flowers—the richness and depth— were his children. He's that proud.

Speaking of proud, there's probably no one in the company more proud of the products, the ethics, the history, or the privilege of working for Polaroid than Gene Donovan, the head security guard at Polaroid's executive building. When he returned from Vietnam in 1968 and had trouble finding a job, he began sweeping floors for Polaroid at midnight. "About a year later, I became a security guard. I knew it was for me. I was given a little bit of responsibility, and I excelled, and then [in 1975] I got the cream-of-the-crop jobs, and then got the creamiest. The chairman says I'm *his* receptionist."

"I never thought of leaving for another job in security. I do it more for pleasure than the money, though I'm well paid." He pauses for a second. "If I won a substantial amount of money in the lottery, I'd still work here. Even if I won a million dollars." Nevertheless, he buys a lottery ticket every single day. He's won *ten times* and advises that you don't pay taxes on prizes of $600 or less. "People make fun of me because I go on vacation every two months, 'cause I've made so much money." Gene's been to Las Vegas, St. Maarten, and Australia. "It's the best place," he says of the latter. "Tropical, desert, mountains. I spent a week in the outback in a four-wheel drive. It was the best thing I've ever done."

He is without a doubt a happy man. Why? "My favorite part of the job is knowing six or seven thousand people personally. I practice knowing their names, and I never forget a face. I call the chairman 'Boss.' I couldn't call him by his first name; I couldn't form the word. Everyone's friendly. I've been here longer than most people, and I've broken them in." At forty, Donovan is one of the most popular people at Polaroid. There's a rumored fan club in his honor, made up of female employees. "I treat women like they're important. I used to date women here, but I don't anymore. I like to keep them guessing." Socially, he is an enigmatic figure. "No one's quite sure what I do, except for the people who are supposed to know. Everyone wants to know about my personal life, but I like to be mysterious."

Gene awakens at 6:00 A.M., feeds his fish and guinea pig, and walks to work every day. (In the snow, too.) His home is two and a half miles away, a thirty-minute walk. "So I'm ready. When it rains I wear my Red Sox hat." His work day begins at 8:00 A.M. He takes a ten-minute walk around the block at 9:15. "I barely take a twenty-minute lunch at 11:15. It makes me kind of nervous to be away. I never, never goof off. When I'm here, I'm here. At four-o'clock I take my tie off." Donovan wears a suit to work, in lieu of the usual security officer's uniform. He is unarmed. "They didn't want a police presence. We both like the tie and jacket." He walks home every day as well, stopping at a pub "to have beverages." He goes to see the Red Sox play whenever he can get free tickets, and he witnessed the [New England] Patriots compete in Super Bowl XX.

"I like Polaroid. Everyone knows that. They've treated me excellently all these years. I've gotten a good benefit package. I like the way things are run. I'm not a complainer. I could see myself retiring from Polaroid."

Gene's loyalty knows no bounds. At a family outing that was held sometime during the eight years Polaroid was suing Kodak for infringement of the instant camera patent, one of Gene's relatives assembled the group for a picture. The camera in her hand was a dreaded Kodak instant camera. "I couldn't allow my picture to be taken with that camera. I just froze up. We were in the middle of the lawsuit."

Pat King could be the *Übermensch*. Eleven years ago, when he arrived at Polaroid from Ohio State University, the company encouraged him to complete his Ph.D. He worked full time while earning his degree full time. "And we had two more kids [in addition to the two he and his wife already had], and I painted the house. In two years."

When he returned to the Boston area from Ohio (he had attended Boston College as an undergraduate), "Polaroid was one of the few 'chemistry companies' around." King never sought a Ph.D. in chemistry in order to teach. "I can't stand chalk dust. It gives me headaches." Yet he does hold occasional seminars at Boston College. Teaching "is typical of chemists as they age. Being on campus gives us the ability to be current and learn about learning. It's a resource." These seminars are not a front for recruiting, since his department has not hired new scientists in the last six or seven years. But "if we met someone terrific, we'd beat the drums to get them here."

In Exploratory Chemical Research, where Pat is a research group leader, "our charter is to do whatever we want. Also, we work with other groups." The group is small. "Two people report to me; that's a good size." Pat likens his leadership in the lab to "Pete Rose as the manager-coach of the Cincinnati Reds. I like to give projects to people with personal goals. People help each other out. I cover weekends." When Dr. Land was at the helm, "you were here all the time. He'd call you if you weren't here. That's the way it was."

Unlike more marketing-driven companies whose targets are the "average consumer," Polaroid has to endure criticism that it's too technically driven. "But we're responding to our customers." In a way, the issue is the old Polaroid versus the new Polaroid, Land's technocracy giving way to the present day's marketocracy. "It's not a problem. Now it's in a nostalgia stage."

Polaroid does not actively encourage interpersonal socializing, and although people from the company fraternize outside headquarters, "the social nucleus is separate from the company. A lot of people make their own beer." King says he and his fellow chemists do manage to achieve a balance in their lives. "I didn't know anything [about] Polaroid until I got here. I'd only heard that this was a great place in terms of job security and intellectual stimulation." Which turned out to be true. Yet "this place doesn't really offer status and prestige like other companies. We have lots of different ladders. A lot of it is just work. Just chemistry. We are in the upper ten percent of available jobs. It's easy to recognize the other ninety percent as being worse. I'm never bored. I absolutely enjoy coming to work every day. My goal may be to get free and have my own company, and then never be free."

Pat King stresses that all good ideas need attention. "You have to somehow find a mechanism for blowing your own horn. [People in the same position] can't notice you when they want to be noticed themselves. Often you're getting noticed anyway. Otherwise, I wouldn't work here. I don't own a résumé. I don't believe in looking back. My eleven years here have been tough but good."

Marcia Schiff is the executive director of the Polaroid Foundation. Well known for its generosity, the foundation annually bequeaths small sums (up to $10,000) to between 450 and 500 beneficiaries. "The way we do philanthropy at Polaroid is not very corporate, but more like a private foundation. Number one, it's employee-driven. Forty to fifty employees determine who gets grants. We've created a model for the way corporate philanthropy should be run. It's an activity that breaks new ground in an exemplary way.

"A company willing to support social responsibility explains why I have worked here my whole life and don't want to leave." Marcia has been with the corporation for twenty-two years, starting as a secretary, first in Dr. Land's office. A desire to "make cameras and film available to poverty groups" brought her closer and closer to the foundation, which she joined in 1971.

Tracing the good works to Dr. Land, Schiff says that Polaroid's philanthropy "adds a component of goodwill at work. It's almost as important as the good work we do outside." In the beginning, "the ethos came from the top down. Now, at our third president, there's been very little change."

In its seventeen years of existence, the Polaroid pie has remained fairly consistently devoted to social and human services (43 percent), higher and adult education (33 percent), arts (14 percent), primary and secondary education (6 percent), and hospitals (3 percent). The foundation has been careful to sidestep issues that could be incendiary to shareholders. "We often pass up things because we can't explain why the corporation should be involved, i.e., abortion. We fund Planned Parenthood in support of a van to help teenagers keep their babies. No one's pushing them to have abortions. We fund information about nuclear war. We try to stay away from politics." In the foundation's 1983 annual report, Schiff and Christopher Ingraham, the foundation's president, wrote, " . . . believing that in an imperfect world we have at least come close to establishing a productive form for giving within the corporate community."

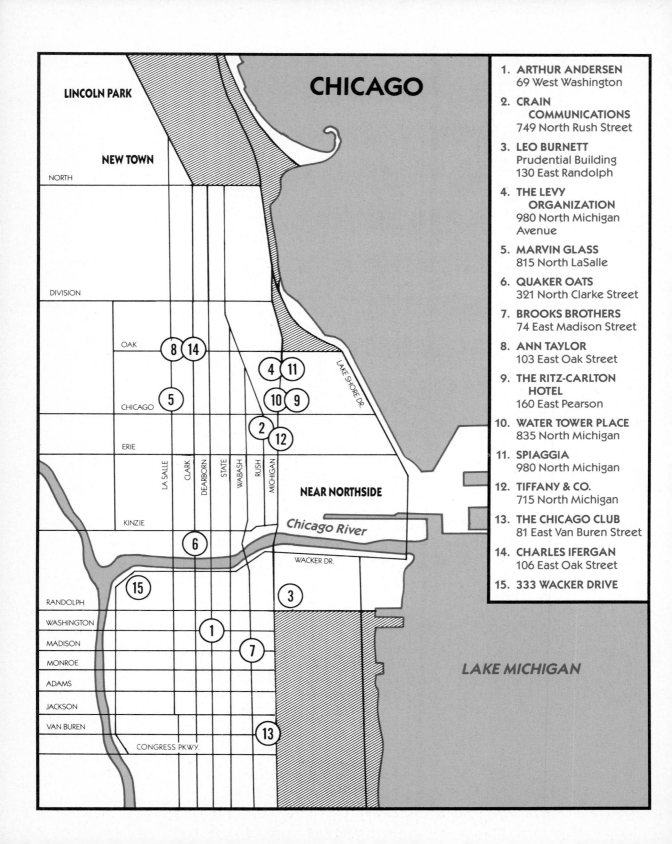

CHICAGO

LINCOLN PARK

NEW TOWN

NORTH

DIVISION

OAK

CHICAGO

ERIE

LA SALLE
CLARK
DEARBORN
STATE
WABASH
RUSH
MICHIGAN

LAKE SHORE DR.

KINZIE

Chicago River

NEAR NORTHSIDE

WACKER DR.

RANDOLPH

WASHINGTON

MADISON

MONROE

ADAMS

JACKSON

VAN BUREN

CONGRESS PKWY.

LAKE MICHIGAN

1. **ARTHUR ANDERSEN**
   69 West Washington

2. **CRAIN COMMUNICATIONS**
   749 North Rush Street

3. **LEO BURNETT**
   Prudential Building
   130 East Randolph

4. **THE LEVY ORGANIZATION**
   980 North Michigan Avenue

5. **MARVIN GLASS**
   815 North LaSalle

6. **QUAKER OATS**
   321 North Clarke Street

7. **BROOKS BROTHERS**
   74 East Madison Street

8. **ANN TAYLOR**
   103 East Oak Street

9. **THE RITZ-CARLTON HOTEL**
   160 East Pearson

10. **WATER TOWER PLACE**
    835 North Michigan

11. **SPIAGGIA**
    980 North Michigan

12. **TIFFANY & CO.**
    715 North Michigan

13. **THE CHICAGO CLUB**
    81 East Van Buren Street

14. **CHARLES IFERGAN**
    106 East Oak Street

15. **333 WACKER DRIVE**

CHICAGO

CHICAGO

Try to consider Chicago without thinking of the fiction of Sinclair Lewis or Theodore Dreiser or Saul Bellow. I defy you. It validates the prose it has inspired. Big, gray, industrial. Beef stockyards. The Mercantile Exchange. The wonderful architecture. Al Capone. The blues. America's "Second City" pulses with an excitement and energy hard to find in most cities in the world. It's a city that's alive day and night.

If cities were people, Chicago would be a man at midlife. His overcoat would flap in the wind, he being too careless and robust to keep it buttoned. He would have worked at three companies by this time and been married to one woman. He'd achieve his potential in the nearest future. In public, he'd be a sports fan, with the abandon of a rowdy in the company of his male buddies. Privately, he'd be a serious, passionate reader—almost a scholar.

Once the country's industrial nexus, Chicago has quietly become Chicago. Your company does not have to use heavy machinery to be taken seriously here. Service industries, no longer considered lightweights, are succeeding.

The city's skyline is glorious. It could serve as a textbook for Architecture 101. The greats designed Chicago, and a visitor here for the first time will be amazed by how many buildings he or she recognizes. It's like walking into the Louvre and seeing the Winged Victory and the Mona Lisa. Probably the most wondrous feature of all is the lake.

Lake Michigan dominates (as a great lake should) with oceanic mass. During the summer it's not unusual to see residents walking the main drag, North Michigan Avenue, in bathing suits. Those wearing business suits don't seem to mind. One can live on the Lake Shore (as people with enough money do) and watch it change with the seasons. North of Chicago, the suburbs bordering the lake are the priciest.

I love the broad, flat A's that identify natives. They give them a place in a country that's increasingly regionless and rootless. (The Bennetonification of our country makes our cities resemble one another.)

When Chicago's political machine was strong-armed by Mayor Richard Daley, its citizens smiled nonetheless, pleased that their city was so clean. Traditionally Democratic, Chicagoans pay attention to governance, even when they feel it's been preordained.

BEST NEIGHBORHOOD WITH DECENT PUBLIC SCHOOLS: Near North (Ogden School): kindergarten to eighth grade)

NICEST NEIGHBORHOOD (BUT YOU'LL PROBABLY HAVE TO SEND YOUR KIDS TO PRIVATE SCHOOL): Lincoln Park

BEST PLACE TO LIVE IF YOU'RE AN ASPIRING ARTIST OR YOU WANT TO LIVE NEAR PEOPLE WHO WEAR ONLY BLACK: Loft Area of River North

BEST NEIGHBORHOODS WITH TAKE-OUT FOOD AND SINGLE PEOPLE WHO ARE ALSO REPUBLICANS: Near North, Lincoln Park, New Town, Lakewood Balmoral area

MOST OVERPRICED COMMUNITIES FOR SUMMER HOMES: This really doesn't apply to Chicago, but the best areas for summer homes near Chicago are Lake Geneva (Wisconsin) and New Buffalo (Michigan)

BEST PUBLIC SCHOOLS: Lincoln School, Ogden School, New Trier, Kenwood Academy, Lane Tech High School

BEST PRIVATE SCHOOLS: Francis W. Parker, The Latin School, Lab School

BEST ALTERNATIVE SCHOOL: LaSalle Language Academy

LIVING ARCHITECTS WHO HAVE MOST INFLUENCED THE CITY'S SKYLINE: Helmut Jahn (Murphy Jahn); Bruce Graham (Skidmore, Owings & Merrill)

MOST POPULAR RESIDENTIAL ARCHITECTS: Tony Grunsfeld, Marvin Ullman, Marvin Herman

SOCIALLY INCLINED REALTORS: Rubloff; LaThomus; Sudler

DECORATORS WHO WOULD DECORATE HOMES PURCHASED THROUGH THOSE REALTORS: Bruce Gregga, Richar Interiors

DEALERS IN THE FINEST, MOST VALUABLE ART: Richard Gray, Bud Holland

TRENDY GALLERIES FOR PEOPLE WHO WEAR ALL BLACK AND HAVE A LOT OF MONEY: Phyllis Kind Gallery, Klein Gallery

MOST EXCLUSIVE GOLF CLUBS: Ontswensia, Indian Hills, Shore Acres

BEST PUBLIC GOLF FACILITY: Cog Hill

MOST EXPENSIVE HEALTH CLUB: East Bank Club

BEST HEALTH CLUB FOR MEETING POTENTIAL MATES: East Bank Club

BEST HOTELS FOR BUSINESS TRIPS: Ritz-Carlton, Park Hyatt, Mayfair Regent, Nikko

BEST HOTELS FOR TRYSTS: Tremont, Whitehall, Raphael

RESTAURANTS KNOWN FOR BEST CUISINE: Spiaggia, Jackie's

BEST RESTAURANT FOR PEOPLE WHO WEAR BLACK: 3rd Coast Coffeehouse and Winebar

BEST RESTAURANTS FOR AN INEXPENSIVE DATE: Uno's or Due's, Ed Debevic's, D.B. Kaplan's

NOISIEST RESTAURANTS (INTIMACY IMPOSSIBLE): Bistro 110, Scoozi, Hard Rock Café

BEST SPORTS BARS: Ditka's, Ultimate Sports Bar, Harry Caray's

BEST DARK BARS: Coq d'Or (Drake Hotel), The Pump Room

BEST GIMMICKY BARS: Ed Debevic's, Ditka's, Butch McGuire's at Christmas

BEST BARS TO IMPRESS A CLIENT: The bar at Spiaggia, the Greenhouse at the Ritz-Carlton, the bar at LaTour

MOST EXCLUSIVE CITY CLUBS: Chicago Club, Casino Club, Commercial Club

FANCIEST WINE STORES WHENCE CEOS PROBABLY STOCK THEIR OWN CELLARS: Louis Glunz, Sam's Liquors, Chicago Wine Company

GOURMET STORES GUARANTEED NOT TO RUN OUT OF GOAT CHEESE OR SUN-DRIED TOMATOES: Convito Italiano, Mitchell Cobey, Zambrana's

NICEST MOM-AND-POP GROCERY STORE: The Big Apple (Lincoln Park)

LARGEST DRUGSTORES WITH MOST REMARKABLE SELECTION: The Walgreen chain of stores

CORPORATE PARTY PLANNER: Carole Drew (Private Dining Rooms of Spiaggia)

HIGH-SOCIETY PARTY PLANNER: Randy Shuster

POWER BARBERS: Drake Hotel Barber Shop, Colin of London, Charles Ifergan (mostly for women)

NEW WAVE HAIRSTYLIST: Gary (Vidal Sassoon)

JUNIOR LEAGUE BEAUTY PARLORS: Bonwit Teller, Elizabeth Arden

PLACE WHERE LADIES WHO LUNCH ARE LIKELY TO HAVE TEA AFTER A HARD DAY OF SHOPPING, VOLUNTEER WORK, AND TENNIS: The Palm Court (Drake Hotel), The Greenhouse (Ritz Carlton), the Mayfair Regent, Saddle & Cycle Club

BEST STORES FOR EXECUTIVE WOMEN: Corporate Level (Carson, Pirie, Scott), Mark Shale,

BEST STORES FOR EXECUTIVE MEN: Mark Shale, Polo

BEST STORES FOR DRESS-UP CLOTHES: Ultimo, Pompian, Neiman-Marcus

BEST SHOPPING RESOURCE FOR PEOPLE WHO WEAR ONLY BLACK CLOTHES: City

DEBUTANTE BALL: Passavant Cotillion

BUSIEST SOCIAL SEASON OF THE YEAR FOR THOSE WHO CARE ABOUT SUCH THINGS:
through Christmas

SOCIAL HIGHLIGHTS: The Zoo Ball, the Consular Ball, the Gem Ball

MOST RELIABLE FLORIST: Anna's

MOST EXOTIC FLORIST: Heffernan-Morgan

TOP JEWELERS FOR RESETTING MOTHER'S EMERALDS: Trabert & Hoeffer, Spauldings

MOST COMPLETE BRIDAL REGISTRIES: Marshall Field, Neiman-Marcus, Crate & Barrel

MOST CREATE BRIDAL REGISTRY: Material Possessions

PROMINENT PHYSICIANS: Dr. Edward Newman (gastroenterology), Dr. Neil Stone (cardiology)

PROMINENT PLASTIC SURGEONS WITH EQUALLY PROMINENT CLIENTELLE: Dr. Thomas Krisek,
Dr. Diane Gerber

GYNECOLOGIST MOST OFTEN QUOTED IN THE LOCAL PRESS: Dr. Melvin Gerbie

PSYCHIATRIST MOST OFTEN QUOTED IN THE LOCAL PRESS: Dr. David Gross

BEST SEAMSTRESS OR TAILOR FOR ALTERATIONS: Marie Rose, The Dress Doctor, Alfred's
Tailoring

POPULAR FACIAL SALON: Ilona of Hungary

POWER TOOLS

MEN'S POWER DRESSING

BROOKS BROTHERS
74 East Madison
Chicago, IL 60602
(312) 263-0100

BEST-SELLING EXECUTIVE SUIT: Three-button, fall weight, navy or charcoal, 100 percent
wool, $545 (three-piece), $465 (two-piece)

POWER SHIRT: White pinpoint button-down, 100 percent cotton, $50

POWER TIE: Red foulard, silk, $25

WOMEN'S POWER DRESSING

ANN TAYLOR
103 East Oak Street
Chicago, IL 60611
(312) 943-5411

Ann Taylor is the place many executive women shop for work wear. Leslie, the store manager, discussed the latest trends in female power dressing:

"The main change in buying trends among executive women is that they are buying more suits and less separates and dresses. But these suits are not the typical, traditional conservative suits—women are picking suits that have a lot more color." The newest colors are "rich and warm and the most popular color this season is pumpkin. Vicuna is selling, as are brown/black combinations. The new suit may be tweedy, but it's not conservative. It will be two-tone and have interesting details like no lapels or a jewel collar. The shorter hemlines are selling, especially among executives in the early twenties to early thirties age range. A large percentage of customers in general are buying shorter hemlines. "Accessories are remaining constant—jewelry, belts, and scarves."

POWER LUNCHES

SPIAGGIA AND CAFÉ SPIAGGIA
980 North Michigan Avenue
Chicago, IL 60610
(312) 280-2764

Café Spiaggia: For a light, informal lunch. The café serves mainly pizzas and calzone and seats fifty-five.

PIZZAS: $8.95
Traditional pizza Margharita with basil and mozzarella; Spiaggia Special Pizza with duck sausage, sage, and goat cheese. All dishes prepared to order.

CALZONES: $8.95
Best is Calzone Spiaggia (escarole, prosciutto, provolone, double-blanched garlic)

ANTIPASTO BAR (seven different selections daily): Assortment of any three, $10.95
Insalata vi mare (calamari, bay scallops, and shrimp with lemon and extra-virgin olive oil); Insalati di Pollo (grilled chicken breasts in pesto sauce with raisins, pine nuts, black olives, and sun-dried tomatoes); Pasta Fredda (cold pasta, gnocchi salad with fresh plum tomatoes, basil, red onion, Bel Paese cheese and extra-virgin olive oil)

HOT AND COLD PASTAS: $8.95–$10.95

ENTREE SALADS: $3.95–$7.95

Spiaggia: Seats 120; formal restaurant.

APPETIZERS: Small pizzas, $6.95

PASTAS: (nine daily plus one daily pasta special): $8.95–$10.95
Favorite Pastas: Pasticcio de Radicchio, $9.95 (pasta layered with grilled radicchio, cream, and parmesan cheese—very rich, often ordered to split); Maltagliati con Anitra, $9.95 (assorted pasta shapes with grilled duck breast, black olives, duck broth, and seasonal vegetables)

BEST LIGHT DISH: Assorted grilled vegetables with fresh mozzarella and tomato vinaigrette, ($12.95)

BEST ENTREES: Two fish dishes ($16.95–$18.95), lamb medallions ($15.95), veal chops ($16.95)

DESSERTS: Cañolli Modo Mio (almond cone and ricotta chocolate chip gelato with orange and pistachio sauce), $6.95; Tiramisu (mascarpone cheese; ladyfingers, espresso, Marsala wine, and chocolate), $5.50; Bianco Mangiare (a white almond cream with caramel and fresh berry sauces), $5.50

ON EXECUTIVES' LUNCHTIME DRINKING HABITS: Executives still drink at lunch, "but in the past two years there has been a switch to wines—we serve very few cocktails. We sell only Italian wines and offer four selected wines by the glass per day [$4.50–$6.00 per glass]. Our wine list has eighty-five additional wines, and there are twenty-two more wines on the reserve list. Most popular are the chardonnays, barolos, and barbarescos."

PROMINENT CLIENTELE: "We are situated at the end of Michigan Avenue, so we are in the heart of the business district. Regular customers travel from all over Chicago to Spiaggia for lunch." Steve Garvey, Burt Reynolds, and Loni Anderson (when they are in town), Jim Thompson (governor of Illinois), top executives from all the major television stations (NBC, ABC, WGN, WTTW), top executives from major investment banks (Salomon Brothers, Goldman Sachs, First Boston), major advertising agencies and public relations firms, people from JMB (real estate), Arthur Andersen, from the top department stores in the area (Saks Fifth Avenue, Marshall Field), and assorted heads of corporations. "Really every major company in the Chicago area."

POWER WATCHES

TIFFANY'S
715 North Michigan Avenue
Chicago, IL 60611
(312) 944-7500

BEST SELLERS AMONG EXECUTIVE MEN: Audemars Piguet, $7,950; most popular model is Day/Date/Moon Face (tells you where the moon is at any time of the month), eighteen-karat gold, leather strap, self-winding.

Patek Philippe, $6,350; most popular model is the Classic—no day, no date, no moon, no second hand—eighteen-karat gold, leather strap, white dial, black Roman numerals, self-winding.

BEST SELLERS AMONG EXECUTIVE WOMEN: Rolex, two-tone, $2,300, and President (all gold), $6,750 (both models are equally popular). "Women tend to go for quartz. We also sell more bracelet watches to women, because women see them as jewelry."

Baume and Mercier, $2,000–$5,000 (some with diamonds, some without). This watch is "lighter than the Rolex, for women who don't want the sporty look."

"Most [executives] buy watches for themselves, or if they're buying them for someone else, it's someone they know pretty intimately, so they know their taste. Of the men who buy watches in the above price range, most own three, four, even five—it's pretty much their only form of jewelry—whereas women, who tend to have a variety of jewelry, generally only own one or two watches."

POWER HAIR

CHARLES IFERGAN
106 East Oak Street
Chicago, IL 60611
(312) 642-4484

Ifergan's salon caters primarily to female executives and is located on the quietly elegant block of stores downtown that most closely resembles Paris's Faubourg St. Honore (although there are a good hamburger spot and movie theater there.

ON TRENDS IN EXECUTIVE HAIR: "Slowly but surely," Ifergan reports, "women cannot be locked into a corporate look anymore. They want to be able to look feminine within a corporate look. I always try to tell my businesswomen not to think of themselves as a male monkey, but as an entity unto themselves. They are female businesswomen. I hate when women try to emulate men. It's not necessary." Charles combines the professional with the tendy. "Men don't change their hairstyles often. They will keep them for many years."

ON PERMS: "Permanents today have become commonplace. They're not a novelty anymore. A man will get a permanent as comfortably as a women. I do not believe that men don't want soft hairstyles. You can have a curly head of hair and still look like an executive."

ON COLORING: To these customers who are seeing more and more gray, "my question is always, does it bother you? If it bothers you, don't question it, try it. More and more men are getting their hair colored. It's a very competitive world, and a youthful image is often the presentation of energy. Executive clients used to like going gray. Today, if you're a doctor or dentist and getting too old, cutomers want someone younger. Wherever there is technology, people tend to go for someone who is not that old." Similarly, "in the business world, women do not want to go gray. Aging is a sign of less productivity. More women will dye their hair than men, but the men's market is getting bigger and bigger."

ON BALDING: "Implant plugs are fabulous today. It's become quite a powerful tool. We refer people to plastic surgeons. We always recommend that customers interview at least three people and then go with the one they're most comfortable with. We have people we recommend, too, for toupees. But they're not as practical. It's very difficult for people to wear toupees. For younger men, we definitely advise the plugs." Overall, men are not as concerned with being bald as they used to be.

ON FACIAL HAIR: "It's out. In the business world, the clean look is better. A little longer hair is much more acceptable than facial hair. Small mustaches are not considered facial hair when they hide weak lips."

ON EXECUTIVE MANNERS: "They know what they want; it's much easier. They are used to making decisions about everything in their lives, so they are more likely to be decisive about their hair. I wouldn't say they're always in a hurry, but their time is precious."

ON NETWORKING IN THE SALON: "Clients do talk to one another. Definitely. Eighty-five percent of our clientele are working women. Very highly professional."

ON MANICURES: "A manicure is time-consuming, and usually women will do it at home themselves. A few men come for manicures, but not as many as women. Men are more neurotic, they bite their nails."

ON HOUSE CALLS: "We do make house calls for sickness, weddings, special occasions. If a client is sick, we always try to help them."

HOURS: Tuesday to Saturday, 9:00 A.M. to 5:00 P.M.; Thursday, 9:00 A.M. to 6:30 P.M.

PROMINENT CLIENTS: The last time Ifergan revealed the names of his important business clients, they were very unhappy. He will, however, divulge his show business people. They include broadcaster Bill Kurtis, Barbara Sinatra (Frank Sinatra brought her in "just last week"), and Judith Krantz (when she was in Chicago). "We're more interested in working women than celebrities. We gear most of our sales and services to that client."

FEES:
Haircut, women (shampoo, cut and blow-dry), $50
Haircut, men (shampoo, cut and blow-dry), $40
Permanent without haircut, $60
Coloring upon consultation, $30–$60
Manicure, $10
Pedicure, $22 ("Executives go for pedicures much more than manicures because it's only once a month, and easy to maintain")
Facials, men and women, $40 ("The men's facial business has been increasing over last five or ten years. The more comfortable men feel using the services of a beauty shop, the more they will use.")

MOTTO: "Let us create a hairstyle that will become a lifestyle."

POWER FACIALS

GEORGETTE KLINGER
Water Tower Place
835 N. Michigan Avenue
Chicago, IL 60611
(312) 787-4300

Georgette Klinger, with shops in New York, Dallas, Beverly Hills, Miami, and Palm Beach in addition to Chicago, caters to the woman (or man) with expendable income who wants to look and feel her (or his) best. The salon offers facials, body massages, manicures, pedicures, overall body treatments, and one-on-one fitness (in some locations) and sells a panoply of (not inexpensive) related products. Klinger's professionals (most of whom have eastern European accents) pamper their clientele in plushly appointed private rooms. A basic facial—for which the salon is most noted—takes about an hour to perform. We spoke to Nancy Joyce, the salon manager, about her executive clients and the treatments they seek.

WHAT PERCENTAGE OF YOUR EXECUTIVE CLIENTS ARE MEN?
  "This is interesting. Throughout the U.S.A., Klinger's clients are about twenty-five percent male. But in Chicago, a full third are men. I don't know why. Women have run out of

ideas for gifts for their husbands and boyfriends. They've bought all the ties and cuff links—what's left? Gift certificates are on the increase as presents." Also, "men are looking for new experiences and are concerned about their looks. So we are getting more and more men, buying series like their wives. The wife will give the husband one free facial as a gift, they come in and love it and buy a series. Ten percent (at least) of the wives bring their husbands."

WHAT KINDS OF TREATMENTS ARE EXECUTIVES COMING IN FOR THESE DAYS?
"Body treatments are the new thing. It's like a body facial and takes a lot of preparation because it involves an herbal body wrap." This treatment takes about an hour and has become popular among men as well as women. "Also scalp treatments. People are more interested in their total health and realize the scalp is just an extension of the face. A healthy scalp will help you keep healthy hair." This treatment also takes about an hour and includes a "vigorous massage. It's good for people, for example, who have breakouts along the hairline (from using too rich shampoo, too much shampooing)." And finally, "pedicures are especially popular with men. We wrap the soles of their feet in paraffin treatment, peel it off, and massage their feet. It's very hedonistic. A great way to relax is to have your hands and feet massaged—men are realizing this. It also takes less time than a full body massage."

IS BIKINI WAXING STILL POPULAR?
"If you're sunning, you're waxing. It's an enduring business. You need a professional, however, and someone who is fast, because it's painful. We are the fastest bikini waxers in the Midwest."

ARE MANY EXECUTIVES HAVING FACIAL PEELING?
"Facial peeling is good for people who are in air-conditioned or centrally heated rooms—stale air environments that dry out the skins. Not everyone who works in an office will need a peel—it depends on the skin type. We recommend a peeling after a facial only if the client needs it—sometimes we can't do a facial without a peel."

DO YOU NOTICE ANY DIFFERENCE BETWEEN EXECUTIVE AND NONEXECUTIVE CLIENTS?
"Yes. Executives are result-oriented, but they aren't looking for magic, they know it's going to take time. They ask more questions—they really want to know how to use things and how they work and why. They call in for information. Nonexecutive clients want more magic. Executive women are more punctual."

HOW OFTEN DO EXECUTIVES COME IN FOR TREATMENTS?
"About once a month for facials and then follow-up at home. Men, too, but men don't want lots of products to take home with them, just one tube of cream. Men buy a series and show up on time."

PROMINENT CLIENTELE: Jane Byrne (former mayor of Chicago), Michael Sneed (columnist for *The Chicago Sun-Times*), Jane Sahlins (Director, International Theater Festival of Chicago), Lucy Salenger (former head of the Illinois Film Office, now a partner in a film production company called the Odeon Group), Robert Goldsborough (mystery writer and editor at *Advertising Age*), Sugar Rautbord (socialite, writer for *Interview Magazine* and co-author of *Girls in High Places*), Linda Simon (Managing Director, Department of Commerce and Community Affairs, Illinois Office of Tourism), Linda Yu (anchorwoman and local ABC affiliate), Taylor Miller (star on *All My Children*), Abra Anderson ("one of the Rockefeller girls," journalist, columnist, and "woman-about-town").

FEES:

1 facial treatment, $60
6 facial treatments, $330
12 facial treatments, $660
18 facial treatments, $990
1 peeling mask, $25
6 peeling masks, $140
12 peeling masks, $300
6 scalp treatments, $270
12 scalp treatments, $540
1 body massage, $50
6 body massages, $300
12 body massages, $600
52 weekly facials, $2,860
1 bikini wax, $17
1 body treatment, $75

ARTHUR
ANDERSEN & CO.

ARTHUR ANDERSEN &CO.

HISTORY & OPERATIONS

Arthur Andersen & Co., if not the largest of the Big Eight accounting firms, is close to it. The firm, first known as Andersen, DeLany & Co., was founded in Chicago in 1913, when Arthur Andersen and his partner, Clarence M. DeLany, bought the Audit Company of Illinois for $4,000 upon its owner's death. Andersen, who had been head of the accounting department at Northwestern University (where he continued to teach courses until 1922), was twenty-three when he passed his CPA exam—making him the youngest CPA in Illinois at the time—and only twenty-eight when he and DeLany acquired the firm.

Andersen, DeLany & Co., which consisted of the eight-person staff from the Audit Company of Illinois and the two new partners, was established to provide a range of general corporate accounting services, including periodic audits, certification of financial statements, investigations for special purposes (such as to determine the advisability of its clients' proposed investments), design and installation of new systems of financial and cost accounting and organization (or the redesign of existing systems), and preparation of reports under the federal income tax law. Fees increased moderately in the firm's first few years of operation, from

$45,400 in 1914 to $67,700 in 1916. In 1918 Clarence DeLany resigned from the firm, and its name was changed to Arthur Andersen & Co.

The first federal income tax (as it's known today) did not become effective until March 1913, and Andersen was among the first experts in the field. In 1917–18, he gave a series of lectures on federal taxes at Northwestern—attended by prominent judges, bankers, lawyers, accountants, and business executives—which added greatly to the firm's reputation and renown. As more clients sought his expertise, the firm's revenues increased significantly, reaching $322,000 in 1920.

The twenties brought a period of rapid expansion to the firm. In 1921 Arthur Andersen & Co. opened an office in Washington, D.C., in order to gain proximity to the Internal Revenue Service. By 1930 the firm had offices in seven U.S. cities, a staff of 378, and annual fees of almost $2 million. But due to the Depression, the firm's business was curtailed and fees sank to $1.5 million in 1932. Between 1934 and 1940, business began to pick up again, and the firm opened four additional offices in the United States.

During World War II, when many companies had contracts with the government for products and services to aid in the war effort, accounting became more complex, taxes increased dramatically, and public accountants took on added importance. Companies that had formerly handled their own accounting internally now sought the services of outside accounting firms. As a result—and despite the fact that at one point more than 50 percent of the firm's permanent staff was in the armed forces—Arthur Andersen & Co. continued to expand, opening four new offices during the war years. In 1947 Arthur Andersen died, and leadership of the firm was assumed by Leonard Spacek, who had started as a junior accountant in 1928 and risen through the ranks to become a partner in 1940.

Arthur Andersen & Co. began a period of rapid and sustained growth during the 1950s. While the firm continued to open many new domestic offices, its most dramatic expansion, starting in the mid-fifties, was overseas. As Arthur Andersen began to extend its reach abroad, it adopted a policy of instituting uniform practices in its offices everywhere in the world. The firm's philosophy was that an Arthur Andersen & Co. office in Guadalajara should be organized in much the same way as one in Chattanooga. And rather than staffing its foreign offices with Americans, it chose to staff them predominantly with local nationals, who were recruited from local universities and offered the same training and the same opportunities for advancement as those recruited in the United States. By 1963 twenty-six Arthur Andersen & Co. offices were in operation in foreign countries. By 1973 (the firm's sixtieth anniversary year), there were an additional twenty-six offices operating abroad, and total personnel outside the United States had grown to almost 3,500. Meanwhile, twenty-seven new offices had been opened in the United States, bringing the 1973 total of Arthur Andersen offices worldwide to ninety-two, with a worldwide staff of 12,320. Fees increased accordingly, and by 1973 the firm's annual revenues had reached $12.7 million.

Arthur Andersen & Co. prides itself on its training school—the Center for Professional Education—which is considered the best in the industry. The company instituted a formal training school in 1940, and in 1970 it purchased a facility in St. Charles, Illinois (forty-five miles from headquarters in downtown Chicago), from St. Dominick's College. The Center for Professional Education has classroom and housing facilities for more than 850 people, and current expansion plans call for the capacity to double by 1989 and reach 3,200 people within the next decade. After spending one to five weeks in their home offices (depending on which division they're in), new recruits go to St. Charles for three to five weeks of training. People at all levels of the firm return to St. Charles at various points in their careers to take one or another of the school's close to seven hundred courses and programs. The firm, which considers the training of new recruits a top priority, spends $195 million per year on its programs.

Today, under the leadership of Duane Kullberg, who joined the firm in 1954 and has been CEO since 1980, Arthur Andersen & Co. employs approximately 40,000 people in its seventy-nine domestic offices and 140 offices abroad. The firm, which has more than doubled in size during the past decade, took in fees of $2.3 billion in 1987. Arthur Andersen & Co. is organized into the following divisions: Accounting and Audit, with 13,300 professionals, which in 1987 accounted for 43 percent of total fees; Management Information Consulting, with roughly 9,200 professionals, which accounted for 36 percent of 1987 fees; and Tax, with nearly 4,800 professionals, which accounted for 21 percent of fees in 1987. The firm serves more than 91,000 clients and boasts "the largest audit practice in the United States" and "the world's largest tax and consulting practices." The firm's literature also states that Arthur Andersen & Co. audits more companies listed on the New York and American stock exchanges and more of the fast-growing young businesses on the *Inc.* 500 list than any other firm. Considered one of the most prestigious public accounting practices in the country, it interviews approximately 35,000 recruits for 3,500 to 4,000 entry-level openings each year.

One of the oldest and most enduring trademarks of Arthur Andersen & Co.'s practice—and probably one of the keys to its success—is the firm's policy of operating with "one voice." This philosophy encompasses everything from the uniform setting-up of offices all over the world, to ensuring that no professionals publicly voice disagreement with one another over a client's accounts, to the consistent training of its accountants. Arthur Andersen professionals work together in teams comprising a partner, a manager, one or two senior accountants, and several staff people. According to the firm, "the team approach not only brings the best available skills to an engagement, it also serves to give younger personnel the benefit of expanding their professional skills by working on a variety of assignments."

(Information provided by Jack Ruane and Walter Billitz, company spokespersons.)

REVENUES: $2.32 billion in fiscal 1987.

EARNINGS: The firm is a private partnership and will not disclose.

OFFICES: 219 offices worldwide, with 79 in the United States and 140 in 49 other countries.

NUMBER OF EMPLOYEES: Close to 40,000 worldwide, with about 21,500 in the United States and the remainder abroad.

AVERAGE AGE OF EMPLOYEES: Information not available.

TURNOVER: Information not available.

RECRUITMENT: Arthur Andersen & Co. recruits at 550 colleges and universities around the world and interviews some 35,000 potential recruits each year. The firm looks for business and accounting majors, MBAs and lawyers, as well as engineering, computer science, and liberal arts majors. Some of the more than two hundred schools the firm recruits from in the United States are: Abilene Christian University, University of Alabama, University of Arizona, Arizona State University, University of Arkansas, Auburn University, Babson College, Baldwin-Wallace College, Bob Jones University, Boston College, Bowling Green State University, University of Chicago, Cornell University, Creighton University, University of Delaware, Duke University, Emory University, Fairfield University, Harvard University, Hofstra University, Indiana University of Pennsylvania, University of Iowa, Johns Hopkins University, Loyola College, University of Massachusetts, Memphis State University, Miami University of Ohio, University of Missouri, University of Missouri at St. Louis, Northern Illinois University, Ohio University, University of Oklahoma, Oklahoma State University, University of Pennsylvania, Pennsylvania State University, University of Pittsburgh, University of Portland, Princeton University, St. Louis University, San Diego State University, University of South Carolina, Southern Methodist University, Texas Tech University, Tulane University, Utah State University, Wake Forest University, Washington University, Washington State University, and Yale University.

NUMBER OF NEW HIRES PER YEAR: More than seven thousand.

RANGE OF STARTING SALARIES: "We have competitive starting salaries. They vary according to the academic degree, background of the applicant and the city of employment. Overtime is paid to all employees up to a salary of $35,000."

POLICY FOR RAISES: "Employees are eligible for annual compensation adjustments based on qualifications and merit."

TRAINING PROGRAMS: "Arthur Andersen & Co. has a Center for Professional Education in St. Charles, Illinois, at which some 1,200 students (during peak season—June to October) are being trained daily to help provide the highest-quality services to our clients. New hires worldwide in audit, tax, and management information consulting attend training from three to five weeks. Partly intended to bridge the transition from academic study to practical application, these courses help provide new professionals with shared experience that introduces the firm culture and emphasizes our commitment to quality service. As careers progress there are formal educational programs that go more deeply into specific areas of learning or skill development."

BENEFITS: "While our benefit programs vary to meet each country's local law and customs, these programs are designed around three primary objectives: to ensure a total compensation arrangement that is fair; to ensure adequate, comprehensive financial protection in the form of medical, disability and death benefits; to provide long-term employees with adequate retirement income benefits in combination with government plan income."

VACATION: "Our regular vacation and public holiday allowances for employees are established to comply with local laws and customs for each country." In the United States, two weeks for the first five years, three weeks after six years, four weeks after eleven years, and four weeks for managers and principals, plus nine regular paid holidays per year. In addition, practice staff are entitled to accrue their first eighty hours of overtime for additional vacation and regular part-time personnel are entitled to vacation based on the number of hours worked.

ADDITIONAL PERKS: The firm has an employee assistance program and a child care reimbursement account in the United States.

BONUSES: "Not applicable."

ANNUAL PARTY: "Each office hosts a social function each year for employees of that office. Large offices may alternatively sponsor one annual social function for segments of the office (such as divisions or other groupings)."

DRESS CODE: "We expect our personnel to dress in a manner that conforms to the standards in the local business community. Generally, men wear business suits and women wear conservative dress or suits."

SOCIAL ATMOSPHERE: "We promote teamwork. As a result, it is fairly common for people working on a project or a client assignment to get together after working hours. However, we strive to maintain a professional work climate to help ensure objectivity in such matters as performance evaluations, promotions, and work assignments."

HIERARCHY: Starts with staff, semi-senior (for accounting and audit only), senior, manager, then principal. People at the manager and principal levels are eligible for election to the partnership, a group of more than 2,100.

HEADQUARTERS: Arthur Andersen & Co., Société Cooperative, the firm's worldwide organization, is headquartered in Geneva, where it is "the coordinating unit for the legally separate Arthur Andersen National Practice Entities throughout the world," and has a headquarters office in Chicago as well.

CHARITABLE CONTRIBUTIONS: "The firm and its employees contribute to hundreds of charitable, educational, cultural, and community welfare organizations through 79 U.S. offices and 140 offices abroad. Most recipient organizations are funded in communities where our firm operates, but national organizations are supported as well. In addition, the Arthur Andersen & Co. Foundation contributes to charitable and cultural organizations. Since many contributions are made through individual offices, a total firmwide figure is not available."

INTERESTED APPLICANTS CAN SEND RÉSUMÉS TO:
Mr. Thomas Nessinger
Director—Recruiting
Arthur Andersen & Co.
69 West Washington Street
Chicago, IL 60602
(312) 580-0033

The *Going to Work* challenge: How to make accounting seem like the most fascinating, glamorous, and fast-paced of fields. Let's try with Arthur Andersen & Co. and see how far we get.

Anyone who has studied accounting or attempted to get a CPA degree (after taking what is known as one of the most brutal of qualifying exams) talks of the prestige affiliated with the "big eight," or the nation's largest public accounting partnerships. It means being initiated into a huge, though selective, fraternity, a vote of confidence in the profession.

Arthur Andersen, based in Geneva and Chicago, employs close to 40,000 employees in fifty countries. More than 2,100 of them are partners, or "owner operators," each with one vote regardless of seniority or the size of their dominion. Duane Kullberg has been with Arthur Andersen for over thirty years, eight of them as chief executive officer. "I was kind of typical," he says. He was raised on a farm in Minnesota, and his parents, who were "very poor, were relatively ambivalent about my attending college." He was a business major, specializing in accounting, at the University of Minnesota. "I got into accounting based on wrong information. I'd heard there was a glut in engineering." A good student, he was recruited by a lot of companies. "I hadn't enjoyed accounting. I chose this company because I respected the recruiters, and because of the prestige." After two years in the military and then marriage, "I went through some maturing." He returned to Arthur Andersen and found "I liked it here better."

Kullberg realizes that "a good recruiter could be the entire key to one's career. In one half hour, you must interpret enthusiastically why this is the place to be. The hardest thing is learning to speak for only three of the thirty minutes." The culture is still reliant on the people who skim the college applicants. "Our people primarily come straight from campus. Their minds haven't been muddled yet. That's the good news. The bad news is, it can get insular." Arthur Andersen has its own way of doing things, unaffected by other organizations' points of view since there are few lateral inductees who can cross-pollinate. "A lot of times you have to reassess the situation and not just apply what happened before. The essential characteristics are there. It makes management easier."

If you open the trademark maple double doors to any Arthur Andersen office, from Detroit to Düsseldorf, "you will feel it's the same. The standards are the same." Arthur Andersen commissioned the design of the doors, and they, heralding the entrance to every single branch office around the world, are the symbol of the company and the icon of which employees and partners are proud. (They were actually designed by Andersen's son-in-law, Vilas Johnson, who was the office manager in Chicago during the fifties and is also credited with initiating college recruiting.)

"Most people forget that there was a person—Arthur Andersen himself. He was a very iconoclastic individual in the profession. His name helps to reinforce the culture." Kullberg and others attribute the present Andersen culture to have been codified by Leonard Spacek, three CEOs ago. "He was the architect of the firm's growth. New ideas are not to make print, but to make change. When you're small, you try everything." In response to the question of how Kullberg will try to imprint the Arthur Andersen culture, he said, "To reinforce the partnership as opposed to reinforcing Kullberg. The different practices within have different personalities. Debates will end in, 'That's not Arthur Andersen.' "

Kullberg maintains, "The best job in the firm is the office managing partner. You can see the results of your efforts. Here, you never know; you can just guess the results." As CEO, "I miss the people contact from the standpoint of doing accounting for clients. My challenge in this job is to not be insular. It's easy for the CEO to feel isolated. I don't just listen to the people closest to me."

Business as usual at Arthur Andersen is based on teamwork. Teams can range in size from two to thirty people managed by a partner. Kullberg says that partnership is the "carrot" that's dangled in front of associates, the track being ten to twelve years long. "Technical knowledge is important, and we assume everyone has it or will gain it. 'Bedside manner' is what counts."

In an attempt to blend into the cultures they are penetrating internationally, Arthur Andersen hires mostly nationals of the countries. "We constantly try not to be seen as an American company with foreign offices. There may be some Americans, but that's because we can't train people fast enough."

Frank Rossi, managing partner—region, confirms, "I can very easily know who my partners are when I travel, even though I don't _know_ them. Our guys travel more professionally. They wear suits. Our guys carry themselves in a certain way. Even on pleasure trips. Our people are very visible. Our people in the Philippines wear the 'barong' [the embroidered, boxy, light-colored shirt you've seen Ferdinand Marcos wear]. We will dress in the most professional, comfortable attire of the place and its environment." Rossi uses the term "awesome" to describe Arthur Andersen and its success. "We have the best people in the world."

Having joined the firm in 1959, Rossi explains why he has stayed so long. "I did very well as a young man. I got responsibility early on. I was always challenged. I never had a dull day.

I have had a wealth of opportunities to leave the firm all these years. Even now. Often for more money. In the final analysis, I never thought I'd have the independence I had here. At Arthur Andersen, I was never beholden to anyone else. It's free of politics. The fact that we retain so many people is amazing because so many get offers for more money."

Rossi discusses the generic fit at the firm. "You must be people-oriented. (Most people think accountants are technically oriented. We take that [ability] for granted.) We encourage our people to take Dale Carnegie. Universities keep asking us how to better create applicants. We say, 'Take less accounting, and take more speech and debate.' " Rossi himself arrived as a Korean War veteran, married and with a family, older and more mature than the newcomers typical of today. His need for security in the fifties implied a willingness to stay and a definite risk aversion. Today's recent college graduates, who have a lighter financial burden, "have no idea or intention of staying. They view their time with us as an apprenticeship or an extension of university training. We understand the résumé-building aspects of coming here, but we have to sell staying."

Clients are the main threats to the longevity of an accountant's tenure. "Anyone who does a reasonably good job for a client might be offered a job [there]. We know that. You cannot become wealthy here. You start with an attractive salary, which can be grown into a comfortable living. No partners will ever be in the *Forbes* 400," he says of the magazine's annual register of the four hundred richest Americans. And that's why people have left.

Cozying up to the client has never been suggested, unlike the practices of other service businesses. "We encourage enough socializing for a good working relationship, but not enough to lose our objectivity. It would not be appropriate for a partner to share a ski condo with the president of a client company. And you're the only one who can judge how your objectivity's been affected." Finally, accounting professionals must rotate clients after seven years.

Most escapees do not jump to other accounting firms; they leave the accounting profession altogether. Of those who leave, many return. "They miss the people. On a day-to-day basis, they may not interface with the same caliber of people. Some have a feeling of emptiness. Our objective is, when people leave, they stay loyal and are great sources of new business contacts. We have a great rapport with our alumni. Few of our people wouldn't influence their firms to use us." The efforts to keep people within Arthur Andersen stop short of turning the environment into a surrogate family, but married couples can work here, "because you can't really discourage it."

Don Baker, whose middle name might as well be "Baylor" for his devotion to his alma mater (Baylor University), is a partner and the managing director of university relations. A former president of the Baylor Alumni Association, he's been with Arthur Andersen since 1955. "They offered me the job of university relations fifteen years ago, but I turned it down. I wanted to wait." He accepted the job in 1984 and has breathlessly returned from a trip to campus when we meet. He presses a button underneath his desk, and his office door automatically closes.

"Last year we interviewed 35,000 recruits on campus to get between 3,500 and 4,000 new people. We visit every accredited school with some reputation." By 1995, he estimates, "we may be hiring eight thousand students per year worldwide." When you take travel expenses and the billable time of interviewing partners into account, recruiting can cost anywhere from "three to four thousand dollars per kid. Desire and self-reliance are key ingredients. The stars anyone can pick out. They have haloes, and bands play."

Baker is concerned with the way business ethics have deteriorated. He calls today's thinking the "Titanic ethic—get mine before the ship sinks." He was not motivated by money when he joined the firm. "My motivation was leaving Mart, Texas. I hardly knew anything about Arthur Andersen, and now I think that was lucky." Citing a general desire for immediate gratification, he says, "I don't think today's hires are willing to wait. I've changed our recruiting pitch. I used to say, 'You could expect partnership in between ten and twelve years.' Now I say, 'I'll show you industry from inside.' "

A round-table discussion of young staff elicits the firm's appeal to outsiders. "It was because of the reputation," says a manager in the tax division who was recruited from law school. A senior staff member in the consulting practice says, "The training and exposure. I wanted training within a business environment, and I wanted exposure to other businesses through consulting." A brand-new staff member in commercial audit says, "I felt Arthur Andersen was personally interested in me. They flew me here [from Tulsa] since I was interested in moving to Chicago." A manager in accounting and audit with an MBA from Northwestern's Kellogg School says her classmates were headed to "glamorous" fields. She chose Arthur Andersen as a way to "see more things and meet more people." It must be added that accounting professors often recommend Arthur Andersen as a good place for their students to work.

The quartet—two men and two women—is conservatively attired. Each wears a white shirt and a dark suit. "The dress code is not written for women." The women are lacking extraneous adornment, and all four are clean-cut and serious. Almost like . . . accountants. "We don't have to wear white shirts," one of the guys says. "No beards [are allowed] in the Chicago office, although mustaches are okay." Suits are required for men.

"Your first impression is that everyone will be alike. Our backgrounds are not that diverse, but our personalities are different." As in any organization, everyone has individual abilities and goals. "To get positive feedback from someone I respect makes me feel good. At an early staff level, we get feedback every four or five days. There's also systematic evaluation. In audit, it's at the end of every engagement [project]." The tax people look to the client's satisfaction above the internal evaluation. "If the client's happy, everything falls into place." This group is happy. Their tenure averages out to five and a half years. So far, Arthur Andersen & Co. has lived up to their expectations. All four are married. Their lives are comfortable.

"Why stay?" One repeats the question. "Money's not everything. I've never had enough enticement [to leave], although all my offers have been for more money." As we go around the table, these four offer their praises of this large firm. "You don't have to sit on people to get things done here. By virtue of people being here, I know they'll get things done. I like the resources and the technical support. I like the independence. It's incredible—like running your own business. I like this better than graduate school. It's more fun. In school, it was self-interest. You had your bright people, and you had your people who were just there. Here we're surrounded by stars. I like to drop the name. First and always I tell people [outside of the office] 'I work at Arthur Andersen.' "

In these accolades, Arthur Andersen sounds very much like any other successful employer. The firm is a good motivator, keeping people here despite richer job offers and getting them to work hard. "This is the hardest I've ever worked. I must be at my top performance. The company's shown me how to work smarter. I feel I'm accomplishing a lot more." The work-week can be a long one. "You'd feel like a schmuck if you left and everyone else stayed. It's a team effort. People are more likely to be seen early than late." Employees in the tax practice typically work ten-hour days. In audit, there are many Saturdays in the office. "I feel I'm giving things up, but not my priorities." The project-to-project nature of a lot of the work allows accountants the satisfaction of job completion.

The focus on making partner is not intense, these staff people contend. Since some people choose a first job at Arthur Andersen as a stepping-stone, partnership is not even an issue for them. "After three to four years as a manager, you're counseled. They let you know by the seventh year [whether you're likely to make partner]."

Moreover, at the cost of becoming partner or making it to the fast track, people at Arthur Andersen advise that "you have to be yourself here. No one could wear a mask for that many hours."

Members of Arthur Andersen's support staff are especially delighted to praise their employer. Even after many years here, they are overwhelmed by the solidity and prestige of the company that took a chance on them. "My husband's parents said, 'Oh! Arthur Andersen! You'll have a great résumé!'" Another says, "I was scared I'd just be a number. I've been treated as an individual. There were times in my life I wasn't regarded as reliable. They give me hope and trust." "Can you imagine getting a thank-you letter for service I did for Johannesburg? It makes me feel good." "My boss senses when I'm ready for a new step. There are always new challenges and a good time."

Arthur Andersen & Co. has the distinction of opening up the middle class to its people, who might not have otherwise had a clear entrée. Steve Samek, a partner and head of the Wholesale Distribution Industry Competence Program, had assumed while in high school, that he would probably pump gas for a living after graduation. From Cicero, Illinois, a poor blue collar town, he recalls, "One day Dad says, 'Let's get you into college.'" It was August 15, 1970. After graduating from Southern Illinois University in three years, his father, a contractor, who had built a house for a manager at Arthur Andersen & Co., suggested he look for a job there. "Now I've written books on strategic planning," Steve says happily.

At lunch with a high-powered group in Chicago led by Paul Wilson, Arthur Andersen's managing partner—human resources, the culture is more explicitly enunciated. "I call it management by planned failure," Barry Wallach says. He's a partner in the tax division. "It's not a question of working smart or hard. The difference is experimenting." Barry's own career began on the very day he had his last college class, March 19, 1970. A member of the army reserve, he says, "As a middle class draft dodge, I did hysterectomies on dogs and cats." After taking his CPA exam, Barry attended law school at night at DePaul. "I found Arthur Andersen was harder than law school. My friends in law school made more money than I, but their work was repetitive. I enjoyed with I was doing. I was admitted to the partnership in 1980."

The lunch bunch touts Arthur Andersen's remarkable growth, from $1 billion to more than $2 billion in the last five years. "We're exploding." On a personal level, "everyone's trying to develop someone to replace them. There's constant incentive." Mentoring relationships exist, and a typical manager works for half a dozen partners. There's talk of competition, though everyone swears it's based on personal motivation and not at all mandated by the corporate culture. "We attrit 93 percent. Only 7 percent stay on to become partner. [Of those who stay,] we'll give you a chance to live well." "My objectives," another partner says, "are to grow my practice. I want to grow faster than the firm. It's partly ego. There's more business out there to be had."

Client satisfaction, of course, is the paramount concern. The senior people talk excitedly about that because they obviously have high-ranking client contact. They are urged to be aggressive, develop new clients and products, and market, market, market. "We each have individual styles. If I can think of something and work it out, it's rare I can't do it. When it works, you keep it. You're driven by what's needed. We're here to solve our clients' problems." As tax laws become more complicated, "the better managers and partners are the ones who'll ask for help. The generalist is obsolete. We must reflect and anticipate economic changes in the world."

There are formalized Arthur Andersen approaches to accounting work. There is an Arthur Andersen audit and an Arthur Andersen tax return. "These mechanisms get things right." There is enormous comfort in being part of a structure that is both roomy and effective. "The most intellectual feat is creating new uses." The freedom to try new techniques is tempered by one's accountability to the client and to the partnership. Obviously, after a decade of experience and the vote of confidence conferred by the partnership, there is less and less fear of risk taking. And the independence that is frequently mentioned is manifested by the fact that "we can afford to lose a client. That's the measure. It takes leadership from the top. You can afford to have integrity at Arthur Andersen." If you think your accountant at Arthur Andersen & Co. will accommodate your desire to have a document backdated, forget it. Call someone else. "I want people to say, 'I have an accountant, but I need the good guys. I'll call Arthur Andersen.' "

"I have to use the word 'exciting,' " one partner gushes when asked to recall his annunciation to partnership. "The partnership is really the start of your career. I'll remember my first partners' meeting as long as I live. There were eighteen hundred people in Dallas, and they were all like me." The camaraderie of the partnership is almost a perk. "If you become a partner at thirty-two, you have thirty years as a partner!"

St. Charles, Illinois, a forty-five-minute drive from downtown headquarters in no traffic, is the home of the Arthur Andersen Center for Professional Education. Housed in a former Benedictine college—St. Dominick's for women—it is an impressive campus filled year round (except for Christmas week) with Arthur Andersen people from all over the world constantly catching up with the latest laws, methods, and tools. The St. Charles campus was purchased in 1970 and now boasts close to 450 employees, about 150 of whom are involved in course development and evaluation, and 300 administration support staff.

Every freshly minted college arrival spends his or her first few weeks in his or her new office, wherever it might be, and then comes here for three to five weeks for training. In 1987 the company spent $195 million in training worldwide, $90 million of which was the participants' billable time away from their offices. While the St. Charles campus has a large share of the international population, another center in Segovia, Spain, handles most of the basic training needs for the European and Middle Eastern employees.

After corporate initiation and training take place, associates, managers, and partners return to St. Charles for programs and classes offered in a course catalogue that rivals that of any major university. True, the range of courses is narrower than one would find in the average accredited school, but there are 118 pages of offerings of programs lasting from one day to three weeks. Courses include "Effective Business Writing" (sixteen hours), "Introduction to Intermediate U.S. Tax School 'B' " (fifty-five hours), "Latin America—Multinational Transactions" (three days), "Auditing Income Taxes: Substantive Auditing Procedures—Income Taxes" (sixteen hours), "Basic Oil and Gas Taxation School" (twenty-four hours), and "U.S. Expatriate Tax Return Preparation" (eleven hours).

Richard Nerad, managing partner—professional education, heads the professional education division. He arrived at St. Charles three years ago after thirty-five years with Arthur Andersen, twenty years of which he spent involved in computer methodology and training in the consulting division. "To have five years left before retirement and get to do this!" he says at midtour through his campus. Unlike his suited colleagues, Nerad, who looks like a teacher or a dean, is attired more casually, and his pace seems perhaps a bit more relaxed. In addition to running the training center, he is developing a permanent art exhibit of the history of Arthur Andersen, including photographs of every single office. The original doors are also here (although the doorjamb is a reproduction). A crescent of flags of different nations represents the homes of the current student body.

"This is the one place in the world that every Arthur Andersen person has in common." On this particular evening, the classrooms are filled. Everyone is dressed for business. People do look pretty much the same, although it's a good bet that the smokers are not American. In the social and dining rooms, students are wearing casual slacks and sweaters. The dress code officially breaks at 6:30 P.M., when the bar opens. It's a graduate school for grown-ups! However, the students loitering are not laughing or carrying on, and there is not the remotest hint of rock and roll or a ride board. You will be pleased to know, however, that romances have been known to blossom here, especially during the universal orientation sessions.

Hailed for four consecutive years at the foremost training curriculum for accountants in the nation, the professional education program's peak season is the summer, when it reaches its (full-bed) capacity of about eight hundred students. The 57-acre campus is being expanded to 147 acres. Dorms are coed. There are recreational facilities. The school day begins at 8:30 A.M. and can go until 9:00 P.M. And homework is assigned. "It truly is a conditioning process that builds the confidence of individuals in themselves and the people they team with," according to Nerad. One student, thoroughly immersed, confessed, "I've got to admit I've had a few auditing dreams since coming here."

CRAIN COMMUNICATIONS INC.

Crain Communications Inc

HISTORY & OPERATIONS

Chicago-based Crain Communications, publishers of flagship *Advertising Age* and twenty-four other trade and consumer newspapers and magazines, was started in Louisville, Kentucky, in 1916 by G. D. Crain, Jr. Born in 1885, Crain always wanted to be a publisher. He started out in the business as a child, buying newspapers from *The Louisville Times* at a penny a piece and selling them to a group of regular customers for two cents. Later he worked as a paperboy for both the *Times* and *The Louisville Herald*. Crain attended Centre College in Danville, Kentucky and graduated in three years with a bachelor's degree and an MA in English. In college, he worked as a semiregular correspondent for the *Times*, and upon graduation he joined the staff of the *Herald*.

The years Crain worked for the *Herald* included stints as a city editor and a sports editor. But he always had an interest in reporting on the business world, and he eventually quit the *Herald* to start a business news writing service. In order to drum up work, Crain sent out a form letter to approximately six hundred trade and business publications. The response was overwhelming, and he put together a list of nearly a hundred papers that wanted either news or feature writing. Within a few years, Crain had hired several reporters to write for the service, and he was ready to launch his own publication.

In 1916, with only a few thousand dollars in capital, Crain started *Hospital Management*, a small trade paper devoted to hospital administration. Readers responded positively, but advertisers were slow to follow, in part because promotional opportunities were limited. Crain concluded that there was a need for a periodical devoted to specialized advertising in business publications, and he accordingly established *Class*—whose name was later changed to *Class & Industrial Advertising* and then later to *Class & Industrial Marketing*—only a month after starting *Hospital Management*.

Both journals enjoyed a modest initial success. Crain ran them with the help of a secretary while continuing to administer and write for his business news service. After six months, he sold the news service to his associates and moved his publishing business to Chicago. There the circulation of the papers gradually grew, and Crain was able to hire additional staff.

By the late twenties, Crain was ready to launch a new paper. His editorial policy for launching each of his publications was to determine an information need and then fulfill it. In 1930 he started *Advertising Age*, the first weekly reporting on advertising industry news. Though there were other advertising industry publications before *Advertising Age*, none had covered strictly news.

By 1933, with the economy weakened by the Depression, *Advertising Age* had suffered three straight years of losses. The other two properties were also losing money. In order to consolidate costs, Crain incorporated *Class* into *Advertising Age*, where it remained for two years before spinning off again on its own. The move increased *Advertising Age*'s circulation, and by the end of 1933 the magazine was breaking even. Its readership was growing. By the mid-1940s it had a paid subscription base of roughly 17,000, and after World War II it had the greatest growth spurt in its history. By the 1960s it was recognized as the undisputed leader in the industry in terms of circulation, advertising volume, and advertising response. (Crain sold *Hospital Management* in 1952. Though the publication was thriving, it competed with too many potential and actual advertisers of *Class* and *Advertising Age*.)

Crain stepped down as president of Crain Communications in 1963, relinquishing that title to Sidney R. Bernstein, who had joined the organization in 1922. Upon Crain's death in 1973, his widow, Gertrude, took over as chairman, his elder son, Rance, became president, and his younger son, Keith, became vice-chairman. At the time Crain died, Crain Communications was publishing five titles in addition to *Advertising Age* and *Class* (which ultimately changed its name to *Business Marketing*). They were *Automotive News*, a Detroit-based automobile industry paper known as "the *Advertising Age* of the automotive industry," *American Dry Cleaner*, *American Laundry Digest*, *Business Insurance*, and *Pensions & Investment Age*.

In 1978 Rance Crain launched *Crain's Chicago Business*, a business weekly that competed with Chicago's two daily papers. Despite the consensus among his colleagues that the paper would fail, it has since grown to be the fifth largest business publication in the country. Crain Communications subsequently launched successful local business weeklies in Cleveland and Detroit and in 1985 started *Crain's New York Business* to see if such a paper could survive in the biggest city of them all. If *New York Business* succeeds—it's expected to turn a profit by 1990 at the latest—Crain Communications intends to launch regional business weeklies all across the country.

Since G. D. Crain's death, Crain Communications has grown from a midsized publisher to a mini-empire made up of twenty-five trade and consumer newspapers and magazines. Today the company employs over a thousand people in twelve offices in the United States, England, Germany, and Japan. Its publications—most of which were launched or acquired between 1973 and 1985—include, in the United States: *Advertising Age*, a weekly with a circulation of nearly 90,000; *Automotive News,* a weekly with a circulation of approximately 66,680; *Auto Week,* a weekly with a circulation of over 181,650; *Business Insurance,* a weekly with a circulation of 48,560; *Business Marketing,* a monthly with a circulation of 43,000; *City & State,* a monthly with a circulation of approximately 30,000; *Crain's Chicago Business,* a weekly with a circulation of approximately 48,930; *Crain's Cleveland Business,* a weekly with a circulation of around 25,000; *Crain's Detroit Business,* a weekly with a circulation of 33,000; *Crain's New York Business,* a weekly with a circulation of 85,000; *Detroit Monthly,* the company's first city lifestyle magazine (it was recently named the best city magazine in the country in its circulation category by a city magazine trade association), with a circulation of 80,000; *Electronic Media,* a weekly with a circulation of 25,270; *Florida Keys Magazine,* published six times a year, with a circulation of approximately 10,000; *Humm's Guide to the Florida Keys,* a quarterly tourist magazine with a circulation of 50,780; *Modern Healthcare,* a fortnightly tabloid with a circulation of approximately 89,070; *Pensions & Investment Age,* a fortnightly tabloid with a circulation of 50,000; *Rubber & Plastic News,* a weekly with a circulation of approximately 15,000; *Tire Business,* a fortnightly tabloid with a circulation of 15,590; *American Clean Car,* a bimonthly with a circulation of 18,500; *American Coin-Op,* a monthly with a circulation of 19,000; *American Drycleaner,* a monthly with a circulation of 26,000; and *American Laundry Digest,* a monthly with a circulation of 13,000. Abroad, there are *European Rubber Journal,* a monthly with a circulation of 8,000; *Urethanes Technology,* a London-based quarterly with a circulation of 4,000, and a recently added newsletter called *Euromarketing.*

In addition to its publications, Crain's holdings include a radio station in the Florida Keys; Crain News Service, a news service that provides business information and features from Crain publications to other media; and Crain Computer Services, which provides a computerized subscription service for business and consumer magazines. The company is privately held, with about 90 percent of the stock in the hands of Gertrude, Rance, and Keith Crain, and the rest is owned by employees and some other family members.

(Information provided by Rance Crain, president of Crain Communications.)

REVENUES: Approximately $130 million in 1987.

EARNINGS: Company is privately held and will not disclose.

OFFICES: Nine in the United States: Chicago headquarters, Detroit, Florida Keys, New York, Washington, D.C., Los Angeles, Cleveland, Akron, Dallas. Three abroad: London, Tokyo, Frankfurt.

NUMBER OF EMPLOYEES: About 1,000, with the vast majority in the United States.

AVERAGE AGE OF EMPLOYEES: Thirty-three.

TURNOVER: 20.7 percent.

RECRUITMENT: None.

NUMBER OF NEW HIRES PER YEAR: For each of the last two years, Crain has hired an average of 200 new employees.

RANGE OF STARTING SALARIES: Depends on the position. Salaries are completely different for editorial, sales, and clerical jobs, but an average range might be $15,000 to $17,000.

POLICY FOR RAISES: Raises are awarded once a year and determined on the basis of cost of living and merit.

TRAINING PROGRAMS: No formal programs.

BENEFITS: Medical insurance, dental insurance, life insurance of double an employee's salary, disability insurance, profit sharing (which averages somewhere between 10 and 15 percent of payroll), pension plan, and educational assistance (if people want to get advanced degrees, the company pays for half of their expenses upon completion of their studies).

VACATION: Two weeks for the first two years, three weeks after three years, four weeks after seven years, and five weeks after fourteen years, in addition to ten regular paid holidays per year.

ADDITIONAL PERKS: Crain Communications awards cash gifts to employees upon their fifth, tenth, fifteenth, and twentieth anniversaries with the company. The company also gives employees money upon marriage or the birth of a child. For editorial people, monthly contests are held for the best articles, and winners receive cash prizes. If employees want to participate in activities such as the New York Marathon, the company provides uniforms and picks up some of the expenses.

BONUSES: All salaried employees receive an automatic annual bonus of two weeks' salary. In addition, the top management staff is eligible for merit bonuses.

ANNUAL PARTY: All the offices hold annual Christmas parties, which are left up to their individual discretion. In Chicago, the party is held in a hotel or restaurant (one year it was at the Chicago Historical Society). The Chicago party is informal and includes hors d'oeuvres and dancing, while the Detroit party is more formal. In addition, the company sponsors special sports days—in Chicago it's Cubs day and in New York it's Mets day—during which employees go to games.

DRESS CODE: "On the editorial side, it's pretty loose. They can wear pretty much what they want to wear unless they have interviews or something like that. For everybody else, it's suit and tie or sports jacket, and comparable dress for women."

SOCIAL ATMOSPHERE: "I would say there's probably a lot of camaraderie among the editorial people. And then the sales people—there's a lot among them too. They get together, socialize, go out for drinks, have fun together. I think people are pretty tight. No question that people form friendships and go out after working hours."

HEADQUARTERS: Crain Communications occupies most of the space in a seven-story, 120,000-square-foot building in Chicago. At present, the building is being refurbished "from head to toe."

CHARITABLE CONTRIBUTIONS: About $350,000 in donations for 1987. Some of the charities included: Boys Club of America, the Metropolitan Museum of Art, WBBM Radio Wreath of Hope, March of Dimes, Salvation Army, Lyric Opera of Chicago, the National Press Foundation, Advertising Council, B'nai B'rith.

INTERESTED APPLICANTS CAN SEND RÉSUMÉS TO:
Crain Communications Inc.
Personnel Department
740 North Rush Street
Chicago, IL 60611
(312) 649-5200

t's too tempting. I can't help myself. I want to be able to use the phrase "Citizen Crain" sometime before the chapter is over. Just let me say it once more. "Citizen Crain." Thank you. I feel much better now.

Crain Communications Inc. is a print media empire, but it lacks the imperial quality of Charles Foster Kane (or indeed William Randolph Hearst). Besides, the Crains do not publish general-interest newspapers. Their fortune has been based on trade magazines and tabloids. The company was founded in 1916, but it wasn't until the mid to late 1980s that Crain entered the more widely recognized news arena through its regional business magazines— *Crain's Detroit, Chicago, New York,* and *Cleveland Business.*

With a roster that now includes consumer publications, too, Crain is still the largest independent trade publisher in the United States. With an eye toward further expansion, the company publishes twenty-three monthlies, weeklies, and fortnightlies domestically and two monthly magazines and a newsletter in Europe, owns a 100,000-watt FM radio station in Florida, and has its own news (syndicate) service. Its best-known publication is *Advertising Age,* the so-called Bible of the industry. (Well, actually it *is* the Bible of the industry.)

Mrs. Gertrude Crain, the widow of founder G. D. Crain, Jr., holds the title of chairman. An attractive woman who looks far younger than her age of seventy-seven, she comes into work at the Chicago headquarters "every day unless I'm traveling." She keeps a schedule that would fatigue a thirty-five-year-old. "I don't do any writing or selling," she says, "but we've got about a thousand employees. I deal with profit sharing, and policy matters I decide on with [my sons] Rance and Keith [the president and vice-chairman, respectively, of the corporation]. I go to association meetings and make myself available to all our publications." The employees of Crain known they have a gem in Mrs. Crain. She is sharp, bright, current, and a witness to some key publishing and advertising history. "I don't concentrate on one publication. I do know *Advertising Age* better than the others. It's my favorite. My husband started it."

Before her marriage, Mrs. Crain worked for NBC in New York. But she got seriously involved in the business only after her husband died. "My husband was a remarkable man. When my husband was alive, I basked in his reflected glory. I was so happy. Now, a few years after his death, I've assumed my own identity." She's a woman of some surprise. Last year, this member of the *Forbes* 400 wanted to pursue a dream in which she got to be a race car driver at the Speedway in Charlotte, North Carolina. Her wish was implemented through the editor of *Auto Week.*

"It was really thrilling," she says, still exhilarated as she exhibits her pictures and press clippings. "They asked me who I wanted to drive with, and I said Paul Newman." He was unavailable, but Mrs. Crain drove seven laps at an average speed of 159 miles per hour. "They're naming a car after me," she giggles. "I never had so much publicity in my life!" She was on *PM Magazine* on a segment that was aired nationally, and she got tons of print coverage. For her ride she wore her usual elegant clothes and a helmet. (It's amusing to picture the expensively tasteful woman burning rubber. Her hair looks professionally coiffed; her suit is accented by a necklace, bracelets, earrings, and rings. Her nails are manicured. She smells good.) "I'm thinking of skydiving as an encore performance."

Rance and Keith were already indentured when their mother arrived at work. "I have a good rapport with my sons. I don't tell them what to do. All decisions are made by the three of us. I must say, I don't think they resent me. We speak every day." They don't see each other every day, though, because Keith runs the substantial Detroit operation (where the corporation's money is handled), and Rance spends half of each week at the company's New York bureau.

The Crains do make a conscious attempt to emulate their founding father. "We try to convey that this is a small family business. We learned that from my husband. He preferred it that way," Mrs. Crain says. Taking their lead from G. D. Crain, Jr., the three Crains in charge also answer their own phones. "The boys still quote him." That is true. Rance says, "At one time our company was going to merge with another company. It made sense. But the guy who ran it drove around in a limousine, and Dad wouldn't deal with him. Dad hated pretension." To almost a remarkable extent, the Crains and the people who work for them evoke G. D. Crain, Jr. His image, his words, his goals are common references.

"We've had women in the business as long as I can remember," Mrs. Crain says. "My husband hired qualified people, not women or men. I'm very anxious for women to progress. I hate to see women pitting themselves against men. I'd rather not be aware of who's male and who's female."

Rance Crain is the editor in chief of *Advertising Age* and one of the magazine's featured columnists in addition to his administrative role. He also looks younger than most people his age (forty-nine). His manner is not at all typical of a corporate president. He's enthusiastic in an unjaded, almost naive way, his pleasures seemingly detached from the bottom line altogether. Reporters have long commented on his rumpled look. He may have trouble keeping his shirt neatly tucked in, but he also doesn't give a hoot about it.

His New York office has the most eclectic art arrangement I've ever seen. A print ad—a picture of Mike Ditka and Dick Butkus—is signed to him. It is the only outwardly personal detail in the gray room. One oil painting seems inspired by Cézanne, another a contemporary painting of fashionably attired models.

He says, "As a kid, all I knew was I wanted to be a reporter. I wanted to write. It was all I was good at." He went off to De Paul University for two years, then transferred to Northwestern's Medill School of Journalism. He became the sports editor of *The Daily Northwestern*. "I immersed myself [in journalism] maybe too much. Twenty-eight years later, I still wonder whether it was too much. I didn't have enough liberal arts."

After graduation, "I read *Advise and Consent,* and I wanted to go to Washington. I asked Dad if I could. All we had in Washington was one guy with *Ad Age.* This guy, Stan Cohen, asked me what I wanted to do—tour the Capitol, the White House, etc. I wanted to write an article. And I did. One of my biggest thrills to this day was when I got to take over the Washington office for three weeks. It was fantastic being in Washington during the sixties. I loved getting scoops and getting good stories." Rance says his favorite job is writing his *Advertising Age* column, "Parting Shot," the point of view of which he describes as "no big deal; just a guy who works hard."

Rance says he didn't feel the need to overcompensate for being the son of the chairman and owner. "I was lucky to establish my own identity early." Being away in Washington helped. "I was not under my father's shadow. It's difficult for kids of famous fathers." After almost two years in the capital, he moved to New York, where he lived for ten years, some of them in the city, some in Connecticut. "I moved back to the Midwest in 1972 and worked with Dad until his death in 1973." At the time, Crain owned seven publications, though heavily dominated by *Advertising Age.*

Rance keeps an apartment in New York, within walking distance of his office. "Culturally Crain New York and Chicago are the same. People are enthusiastic about what we're doing. They appreciate that we hire them as professionals and leave them alone. That's the playback I get from these guys."

The source of the laissez-faire culture? "It all comes down to my being lazy," Rance concedes. "I'd rather just hire good people—bright, curious journalists—with confidence and trust them. They don't have to have backgrounds in the fields they cover. Clark Bell is the editor of *Modern Healthcare*. He knew nothing about the area. The advantage was that he wasn't a lackey of the industry." He pauses. "I have no conscious game plan. Ever. I hope I never do."

Rance continues, "I'm not obsessed by details, so I'm perfectly happy to hire people who are obsessed by details. I have no goals. I go on vacation and don't go into the office. I'm not a type A; I'm not a driven man."

Rance says, "My brother is not at all like me. He's a more bottom line—oriented business-man." What Rance did not mention was that they don't even look like brothers. Rance is dark and bespectacled, while Keith is fairer and larger. Well, they are both tall. Keith is in Chicago when we meet. He also joined the business after graduating from Northwestern and worked on a publication called *Advertising and Sales Promotion Magazine,* which no longer exists. "I hadn't yet hit my stride. In 1971 I moved to Detroit with the purchase of *Automotive News.* I really like it there."

He explains that the business is divided. "You have to think of it as two: business—printing contracts, pension plans, vacation schedules, etc.—and magazine publishing. It [the latter] is more fun. Rance and I split it." Keith likes to think of himself as a publisher. "I publish about five or six publications. That's what I like best. I get stuck with a lot of boring business stuff, so I hired a senior vice-president of operations."

Isn't it hard to be impartial? He must have a favorite magazine. "Heaven forbid your having a favorite publication. Heaven forbid a line of demarcation. We get involved with everything. If there were a magazine that bored us, say *Widget Age,*" he invents, "I'd look at Rance and say, 'I don't want it.' Even though it's profitable." Obviously, though, if you were a member of the widget industry, you would appreciate such a trade publication. Some of Keith's responsibilities include *Tire Business, American Clean Car* for the carwash trade, *American Drycleaner, Pensions & Investment Age, American Coin-Op,* "serving the business needs of owners and operators of coin-operated washing, drying, and related services," and *European Rubber Journal,* a monthly. "We're good at the specialized customer. We have focused publications."

Keith says the family is careful about writing even the most sophisticated journals in plain English. "All of us have no problem saying, 'I have a problem. I don't get it.' No publications are written in technicalese." Which makes it easier to move reporters and editors around the company. "There's quite a bit of lateral movement. The new editor of *City & State* ["for management-level executive and financial officers within state, county and local government and government agencies . . . circulation about 30,000"] used to be the senior editor of *Electronic Media.*"

Keith tells me about his first move after acquiring *Automotive News* (founded in 1925, circulation 66,680). "I ran a two-page spread in *Advertising Age* [circulation 90,000]. The left side was a picture of Henry Ford, and the right side said, 'The trade paper the chairman reads.'" The anecdote points directly to a moral dilemma that must be at the heart of the trade publishing business. Can you run editorial with integrity if the subjects of your articles are your advertisers? "As a publisher, we stand up and write the story that must be written. You've got to tell your people, 'Now, I know this guy runs fifty-two pages of advertising, but write the story that needs to be done.' We don't care if we lose ad pages. We've lost some before. It's the price of doing business."

Keith, a confessed multimillionaire, describes his company—as Rance did months before—in the most innocent of ways. "We're a small family business," he says. "It's Mom and the two kids. You don't think about a thousand people: you think of small units." Since the bulk of Crain's employees are divided pretty evenly among Chicago, New York, and Detroit, the ambience stays personal.

Joe Cappo has become an influential man in the business world. He is a vice-president of

Crain and the publisher of *Crain's Chicago Business,* one of the brothers' most successful launches. (You can hear Joe hosting a business talk show on both PanAmerican World Airlines' and American Airlines' audio services, and on WLOO-FM radio in Chicago.) A native of Chicago, he majored in economics and philosophy at De Paul. He was the sports editor of the *De Paulian* and the student body president. "I couldn't get a job as a philosopher," he says, so he enlisted in the Army. Actually, he was drafted. After his discharge, he got his first job through an ad in a newspaper; a chain of North Shore suburban papers was looking for a reporter. From there it was a job with *The Chicago Daily News* on the midnight shift. "City Hall, the morgue, the state of Illinois building, the police department, drug and prostitution raids, etc. I covered the Richard Speck trial, the Beatles' first tour, the 1968 Democratic convention. I don't know how good or bad a reporter I was, but I knew I was working for a major daily.

"In September 1968 I moved to the financial section in order to work days. This was before business was considered 'sexy.'" Because *The Daily News* was an afternoon paper, it published the closing stock prices, and so it had a lot of business readers. The newspaper folded in 1978, but not before Cappo discovered he had a feel for business writing. He joined *Crain's Chicago Business* about two months later "as 'editor at large.'"

"I'm a professional publisher now," he says after nine years with that responsibility, "and I think a damn good one. I don't think I could have done this for a larger company." *Crain's Chicago Business* is so much a part of the business scene in Chicago that a reporter from the magazine will be included in any germane press conference, business show, or convention in the area. *CCB*'s most popular issue each year is its annual "The Fortunate 100"—a listing of Chicago's best-paid businesspeople.

On this blustery, cold day we walk from Crain's headquarters to a nearby restaurant, where Joe is greeted by several people. Being a publisher at Crain does not mean having to fit a mold. "All the publishers in the company do things differently and come from different backgrounds, many from advertising. We're each autonomous. I hire and fire and make decisions. As long as I do a good job, they leave me alone. I run my publication. It's wonderful being the boss. I like the freedom. I go to the board once a year and talk to them about corporate issues."

Bob Niesse is the Midwest sales manager of *Business Insurance* (circulation 48,560). He describes himself when he was younger as "a fraternity guy at Indiana University—I wasn't a revolutionary, but I didn't want to serve in Vietnam. I enjoyed myself." After graduation in 1967, he got a job at a fairly desirable company: IBM. He left within his first two months, during training. "I didn't like the regimentation, the white shirts. The technicalities were a turn-off. I wanted to hit the streets, not learn wiring. They were going to place me back in Indianapolis. That was the straw that broke the camel's back."

Voting against the familiar, Niesse moved to Chicago, got a room at the "Y," and found a job immediately at the *Tribune.* "There was a two-week training session, and that was it; I had my own territory. It was such a great door opener to the city." He sold classified ads at first, then was promoted to display ads in the retail department. Discovering that "magazine sales in general pay better than newspaper sales," after three and a half years Bob left to become the advertising manager of a high-tech magazine. "I didn't check them out thoroughly first," he admits, "and I found out I was the fourth or fifth ad manager in one year, and they weren't even a distant second in the field. I was pissed off."

In 1969 Niesse found a job at *Business Insurance,* a field in which he had no training, which concerned no one. "I never felt—and still don't feel—that I'm in the insurance business. I'm in the publishing business. I'm a marketing consultant. We're the most efficient way to reach the audience and help their business." Since the magazine had been launched just the year before, "at first I had to educate people—especially [advertising] agency people about our business: corporate insurance and pensions. I turned my newness into an advantage. I'd tell the client, 'Help me. I'm the new kid on the block.' "

Bob says he never gave much thought to whether Crain would be a long-term career move or a short hiatus. The positive initial signs were "no training program at Crain, and early independence. It was a happy marriage. I never planned it, but I can't envision selling anything else. It's a good company. It went through explosive growth after G. D. Crain died."

He likes the way the company is run. "Crain is very ethical. There's no variation, no cutting on the [ad] rate card [a practice apparently common in the industry]." Furthermore, "we'll take potshots at our advertisers. We'll publish ten great articles [about their company] and they'll never say anything, and then we'll print one small negative piece, and they complain bitterly.

"We have a hell of a lot of autonomy. I don't know what goes on in the board of directors meetings. I don't think they meddle with the publishers. I don't think of my publisher or editor meddling with me. I think of my territory as my own entrepreneurial profit center." Niesse tells potential customers, "I'm not here to sell you advertising; I'm here to help you with your business." He mentions that this persuasive argument plus Crain's excellent reputation usually do the trick.

"There is a Church and State at Crain. I won't talk to the client about editorial. I'm only involved in advertising. I can't speak for our editors, and I prefer not to. I can talk about our market effectiveness and our reach, and the purchase power of our customers."

As at most publications, Niesse says, the classic conflict between editorial and business rears its head here. "There's a little rivalry between editorial and business." The latter think the former "are in it for the glory," and the former think the latter "are only in it for the money." He generalizes: "the ad people are more gregarious and social; the editorial are sensitive and poor. Editorial does a good job, and they're obviously less motivated by money than the ad people are. *I* never get any recognition—I get commissions, not a pat on the back."

Niesse's been around other Crain offices, and he thinks Chicago is the most collegial. "It *is* like a family in lots of ways. People get to know each other well, not like at some large corporation. When I got here, the receptionist's son and husband worked here. Lots of children of employees work here. Why not hire those people? There's a better chance of that person being a better employee. People do get fired, but people think of the individuals and consider them friends."

LEO BURNETT COMPANY, INC.

HISTORY & OPERATIONS

Leo Burnett, Company, Inc., an advertising agency named after its founder, opened shop in Chicago in 1935. It was the middle of the Depression, and the fledgling agency had only $12,000 in capital, eight employees, and three clients on its roster. In an attempt to brighten up the offices, Burnett's receptionist set out a bowl of apples on her desk each morning to be handed out to anyone who wanted one—a generous and optimistic gesture. The apples became (and remain) the agency's trademark and are still distributed daily. During its first year of operation, Leo Burnett's biggest client, the Minnesota Valley Canning Co. (today's Green Giant) was crippled by a severe drought. As a result, the agency took in only $600,000 in billings that year.

Originally from St. Johns, Michigan, Leo Burnett came to be known as one of the few true originals in the advertising industry. He began his career in journalism as a reporter on *The Peoria Journal* and later moved to Detroit, where he got his first taste of advertising working for the Cadillac Motor Company. From there, Burnett moved to Chicago to start his own agency.

Leo Burnett's goal was to produce the best advertising in the world, bar none. Early in the agency's history, Burnett gained a reputation—which fueled the agency's rapid growth—of being able to understand his clients and their particular needs. Each client's campaigns were created around what Burnett referred to as "the inherent drama" in a product. The aim of each campaign was to get people to remark on the product, rather than on the advertising itself. And the agency measured the success of a given campaign solely in terms of how well a product subsequently sold. Burnett's sensibility (and consequently the agency's) leaned toward "warm sell sentimentality" with a broad geographic and demographic appeal.

In 1940 Leo Burnett Company landed its first $1 million-plus account: the American Meat Institute. By 1945 the agency employed more than a hundred people and had annual billings in excess of $7 million. In 1946 Burnett opened a production office in Hollywood (which has since moved across the street to Los Angeles), and in 1947 it passed the $10 million mark in billings and was ranked twenty-sixth in *Advertising Age*'s list of U.S. agencies. In 1950 billings topped $22 million and Leo Burnett became the largest advertising agency in Chicago. In 1952 Burnett's influence spread to Canada with the opening of a Toronto office. By 1956 it had surpassed $100 million in billings, and in 1961, with the purchase of a controlling interest in Leggett-Nicholson and Partners, Ltd., a London agency, it extended its reach overseas.

By 1965, when the agency celebrated its thirtieth anniversary, Leo Burnett had amassed a list of heavyweight clients, including Pillsbury Company; Kellogg Company; Procter & Gamble Company; Phillip Morris, Inc.; Maytag Company; Allstate Insurance Companies; Star-Kist Foods, Inc.; Union Carbide Corporation; and United Airlines, all of which are still on its client list.

In 1967 Leo Burnett retired from active management of the agency. In 1969 the firm merged with the London Press Exchange International Network, resulting in thirty-one Burnett offices in twenty-one countries around the world. Leo Burnett died in 1971. Although mourning his loss, the agency continued to grow, and by 1985 Leo Burnett USA's billings—all emanating out of Chicago—totaled $1.13 billion, the first time a single advertising office exceeded the $1 billion billings mark.

Leo Burnett Company has come to be known for creating some of the most enduring advertising campaigns in the industry's history. Its reputation is based in part on the longevity of its commercial creations—the Marlboro Man, the Jolly Green Giant, Charlie the Tuna, Morris the Cat, Tony the Tiger, the Pillsbury Doughboy, and the lonely Maytag repairman—and client relationships. The agency, which is considered to be one of the best and most desirable to work for in the country, draws a surfeit of talented people eager to join its prestigious ranks; close to 5,500 people apply for fifty to sixty new entry-level positions per year.

Today, under the leadership of Leo Burnett's chairman, Hall "Cap" Adams, who joined the company in 1956, the agency has fifty offices in forty-three countries. Burnett, which serves fewer clients than most other top agencies (just twenty-eight in the United States), limits its client roster in order to avoid spreading itself too thin. It represents 226 major product brands, fifty-one (or 22 percent) of which are ranked number one or two in their product categories. Of the agency's approximately 4,727 employees worldwide, 1,879 work in the USA division and 2,648 work in the international division. The agency is the only major player in the industry to have only one full service American office—in Chicago at that—and no real presence in New York City, save a production office.

In 1987 Leo Burnett was ranked as the tenth largest agency in the United States by worldwide gross income, with worldwide billings of $2.46 billion. The agency is privately held, and all of its stockholders are active full-time employees.

(Information provided by Wally Peterson, agency spokesperson.)

RANKING: Tenth largest in the United States by worldwide gross billings, according to *Advertising Age*'s 1987 statistics.

BILLINGS: Worldwide, Leo Burnett's billings were $2.46 billion in 1987. Leo Burnett USA had billings of $1.549 billion, and Leo Burnett International billed $911 million.

EARNINGS: The agency is private and will not disclose.

OFFICES: Leo Burnett has headquarters in Chicago, for a total of fifty offices in the following forty-three countries: Argentina, Australia, Bahrain, Belgium, Brazil, Canada, Chile, Colombia, Denmark, Dominican Republic, Ecuador, Egypt, France, West Germany, Greece, Guatemala, Hong Kong, India, Indonesia, Italy, Japan, Korea, Kuwait, Lebanon, Malaysia, Mexico, the Netherlands, New Zealand, Panama, Peru, Philippines, Puerto Rico, Saudi Arabia, Singapore, Spain, Switzerland, Taiwan, Thailand, Turkey, United Arab Emirates, United Kingdom, United States, Venezuela. Furthermore, though Burnett maintains small production offices in Detroit, Los Angeles, and New York, the company considers only Chicago in the above list.

NUMBER OF EMPLOYEES: 4,727 worldwide. Of the 1,879 who work in the United States, 1,788 are located in the Chicago headquarters.

AVERAGE AGE OF EMPLOYEES: Thirty-seven.

TURNOVER: Information not available.

RECRUITMENT: Leo Burnett Co. recruits at different schools for each of its major departments. For the most part, it looks for promising liberal arts students, though some MBAs are recruited for client service. The four main departments recruit primarily at the following schools: *Client Service:* Amherst College, Brown University, University of Chicago, Dartmouth College, Denison University, DePaul University, Duke University, Emory University, College of the Holy Cross, University of Illinois, Indiana University, University of Michigan, Michigan State University, University of North Carolina, Northwestern University, Notre Dame University, University of Virginia. *Research:* Boston University, University of Chicago, University of Illinois, Michigan State University, Northwestern University, Ohio State University. *Creative:* The Art Center, Portfolio Center, Pratt Institute, the School of Visual Arts, Syracuse University, University of Texas at Austin. *Media:* University of Chicago, University of Illinois, Indiana University, University of Iowa, Miami University, University of Michigan, Michigan State University, Northwestern University, Notre Dame University, University of Texas, University of Wisconsin at Madison.

NUMBER OF NEW HIRES PER YEAR: 280 in 1986 and 337 in 1987. (Of those, 138 filled new positions.)

RANGE OF STARTING SALARIES: "Very confidential." The agency will not disclose figures.

POLICY FOR RAISES: Depends on the department and the employee. The agency will not disclose its specific raise policy.

TRAINING PROGRAMS: Vary by department. Non-MBAs who are hired for the client service department spend between one and two years working in the media department, where they learn that end of the business through on-the-job training. Afterward, they move to client service, where they become assistant account executives, learning on the job and attending monthly seminars. MBAs hired for client service go directly into a client service training program, where they, too, learn on the job under the direction of a supervisor who monitors their progress, in addition to attending monthly seminars. Each of the other major departments has its own set of seminars. All employees (except for support staff and creative people) are encouraged to attend the client service seminars as well as those offered in their own departments. Leo Burnett has recently launched an experimental training program for the creatives called the "Rotating Option Program," which the agency has adopted on a permanent basis.

BENEFITS: Comprehensive major medical and dental insurance, participation in a health maintenance organization, life insurance, long-term disability insurance, supplemental disability income, accidental death and dismemberment insurance, travel accident insurance, profit-sharing plan, pension plan, and tuition reimbursement for any course or degree program that will benefit an employee's career at the agency (and terms are loosely defined).

VACATION Two weeks after one year, three weeks after three years, four weeks after ten years, five weeks after twenty years and six weeks after twenty-five years, in addition to ten regular paid holidays per year.

ADDITIONAL PERKS: An adoptive aid program that pays up to $3,000 to help an employee adopt a child. All employees traveling on business fly first class. (If client United Airlines flies that route, so much the better.) And, on the agency's anniversary (August 5), each employee around the world receives a dollar for every year the agency has been in business ($53 apiece in 1988). There is a special theme for the day. In 1987 it was "52 years of playing our cards right." When employees arrived at work that morning, there were genuine tarot card readers in the lobby and magicians doing card tricks. Upstairs, everyone received a gift—a "good quality" wooden box containing two decks of playing cards embossed with the Leo Burnett logo and slogan.

BONUSES All employees are eligible. Although Leo Burnett will not reveal its specific policy for awarding bonuses, the word is that they're generous, very generous—rumored to be as high as 15 to 20 percent of salary.

ANNUAL PARTIES: The agency hosts two lavish annual parties. In December the Burnett breakfast is held for all U.S.A. employees at a hotel in downtown Chicago. After breakfast, management discusses the agency's performance in the past year, and after that they screen commercials and see print ads of their best work over the year. A "Black Pencil Award" (an outsized black pencil mounted on a base—Leo Burnett always wrote with a black pencil) is presented to each Burnetter who has contributed to the creation of superior advertising (the corporate mission). Then employees return to the office, where their bosses hand out bonuses to everyone. From there, groups go out for lunch, and then they go off to local bars, where they drink and dance and celebrate the past year. And in August the "Apple Blast" is held for all Chicago employees. They go to Indian Lakes Resort, outside Chicago, where they can choose among such activities as swimming, miniature golf, volleyball, badminton, tennis, and poker. Then there's a huge dinner at which everyone gets a commemorative gift—in 1987 it was a pair of sunglasses on a cord, with a tiny little apple embossed on one of the earpieces—after which prizes are awarded to the winners of the day's competitions. In addition, door prizes associated with the agency's clients (United Airlines tickets, McDonald's gift certificates, a Maytag dishwasher, Samsonite Luggage, etc.) are given out, and everyone present is eligible to win.

AVERAGE WORK DAY Official hours are 9:00 A.M. to 5:00 P.M., "but we're hard workers and a lot of overtime is put in."

DRESS CODE: There is no stated dress code, "but it's kind of unofficial." People in the Client Service, Media, and Research Departments tend to dress in traditional business suits ("but business suits with a flair")—that goes for both men and women—or slightly more casually if they're not meeting with a client. For people in the Creative Department, "let's just say that when you get on the elevator you know who's Creative and who's not." They wear anything from blue jeans with sports jackets to shorts, though the latter are "kind of discouraged."

SOCIAL ATMOSPHERE: "A very warm and giving atmosphere. We're bound together by a common cause. We're inspired by Leo Burnett's legacy. We believe in it. People are friendly and helpful, and even though the agency is rather large and it's impossible to get to know everyone, there still is a feeling of unity and family that comes from working toward the same goals." Many employees do socialize after working hours. "There's a bar downstairs called the Chicago Bar and Grill. You go in any evening, and you'll find a lot of Burnett people."

AGENCY LOGO AND MOTTO: A hand reaching for the stars, because, in the words of Leo Burnett himself, "When you reach for the stars, you may not quite get one, but you won't come up with a handful of mud either."

NUMBER OF CLIENTS: Twenty-eight, twelve of which have been with the agency twenty-five years or more and seventeen of which have been with the agency ten years or more.

NUMBER OF APPLES HANDED OUT PER YEAR: In 1987 Leo Burnett gave out 447,445 apples worldwide, 318,732 of those in the Chicago office alone.

HEADQUARTERS: The agency currently occupies thirteen floors of Chicago's Prudential Building, with 385,968 square feet of office space. Burnett is constructing a new headquarters, at 35 West Wacker Drive, which is scheduled to open in early 1989. The agency will own the new structure and occupy about half of it.

CHARITABLE ACTIVITIES: The agency has a matching gifts policy through which it will match gifts up to $3,000 made by full-time employees to eligible institutions (basically any nonprofit organization recognized by the IRS as tax exempt, with the exception of religious organizations, political parties, and the Crusade of Mercy, to which the agency contributes generously on its own).

INTERESTED APPLICANTS CAN SEND RÉSUMÉS TO:
Employee Relations
Leo Burnett Company, Inc.
Prudential Plaza
Chicago, IL 60601
(312) 565-5959

Much as we hate to traffic in clichés, let us turn our attention to the Saul Steinberg poster of the New Yorker's view of the world. Imagine this same map, with its geographic axis intact, to be the advertising agency view of the world. While New York would remain dominant, white out the name "Chicago" and replace it with the name "Leo Burnett." This little illustration should be a pretty fair indicator of the power, the influence, and the size of this midwestern-international advertising agency, currently ranked tenth largest in the United States, by worldwide gross incomes. And that's not due to mergers or takeovers, either.

Leo Burnett is famous for lots of reasons: Tony the Tiger, the Marlboro Man, the Jolly Green Giant, Morris the Cat, the Keebler Elves, Ronald McDonald, Charlie the Tuna, the lonely Maytag repairman, and the Pillsbury Doughboy, to drop the names of some of the more familiar characters. Leo Burnett is also famous for having more long-term relationships with clients than any other agency in the country—nay, the free world—and this in a business so desperate to stay ahead of trends that the threshold for continuity is notoriously low. The roster of clients is impressive, to say the least. They are listed here along with the year they became Burnett clients: Allstate Insurance, 1957; Amurol Products Company (a wholly owned associated company of the William J. Wrigley Company), 1988; Beatrice Foods, 1983; Black & Decker, 1987; Commonwealth Edison Company, 1954; First Brands Corporation, 1961; General Motors Corporation, 1934; Harris Trust & Savings Bank, 1952; H. J. Heinz Company, 1974; Hewlett-Packard Company, 1984; Keebler Company, 1968; Kellogg Company, 1949; Kraft, Inc., 1984; Maxell Corporation (Clarion Cosmetics), 1988; Maytag Company, 1955; McDonald's Corporation, 1982; McDonald's Owners of Chicago Land and Northwest Indiana, 1985; Miller Brewing Company, 1982; Mrs. Smith's Frozen Foods Company, 1980; Phillip Morris, Inc., 1954; Pillsbury Company, 1944 (and its subsidiary the Green Giant Company, 1935); Procter & Gamble Company, 1952; Schenley Industries, Inc., 1968; Seven-Up Company, 1985; Star-Kist Foods, Inc., 1958; Talaction, 1987; UNOCAL Corporation, 1938; and United Airlines, 1965. Worldwide, 4,727 employees handle these twenty-eight clients, who consider this to be a favorable ratio.

Many of the approximately 1,788 employees who work for Leo Burnett in its Prudential Building headquarters spent a significant portion of their pre-Burnett days dreaming of working there. As residents of the Midwest, they were already acquainted with the agency in some way—through people who worked there, through the agency's work, or because it is known as a high-paying company. Advertising is a field that sounds interesting, but until you actually start working in it, you might not understand it. In the words of one account supervisor, "Advertising is the perfect career for someone who doesn't know what he or she wants to do." Another claims that advertising is "a good place for people who want to do too much." Leo Burnett's appeal transcends making ads or selling cereal. It's a fine company filled with contented folks who hope they can stay there a long time. And yes, they do good solid work, too.

Employees call themselves "Burnetters." Burnetters work hard. In part, it's the culture, which turns normal people into workaholics. Partially it's the implicit peer pressure of fanatics working in the office next door. John Kinsella, Burnett's ex-chairman of the board and chief executive officer, says, "Coming in early and staying late for the sake of it is nuts. There is pressure to turn out superlative work. That becomes a strict taskmaster. If you can do it better, you should. There is that kind of pressure. I like it."

People a little lower on the totem pole have their own reasons for the long hours and the hard work. For one thing, "you never have to do anything long enough to get bored." Each campaign feels different, "even if it's similar to commercials done five years ago," and Burnetters are able to feel their imprint on every piece of work they do. Even if it's just adjusting the size of the Surgeon General's warning in a newspaper ad for Merit cigarettes. For another, despite the agency's large size (for this industry), people are divided up into groups of approximately twenty with which they identify. No matter which department—Client (a.k.a. Account) Service, Media, Creative, Production, Research, or the Mailroom—employees develop a fierce loyalty to their group, which becomes, naturally, a surrogate family, with its attendant ups and downs, both professional and emotional. You naturally identify with your group, which takes the name of its leader.

"Burnett is like a Notre Dame football game," a creative (respectable nickname for copy-writer or art director) explains. "I'm in the Bell group," he said in the days when Creative Director Ted Bell still led a gang. Today Bell is also president of Leo Burnett USA and a smooth and charming man who, contrary to the casual attire that usually clads copywriters, has the sartorial splendor of a banker, which has been emulated by many who've worked closely with him. The writer added, "One girl [in Creative] asked me, 'Why do I feel I work for a bowling team and you work for a yacht club?' "

Within these little families or teams, close partnerships exist, especially in the Creative department. Most writers and art directors are paired for as long as they can or want to work together. Some teams are even recruited together. This becomes more like marriage than like fraternal twins. "It's a matter of clicking or personality," one of these business spouses says. "You spend so much time together, some of it screaming." If the pairing doesn't work out, however, all you have to do is see the creative director, and you'll be matched up with someone else. Some people prefer monogamy or serial monogamy; others choose to play the field.

All this warm family gestalt belies the fact that this is a seriously competitive company. With a nod to the prevailing ethos of the business, there is a constant, albeit minor, fear that your work will be inferior, the client will leave, and you will be fired. Given Burnett's track record, this is highly unlikely, but no one dares get smug. Even Burnetters with gold-and-diamond watches (members of the Fifteen-Year Club) who haven't missed a day of work and who have been promoted steadily admit to having lost a night or two's sleep with worry every so often. A senior art director confesses, "People always worry about getting canned. We do have a lot of competition, which is stimulating if you win more than you lose." A media director with a quarter of a century at Burnett under his belt verbally crosses his fingers that he can stay until his retirement. Kinsella says, "Panic helps the work." He clearly recognizes the existence of the underlying nervousness but maintains that "a lot of worry and paranoia is brought on by oneself. We absorb people. If we lost an account, you don't go off to the streets; we're more benevolent." Besides he says, "there's no stigma in this business if you're a creative who's fired."

Creatives who succeed may be astonished to find they have won a "Black Pencil Award," the agency's version of the Oscar. It's quite selective, and since there's no open nomination committee, winners squeal at the annual breakfast when they hear their names announced. The black pencil is another Burnettian image—it was Mr. Burnett's implement of choice when he wrote copy.

Again and again Mr. Burnett's vision and philosophy are evoked both by those who knew him and just as often by those who did not. Pride in the agency's history is almost a perk of one's job. It is, furthermore, inconceivable to go out in Chicago and not make a positive impression with the news that you are a Burnetter.

Interestingly, Burnetters seem to take their client's side before they take their own into consideration. They believe in service—they really do—and are somehow able to push their egos out of the way. If a conflict were to develop between the creative team and the client, and the creatives could not sell their approach, that would be that. No hard feelings. He who pays the bills triumphs. "When an account wants a new campaign," a writer explains, "the group leader will assign the project to two or three teams. The best one wins. You always hope the best campaign wins. You don't take it personally." What about striking a compromise? "You never merge the approaches of different teams. That's a nightmare!"

Simply learning how to work with clients is an unspoken requirement. According to Burnetters, a "good client" is someone who "believes in advertising." (So is a client who is straight and honest, works well with the team, and pays his bills.) "Bad" clients are closed-minded and are sometimes reluctant to take the advice of their advertising agency. "We're marketing consultants," a true blue Burnetter says. "We have recommended that some clients pull money away from advertisements and put it into promotion. We don't regard it as losing money; we see it as helping the client."

Client Service is considered to be the department that is hardest on people. If ever anyone could feel entangled in the middle of the sometimes murky client-agency relationship, it is in this crowd. In addition to identifying with their own in-house group, these people are so loyal to the brands they represent, they really have two masters. Leo Burnett has a training program called the Client Service Development Program, which is considered to be one of the best in the land. It can last between twelve and eighteen months, much of it spent in Media Services if you arrive bearing only a BA. Graduates call it " 'boot camp' with hard work and hard play. There are a lot of hormones. Everyone's between the ages of twenty-one and twenty-five." Furthermore, every new recruit is assigned to an adviser, who can help the transition to Burnett.

It's important to communicate to you, the reader, the "problems of balance" on which many Burnetters thrive. "It's not overly healthy, but we are obsessive. We like stress. Sometimes the company expects too much of you. Sometimes they ask you to skip vacations." Think back to the 1986 Garry Marshall movie *Nothing in Common,* in which Tom Hanks played a harried creative director at an unnamed Chicago agency. Though he was cinematically cutely overworked, he was under constant threats to his well-being. He had to please his boss and his client, and he had almost no time for his personal life.

As a service industry, advertising often reeks of franticness. Any idea or piece of paper that goes to the client from a junior employee has to be approved internally by at least someone or some board. It may be cat food and not neurosurgery, but the pandemonium feeds the sense that these activities are important. Being asked to stay late means you are essential to the process. The whole team is needed. Millions of dollars could easily be at stake, after all.

Sometimes the intensity can reach toxic levels. "After an intense period of seven A.M. to seven P.M., seven days a week, I thought something was wrong." The most successful advertising people will tell you it's important to have a life outside the agency, if for no other reason than to be exposed to new stimuli to bring back to the office. Self-doubt can set in. "One thing I don't like is, I don't feel I'm directly helping people," one executive admits. "It doesn't crop up too often—just New Year's Eve."

Creatively, Burnett provides unprecedented security, if not the license to break established styles and do avant-garde ads. You know if you work on the Keebler account that you've got to include those animated elves. You know the Marlboro Man will appear in the print campaign for your cigarettes. You might think this dulls your personal contribution to the archives, but it's a great way to build a portfolio and learn the nuts and bolts of advertising. But is it the advertising kids will talk about after watching a commercial aired during *Saturday Night Live?* Probably not.

"Some young creatives might not want to come here," says one who has made her peace with work on the United Airlines and McDonald's accounts. "We're not hip. We have old [as in not new, as opposed to not young] clients who like to continue the same campaigns. The challenge is to *make* it new." To be fair, Burnett keeps collecting enough awards to reinforce their approach.

Burnett handles a substantial amount of package goods. These include Kraft Velveeta, Salada tea, Eggo frozen waffles, Whitney yogurt, Heinz ketchup, Mrs. Smith's pies, 9 Lives cat food, Glad bags, Secret deodorant, Gleem toothpaste, Jolly Green Giant vegetables, and Kellogg's Raisin Bran. To the agency, package goods mean "larger budgets and overall resources, more sophisticated clients, do-able research, and a slower pace." And more conservative clients.

It's Advertising with a capital "A," the kind that lost vogue during the late sixties and early seventies. "When I was in college in the seventies," an account woman said, "advertising was a four-letter word. When I was recruited here from school, I couldn't decide whether it was Burnett or the business that finally grabbed me." At twenty-four, she was responsible for a piece of business worth $8 million. Today, she is a recruiter herself.

In advertising, the executive producer is the person who actually supervises the commercial shoots, bidding out the jobs, hiring the director, and so on, all the way through to a polished piece of video. One identifies himself as a "child of the sixties. The week before my interviews here, I had waist-length hair and an earring. The last thing I thought I'd ever do was advertising—it was selling out. The only reason I majored in radio, TV, and film was because it had no language requirement." Having heard of Burnett from a cameraman, he was hired as a junior producer seven years ago. That meant a lot of time in postproduction, specifically editing. "Burnett is the only agency with a training program for producers. A good producer deals with people and has to be organized and attend to details. You schedule and hire. I think I have one of the easiest jobs in the business, because I hate shitwork, and there's none. A lot of nights I'm here till eight, nine, ten, or eleven P.M. Then, I go running to let off steam." (Often when he's on a shoot, that means he's running in Los Angeles, the goal of every producer working in the Chicago winter. You can spot them at the Beverly Hills Hotel all winter, looking very busy and very tanned.)

Even the receptionists become fanatics. "You pick up stress from the environment. For a new pitch"—selling the agency to a new client or a new campaign to an old client—"everyone's keyed up. I pick things up," a twenty-four-year veteran says. "I hear things. I try to be very careful about what I say." Then again, working on the fifteenth floor, the executive suite, she has gotten to see Jimmy Durante, William "Refrigerator" Perry, Gene Kelly, Morris the Cat, and "the Marlboro Man was in last week. He's a real cowboy; dressed right."

When the management of Leo Burnett is not cracking the whip, it spends a lot of time and money perpetuating traditions started by Mr. Burnett and celebrating the success of the agency. When the agency opened its doors in August 1935, the receptionist set out a bowl of apples. This attracted a good deal of attention during the Depression, and the apple has consequently become one of the company's symbols. To this day, over a thousand apples are given away every day, almost half a million a year worldwide. They sit on receptionists' desks on every floor, arriving with the first mail delivery. In the last ten years, the Chicago offices have given away in excess of two million apples.

On the annual anniversary of the founding of the agency, Leo Burnett gives every employee a dollar for every year of the company's existence. Since 1935 the wad has gotten quite plump, but that's small apples compared to the degree of attention given the celebration itself. (Employees love to reminisce about year forty-eight—1983. That was when the lobby of the Prudential Building was transformed into "WLBC," hosted by radio personality Casey Kasem. Every employee was given a small apple-shaped radio on which to hear the shortwave frequency program, forty-eight years of Leo Burnett jingles.) At noon, everyone is traditionally given the rest of the day off, although most people choose to revel together in their groups. One year there was a circus. Creative teams are assigned to pick a theme and design the event, almost as if it were another ad campaign.

Bonus Day is another highlight. Held at the end of the year, generous bonus checks are distributed at a lavish breakfast party. One Creative remembers last year's breakfast with shame. "I lost my blue blazer, my bonus check, and my self-respect the same day."

People praise Burnett for being a "first-class company." That phrase was repeated several times during my two-day visit. In the most literal sense, this means everyone traveling for business flies first class, even if they're just going to Cincinnati. United Airlines, a client, as you will recall, since 1965, is the airline of choice, but if United doesn't fly where you have to go, you go first class on the available carrier. Second, if you are entitled to a cash reimbursement, you are trusted. "You don't have to prove you drank a Coke to get your quarter back," says someone who is thrilled after years of receipt hoarding for another employer.

Many BAs in Client and Media Services are studying for their MBAs at night through the generosity of Burnett's tuition reimbursement program. Luckily, two of the country's highest-ranking graduate schools of business, the Kellogg School (yes, a relation of the Battle Creek Kellogg's) at Northwestern University and the University of Chicago, have part-time programs within close distance of the office. If you can prove other studies are necessary for your professional development ("and we're lenient," says a representative of employee relations, which okays "anything that's remotely job-related"), Burnett will pay for them as well, up to 75 percent or $3,000.

Presenting your work, whether it's research on consumers, a media plan, or campaign strategy, is vital to ensuring your success in advertising. Those who excel in speech making are sometimes able to steal the thunder from good workers who shy away from the spotlight. Presenting your own ideas to the client is considered a coup, as well as a way to guarantee you credit and attention. Burnett will send interested employees in Client Services who need coaching to the Second City Players Workshop. There, at the well-known comedy troupe, thinking on one's feet is taught and paid for.

Officially, there is no dress code here. Unofficially, executive women wear "dresses, sensible purchases, like from a 'good sale' at Lord & Taylor. No funky jewelry like Ylang Ylang, more like Miss Illinois accessories. Guys wear such a uniform it's scary," claims a tour guide, anxious to stand out just a tad. "They all wear blue sixty-forty shirts [60 percent cotton to 40 percent polyester]; a yellow tie from anywhere. Nobody wears three-button suits," is said apologetically, and they wear "tassle Florsheims. They mean well. They are nice people with nice parents."

A word about Chicago. "Leo Burnett is proudly midwestern." It is the only major agency without a New York City presence. (A small production office is not even a proxy.) "Part of staying *here* is, I don't want to live *there*." One ex-New Yorker admits, "I was worried about being out of the mainstream, but Leo Burnett is solid . . . around the world." John Kinsella has the last word on the subject. "I don't give a rat's rear end about New York, and vice versa. There are not two sets of criteria. They may think of us as farmers or conservatives, but we can really do something out here. Or tell people to jump in a lake."

The Five-Year Club has 986 members. Each woman member receives a gold bracelet with an apple charm. Men get ties. Burnett's Ten-Year Club has 536 members. Women choose either earrings or a pendant; men get ties. The 301 members of the Fifteen-Year Club get gold-and-diamond watches. "People wear them every day. Management presents them at a luncheon where they give a speech about you. They've researched you." Members of both sexes of the Twenty-, Twenty-five, and Thirty-Year Clubs receive, in dollars, 100 times the number of years they've put in. And no one stays just for his or her $3,000. These are employees who want to stay forever.

In the outgoing mailroom—a promotion from incoming—a young man talks about his plans for the future. "I plan to move up. I plan to work my way up to CEO. There's no stopping until then. I'm taking initiative and absorbing everything. Now I'm a traffic supervisor. Outgoing is pressured. A hazardous mess-up could cost you your job. We have sensitive materials and deadlines. But I always tease people and say, 'One day I will be your boss.' "

Interview:

KATIE GOLDSTEIN, RESEARCH VICE-PRESIDENT

Thirty-one year-old Katie first arrived at Leo Burnett for an internship during her junior year at Oberlin College, a small, private citadel of the liberal arts outside Cleveland. A native of Chicago, she is now vice-president, group research director, with eight promotions in as many years.

"I had no idea this world existed," she says from her bright office. "Until I discovered Leo Burnett, I thought I'd go into law or social work. Oberlin had nothing to do with business." Today, as a self-proclaimed "lifer," she regards Burnett as "almost like Oberlin grown up." Her evolution into liferhood is especially interesting, since her college and cultural roots would not immediately suggest she'd turn into a midwestern corporate female. She has not, however, forsaken her long, curly hair.

"Advertising did change me into a new person. I was an [suburban] Oak Park Zionist socialist. Now I'm a capitalist tool. My attitudes have softened. We're not bamboozlers, and I now accept that. We don't create needs; we reflect them. Now I know that while profits are still important, people are important, and you can't force people to do what they won't do."

Like many of her colleagues at the agency, Goldstein says that "Burnett's been good to me." Unlike others, she expands upon that phrase. "They gave me a career which uses my skills. When I describe what I do and my skills, I'm in diplomacy, politics, sociology, anthropology, psychology, communications, and sales. This job is as close as I get to the liberal arts.

"Burnett has taught me the business of advertising. I haven't disappointed them either. They recognize me and my contributions and reward me well monetarily and with promotions. After two years, they let me present research to a client at new business pitches. If you ask me, 'Do you design studies?' I do that all the time. If you ask me, 'How did you learn to do that?' I'd have to say, 'I have no idea.' John Kinsella knows my name. Norm Muse [Burnett's ex-chairman of the board] talks to me at parties. There's a sense of camaraderie despite the size."

Katie's observations coincide with those of the majority of her co-workers. When a culture is this entrenched, it can only reflect a consistency of thought that trickles down from the top. "Our culture is self-perpetuating. We hire people like ourselves—we butt in, we care, we're fanatic."

Goldstein likes the people at Burnett. "All my best friends are here," she says with a little surprise in her voice. A single woman, she has forced herself to wonder whether the devotion and time she has put into her work at the agency has distracted her from an agenda with marriage on the list. "The demands of work don't prevent me from being married. If I were doing something else, maybe I'd worry more if I were single, but my life wouldn't be so rich."

THE LEVY ORGANIZATION

The Levy Organization

HISTORY & OPERATIONS

The Levy Organization had an inauspicious start in 1976, when the brothers Levy—Larry and Mark—along with a group of investors opened a delicatessen called D. B. Kaplan's in Chicago's then practically deserted Water Tower Place (a downtown skyscraper-cum-mall). They thought it would be fun. But the restaurant, which was poorly run, flopped. After six months the Levys bought out their partner, and Mark, the younger of the brothers, quit his job as a corporate insurance broker to work in the restaurant full time. With the help of his mother Eadie's recipes, Mark turned the business around, and within several months it was earning a profit.

In 1978, The Levy Organization, with two employees—Larry and Mark Levy—was born. Larry, the chairman of the board and a born entrepreneur (his mother remembers when, as a six-year-old, he used to take her old magazines and sell them to the neighbors), had already built up a successful real estate development business, which he continued to operate as part of the Levy Organization. Mark, the organization's president, devoted himself full time to the restaurant business. The company grew rapidly (there are now more than 2,500 employees) and continues to expand.

The Levy Organization is divided into two divisions: real estate and food services, officially called "The Levy Restaurants," with the vast majority of employees working for the latter. The real estate development group has been responsible for the development, planning, construction, marketing, leasing, and property management of major development projects in the Chicago area. Among these are: Woodfield Lake Office Campus, a $200 million, 103-acre development in Schaumberg, Illinois, which offers 1½ million square feet of office and commercial space; One Magnificent Mile, a $120 million commercial and residential sky-scraper on Chicago's Lake Shore Drive, which the Levys sold in the summer of 1986 though still manage; the Chicago North Loop Redevelopment Project, a joint venture for mixed-use development in Chicago's downtown retail district which will include an enclosed shopping mall and 1.8 million square feet of office space; and Butterfield, a 1,600-acre multiuse land development near Aurora, Illinois, for residential, industrial, and office space. In addition, the division acts as sole real estate consultant to the Chicago Mercantile Exchange.

But the restaurants are more or less the soul of The Levy Organization. Each one (and there are now twenty-seven food service operations in Chicago, three in Pittsburgh, and two on Pleasure Island at Disney World in Florida) is unique in both ambience and cuisine. According to Larry, "We've discovered that we're at our best when we're doing something original." The food at the restaurants spans the gastronomical spectrum from deli to haute Italian to ham-burgers to barbecue to Mexican to gourmet fast food to French bistro to their new pan-Asian restaurant, which offers a wide variety of Oriental cuisines. Selected employees of the restaurant division travel the country and the world in search of new ideas and new foods. In addition to their restaurants and fast food services, the Levys are the exclusive caterers for the Chicago Cubs, the White Sox, the Bulls (in which they used to have an ownership share), the Ravinia Summer Music Festival, the Goodman Theater, and the Lincoln Park Zoo.

(Information provided by Larry Levy, Chairman of the Board.)

REVENUES: The company is privately held, and the figures are not published. Larry Levy: "We don't talk about that."

EARNINGS: The firm will not disclose.

NUMBER OF FOOD SERVICE OPERATIONS: Thirty-two.

NUMBER OF REAL ESTATE DEVELOPMENT PROJECTS: Four.

NUMBER OF EMPLOYEES: Approximately 2,500 throughout the organization. Of those, only fifteen or sixteen are employed full time in the real estate division.

AVERAGE AGE OF EMPLOYEES: Corporate staff: thirty-two to thirty-three; restaurant managers: twenty-six to twenty-seven.

TURNOVER: No exact figures available, but the organization's turnover statistics at both the hourly and salaried levels are substantially lower than industry averages.

RECRUITMENT: The restaurant group recruits heavily at the following hotel and restaurant schools: Cornell University, The Culinary Institute of America, Denver University, Michigan State University, and Johnson & Wales (Rhode Island).

NUMBERS OF NEW HIRES PER YEAR: Around three or four hundred, maybe five hundred, depending on the year, all for positions in the restaurant group. The organization is not currently hiring people for the real estate division and hasn't been for some time.

RANGE OF STARTING SALARIES: $18,000–$20,000 for recent college graduates with hotel/restaurant majors; $20,000–$25,000 for restaurant managers with some industry experience.

POLICY FOR RAISES: Restaurant operations staff (managers and hourly employees) are evaluated every six months and are eligible for raises at those times. Corporate staff people are evaluated annually, and salary increases occur then.

TRAINING PROGRAMS: There are training programs which are structured but loose enough to allow for individuality. They are hands-on in nature and involve working in every hourly position in the restaurant.

INTERNSHIPS: The organization offers "the best summer jobs in the industry," with paid internships at Wrigley Field, Ravinia Music Festival, and Comisky (White Sox) Park. They also offer internships for summer training in restaurant management. Many of their best recruits have started out in one or another of these summer job programs.

BENEFITS: *Management and corporate staff:* Health insurance, dental insurance, life insurance, and long-term disability—all company paid. *Hourly employees:* Health insurance, dental insurance, and life insurance are available to all employees; the company's contribution is based on seniority.

VACATION: *Management and corporate staff:* Two weeks after one year, three weeks after five years, four weeks after ten years. *Hourly employees:* One week after one year, two weeks after two years, three weeks after six years.

ADDITIONAL PERKS: *Management and corporate staff:* Free tickets to White Sox games, Cubs games, and Ravinia Music Festival events. A $50-per-month dining allowance to keep abreast of industry competition. Fifty to 100 percent complimentary privileges, depending on position, for employees and guests at Levy restaurants. Additional bonus program and travel coupons available to restaurant managers meeting quarterly and annual objectives. *Hourly employees:* Dining discount cards that entitle employees and guests to a 25 percent discount at all Levy restaurants. Complimentary dinner for two on the anniversary of employment. The company also has an arrangement with a health club to offer employee memberships at corporate rates.

BONUSES: All corporate and management staff get Christmas bonuses.

ANNUAL PARTY: Every restaurant has a staff Christmas party, and Larry Levy throws one at his house for the corporate staff and restaurant managers.

AVERAGE WORKDAY: For restaurant workers, shifts vary. For the corporate staff, generally 9:00 A.M. to 7:00 P.M. or 8:00 A.M. to 6:00 P.M.

DRESS CODE: According to Larry Levy, there is no dress code, and people can wear whatever they want, except, of course, in the restaurants, where servers dress in uniforms. However, according to the director of human resources, Larry wears whatever he wants (which generally means casual clothes from Polo), and the rest of the corporate staff dress fairly conservatively —women in skirts, slacks, or dresses, men in jackets or suits and ties.

SOCIAL ATMOSPHERE: People socialize *all the time* (this according to Larry) both in and out of work. "Our first rule of hiring is that we only hire nice people." Romantic relationships are not discouraged, and there have been several marriages to the organization's credit.

HEADQUARTERS: The Levy Organization leases space in the One Magnificent Mile building they developed on North Michigan Avenue. Its 20,000 square feet of office space (a floor and a half) are located on low floors overlooking the Oak Street Beach (the most popular beach in Chicago).

CHARITABLE CONTRIBUTIONS: The company will not disclose the amount of its donations. "We're a small entrepreneurial company, giving by personal interests." The Levys' charitable priorities include "disadvantaged city people, handicapped people, and helping our own people." Among the causes receiving donations are the Better Boys Foundation, Access Living, and the Jewish United Fund. In addition, the company often donates dinners at Levy restaurants to charity auctions.

INTERESTED APPLICANTS CAN SEND RÉSUMÉS TO:
The Levy Organization
980 North Michigan Avenue
Suite 400
Chicago, IL 60611
(312) 664–8200

W hen Larry and Mark Levy succeed, you're pleased for them. When they talk of their wins, you beam. And when they reveal their plans for the future, you believe them. The Levys, brothers from St. Louis, have in short order established themselves as a force to be reckoned with in the real estate development and restaurant businesses in Chicago. As the chairman of the board and president, respectively, of The Levy Organization, they have changed the skyline of their new city and the waistlines of their fellow citizens.

You've already read their corporate history. It's a story the Levys enjoy repeating, and one that sounds so simple and sensible, you wonder why you are not an entrepreneurial millionaire. But you are not jealous. They give business a good name. In their modern, art-filled offices in their flagship property—the splendid One Magnificent Mile—they talk about their work as their eyes dart back and forth to the Quotron machine in Larry's office. (They are serious investors in the stock market, and on this day, a dramatic one on Wall Street, their broker is calling them at intervals of roughly twenty minutes.)

"We've always been close. We have perfect chemistry. We're both good on our own, but together we're unbelievable." It's not really important who's speaking here, although it's probably Larry, the more garrulous of the two. Larry and Mark live two blocks from each other, drive to the office together every day, leave together, and usually speak on the phone each night before retiring. They are devoted family men, often naming restaurants after wives or children or their mother, Eadie, who works quite closely with her sons.

Although both brothers attended business school, Larry earning his MBA from Northwestern's Kellogg School and Mark dropping out of Washington University just a few credits shy of his degree, there is something rather unorthodox about them. While it is believable that they are great negotiators and single-minded in their pursuit of a deal, they enjoy what they do too much, pausing to pinch themselves rather than humorlessly going on to the next point on their agendas. "I always felt we were living a fantasy."

Next, they are so involved in their children that, if anything, their work may come second. (As much as Larry wants you to love the ravioli at Spiaggia, his top-of-the-line restaurant, he wants you to meet his son, Ari, a nine-year-old who loves lobster and calamari soup, soft shell crabs, and seems to prefer crème brulée to a Twinkie. He is absolutely Larry's proudest achievement. Larry's wife, Carol, has three sons from a previous marriage, all of whom Larry has raised since they were small and whom he regards as his sons, not stepsons.)

Then there is the issue of appearance. Larry helps support Ralph Lauren by wearing clothes from the Polo Shop on the ground floor of the Magnificent Mile building (also known as 980 North Michigan Avenue). Mark won't wear a tie. He just won't. On the gala occasion of the Chicago Theatre's reopening, Mark Levy was one of the few men who didn't wear black tie. He doesn't own it and doesn't like it. (He wore his customary button-down shirt, khakis, and vest.)

Finally, as has been documented before, the premier accolade in the Levy lexicon is not "shrewd," "brilliant," "rich," or "tough." It's "nice." Mark and Larry are nice guys who value personal relationships over dollar signs. It's reassuring they don't have to make sacrifices.

Today will be almost a typical day, if there is such a thing, of running around to the different Chicago restaurants and food services (gourmet cafeterias, ice cream shops, pizzerias, etc.) in a chauffeured 1985 Buick Le Sabre. Mark is technically in charge of the food business, but that doesn't mean Larry is not intimately, even spiritually, involved. They point out the essential differences between food in their city and food in New York, San Francisco, Dallas, Washington, Boston, and Los Angeles. "The term 'hot' is meaningless in Chicago. 'Good' is what matters here." This is not to say that trendy cuisine will not have its followers here, but Chicago is still basically a meat-and-potatoes city, heavy on the beef. As of 1987, none of the major food entrepreneurs in town had opened a sushi bar. Thai and Vietnamese restaurants are not the rage, although the Levys travel on extensive eating tours around the country and the world, and are certainly not averse to testing new foods. But to be avant-garde is not their mission. They like serving food they like—and think Chicagoans will like—in pleasant and interesting settings. Not that it's all steaks and chops. The Levys have tasted success with their two Dos Hermanos restaurants, which offer Mexican cooking. They serve ribs at Randall's, country French cuisine at Bistro 110, and wok-charred tuna at Eurasia, their new pan-Asian restaurant.

Today it's french fries at Bencher's (dark walls, brass fixtures), matzoh ball soup and corned beef sandwiches at Mrs. Levy's Delicatessen (brightly tiled, butcher block), a danish and a chocolate turtle donut (95 cents) at Terry's Old Fashioned Donuts, Blueberry Hill ice cream at the Great Midwestern Ice Cream Company (all located in the Sears Tower), then it's time for lunch at the Chestnut Street Grill (art nouveau woodwork), their seafood restaurant at Water Tower Place.

The Levys take small bites. They don't finish what's on their plates. If you tattletale to their mother, she just smiles. Petite Eadie Levy, one of the hostesses at the Chestnut Street Grill, moonlights as adviser to the delicatessen that bears her name, in addition to posing with local and imported celebrities for posterity on the walls of the deli. (A life-size cutout of Eadie, à la Ronald Reagan, allows visitors to get their pictures taken with her. She is something of a cult figure.) She doesn't finish her meal, either. Their visitor, not schooled in the art of tasting, embarrasses herself by finishing all food in sight. [Author's note: Only to be polite.] Salad, swordfish and the coup de grâce, cappuccino ice cream: "A house specialty which uniquely blends chocolate and coffee ice cream, laced with bits of toffee." Bliss.

Eadie Levy moved to Chicago in 1979 to be close to her sons. "I never worked a day in my life. I married at eighteen." Eadie earned her stripes in the kitchen at home in St. Louis, where her husband had been in the record business. "I used to cook for the recording artists. Eydie Gormé spent a weekend with us. (She rode Mark's bike and fell.) Paul Anka wore Larry's letter sweater." When Mark worked full time at D. B. Kaplan's, he used to call his ma twice a day for recipes. As a new employee of the Levy Organization, "I'd go in the kitchens and advise people. They used lots of my recipes. I must have done okay, because they promoted me.

"I was never my own person. I was a late bloomer. I was one of seven siblings, then I was Paul's wife, then Larry and Mark's mother. If you knew me before, I was so shy. I don't mean to boast about myself, but I found qualities in myself I didn't know I had."

All mothers are proud of their children, but for Eadie Levy, being proud is such a big part of who she is, it's almost a hobby. "Larry worked his way through college because he *wanted* to. Everything they have, they got themselves. I always say, 'I lucked out.' I see them every day. Have you noticed how the two of them get along? Mark really idolizes Larry. Their kids are well behaved. I'm so overwhelmed and embarrassed by it all. Larry and Mark and their families have been so wonderful to me. I was a widow for six years, and they took me everywhere. Then I met my husband, Bob! When Bob and I walk down the street, people say, 'Hi, Eadie!' "

Eadie works at the Chestnut Street Grill five days a week, down from six. "It's very important that I'm there. People ask for me. The harder a time a customer gives me, the sweeter I am." Her hours are nine to six. "When I'm not working, I'm a taster," she says. "I notice service and how long it takes."

T hroughout the tour, Mark and Larry greet their employees by name, be they busboys, chefs, waiters, or maître d's. And all these folks call them by their first names as well. Mark occasionally disappears and returns with a report from Wall Street. Pandemonium has struck. It's time to go to the "Merc," Chicago's Mercantile Exchange.

In 1979, the exchange decided to move from its original quarters to something newer in the 10–30 Wacker Drive vicinity. Its management approached Larry Levy because, according to one of his associates, "he had the reputation for being the hottest thing in town at the time. Larry told them they needed a consultant, not a broker, and they agreed and hired him to consult." The site, a parking lot, was procured, and the Merc built twin buildings that opened in 1983.

Holly Youngholm, The Levy Organization's vice-president for real estate, greets the Levys this afternoon, wearing a stylish business suit and her hair in a twist. She is thirty-one years old and a great favorite of the brothers, who hired her when she was twenty-three. When the Levys got the Merc account, Holly asked to be assigned to it. Larry demurred, saying she'd be dealing with aggressive, macho males "who'd eat me alive. I persisted. I attended the first meeting with Larry. The head of the Merc asked me to take notes. I said I would if he'd type them up." Larry still laughs when he thinks back to that meeting eight years ago. The exchange has since renewed the Levys' original three-year contract.

Not only does The Levy Organization lease the office space here (for healthy fees), it also owns and operates the buildings' concession stands, selling everything from sandwiches to Chicago Bears memorabilia. In a glassed-in lounge above the trading floor, it is impossible to ignore the frantic hair pulling and histrionics demonstrated by the traders in their smocks.

The semiotics of these gestures could make Umberto Eco spin. Mark Levy disappears again. It's a dark day in investment land, the Dow-Jones dropping 86.61 points. Through the vigilance of Mark and his broker, the Levys have survived the fall, even making a profit on a quick transaction of that morning. Rumors of window jumping will persist until the evening news puts all in its proper perspective, but now it's time for a tasting at Spiaggia (postmodern, elegant, flower-filled, thirty-four-foot plate glass windows), where Tony (Head Chef Anthony Mantuano) will present a menu of Oriental dishes for the Levys to try, in anticipation of their new Pan-Asian restaurant, Eurasia.

The session is attended by Mark and Larry, Cathy Mantuano, Tony's wife and the captain of Spiaggia, Eadie Levy, and her husband, Bob Abrams. (They live upstairs in a condo in the Magnificent Mile building and are about to leave on a belated honeymoon to the Far East the next day.) Tony distributes photocopies of his handwritten menu. Accompanied by the appropriate wines and presented on china which is being considered for use at Eurasia, the dishes include "Veal chop marinated with Chinese five spice powder, soy, ginger. Charcoal grilled, served with sauce of soy, rice wine (Mirin), ginger, peanut oil, and black and white sesame seeds"; "Smoked chicken wonton ravioli with coriander, basil pesto with peanuts"; "Steamed halibut with dressing of soy and sesame oil sprinkled over and scallion threads and fresh coriander." The group oohs and ahs. No one finishes the morsels served to them. Everyone's opinion is solicited. Then Mark asks Tony to sauté some fresh foie gras. Its richness is a painful reminder that dinner is just an hour away. [Author's note: This is a tough gig.]

But not before a discussion with Tony and Cathy Mantuano. Seven years ago, Tony and Cathy were living together in Milwaukee, where he was working as a sous-chef and she was waitressing (at the same restaurant) while going to school. When he "realized I needed to develop my own style—Italian—and it couldn't be in Milwaukee," he put together his résumé and mailed it to restaurants all over the country. Tony found a job at an Italian restaurant in Chicago, and Kathy found a job at the Levys' Dos Hermanos in the Water Tower Place (informal, bright orange, fajitas bar).

Cathy's background was in "formal service," and after a year and a half, she requested to move to the Chestnut Street Grill. "I was nervous," she says. "I hadn't done formal service in a long time." Her wish was granted, she got to know Mark and Larry, married Tony, and honeymooned in Italy. "Mark and Larry were always very friendly. It was a great place to work, good money, good food quality. I didn't feel I was working for a chain. I had worked for a corporation before and had never had contact with the owners. [Here] everyone knows everyone. It's family."

In 1982, through the wife of another Levy employee, Cathy heard rumors of a new restaurant, which would eventually become Spiaggia. Tony, unhappy at his job, got an interview with Bill Post, Levy's executive vice-president of food services. "At the time there was no appreciation of northern Italian cuisine. I had ideas of what the place should be: wood-burning ovens, fresh-made pastas. Everything I mentioned, Bill's face lit up. It was like fate. We agreed on everything: no veal parmagiana or fettucini Alfredo." Still, The Levy Organization needed to try Tony's cooking and see whether his execution lived up to his vision.

Neither Tony nor Cathy will ever forget that meal or the pressure they felt to make it perfect. Using the kitchen of Randall's, the Levys' barbecue restaurant (black-and-white and spare, filled with a rotating art collection), Tony and his assistant prepared about a dozen items for Larry, Mark, Bill, and Tom Heymann, Food Services' young president. They remember that the menu included a grilled fish, sautéed escarole ("still on the menu today"), a veal chop, and several pasta dishes. Cathy served and explained every dish. The Mantuanos selected Italian wines to complement the food.

"After dinner," Tony recalls, "they called me in and said, 'It was really special; you're great.' " That Saturday at lunch at the Chestnut Street Grill, they offered Tony the job of chef at the as yet unnamed restaurant in the as yet unbuilt One Magnificent Mile. Larry and Mark were a little nervous, as they were about to break even bigger news to the couple. The Levys explained to the Mantuanos that the offer was contingent on their going to Italy for a year— all expenses paid—to polish Tony's cooking skills by apprenticing in restaurants there. "They said, 'Your wife can go with you, and she will be a captain at the new restaurant.' It was a once-in-a-lifetime dream come true—all that stuff," Tony gushes. A further thrill was provided by a huge picture of (Tony's) grilled fish and escarole on the construction site of One Magnificent Mile. Mantuano was still working elsewhere, and he passed it every day going to work; it was his secret.

"We took crash courses in Italian before we left, although we were familiar with the language from our grandparents. We cooked a 'before' dinner before we left at Larry's house," and while they were in Italy, Larry and Mark called Tony once a week to get his input on the new restaurant. "Mark and Larry and their wives came to the restaurant in Mantua. We were so happy to see them and to speak English! We didn't make any money, but we had everything taken care of." They prepared an "after" dinner chez Larry when they returned.

"When I took the job, I knew it could be big," says Tony. "I knew I'd be doing something that had never been done in Chicago." With his signature emblazoned across Spiaggia's menu, the Levys have certainly shared the credit for the restaurant's success with their young chef. Now that chefs are becoming celebrities in their own right, does Tony have any desire to capitalize on his name even further? "I don't know what would tempt me, frankly. I'm not interested in moving. I'm on the corner of Oak and Michigan."

Cathy is as grateful as her husband. "The Levys offered me management. They offered me opportunities to grow." They also let her work at Spiaggia right off the bat. Cathy: "Working together makes me relaxed. Our life centers around food. We always talk about food. We try not to talk about business." Tony: "Sometimes Cathy will bring something up, and I have to say, 'That's the last thing we'll say about Spiaggia.' " Their work week is five days, with Tony cooking every night and supervising a work force of seventeen in the kitchen. (The total kitchen staff numbers forty-five.) "We eat mostly here. We cook at home maybe three times a year." When Cathy wanted to return to school, she was told by the Levys, "We'll split it with you."

Amy Benecki is another young person with an exalted title and set of responsibilities. At thirty-one, she has been the chef de cuisine of The Levy Organization for two years, maintaining standards and revising menus throughout the system. With her BFA in textiles from Indiana University, Amy, who comes from a small town in southern Illinois, decided to take the one-year course at the Cordon Bleu in London. "I came to food by accident," she says in her office, wearing her *toque.* "I wanted to be with people. And art doesn't have a right or wrong, unlike cooking, which does have a right or wrong." After she finished her program, she landed a job at Le Gavroche, London's only three-star restaurant. From there it was back home, where, pursuing a recommendation of André Soltner, the chef-proprietor of New York's four-star Lutèce Restaurant, she applied for a job at Le Français, one of the country's great French restaurants, located about thirty miles outside of Chicago in Wheeling. When the owner offered her the job of pastry chef over the phone, "I thought it was a joke. I thought it was my older brother speaking with a phony French accent." The job was no joke and required twelve-hour days, six days a week. "I didn't love it. I couldn't have a social life. Everyone thought it was glamorous, but it was the furthest thing from that." Amy later worked at a gourmet store that was patronized by Larry Levy.

"One day he said who he was. I said who I was. He hired me to become the corporate chef." She was twenty-six. Amy probably could have named her job with the Levys. "There's nothing I want to run. I'm always doing different things. It's creative. If you believe in it and enjoy it, you get 'Levyfied.' " The Levys send Amy around the world to eat. She's another satisfied employee.

Bob King worked at WMAQ-AM in Chicago when Bob Pittman (see p. 527) was its program director. From answering the phones he became a "weekend overnight" person. Then he moved to WKQX-FM, the "number one rock station in the United States." He is tall and handsome and the head bartender at Hillary's, the premiere bar at the Water Tower Place. "I got disenchanted with radio. Ultimately, I got fired, as all people do." Although he was a certified on-air personality, Bob broke totally from radio ten years ago.

King knew Levy Restaurants' then vice-president Tom Heymann's brother. Having put himself through school by tending bar, Bob asked for a job and ended up working for the Levys during intermissions at the Drury Lane Theatre in the Water Tower Place concession a few nights a week. Since he wasn't earning enough to live on, "I convinced the manager of Hillary's that I was a really great bartender and that I should be tending the big bar. He agreed.

"A machine can make a cocktail. [The secret of a successful bar is] the whole delivery. You should get more than just a drink. Hillary's—in my perception—was the Levy's first big statement in restaurants, and they attracted a very smart group which is incredibly loyal. In terms of the industry, the Levys are extremely fair, especially in an industry that's notorious for lowballing.

"I've turned down twenty general managerships. For several years I had the title of director of liquor purchasing." King was never enamored of the name, and it went away. "I'm still the de facto beverage guy. I help set up new bars. I don't do this while I'm waiting for my big acting break." King, whose voice if not face is recognized, is always asked when he'll return to radio. He still does voice-overs and narrations for books for the blind. "I know what I don't want to do or what is not for me. I know that at what I do, I am the best. It's a job, and the people who work for me think of it as a job. It gets routine, but what job doesn't?" Bob has serious responsibilities. His bar generates almost $2 million in business per year.

King wields a lot of influence on the look of the bartenders and the service staff. In the summer, they're in their Hawaiian shirt phase, in the winter it's a "very Ivy League" green-and-white-striped button-down shirt with Hillary's monogram on the pocket, "our fifth or sixth uniform look. Why? In a neo-Prohibitionist atmosphere and given liquor's profitability, we're not going to go topless, but we have to create consumptional fun. You can have a couple of drinks, and I won't tell your preacher." The brothers Levy say they come to Hillary's every day after work.

Larry and Mark say, "One occupational hazard of the restaurant business is, you're never not scared." Yet they entered the industry with just their common sense. And the Levys have made a remarkable commitment to hiring fresh young talent rather than industry veterans. "We have a history of bringing people right out of school to push us." Larry chairs the Chicago Rhodes Scholars Committee and finds himself overwhelmed by the terrific college students he meets. (Two years ago one of his employees made the finals.) "The most amazing thing to me," Larry reflects, "is that we're considered heroes by black and Hispanic people. A job is part of someone's dignity. It's part of their motivation."

The real estate aspect of the business always involved greater financial risk. "I remember when I realized it wasn't a fluke anymore. Exactly the moment. It was when I sold my interest in One Magnificent Mile." The Levys still manage the property and keep their offices in it, but it's not just the Levys' anymore.

I eat dinner at Randall's with three of the young executives on whom the Levys took chances. Donna Crane Chudacoff, who is twenty-seven, is vice-president and director of marketing and promotions. She spent the summer between her first and second years at Northwestern's business school working for the Levys in operations and, after some finagling, marketing. Tom Heymann offered to hire her full time without her MBA, but she finished school before returning to The Levy Organization.

Bill Post entered the hospitality field as a twelve-year-old caddying at his local country club for $1.56 an hour. At the University of Houston, he "tailored school for my career," with a major in hotel and restaurant management. He graduated in 1976. He also bartended at the Astrodome, "the largest bar in the United States." Returning home to Chicago after a few years in the hotel business, "I had heard of these two guys named Mark and Larry Levy in 1978 and heard everything they touched turned to gold. Mark didn't want to hire me. I had to pester him. I showed up for my third interview in a suit and tie—I didn't even catch on."

Post was able to persuade Mark to give him a job as the floor manager at D. B. Kaplan's. When the Levys saw he was accountable for the restaurant's single most profitable day— $84,000, in August 1979—"I got two raises in one day!" After eight months, he moved up to the Chestnut Street Grill. Tom Heymann recommended that Bill be promoted to general manager there. From that position, Bill was "offered good, serious jobs, and I was tempted by them. I told Mark I'd gotten a good offer but that I wanted to stay within the organization. So Mark struck a deal with me. I was so happy, I proposed to my wife that night. And we were married five weeks later."

Of his bosses, Post says, "Mark and Larry give you latitude and autonomy. Autonomy is the motivator." As executive vice-president of the Food Service Group, Post is in charge of operations and procedures.

Tom Heymann's career is the stuff business books are made of. Heymann met Larry Levy when he was a nineteen-year-old sophomore at Northwestern trying to get him to buy an ad for D. B. Kaplan's in a flyer he helped publish. At the time The Levy Organization was not yet born. "I decided then and there I wanted to grow up to be Larry Levy. I wanted to work for him in real estate." While in school, Tom would call Larry to keep in touch. "My sister was one of his bankers. Larry was open to hearing from me. I tried to work part time for Larry my senior year; I felt the real estate business was right for me. Larry suggested I meet Mark.

"Mark laid out plans for opening new restaurants. It sounded glamorous. I was twenty. Mark said I could come and work for them in either business. I decided to work for Mark. I felt the restaurant business was better suited to a twenty-year-old." In Tom's first year he worked full time for the Levys (at $250 per week) while attending school full time (four courses per week). Heymann also got his BA in economics.

"I had a real credibility problem in the business at twenty. I was hired as Mark's assistant. Then one day, about three or four months later, he handed me a business card that said I was a vice-president." Some people were jealous of him. "First I was 'Mark's little whiz kid from Northwestern.' Everyone else had come up through waitressing, et cetera." With his young face, Tom's chronological age probably didn't matter too much anyway. "Now I'm the old man in the group. At thirty-one." Heymann is the president of the Food Service Group, a title he earned at twenty-six. "If anyone had asked me four years ago where I'd be, I'd never have said this."

He describes the brothers' division of labor as "a division of interest. The brother who is most interested in a project takes care of it. They really complement each other. If they lose interest, you get a chance to take it over." He, Donna, and Bill describe a work environment that is social and warm, abetted by spouses who know each other and close friendships throughout. The word is that there is no jockeying for Levy approval and almost no internal politics. Larry and Mark take an interest in their people that transcends business. Corporate officers, all younger than their bosses, will confide in Larry and Mark, who know of the dating and courtship trials and joys that befall their troops. Certainly, the restaurants themselves provide a comfortable setting for gathering, goofing off, and intimacy. Any officer with the rank of general manager or above gets an "A" card, entitling them to eat (with guests) free of charge at all Levy restaurants as often as they like, assuming they won't abuse it. Managers get a "B" card, giving them 50 percent off meals for two, prorated for larger groups. Nonmanagerial staff receive discount coupons, varying according to number of years of service.

New deals for new restaurants are burgeoning daily, including two restaurants at Disney World's "Pleasure Island," a fantasy nightspot for adults. The Levy Organization was chosen after an international search. Their two facilities—the Portobello Yacht Club, serving Italian seafood, and the Fireworks Factory, offering an all-you-can-eat barbecue—have been mythologized by the Disney people like their other fairy tales. They are slated to open in December 1988.

The Levys bought Eastern Newsstands, the country's largest chain of news concessions, in April 1988. (This means Larry and Mark will operate eighteen stands in Rockefeller Center alone.) The Levys must contend with the fact that two decent guys, who prize niceness over all other virtues, are moguls. By next week they could own a chain of hotels or a newspaper (in fact, they published, for about six months, a small daily called *The Daily Market Digest*, Chicago's only afternoon stock market report/newspaper). They have a human resources office. And, having created a separate entity in The Levy Restaurants, they have a brand-new mission statement:

"The Levy Organization provides an entrepreneurial home where talented people create, develop and manage business enterprises with a commitment to quality and distinction. We seek to anticipate and recognize opportunities which meet the demands of a constantly changing world. In partnership with our employees and business associates we strive to become leaders and innovators in our chosen fields."

It's only fair to let Eadie Levy have the last word. "To me the most wonderful thing is how they conduct themselves. They still remove their shoes when they come in the house."

MARVIN GLASS & ASSOCIATES

HISTORY & OPERATIONS

Marvin Glass & Associates, an independent inventor and designer of games, dolls, and toys, was founded in Chicago in 1950 by designer Marvin Glass and several partners. Glass began making toys as a child, for his neighborhood playmates. (His juvenile efforts included a tank big enough to sit in and a submarine that shot wooden torpedoes.) After graduating from the University of Chicago in 1935 with degrees in psychology and fine arts, Glass took a job designing window and counter advertising displays. He didn't like it. For lack of a more appealing alternative, he decided to parlay his childhood hobby into a vocation and strike out on his own.

Glass borrowed a little money from friends and set up living quarters and a tiny machine shop in the sleazy Alexandria Hotel in downtown Chicago. His shop was so small that he had to keep it running sixteen hours a day in order to keep up with his work. When Glass started out, his dream was to create a fantasy world for children. His first toy, Tiny Town Theater, was a projector used to illuminate comic strips. Glass sold the design outright for $500 to a manufacturer, who in turn made a quick $30,000 in sales. As a result, Glass subsequently insisted on royalty arrangements for all of his inventions.

Early in the firm's history, it lost hundreds of thousands of dollars making religious decorations for Christmas trees, and soon afterward, Glass decided to give up making toys entirely and to license all his company's designs to manufacturers instead. In 1952 Marvin Glass & Associates more than recouped its losses when Glass came up with a novelty toy called Busy Biddee Hen, a plastic hen that laid eggs (marbles) when its tail was pressed. It was the first of his designs to turn a significant profit.

In 1960 Marvin Glass & Associates came out with its first major commercial hit, Mr. Machine, a large transparent plastic wind-up robot manufactured by the Ideal Toy Company. The idea for the toy reportedly came out of a fight between Glass and one of his wives—Glass was married four times, twice to the same woman—who accused him of being a machine. Glass claimed that the wind-up robot was a metaphor for modern man. "It's transparent, screams, and makes a lot of motion without doing anything." Mr. Machine helped make Marvin Glass & Associates the foremost independent designer in the toy industry. Included among the firm's other early creations were Super Specs, footwide glasses; Kissy Doll, a doll that kissed; King Zor, a mechanical dinosaur that bellowed and lunged when shot with a dart gun; Odd Ogg, a plastic turtle/frog that played competitive catch (if a child hit the toy's belly with a ball, it would meekly return the ball; if the child hit the toy's flipper, Odd Ogg stuck out its tongue and made disgusting noises); and Mousetrap (the first three-dimensional board game), a highly successful game in the style of Rube Goldberg, that used marbles to trap a plastic mouse.

After President Kennedy's assassination, Glass refused to design any more toys that simulated violence. He discarded a line of his own toys already in design and pressed manufacturers and other toy designers to do the same.

By 1964 Marvin Glass & Associates had grown to a staff of more than forty artists, designers, and engineers. That year, the firm moved to its own two-story building on LaSalle Street, which was eventually expanded to about 25,000 square feet, including an employee recreation and game room. In the late sixties, toy manufacturers were selling $100 million of the company's toys each year—5 percent of which the firm received in royalties—and by 1970 Marvin Glass & Associates' toys and games accounted for more than 5 percent of all toy sales. Glass insisted that his logo—two silhouetted children and Glass's initials—appear on all his toys, and he thus became the only free-lance toy inventor in the world to earn that signature distinction. Among the toy manufacturers producing his designs were Parker Brothers, Milton Bradley, Playskool, Romper Room, Hasbro, Ideal, Kenner, Schaper, Horsman, Munro, GAF View-Master, Rainbow Crafts, Lakeside, and Britain's Denys-Fisher Group.

Marvin Glass died in 1974, leaving the management of the business in the hands of his five partners. Since his death, Marvin Glass & Associates has grown to a staff of seventy-five designers, engineers, sculptors, artists, and model makers and is now the largest firm of its kind in the world.

One of the trademarks of the toy profession is its secrecy. In order to thwart industrial spies, the company has always carefully guarded its designs, monitoring all visitors with a video security system and keeping its workshops and design studios off limits to everyone except authorized staff members. Before the firm shows a client a new design, the manufacturer must sign a nondisclosure agreement guaranteeing that if it turns down a toy, it won't produce anything similar to it.

The company's big hits—in addition to Mr. Machine and Mousetrap—have included Rock 'em Sock 'em Robots, Time Bomb, Hands Down, Operation, Lite Brite, Talking View Master, Masterpiece Game, S.S.P. Racer, Tip It, Evel Knievel Motorcycle, and Simon, the first computer-generated game. The firm's products fall into the following broad categories: games, toys, dolls, vehicles, preschool, and novelties.

The holder of over 850 patents, Marvin Glass & Associates has more patents to its credit than any other private company in this country.

(Information provided by Jeffrey Breslow, managing partner.)

REVENUES: Firm is privately held and will not disclose.

EARNINGS: Firm will not disclose.

OFFICES: One in Chicago.

NUMBER OF EMPLOYEES: About seventy-five.

AVERAGE AGE OF EMPLOYEES: Approximately mid-thirties.

TURNOVER: "Relatively small." Between three and four employees leave each year.

RECRUITMENT: The company regularly recruits at the University of Illinois (Champaign-Urbana and Chicago Circle campuses) and the Cleveland Institute of Art. "We look for graduates in industrial design with a bachelor of fine arts degree."

JOB CATEGORIES: Electronic engineer, sculptor, model maker (technical and plastics specialists), graphic artist, legal, financial, clerical, maintenance worker. The majority of employees are called "toy designers," following this hierarchy: assistant designer, designer, senior designer, assistant product manager, product manager, senior product manager.

NUMBER OF NEW HIRES PER YEAR: Four to six.

RANGE OF STARTING SALARIES: "Entry level for recent graduates is comparable to the rest of the industry. Starting designers with work experience may be higher, commensurate with their experience."

POLICY FOR RAISES: "Raises are given out periodically during the year. Some exceptional employees may be reviewed and raised frequently during a year. Everyone is reviewed a minimum of once a year."

TRAINING PROGRAMS: No formal programs—new employees learn on the job. "We seek self-motivated individuals who are self-starters."

BENEFITS: According to Managing Partner Jeffrey Breslow, "Marvin Glass & Associates pays for hospitalization costs, a life insurance policy, major medical coverage, and an extensive profit-sharing plan. Also, subsidized parking and free doughnuts and coffee."

VACATION: Two weeks after one year, three weeks after seven years. "All regular national holidays are paid for and given off."

ADDITIONAL PERKS: "We have a workout gym complete with equipment, a recreation facility with a pool table, a kitchen for employees, a beautiful working environment, and an outdoor café and dining room." The partners have their own dining room, where a hot lunch is prepared daily by a chef. (Nonpartners are often invited.)

BONUSES: All employees are eligible, and bonuses are awarded on a merit basis. "They are always given at the year end and often at other times during the year. Bonuses cover a wide range and in some cases can be as high as 50 percent of an employee's salary, totally dependent on performance."

ANNUAL PARTIES: The company hosts an annual Christmas party, a summer picnic, "and often other events throughout the year, such as Halloween parties, baseball games, parking lot picnics, and boat cruises." The Christmas party is held at a different place every year—sometimes in hotel ballrooms, sometimes in small Chicago nightclubs; one year the company rented a private loft. "What we try to do is vary it every year. We find that if you hold the same function year after year, there ceases to be the same magic for people." The party is dressy (though not black tie) and employees and their spouses, girlfriends, or boyfriends are invited. It takes place in the evening, and guests eat dinner and dance to a live band. One year the firm hired a midget dressed in a Santa Claus suit, who distributed gifts to all the women. ("He was very funny.") The annual summer picnic is usually held at some kind of private campground for employees and their families (including children). Employees plan events such as egg tosses and the like, and the company provides a meal. "There's food, pop, games, and prizes."

AVERAGE WORK DAY: Office hours are 7:00 A.M. to 4:30 P.M., though some people come in earlier and stay later.

DRESS CODE: No dress code. "Most employees dress casually. However, during client product presentations appropriate attire is required."

SOCIAL ATMOSPHERE: "The employees generally socialize together. They do get together frequently after work and spend off-hours together."

HEADQUARTERS: "Our facility is in one two-story building, which is about 25,000 square feet."

NUMBER OF NEW TOYS ON THE MARKET PER YEAR: Thirty to forty.

BIGGEST HIT EVER: Simon (1978), an electronic game that uses tones and light sequences to pit players' memories against the memory of a microcomputer. Simon always wins; it's a matter of how long players can stay alive. Manufactured by Milton Bradley.

CHARITABLE CONTRIBUTIONS: Firm will not disclose. Its main areas of giving are children's charities, cancer research and scholarship funds at several universities.

INTERESTED APPLICANTS CAN SEND RÉSUMÉS TO:
Marvin Glass & Associates
815 N. LaSalle Street
Chicago, IL 60610
(312) 664-8855

There is probably no one in the world who wouldn't want to work for Marvin Glass & Associates at one time or another. This deliberately well-kept secret, a think tank of sorts in Chicago, is in the business of inventing toys, games, and dolls. It is populated with grown-ups who have a lovely childlike appreciation of what children like—men who can lovingly snuggle with dolls, people who can see the world through the eyes of a three-year-old. Everyone takes his or her work seriously, which is part of the company's appeal.

Like most trend marketers, Marvin Glass works on a calendar that's two years ahead of time. Most of the company's thirty-five designers have a specialty, be it "boys' toys," board games, dolls, electronic or computer-operated toys, or preschool. While they will work on any idea that seems promising, they will also keep in mind the needs of say, Hasbro, for Christmas 1990. While every work station is filled with happy toys and designs, this seems less like Santa's workshop than it does a business. No one seems surprised that they discovered Marvin Glass, nor indeed that such a place exists. People at Marvin Glass were born to work at Marvin Glass, and in various ways all prepared for their careers here.

Many Chicagoans have heard of the company but only vaguely know what it does. They feel excluded by what they perceive as a mania for privacy. True, work in progress must be covered before outsiders visit, and there is serious security protecting the Marvin Glass building, but the partners and employees are an easy and open bunch of people.

It is a partnership comprising four senior people who own and operate the business. They were the heirs to the business when Marvin Glass himself ran the show. (He died in 1974, with the partners at his bedside.) Jeffrey Breslow is the managing partner. "We've all grown up together," he says. "One retired last year after twenty-five years, three have been here twenty-one years, and one has been here fourteen years. Once you're here, you don't want to leave." In fact, the partners don't like to leave during the day, even for lunch. Indeed, a Chinese chef prepares terrific three-course meals in a dining room to which clients, designers, and engineers are sometimes invited. Lunch resembles going home, minus Mom. It's four brothers who share a comfortable fondness and familiarity. When they're not talking about work, stories about wives and kids abound; everyone is a surrogate uncle to his partners' children.

Jeffrey studied industrial design at the University of Illinois, where he made one toy project. As a student, he won a patent for a design for modular furniture. A classmate had an uncle at Marvin Glass, which is how Breslow discovered the company. He couldn't get an interview there when he graduated, so he ended up designing hospital supplies for two years. With a portfolio that included a toy already in the marketplace, he returned to see Marvin. "There was no way he wasn't going to hire me."

Glass was so powerful an influence that everyone who knew him still feels a need to talk about him. "He was a real genius, a father image to all of us at one time or another. He could be mean and vicious and loving and had a twinkle in his eye. He had a level of enthusiasm that was contagious. He was a driven man. He married four times. Nothing mattered to him but work." The respect for Marvin does not interfere with a resigned tolerance for his volatility. Fourteen years after his demise, employees still retell vivid anecdotes that illustrate how difficult he could be.

"We used to work all night sometimes—all-nighters. He'd do that deliberately. If we had six great toys to present the next day to a client, at six P.M. he'd want to create a new one. It could take all night. Three-day weekends were the worst for him. [He'd summon us to] his house talking toys."

When Glass was alive the company employed thirty to forty people. Today there are seventy-five, and it's still growing. The firm's handsome two-story limestone structure on LaSalle Street, which Marvin had built, is filled with an eclectic art collection. The introduction is by way of a Frederic Remington bronze, a large portrait of Marvin Glass painted by Marlene Breslow, and an eight-by-twelve-foot Leroy Nieman canvas. The reception office is extravagantly outfitted with modern and art deco furniture. One wall is a huge aquarium, there are several large paintings (one of which looks like a Rousseau; the other is a Nieman), a Tiffany lamp, a tall, enameled baroque Fabergé clock, silk water lilies floating in a water-filled bowl, and an imposing Lalique crystal table. Hidden in tortoiseshell-like cabinets are some of the toys that have financed this luxury. They are almost incongruous in this setting. "Customers come here to meet with designers. We have no salesmen. Designers get to present their own ideas."

Not every toy gets as far as a customer presentation. When a product is designed, "one of the partners must believe in the project to get it worked on. More support means more money and more people." Approximately two to three thousand ideas are dreamed up per year, and about 1,000–1,300 of them are interesting enough to merit being recorded into the logbook with job numbers. These will go forward to sketches or mock-ups. Of these, 150 to 200 will advance from here. Then a team comprised of a senior product manager, a product manager, and designers work to completion. Forty or fifty games and toys will be sold, and of those, chances are that eight to ten will be successful, enabling Marvin Glass to reap a healthy enough profit to make the partners prosper and keep the company comfortably in the black. Marvin Glass does not sell its inventions outright; it licenses them on a long-term exclusive basis. The company will not accept solicitations of ideas. "We don't buy anything. And we return ideas unopened. We don't look or talk to anyone." The firm's clients include every major toy manufacturer in the country, and many of the minors, too. "A client won't direct us and say, 'We need a doll to do this.' That would be throwing a wrench at us," a senior product manager explains. "We pay all the [development] bills until the presentation, so there's no priority."

John Fertig admits, "I never even heard of this company, either. It keeps a very low profile in the public, although it's well known in the industry." After graduating from the Cleveland Institute of Art, Fertig had hoped to work in the automobile industry, but his senior thesis had been a toy project. "I called Marvin Glass after blindly finding their name in a phone book under 'Toy Design.' I came in for an interview and got hired on the spot. Now I'm glad [I didn't end up in Detroit], because this fits my personality better. I love animals and movies, and have a toy tarantula. The partners are nice guys. For me it was, 'Here you are. Welcome.' Once you get here, you've got to catch up with the toy market." John's specialty is in boys' toys, for ages three to twelve. "I tried girls', but not everything I do works."

He awakens on 'school days' around 5:15 A.M. His commute from the suburbs takes one and a half hours, including the twenty-minute walk he always takes (even when it's freezing) from the train station to work. He arrives at the office at 7:00 A.M. and leaves at 4:00 P.M. and rarely works on weekends, except for special assignments. But, as other designers here will claim, "toys are always in the back of my head." Fertig has, however, experienced the inventor's equivalent of the dreaded writer's block.

"It's very tough when you're not coming up with ideas. It's horrible to sit there when other people are working hard. It doesn't happen often." While it might seem reasonable for Fertig to summon his muses at home, in his garage, or by a lake, this won't happen. "I couldn't, because of the confidentiality of the business."

Luckily, many of John's close friends from school are also inventors at Marvin Glass, so he is able to have a social life and talk about work uninhibitedly. If not for this, he might have to make up an alibi at cocktail parties. For a company which practices some strict codes, Marvin Glass's culture is otherwise pretty loose. Fertig raves about "the unlimited freedom. I check in with partners—whenever. We create our own comfort here." The other side of the coin means that as a relatively unimpeded young designer, "you've constantly got to prove yourself. That's how to get what you want. When I first got here, I had an idea I was crazy about. They all said no. It hurt my feelings, but it pushed me more. I made a mock-up, and some partners liked it. Whenever they made a presentation, I'd hang around with my mock-up and try to present it." He suggests that the kinds of people who could not fit in would be "people who get bummed out or people who can't handle the freedom and get lazy and goof off."

Besides learning how to sell himself, John has been able to immerse himself in his favorite things: nature, comic books, movies—especially science fiction—music, and cable TV. "If I hadn't gotten a job here I'd be designing car treads for B. F. Goodrich. I imagine staying here [for the long haul]. It's really neat to see how kids like toys. It's rewarding. I observe people in stores. You'd be amazed how many people are into toys." As a kid his favorite toy was his G.I. Joe doll.

Ginnie Bala is a tall, ebullient woman whose background is in the fashion industry and graphic design. After a stint on Seventh Avenue, she returned home to Chicago and happened to see an astrologer, who predicted it was "time for a big change. I had heard of Marvin Glass years ago but never thought of myself as a designer. I didn't really know what to expect. I came here to pay off my charge cards, and for a good salary. I still go, 'I don't know what the heck I'm doing.' But I've always had the attitude of trying things. You go around only once in this world."

Her introduction to Marvin Glass & Associates was hardly belabored. "They gave me a desk and said, 'Here's a project.' There's so much creative freedom. Sometimes it's, 'Gosh—what do we do now?' There's no right or wrong. There's a self-imposed discipline around here. Most people want to achieve and produce. I think there is competition here. Most creative people are insecure and wonder, 'When will the well dry up?' "

After four years with the company, Ginnie has been Glassified. She allows that she thinks about toys *all the time*. "It doesn't ever stop. An idea can start at one place and end up completely differently. I'm looking into 3-D for the first time." Working here requires collaboration with model makers and a receptivity to change. It requires defending your ideas, a familiarity with the toy industry, and the ability to juggle several projects at once. "A lot of people say it's the closest thing to not working," which is why Ginnie rarely tells people she's a toy designer. When people ask her what she does, "I just answer 'I'm a designer,' because when you say 'toy designer,' people say, 'Ooh! That must be so much fun!' "

Obviously, Ginnie regards her work as seriously as any lawyer, accountant, or brand manager. "I'm still overwhelmed by what I'm learning. I owe good work to myself and the people who hired me. Every day I worry they're going to can me. [Author's note: I've been reassured that no one makes her feel this way except herself.] You experience the highest of highs when a prototype goes out [to a client], and the lowest of lows when it comes back. It doesn't feel it's really happening until you see it on a store shelf. You have to get used to that. It takes two years to hit the shelves. Sometimes I wish there were more feedback. Ninety percent of what we do, we throw away." One of her biggest successes has been Mattel's The Puttins, a group of soft plush characters for very young children. "I can say, 'Ooh! I did okay today.' "

"Of all the jobs I've had, this is the weirdest, the most challenging, and the best. It's a strange job. Toy designers are a different breed who never wanted to grow up." Ginnie's mom invited creativity when her daughter was little. "She gave me a paintbrush and a can of water and said, 'Paint the sidewalk.' We sculpted toy food out of chewing gum." Ginnie still plays with her Barbie doll. "One of my ambitions is to make toys fun again.

"This business keeps you young." Plus, Ginnie has a nine-year-old daughter. "She's more mature than I am. Having a kid keeps you in touch with childhood. She loves toys. I don't design with her especially in mind; I know what she likes. They've let her in here a few times. But of course," she cracks, "they search her when she leaves."

Balancing her home life with her work life is Ginnie's greatest source of stress. A single mother, her social life centers around her colleagues. "We have parties and outings—go to the horse track, Cubs' games, boat trips. This *is* family. I look forward to coming here every day."

Don Rosenwinkel is another employee who was hired on the spot. That was ten years ago, direct from the University of Illinois, when he was the first person hired straight from college. "Now we almost exclusively hire new college grads." A native Chicagoan, he, too, stumbled onto Marvin Glass & Associates accidentally, while looking for a job as an industrial designer. "You get used to this, and you don't want to design toasters. I've forgotten how to draw toasters, and our thought processes work differently. We pretty much cater to people twelve years old and younger."

Don repeats the thoughts of Jeff, John, and Ginnie. There appears to be a unifying culture here, as each employee confirms the notion of his or her peers. "The highs are incredible. When you see your toy on TV or walk down the aisles of Toys 'R' Us and realize you've put so many people to work." Nevertheless, "in the ten years I've been here, a thousand times I worry I'll never have a good idea, and then the next day in the shower I get a good one and have something to do for a few weeks. It's a process, not a miracle that falls out of the sky."

Simon, the first computer chip game. Operation. Mousetrap. Bingo Bear. These are some of the sophisticated means through which Marvin Glass & Associates makes a good living for seventy-five people. And their children.

In addition to bathroom epiphanies, there are formal brainstorming sessions "that help you later when you go to your desk. Big ideas don't happen in those meetings." It seems that during one's first couple of years at Marvin Glass, thinking about toys is a self-conscious effort, filled with "Aha!" experiences and panic. After a while, these thoughts get expropriated by the subconscious, and life becomes a little more "normal."

"Getting this job is like a ton of bricks being placed on your shoulder. Initiation is more like a hazing period. They think the cream will rise to the top and try to weed you out at first. You know within a month who'll make it. You have to work fast." Don's first project was a mechanical bow and arrow. He made that prototype within his first two weeks. "My second idea got me almost laughed out of the conference room. You get a thick skin soon. If only one or two of my ideas make it to Toy Fair out of a hundred per year . . . you've got to get used to it." Some advice for the newcomer: "Grab all the glory while you can."

Don tries his hand in every category of Marvin Glass's repertoire. In his mind there are thirteen divisions, including board games, plastic action games, strategy games, activity toys, large baby dolls, preschool toys, novelty toys, vehicles, girls' figures, boys' action figures, adult games, family room games, and electronic games or toys. "My personal goal is that by the time I leave the toy industry, I'd like to have sold at least one product in each category." His proudest contribution so far: Zany Zappers, which are light-emitting diode (LED) sunglasses. In other words, they blink. "I developed them within my first six months here. The idea was killed in an internal brainstorming meeting. But if you feel strongly enough about an idea, do it, no matter who says no. You won't get fired." It took two years to make a successful prototype, and then "they were sold within the next hour, which is very fast for this industry. They sold many millions of pairs." Rosenwinkel also created Mr. Gameshow (see p. 156).

Don says the secret to Marvin Glass & Associates' smooth functioning is that "we've got a lot of almost brilliant people. They're winners and would be good at almost anything else."

Carol Snyder has worked at Marvin Glass for four and a half years. Although she earned her BFA in painting at the Kansas City Art Institute, it was through her sewing that she earned a living, making quilts to put her then husband through school. A friend at Playskool hired Carol to do free-lance sewing, and when the vice-president of research and development at

Playskool asked to meet her, Snyder brought samples of her work in a garbage bag and a shoebox. She now laughs at her lack of professionalism. "It was irrelevant, because I got a job as a part-time designer."

Although Marvin Glass had worked with Playskool and some employees of the latter had defected to the former, Carol had had no contact with MGA. After six years, she interviewed here ("on the sly") when it was rumored that Playskool was being sold to Hasbro, necessitating a move from Chicago to Pawtucket, Rhode Island. People at Marvin Glass "have been very nice. Before arriving I'd heard horror stories about this place—competitiveness, constant pressure, cracking the whip. It feels competitive because of the broad range of clients. The pace you work at is determined by who's coming in and what they want to see. If you don't show your product by a certain time, you may have to wait a year. That's when it's stressful. Fisher-Price is closing its Christmas 1990 line in December 1988." Snyder's specialty is infant and preschool.

Some designers work in pairs, like a creative team in an advertising agency. Having discovered a fruitful collaboration, they'll be in partnership for years. Other designers rove around, working with various partners, soloing on some projects. Carol prefers to work alone in her own office, although she does get pulled into other projects.

Having a child is an asset, but interestingly, "having children shows me what's useless, not what to do. Kids of toy people have fewer toys than kids of nontoy people." Unlike Ginnie, Carol does admit to her profession when she meets new nontoy people. Not surprisingly, her confessees completely misunderstand that designing toys is a job. "Most people are at a loss because they usually haven't met a toy designer. I have to describe what goes into making a toy. It begins to sound a lot more like work."

Of all the toy makers at Marvin Glass, Terry Webb may be the only one who found his job through an employment agency. A sixteen-year veteran, he is a model maker, having previously spent a number of years as a journeyman pattern maker in the metal business. "I walked in here and thought it was perfect for a kid at heart. My first project was a road racing set. I fit in right away. Marvin liked me and gave me a few raises in my first year. I realized I wouldn't be returning to my union."

When Terry arrived at Marvin Glass he was one of the youngest. "Now, at forty-three, I'm one of the older people here." Still, he never thought he'd spend his career making toy prototypes. "The great thing is following an idea from its conception to the shelves of Toys 'R' Us. You get a great feeling of satisfaction knowing you were an integral part. If I have to work for a living, I'd rather be here than anywhere else on a daily basis." One of Webb's achievements was developing Simon. He designed its case, buttons, and pivot. Requiring manual dexterity as well as hand-eye coordination, Simon is now used by Terry "as a sobriety test at my bar." If his guests can't win at the game, he won't let them drive home. A large, muscular man, Webb once played semipro football for the Blue Island Blues, outside Chicago. To stay in shape, he works out three days a week in the weight room on MGA's ground floor.

What's it like to be a partner? Howard Morrison, one of the four, says, "All the partners are partners because of their talent as designers, not as businessmen. We became very dependable as creators of money-making toys." A member of the twenty-one-year club, Howard had been a chief engineer in the electronics industry before making a cold call to Marvin himself. He was also hired on the spot.

"It was like proposing marriage on a first date." Then, as now, orientation lacks spoon feeding. "The honeymoon is tough. Everyone is given a table. Everyone else is willing to help —they've been there before and no one bothers them for a month. We give them toy catalogues, send them out to Toys 'R' Us every night, and get them acclimated.

"If a young person needs direction, this is the wrong place to be. We look for self-directed young people who don't need petting and can handle criticism." Structurally, while there is a nominal hierarchy and one can advance from assistant designer to designer to senior designer to product manager to senior product manager to partner, "there is no chain of command, no organizational chart, no list of procedures. You do what you want. If Rouben [another partner and the resident doll expert] said he was dying to do a certain doll and none of us liked it, God bless him, he could do it." In other words, partners are working designers. They are, however, responsible for being the front guys, who manage and maintain relationships with clients. "Just because an idea is mine doesn't mean I can carry it out," Morrison avers. "Partners sometimes assign a mix of stuff they get excited about. That's a major strength of the company. There are no politics here. We're designers and get gratification from each accomplishment."

Besides the prototypes, the large work areas, the machinery, the dining room, and an incredible futuristic guest bathroom heralded by life-sized mannequins (which has a door that slides open like a door on the spaceship *Enterprise,* but inside looks like a dressing room in a Hollywood mansion), there is a small area that looks exactly like what it is: the accounting and payroll departments, also known as the front office.

Mary Ann Kotowicz's title is something like "chief money person," and she has fifteen years at Marvin Glass under her belt. As an accountant for a small company on the South Side of Chicago, she "didn't even want to work in this tony neighborhood. But as soon as I got up the stairs, I hoped they'd hire me. Everything was just first class: the wrought-iron staircase, the sculpture, the way you got greeted." She was put in touch with the company through an employment agency, and after her interview she was given an accounting test—over the telephone.

As a nondesigner, it took Mary Ann a while to feel she was in the thick of things. With its passion for confidentiality—the toy industry is notoriously tainted with sabotage and idea thieves—Marvin Glass does not easily permit access to the design area to strangers. [Author's note: When I visited, an announcement came over the PA system alerting designers to my tour of the premises and asking them to cover their desks. Not a single worktable or project in progress was visible.] "It used to be taboo to hang out with designers. It took four years for me to be allowed into the design area. I probably could have gone in earlier had I pushed it.

"There's not a day you don't have a good laugh. You've got such nuts around here. That's why I've stayed. I enjoy my work. The designers come into my office with some crazy mock-up or story. I'm posting receipts for Rock 'em Sock 'em Robots—that's fun right there. The names make you smile, and I'm familiar with the products. They ask me my opinions as a typical consumer. 'Would you buy this doll?' They spoil you. When I was sick for a week, they sent flowers and toys, and they all called. And no one gets bonuses like we do."

MARVIN GLASS GOES TO HOLLYWOOD

M r. Gameshow is a cross between TV host Wink Martindale and the unused nailbrush lying by your sink. He is a plastic-bodied, computer-operated quizmaster that is programmed to play ten different games with up to four different contestants. About a foot tall, he retails for approximately a hundred dollars, tuxedo included. He was invented by Marvin Glass & Associates and is licensed to Galoob, a toy manufacturer located in San Francisco.

You may have seen Mr. Gameshow on television when every feature reporter around the country covered the industry's annual Toy Fair in 1987. You might have caught his appearances (sharing a box with television's popular stuffed alien, Alf) on the syndicated program *The New Hollywood Squares.* Mr. Gameshow transforms the smarmy, self-involved TV host into something closer to art. He's frozen in a permanent grin, his eyes roll as if witness to a game show epiphany. He's apt to scream something about lunch, babe. *Très* Hollywood.

Today Mr. Gameshow is *in* Hollywood, in fact, to talk to the network executives about his own daytime show. For real. This meeting is taking place in the Beverly Boulevard offices of Passeta Productions (producers of the Academy Award shows, among others), Mr. Gameshow's producers. They have a development deal. Jeffrey Breslow, Marvin Glass's managing partner, David Capper, Galoob's vice-president of marketing, and Dan Schrier, Mr. Gameshow's big-time talent agent from ICM, are on hand for the run-through, to be presented to the game show brass of ABC.

Breslow, one of two people wearing a suit, has brought along Mr. Gameshow's actual TV-sized head. It's still unpainted but relatively lifelike. Though Mr. Gameshow's TV career is still not ensured, he is being built in Valencia, California, to be approximately four feet tall. Jeff tells the assemblage, "This is a toy that is totally alive," and, while a caricature, he is as animated as anyone else in the room.

Mr. Gameshow is holding forth from a white plastic podium in a converted office. Without even trying, he is definitely a scene stealer and detracts from even the glowy pastel presence of Sharrie Paulson, Miss California of 1983, his cohost. About eighteen people are crammed in to watch this live audition, and excitement is in the air.

"Hi, Mr. Gameshow, you're looking spiffy today!" is Miss California's opening line. Mr. Gameshow, in a brief spurt of modesty, asks his own Vanna to call him "M.G." The crowd goes wild. With four actors portraying celebrity contestants Phyllis Diller, Howie Mandel, and two civilian contestants, the game begins. M.G.'s game is essentially of the word game genre (à la "Cross Wits," "Tic Tac Dough," "The $25,000 Pyramid," et al.), wherein both partners see a board with six words printed on it. One partner gives clues for what would be sensible pairings of words. The partner who "receives" must figure out which words go with which other words, in the proper order. All correct guesses are worth $50. Each turn takes thirty seconds.

For example, the following board is used:

TOP	DOG	LONG
GUN	SHOT	LEASH

Clues might include "the name of a Tom Cruise movie," "what you use to walk your dog," "when something isn't a sure thing, it's a . . . ." After the "Phyllis Diller" team does well its first time up, M.G. encourages them by saying, "That was really adequate."

While actual commercials are not pantomimed, M.G.'s producers keep the clock going and pause during the appropriate breaks. This is the only time when Mr. Gameshow seems like a plastic toy. There are no wisecracks, no "enough about me; what do *you* think of me?", no careening eyeballs.

Round two proceeds, and when Mr. Gameshow utters a spontaneous "I've got eyes in the back of my head," he provokes convulsion-quality hysteria. (It was ad-libbed by the comic who is the voice of M.G., Murray Langston, better known from his days as "the unknown comic" on Chuck Barris's *The Gong Show*. He's gone from wearing a bag on his head to speaking for a mechanized plastic doll, and he's none the worse for wear. He's not even unattractive.) Apparently, this run-through has been thoroughly rehearsed, and while Murray could crack jokes at random, I suppose that's not part of his job description.

When the mock Phyllis Diller and her partner win the game, they are placed in the winner's circle and have the opportunity to win even more big money. The final round is shown on a specially rigged TV and is something like *Password*'s "Lightning Round." In any case, mock-Phyllis and the contestant win, the winner actually screams, and they hug. It's just like a real show until M.G. says good-bye. Then you remember the point.

The ABC people prepare for the post-run-through meeting. As the crowd thins out, one of the actresses says to the producers, "Don't forget my name, you guys, or my face. You have my number." It's a wistful departure. Suddenly, it's just Mr. Gameshow and me left in the room, while the producers, manufacturers, agents, creators, and network people convene behind the closed doors of the office of the absent Marty Passetta, head of the company and executive producer of the show.

When it's all over, rumor has it that Sharrie's career is sewn up. The producers want to sign her and Murray to long-term contracts. Although they "liked the interaction," the ABC people want the show rethought a bit to include Mr. Gameshow in more of the quiz part of the show. Everyone wants to know when the larger Mr. Gameshow will be completed. Jeff Breslow, who flew from Chicago for this meeting, adds that a second set of legs—in a sitting position—is being made (as well as M.G.'s standing legs) for M.G.'s appearances on talk shows like Johnny Carson's.

After being hustled and seduced, no promise of a deal has been offered the toy makers. And you can see that show business has been committed all over Jeff Breslow's face, clouded by disappointment.

Passetta's people promise ABC they can deliver a new show in ten days.

EPILOGUE

As *Going to Work* was being put to bed (in April 1988), Marvin Glass & Associates was closing its doors. Although by far the most successful company in its industry, according to the original partnership agreement written in 1974, the company was directed to dissolve at the point at which less than four of the original eleven partners were still at the helm. Jeffrey Breslow, Howard Morrison, and Rouben Terzian—the remaining partners—opened the doors to a new firm, Breslow, Morrison, Terzian & Associates, Inc., in May 1988.

Breslow, Morrison, Terzian & Associates, Inc.

750 North Orleans Street

Chicago, IL 60610

(312) 440-1044

THE QUAKER OATS COMPANY

HISTORY & OPERATIONS

The Quaker Oats Company began before the turn of the century as an uneasy alliance among three independent millers who joined together to form the world's largest oats company. Ferdinand Schumacher, a German immigrant, was the first to introduce Americans to oatmeal as a cheap and nutritious alternative to heavy, multicourse breakfasts. He established a national market for oats and was soon faced with a number of competitors. When Schumacher's Ohio mill burned down in 1886 and his oats no longer dominated the market, his rivals rushed in to fill the gap, almost driving one another out of business with price wars. In 1891, after several failed attempts, the seven largest cereal mills in the country banded together to form the American Cereal Company, based in Iowa and led by Schumacher (who by then had reorganized), Robert Stuart, and Henry Parsons Crowell.

The new company performed well, acquiring other cereal companies and diversifying into related cereal products and animal feed. The oats were sold under the name "Quaker," the first American trademark for a cereal—the trademark had been registered in 1877 by Henry Parsons Crowell, when he was still an independent miller—and packaged in brightly colored cartons adorned with the now famous picture of the cereal's jolly namesake. From the outset, the company's success was as attributable to the pervasiveness of its advertising as it was to the quality of its products. Crowell pioneered merchandising techniques at a time when most food products were sold in general stores from unmarked bins. The effectiveness of its many campaigns—Quaker's original advertisements, mostly created by Crowell, linked the consumption of Quaker Oats to favorable results ranging from vastly improved health to success in romantic relationships—were evidenced by its growth in its early years. Crowell established an international market for the brand name product, yet despite the company's success, there was in-fighting among Schumacher—who mistrusted Crowell's methods—and Stuart and Crowell. Tensions came to a head in 1899, when Stuart and Crowell managed to depose Schumacher in a fierce proxy fight.

In 1901 the American Cereal Company was restructured and incorporated as the Quaker Oats Company—based in Chicago—and all the company's products were consolidated under the Quaker name. Twenty years of growth and diversification followed, during which time the company became the country's leader in livestock feeds as well as oatmeal, and developed a number of ready-to-eat cereals, including puffed wheat and puffed rice. In 1901 the company's revenues were $15.79 million, and by 1910 that figure had increased to $25.6 million. During World War I, when food was scarce, sales reached a high of $123 million (an artificial peak which was not surpassed until 1926). In 1920, when a sudden world economic depression coincided with an oversupply in grains, the company came close to folding.

In 1922 Robert Stuart's son John was elected president of the company. During his tenure, the company diversified into pet foods (Ken-L-Ration for dogs and Puss'n Boots for cats), chemicals (furfural, a by-product of oats with a number of industrial uses), and ready-mixed pancake flours (Aunt Jemima, which Quaker purchased in 1926). In 1942, John Stuart became CEO and chairman of the board and his brother Douglas took over as president. Quaker's annual revenues had reached $90 million. Again, its growth during those years was spurred largely by aggressive promotion of the Quaker brand names, including the sponsoring of popular radio programs and premium giveaways with the purchase of Quaker products.

During the World War II, Quaker's Nebraska plant was converted into a bomb-loading complex to aid in the war effort. After the war the company continued to expand. By the time John Stuart retired as chairman in 1956, Quaker's annual revenues had reached $277 million on two hundred different products, of which foreign sales were $72 million. In 1965 the company employed 10,000 workers—6,500 in the United States and the rest abroad. By 1966 worldwide annual sales had reached almost $500 million, more than 25 percent of which came from overseas sales. Quaker Oats was the largest-selling breakfast cereal in the world, and the company was one of the foremost manufacturers of cereals anywhere. (New brand names included Life cereal and Cap'n Crunch.) The dog and cat food lines were leaders in their fields in total sales, and the company remained one of the largest manufacturers of livestock and poultry feed. Quaker had also entered the frozen food market with Aunt Jemima frozen waffles and other toaster products. Worldwide, Quaker was the largest seller of corn meal, hominy grits, and other dry-milled corn products.

In 1969 Quaker entered the toy business with the purchase of the Fisher-Price company, located in East Aurora, New York. During the seventies, the company continued to diversify, broadening its food lines, getting into some nonfood products, and acquiring a number of international food businesses. During the early 1980s, Quaker sold off its chemical division and diversified into specialty retail sales through several acquisitions. Quaker purchased Brookstone, a supplier of tools, Jos A. Bank Clothiers, a budget version of Brooks Brothers, and Eyelab, a New Jersey–based eyewear chain. In 1983 Quaker bought Stokely-Van Camp—whose main products are canned pork and beans and Gatorade—for $238 million.

In 1986, under the leadership of William Smithburg, who became CEO in 1981 and chairman two years later (Smithburg took over from Robert D. Stuart, Jr., the last in line of the founding family), Quaker divested itself of its specialty retail businesses in order to refocus on its basic businesses: toys and grocery products. That year, the company made two major acquisitions. Golden Grain Macaroni Company, whose product lines include pasta products, Rice-a-Roni, Noodle-Roni, and Ghirardelli Chocolates, was purchased for $275 million and takes Quaker beyond its line of predominantly breakfast products. Anderson, Clayton & Company, which owns Gaines pet food, Chiffon margarine, and Seven Seas Salad Dressings, was acquired through a hostile takeover—not Quaker's usual style—for $800 million. Quaker bought the company in order to add Gaines pet foods to its existing pet food lines and thus be in a position to compete with Ralston Purina, the number one company in the pet food market. (Quaker has since sold off Anderson, Clayton's other divisions to Kraft.) With the purchase of Gaines, Quaker moved from fifth to second place in the pet food field.

Today, Quaker employs approximately 29,000 people worldwide, with about 19,500 in the United States and the remainder abroad. It has offices and plants in seventeen countries, in addition to the United States. The company saw $4.4 billion in revenues in 1987, approximately 30 percent of which was generated by foreign sales. Quaker Oatmeal, which is now available in thirteen flavors—regular; apples and cinnamon; raisins and spice; maple and brown sugar; honey and graham; bran and raisins; cinnamon and spice; cinnamon, raisins, and almonds; peaches and cream; strawberries and cream; blueberries and cream; bananas and cream; and raisins, dates, and walnuts—is still one of the company's most profitable products.

In July 1987, after more than thirty years in Chicago's massive Merchandise Mart building, Quaker moved into its new headquarters. Quaker Towers, designed by the architectural firm of Skidmore, Owings and Merrill, is situated on the north bank of the Chicago River. The 850,000-square-foot building takes full advantage of its riverfront location, with terraces on the riverbank side, parklike grounds, many trees, and walkways along the river. Quaker, which occupies most of seventeen floors in the thirty-five-story building, has its own employee cafeteria with an adjoining terrace where employees can eat lunch during the warm months. The building is connected to the Nikko Hotel, which has a health club where Quaker employees can get memberships at a discount.

(Information provided by Ron Bottrell, company spokesman.)

1987 *Fortune* 500 RANKING: 93rd among all companies, fourteenth among food companies.

REVENUES: $4.4 billion in 1987.

NET INCOME: $243.9 million in 1987.

INITIAL PUBLIC OFFERING: Public since its incorporation in 1901.

NUMBER OF SHAREHOLDERS: 38,000

OFFICES: The company has offices and manufacturing facilities in seventeen countries in addition to the United States: Argentina, Belgium, Brazil, Canada, Colombia, Denmark, England, France, West Germany, Guatemala, Italy, Malaysia, Mexico, the Netherlands, Scotland, Spain, and Venezuela. Quaker products are on sale virtually all over the free world.

NUMBER OF EMPLOYEES: Quaker employs approximately 29,000 people worldwide, with about 19,500 in the United States and the rest abroad.

AVERAGE AGE OF EMPLOYEES: Though the company does not calculate that figure, their hunch is that it's in the early thirties, though there's no research to back it up.

TURNOVER: Varies from location to location and year to year, depending on the job market, the general economic climate, and additional factors. The average is about 10 percent.

RECRUITMENT: Quaker does have a program, and the number of target schools fluctuates annually, between thirty-five and forty. The company recruits at "the top schools for the disciplines we're looking at," including accounting schools, business schools for MBAs, and law schools. "The rankings for those are pretty well known."

NUMBER OF NEW HIRES PER YEAR: Recent college graduates: 150 to 200; employees in general: as many as four thousand.

RANGE OF STARTING SALARIES: "I can't really quantify that other than to say we're competitive for the function."

POLICY FOR RAISES: Employees are subject to performance reviews on an annual basis, and raises are awarded on merit.

TRAINING PROGRAMS: There are no formal programs that all new hires go through. "Basically it's on-the-job kind of training to familiarize new employees with their particular jobs, rather than on a broad basis."

BENEFITS: Medical insurance (including a unique feature known as the "Health Incentive Plan," which gives employees an allowance of up to $380 for certain health expenses; if they do not incur those expenses over the course of a year, they receive the balance in cash), dental insurance, life insurance, accident insurance, disability insurance, profit-sharing plan, employee stock ownership plan, retirement plan, tuition reimbursement for courses that benefit an employee's career at Quaker, student loan program for dependent children and spouses, and college scholarship program for dependents (determined on a competitive basis).

VACATION: Two weeks after one year, three weeks after five years, four weeks after fifteen years, five weeks after twenty-five years, plus eight paid holidays and two personal days each year.

ADDITIONAL PERKS: From mid-May through Labor Day, employees work "summer hours," which means slightly longer hours during the week and only half days each Friday.

BONUSES: All salaried employees are eligible for bonuses, which are determined by department heads on the basis of performance. Usually department heads have a set amount to work with, from which they allot bonuses.

ANNUAL PARTY: The company hosts an annual picnic for employees and their families, which includes people from headquarters and from Quaker's research laboratory in the Chicago suburbs. The party is thrown at a Chicago area amusement park. Employees congregate for a meal and socializing, after which they have the run of the park.

AVERAGE WORKDAY: 8:30 A.M. to 4:45 P.M. During the summer months employees work either 8:00 A.M. to 4:45 P.M. or 8:30 A.M. to 5:15 P.M. Monday through Thursday, and then take Friday afternoons off.

DRESS CODE: "A dress code isn't really emphasized, and there are no written guidelines. For the most part, employees dress conservatively and appropriately." Meaning suits for the men and suits, dresses, or skirts for women, who almost never wear slacks.

SOCIAL ATMOSPHERE: "It varies from department to department. There's a great deal of fraternization among some of the younger employees in certain departments. In large departments, where there are many people similar in terms of age, backgrounds, job descriptions, and home neighborhoods, there is a lot of socializing. But Chicago is a commuter city, so people who commute from the suburbs might not be in that category."

HEADQUARTERS: Quaker occupies seventeen floors—it shares space on two of the floors with other firms—of Quaker Towers, its new 850,000-square-foot, thirty-five-story building situated on the north bank of the Chicago River.

RESEARCH AND DEVELOPMENT: Usually about 1 percent of total revenues is spent on R & D.

NUMBER OF PRODUCTS: Quaker produces more than 500 grocery products worldwide (not including Fisher-Price's 225 products).

NUMBER OF NEW PRODUCTS PER YEAR: About twenty grocery products in the United States. Fisher-Price introduces as many as fifty new toys each year.

MOST POPULAR GROCERY PRODUCT: Gatorade, which in 1987 surpassed oatmeal, the company's best seller for 109 years.

CHARITABLE CONTRIBUTIONS: In 1987 the Quaker Foundation dispersed $2.6 million in direct grants to 1,500 organizations. The company contributed an additional $4.8 million in product donations (including food banks) and other cash contributions, a portion of which was donated as part of the foundation's matching gifts program. Quaker will match, on a three-for-one basis, an employee's donation to a charity of his or her choice, up to $300. (Quaker was the first company in the United States to offer its employees a three-for-one matching contribution.) From $301 to $2,000, the foundation will match an employee's donation on a one-for-one basis. Employees can apply the matching gifts policy to as many charities as they want.

INTERESTED APPLICANTS CAN SEND RÉSUMÉS TO:
Placement Office
The Quaker Oats Company
P.O. Box 9001, Suite 13-11
Chicago, IL 60604
(312) 222-7111

The Quaker Oats Company is an all-American can-do company. Under its new, rejuvenated management, Quaker has grown from thirteen brands to more than thirty-five brands in less than ten years. It is quickly losing its stodgy image, which was due in part to its premiere product, oats, which seems old-fashioned, and in part to its logo, a Quaker circa 1877. As it grows, it is both cutting back on staff and deepening the layers of management. But Quaker Oats is faring well in its eighth decade since its incorporation.

Chairman and Chief Executive Officer Bill (called by his first name by one and all) Smithburg has a message. He is credited with galvanizing the new, action-oriented Quaker Oats. He demurs. "Change here is not static between epochs of CEOs. It's evolutionary, started by our predecessors." He began his tenure as leader "by establishing financial objectives. You'd think every company does this. They don't." Further, "you must live it. We set goals for every single manager in the company. Not just quantitative, qualitative. What have you done to create innovation and to develop those underneath you? It's remarkably easy for people to fall into a rut of numbers."

"We're in mature businesses," he says in his conference room, which features a painting by Edgar Buonagurio. "The difference is how we execute. Everyone's bright and motivated. The status quo is not acceptable. We're not a paternalistic organization. We're professional managers who want to prosper on behalf of our shareholders."

Smithburg wants people who work at Quaker Oats to be treated fairly. "It rarely happens that someone with high potential quits. It means they haven't gotten feedback. It did happen recently, and it made me go through the roof. A bad product I can live with; losing good people is the worst loss."

Bill Smithburg doesn't tolerate buzzwords. He doesn't like to institutionalize his policy, for fear of sounding glib. "I don't look at {my role] as 'managing people,' he says, "I think of it as managing *with* people. I learned this lesson in 1979–81: You can't accomplish changes in a manual."

His aim is "to maintain old good things and blend them with good things of newly acquired companies." Since he's held the reins, Quaker has bought Golden Grain, makers of Rice-a-Roni, "a close, family-held, private company," and Stokely-Van Camp, manufacturers of pork and beans and Gatorade. "We are trying to evolve the company. This company has made the transition from a family-managed and -owned company to public ownership and management."

One of the long-held principles of the original management has been "being a good corporate citizen. Quaker has had a great relationship with the unions for decades. We can't be activist on all issues." He describes the culture by citing its three main attributes. "Motivation to get up in the morning, enthusiasm to enjoy it, and willingness to take prudent risks. If you're not in sync with the culture, you should leave." Quaker Oats is not a one-man show, no matter how much people try to please their chairman. The Senior Management Committee is made up of ten people who meet every two weeks, and it reviews all business. "Nine of the ten have worked together an average of seventeen years or more."

Smithburg's advice to employees who want to do well here, or anywhere, for that matter, is "Broaden yourself. Don't just socialize with your own group. I don't know how many hours a person *should* work." The appearance of working late will not win any points from him. "If someone was on an extended maternity leave, we'd put a computer in her home, if it were appropriate."

Janet Cooper, Quaker Oats' director of corporate finance, says, "Having a young, vibrant CEO has changed things." She came here from one of the world's largest industrial companies, where she was forced to be a specialist. In contrast, "Quaker seemed to offer a variety of opportunities. The company is thirsty for people and ideas and doing new things. They don't fire you when you make mistakes. Bill Smithburg goes on record as a risk taker. He expects mistakes and encourages successes." She pauses. "It's an encouraging system. Quaker {which is how employees always refer to their company] doesn't accept failure because they *like* us; it's just realism. The atmosphere changes; not the culture."

Janet is joined by Barbara Allen, a vice-president in product management (snacks). "As we grow, enough of us remember the old prebureaucracy days and fight it. We're like Chicago: We're large and realize it, but deny it."

The folks at Quaker Oats—one of the city's major corporations—perhaps have a sense that they have not made a dent in Chicago's consciousness due to the fact that they never had their own building. Lo these many years, Quaker occupied a few floors in the Kennedy family-owned Merchandise Mart, one of old Chicago's foremost commercial buildings. But by the time this book is in your hands, Quaker Towers at 321 Clark Street will have been open for business for about a year "and will make Quaker's Chicago identity. Often people don't realize it's here." It's just not the same as having a space of your own that can be a landmark as well as part of a city's culture: "Meet me in front of Quaker Towers."

Barb entered the University of Chicago Business School without a sense of what she would do with her MBA. She was a summer intern at Quaker Oats "and just stayed on. I finished my MBA at night. Being here confirmed my interest in marketing. When they offered me a summer job after my first year of grad school, I figured I'd end up here anyway.

"They operate as I do—through people. It's a challenging environment which trusts me. They enjoy having your point of view . . . although they may not always agree with you." She touts the limitless access to top decision makers. "It's informal. You bump into people like Bill Smithburg or Frank Morgan [the president and chief operating officer]."

Accepting the company's values is key to a fruitful affiliation with Quaker. Barb and Janet enumerate: "Hardworking, ethical, humanistic. Liking the products helps. People identify with the products." They admit that their attitudes toward consumerism have changed since joining the country's 93rd largest company (in the 1987 *Fortune* 500). For one thing, they are brand loyal. "I don't eat competitive products. I do little things like straightening out grocery store shelves. I talk to store managers. I'm more likely to try new products; I don't need to wait for the advertising. I'm more aware of nutrition."

Quaker Oats provides a full life for those who work there. "The people I work with, I genuinely like. I've taken vacations with them. Young people in marketing who have no family in the area, their whole lives are filled with Quaker people. Is there a sense of competition? Yes. But there's more teamwork than cutthroat." People are not expected to kill themselves for their jobs. The company "does allow for a personal life. You don't need to work eighty hours a week. You can easily do fine at a fifty-eight-hour workweek. We're not process-oriented; we're just results-oriented. Smithburg feels if you're here seven days a week, something's wrong."

Barb Allen remembers when she first became pregnant nine years ago. "When I first told Quaker, they were puzzled. They assumed my personal life wouldn't interfere with my work life." Obviously, her career didn't suffer. "They don't take away from your career mobility if you can't move. If there were a crisis at work, I'd leave home on Saturday. I'm lousy at prioritizing, and I'd like to do everything." Both times she was pregnant, she went to the office the day she gave birth. "I didn't take advantage of the company. I took six weeks off, as promised." A live-in housekeeper takes care of Allen's two children during the day; otherwise it's a matter of trade-offs. "Haircuts and working out, reading and going to the movies are out. I have my work and my family."

Nevertheless, being a woman at Quaker is "nonissue. The guy I work for never seemed to notice I was a woman. He thought I wore pants." Debbie Kelly, the vice-president of corporate affairs, is presently the most senior woman in the organization, just under the Senior Management Committee. She is regarded as proof that the company will promote women as high up as possible. Calling the company "sex-blind," Janet Cooper says she's become more ambitious the longer she's been here. "I always thought I'd run a division. As you get closer to your objectives, it seems more realistic."

When you walk from office to office, it is likely that your first reaction is, "How does anyone find his way around?" A stack of Mama Celeste pizza boxes, a pile of Cap'n Crunch, or bottles of Aunt Jemima syrup may be your best clue as to who works where.

David Bere has a microwave oven in his office. As the director of new areas, he needs it for product tasting. With a BA and MBA from Indiana University, his story of finding work at Quaker Oats is the stuff of business writers' dream. It was 1977. "I originally arrived as the escort of a girlfriend who was interviewing. I saw the Quaker promotional film *Wherever the Sun Rises,* and I liked it. I visited personnel. My girlfriend didn't get hired. We split up." As a matter of fact, Quaker Oats fit into the profile of what Bere was looking for. He wanted "to live in the Chicago area and work in brand management." It's inconceivable that he could have landed here more fortuitously.

After spending five years according to plan—one year as a marketing assistant, two years as an assistant brand manager, and two years as a brand manager (on Cap'n Crunch), David was tapped to become a White House Fellow, a year-long federal appointment as a cabinet-level aide, awarded to exceptional young executives and leaders, providing them with high-octane government experience. "Quaker gave me a lot of support. They made a big deal about it and guaranteed me a job afterward." When Dave returned in 1984, he was sent to Cedar Rapids, Iowa, to be a plant superintendent. "I had to explain it to my wife, Karen. She thought I was a big deal White House Fellow, and here I'm in Cedar Rapids. We were a little shocked." The pleasant surprise was that as opposed to "being just a peon here"—his tongue is pressing the inside of his cheek—"being the plant super was like being the executive vice-president of a small company.

"The company told me they wanted me to get experience outside of marketing. Here, you get lots of MBAs who all want to be president. At the plant, the job isn't the most important thing in [the workers'] lives. They're good workers. They taught me the human implications of business decisions. Here in [headquarters], it's a joke. When you actually have to lay off people affected by a bad decision . . . " his voice trails off.

The Beres bought a house and settled down in Cedar Rapids. He characterizes their life there as " 'nice.' The head of the plant in Cedar Rapids is more influential in Iowa government and politics than Smithburg is in Illinois." Thirteen months later, Bere was summoned back to Chicago for a promotion. "I would have liked to have stayed longer." Quaker Oats bought the house back from him.

Moving around in the company has made David feel like a part of it. "I always felt anything I did would have an impact on the company. What I like best is that you can make a contribution and be a part of the team. What Dave Bere thinks makes a difference. Quaker was considered sleepy when I came here, and now people want to work here. It makes you proud."

Teamwork notwithstanding, he amends, "I must admit, sometimes I think of senior management as 'them.' We all know who 'they' are. You get to know everyone from the Polish cleaning ladies to Bill Smithburg. Because we're horizontal." Before the move, most corporate employees worked on two humongous floors. ("I'm worried when we move to our new building it will change. Top management will be isolated. It will put our culture to the test.")

The job "they" gave Bere in new areas has been the most fun. "For the first time in my career, I'm doing strategic thinking and planning. I have a lot of exposure to senior management. I'm positive there were a lot of people who were better qualified, but they—really Frank Morgan—felt I could handle it. I think I will stay here. I'm happy." Having been a White House Fellow made Dave realize that he has options. The two he would perhaps consider would be consulting and politics. "I did a lot of soul searching. And working for a corporation makes me happy." (So do community activities. Bere works at a center for alcoholic women after hours.) "Quaker's values are important. If there were inconsistencies, I'd reassess my future. I see myself as the president of the company. But so does everyone else. It doesn't drive me. I have an excellent chance at running a division in the next five to seven years."

His favorite product to eat? Quaker Chewy Granola Bars. "It's embarrassing not to be a breakfast person at a breakfast company."

Jan Relford attended Ball State University (at the same time as David Letterman), where he earned his BS and MS in physical chemistry. He joined Quaker in 1974 as a lab supervisor and is now the director of quality assurance for the Grocery Specialties Division. His office contains a large variety of products.

As a "quasi scientist [his words] I represent the technical side of the management team. It means I know nothing about business." Jan always wanted to work in the space program, but "I graduated during the recession of NASA. I watched the moon walk on an ancient Motorola I inherited from my wife's parents in Muncie while I was in grad school." He moved to Chicago to work for a small pharmaceutical company. From there, he found his way to Quaker's Rockford, Illinois, lab, where pet food (Ken-L-Ration and others) is made. "When I told my friends I went to pet foods, they thought I'd gotten fired, but as a chemist, it's very fascinating." Jan observed Quaker's senior management from afar and assessed it as "excellent." Furthermore, "the work was challenging and interesting. It was a fast time for the pet food industry. We introduced Tender Chunks. We built a new plant in Lawrence, Kansas. I got the feeling I left something there, and I got a lot of information. I've got to keep it even. Maybe I should give a little more. It's like a bank. You put in to get out."

Quaker Oats maintains a kennel in nearby Barrington, "geared to middle-aged dogs. There are over two hundred dogs—all major breeds, including mutts. We look to see how dogs respond to fat content, the amount of moisture, grain, and protein." When queried, Relford admits he's tasted a hard dog biscuit.

Claiming "each job improves upon your last one," Relford has gained a greater understanding of Quaker Oats as he has moved around. "Quaker is communicative. You *know* what's expected, where the company wants to go. They publicize it—in the quarterly and annual reports. You can figure out your place. And you're generally right. Without clear direction [from the top], that could be lost. You can go off on a tangent, as long as you're a doer and a team player.

"Maybe that's why I like it here. They think the way I do. They're results-oriented." Without being heavy-handed, it is worth noting that the corporation described by its employees in various positions and divisions is consistent. "When you're four hundred miles away from headquarters and see it, it's consistent." A scientist and a strategic planner, using their own methods of expression, talk about what is clearly the same place, with the same regard for certain prized qualities. Take the notion of risk. Relford says, "We throw this term out a lot. I assume I take the same amount of *risk* as a marketing person, but the definition must be altered. We [in quality assurance] can't take risks.

"We're a marketing company. There's no doubt about that. But we need a research and development component to stay alive. There's respect for scientists on the team." Relford says, "I certainly have my hands full here. I'm moving a lot of programs along, working on plants, logistics, and sanitation design. I work with researchers, engineers."

After the products reach the manufacturing stage, they are no longer tested. "We test diligently at the beginning of products. I'm strong on ethics, almost to the point of being a consumer advocate. Quaker is only as good as its weakest link. I've been impressed with a lot of the positions at Quaker. Nothing's been allowed to slide, as often happens with big success. It's Smithburg. I hope to stay at Quaker."

Phyllis Douglass, a manager in human resources, has been with Quaker since December 1984. A member of the Wellesley College class of 1977—"I was convinced that I was the one to round out the curve"—she came to the company after a career in commercial banking. There she worked in the human resources area initially, but "for a year and a half I was put through the loan officer training program, and I missed people." Although she had been told she had a great future at the bank and she had reached the level of an assistant vice-president, "I was ready for a change. I wasn't quite thirty. I had done a lot and couldn't see what would be next. The bank was comfortable and I liked the people, but I began to feel like I was the last person at the party.

"Right away, this place felt great!" At Quaker, Phyllis runs college recruiting in marketing, from the entry level and up in brand management. "My mother was a social worker. I said I wanted to help people. Mother said, 'Come on!' She realized that this is the perfect job for me."

For those applicants without MBAs, the company has a two-year program called "Marketing Associates," which is more structured than the MBA training programs. In 1987 two associates were hired from a pool of thirty-three finalists. "This is a forward-thinking company in terms of employees and benefits. Quaker has an outstanding reputation on campus," she says. "The company, products, and people. You hear, 'Neat company. I was raised on it.' " Douglass looks for students at Brown, Princeton, Wellesley, Wharton (at Penn), and Yale. "Students have a realistic view of work," she says. "People are very active in extracurricular activities, leadership, and entrepreneurial ventures."

Among MBAs, Quaker sees a self-screening applicant pool, those who specifically want to be in the food business or, more generally, consumer package goods. "Our major competition is from General Foods, General Mills [see p. 373], Frito-Lay, and PepsiCo. We don't *not* hire people because they didn't go to the 'right' school. We don't want to be homogeneous." Nevertheless, Quaker has to foster a relationship with some graduate schools, and visits Atlanta University (primarily for black students), the University of Chicago, Harvard University, Indiana University, the Kellogg School at Northwestern, the University of Michigan, the University of North Carolina, Stanford University, the University of Texas, Amos Tuck at Dartmouth College, and the University of Virginia.

Barbara Barrow came straight from Princeton (her BA is in literature) into the Marketing Associates program. When she was a brand manager in Presweetened Cereals (she's now a senior manager of corporate communications), she said, "You have to think like a kid." Her office was decorated in Cap'n Crunch. "I have to step down and think I'm nine years old again," she said when we met. "Would I think this was cool?" Besides extensive testing with her young consumers, Barb immersed herself in her product. "It's good. It has 'crunch power.' "

As the president of her class at Princeton, Barrow had plenty of options. She was originally headed to Morgan Stanley's training program—"I figured I'd allow the bank to send me to business school"—except she knew she was really interested in marketing. Then Procter & Gamble tried to recruit her. "I didn't try hard at P and G," she confesses. "I blew the interview and didn't get an offer. I realized by the end of the day that brand management *was* what I wanted." A native of Evanston, Illinois, Barb entered the associates program "immediately," in its third year. "There were three people that year. It was great."

Those two years are divided thus: the first year and a half as an assistant in marketing, and the last six months in fieldwork—two months in sales, two months in operations, and two months as an analyst in marketing research. "You get a sense of how your job affects consumers' decisions. In a perfect world, people make rational decisions, but . . .'" The liberal arts student should not fear the real world of brand management: "You do a lot with numbers, but it's really good judgment and common sense—nothing fancy," Barrow says. "There is complicated stuff, but your team can help you interpret. Obviously, it's important that you make your numbers. It's the most important part of your job. You try to make the best guess you can possibly make. It's in your best interest." If you thought that people in the training phase are just window dressing, think again. "You see hiring and firing decisions based on the numbers you've given operations."

After two years Barrow moved to Van Camp for a year as brand manager, right after the business was acquired by Quaker. "The business was in excellent shape. I got to try some things. I learned to say to my boss, 'I'm going to try this,' not 'Do you think we could do this?' " Barb thought of new products to add to the pork-and-bean line, notably Italian-style pork and beans. "I proposed [it] to my boss and my boss's boss. Our customer is blue collar. He's interested in price, not brand loyalty. At first I didn't get a lot of encouragement, because of all the money [making and testing new products would require]. What you're able to accomplish is a function of how hard you push for things. It wasn't, 'No, Barb. No money.'

"Why did I push? They were smart people and good marketers, and it was a question of waiting for the right time." A moment later, she adds, "I like to argue. It's a challenge to convince people. I've fought a lot of battles and lost. That's how you learn.

"I finally convinced my boss." Although Barb moved away from Van Camp in 1985, she says she's "real proud of it. We have the number one share in the marketplace. If I hadn't been there, it wouldn't have happened that way."

And then she was promoted to the "Crunch Squad Headquarters." "I think Quaker allows you to make your own decisions, and you get to see if they work or not. You get better over time. There are lots of checks and balances. No one will let you go out on a limb, but you can take a calculated risk. Understanding _why_ something doesn't work" is almost as valuable as finding something that does.

Quaker launched the massive "Where's the Cap'n?" campaign in 1985 which transformed the cereal from a cult favorite to headline status. Mary Whalen, a group manager in promotions, calls the effort the "Who shot J.R.?, for nine-year-olds." [Author's note: In case you didn't know, the Cap'n was found in the Milky Way.] Everyone associated with the Cap'n has an enthusiasm—being part of a winning team—that is youthful and genuine. Just for fun, the Crunch Squad goes to supermarkets to watch people shop. They have Cap'n Crunch clipboards, lamps, and beach towels in their offices. And they enjoy the cereal itself. Some will go so far as to have it for supper. "It looks like a Cap'n Crunch night" is a not atypical refrain.

When Deborah Lathen meets a stranger who asks her what she does for a living, she says, "I'm an attorney." A native of Elgin, Illinois, Lathen attended Cornell as an undergraduate, then Harvard Law School, and worked at two private firms before joining Quaker Oats in 1982. "I heard it was a good place to work for. A good place if you have to work for a living." Without a single connection, Deborah wrote a letter—"blind"—to the general counsel's office. Obviously, it paid off.

There are nineteen lawyers in Quaker's legal department. "I do now pretty much what I did at the firm, but it's more fun since I can give the crappy stuff to our outside counsel. I do litigation. It's not nine to five. I travel like crazy; I took eight business trips in the last two weeks. I spend much more than 50 percent of my time not in Chicago. I prefer the direct client contact here. You have to see these people every day. They grab you in the cafeteria and say, 'Will we win?' "

If she had stayed in private practice, Deborah would be a partner by now. "I'm not envious of them, but they make more money. I don't have to worry about billable hours or new clients." If she had her druthers, Lathen would be French. "My fantasy is to live in Paris before I die. It has nothing to do with Quaker." She is satisfied professionally, but that sort of worries her. "My biggest fear is not leaving. It's too comfortable. I like smart people, and here they're really smart. It's so exhilarating, and I like to win."

Her department is made up of people "all pretty much the same age with the same interests." Socializing is voluntary and practiced. "We're not coerced. It's not, 'We're having a picnic and you're *going*.' There've been at least three couples who got married since I arrived at Quaker. Lots of couples. It's a natural thing. Some of my best friends work at Quaker."

The exuberant attorney lives with her job. "I dream about this case! I'm serious! I dream about dog food!"

Tom Phillips is the vice-president of corporate programs. This means he administers the Quaker Oats Foundation. He came from General Foods and has so far spent half of his career at the corporation in Sales. "When Quaker loaned me for six months to the United Way campaign, I got so impressed with how involved the corporation was in nonprofit giving that I expressed an interest in getting into this general neighborhood. The key emphasis in giving is on communities where Quaker has facilities: Chicago, East Aurora, New York, Cedar Rapids, Iowa, et cetera." Quaker's matching policy is generous; the company donates three times what an employee donates, in gifts up to $300.

The pitfalls of giving away a corporation's money are many and have been delineated elsewhere. Tom says, "Yearning to be a goody-goody can get the company into trouble." You need to temper your "goodheartedness with good management techniques." Although he's no longer accountable for profit and loss, "there's a fiscal responsibility. I don't feel *not* a part of Quaker, but it's a different group of co-workers." Giving has been institutionalized at Quaker for forty years, and 1988 is the twenty-fourth year of increased funds. "Last year the corporation gave more than three percent of its pretax income to charity."

It starts at the top. Bill Smithburg, an alumnus of Northwestern's Kellogg School of Business, is a trustee of the university. "Quaker has made a substantial contribution to Northwestern, not because he said so, but because it fits our profile."

Jim Sullivan, another alumnus of the marketing assistant program, became the director of investor relations four years after his arrival at the company. Before that, he was the brand manager on Granola Dipps, Quaker's ultimate snack bar—a granola bar dipped in chocolate. (Since then, he's been named the director of product management for pet foods.) We're speaking in his office, although he's out of town and I'm on his phone.

An Army brat who calls Falls Church, Virginia, his hometown, he says, "I always had an image of Chicago as a place to work. It has a sense of power and majesty, a can-do attitude, less pessimistic than the East Coast." Quaker Oats was the last job interview he scheduled during his final year at the University of Virginia Business School. It was the day after "Plannning Party," when the marketing department announces its new plans. Everybody had celebrated the night before at a Mexican restaurant. "Everyone was nice," he remembers, "but quiet. It turned out that everyone was still recovering from the party. I thought it was a good place. They had celebrated a good thing the night before." Each person Jim met during his day of interviews is still with Quaker.

When he was turning thirty and thinking about his future, Sullivan became "tired of marketing. I was burning out. I wasn't looking at marketing as a profession. I knew promotions were awhile off, and I entered a year-long reverie. The edge I had at the beginning was lost. I decided that whatever I wanted to do, I should do it at Quaker. The chairman and president knew my name after just four years." Investor Relations, which he sought on a tip from Vice-President Debbie Kelly, "is a financial job without my being a financial whiz. My move away from marketing was countercultural."

Jim sees himself as an example. If he succeeds, others may take his lead. "I have more people looking out for me. I'm a test." At thirty-two, his life has exceeded his expectations. "I never thought I'd be so successful so fast. I feel I have a pretty good future. The bad part is that I never thought I'd give so much. There's less time for my marriage.

"Quaker is well known as an ethical company. I'm never embarrassed about what to tell Mom. We have nothing in South Africa. No investments. No operations."

Philip Marineau was released by the Army on a Friday in 1972 and started working for Quaker Oats the following Monday. Having joined the ROTC program at Georgetown University, he was able to go to graduate school, although he didn't know what he wanted to study. "I knew I wouldn't be a doctor," he says, "and law had no appeal. I guess I was headed toward a Ph.D. in history," although that didn't sound as if it could culminate in the kind of remuneration Marineau wanted.

"My future wife was a copywriter. She said, 'You'd be perfect for brand management' and gave me a book. I read it and said 'Eureka! This is for me!'" Philip thought it sounded like the perfect career for a "dilettante; a generalist's job with a lot of influence." When he was told that he'd need an MBA, he was back in business. "The days of job avoidance," he says wistfully. He chose Northwestern for its strong marketing emphasis.

"If you wanted Chicago and brand management in Chicago, to me there was only one real choice: Quaker Oats. I wrote them a letter and called for an interview. I was hired for a showcase position in sales, since marketing was filled up." Since 1972 Marineau has held eleven positions, most recently as executive vice-president, Grocery Specialties and Market Development. ("My son says I'm the president of Gatorade.")

While he was in college, Philip worked for a man who started his own company. "I watched his business grow until it was a $20 million business. He would work until he could work no more and then went to sleep. I saw all the sacrifices he made." That experience left a deep impression on Marineau, who always considered himself ambitious but "saw it wasn't worth it to give up" the rest of his life. "I don't work weekends, I don't work nights. I coach Little League and basketball."

His success has not made him less desirous of future success, however. "I feel more competitive *now*. I take pride in my versus others' businesses. I'd love to be chairman of the Quaker Oats Company. I don't spend a lot of time thinking about it. You don't have to in order to succeed." His own competitiveness is not directed toward his colleagues. "They're not rivals; they're best buddies. Nothing's cutthroat. I'd feel terrible to compete with a best friend."

Calling some divisions' structures "flatter and others more pyramidal," Philip has up to now "marketed every product Quaker Oats has marketed except Golden Grain. Of course you have your favorites." His are Cap'n Crunch and Gatorade.

His experience of being somewhat less than directed in what he wanted to do for a living would be the exception now. "It's more competitive to get a job like this today. People are more programmed to do this rather than the serendipitous way I did. They are more serious and mature. Others who started at Quaker when I did had a similar experience. We entered later in our late twenties and early thirties. I've never ever worried about losing a job.

"The worst thing you can do is say, 'I.' We're team-oriented." Marineau thinks the qualities needed for corporate success are "a degree of intensity, a problem-solving orientation, creativity, and rational skills. The thing that's kept me here, more than anything else, is how rational it is. I have never ever been turned down with a good idea."

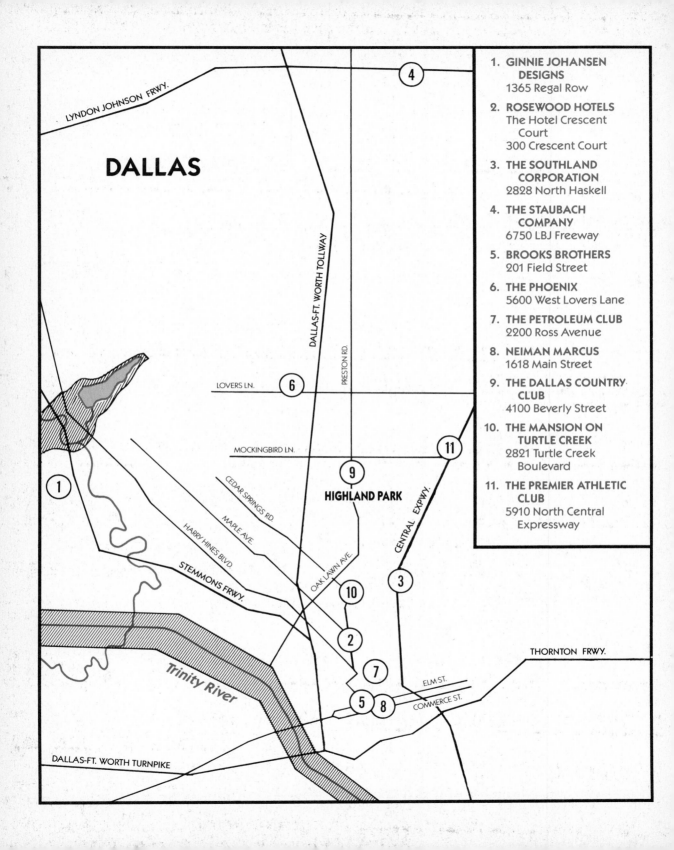

DALLAS

LYNDON JOHNSON FRWY.

DALLAS-FT. WORTH TOLLWAY

PRESTON RD.

LOVERS LN. ⑥

MOCKINGBIRD LN. ⑪

⑨

HIGHLAND PARK

CEDAR SPRINGS RD.

MAPLE AVE.

HARRY HINES BLVD.

OAK LAWN AVE.

CENTRAL EXPWY.

STEMMONS FRWY.

① ⑩

③

② ⑦

⑤ ⑧

ELM ST.

COMMERCE ST.

THORNTON FRWY.

Trinity River

④

DALLAS-FT. WORTH TURNPIKE

1. **GINNIE JOHANSEN DESIGNS**
   1365 Regal Row

2. **ROSEWOOD HOTELS**
   The Hotel Crescent Court
   300 Crescent Court

3. **THE SOUTHLAND CORPORATION**
   2828 North Haskell

4. **THE STAUBACH COMPANY**
   6750 LBJ Freeway

5. **BROOKS BROTHERS**
   201 Field Street

6. **THE PHOENIX**
   5600 West Lovers Lane

7. **THE PETROLEUM CLUB**
   2200 Ross Avenue

8. **NEIMAN MARCUS**
   1618 Main Street

9. **THE DALLAS COUNTRY CLUB**
   4100 Beverly Street

10. **THE MANSION ON TURTLE CREEK**
    2821 Turtle Creek Boulevard

11. **THE PREMIER ATHLETIC CLUB**
    5910 North Central Expressway

DALLAS

DALLAS

Once upon a time not so very long ago it was possible to feel that Dallas was a land of enchantment. People lived it up, whooped it up, and had that J. R. Ewing larger-than-life perspective about the Longhorn State. They wore seven-league boots fashioned out of the most expensive, exotic leathers—ostrich, lizard, and eel. Then the oil business suffered, primarily affecting Houston but making Dallasites more cautious. Not so cautious, however, that they stopped building mammoth edifices—Trammel Crowe's Infomart, Rosewood's Crescent Court, and Southland's new headquarters—in addition to the underleased existing properties all over town. (The latter two, as you will see, were built in what may well be the largest excavated holes in this country.)

Today a spin through Dallas will evince a sharper dichotomy between the superrich and the middle class. It seems that almost every major office building and complex sports a "For Sale" or "For Lease" sign. Reality has dropped anchor in the real estate market, and the exhibitions of conspicuous consumption are more infrequent and less loud. The "Big D" has adopted a wait-and-see posture.

Meantime, life continues. True, SMU may not have a football team for a while, but there is still a quiet exuberance to this southwestern capital.

One can also find old-time religion here. If Dallas isn't the buckle of the Bible belt, it's at least one of the holes. There seem to be great extremes here; the devout and the good ol' boys and their gals lead lives that point them down separate paths. For the religiously inclined, Bible groups are the linchpins of their agendas. They may be sponsored by their offices or their churches, or formed by flocks of friends. For those of divergent interests and deep pockets, champagne may be the nectar of choice. Their Dallas might be called "Sodom," and they rely on specialists like *the* architect, *the* party planner, *the* florist, and so on to handle all the details of their decadence.

BEST NEIGHBORHOODS WITH DECENT PUBLIC SCHOOLS: Park Cities, Richardson

NICEST NEIGHBORHOOD (BUT YOU'LL PROBABLY HAVE TO SEND YOUR KIDS TO PRIVATE SCHOOL): North Dallas

BEST PLACE TO LIVE IF YOU'RE AN ASPIRING ARTIST OR YOU WANT TO LIVE NEAR PEOPLE WHO WEAR ONLY BLACK: Deep Ellum

BEST NEIGHBORHOODS WITH TAKE-OUT FOOD AND SINGLE PEOPLE WHO ARE ALSO REPUBLI-CANS: Inwood/Lovers Lane, Lower Greenville

MOST OVERPRICED COMMUNITY FOR SUMMER HOMES: Lakeway

BEST PUBLIC SCHOOLS: Highland Park, Richardson High School

BEST PRIVATE SCHOOLS: Hockaday (for girls); St. Mark's (for boys); Greenhill

BEST ALTERNATIVE SCHOOLS: The Episcopal School of Dallas; DISD (Dallas Independent School District) Magnet Schools

ARCHITECT WHO HAS MOST INFLUENCED THE CITY'S SKYLINE: Philip Johnson

SOCIALLY INCLINED REALTORS: Ellen Terry, Abio & Adleta, Allie Beth Allman

DECORATORS WHO WOULD DECORATE HOMES PURCHASED THROUGH THAT REALTOR: Tricia Wilson, Marilyn Rolnick

DEALERS IN THE FINEST, MOST VALUABLE ART: Crescent Galleries (Cresent Court Hotel)

MOST EXCLUSIVE GOLF CLUBS: Dallas Country Club, Brookhollow Country Club, Northwood Country Club, Preston Trails (doesn't allow women)

BEST PUBLIC GOLF FACILITY: Bear Creek

MOST EXPENSIVE HEALTH CLUB: Spa (Hotel Crescent Court)

MOST SERIOUS HEALTH CLUB: The Copper Clinic (credited with popularizing aerobics.)

BEST HEALTH CLUBS FOR MEETING POTENTIAL MATES: International Athletic Club, The Premier Club

BEST HOTELS FOR BUSINESS TRIPS: Mansion on Turtle Creek, Crescent, Loewe's Anatole

BEST HOTELS FOR TRYSTS: Crescent, any Holiday Inn

RESTAURANTS KNOWN FOR BEST CUISINE: Mansion on Turtle Creek, Routh Street Café, San Simeon, Riviera

BEST RESTAURANTS FOR PEOPLE WHO WEAR BLACK: Café Margaux, Nero's, Sfuzzi, The Hard Rock Café

BEST RESTAURANTS FOR AN INEXPENSIVE DATE: Massimo's, Houston's, Chiquita's

NOISIEST RESTAURANT (INTIMACY IMPOSSIBLE): Dakota's

BEST SPORTS BAR: Humperdink's

BEST DARK BAR: Dave & Buster's

BEST GIMMICKY BAR: The Palm

BEST BARS TO IMPRESS A CLIENT: Bar at the Mansion, Beau Nash (Crescent Hotel)

MOST EXCLUSIVE CITY CLUBS: Dallas Club, Tower Club, Petroleum Club

FANCIEST WINE STORE WHENCE CEOS PROBABLY STOCK THEIR OWN CELLARS: Marty's

GOURMET STORES GUARANTEED NOT TO RUN OUT OF GOAT CHEESE OR SUN-DRIED TOMA-TOES: Simon David, Marty's

LARGEST DRUGSTORE WITH MOST REMARKABLE SELECTION: Page Drugs

HIGH-SOCIETY PARTY PLANNERS: Ann Draper; Wendy Moss and Mark Seale

POWER HAIR: The Phoenix

JUNIOR LEAGUE BEAUTY PARLOR: Paul Neinast

PLACES WHERE LADIES WHO LUNCH ARE LIKELY TO HAVE TEA AFTER A HARD DAY OF SHOPPING, VOLUNTEER WORK, AND TENNIS: Mansion on Turtle Creek, Adolphus Hotel

BEST STORE FOR EXECUTIVE WOMEN: Mark Shale

BEST STORES FOR EXECUTIVE MEN: Culwell & Sons, Marvin Brown

BEST STORES FOR DRESS-UP CLOTHES: Gazebo (for women), Loretta Blum (for women), Lou Lattimore (for women), Neiman-Marcus (for men)

BEST SHOPPING RESOURCE FOR PEOPLE WHO WEAR ONLY BLACK CLOTHES: The Gazebo

DEBUTANTE BALL: Idlewild

BUSIEST SOCIAL SEASON OF THE YEAR FOR THOSE WHO CARE ABOUT SUCH THINGS: Fall

SOCIAL HIGHLIGHT: Crystal Charity Ball

MOST RELIABLE FLORIST: Carren's

MOST EXOTIC FLORIST: The Potted Palm, Zen

TOP JEWELER FOR RESETTING MOTHER'S EMERALDS: Bachendorf's

MOST COMPLETE BRIDAL REGISTRY: Neiman-Marcus

PROMINENT PLASTIC SURGEON WITH EQUALLY PROMINENT CLIENTELE: Dr. Mark Lemon

PSYCHIATRIST MOST OFTEN QUOTED IN THE LOCAL PRESS: Dr. Kenneth Altshuler

POPULAR FACIAL SALON: Elizabeth Arden

POWER TOOLS

MEN'S POWER DRESSING

BROOKS BROTHERS
201 Field Street
Dallas, TX 75270
(214) 748-4700

BEST-SELLING EXECUTIVE SUIT: Three-button, tropical weight, navy or gray, 100 percent wool, $425

POWER SHIRT: Pinpoint oxford button-down, white, 100 percent cotton, $50

POWER TIE: Foulard, burgundy, 100 percent silk, $25

POWER EATING

BEAU NASH at the Crescent Hotel
400 Crescent Court
Dallas, TX 75201
(214) 871-5186

The Beau Nash, among the toniest eateries in Dallas, is located in the Crescent Hotel, one of the holdings of the Rosewood Hotel Corporation (see p. 192). Like everything else that bears the stamp of Caroline Rose Hunt, the restaurant offers the best that money can buy. According to Donna Derryberry, the Beau Nash's public relations coordinator, "We use only fresh ingredients—we don't even have a freezer except for the sorbets. And all our meat is approved by the American Heart Association as it has twenty-five percent less cholesterol."

EXECUTIVE BREAKFAST: "One of our most popular items is homemade granola with Texas honey," $4.25; $3.50 extra for a bowl of fresh fruit with it.
"The poached eggs benedict with grilled chicken breast is also a big hit." (Poached eggs, grilled chicken breast, and Canadian bacon on an English muffin with a tomato herb hollandaise sauce, served with fresh raspberries and blueberries), $7.50.
"We have our own bakery and bake fresh warm muffins, breads, and Danish for breakfast. We're so health-conscious here in Dallas and work out so much, we can eat whatever we like."

EXECUTIVE LUNCH: "For lunch, we have three very popular items":
Crescent cobb salad (iceberg and radicchio with eggs, apple-smoked bacon, avocado, tomato, light Dijon mustard vinaigrette), $8.95
Grilled pineapple and chicken salad with honey mustard dressing and toasted macadamia nuts, $9.25
Special house pizza (with smoked salmon, caviar, and sour cream), $10.95

ON EXECUTIVES' LUNCHTIME DRINKING HABITS: "They wait until the cocktail hour. We sell a lot of iced passion fruit tea. Concocted by our chef, it is made of passion fruit, orange juice, and lemon juice concentrates mixed with passion fruit tea" ($2.00).

PROMINENT CLIENTELE: "In the Crescent Hotel complex is an office tower, shops, and a gallery. Tenants in the office tower include Goldman Sachs, Smith Barney, and Tracy Locke. All of their executives frequent the Beau Nash. Plus we are popular with the downtown Dallas crowd."

POWER WATCHES

RICHARD EISEMAN JEWELS at Frost Brothers
P.O. Box 31187   330 N. Park Center
Dallas, TX 75231   Dallas, TX 75225
(214) 369-7300

BEST SELLER AMONG EXECUTIVE MEN: Ebel Beluga, $4,250–$11,000; eighteen-karat, yellow gold watch, leather strap with a deployant buckle (all in one piece, like a bracelet watch with a leather strap), date, and a variety of unusual dials from white with gold Roman numerals to a deep blue dial with cabochon sapphires.

Audemars-Piquet, $16,000; Perpetual Calendar Strap Watch, eighteen-karat gold, entirely hand-made, with month and year (self-correcting for leap years until 2011) and a crocodile strap.

BEST SELLER AMONG EXECUTIVE WOMEN: Lady's gold bracelet Beluga, $8,000; mate to the gentlemen's watch, except with an eighteen-karat gold bracelet, no date, no second hand.

Mini, $3,300; eighteen-karat, yellow gold and stainless steel bracelet watch with a diamond bezel and a diamond dial. No day, no date, very feminine, yet it's "a sports watch that doesn't look like a sports watch, made for a very active, on-the-go person."

Richard Eiseman Jr., elaborates:
"The women executives definitely buy the watches for themselves—they're decision makers, and they enjoy making the decision on a watch. It's a personal signature. On the other hand, women enjoy giving gifts to men, and there is a very limited amount of jewelry a man enjoys receiving. One of those things is a watch. We have more women who give men watches than men who give them to women. About fifty percent of our male executive clients buy watches for themselves, and about fifty percent get them as gifts from women.
"Most of our male clients own more than one watch, though we have a whole range—from someone buying his first fine watch, to men who are adding to their collection who might have five, ten, twenty. One of our clients, who enjoys collecting special timepieces, owns in excess of one hundred. Most of our female executive clients also own more than one watch. Women will have a dressy evening watch, a work watch, and a sporty watch—a minimum of three. If she's very fashion-conscious, she might have a watch with a pearl bracelet because she accessorizes a lot and wants a pearl watch to go with the pearl jewelry in her collection. We always suggest that women buy a handsome diamond bracelet as a 'must' accessory to a fine lady's timepiece. A lot of women take us up on the suggestion."

POWER INTERIOR DESIGN

TRICIA WILSON
3811 Turtle Creek Boulevard, Suit 1500
Dallas, TX 75219
(214) 521-6753

Tricia Wilson, cited in the *Going to Work* survey as one of the best known interior decorators in Dallas, is well versed in designing the executive home. "People rely on our reputation and hire us accordingly." Her clientele is primarily comprised of "older, wealthy" types who "want the best of everything." However, "We work with any budget and any size job to accommodate our client's needs." We spoke to Ms. Wilson's public relations representative, Connie Campbell, who offered some observations on the homes and decorating habits of the firm's executive clients.

IS THERE ANY PARTICULAR STYLE OF INTERIOR DESIGN THAT YOUR EXECUTIVE CLIENTS SEEM TO PREFER?
   "We can design for any market taste in upper-end homes, hotels, and resorts. Taste levels in the residential market run the gamut from very contemporary to very traditional. However, the majority of [executive] residential clients tend toward traditional."

WHAT'S THE SIZE OF THE AVERAGE DALLAS EXECUTIVE HOME?
   "Mansions."

DO EXECUTIVES GENERALLY WANT MORE OR LESS INPUT INTO THEIR INTERIOR DESIGN THAN NONEXECUTIVE CLIENTS?
   "It varies. Each client is different—some leave it totally up to Tricia, others want to be personally involved in every single choice."

DO EXECUTIVE CLIENTS HAVE TRICIA WILSON PICK OUT THEIR ARTWORKS?
   "The majority look to the designer for input, unlike New York clients. Many people like Tricia and trust her judgment to help them choose artworks."

DO EXECUTIVE CLIENTS SEEM OUT TO IMPRESS WHEN CHOOSING THE DECOR FOR THEIR HOMES?
   "Yes. Especially in Dallas, where you show all you have. It's very important to have the best, even if it means purchasing less."

POWER HAIR

THE PHOENIX
5600 West Lovers Lane
Dallas, TX 75209
(214) 352-8411

The Phoenix, with eighteen hairdressers, eight manicurists, a facial department, a makeup department, and a pedicurist, is the salon of choice for many Dallas executives. We interviewed William James Canoway—who goes by the name of Bill James professionally—one of the Phoenix's top haircutters, about his executive clientele:

ON TRENDS IN EXECUTIVE HAIR: "I think most executives keep a style for one or two years. Styles tend to last that long. Right now, women are choosing a kind of loose curl—a casual style. Shoulder-length hair is very fashionable at this time. We like to give executive women a hand-dried look—we blow the hair on low heat and create a sort of messy look."

ON PERMS: "You definitely need a perm for this look. Not a tight perm—that was popular a few years ago—but something more than a body wave. Basically, the current shoulder-length, loose curl style is an evolution from the bob. Women have let their bobs grow out, added a perm, and created a longer, softer, more casual but manageable look."

ON COLORING: "Very few women or men can carry off gray hair. If you are very beautiful and have beautiful hair, then sure, keep it, but for most clients I recommend coloring. We mainly highlight hair, no drastic color change, but add a light gold brown to brown hair, covering the gray with a permanent dye. This will have to be touched up every five to six weeks or so."

ON BALDING: "I recommend Monoxidil, by Upjohn. It is the only product on the market that is FDA-approved, the only product that is allowed to advertise worldwide to actually grow hair. It's prescription-only, so you have to go to a dermatologist to get a prescription. It actually does work. They discovered it five or six years ago in a medication for high blood pressure. They found that women who were using it were growing hair on their faces and chests. So they created a liquid from it that you use externally."

ON FACIAL HAIR: "Facial hair is not very popular anymore. Beards are not acceptable for executives, but mustaches are still quite popular."

ON EXECUTIVE MANNERS: "They have less time because they have very busy schedules, and their time is more valuable, but they must maintain their appearance. They tend to keep more regular appointments than nonexecutive clients."

ON NETWORKING IN THE SALON: "Not really. We do get a lot of top oil executives, so sure, if two of them are sitting side by side in the salon, they will talk shop. People always talk shop."

PROMINENT CLIENTS: "Victoria Principal comes in for manicures, and we have many top oil executives. This is Dallas. Our salon is located in a very prestigious area, and our clients tend to be the cream of the crop in their professions."

FEES:
Haircut, $30 average
Set or blow-dry, $20
Average haircut with set and blow-dry, $50
Permanents, $100
Highlighting, $100
Coloring (mostly highlighting), $100
Manicure, $15
Pedicure, $30

Hours: Monday to Saturday, 8:30 A.M. to 6:00 P.M. Open till 9:00 p.m. Wednesday and Thursday

POWER PARTY PLANNERS

AN AFFAIR TO REMEMBER, INC.
4707 Wildwood Road
Dallas, Texas 75209
(214) 357-0013, 357-5401

Whether referred to as An Affair to Remember or simply Wendy Moss, the producer of some of the most lavish parties *Going to Work* has ever heard of, the party planner is a Dallas institution. Wendy Moss is gaining a national reputation for sparing no detail or expense to create the most memorable and original events. We talked to Mark Seal, who is Wendy Moss's partner and husband.

The business was started in 1979, when Wendy, daughter of actress Jane Withers, was flown to Acapulco by a friend, for her thirtieth birthday. Wendy wanted to reciprocate. She did, and soon people started calling her to choreograph her brand of entertaining extravagance for them. "Most of the time our clients want us to dream for them," Seal says, although "we don't insist on creative control." An Affair to Remember will not, however, do "cookie cutter weddings"; only a wedding they determine will be unique. "Once we get involved, it's our whole life. We come in with actual blueprint renderings," he adds, demonstrating the seriousness of the operations. An Affair to Remember stores props, dance floors, furniture, costumes, pianos, etc., in its 20,000-square-foot scenery shop. With a full-time staff of ten and freelance magicians, "Wendy pushes everyone to their limits."

"Our style is Texas extravagance, which we can import anywhere." Besides, "a lot of times Texas is not that different. The wealthy are still willing to go the extra distance," Mark says, even of the postcrash days. They've been so busy that "we've been trying to take a rest . . . for eight years." The company works for individuals and corporate clients.

Memorable past events:

"We did a debutante party in 1983—a good year for Texas—for two sisters from Fort Worth. The theme was 'A Walk Down Route 66.' The invitation was a record album cover with a photograph of the girls sitting in a '56 T-bird, drinking Dom Perignon on Route 66. There was a black market for those invitations." Wendy and her team of experts converted the Ridgely Country Club into Route 66 and its various intersections. Guests arrived in "Chicago" and walked down a lit "highway" from the Windy City to Los Angeles. En route, the food and drink represented the various regions Route 66 travels. The party featured ten bands and James Brown. Mark will only say that this deb party cost "several hundreds of thousands of dollars."

A Dallas banker and his wife wanted to throw themselves a fiftieth wedding anniversary party. They had been married in a cathedral in Acapulco. Naturally, Wendy and team traveled to Mexico to take notes. The couple were knocked out when they showed up at the Fairmont Hotel in downtown Dallas on the appointed evening. Moss et al. had literally re-created the cathedral in the hotel, with a green marble dance floor, palm trees—and "none of the bad stuff of Acapulco."

Fifteen hundred guests attended the world premier of *Benji the Hunted,* the Disney movie made produced and directed by Dallasite Joe Camp. Wendy read the shooting script while in hospital, recovering from back surgery. Since the movie is set in the Oregon woods, she put up 27,000 square feet of tents, filling them with "bark mulch, thousands of flowers and trees, with a trail of Benji's footprints. Benji was there, too."

FEES: Wendy Moss's minimum consultation fee is $150 an hour. Minimum all-inclusive cost for a party: $10,000.

GINNIE JOHANSEN DESIGNS, INC.

GINNIE JOHANSEN DESIGNS, INC.

GINNIE JOHANSEN DESIGNS, INC.

HISTORY & OPERATIONS

Ginnie Johansen Designs Inc., was founded in 1978 on the basis of a single fashion accessory designed by an eighteen-year-old college freshman. In her first year at Sophie Newcomb College in New Orleans, Ginnie Johansen needed a belt to match her khaki slacks and pink Izod shirt. After failing to find what she wanted in the stores, she bought some ribbon and a buckle, pieced together a webbed belt on the sewing machine in her Dallas home, and fitted it with a Velcro closure that made it one size fits all. When her college friends admired the belt's design, Johansen figured she had a potential business.

Viewing the venture as a summer job, Ginnie set about making a number of belts in a wide range of colors. But she soon realized it was too much for her to do alone. She approached her father, Gerry Johansen, who had recently become a management consultant after years as a top corporate executive, and he suggested that she test the market outside of Dallas. Ginnie took sample belts to stores in Austin, San Antonio, and Waco. When she came home with $1,500 in orders, her father started taking her business idea seriously and arranged a meeting with a manufacturer.

Ginnie and her father drew up a business plan and each contributed $12,000—Ginnie's portion came from her college trust fund—to start a company. Within six weeks after Ginnie made the original belt, Ginnie Johansen, Inc.—the company was renamed Ginnie Johansen Designs, Inc., in 1987 to emphasize that it's a design firm—had telephone orders from stores in twenty-three states. (Ginnie did not return to New Orleans the following September.) Instead she concentrated on the creative end of her new company, gradually learning the business side from her father. In 1979 annual sales were $350,000.

The Johansens soon expanded the company's belt line to encompass a full line of "better" women's accessories, including more belts, scarves, and other types of neckwear. In 1980 annual revenues jumped to $1.7 million, and they've continued to increase every year since.

By 1981, Ginnie and Gerry Johansen were running a $3 million company with a base of 1,800 specialty store accounts and twenty-five employees, most of whom were women in their early twenties with backgrounds similar to Ginnie's. In 1982 sales increased to $6 million, in 1983 they were at $7.2 million, and in 1984, after an unsuccessful experiment in dress manufacturing, they again increased to $9.2 million. By the age of twenty-four, Ginnie, as president of her own company, was earning a salary of over $100,000 per year. That same year, President Reagan selected Ginnie Johansen, Inc., as one of three small companies that exemplified the entrepreneurial spirit of America.

In 1985 Chuck Griffin, who had twenty-five years of executive retail experience, was hired as president of the company with a partial ownership stake. Ginnie became chairman of the board and Gerry remained as chief executive officer. That year, Ginnie Johansen, Inc., launched a full line of jewelry and a signature cologne, Ginnie Johansen, which the company positioned as a "liquid accessory" to be sold with other Ginnie Johansen accessories rather than at fragrance counters. In 1985 sales reached $10 million and the company's staff doubled from fifty to a hundred employees.

Ginnie Johansen Designs has flourished in part because the company was fortuitously launched at the beginning of the women's accessories boom, and in part because of its unique marketing strategy. Unlike most accessory manufacturers—which use free-lance sales representatives—the company hires its own sales reps on an exclusive basis. And instead of going after large department store accounts, the sales team approaches small to medium-sized better specialty stores and specialty department stores like Mark Shale, Hartmarx Specialty Stores, and Nordstrom's boutique for executive women called "Tailored Woman." In addition, the company has a policy of communicating directly with the stores' salesclerks—who are responsible for pushing merchandise—by means of quarterly newsletters and regularly updated brochures that illustrate various ways to tie a Ginnie Johansen scarf. (These are sold to retailers for fifteen cents apiece and then given away free to customers who make significant purchases.) In order to make the Ginnie Johansen line stand out, the company designs its own display units and sells them to stores at cost. This way the merchandise doesn't compete in cases and racks with other lines.

Today Ginnie Johansen (now Mrs. Wayne Johnson) works only part time in order to spend time raising her two young daughters. The company employs approximately 150 staffers, counting on-site people, a twenty-seven woman sales force (plus three additional floating sales reps called "reps at large"), and about thirty-five people who are employed at the company's Dallas manufacturing plant, which makes roughly 30–33 percent of Ginnie Johansen products. (Fabrics are designed by the company's design team and are woven or silkscreened in Italy or the Orient, while the accessories are all manufactured in the United States.)

In 1987 Ginnie Johansen Designs launched a scented body lotion, along with a new line of hair accessories and belts for "large-sized ladies." The company also launched a line of scarves called The Gallery Collection, which are inspired by works of art. In 1987 revenues reached

$16 million. The company is privately held by Ginnie and Gerry Johansen and Chuck Griffin, and there are no current plans to go public.

(Information provided by Kathi Johnson, company spokesperson.)

REVENUES: $16 million in 1987.

EARNINGS: Firm is private and will not disclose.

ACCOUNTS: Approximately 1,900 specialty stores and specialty boutiques within department stores throughout the fifty states.

NUMBER OF EMPLOYEES: Approximately 150.

DEMOGRAPHICS OF EMPLOYEES: Ninety percent are women, and 70–75 percent are under the age of thirty.

TURNOVER: Negligible.

RECRUITMENT: None.

NUMBER OF NEW HIRES PER YEAR: Average of ten since 1985, when staff doubled from fifty to a hundred.

RANGE OF STARTING SALARIES: $13,000–$17,000 per year.

POLICY FOR RAISES: Every six months, managers conduct a performance review with their employees. In preparation for that review, employees fill out forms on which they evaluate their own strengths and weaknesses, discuss those areas they would like to develop, evaluate their relationships with their managers, make suggestions for the benefit and growth of the company, and set long-term goals for themselves. This form serves as the basis for discussion between employees and their managers. Reviews take place in July and December, and raises are typically awarded in December on the basis of the company's success as well as an individual employee's performance. It is possible for an employee who has performed sensationally to get a raise twice in a single year, and it is also possible for an employee not to get an annual raise.

TRAINING PROGRAMS: Sales representatives—who work exclusively for Ginnie Johansen and are paid both salary and commission—are expected to know much more about the line than is generally the case for reps at other companies (most of whom sell more than one line). New reps go through a two-week program that teaches them everything from how to fill out an order form to how to tie the scarves and how to promote the line. Though this is the only formalized training program, the company offers ongoing training to people at all levels of management through guest speakers, videotapes, and regular training with outside management consultants and psychologists.

BENEFITS: Medical and dental insurance, both of which are contributory (dependent coverage is available at extra cost), life insurance in the amount of an employee's annual salary, long-term disability, tuition reimbursement of 50 percent of the cost of any course that relates directly to an employee's career, and generous paid maternity leave, the amount of which depends on an employee's tenure with the company. The company is looking into HMOs (which are currently an option on the dental insurance), and plans for a day care program are also in the works.

VACATION: Two weeks after one year, three weeks after five years, plus nine regular paid holidays. The company closes down during the week between Christmas and New Year's. There are two paid holidays during that week, and employees are expected either to take part of their vacation time to cover the other three days or to take the days off unpaid.

ADDITIONAL PERKS: All employees are offered a discount of 40 percent off wholesale on all Ginnie Johansen products.

BONUSES: Awarded on the basis of merit; all employees are eligible. The size of bonuses depends on how well the company is doing.

ANNUAL PARTIES: The company hosts two major parties in conjunction with their launching of the spring and fall lines in March and October. The parties are for everyone in the company and their spouses or guests and consist of a fashion show, cocktails, hors d'oeuvres, and entertainment. In addition, the company throws less formal pot luck or catered parties at Thanksgiving, Christmas, Halloween (everyone dresses up and a prize is given for the best costume), and Valentine's Day (when they vote for "Sweetheart of the Year," who wins a gift certificate for Ginnie Johansen products). On the day Ginnie's first baby was born, Gerry Johansen brought cases of champagne into the office and everyone quit early to celebrate. And on an employee's fifth anniversary with the company, they'll throw a small afternoon party with wine and cake.

AVERAGE WORKDAY: 8:30 A.M. to 5:30 P.M. When deadlines are imminent, people will come in early, stay late, and work weekends.

DRESS CODE: The dress is "very fashionable, but very informal and relaxed." Other than for those in shipping, the line is drawn at jeans. Employees who come into contact with the public are required to wear Ginnie Johansen accessories, and all other employees are encouraged to wear them.

SOCIAL ATMOSPHERE: The environment is very familylike, and "the company is interested in employees as people, not just workers." Many people socialize with one another on the outside.

BIGGEST SELLER: Scarves, which account for about 35 percent of sales.

RETAIL PRICE RANGES: Scarves $22–$75; belts $22–$68; jewelry $12–$55; fragrance $14–$25; hair accessories $6–$30.

MAJOR ACCOUNTS: Nordstrom's, Mark Shale, Hartmarx, She.

HEADQUARTERS: Ginnie Johansen Designs, Inc., is headquartered in a single-story facility in the Market District of Dallas. The company occupies 45,000 square feet of space, including a receiving dock. The whole operation is housed in that building, with the exception of a manufacturing plant (where the company makes between 30 and 33 percent of its products) which is also located in Dallas.

CHARITABLE CONTRIBUTIONS: In 1987 the company donated approximately $300,000 in cash and products. Corporate donations accounted for about $150,000 of that, with the majority going to Dallas organizations supporting civic and artistic causes. In addition, Ginnie Johansen Designs, Inc., donated another $150,000 in accessories through each of its approximately 1,900 accounts around the country. The company invites its retailers to donate accessories to the charities of their choice. The contribution is announced in a press release, which is sent to local newspapers, and Ginnie Johansen Designs shares credit for the gift. The accessories are either surplus or "distressed" goods rather than current merchandise. Also, the company participates in the Dallas United Way through employee donations (or payroll deduction). In 1988 approximately 88 percent of Ginnie Johansen employees are contributing to the Dallas United Way.

INTERESTED APPLICANTS CAN SEND RÉSUMÉS TO:
Ginnie Johansen Designs, Inc.
Personnel Department
1365 Regal Row
Dallas, TX 75247
(214) 631-1180

The story of the evolution of Ginnie Johansen's company is as mythologized for employees as the story of how Mommy and Daddy first met. Part of believing in the company is a familiarity with the Johansen family and, even more, a sense of belonging to it.

Ginnie Johansen, a tall, vivacious brunette from Highland Park—Dallas's premier residential area—set off to New Orleans in the fall of 1978 to become a freshman at Sophie Newcomb College, Tulane's sister school. She didn't like it. She recalls verbatim the letter she wrote her parents that spring: "Dear Mom and Dad, I don't really like this school and I want to come home to Dallas and work in the fashion industry in Dallas, the fashion capital of the Southwest."

One of the factors contributing to Ginnie's disenchantment was the lack of good accessories in New Orleans. She had a favorite webbed belt that she wore out during that fateful freshman year, and she was unable to replace it. As legend has it, the following summer she constructed a crude version of the belt, using a Velcro fastener, which she and her sister Jane schlepped around to women's specialty shops in Waco, Austin, San Antonio, and Dallas. They returned with $1,500 in orders and a business. (Ginnie never returned to Sophie Newcomb, but did enroll for a time at Southern Methodist University.)

Walk into corporate headquarters ten years later, and you'd be surprised to see such well-dressed and authoritatively accessorized businesspeople working in such plain surroundings. Though they will have moved by publication time into one large but homely building, the genteel people who work here look like it might be accidental—their offices were situated in a trio of barrackslike buildings you could imagine a young lieutenant's wife decorating with bright colors. Not to mention that such well-dressed young women—the average age of design staff is twenty-eight—work at all. They don't look as if they have to.

Ginnie is a pious Christian. She attributes much of her success to her faith. "I don't use finances as the barometer of my success, although I am well off," she says. "My barometer is my relationship with God, being a good Christian woman." Now that Ginnie can add "mother" to her list of accomplishments, she works part time, a minimum of two days a week at the office and in fact will be a less influential spirit than she was in the first pioneering years of her company. Yet the division leaders, who were hired when she was dominant, carry her sensibilities about them like a silk scarf. (Scarves make up 35 percent— the largest share—of Ginnie Johansen's business.) Being born again is most certainly not required of new employees, though there is something quietly Christian that permeates the atmosphere. Perhaps "Christian" is not the proper word. Yet in moments of frustration four-letter words would be inappropriate; something along the lines of "Jiminy Cricket" or "Darn it!" might be better. There is no pressure to join Ginnie's "yuppie Bible study group," no real proselytizing, but proximity to someone of such extreme piety might encourage colleagues to give religion a thought now and then. "I have religious convictions," one employee confesses, "but they're private." During a meeting with an adviser, Ginnie interrupted her train of thought with a reminder. "I took the liberty of titling your talk to our study group next week," she told him. "I've called it 'Death to Life; Soul to Jesus.' " Then it was back to business.

Several of the most senior employees were sorority sisters of Ginnie's when she transferred to Southern Methodist University. Laura Koenig Young is the senior vice-president of sales and merchandising. She graduated from Southern Methodist University in 1980 with a degree in business and marketing. While interviewing for jobs in Dallas the following fall, she ran into Ginnie at a surprise party. "We were both Kappas," she recalls, "and she asked me what I wanted to do." Ginnie asked Laura to send her father, Gerry, a copy of her résumé.

"Gerry called me at home at ten A.M. on a Saturday and asked me to meet him for brunch at eleven-thirty. I met him at the office and drove him to the airport. I had a wedding to go to at one, so I was all dressed up." Six years later, a very pregnant Young reminisced about her first year at Ginnie Johansen. "There were only about ten people here when I started; I don't know what they called my first job. I had to solicit orders over the telephone. It wasn't easy, though most people had seen the product. The belt." The following year Laura was one of three sales representatives for the Southwest. She had to travel four or five days a week, fifty weeks per year, and then have a sales meeting every Friday or Saturday with Gerry. She was traveling to Fort Worth, Waco, Austin, Houston, and East Texas by car, and she was involved with a man—the fellow she later married. "When I look for sales reps, " she says, "one of the things I like is when they have a nice relationship so they're not anxious about when they leave town. When some of the girls have left it's been because of men."

When Laura was promoted, she was able to hire an ex-roommate, who is still with the company. "Now we have our own sales force of thirty full-time employees, three of which are sales reps-at-large. Most are under thirty-two years old. And of all of them are women." Although she is charged with the ability to "hire, fire, whatever," Laura doesn't spend time thinking about her "power." "I don't feel anything—it's just the way it is. After a couple of years there was no doubt in my mind that this wasn't going to be my career. I consider myself an executive in an entrepreneurial environment." Laura Young was planning to lead the national sales meeting three weeks after her baby was due. "Women here make a tremendous difference. A woman salesperson is a walking model for us. I mean, if you've got on gorgeous earrings, scarf, belt, et cetera . . . And most of the buyers are women."

The women of Ginnie Johansen work together happily and well. There are moments when it's surprising no one is humming—the same tune. "Ginnie and I were classmates at Highland Park High School," says Tricia Mattil, the marketing vice-president—a chic, attractive twenty-nine-year-old. "We ran into each other at a party in 1981. She interviewed me a few months later, and I started the following spring." Tricia's previous experience had been in department store retailing. She was disappointed with all the time spent on the phone; she had thought retailing was a good "people" business. She wanted something smaller.

"I saw this as a young, small company that had unbelievable potential. I could see it in front of my eyes. I liked the people: They were personable and motivated. We had similar backgrounds. We worked hard but had fun."

Satisfaction (with the company) could be the name of the tune issuing forth from the well-made-up lips of the Ginnie Johansen team. "This is my standard for what a business should be. This is all I know. When I hire new people, they can't believe it." While Ginnie Johansen employees regard one another as "good friends," socializing after work is up to individuals and not a strict aspect of the culture. Now with about a hundred fifty employees, it still feels like the small family business it was ten years ago.

Ms. Young tries to think of any casualties. "There were two little girls on the West Coast. They were rebels and left Ginnie Johansen. Later they called to say they loved it and appreciated the training they got here."

"I'd heard Mr. Johansen was so tough that I'd never have any time for myself or any privacy," one veteran recounts. "People who are happy here put high standards on themselves. The expectation is that you will determine your goals. We know where the company is going, and it's up to you to figure out your place in that." You get the feeling that these were the kind of well-organized sorority sisters who actually began working on term papers the week they were assigned. Their reliance on their looks belies that this business is made up of hard work, not frivolity.

"We don't take any runaround. We are direct. That doesn't mean feelings don't get hurt at times," one contented employee says. Because this is a fairly homogeneous environment, the atmosphere is informal—we're talking about a building on the outer perimeter of Dallas, after all. "We try to make a point of 'no Chinese walls' around here. We hope everyone feels they can speak with everyone else. You'll never hear someone say, 'That's not my job.' When you fail, you move on."

Because this is a company in a growth mode, objectives are emphasized, and employees are reviewed formally twice a year. "I try to make it a point with my girls not to wait until review time to let them know how they're doing," one manager explains. "There should be no surprises."

All this talk of "girls" and use of the feminine pronoun could result in a misunderstanding. Make no mistake; Ginnie Johansen is an equal opportunity employer: two men stand at the helm of the business.

Gerry Johansen, Ginnie's dad, had a consulting business and was chief strategist of his daughter's belt company when it looked like a part-time business. While he still holds the title of chief executive officer, Gerry is able to delegate more and work on other projects that fascinate him. Chuck Griffin, a veteran of twenty-five years in retailing, is president of Ginnie Johansen and brings with him the savvy and language of fashion, long considered one of the most competitive industries.

Both are regarded somewhat as gurus by company members. The women are deferential to them, not because of their sex, but out of respect to their experience and previous successes. Chuck regards Ginnie Johansen as a "sales and marketing company with a product, not the other way around. You can't just be a cute girl wearing the stuff and sell," he continues. "That used to work. But look around: Topsy's grown up. It happened overnight. When an account grows from $4,000 to $20,000, you've got to pay attention."

Chuck has the sunny demeanor of someone who's just experienced freedom for the first time —and loves it—in this case, escape from a rigid corporate environment. "This is so much damn fun! To hear a vendor say, 'I sold all your scarves!'"

Gerry is a philosopher, constantly conjuring up new business and philanthropic ideas. He phrases them with the eloquence of someone who gets quoted a lot. "Business is my business," he might say. "And if Ginnie wants to do it, I owe it to her to help her." Or "When people start out in business, their great strength is their ignorance. A friend told me, 'If you had grown up in the garment business, you would have failed. Your techniques would never have worked.' "

The plan is to keep Ginnie Johansen private. The first year's goal was $100,000 in sales. This was surpassed by $250,000. The following year (1980), Ginnie Johansen grossed $1.75 million. In 1986 that figure exceeded $12 million and in 1987 it reached $16 million. Not bad for belts, scarves, costume jewelry, hair accessories, and a small fragrance line. Gerry's "ballpark goal is thirty million dollars by 1991. To remain a small company, we pretty much know what we're going to do. We were initially a belt company. Then we decided to design our own fabrics and ribbons. No one told us not to."

A foray into dress manufacturing failed, thus "we never take success for granted." Ginnie Johansen's designs are available at about 1,900 "better women's" retail stores, with service the value-added component. The most popular service item is an illustrated booklet, selling to retailers for fifteen cents and distributed free to customers, that demonstrates how to tie scarves in a variety of ways. (Yes, bow ties included.) Aside from the fanatically service-minded Nordstrom's department stores, general department stores are avoided, since the Johansen philosophy is to display accessories integrated into outfits, and not just strewn about on another counter in the accessories department on the first floor of a big store. Besides, the accessories department is considered by most stores to be an entry-level selling position.

Designs of all products are divided into four categories: "Traditional Professional," "Traditional Classic," "Traditional Updated," and "Updated." Designers do what they do everywhere: they keep their eyes open, and they travel a lot, to both color and fabric workshops and manufacturers in the United States, Europe, and the Orient. Some of the products are actually manufactured by Ginnie Johansen in a small warehouse not far from the main building. There, about thirty people put belts together by hand.

One employee, who's been with the company approximately six years, her longest stint anywhere, says, "I had to adjust my attitude at first. I went through a rocky period. I had to deal with things the way they were and not the way I wanted them to be." But her point of view has rotated 360 degrees. "I have never gone out and looked for another job since I got here. What opportunities! To see it grow! It's not the garment business I'm attracted to, it's the people and my job."

Interview:

GINNIE JOHANSEN JOHNSON

*G*innie Johansen Johnson sweeps into the office on a nonoffice day with her tiny daughter, Elizabeth. She's in the rare position of "having it all," since her business can survive without her constant presence. She's on the two-day-a-week plan. Ginnie Johansen Designs, a private company making and marketing women's fashion accessories, is thriving due to the leadership of Chuck Griffin and the man Ginnie refers to as "Daddy," Gerry Johansen. Ginnie must be almost six feet tall, and she is a natural salesperson of her wares. She may dress a tad more fashion forwardly than most of her customers, but there's no reason she couldn't combine, say, a Joan Vass knitted outfit with one of her scarves and a pair of silver-toned earrings that she designed.

Ginnie seems not to be motivated by money. She grew up in a well-heeled Dallas neighborhood, and by all accounts she will profit enormously in the coming decade. She says that that hardly matters to her. What counts is being a good Christian. "I was so fortunate to know at a young age what matters. I became a Christian as a freshman in high school." A mere six weeks after she returned home from her freshman year in college, she met her future husband, Wayne, at a Kappa–Phi Delta mixer at SMU. "It all fell into place. I realized God looked out for me." When the listener expressed surprise that born-agains can meet at mixers (where alcohol is served), she replied, "This is the Bible Belt. You'd be surprised. About 60 percent of my Kappa group is Christian. Wayne became a Christian in high school through a dental hygienist in St. Louis who wrote him a five-page letter."

Responsibly, she says, "I need to stand for the company, and not everyone in the company is a Christian. I just feel like a healthy, normal person. I try not to take anyone for granted, and to hire good people who will hire other good people.

"You can be a good businessperson, but if you don't have a good personality and values, you don't stay here. Daddy and I are both part time. The company is more or less running itself. Daddy, with his wisdom, makes a significant contribution, and we're having the best year ever. At this point I feel I'm a contributor, not a leader."

Ginnie has discussed her role with Daddy and Chuck, and they have agreed that she can be most valuable in a public relations capacity. "I've had the benefit of so many business professionals. I enjoy going out there." But most important, her main focus is motherhood. "Work is an accent. I didn't realize how much my identity was wrapped up in the company. It was the Lord who allowed me to make character changes. He allowed me to become a mom," says Mrs. Johnson, who recently became a mother for the second time.

ROSEWOOD
HOTELS

ROSEWOOD

HOTELS, INC.

HISTORY & OPERATIONS

Caroline Rose Hunt, the younger daughter of the late flamboyant oil billionaire H. L. Hunt, is estimated to be worth more than $1 billion, and as such is one of the richest people in the country. (She began using her maiden name in 1987, when she separated from her husband, Hugo Schoellkopf.) Yet despite her immense wealth, she always led a low-profile life, devoting herself to the duties of raising a family, serving on various charities, and taking an active role in her church. Rosewood, the corporation formed with Mrs. Hunt's trust fund—the name of which comes from her middle name, "Rose," coupled with her affinity for nature, "wood"—and headed by her and her children, includes among its holdings an insurance company, a savings and loan company, a real estate company, a coal company, an exotic game ranch, farms, ranches, and an aircraft company. However, until fairly recently, Caroline Hunt never had much to do with the day-to-day operations of these various enterprises.

All that changed in 1979, when Rosewood purchased the Sheppard King Mansion, one of the last great mansions in Dallas, for $1.6 million. The purchase, acquired for largely sentimental reasons—the mansion was about to be razed to make room for commercial development —was originally considered just another property for the real estate company. Then Mrs. Hunt and her children decided that the mansion should be converted into a hotel, the management of which they would turn over to a large hotel group. However, the more they thought about it, the more it appealed to them to hold on to the Mansion and manage it themselves, endowing the new hotel with the Hunt stamp of quality. The family did just that, and Rosewood Hotels, a builder and acquirer of moderately sized, immoderately luxurious hotel properties, was launched.

The company hired Robert Zimmer, who had built a reputation designing luxury resorts in exotic locales—most recently in Bahrain—to head the design team for its new hotel. Zimmer became Rosewood Hotels' first employee and was eventually appointed as its president. Rosewood turned the Sheppard King Mansion into a posh, high-priced restaurant (August 1980) and built a nine-story, 143-room luxury hotel adjacent to it. It opened in February 1981. Total cost: $20 million. With a publicity campaign starring Caroline Hunt, the new Mansion on Turtle Creek was an immediate success.

Thus armed, Rosewood Hotels turned to another venture—this time built from scratch—in Houston. The Remington Hotel was launched in 1982 with a $100,000 gala that included "Twenty-Four Karat Soup" made with a sprinkling of real gold flakes. At a cost of approximately $200,000 per room, the Remington was, at the time, among the most expensive hotels ever built. (The hotel failed to prosper in the glutted Houston market, and in 1985 Rosewood sold it to the Criswell Development Company at a substantial loss. Rosewood continued to manage the Remington until the beginning of 1987, when the hotel was sold to the Southmark Corporation of Dallas.) Also in 1982, after months of tense negotiations, Rosewood won a closed bidding war against (the as yet unindicted) legendary securities wheeler-dealer Ivan Boesky and purchased the Hotel Bel-Air in California for $22,729,000, only $8,000 more than his bid. Rosewood made renovations, added new rooms (for a total of ninety-two), and relandscaped the eleven-acre property for a total cost of $36 million, and the Bel-Air, which had always had a reputation as a top-drawer hotel, thrived. It is currently Rosewood's most profitable hotel.

Rosewood next set its sights on Hawaii, and in 1984 the company purchased the Hotel Hana-Maui, located on the island of Maui and situated on a 4,500-acre ranch called the Hana Ranch. The total cost of the sixty-six-room resort, including a purchase price of $25 million and subsequent renovations, was $33.23 million. Rosewood is currently adding a health spa to the property, which will open in 1989.

Rosewood built a second luxury hotel in Dallas, the Hotel Crescent Court, within the Crescent Court complex, which was designed by architects Philip Johnson and John Burgee and completed in 1986. Another lavish gala—food provided by celebrity chefs Wolfgang (Spago) Puck and Larry (An American Place) Forgione—with a guest list of 3,700 kicked off its opening. At a cost of $293,577 per room, the Crescent was even more expensive to build than the Remington. The enormous complex includes the 218-room hotel, a nineteen-story office tower with 1.2 million square feet of space and 175,000 square feet of upscale shops, restaurants, and art galleries. The Crescent also has a European-style health club and spa, a nightclub, and a private dining club. At present, the Crescent office towers are 78 percent occupied and the rental space is 65 percent occupied.

In addition to its hotel properties, Rosewood Hotels owns ZEN Concepts, Inc., a nursery and chain of shops that was originally established as a floral design studio to provide the hotels with fresh flowers, a Rosewood trademark. ZEN grew with Rosewood, and today it not only provides all Rosewood Hotels with flowers, many of which are grown on the Hana Ranch, but it also landscapes and maintains the hotels' grounds. ZEN now has full-fledged operations in

Dallas—ZEN Dallas—and Los Angeles—ZEN Los Angeles, and Hana Tropicals at Hana Ranch—and provides services to outside clients as well.

Today Rosewood Hotels employs a staff of 1,414, including the forty-seven staff people at ZEN. The company is currently building a ninety-five-room hotel and seven-story office building in the Georgetown section of Washington, D.C., scheduled to open in early 1990. Rosewood Georgetown (the project's working name) will include twenty-one suites, a public and a private restaurant, boutiques, and a landscaped botanical conservatory linking the hotel with the office building, at a total cost of approximately $60 million. Rosewood has a seven-year, $250 million development program through which it will explore sites in New York City, Chicago, and San Francisco.

According to the Rosewood philosophy, part of building and sustaining an image as a luxury hotel requires hiring "good-looking and graceful help." Another prerequisite is offering a list of basic luxuries. Every guest who checks into a Rosewood Hotel is entitled to the following: a complimentary limousine (within a two-mile radius); a shoe shine; valet parking and a car wash; same-day pressing and laundry; terry cloth robes in each room; fancy soaps, chocolates, and mineral water; newspapers (both local and national); twenty-four-hour room service (which comes with a flower); a stereo system (only in suites); full concierge services (including getting tickets for the theater, local ball games, and the like, making reservations for guests at other hotels, or anything else a guest may require); special meals for anyone on a special diet; bedboards for people with bad backs; and airport pickup (at an extra charge). Furthermore, Rosewood keeps personal files on all "transient, corporate, and potentially returning guests" that include their company, their address, their telephone numbers, their credit card information, any special requests such as down pillows, special soap, and so on, the rates they have paid on past visits, and the rooms they have stayed in previously. These services obviously come at a cost. The nightly charge and average occupancy rate for rooms in the Rosewood hotels are: The Mansion on Turtle Creek: $160–$845, 60 percent; Hotel Bel-Air: $190–$1,500, 85.5 percent; Hotel Hana-Maui: $263–$701, 73.2 percent; and the Hotel Crescent Court: $130–$950, 55.5 percent.

(Information provided by Robert Zimmer, president and CEO, and Pat Donahoe, company spokesperson.)

REVENUES: $51 million in 1987.

EARNINGS: Information not available.

NUMBER OF EMPLOYEES: 1,414, including about thirty-five corporate employees.

AVERAGE AGE OF EMPLOYEES: Information not available.

TURNOVER: Information not available.

RECRUITMENT: "Past recruitment trips have been to Cornell University; sometimes to the Culinary Institute of America."

NUMBER OF NEW HIRES PER YEAR: No average figure. The number of hires differs according to the company's activities—such as launching a new hotel.

RANGE OF STARTING SALARIES: $20,000–$30,000 per year for beginning to middle management.

POLICY FOR RAISES: "Salary increases/performance reviews are usually done on an annual basis."

TRAINING PROGRAMS: None.

BENEFITS: Health and life insurance, dental coverage, long-term disability insurance, pension program, thrift savings plan, employee wellness program and tuition reimbursement (for two college-level courses per semester for individual classes or degree plans that contribute to an employee's "potential with the company"; in order to be reimbursed, an employee must receive a C or better for undergraduate courses and a B or better for graduate studies).

VACATION: Two weeks after one year, three weeks after five years, four weeks after ten years.

ADDITIONAL PERKS: Employee cafeterias; employee discounts at the hotels: After one year of service, employees are entitled to a 70 percent discount on retail food and beverage prices, a 40 percent merchandise discount, a 50 percent discount on ZEN floral arrangements, and a 70 percent discount on retail customer room rates. After three years of service, employees receive complimentary room accommodations up to forty nights per year and a 70 percent discount on hotel laundry, phone, and other incidentals.

BONUSES: Bonuses are awarded at the managerial level and up. Executives at the individual hotel properties receive automatic bonuses within a predetermined range. Department heads and key managers receive bonuses based on merit.

ANNUAL PARTY: Each of the hotels hosts an annual Christmas party for staff, and the company also throws employee picnics.

DRESS CODE: "Corporate: business attire; hotels: uniforms or front office appearance."

SOCIAL ATMOSPHERE: "Creative, synergistic, and high energy level."

VALUE OF ART COLLECTIONS AT HOTELS: The Mansion on Turtle Creek: $300,000; Hotel Bel-Air: $200,000; Hotel Hana-Maui: $100,000 (in process of being purchased); Hotel Crescent Court: $501,193. Name artists include David Hockney, John James Audubon, and Frederic Remington.

HEADQUARTERS: Rosewood Hotels occupies 19,000 square feet of office space on the tenth floor of the Crescent Office Towers.

CHARITABLE CONTRIBUTIONS: "$14,000 budgeted." Most of the company's large contributions come from the Rosewood Corporation rather than the hotel group. Rosewood Hotels' donations are generally in the form of weekend hotel packages and complimentary meals and are given to diverse philanthropic organizations.

INTERESTED APPLICANTS CAN SEND RÉSUMÉS TO:
Rosewood Hotels
Personnel Department
3000 Crescent Court
Dallas, TX 75201
(214) 871-5400

If you tried to imagine the kind of hotel owned by America's second richest woman (second only to her elder sister), you might imagine something reasonably close to Dallas's Mansion on Turtle Creek, Los Angeles's Hotel Bel-Air, or the Hotel Hana-Maui on the Hawaiian island of Maui. Good for you. These are lodgings of fantasy with profusions of gloriously scented exotic flowers, objets d'art you'd be proud to display in your own home, and so much marble formality, you might be tempted to dress for dinner—when you're just ordering room service. These are hotels familiar to the viewers of Robin Leach's *Lifestyles of the Rich and Famous*.

Several years ago, Caroline Rose Hunt—formerly Caroline Hunt Schoellkopf—daughter of legendary Texas oilman H. L. Hunt (and sister of the Hunt brothers, who manipulated the silver market a few years back), decided to go into the hotel business at the age of sixty, using part of what *Forbes* magazine estimates to be a $1.3 billion trust fund. It's hard to believe anyone could turn a profit on a property that cost $293,577 per room for its 218 rooms and that for its grand opening ordered $200,000 worth of flowers (not to mention caviar, champagne, etc., for 3,700 guests). But she believed, and in April 1986 she opened her new Hotel Crescent Court (and complex) a short distance from her flagship hotel, the Mansion on Turtle Creek. As has been documented many times since then, the gala Crescent and its gala celebrations happened in the midst of Dallas's serious real estate–driven financial crisis, which has, among other casualties, left the occupancy rate at local hotels at approximately 58 percent.

Nevertheless, Rosewood Hotels, a division of Rosewood Properties, is a bottom line business.

Robert Zimmer, the first employee of Rosewood, is also the company's president and CEO. A graduate of the Hyatt, Hilton, and Regent hotels with eight years in southeast Asia to his credit, he was interviewed by Mrs. Hunt's family at the Dallas Country Club in February 1979 and hired on the spot. His mandate was to build—if you will excuse the expression—luxury hotels. "I hate the word 'luxury,' " he says over a four-star breakfast at the Mansion, "and I never use the word." Zimmer prefers "Understated. Balance. Panache. Style. Proportion. Grace." He gestures around the elegant dining room. "Look at this hotel; nothing shouts at you." Indeed, were it not for a few hearty businessmen enjoying their fresh-squeezed grapefruit juice, exquisitely presented berries, and flapjacks and sausage, you would feel squeamish about raising your voice above a whisper.

"People think of this company as a whim of a billionaire. They don't understand. We're a profit-making center." Nevertheless, Rosewood's goal is not to be the biggest, it's to be the best. Since 1980 the company has established the Mansion, the Crescent Court, and the Remington and has purchased and renovated the Bel-Air and the Hotel Hana-Maui. (It has since sold the Remington.) Situated on prime waterfront property in the Georgetown section of Washington, D.C., Rosewood Georgetown (working name) is scheduled to open in early 1990, and Chicago, New York City, and San Francisco are also on the hit list.

Hotels allowed to use the label "luxe" can be categorized comme ça: No more than 150 rooms, a high staff-to-guest ratio, an amenities package (at the Crescent Court, that means Chanel products), high-quality phone service, concierge service, room upkeep, and, in general, high standards of service. (Technically, the Hotel Crescent Court, at 218 rooms, is classified as a "deluxe corporate hotel.") Some Rosewood signature services: All laundry is delivered packaged in pretty wicker trays, looking like gifts of gourmet foods. Extra boxes of tissues and rolls of toilet tissue are stashed away in closets, gift-wrapped in paper and ribbon (I swear). [Author's note: It's always disappointing to realize that this is just—after all—waste paper. I always get carried away and hope the last visiting billionaire left a little something by accident, which he'd want me to keep since I was so honest and sweet.]

The Mansion was a clear success from the beginning. With kingly beginnings (the shell was originally the Sheppard King mansion), it has 129 guest rooms and 14 suites. It is no accident that European-born and -trained managing directors run Rosewood's hotels. At the Mansion, the man in charge at the time of my visit is Alexander de Toth. [Author's note: The new managing director is Atef Mankarios. Alexander de Toth is now running the Remington.] His staff—his "trademark"—is characterized by exceptionally pleasant young people who appear to be and are, in his words, "from good families. They know how to behave. What we look for in hires are not hotel alumni but college graduates or people with people contacts. They're young, naturally friendly, and cross-trained—they must be able to do all jobs. The success of the hotel is due to them, and we tell them that all the time. We get the family together once a month," he says, referring to his 350 employees, who make up an impressive 2.5-to-one staff-to-guest ratio.

The term "family" is used all the time by people at all levels of the organization. "Family" does not imply the Hunts, or the Sandses (Mrs. Hunt's children from her first marriage). It is the Rosewood family, and employees seem so sincere in their embrace of this concept that it contributes to their happiness and longevity. Bob Zimmer is given credit for presenting a family-employer model, and employees are loath to leave the family.

Abel, the Mansion's chief executive steward, had "heard of the mystique of the Mansion." When he was offered a job here, he considered it the "chance of a lifetime. It's like a big family," he adds. "Everyone from a dishwasher to the general manager helps out. It makes people feel good when the president says hello to a dishwasher. Everyone has a future here. I turned twenty-seven two months ago, and the hotel business is where I want to spend my life. There's no reason ever to leave Rosewood, the Cadillac of the industry." (He's now pushing thirty.)

Certainly, part of what makes working here interesting is the proximity to rich people. And not just people *with* money, but people who *behave* rich. A luncheon at the Mansion is an occasion for the best furs and jewels. The parking lot is a tribute to German engineering mixed with a healthy dose of Rolls-Royces and Jaguars. It is the rich as they are portrayed in movies and television, but it is very real here and part of the fun. "We give lessons, seminars in how to address royalty. When the King of Norway comes in the door, you don't say 'Howdy!'"

Twenty-nine-year-old Vickie was the head concierge at the Mansion. She started at another hotel in Dallas that was first-rate but part of a large chain. "It was not for me," she said in the foyer, near the ever-present roaring fire in the hearth. "It was too corporate. A friend called and said, 'Vickie, you've just got to see the Mansion.' It bit me. This was a beautiful place. The lobby wasn't even finished. I felt close to what they wanted—the philosophy—and felt that due to the small size, their goals were attainable. It was dedication to the guest." Because she was late in submitting her application, the only job available to Vickie was as a reservationist, for which she was overqualified.

It was Mr. de Toth who encouraged her to move to the concierge desk. "We're encouraged to know our guests' names. We have a guest history program" in which guests' preferences and frequency of visits are recorded. "We're encouraged to read the papers and *Town and Country* to keep up. If a Dallas society person brings a guest in, they'll call us and alert us. We try to treat almost all our guests as VIPs or friends of Mrs. Hunt. They may not look like a wealthy person, but you never know. It's challenging."

At her tenth high school reunion, the Dallas native was surrounded by friends who'd achieved professional success. "Everyone thought *my* job was exciting and thought I was happiest. Guests think this job is happy, and we are. I am by nature a polite person, because I like to be treated that way. The pay is fine and guests pay you and compliment you, and you feel wonderful. Everything I do is based on what's good for the hotel. I don't think, 'What's good for Vickie?' Working here is a humbling experience. I like when people say, 'The Mansion did it.' " She cites one of those travel emergencies that can either cement or destroy the loyalty of a guest. "A woman wanted Christian Dior graphite gray panty hose, and I had some in my apartment. You learn to think solutions, not 'What am I going to do?' "

The job has taught Vickie "ease. Famous people are normal people. They can be so together, I can't always express it in words. I feel the Rosewood philosophy. I try to mold myself around that. Mr. Zimmer and Mrs. Hunt are so unaffected . . ." Out of gratitude to her mentors, Vickie applied to the Clef d'Or (Gold Key), the international society of concierges, which has only sixty members. "I wanted to do it for them. I wanted to wear my keys for the Mansion." In addition to her written application, she needed two recommendations.

As the head concierge, Vickie supervised a staff of eight, including six bellmen. "I try to be positive during the most stressful moments. I'm a role model to my staff. Concierges are asked for the impossible all the time, and we love to surprise our guests with what we can do."

Thomas Axmacher was the resident manager of the Crescent Court at its opening. He'd spent ten years at the world-renowned Brenner Park Hotel and spa in Baden-Baden, West Germany. "I thought I knew it all," he said about running a hotel, "but operations in the States are completely different from Europe. Here, an SMU student might take one job and know nothing of the rest of the picture. There you might spend three years, practically unpaid, as an apprentice, learning all about the hotel. Europeans stay in jobs for years. In America, once you've trained somebody, they leave. [Author's note: Ironically Axmacher defected to another hotel in late 1987.] The ideal combination is European food and beverage service and guest-related services, mixed with American controlling, sales, accounting, and computers."

I spent a week at the Crescent, and Axmacher seemed omnipresent. He was in the spa, in the restaurant, in the lobby—he'd never leave. "When it comes to a private life in the hotel business, you can forget it," he says. "Even if you leave at midnight, you have guilty feelings, and when you arrive at seven A.M. you feel guilty. It doesn't close at five P.M. like most businesses." Indeed, in a labor-intensive industry such as this, quality must be maintained twenty-four hours a day.

Designed by Philip Johnson and John Burgee, the Crescent is an imposing walled city-within-a-city that started out as "the largest excavation west of the Mississippi." Ten acres. Really. (Author's note: Southland's hole would soon supplant this.) The parking space for the hotel, retail shops, and an office building accommodates 4,500 cars—again, the largest in the world.

Hiram, a bellman at the Crescent, is sitting in a suite for his interview. "It makes me so nervous sitting here in street clothes," he says, lighting a cigarette. He has worked for Rosewood "on and off for five years," starting out at the Mansion, where he trained under Alexander de Toth. He is so well liked that when he has an urge to take a chunk of time off to travel or write (he's finished several screenplays), he gets a sabbatical. He spent a year in Italy and Geneva. "Mr. Zimmer was nice about leaving the door open. He said at lunch one day, 'Hiram likes to travel, and he will probably travel again, but we hope he'll come back.' He says 'family,' and he means it." [Author's note: In October, 1987, Hiram in fact left Rosewood—possibly for good—to start his own business selling carpet cleaning chemicals. The Hotel Crescent Court is one of his customers.]

Hiram analyzes the clientele of both Dallas properties. "The Mansion is for the quiet rich. The Crescent is for the not-so-quiet rich. Working here is fun. It's like going to a party. You dress each day and wait to see who'll show up. I've unrolled the red carpet for Queen Noor," he says, recalling a highlight. "I've escorted Julia Child to the restaurant and escorted John Travolta through mobs. You can't even let celebrities know you know them. You can't fawn.

"I suppose it *is* glamorous," he says, as if he'd never considered the notion before. "No two days are ever the same. In Guest Services [the belldesk] we're the guests' friends. We *are* the hotel." Actually, he's correct. If your bellman forgot to point out the thermostat or offer to fetch ice, you would think less of the hotel. You don't ordinarily call the vice-president of corporate planning to look at the five-year plan in order to decide whether the hotel is worth checking into. In a service business, the people downstairs who have direct contact with the guests are the people who matter most.

"It's a tough company to work for. There's very little room for error. Little tiny things aren't acceptable. Too much is at stake. When Mr. Zimmer and Mr. de Toth pick up a leaf from the floor, you feel so small."

The degree of wealth and opulence among the upper reaches of Dallas could turn a person's head. Yet even in this context, the Hunt money impresses. Marti Chalk, a vice-president and the director of corporate and developmental finance, handles accounting, planning, and cash flows. She could take her profession anywhere but likes Rosewood for its international flavor and changing profile. " 'Rosewood Hotels' suggests beauty and enchantment," she says. "I still like to walk into the lobby of the Mansion. I appreciate it more every time." Chalk started working for Rosewood before it was named. She found her job through the husband of a friend who worked for Hunt Properties, the original holding company.

"You don't think of working for billionaires; you think of working for a company. It wouldn't be the same as working for Holiday Inn because of the numbers. I appreciate each room and feel very proud." [Author's note: Don't forget that some of the rooms we're talking about cost in excess of a quarter of a million dollars apiece.] The corporate staff is made up of only about thirty-five people, located on the tenth floor of the Crescent Office Towers. "I appreciate a small company. On a given day, I interact with ten or fifteen employees. With growth you have to have more rules, and things would be a little tougher. It's a flexible place to work. People take care of their responsibilities and don't look over your shoulder." Marti also likes the foreign influence. "There's something romantic about a foreign accent, and sometimes you'll have four different accents in one meeting.

"This is a very fair company as far as salaries, benefits. It's a good atmosphere, with wonderful offices, furnishings, and surroundings. I can have lunch and dinner at the hotels, but I don't abuse it. I take my girls to lunch at the Mansion. It's a treat for them." But what about all the money? She is the one, after all, who writes the checks. Chalk is pretty nonchalant about it, citing figures like the $60 million budget for the Rosewood Georgetown, which has only about ninety-five guest rooms and the $45 million budget for the Crescent Court. "This is how the other five to ten percent lives," she rationalizes. "The biggest check I've ever signed was for ten million dollars. It felt like a ten-dollar check."

No description of Rosewood would be complete without including ZEN Concepts, a wholly owned subsidiary of Rosewood Hotels. "Bob Zimmer had an idea," relates Rick Duran, ZEN's ex-design director. "Flowers played such an important role in the ambience of the hotels." Zimmer wanted an in-house florist. In 1982, while the Remington was under construction, he approached his favorite florists at the Village Gardener in Highland Park (Dallas's nicest neighborhood) to see about handling the Houston account. At the same time, Rick wanted to leave the shop and work directly for Rosewood. The Floral Services Division of Rosewood Hotels was established. Its first office contained just Rick and Judy Coche, his partner, in an 800-square-foot office with one round table and two phones.

Now they inhabit their own handsome building, with one room devoted to vases and planters, another to exotic flora, and a third to a library of flower books. There is a bustling group of employees here. In just five years, the Floral Services Division has had revenues of approximately $5 million, proof that Midas touches tangents, too.

The flowers are breathtaking. ZEN took a vow to ignore daisies, chrysanthemums, baby's breath, carnations, and any flower that's dyed or artificial. Order your FTD "tickler" bouquet elsewhere. The lobbies of all the Rosewood hotels are fragrant and dramatic, each dominated by a towering urn of flowers and branches. In every possible corner there are tiny little blossoms or unusual-looking plants that add to the rarefied ambience. All the rooms have bud vases, and room service is likely to include a lovely flower on the tray. In addition to flowers imported from Holland, the world flower market, orchids for Rosewood are grown on the premises of the Hana Ranch, the Hawaiian property.

In addition to flowers, ZEN now has a landscaping service that employs twenty designers. ZEN sells flowers at the retail level at its own studios, and bids for jobs on the outside. The Bel-Air ZEN did the flowers for Metro-Goldwyn-Mayer's Diamond Jubilee. All ZENs supply local restaurants, banquets, and so on. "It's the best of both worlds," Rick says. "We'd already had our own business, and we didn't want to do it again." He and Judy are genuine entrepreneurs but don't have to bear the personal financial burden. "Altogether Rosewood's our biggest customer, and its connections have gotten us a lot of work. We have freedom, but we have security and corporate benefits."

One last thing: How did ZEN get its name? A contest to find the right one was held among Rosewood employees. The prize was a free orchid plant. ZEN seemed right because of the "ZEN Buddhist ideal. The attainment of perfection through simplicity." The winner, judged by Bob Zimmer, was Bob Zimmer. He won the plant.

Interview:
DEAN FEARING, EXECUTIVE CHEF

At thirty-three, Dean Fearing is coming to terms with his celebrity chef status. His cookbook, *The Mansion on Turtle Creek Cookbook,* was published by Weidenfeld and Nicolson in 1987. It can be said without hesitation that he is a master architect of what is known as the new Southwest cuisine. His building materials: roasted yellow bell peppers, chili cream, tortilla soup, corn cakes. Fearing is the executive chef of the restaurant at The Mansion on Turtle Creek, Rosewood's flagship property. But rather than regarding himself as an executive in the hostelry industry, he says, "I accept this as a restaurant in a small hotel. Almost ninety percent of the clientele is local. People don't have to walk through the lobby to get to the restaurant, which is the best thing they could've done."

It's not that Dean has an innate antipathy toward hotels. He got his first job in the hospitality business as a result of his dad being a hotel general manager. "I started cooking at Holiday and Ramada Inns, where my dad worked. I hated it. To them, cooking dessert was thawing a frozen dessert. I wanted to be a musician." As he got older, Fearing realized it was time to plan for a real career, and he found an apprenticeship with a chef who was a graduate and advocate of the Culinary Institute of America—the *other* CIA. Dean "saw the skill, technique, and professionalism in the business" and made tracks for the CIA in Poughkeepsie, New York.

There he felt his calling. "My true love is sauces. It takes method. It is one of the most important functions in a restaurant—that's how you tell if a restaurant is good. it's a real special skill that not everyone can master." As one of the States' only academies of haute cuisine, the CIA is very competitive. It is where fine restaurant chains, hotels, corporations, and individual restaurants recruit, and, when graduating, Dean sought a job at Cincinnati's five-star Maisonette restaurant, one of the toughest placements.

When they called him for an interview, "I didn't own a suit. I borrowed my brother's black suit, which was two sizes too big, and the vent was ripped. I had brown shoes, my uncle's tie, and a light blue shirt. Nothing matched. My God! It was big time for me." He laughingly remembers his anxiety. He was interviewed by the restaurant's owner and sent outside to wait for the decision. "They said it would be a few minutes, and it turned into forty-five minutes. Then they needed to see me again. They asked me a lot of personal questions and food questions. They made a big deal about the interview, like I was going to be the executive sous-chef. I was only applying for a five-dollar-an-hour saucier job."

Projecting his career at one-year intervals, he moved to Dallas's Fairmont Hotel as the saucier at its fancy Pyramid Room. It was at this time that the Mansion was opening up. The buzz in town about the Mansion was positive, and, like many of his colleagues, he drove over to talk about working in its kitchen. "The chef asked, 'What position do you want?' I said, 'Saucier.' He said, 'Where do you work?' I said, 'Pyramid.' He said, 'You're hired.' I got three friends in, too." That was ten years ago.

When he'd been at the Mansion a few years, Dean was tapped to be the chef at a new restaurant, Agnew's. He was only twenty-six years old. "It was the opportunity to open Dallas's first new American restaurant. [Food critic] Craig Claiborne came down and wrote us up, which helped. We were pioneers, legends in town," he says in a voice that's bemused, not blustery. "The new Southwest cuisine actually started here, in [suburban] Addison, Texas. We had five stars within six weeks and kept the rating over the next couple of years."

One day, Bob Zimmer, Rosewood's president, called Fearing and said, " 'We'd like you to come back to the family.' I couldn't turn down the Mansion." Besides, the offer was as head chef. He has held that position for the last three and a half years, and today his name is mentioned in the same league as Wolfgang Puck of Spago in Los Angeles ("my godfather in this business"), Jonathan Waxman of JW in New York, Brad Ogden of San Francisco's Campton Place Restaurant, Stephan Pyles of Dallas's Routh Street Café, and Anne Rosenzweig of Arcadia and the "21" Club in New York. "I don't think about being well known," he says, wearing his whites in a tiny office off the kitchen. "I can't let it go to my head." He says the relationships among these (star) chefs are forged of friendship, sympathy, and assistance.

Fearing's stint at Agnew's seems to have knocked the need to pursue new entrepreneurial ventures out of his system, although with his name recognition, he is frequently approached by restaurateurs who think he can lure business. "I'm just content to be at one place. It's less fun if you're stretched too thin. I want to cook good food and create good things."

THE SOUTHLAND CORPORATION

HISTORY & OPERATIONS

The Southland Corporation, founders of 7-Eleven and the world's largest operator and franchiser of convenience stores, was founded in Dallas, Texas, in 1927 as an ice manufacturing and retail company called the Southland Ice Company. During the company's first year, an enterprising ice station operator began selling items such as eggs, milk, and bread. When he handed over the profits to Joe C. Thompson, one of Southland's original directors, Thompson decided to expand all of the company's outlets to include more of such items. Not only would the new strategy increase revenues, it would enable the ice stations, which generally closed down during the winter, to operate year round. Hence the birth of convenience stores.

The company named the new operations Tote'm Stores, and while the convenience items sold well, the majority of revenues and profits came from the ice business. By the end of 1931, when Joe Thompson became president of Southland, there were more than thirty stores in operation around Dallas and Fort Worth and the company had acquired a number of new ice plants. In 1932 Southland was forced to declare bankruptcy when its main investor fell victim to the Depression. The company, which came close to folding, remained in receivership until 1934.

In 1936 the company founded Oak Farms Dairies to provide its own stores as well as outside operations with dairy products. By 1939 there were sixty Tote'm Stores and the sale of convenience items had surpassed those of the ice business by a wide margin. During World War II, the stores flourished and the ice business revived as well, prompting Southland to expand further. In 1945 the company was officially renamed The Southland Corporation. The following year, Southland renamed its seventy-four convenience stores, which were to operate from 7:00 A.M. to 11:00 P.M., 7-Elevens.

In 1950 Southland opened the first 7-Elevens outside the Dallas–Fort Worth area, and by 1952 there were one hundred stores in operation throughout Texas. In 1954, when the profits of 7-Eleven stores reached $1 million for the first time, Thompson decided to open stores outside the state. In the meantime, the company expanded its dairy operations, while the ice operations continued to bring in revenues. In 1958 Southland celebrated the opening of its three hundredth 7-Eleven, with stores in operation in Texas, Florida, and Washington, D.C. By the end of 1960, more new markets had been penetrated and there were 591 7-Elevens.

When Joe C. Thompson died in 1961 at the age of sixty, his son John, a Southland executive since 1948, took over the reins and orchestrated the most rapid expansion program in this private company's history. 7-Elevens were opened all over the country, and new dairy operations were acquired in regions outside Texas. By the end of 1963, there were 1,052 7-Eleven stores in approximately 250 cities and towns in America. In 1967 Southland's revenues passed the half-billion-dollar mark, and by the end of the decade, there were 3,537 stores in operation —36 percent of them franchises—with a total of more than a million customers each day. During the sixties, the company also acquired 115 Gristede Brothers supermarkets (which were sold in 1986) and 145 Barricini Candy Company stores in the Northeast. The first Canadian 7-Eleven was opened in 1969, and by the end of the year Southland was operating in thirty-eight states, the District of Columbia, and three provinces of Canada. The company's dairy operations, which were distributing products in twenty-two states and the District of Columbia, had sales of almost $200 million by the end of the decade.

In 1971 Southland's sales exceeded $1 billion. Over the next two years, the company expanded overseas through the purchase of a half ownership stake in a number of specialty shops and grocery stores in England, Scotland, and Wales. By the time it was listed on the New York Stock Exchange in 1972, Southland had also begun experimenting with the sale of self-service gasoline at selected 7-Elevens. Though the retail gasoline business started gradually, it took off during the oil embargo of the seventies, when the major oil companies shut down their neighborhood stations to open bigger outlets on busy thoroughfares. When Southland experimented with opening 7-Elevens on corner lots the gas stations had occupied, store sales shot up a remarkable 50 percent. Thereafter, the company adopted a policy of opening most new 7-Elevens on corners and including gasoline service. In 1974, 7-Elevens were introduced in Japan through the first area franchises in overseas markets. In 1976 the company's revenues reached $2 billion.

Throughout the late seventies and eighties, Southland opened more 7-Elevens, both domestically and in foreign markets. In 1978 it acquired Chief Auto Parts, the country's largest retail chain of automobile replacement parts. In 1983, with its gasoline retail business flourishing, Southland purchased Citgo Petroleum Corporation and became a gasoline wholesaler as well. (In 1986 it sold half its stake in Citgo.) Today Southland is the largest independent gasoline retailer in the country.

Under the leadership of John Thompson, chairman, and his younger brother Jere, president and CEO, Southland currently employs 59,000 people. In June 1987, its worldwide holdings included 8,200 7-Eleven stores in forty-nine states—roughly 60 percent of which are company-owned, and the other 40 percent of which are franchises—sixty-eight Svenska/7-Eleven stores in Sweden, and an equity interest in sixty-one Super Siete stores in Mexico. The following foreign stores are operated by area license: 2,924 in Japan, 183 in Hong Kong, 119 in Australia, 122 in Taiwan, 52 in Great Britain, 44 in Singapore, 31 in Malaysia, 3 in the Philippines, and 1 in Norway. Other holdings: 465 Chief Auto Parts Stores; 346 High's Dairy stores; 163 Quik Mart gasoline/convenience stores and Super-7 multipump self-service gasoline outlets; the Dairies Group, which markets products under a number of regional brand names in forty-six states, the District of Columbia, Canada, Guam, and the Caribbean; Reddy-Ice, the largest manufacturer of crushed ice in the world; and a number of other store-related operations, including five distribution centers that distribute products to Southland and non-Southland stores.

In July 1987, after Southland was threatened with a hostile takeover attempt by Canadian corporate raider Samuel Belzberg, the Thompson brothers announced plans to take the company private again in a $4 billion leveraged buyout. To finance the LBO, Southland announced it would divest itself of the majority of its non–convenience store businesses. At press time, Southland was in the process of selling off the Dairies Group, Chief Auto Parts, Reddy-Ice, Tidel Systems (which make cash controller machines), Southland Chemical/Food Labs, the Snack Foods Division, one thousand convenience stores in the United States, and MovieQuik. The sales should be consummated by the end of 1988.

What remains are more than seven thousand 7-Eleven stores in the United States and Canada, slightly less than half of which are operated by franchisees, as well as the international operations, which now also include stores in Panama and Ireland as well as an equity interest in convenience stores in the United Kingdom, Spain, and Puerto Rico. (In all, affiliates and area licensees operate more than 4,100 7-Eleven stores in sixteen foreign countries.) Southland still owns five distribution centers, six fast food production facilities, a 50 percent interest in Citgo Petroleum Corporation, High's Dairy Stores (regional convenience stores mostly in Virginia and Maryland), Quik Mart (high-volume gasoline and mini-convenience stores), and Super-7 (self-service gasoline outlets on the West Coast).

Southland dug the biggest hole in Texas's history for the construction of its new headquarters, which the company is scheduled to begin to occupy at the end of 1988. The hole, which required the excavation of 790,000 cubic yards of rock and dirt, was ninety feet deep and covered an area of approximately twelve acres. (Rosewood's hole—see p. 192, dug earlier, was about ten acres in size.)

(Information supplied by John Singleton, Pat Lagow, and Markeeta McNatt, company spokespersons.)

REVENUES: Store sales for 1987 exceeded $8 billion. "Total yearly revenues for the corporation are not available due to change to purchase accounting on August 1."

EARNINGS: $90.1 million for the first seven months of 1987. For the last five months, Southland reported a not unexpected net loss of $149.7 million. "Due to LBO-related accounting restatements, results from the two periods in 1987 are not comparable and cannot be added to achieve 1987 full-year financial results or compare with 1986 results," which were $200.4 million.

INITIAL PUBLIC OFFERING: Though some shares were traded earlier, Southland stock was first listed on the New York Stock Exchange in 1972. The company was taken private again in late 1987.

NUMBER OF SHAREHOLDERS: 8,288 as of June 4, 1987. But as of publication, the company is privately owned by Jere, John, and Joe Thompson, Jr., and some preferred shareholders.

NUMBER OF EMPLOYEES: 59,000 in the United States and Canada.

AVERAGE AGE OF EMPLOYEES: Information not available.

TURNOVER: The company considers this proprietary information. However, turnover in entry-level store positions is high.

RECRUITMENT: Southland has no college recruitment program at the corporate level; however, individual divisions do participate in job fairs, etc., for college students.

NUMBER OF NEW HIRES PER YEAR: Company will not disclose.

RANGE OF STARTING SALARIES: Company will not disclose. "We have starting salaries that are competitive with other companies in our industry."

POLICY FOR RAISES: "We have a merit system which is very similar to our competitors'." Southland will not provide further details.

TRAINING PROGRAMS: "We offer a variety of training programs that range from basic skills training—computer courses and so forth—to executive development."

BENEFITS: The company considers this information proprietary. "We have above-average benefits for the retailing sector. They include profit sharing, group insurance, holidays, et cetera."

VACATION: Two weeks after one year, three weeks after five years, four weeks after ten years, in addition to ten regular paid holidays per year.

ADDITIONAL PERKS: "We're not going to address that at all." Nevertheless, *Going to Work* learned of Southland's subsidized vacation grounds in Hot Springs, Arkansas. It's available to employees after one year's service.

BONUSES: Company does have a bonus program and all salaried employees are eligible. "Bonuses are based on profit goals within company subgroups."

ANNUAL PARTY: Nothing at the corporate level, though some divisions host their own parties.

AVERAGE WORKDAY: 8:00 A.M. to 4:45 P.M. for corporate employees. 7-Elevens run on a series of shifts which differ by area and store.

DRESS CODE: "It's a local option kind of situation. We do have a dress code, but it's very loose. Its really up to the area managers and division heads to determine what's appropriate. In the corporate office, it's standard business attire."

SOCIAL ATMOSPHERE: "The best way to sum it up is to say that Southland has a family-type environment."

NUMBER OF CONVENIENCE STORES: Over 7,000.

NUMBER OF HOT DOGS SOLD IN 7-ELEVENS EACH YEAR: 7-Eleven, the largest retailer of frankfurters in the country, sells over 9 million pounds of them per year.

MOST POPULAR FLAVORS OF SLURPEES: For the uninitiated, a Slurpee, 7-Eleven's signature beverage, is a carbonated iced drink that is slurped through a straw. The most popular Slurpee flavors are Coca-Cola and cherry, in that order.

NUMBER OF 7-ELEVEN SHOPPERS: Over 7 million per day in the United States and Canada.

HEADQUARTERS: Until the end of 1988, Southland will house approximately 1,200 corporate employees in a cluster of fourteen buildings—the tallest is eleven stories—it owns and manages. New headquarters, just north of downtown Dallas, should be open by Thanksgiving and will consist of one enormous building, forty-two stories high. A second tower will eventually be built next door. The site is known as Cityplace.

CHARITABLE CONTRIBUTIONS: "The management of The Southland Corporation believes in good corporate citizenship and demonstrates this in many ways. The company and its 59,000 employees and franchisees are active in social and community programs. As a major sponsor of the annual Jerry Lewis Labor Day Telethon for the Muscular Dystrophy Association, Southland has raised more than $53 million for the campaign in twelve years. Financial support for education is also a high priority. Southland, through its various divisions, has sponsored grants, scholarships, and awards throughout the nation."

OTHER: In 1984 Southland and 7-Eleven cosponsored the summer Olympics in Los Angeles. The company constructed an Olympic cycling stadium known as the 7-Eleven Velodrome, at the California State University campus at Dominguez Hills, where the cycling competition took place. After the Olympics, Southland donated the velodrome to the citizens of California. The company also built an identical velodrome at the U.S. Olympic Committee Training Center in Colorado Springs, Colorado, for training use by the U.S. Olympic cycling team. Since 1981 Southland has had its own 7-Eleven cycling team, which has competed all over the world. Eric Heiden is the team captain. There are both professional and amateur riders on the team, with five women and seven men in the latter category, all of them candidates for the Olympics. In 1986 the 7-Eleven team was the first American team to compete in the Tour de France, where two of its riders won different certain stages of the race.

INTERESTED APPLICANTS CAN SEND RÉSUMÉS TO:
Corporate Personnel
The Southland Corporation
Box 719
Dallas, TX 75221
(214) 828-7011

The Southland Corporation of Dallas is best known as the parent company of the 7-Eleven convenience store chain. Privately owned, then taken public, it is once again owned by three Thompson brothers, John, Jere, and Joe C. Jr., who are the sons of one of the founders of the company. (Joe Jr. is a part owner and a member of the board of directors. Unlike his brothers, he is not a corporate officer and therefore not as involved in day-to-day operations.) The corporate headquarters do not resemble a twenty-four-hour convenience store; rather, they are a group of fourteen buildings that are extremely unobtrusive on the Dallas skyline. The low profile will disappear soon, however, when the company moves into Cityplace, its new headquarters, located in what was allegedly "the largest hole ever dug in the state of Texas for a building excavation."

There is something upbeat about this quintessentially American organization. Employees are treated to flashy incentive programs like 1986's "Thanks a Million," in which "one lucky store manager or franchisee would win $1 million." The winner, Debra Wilson, a five-year veteran of the company, is a store manager in Plano, Texas. She will receive $50,000 (before taxes) for twenty years. She has not quit her job. The "Gold Key" program awards those who have provided "outstanding service over and above the call of duty." ("It's very prestigious," an employee offers.) This is a company that trades in the American dream. If you've shopped at a 7-Eleven lately, you may have noticed a proliferation of immigrant employees. Management calls them "new Americans." Southland gives these people a chance at more than a job. They instill in them an entrepreneurial can-do attitude. Maybe you've seen the Thompson brothers handing over a megabuck check to Jerry Lewis on his Labor Day Telethon. (Southland has raised over $53 million for muscular dystrophy over twelve years, in addition to supporting other causes.) The company promotes philanthropy among its employees this way, and it shows the country that Southland is a good corporate citizen. The company was also a major sponsor of the 1984 Los Angeles summer Olympics.

A spokesman for the company boasts, "7-Eleven has become a national institution." Well, there are over seven thousand stores in the United States and Canada. "We take a lot of pride," he adds, grinning, "in being the largest convenience store in America. And we will grow." Employees are offered a range of career possibilities. "A 7-Eleven division manager is autonomous. There are eighteen operating divisions across the United States. He's running a five hundred million dollar business. It is very likely a division manager started out as a clerk."

People at 7-Eleven speak in terms of "we." "*We* all feel good about our compensation," they'll say, and "*We* feel a kinship because *we*'ve all worked in a store. It's like a family. The company treats people right." In fact, every single salaried employee spends one week a year in an actual store. They say, "*We* love it."

One voice among Southland's 59,000 employees says, "There's a feeling of smallness. I don't think of Southland as huge because I know everyone I come into contact with. We know every store manager in our district." CEO Jere [pronounced "Jerry"] Thompson is praised for knowing every custodian's first name.

Allen Peterson was a training store manager in the Dallas–Fort Worth division training new area store employees in a store/classroom with two cash registers when we met. (He has since been promoted to supervisor in Mesquite, Texas.) He said, "Clerks in this area start at $4.50 an hour [compared to the current minimum wage of $3.35]. Their first opportunity for increase is sixty days later, and every six months thereafter. They can make as much as sixty-five cents an hour raise in the first eight months." Seven years ago he was working for Burger King. His wife was on board at 7-Eleven, "and the company was on the up and up. Burger King seemed stagnant." Since he joined Southland, Allen's been with five different stores. "I developed a reputation for good store management, and they liked the way I ran things." He says he gets "lots of visits" from management. "I'm rarely left alone. The Thompsons have been here. I call them 'Mr. Thompson.' They're quick to come back with 'You can call me John.' I don't know them well enough to consider them role models. I know people who've grown up with Southland, and they say good things about them. They're real people.

"I run my own business, basically. I have independence, and if I do a reasonably good job, I'm left alone. My mark is on my people, and my people are individuals. Every store has my personality. My style is very people-oriented. I've created a lot of credibility with my people. When I say something will happen, it does. My employees can count on review on time and on their raises being processed on time."

He relies on the Division Advisory Council (DAC) for new operational ideas, such as pricing individual cans or bottles of six-pack soft drinks. "Now they're labeled on shelves, not on each one. It saves one and a half to two hours a day." Other innovations are developed regionally. "If there's a fad in town, the store manager is at liberty to try it," a corporate official says. 7-Eleven's trademark beverage presentations, the Slurpee and Big Gulp—thirty-two and forty-eight ounces, respectively, of ice-filled drinks—were the idea of a Dallas employee. "People listen. It takes two years from the suggestion to national rollout. That's how popcorn machines got started. If it works on a local level within a limited time frame, they do it. Space [in the stores] is precious. You don't invest in bad ideas again and again." And there are opportunities to rethink merchandising ideas. For example, a former store staple, cigarette rolling papers, are no longer sold by the chain.

Allen thinks that "someday I'd like to run my own business. My wife and I are saving to buy a 7-Eleven franchise in southern California." A total 7-Elevenophile, he favors cherry Slurpees and says the hot dogs are "very tempting." Both store clerks and managers are entitled to free beverages on the job, but they must buy any food they eat. Employees of 7-Eleven usually buy their groceries at supermarkets. "You can eat on the job, but there are no breaks." The workday is made up of three shifts of eight solid, unbroken hours apiece. Sometimes only one clerk will be on the premises.

Ken Wolfe never imagined he'd be working for 7-Eleven. A graduate of Texas Lutheran College, he, too, discovered the company through his wife, who'd worked here first. "This is a lifetime career move," he says in his Dallas store. But he won't be satisfied spending his whole career in the stores. He's looking for an upper management position in the corporation eventually. "You get noticed by doing a good job. Upper management is in the stores regularly, sometimes with advance notice."

Wolfe's on his feet all day long. "You get used to standing and not taking breaks." Of his first two and a half years, "I went out to lunch four times," he calculates. I almost always bring my own lunch. I'm cheap. I usually drink water. There's one chair in the back room, and one bathroom." In other words, his days really are confined to his store. Thirty-three years of age and now a father, Ken, a store manager, says, "This is the most challenging job I've had. You do basically the same stuff, but people and their needs are different. You never get bored." He figures it'll take him between one and three years to be promoted to a desk job. "A lot depends on when positions will be available. I'm too realistic to dream."

Allen Walker is one of Southland's thirty lawyers. She (that's right) had never worked in private practice. After three years with the federal government and a position as the counsel for East Texas State University, a headhunter approached her to come here. "It was a rather extensive interviewing process," she remembers of her arrival seven years ago. "I was the tenth attorney hired."

Allen, who met her husband at SMU law school, says, "Maybe the reason so many women become in-house counsel is because law firms are not open to women. I like to avoid billing, et cetera. I don't have to do administrative work, and I don't have to recruit. I get to practice a lot of law. My client is Southland, and I can treat everyone equally. It makes me a more fair lawyer."

There is no one way that corporations regard their in-house legal departments. Some create departments with the same hierarchical structures found in law firms. Others, like Southland, maintain an office of generalists, more or less. "We're not really sectionalized, but each of us has a concentration informally. A lot depends on who you report to. It helps to despecialize, so someone can cover for you." Southland also has plenty of work for outside counsel, most often in litigation.

"Just in the last few years we've divided up into a more supervisory structure. We needed tiers. Because we've grown so fast, titles change fast. They are not regulated by years here." First comes attorney, then general attorney, senior staff attorney (Allen's title), assistant supervising attorney, supervising attorney, assistant general counsel (of which there are two), and, heading the legal pyramid, general counsel. "There must be enough satisfaction, because we've all stayed. We all would've been partners by now [had we been in private practice]. Only two of the original ten aren't still here. They got married and moved East."

The Walkers have two children. The older one was born before Allen joined Southland; when her second child was born, she took off three weeks before returning full time. "Time expands to fit your needs. If I had three days to make a bed, I'd do it the last hour of the third day." She arrives at the office before 8:00 A.M., and "I walk out at 6:00 P.M. I will do two or three hours of work at home two or three days a week. I would have a hard time traveling. I don't want to. My travel is elective."

Allen mentions that the department is still recruiting and expanding. No one is hired directly from law school. Applicants need one or more likely two years of professional work before they're eligible to join. "People applying should just walk around and visit," she advises. "They'll meet with a lot of different lawyers. I don't know that they're expected to know a lot about Southland; it's always a pleasant surprise when they do.

"We produce very high quality work." Although the legal department is free of the stress incurred by the partnership track at law firms, Walker says there is pressure on the job. "You don't have to do a lot of big deals to feel it. Whether it's a $250 deal or a two-million-dollar deal, it's equally important. The addition of lawyers isn't going to lessen our work loads. I cannot—do not—delegate work to junior lawyers. If I'm given work, I do it. I don't know their work loads."

In 1986 the law staff established an "elaborate" review system. Every lawyer is reviewed by his or her supervising attorney plus four or five others. "It was very beneficial to me," Allen reports. "It was nice to see how I was perceived. I'm aware of some weaknesses, and I went over them in detail. We set goals with a time limit, and they're being taken very seriously. If I did have a complaint, it would be listened to."

Walker advances the idea of Southland as a family organization. "It's sponsored by the Thompsons. People take care of each other. So many people, including the Thompsons, are on a first-name basis. Titles are important, but what you do is more important than the title. Titles aren't put on memos. Memos begin with 'Dear ———' and end with 'Very truly yours.' It's a personal place. The Thompsons' father made a big deal of knowing everyone. In Dallas, at least, John and Jere [Thompson] would be recognized by store employees. They're very visible. A lot of people pick up their own phones; not their secretaries." (By the way, every lawyer has his or her own secretary, and every two paralegals share one secretary.)

Divisions run their own college recruiting programs. MBAs might consider a career at Southland, too. "Business students might think of IBM or Xerox first. But if you know someone who works here, you'd think about it."

Despite other holdings, including Citgo, once wholly owned and now only partially so, the stores are central to a culture that seems to rise from the bottom and trickle down from the top simultaneously, and meet—over a Slurpee—somewhere in the middle. "It's a people business with people skills," a divisional personnel director says. "Different companies have different benefits for different jobs. Here, everyone's the same. College degree holders start out as clerks, too. You have to learn the business from the bottom up. Insurance starts seven days after *anyone* starts. Profit sharing starts after one year, whether you're full time or part time. There's a tuition reimbursement program for people who work thirty-two hours a week or more. If you study something that could apply to your next job, submit it to a committee. The company has a vacation area, Buena Vista, in Hot Springs, Arkansas, a hotel and cottage with pools, open to anyone who's been here a year at a fifty percent discount."

Perhaps the most zealous of all are the store managers. One of them volunteers, "We spend a lot of time and money teaching people to say thanks. If you're open twenty-four hours a day, you can work at night. You [the typical 7-Eleven store manager] have to visit at night, too. Make the night shift feel they're important. A good store manager will arrive early—six or six-thirty A.M.—to be with the night people." Each group of six stores has a supervisor, who visits each store *every day*. "You foster and reinforce the atmosphere." In the north Texas area, the average salary of a "certified store manager" is about $27,000 a year. But don't kid yourself; managers have been able to get, if not rich, quite comfortable from their jobs. More than a few drive new luxury cars. "My brother-in-law worked here," a store manager says, "and I liked his style, the way he lived—his new car and new house. I went to the district office and got interviewed."

The average 7-Eleven customer might not realize it when stopping in late one night for cigarettes, a Slim Jim, Pepto-Bismol, or a video rental, but the stores look the same for a reason. Once ensconced in the fluorescent pristineness of a 7-Eleven, be it in Anchorage or in Boca Raton, you can find exactly what you're looking for. Employees hustle to keep their stores clean and orderly. The service is supposed to be: "nice and fast. If you don't like our customers, don't be here."

The stores' beefed-up security system has been the subject of a lot of attention. Comedian Jay Leno says these stores are "where twenty thousand dollars' worth of cameras protect twenty dollars' worth of Twinkies." Without the use of weapons, "Our stores are the leaders in comprehensive security. We developed the standard for the industry. Our incident rate drops annually as it grows elsewhere. 7-Eleven has advertised that it's not a target for crime."

Essentially, the system forbids more than thirty dollars to be in the cash register at a time. "More is in violation of company policy." When there's more cash than that, it gets deposited, vacuum-sucked directly into a locked safe. The average turnaround of twenty dollars takes twelve minutes, "too long for a criminal to wait. They'll abandon it. Paramount in everything we do is the clerks' and customers' safety."

Toki came to this country twenty years ago from her native Korea. She's been a store manager in North Dallas for nine years. She drives her own Cadillac Seville. "I think I'll stay here until I'm sixty-five," the thirty-six-year-old says. "If someone offered me a hundred thousand dollars, I would stay. I enjoy it. The money's important, too. Even if I win a million dollars, I'll still be here at Southland." (She's alluding to a 7-Eleven store manager in New Jersey who, after winning the state lottery, did not leave her job, a fantastic publicity coup for the company. When, defying all the odds, she won a second time, she finally quit.) In addition to her salary, Toki's eligible for bonuses based on her profits.

Southland's culture is entrenched. Can there be any doubt? Too many people from too many disparate departments and backgrounds have too many similar things to say about their company. Far from thinking they were all coached beforehand, it would appear that the organization sends out its messages loud and clear. WE ARE HAPPY. YOU ARE PART OF OUR FAMILY. SPEND THE REST OF YOUR LIFE WITH US. In 1988 any comparison between corporation and family constitutes the loftiest of accolades. Even the Southland quarterly publication for employees and franchisees is called *The Southland Family*. And the constant soothing presence of the Thompson brothers makes it official.

"I feel I'm at the best. It seems anyplace you go from here is going downhill," a public relations person says. "I'm not naive enough to think everyone would be happy here. But I can't think why not." The positiveness that radiates from Southland employees seems like fallout from a Dale Carnegie course, which in fact is a recommended part of the curriculum of Southland's Corporate Training Center. People say the right things. They sound like they care. "We don't set up people to fail; we set them up to succeed." An employee assistance program provides confidential phone counseling and three sessions with a professional counselor free of charge.

Clark Matthews is Southland's senior executive vice-president and chief financial officer. A former practicing lawyer, he joined the company in August 1965. We meet at the Tower Club, a private downtown club, populated that day by only Southland employees. We have a view of part of downtown and can see the cranes and construction surrounding Cityplace. "The company listens to people. It's a friendly work environment. The personality of the company is a reflection of the Thompsons' father and his sons. John's and Jere's strong personalities filter through layers of management. Close communication is our biggest challenge and our biggest opportunity."

Lest you think this is just a company of hand holding and cosseting, 7-Eleven throws some American-style competition into the mix. Since stores get access to their own profit and loss information "and how it compares to their group's other stores, competition does exist."

Matthews is excited about the new ticketing service at 7-Eleven. Southland purchased TicketQuik, a "self-service ticketing machine still in the development stage," from the Pritzker family (Hyatt Hotels) of Chicago. "It will be a self-operating service, twenty-four hours a day. You can touch a screen with graphics that will take cash or credit cards, give change, pick out your seats, print up your tickets, and show directions to arenas." The service will primarily sell tickets to sporting events and concerts. "Tests say that people would buy thirty to forty percent more tickets if they bought them at 7-Elevens. We've committed ten million dollars to its development."

THE
STAUBACH
COMPANY

HISTORY & OPERATIONS

Roger "the Dodger" Staubach embarked on a career in real estate while serving as star quarterback for the Dallas Cowboys. In 1970, a year after he joined the team, Staubach took a job at the Henry S. Miller Co. in Dallas, selling insurance during his off-season. After acquiring two years of sales experience, Staubach asked to work for the company's real estate division. The management granted his request with reluctance—they worried that a football star might not be taken seriously as a real estate broker—but Staubach quickly became one of the company's top producers. In 1977, when Dallas was experiencing a growth spurt and the real estate market was booming, Staubach and Robert Holloway, Jr., a colleague at Henry S. Miller, left to start their own business, the Holloway-Staubach Corporation.

Staubach split his time between his athletic career and his company until 1980, when he retired from the Cowboys. He then divided his time among the company, television commercials (primarily his endorsements for Rolaids), his ownership of a chain of fast food chicken restaurants in Cincinnati (where he grew up), and a stint as a sportscaster for CBS. In 1982 Staubach relinquished all his other obligations to devote himself full time to real estate. He bought out Holloway's interest in the firm—on amicable terms—and in January 1983 he established The Staubach Company.

The Holloway-Staubach Corporation had specialized in development—the high-stakes side of real estate—as well as the brokerage and leasing of commercial space. Part of the reason Staubach and Holloway parted was that Holloway wanted to push the company in the direction of development, while Staubach preferred to concentrate on brokerage and leasing, the less risky and more customer-oriented end of the business. The Staubach Company, though a full-service company with some modest development activity, grew primarily as a result of tenant service. It was among the first real estate firms in the country to solely represent a tenant's interests in finding and leasing office space while refusing to have any involvement in the landlord's end of the deal. The company's methods proved successful, and, benefiting additionally from its founder's fame and good name, The Staubach Company expanded more quickly than Staubach had anticipated. It continued to flourish even after 1984, when the overextended Dallas real estate market began to soften.

In 1983 The Staubach Company had revenues of $1.05 million and twenty employees. Revenues more than doubled to $2.8 million in 1984, and almost doubled again to $5.45 million in 1985. That year, the firm was ranked ninety-first (first among Texas companies) on the *Inc.* 500 list of the fastest-growing privately held U.S. companies. In 1986 revenues increased to $10.6 million and the staff grew to 150. And in 1987 the employee count increased to 190 and the firm saw revenues of close to $15 million. Among the more than 150 commercial clients the firm represents are American Express, AT&T, Control Data, Ernst & Whinney, Ford Motor Credit, Hospital Corporation of America, McDonald's Corporation, MCI, and Texas Instruments.

At the end of 1986, when the company already had dealings in markets outside of Texas, Staubach made a land investment in Atlanta. In 1987 the organization established offices in Washington, D.C., and Nashville, and Fort Lauderdale, Florida. In 1988 it opened an office in Orange County, California. An Atlanta office is scheduled for 1989, Chicago in 1990, and a New York office is also slated to open within the next couple of years.

The Staubach Company is structured into the following divisions: Corporate Services, which provides tenant representation for corporate users of office and industrial space and accounts for roughly 60 percent of revenues; the Retail Services Division, which provides the same services as the corporate service group but in the retail sector and contributes 15 percent of total revenues; Staubach Investments, Inc. which syndicates land and accounts for about 10 percent of revenues; and Assets Services, which contributes about 15 percent of revenues and is split into the following subdivisions: Asset Management Services (a consulting practice), Land and Income Property Division (which puts together buyers and sellers for a brokerage fee), and the Residential Development Management division (which primarily develops and manages apartments). Pension Advisory Services, a division that was started in 1987, acts in a fiduciary capacity for investing pension funds in real estate. In 1987 the firm leased $263 million worth of commercial space.

(Information supplied by Jim Leslie, chief financial officer.)

REVENUES: Approximately $14.9 million in fiscal 1987.

EARNINGS: The company is privately held and will not disclose.

OFFICES: Headquarters in Dallas and offices in Fort Lauderdale, Nashville, Washington, D.C., and Orange County, California. Over the next two years, the company plans to open additional offices in New York, Chicago, and Atlanta.

NUMBER OF EMPLOYEES: 190, which includes independent contractors as well as full-time employees. Personnel are divided roughly in half between the service side and the assets side of the business.

AVERAGE AGE OF EMPLOYEES: Thirty-two.

TURNOVER: About 13 percent, which is low by industry standards.

RECRUITMENT: The firm recruited for the first time in February 1988 at the Harvard Business School. Beginning fall 1988, the program is expanding to the business schools at the University of Michigan, Stanford University and two others, as yet undetermined. Right now The Staubach Company is recruiting primarily in the area of Corporate Services. At present, more than half of the new brokers hired have MBAs, and the company has been replacing some brokers who don't have MBAs with people who do.

NUMBER OF NEW HIRES PER YEAR: About thirty, though that number should increase as the company opens new offices.

RANGE OF STARTING SALARIES: Entry-level salaries for asset people, almost all of whom work on straight salary (plus bonus), range from $13,000 to $30,000. Beginning brokers—all brokers work solely on commission—can expect to earn $40,000–$60,000.

POLICY FOR RAISES: All employees are reviewed every December, and raises are generally comparable to the cost of living index.

TRAINING PROGRAMS: No formal programs, but new employees undergo a lot of on-the-job training, and the company sponsors several one- and two-day internal seminars for all employees on an ongoing basis.

BENEFITS: Health insurance, dental insurance, life insurance (in varying amounts, depending on position), and long-term disability insurance. The company pays all the above costs for employees and their dependents. The company also has a profit-sharing plan, determined at the end of the fiscal year. It takes six years to be vested. If employees leave after six years, they can withdraw all the money the company has contributed for them. If they leave before that time, they get a prorated amount—20 percent after two years and an additional 20 percent for every additional year. The company encourages all its professionals to get their professional designation in whatever capacity they serve—such as CPA for accountants and CPM for property managers—but it doesn't usually pay for that unless an employee has strongly demonstrated his or her abilities. Reimbursement is determined on a case-by-case basis.

VACATION: Two weeks the first year, three weeks after five years, in addition to ten regular paid holidays.

ADDITIONAL PERKS: Free parking for all employees as well as a company-sponsored employee discount at the Aerobics Activity Center in Dallas. Six weeks per year, usually in the spring, the company offers morning Bible classes (7:30 A.M. to 8:30 A.M.), which are generally attended by 40–50 percent of the employees.

BONUSES: In December All employees are awarded bonuses that reflect the profitability of the firm. Awards are given to the top five producers and to goal achievers, those who have met or exceeded the financial goals they set for themselves for the year. The top producer gets to attend the Super Bowl with Roger Staubach, and all five top producers get rings inset with diamonds corresponding to the number of years they've been among the top five (the more years, the more diamonds). Goal achievers receive some type of "not too terribly gaudy" memento they can display in their offices.

ANNUAL PARTIES: Two per year. The company hosts an annual picnic in the fall, including various athletic events, for employees and their families. Also, the week before the Super Bowl there's a black tie awards banquet for all employees and their spouses.

AVERAGE WORKDAY: Official company hours are 8:00 A.M. to 5:00 P.M. Most people, including support staff, work between forty-five and fifty hours per week.

DRESS CODE: "Professional." Men wear suits and ties and, for the most part, white shirts; women wear suits or dresses, no slacks.

SOCIAL ATMOSPHERE: "Very cordial and very friendly." Some people socialize with one another after office hours, but everyone has his or her own life, too. "I don't want you to think, 'Hey, everything's great, we just can't spend enough time with each other.' Everyone has their families and their own personal pursuits outside of the company."

HEADQUARTERS: The Staubach Company occupies approximately 22,000 square feet of space in a two-story north Dallas building set on a creek. The company used to own the building, which is one of five in a corporate park, but it was sold in 1982. The Staubach offices are located on the first floor.

CHARITABLE CONTRIBUTIONS: Historically, the company has contributed between 10 and 15 percent of net income to charity. Among those it regularly supports are the Salvation Army, American Cancer Society, Leukemia Society, Fellowship of Christian Athletes, United Way, and several local organizations.

INTERESTED APPLICANTS CAN SEND RÉSUMÉS TO:
The Staubach Company
Vice-president of Administration
6750 LBJ Freeway, Suite 1100
Dallas, TX 75240
(214) 385-0500

So you think Roger Staubach's main source of income is his residuals from the manufacturers of Rolaids? Wrong. The Staubach Company, based in Dallas, is a major player in commercial real estate. Our visit took place after Dallas's fortunes started to sour—when the huge superstructures that dotted the city's horizon looked shiny unoccupied instead of shiny new. The company's headquarters are located in one of the shiny, well-designed corporate parks and are filled with clean-cut, well-spoken, aggressive salespeople who, for a million reasons, are competitors.

It was once said, "Real estate is to Dallas as automotives are to Detroit. And Trammel Crowe [Dallas's most successful practitioner] is the Henry Ford of real estate." Now it is an even more apt comparison. Detroit has been on the mend from a seemingly relentless period of hard times that began during the oil crisis of the 1970s and was perpetuated by the feeling that foreign-made cars were superior in value, craftsmanship, and design (not to mention automatic prestige). Dallas, a boastful success story, built one huge building atop another in striking defiance of any lean years and laughed as Houston, Texas's oil capital, started to collapse. In the metropolitan area two gargantuan holes were dug that were successively termed "the largest hole in Texas." (One, which became the Crescent complex, belongs to Rosewood [see p. 192], and the other, Cityplace, is part of the Southland empire [see p. 202.) But Staubach's universe is not restricted to Dallas, and there is a willingness to see through this crisis and develop authority in other areas.

Real estate salesmen, the object of David Mamet's Pulitzer Prize–winning play, *Glengarry Glen Ross*, are not objects of sympathy. "Historically," explains a Staubach employee, "we're one step above used car salesmen. Those guys on TV who are not educated, but very flashy." Pinky rings and hacking customers would not be consistent with the culture established by Roger Staubach, a soft-spoken, modest graduate of the U.S. Naval Academy, Heisman Trophy winner, ex–Dallas Cowboy superstar, father of five, and pious Catholic. Salespeople at Staubach have all kinds of advanced degrees, dress like attorneys, and sometimes marvel at the fact that they actually ended up in real estate.

Jim Leslie, chief financial officer, earned his MBA at the University of Michigan. A Nebraska native, he moved to Dallas in search of a more pleasing climate, having passed his CPA exam. He joined Coopers & Lybrand, a Big Eight public accounting firm, where he focused on real estate, "as a stepping-stone." "It's funny; you go to business school, you're geared to be president, and then you're underemployed." When he was twenty-six, "this opportunity came up with Rog." He was hired as CFO for a company that totaled twenty employees. "It was a calculated risk. In the worst case, I'd go back to Coopers," he says from his comfortable office six years later. Today the Staubach Company employs 190.

What made the risk so much more palatable was the opportunity to work with Staubach, a Dallas hero and civic leader. In a city where people are not afraid to voice their opinions, Roger Staubach gets high marks from all corners. People like knowing him. "Investors have faith in him." Of course, this is not enough to maintain a profitable organization. "Initially there was some skepticism about Roger as a businessman. He had to develop some consistency in business and not be an ex-jock." When Staubach was a partner in Staubach-Holloway, it was suggested that "Holloway was the brains; Staubach the flash." With good references and some promotion, that notion has been eliminated. The company's slogan is "You know the name, but do you know the company?" Simply stated, Staubach's celebrity in Texas cannot be underestimated.

"A lot of people in the Dallas real estate community think Roger can't write a lease. But a lot of doors easily open to him. He's 'Mr. Clean' and does have a very good business head. He wants to be known as the guy you can count on. I'm sure he's a millionaire many times over, and he doesn't need this company, but his past as a football player made him competitive. He doesn't go out of his way to toot his own horn."

That's okay; his team will do that for him. When employees are asked about their jobs and the way business is conducted in the modern halls of The Staubach Company, it is rare for them to answer in a way that doesn't include a tribute to Roger Staubach, the man. Perhaps this is due to a career filled with so many questions about What He's Like that employees take on the added task of public relations. Even if you are not curious about Roger Staubach, you will learn about him through his proud and practiced employees.

Staubach's company, which is regarded as "conservative" by other local real estate people, means to concentrate on service as much as brokerage. "If we were just in the asset side of business we'd have to diversify geographically [à la other real estate heavies in Dallas]. But this is a great time. Service is up. Our leasing group's really strong, so we're not under pressure to leave Dallas." (Expansion outside Texas, however, is under way.) Asset-side employees are rewarded with salaries, and service-side people earn commissions. "Every time you set up a new property, it's like a separate business. The person who's created the ideas gets part ownership." Everyone at Staubach feels the pressure to "enhance."

Professionals at Staubach are not of the my-car-is-my-office genre; they tout their reliance on sound planning. "Every year we revise the five-year plan." Hiring is also based on a master plan. "We look for people with high morality and ethics, people with pretty good spiritual lives, but we're not preaching or forcing Bible studies or anything like this. Not one religion." But Staubach's deep piety "gets picked up, and we may attract this kind of person. It's real subtle; you just live your life around your spiritual life."

Gary Polozola, Staubach's vice-president of operations, is a relative newcomer to the company, although an old acquaintance of Roger's. After attending a seminary-affiliated high school, he played varsity baseball in college and was in the semipros after that. He, too, cites the sense of integrity and morality as a trademark of the organization. Furthermore, he regards a solid education as the best training possible. "Believe it or not, a young person needs good grades, to be well rounded and involved in extracurricular activities. You'd think these skills are way out, but speaking Japanese, being an attorney, having worked in acquisitions, or a long-term experience at IBM would all be relevant to real estate. We have an array of people who are entrepreneurs." When asked what he looks for in an interview that would indicate an applicant's "fit," Polozola echoes Supreme Court Justice Potter Stewart's 1981 definition of pornography: " 'I know it when I see it.' There's something about their eyes, a smile that says, 'I can be very good,' even the way they dress." Gary guarantees he'll see any applicant who approaches him, even if there are no positions open.

Aside from proximity to Roger Staubach, part of the allure of working here is the feeling that you are in control of your life. "We're all independent contractors. We're here because we don't want an eight-to-three [workday], six-sick-days environment. We're a group of people who don't want to be managed." This from Susan Gideon Arledge, an honor-festooned broker who is ranked among Staubach's Top Five Producers, an annual ranking of roughly thirty-nine brokers, and 1987's Top Achiever. "You report to him. [Any doubt who "he" is?] There are no levels of supervision. People must be motivated and disciplined. The tarnished image of commercial real estate is ameliorated by Roger."

Susan, who was listed in the 1981 and 1982 directory *Outstanding Young Women in America,* remembered her initial considerations when she thought about joining The Staubach Company. "I didn't want to deal with residential [real estate], because that's based on emotional decisions. To start out, you have to have a sense of confidence or be an idiot. Roger was just starting. There weren't ways of doing things that I'd have to fight or obey. And I wanted to have control over my own financial destiny.

"People fail at this business because they don't understand about not making a salary. You do not know from year to year what you'll earn. You must tolerate volatility. Brokers get no corporate titles. They get no structure, other than making money." The only possible structure offered by Staubach is the annual goal review. Each broker meets with Staubach and Jim Leslie to determine his or her individual goal. "You must produce to meet the corporate goals and pay overhead." On the other hand, "If you coasted or didn't work, Roger wouldn't ask you to leave. He's got a soft spot.

"Roger's a good example of having money and integrity. He's got a lot of money, but he's very family-oriented. He's not out of touch or unreal, but he has his life in proper perspective. Roger preaches balance in his life."

Susan continues, "We tend to have a type of person. Roger wants this company to be different from the industry [norm], to overcome the image of commercial real estate. Roger preaches that the needs of the client come first. If your sole goal is to make money to the negligence of your client, you wouldn't last long. We either have people who fit in, or they leave on their own. Personal feelings about Roger keep me here."

We are now driving to Dallas's Aerobics Activity Center, an impressive fitness club designed by Dr. Kenneth Cooper, *the* guru of aerobics, where the company maintains a corporate membership. Did I mention that we were driving in Susan's blue BMW 733i, which is outfitted with a car phone? "The car phone is the tool of your trade," she says in a no-nonsense way. "It's nothing special in real estate. I can buy two extra hours in a day sometimes. I don't think there's as much conspicuous consumption in our company. There's less need to prove yourself.

"Everyone's positive here. There's not one person I wouldn't go to for help; I trust everyone. Roger's moral fiber, his religious beliefs—people are cut from the same moral mold. The sense of spirit and the team is why I haven't started my own company. I don't want managerial headaches. I can do what I enjoy: real estate transactions."

Being a female broker in an overwhelmingly male business "is neither an advantage nor a disadvantage," Arledge says. "Eighty-five to ninety percent of the decision makers are male. Your credentials speak for themselves." (Sometimes, when desperation sets in, Arledge admits that desperate measures are needed to win a client. These include autographed footballs and photographs of ex-quarterback Staubach.) Susan makes no fashion concessions to corporate America. She wears her hair shoulder length, sports a professional-looking makeup job, and accentuates her femininity. She seems to be one of the "having it all" women we read about but seldom meet. She lives seven minutes away from the office. She arrives for work at 7:30 A.M. and stays until 5:30 P.M., then works out daily at the Aerobics Activity Center. She is married to a car salesman and is the mother of a preschooler.

"I took five days off after the birth of my son on December 26, 1984. I was in the office on December 30." A full-time live-in nanny solves the day care problem. "Work is really fun. I don't think of it as work, just as a hobby I enjoy. And the aerobics gives me emotional freedom. You have to be driven. It's not a desire to be rich. It's an inner drive. I like that we're selling services, not just a product. It's more of a challenge. It's hard for people to buy the intangible."

Susan Arledge may not be the most competitive woman working for the Staubach Company. In all fairness, that title probably belongs to Ka (pronounced "Kay") Cotter, the only broker who's been in the Top Five Producers every year since the award was founded and was the Top Achiever for 1986. (On January 1, 1988, she was promoted to executive vice-president, managing the Dallas office, and is no longer a broker.) In addition to this success, which nets her personal wealth plus a share in Staubach Company equity, she concedes, "There's a competition to know Roger. In and out of the office. Roger doesn't want people to work here for *him.* People have actually said, 'I want to work with Roger Staubach—he'll make my career!' I'm fortunate for the years I've been here, because they can't take that away from me." Ka met Staubach when she was a residential real estate broker and she listed and sold his old house in forty-eight hours. Previously, she had been a salesperson at IBM, a teacher, and a housewife.

If there is a downside to her job, it's "making time for my family. It's hurt business, because I'm very competitive." But Cotter loves her job. "I give more to clients than they know. The struggle is how to commit hours and to balance work and home. When you work real hard, you know how much you do—otherwise there'd be no tops on the trees."

John Amend's picture is printed on a glossy flier announcing him as 1985's Top Achiever. A former college athlete at Oklahoma University and its rival University of Texas, he started his professional life as an accountant. "That was my daddy's idea. I was in it for five years and tried to get out of it for two. I finally convinced a finance company to hire me. I was the president at twenty-eight. Don't be too impressed; there were only forty-five employees." When it became obvious Amend would never gain any ownership, he left. "I saw my dad deprived when he hit his fifties, and I didn't want that to happen to me."

From there he mastered marketing and sales through door-to-door sales. "I saw these fourth-grade guys making all this money," he recalls laughingly. "I sold Saladmaster—a package of china, crystal, cutlery, and flatware—for a thousand dollars to single women. I'd make three appointments a night. I made more money doing this than I did as president of the finance company."

Recognizing his taste for entrepreneurship, John decided to consider real estate, "one of the last frontiers of entrepreneurial enterprise. The strongest requirement for real estate is to fog a mirror." In other words, none. "A little old lady can sell an office building. It's a joke.

"The industry has few controls and so very little professional development. At Staubach, we internally regulate it. Roger's integrity is unassailed. I never have to prove I'm honest. On a big deal you need more than integrity and an ex–pro football player. You need good people. My efforts are the result of twenty-five other people I work with. You are looking at the most unusual real estate services company in the business."

Although his recognition is validated by his financial compensation, Amend swears it's not the money that keeps him going. "I'd rather win than get paid." But it's definitely big buck time. His first big deal, concluded four years ago, was a $10 million lease. Now he's closing a $500 million deal. "It's not the money. It's doing things that haven't been done before. I have to struggle with the feeling of 'What's next?' Looking for satisfaction can be a disease. You can achieve and achieve, but what's next?" he repeats.

"I'm competitive. I want to be the very, very best I can be. I'm a Type A obsessive-compulsive," he says amid the pandemonium of his office, including a ringing phone and a visiting daughter. "I like those underdog movies. *Valdez Is Coming* is my favorite." He identifies with Roy Hobbs, the baseball player portrayed by Robert Redford in *The Natural*.

Amend reiterates the gospel according to Staubach: The company is atypical. Business is performed a bit differently from the norm. "The only way my clients can distinguish me from seven hundred other guys is to spend time with me. Otherwise, we don't have a commonality of purpose. I don't want to hire an experienced real estate guy anymore, because we'd have to de-train him."

And what about Roger Staubach? "He's the greatest guy I've ever met in my life. He's a great leader. It's not hero worship, either. Life is too short to worship the almighty dollar, but Roger and I believe in a higher existence. I want to be around people whose values I share. We're partners. He's like a brother to me. It's a relationship money can't buy.

"You see the man. He's happy. I'd like to be like him. He doesn't take drugs or chase women, and it rubs off on people. His life must be filled with peace. I'm personally a spiritual person, or at least I try to be. I think people are better for having met him."

Ever since Roger Staubach left the NFL, there's been talk of his running for political office. Although an engineering major, his Naval Academy thesis was on the Bolshevik revolution, and he's maintained his interest in foreign policy over the years, "although I'm not a fanatic." His postgraduate year was spent in Vietnam. He is a conservative Republican who, according to a colleague, "speaks with Reagan once a month, and to Bush more than that."

"I definitely believe there's a Communist game plan," he says firmly in his large but relatively unadorned corner office. "It's the enemy of freedom. I've read Marx. I'm about as well read as any ex-athlete who's in real estate. I'm really enlightened." Real estate is his business, and that is why we are talking today, but his interest in politics is keen enough that it doesn't take long to divert his attention. Staubach's campaigning for President Reagan in 1980 "really fueled gossip about my political ambitions. I really don't have the desire to enter politics now. Maybe someday, as a businessman, not as an ex-athlete, when my children are older. You have a responsibility in public. Power, ego, identity—I've had those things. You've got to be ready for it. I'm not afraid to speak my mind. I'm a fierce competitor as an athlete, but I'm pretty darn objective as a guy."

On his leadership of others, Staubach says, "I'm not trying to place my morality on other people. We have people of different faiths. I have strong Christian beliefs." He claims that piety is not a prerequisite for employment. "I'd hire an atheist who's honest and works hard. I'd try," he adds, "to change his mind. I don't specifically ask, 'Are you a Christian?' We have Jewish people. I believe in Jesus Christ. You need a basic foundation. I want to hire people who work hard and want to be successful. We're not a nonprofit organization. I wouldn't tolerate anyone messing around with other people's husbands and wives or drugs."

Roger's been called "Mr. Clean," a "goody two-shoes," "squeaky clean," and "too good to be true." In addition to running his business, he is involved in charitable and civic activities, including the Fellowship of Christian Athletes, the Salvation Army Advisory Board, the No Greater Love Program, the Young Presidents Organization, and the Dallas Assembly, and he serves on other companies' boards of directors. He always maintains, however, that his family comes first. "The [collective] priority *is* the family. Even for secretaries. The balance is important, especially for women. I don't think many drop their kids off at day care." It is said that Roger once canceled a dinner with Ronald Reagan to spend time with one of his daughters. "It is more important than our business."

Besides Staubach being the kind of person we all wish we could lean on, or at least wish we knew, his style of business reflects a faith in people. It reflects a commitment to service and loyalty toward one's customers. "Business is cutthroat. You don't have to be cutthroat, you have to be tough. I enjoy managing actively. In business, you have to let people know where you stand. Especially if you're a Christian. Sometimes we're our own worst enemy. What we say and what we do are not always the same thing. We must make money without stepping on others." The struggle is between morals and business. Although none of the other employees mentions it and some evade the question, The Staubach Company holds "intermittent Bible studies in the mornings and gets a fifty percent turnout."

Ka Cotter sees Roger's life in ten-year cycles, more or less: his college and military career; his tenure as a Dallas Cowboy, during which time he was hailed as "this country's greatest sports hero" with ninety-six victories, eleven in playoff games and two in Super Bowls; and now his real estate decade. He's not ready to quit the business . . . yet. "I haven't experienced [in business] the total satisfaction of walking off the field having won the Super Bowl," he says at the end of the day, getting ready for dinner at home.

Interview:

TONY WAINWRIGHT

C. Anthony Wainwright, the president and chief operating officer of the Bloom Companies, New York and Dallas (number fifty-four in *Advertising Age's* 1987 ranking) and the chief executive officer of the Bloom Agency in Dallas, can't sleep. Since he's been in charge of these combined agencies, they've grown like crazy—from local to national agencies, with billings almost reaching $200 million—often due to campaigns he dreams up late at night. When he's not writing one of the two books he has under contract at the moment or working on a screenplay or a column for *Advertising Age,* he's flying around the country, maintaining an interesting schedule. He goes to sleep at 9:00 or 9:30 P.M. at the latest, to wake again at midnight. His most fruitful creative time is then, from midnight till 2:00 A.M., when he retires again, and during other breaks until dawn. He wakes at 4:30 A.M. He arrives at the office before 6:00 A.M. He sticks to this schedule even during business trips, which he makes about three times a week. Tony figures he logs about 600,000 air miles per year, most of them on American Airlines. He's got over 2 million miles on their AAdvantage program for frequent flyers.

Meeting Wainright—compact, fit, sandy-haired, fifty-four years of age, patiently tamping his pipe—you are confronted by a warm, calm man. He doesn't seem like an insomniac. After enthusiastically describing the plot of a suspense tale he's writing, he changes gears and mentions a new business pitch that might be taking place within the next few days. And then another aside. He seems completely at ease with being overextended, overtaxed and overworked. [Author's note: I don't think he realizes this is unusual.]

"My job comes first," he says. "So I get that done. The only way I can get the other stuff done is because I have more time than other people. I'm sure I have four more hours a day than anyone else." Well, sure, the other four hours when most people are sleeping. "That's when I write. It doesn't interfere with my job."

When he takes vacations with his wife, Mary Beth, who sleeps and wakes the way most normal people do, he brings work along but touts them as wonderful rests. When Tony is enthusiastic, the word "terrific" bubbles out of him like carbonated soda out of a shaken can.

Under Wainwright's leadership, Bloom won that most desirable of accounts—a car—Alfa Romeo. (It was asked to compete for Nissan, the single largest automobile account, when it left J. Walter Thompson in 1987, and for Porsche, when it left Chiat/Day (see p. 287), because it had won Nissan. Bloom declined both out of loyalty to Alfa Romeo.) Bloom represents Maybelline, Murine, Poli-Grip, Pentax Cameras, Carnation, Tropical Blend sun care products, Solarcaine, Airwick household products, and Church's fried chicken, among others. (The last was helped by the recruitment of Seth Werner, the art director behind the award-winning California Raisin Board claymation campaign.)

Born in Los Angeles, Wainwright attended the University of Colorado, graduating with a degree in journalism in 1955. He was headed toward a career as a reporter, but "the only job I was offered was at a small newspaper in, I think, Cody, Wyoming. I didn't want to move there. I went back to Chicago, which was home at the time, and when I couldn't get a job at the *Tribune* or the *Sun-Times,* I knocked on doors." His first job was at McCann-Erickson in Chicago, working as an assistant director and producer of radio and television commercials for Swift & Company, Helene Curtis, and others. His next position, as a copywriter, was pivotal, for it was at Leo Burnett, where he got to work with the man himself. He worked on the Green Giant account and is given credit for helping to develop the Marlboro Man. As headhunters called, Wainwright moved up and away to N. W. Ayer & Son and then Grey Advertising, both in Chicago.

By this point he had achieved financial independence. Did he reconsider journalism? "No. I liked advertising, and I was good at it. Most people stumble into what they do, anyway. Besides, if I'd pursued journalism, I'd have had to have been a newspaper reporter. I would have wanted to be a columnist, and there are only about fourteen of them in the world. I'm not Jimmy Breslin, and I'm not Tom Wicker."

In 1969, wanting to work for himself, he started a company that developed new products for big companies. Wainwright's first assignment was for Plough (whose account Bloom handles today). "It gave me the courage to quit my job." Later, when he refused to move to Plough's Memphis headquarters, Mr. Plough fired him. "Then he hired me about three years later." While sharing a small two-room office with a secretary, Wainright got a visit from an officer of Richardson-Vicks. He offered Wainwright a one-year contract, which got his business rolling. Wainwright ended up going to Paris to write the original copy for Oil of Olay: "Women of the world discover the secret of Oil of Olay." It ran for years in the United Kingdom, Germany, and Canada. When Richardson-Vicks introduced the product in the United States, it took the account away from Wainwright and gave it to a larger agency.

As a product creator, Wainwright invented what is now known as Freshen-Up Gum. "I called it 'liquicenter gum,'" he says. The job was "to look for opportunities in new areas—acquisitions, really and to move the companies where they wanted to be. I did extremely well. After about three years I had five people working for me, then I brought in Spaeth and Wright.

"The upside was, it was fun and well paying. The downside was, once you'd done it [finished a project], it was over and you had to worry about replacing the business." Wainwright, Spaeth and Wright added conventional advertising accounts in addition to creating new products and new product categories until 1978.

Then the Marschalk Company lured him to New York with the offer of being the large agency's executive vice-president and general manager. He oversaw the Heublein, Minute Maid, Coca-Cola, and Stroh's accounts there, with an eye to increasing *their* business. Bob Bloom lured him to Dallas in 1980.

He can't believe the company he keeps in the Big D. His circle includes the names of the mighty raiders and family dynasties we read about in the business pages. Wainwright is involved in community activities on a high level. Politicians seek his advice, and he's given his time and ideas to candidates when solicited. He worked on Annette Strauss's winning campaign for mayor of Dallas. He worked on Governor Mark White's campaign for reelection. Two candidates for the Democratic presidential nomination made detours to Dallas to meet with him and solicit his help. He loses his placid facade when talking about his two main philanthropies, Baylor Hospital's Digestive Disease Center—"We've raised $2.7 million for expansion!"—and Boy's Hope, a network of inner city homes for orphaned boys.

Wainwright is a member of several boards of directors, including Horn & Hardart, Texas Commerce Bank, American Woodmark, and Tony Roma Corporation. He is one of several owners of KYRS, a country-western radio station in Corpus Christi, number one in its market.

He believes in people and in their potential to master their circumstances. As a child, he was undersized and the fodder of bullies. He studied karate and became a black belt, defending himself in actual life-threatening circumstances. His books, too, show an indomitable spirit. In 1962, after the death of his eight-month-old daughter, looking for solace, Wainwright wrote to a thousand dignitaries—Somerset Maugham, Eleanor Roosevelt, and Dr. Albert Schweitzer, among others—inquiring whether they'd ever been tried by tragedy or pain. The results were compiled in *Moments of Truth,* now in its second edition. A column for *Advertising Age,* "You will win if you have will to win," will be expanded to book length. He writes,

"When I had a small agency, one of my major clients asked to meet me at the airport. He represented one third of my billings. I was given the bad news. We had done a good job, but we were too small for the growing brand business. We were terminated. That night I sat up thinking.

"Refusing to allow myself to be depressed, I made up lists of new business prospects. We replaced the lost business in two months. . . . Most successful people have failed at least once. They seem to have an inner drive that gives them the strength to start over."

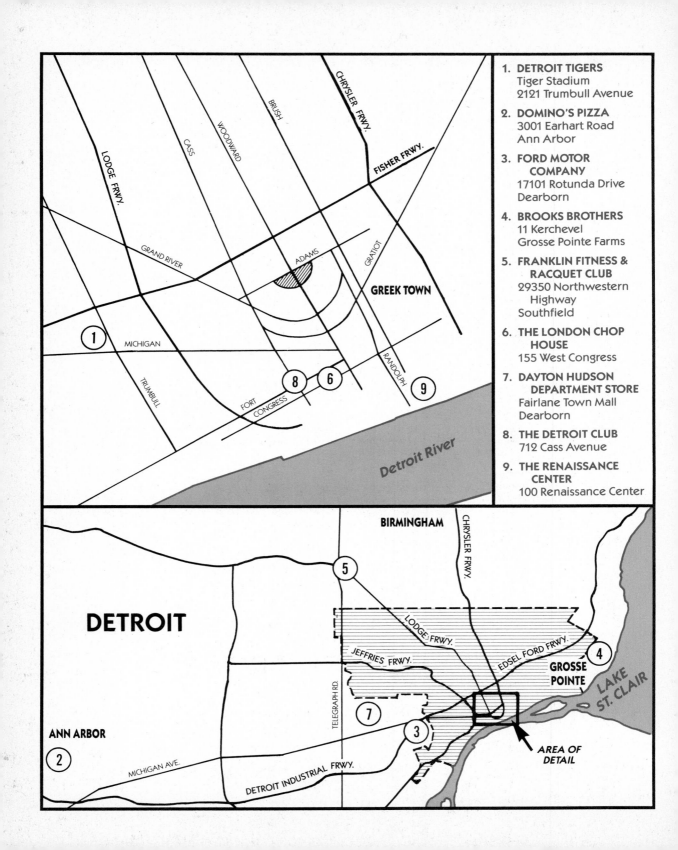

1. **DETROIT TIGERS**
   Tiger Stadium
   2121 Trumbull Avenue

2. **DOMINO'S PIZZA**
   3001 Earhart Road
   Ann Arbor

3. **FORD MOTOR
   COMPANY**
   17101 Rotunda Drive
   Dearborn

4. **BROOKS BROTHERS**
   11 Kerchevel
   Grosse Pointe Farms

5. **FRANKLIN FITNESS &
   RACQUET CLUB**
   29350 Northwestern
      Highway
   Southfield

6. **THE LONDON CHOP
   HOUSE**
   155 West Congress

7. **DAYTON HUDSON
   DEPARTMENT STORE**
   Fairlane Town Mall
   Dearborn

8. **THE DETROIT CLUB**
   712 Cass Avenue

9. **THE RENAISSANCE
   CENTER**
   100 Renaissance Center

GREEK TOWN

Detroit River

DETROIT

BIRMINGHAM

CHRYSLER FRWY.

LODGE FRWY.

JEFFRIES FRWY.

EDSEL FORD FRWY.

GROSSE
POINTE

LAKE
ST. CLAIR

TELEGRAPH RD.

ANN ARBOR

MICHIGAN AVE.

DETROIT INDUSTRIAL FRWY.

AREA OF
DETAIL

DETROIT

DETROIT

The victim of bad press (I have heard the complaint that airports don't advertise Detroit [or Michigan] as the vacation spot it ought to be, unlike the endless posters for say, Florida or New York City), Detroit is an acquired taste for transplants and the object of its natives' fierce love and pride.

Of course, home is best to most Americans, but civic pride seems boundless in the Motor City—racial disquietude, economic fragility and a high crime rate notwithstanding.

Michiganders, for example, *love* the Detroit Tigers. They love their cars. Made in America *means* something in this ethnic potpourri, and it would seem almost bad manners to drive an import. This is the industry that fuels the city (and the country, to a not insignificant extent), and as the employer of record, which has helped bring immigrants into the middle class, it is to be respected and feared.

The auto business (and its ancillary industries) is a man's business, if only because those in power tend to hire younger versions of themselves as their replacements. (Also, there are more boy car nuts than girl car nuts.) Consequently, women haven't penetrated the highest corporate levels of Detroit. Needless to say, there are other industries in Detroit where this is not the case, but women in Detroit don't flex their collective managerial muscle with the same agility as their sisters in other cities.

They look more feminine, for one thing—more pastels, more ruffled collars and shirt fronts, more iridescent eye shadow, more frosted nail polish.

They are more willing to use the term "boss" to describe the person to whom they report, rather than to describe their working relationship in a more cooperative, collaborative way. They accept the hierarchical authority in which they've been placed with contentment. They're pretty happy with the way things are.

But look, let's not have any trouble.

The contrasts between rich and poor in the metropolitan area have—as is the trend everywhere—become more pronounced than ever in the past decade. Parts of the city, like the housing projects, are hard for even the most stalwart Detroit boosters to praise. Across town, in communities you've heard of—Grosse Point being the most famous, Birmingham, Bloomfield Hills—homes are frequently estates and women's work can be lunch.

The waning middle is a great place to raise a family, and the University of Michigan in nearby Ann Arbor is one of the country's great universities. (No need to modify it with "public." It stands alone.)

BEST NEIGHBORHOODS WITH DECENT PUBLIC SCHOOLS: Grosse Pointe, Birmingham, Bloomfield Hills

NICEST NEIGHBORHOODS (BUT YOU'LL PROBABLY HAVE TO SEND YOUR KIDS TO PRIVATE SCHOOL): St. Claire Shores, Ann Arbor, Indian Village, Detroit Riverfront

BEST PLACES TO LIVE IF YOU'RE AN ASPIRING ARTIST OR YOU WANT TO LIVE NEAR PEOPLE WHO WEAR ONLY BLACK: Greektown, Ann Arbor, Cross Corridor Lofts

BEST NEIGHBORHOOD WITH TAKE-OUT FOOD AND SINGLE PEOPLE WHO ARE ALSO REPUBLICANS: Birmingham

MOST OVERPRICED COMMUNITIES FOR SUMMER HOMES: Petosky, Saugatuk, Traverse City, Macinac Island

BEST PUBLIC SCHOOLS: Gross Pointe, Birmingham, Bloomfield Hills

BEST PRIVATE SCHOOLS: Cranbrook Academy; Grosse Pointe Academy, University—Legett, Detroit Country Day

BEST ALTERNATIVE SCHOOLS: Rolper School

ARCHITECT WHO HAS MOST INFLUENCED THE CITY'S SKYLINE: John Portman; Albert Kahn

MOST POPULAR RESIDENTIAL ARCHITECTS: William Kessler & Associates

SOCIALLY INCLINED REALTOR: Jim Saros

DEALERS IN THE FINEST, MOST VALUABLE ART: Dumouchelle Art Galleries

TRENDY GALLERIES FOR PEOPLE WHO WEAR ALL BLACK AND HAVE A LOT OF MONEY: Detroit Focus gallery (Detroit), One One Eight Gallery (Ann Arbor), Detroit Artists' Market (Detroit), Habitat (Lathrup Village)

MOST EXCLUSIVE GOLF CLUBS: The Detroit Country Club, Oakland Hills Country Club

BEST PUBLIC GOLF FACILITY: Kensington Metro Park

MOST EXPENSIVE HEALTH CLUB: Franklin Fitness & Racquet Club

BEST HEALTH CLUB FOR MEETING POTENTIAL MATES: Vic Tanney's (Somerset Mall)

BEST HOTELS FOR BUSINESS TRIPS: Hyatt Regency (Dearborn)

BEST HOTELS FOR TRYSTS: St. Claire Inn (St. Claire)

RESTAURANTS KNOWN FOR BEST CUISINE: Van Dyke Place (Detroit), The Whitney (Detroit), Golden Mushroom (Southfield), Chez Raphael (Novi)

BEST RESTAURANTS FOR PEOPLE WHO WEAR BLACK: Seva (Ann Arbor), Koreana (Detroit), Wong's Eatery (Windsor, Ontario), Wah Court (Windsor, Ontario), The Appe' teaser (Birmingham), The Money Tree (Detroit)

BEST RESTAURANTS FOR AN INEXPENSIVE DATE: Lido (St. Claire Shores), Mexican Village (Detroit), Britts (Detroit) (for lunch)

NOISIEST RESTAURANTS (INTIMACY IMPOSSIBLE): Brownie's by the Lake (St. Claire Shores), Sparky Herbert's (Grosse Pointe)

BEST SPORTS BARS: H. C. Lindell (Detroit), Nemo's (near Tiger Stadium), Hummer (Detroit)

BEST DARK BARS: Footlights, The Caucus Club (Detroit), Boker's Keyboard Lounge (Detroit)

BEST GIMMICKY BARS: Woodbridge Tavern, The Cadieux Café (has Belgian Feather Bowling) Detroit; Club Taboo, Detroit

BEST BAR TO IMPRESS A CLIENT: Bar at the London Chop House (Detroit)

MOST EXCLUSIVE CITY CLUBS: The Detroit Club, The Detroit Athletic Club; The Little Club (Grosse Pointe)

FANCIEST WINE STORES WHENCE CEOS PROBABLY STOCK THEIR OWN CELLARS: The Vintage Pointe (Grosse Pointe), Merchant of Vino (Birmingham)

GOURMET STORES GUARANTEED NOT TO RUN OUT OF GOAT CHEESE OR SUN-DRIED TOMATOES: Merchant of Vino (Birmingham), The Merry Mouse (Grosse Pointe), R. Hirt Jr., Company (Eastern Market)

NICEST MOM-AND-POP GROCERY STORES: Hamlin's (Grosse Pointe), any Polish shop along Joseph Campeau Boulevard in Hamtramck

LARGEST DRUGSTORE WITH MOST REMARKABLE SELECTION: Meyer's Thrifty Acres.

CORPORATE PARTY PLANNERS: The Gourmet House (St. Claire Shores) (they fed the Pope)

HIGH-SOCIETY PARTY PLANNERS: Tom & Diane Schoeneth

POWER BARBERS: Barbers at General Motors and Ford

JUNIOR LEAGUE BEAUTY PARLORS: Maier Werner Beauty Salon (Grosse Pointe)

PLACE WHERE LADIES WHO LUNCH ARE LIKELY TO HAVE TEA AFTER A HARD DAY OF SHOP-PING, VOLUNTEER WORK, AND TENNIS: Jacobson's Tea Room (Jacobson's Department Stores)

BEST STORES FOR EXECUTIVE WOMEN: Lynn Portnoy (Detroit)

BEST STORES FOR EXECUTIVE MEN: Brooks Brothers (Detroit), Van Boven's (Detrroit), E. J. Hickey (Grosse Pointe)

BEST STORES FOR DRESS-UP CLOTHES: Roz & Sherm (Birmingham), Linda Dresner (Birmingham)

BEST SHOPPING RESOURCE FOR PEOPLE WHO WEAR ONLY BLACK CLOTHES: Corporation Cortino (West Bloomfield)

DEBUTANTE BALL: None—individual coming-out parties

BUSIEST SOCIAL SEASON OF THE YEAR FOR THOSE WHO CARE ABOUT SUCH THINGS: Thanksgiving to Christmas

SOCIAL HIGHLIGHT: Detroit Institute of Arts Under the Stars Gala (November)

TOP JEWELERS FOR RESETTING MOTHER'S EMERALDS: Pongracz Jewelers & Silversmith (Grosse Pointe), Matthew Hoffman (Ann Arbor)

MOST COMPLETE BRIDAL REGISTRIES: Jacobson's Department Stores, Hudson's Department Stores

PSYCHIATRIST MOST OFTEN QUOTED IN THE LOCAL PRESS: Dr. Emanuel Tonoi

BEST SEAMSTRESS OR TAILOR FOR CUSTOM TAILORING: Antonio Rimanelli (Grosse Pointe), Polyzois (Grosse Pointe)

POPULAR FACIAL SALONS: Bloomie's Face and Body Salon (Bloomfield)

POWER TOOLS

MEN'S POWER DRESSING

BROOKS BROTHERS
11 Kerchevel
Grosse Pointe Farms, MI 48236
(313) 886-2300

BEST-SELLING EXECUTIVE SUIT: Medium gray, midweight, 100 percent wool, solid gray or pinstripe on gray, $430

POWER SHIRT: Pinpoint oxford cloth, button-down collar, 100 percent cotton, white or blue, $46

POWER TIE: Silk burgundy foulard, $22

ANTONIO RIMANELLI
20335 Mack Avenue
Grosse Pointe, MI 48236
(313) 882-0173

Antonio Rimanelli caters to the executive man and carries a range of suits from relatively inexpensive ready-to-wear, to designer labels, to custom-made. In the latter category, Rimanelli fits custom suits for men who fall into two groups: those who are hard-to-fit and those with money who "always dreamed of being able to afford a custom suit. This is a realization that they've finally made it." We spoke to Rimanelli about his executive clientele:

TELL US ABOUT YOUR EXECUTIVE CLIENTS AND THE KINDS OF SUITS THEY BUY.

"Younger men usually buy readymade suits. Our best-sellers in this category are HartMarx, Cricketeer, and Stanley Blacker. We also carry designer labels in the more expensive area—Ralph Lauren, Donald Brooks, and Oscar de la Renta—but the average executive is somewhat reluctant to spend more than $300 per suit, so he prefers to have a variety of suits rather than a custom suit costing upwards of $800. The average age for custom suits is mid-forties to mid-fifties."

WHAT STYLES DO YOUR EXECUTIVE CUSTOMERS BUY FOR THEMSELVES?

"They are most interested in a more conservative silhouette—natural shoulders, notched lapels, single-breasted—to give a serious impression when going to the office."

DO MANY EXECUTIVES WANT, FOR INSTANCE, AN ARMANI SUIT, IN ORDER TO WEAR SOMETHING THAT CLEARLY COSTS A LOT OF MONEY?

"Well, not really. However, we just started carrying his line. Let's face it, we are somewhat brainwashed in our society—slaves to the advertisers. But what's the point of buying an Armani suit if it doesn't look well on you just so people know how much you spent? It might be the case, I think, if the label were on your fanny. But it's inside the jacket."

WOMEN'S POWER DRESSING

LINDA DRESNER
299 West Maple Road
Birmingham, MI 48011
(313) 642-4999

Linda Dresner, the chic Michigan boutique, outfits both sexes, with a heavy emphasis on women. Known for "incomparable personal service," the store keeps a page on each of its customers that notes her (or his) stylistic preferences and past purchases. Such service comes at a price; the *average* purchase at the store is a whopping $1,500. Linda Dresner herself serves as the shop's sole buyer, and most customers come in at the beginning of each season to preview the new lines. The store has 9,000 square feet of selling space.

We spoke to Lou Plotkin, the store's manager, who told us that the average executive customer is thirty-five to fifty-five years old, and most executive customers are doctors and lawyers. The store's best-selling designers are Luciano Soprani, Yoshi Yamamoto, Comme des Garcons, and Jean Muir ("we do a tremendous business with Jean Muir for the executive" for women's daytime wear starting at $800 for classic wool jersey wool crêpes, and cashmere dresses and suits), and Vicky Tiel and Chloë for cocktail wear. Hot-selling accessories include Prada and Maxine for handbags (average sale: $500), Kieselstein-Cord belts ("we can't keep them in stock"), and, especially popular this year, wide alligator belts with sterling silver buckles ($1,200).

POWER WATCHES

SCHUBOT
3001 Big Beaver West
Suite 112
Troy, MI 48084
(313) 649-1122

BEST SELLER AMONG EXECUTIVE MEN: Patek-Philippe, $5,100–$14,000; round face with coin edge, perfectly plain, waterproof, mechanical, eighteen-karat gold. "For a top executive who does not want to be overflashy or ostentatious." Comes with either a leather strap ($5,100) or a gold bracelet ($14,000) and either a blue or brown dial.

Piaget Dancer, $11,900; gold bracelet, link type, very thin, "not real heavy—a good weight but not as heavy as the Polo, which was the big model a few years ago."

BEST SELLER AMONG EXECUTIVE WOMEN: Cartier Panther, $8,000–$13,500; Cartier gold bracelet watch, usually has either Roman numeral or mother-of-pearl sunburst dial, either plain or with diamonds around the edge (choice of one or two rows of diamonds). "It's a thin, very traditional watch."

Piaget Dancer, $8,900–$25,000; looks the same as the man's version, only smaller, and comes with round or square face. "In square, the watch is the same width as the bracelet." Comes with or without diamonds.

"We find that the executives are looking for dressy, not too thick, not ostentatious, but elegant watches. They're looking for quality, and people who know quality will recognize it. I can say without being contradicted that we have a selection of watches that no other place in the world has."

"The most popular all-around watch is probably the Rolex, for both men and women. It's more for when someone first makes it. They buy a Cadillac and a Rolex. Everyone knows what a Rolex is worth. When they're buying the Patek-Philippe, no one really understands it unless they know watches. In addition to having the sport watches, people buy dress watches because when they go out in the evening they like to have a dress watch."

DO MOST MEN BUY WATCHES FOR THEMSELVES OR RECEIVE THEM AS PRESENTS?
"It's a combination. About fifty-fifty."

DO MOST WOMEN BUY WATCHES FOR THEMSELVES OR RECEIVE THEM AS PRESENTS?
"Up until now, the women haven't really bought too many for themselves. More and more women are buying watches for themselves. Men have many things to buy for women, and women don't have many to buy for men. Women love buying men a watch. There's watches, cuff links, bracelets, but not many things. Women change their jewelry all the time. A man can buy a woman many different rings, and she can wear them all at different times. Men don't change that often. If they get a ring, it's a ring they love and they'll wear it all the time."

DO MOST OF THESE EXECUTIVES HAVE MORE THAN ONE WATCH?
"Most of our customers, both men and women, have several watches. We had one couple where the man and woman each bought watches for each other on their anniversary for twenty-

two years. They had twenty-two different watches—rubies and diamonds, emeralds and diamonds, little tiny watches, great big watches. She passed away, and he's now buying watches for his children."

EXECUTIVE FITNESS

FRANKLIN FITNESS AND RACQUET CLUB
29350 Northwestern Highway
Southfield, MI 48034
(313) 352-8000

We talked to Dave Holderness, manager.

WHAT PERCENTAGE OF YOUR CLIENTELE WOULD YOU SAY ARE EXECUTIVES?

Of 7,000 members, "a very, very high percentage. Two reasons: one being that our pricing is such that we do not have the lower-income people involved. We're probably the highest-cost club in the metropolitan area. So we probably have eighty percent executives."

OF THOSE, WHAT PERCENTAGE ARE MEN?

"Almost equal. The only reason that it would be a little less than equal—let's say fifty-five percent men, forty-five percent women—is that during the day the club has a lot of women tennis players. I have to assume that the majority of those daytime women tennis players are housewives. But the tennis players are only about thirty percent of our membership."

WHAT SERVICES, ACTIVITIES, AND EQUIPMENT DOES THE CLUB OFFER?

"Tennis, racquetball, squash, handball, Wally Ball (a midwestern sport played on a racquetball court with a volleyball net), swimming, aerobics, free weights, Nautilus," and lots of other equipment. Stationary bikes, Stairmaster machine, treadmill, rowing machines, cross-country skiiing simulator, and recumbent bicycle (lying flat on your back and pedaling). "We have a fitness evaluation department. Members can come in as often as they want to check where they're at." Other services: babysitting (free); full-service restaurant ("a healthy menu, not a health food restaurant; in other words, we're very conscious of the amount of fats in food and what kinds of foods we serve, but you can go in there and get a hamburger"), massage, suntanning, steam rooms, saunas, whirlpools (one coed, then a men's and a woman's in each locker room), a card room, game room, water aerobics, swimming lessons, twenty indoor tennis courts with tennis pros, sixteen racquetball courts, two squash courts, one-on-one training (for beginners only), twenty-four tennis pros, eighteen aerobics instructors, twelve fitness insrructors, four swimming instructors, two racquetball/squash instructors.

WHAT DIFFERENCES DO YOU OBSERVE BETWEEN YOUR EXECUTIVE AND NONEXECUTIVE CLIENTS?

"No difference. They're more dedicated to keeping themselves in physically good condition. They come more often."

DO EXECUTIVES SEEM TO PREFER CERTAIN TYPES OF EXERCISE OVER OTHER TYPES?

"I would say that they tend to be more involved in the physical aspect than in the gamesmanship aspect. And not to a great degree, I don't want to mislead you in any way, but they seem to be more involved with getting themselves in shape than, let's say, playing racquetball. They go more toward machines, aerobics, cardiovascular (which has grown by leaps and bounds in the last year and a half)."

DO EXECUTIVES MINGLE AND DATE (OR SOMETHING ALONG THOSE LINES)?

"It is a very social club. That's one of the reasons that we have the full restaurant and bar. There is a lot of comingling in there. And downstairs (the workout area) there's a large lounge with a large-screen TV, and a lot of socializing goes on there as well. They do meet each other and date. We have a very high social aspect in this club."

DO THEY NETWORK IN THE GYM?

"Of course, I don't listen in on conversations, but there seems to be a lot right in the workout rooms themselves. You don't always have to be out of breath when you're doing cardiovascular and a lot of conversations go on. Whether it's business or social, I really couldn't say."

FEES: The initiation fee is $500. Dues are $65 per month. Executives tend to come in in the mornings and at noon, and 4:30 in the evening it starts very heavy again with executives. Morning: in from 6:00 to 9:30, in at noon for an hour, again starting at about 4:30.

HOURS:
6:00 A.M. to 11:00 P.M., Monday to Friday;
6:00 A.M. to 10:00 P.M., Saturday and Sunday.

POWER SWING

KENSINGTON METRO PARK
2240 West Bunol Road
Milford, MI 48042
(313) 685-1561

We spoke to Brian L. Kelly, the director of operations of one of Detroit's premier public parks.

Kensington, which was rated "one of the top ten golf courses in Southeast Michigan by the *Detroit Free Press*," is probably the facility closest to downtown Detroit—about thirty-five miles away—and convenient to residential neighborhoods Brighton and Millford. "We are probably best known for our exceptional maintenance program," Kelly says. "The courses are kept in fantastic shape."

The park, situated on 4,300 acres, includes two beaches, a nature and farm center (complete with animals in their native habitats, golf courses, a snack bar, restrooms, and lockers for daily use). (No showers, though.) Approximately 250–260 golfers play here on a daily basis in season.

FEES: Since Kensington is open to the public, with no membership group, fees are charged on a per-day basis:
18 holes: $11.00 on weekdays; $13.00 on weekends
9 holes: $7.00 on weekdays, $8.00 on weekends

THE
DETROIT
BASEBALL
CLUB

HISTORY & OPERATIONS

The Detroit Tigers, a subsidiary of The Detroit Baseball Club, originally became a major league team in 1881, when they joined the National League. [Until 1895, when they were dubbed "Tigers," Detroit's team was variously called "the Detroits," the "Wolverines," and the "Creams."] At that time, organized baseball had been played in the United States for roughly twenty-five years. In 1887 the team won the National League pennant and then toured the country in a fifteen-game postseason series against the St. Louis Browns, the champions of the American Association (which later merged with the National League), in what was the first predecessor of a World Series. Detroit won the series ten games to five. The following year, the team dropped out of the major leagues.

The Tigers reappeared in 1901 as charter members of the newly formed American League. In 1905 they paid $500 to a minor league team based in Georgia—$200 on immediate delivery—to buy a promising young outfielder named Ty Cobb. Cobb, who was dubbed "the Georgia Peach," became a superstar. In 1907 he led the Tigers to the first of three consecutive American league pennants, though the Tigers lost in the World Series each of those years: to the Chicago Cubs in 1907 and 1908, four games to zero and four games to one, respectively, and to the Pittsburgh Pirates in 1909, four games to three. Cobb, who played with the Tigers until 1926 and served as the team's manager from 1921 to 1926, is considered to be one of the most outstanding players in the history of the game. In 1936 he was among the first group of players to be elected to the Baseball Hall of Fame. He led the league in batting for nine consecutive years, a record that is still unsurpassed, and then, after a one-year hiatus, led again for three more years. His record for the most base hits ever (4,191) stood until 1985, when it was bested by Pete Rose.

In 1934 the Tigers won the American League pennant again. It was their first year being managed by Mickey Cochrane, also named the American League's Most Valuable Player that year, who played with the team as its star catcher from 1934 to 1937. Though they lost the 1934 World Series to the St. Louis Cardinals, four games to three, the Tigers won the pennant again in 1935 and went on to win their first World Series against the Chicago Cubs, four games to two. The team had a number of superb players during this period, including future Hall of Famers Hank Greenberg (1930–46), a first baseman and outfielder who was named the American League's Most Valuable Player in 1935—(Greenberg actually broke his wrist in the second game of the series and couldn't play for the remainder), outfielder Earl Averill (1939–40), outfielder Goose Goslin (1934–37), infielder Charlie Gehringer (1924–42), Cochrane, and pitcher "Schoolboy" Rowe (not a Hall of Famer).

In 1940 the Tigers won the pennant but lost the World Series to the Cincinnati Reds, four games to three. They won the pennant again in 1945, and this time won their second World Series against the Chicago Cubs, four games to three. Hank Greenberg, who had just returned from the Army, again helped lead his team to victory. (In 1941 Greenberg had been the first American League player to be drafted into military service.) Twenty-three years later, in 1968, the Tigers won the pennant again, and again went on to win the World Series, this time against the St. Louis Cardinals. Al Kaline (1953–74), an outfielder who was elected to the Hall of Fame in 1980, was a Tiger superstar for sixteen years before getting his first chance to play in a series. Mickey Lollich, an ace pitcher, led the team back from a three-to-one game deficit to win the series four games to three. The Tigers won the pennant once more, in 1984, and went on to an easy victory against the San Diego Padres in the World Series, four games to one. Stars that year included the "Detroit Four": catcher Lance Parrish, second baseman Lou Whitaker, shortstop Alan Trammell, and centerfielder Chet Lemmon, as well as Willie Hernandez, a left-handed relief pitcher who was named the Most Valuable Player of the American League that year and also won the Cy Young award. (It was Hernandez's first year with the Tigers.) In 1987 the Tigers won the American League Eastern Division with ninety-eight wins and sixty-four losses, finishing two games ahead of the Toronto Blue Jays. Although they did not reach the pennant race, they led the major leagues in home runs with 225—the most of any team since 1965.

The Tigers have played on the same field since they became members of the American League in 1901. Originally known as Bennett Park, it became Navin Field in 1912 (after Frank J. Navin, Tigers president from 1908 to 1935); Briggs Stadium in 1938 (after Walter O. Briggs, Sr., president from 1936 to 1952, and his son Walter O. Briggs, Jr., president from 1952 to 1956); and Tiger Stadium in 1961. The team has conducted its spring training in Lakeland, Florida, ever since 1946.

The Tigers are regarded as one of the best-run franchises in professional sports. The team has had eleven presidents in its history in the American League and is currently headed by a three-man board of directors made up of John E. Fetzer, chairman of the board, Thomas S. Monaghan, vice-chairman and owner, and James A. Campbell, president and chief executive officer. In 1983, Fetzer, who was the sole owner of the Tigers from 1961 to 1983, sold the team to pizza king Monaghan (see p. 247) for $53 million, the highest price ever paid for a baseball team. Monaghan, who grew up in Michigan in an orphanage and regarded his once-a-year trip to see the Tigers as one of the few highlights of his childhood years, had always dreamed of owning the team. His fantasy was more than fulfilled when the Tigers won the World Series in his first full year of ownership. Campbell, who has devoted his entire career to The Detroit Baseball Club, joined the team in 1949 as the business manager of the Thomasville, Georgia, farm team (which was then owned by the Tigers) and rose through the ranks to become president and chief executive officer of the whole organization in 1961.

The executive board makes all the major decisions for the team. Financial decisions are the domain of Vice-President Bill Haase and Vice-President for Finance Alex Callam. Baseball operations, including decisions regarding scouting and the development of players, are run by Bill Lajoie, the Tigers' vice-president and general manager, and Joe McDonald, vice-president of player procurement and development. Rounding out the quintet of vice-presidents, is Jeff Odenwald, vice-president of marketing, radio, TV, and public relations. The team itself is managed by George "Sparky" Anderson, "the dean of American League managers" and the only manager who led World Series–winning teams in both major leagues (the Cincinnati Reds in 1975 and 1976, the Tigers in 1984). The remaining administrative staff, roughly forty people, cover the following areas: stadium operations, tickets, minor leagues, and computers.

In contrast to most major league teams, the Tigers almost always turn a profit. This is partly due to the fact that Detroit is a baseball-crazy city (in general, half of a team's revenues come from ticket sales and concessions, while the other half comes from TV and radio contracts) and partly because the Tigers, rather than paying enormous sums to attract free agents, groom most of their star players in their farm team system. (One notable exception was infielder Darrell Evans, whom the team acquired as a free agent for their championship 1984 season.) The Tigers have five minor league affiliates (which are run by contract agreements— *not* owned): Bristol, Virginia (rookie league); Gastonia, North Carolina (Class A); Lakeland, Florida (Class A); Glens Falls, New York (Class AA); and Nashville, Tennessee (Class AAA). As a general rule, players start out in the rookie league and move up through successive teams (obviously, depending on their ability). Those who make it to the Class AAA team are eligible for recruitment into the major leagues, although players can technically be recruited into the majors at any stage. It takes an average of ten years for the team to build a championship player—in fact, the average age of Tigers' players is thirty-two, which is old for baseball— and part of its long-term strategy is to add two or three players from the minors each year. Because so many of the team's members have been involved with the Tigers from the start of their careers, the club has more of a "family" atmosphere than most major league teams.

An average of 1.5 million loyal fans turn out each year to watch the Tigers play. The team has had an outstanding history. Twenty-one of its players have thus far been elected to the Hall of Fame. And the Tigers are second only to the New York Yankees in terms of total victories: 6,986 between 1901, when they joined the American League, and the end of the 1987 season.

(Information supplied by Jim Campbell, president and CEO, and Greg Shea, team spokesperson.)

REVENUES: "Satisfactory." The team will not disclose.

EARNINGS: "Satisfactory." Again, the team will not disclose.

NUMBER OF EMPLOYEES: Approximately six hundred, including the forty-person administrative staff, minor league managers, vendors, ushers, guards, watchmen, and "on and on." Some of these are seasonal employees, some are hired on a daily basis, some on a monthly basis, and some work year round.

NUMBER OF PLAYERS: Forty under major league contracts (twenty-four players from opening day through August 31; forty players from September 1 through end of season) and 120 with the minor league affiliates.

AVERAGE AGE OF EMPLOYEES: Information not available. "There's a wide variance."

AVERAGE AGE OF CLUB'S MAJOR LEAGUE PLAYERS: Thirty-two.

TURNOVER: Very low for full-time staff, 25 percent for players, and fairly high for seasonal, monthly, and daily staff.

RECRUITMENT: The team does not have a college recruitment program. Most players enter the farm system from high school.

NUMBER OF NEW HIRES PER YEAR: The club hires between forty and fifty new players per year into its farm system. For administrative staff, maybe two to three new people a year, although some years they don't hire anyone. "We take pride in the fact that our key employees stay with us a long time." The number of temporary staff people varies widely from year to year.

RANGE OF STARTING SALARIES: Information not available. "It varies because there are so many different positions."

SALARIES FOR PLAYERS: Beginning players starting out in the farm system earn $700 per month. The average salary for major league players is approximately $450,000 per year.

POLICY FOR RAISES: Administrative employees are reviewed at the end of the year, and there is no set pattern for raises. For players on long-term contracts: "We'd like to think we base raises on performance, but players get them through negotiation, arbitration (many players are represented by agents), and all various ways."

TRAINING PROGRAMS: No formal programs (other than the farm system).

SEASON DATES: Roughly April 1 to October 1.

BENEFITS: *Administrative people:* a pension plan ("one of the best in baseball"), medical, dental, hospital, and life insurance, a stock program, and a 401(k) program. *Players:* a pension plan that "includes hospitalization and so forth, and is probably the finest in the country." As far as pensions are concerned, a player with ten years of major league service can retire at the age of sixty at $90,000 per year. "That ain't bad."

VACATION: For administrative people, a month to six weeks per year. "Tenure is involved."

ADDITIONAL PERKS: All administrative people get free tickets to Tigers games. Full-time employees have their own dining room, where meals are served gratis year-round, and parking is available on the premises.

BONUSES: Automatically awarded to all administrative staff people once a year; size depends upon the team's profitability.

ANNUAL PARTY: None. In the words of Jim Campbell, the Tigers CEO: "I'm an old Scrooge. We have get-togethers, but nothing you would call 'the annual picnic.' "

DRESS CODE: "Men wear coats and ties to the office. Women wear dresses." Players wear uniforms.

SOCIAL ATMOSPHERE: "Well, it's good. We're not General Motors; we're talking about a very small office. People are very friendly. We have a nice relationship here. But I wouldn't say people party a lot or have parties, like at some companies. We don't. It's all business."

HEADQUARTERS: Located in a two-story building attached to Tiger Stadium. Across the street, there's another building that houses the bookkeeping department and part of the public relations department. Additional temporary facility in Lakeland, Florida, during spring training.

CHARITABLE CONTRIBUTIONS: Although there is involvement at both the team and the individual level, the Tigers have not quantified the value of their donations. Most activities involve free admission to baseball games—on the two Safety Patrol days—for grade schoolers of southeast Michigan, and on Courtesy days—for nonprofit groups. Sparky Anderson started CATCH—Concerned Athletes Team for Children's and Henry Ford's Hospital—and organizes auctions of sports souvenirs to raise money, and Frank Tonana, Alan Trammell, and Matt Nokes are players involved in the battle against cystic fibrosis. (Many players lend their names to fund drives.)

RECORDED INFORMATION NUMBER: (313) 963-9944

INTERESTED APPLICANTS CAN SEND RÉSUMÉS TO:
Mr. William E. Haase
Vice-President for Operations
The Detroit Baseball Club
2121 Trumbull Avenue
Detroit, MI 48216
(313) 962-4000

I t's a man's world here in Detroit. This industrial city on the Detroit River is an autotocracy, where the car and his manufacturer are king. And when it's time to relax, guys head out to Tiger Stadium to see their beloved Detroit Tigers play ball.

The front office of The Detroit Baseball Club, owner of the Tigers, is the focus of this story. It's a full-fledged year-round business. Jim Campbell, the Club's president and chief executive officer, says, "We operate on a business basis. We're not a hobby. We attempt to run a prudent business. We've never lost money, and for that we're proud. Players call me cheap." He hates it when sportswriters call him cheap, though. "They don't know the whole story." Campbell, a lifelong sports fan, has worked for this team his entire working life.

After graduating from Ohio State University in 1945 and four years in the service, his next-door neighbor, Mrs. Parker, told Campbell that if her husband had been alive, he'd have loved to help Jim find a job. Parker had been a friend of Billy Evans, the general manager of the Tigers. "Within hours of Mrs. Parker's call [to Evans], I was invited to Detroit. When I thought this was what I wanted to do, I asked George Trautman, a former coach at Ohio State and former general manager of the Tigers [who had also recommended Campbell to Evans] for his advice. He told me about what I'd run into. The first thing you've got to get over is wanting to be a player. I had played for three years at Ohio State, but I was an average college player. My whole life was always sports. (What I'm saying to you is that I was a C student.) I got over it right quick. I was twenty-six years old." Evans gave Campbell a job in Thomasville, Georgia, "the lowest rung on the Detroit Tigers Farm System" (now no longer a part of the system).

When Campbell talks, his eyes sparkle, and though he is remembering almost forty years back, the details are so vivid they seem recent. "Our opening day in 1950, the Georgia ballpark burned down. I got local convicts to clean the debris, and I borrowed bleachers—I said anything else would be easier." As he gained seniority, Campbell moved up in the club through farm teams in Toledo and Buffalo, finally reaching Detroit in 1953. "Billy Evans was not my mentor, although he was kind and generous in hiring me. Many people have helped me, but my number one is John Fetzer [the club's current chairman of the board and former owner]. I've observed him as a businessman. He's a great role model."

Campbell became the Tigers' general manager twenty-six years ago, which forced him to become a public personality in this city, accountable to the fans in good times and bad. "The baseball fan wants to win, and you can't fault him. When things don't go good, you've got to accept criticism." Campbell is so visible in Detroit that a simple activity like eating dinner at a restaurant can be filled with constant intrusions and remonstrations. When the team is playing at home, he'll usually just grab a hot dog with Alice, his secretary of many years—her career predates Campbell's; Alice Sloane started in 1946, giving her the longest tenure at the club—before heading to his seat for the game. "I think I've operated one club in a city longer than anyone else in the business today. I've become known to the public. It's not the same as the star-type athlete. But I do represent the ball club.

"I knew the Detroit Tigers was a career for me in the mid to late fifties, when another organization offered me a job. I felt loyal to Mr. Fetzer—I didn't have a contract or anything —and since that time I've had a few overtures and they didn't interest me at all." Sitting in his office at Tiger Stadium one quiet off-season Saturday morning, Campbell is a picture of loyalty and a repository of memories and information. He appears to be one of the lucky who found and secured a place with the company of his dreams right off the bat—pardon the expression. "This has been my home, my love, and I take great pride in it. I owe so much of that to Mr. Fetzer. He doesn't beat on you, he doesn't second-guess you." Campbell's brand of devotion hasn't been without its cost. "I had a wife who divorced me. She said, 'Isn't it the truth that you love baseball, Ohio State, and me in that order?' I said yes. I was probably not a good husband, I didn't have children, and maybe I spent too much time here. I've been called a workaholic, but it's not work to me. I love it. Look—I'm here Saturday morning! Today I could raise my hand to God and say there's never been a morning I didn't want to rush to work. I enjoy the people I work with. I don't think people in the front office confuse their roles in life with the players'. They see them come and go."

Financially, The Detroit Baseball Club is well run. "We run a staid baseball operation. We sell baseball and nothing but baseball—no giveaways or fireworks."

Bill Haase is the club's vice-president for operations. With an accounting degree from Western Michigan University, he went to work for a copper and brass company. But "things weren't moving along fast enough. I wrote a letter to the commissioner of baseball in New York in 1975." A response from the commissioner's office stated that there were no openings at the time, but it might be smart to check with the clubs themselves. "I figured I'd start with the Tigers. They were my hometown team. My letter and résumé hit Jim Campbell's desk when they were looking for an accountant." Haase started in July 1975 as the club's auditor and became business manager in 1976 and vice-president of operations in 1978. "People see the glamorous side of the job, and it's there. There's nothing like going through the 1984 season [the last time the Tigers won the World Series]. But it's very demanding: a lot of work and a lot of time away from your family. We put in sixteen-hour days, from early in the morning till after the game is over. From July 14 to August 29 we only have four days off. We work weekends. A sports business isn't like other businesses. Even with my background, I had to relearn. You must make decisions faster during the season. We sell a different kind of product; we have to market differently."

"During our renovation process here, we had to close the upper bleachers. Lots of letters came in from people who felt *their* bleachers were closed off to them. The emotional component is bigger these last five or six years. People always identify with their team, but it's been more so." So, too, the people actively engaged in the business of baseball (in this front office). "Very few people today haven't had some personal experience with baseball—touched a ball, swung a bat, et cetera."

As you might have guessed, Haase also feels he has the greatest job in the world. It's like his childhood fantasies come true. "I have been a sports fan all my life—baseball especially. It's amazing to be sitting here after remembering walking down Michigan Avenue and coming to the stadium. Sometimes I still have to pinch myself."

But Haase must watch the bottom line. "We're in the black. Some years it's just on the borderline. Very seldom are we able to invest our profit." When Detroit won the World Series, it meant big business for the city. Every camera crew, every souvenir sold, every booked-up hotel, and every parking meter brought revenue to the city and the club. In 1987 "we drew 2,162,830 people during home games." That was the seventh largest crowd for an American League team." Ticket prices range from $4.00 to $10.50, which covers everything from the club's salaries to fixed operating expenses. "Memorabilia isn't that much of a revenue producer. TV and radio contracts and gate sales generate more. All teams that qualify for the playoffs and the Series participate in a pool of money. Would you rather win the World Series in four games or lose in seven? The pool only starts to pay after the fourth game.

"I am a businessman; there's no doubt about it." Yet, if Haase were at a dinner party or on a plane next to a stranger, he would identify himself by saying, "I work for the Detroit Tigers." "It's nice to get a reaction from people. I love to talk baseball. I never tire of talking about it." However, "if they think I can do special favors for them, it turns me off. Then I don't broadcast where I work. Also, people have a tendency to give suggestions or complain about the team. Everyone has a right to their opinion, but I just don't want to hear it."

Haase maintains that in order to work for the club you do not have to be a baseball fanatic. "But I can't envision working without it. My colleagues love baseball. It *is* hard on wives. Families suffer—there's no doubt about it. There are lots of things I wished I could have done with my son, but I didn't have time." To work here [or probably at any ball club], "you must have the support and understanding of your family." Don't forget that the office needs to win as much as the players do. The sting of competition never goes away. It's not just running an office and a business; it's winning. "The drive to win takes up a lot of time," although Haase and others in the club's administration claim they can simply enjoy watching a ball game, regardless of the outcome. "We don't cheer," says Campbell. "It's very quiet where we—Bill Lajoie [the current general manager], Alice, and I—sit. But you can't lose your love of winning."

The Detroit Ball Club administration features an all-male roster in executive positions.

There are women in supporting roles. Since this entire group comprises only about forty full-time people, there is really no job overlap, and, with a narrow power pyramid, there is not a lot of competition for jobs. Furthermore, job turnover is so low that waging a political war within the ranks would be futile. Haase says that working for an externally competitive company does not make for internal competition. "I never perceived the Tigers as a laddered environment. And unlike Apple and IBM, we can't be happy if our competitors go out of business. We need a long season. We want them to succeed in business but fail on the field with us." Campbell reiterates, "My counterparts, other baseball executives, are my dearest friends, but we each want to win in the worst way. Competition's wonderful. It's a way of life."

Is it fair to try to codify a corporate culture at the club? Haase says, "There is one, and there isn't one. We have a family here." Campbell reminds us that "all full-time employees have a little equity in the company. Tom Monaghan put that in." Monaghan, the owner of Domino's Pizza (see p. 247) bought the club in 1983. "If we have good years, we give bonuses. We have the best pension plan of any baseball club, and we serve a good meal here every day at noon.

"The great majority of our employees like baseball. They're not all baseball nuts, or anything like that. All employees get free tickets to all home games. The girls in the office get to know the wives. Eddie Yost's (infielder, 1959–60) wife, Patricia, worked in the office. Our trainer once married one of our girls."

Dan Petry wears number 46 on his uniform. A right-handed pitcher originally from Palo Alto, California, he joined the organization in a draft in 1976—he was the Tigers' fourth pick—and entered the Big League in 1979. He's going to play this particular evening but calmly talks about his team and his sport. [Author's note: Petry is twenty-eight years old at the time of the interview, though he seems older and more poised than his years. I realize that he is married and has a child, giving him the maturity of responsibility. Also, I had forgotten that major league athletes are pros at being interviewed. Of all the employees I interviewed for this book, they are the only ones who must include interviews in their job descriptions.]

"I'm just one of those people who feels loyalty," he says simply. "They drafted me out of high school in Anaheim, California. I was seventeen. They may have seen something in me that others never saw. I like playing here." With one's record and club trades determining one's career and home base, Petry recognizes he might not always be a Tiger. "There's no guarantee I'll stay here, but these are my friends. When I was first signed, I thought I was king. Then I found out pretty quick I was not; everyone's hot stuff.

"It was a lifelong dream. Any kid in America (or Mexico, Puerto Rico, or the Dominican Republic) wants to play baseball." When Dan was a kid, his parents presented him with a basket filled with the tools of the major sports: a football, a baseball, and a basketball. "Afterward, my Dad and I would fly a kite and talk about stuff.

"I was a late maturer freshman year of high school. My voice hadn't changed; I wasn't a man yet. I got beat up in football. If I had to do it all over again, and knew it'd turn out like this"—today, Petry is a healthy six feet four inches and weighs in at 200 pounds—"I'd definitely play football. It's a great game." But back to baseball.

"I never regretted not going to college, but it was a scary moment" [casting his future at seventeen]. "I can remember it as if it were yesterday. I had to have my parents sign my letter of intent. I had been told by the coaches at high school the recruiters would give me a hundred thousand dollars, and the scout offered a lot less money. But I was given a chance to dream. And I thought, 'I'm gonna buy my parents a house.' "

Although he was recruited by the Detroit Tigers, Petry didn't start in Detroit. "The farm system feels like a farm system. They dangle playing with the Detroit Tigers in front of you as an incentive, but the odds aren't good. I remember the day Sparky Anderson [the Tigers' celebrated field manager] called me up here. I wasn't tearing up in triple A. It was a total surprise. Even if it had only been one day, I could have said, 'I pitched in the majors.' But I stayed. I was the youngest for approximately three years up here. I'm still one of the youngest, but I'm kind of middle-aged. I've been around a while."

Dan has finally bought himself a house in suburban Detroit. At last he feels that Detroit, where he lives essentially only half the year, and at that only during home games, is home. He is grounded, in the best sense of the word. "The minor leagues are lonely. That's why people call their parents so much. That's why people get married so young—because of the support and all the time alone." In the majors, Petry is definitely one of the boys. "You're spending so much time together. We're a pretty close-knit group of people. The assholes are gone. We won a world championship and have a good group."

When the group goes on the road—in first class when using commercial jets (about 50 percent of the time) or in a chartered plane—they must wear jackets and ties. It's a rule. People hang out in the cliques that form around position. "Pitchers hang out with pitchers. On the road, when the game ends at ten P.M., everyone doesn't just go back to the hotel, call their wives, and watch Johnny Carson. We're still wound up and need to have fun, especially after a good game." Petry adds, "Most people prefer, at least I do, being home."

It is sometimes difficult to reconcile the intensity of being in the thick of competition half the year with the rest of the year's relative inactivity. Unlike other Tigers, Dan does not have an off-season job, although Jim Campbell has encouraged him to start thinking about what he'd like to do . . . you know, later. "I've never been anxious for a season to end, but when it does, I rush home to California [where his parents still live], then, after two weeks, I get anxious to start again. What will I do afterward?

"The average length of time in the big leagues is three years." Obviously, Petry has exceeded the norm. He's going on his second decade. "For every Tommy John with twenty years in the majors, there's a guy who plays for a month. I'd love to pitch till I'm thirty-five. It's conceivable. At thirty-five I'd love to work here in the office. I know there's not as much money, but I could maintain the same lifestyle."

Certainly the salaries earned by major league stars are substantial enough that by retirement, ball players should be able to regroup without fear. "To make about three to four hundred thousand dollars for fifteen years—that's a lot. A lot of the guys indulge themselves in fancy cars. Mercedes and BMWs are the most popular. But not me. Most people aren't reckless with the money. We've heard too many horror stories. People are more scared of losing it."

Dan says his dreams, as well as those of many of his teammates, are not of the financial variety. "We're very traditional-minded. We still have Ty Cobb's photo on the wall. Making the Hall of Fame is what it's all about. Playing to be good. Guys have pride. I want to be the guy whose picture is on the wall. The first time a kid asked for my autograph, it embarrassed me. But it's what it's all about. I know how I felt about Nolan Ryan [one of the greatest pitchers of all time, currently playing with the Houston Astros], so I imagine how the kids look up to me." [Author's note: Dan Petry was traded to the California Angels after the 1987 season.]

Although it's not a full-time, year-round job, Dr. Clarence Livingood, the team's physician, takes his role very seriously. "I've always been a baseball fan. I could name for you right now the starting lineup for the Philadelphia Athletics in the thirties." A dermatologist by training, he was approached by Messrs. Fetzer and Campbell in the early sixties. His specialty notwithstanding, "I'm more or less the family doctor for the whole team and their families. I'm on call. I get an average of two or three telephone calls a day." Medically, Dr. Livingood says, "We're relatively conservative. This doesn't mean we're slow. We make decisions quickly. We operate on fifteen to twenty percent of the team each year."

Dr. Livingood is based at the Henry Ford Hospital, although he is officially retired from it. He's at his hospital office from nine to five most days, but he says, "My time is my own. My main source of income is from the American Association of Dermatologists." His main source of pleasure is the Detroit Tigers. "I've enjoyed knowing the players. I've become good friends with their wives. I've always had close relationships with the managers." He is required to spend half his weekends with the team, from April to October, including the first week or so the players spend in Lakeland, Florida (the site of their spring training). He, too, admits that working for the team demands an enormous amount of time, which "has been taken away from my family." Indeed, this seems to be a problem for all members of the (extended) Tiger family, requiring a new set of priorities and tremendous understanding from the nuclear families of the individuals involved.

On the subject of drug testing (advocated by Commissioner of Baseball, Peter Ueberroth): Livingood believes "Everyone should be tested—the players, the front office, the coaches, the doctors." President Campbell is "for drug testing one hundred percent. Players are role models, and they know it. If they don't agree, they should look for other employment." Dan Petry says, "Management really wants drug testing. Players don't. It's really sad. Players want to cooperate and clear things up, but not to subject themselves to the tests. You know you don't use cocaine."

Dan Ewald is the Tigers' director of public relations. A former sportswriter who covered the team for *The Detroit News,* he describes the ambience in the front office as "intimate. Everyone knows everybody. I like that. We have a professional, businesslike decor here, and yet it's slightly more informal. I appreciate this." (The offices, aging comfortably, are not better appointed than, say, the offices of a university athletic department. Opaque glass partitions, old metal and wooden desks, blackboards in some rooms, and, aside from a club room outfitted with a bar and little tables, no frills at all.) "It could be just me," Ewald says, "but I like to pass a joke around. I have freedom. Sometimes you feel you're not doing anything, not feeling productive, but every company needs someone for bouncing ideas."

One of Ewald's tasks is approving television commercials that use Detroit players in uniform. "I don't think I've ever dissuaded anyone from doing a commercial. I allow players to do a commercial if it is in good taste, like [number 13, catcher] Lance Parrish for Ford. We don't charge the company. The Tigers enjoy their image of stability and tradition. Any adverse effects of an endorsement are measured by the number of zeros after the dollar sign."

We hate to belabor a point, but Ewald also mentions the amount of time taken up with the business of baseball. "Working here can have a serious effect on personal relationships. We arrive at nine A.M. Most games start at 7:35 P.M., they're three-hour games, and we might not get out until midnight." As far as a personal life is concerned, "you've got to decide whether you can do this or not. Obviously, there are advantages. If you don't love it, you don't get into it. I get a lot of letters from people who want jobs. They don't think working here is like working. But baseball requires sacrifices."

Jim Campbell has confronted a different sort of attitude in applicants he's met. "When I went to work for the Tigers," he recalls, "I don't think I knew what I was going to earn. Until I arrived at Thomasville, I didn't ask. Nowadays, if you talk to some kids, this is the first thing they ask about. 'Do you have a dental plan? Pension, hospitalization?' I don't blame them; they hear it from their parents."

Pio DiSalvo is the trainer of the Detroit team. He's been with the organization since 1970, when he came from a Boston Red Sox farm team in North Carolina. "Being a trainer in the Major League is the highlight, the pinnacle of my career. There are only twenty-six head trainers."

On a home game day, DiSalvo arrives at the stadium between 9:00 and 9:30 A.M. He likes to be there approximately an hour and a half before the players get in, "to set up the training room, do the daily injury reports, odds and ends, and get myself together." Before the game begins at 1:30, he must care for the team using tape, massage, ultrasound, heat treatment, ice massage, and whirlpool. The most common ailments in baseball are twists or tendonitis in the shoulder, elbow, knees, and ankles. "This year is the 'Year of the Wrist.' Everyone seems to have a wrist problem." As far as eating goes, "not eating is a fallacy. I try to get the guys to eat a good, balanced meal with a lot of carbohydrates two to three hours before a game."

"The players treat me well," Pio says. "I sit in the dugout with my medical bags and supplies. I've known them a long time. The best thing about my job is that I love it." There is no reason to doubt the smiling DiSalvo's sincerity. "I like baseball and the people I work for and with. Otherwise, it'd be a very aggravating job. It's a demanding job from start to finish. A player could call you anytime, almost twenty-four hours a day." DiSalvo, who is single, says, "I probably spend most of my time at the club. I bought a home one and a half years ago, and now I'm learning to feel at home." Although his work calendar doesn't technically include the winter, "I have an annual salary, and I can draw it any way I like. [He takes it year round.] Not many people in the club stay here in off-season. The only guys who stay are northern guys. I'm available to work with them."

DiSalvo's advice to future athletic trainers? "Be prepared to spend a lot of time and a lot of hours. You must like traveling. Do not expect to make a lot of money. Don't resent the players' high salaries. We laugh together." Like the players who survived the 1984 World Series, Pio wears a gold-and-diamond ring—the World Series ring. "Everybody in field service got one. So did the front office. We wear them every day."

Finally, we come to Bill Lajoie, who was named general manager (in addition to vice-president) of The Detroit Baseball Club in 1983, right after it was sold to Tom Monaghan. An ex–minor leaguer, Lajoie has been with the Tigers for only twenty years, starting as a part-time scout. "Since Jim Campbell's been here, [the front office has been filled] with mostly people from this area. If their roots are here, they're likely to put in longer hours. I haven't had a whole week off since I started here. The most has been three to four days . . . ever." Even if Lajoie wants to go out for dinner, he is the general manager, after all, and this is Detroit, after all, a city deeply involved in its team, win or lose. "There aren't many places you can go in Detroit where people *don't* talk about baseball. I get at least two or three letters a week about what I should do with the ball club. If you answer some of them, you won't stop the correspondence."

Lajoie describes his annual schedule: January and February are when he deals with the contracts for the new season. Spring training begins in early March and lasts about a month.

"That's when we settle on our opening roster. During the season [April to October], I attend home games and go to the minor league games. The fall is the trading period. My favorite time of year is October, for the league playoffs, the World Series, and the [sportwide] General Managers' Meeting. In November we go to Puerto Rico and the Dominican Republic checking out the young players. Trading lasts all winter."

Trading a player can be awful, "especially when they don't want to go. I show players respect; I'm honest with them." It's worse when you consider a player a friend, and vice versa. "They usually know when it's over. We have a 25 percent turnover each year, which is consistent with the league average. When players have kids under the age of five, it's easier to move. When I played in the minor leagues," Lajoie points out, "I said if I didn't make the majors by the time our oldest child was school-aged, I'd quit. And I did."

Nothing is quite so painful, however, as terminating a minor league player. "It's not nice. They're living in a dorm. You make an announcement over the PA system, calling eight or nine names. It's not good," he apologizes. "I try to time it so the other players are on the field. And we try to get them on a plane within a few hours. They sign a release paper, and it's over in three to five minutes." The system isn't meant to be cruel; it's simply the way it's done.

Lajoie attends home games, but "more as an observer and an evaluator. It's part of my job, rather than a break. It's not for pleasure. I don't get nervous before a game. I do get a surge of excitement before the pennant, or during the Series."

The last word, on life after the Tigers, belongs to CEO Campbell. "I think the worst disservice you can do to any company is to stay too long. Just because some old goat wanted to stay—it's your own foolishness. One of my main responsibilities is to prepare an orderly transition from the Fetzer-Campbell-Monaghan administration to the Monaghan administration. I don't know how many years I have. It's up to Tom [Monaghan]. Everyone writes books, and that's something I wouldn't do. I've been so fortunate to work with such good people and good friends, hard workers."

DOMINO'S PIZZA, INC.

HISTORY & OPERATIONS

Tom Monaghan started Domino's Pizza, Inc.—now an empire of close to $2 billion in yearly revenues—from an out-of-business pizza parlor in Ypsilanti, Michigan, called DomiNick's. The path to prosperity was not easy, and the story of Monaghan's astounding business success is almost inseparable from that of his personal history.

After his father died when Monaghan was four years old, his mother, who couldn't afford to support a family, sent him and his brother to an orphanage, followed by a series of temporary homes. Monaghan, who aspired to be a Catholic priest until, as a teenager, he was expelled from a seminary for misbehavior, determined to make a success of himself. He served a two-year stint in the Marines in order to afford a college education but was bilked out of his entire savings when he handed them over to a con man posing as an oil man. Forced to abandon college, he scraped together $900 from odd jobs, and in partnership with his brother bought DomiNick's pizza parlor in 1960.

Monaghan taught himself the pizza delivery business from scratch and managed to make a success of DomiNick's, even after his brother pulled out of their partnership. He formed a new partnership with a veteran restaurateur and within three years had opened up several other local stores. After this period of trial and error, during which he experimented with various types of locations and menu items, Monaghan arrived at a threefold strategy: to expand by opening stores in college towns, as students were his most reliable customers; to deliver pizzas *hot* in under thirty minutes; and to offer nothing but pizza. Monaghan dissolved his second partnership at considerable financial loss, when he decided his partner was inept as well as greedy. In 1965 he named his business Domino's.

By the end of 1967, Monaghan had four stores—one of them a franchise—150 employees, and $50,000 in annual profits. Then in 1968 the Ypsilanti headquarters caught fire and burned to the ground. All of Monaghan's business records were lost, and he incurred $150,000 in supply and repair costs. Though the company was almost wiped out, he again picked up the pieces and forged on. By this time Monaghan's goal was to open stores all across the country.

Domino's grew throughout most of the seventies, yet was again confronted with calamity when Amstar, the owners of Domino Sugar, sued for violation of their trademark. In 1980, after a lengthy and costly legal battle, Domino's Pizza won the right to retain its name. By this time Monaghan had approximately 230 stores; future growth, both domestic and international, was virtually uninhibited.

Today, Domino's Pizza has approximately 4,500 stores in the United States and abroad— and the company is still adding an average of one and a half to two stores each day—and more than a hundred thousand employees. Annual company revenues reached $1.8 billion in 1987, and Monaghan himself—who purchased the Detroit Tigers in 1983 for $53 million—is estimated to be worth more than $250 million. The company's international holdings include franchises in Canada, Australia, West Germany, the United Kingdom, Hong Kong, and Japan. Company headquarters in Michigan are now housed in a brand-new $300 million office complex inspired by Frank Lloyd Wright (one of Monaghan's greatest heroes) called Domino's Farms. Monaghan's goal is to have ten thousand stores in operation by 1990, each generating an average of $1 million annually for total yearly revenues of $10 billion. He sees the biggest potential for growth in foreign markets.

Domino's Pizza International, Inc., is split into three main divisions: Domino's Pizza, Inc., (DPI), which handles the stores; Domino's Pizza Distribution Corp. (DPD), which handles all the food commissaries (about twenty-seven around the country), including all equipment and supplies for the stores, and the Emporium, which sells T-shirts, jackets, hats, etc., with the Domino's logo; and TSM Properties, Inc. (Monaghan's initials), which is Domino's real estate holding company for all corporate buildings. The company still has a firm policy of delivering pizza hot within thirty minutes, or the customer gets three dollars off. Approximately two thirds of Domino's domestic stores are owned by franchisees, roughly 98 percent of whom are former Domino's employees. Though the company occasionally test markets new items (like breakfast pizzas called "bakeups"), so far none has been incorporated into the menu, and for the time being Domino's is sticking exclusively to pizza.

(Information provided by Ron Hingst, Kathi Seglund, Laura Johnstone, and Bill Kearns, company spokespersons.)

REVENUES: For DPI, $1.8 billion in 1987; for DPD Corp., $593 million.

EARNINGS: For DPD Corp., $18 million in profits before taxes in 1987.

NUMBER OF STORES: Approximately 4,450 in the United States and abroad.

FOREIGN MARKETS: Canada, Australia, West Germany, the United Kingdom, Japan, and Hong Kong.

NUMBER OF EMPLOYEES: Approximately 900 people work at Domino's Farms headquarters, and 150,000 work in the Domino's system, including those who work full time or part time in the stores.

AVERAGE AGE OF EMPLOYEES: Information not available.

TURNOVER: Information not available.

RECRUITMENT: Domino's "targets every school in the country." Though it does not visit campuses, its regional offices are responsible for the schools in their areas.

NUMBER OF NEW HIRES PER YEAR: Company keeps no records, given that their franchisees are in business for themselves and do not give the corporation their hiring figures.

RANGE OF STARTING SALARIES: "Minimum wage and up."

POLICY FOR RAISES: Employees are reviewed every year, and raises are "dictated by performance."

TRAINING PROGRAMS: Tom Monaghan established the "College of Pizzerology," which is essentially a national pizza-making training program, optional for all Domino's employees and taught in Ann Arbor and at selected sites around the country. Upon completing the one-year program, which students take while working, employees earn a diploma and a degree. Individual Domino's stores have training programs for all new hires. Corporate headquarters has no training programs.

BONUSES: DPD Corp. has national performance objectives, and every team member [employee] has his or her individual performance objectives. When these goals are achieved, team members are paid bonuses—every twenty-eight days! Twenty percent of Distribution Corp.'s profits are put aside for this purpose.

BENEFITS: Medical, dental, and life insurance.

ADDITIONAL PERKS: Domino's Farms has a gym where employees can exercise as well as a chapel where they can opt to attend daily religious services. A pizza store on the premises delivers pizzas right to employees' desks.

VACATION: *For corporate staff:* one week after six months, two weeks after one year, one and a half days per month after four years, and one and two thirds days per month after seven years, in addition to eight and a half regular paid holidays per year. *For store employees:* Stores are closed on Thanksgiving day, Christmas Eve, and Christmas Day. Store managers receive paid vacation, the amount of which varies by region.

INCENTIVE AND REWARDS PROGRAMS: Each region—the company divides the country into four geographic areas—hosts an annual awards celebration for top performing managers, store people, and franchisees. Regional winners then compete against one another in a national awards competition held in Ann Arbor, called the Distribution Olympics. DPD Corp. also offers three major awards during the Distribution Olympics: the Kelley Hannan Award (named after a former commissary manager); the President's Award, a plaque awarded by DPD Corp. President Don Vlcek to an employee (or employees) who has helped Domino's Distribution succeed; and the Bob Ulrich Award, a solid-gold ring with a black Domino's Pizza logo, for the employee(s) who has come up with an innovative idea that has "taken Domino's on a on a quantum leap." The company also runs a competition called Two-Tray Time: the fastest regional pizza makers compete in the nationals, and then the company appoints the fastest pizza maker in the organization for the year. All of the above are celebratory events for employees and their families. The company has a program through which store managers—if they fulfill all their duties in a given year—are awarded an all-expenses-paid trip for themselves and a guest to a company-owned lodge on Drummond Island in Michigan.

ANNUAL PARTY: Tom Monaghan throws a Christmas party each year for all Domino's Farms employees. There is no alcohol [on the premises—ever], but lots of food and gifts for all.

AVERAGE WORK DAY: The stores are open roughly from 4:00 P.M. to midnight (though that depends on area); at headquarters the average workday is 8:30 A.M. to 5:30 P.M.

DRESS CODE: At the stores: uniforms (standard issue throughout the country), at headquarters: business attire—men in suits and ties and women in comparable business dress.

SOCIAL ATMOSPHERE: The atmosphere at Domino's is "less bureaucratic than at most large companies and reflects Tom Monaghan's priorities, which include a good social life, physical fitness, a good religious life, and financial gain." There are many regular social activities for employees, such as once-monthly "eye-openers," when one of the departments at headquarters supplies coffee, juice, and doughnuts in a casual atmosphere designed to encourage social interaction. "At the stores, the atmosphere is geared to competition and having fun."

EMPLOYEE DISCOUNT ON DOMINO'S PIZZA: None.

NUMBER OF PIZZAS SOLD PER YEAR: 200 million in 1987.

MOST SUCCESSFUL FRANCHISEE: Frank Meeks of Washington, D.C., whose eighteen stores average $30,000–$35,000 per week in sales.

MOST POPULAR TOPPINGS ON DOMINO'S PIZZA: Pepperoni, mushrooms, sausage.

HEADQUARTERS: The company's headquarters, Domino's Farms, are situated on about eight hundred acres in Ann Arbor, Michigan. There are four "low-slung" office buildings, inspired by architect Frank Lloyd Wright, surrounded by a working farm. The grounds include an employee cafeteria, a gymnasium, a barbershop, a hair salon, a dry cleaner, a tailor, a bank machine, and an athletic supplies store, all for the use of the approximately 900 employees housed there. In addition, there is a pizza store, open to the public. The site is increasingly popular with tourists. A petting barn—with cows, pigs, horses, ducks, rabbits, sheep, and some more rare breeds—is popular with children. Domino's 1987 Christmas light display attracted about 250,000 people.

CHARITABLE CONTRIBUTIONS: Approximately $500,000 to $750,000 in 1987 from the corporation and the thirteen regional offices. Money was donated to the University of Michigan, a mission in Honduras, efforts to save Frank Lloyd Wright works, the arts in general, and Project Concern, a nonprofit group that helps Third World countries better their quality of life.

INTERESTED APPLICANTS CAN SEND RÉSUMÉS TO:
Domino's Pizza, Inc.
30 Frank Lloyd Wright Drive
Ann Arbor, Michigan 48106
(313) 668-7450

The 1986 National Olympics took place on an overcast May 13, in a convention park in Dearborn, Michigan. You didn't know 1986 was an Olympic year? If you worked for Domino's Pizza Distribution Corp. (DPD), you'd know that since 1985 every year has been olympic in scope. Each employee is eligible to compete on a local level, without missing a day's work. Why? Instead of the shot put, the fifty-yard dash, tobogganing, and the ever-popular luge, turn to the 1986 Distribution Olympics and National Awards Convention's slickly printed program, *Rally of Champions.* Our events include: Receptionist/Secretary ("A one-person event testing for communication skills, handling of inquiries, and general clerical abilities"); Veggie Slicing ("A one-person event judging participants on quality and quantity of vegetables, individual appearance, and sanitation"); and Dough Making and Catching ("A two-person event testing for dough quality and handling procedures, efficiency, and professional image"). Doing one's job well is enough to merit olympic consideration. Once you've reached the Nationals, you are part of the National Awards Convention, which, since 1987, has been held at Domino's Farms.

Domino's Distrubution's America is divided into four regions: Soignet, Gordon, Fulp, and Home Office (located in Ann Arbor, Michigan, for our Olympic purposes known as Equipment & Supply). Soignet, Gordon, and Fulp are the names of the respective regional managers. Each region includes Domino's National Commissaries (DNC).

Domino's is America's fastest-growing fast food company. Founded in Ann Arbor, Michigan, in 1960 by Tom Monaghan—winner of the 1986 Horatio Alger award—its claim to fame is that by sticking to one thing, product enhanced by service—in this case home-delivered pizza—one can own a huge share of the market. Domino's dominance hails from college towns, the places where pizza becomes a necessity and dorm delivery is a dream come true.

At the Fairlane Manor in Dearborn, Michigan, the massive ballroom is divided into areas circumscribed by free-standing bleachers and some of Tom Monaghan's collection (250-plus and growing) of antique cars, known as "Tom's babies," which team members— "You could get wiped out for saying 'employees,' " says a cultural attaché—love to see frequently, and which seem to travel almost as much as their owner does. Since Monaghan is also the owner of the Detroit Tigers baseball club, Tigers stuff vies for about a third of the display space. Each indoor event is monitored by a professional-sounding announcer who does Bert Parks proud. Although it is sometimes hard to concentrate amid the conflicting sounds, one can hear phrases like "Born in Tennesssee . . . loves the family atmosphere . . . thanks, Domino's . . ." Further confusion and noise are provided by the steady honk of party blowers decorated with the Domino's logo, which permanently dangle out of the mouths of revelers like a cigarette stuck to George Raft's lower lip. Most attendees are in casual dress—slacks and sports shirts for both sexes—some, again, designed by Domino's. Those men wearing business suits appear to be senior executives. Occasionally one can see young children quietly doing their homework, since the festivities take place over three weekdays.

The annual Distribution Olympics are the apotheosis of corporate pride. Each region has supplied boosters in additon to competitors and spirited banners: "DNC Houston: We don't deliver food, we deliver peace of mind. We Care ♥." Many participants live within the area, so only two hundred people have actually been flown into Detroit, but everyone is put up at the nearby Hyatt Regency since the days are long and intense. This year's celebrations cost $750,000, and while that doesn't include pizza, there are plenty of refreshments.

One of the more subdued competitions (since cheering would interfere with the contestants' work) is the Team Leader competition, "A one-person event with participants judged on problem solving, people skills, leadership ability and knowledge of company mission." ("We never say 'front line supervisor,' just 'team leader.' ") The regional champs are placed in typical scenarios that might confront them in real life, and are judged by four judges, three from DNC, plus guest judge Reuben Harris of The Tom Peters Group. (Events are judged by an average of three judges.)

In a realistic situation, except for the audience, team leaders deal with issues such as: "I need to feel more like a team member"; "I need a new pair of scissors"; an irate phone call; a career review; a private counseling session with a team member confessing to a drug problem ("Tell me how you feel . . ."); and a solicitation for a raise. The winner in this event—and all others—is to be announced the next morning during the awards banquet.

During Veggie Slicing, the judges take their mandate seriously, as they crouch over the sliced onions and walk around the slicing arena. One contestant, Levan Davidson, Gordon Region, DNC Kentucky, was born in Vietnam, arrived in the States in 1975, and has been employed by Domino's since 1981. She has three children and "likes to bowl, shop when she has the money, cook, and sew." Levan has also won a Perfect Attendance Award. All veggie slicers, male and female, must wear hairnets as part of their uniform, and although one of their criteria is speed, they organize and deliberate solemnly.

Don Vlcek is the president of Domino's Pizza Distribution Corp., a position he has held since he joined the company in 1978, and vice-president of Domino's Pizza, Inc. According to his press release, "he demonstrated his leadership as the company grew from a liability—losing $380,000 the year he arrived—to the single largest profit-making subsidiary for Domino's Pizza, Inc. In each of the seven years under his leadership, Distribution has shown a profit and now averages over $330 million in sales ($15 million in profit)." [Author's note: That was two years ago.]

Vlcek (pronounced "Volcheck") was introduced to Domino's as a customer "because they were the only pizza deliverers who made pizza with green olives." What you will not see in any press release are Vlcek's personal pizza peeves. "The thing that offends me most is bad pizza," says this once- or twice-a-week pizza eater who, to lose weight, hunts grouse during the appropriate season. "I don't like onions and green peppers. Or most cooked vegetables." Don does like anchovies, however.

In 1978 a box salesman who knew Tom Monaghan called Don about Domino's. "Tom's assistant said that Barney [the box salesman] said I could walk on water. We went to Travis Point Country Club. I thought, 'God! A country club!' We talked about our dreams. He said the last guy made forty thousand dollars. I liked his honesty. He said, 'I'll pay you thirty thousand and work you up to forty thousand in one year.'

"I did a day of executive testing. I loved it! I had a ball! The assessment said, 'This guy's ready for senior management.' " Vlcek met Monaghan at the eye doctor's office and was offered a job. "I didn't realize my title was 'president'; I thought it would be 'general manager.'

Tom said, 'Think of it as your own company,' and the title opened a lot of doors with suppliers."

Don's domain was then referred to as Domino's National Commissary Holding Corporation, known as the "Holding Corp." "It was a mess. I changed the name every year. In 1979 it was Domino's National Commissaries, in 1980 Domino's National Consolidated Services, which didn't last a year, and in 1981 Domino's Pizza Distribution. It became a company joke. People would say I had an identity problem."

In the ten years since Don's arrival at Domino's, the company has attempted variations on a theme. "We tried breakfast—small pizzas with scrambled eggs and cheese with bacon and tomatoes; and sweet ones with cream cheese, apples or blueberries, and streusel toppings." Since Domino's has no restaurants, only a delivery business, breakfast had to be ordered one night in advance. For $4.95, customers in the test markets would get a wake-up call and delivery of their breakfast pizza, orange juice or coffee, and a copy of *USA Today*. Breakfast at Domino's lasted six months. A "taco experiment" was less successful. Other digressions from the original concept have focused on establishing a presence in noncollege towns, where business would be stable over the summer. "Nothing scares us."

(Jeff DeGraff, Domino's director of communication and education, says, "While other companies try to add to their menus, we streamline ours. We only offer two sizes of pizza. And Monaghan only wants to sell one size. We only offer one kind of pop [in corporate-owned stores]: Coke. That's it. My concern is that we make the best generic product. We always come out ahead in taste tests.")

Don Vlcek considers Domino's to be his surrogate family, but, he says, "I have been over my head from day one. I still am. The day I stop thinking that, I'll be dead meat. I always tell people where I'm weak. If I say something that's not right and find out, I've got to apologize. My plan is to be flexible." DPD's executive management team is called its "coaching staff." "We were thinking of calling ourselves 'cheerleaders,' but some guys thought it was too female." The coaching staff is comprised of three regional managers, two general managers and Vlcek. "Sometimes I just shake people up," Vlcek admits. "The coaching staff knows when I'm about to blow. Then they step in."

Domino's is a nonunion shop. Vlcek says the folks most threatened by union encroachment are truck drivers. "There's danger at truck stops. We grew so fast! We didn't have a semi until 1982; now we have more than two hundred." Don says that problems are to be laughed about, and that he prefers to talk about screwups rather than solutions. His approach to running DPD is informal. "I like to be called Don. I don't like people kissing my rear end."

DPD's Olympics originated with one regional manager's idea of holding the awards banquet during the Los Angeles Summer Olympics. Furthermore, it was regarded as an antidote to low employee motivation. The first activities, attempted on a regional level, began in March 1985. "Some commissaries were cynical and just asked everyone if they wanted to attend. Whereas in Houston, we had a guy with a torch running through our corporate park. I started to cry on the steps. If a genie came to me last year and asked me what job I'd want, it would be mine.

"Last year maybe two or three people who won the Distribution Olympics thought their lives would be made, and they had a rude awakening. Their work slowed down, and some of the supervisors felt they couldn't reprimand them since they were Olympic winners. Most winners are still with us. Some didn't compete this year to allow others the chance. But I want two- and three-time winners to be beaten. I want tradition. I would put a dollar value on loyalty and hard work. Youth likes fun. So if you can tie fun to tradition, then people have a ball."

After a buffet dinner at the Hyatt featuring foods from different parts of the country and a short but forceful speech by Tom Peters, the stage is cleared for the Domino's Partners event ("A two-person event emulating *The Newlywed Game*"). It's hosted quite competently by Brian Hickey, a competitor in the Team Leader event from Equipment & Supply with a swell of Chuck Barris-like theme music, and the finalists have apparently prepared for this event no less assiduously than contestants in the other events.

The three regions plus E&S have sent couples to the Nationals. Questions range from facts and trivia about the company to intimate details about each other:

"How much business do you think Distribution will do in 1986?"

"What is your partner's most disgusting personal habit?"

"Does your partner think his or her team leader is most like: (a) Bozo the Clown; (b) Count Dracula; (c) Winnie the Pooh?"

"Would the men ever buy anything from Frederick's of Hollywood?"

"How much of your home time does your partner spend talking about Domino's: (a) 10 percent; (b) 25 percent; (c) 35 percent or more?"

"Before we bring back our partners, a message from our sponsor."

Here three Domino's thespians wearing backpacks simulate a camping trip. "We should never have left Skunk Camp"—an advanced managing seminar run by Tom Peters warmly and publicly embraced by Tom Monaghan and thus the senior people at Domino's, (see p. 675.)—they moan, in deference to Tom Peters, Domino's nonstaff guru. They build a fire and pull out cookbooks, a baseball mitt, a woman's negligee, a smoke alarm, a telephone, a basketball, and a stethoscope from their packs. Suddenly, in the distance, they hear the familiar and comforting hum of Domino's theme music as a grizzly bear approaches. One guy runs out, and after the others struggle with the killer mammal, the escapee returns with a box of pizza. "They'll give a franchise to anybody" is the tag line of this live action commercial, which, to the audience, is the most hilarious thing they've ever seen, or almost as funny as Gordon Region's Rod and Becky Petterson, DNC Illinois, who are this particular game's Bickersons, disagreeing and slapping each other as they fail to score.

Ultimately, Soignet Region's Frank and Barbara Caputo, DNC North Carolina, win the game. Their pictures and biographies appear in the *Rally of Champions* booklet. "Frank and Barbara have been married over two and a half years. Barbara has always been supportive of Frank during his two years of being a Delivery & Service team member. Barbara's the office manager at a medical office and works hard to meet her family's needs as well. Frank and Barbara are a good example of a team that works well together. Preparing for the Olympics, they spent their spare time studying, reading, asking questions and concentrating to win. Frank succeeded terrifically, winning this event and the Team Leader and Traffic Management categories!"

The Rally of Champions itself takes place the following morning. Although it's 10:00 A.M., tuxedos are in evidence, and women are wearing cocktail party–caliber outfits. Don Vlcek, the master of ceremonies, introduces "my team leader, Tom Monaghan." Although Monaghan attended dinner the previous evening, this is his first official public appearance in Dearborn. He receives a standing ovation. Monaghan also gets applause with the statement that "workers count the most. Another thing I like about these people—you people—your positiveness. I like it because there's so much negativeness. We had a gal in our Chicago office who stole between three and six hundred thousand dollars from us. That'll cost us about $1.4 million. Sales are down, and there's more competition from Pizza Hut, Little Caesar's, and McDonald's. But I have two teenage daughters, I've got my family, my health, my faith, and a job I enjoy going to every day. That's rich." More applause.

Monaghan relates his initial youthful ambition to become an architect. A devoted fan of Frank Lloyd Wright, he's had Domino's headquarters designed in a homage to Wright. He's bought up so much of Wright's furniture and decorations that he's reportedly raised the prices and values of anything Wright designed—singlehandedly. Employees who know nothing about architects know, at the very least, that Frank Lloyd Wright was a great one.

"I wanted to be an architect. I would have graduated and been able to take exams in my thirties, which was frustrating for a guy as ambitious as I. I didn't want to go into the pizza business. I was still trying to be an architect. I figured a pizza store would pay my way to architecture school. But since I was in the pizza business, I tried to make it the best I could do. And I did, didn't I?" Thunderous applause.

"We have suffered a lot of divorces in this company. I think your marriage is the most important decision you ever make in your life. The other [important decision] is the chance to take dope. And you say yes or you say no. If you make the wrong decision, I tell you, you're stuck.

"I mean, my wife and I are as opposite as you can get. A few years ago, we went to see a marriage counselor when the friction was high. It cost a hundred dollars an hour. I mean, she doesn't like Frank Lloyd Wright. She won't live in a house he designed. She hates sports. She hates physical fitness. Now we take ten to fifteen minutes every day to talk."

"Tom Monaghan is the conscience of the company," a team leader says. 'We all know what he would do in a situation. He has a strong Judeo-Christian ethic."

A beautifully produced slide show of the last two days' activities, accompanied by rousing music (the Pointer Sisters' "I'm So Excited" and Glenn Frey's "The Heat Is On"), ignites the room as attendees, their families, and the coaching staff get to see themselves on screen. They scream when they see themselves and their friends. Tigerabilia and race cars punctuate scenes of Olympic events. In fact, everyone likes what they see so much that Don Vlcek shows it a second time. Some team members are whipped into a frenzy. Now it's time to present the awards.

A three-tiered platform, very Olympic, commands center stage. Aside from Frank and Barbara Caputo, no winners have been announced until now. The projection screen shows the interlinking circles that make the Olympic motif, and although people are sitting at lunch tables in Dearborn, Michigan, everything else is in perfect mimicry of the athletic championship, from the music to the bronze, silver, and gold medals and the way they are presented. All finalists are escorted to the stage by comely young people. Contestants are reserved and anxious. Everyone gets standing ovations. First-place winners are presented with red Domino's sports jackets.

"Tom, I'd like to thank you for opening a pizza store, because I am a true believer. And I'd like to thank my wife."

Gold medalists win $4,000 apiece, in addition to gold commemorative rings and their medals and jackets. In the dough-making event, a two-person team event and the most important event, "since dough is the only product we make ourselves," winners each receive $6,000 in cash plus an additional $4,000 apiece in prizes. Silver medalists win silver rings to match their medals, and bronze winners get medals as well as silver rings. One first-place winner says, "I'm going to be a father in about eight weeks, and this'll help a lot."

"They've treated me like a human being like no other company," says the winner of the

Driving event, Greg Henry of Gordon Region, DNC Delaware, a real favorite today having come in second last year. He spent thirteen and a half years driving for other companies before joining Domino's in 1982. "Thanks, Domino's. I love you." There's not a dry eye in the house.

Domino's has a saying, "Experts aren't." The company has midwestern roots and values that set it apart from the *Fortune* 500 mentality. "There are only two MBAs in Distribution. We don't read *The Wall Street Journal* or consult with business schools. We take tremendous pride in being amateurs and misfits. We don't pay you to think a certain way; we pay you to think. You get moved up real quick if you're good. If you're here a year, you might be promoted three times, and over your head. If you're the greatest tray scraper but only finished ninth grade, we'll help you read a ledger." Jeff DeGraff repeats the statement he believes got him his job at Domino's. He told his interviewer, "I'm a left-wing Democrat. My father's a Socialist. I hate MBAs." His interviewer said, "So? Me, too."

Team leaders must get their hands dirty. That means making dough at commissaries around the country and being available to all team members. "If you're at your desk more than three days a week, you're not doing your job, damn it." DeGraff urges prospective Domino's people to think about the following: "If you're great at what you do but easily intimidated, don't work here. You better come prepared to play. With your shoes tied. It's still a boys' network. Tom believes in women [executives], but it'll be a while. The idea of champions is very real here; not for wimps."

It is published in the back of the Rally booklet, printed on parchment, and included in Domino's press kit. It's the mission statement of Distribution, called "Mission Possible." An adherent says, "Breaking it is like the only reason you'd get fired." It says:

"◆ Customer's belief that we're the best place to shop for their needs

"◆ Team members who can't think of a better company to work for

"◆ Community (government) that considers us a fine example of what business should be

"◆ Parent company proud to have us as their best performing area

"◆ Suppliers excited enough to call us their favorite account

"◆ Result in our attaining those key operational goals so necessary for our future."

FORD
MOTOR
COMPANY

HISTORY & OPERATIONS

Ford Motor Company, the oldest car manufacturer in the United States, was founded in 1903 with "an abundance of faith" and $28,000 in cash scraped together by twelve investors. Eighty other automobile companies were started in the same year in the United States. At the time of its incorporation, Ford was a tiny operation run from a converted Detroit wagon factory and staffed with ten employees. Its first car was the 1903 Model A, and subsequent models were named sequentially for letters in the alphabet. A month after its start-up, with an inventory of about 650 unsold Model As, the new company had all but run through its capital (it had $223.65 left in the bank). Ford was saved from insolvency by the fortuitous arrival of an $850 check—for a Model A Runabout—from a Chicago dentist named Pfennig, the first person ever to buy a Ford car.

Henry Ford, the industrial genius behind the Ford Motor Company, founded the company with a guiding dream: to build a simple but durable car priced low enough to be within financial reach of virtually every working person. The Model T, which was introduced in 1909, became that car. It cost $260 without extras—they jacked up the average price to about

$400—and sold so rapidly that production could not keep up with demand. In 1913, after nearly three years of development, Henry Ford and his staff devised a moving assembly line system, the first of its kind, that enabled the company to speed up production and meet consumer demands. In 1914 Henry Ford surprised the business world by announcing that he would pay his workers five dollars per day for an eight-hour shift, as opposed to the standard wage of $2.34 for a nine-hour day. His rationale was that if he paid them well enough, his employees would be able to afford one of his cars.

In 1919 Henry Ford, who already owned 58 percent of Ford stock, bought out all of the outside stockholders: the Dodge brothers, who owned 2,000 shares, which Ford purchased for $25 million; John W. Anderson, who had 1,000 shares worth $12.5 million; the heirs of the Gray family, who owned 2,100 shares, for which they received $26.25 million; H. H. Rackham, whose 1,000 shares sold for $12.5 million; James Couzens, who had 2,180 shares, which sold for $29,308,857.90; and Rosetta Hauss, whose twenty shares were worth $262,036.67. At the time Ford purchased the remaining stock, his company was earning roughly $60 million per year.

Edsel B. Ford, Henry's son, succeeded his father as president of Ford Motor Company in 1919, and the company expanded into the production of trucks and tractors. In 1922 Ford purchased the Lincoln Motor Company for $8 million. Ford continued its rapid expansion until the start of World War II, when civilian car production was halted and the company turned over its manufacturing facilities to the production of bombers, jeeps, and aircraft engines. In the postwar years, Ford was losing money fast. Under the new presidency, of Henry Ford II, the founder's young grandson, the company lost $50 million in the first seven months of 1946. Ford did manage to finish the year with $2,000 in earnings. Four years later that profit margin increased to $265 million. This resurgence was achieved through a re-building program that has been called the most phenomenal comeback in U.S. industrial history.

Henry Ford I died in 1947 at the age of 83. In 1956 Ford went public. Business prospered until the recession of the 1970s precipitated a sharp decline.

When fuel economy became a major industry issue, both General Motors and Chrysler (Ford's main competitors) got a lead on Ford in downsizing their cars. Ford was also slow to introduce front wheel drive and to update its conservative, unpopular styling. And to make matters worse, during the seventies Ford was labeled a manufacturer of substandard quality. Sales diminished substantially, and Ford was forced to close plants and to lay off some 30 percent of its North American staff. But, as in the past, the company was able to make a remarkable comeback. It managed to cut almost $3 billion from its worldwide operating costs while making substantial improvements in the quality of its cars. Furthermore, in a coopera-tive effort with the United Auto Workers Union to improve management-employee relations, Ford initiated its Employee Involvement Program, through which employees work together to solve problems and offer the company suggestions. The company attributes much of the credit for its 59 percent improvement in quality since 1980 to contributions made by workers through this program.

Though Ford is best known for its automobiles, a substantial percentage of company revenues comes from its Diversified Products Operations (DPO), which was formed in 1955. The division includes Ford Aerospace & Communications Corporation, a leading high-technology company; metal and glass operations that would, on their own, rank with the nation's largest; the Electrical and Electronics Division, a premier force in automotive tech-nology; and substantial farm machinery, climate control systems, castings, paint, plastics, vinyl, and microelectronics businesses. The total sales of DPO alone would place it well up in the *Fortune* 100.

Henry Ford II stepped down as chairman in 1979, paving the way for the first nonfamily member in that office. (He was still a member of the board and officially an employee until 1982.)

Today, under the leadership of CEO Donald Petersen and Vice-chairman and COO Harold ("Red") Poling, Ford has won renewed esteem, both externally and internally. According to company research, Ford's 1986 models ranked 13 percent higher in quality than Chrysler's and 16 percent higher than General Motors'. (Chrysler later challenged those findings, and the dispute was referred to the National Advertising Division of the Better Business Bureau. The issue was decided in Ford's favor on April 16, 1987.) In 1987 Ford sold close to 4 million vehicles in the United States and Canada, and approximately 6 million worldwide. The Escort, the company's best-selling model, has been the best-selling car in the world for six years. (Ironically, Ford loses money on each Escort sold, as it's priced very low to compete with Japanese cars.) And Ford has sold more cars overseas than any other American manufacturer for twenty-three consecutive years. In 1986, for the first time since 1924, it was the most profitable automobile company in America, with overall earnings of $3.3 billion. That was the first time in more than sixty years that Ford, the number two car company in the United States, was more profitable than its archrival General Motors (which earned $2.95 billion that year). With profits of $4.6 billion in 1987, Ford soundly beat its competitors again. (General Motors earned $3.6 billion in 1987, and Chrysler earned $1.3 billion.)

Henry Ford II died on September 29, 1987. His son Edsel B. Ford II was appointed general sales manager, Lincoln-Mercury Division, on June 1, 1987, and remains one of three Fords on the board of directors.

(Information provided by Jay Meisenhelder, Tom Foote, George Trainer, and Al Chambers, company spokesmen.)

1987 *Fortune* 500 RANKING: Third.

REVENUES: In 1987, worldwide sales were $71.6 billion, up 14 percent from 1986.

EARNINGS: $4.6 billion in net income in 1987, or $9.05 per share.

INITIAL PUBLIC OFFERING: 1956.

NUMBER OF SHAREHOLDERS: 260,000.

NUMBER OF DEALERSHIPS: 10,550 car and truck dealers worldwide, including more than 5,500 in the United States.

NUMBER OF FACTORIES: Over 160 worldwide.

NUMBER OF EMPLOYEES: 350,100 worldwide, with 180,700 employed in the United States.

AVERAGE AGE OF EMPLOYEES: For hourly workers, the average age is 41.1 years, with 17.4 years of service. The company does not keep figures on its salaried employees.

TURNOVER: 6,335 United States employees retired in 1987.

RECRUITMENT: Ford recruits at over a hundred colleges and universities in the United States.

NUMBER OF NEW HIRES PER YEAR: In 1986, Ford hired 5,500 new employees. The 1987 figures are not available. The company hires an average of 1,100 college graduates per year.

RANGE OF STARTING SALARIES: "The range of starting salaries is competitive with other major firms recruiting college graduates." The company will not give out figures.

POLICY FOR RAISES: Salaried employees receive raises based on merit. The timing and amount of the raise depend upon an employee's performance.

BONUSES: Ford's supplemental compensation has been in place for more than thirty years. Eligible managers receive bonuses providing the company's profitability formulas are sufficient.

TRAINING PROGRAMS: Most new job assignments involve on-the-job training, which may be supplemented with off-site classroom training. The Ford College Graduate Training Program provides recent college graduates with a variety of assignments throughout the company in their first two years of work. The program is designed so that new hires will have the background to pave their individual career paths at Ford.

BENEFITS: Major medical and dental insurance, maternity/paternity leave, tuition reimbursement, profit sharing, pension plan, and stock options for certain executives. The company pays relocation and moving expenses for employees who move for work. The benefits are much the same for hourly and salaried employees, though not entirely uniform.

EMPLOYEE DISCOUNT ON FORD CARS: Approximately dealer cost.

ADDITIONAL PERKS: Those of middle management status and above are entitled to lease two Fords of their choice per year (at a reduced cost). In addition to those two cars, "top-level executives are encouraged to drive Fords of all sizes and product lines for evaluation purposes, and generally rotate these cars twice a year." Greenfield Village, a restored museum town and a pet project of "Henry the First," is nestled in the middle of Ford territory in Dearborn. It contains Henry Ford's birthplace, Orville and Wilbur Wright's bicycle shop, Thomas Edison's Menlo Park laboratory, and other highlights of the American Industrial Revolution.

VACATION: For hourly workers, vacation is on a sliding scale, from forty hours the first year to two hundred hours for twenty or more years. For salaried employees, vacation starts at two weeks the first year and goes up to twenty-five days after twenty years.

ANNUAL PARTY: There is a variety of events, ranging from private parties to those sponsored by the corporation, at all levels and in all divisions of Ford.

AVERAGE WORKDAY: 8:00 A.M. to 5:00 P.M., "with some casual overtime expected of salaried employees at higher levels." Shifts for hourly workers vary.

DRESS CODE: For salaried workers, "corporate conservative."

SOCIAL ATMOSPHERE: Depending upon where in the company one works, one can count on a range of possibilities.

JOINT VENTURES: Ford is currently involved in a number of projects with Mazda, including the Mercury Tracer, the Ford Festiva, and a compact, called the Probe, built at Ford's Flat Rock, Michigan, plant. The company owns 10 percent of Kia Motor Corporation, a Korean manufacturer that produces the Ford Festiva. Ford is involved in a joint venture with Iveco to manufacture heavy trucks in Britain. And Ford and Volkswagen have announced a cooperative venture in Brazil and Argentina called Autolatina.

COMPANY MISSION AND GUIDING PRINCIPLES: (Following is Ford's mission statement, a laminated, pocket-sized copy of which is distributed to every employee):

MISSION: Ford Motor Company is a worldwide leader in automotive and automotive-related products and services as well as in newer industries such as aerospace, communications and financial services. Our mission is to improve continually our products and services to meet our customers' needs, allowing us to prosper as a business and to provide a reasonable return for our stockholders, the owners of our business.

VALUES: How we accomplish our mission is as important as the mission itself. Fundamental to success for the Company are these basic values:

⬩ People—Our people are the source of our strength. They provide our corporate intelligence and determine our reputation and vitality. Involvement and teamwork are our core human values.

⬩ Products—Our products are the end result of our efforts, and they should be the best in serving customers worldwide. As our products are viewed, so are we viewed.

⬩ Profits—Profits are the ultimate measure of how efficiently we provide customers with the best products for their needs. Profits are required to survive and grow.

GUIDING PRINCIPLES:

⬩ Quality comes first—To achieve customer satisfaction, the quality of our products and services must be our number one priority.

⬩ Customers are the focus of everything we do—Our work must be done with our customers in mind, providing better products and services than our competition.

⬩ Continuous improvement is essential to our success—We must strive for excellence in everything we do: in our products, in their safety and value—and in our services, our human relations, our competitiveness, and our profitability.

⬩ Employee involvement is our way of life—We are a team. We must treat each other with trust and respect.

⬩ Dealers and suppliers are our partners—The Company must maintain mutually beneficial relationships with dealers, suppliers, and our other business associates.

⬩ Integrity is never compromised—The conduct of our Company worldwide must be pursued in a manner that is socially responsible and commands respect for its integrity and for its positive contributions to society. Our doors are open to men and women alike without discrimination and without regard to ethnic origin or personal beliefs.

BEST-SELLING VEHICLES OF 1987: (1) F-Series pickup truck (550,125 units); (2) Escort (392,360); (3) Taurus (354,971); (4) Ranger compact pickup (305,295); (5) Tempo (219,296).

HEADQUARTERS: Ford's World Headquarters, "the glass house," home to almost 2,000 employees, is 923,030 square feet, twelve stories high (plus a two-story penthouse) and located in Dearborn, Michigan, in a ninety-acre landscaped site that also contains a "world-famous" arboretum. All told, Ford has about fifty major buildings in the Detroit area, including offices and factories.

CHARITABLE CONTRIBUTIONS: In 1987, Ford Motor Company, through its corporate contributions and Ford Motor Company Fund contributions, donated $22.16 million to a range of charities in the following areas: education; health and welfare; civic activities and public policy groups; the arts and humanities; and U.S. and international relations programs. Almost 35 percent (the largest chunk) went to educational programs and facilities.

INTERESTED APPLICANTS CAN SEND RÉSUMÉS TO:

Corporate Recruitment Manager
Ford Motor Company
Central Placement Services—Room 50
Box CL
The American Road
Dearborn, MI 48121
(313) 322-3000

Welcome to Detroit. Look at the cars that accompany you on your drive from the airport. You will see a lot of domestic automobiles, almost no imported wheels. Driving a foreign car would almost be an affront in the Motor City, where more people truly understand cars than anywhere else outside Japan. If Detroit is filled with car nuts—it is a one-industry town, don't forget—then the nuttiest of all work for Ford. A longtime manager says, "Every red-blooded American guy buys a car and wants to tinker with it. By the same token, many would like to work here."

Ford is huge, industrial, serious. The company has won the American car contest for the second consecutive year. The mood is up. The company is hot. Ford's pickup truck has become the best-selling vehicle in the United States. The Escort is the best-selling, most popular car in the world. (Princess Diana drives an Escort Cabriolet convertible.) It's a good time for a visit—one week before the Detroit Grand Prix, the city's annual sporting event and celebration, largely sponsored by Ford. And the company's 350,100 employees are breathing a new and different collective sigh of relief: The old corporate culture—management by fear, old boy network, playing the political game—has finally toppled. The culture is dead; long live the culture.

The result of a study that was begun at the end of Henry Ford II's regime, Ford is now a better place in which to work, and—most important—more humane. People matter more, and they say they feel it.

Old Ford people, who are very much aware of working for a family business, sometimes refer to their company as "Ford's." "It was Henry Ford and then God beneath him." Now that the company is run by a non-Ford, the son of a poor farmer, the new Ford is firmly in place.

Joseph Kordick was an integral part of the transition. He says at lunch in a private exeeutive dining room (the china wears the Ford logo), "Our team is a pumped-up bunch of people." Kordick, a thirty-four-year Ford man, joined the Ford Parts and Service Division on April 1, 1985, as its general manager, the top divisional position. (He's since added vice-president to his title.) He's a smiling, genial fellow. "I followed twenty-five years of autocratic leaders. I'm a devotee of my friend Leo Buscaglia. I'm a touchy-feely kind of guy, a hugger." Beryl Goldsweig, the public relations person who works most closely with Kordick, confirms that Kordick hugged before the culture made room for hugs.

He continues, "This is the most loving and caring division of Ford, and that's nifty. I think this place is loving and caring. I've talked about my relationship with God, and I'd like to help people. I think anyone could be happy here." Obviously, this is big big _big_ business. Parts and Service occupies one building and an annex containing approximately two thousand people. The entire Parts and Service universe totals more than 7,600 employees. "All of us are here to make money," Kordick reasons. "Otherwise we'd be in the ministry." He speaks frequently of his devotion to God. "If God loves me with my warts and all, he really loves me. I wake up with two prayers every day: I thank the Lord for the lady I've slept with for thirty-six years—a saint—and I hope I have a positive impact on one person each day. One person this year committed himself to Jesus Christ at my desk."

Kordick's devotion to the old Ford is nothing compared to his pride in the company today. He pulls from his breast pocket the miniature version of the company Mission, and Guiding Principles.

"At old Ford, we acted like second-class citizens and were. Not now. In 1984 our turnover rate was seventeen percent; today it's four percent." One of the larger profit centers at Ford, "this division's attitude rubs off on other divisions. Our division was looked down on once."

Kordick's own management style requires him to make personal contact with as many employees as he can. He begins every workday morning with personal phone calls to employees celebrating their twenty-fifth anniversaries with Ford. "It sets the tone for the day. I don't think anyone else here does it." He has instituted a highly regarded program dubbed "Koffee with Kordick—I get twelve to fifteen people in the organization and just talk. The executive secretaries complained about the ladies' rooms and the lack of an on-premise nurse." Kordick followed up, and shortly thereafter the nurse saved the life of an employee suffering a heart attack. The company had a luncheon for the employee's family when he recovered. "We try to create an environment that for eight to ten hours a day will be like what employees will return to at ·night." No one is keeping score, but in his first year as general manager of Parts and Service, seventy-three people approached Joe to confide in him about nonwork issues. Since that time, a company spokesperson confirms, "he has been approached quite literally by hundreds of people. People approach him—not only in his office, but by mail and telephone and on his visits around the country." He admits that in hiring he selects "people who reflect my personality."

Even though the old culture is criticized—gently, "Ford has a large reservoir of goodwill of the employees." In part, natives of the area are dependent on the automobile industry and rely on the generosity of the local enterprises, and in part, many are sons—and a few daughters —of men who worked in the business their whole careers. It makes sense to like the corporation that supports you and your family. John Stewart in the personnel department says that when he arrived thirty-two years ago, he perceived Ford as the locus of his career. "My father worked for General Motors all of his working life, and he thought Ford was a better bet in terms of fast growth. My dad didn't see Ford as the enemy." After a moment Stewart says, "Thirty years have gone by like that," and he snaps his fingers.

In Detroit, people *do* rather than think about what they might do. The economy doesn't allow for pause. It is quite easy to imagine that before you know it, your career has *happened*. Almost by itself. Until recently, Stewart explains, most often job changes were not determined by the one moving around, but rather by one's supervisors. They came "as a result of being recognized by others." Ford's effort to allow its people to feel they were more in control of their careers has been mammoth.

CEO Donald Petersen and Vice-chairman Harold "Red" Poling knew they had to work to improve the mood of their people. "At one point, the relationships between management and laborers were adversarial. There used to be a time that a mistake would result in a bashing. It was about control. Now there's less control and more delegation; employees will take more risks." A committee was formed to draw up the Company Mission statement, and the culture is evolving. Everyone gives credit to the men at the top. "If the top won't change, the bottom can't" is an opinion that is widely expressed.

It is not possible to overstate the new culture or its impact. It is important to let Ford's people revel in their positive feelings because they probably did not voice their discontent in the old days.

"People used to rise to the top through their functions and had little appreciation for other areas and what other people did," says Dick Hartshorn, the technical planning manager of the Executive Development Center (EDC). His group coaches, or perhaps it's more apt to say it *facilitates,* discussions with the top 2,128 people in the corporation worldwide—from upper middle management on up—on "Fordliness." "We were determined to change Ford's executives in some way. We interviewed two hundred people around the world in management ranks to understand their frustrations and concerns. The culture of the company recognized last year that the change goes beyond the cosmetic." The EDC program is run by thirteen people, all of whom left other jobs at various places in the Ford galaxy: engineering, research, finance, and so on. Outside experts, including a business philosopher and a licensed therapist, come in regularly. (Dick himself is a metallurgist who spent years working at General Motors, at each of their foundries. His name is on two or more patents. He also got his master's degree in instructional design.)

For seventeen weeks during the year, groups of forty-nine executives, 15 percent of them non-American, come to the Renaissance Center in downtown Detroit for a "5½-day, well-packed program dealing with Ford issues in the Ford way." Hartshorn's constituency spans seven levels of executives, who attend in sports clothes, the ambience informal. "The bulk of what they learn, they learn from each other," Dick says in his office overlooking the water. "The process depends on the group; the content is stable. It's not esoteric. We ought to run this thing as if it were our own business."

Two rules govern the program: First, every participant must live in whichever local hotel is used for lodging, even if he lives nearby; and second, no one may make or receive phone calls during the day except for family emergencies. "Business is not an emergency." However, attendees may use their two-hour lunch periods to call their offices. "We ask them to leave their rank at the door."

On Friday, as the seminar draws to a close, "Don Petersen usually comes to talk to the group. Ninety percent of the time. Or Poling. They talk about commitment. It shows the sincerity of our corporate executives." Then, at the end of each session, groups are required to write a memo offering feedback to Ford's Policy and Strategy Committee. "It's not just a new way to beat people up," Hartshorn explains. He quotes the comic strip *Pogo:* " 'We have met the enemy, and he is us.' " "The outcome is that people are better prepared to do their jobs." Over the first two years of the EDC program, Dick has seen the groups change in the same ways. "Most groups end up at the same place. Groups with more young people tend to get intense sooner. By Friday there's a marvelous introspection."

Dr. Nancy Badore works with Hartshorn as the program development director of the EDC. While completing her Ph.D. in community social psychology at Boston College, she began commuting to Detroit when her husband, "who had a passion for cars," took a position at Chrysler. She moved here in 1979. Badore confesses that her initial attitude toward industry was "naive: dumb people worked in industry and smart people were academics. Even Peter Drucker," she says, citing one of academia's business gurus, "says, 'The auto industry is humorless.' " Nevertheless, when a friend told her that Ford wanted to hire a psychologist, she applied for the position. "It was so bewildering. I just wanted a job. I didn't want to be just another unemployed Ph.D. I would do whatever it took to get an A in life."

Nancy found herself in Ford's Flat Rock, Michigan, foundry as an industrial relations analyst looking for the answer to the question "What does it feel like working at Ford?" This facility "got the lowest marks in issues of career. It was old-style Ford—they planned and moved people around and didn't let you move on your own." The foundry, home to three to four thousand people, "felt like family. It was old-fashioned. It was midwestern, and rough and tumble.

"In my mind, if I hadn't had such a good time, I wouldn't have done such good work." Nancy's next job was at Ford's World Headquarters in Dearborn, working on the Employee Involvement Program. "This job really affected the company. I saw a different side from the plant. It was like beer drinkers looking at the guys whose drinks had parasols in them. The staff behaved patronizingly toward the plant. But from the plant point of view, there was greater status being in the plant."

What was Nancy's purpose at the corporation? "I still had not figured out what I wanted to do in the world of work," she confesses. "Nothing I was doing at Ford was what I had been hired to do. I've made up every single job I've had. I knew I adored seminars. I enjoyed arguments and preparing for them. I could have been a good quantitative psychologist, but I'm having the time of my life and I'm on the way to being great. I'm being me."

"We're in the business of change." In her first years with the company, Badore felt "we were the only ones who were going through change." That in itself has, um, changed. "People who can't deal with change will find it a less comfortable place in which to work. No one is expected to change overnight. It's not change for change's sake; it's much more real.

"What business has a game plan? Ford needs the kind of people who can make a difference. I try to release people into what they're good at. The larger the comany, the more clearly its purpose must be stated. You are entitled to good feelings because you've been part of the process—even if you're not part of the production."

Nancy started by getting a fix on the old Ford and who it attracted. "I asked the right questions, so I'd get taken seriously." The guys "who succeeded under the old regime had the drill sergeant persona. You had to look like you could take it. There was a macho criterion. In many cases, they didn't behave that way at home or outside work. Each one had an 'Aha' story about when they committed themselves to success at Ford. Some ran two-billion-dollar divisions." Another subspecies was drawn to Ford in its early days, maintaining another personality strain. "A lot of good guys were like Wyatt Earps. Later, some were ex-FBI agents. They were squeaky clean—they overdid it—to prove the system was honest. They had a fear of looking bad. They were the gung ho elite." Still others in the company reveal ancient "horror stories—finding out you were fired by finding your lock's been changed and your stuff was outside on the floor . . . because you didn't wash your boss's car."

Badore is pleased to tell you that now people "know they can be more fully themselves. There are about 350,000 people here, and you don't want to throw them all out. You don't want everyone to make an about-face. But you better be right."

It is safe to say that 50 percent of the working population prefers stability to mobility. "When asked 'If you're not getting a promotion, do you want to move?' 50 percent said, 'No, thank you.' One must evaluate oneself."

The size of Ford can be intimidating to potential employees. "They have an exaggerated notion of the scariness of Ford. It's like facing down a bully." In a funny way, those are the people who will be especially useful to the company. "There is a definite sign that the culture has changed and that they want a different kind of person, who reflects that change.

"Change is what's kept me here," she continues. "I've gotten some job nibbles to do the same thing elsewhere, but I wouldn't leave for anything. I'm growing a school, a team, here. It's like watching the beginning of the American Revolution. I get lumps in my throat over Ford commercials. You'd never expect this lump in *this* throat," she laughs.

Employees have always believed in management's basic good intentions, even when those were obfuscated by harder times. "The personality of Ford is fundamentally a company that has had strong underpinnings of placing high value on employees, which it is trying to reestablish. We have a reasonably good image." The introduction of career planning may have been late at Ford because during its biggest growth period, from the late fifties to the seventies, 2,500 college graduates were hired per year. "Now things have changed dramatically." The automobile industry suffered a tremendous slump in the late seventies due to the oil crisis, the recession, and the "quality crisis," which led to increasing Japanese preeminence. It came tumbling down on Ford in 1980.

According to John Stewart, the corporation has decided "to move the burden of career development from Ford to the individuals. We owe them some things; no question about it. We looked at what other companies did and decided to do it in house. Now the program is operational and has five full-time people.

"The culture that Petersen and Poling want to have is not quite there. People do carry the cards [with the Mission and Guiding Principles Statement printed on them] around. The real intent is to communicate."

Jim Bakken is the vice-president for Corporate Quality and Engineering. His office is on the twelfth floor—senior executive territory—of Ford's World Headquarters on the American Road in Dearborn. With a degree in engineering from the University of Wisconsin, he arrived at Ford as part of their first college recruitment program, forty-three years ago. "Within three years, the original recruitment group was cut in half. (Iacocca was one of the last to go.) Progress kept me here. Challenge and opportunity came at frequent enough intervals. At various times I've managed six manufacturing divisions of the company.

"Also," Bakken emphasizes, "the company's commitment to me" has made it unlikely that he would ever have left Ford. The company sponsored him as a prestigious Sloan Fellow at MIT in 1962. "It was a fairly strong signal from the company. They felt a few dollars invested in me would be worth it.

"I've really liked every job I've been on." Whether or not he admits to any of the responsibility, Bakken is certainly one of the "catalytic agents" of the cultural change. "A company is no different from someone going to the races. You select from all in the field. A company can't pay attention to everyone. We do a reasonable job of it, and are doing better.

"Any company is in continuous cultural change," he says. "During hard times in 1979, we needed a direction. [Ex-CEO] Philip Caldwell's priority list was topped by 'quality.' At that time, quality meant how something measured up to preset specifications. We looked for a new culture, and we found Dr. Demming, an expert on quality, who turned Japan around after the war." To make the point stronger, Bakken adds, "The highest quality award given annually in Japan is called the Demming Award. We heard about him on an NBC *White Paper*: 'If Japan Can, Why Can't We?' He worked closely with us and became our mentor.

"Americans measure success against a fixed standard. The Japanese have increasingly higher standards. At the beginning of the seventies, the U.S. and Japanese auto industries were at the same point. By the end of the decade, they were ahead of us. Demming looked for the bonfire, the prairie fire that would turn America around."

Bakken is not the only executive who invokes the moment the Mission, Values, and Guiding Principles were announced for the first time to the operating staff. "It was Mr. Ford II in Boca Raton, Florida. [It was part of his farewell speech in 1982.] He said, 'I want to leave you with more than good wishes.' His desire made a strong impact."

The statement is the result of two years' work, and it is certainly impressive that so many employees seem to carry the laminated card in their pockets (or, at the very furthest away, in their desk or briefcase) and the statement is framed on many walls in every building, should one need a refresher. "How do [the cards] affect your daily life?" Bakken repeats the question. "They help you deal with a deviant. They give you—by pulling out your card—the opportunity to say, 'We should really think about your action in terms of our guiding principles.'" The card seems imbued with some kind of management magic.

Reliance on a printed card may be due, Bakken thinks, to the changes in the basic midwestern work ethic. Perhaps it's because his generation experienced the Depression. "This generation is more realistic. Many recognize there's more to life than just one's occupation. There's family and self—equally or more important. I give them very high marks for that. Many of us with tremendous loyalty to the company shortchanged our family and society. One year I worked 351 days out of 365. Not because the company asked me to, but because I felt I needed to be here. Maybe it was a bit of an ego trip—I thought the company couldn't manage without me. Meanwhile, my wife raised our kids."

The Mission and Guiding Principles does not enunciate social behavior. And Ford does not especially foster a social environment. "The fast track is business-oriented. People are civil to one another in the business sense. You have to be people-oriented; I'm convinced of that."

We are now at the Wayne Assembly Plant. It is possibly the size of a small country. It has a population of approximately 3,300 people. In two eight-hour shifts plus overtime, 1,064 Escorts per day, or sixty-six cars per hour, come off the line. ("And we're not the only ones who make Escorts".) It takes eighteen hours to make a single car. Our host is Mary Ellen Plante, a young engineer who knows her way around Wayne's 1,994,000 square feet.

The cavernous plant has classrooms on the premises, where, at an employee's request, he or she can study remedial reading and writing, computer training, and Dale Carnegie programs. Over ten thousand people companywide have been trained on the computer during their breaks, at Ford's expense. There are even graduation ceremonies. TV monitors, the antennae of the Ford Communication Network, punctuate some walls. A huge satellite network, it broadcasts news, trivia, and a stock report in addition to live teleconferencing. Ford's annual shareholders' meeting is aired live. (And lots of employees are shareholders. Ford subsidizes sixty cents of every dollar invested up to 15 percent of base pay.)

Mary Ellen demonstrates CAD-CAM (Computer-Aided Design—Computer-Assisted Manufacturing) and how "Ford's cars are completely designed with computer graphics." With a light pen touching her monitor, she can rotate a design. It looks like fun. [Author's note: Even better than an Etch-a-Sketch.]

As we enter the assembly area, a large sign announces "Build it as though you are buying it!" We put on goggles. Mary Ellen says, "It blows your mind when you think, 'Gosh! How many parts go into a car! And that they all get done, and get done right!'" A graduate of Michigan State University, she's been with Ford since 1984, entering the two-year Stamping and Assembly Engineering Development training program for mechanical and electrical engineers. The first year is spent in a stamping plant and the second year in an assembly plant. "I had no intentions at all of working in the auto industry. While I was in college, the industry was in trouble. Ford's getting leaner meant I wouldn't be bored. I was impressed with the people I met from Body and Assembly. People here are like, 'Okay, let's get tough.'"

It is noisy. The machinery is big. There are robots, but not the kind that can serve drinks. It is colder in the assembly area than outside and, for the most part, pretty dark. What is not visible is the computer that is masterminding this relentless building. Different models are made on the same assembly line, and miraculously they come out right. A red car comes by and gets fitted with a red interior. "Once a week they build a car and take it apart to check the welding." Most of the workers are men, many of them wearing stereo headphones, half tuned out, half tuned in. Sparks fly during certain procedures, but the guys couldn't be more blasé. Many of them are smoking cigarettes. At regular intervals, lunch tables and vending machines are nestled under the dinosaurlike machines, and this is where many employees eat. They get a half-hour break every four hours. Downtime "is a no-no."

This is how car bodies get painted. [Until the interiors and engines are installed, cars cannot correctly be called cars.] First, car bodies are cleaned by hand with sponges and a solvent. Then they are sprayed with phosphate to make the electrocoat ("E-coat") stick and improve anticorrosion performance. After the E-coat dip, the bodies pass through an E-coat oven. Next, they enter a body primer booth, where primer coats are sprayed on automatically. This is followed by the primer coat oven. Car bodies then move into a special chamber with a grilled floor. A team of two sprays the color, predetermined by a computer, over the car body interiors, while the exterior paint is applied automatically. Each car body gets two coats of color followed by two clear coats of varnish. After each car body, the painting machine purges itself of the old color before the new car body arrives. "The painters are at the top end of the assembly workers." They wear jumpsuits and hairnets in their glassed-in compartment.

The sound of music informs you that you have entered the trim department. Still, the stereo only provides background. Barbra Streisand singing "The Way We Were" sounds ridiculously small and human.

At the end of the line, a battery of fellows grabs each car and drives it off to a train—whose terminus is right inside the building—a trailer, or the dealership across the street. "A bunch of cars gets driven home and back by managers each evening to evaluate them." Whenever the plant is open (which is usually twenty-four hours a day), a full-time physician, who is able to handle more sophisticated problems than the usual company infirmary, is present. The Wayne Assembly Plant shuts down twice a year for Christmas week and two weeks in July "when all changes are made," when the machines are retooled for new parts, etc. Proudly Mary Ellen proclaims, "Ford has nineteen assembly plants like this in North America."

Every time Ford conducts a crash barrier test, it spends in the neighborhood of $25,000, *plus* the cost of the car it wrecks. These are deliberately violent acts. No matter how many times they are performed, the preparation takes a whole week and the documentation is thorough. Dummies with chamois faces are strapped into the Tempo that will be the subject of today's passive restraint test. The car, aided by pulleys, will go 525 feet at thirty-five miles per hour and crash into a special barrier outfitted with cameras. ("Federal standards are less strict than Ford's," we're told. The government requires only a thirty-mile-per-hour crash, but "the difference between thirty and thirty-five miles per hour is more than thirty percent.") The car is emptied of gasoline and replaced with Stoddard solvent, which is red and thus more visible.

Just before takeoff, the dummies' faces and legs are painted red, blue, orange, and green, so that the wet paint will make contact with the interior of the car and the affected parts of the body will be identified. The dummies being used today—they sit around like so many George Segal sculptures—are composites: heads, torsos, legs that don't quite match. The dummy room, officially called the "anthropomorphic test device laboratory," in which body parts are separated, looks like a torture chamber. The standard male dummy is 5'10" and weighs 170 pounds with instrumentation. The female is 5' and 105 pounds with the instruments. (New top-of-the-line dummies have been ordered. They cost $25,000 apiece. The instrumentation adds approximately $40,000 to the price.

As is true of so much at Ford, the testing building is also huge, with room for an audience. This is the 6,081st car to be crashed. "There are about 283 tests per year," Jim Maxwell says, meaning that about 283 cars are mashed up annually. They're not always Fords. "Our object is to crash a vehicle and have the data in one hour. It helps the designers."

Two thousand feet of sixteen-millimeter color film will be shot during the test, which will last only a few seconds. In addition to the cameras in the barrier, in the test car, all along the runway, and suspended from the ceiling, there are several photographers shooting motion pictures and a still photographer at the site as well. It feels like a rocket launch. It looks like a rocket launch. Observers cannot even stand at the same level as the test in progress. One viewing area is a room suspended exactly above the barrier in a glassed-in computer center. It reverberates slightly when the car hits.

W orking for Ford, or at least visiting Ford, is much more about process than about fit. Do you love cars? Do you want to be around cars all the time? Do you want a reserved parking space? Then you have to drive a Ford. That's called incentive.

The informed car lover can have no greater ambition than to design the cars themselves. Most of Ford's design studio is off limits to the public, but the concept cars—the fantasymobiles of the design staff—are displayed in what is essentially a showroom and a showpiece. In the past year, Ford's streamlined designs, touted for their sleek, clean aerodynamics, have led the industry domestically. Even the company's rivals must admit to being influenced by Ford. Sadly, none of these prototypes ever makes it to production. "There are three reasons to do concept cars," explains designer Bud Magaldi. "To allow designers and engineers to stretch and dream; to help share this with management and bring them on board to decide new trends; and to share with the public via auto shows." These cars are as well traveled as any celebrity on a promotional tour, and probably more popular. (They are not presently writing diet books.)

The Probe 5 is the newest of the new models. It has a pointed nose, it's very sleek, and it is "more efficient than an F-15 fighter." Some of its cooler features include a holographic speedometer, which allows the motorist to check his speed without looking down at a dashboard, a computerized map that looks like a video game, shows you exactly where you are, and points you where you're going, and great legroom.

"Most designers have gas in their blood. They just happen to love cars more than other stuff."

What if you *like* cars more than you love them, and you like the idea of working for Ford but you're not an engineer? Obviously, there are a number of places where you could work in a white collar without significant auto/mechanical/technical expertise. Ford's legal department comprises about 150 attorneys, who enjoy a range of work that spans real estate, patent, libel, and even pro bono cases. Lassie Wildern, who joined the department straight from law school in 1977, says, "First-year associates at firms don't get to practice law, unlike here." Besides legal, there's labor relations, finance (where most of the MBAs work), investor relations, college recruiting, personnel, marketing, corporate strategy, purchasing and supply, employee communications, and news and public affairs.

Many members of these staffs chose Ford for reasons other than the obvious. They were not car nuts. That this was the legacy of Henry Ford, the maker of the Model T and the Mustang, was secondary. They liked the people they met during their interviews, the jobs for which they applied sounded interesting, and they liked the fact that public opinion of the manufacturer was warming up. Soon autophilia kicks in. "You get bitten by the bug. Not just because it's a car, but because it's your end product." Obviously, the company is too large to allow for every employee to identify with every other employee, or even for everyone to have a sense of what other people do. "I couldn't tell you what other staffs did or where they lived," a corporate staff member says. "When we first sat down together, people couldn't understand each other's language. Now there's a greater awareness. I see myself as part of a service organization, rather than just part of my staff."

Corporate staff members think that adjusting to Ford's cultural transition was probably most difficult for "people in their forties; not older or younger"—company people who've been with Ford for about twenty years. "The most encouraging thing is, we're not picking up the bad habits we divested. We're retraining people; we're staying humane."

What else? What else? Writing about Ford presents innumerable frustrations. How can one distill the experiences of 350,100 people into a short chapter? And a chapter focused on the corporate side, at that? How do you analyze the responses of employees who, when asked how they feel about their work, talk about what they do? In eight or so days at the nation's third largest industrial corporation, I met with about seventy employees in various walks of Ford life. I saw Ford's Cray supercomputer, which, at a cost of $8 million, is the most powerful information processing machine in the world. It takes a month to build a single system. The room had to be built around the computer, which resembles the turquoise Naugahyde banquettes that decorate bowling alleys.

Let's return to the issue of size. As long as you don't feel one of 350,100, you won't be daunted or dwarfed. Besides, you are not choosing a career in an industry that is led by small, boutique-y upstarts. "When you come to work for Ford Motor, you're in awe because of the size. Some awe goes away because you start to understand the industry. Then you don't leave. You get gas in your blood." John Stewart says, "Ford becomes divided into workable units. You make damn sure that the clerical staff is part of the team decision making. There's smallness within the bigness, and it's more challenging to get things done here." It must be a comfort knowing that you work for one of the most recognizable names in business anywhere. ("The two best recognized logos worldwide are Coca-Cola and Ford. But Ford in pronounceable in every language.")

Ford's National Service Training Center boasts five shop classrooms for technical service people. Some thirty thousand people come in from around the country to familiarize themselves with the new models and their innards. (Dealers pay the cost of their technicians' trips.) Some of the fellows going through the program maintain that they feel better about working at the new Ford; that even though they work off site, "these days we have a chairman of the board who'll address us in shirtsleeves. It never would have happened before. They brought themselves down to the masses." For the record, the term "mechanic" is "outdated, stigmatized." The preferred title is "technician," or better, "technical support person."

OASIS stands for On-line Automotive Service Information Systems. Started in 1985 with computers and Touch-Tone phones in participating dealerships, it allows the dealers to get an immediate diagnosis for a vehicle with problems. It was developed by the service research and development people. "OASIS has caused several groups to be thrown together, and we pulled it off. We're very proud of it. It's our baby." OASIS is an optional program. Its progenitors never thought it would be accepted so quickly or so widely. "They're using it five times more than we expected. Fifty-two hundred dealers are using it now, and we didn't beat them up or anything."

As OASIS's creators go on to future projects, they are concerned about its next caretakers. "Is another group going to take as good care of it? We can't work on it indefinitely, but we have to make it great." Because the service research and development teams were allowed freedom in this program, they feel the pride of ownership. They care about their work and feel a tremendous debt to Ford for its trust, with, again, a nod toward the new culture for allowing OASIS to happen. "We are self-motivated, and we enjoy our success. OASIS allows for instant gratification. We've helped save the company $35 million."

What else? What else? Oh yes, the Diversified Product Technical Center, a focal point of Diversified Product Operations (DPO), is one of Ford's most high-tech facilities. Here are the laboratories whence climate control, audio products, antilock braking, electronic suspension, et al. are developed. There are approximately 85,000 people in the whole DPO, about 1,200 in the DPTC), and it is growing. Each group has its own research and development labs in immediate proximity to its offices. It's like a graduate school. What's more, there are classrooms, called "learning centers," in the building that are actually connected through closed circuit television, to the University of Michigan in Ann Arbor. Using a telephone and watching the screen, an employee can actually earn a graduate degree in, for example, electrical engineering, without ever having to leave the building.

Employees can also study German, Portuguese, Spanish, and Japanese and take self-improvement classes via an extensive videotape library. "You can use company time, but budgeted and disciplined. The learning center is constantly in use. This room is a highlight for new employees." DPO lives in one of the newer edifices at Ford, built in 1980, but "its technology and thinking are newer. It's not 1980-oriented, it's 1990, '91, '92. We have a progressive image within the company as a whole. People in this building see themselves as the elite of engineers." DPO is a highly coveted area with a sense of management's benediction. Life within this elite facility features flextime, under which employees can start their days anytime between 7:00 and 8:30 A.M. and leave 8½ hours later, the extra half hour going for lunch. "But no one looks over your shoulder."

The design group's Probe 5 is pretty nifty, but DPO has its own *pièce de résistance* in the

Concept 100 vehicle. The body was actually fashioned at the Design Center in 1983, but the instrumentation is created here. Dramatically displayed in the middle of a white room, it's a canvas for future advances and amenities. With its pigskin interior, it is comfortable, plush, and rich. (Well, it did cost $500,000; what do you expect?) How about keyless ignition ("which doesn't pass safety regulations")? Voice control and voice command? No door handles? "A lot of ideas have been incorporated into our cars."

This might be the right time to tell you that the development of a new car takes five years. Some of the really wonderful features developed by Ford that don't come into conflict with government standards are not always integrated quickly, because new equipment means new machines and gobs of money. Some features are held until it's time for serious redesigning.

Sales and Operations is made up of people who, unlike designers, could work anywhere. "It isn't that technical; we're selling ourselves and the business." Yes, they have a special affinity for cars and the automobile business. The salespeople are headquartered downtown in the Renaissance Center, but all of them have put in time elsewhere. One of the caveats of accepting a job in sales at Ford is that you must be prepared to move. It comes up in every single job interview. "If you're in sales, you might move more than anyone else." Upon hearing the warning, if an applicant responds negatively, chances are he or she will not be hired. "That's very bad. You can say you don't want to move, but then what's the point? The company's not deaf and blind—if you have personal problems . . ." Essentially, the willingness to relocate is proof of one's loyalty to the organization.

"Two-career couples can't work. There are lots of commuting couples, split couples, and a high divorce rate. One of the major problems we have is keeping women. We hire 40 percent women, but with transfers and travel it's hard. It's hard to find a guy [husband or boyfriend] who will move. By the time you make it to regional manager, you've proven your devotion." This may all sound quite harsh, but remember, everyone's been alerted. The salespeople assembled today are pretty cheerful about the courses their lives have taken.

A young woman says, "I realized I was interested in cars, so I wrote to Ford. I realized that the whole industry looks to Ford for its management and training program." Another is thrilled that Ford paid for her MBA. Plus, "Detroit is better than I thought it would be." Mary is married to a fellow who was the ultimate supporter of her ambition. "He's given up his career. We're thinking of having kids, and he said he'd stay at home." Connie is involved with a guy who lives in St. Louis. "I want to see how well I do [before I request a transfer to St. Louis]. I think I'll be very successful. Ford tells you your potential."

Ray Fregia, a father of two, says, "My kids are constantly aware that this [moving] can happen again and again, but we try to upgrade our style of living each time." The Fregias lived in Utah, Wyoming, and Illinois before coming back to Detroit. (They've since moved to Seattle, Ray having been promoted to general field manager position there.) A black family, they were in a tiny minority in Salt Lake City. "I didn't think I'd like it, but after five years, I did." Their elder child is a teenager, at the age most traumatized by uprooting. "I tell them, 'Don't get settled.' It's a constant reminder. We move to transient neighborhoods. It makes them more well-rounded."

This group professes no regrets. "Ford's taken a chance on me," one says, "and taken my feelings into account. I think the company is compassionate." It probably would not surprise you that as salespeople, their language is upbeat, their "people skills" refined.

"What is a Ford person?" Vice-chairman and COO Poling's answer is "Someone who is intelligent, highly motivated, and interested in working together as a team. You learn team building from sports. What you need in a corporation is a team effort. What we had were individual organizations working well, but not effectively. It's getting better." Team spirit notwithstanding, Poling agrees that Ford is a competitive environment, though no more so than life itself. But is it a place of individuals competing and winning for themselves? Are there stars soaring above the top 10 percent of the Ford universe? "God, I hope we don't have stars; we have leaders. Star systems have problems. Shooting stars play out."

Poling has been with Ford since 1950, including stints as the head of Ford Europe and Ford North America, where he was known as "Mr. Quality." "I never awakened in the morning and thought, 'God, do I have to go to work today?' In the early eighties some of the days were unpleasant. I don't sleep well laying off people, but you're doing the best you can." For Poling, being an effective leader has not meant wondering how to run a company of this magnitude or learning to trust his judgment. "I never think of it that way. I just handle it."

The subject of Japan must come up in any conversation with a senior manager of an American automobile company. "Our equity with Mazda, built up over eight or nine years, indicated we can work together with the Japanese. Two trading partners like us should not be in the position we're in with Japan. An industrial society should not give up an industrial base."

Still, Ford wants to win. "You can't depend on the loyalty of Americans. You must earn it. We're marketing aggressively on the luxury end. We're promoting the 'Buy American' philosophy."

Poling claims the new Ford is a place where "if something went wrong, you're not looking for the person responsible, you're looking for a solution." He is clearly a role model for his people, a responsibility he interprets as "All you can do is establish what your values are and then live them day to day. What you do speaks louder than what you say." He holds consistency, dependability, and predictability in high esteem. "You can't vacillate. People try to outguess you."

Donald Petersen is Ford Motor Company's chairman and chief executive officer, positions he has held since February 1, 1985. He grew up in a family too poor to own a car and joined the company in 1949 with an MBA from Stanford. "I never had a specific goal in the career sense," he says at lunch. "I didn't set out to reach a certain level or run a certain piece of the organization. I knew I had to develop skills that I knew I didn't have. It was relatively very recently that I saw myself as the leader of people at Ford."

He is lean, tan, and very amiable. He admits he "did better at staying in touch with people when I was president. There's lots of stuff only the chairman must do." Consequently, he sometimes gets groups together for lunch "without agendas. I ask, 'How are you all doing?'"

Petersen is proud of the Mission and Guiding Principles, conscious that it "was written in a sufficiently generic way to not have to make major changes." That does not mean that Ford is finished with its sweeping cultural renovations. "Personal review change is imminent" and would mean moving away from personal achievements toward team achievements. "I'm not clear at all whether we have the right organization now, or how it could be. I think a lot about whether we could eliminate vagueness and layers in our hierarchy." However, "despite changes, the organizations have remained stable."

The pressures of being CEO of the fourth largest industrial corporation in the world—the third largest in the United States—must be daunting. Is Petersen scared? "No." Worried? "Yes." Is he ever overwhelmed by it all? "I'm certainly surprised, but by and large, I'm comfortable, which by and large surprises me." Moreover, he sees no "they" and "us" in the 350,100. "There is no 'they,' no divergence between Donald Petersen's point of view and Ford's teams' conclusion. *They are we,*" he adds passionately.

"I love cars; I love to drive." His first Ford was a '34 or '35. He bought a 1948 sedan that he drove to Stanford and has a fondness for a 1950 Ford convertible in chartreuse and black with a V-8 engine. "I always got twenty miles per gallon," he recalls. And yes, Donald Petersen passed his road test on his first try.

THE TEST DRIVE

Jackie Stewart is here, tearing up the track in his role as consultant and troubleshooter for Ford. His affiliation has spanned eight years, and the people of Ford who see him regularly are still starstruck. "He knows his stuff," one manager says admiringly. "The cars we market as 'high performance' all have his stamp on them." Stewart spends most of his time with the Mustang, Thunderbird, and Merkur.

Although the famed racer is "cheerful" about his obligation to spend thirty days a year in Dearborn, today is a bit more special than the other twenty-nine: Today is his first turn with the finished 1987 prototypes, the finished models of the cars whose development he has helped guide. The sounds of the screeching of brakes are menacing, but music to the ears of the audience of engineers, designers, and press people, who no longer have to worry about industry spies perching in the trees adjoining the track, the site of a former airport. (It's too late for rival car manufacturers to do anything with the photographs taken by their spies. As far as the calendar is concerned, it would be another couple of years at the earliest that styling details garnered today could be assimilated. Because of the enormous efforts, time, and expense required to redesign machinery to make new cars it would take too long to integrate the new designs for the next season.)

Jackie Stewart drives the handling course and the braking course. He averages about 120 miles per hour. When he is finished and the crowd has dispersed, it is my turn.

I procured my New York State driver's license a mere three weeks before my visit to Ford. A lifelong Manhattan resident, I probably would have perpetuated my vehicular handicap indefinitely had I not been offered one of the plums of a visit to Detroit: an (unsolicited) opportunity to test-drive. When I mentioned my unlicensed state to the Ford News Department—the group responsible for handling my visit—their reaction was as though I'd denounced America, democracy, and capitalism. After having left a mildly positive impression with the Ford brass through letters and phone conversations, I could almost hear the disgust welling up in the belly of the organization. I promised to arrive, license in hand, by June 15.

I spent April and May taking driving lessons, double and triple sessions during which I drove my instructor around the island of Manhattan in order for him to do his errands. There were mysterious drop-offs on Fifty-seventh Street and Sixth Avenue, numerous trips to the dry cleaners on Lenox Avenue and 115th Streeet, lunch runs where he picked up steaming containers of pungent sauerkraut and brats in Yorkville, New York's German neighborhood—my instructor's ability to eat during my lessons filled me with confidence, actually—and one unplanned opportunity to drive my mother, seen trying to hail a taxi, to the hairdresser.

My last lesson ended about a half hour before my road test. I believe I had the shakes. En route to the testing area, my teacher and I picked up another student, who claimed to have had a license in her previous country of residence but who nevertheless was more nervous than I. But she wasn't about to prove herself at Ford's proving grounds. I felt I had my credibility at stake.

Although my teacher felt my chances of passing were only pretty good, he thought it was worth a try. Besides, driving schools buy up a lot of prime testing time, and he had plenty of slots for sale the following week. I succeeded, however, without a single demerit. My teacher seemed only nominally pleased, but he did allow me to make a single phone call from his car phone to alert the person of my choice. (I didn't call the Ford News Department, since it was long distance.) My cotest taker also passed. Her call, suffused with tears of joy, was to her mother.

It would be a mistake to belabor the point, but when I left for Detroit, I did not have the pleasure of bringing a driver's license with me; just the now-weathered scrap of paper that was my learner's permit, stamped "Approved." I waved it at my friends at Ford, who smiled pityingly while taking me to the former hangar that served as the test track's offices.

My host was Jim McCraw, a former executive editor of *Motor Trend Magazine* currently working in the Ford public affairs department. Over coffee, Jim prepared me for my test drive. Knowing nothing whatsoever about automobiles (other than my grandmother's warning that even if the car is parked with its ignition off, if you jump up and down in the back seat anxious to get going, the car will move and you will die), I found myself nodding my comprehension to information that might as well have been explained in a non-Romance language. I accepted the knowledge about antilock braking systems, the batteries of tests undergone by the machines, and so on, as if I were watching Japanese game shows on cable TV (they happen to be quite entertaining).

The track emptied, Jim invited me to choose a car and go for a spin. Having never driven a car without dual controls, I offered him the opportunity of coming along for the ride. I was only too happy to accept the crash helmet one must wear on the track. It accessorized my linen suit very nicely, although it crushed my earrings to my head. I decided to start with the Mustang. We strapped ourselves in.

White and sleek (the Mustang, I mean), I was delighted by the car's handling. It took the curves with ease. I felt like Jackie Stewart, so comfortable was I behind the wheel. This was the first time I could drive for the pleasure of it, and not stop for traffic or sauerbrauten. Zooming around and around, I finally had the temerity to look at the speedometer to check my intrepidness: forty miles per hour. I was flying!

Then the Thunderbird. Such grace in motion! (The car, I mean.) The Merkur—sophistication and ergonomic prowess! (And the car looked good, too.) While Jim wanly praised my expertise, I thought by this point he would like to take the wheel. I could have driven all day, the creasing of my linen ensemble be damned.

We switched seats. I think he averaged eighty-five or ninety miles per hour. It was too fast to take notes. He was able to talk and drive simultaneously. While waiting for my life to begin flashing in front of my eyes, I wondered when my actual license would come in the mail. Then I remembered I would be summoned to the New York Department of Motor Vehicles, where I would be the oldest native American waiting on a daylong line for a *first* license, and that perhaps by Labor Day or maybe Thanksgiving I would find in my mailbox —if I survived—the ugly photograph ID card. And why be coy? That has turned out to be my license's primary purpose. Although I still go through life taking taxis through Iowa ($50 from Des Moines to Ames, approximately forty miles) and Beverly Hills ($8.50 from the Beverly Hills Hotel to the Beverly Wilshire, one quarter mile), I know I am able to cash a check anywhere.

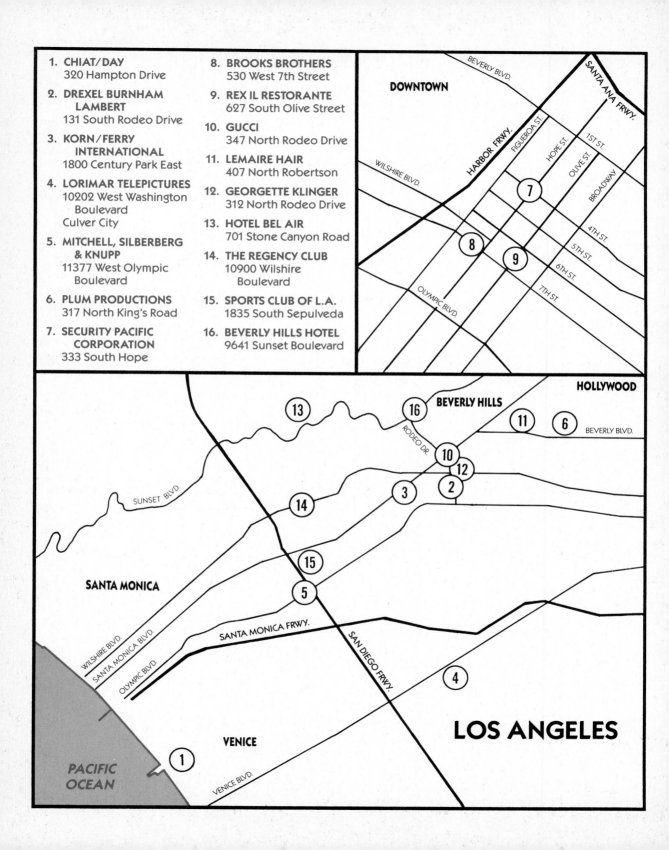

1. **CHIAT/DAY**
   320 Hampton Drive

2. **DREXEL BURNHAM LAMBERT**
   131 South Rodeo Drive

3. **KORN/FERRY INTERNATIONAL**
   1800 Century Park East

4. **LORIMAR TELEPICTURES**
   10202 West Washington Boulevard
   Culver City

5. **MITCHELL, SILBERBERG & KNUPP**
   11377 West Olympic Boulevard

6. **PLUM PRODUCTIONS**
   317 North King's Road

7. **SECURITY PACIFIC CORPORATION**
   333 South Hope

8. **BROOKS BROTHERS**
   530 West 7th Street

9. **REX IL RESTORANTE**
   627 South Olive Street

10. **GUCCI**
    347 North Rodeo Drive

11. **LEMAIRE HAIR**
    407 North Robertson

12. **GEORGETTE KLINGER**
    312 North Rodeo Drive

13. **HOTEL BEL AIR**
    701 Stone Canyon Road

14. **THE REGENCY CLUB**
    10900 Wilshire Boulevard

15. **SPORTS CLUB OF L.A.**
    1835 South Sepulveda

16. **BEVERLY HILLS HOTEL**
    9641 Sunset Boulevard

DOWNTOWN

LOS ANGELES

LOS ANGELES

LOS ANGELES

S ince you won't read this elsewhere in *Going to Work,* let's just add one simple fact about
Los Angeles. It's a one-industry town. Say it yourself. "It's a one-industry town."
Everybody! "It's a one-industry town." At least, it might as well be. The name Los Angeles
doesn't conjure up, for example, the floor-covering business, or insurance, or oil (except to
students at Beverly Hills High, who, appropriately, have a real oil well on their property), or
anything but show business. And while the biz has a certain charmed way of sneaking up on
you and taking over (you may be eating lunch with a banker, but the guy at the next table is
Burt Reynolds, so what are you going to do?), in fact it generates lower revenues than any of
the industries listed above. In fact, far lower. All this by way of an explanation.

Only one company in this book, Lorimar Telepictures, is expressly involved in entertainment. (Another, the law firm of Mitchell, Silberberg & Knupp, has a major entertainment
practice.) The others—Chiat/Day, Security Pacific, and Plum Productions, and so on—are
serious businesses that might brush with fame but are filled with people who don't really care
about it. Why belabor the point? It's just because up until I researched companies for this

book, I had almost never made contact with *anyone* in L.A. who was not in show business. Or related to someone in same.

It is refreshing to discover serious businesspeople who don't care about the biz. This must sound naive, but it gives one the sense that real lives happen in southern California without limousines or Technicolor touches.

I've developed a rather insignificantly significant theory about corporate life in Los Angeles: It is less stressful to go to work in good weather than it is in inclement weather. It's rarely dark during office hours. This idea comes out of visiting offices on both coasts of several bicoastal organizations. Lorimar Telepictures, Drexel Burnham Lambert, Korn/Ferry [Author's note: These last two chapters are grouped with New York companies.] Chiat/Day—life seems simpler, less somber, and (I'm willing to say it's my own personal take on what I've seen) less serious. People still work hard and for the same stakes, but the approach is more casual. You cannot worry about being a creaseless executive when you spend a couple of hours each day in your car.

Oh, yes—the car thing. An increasingly evident obnoxious habit is referring to one's car by its make. "I've got to take the Mercedes to the mechanic." "We took the Roller [cute for Rolls-Royce] to the beach." "Let's go in my Porsche." No one uses the word "car" anymore. Can Angelenos really be that insecure? When someone in the public eye or the *Forbes* 400 is seen driving less than a top-of-the-line import, it is commented upon as if that person were rather brave, eccentric, or driving a rented car—their Porsche/Jaguar/Mercedes/BMW must have been at the mechanic's.

Interestingly, southern Californians engage in the active proselytizing of out-of-staters to a degree one finds nowhere else except in Utah or in some airport terminals. They will ask the out-of-town business traveler "When are you moving here?" and before the visitor is able to answer, the Californian is already assaulting him or her with a list of reasons why his hometown is unlivable and why the quality of life in L.A. is without peer. (This activity abates somewhat just after earthquakes, mudslides, brushfires, killing sprees, and other assorted natural disasters.)

A final note: In the unlikely event that you could ever possibly procure a reservation for dinner at Spago, the celebrated restaurant, at *dinnertime* (if you haven't heard of Spago until now, chances are you will never eat there) you would see that the food really is good. As of publication time, Spago is not open for lunch.

BEST NEIGHBORHOODS WITH DECENT PUBLIC SCHOOLS: Beverly Hills, Santa Monica

NICEST NEIGHBORHOODS (BUT YOU'LL PROBABLY HAVE TO SEND YOUR KIDS TO PRIVATE SCHOOL): Holmby Hills, Bel Air, Brentwood, Encino

BEST PLACE TO LIVE IF YOU'RE AN ASPIRING ARTIST OR YOU WANT TO LIVE NEAR PEOPLE WHO WEAR ONLY BLACK: Venice

BEST NEIGHBORHOOD WITH TAKE-OUT FOOD AND SINGLE PEOPLE WHO ARE ALSO REPUBLICANS: West Hollywood

MOST OVERPRICED COMMUNITY FOR SUMMER HOMES: Malibu

BEST PUBLIC SCHOOLS: Beverly Hills, Santa Monica

BEST PRIVATE SCHOOLS: Crossroads (lower school), John Thomas Dye (lower school), Center for Early Education (lower school), Brentwood (coed), Crossroads (coed), Harvard (boys' high school—home of the Billionaire Boys Club), Westlake (girls' high school), Marlborough (girls' high school), in the Valley: Oakwood & Buckley (coed, all grades)

ARCHITECT WHO HAS MOST INFLUENCED THE CITY'S SKYLINE: Frank Ghery

MOST POPULAR RESIDENTIAL ARCHITECT: Alberto Lensi

SOCIALLY INCLINED REALTORS: Jon Douglas, Fred Sands

DECORATORS WHO WOULD DECORATE HOMES PURCHASED THROUGH THAT REALTOR: Barbara Windom, Leslie Zinberg

DEALER IN THE FINEST, MOST VALUABLE ART: Margo Leavin

TRENDY GALLERIES FOR PEOPLE WHO WEAR ALL BLACK AND HAVE A LOT OF MONEY: Corcoran, L.A. Louver, Margo Leavin

MOST EXCLUSIVE GOLF CLUB: Los Angeles Country Club

BEST PUBLIC GOLF FACILITIES: Wilson (Griffin Park); Rancho

MOST EXPENSIVE HEALTH CLUB: L.A. Sports Club

BEST HEALTH CLUB FOR MEETING POTENTIAL MATES: L.A. Sports Club

BEST HOTELS FOR BUSINESS TRIPS: Century Plaza, Century Tower, Beverly Wilshire, Four Seasons

RESTAURANTS KNOWN FOR BEST CUISINE: Spago, Chinois

BEST RESTAURANT FOR PEOPLE WHO WEAR BLACK: West Beach Café

BEST RESTAURANT FOR AN INEXPENSIVE DATE: Ed Debevic (dinner)

NOISIEST RESTAURANT (INTIMACY IMPOSSIBLE): Dan Tana

BEST DARK BAR: Polo Lounge

BEST GIMMICKY BAR: Rebecca's

BEST BAR TO IMPRESS A CLIENT: Polo Lounge

MOST EXCLUSIVE CITY CLUBS: Regency Club, Jonathan Club

FANCIEST WINE STORES WHENCE CEOS PROBABLY STOCK THEIR OWN CELLARS: Wally's Wine Merchant

GOURMET STORES GUARANTEED NOT TO RUN OUT OF GOAT CHEESE OR SUN-DRIED TOMA-TOES: Irvine Ranch, Mrs. Gooch

NICEST MOM-AND-POP GROCERY STORES: Owen's, Arrow

LARGEST DRUGSTORE WITH MOST REMARKABLE SELECTION: Rexall at Dart Square, Thrifty

CORPORATE PARTY PLANNERS: Rowoco, Along Came Mary

HIGH-SOCIETY PARTY PLANNER: Parties Plus

POWER BARBERS: LeMaire, Little Joe

NEW WAVE HAIRSTYLIST: Jill (Taboo)

JUNIOR LEAGUE BEAUTY PARLOR: Elizabeth Arden

PLACES WHERE LADIES WHO LUNCH ARE LIKELY TO HAVE TEA AFER A HARD DAY OF SHOP-PING, VOLUNTEER WORK, AND TENNIS: Bistro Garden; Trumps

BEST STORES FOR EXECUTIVE WOMEN: Carroll & Co., Allan Austin, Polo

BEST STORES FOR EXECUTIVE MEN: Polo, Carroll & Co.

BEST STORES FOR DRESS-UP CLOTHES: Giorgio, Suite 101, The Alley, Eleanor Keeshan

BEST SHOPPING RESOURCE FOR PEOPLE WHO WEAR ONLY BLACK CLOTHES: Maxfield Bleu

DEBUTANTE BALL: At the Crystal Room at the Beverly Hills Hotel

MOST RELIABLE FLORIST: Harry Findlay

MOST EXOTIC FLORIST: David Jones

TOP JEWELERS FOR RESETTING MOTHER'S EMERALDS: Regency; Fred Joaille

MOST COMPLETE BRIDAL REGISTRIES: Geary's, Robinson's

PROMINENT PHYSICIANS: Dr. Robert Huizenga, Dr. Laurence Seigler

PROMINENT PLASTIC SURGEONS WITH EQUALLY PROMINENT CLIENTELE: Dr. Frank Kamer, Dr. Harry Glassman (married to actress and Jhirmack spokesperson Victoria Principal), Dr. Steven Zax

GYNECOLOGIST MOST OFTEN QUOTED IN THE LOCAL PRESS: Dr. Art Ulene (appears on *Today*)

BEST SEAMSTRESS OR TAILOR FOR ALTERATIONS: Charles the Tailor (on Dayton Way)

BEST SEAMSTRESS OR TAILOR FOR CUSTOM TAILORING: Arnold Fiddler

POPULAR FACIAL SALONS: Aida Thibiant, Aida Grey, Georgette Klinger

POWER TOOLS

MEN'S POWER DRESSING

BROOKS BROTHERS
530 West 7th Street
Los Angeles, CA
(213) 620-9500

BEST-SELLING EXECUTIVE SUIT: Three-button, midweight, gray or navy, 100 percent wool, $450

POWER SHIRT: Pinpoint button-down, white, 100 percent cotton, $50

POWER TIE: Foulard, maroon or navy (50/50 split), 100 percent silk, $25

REX IL RISTORANTE
627 South Olive Street
Los Angeles, CA 90014
(213) 627-2300

FIRST COURSES:
Pheasant salad, $14.00
Fettucine with porcini mushrooms, $14.00
Pagliolini with fresh white truffles, $22.00

SECOND COURSES:
John Dory (fish) with broccoli and truffle oil, $24.00
Fresh Mediterranean shrimp served in shell with butter and herbs, $24.00
Medallion of veal with sweetbreads and artichokes, $27.00
Veal cutlet in morel mushroom sauce, $25.00
Filet of lamb in red wine sauce with fennel au gratin, $25.00

DESSERTS:
Soft gianduia ice cream with caramel sauce, $7.00
pistachio pie with prunes in port wine, $8.00
Coffee chocolate cake with ice cream, $8.00
Vanilla and cocoa Bavarian cream with mint sauce, $7.00

PROMINENT CLIENTELE: "I cannot give you that. I don't know if they're happy to be mentioned."

LE DÔME
8720 Sunset Boulevard
Los Angeles, CA 90069
(213) 659-6919

APPETIZERS:
Fish soup, $5.50
Shop salad, $6.50

MAIN COURSES:
Hot duck salad, $16.00
Chinese air-dried duck, $15.00
Meat loaf, $12.50
Ahi tuna, $12.50
Original cobb salad, $11.00
Roasted vertical chicken on a bed of lettuce, $12.50

DESSERTS:
Individual pastries, $5.00

PROMINENT CLIENTELE: Michael Ovitz (head of CAA and often called "the most powerful man in Hollywood"); Marilyn Grabowski (*Playboy*); Shelly Berger, Sylvester Stallone, Jake Bloom (lawyer), David Guyler (writer), Irving ("Swifty") Lazar, Jackie Collins, John Gaines

POWER ACCESSORIES

GUCCI
347 North Rodeo Drive
Beverly Hills, CA 90210
(213) 278-3451

MOST POPULAR MEN'S SHOE: Gucci loafer, $195

MOST POPULAR WOMEN'S SHOE: Classic pump, low cut, two- to two-and-a-half inch heel, in all colors, $195

BRIEF CASES (MEN'S AND WOMEN'S): Top of the line is their crocodile briefcase, which sells mostly to advertising people—"people who can get away with being more flashy"—$6,800

EXECUTIVE MISCELLANY: Watches (men's and women's), $175–$450; belts (men's), $95–$250

BUYING AN EXECUTIVE HOME

FRED SANDS
9400 Santa Monica Boulevard
Beverly Hills, CA 90210
(213) 278-1345

Fred Sands, which has seventeen offices scattered around southern California, is the second largest privately owned realty company in California and the fifth largest in the country. The firm represents an enormous range of listings, from $80,000 condominiums to $20 million homes. We spoke to Lonna Presser, a young realtor who has done remarkably well in her first year with the firm. Her clientele is equally divided between executives and foreign investors.

WHAT NEIGHBORHOODS ARE EXECUTIVES CHOOSING TO LIVE IN?

"Executives are not the wealthiest around here. It's really the investors who are the wealthiest. The older executives [who have more money] are more likely to go for very expensive properties. The younger ones—a lot of them can't even afford Beverly Hills, where a small house goes for $400,000 to $600,000." The prime Los Angeles neighborhoods and price ranges of average homes there are: Old Bel Air ($2 million to $9 million); north of Sunset ($3 million to $6 million or $7 million); Holmby Hills ($1.5 million to $10 million); Brentwood Park ("a very classy area," $1 million to $2.5 million), Pacific Palisades (a new up-and-coming neighborhood," $500,000 to $1.5 million); Malibu ($500,000 to $1.5 million); Santa Monica ($400,000 to $1.5 million); Beverlywood (where a lot of young yuppies go, $350,000 to $600,000); Cheviot Hills ($400,000 to $900,000), Wilshire Corridor (for "exclusive condominiums with beautiful views," $350,000 to $9 million), Beverly Hills Post Office ($450,000 to $2 million), and Trousdale ($1 million to $5 million)

GIVEN THE ABOVE, WHAT IS THE AVERAGE PRICE RANGE FOR AN EXECUTIVE HOME?

Young executives, $350,000 to $400,000; middle-aged executives, $800,000; older executives, "If they're really affluent, then $1.5 million."

WHAT ARE THEIR PRIORITIES WHEN SEEKING A HOME?

"Priority is location, usually. Because they want to be centralized, and they want a property that's going up in value. Most people don't buy homes they like out here. They buy an ugly home, fix it up and sell it, and then buy their dream house. Most buy what they can afford.

Only people who are very affluent can find a beautiful home. Most want a prestigious location. After that, if they can afford it, they want a house with the most land they can get. (But here they can't get much land because it's too expensive.) The last priority is the house itself, because if you have a lot and it goes up in value you can trade it in for a better house."

WHAT KINDS OF EXTRA FEATURES ARE IMPORTANT TO EXECUTIVES?

"The most important features are gourmet kitchens and master suites with his-and-hers baths, marble, and the works. Then come a pool and tennis court."

ARE EXECUTIVE COUPLES WITH CHILDREN CHOOSING NEIGHBORHOODS WITH GOOD PUBLIC SCHOOLS, OR DO THEY SEND THEIR KIDS TO PRIVATE SCHOOLS?

"They send their children to public schools, and neighborhoods are important. Beverly Hills High is the top school—it's like a private school."

ARE YOUR EXECUTIVE CLIENTS DIFFERENT FROM YOUR NONEXECUTIVE CLIENTS?

"Yes. They usually can't afford the same kind of house. Also, they're usually really nervous about buying a house—more so than other people. Other people usually find a property—they know the area they want—and they buy. Executives are usually more cautious. In this market you have to move fast. A lot of executives are afraid. By the time they think about it and discuss it with their spouses, the house is sold. It takes executives an average of six months to buy. Other clients will usually buy right away. I have to take executives on for six months so they'll believe me and believe that the market is like I say it is. When they miss out on deals, they say, 'Why didn't I listen to you?' After about six months they trust me, and they jump on deals when I tell them to."

HAVE YOU NOTICED A SLUMP IN THE MARKET SINCE "BLACK MONDAY"?

"Actually, I've noticed an increase in the market. I was shocked, but that's what I see. Everyone's calling me, they want a house. They see houses as a sound investment. People are still buying houses to fix them up and sell them. The market is still going up. I see houses that are not even on the market and they're selling, so to me, that's a hot market."

POWER HAIR

LEMAIRE/HAIR
407 N. Robertson Avenue
Los Angeles, CA 90048
(213) 276-1635

Resembling a new wave shrine with its shiny, geometrically patterned floor and stained glass crosses, LeMaire/Hair is a testimony to the power-savvy magic of LeMaire, the power haircutter to the decision makers in Hollywood. With a roster of clients who can give and take meetings wherever they please, thank you, LeMaire demands they not take anything too seriously in her Robertson Avenue lair.

ADVICE TO CLIENTS: "Keep your eyes on the floor."

ADVICE TO BALDING CLIENTS: "Be bald and be proud!"

ON PERMS: "Chemical interference can get in the way of decisions."

ON EXECUTIVE HAIR: "People in the business tend to gray easier than most other people, and they love their gray. It's a sign of wisdom." When guys come in who part their hair way over their ears to cover bald: I call it the 'imposter do.' I trim it first to liberate them from hair bondage."

ON NETWORKING IN THE SALON: "I've seen lunch be made; I've seen auditions happen. Some people don't like to be seen in public with their hair wet, because mostly they do business with people with dry hair."

ON THE DIFFERENCES BETWEEN MEN AND WOMEN STUDIO EXECUTIVES: "They can be equally demanding, because if your hair looks rotten it's hard to be effective."

PROMINENT CLIENTS: PRODUCERS AND STUDIO PRESIDENTS: Jeffrey Katzenberg (Disney); Keith Barish (Taft-Barish); Craig Baumgarten (independent producer); Richard Fischoff (Jaffe/Lansing); Dawn Steele (Paramount); Irwin Winkler (independent producer); Bob Lawrence (U.A.) David Kirkpatrick (WEG); Jon Tarnoff (Delaurentiis Films). DIRECTORS: Brian de-Palma (*The Untouchables*); Costa-Gavras (*Z*); Rob Cohen. ACTORS: Stephanie Powers, Keith Gordon, Tatum O'Neal, Helen Slater, Joanna Kerns, John Laroquette, Alan Thicke. AGENTS: Jim Wiatt (ICM), Marty Bauer. POWER WIVES: Margo Winkler, Randee Wiatt. FINANCIER: Max Palevsky.

MOTTO: "I never met a head I didn't like."

FEES:
First haircut, women, $75 and up
Haircut, women, $60
Haircut, men, $50
(Double for at-home or at-office cuts)
Permanent, $85
Coloring, $35
Streaking, $85 and up
Tension-reducing scalp treatment (usually fifteen minutes, performed by Miss Mary), $1 per minute; "the only quarter hour of peace my clients can allow themselves."

CHIAT/ DAY INC., ADVERTISING

Chiat/Day

HISTORY & OPERATIONS

Chiat/Day, a bicoastal advertising agency known for its provocative "breakthrough" work, was founded in 1968, when Jay Chiat and Guy Day merged their tiny Los Angeles—based agencies. When Chiat merged with Day, both were involved primarily with advertising technical products such as semiconductors. In an attempt to woo consumer product accounts through reverse psychology, the partners took out an ad that asked, "Who Says Chiat/Day Doesn't Do Technical Advertising?" Despite early efforts to break into the area of consumer products, it took years to attract the kinds of clients Day and Chiat wanted.

The agency got a false start in the right direction in the early seventies, when Honda hired it to create the advertising for one of its small, low-powered cars. But when Honda grew bigger, it yanked the account from Chiat/Day. The incident was traumatic for the agency, which was more or less stalled until 1978, when it won the Yahama Motor Corporation account, followed by Olympia Beer. At that point it started growing again, and since then it hasn't stopped.

Chiat/Day's unconventional approach to advertising is perhaps best illustrated by two campaigns the agency created in the mid-1980s. The first, for Apple Computer (see p. 642), is epitomized by a commercial that officially aired only once on national television, during the 1984 Super Bowl, in addition to a few times in eleven regional markets. The sixty-second advertisement, designed for the grand introduction of the Macintosh computer, was in keeping with Apple's strategy of "event marketing"—making the launch of each new product into a media event. Based on the theme of George Orwell's *1984,* it showed a young woman in running gear trying to triumph over the "thought police" in a large assembly. At the end of her desperate run, she hurls a sledgehammer through a large television screen depicting Big Brother, a not-so-subtle metaphor for IBM. The ad was so controversial that Apple almost canceled it just days before it was scheduled to air, and with strident proponents as well as detractors, it became one of the most talked-about commercials in the advertising industry in recent years.

Chiat/Day's campaign for Nike, though less dramatic, was equally innovative and effective. Launched during the 1984 summer Olympics, the effort consisted of billboards, print ads, and television spots featuring both famous and unknown athletes (among them Olympic long jumper Carl Lewis, marathon winner Joan Benoit, Los Angeles Dodger Steve Sax, tennis star John McEnroe, and Olympic runner Mary Decker). The billboards and magazine ads consisted of artistic, attention-grabbing photographs, while the television commercials were action vignettes, the most outstanding of which cut rock video–style to the Randy Newman song "I Love L.A." and starred Newman himself. Nike's name was added so quietly it appeared to be an afterthought—a dramatic departure from standard advertising formulas. The company's logo was unobtrusively stuck into the corner of a billboard or television screen. (In broadcast venues, the name Nike was never heard.) Although the emphasis was on the athletes, the company's message got across. Within six months after the campaign was introduced in Los Angeles, Nike's sales there increased by 30 percent.

Chiat/Day's methods for creating commercials, like the commercials themselves, depart from traditional advertising techniques. In 1981 it was the first of only a few American agencies to dispense with research departments and form account planning departments in their stead. Account planning, which was introduced by the British more than ten years before Chiat/Day brought it to the United States, stresses an integrated approach to consumer research. Proponents of this strategy maintain that most U.S. advertising research departments feed market information to the rest of an account team sporadically or sometimes not until after a commercial idea has already been executed and thus fail to infuse campaigns with the consumers' point of view. Account Planning departments work closely with the rest of an advertising team throughout the entire creative process, using their research to introduce the perspective of "the man on the street." Like researchers, account planners are supposed to keep up with consumers on a daily basis, amassing information on a given target audience by moderating focus groups and conducting one-on-one interviews and mail and telephone surveys. Chiat/Day employs roughly two account planners for every account.

Chiat/Day also strives to involve its clients as well as everyone on its staff in the creative process. Rather than presenting completed campaign ideas for a client to either approve or reject, the agency works closely with its clients to come up with ideas that will satisfy both parties (i.e., the current Nissan campaign, which appears to be a filmed Chiat/Day brainstorming session). Internally, it eschews distinctions of hierarchy and department, believing that a good idea can (and should) be generated by anyone in the ranks. This egalitarian philosophy, which is evidenced by the absence of fully enclosed offices—the offices are separated from one another by low barriers, and even conference rooms are enclosed in glass—applies to everyone, including Jay Chiat himself (who reportedly gets his own coffee and answers his own telephone).

At Chiat/Day, employees are expected to put in long hours—so long that at one point employees printed up T-shirts that read "Chiat/Day and Night." And although salaries are reputedly not on a par with those at other agencies of similar size, Chiat/Day gets more than its share of eager applicants seeking the opportunity to join the mission. The agency has a reputation for caring more abut the quality of its output than about its revenues, and it will go so far as to resign from accounts on which it feels its creativity is constrained. As a result of its emphasis on innovation and quality, the agency has won more awards than most agencies ten times it size. Chiat/Day claims to have won more awards per client than any other major ad agency in the world.

Today, Chiat/Day employs 482 people in its offices in Los Angeles, New York (opened in 1981), and San Francisco (opened in 1980). In 1987 billings were $350 million and gross income was $52.5 million, ranking it twenty-fifth in size in *Advertising Age*'s listing. The agency's roster of forty-one clients includes Christian Dior, Drexel Burnham Lambert (see p. 459), Gaines Food, Mitsubishi, the Whitney Museum of American Art, California Cooler, Gillette Oral-B Laboratories, Intel Corporation, 3M Recording Products Division (see p. 390), U. C. Berkeley Foundation, Reebok International, and Nissan Motor Corporation. (In 1986, the agency lost both the Apple and Nike accounts.)

In 1987 Chiat/Day acquired Jessica Dee Communications, a Manhattan-based public relations firm which now has twenty-seven employees. The move was the first in a number of planned acquisitions of nonadvertising businesses that will be purchased through Chiat/Day Marketing Communications, a New York–based subsidiary of Chiat/Day.

Chiat/Day is privately held, and employees own stock in the agency.

(Information provided by Carol Siodmak, assistant to Jay Chiat.)

Advertising Age RANKING: Twenty-fifth largest agency in terms of worldwide gross income.

BILLINGS: $350 million in 1987.

EARNINGS: Gross income was $52.5 million in 1987, and the agency's operating margin was $11,025,000.

OFFICES: In Los Angeles, New York, and San Francisco, in addition to Jessica Dee Communications in New York.

NUMBER OF EMPLOYEES: 509 total: 216 in Los Angeles, 148 in New York, 118 in San Francisco, for combined 482, and twenty-seven at Jessica Dee Communications.

AVERAGE AGE OF EMPLOYEES: Thirty-one.

TURNOVER: Information not available.

RECRUITMENT: The agency does not actively recruit.

NUMBER OF NEW HIRES PER YEAR: Approximately ninety-one.

RANGE OF STARTING SALARIES: Secretary: $15,000–$18,000; account coordinator: $15,000–$18,000. Starting account executives: $28,000–$35,000, depending on experience.

POLICY FOR RAISES: Awarded annually on the basis of performance.

TRAINING PROGRAMS: Employees are taught the Wang computer system through self-teaching computer programs. There are several.

BENEFITS: Medical and dental insurance (four different plans), employee stock ownership plan, profitsharing, 401(k) pretax savings plan, long-term disability insurance, life insurance, and 50 percent tuition reimbursement for courses that help an employee's current position or future goals with the agency.

VACATION: Two weeks after one year, three weeks after three years, four weeks after five years, plus 10½ regular paid holidays per year.

ADDITIONAL PERKS: Exercise facilities (only in New York) and a discount on some client company products.

BONUSES: All employees are eligible for bonuses, which are determined by merit.

ANNUAL PARTIES: Each office has an annual Christmas party, an annual picnic, and occasional special event parties after working hard on a big pitch. Parties at the various offices differ. For Los Angeles headquarters, the Christmas party is "very grand." The agency rents different locations—one year it was the Batman Mansion in Pasadena, where the television series *Batman* used to be filmed, another year it was the Hollywood Paladium—and hires a live band (past entertainment: Jack Mack and the Heart Attack). The event is semiformal "but everyone ends up with their shoes off anyway" and includes dinner and dancing for employees and their guests. For the last few years the Los Angeles headquarters' summer picnic has been held at the Calamigos Ranch in Malibu. The agency rents out the entire ranch, and employees and their families ride horses, participate in games (egg tosses, balloon races, three-legged races, etc.), and go out on a lake in pedal boats. The picnic has "really good food" and a live band. Los Angeles headquarters threw a special party after working for months to retain (but losing) the Apple account, and another party after winning the Nissan account. The Apple party took place at a Venice Beach restaurant and included a catered dinner, live music, and dancing. The Nissan party was a catered party held in a big tent pitched on the beach at Jay Chiat's house.

DRESS CODE: "Casual, but no shorts."

AVERAGE WORKDAY: Officially, "7.5 hours a day, on average, although many people stay later and work weekends, depending on their workload."

SOCIAL ATMOSPHERE: "There is a good social atmosphere. The agency is very casual, and there is a lot of open communication. Employees fraternize after work and on weekends."

HEADQUARTERS: In January 1988 Chiat/Day relocated its Los Angeles headquarters to "one large building" in Venice Beach. Located in an old three-story warehouse that the agency leases from Antioch College, the new offices are in one enormous room with skylights and occupy 55,000 square feet of space. Frank Gehry designed the interior, and "everything sprouts out of the ground. The main conference room is a wooden fish with metal scales." Late in 1988 Chiat/Day also took over the building next door (also leased from Antioch).

CHARITABLE CONTRIBUTIONS: $131,000 in 1987. Areas of donation vary.

INTERESTED APPLICANTS CAN SEND RÉSUMÉS TO:
Chiat/Day inc., Advertising
320 Hampton Street
Venice, CA 90291
Attention: Personnel Department
(213) 314-5000

To: Everyone
From: Lisa

CHIAT/
DAY INC.,
ADVERTISING

_291_

This is the memo style of the people of Chiat/Day, one of the country's most trend-conscious advertising boutiques. (For the record, memos were eliminated in a memo issued by the CEO.) The agency still best known for introducing the Apple Macintosh to the public, and for its Nike commercials (although, as discussed, both accounts have since departed) is based in Los Angeles and New York, with a smaller office in San Francisco, and is almost as memorable for its corporate culture. Let's start with its two most important offices.

The New York office, on lower Fifth Avenue, was selected initially for its away-from-Madison-Avenue-high-rent location, though it is now a chic work neighborhood. It is bright and art-filled, an exemplar of how hip a business can be. A beautiful patio filled with greenery and lattice work is used for lunch and meetings. "I was knocked out by the office," said an account person, recalling his first impression. "This office is beyond open—it's collegiate and collegial. There were Macintoshes on every desk." A small training room upstairs, filled with Nautilus equipment and "training assistants" (trainers), gets a lot of use. (The first two sessions of one-to-one training are courtesy of Chiat/Day. Subsequent workouts cost $35 an hour, but anyone is free to use the machinery when they like at no charge.)

The Los Angeles office is in transition. It moved after a prolonged delay—from the second floor of the downtown Biltmore Hotel to its new temporary building on Venice Beach. Chiat/Day's ultimate headquarters, with a planned move-in-date in the early 1990s, was designed by famed L.A. architect Frank Gehry, with a Claes Oldenburg entrance—a giant pair of binoculars that includes two conference rooms and an observation deck.

Chiat/Day is the brainchild of veteran adman Jay Chiat, an iconoclastic New-Yorker-turned-Californian-turned-bicoastalian. His people echo his desire for great advertising and, in fact, create it.

Perhaps you recall the Pizza Hut campaign for 1985–86, a twist on the usual celebrity endorsement, featuring beautifully shot close-ups of Martin Mull, Roseanne Barr, Rita Moreno, and the MacKenzie Brothers—SCTV's Dave Thomas and Rick Moranis—talking about their feelings about pizza. They were backlit, calming, and real. Or perhaps you stopped to watch a hard hat–wearing construction worker chew the living daylights out of a piece of Bazooka bubble gum. Remember the dramatic arena setting for the introduction of "Lazer Tag," the best-selling game of Christmas 1987 from Worlds of Wonder, which makes the game look appealing to grown-ups as well as kids? Randy Newman driving around Los Angeles in a red convertible, singing the joys of his city in Nike's "I Love L.A." commercial, with athletes Carl Lewis, John McEnroe, and Mary Decker unobtrusively peeking in? These commercials are really short movies. And in fact, Chiat/Day has persuaded feature film directors to take a go at these thirty- and sixty-second gems. (Steven Spielberg shot his own commercial for his _Amazing Stories_ television series on NBC; Ridley [_Blade Runner_] Scott shot the famous _1984_ spot for Apple; Adrian [_Fatal Attraction_] Lyne shot a lot of other Apple spots; and Tony [_Top Gun_] Scott shot many Priazzo pizza commercials.

Whether you're in New York, L.A., or any other place where more than one Chiat/Day person congregates, you may hear the phrase _"very_ Chiat/Day," and it won't take long to figure out what that means. The company has assembled a bunch of hard-working young people who believe they are engaged in important work. "I didn't come here to do compromise advertising" is a common rebuke. They bring with them talent and energy as well as an attitude that's —well—very Chiat/Day.

A recent agency brochure illustrates the point well:

WHAT IT FEELS LIKE TO WORK WITH CHIAT/DAY

It feels different.

Is that different "good" or different "bad"?

Well, that depends on how you want to work with your advertising agency. Because
believe us, you will be working if you hire Chiat/Day.

Let us elaborate.

The perception is that Chiat/Day clients get bullied into buying an idea, done the Chiat/
Day way.

And please, no comments about the size of the logo.

The fact is, our clients bully themselves into buying ads. Because they get much more
involved with their advertising than ever before.

From strategy through to creative development.

While we get more involved in our clients' marketing than most of them would have
expected.

All this by way of a series of fenceless free-for-alls that we call "creative work sessions."

Which is where the part about your working comes into play.

Everyone is a participant. No matter who.

Everyone says what they think. No matter what.

It isn't a session for massaging creative egos.

And so on for three more pages.

Christine Donohoe is the manager of print production in Los Angeles. She found work in advertising "through a fluke" and ended up in production at Young and Rubican (see p. 588) in L.A. After two and a half years, she heard of an opening at Chiat/Day. She did wonder briefly whether another area of agency work would be better for her. "A lot of people just fall into print production, waiting for other jobs. As it turned out for me, print production is okay for me. It satisfies my creative side and business side. I look around the agency, and frankly, I don't think there's another place I'd like to work.

"I'm included in meetings and asked for my input, not because of politeness but because they respect me. I am involved from the very beginning. The art director calls me from a shoot. They basically told me I saved their asses on Porsche." Christine finished two years of junior college. She was hired at the agency when she was twenty and was named head of the print department (four people) at twenty-three. "They're all older. I keep my age quiet. I sort of grew up here," she says at the ripe age of twenty-four.

"I learned the right way to do things at Y and R. I came here and learned the wrong way and turned it around. I went from buttoned-up to loose and cool." She's wearing a purple blouse and white skirt, modest gold jewelry, and a glossy manicure. "Dressing conservatively at Y and R helped me hide my age. Here I'm sloppy." In the summer, she says, people dress more casually, often in Chiat/Day T-shirts that broadcast the motto "Good enough is not enough."

Whether it's her youth or her ambition, Donohoe is driven hard to prove herself. "I make things perfect. I work as hard as possible. Knowing the art director busted his tail doing it makes me want to the do the same. I have a responsibility to my co-workers, the agency, and the account. I'm the last person to get a job, so chances are it'll be at the end of the day. It's not a constant that I have to be here late at night. Only when there's something to do." When a job is at the printers, though, she'll be there, too, often until 2:00 A.M.

Christine has experienced some hard times at Chiat/Day. "When Apple and Nike left, the morale was low. We had all doubled up, so when they left, we were at a normal staffing level. No one had to leave. It was a little bit of a relief." She admits to being "very Chiat/Day." "I'm certainly comfortable here. I'm bored with the drive [it takes her an hour each way to commute] but not the work. I just bought a house in the San Fernando Valley. I think about work during the drive and most other times. It never ends."

The alleged heavy-duty socializing that employees talk of is less involving for Christine than is used to be. "Maybe eight times in three years I've had drinks with colleagues after work. A bunch of us girls went to Palm Springs after Apple left the agency. You have to get to know people well. Chiat values teach you that you're all neat people.

"The early days were like family. When I first got here, they checked me out. Like a family." In fact, others have called the interview process "more like pledging a fraternity than being interviewed for a job." Issues that arise during the long-winded procedure have a lot to do with the kind of person you are. "Creatives wanted references from previous creatives I'd worked with," an account guy says. "They didn't know if I'd be able to fight for them. It seemed like everyone in the whole office interviewed me. I'm glad there are only 148 in New York."

New employees are introduced to the essence of Chiat/Day at the "New Employee Breakfast," held once a month. Among the lessons: Hard work is expected of you, and "Do what it takes to get it done." Another guy says, "It's just like a revival meeting."

Chiat/Day—what it is and what it isn't—will always be the subject of endless consideration by its teams and its observers. "Jay is the architect of the sensibility, and very conscious about it. People will say, 'This is not an accident.' " CEO Jay Chiat designated his agency to be creative-driven from the start, inspired, he's written, by the late creative risk taker and agency head Bill Bernbach. And that's certainly its reputation. "You are what you're perceived to be" is one of his maxims. In his dramatic bachelor-pad town house in the Murray Hill section of Manhattan, Chiat, attired in all black, says, "I try to convince everyone here that they are creative. I make sure people don't feel blocked. My job is to keep the place changing."

Between slugs of bottled water, he says, "I'm a tough guy to please." (This is confirmed by his employees on both coasts.) "I can see every flaw in every commercial." His temper is incendiary, according to legend, "but stories about it always end with, 'but that's Jay.' "

Opening a New York presence after achieving black sheep heroics in California "helped Chiat/Day's perceptions as a national agency. And we're the only West Coast agency that's survived in New York." At first it seemed the New York office was Los Angeles's stepchild. The attention-getting, sexy accounts stayed west—Nike, Apple, Pizza Hut, Porsche—while New York started out with the less flashy L.A. clients whose headquarters were in New York: Suntory and Fotomat. Next came New York Air (now defunct) and Holland America Cruises. When L.A. lost some of its premiere accounts, the balance changed, and now New York is growing at a faster clip. Today the New York roster includes the Arrow Shirt Company, Christian Dior, Kitchens of Sara Lee, National Car Rental, William Grant & Sons (a distiller), NYNEX Corporation, Drexel Burnham Lambert (see p. 459), Quaker Oats (see p. 159), Reebok, and the Whitney Museum. Although most people stay in the city where they joined the agency, Chiat and his senior teams travel back and forth—he commutes from coast to coast every week—and he says, "You can't tell the difference between the different offices."

Rick Boyko's five years with Chiat/Day Los Angeles make for a tenure that's "the longest I've been anywhere." This art director's résumé includes short tours of duty at Leo Burnett (see

p. 123), Tatham-Laird & Kudner, Benton & Bowles, and N. W. Ayer. The native Californian reached his Chicago threshold after about ten years. "It was time to leave. I knew what I wanted to do wasn't being done in Chicago. Everything was research-oriented. When I looked at the awards books, most of them were being won by western agencies. A lot of clients here don't care about research." His goal was Chiat/Day, but with no positions available for art directors, Rick took a job with another Los Angeles agency.

Although he'd been unhappy at other agencies, Boyko never thought he was pursuing a career in the wrong industry; he just figured he couldn't fit in at most places. "Chiat is very familiar, much smaller than the other agencies I've worked for. And it's not adversarial between departments. We make strategies here with everyone in the room." Talking about "good advertising" as the collective product and goal of the 216-person L.A. staff, Boyko doesn't seem to be intransigent on the subject of the creative/client struggle. "If there is a disagreement between what we see or a client sees, we'll compromise. If it's too watered down, we'll try something new. We're never so far apart that there's an argument. Clients don't come here for a 'P and G account.' " (In other words, if it's standard advertising you're after, Chiat/Day is not the agency for you.)

"We try to make the product we're selling do better. If the cash register rings, then we've been very successful. You don't feel happy if you have a great piece of art and 99 percent think the product is shit. Since we're on the edge, there is a perception about us that we're aloof and just trying to make art." Rick attributes that attitude to jealousy. Chiat/Day does seem to win more than a fair share of awards, as far as other agencies are concerned. "To be able to have clients go out on the edge with you . . . "

Boyko doesn't talk about life after Chiat/Day. He doesn't whip out a screenplay or a dream of directing rock videos, unlike many creatives in the business. He likes working here because "there are better people at the top who understand how it works. If I'm not happy here, I'm not happy at home. Anyone working at Chiat could command a much higher salary elsewhere, but I'd rather be happy. I have been able to develop a body of work" of which he is proud. "I'd never be able to do what I do elsewhere."

Patrick Sherwood, blond and ebullient, ran account management in the Los Angeles office. In his shirtsleeves, this former junior and senior high school teacher communicated his enthusiasm for his business and his company. "I still get a rush going on a shoot," he confesses. "It's as close as you get to the movies, a suspension of all the crap."

While quite removed from teaching social studies to teenagers, advertising was the business of Sherwood's dad, so it was familiar to Pat, plus "it had a sense of glamour—because of TV—and it was cool and intriguing. So many people watch commercials." Without experience in the field, he was able to get a job at another major agency, on a (big money) car account. "It didn't require knowledge of advertising; just stamina. I could move paper, keep clients happy, et cetera. I don't think I learned a lot about advertising until Chiat/Day." [Author's note: In April 1987 he took that knowledge to Foote, Cone & Belding Communications.]

Pat joined the San Francisco office in 1983. "I learned discipline, systems, getting along with people." His first twenty-two months were spent commuting between San Francisco and Los Angeles. "I became more sensitive to the creative product, which, ironically, made me a more strategic thinker. This is a creative-driven company, which makes it more demanding for account people." He says account people must overcome the feeling that they are secondary to the creatives, while simultaneously acknowledging that creative rules the roost. "Account people are like eunuchs or handmaidens to creative. I try to talk to groups about the role of account in a place like Chiat/Day. This is a creative—he pauses to add, "all capitals—CREATIVE house. I get shit for wearing a suit. I say this to everyone we interview: 'There is, bar none, no other place where being an account person is this difficult. It can be diminishing. You don't want to overthink it.' "

But, courage, prospective account guys and gals: "The client sees the agency through the account people first." More than a willingness to work in a club dominated by creatives, you need to love good advertising. "I want to see that somebody's chest swells when their ad's on TV. Mine does," Sherwood admits. "The room should stop. Without passion they won't be able to encourage clients. A good fit feels a part of advertising and doesn't just view it scientifically."

Citing top management, specifically Jay Chiat, a fellow "suit," and Creative Director Lee Clow, Sherwood says, "If they were to leave, it would certainly be a different company. There's something about our culture and the way it flows from the top which allows us to do great work." In Pat's case, four months after being handed the reins to the Pizza Hut account, he was made head of account management. "Sometimes I have to just go outside and take a deep breath. I show my group that our role is a meaningful one."

The reputation for grueling work and long hours, embodied in the nickname "Chiat/Day and Night" and the joke with the bitter taste "If you don't come in on Saturday, don't bother coming in on Sunday," is also deserved, though no one is really sure from whence it came. It permeates all offices. "Since I've been at Chiat/Day," Pat says, "I've never had to tell anybody to work late and gotten grief. It's not printed up. It's not what it takes. You won't get fired. [But] if you're a good manager, you get people to work."

Most people talk of the peer pressure of the teams egging one another on to new heights of hard work. Guilt is another component. "It's the sense of the team. You're really going to help out. Account people will do it, traffic people will spend the weekend. We'll do whatever it takes." (A further incentive is provided by "a pool of money for spot bonuses.") Creatives are judged every day, which is certainly another motivator, and since accepted campaigns are on display both in the media and throughout the offices, there is a tacit competition to do the best work possible.

The language of some Chiat/Day-ers is relentlessly laced with "awesome," "great advertising," and "excellence." It is the jargon of the hip entrepreneur—the capitalist who goes on exotic treks during vacation, the member of a two-career couple who is never home, the business jock with unlimited frequent flyer miles who listens to self-help tapes while tooling around in his or her Porsche—pronounced with two syllables. (Although with Chiat/Day's win of the $150 million Nissan account, Porsche left the agency and the yuppies of Chiat/Day will probably be expected to retire their expensive wheels.) Some of the "very Chiat/Day" sentiments you might hear around the offices are "In five years we'll be even more awesome" or "As long as there are people who want Rolls-Royces, there's a place for Chiat/Day" or the phrase "this radical pursuit of greatness or memorableness."

It's clearly not the agency for just anyone. You must buy the attitude and the attendant dialect to fit in. You must believe you and your brethren are engaged in something different and more special than the missions of all other agencies. "A lot of them actually love advertising," a cynic says. "But a lot of them think they're in fine arts. They think they just do creative work, and don't think of this as a business. I always want to say, 'Kids, give me a break.'" Everyone I spoke with speculated they could never work for another agency after the Chiat/Day experience. (Well, perhaps they could start their own shop.) [Author's note: I obviously forgot to ask Pat Sherwood.]

Greg Helm is the vice-president and general manager of Chiat/Day's Los Angeles office. He comes across as more low-key than the others I've met, though certainly not less committed. With a degree in economics from Notre Dame, his is the most conventional nonagency background of the bunch. He worked for a bank in Kansas City before seeking his fortune on the West Coast. He was recruited by Jay Chiat for the San Francisco office after five years at other, larger agencies. "I left my previous employer because their advertising was boring, safe, and not fun."

He was made general manager of the L.A. office at thirty-eight. "I didn't know it was coming at all. I never asked for it. The best way to get ahead at Chiat/Day is not to try to get ahead. Avoid politics. Political people don't get ahead. [Consequently], your political skills tend to atrophy." A veteran of several other major agencies disagrees. "It's up to *you* to get attention. You've got to carbon the right people and hope the top people attend your meetings and you say bright things. They say it's not political, and that it's different from other agencies," but this fellow is a bit skeptical. Since the agency is small, however, "you can promote your interests by yourself."

Helm describes the people he works with, in an attempt to evince the culture of the company: "They are smart, energetic, slightly obnoxious in the cause. They believe their advertising and try every time to do the best." In the recruiting process, one's "energy level is really the biggest discriminator—it can compensate for a lack of traditional education." [Read: a young bunch, some of whom didn't attend or graduate from college.] For emphasis he adds, "We really have this charter. People on the outside realize they're Chiat/Day people. If you're not a strong personality, you could be in awe—which is exactly what you shouldn't be."

Greg prefers the term "Chiat/Day-like" to "very Chiat/Day." The former "describes an aggressive point of view, and it's the way you describe our ads. Sometimes I say an ad is good, and I get corrected. 'They're great!' " This is a giveaway that Helm comes from the account side, the spawning ground of all general managers. Yet, when it comes to the eventual passing of the CEO mantle, "I don't believe that Chiat/Day will ever have a top officer *not* come from Creative," he says evenly. "It gives the wrong message."

Nevertheless, if you hesitate about contributing to the creative process, look elsewhere. "If you don't pull your weight, we return you to your donor institution.

"We've built the place to be heard. We prohibit mail to be delivered to employees. We have a mailroom so that people move around. You're not allowed to let your secretaries pick your mail up for you. At this agency, the buck stops with Creative, but the ads are king. Everybody should feel they're making ads—not by coming up with ideas, but by sitting in on the process so you feel you own it.

"We hold up a brilliant concept and say, 'What's better?' " Helm admits he works in a stressful environment. "One breakthrough idea takes away so much stress, you can't believe it. All your arteries are blown free with a great idea. It's a trade-off."

No one has a franchise on stress. This is an office filled with as many shards of broken marriages as ongoing strong ones. "Work is number one," Helm says, speaking for his 216 people. "It is hard for us to strike a balance." Employees are encouraged to share credit. "Every once in a while, you go to a presentation and someone says 'I' a lot. It's no good. We do reward individuals, but we treat everyone the same. People at the top don't take credit for everything. We probably have one of the largest corporate egos around. It keeps individual egos at bay."

Has there been talk of selling Chiat/Day to a larger agency or a holding group one day? "It'd be like Texas selling itself to Alaska, or Stanford selling itself to Harvard."

CHIAT/DAY AND THE NISSAN ACCOUNT

In 1986, within one week, Chiat/Day lost two of its biggest accounts—Apple Computer, Inc., and Nike—at a reported cost of about $35 million, or roughly 12 percent of billings, and a heavy emotional toll. When the Nissan Motor Corporation dropped its longtime agency, J. Walter Thompson, in May 1987, leaving the biggest advertising account in recent history up for grabs, Chiat/Day saw an opportunity to recoup billings and repair its bruised reputation. For nearly two months, agency staffers camped out in the Biltmore Hotel in Los Angeles, scrambling to come up with a winning campaign for the car maker. Chairman Jay Chiat presided over the team, rejecting one slogan after another. Among the losers: "The People's Car" and "The Official Car of the Human Race."

On June 19 Nissan narrowed the field to three finalists. (The others were Chicago-based Tatham-Laird & Kudner and the Los Angeles office of Ogilvy & Mather, which ultimately dropped out, allegedly because they didn't want to risk alienating another of their clients, the Ford Motor Company.)

Chiat/Day presented the campaign to Nissan on July 30 and won the account on August 3 with "We've Got a Way to Move You." Nissan was not only impressed with Chiat/Day's slogan and presentation—after the Chiat/Day team presented its idea, the Nissan staff burst into applause—but by the agency's eagerness to work closely with Nissan's marketing staff.

By the time Chiat's campaign hit the air in late 1987, the slogan had been changed to "Built for the Toughest Race of All: The Human Race."

In winning the $150 million Nissan account, which cost the agency an estimated $250,000, Chiat/Day has entered a different league and received an incalculable boost to its reputation. Ranked as the thirty-first largest agency in the United States in 1986, with the new business, it moved up to twenty-fifth largest in 1987.

LORIMAR
TELEPICTURES
CORPORATION

LORIMAR TELEPICTURES
CORPORATION

HISTORY & OPERATIONS

Lorimar Telepictures, a producer and distributor of television programs, home videos, and movies, was formed in February 1986 with the merger of two television giants—Los Angeles–based Lorimar, Inc., and New York–based Telepictures Corporation. Lorimar, founded in 1969, is a major producer of network television programs (series, made-for-television movies, and miniseries) and a minor producer of theatrical films. Its best-known programs include *The Waltons* and the hit nighttime soap operas *Dallas, Falcon Crest,* and *Knots Landing.* Telepictures was founded in 1978 to distribute other producers' programs in syndication. The company sold network reruns, old TV movies, and first-run syndication shows (original programs produced independently of the networks and sold to individual television stations). In 1981 Telepictures began producing its own first-run syndication shows, the most successful of them a children's cartoon series called *Thundercats.*

In 1985, after several days of negotiations, the managements of Lorimar and Telepictures determined that their companies were a good fit. With Telepictures' distribution expertise, Lorimar could sell reruns of its shows in syndication without paying costly distribution fees;

and with Lorimar's network connections—most of its biggest hits have been for CBS— Telepictures could produce and later syndicate network programming. Though Lorimar technically merged into Telepictures, it ended up on top. Merv Adelson, one of the three cofounders of Lorimar and its former head, became chairman and CEO of the newly formed company. Lorimar Telepictures' holdings at the time of the 1986 merger (in addition to its television programs and films) included, from Lorimar: Karl-Lorimar Video, a home video producer and distributor best known for the Jane Fonda exercise tapes, and Bozell, Jacobs, Kenyon & Eckhardt, a fast-growing advertising and public relations agency ranked twelfth in U.S. billings in 1985; from Telepictures: five small television stations, their syndication business, and a magazine publishing concern that owned 75 percent of *US* magazine and published children's magazines such as *The Muppets Magazine* and *Barbie, The Magazine for Girls.*

In its first year of cooperation, Lorimar Telepictures suffered several setbacks that cost the company money and caused it considerable embarrassment. First, in an attempt to diversify into a broad-based television concern, the company attempted to acquire seven additional television stations at a cost of $1.85 billion. After months of negotiations during which the structure and price of the deal changed a number of times, Lorimar Telepictures backed off, stating that the cost of the acquisition was too high. Then three executives of its home video concern resigned after the company discovered that they had profited from an unethical arrangement with one of the video unit's subcontractors.

In mid-1987, after posting a $63 million loss for the fiscal year, Lorimar Telepictures announced it would restructure to focus on its core business of making and distributing television shows, videos, and movies. As part of the restructuring, the company announced it would sell its television stations, its publishing business, and its advertising agencies. (Earlier that year, Bozell, Jacobs, Kenyon & Eckhardt had acquired a small agency called Poppe Tyson.) The deal to divest the advertising concerns was closed on February 19, 1988, when the management of BJK&E bought themselves back. The children's magazines were sold to their management in August 1987. (*US* magazine was in the midst of negotiations in the spring of 1988.) With regard to its core entertainment business, Lorimar Telepictures announced plans to become a major theatrical film producer and distributor in 1987. Before the merger, Lorimar had been involved in the development, production, or coproduction of twenty-four movies. Though a few of them were hits—among them the Academy Award–winning *Being There* (1979)—Lorimar ultimately lost a reported $12 million on its film ventures. In 1986 the company purchased the MGM studio lot in Culver City to serve as its own production site and headquarters. And over the following year, Lorimar Telepictures set up a distribution system to place its own films in theaters and charge independent producers to distribute their films. In its 1987 announcement, the company stated that it planned to release ten films by the following winter—seven of its own productions or coproductions and three acquired from outside producers. (The first two releases were *The Fourth Protocol,* an independent British production distributed by Lorimar Telepictures, and *Orphans,* its first inhouse production, starring Albert Finney and directed by Alan Pakula.) Eventually, Lorimar Telepictures hopes to release fifteen films a year, which would put it in the same league as the major studios. Though the strategy is very risky—many start-up film production companies have flopped, and most films fail to recoup the cost of production—the success of the company's television enterprises should provide financial protection in the event that it has to struggle.

Lorimar Telepictures is headquartered in Culver City, California, and New York City. The company is made up of the following divisions: Lorimar Television, which produces television series, made-for-television movies, and miniseries for network, pay/cable, and syndicated television; Lorimar Syndication, which markets and licenses Lorimar-produced and -acquired entertainment programs to the domestic television syndication and pay/cable markets; Lorimar International, which distributes the company's productions and those acquired from outside producers to more than a hundred international television markets; Lorimar Film Entertainment, which oversees the production of theatrical feature films and the domestic distribution of features; Lorimar Home Video, which produces, acquires, manufactures, markets, and distributes prerecorded video software for the home video market; The Brillstein Company (a wholly owned subsidiary acquired in 1987), which produces television programs and films and manages talent; Lorimar Music, which is responsible for all music publishing activities and music use and development, and provides music production for the company's television programs and movies; News Information Weekly Service, a syndicated video news service delivered twice weekly by satellite and videotape to more than 125 U.S. and Canadian television markets and forty foreign countries; DIR Broadcasting, a radio production company, which produces, among other shows, Rick Dees' Top Forty Program; and California Video Center, a videotape production and postproduction facility.

During the 1987–88 television season, Lorimar Telepictures had eight series on the networks' prime time schedules and three possible midseason replacements, more than any other program supplier. The eight prime time series were: *Dallas* (eleventh season), *Knots Landing* (ninth season), *Falcon Crest* (seventh season), *Valerie's Family* (third season), *Perfect Strangers* (third season), *Our House* (second season), *Max Headroom: 20 Minutes into the Future* (which was canceled midway into its second season), and *Full House* (premiere season); the three replacements were *Hot House, B-Men,* and *Aaron's Way* (the last premiered in March 1988). In addition, The Brillstein Company provided the networks with *Alf, The Days and Nights of Molly Dodd,* and *The Slap Maxwell Story,* and supplied *It's Garry Shandling's Show* to Showtime and Fox Broadcasting. The company's first-run syndication programs for the season were: *Love Connection* (fifth season), *The People's Court* (seventh season), *Superior Court* (second season), three cartoons from Rankin/Bass Productions—*Thundercats* (third season), *SilverHawks* (second season), and *The Comic Strip* (premiere season), and three half-hour comedies, *It's a Living, Mama's Family,* and the premiere of *She's the Sheriff.*

By mid-1988, Lorimar Telepictures was considered an attractive candidate for acquisition, with several entertainment companies in pursuit.

(Information provided by Barbara Brogliatti and Amy Quinn, company spokespersons.)

REVENUES: $767 million in fiscal 1987.

EARNINGS: The company lost $58 million in fiscal 1987.

INITIAL PUBLIC OFFERING: Public from its inception in 1986.

NUMBER OF SHARES OUTSTANDING: 45,336,864 as of December 31, 1987.

OFFICES: The company maintains offices in Los Angeles, New York, Chicago, Dallas, and Atlanta.

NUMBER OF EMPLOYEES: The core staff of full-time people is approximately 1,750. When the company has shows in production, that number can be increased by up to 1,000.

AVERAGE AGE OF EMPLOYEES: Information not available.

TURNOVER: "Comparable to industry standards."

RECRUITMENT: The company currently has an informal recruitment program and is in the process of developing a more formal one to suit its changing needs. For now, the company has a policy of granting interviews with any recent graduate referred either by one of its managers or by a school with which a manager is affiliated. "When you have good people in the company, you look to them to find people that are either as good or better than they are." The company also has summer and school-year internship programs. (The number of interns fluctuates from year to year.) "In terms of educational backgrounds, we obviously look for the most diverse group of people we can find. We want people who not only have an interest in working in show business, but who want to be at Lorimar Telepictures. Those are the people who will get the most out of working here."

NEW HIRES PER YEAR: No average figures. "Whatever the marketplace demands. Rules don't apply to this corporation as they might to Xerox or someplace else."

RANGE OF STARTING SALARIES: The company can't quote a range. "It depends on the skills involved. Salaries match industry standards," which span from $300 a week to $3,000,000 for a movie star salary.

POLICY FOR RAISES: Employees are reviewed annually, and raises are awarded according to a combination of factors. Merit is heavily weighted.

TRAINING PROGRAMS: No formal programs aside from internships. All training is hands-on. "We have people do it with supervision. You're not just here to observe, you're part of the process."

BENEFITS: "Above and beyond industry standards. We have dental coverage that other companies don't even *think* about." Specific benefits include maternity leave, tuition reimbursement for career-related courses, and a day care program that the company is looking to expand.

VACATION: "Standard, depending on length of employment."

ADDITIONAL PERKS: The company pays for employees to take classes on its mainframe computer and encourages them to borrow computer equipment for extended periods of time. Employees get first priority seating for company programs taped in front of a live audience. Lorimar offers two free film screenings every Monday night (of company-made and others' movies) and holds special employee screenings of new company shows (both television and movies). Optional stress management courses are offered during lunch hour, and the company is looking into other types of speaker forums. Whenever major company events occur, Lorimar's public affairs department distributes in-house news bulletins to all employees.

BONUSES: "There is a reward policy." Different divisions have different methods of remuneration.

ANNUAL PARTY: The company puts together focus groups comprised of randomly selected employees at different levels to see what kinds of parties and functions employees favor. "We try to be open about changing it. A lot of employees might feel a Christmas party is a burden." Normally, the company hosts a Christmas party and an employee picnic, both of which are held outside the Lorimar lot and are open to all employees. "But that could change."

AVERAGE WORKDAY: Varies among production staff and management. "We try to be flexible, because we want people to be fresh and on their toes, but it's standard industry—a lot of long hours for little pay. People in show business are willing to devote those long hours, and we don't hear a lot of *kvetching*."

DRESS CODE: None.

SOCIAL ATMOSPHERE: "Very warm and friendly. The company has gone to great expense to create areas of fraternization (where employees can congregate) during free time. The lot is not restricted in any way." People get together after working hours "more than you would find in a lot of other industries."

HEADQUARTERS: On the old MGM lot, which is currently undergoing massive reconstruction (a million square feet of building improvements). The lot is forty-four acres and has twenty-four sound stages, a barber shop, a shoe repair shop, a company store, and bank tellers. A free tram runs all day at fifteen-minute intervals.

CHARITABLE CONTRIBUTIONS: The company will not disclose figures. "For us to give a dollar amount only opens us up to hundreds of people asking for money." Lorimar Telepictures donates to the Motion Picture Home (a retirement home for film personnel), children's organizations, the Museum of Broadcasting, the homeless (shelters and food), AIDS research and care, and child abuse. "Not only do we make these contributions, but we try to have as much public service orientation as we can possibly squeeze into our various television shows and movies. Virtually all of the talent we use on the shows does public service announcements. They're probably one of our greatest charity-related assets. We do the scheduling and make sure they have the scripts and rehearsal time."

OTHER: The company does not conduct business in or with South Africa. This is company policy.

INTERESTED APPLICANTS CAN SEND RÉSUMÉS TO:
Human Resources Department
Lorimar Telepictures
10202 West Washington Boulevard
Culver City, CA 90230
(213) 202-2000

What's going on at Lorimar Telepictures, anyway? First there was Lorimar, Inc., founded in 1969, one of the most prolific forces in prime time television, creators of *The Waltons, Dallas, Knots Landing, Falcon Crest,* and most of the made-for-television movies in which the costumes rate almost as much publicity as the stars who wear them. Lorimar reflected its Los Angeles base, and the people who ran it were seated in high-visibility "face tables" at the power restaurants of their choice. They've been in the biz long enough to know and be known. Then there were the fellows of Telepictures Corporation, four guys from the East Coast who were escapees from traditional, big-time corporate life and figured that television syndication was a good business. They opened their doors in 1978. Their base of operations was in New York, in offices that were most definitely not opulent.

So in 1986 the two companies merged in the spirit of symbiosis and bicoastality. Culturally, they claimed, they were compatible. Lorimar was Hollywood; Telepictures was eastern. The new company bought the MGM Studio lot in Culver City, California, and moved into spiffier

New York offices near the United Nations. And then it swelled. For a time it seemed that Lorimar Telepictures was involved in every imaginable form of business related to communications. It owned television stations, network shows, syndicated shows, cable shows, magazines, radio programming, advertising agencies, and a news service. By mid-1987, however, rumors of spin-offs and divestitures were rife. Were the two entities about to split after a year of marriage? Would they sell Bozell, Jacobs, Kenyon & Eckhardt? Would they sell off their television stations? *US* magazine? Since the structures of companies have become more flexible, if not downright amorphous, it is not possible to provide absolute answers for the fate of Lorimar Telepictures (or, indeed, any other corporation). But by publication time, the company was still supplying more product to the broadcast media than any other production company in the country. So far, so good.

A bit of Telepictures history: Michael Garin arrived at Time Inc. after working on *The Harvard Crimson.* A native Long Islander, he says, "When I entered Harvard, I had a very fixed sense of my opportunities in life, of what was available to Jews. When I left Harvard, I learned that the only limitations were ones I'd created." He majored in economics, "but I did the classic liberal arts. I only took four and a half economics classes.

"Personally, I feel very fortunate I didn't get an MBA. I was originally going to go straight to Harvard Business School, but I was offered a job as the assistant to the publisher of *Fortune,* which is usually an MBA position. In business school you're learning solutions to problems other people have had. The MBA doesn't have a special attraction for me."

One can perhaps detect a residue of Harvard in the pipe Michael smokes or in his argyle socks and wool cardigan, but to make anything of those accoutrements would be to make too much. When he returned to New York to embark on his "real life," he studied at night at the New School for his master's degree in philosophy. He is introspective and soft-spoken, and in his attentiveness he nods vigorously and murmurs his assent.

At Time Inc. he remained on the business side (formally known as the state of the church/ state relationship between business and editorial), working also for *Time* and for the short-lived Time-Life Films. Garin lasted ten years.

"I left because I was unhappy," he says simply. He was trying to reconcile the discrepancies between his unhappiness and the professional status and comfortable quality of life the huge media company afforded him. "I ran into Michael Solomon {a former careerist at MCA}. He said, 'How are things?' I said, 'Terrible.' He said, 'Why don't we start a company?' We saw a real niche for ourselves in distribution." They acquired the American Film Theatre library from Time-Life and a keyhold on Latin American distribution for other independent producers.

On September 8, 1978, Telepictures was born. It was composed of people who were wondering what the hell they were doing. "The very first day was a profound experience. We'd each worked for such big companies. All of a sudden you weren't 'Michael Garin of Time Inc.,' you were just Michael Garin. You were naked. What you were was a product of skills and ambitions."

The partnership knew it had harnessed intelligence and ambition, but—begging your indulgence as I overstate the following—the comfort of working for a big, successful company was gone. The money and reputation on the line was no longer that of a *Fortune* 500 institution. Michael suggests, "I think that's why people accept less-than-tolerable situations.

"We had confidence that what we'd do would work. We didn't know which exact path would lead to results. We've worked very hard, and that's probably why we're so successful. We've tried to create an environment where people feel a sense of creating their destinies, by example and by performance."

As refugees of companies that didn't provide the satisfaction they expected, the Telepictures leadership knew there were aspects of big business they wanted to borrow and others they wanted to avoid. "For us, creating a culture was very conscious. We wanted to create an environment where we could spend the rest of our lives and attract competent people." Garin says that even companies that don't devote time and attention to their organizational styles have them. " 'Corporate culture' is a buzzword. It's 'organizational culture.' People had personalities before Freud."

Telepictures' central operating device was similar, in form, to a town meeting. "Our principal mechanism was the 'management meeting.' We stopped the company every ninety days and talked organizational strategy and individual performances. It was companywide and gave everyone a sense of participation and the understanding of why we were doing things. We couldn't talk behind peoples' backs. They were grueling—nine A.M. till midnight."

By the time Telepictures had grown enough to merit two divisions for international and domestic distribution and had gotten involved in nontheatrical projects, broadcasting, and publishing, the management meetings had bloated into three-day events. "They short-circuited the system. Now we do it differently, because we'll be an $800 million company this year." (When Garin left Time Inc., that company's revenues were in the neighborhood of $400 million. For the curious, Time Inc. is now a $4 billion–plus company.)

"I don't think we've ever said we want to be a certain size; our growth has vastly exceeded our expectations. Our early interest was survival. We told the rest of the world we were better marketers and honest accounters. We saw businesses we were interested in. We were over the struggle when we got the rights to distribute *Here's Lucy* [one of Lucille Ball's later television series, costarring her children and actor Gale Gordon]." That meant 144 episodes. "We took one year. We grossed fifteen million dollars."

Rather than having a narrow pyramidlike administration, the founders of Telepictures created a consensual hierarchy. They created the office of the president, made up of Garin, Solomon, Dick Robertson, and David Salzman. "Titles here didn't necessarily reflect responsibilities. The four principals made the same salary and got the same bonuses." Although Lorimar Telepictures has a chairman and chief executive officer, Merv Adelson, the office of the president remains intact. "The principals themselves are so different," Garin says. "There's no uniformity. No one to emulate. Evenhandedness is achieved at the top level." Garin and Solomon have stayed in New York, while Salzman and Robertson moved to the West Coast. "The focus of our company has really shifted to Los Angeles. I live in New York by choice."

The merger between Telepictures and Lorimar took only about three weeks from start to finish. "Our only concern was maintaining the character of the company. We try to push decision making down low. We try to keep paper to a minimum. Until the merger, we had a mandatory sabbatical program." (Telepictures' plan was to offer three-month paid leaves to all employees who'd spent seven consecutive years with the company and six month leaves for the principals with the same length of service.) "We will reinstate the program. If the merger hadn't occurred," Garin adds, "I wouldn't be here." His plans for his half year included travel to the Caribbean Island of Tortola, where he owns a house, and trips to Africa, the Middle East, the South of France, and Norway, where his wife is from. He did manage his month in Africa before he was called back.

"We try to keep middle management to a minimum. That's where most politics exist. We're laissez-faire. We don't work people. They do what they want. We have a very low turnover. We have two categories of people: those who've worked elsewhere and know how good they've got it, and those who've only worked here. This is a self-reinforcing process, and it is fulfilling."

Dick Robertson seems as much at home in California as Garin is in New York. He moved here from New York ten years ago and claims he loves it. Large and athletic, he wears khaki pants, a pink polo shirt—from New York's Paul Stuart—and a beard. He also wears a family crest signet ring. Aha! He's a displaced Easterner, a slight, soft Virginia accent the only tip-off. As he strides through Lorimar's commissary, his walk is interrupted constantly by employees, aspiring employees (two kids who've come to spend the day in interviews send strawberries to the table), and sundry well-wishers. He's probably the most important guy on the lot in this room at the moment. He smiles the smile of the successful and in the verbal equivalent of pinching himself says in a voice of incredulity, "We own this! Clark Gable ate here when this was MGM. I get goosebumps!"

Growing up in Norfolk, Virginia, Robertson knew he wanted to work in advertising. He majored in it at Virginia Commonwealth University in Richmond. He not only remembers all his early successes as an advertising salesman, he remembers the rates he charged and the profits he made. During his college career (1963–67), he earned $5,000–$7,000 a year working part time. "I always had a burning desire to succeed professionally and an inferiority complex from not going to a high-powered school."

The first indication Robertson had that he would have the opportunity to do well was in 1969, when he was "the first young guy ever hired by NBC in D.C. in sales." WRC, the network affiliate, took a chance on him, assigning Dick to retail accounts. Since his first week happened to coincide with Sears' decision to launch a test marketing drive in Washington, Robertson's stock was launched as well.

"I got promoted to San Francisco in National Spot Sales. I had a peacock on my bumper. I felt pride in belonging to a big, fancy company. I was competing with New Yorkers from high-powered schools."

By the age of twenty-five, he had moved again, this time to Cleveland. ("It takes about six months to forgive a new city for not being the old one.") Robertson's name was known in the ad sales circuit based in New York. "A certain group of guys in New York were pissed off that I hadn't taken the proper route. I was already in management." In 1973, he was offered a job in New York. "I said, 'You win. I'll go to New York and get it out of the way.' I wanted big time network television."

Afterward, Robertson moved to Chicago, where he spent four mostly happy years with CBS. Toward the end—as a vice-president—he became disgruntled. "When certain companies get very big, they lose sight of entrepreneurialism. Here I was, this young guy, and I had success and financial security burning in my blood. They were trying to suppress me. I said to my wife, 'I'm thirty-two and a big black rocket ship takes off every morning at West Fifty-second Street, with me or without me." He was referring to CBS's corporate headquarters, a dark granite building known as "Black Rock."

"I decided it was not for me. I wasn't against the people I worked with. It was like the Peggy Lee song, 'Is this all there is?' I had a three-bedroom co-op at the [chichi] U.N. Plaza, a Mercedes-Benz, a CBS American Express Card, and a membership to a country club in Bronxville [one of New York's more elegant suburban communities]. I thought this would fill my life."

In the midst of his growing dissatisfaction, Robertson and his wife were guests at a dinner party in Bronxville. So was a fellow named Michael Garin. At the table, "someone made a racist remark about black management. I decided not to say anything—I was a guest at the party. But Michael said everything I wanted to: 'You ignorant . . . et cetera.' I wanted to kiss Michael Garin on the lips! We had lunch the next day. He offered me a job then and there at Telepictures. I quit CBS thirty days later. I was a laughingstock."

Who's laughing now? As a manager in charge of domestic distribution, Robertson can allow his people the freedom he was deprived when he worked for the networks. "Young people don't know how good it is, since they can't compare it to more conventionally run companies. We hire horses to run their own races. I don't care if you wear tennis shoes or cowboy hats. To try to make you wear blue suits . . . this is at the spine of who we are. It's a self-esteem issue. To reach your own potential and make a lot of money with a lot of yuks and feelings. We don't take ourselves seriously; we take our work seriously. We give people long leashes."

Unlike the production side of Lorimar Telepictures, selling requires an intimate sense of human psychology. It's rewarding, because results are known instantaneously, as opposed to all the waiting that's done in the entertainment business. You may have six weeks to write a screenplay, but the studio gets three months in which to read it. You may produce a pilot and wait months until the network proffers its verdict. You may send a script to an actor, who won't get around to it until he's finished shooting his next two features.

Dick calls the syndication business—now only a fraction of Lorimar Telepictures' enterprise —"sales-driven, not production-driven. Going into a city is like Iwo Jima warfare. I've seen people lose a sale after it closed." He talks about figuring out "when 'no' means 'no.' Sometimes 'maybe' is a disguised 'no.' Why do people accept 'maybes'? They have a fear of 'no.' We tell people, 'We're not there to be liked, but to make the sale. After the sale, you leave the office, or you leave town.'"

David Salzman's goals as a youth were not to sell, advertise, or even make television or movies. "My goal in life was to go to Columbia," the Brooklyn native says. "But I couldn't stand the idea of working in the Catskills for spending money another year." He ended up as an English major at Brooklyn College, which was much more affordable and commutable. There, his dream once again was to attend Columbia, this time at the graduate School of Journalism. Meanwhile, he'd gotten a job at the now defunct *Herald Tribune*. He was a copyboy, and then a reporter. A writer there to whom he looked up, film critic Judith Crist, advised Salzman to go into TV. Although he was accepted at Columbia, he was told that Wayne State University in Detroit had the best TV graduate program in the country, so he dashed the Columbia dream and moved to the Midwest on a scholarship.

Apparently it was the right decision. In Detroit, David started producing and hosting television shows. He worked on the first UHF independent station. "It was an instant success. We added five other stations." Quickly establishing stations in other cities, Salzman became known as "one of the boy wonders. I lived, slept TV. I didn't date." The trade-off was that "as you became better known, other companies wanted you." Westinghouse hired him to be the manager of KDKA, their Pittsburgh station, known as the flagship of their entire network. From there he was moved to their Philadelphia station, KYW, and then back to KDKA, this time as vice-president and general manager. "It was two years of heaven," he recalls. "Nothing I ever do could ever be so fulfilling. The power of the station was awesome—we had a forty to fifty share [the percentage of television viewers who are actually watching the show—*even Cosby should be so lucky*] on everything."

By the time he was thirty, Salzman was the chairman of Group W (Westinghouse) Productions. He moved to New York and had to deal with legal, financial, and real estate issues, as well as production. When Westinghouse decided to move to the West Coast four and a half years later (1969), Salzman moved, too, along with *PM Magazine, The Mike Douglas Show, Hour Magazine,* and a hundred staffers.

In Los Angeles, he created the independent News Information Weekly Service. "It was the first TV electronic news service outside a network. I knew what small stations needed and couldn't afford, e.g., health reports with Dr. Art Ulene. Within six months we had a hundred stations. It's my proudest creation." In fact, NIWS is still a functioning arm of Lorimar Telepictures.

"I met the Telepictures people through NIWS. I loved these guys, who were refugees from other corporations. We played without a net for six years. We borrowed money from our parents and grandparents. We sold our children's savings bonds." In the seventh year "we bought TV stations." A member of the office of the president, and the president of Lorimar Television, Salzman says, 'I'm the luckiest man on earth. I love what I do.

"This is a special company. We're perceived as a giant, but we're not a monolith; we're a lot of little companies." Any way you look at it, Lorimar Telepictures is still the largest vendor of shows that make it to the air. In 1987–88 that means eleven prime time network shows, nine in first-run syndication, and the critically acclaimed Showtime series, *It's Garry Shandling's Show.*

In Salzman's eyes, it's the collective concern of his colleagues that matters most. "We all have a fundamental need to be a part of something. I call it 'family.' You look for new structures and a new family. People care so much; I get goosepimples just thinking about it."

K arl Kuechenmeister became a Navy pilot after graduating from Dickenson College with a major in history. He says he "had no clue" about what he could do in the real world. "I didn't want to go into the business world, thank you." After the service, he went to Emerson College, "which I used as a trade school to get into the TV business. I didn't know what [I'd do] in broadcasting, but I knew [I wanted] broadcasting." He got a job at CBS in New York as a sales development analyst.

"I moved to the Chicago sales office. It was a faster way to become a salesman. There was more money, more people contact, out of the office, and I was ready to roll." Karl did very well there, but after four years, his progress was stymied. "To this day, my biggest disappointment in my business life was being passed over as an account executive for someone who'd been fired by NBC who had twenty years' experience. I called NBC, knowing they had lost a guy. It was like a trade.

"Even some NBC people thought I was nuts to leave CBS. It was January 1977, and NBC was in third place. No one could understand why a 'CBS type' like me would move." Karl thrived. He stayed in Chicago for two and a half years, moved to Los Angeles and a position as vice-president of western sales, and back to New York in sports sales. "We had baseball, football, the NCAA. It is a *Boys' Life* dream column." (The job also meant "a lot of babysitting drunken guys; a nonstop party.)

In March 1982 Kuechenmeister became the vice-president of daytime (10:00 A.M. to 4:00 P.M. Monday to Friday; 8:00 A.M. to 1:00 P.M. Saturday) sales. In March 1983 he traveled to Los Angeles to see some toy advertisers. "I called Dick Robertson," a friend and mentor from his Chicago days. "I arrived at his office at 5:30 on Thursday night. Telepictures was in the trades a lot, because of their success with *People's Court*. I didn't go for a job interview; I was visiting an old friend.

"They needed someone else. In Dick's words, 'You know, someone who's worked in New York, Chicago, L.A. . . .' I said, 'What are you saying?' He said, 'Would you be interested in this job?' I said, 'I want this job.' I asked for ten thousand dollars more than I was getting [at NBC]. I didn't go for the jugular. I spent four hours at Dick's office.

"By 9:30 Monday morning, I was in Garin's office. Everything was right. I met Michael Garin and Michael Solomon. At NATPE [the syndication convention] I was approved. Dick said, 'Don't make NBC angry; we sell to them.' Ten days later, I was at Telepictures. It was like everyone knew I'd be hired except me.

"A lot of people didn't understand the move. The bottom line was, I didn't feel I fit in at NBC. I didn't go out of my way to fit in. Obviously, I did a good job and fit in with senior sales management." During his last six months at NBC, Karl experienced a period of malaise and self-examination. "Did I want to move to the Sunbelt and work at a [TV] station? Did I want to leave TV? I didn't want to hang in there until I was fifty, sixty-five, and be unhappy. I discussed this with my fiancée and with friends. I decided I liked the TV business."

Those first months at Telepictures must have been like the feeling you get when you finally get to take off an uncomfortable pair of shoes after a long day of walking and blisters. "When I was good at network sales, I said to myself, 'I could do this with one eye closed and one arm tied behind my back.' " At Telepictures, "I liked the company from the time I was a recruit. Dick would say to me, 'Hey, Carlos—look at these numbers, look at these tapes!' Things got done. Fast. I saw an organization that was freewheeling. We wanted to control our own destiny. That ethic was not so much said as shown."

The merger with Lorimar concerned Kuechenmeister. "We were afraid of changes to a certain extent, and there was a group of us at a certain middle level who said, 'Well, I guess it's over.' They didn't ask us; they just did it." Karl remembers the day he first heard the official word on the merger. "It was September 25, 1985, the same day as Hurricane Gloria. People at Telepictures were anxious, as were their counterparts at Lorimar. Who was buying whom?" As he sees it, the choice was "to be on the board of a seven hundred million dollar company now, or wait to build one."

Karl enumerates each company's assets as of the announcement. "It was complementary. Lorimar was a major network TV producer; we were a successful player in syndication. We had magazines, they didn't. We had missed the boat on home video. [Lorimar Home Video, né Karl-Lorimar—for former company president Stuart Karl, whose company was acquired by Lorimar—made its name and money with the Jane Fonda Workout series.] We had media sales and they did not. We had TV stations, and they did not. Lorimar had Kenyon & Eckhardt and, by the time of our agreement, Bozell.

"As we got bigger—and don't get me wrong, getting bigger is what it's all about—the spirit got lost; it's a necessary evil. When I came here, we had 260 thirty-second commercials we had to sell. By my second season [six months later] I had 1,560 thirty-second spots. By 1987 it grew by two thousand percent. And for the 1988–89 season, I've got 11,300 thirty-seconds to sell.

"I think Telepictures people have changed since the merger. But I don't think I've changed that much. They didn't have my function, and I tried to let my performance speak for me. Lorimar has been changed by Telepicture's communication, the open office. They've opened up a lot from their traditional hierarchy."

Kuechenmeister feels a brand of pride as the president of Media Sales for Lorimar Syndication that he never felt in any of his previous jobs. "Every person in the department is my hire. It's my department. I've managed its growth." Media Sales is a department of fourteen, concentrated in New York with eleven people there, two in Chicago, and one in Los Angeles. "I like it; it's very exciting. I've spent fifteen and a half years in the business so far. I want to stay with this career. I envision doing this another six years. I'm forty-one now, and a pension is available at forty-seven. It's great for my mental health."

Leah Rosovsky McIntosh used to be a member of the New York staff, as the vice-president of Special Projects. She has an MBA from Harvard. "There are few MBAs here. Until the merger, there were very few. I was 'corporate fat.' Lorimar Telepictures is not looking for MBAs, but there's no antipathy toward them. Industry experience is more important."

The merger with Lorimar occupied a lot of her time. "I regarded merger issues as generic. The business logic was overwhelming. The fit made sense. There were no deep philosophical differences." Still, "it always takes a while to get over us-them thinking. It took a year to work it through completely. I had presumed it would have taken longer."

She said that any hesitancy to embrace the merger was a symptom of "what people felt they got or didn't get. Corporately, we like to see ourselves as one company." Stylistically, McIntosh believed, the only real differences between the two organizations were the usual New York–Los Angeles discrepancies, nothing more.

"The Executive Committee [Today made up of Chairman and CEO Merv Adelson, presidents Garin, Solomon, Robertson, and Salzman, CFO Tony Young, Richard Dalbeck, and Bernie Brillstein] is trying to figure out who we are. We're a major entertainment company, which is what we want to be. We're intelligent about it. We do strategic growth according to the businesses. We recognize cycles. We've decided to be big," she explains. "That's good. I sometimes find it hard to believe the small company I joined is so big.

"This company is one of the most consensus-run places I've ever seen. Decisions are made by groups, and the priority is to get people to buy into ideas before they're presented. As a small organization, Telepictures had a reaction against previous environments. My own experience is that I've worked for very decent, good people."

Scott Carlin also joined the organization through Telepictures. His elementary school in Connecticut was the recipient of old TV equipment donated by CBS which formed a little studio. That exposure made Scott want to work in television. While at the University of Colorado studying journalism, he wrote "a starry-eyed letter to Fred Silverman. It was his heyday at ABC. I got a phone call four weeks later from the director of program administration, ABC network in New York." When the caller announced himself to Carlin, Scott thought he was joking. "I said, 'Oh, yeah?' We talked for forty minutes. He said I should leave school and get job experience right away. The next day I knocked on doors at every TV station in Denver."

He got an internship at KOA, then Denver's NBC affiliate. "I was a full-time slave for three months in the news department. It was a nonunion shop. I was allowed to do everything —edit, write, produce." After college, Carlin found a job with a news consulting firm in Cedar Rapids, Iowa. "For anyone young, single—forget about hungry—there's nothing there. Guys cruise in Chevys. It's like *Happy Days*." To fill his free time, Scott played semiprofessional football. Otherwise, "I was going home by myself to a one-room apartment. I was leading the life of Ivan Denisovitch there." Obviously, he had to get out of Iowa.

He had an idea for a new business, nurtured at the Tarrytown Center and School for Entrepreneurs. In 1979 he sold the idea, was offered a hearty sum of money and, best of all, got to move to New York. Within six months, Scott's new business crumbled.

"I knew I could sell; I'd always sold myself. I had read about Telepictures. Something just rang true about the two guys [Michael G. and Michael S.] and their approach. I contacted the

Michaels by letter. At that time I had little to sell, but I decided I was going to work there."
David Salzman had just joined the corporate family. Scott flew out to Los Angeles to meet
with him in June 1980. "We hit it off. A few days later, he offered me a job.

"I was hired for production, but I turned him down. It was the toughest decision I had to
make. I wanted to sell. It was the fastest track professionally and financially. I said to Salzman,
'I want to work for you in the worst possible way.' Garin said it was a big mistake. [It would
have been worth taking a non-first-choice job] to get my foot in the door."

Carlin was still unemployed by the fall of that year. "I continued to stay in touch with
them." He admits to having had second thoughts about his decision. Impulsively, he called
Dick Robertson and succeeded in pulling him out of a meeting he was having in Salt Lake
City. "I gave him my best pitch. He hired me—for much less money—almost a fifty percent
cut. I took it.

"I was hired as an account executive. It felt right." Carlin was confronted with the fact that
many of his accounts had never heard of his company. "Telewho?" he was asked again and
again. But the timing couldn't have been more propitious. Scott was practically in the room
when the Telepictures syndication business was hatched. "The rights to *Here's Lucy* were up for
grabs for the first time. We were in the position of needing product. We outbid the others
and mortgaged the company to get the rights. People thought we'd never do it, but the twelve-
million-plus dollars in sales put us on the map and gave us wherewithal."

Scott is now the president of first-run syndication Lorimar Television. "Premerger, that was
the entire company." His jurisdiction encompasses, among others, *The People's Court, Superior
Court,* and *The Love Connection.* Other first-run syndicated shows include the original sitcoms
It's a Living, Mama's Family, and *She's the Sheriff,* starring Suzanne Somers. Finally, Lorimar
Telepictures is active in children's programming, offering *Thundercats, SilverHawks, Comic
Strip,* and the new and improved *Gumby,* premiering in fall 1988.

Carlin on the merger: "It feels different. I look at it as if it were time for us to grow up. To
go through the transition from little lean guys—Davids—into Goliaths. We achieved what
we dreamed of, and more, eight years ago. The merger put us ahead. We're a sales-driven
company even after the merger. Syndication is the tail that wags the dog. Sometimes we're
like the dog that grabs your leg and won't let go."

Scott says that based on his experience and the experiences of his colleagues, he appreciates
Lorimar Telepictures' iconoclasm. "Everyone operates with autonomy. We have the freedom
to do what we want or what we have to do. Some people like more structure than is available
here. Some people don't appreciate it, not having worked elsewhere."

F inally, it's time to meet someone who actually came from Lorimar. [Author's note: It's
not my fault that just about every time I tried to see Lorimar-bred employees or free-
lancers, they were out of town or had no time. But not Julie Waxman. We had an appointment, and she kept it.]

When Julie joined the company in 1972, there were only eight people at Lorimar. After
graduating from the University of Michigan with a degree in business, she moved to Boston,
where she spent a few years as a junior securities analyst. "It was good but stodgy," she says,
not mentioning the name of her firm. She also started "a little theater with a friend" and then
moved to the West Coast. "I was job jumping, to feel my way," she says, not a bad idea for
anyone (unless they're in a hurry). "I had family in L.A., I liked the weather, I'd had five or
six roommates who'd gotten married, and I felt like moving."

Her first job was as the production coordinator for a new show called *The Waltons,* Lorimar's first network series. Waxman got there in time to work on the first episode. From this program she moved onto others, including pilots and movies-of-the-week. She was now the assistant to the head of production.

After four years, Julie did something rather unusual. She moved into the business side of Lorimar. "Looking ahead, I didn't know where my production experience would lead me. Everybody wants to be a producer in this town. I didn't belong to a union, and then Lorimar was so small, I didn't expect it to grow." It never occurred to her to leave the company for a production job elsewhere. Besides, she says, "I didn't see myself as a creative person. Most producers then were writing producers." (To this day, producers who are also writers are favored in TV.)

Business affairs, as it's known in the industry, the division that supervises legal and financial matters, "prefers lawyers, but this company has no bias." Julie did not go to law school, but she enrolled in one course in contracts. "You don't need a degree to negotiate. A lot is common sense, knowing the marketplace and the people. At certain times I have to defer to lawyers.

"In the beginning of my time in business affairs, I missed production and being part of that excitement, but I stuck with it." Waxman is married to writer-producer Seth Freeman, who a few years ago created a series called *The Best Times.* At the very least, Julie was surrounded by production, if not in the thick of it herself.

"This area is action. There are opportunities to grow. The business end of the business keeps changing. Lawyers, agents, and studios become more sophisticated. Lorimar has become a bigger company, and the paperwork is more detailed. When I started, deals were in short form and handshakes. Now performers have agents, lawyers, business managers, and personal managers." But the more complicated the rules and deals get, Waxman believes that people skills are still the most important assets for business affairs. "The variable in a deal is still the individual. You're dealing with a lot of egos. You develop good relationships in the industry and know who to call, who to ask."

Julie works exclusively in television business affairs. She has her hands in merchandising, ancillary matters, license fees to the networks, overall and term deals (for producers who work exclusively on the lot), rights acquisitions, and talent deals. In addition to her, Lorimar Television's business affairs staff is made up of seven people who negotiate, two financial administrators, and support staff. "The workload is enormous." Her workdays are about nine hours long, shorter since she became a mother. In an industry where social lives blur [Authors note: uncomfortably] into professional lives, Waxman has streamlined the social aspects of her work obligations to a minimum. She'll do lunches, but breakfasts must be spent at home with her daughter.

Not surprisingly, the work can be very adversarial. (Of course, that's the way outsiders perceive it. Witness actress Valerie Harper's ouster from her own series by NBC and Lorimar Telepictures.) Waxman maintains, "You always think you're being reasonable. I have my bad days when nothing seems to go right." She certainly doesn't have a tough edge. The many photographs of her pretty young daughter nullify the businesslike sensibility that permeates the corridor where she works.

She sums up her feelings toward her business. "You deal with a small group of people again and again. My attitude is that it doesn't pay to alienate people. That's not to say there aren't mornings when I wake up at three A.M. This is a competitive environment. There's always so much urgency. You must be fast—the bidding can be stiff, and you must be poised to respond quickly. There are days when I say, 'I've had it; what an asshole!' but I can shut it out when I'm with my daughter.

"This is a young person's business. It can consume you and take everything you can give."

With her experience, longevity, and reputation in business affairs at a growing company,

Julie could find another job without trouble. (She's now senior vice-president of business affairs.) "I have had other offers," she admits. "I've evaluated the pros and cons and felt that many of my needs were satisfied here." She points out that as a native of Cincinnati, her ethos is midwestern, stable. "I was raised in one house." And with Lorimar's growth and merger, the company can provide new challenges.

"I've had a wait-and-see attitude. The bottom line is, I like coming into work and I like the people I work with. I'm not saying I'm a lifer. For me, this is a good place to be. I'm comfortable and I'm stimulated. Without moving, I feel I'm working for a new company. It took a year, but I see it now as a blended company. In the beginning it was them-us. The people are different, with different styles and dynamics. They are very energetic. I'm impressed with the people I work with. They're smart and they care, and they're fun and hardworking."

Interview:
BERNIE BRILLSTEIN

*B*ernie Brillstein is the newest principal of Lorimar Telepictures. Well known as a talent manager, he enjoyed official "consultant" status for three years before selling his company, The Brillstein Company, to Lorimar Telepictures and becoming the chairman of Lorimar Film Entertainment. Still based in his Brillstein Company offices in Beverly Hills, Brillstein is an ebullient, funny, Falstaffian figure complete with beard, wearing a velour sweatsuit, the apotheosis of what we think an entertainment tycoon should be. He is what would have been called by those inventive people who write for *Reader's Digest* a "colorful character." He is one of Hollywood's most persuasive success stories. His office is crammed with so much memorabilia that it's distracting. Posters of his production compete with gold and platinum records, all hung on suede-covered walls. He's told his life story so many times that today's version is abbreviated.

The son of a showbiz family, Brillstein graduated from New York University in 1953 before heading off to the Navy and England. He put on shows there. [Author's note: From here on in, I'm just going to copy my notes. They're in my own patented form of shorthand. Do not try it yourself without proper instruction.] "First job at station. WGTH—hated it. Hartford. Sold time. First take-home pay $32.81. William Morris—mailroom. Got out of mailroom fastest. 4½ weeks →. Sec'y at Publicity. → commercials → daytime → became asst. to head of TV packaging (Asst. Wally Jordan). Took shorthand at course. Gregg method & typing. Started resenting Wm. Morris. Wasn't rebelling, but as a big guy, wore sweaters.

"1964. After MCA broke up, Martin Kummer Agency brought Brillstein in $25,000—partnership on all new bus. 1965. Brought Jerry Weintraub in. Signed Jim Henson 1959–60 at Wm. Morris.

"1967. Moved to L.A. April 1. Opened Management III. Jerry & Marty said 'sign stars' but stars didn't want to sign.

"*Hee Haw*—started me in packaging. Now 20 yrs. Couldn't sell Muppet shows. *Hee Haw,* country *Laugh-In*—that's why I made the big bucks. 1969 split Mgmt III. The most any of us made there was $35,000. When big star leaves first mgr. they never do well—A mgr. is a best friend.

"Why I've done well: To handle neurosis of funny mind—comedy. If I weren't crazy, couldn't handle comedians. Talent could be killed by rejection.

"Mgmt.—to get employment. My job is to know what to do & take advantage of it.

"1975—*Saturday Night Live.* I'm now an atomic scientist.

"1976—*The Muppet Show.* Then, the movie business—Worst bus. in the world—television is gentleman's business compared to movie.

"2 yrs. ago real bored. 50 or 60 clients—Nicest thing I've done in 3 yrs. was putting Richard Dreyfuss back in bus.

"Got real tired—

"*Buffalo Bill.* Thought it was time to do it myself. Was consultant to Telepix. 7-8 mos. ago, became Chmn. of Film Div. Have mgmt. co. & Board of LT. 2½ days apiece."

Brillstein enjoys being a part of a big company after all these years on his own. "Having not been in corporate America since 1963, I see nothing's changed, just the people. The nice thing about a big company is, I don't have to sell it. We do sell to ourselves. [Not to mention that many of The Brillstein Company's clients have deals with Lorimar Telepictures.] Ever since I've gone to Lorimar, everything has turned to gold. I needed a new challenge after thirty-five years of experience. To take guys of sixty-five [Bernie is fifty-seven] and put them to pasture is stupid."

Bernie Brillstein made his mark representing funny people. Funny people who become—under his direction—funny *famous* people. Besides handling Dan Ackroyd, Garry Shandling, Richard Dreyfuss, Jim Belushi, Dabney Coleman, Peter Falk, Lorne Michaels, Bronson Pinchot, Jim Henson, and many other former and present "Not Ready for Prime Time Players," Brillstein is also the executive producer of *It's Garry Shandling's Show, The Days and Nights of Molly Dodd, Alf,* and *The Slap Maxwell Story.* He has also produced *Ghostbusters, The Blues Brothers, Dragnet,* and other features. You might notice their common denominators. All three starred (or costarred) Dan Ackroyd, and they grossed in the megabuck stratosphere. "Certain movies are almost sure things," Brillstein feels. "I knew *Ghostbusters* was a good idea—and the movie made over two hundred million dollars. And I'm not a genius." He is regarded as a strong producer who takes his role seriously and gets involved actively. He fights for big fees for his clients and consequently earns some for himself.

He plans on making six to eight movies his first year as chairman, including *It's Garry Shandling's Movie,* and *Penn and Teller Get Murdered.* "I'm going to try to bring back the studio system," he says.

"Until I went to Lorimar, I came home at five-thirty every night to eat with my kids." He has five children aged twenty-nine, nineteen, fifteen, nine, and five.

EPILOGUE

Michael Garin announced his resignation from Lorimar Telepictures on May 6, 1988. On May 10, 1988, Warner Communications agreed to acquire Lorimar Telepictures for $1.2 billion. Although a previous attempt by these two entities to wed fell apart, both organizations were optimistic that they would conclude this transaction as *Going to Work* was going to press.

MITCHELL, SILBERBERG & KNUPP

LAW OFFICES

MITCHELL, SILBERBERG & KNUPP

A PARTNERSHIP OF PROFESSIONAL CORPORATIONS

HISTORY & OPERATIONS

Shepard Mitchell, a graduate of the University of Michigan Law School, and Mendel R. Silberberg, a graduate of Stanford Law School, were fresh out of school when, in 1907, Los Angeles lawyer John Kemp hired them into his firm. A year later Kemp brought his son into the firm, and Mitchell and Silberberg, who were strongly averse to nepotism, left on principle to start their own practice. When Mitchell and Silberberg founded Mitchell & Silberberg in 1908—the firm is one of the oldest in Los Angeles—they were only two years out of law school and had no visible means of support.

The partners struggled at first, serving their own papers and subsisting mainly by frequenting restaurants that provided free lunch with a nickel glass of beer. Silberberg—who was reputed to have had a winning personality—attracted a number of clients, and the firm gradually cultivated a practice. Two of Mitchell & Silberberg's most significant early clients were in the film business. When the partners acquired Columbia Pictures as a client, several Mitchell & Silberberg lawyers went to work full time on the Columbia lot. Shortly thereafter, RKO Pictures sought the firm's services and hired Mitchell & Silberberg lawyers to work full time at its studio.

By the early thirties, the firm's practice had grown enough so that the partners could no longer handle all of the litigation work by themselves. In 1932, the outstanding trial lawyer Guy Knupp joined as a partner, and the firm's name was changed to Mitchell, Silberberg & Knupp. Knupp, who had been a classmate of Silberberg's at Stanford Law School, had built a reputation as one of the best water lawyers in California, at a time when water rights were being litigated in the state. (At one point, Lester Roth became a partner and the firm's name was changed to Mitchell, Silberberg, Roth & Knupp. When Roth left to become vice-president of Columbia Pictures, the name was permanently changed back to Mitchell, Silberberg & Knupp.) In the mid-thirties the firm added a third important client—Pacific Mutual Life Insurance Company—which became a mainstay of its business during the difficult Depression years. During the decade, Mitchell, Silberberg & Knupp became known for its corporate work in addition to its entertainment practice.

Despite its increasing work load, the firm remained relatively small in its early decades, and by 1944 it still had only eight lawyers. By the sixties, that number had grown to twenty-two. Silberberg—who had been a member of the Republican National Committee, active in the Hoover administration and a close associate of Earl Warren and Richard Nixon—died in 1965 after a two-year illness. Mitchell had retired earlier, and Knupp left two years after Silberberg's death.

The firm underwent the greatest growth spurt in its history in the years following the departure of the name partners. In 1967 it acquired Freston & Files. Once the biggest law firm in Los Angeles, Freston & Files was down to about five lawyers when Mitchell, Silberberg & Knupp took it over. During the seventies, it added a labor law department, which is now a key area of its practice.

Today, Mitchell, Silberberg & Knupp has 114 lawyers—fifty-two of them partners with the remaining sixty-two associates. Though the firm is still known primarily as an entertainment firm, it has a wide general practice and entertainment is no longer its largest division. The firm is organized into six practice areas: Litigation, Corporate, Tax, Labor, Motion Pictures & Television, and Music. Litigation is the largest department with approximately forty lawyers, Corporate has twenty-two, both Labor and Tax have about twelve, Music has nine, and Motion Pictures & Television has about fifteen. The firm's clients range in size from *Fortune* 500 corporations and major banks and institutions to smaller start-up companies and individual entrepreneurs and artists. Some of the clients of the firm's six departments are: Litigation: The International Olympic Committee, the International Amateur Athletic Federation; Corporate: Dataproducts Corporation, Financial Corporation of America, Fairmont Financial, Inc., Diceon Electronics, Inc., Bank of America, Occidental Petroleum Corporation, and the Arden Group, Inc.; Tax: the National Hockey League; Labor: Cedars-Sinai Medical Center, St. John's Hospital, Children's Hospital; Motion Pictures: Paramount Pictures, Tri-Star Pictures, Paul Newman, Jack Nicholson; Music: A&M Records, Chrysalis Records, George Benson, the Motels, David Lee Roth, the Rolling Stones.

The firm is known for its informal work environment and the high level of responsibility it gives its young associates. In a 1986 poll by *The American Lawyer,* which surveyed members of the law school classes of 1982 and 1983 on their satisfaction with their firms, Mitchell, Silberberg & Knupp came out on top of all other firms across the country. New associates are generally hired for a specific department on the basis of their expressed preferences, and although the skills of the various practice areas are integrated in particular cases, associates don't normally rotate among practice groups. (However, if an associate is unhappy in the practice area that he or she has initially chosen, the firm allows changes.) New associates are involved in all aspects of a given case and assume active responsibility and client contact from the outset of their tenure with the firm.

The track from first-year associate to partner normally takes about seven years (at most firms it's closer to eight years, and in fact, earlier in the firm's history it took between eight and nine years), and associates are first informed of their partnership prospects after their third year with the firm.

All the members of Mitchell, Silberberg & Knupp's partnership have an equal vote in the administration of the firm. The firm's day-to-day administrative decisions are handled by a management committee elected by the partners, and all the firm's lawyers are invited to attend management committee meetings.

Mitchell, Silberberg & Knupp encourages its lawyers to take on pro bono work. Among the firm's most enduring traditions are a Friday afternoon cocktail party and weekly departmental luncheons.

(Information provided by Stuart Linnick, partner, and Robert Block, Esq.)

REVENUES: Firm is private and will not disclose.

EARNINGS: Firm will not disclose.

OFFICES: Headquarters in Los Angeles and an additional office in London with only one lawyer. (The firm plans to enlarge its London presence in the forseeable future.)

NUMBER OF EMPLOYEES: 288; 114 attorneys (52 partners and 62 associates), 24 paralegals, and 150 support staff.

AVERAGE AGE OF EMPLOYEES: For associates the average age is roughly twenty-eight; for all attorneys, it's probably around thirty-eight.

TURNOVER: For attorneys, probably around 4–5 percent per year.

RECRUITMENT: The firm recruits at ten law schools: Boalt (University of California at Berkeley), University of California at Los Angeles, Columbia University, Georgetown University, Harvard University, University of Michigan, New York University, University of Southern California, Stanford University, and Yale University. "Although we also consider applications from law students at other schools. We generally are seeking candidates in the top ten to fifteen percent of their classes."

NUMBER OF NEW HIRES PER YEAR: Twelve to fifteen entry-level attorneys.

RANGE OF STARTING SALARIES: In 1987 first-year attorneys earned $52,000.

POLICY FOR RAISES: "Associate attorneys receive a raise annually to the next tier in the salary structure; the overall structure is reevaluated annually with adjustments made in accordance with market considerations.

SUMMER ASSOCIATE PROGRAM: The firm hires fifteen to eighteen summer associates—students who have completed their second year of law school or those who want summer experience before taking a judicial clerkship—each year. Summer associates, who generally spend about ten weeks with the firm, are given a broad exposure to the different areas of Mitchell, Silberberg & Knupp's practice. Their work includes research and writing as well as assisting in the preparation of contracts and pleadings, court attendance (with a firm member), labor negotiations, and conferences with clients and other lawyers. The intention is to give them a clear idea of what it's like working for the firm. The 1987 summer salary was $900 per week. (In 1988 it ranged from $1,000 to $1,100 per week.) Roughly half of 1987's twenty summer associates have joined the firm full time.

BENEFITS: *Attorneys:* medical and dental insurance, life insurance, paid parking, bar stipend (since the California bar exam is so tough, new lawyers are given five weeks off at full salary for it), moving allowance, and paid continuing education. *Support staff:* medical, life and dental insurance, pension, and profit sharing.

VACATION: *Lawyers:* three weeks per year for associates and four weeks per year for partners, in addition to ten regular paid holidays per year. *Support staff:* two weeks the first three years, three weeks after three years, plus eight sick days the first two years and eleven after the third year (if employees don't use their sick days, they get paid for them), plus ten regular paid holidays per year.

ADDITIONAL PERKS: In and around MS&K's own building, there are exercise facilities (including weight equipment, tennis courts, and a basketball court), and when associates make partner they're given the opportunity to become equity participants in the building.

BONUSES: Beginning in their second year, associates are eligible for bonuses. The only criterion is that the associates must bill a minimum of 1,850 hours, in which case the bonus is awarded automatically. (Associates are not required to bill 1,850 hours unless they want this bonus.)

ANNUAL PARTIES: The firm has an annual Christmas party for all employees and an annual picnic or similar event for employees and their families. The Christmas party is held at Hillcrest Country Club and is "quite a feast." The party is informal—it's generally held on a weeknight, and the staff goes straight from the office—and includes cocktails, a buffet dinner, and sometimes a couple of skits. "We're a talented group of people here." The annual picnic is hosted at different places each year. Once it was held at a day camp with a big water slide and all kinds of athletic facilities. Employees participate in sports and games, as well as talent contests in which people sing, play musical instruments, etc. In addition, the firm hosts periodic social events for the attorneys.

DRESS CODE: No stated dress code, but attorneys tend to wear business attire (e.g., suits, dresses). The entertainment lawyers tend to dress more casually.

AVERAGE WORKDAY: Official hours are 9:00 A.M. to 5:15 P.M., but the lawyers' hours are considerably longer. "I don't know anyone who leaves at 5:15."

SOCIAL ATMOSPHERE: "Among the attorneys, the social atmosphere is very informal, friendly, and collegial. Attorneys do tend to fraternize with each other after work."

HEADQUARTERS: The firm occupies six floors of its own West Los Angeles building (not including its file room in the basement).

CHARITABLE CONTRIBUTIONS: Firm will not disclose.

INTERESTED APPLICANTS CAN SEND RÉSUMÉS TO:
(For attorney positions:)
Mitchell, Silberberg & Knupp
Attention: Laurel Travers
11377 West Olympic Boulevard
Los Angeles, CA 90064
(For nonattorney positions:)

Mitchell, Silberberg & Knupp
Attention: Diane Chase
11377 West Olympic Boulevard
Los Angeles, CA 90064
(213) 312-2000

I f law firms, like any service business, make their clients comfortable by aping the people they serve, then Los Angeles's Mitchell, Silberberg & Knupp may be three firms in one: it's a labor firm, with shirtsleeves rolled and ties loosened a bit; it's a corporate firm, with conservatively attired advisers and litigators; and it's probably best known as an entertainment firm with a contingent of casually dressed producer/director/actor lookalikes. All three practices compatibly interact and coexist, and, according to *The American Lawyer*'s 1986 national survey of law associates' satisfaction, Mitchell, Silberberg & Knupp comes out at the very top.

The attorneys I met at Mitchell, Silberberg & Knupp seem to work there because they want to, not because they have to, not because they see law school as an investment and feel stuck. Even the young, typically overworked associates do not despair of their careers or their chances of making partner.

Ed Rubin has been with the firm since 1940, although he went on a military hiatus from 1941 to 1949. A specialist in entertainment, copyright, and intellectual property, his initial exposure to these areas was via Columbia and RKO Pictures, which used MS&K in lieu of staffing their own legal departments. "You didn't hear the phrase 'entertainment law' until the late fifties," he says from his large, beige corner office with terrace, restrainedly festooned with entertainment memorabilia. (A prominently displayed poster for the movie *Hoppy Serves a Writ* is framed on a wall near a collage featuring *Gone with the Wind,* Douglas Fairbanks, Jr., Charlie Chaplin, and an Oscar statuette.) He recalls that the first seminar on entertainment law, sponsored by the University of Southern California and the Beverly Hills Bar Association was in 1954–55. The practice has grown, beginning with motion pictures and moving into television, then music, and now even sports.

Rubin says one of the differences between associates of his day and today's young lawyers is that the latter have *studied* entertainment law, an impossibility forty years ago. Furthermore, "there's a great deal of transiency. There's a greater demand for lawyers in the entertainment field than ever before; more house counsel opportunities between the networks, independent producers, et cetera. In the past, the post-Depression mentality meant keeping a job."

Rubin, who was born in 1912, avers that entertainment clients are generally "much younger, especially those in music, than any other clients. The relevant thing is whether you still have your marbles, not whether you enjoy your client's work. My age is such that many people of it wouldn't work full time, or at all."

Arthur Groman arrived at MS&K just a few years after Rubin. He says, "My mother told me when I was eight years old I told everyone I'd be a lawyer, which baffles me. There were no lawyers in the family, or role models." When pressed, Groman thinks he might have been inspired by the president of his family's temple, who was a great speaker. Then, "I took Latin in the seventh grade because I thought lawyers did that." At USC as an undergraduate, Groman was the president of the debate squad, and had plenty of chances to polish his oratorical skills.

"I've been very lucky in my career," he says from his clubby-looking office. He's represented "at one time or another, every studio," Norton Simon, Armand Hammer—"I helped Dr. Hammer buy Occidental Petroleum," of which Groman is the oldest board member—and RKO pictures chairman Howard Hughes—"I tried the only case he actually showed up for in a suit against the writer Paul Jericho. It was a difficult decision." Jericho sued Hughes for screen credit for the screenplay he wrote for *The Las Vegas Story.* Groman won. He is the litigator who represented Mick Jagger in his divorce proceedings against the team of Marvin Mitchelson and Bianca Jagger. Groman's enthusiasm makes him seem younger than his seventy-five years. He recounts the story of the biggest case he handled as a young trial lawyer, involving the 3-D process. "It was down to a question of credibility. I was able to impeach the plaintiff so many times, and materially. The judge told the plaintiff, 'I don't believe you.' That's like being crowned the King of England!"

As the dean of the firm, Groman is approached by more clients than he can represent. "It is necessary to delegate and to persuade clients that in some cases my partners can do as good a job as I can. Young lawyers get so fired up!" He says many more suits are settled than are actually tried in court. "But still, sometimes during a cross-examination, something happens that's so dramatic. . . . My wife tells me during a trial I can't be talked to. When I was a young lawyer, I could prepare a complaint, do depositions, try a case, et cetera, for twelve thousand dollars. [Now] litigation may be so costly that it will price itself out of existence."

Groman has witnessed countless changes in the life of the firm. "The seniors no longer run the management committee; often younger lawyers decide. Certainly there's not the reverance for seniors [that was manifest during the early years]. Until I was made partner, I called Mr. Silberberg 'Mr. Silberberg.' Now a first-year associate calls me 'Arthur.'" When asked if he had wanted to be a name partner of the firm, i.e., "Mitchell, Silberberg, Knupp & Groman," he says laughingly, "I'd rather explain why I'm not a name partner than defend why I am one."

After thirteen years at MS&K, Deborah Koepfler describes her firm as having "a liberal, entrepreneurial, and somewhat chaotic atmosphere." Her identity upon arrival was SDS. Her mentor was a Young Republican. "He thought I was left of Che Guevara, and I thought he was right of Genghis Khan. We had a peaceful coexistence." Despite the heterogeneity within, she thinks the world at large sees Mitchell, Silberberg & Knupp as homogeneous. "Outside adversaries think we're large, traditional, influential, old, and effective. That's true, but they don't *know* us." A partner in the labor department, she says each practice has a personality that's a variation on a theme. Labor's particulars: "Easy, laid-back, pretty happy group of people; intellectually well regarded; a poorly dressed, bad-taste group. If you saw Laura Lofton [an associate in the corporate department] and me together, you'd think I cleaned her house."

When we meet, Deborah is pregnant, the deed perpetrated by another partner at the firm —her husband. They find working together comfortable, and Koepfler thinks that being a woman at MS&K is a nonissue. "Sex is irrelevant. This is one of the most flexible environments to be a mother and have your own life. There are all kinds of maternity leaves, and they don't affect partnership. I took six months off for a fertility program. We used to have women's lunches here, and it was such a joke. We didn't have that much in common [just because we were female]." The question of sex certainly did not arise during her quest for partnership. "There isn't competition for partner," she says forcefully. "If you are good, you become partner. My whole class became partner, and are all still here except for one who's left to work for a client." Her accession came after only five and a half years. "I think five and a half is too fast. It takes a while to acquire all the skills. The trend now is toward six and a half to seven years.

"Being made partner was no big deal. I never really thought about it. When I saw everyone else overwhelmed, I figured I might not be something I'm supposed to be. I would have been destroyed," she admits, "if I'd been turned down.

"We're very collegial, in an old boys' sense. We're a real team, even between two people on the same partner track. We're like a sports team competing together. If we compete among ourselves, we're depleting our own resources. A victory is great. We really love to share that. People who are ballbusters won't fit in."

Somehow, mysteriously, your seniors and partners become apprised of all work that is done at the firm. No one has to resort to active carboning, etc., to win notice. Koepfler maintains, "My own career has been aggressively promoted. I got exciting cases early on that gave me a lot of visibility." Deborah says money and public recognition are not what get people to come in in the morning. "The younger you are, the more you need approval. The messages don't need to be banners. If you're honest and know your craft, you know when you're fucking up or when you're doing well. I'm at a stage in collective bargaining when you know you're good. There's self-assessment. I always felt that I was being forced to stretch and I still do."

She admits she's "not the world's biggest client-getter, but because I was one of the first women management lawyers, I have good visibility and get inquiries. As a labor lawyer, you learn a lot about other jobs." Through the words of mouth of satisfied customers, she's worked extensively in the computer and hospital industries. "I wear a different hat for different clients in the same industry. You have to be a chameleon, and I'm not good at it."

Koepfler seems to truly enjoy her work. In addition to her practice, she's published "quite a bit, and I speak frequently—about twenty-five times a year. [The work] does get repetitive; many problems are so avoidable, and sometimes you think you've already taught people to solve them." In her civilian life, "none of my social friends are lawyers. None of them have seen me with nylons or earrings. For my first day of work I thought I looked pretty good. I was wearing new Levi's corduroy pants and a matching jacket. New shoes."

Who might be suited to a career at Mitchell, Silberberg & Knupp? Deborah lists the following abilities and qualities: "One, hard work—not the nine-to-five kind. Two, social skills. There's no room for 'library lawyers.' We've bypassed people with top credentials because of rudeness, et cetera. Three, spark. That you really enjoy and care. The client likes to think you're enthusiastic. Four, a certain level of physical appearance, like having your fly zipped and good personal hygiene. Five, a sense of reality about your own abilities. To crave learning. Maybe that should be number six.

"But I just do it because it's fun. I'm overwhelmed by what I'm paid. We're very lucky."

Dan Petrocelli joined the firm in 1981. The New Jersey native went West ten years earlier to attend UCLA, where he majored in music and economics. Working for a bank, "I went to law school at night at a school that would not typically have been recruited here, Southwestern University. I got obsessed, did very well, and interviewed at all big firms." He clerked at MS&K during his second summer and chose the firm without hesitation.

A member of the litigation department, he says, "I came here with some perceptions in mind that have been borne out. It's an open environment. Young people have a lot to say about what goes on here. There's never been a time when a partner said to me late Friday night, 'I need this first thing Monday morning.' He'd be here with me. They're not yachting when they delegate. Young associates are given a great deal of responsibility and put on the front lines. People have been fair, nice, and good to me.

"There's individualism and tolerance. There's freedom of choice and expression. There's no political or philosophical strain. If anything, we're probably more liberal. I was turned off by conservative firms where the style [of the seniors] was all emulated. I realized I'd be spending most of my life here. With a diversified practice, I could dabble in other industries. I've become a jack-of-all-trades. Plus, I want to practice at the highest level."

Petrocelli has helped run the summer associate program. He attempts to teach the values of Mitchell, Silberberg & Knupp during this abbreviated apprenticeship. "The least effective way of communicating values is by telling them. We try to get the summer people more involved. Let 'em see what it's like—lunch, cocktail hours, b.s.-ing in the hall. We welcome them to see us as we are."

Dan was up for partnership in April 1987. "First- and second-year associates don't feel any pressure [about making partner]. It's too far off. As a young litigator, you're learning, and you're overwhelmed by the enormity of work and proving you can do it well. You're learning to get along with the people at the firm. You're intimidated by everything: the courts, your seniors, the opposing counsel.

"In the third year, the pressure changes. You start becoming anxious about the partnership. By your third or fourth year, if it's not for you, you should leave." By then, presumably, you have more confidence in your abilities and goals. "Everyone we hire, we think will be partnership material. There's no competition for partnership slots. There's no quota; you do good work, fit into the firm, and make partner. It's a foregone conclusion you're going to make it. It should never have an element of surprise or suspense."

Petrocelli clearly has the long term in mind. "I want to be a career lawyer. I don't think my life will change when or if I make partner. You get a bigger office, which I just got, and some remuneration. There's not a big difference between a senior associate and a junior partner." [Petrocelli is now a partner.]

Managed by a formal review process, the litigation department, currently made up of about forty lawyers, is the largest group at MS&K. "Associates are instrumental in determining the review. Young people have a lot to say about governance and what's done with them." This is a theme that constantly resonates around MS&K's offices. The associates don't feel trashed or quashed by the partnership. They have control over their destinies and confer with their seniors before policy is made. "Weekly meetings of the department are great. We share a lot of camaraderie." Dan says he never worked in any other department here, "so I don't know if it's so elsewhere in the firm. As lawyers, I think our department is aggressive. As people, we're very friendly." A cocktail party for all lawyers every Friday adds to the conviviality, and it's open to the whole firm (staff and paralegals) every two or three weeks. It is here that you see MS&K's various personalities. By essentially just looking around the room, you can detect the various practices through the mannerisms and appearances of the assemblage.

Though earning a comfortable living, associate Steve Warren has supplemented his income through a secondary television career: Through apppearances on the quiz shows *Sale of the Century* and *Tic Tac Dough,* he earned himself, while a summer associate, a handy $76,000. (He's not the only moonlighter. Dana Cook, another young associate, won $33,000 on *Trivia Trap.*) Working in the entertainment department, Warren is aware that the visibility of that practice sometimes overshadows that of the rest of the firm. Stuart Linnick, the head of the Labor Department, says, "We need more corporate, litigation, and labor lawyers." For all the summer people whose expressed interest is show business—"trying to hide their entertainment ambitions," adds Steve Warren—they are urged to have open minds. "Don't say it. You could change your mind during the summer."

Throughout the day, members of the Labor Department quietly lobby for their group. Murmurings of how small and friendly it is permeate even their small talk. Stu Linnick is a native New Yorker who was made a partner in his early thirties at the eminent New York firm of Phillips, Nizer. By his thirty-ninth birthday, "I looked around and said, 'Is this it?' " With a mentor in Mitchell's Labor Department leader Harry Keaton, he chucked New York and found himself having to tough out the bar exam once again. "It staved off a midlife crisis." Though he still smokes a pipe and misses parts of Gotham, he is one happy Californian labor lawyer. "Everyone likes each other," he says gleefully. But the ambience of the firm at large is relaxed and friendly. Labor Department member Bill Cole's best friends from high school and law school work with him here.

Tom Lambert is a senior partner in Litigation. He joined MS&K in 1971. He talks about the trendiness of the different practices within the profession. "The nonlegal community sees litigation as 'hot.' " What could be trendier than white collar criminal work? The firm sees plenty of those cases. "A lawyer has an obligation to defend his client. It's not for you to decide guilt—it's for the judge and jury to decide. What if you know your client is lying? Many would say withdraw from the case. It depends on your attitude toward advocacy. You must be committed to the system. We don't take murderers or rapists." As for corporate litigation, "it is incorrect to think that companies are less emotional than individuals. Now the corporate side is more desirable than the litigation side." Lambert admits that "the overwhelming number" of law students who approach MS&K "want entertainment."

Furthermore, cities are prey to trends as well. Los Angeles is popular "and sells itself; we probably had some summer clerks who just wanted to see what the West Coast was like, and we have good experience with those." The firm likes to hire non–Los Angelenos as summer clerks. Tom says the Sunbelt was hot a few years ago, but that Dallas and Houston "are dead now."

Pat Benson, a chic litigation partner, recalls that when she interviewed for her job in 1974, "the first question I asked was about pro bono work. I laid down the gauntlet. Now when I hear that during an interview, I want to hug the applicant." Lambert also remembers fielding many queries about pro bono in the late sixties and early seventies, and then not again until recently.

Pat was the second female full-time associate at MS&K. (By the way, she mentions, "No one refers to this firm by name," and by golly, she's right, at least today when everyone says simply, "the firm.") After two years at Smith and a BA from Stanford, this Los Angeles native ("but I'm spiritually bicoastal") matriculated at the USC Law School. "I never thought I'd end up in L.A., but it didn't occur to me that USC was [perceived as] a national institution, and could get me East. I chose Mitchell, Silberberg because it was on the west side of town and my car wasn't air-conditioned. I didn't really even want to work here."

After fourteen years, though, Pat likes her life at the firm. "The firm has been real good to us as women." Married to a criminal lawyer who has his own firm, she says, "There are no kids in our plan. I'm the only woman here without maternity leave or children." She fervently believes "everyone is entitled to a defense." She travels like crazy and tries to restrict her legal life to the office.

"I don't like talking about work at home. It depends on what crisis is brewing on whether I can leave it at the office," the slim brunette says. "I go to the gym three times a week, play 'dumb blond' music, and turn my brain off. The music helps."

Hayward Kaiser started at Mitchell, Silberberg & Knupp as a part-time student during his first year at UCLA Law School. He showed up with "very long hair, which I didn't cut, and a beard." He finds pictures from a 1973 outing that attest to this fact. From Walnut Creek, California, outside San Francisco, he always thought he'd return to the Bay Area, "but prestigious, old-line firms there didn't want to hire me. I decided if I wanted L.A., it would be *here,* otherwise I'd go back to San Francisco."

In the contest of San Francisco versus Mitchell, Silberberg & Knupp, "I made a permanent decision to call L.A. home. It was an emotional adjustment." Kaiser, like Arthur Groman, wanted to be a lawyer from the time he was small. "In the fifth grade my teacher asked me what I wanted to be, and I said I wanted to go to UCLA and be a lawyer.

"Being in trial is fun." It only took Hayward a year and a half to two years before he had his own trial. "Unfortunately, with the system in place, we're not spending enough time in trial. There's too much time spent on discovery [the process of determining the adversary's case through interrogatories, depositions, etc.]. Lots of lawyers who are discovery smart are not trial smart. One of the problems is that we're hardly ever on trial. [Only] five percent of my cases ever get to court.

"Trial lawyers want to go to trial right away. It's not justice to bring a suit four years after the breach and not go to trial for five years. My solution? One, a one-year statute of limitations. (If you want to sue, do it in a year.) Two, go to trial in one year. Three, loser pays all court and attorneys' fees. Four, extremely limited discovery. Five, appoint more judges at higher pay. Six, federal system: one judge for the entire case."

When discoursing on the frustrations and joys of litigation, Kaiser sounds and looks like a lawyer, but when organizing the beer and food selections for a baseball game on TV that evening, he seems like . . . a guy. His hair is still longish, and he is relaxed organizing his social activity in front of the reporter. But again, let Hayward reflect the culture of the firm where he has grown up. Nobody is uncomfortable about letting their real lives show through. You can be whatever or whomever you are here at this firm no one refers to by name. (Okay, some call it "Mitchell.")

You might not expect to meet someone like Jimmy Blancarte at an "old-line, conservative law firm." Though a partner in Litigation, "my personal clients are in entertainment, and I follow them." One client is comedian Bob Zmuda, the mastermind behind *Comic Relief,* the comic marathon that raises millions of dollars of aid for the homeless. Blancarte represented *Comic Relief* itself, making deals with HBO and Lorimar (see p. 298) for the videocassette. He is particularly close to Chicano comedian/actor Paul Rodriguez. "I'm actually better-looking and taller than he is." In a 1986 pilot for ABC, called *Hardesty House,* about five UCLA-trained lawyers living and working together in a 1986-style cooperative, Rodriguez actually played a Hispanic entertainment lawyer, based on . . . you got it.

Blancarte seems to be having a ball. "I consider myself a fun guy with fun clients. I chose this firm because they seemed the most progressive, for a large firm, and allowed me to do my social and political stuff. Now I have a level of public visibility."

PLUM
PRODUCTIONS

HISTORY & OPERATIONS

Plum Productions, which produces commercials for advertising agencies on an independent, free-lance basis, is six years old. The company was founded in 1982 by producer-entrepreneur Chuck Sloan, who is now Plum's president and executive producer, in conjunction with Eric Saarinen, the director of the company (and the commercials), a cinematographer. Chuck Sloan started the company with $10,000 scraped together from cash advances on his and six friends' credit cards. "It's the American way." The first year they made $500,000 in revenues ($40,000 in profits), the second year revenues grew to $3 million, and in the third the business made $5.5 million. Plum's revenues dipped to $2.6 million in 1986 and then rose to $3.4 million in 1987. Profits both those years were in excess of $500,000.

Plum employs six full-time staff people, which, for the time being, is just the right number. In addition, approximately a hundred free-lance production people work for the company on a consistent basis. Plum's commercial reel (and corresponding advertising agencies) includes, among other clients, Porsche for Chiat/Day, Los Angeles (see p. 287); Honda motorcycles for Dailey & Associates, Los Angeles; Miller Beer for J. Walter Thompson, New York; United

Airlines for Leo Burnett, Chicago (see p. 123); Chevrolet for Campbell Ewald, Detroit; Chevron for J. Walter Thompson, New York; Gaines Gravy Train for Chiat/Day, New York; Coca-Cola International for McCann-Erickson, New York. The company's biggest budget for a shoot was over $1 million for Chevrolet; the smallest, when it was just starting out, was $19,000 for *The San Diego Tribune*. Plum prefers large-scale logistical productions, and it will turn down work it doesn't feel is right for it. Eric Saarinen's strength is primarily visual, but if the company doesn't feel a storyboard for a commercial has a strong advertising concept and the advertising agency isn't willing to make appropriate changes, Plum won't produce it.

In 1986 Chuck Sloan started a spin-off commercial company called Blue Goose, which is known in the industry as a "tabletop" company. While Plum specializes in live action major productions, Blue Goose will do product and food shooting. So far the new company has also been successful, and Chuck Sloan has no present plans for further expansion.

(Information provided by Chuck Sloan, founder.)

REVENUES: $3.4 million in fiscal 1987.

NUMBER OF EMPLOYEES: Six full-time, permanent employees, approximately a hundred free-lancers employed on a regular basis.

LIKELIHOOD OF NEW FULL-TIME HIRES: Slim to nil in the foreseeable future.

RECRUITMENT: None.

RANGE OF SALARIES: From $18,000 for their receptionist/typist to $400,000 for the director. No figures on the president.

POLICY FOR RAISES: "Freewheeling."

TRAINING PROGRAMS: None.

BENEFITS: Insurance policy and major medical and dental insurance.

VACATION: "What we do is, I encourage people to take off during slow periods. It usually works out to about four weeks per year per employee. Regular paid holidays depend on our production schedule, except for obvious ones like the Fourth of July."

ADDITIONAL PERKS: You get to work in a real house with skylights.

BONUSES: Awarded to each full-time staff person, depending upon how well the company is doing and what kind of mood Chuck is in.

ANNUAL PARTY: Plum's first company picnic took place in spring 1987 and included the regular free-lancers as well as the full-time staff. There are currently no plans to make it an annual event. The permanent staff not infrequently go to the theater and various sporting events together.

AVERAGE WORKDAY: 8:30 A.M. to 6:00 P.M.

DRESS CODE: Anything you want. It's extremely casual. A very California beach company. "We're surfers and balloonists."

SOCIAL ATMOSPHERE: "Like a family."

CORPORATE PHILOSOPHY: "We work for love and money."

FAVORITE RESTAURANTS FOR CLIENT ENTERTAINING: The Ivy in Santa Monica or the Mandarette Café across the street.

HEADQUARTERS: Plum was headquartered in a charming three-bedroom Spanish house converted into offices, with approximately 3,500 square feet plus storage garages. Unfortunately, on March 4, 1988, this house burned to the ground. (The fire occurred at 2:00 or 3:00 A.M. "What wasn't destroyed by fire was destroyed by smoke, and the few things that were left were destroyed by the fire department." No one was hurt.) Plum, which immediately began operating out of temporary headquarters, planned to rebuild on the same site, and they should be moved back in by publication time.

CHARITABLE CONTRIBUTIONS: The company helps the homeless in Ocean Park (around Santa Monica) financially and through collecting clothes for donation, "but we don't do enough." Favorite charities are the Liberty Hill Fund and the Foundation for the Junior Blind.

SHOULD PEOPLE BOTHER TO APPLY?: "Yes, we would be interested in seeing what kinds of résumés come in. And who knows?"

INTERESTED APPLICANTS CAN SEND RÉSUMÉS TO:
Chuck Sloan
Plum Productions
317 North Kings Road
Los Angeles, CA 90048
(213) 658-7586

No one said you had to work in an enormous office to be part of corporate America. No one said you had to wear a suit and spend hours billing all your hours. No one said corporate America couldn't have a barbecue in its backyard. Welcome to Plum Productions, a commercial production company in Los Angeles.

Plum is essentially the marriage of two happily married couples: Eric Saarinen, director and cinematographer, and Toni Saarinen, business procurer, and Chuck Sloan, film entrepreneur, whose wife, writer Holly Goldberg Sloan, is an occasional production coordinator. With two permanent staff people in the cool-o stucco house they've bought in Hollywood, some permanent outside assistants, and some project-to-project free-lancers, you've got the entire organizational chart.

Nancy Walker wanted to come to L.A. after she graduated from Northern Colorado University. A technical theater major, she dreamed of getting production work here. She packed up her Honda Civic and impulsively followed the road to Hollywood, where her first job was checking cars as part of the 'bomb squad' at the 1984 summer Olympics. Relying on classified ads in the trade publications (*Variety, Hollywood Reporter,* and *Back Stage*), she interviewed for a job as office manager at Plum on a Saturday and started the following Monday. "At the time I was manager of myself. I did everything myself. Now I'm also the production coordinator." It takes no great intuition to see how pleased Nancy is with her job at this cozy company. She has learned to be resourceful and takes pride in her increased skills and responsibility. Certainly at a larger company she might not have had the range of duties and crisis management so often associated with film and video production. "The pandemonium is exciting," she bubbles, wearing pastel jeans, a plaid shirt, and sneakers, a not atypical Plum work uniform. "I learned I'm not a nine-to-five-type person. I work well under pressure—that's how you get it done. I have a sense of accomplishment.

"This job forces you to think on your feet. My gosh! When I think of the alternatives! Sometimes I'm prepping here. Or wrapping a job, or both, back to back." At this moment, Holly Goldberg Sloan walks in with her baby son, Max. Nancy leaves her desk and cuddles the red-haired infant. It's not part of her job description, but it's part of the (somewhat unconsciously) informal and intimate atmosphere at Plum. As a young single woman from out of town, Nancy has been embraced by the two founding couples, who see her very much as a surrogate younger sister. "L.A. was overwhelming at first. I hated it. My support system was back at home. I have an aunt and uncle here, but it took a good five months to adjust and feel that this was where I lived. The first thing I did was buy Thomas Brothers maps [the ubiquitous spiral-bound thick books of maps that even natives keep in their cars]." Her universe was circumscribed by Plum people. Then she enrolled in UCLA extension classes and karate classes as a way of meeting new people, and has joined a philosophy discussion group.

"Their whole philosophy here is so excellent. We don't accept work that we think someone else can do better. Eric was offered a series of commericals that had to be shot underwater and he even said he'd do it, but might not be the best. Everyone cares about quality." In the remote case that Nancy doesn't realize how highly she is regarded, let her read it here. "Two people could do her jobs, and not as well." This is Chuck Sloan speaking. "We have a responsibility to not let her down. When we do well, we give her a bonus. But if we don't, her salary won't kill us. We pay for every class she takes."

Nancy has given thought to leaving the world of commercials for feature films. Certainly it's difficult to be surrounded by heavy-duty show business and have only a toe dipped into it. After all, Hollywood can even make a game show host's chiropractor yearn for and feel entitled to a development deal with a studio or production company. And make him feel lousy if he can't get one. "Hollywood big time is in the back of my mind sometimes. But technically, commercials are the playgrounds for features. They are fast. Everyone's *so* excited a hundred and fifty percent of the time. And there's a large pool of talent. You can get the gaffer who is *the best* with trucks—specialists." One final thought: "I'm going to be here awhile because the people are so good. I'm so glad I don't feel like 'Oh, I've got to go to work.' "

Donna has been an aerobics instructor off and on since she was sixteen. She modeled and aerobicized her way around Europe, landing in Parma, Italy, where she was a "local celebrity. I had my own radio show, called *California American Girl.* It was right after the movie *Flashdance* was released. Everything I had ever dreamed of came true, but I left because I missed home [L.A.]."

She found her job as Plum's receptionist in *The Hollywood Reporter.* "First I interviewed with Nancy, then with Chuck. I could only type a little, but I guess I could do phones, and they wanted someone with a good appearance. I was chosen out of eighty people. They sent me to typing classes."

Her first day of work was "really scary. I was hoping they'd like me. I had never worked in an office-type situation before. Nancy and I are like friends. We talk about stuff and see each other outside and stuff."

Donna had been with Plum a year when we met and still managed to teach seven aerobics classes a week at Richard Simmons' school in the Valley, as well as selling roses at night in bars and restaurants. But her year revised her ambitions. "This is my career, and this is a steppingstone for me to get into commercial productions. Chuck says that that's where the money is. I want to get established. I'm very career-oriented.

"I love the people here and get along real well with them. Toni helps me whenever she can.

I love Eric's work; it's excellent. I love this house," she says of the renovated one-story, three-bedroom house with its open living room with fireplace, modern kitchen, and trim front yard. "It would be the perfect example of a first house, with one baby." (Donna's no longer at Plum.)

Merle works at Plum every Tuesday. She is the company's bookkeeper and says in a voice that rings with sincerity, "They can count on me! I have another client that I see on the fifteenth and thirtieth of every month. If those dates fall on Tuesdays, I'll go there on the fourteenth and twenty-ninth. I don't work on my birthday, though, even if it falls on a Tuesday. I'm very happy here, quite honestly. I'm satisfied with my work. I used to be able to fit it all in in one day. Now as their business has grown, I might need two days a week."

Merle had been a staff bookkeeper for several years, but she felt unappreciated and deprived of one of her pleasures: travel. As a permanent temporary, she can travel frequently to follow her two passions: hot air ballooning (she takes at least two major trips per year for that) and baseball, "the big love. The Dodgers are my team now, but I fell in love when we got the Twins," says the native Minnesotan. "Everyone knows my favorite player is Harmon Kille-brew. I went to Cooperstown [N.Y., the Baseball Hall of Fame] for his induction. I go to at least twenty to twenty-five games a year." She has no trouble getting tickets to World Series games and has attended many, whether or not her favorites are playing. A highlight was witnessing Reggie Jackson's strikeout in 1978. But back to work.

"I love working with numbers, and I always know whether I'm right or not. I only charge quality time. If I'm doing books while watching TV, I can earn some money, but I know how long a job will take." As for Plum, "I feel a part of it. When I see our commercials on TV, I get a kick out of it."

Eric Saarinen had been a cameraman for fifteen years. As such, he had to "take orders from the director. I'd never been in the Army, either. When you shot, you'd have to lobotomize yourself. It was boring and frustrating, but I learned from other people's mistakes."

Eric gave his reel of short films and industrials to Toni, who was working for Coast, a big production house in Los Angeles. And that firm unbeknownst to Saarinen, sent it on to a small advertising agency in San Diego with the notation "camera-director." He won an assignment, not knowing what the job was, never having directed a commercial. "Coast called me in for casting and wardrobe. Yikes! I didn't even know I had the job." The client was the San Diego Zoo, the stars—its animals. "I told them, 'No problem.' It wasn't even my decision to direct," he says. The campaign, called "Under Your Nose,"—which grew to six commercials—won awards for its director, Eric Saarinen, and its producer, Chuck Sloan.

"Chuck produced the series out of his house, and it was so much fun. When you're a cameraman, you can be replaced. A cameraman is asked about wardrobe, but no one cares about his opinion. Not a director; they're irreplaceable."

With a background in art and a father famous for his vision—he was the architect and designer Eero Saarinen—Eric spent the sixties traveling around with his movie camera. He was on the stage of the Ambassador Hotel in L.A. when Robert Kennedy was shot. (Although the footage has been seen and incorporated into the body of documentation of that event, it mysteriously disappeared from his possession.) He shot the Rolling Stones' documentary, *Gimme Shelter*. He also shot all of Albert Brooks's feature film comedies.

These days it's impossible to read an interview with a commercial director who doesn't speak of his dream of directing feature films. Many film directors werre introduced to their audiences by Madison Avenue: Steve *(Arthur)* Gordon, Ridley *(Alien)* Scott, Tony *(Top Gun)* Scott, Alan *(Angel Heart)* Parker, Adrien *(Fatal Attraction)* Lyne. It is almost shocking, therefore, to hear Saarinen talk about his goals behind the lens. "I don't want to shoot features anymore. I hate them. They take you away from your family, from real life." Eric and Toni now have two small sons, Evan, who is three weeks younger than Max Sloan, and Elliott, who is three weeks younger than Calvin Sloan. "I much prefer commercials. A one-day shoot means a week of my time (and more for Nancy). A two-day shoot means two weeks. Unlike features, there's immediate gratification. You shoot the commercial one week, and you see it the next week. That's great."

Saarinen bids for jobs against some of the world's most esteemed cinematographers—the class of cameramen with unpronounceable names who routinely win Academy Awards. But the thing is, increasingly, Eric's winning the commissions. "I'm extremely competitive. A lot of it is being able to describe a shot." As an example, he cites, " 'Alpine glow.' Agencies go nuts when you say it. It means the soft, golden light when the sun goes down." This is not a guy who's vocabulary is populated by "baby" and "hot." Unlike many visually oriented people, Saarinen is verbally expressive, too. "They can trot me out on a leash. I think of paintings. Vermeer's my favorite painter."

Saarinen's work is painterly, or perhaps moviely. His commercials look rich and cinematic. No kids hovering over cereal or toilet bowls for him. Toni says, "He's really an artist—nothing ends up the way it started." But Eric is quite focused on being a good businessman. "Your work may be great, but if it's not national, so what?" Toni is proud of him. "He can grow within the business. He's profitable. He always comes within the budget.

"The toughest part of starting the company was getting creatives and producers [agency people] just to see our reel. It is hard to establish credibility. Now we have friends and contacts, and they know what to expect." As of this moment, Plum's reel includes a series of commercials for J. Walter Thompson, McCann-Erickson, Foote, Cone, & Belding, Leo Burnett, Grey Advertising, and Chiat/Day.

Eric would prefer to be selected for the "right reasons—my reel—rather than the wrong ones—a lottery, which is debilitating. I try to bring something more to the commercials; I try to do better than they anticipate. I shoot commercials in the rain and pretend that it's sunny. Our reel is what we do, not what they do." Advertising agencies don't expect a final cut from the directors; "usually just raw footage. They don't pay me for a cut, but I ask for it. I'm a filmmaker."

The partnership between Eric and Chuck appears to be rather problem-free. Saarinen says, "It's all Chuck. He takes all the financial risks. I feel beholden to him. I had some money before, but now . . . we make a lot of money." He is so modest and matter-of-fact that he talks about finances like someone who doesn't know what to do with all his success. He's giving some thought to taking a course offered by the Directors' Guild of America on how to deal with Sudden Success Syndrome.

Chuck Sloan enlisted in the army and arrived in Germany with Elvis Presley, whom he met twice. Although a Hollywood High School dropout, he attended Valley Junior College, where starting his own businesses seemed unavoidable. As a student entrepreneur, he started two companies a year, from construction to parking lots. "My survival was never working for anyone. I never really fit into structures and authority."

His introduction to production work came after a period of "bumming around." Sloan's best friend, a propmaster, needed help for a beer commercial. "That meant providing cold beer. There are tricks in the beer business, though: how to chill glasses, how to pour, how to show beer on camera. I made $1,500 a week for a six-week shoot. I observed other people and their jobs and was offered a staff position as a propmaster-producer.

"Everything I had done was applicable to this. The job was finding solutions to crises." Within four years Sloan had his own production company with fourteen directors, making it one of the largest in the business.

In 1982, flat broke, ("I was involved with a motion picture project that went sour, and I went sour with it") Chuck met Holly Goldberg, his wife-to-be, and received a phone call from Eric Saarinen, a young director who needed a producer for a series of commercials he'd been commissioned to do for the San Diego Zoo. "It was karmic," Chuck recalls. "This is a director-oriented business. Eric was obviously new to directing, but he was a natural. And we had fun working together."

Thus, the beginnings of Plum, named by Holly. "It was like an Andy Hardy movie. It wasn't planned. We all liked each other, and it evolved. It was as if a light bulb went off over our heads. All of a sudden we got an office and had to borrow ten thousand dollars on our credit cards to have a cash flow for our first job." While many successful companies are the result of long-term planning, organizational charts, and mission statements, no one says you can't start one on the spur of the moment, just because you and your friends like to work together.

Holly's philosophy is "We all brought our little ingredients to our soup. We're two small families, with two small babies apiece. There's a partnership between Eric and us, even though we own it. We're different. He's the filmmaker, and Sloan's the businessman. The Sloans and the Saarinens have a similar sense of esthetics. We all have fun together. It is like a marriage. We've got to work at it. We must collaborate and communicate."

Sloan speaks. "After a year Toni came here to sell. We had a low overhead—our sales reps got commissions but worked out of their homes. We put our money in front of the camera." When talking about Plum, Sloan, who looks like a sunburnt yachtsman and talks like a sailor, sounds like the company president he is. "We were cost-effective. We had two phases of pricing. Now, after a few years, we're earning hundreds of thousands."

Obviously, the prospering Plum has the option of growing, of hiring more personnel, of doing some aggressive marketing, of accepting all work that comes its way. "We have directors approaching us all the time. Maybe we'd hire a second director, but we wouldn't hire a third. It's very important for Eric to feel as good about another director as I would. We couldn't have a conflict with Eric's style. Adding another director doesn't double your problems; it quadruples them.

"We're learning to be satisfied as a small company," Chuck says. "Which is philosophically different from a large one. This is not our whole lives. Longevity is the quality of work, not the quantity. I don't want to be miserable en route to the bank. How much money do you need? We make enough money. We definitely earn within the top one percent in our field, and this is so *uncorporate* America. What we need is the time to spend the money. This has satisfied me on a personal level, too. We go out and do our jobs. I'm really happy with the way it's turned out."

SECURITY PACIFIC CORPORATION

SECURITY PACIFIC CORPORATION

HISTORY & OPERATIONS

Security Pacific Corporation, the holding company for California's second largest and the country's seventh-largest bank (in addition to diverse international financial services operations), was formed from the mergers of several California banks. The first occurred in 1929, when Los Angeles First National Trust and Savings Bank merged with Security Trust and Savings Bank to form Security–First National Bank of Los Angeles. Unlike many other states, California permitted banks to open statewide branches, and both banks had proliferated accordingly. At the time of the merger, Los Angeles First National, which was founded by local entrepreneur Hiram Mabury in 1875, had ninety-four branches in the southern half of the state. Security Trust and Savings Bank, founded by Joseph Satori in 1889, had grown to forty-eight branches in Los Angeles and Orange County. After the merger, with more than $600 million in assets and over 142 branches covering the entire southern portion of California, Security–First National was among the ten largest banks in the country.

Over the next twenty years, including the Depression and World War II, the bank held off on further growth. During the fifties, Security–First National began expanding by opening new branches and acquiring other banks. It first merged with the Citizens Bank of Riverside, founded in 1903, and then with the Security Trust and Savings Bank of San Diego, which was started by merchant Abraham Blochman in 1893 as the Blochman Banking Company. The mergers added forty-five branches. Also during the decade, Security–First National merged with the Farmers and Merchants Bank, the oldest of its components. It was founded in 1871 by John G. Downey—a dry goods merchant who became a banker because he possessed the only safe in town—and his partner, Isaias W. Hellman.

In 1968, under a new management trio comprised of Chairman and CEO Frederick Larkin, Jr., President Carl Hartnack, and Head of International and Corporate Banking Richard Flamson III, Security–First National adopted a threefold strategy for further growth: It expanded its corporate banking activities, aggressively pursuing customers in the East and Midwest, in order to better serve large corporations; it began expanding overseas in order to participate more fully in international finance and better serve multinational companies; and it expanded into northern California in order to become a statewide bank.

As the first step in its northern expansion, Security–First National merged with Pacific National Bank of San Francisco, the largest single-office bank in the western part of the country, to form Security Pacific National Bank (its permanent name). The bank has continued to expand its California presence by merging with a number of additional regional banks. And the bank expanded internationally to twenty-six foreign countries—primarily in the Pacific Rim—among them Hong Kong, Japan, Singapore, the Philippines, Switzerland, the United Kingdom, Belgium, West Germany, New Zealand, and Canada.

In 1971 the Security Pacific management formed the Security Pacific Corporation as a holding company for the bank—a move which left the holding company free to diversify into nontraditional banking services. Since then, Security Pacific has diversified more ambitiously and aggressively than most of the country's larger banks into a broad range of financial services.

Richard Flamson III, who joined Security–First National upon his graduation from college in 1955, took over as president and CEO in 1978. In 1980, as chairman, Flamson continued diversifying the bank's services according to a cautious, step-by-step acquisition strategy. As illustrated by Flamson's catchphrase, "We don't bet the bank," Security Pacific never makes an acquisition large enough to devastate the company if it turns out to be a mistake. The corporation starts out slowly when it enters a new area of financial services, normally by opening a single office in a particular field. If the office thrives, the corporation opens additional offices, and if expansion proves successful, it acquires companies in the field. Under this diversification strategy, Security Pacific Corporation has entered into numerous and disparate nonbanking businesses, including venture capital, leasing, discount brokerage, insurance, mortgage banking, corporate and government bond dealing, data processing services, and stockbrokering in London.

Flamson structured Security Pacific Corporation to resemble a loosely knit confederation of entrepreneurial businesses. Rather than expanding to create an integrated network, the bank enters new businesses only if they can be profitable on their own—almost as if they were freestanding companies. As part of a plan to encourage entrepreneurial initiative among the corporation's top executives, Flamson instituted an incentive compensation program through which a substantial portion of executives' earnings come from performance-determined bonuses.

In recent years, Security Pacific Corporation has been making acquisitions outside of California, initially to expand its banking network throughout the West. In 1986 it acquired Arizona BancWest, the second largest bank in Arizona. In 1987 it acquired Rainier Bank, the second largest bank in the state of Washington and—with assets of $9.3 billion at year's end —among the top banks in the West. That year, the company also acquired Orbanco, now

Orbanco, now Oregon BanCorp, the fourth largest bank in Oregon (with $1 billion in assets), and agreed to acquire the Nevada National Bank Corporation, the holding company for Nevada National Bank, the third largest bank in Nevada (with $640 million in assets) (estimated closing: January 1, 1989). In February 1988 Security Pacific announced plans to purchase Hibernia Bank, the oldest state-chartered bank in California. Flamson, who believes that Congress will loosen restrictions on interstate banking in the near future, ultimately intends to extend Security Pacific's network of banking operations across the country.

Today, with 43,300 employees working in 1,350 offices around the world, Security Pacific Corporation has assets of roughly $73 billion and ranks as the seventh largest bank holding company in the country and the country's second largest branch bank. The bank is organized into three primary business groups, each of which contributes roughly a third of total earnings: The California Banking and Real Estate Industries System, which provides consumer and commercial banking and financial services in California and administers the company's commercial real estate operations throughout the country. The division is subdivided into the California Commercial Group, the Bank-Related Business Division, and the Real Estate Industries Group. The Merchant Bank administers the worldwide activities of the corporation and the bank in the areas of wholesale banking, capital markets, investments and securities. It provides both banking and nonbanking services domestically and internationally to businesses, governments, and other institutions, including lending, advising, and securities-related activities such as trading, brokerage, and processing. The Financial Services System, which is involved in leasing, consumer and commercial financing, venture capital, discount brokerage, and credit insurance activities. The system is made up of the Consumer Services Group, the Commercial Finance and Leasing Group, and the Venture Capital Group. An additional part of the organization is the Security Pacific Automation Company, which develops advanced technology systems for the company's worldwide activities and oversees all of its data processing functions.

(Information provided by Michael Bandick and Ed Hoffer, bank spokesmen.)

TOTAL ASSETS: $72.8 billion as of December 31, 1987.

EARNINGS: $15.7 million in net income in 1987. "Excluding the lower developing countries reserve addition, earnings would have been $518.3 million, which would have represented a 14 percent increase from 1986."

OFFICES: 600 banking offices in California, 300 banking offices in Oregon, Arizona, and Washington, and 450 additional locations in forty-six states and twenty-seven foreign countries.

NUMBER OF EMPLOYEES: 43,300 worldwide.

AVERAGE AGE OF EMPLOYEES: Security Pacific does not keep figures. "The corporation is so big that average age isn't relevant."

TURNOVER: Company will not disclose.

RECRUITMENT: The only part of the company that consistently recruits is the Merchant Bank, which looks for MBAs "at only a handful of schools." The bank also visits colleges throughout

California and the rest of the country, but recruitment is handled locally and is too decentralized for the company to mention individual schools.

NUMBER OF NEW HIRES PER YEAR: Information not available. "It depends on the year."

RANGE OF STARTING SALARIES: The bank will not disclose. "We hire everything from tellers to Harvard MBAs. There's such a diversity of entry-level positions that there's also a diversity of starting salaries. Our salaries are competitive with industry standards. That's what we base them on."

POLICY FOR RAISES: "The frequency and amount of each raise are determined on annual performance reviews and based solely on merit—no cost-of-living increases. Depending on your performance review you get X percent, and you're eligible for another raise in X months. It's not only a difference in amount, but a difference in eligibility for the next raise."

TRAINING PROGRAMS: "In every case, yes. But at the same time, it's so diverse that there's no specific 'Welcome to Security Pacific.' Different positions have different training programs, and they're all done on a decentralized basis."

BENEFITS: The bank offers a number of plans and employees choose their options depending on their situation. "It's a cafeteria plan. Employees are allotted a certain amount of benefit dollars, and they allocate them to whatever benefits they want." The amount each employee is granted depends on his or her position. If employees choose benefits that exceed their allotment, the difference is taken out of their paychecks. If they choose benefits that cost less than their allotment, that amount is added to their paychecks.

VACATION: "It's based on salary level and seniority and is too complicated to explain." Plus eleven or twelve regular paid holidays per year.

ADDITIONAL PERKS: Tuition reimbursement in the field of financial services. An employee loan division where employees receive discounts on interest rates and other sorts of banking fees. "Thrift Plus," where pretax or posttax income can be "invested" in any or all of four funds that are managed by the company; after two years of employment, the company matches funds in that program. At the position of first vice-president and above, employees are eligible for stock options. Parking, health clubs, etc., are left up to the discretion of the specific unit. For example, at Security Pacific Plaza, employees get subsidized parking. Rather than the normal rate of $160 per month, employees pay only $35. Also, the company has one of the most comprehensive counseling referral services of any corporation in the country. Through their Employee Assistance Program, employees can seek a full range of professional counseling services with complete anonymity. The company also has a program called "P.S. Can We Talk?" which provides peer counseling led by other employees in the corporation who have dealt with problems similar to theirs.

BONUSES: The company has what it calls "incentive compensation," which is based on merit and handled by some individual units.

ANNUAL PARTY: No companywide parties. "On lower levels, meaning in individual departments or even in an entire region, there's a strong push for that kind of fraternization. However, the corporation is too big to make generalizations. Parties range from everything from golf tournaments to Saturday picnics to Christmas parties."

DRESS CODE: "Conservative business attire."

SOCIAL ATMOSPHERE: Again, the corporation is too big to generalize. "It differs by department. There is a great deal of off-hours socializing among various factions within the company."

AVERAGE WORKDAY: "An average shift is eight hours. That's what personnel would say. But again, you can't generalize. Obviously, it depends on individual work load."

HEADQUARTERS: The company leases thirteen floors in Security Pacific Plaza, a fifty-five story building in downtown Los Angeles. The plaza itself is a rectangular space, with the building on one side and the remainder a grassy, tree-lined area that overlooks "the equivalent of an outdoor atrium." Between the grassy area and the building itself is a huge red Alexander Calder sculpture called *Four Arches*. In addition, the bank leases a twenty-nine-story building directly across the Harbor Freeway on Beaudry Street.

CHARITABLE CONTRIBUTIONS: $5.4 million in 1987. The corporation generally gives to California charities and is "heavily committed to supporting the United Way as well as other organizations in other areas." The Security Pacific Foundation gives cash awards of $1,000 and up to over a thousand recipients.

INTERESTED APPLICANTS CAN SEND RÉSUMÉS TO:
Security Pacific Corporation
Recruiting
333 South Hope, W17-25
Los Angeles, CA 90071
(213) 345-6211

You've seen the sculpture—*Four Arches,* the giant (63-by-57⅜-by-40¼-foot) red (to be more correct, "Calder red") painted steel sculpture (to be more correct, it's a stabile) by Alexander Calder that has become a landmark among monumental works that grace corporate headquarters. Now meet the building. The location is downtown Los Angeles. The company: Security Pacific Corporation, holding company of Security Pacific Bank and the second largest branch bank in the country.

The art collection is only one indication of the priorities of the company within. (The list of artists represented runs to seven pages, four columns to a page.) Security Pacific appears to care about the quality of life of the people who work there. (The coffee table–sized book with selections from the collection says, "In 1982 a reevaluation of Security Pacific's collection took place. An increase in automated banking had cut down the need for large-scale works. Smaller, more intimate pieces are now being purchased. Art is being recycled to new locations as buildings are remodeled or other spaces are developed.") Security Pacific has a pronounced interest in human resources, which provides extensive services to employees.

Tony Kramer is a vice-president in human resources, and he's been with the bank for eighteen years. Loyal to his function, if a stranger were to ask him what he did for a living, he'd say, "I work for a bank in personnel." In fact, he devotes much of his time and energy to Security Pacific's Employee Assistance Program (EAP), "a generic title for a program that's supposed to retain valuable employees and enhance their value and their success for the benefit of them and the bank and the community." He created the program fourteen years ago, and it was one of the first in the country. Kramer says it sees two "customer populations": 60

percent are employees looking for advice and wanting to get involved in community activities, and 40 percent seek help for personal problems. "We provide a structure and support for future steps. It's a personal process to help them keep their jobs. It's not, 'Take a number.' "

Approximately 700–1,000 employees take advantage of the service, "all on a voluntary basis, half are self-referrals and half are supervisor referrals. If they don't come here, the office can't find them," Kramer laments. "We must present a reasonable picture of the office when they're well, so that when they're not, they'll approach us." Tony's strategy for positive PR for the EAP consists of giving talks to various bank groups. In 1987 the office gave 129 talks to more than four thousand people (a little less than one fifth of Security Pacific's California population). "It's not uncommon for someone to call—having heard an office member speak years ago—when they get stuck." Clearly, making the initial phone call is not easy. Although confidentiality is assured, seeking counsel is an acknowledgment of a problem that may have gone unreported for a long time. Kramer says that many calls begin with the preamble, " 'I never thought I'd be giving you a call.' I'm the first step. I give an affirmation that they can feel badly.

"On a self-referral, no one in the organization is made aware of the phone call without the caller's permission. When a supervisor calls, we'll say, 'Yes, he [your employee] called.' We don't reveal the nature of the problem. We ask the supervisor to support the employee's progress—they need to give good feedback."

Interestingly, the majority (65 percent) of the calls are about marriage and family-related issues and 20 percent are problems related to alcohol and drugs. "Very often the person hasn't verbalized this before. We help them focus on the precipitating event or situation. We don't promise them a magic answer.

"When people first call, it's to arrange a good time to talk. We'll accept a collect call from a pay phone [to ensure anonymity] or call them in the evening [to ensure privacy] or meet them in a nonbank environment [to ensure support]. A twenty-four-hour hotline overdramatizes the situation into catastrophe. These are not emergency calls. If you're feeling terrible and talk to someone with respect for you and your problems, it makes you feel okay for one to three days. We don't ask names. They volunteer them."

Kramer has a master's degree in education and counseling guidance. His colleagues have advanced degrees in family guidance, alcoholism, and related areas. A well-organized and extensive peer support program developed by the human resources team, called "P.S. Can We Talk?" is the talk of human resources circles. Security Pacific has developed a network of employees who've survived crises, addictions, traumas, or just run-of-the-mill anxiety and are willing to help others going through them. "I feel that peer support will be widely imitated," Kramer says. "It's economical, and it's good culture."

Why does the EAP mean so much to him and the bank? "There's so little sense of community outside the job. This provides continuity. We spend most of our awake time at the office. And Security Pacific wants to be a good corporate citizen." He believes that in a few years, the EAP will become standard operating procedure for all concerned companies. Who can afford not to care about their employees?

On a lighter note, human resources is also responsible for career counseling, which is a different task in the eighties than it was in previous decades. "What used to be a thirty-five-year career is now six five- or six-year careers."

Michael Bandick and Rosi Cordoba are two young people who started their careers at Security Pacific. (Bandick has since moved on.) During college at California Polytechnic State University at San Luis Obispo and the University of Southern California, respectively, they had paid internships in the bank in corporate communications. Neither had a banking background or had studied business. They say the transition from intern to "real employee" means a stronger commitment to the organization. "It's different. I know if I see an article on banking, I have to read it. That's fun." It's also fun for them to be part of a well-respected corporation in which they can feel like grown-ups. Rosi comments on the conservative wardrobe she's felt compelled to wear. "At first I had a lot of neat stuff I knew I'd never wear here. It wasn't a problem." Mike appreciates how his new attire ages him. "Being younger, it makes me seem more serious. It helps. I don't have a commanding voice over the phone."

Mike and Rosi have expressed high hopes for their careers. "I want my criteria to be met," one of them says. "The most important one is excitement. Things here change fast. I wanted to work for people I could respect and learn from. The second I feel I'm a leg up on people, I stop listening." Their lack of financial background has not been a problem. "We pick up enough to be able to explain stuff. If I came here without the internship, you could believe I'd be up till two A.M. [cramming]. As an intern, you can do no wrong. They don't expect much." The bank hires approximately ten interns a year to handle internal and external communications, two at a time all the time. "It's not a farm system. It didn't look like there'd be spots for us at first."

Interning helps you get to know who the players are. The employee phone directory is as thick as the metropolitan phone book. It's bewildering. When they read through the list of approximately 43,300 people, they want to know "Who does what and are they on the fast track? Now [within their first few months as salaried employees] we're pretty much up to speed. We really feel a part of it—since we're in the head office and responsive to the movements of the company as a company." Mike says, "I don't feel like one of 35,000. You can actually boil down decision makers and newsmakers to a manageable number. There's a certain facelessness to the lower ranks, but it's less anonymous than most college campuses."

Corporate Communications, where Mike worked, requires a great deal of writing and accountability. "The buck stops here. We'll explain, package, et cetera, on a no-credit-for-us basis. It adds up, but it's hard to count." As for the writing, he cautioned, "If you don't like writing, forget interning." He was the associate editor of *Security News,* the bank's flagship publication. It's a bimonthly distributed by mail to every employee. Most of his articles did not carry his byline. "I worked for the college newspaper; it was a thrill to see my name in print." But then again, he didn't have a corporate publisher or have to wear a suit in college. Bandick described *California Banker,* another in-house publication, as "kind of wow, splashy." It is circulated only in the banking system. "It's coffee table material." It's a well-designed monthly detailing promotions, birthdays, and other light news, and distributed within the retail banking system, with some copies available to customers. Mike said, "I write in different styles for both."

Rosi's in External Communications (press relations). She does a lot of reading and pitches stories to the press. Every morning starts with her gathering general and financial news and the Dow-Jones averages off the wire services and from the morning papers, which she distills into a one-pager called *MorningLine,* which is distributed around the whole company and is on most people's desks by the time they arrive. "It used to take two hours. Now it takes forty minutes," she says happily. She repeats the task every afternoon for *NoonLine.*

Cordoba is also attached to the automation group. "I never thought I'd read computer magazines! I'm picking up a lot of terms, market information, and names. Any information that goes out [of the bank] is filtered through this office. We're careful to balance everything. We're not going to release a press release on a new product the same day as our earnings report.

"Security Pacific is in every title. Even if it's only a name, it implies their support. We are connected. Our reputation and billions back it up." She says she feels a real loyalty toward this organization. "But I didn't become loyal the first day. It was gradual. At first, it's easy to get real positive real fast. It's a head rush to see your own name on stationery or a folder with the company logo. I feel an intangible, 'This is your life. It's started.' " Both Rosi and Mike were elevated to officer level their first month, which is unusual. "Now we have 'business card clout.' Like, here you go. [Rosi also finds the dramatically subsidized parking for employees, which she was not entitled to as an intern, "thrilling."] We're the youngest, but we're taken seriously. I worked really hard in college, too. It's different here because we don't get graded right away. People send memos saying, 'Good job.' It means more."

Because they feel the bank has vested them with responsibility and respect, they are conscientious about proving their worth. "There's no homework, but I do take stuff home. Because I want to."

Vernon Crowder is a vice-president and economist at Security Pacific. Raised in Pasadena, he lost his eyesight at the age of ten or twelve. The only indication that he is blind comes from the presence of Klodi, his Seeing Eye dog. And the fact that Vernon talks about it. When he enrolled at the University of California at Riverside, he became a psychology major in order to be a counselor, but when he found he did better in economics and enjoyed it more, he switched. Besides, he says, "I had a low tolerance for people who didn't help themselves." After earning his bachelor's degree, he stayed on for his MBA. "In hindsight, it would have been better to go to a big-name school. At that time, I knew of no other blind people who were MBAs. How do you get a job? How do you show people you can do it? It's no problem not seeing to solve problems. The problem was proving that."

When Crowder finished business school in 1975, it was during the recession and a record 10½ percent unemployment. "I didn't indicate my blindness on my résumé during my first job search. It was a mistake. It was better the next round without the shock value. I had very few interviews, but the ones I had were very serious." Vernon did not want to stay in Los Angeles. He was aiming for San Francisco or Denver. "I didn't think of banking. I thought about personnel and labor relations or marketing."

He couldn't find a job. "In school I had felt brave and pretty damn confident. I figured I could pretty much do what I wanted. During those ten and a half months of unemployment, I was feeling pretty beat up. I was scared. I was newly married and running out of money. I was rethinking my plans." Why was he having trouble getting work? "It's very hard to get honest assessments from people," he says.

He found his way to Security Pacific through a tenacious vice-president in Market Research, "one of the few black SVPs here, a twenty-year Army retiree. I feel I owe the guy who hired me a lot. I must stand by him. He wanted to hire me based on my résumé. He couldn't hire me himself. He needed a department." Which was Economic Research. "I got tired of being asked the same questions, but it showed me I could sell anything. The guys who hired me did it as work, but also as an experiment." It was 1976.

"I had total responsibility for big projects. My boss helped me through." Then the divisional structure changed, Market Research began reporting to the Marketing Department, and Vernon's boss was no longer his boss. Vernon continued in Economic Research. "I had to learn to do my job with minimal support. My wife helped, too. We had to get into a routine. Getting dressed. Arriving here early. I had to move to work here. I came here out of boxes. There were a lot of changes and adjustments at once. Our arrangement was, I clean; my wife cooks. I still don't know where stuff is. If my wife ever leaves me, I hope she marks everything."

Crowder was wary of becoming the token blind guy. "At first, I impressed people. If you can walk and talk, you impress people. I was 'the blind person.' As soon as I worked with people and they saw I could contribute, they appreciated me." He became a troubleshooter for the bank, specializing in agriculture without the benefit of a single agriculture class. "I'm now considered an agricultural economist and an agricultural analyst for the bank. Now they think they'll hire other blind people because of me. You've got to look normal, dress well, and make people forget you're blind." While he does not feel he's on display here, Vernon mentions that "the bank is very careful about having me appear in stuff like this, in interviews."

He confesses that his career at the bank suffered a setback three years before. "It was due to a manager who was intimidated by me. Essentially, I blew it. Even though I consider him to be a poor manager and insecure, I didn't adapt to him. And he's not uncommon. Those who can't take honest criticism certainly can't give it."

Crowder had been with the bank ten years when we met. "While I have a lot of respect here, it's time to go. I'm burned out. There's salary room, but if I get more raises, I'll be priced out of other jobs. And I'm oriented toward security and am scared to do something I might fail at. I'm not a real live economist and don't want to be one. I'm not real skilled in the agricultural thing. I'm not an agronomist." He wants to try being a credit officer. "I'm looking to like work. Everyone knows I can do this, but I can't read financials." He has stayed put, thus far, anyway, because "it's an asset having been respected here." He's unsure of his real value to the bank. "I can't tell you I've managed twenty people . . . "

Kathy, Chuck and Kit, work with Marcia Gold-Levenson in the Foreign Exchange Department. [Author's note: WARNING: *The culture they are about to describe is not an accurate reflection of the entire bank.* I REPEAT: *The culture they are about to describe is not an accurate reflection of the entire bank.*] They work in a trading room that has all the frenzy and excitement of a live auction. It's very much a world unto its own, with a different schedule, pulse, and feel from the "regular" retail bank. "It's not like working in a bank" is the consensus of the group. Marcia says, "The people in this room don't fit traditional banking. There's constant pressure. You never know what your day will be like. I don't feel I'm a banker. I couldn't work in credit. It would drive me up a wall."

Everyone agrees that the entrepreneurial spirit is alive. "You're doing it for yourself. We're rewarded in bonuses. The rest of the bank is catching up to us. We're not totally isolated. We know others."

What do they do? "We buy and sell contracts of foreign currency. We do everything from traveler's checks to multinationals needing money. We solicit customers. Over the phone, from the president of a company to a treasury analyst to someone's secretary. We physically call on customers at lunches, speeches, special events." Since cash, even that minted in other countries, usually has a nonnegotiable value, Security Pacific can't offer it for different prices, much as it might like to. Its competitive edge is in service. "It's a service-and-personality business, and we have better service." Someone's come up with a good phrase that will work perfectly here. "We're international trade marketers."

They draw distinctions between what they do as international trade marketers and what the traders do. "We're divorced from trading. We maintain relationships; they don't. Their pressure is net profit and loss; ours is pleasing our customers." Yet everyone here feels his or her first allegiance is to the bank, *then* to the customers. "We take a longer-term approach. The majority of corporate customers don't speculate. We can service better with global banks. Traders accuse us of servicing our customers more than them. Traders make money based on opportunity that's brought to them. The in-house rivalry between us and them is in most trading rooms. It's the nature of the business." The floor is home to nine people in marketing and twelve of the dreaded traders.

"This department isn't known for a lot of 'please and thank-yous.' The market doesn't wait for you. You must be very aggressive. The job makes you less patient. It makes you more opinionated. You become more confident or act more confident. You exude it from a sales standpoint."

Could anyone do whatever it is they do? "A lot is gut feel," someone answers. "Some people are gifted. You don't last in this business without a knack. That, they don't teach. It's like handicapping a race. You know how the market thinks. It's not like gambling," someone else clarifies, "it's like an apprenticeship. We should be more than 50 percent sure. You should be one step ahead—no more—of the stock market." Everyone in the room groans at the mention of "Black Friday," September 23, 1984, "the most volatile day in the Deutsche mark." (My visit predated "Black Monday," October 19, 1987.) No confidence, knack, talent, or bookie could have predicted the wily currency that day. "You feel terrible if it doesn't work. You know you tried your best; it's the human factor. You're only as good as your last trade. Just try to make it back. Our management is confident in us. You could have a month filled with bad luck, but we're probably not alone." Conflicts do arise when one customer wants the market to go one way and another is counting on the reverse. Oh, well.

Another voice. "Security Pacific is more progressive. They'll let you do stuff if you prove its profitability. They allow you to experiment. Cause and effect aren't always visible or in place. I think all my ideas were tried out. Security Pacific is making leaps and bounds as a merchant bank. We try for creativity."

Interview:

MARTIN RANSOHOFF, PRODUCER

A lot of people who make deals with film producer Martin Ransohoff may have no idea that he was responsible for TV's *Mr. Ed, Green Acres,* and *The Beverly Hillbillies,* to name a few of the huge hits he enjoyed as the founder and CEO of Filmways. (Think back to hearing Ellie Mae, actress Donna Douglas, cheering you good-bye, saying in her twang, "This has been a Filmways Presentation!") We are talking in the Beverly Hills offices of Albacore Productions, Ransohoff's production company. (He has another suite of offices on the Columbia Pictures lot in Burbank.) Sparsely furnished, with just a few framed stills on the wall, most of them of his movie *Class,* Marty is, as usual, dressed casually in khakis and a plaid sports shirt.

Born in New Orleans and raised in Connecticut, Marty attended Colgate University, class of 1949. As a history and English major, he says, "A super liberal arts college was real important to me—with the emphasis on the 'liberal.' I was much more able to handle the bullshit courses, hair frizzing and basket weaving. Language was 'mild Spanish.'" He remembers one economics class in particular, in which the professor asked his students how many of them expected to earn ten thousand dollars one day. Ransohoff was one of the few who did not raise his hand.

His brutal winters in upstate New York were interrupted by a call to action: He was summoned by Cecil "Scoop" Wilkenson, the executive director of the national Phi Gamma Deltas, to spend his last term at Louisiana State University colonizing (setting up, for all you non-Greeks) the Phi Gamma fraternity. Marty was chosen because he'd been born in New Orleans. "It was absurd, because—as I pointed out—I hadn't been in New Orleans since I was six." Since Colgate's dean was a Phi Gam, Ransohoff was given a residential waiver. "The call came in January, and I was starting out toward my car, which I could not see. It was quite a madcap idea." It was Ransohoff's first experience at fund raising, tracking Phi Gams who lived in the Baton Rouge area to finance a new frat house.

After graduation, the (then popular) idea of becoming a traveling sales rep "driving a business coupe filled with Vick's bottles and Crisco" was clearly not a first choice. "A number of companies put you in the coupe, and that's how you spent your next two years. When you have no skills, like me, there's a horror that takes over. I didn't want a Vick's jar on my door. I had logo shyness."

Wall Street did not beckon the young Ransohoff, either. "It was where a lot of losers went. There were just so many things a guy like me could do." The most palatable option was joining the training program of an advertising agency, but Marty took it one step further and thought he'd have a better experience in the mailroom. "I answered the question 'What do you do?' with 'The training program at Y&R.' I never mentioned the mailroom."

Getting bored after three or four months, Marty found out that graduation from the mailroom meant "counting Schlitz cans on Broadway. I couldn't handle it. I counted Schlitz cans in a deli on Amsterdam Avenue and said, 'To hell with it.' 'Market research,'" he says with a harrumph. "I started to think of that business coupe with fondness."

Working in advertising with a fraternity brother and selling cars at a Ford dealership netted Ransohoff enough money to go to Europe on a tramp steamer ($110 one way). He lived on the continent for eight months, his room costing eight dollars a week, with board less than twenty dollars. During a road trip with a friend, he made the startling decision that he wanted to go into broadcasting. It was 1951. He returned to the States to find himself part of an enormous peer upheaval: His buddies were getting married and having kids.

Now married himself, at twenty-three Ransohoff found a job at Caravelle, "an old documentary/training film company. I was a film salesman and 'producer,' which meant 'sales.' We made training films and TV commercials. They put me on commission. I made a lot of money. I got the Ford account. I earned between twenty and twenty-five thousand dollars. Then I got into a hassle with them over money. I got pissed off and left. I formed Filmways as a TV commercial production house in 1952. I was twenty-four. What happened at Caravelle did not happen at Filmways. Lesson: Whenever I had successful guys working for me, I paid them as much as I possibly could. I remembered my experience and getting fed up. I had delivered for them, and instead of giving me a bonus, they hassled me. I often wondered what would have happened to me if they had treated me well."

Filmways started small. With partner Ed Kasper, "we had a 16 mm print lab, and an office and a phone and a secretary. I had a pregnant wife who was not working, living in a snappy $12,000 house in Noroton, Connecticut, and I was broke. I didn't know fucko when I walked out of Caravelle." From 1952 to 1959, Filmways grossed about $3--$4 million. In 1969 that figure grew to $100 million. "Don't forget," Marty adds, "I never raised my hand in economics class expecting to earn ten thousand dollars."

What made Filmways so successful? In 1957 we took a 1957 or 1958 Ford for test drives around the world. We started in Detroit and ended in Detroit." Twenty-six commercials came out of that mileage, including the world's first $1 million commercial shoot. And who were the guys at Ford who worked with Ransohoff? Lee Iacocca and Robert McNamara. "Selling our commercials through J. Walter Thompson, our clients were Ted Bates, JWT, Benton & Bowles, D'Arcy, N. W. Ayer, and Foote, Cone and Belding. Why? We were good.

"I was a two-martini guy at '21' [the '21' Club]. I did the full Madison Avenue trip. I had to grind. We moved to a snappy $19,000 house on a half acre in West Norwalk [Connecticut].

"I had a break because I had lost a lot of hair. So I could stretch my real age. The Ford guys would have had heart attacks if they knew I was twenty-nine."

Seven years later, Ransohoff took Filmways public. "I was thirty or thirty-one when it went public, and I think I was the youngest head of a listed company on the American and maybe New York Stock Exchange. We got a lot of attention. We were the first non–movie company in this area (commercial production) to go public."

Until Filmways' 1PO, Ransohoff maintains he never had a master plan. "The commercial thing was tedious, repetitious. The movie thing didn't appeal to me. Hollywood? No one from Connecticut came here. Why? We weren't related to anyone. 'The industry was impenetrable,' went the myth." Which is not to say he minded Los Angeles. "We had a West Coast operation. I always liked it. I'd come out here in the winter. I directed commercials here myself." His next goal was to "expand into programming." The Ransohoff family, now numbering six, was living on a wooded acre in Darien with a pool and cost $58,000. Marty bought out his partner.

"I'd love to say 'I mapped it out,' but I didn't. I didn't go to Harvard Business School or Wharton."

In 1959 Warner Brothers proposed a joint venture with Filmways. "I was spending time out here, and the guys weren't so awesome. They made movies that were 140 minutes longer than ours." Filmways established its own studio in a former Gristede's supermarket warehouse on 127th Street and Second Avenue in Manhattan. Not exactly an up-and-coming neighborhood. "We didn't go across the street for lunch. We made $150,000 the first year. It was cooking. I have a theory that if you're really good at something and banging away at it," you'll make it. "I had no relatives in the business, no contacts, no fucking breaks, nothing. The concept was that I was a bum, a disaster, had nothing going for me. My sister was bright. My brother was an engineer. My father was in the coffee-importing business. I didn't know what I wanted, but I didn't want that, and he couldn't understand it. He said, 'It'll all be yours.'

"I was a black sheep. I didn't give a shit. I didn't have a chance to plan; it was all blind faith. I had to hustle my ass. My plan was to avoid the business coupe. I kept having this image of picking up a date with the fucking stars and a half moon"—the Procter & Gamble logo.

In 1960–61 a pilot for a TV show called *Mr. Ed* did not sell. Ransohoff had worked with actors Alan Young and Connie Hines in commercials, and he shot a new opening with them. It has not been revealed until now that the voice of Mr. Ed was Western star Rocky Lane, who didn't want his name disclosed. When the show was picked up by CBS after a year in syndication, the network aired it before *Lassie,* its megahit on Sunday evenings.

Concurrently Marty started producing films, starting with *Boys' Night Out,* starring Kim Novak, James Garner, and Tony Randall. It went before the cameras at the same time as the talking horse.

Firmly entrenched in television comedy, Filmways went on to make *The Beverly Hillbillies,* at one time the highest-rated program on network television, with a 60 share and a 41 rating. The initial impetus was a question of Marty's: What about the people between the mountains—the Appalachians and the Rockies? At lunch at Hollywood's Brown Derby restaurant, Ransohoff asked Paul Henning, a writer from the Ozarks who had written the *Fibber McGee and Molly* series for radio, if he would consider writing a pilot. "He said he didn't want to shoot in weed patches, but he'd take one of those families to Beverly Hills. I committed to a pilot with no script to CBS on Henning's name and the appeal to a broad section of the U.S."

In 1963 CBS's Wednesday night lineup featured the Hillbillies at nine, Dick Van Dyke at 9:30, and Danny Kaye at ten. "We virtually destroyed NBC's shows, which had dominated the night. We turned the night around and changed the CBS/NBC balance." *Petticoat Junction* and *Green Acres* followed, American audiences having a seemingly insatiable thirst for *la vie hillbillie.* All of a sudden there were nine hillbilly shows on the air.

Marty Ransohoff moved to Los Angeles in 1961 and left Filmways in 1972, having at one time produced seven shows simultaneously. It was twenty years to the day after he had started the company. "It got so big, I couldn't stay and run it and give time to the motion picture business.

I had to make a choice, and I tried to replace myself. It didn't work. I wanted to make films *and* TV.

"Strangely, the company's interests and mine had become incompatible." Thus, Martin Ransohoff Productions was formed in 1972. While the company's first motion picture was *The White Dawn,* starring Timothy Bottoms, Lou Gossett, and Warren Oates, it was Marty's twenty-seventh film, he estimates.

Although moviemaking was not new to him, Ransohoff describes his first year alone as "a jolt. When you go from thirty-three phone calls a day to fourteen it's a wind-down. A lot of pressure and dreary shit stopped. I knew it was the right thing to do."

One of the industry's most prolific producers, Ransohoff has made over forty-five pictures to date. "I've been through studio shake-ups and seen the folly of otherwise bright guys who have an incredible belief in their inability to be replaced. The bottom line is, you're an employee and you are subject to the vagaries of the people who buy tickets. Without tickets, you are really replaceable. All the fucking studio head is, is an employee. He's *very* lucky if he's four for ten of the films he makes. It's tough. People who are coming into this business better fucking well understand it. Personally, I feel you better love movies to put up with all the bullshit and nonsense."

The publicness of the entertainment industry doesn't help matters, either. "Anything big that happens here gets worldwide—not trade—attention. It's a fishbowl. The industry gets much more attention than it deserves."

In 1987 Marty produced *The Big Town* and *Switching Channels,* his remake of the classic Hecht-MacArthur *Front Page,* with Kathleen Turner, Burt Reynolds, and Christopher Reeve. He has been associated with Columbia Pictures on a non-exclusive basis for the last eleven years. His ordinary diet consists of two films per year. His menu for 1988 should consist of three productions, *Smoke,* starring Burt Reynolds, Theresa Russell, and Ned Beatty, *Passage* with Kris Kristofferson, JoBeth Williams, and Brian Keith, and a sequel to his hit *Jagged Edge.*

Although he maintains no official filmography—"it's not really important to me"—Marty thinks his movies have garnered maybe twenty Academy Award nominations and perhaps five or six oscars.

Some of the films made by Marty Ransohoff include:

Save the Tiger	*Jagged Edge*
The Sandpiper	*Class*
The Americanization of Emily	*White Dawn*
Silver Streak	*Boys' Night Out*
The Wanderers	*Ten Rillington Place*
Catch-22	*See No Evil*
The Cincinnati Kid	*Castle Keep*
The Loved One	*Switching Channels*
Hanky Panky	*The Big Town*
King Lear	

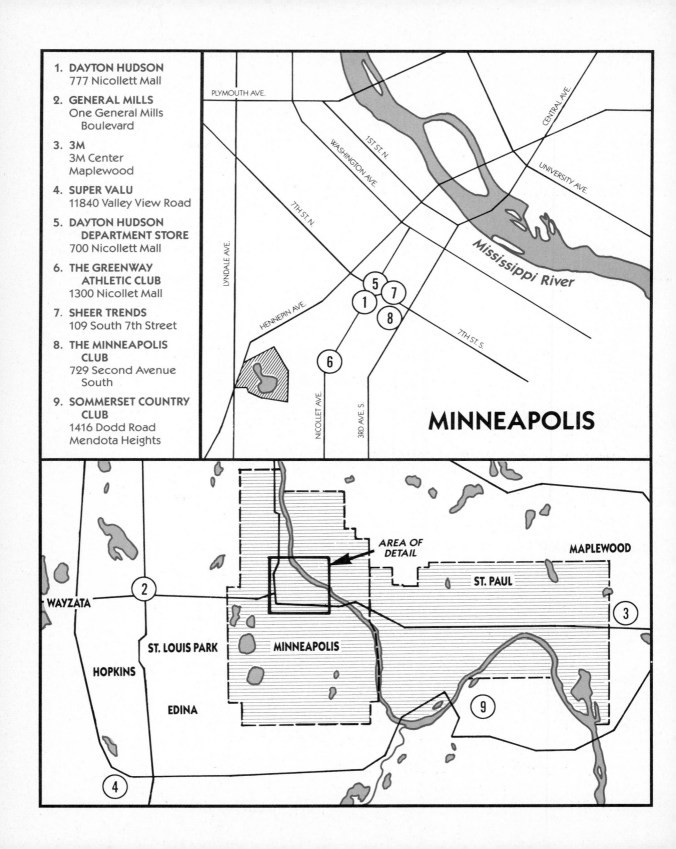

1. **DAYTON HUDSON**
   777 Nicollett Mall

2. **GENERAL MILLS**
   One General Mills
   Boulevard

3. **3M**
   3M Center
   Maplewood

4. **SUPER VALU**
   11840 Valley View Road

5. **DAYTON HUDSON
   DEPARTMENT STORE**
   700 Nicollett Mall

6. **THE GREENWAY
   ATHLETIC CLUB**
   1300 Nicollet Mall

7. **SHEER TRENDS**
   109 South 7th Street

8. **THE MINNEAPOLIS
   CLUB**
   729 Second Avenue
   South

9. **SOMMERSET COUNTRY
   CLUB**
   1416 Dodd Road
   Mendota Heights

PLYMOUTH AVE.

1ST ST. N.

WASHINGTON AVE.

CENTRAL AVE.

UNIVERSITY AVE.

7TH ST. N

LYNDALE AVE.

HENNEPIN AVE.

Mississippi River

7TH ST. S.

NICOLLET AVE.

3RD AVE. S.

MINNEAPOLIS

AREA OF
DETAIL

MAPLEWOOD

ST. PAUL

WAYZATA

ST. LOUIS PARK

MINNEAPOLIS

HOPKINS

EDINA

MINNEAPOLIS—
ST. PAUL

MINNEAPOLIS—
ST. PAUL

To most people, the best thing about the Twin Cities may not be the photo booth in the corner of the bottom floor of the Woolworth's in the IDS Center in downtown Minneapolis. Then again, it might. It takes beautiful sepia-toned pictures—·four for a dollar—that are absolutely suitable for framing. (The people who work the cash register nearest to the booth are also agreeable about making change.)

No, probably the machine is overlooked in examining Minneapolis's and St. Paul's vast riches: an ecologically sound environment, a high quality of life, a thoughtful populace, and maybe the single most exciting cultural life of anyplace between the coasts. The Guthrie Theatre, the Walker Art Gallery, and Lake Wobegone are famous, but the artist's life is more than imagined; it can be a fulfilling existence here. Locals celebrate local talent, in addition to being able to import artists and their works from other provinces. Minnesotans protect and promote their natural resources and their cultural resources with equal enthusiasm.

Corporately, Minneapolis and St. Paul make sense. They are a safe haven for businesses with a social consciousness, a headquarters for headquarters. Dayton Hudson, 3M, Control Data,

Super Valu, General Mills—they're nice companies filled in most instances with employees willing to devote their entire careers to them—as their partners did before them. Many of these folks attended the University of Minnesota with combined enrollment of its five campuses —has a student population of 52,152; the nation's largest—(alma mater of Hubert Humphrey, Loni Anderson, Warren Burger, and briefly (for one unconfirmable quarter) the academic focus of Robert Zimmerman's—Bob Dylan's—life). If one believes in auras, color the Minnesotans' a shade of rosy contentment.

Trends do take a tad longer to root here. You will find hair mousse to be as familiar to Minnesotans as arugula salad—newish and interesting. Fancy imported cars notwithstanding, there is a modesty here, as well as big money.

The downtown is again reasserting itself as a residential neighborhood, abetted by tunnels and covered passageways to shield against winter. (You remember Minnesota winters; when Mary's car wouldn't start, she'd get Rhoda to drive her to work . . . and vice versa.) St. Paul is enjoying a renaissance and is being upgraded from its second city status—at least by the families moving there to take advantage of better real estate values.

To be blunt, the rich of the Twin Cities live in suburban Minneapolis, specifically in Edina and Wayzata. This is the country club–country squire set, who may go duck hunting or at least collect objects adorned with the image of the duck for their large homes. (Hometown "boy" Prince, né Prince Roger Nelson—that small, wiry rock 'n' roll androgene and patron of other likeminded small, wiry androgenes, all given to rococo Edwardian attire—probably has abandoned the duck motif at the present time.)

What else? The Minnesota Twins won the National League Pennant and the World Series in 1987, as you know. The Hormel meat packing plant, site of the long and painful strike by its workers, is located here in Austin. Minnesotans do interesting things with their native-grown wild rice. The source of the Mississippi River is here, too. It's narrow. You can tiptoe over it. Go ahead . . . it's fun.

BEST NEIGHBORHOODS WITH DECENT PUBLIC SCHOOLS: Edina, Hopkins, Wayzata, Burasville

NICEST NEIGHBORHOOD (BUT YOU'LL PROBABLY HAVE TO SEND YOUR KIDS TO PRIVATE SCHOOL): Kenwood

BEST PLACES TO LIVE IF YOU'RE AN ASPIRING ARTIST OR YOU WANT TO LIVE NEAR PEOPLE WHO WEAR ONLY BLACK: Uptown (Lake and Hennepin), Warehouse District

BEST NEIGHBORHOOD WITH TAKE-OUT FOOD AND SINGLE PEOPLE WHO ARE ALSO REPUBLICANS: Uptown

MOST OVERPRICED COMMUNITY FOR SUMMER HOMES: Lake Minnetonka

BEST PUBLIC SCHOOLS: Edina, Hopkins St. Louis Park, Burasville, Wayzata

BEST PRIVATE SCHOOLS: Breck (coed, all grades), Blake (coed, all grades), St. Paul Academy (coed, all grades), Visitation (girls, all grades), St. Thomas Academy (boys, all grades)

BEST ALTERNATIVE SCHOOLS: Most Twin Cities School districts have solid alternative programs and magnet schools

ARCHITECT WHO HAS MOST INFLUENCED THE CITY'S SKYLINE: Philip Johnson

MOST POPULAR RESIDENTIAL ARCHITECTS: Hammel, Green, Abrahamson; Loren Ahles; Rich Varda

SOCIALLY INCLINED REALTOR: Fran Davis (Merrill Lynch)

DECORATOR WHO WOULD DECORATE HOMES PURCHASED THROUGH THAT REALTOR: Interior Design Studio at Dayton's

DEALER'S IN THE FINEST, MOST VALUABLE ART: Thompson Gallery, John Stoler, Dolly Fiterman (Gallery One)

TRENDY GALLERIES FOR PEOPLE WHO WEAR ALL BLACK AND HAVE A LOT OF MONEY: Artbanque

MOST EXCLUSIVE GOLF CLUB: Somerset

BEST PUBLIC GOLF FACILITY: Bunker Hills

MOST EXPENSIVE HEALTH CLUB: The Marsh

BEST HEALTH CLUB FOR MEETING POTENTIAL MATES: Greenway Athletic Club

BEST HOTEL FOR BUSINESS TRIPS: Radisson Plaza

BEST HOTEL FOR TRYSTS: Whitney

RESTAURANTS KNOWN FOR BEST CUISINE: Nigel's, 510, Lucia's

BEST RESTAURANT FOR PEOPLE WHO WEAR BLACK: Monte Carlo

BEST RESTAURANT FOR AN INEXPENSIVE DATE: Fuddruckers

NOISIEST RESTAURANT (INTIMACY IMPOSSIBLE): Monte Carlo

BEST SPORTS BAR: Champs

BEST DARK BAR: Chance's Lounge

BEST GIMMICKY BAR: Jukebox Saturday Night

BEST BAR TO IMPRESS A CLIENT: Cleo's (IDS Tower)

MOST EXCLUSIVE CITY CLUB: Minneapolis Club

FANCIEST WINE STORE WHENCE CEOS PROBABLY STOCK THEIR OWN CELLARS: Haskell's

GOURMET STORE GUARANTEED NOT TO RUN OUT OF GOAT CHEESE OR SUN-DRIED TOMATOES: Byerly's

NICEST MOM-AND-POP GROCERY STORE: Market on the Green

LARGEST DRUGSTORE WITH MOST REMARKABLE SELECTION: Burch Pharmacy

CORPORATE PARTY PLANNER: Patty Meshbesken

HIGH-SOCIETY PARTY PLANNER: Patty Meshbesken

POWER BARBER: Dave Voss at Sheer Trends

NEW WAVE HAIR STYLIST: Avant

JUNIOR LEAGUE BEAUTY PARLORS: Rocco Altobelli, Horst

PLACE WHERE LADIES WHO LUNCH ARE LIKELY TO HAVE TEA AFTER A HARD DAY OF SHOPPING, VOLUNTEER WORK, AND TENNIS: Hyde Park (St. Paul)

BEST STORES FOR EXECUTIVE WOMEN: Dayton's Department Store, Harold

BEST STORES FOR EXECUTIVE MEN: Dayton's Department Store, Mark Shale

BEST STORES FOR DRESS-UP CLOTHES: Dayton's Department Store, Harold

BEST SHOPPING RESOURCE FOR PEOPLE WHO WEAR ONLY BLACK CLOTHES: Dayton's Department Store

DEBUTANTE BALL: None

BUSIEST SOCIAL SEASON OF THE YEAR FOR THOSE WHO CARE ABOUT SUCH THINGS: Spring

SOCIAL HIGHLIGHTS: Symphony Ball, Children's Theatre Benefit

MOST RELIABLE FLORISTS: Bachman's, Butterfields

MOST EXOTIC FLORIST: Audrey's Linden Hills Florists

TOP JEWELERS FOR RESETTING MOTHER'S EMERALDS: Hudson's

MOST COMPLETE BRIDAL REGISTRIES: Dayton's Department Store

PROMINENT PHYSICIANS: Dr. K. James Ehlen, Dr. Harold Katkov

PROMINENT PLASTIC SURGEON WITH EQUALLY PROMINENT CLIENTELE: Carter

GYNECOLOGIST MOST OFTEN QUOTED IN THE LOCAL PRESS: Dr. Ronald Peterson

PSYCHIATRISTS MOST OFTEN QUOTED IN THE LOCAL PRESS: Dr. Donald Mayberg, Dr. Lee Beecher

BEST SEAMSTRESS OR TAILOR FOR ALTERATIONS: Pauline Malmberg

BEST SEAMSTESS OR TAILOR FOR CUSTOM TAILORING: Walter Miskew

POPULAR FACIAL SALONS: Glenby's (Dayton's Department Store)

POWER TOOLS

MEN'S POWER DRESSING

BROOKS BROTHERS
80 South 8th Street
Minneapolis, MN 55402
(612) 338-6600

BEST-SELLING EXECUTIVE SUIT: Solid navy or gray, lightweight, 100 percent wool, $315–$460 (70 percent are three-button style)

POWER SHIRT: Divided evenly among solid white, solid blue, and blue-and-white-striped. In 100 percent cotton oxford cloth ($40–$42) and 100 percent cotton pinpoint ($50–$55)

POWER TIE: Burgundy-and-navy rep stripe, 100 percent silk, $25

WOMEN'S POWER DRESSING

TALBOT'S
80 E. 8th St.
Minneapolis, MN 55402
(612) 333-2482

TALBOT'S CAREER WOMAN CATALOGUE

Talbot's has been a popular source for traditional women's clothing for many years, and with the influx of numbers of women into the workplace during the seventies, it was natural that the store would develop a line of conservative clothing designed for the working woman. For the last four years, Talbot's has produced a catalogue for career women that comes out five times per year. The total circulation of the five books is about ten million all across the country. We spoke to Rebecca Jewett, Talbot's, about trends in women's career dressing.

WHAT CHANGES HAVE YOU OBSERVED IN CAREER WOMEN'S DRESSING OVER THE LAST SEVERAL YEARS?
"The kinds of things that currently sell well in the book [Talbot's Career Woman Catalogue] are very polished dresses. That certainly is a category which has changed over the last three years. Before that, the trend was more toward skirts and blouses. Now the book is much more oriented toward very polished executive dresses. Books from three years ago had 'little man' suits with floppy bow ties. Women aren't purchasing those much anymore."

WHAT KINDS OF COLORS ARE CURRENTLY POPULAR WITH EXECUTIVE WOMEN?
"The total look is no more sophisticated than it used to be, although there hasn't really been a dramatic change in color. This fall [1987] cognac [tobacco brown] and sage [dusty green] are very popular. Colors are getting more sophisticated, and executive women buy both solids and prints."

WHAT'S HAPPENING WITH HEMLINES? DO WORKING WOMEN SEEM TO BE FOLLOWING THE TREND TOWARD SHORTER SKIRTS?
"We're currently showing knee-length skirts, and women seem to be buying them. They're also buying longer skirts. The two most popular looks are long and full circle skirts, and short straight skirts. Women have more choices now. I doubt that skirts will get really short like they were in the sixties, but certainly knee length is appropriate for work."

ARE THEY STILL BUYING JACKETS?
"Yes. Women are still buying jackets, with both circle skirts and short straight skirts."

WHAT KINDS OF FABRICS DO THEY CHOOSE?
"Executive women go for both natural and blended fibers."

WHAT KINDS OF ACCESSORIES DO YOU SELL, AND HAVE THOSE CHANGED OVER THE LAST SEVERAL YEARS?
"We sell handbags, shoes, jewelry, and scarves. Jewelry is more clunky than it used to be. We put together total looks [in the catalogues], and women do buy the accessories we show with outfits."

BEST-SELLING ITEMS?

Straight knee-length skirts, $84

Unstructured blazers (to go with the skirts), $152

Dresses ("a very hot category"), $100–$200

Shoes ("They wear both high-heeled and low-heeled shoes to work, as well as boots"), $75–$225

EXECUTIVE FITNESS

THE GREENWAY ATHLETIC CLUB

1300 Nicollet Mall

Minneapolis, MN 55403

(612) 343-3131

HOURS: 6:00 A.M.–11:00 P.M., Monday through Friday

8:30 A.M.–8:00 P.M., Saturday and Sunday

Located in downtown Mineapolis in the Hyatt Regency Hotel, the Greenway Athletic Club is conveniently close to work for its executive clientele. According to Barbara Long, the assistant to the general manager, "We have a full restaurant and bar in the club to allow for great networking to occur at power lunches after a noontime workout, or over a couple of beers in the evening after a league basketball game." Greenway's facilities include four indoor tennis courts, eight racquetball courts, two squash courts, an outdoor track, two outdoor paddle ball courts, a swimming pool, a full gym with basketball and volleyball courts, an aerobics studio, full fitness Eagle weight training, Universal/free weights, a treadmill, a life cycle/life rower, a Stairmaster, a steam room, a sauna and a whirlpool for men, a sauna and a whirlpool for women, and a masseur/masseuse on duty from 10:00 A.M. to 9:00 P.M.

In addition, the club has many special features: fitness testing—computerized "Micro-Fit" administered by a certified member of the American College of Sports Medicine; volleyball clinics given by the Minnesota Monarchs, a professional women's volleyball team; a basketball league connected to Minneapolis area law firms; water aerobics classes; special aerobic and basketball flooring designed to reduce stress on limbs; biweekly consultations available with a physical therapist; child care Tuesday through Thursday nights and Saturday mornings.

The ratio of male to female members at the club is two to one. Fifty percent of the members have an annual income of $65,000 or more. The biggest areas of interest to the club's executive members are racquetball, (85 percent men, 15 percent women), indoor tennis (50 percent men, 50 percent women), aerobics (50 percent men, 50 percent women), and cardiovascular workouts. Most executives use the club between 11:30 A.M. and 1:30 P.M. and between 4:30 and 7:30 P.M.

FEES: Single membership $275 initiation plus $60 per month for women and $65 per month for men

Couple membership: $325 initiation plus $85 per month

Child's membership: $10 per month per child

The club also offers a prime time membership at a 30 percent discount on the intiation fee plus $45 per month. Prime time members can use the club all hours except 11:30 A.M. to 1:30 P.M. and 4:30 to 7:30 P.M., Monday through Friday.

POWER HAIR

SHEER TRENDS
109 South 7th Street, Room 200
Minneapolis, MN 55402
(612) 333-3329

We spoke to Dave Voss, one of the owners of Sheer Trends. Thirty percent of his clientele is made of executives, and 90 percent of these are men. The shop offers its male clients privacy —all cuts are given in private booths.

ON TRENDS IN EXECUTIVE HAIR: "Traditional hairstyles are continuing to prevail both at work and in private life."

ON GOING GRAY: "They accept their gray hairs and are not interested in changing nature."

ON BALDING: "Hairpieces are the common solution to those balding clients who feel self-conscious about their hair loss."

ON FACIAL HAIR FOR EXECUTIVES: "It's out."

ON MANICURES: "Manicures are popular with women executives. A few male executives do indulge in this service as well, but only a small percentage."

ON POWER HAIR IN GENERAL: "As you can see, the attitudes toward power hair dressing in the Minneapolis/St. Paul area are consistent with the matter-of-fact feeling one receives from the Minnesota executives."

MOTTO: "We try to be nice."

BUYING THE EXECUTIVE HOME

MERRILL LYNCH
2622 West Lake Street
Minneapolis, MN 55416
(612) 920-5605

We spoke to realtor Mary Finnegan.

WHAT IS THE AVERAGE PRICE OF AN EXECUTIVE HOME IN MINNEAPOLIS?
   "The average purchase price in the suburbs is $180,000 to $200,000. Prices *are* going up."

WHERE DO EXECUTIVES PREFER TO LIVE:
   "There's a split of allegience as to the preference in areas. Either they want to be in the outer and inner rings—the suburbs—where new homes abound (Tudor style is popular, and a few planned communities, including recreation facilities, are to be found) or the city 'Lakes' areas—Lake Calhoun, Cedar Lake, Lake Harriett—where they find existing homes dating from the early 1900s to about 1940, in varying styles from Victorian, Colonial, and Tudor. Here they'll spend an average of $250,000 for a home. Young executives buying their first, or possibly second, home are more apt to buy in the city or the first ring of the suburbs and spend an average of $150,000–$170,000. They generally know what they want and will pay a premium to move into a house in good condition. Not too many are interested in fix-me-ups."

WHAT ARE THEIR PRIORITIES WHEN SELECTING A HOME:

"On the whole, a great, modernized kitchen is desired by 90 percent of all executives and 70 percent are interested in Jacuzzi/marble baths as amenities. Other important amenities for the executives are (a) an extra room on the first floor for a study or an office, (b) a large master bath connecting to the master bedroom, (c) double and triple garages, (d) a strong neighborhood, and (e) good schools."

DO EXECUTIVES WANT EXTRA FEATURES, SUCH AS SWIMMING POOLS AND TENNIS COURTS?

"Swimming pools and tennis courts are not conducive to the type of climate we have. And don't forget, the lakes are prevalent."

DAYTON HUDSON CORPORATION

HISTORY & OPERATIONS

Dayton Hudson Corporation, the sixth largest general merchandise retailer in the country, was formed in 1969 with the merger of two family-run corporations, each the dominant retailer in its market. The J. L. Hudson Company was founded in 1881 in Detroit and owned department stores there, and later shopping malls. The Dayton Company (which later became the Dayton Corporation) was founded in 1902 by George Draper Dayton, who started out as a dry goods seller in downtown Minneapolis. In 1929 the Dayton Company acquired J. L. Hudson & Son, a prominent Minneapolis jeweler. Until the end of World War II, Dayton had only one department store.

After World War II, with the business in the hands of Dayton's five grandsons, the company opened a string of Minnesota shopping centers, each featuring a Dayton's department store. (One of these, launched in the Minneapolis suburb of Southland in 1956, became the first fully enclosed, bilevel shopping mall in the world.) In 1962, with the opening of three Target Stores—massive discount operations that offer everything from clothing to electronics—the Dayton Company moved beyond traditional department stores into discount retailing. In 1966 it entered the field of specialty retailing with the creation of B. Dalton Booksellers, a chain of bookstores primarily located in shopping malls. In 1967 the Dayton Corporation went public, and over the next two years, it broadened its holdings through the acquisition of a number of retail operations in markets across the country. Purchases included Sureve and Co., a San Francisco jeweler, in 1967; Pickwick Book Shops, Los Angeles, in 1968; two department store companies—Lipmans in Oregon and Diamond's in Arizona—in 1968; J. E. Caldwell, Philadelphia jeweler, in 1969; Lechmere, a Boston-based appliances and electronics dealer, in 1969.

When, in 1969, the Dayton Corporation merged with the J. L. Hudson Company, the Dayton Hudson Corporation became the fourteenth largest general merchandise retailer in the country. In the early seventies, it enlarged its existing retail businesses with the purchase of jewelers in Chicago and San Diego (C. D. Peacock, Inc., and J. Jessop and Sons, respectively), Team Central, a Minneapolis franchiser of electronics equipment stores, and John A. Brown, an Oklahoma department store company. In 1971 the company passed $1 billion in annual revenues, and by 1973 it had become the eleventh largest general merchandise retailer in the country.

In the mid-1970s, with Target Stores generating more revenues than any of its other operations, Dayton Hudson focused its growth strategy on discount retailing. Accordingly, in 1978 it merged with Mervyn's, a California-based discount department store chain that features relatively inexpensive clothing of a higher quality than that offered at most discount stores. (The Mervyn's merger made Dayton Hudson the second largest department store in the country and the seventh largest general merchandise retailer.) That same year, the company sold its nine regional shopping centers and bowed out of real estate. Between 1979 and 1984, with its lucrative discount operations fueling its growth, Dayton Hudson expanded exponentially. By 1982 Target Stores' annual sales exceeded $2 billion and contributed 46 percent of the company's total revenues, and Mervyn's reached $1 billion and contributed 25 percent of revenues. By 1984 Dayton Hudson was the fifth largest general merchandise retailer in the country, with over 1,200 stores nationwide. That year, in an attempt to compete against the discount booksellers that were sapping profits from B. Dalton's, which sells its goods at full retail prices, the company expanded its Pickwick's discount bookstores with a limited selection and a minimum of service.

Beginning in 1979, the company started to shed its less profitable operations. (This trend culminated in 1986 with the sale of B. Dalton's, which was by then the country's second largest bookstore chain with 777 stores in forty-eight states, to Barnes & Noble, the country's third largest bookstore chain.) In 1984 the corporation merged the Dayton and Hudson department stores into the Dayton Hudson Department Store Company, the largest individual department store company in the country. In 1986 Dayton Hudson launched R. G. Branden's, a chain of upscale housewares stores that sells everything from kitchen gadgets to bed sheets, in Georgia and Florida.

Today, under the leadership of Kenneth A. Macke, who joined the company in 1961 as a management trainee and rose through the ranks to become president in 1981 and chairman and CEO in 1983, the company employs 130,000 people in 583 stores across the country and is again the seventh largest general merchandise retailer in the country. (The company has slipped in the rankings due to a spate of mergers among other retailers in recent years.) In 1987 revenues reached $10.7 billion, with 50 percent contributed by Target Stores, 30 percent contributed by Mervyn's, 14 percent contributed by the Dayton Hudson Department Store Company, and 6 percent contributed by Lechmere. (No calculation exists for R. G. Branden's, as those stores are still in the test stage.)

Dayton Hudson has won a reputation as one of the best-managed companies in the country. Among all other major department store companies, it has been the leader in repositioning itself in newly developed, fast-growing retail markets. The corporation is also regarded both by the communities in which it maintains a presence and by its own employees as fair, honest and extremely generous. It has one of the most liberal return policies of any retailer anywhere, and its humane corporate policies and opportunities for advancement have engendered fierce loyalty among its full-time employees. In addition, Dayton Hudson is among the top corporate donors to charity in the country. Since 1946 the company has donated 5 percent of its pretax income to community programs, mostly in the area of social action and the arts. Total donations in 1987 equaled $19 million.

Due to its stellar reputation (and the fact that it employs 34,000 Minnesota residents), when Dayton Hudson was threatened with a hostile takeover by the Dart Group of Washington, D.C., in 1987, the Minnesota state legislature quickly passed strong antitakeover laws to ensure that the company was able to preserve its independence.

In 1987 Dayton Hudson announced a five-year strategy for growth. (The company updates its expansion plans every five years.) The corporation is spending $5 billion on expansion between 1987 and 1991, 85 percent of which will go to Target Stores and Mervyn's, with the remaining 15 percent earmarked for the department store company for remodeling and to test new store formats. The company projects that Target Stores will grow at an annual rate of 16 percent in terms of square footage—the means by which retailers measure growth—and Mervyn's will increase by 13 percent annually. Lechmere's will also receive money for expansion, and R. G. Branden's plans to add eleven new stores by 1989.

(Information provided by Rod Bib, company spokesman.)

REVENUES: $10.7 billion in 1987.

EARNINGS: $288.4 million in net earnings in 1987.

INITIAL PUBLIC OFFERING: The Dayton Company went public in 1967, and Dayton Hudson has been public since its inception in 1969.

NUMBER OF SHAREHOLDERS: 15,500

NUMBER OF STORES: 583. 317 Target Stores in twenty-four states, which contributed 50 percent of total revenues; 199 Mervyn's in thirteen states, which contribute 30 percent of total revenues; thirty-seven Dayton Hudson Department Stores in seven states, which contribute 14 percent of total revenues; twenty-four Lechmeres in eight states, which contribute 6 percent of total revenues; and six R. G. Branden's in Florida and Georgia (percentage of revenues has not been calculated).

NUMBER OF EMPLOYEES: Roughly 130,000, all in the United States. Target has approximately 55,000 employees; Mervyn's has approximately 46,000; Dayton Hudson Department Stores Company has approximately 24,000; and Lechmere has approximately 5,000. (Figures on R. G. Branden's were not available.)

AVERAGE AGE OF EMPLOYEES: Company does not keep figures, and average age is not a particularly relevant statistic for them.

TURNOVER: "Comparable to industry norms." Because the company has such a large part-time work force, it doesn't keep turnover figures.

RECRUITMENT: Each company in the Dayton Hudson Corporation develops its own recruiting program. Overall, campus recruiting is conducted at thirty to forty colleges. "We recruit at major schools on the West Coast and in the Midwest, where the bulk of our stores are located." Students targeted are those with business, accounting, marketing, and liberal arts backgrounds.

NUMBER OF NEW HIRES PER YEAR: "In the thousands." Sixty-five percent of the total workforce are part-time employees working in the stores. The company can't give a more specific average.

RANGE OF STARTING SALARIES: "Competitive in the marketplace. For example, professional trainees might start in the high teens to mid-twenties."

POLICY FOR RAISES: The company has regularly scheduled salary reviews at least once a year, and raises are based on performance.

TRAINING PROGRAMS: "We have a wide range of formal training programs at all levels. The primary focus is on people who work in the stores, such as sales consultants, store employees, and store managers. We also have programs available for the professional management staff."

BENEFITS: "We have a highly competitive package including medical, dental, life, and disability insurance, and a retirement plan. Some of our operating companies offer tuition reimbursement for courses that benefit an employee's career at Dayton Hudson."

VACATION: "Varies by individual company and length of service. We do have a competitive vacation policy."

ADDITIONAL PERKS: "Discounts on merchandise that vary by individual operating company and types of merchandise."

BONUSES: Company will not disclose.

ANNUAL PARTIES: There are no companywide parties—they're left up to the discretion of the individual stores. The corporate staff has an annual getaway in the summer, "devoted to both business and play. We go to a place called the Lafayette Club on Lake Minnetonka. It's a day just for employees. We have meetings in the morning, and in the afternoon we play tennis, golf, softball, go on boat rides, jog, et cetera." An outdoor lunch is provided. The corporate staff also hosts an annual Christmas party, usually held in the corporate offices. It's an informal social gathering for employees only, which takes place in the afternoon. Hors d'oeuvres are served.

AVERAGE WORKDAY: Official hours for the corporate staff are 8:00 A.M. to 5:00 P.M., though a lot of people put in longer days. Hours for the operating companies and stores differ. "I think people work pretty hard here."

DRESS CODE: "It varies on specifics by individual operating company, but generally we would expect professional dress as appropriate for position."

SOCIAL ATMOSPHERE: "Impossible to describe in general terms."

HEADQUARTERS: Dayton Hudson leases five floors in the IDS Tower in downtown Minneapolis, a high rise that used to be the tallest building in the city. Approximately 180 corporate employees are housed there.

CHARITABLE CONTRIBUTIONS: Since 1946 the company has donated 5 percent of its pretax income to community programs, mostly in the area of social action and the arts. Total donations in 1987 equaled more than $19 million, of which 40 percent went to social action, 40 percent went to the arts, and 20 percent went to miscellaneous causes.

Corporate Personnel Department
Dayton Hudson Corporation
777 Nicollet Mall
Minneapolis, MN 55402
(612) 370-6948

Dayton Hudson's clout in the Midwest in general and Minnesota in particular cannot be overestimated. The retailing giant recently had the laws of Minnesota changed—within a week—in order to stymie a takeover effort. But you can accomplish the impossible when you are known as the good guys.

Dayton Hudson is among the most generous corporate contributors in America in terms of pretax dollars to charity—5 percent. While the philanthropic tradition of the Dayton brothers is not a lure for job seekers who, after all, need a place to work, it is one of the nice sidelights of a job. Furthermore, telling people in Minnesota and Michigan, the company's two main locations, that you work for Dayton Hudson is rewarded by a knowing smile and appreciation. Call it corny; when you see the corporate logo on public television or at the art museum or the local theater, it becomes an unavoidable fact that Dayton Hudson is a good citizen.

When we met, Bruce Allbright was the chairman and CEO of Target Stores, Dayton Hudson's midwestern discount chain. (It does operate in twenty-four states, and Mervyn's, the other discount retailer belonging to the corporation, is based in northern California.) While getting his degree in economics at Vanderbilt University, Allbright worked in a training program at Genesco in Nashville. His goal was eventually engineering, but retailing seemed like a natural since his grandfather was a store owner. Seventeen years ago, when he joined this corporation, it was as head of Dayton Hudson's B. Dalton bookstore chain, sold in 1986 to Barnes & Noble. "I never had so much fun," he says over coffee. "B. Dalton had innumerable Ph.Ds just there for a tiny bit of money to hang around books. They got turned on to business. I was the only one without a beard, the only one who supported Nixon, and the only one over forty." Allbright confesses it was as the head of the nation's second largest book retailer (after Waldenbooks) that "I read fewer books than I ever had in my life."

The prestige of working for the Daytons and their reputation of professionalism is what brought him to Minneapolis, not the reputed community involvement. "I thought it [philanthropy] was crazy my first two, three years. Now I feel it's fantastic. I'm not sure anyone decides to come to Dayton Hudson because of the philanthropy. But it probably helps keep them. The company is a good guy."

Allbright next became the president of Target Stores. "Tasks are transferable in retailing," he explains. "The nomenclature varies from business to business; shoes to books to electronics." When an "attractive opportunity" opened up elsewhere for Allbright, he left "to do the impossible. If I did well, it would have been great; otherwise no one would notice," he rationalized. "The moment [my new employer] closed down, Dayton Hudson called me to offer me a new job." Not only that, they gave him a promotion in his absence. He assumed the position of Target's vice-chairman. The following year he was promoted to the chief executive position.

It is evident that Allbright is not loving his work simply for the purpose of this interview. "It's the only industry with immediacy. I know this morning how we did yesterday. It's exciting." (In October 1987 Allbright became president of the Dayton Hudson Corporation.)

Every September Allbright and company receive the capital allocation they requested the previous June. Target's growth is aggressive. With 225 stores already in operation, they opened twenty-one new stores in 1986 and seventy-one in 1987. "Customer loyalty is over-rated. You've got to keep earning their business."

Roger Goddu is Target's "Mr. Gung-ho." He arrived in the Twin Cities in 1979 "on a hunch," after having spent about a dozen years with other prestige retailers. He was betting on discount marketing's nascent respectability. "People didn't leave department stores for discount stores. By 1982 it became a legitimate retail career path. In hindsight, it turned out to be a great decision." Now he's Target's senior vice-president and the general merchandise manager of hard lines. "There's no more stigma. Today, I think it's in vogue to be thrifty. You see Rolls-Royces at warehouse stores."

Goddu continues, "At some point you have to cast your own vote. I came to Target to be in a growth company." He was reassured by Dayton Hudson's CEO, Kenneth Macke. "I asked him the question, 'What's the mix between soft lines and hard lines?' He said, 'Whatever the customer says. We let the customer vote.' Previous companies where I worked told the customer what the customer wanted and manipulated him.

"As we get big, we've got to stay close to the customer. It's not that hard to figure him out. We never say we can't carry something because we don't make money on it. We accept returns—even without receipts—even if they were not purchased here."

Goddu describes Target's corporate structure as one based on meetings. "We're management by consensus. Every Monday at three o'clock we have a staff meeting." It lasts until 6:00 P.M. "*Every* Monday," he emphasizes, "like religion. There are few things that can't wait until then. Our year is divided into weekly deadlines."

Roger is passionate, hard-working, and the kind of employee who tries to do better. After graduating from the University of Toledo, he characterized himself as "ambitious." Although Dayton Hudson looks at planning in five-year chunks, Goddu admits "I can't say I plan for my own career for five years. Once you find yourself at the 'right' employer, you stop worrying about your career. I can honestly say that Target is the right place for me. If you're comfortable with the people, you'll be comfortable with the corporation. The corporate culture is the same throughout the operating companies. We're more progressive than most."

Dayton Hudson's planning is astonishingly comprehensive. It includes two performance review periods per year that involve more than simply talking about one's goals. "We identify our backups throughout the year." The "Manpower Planning Process" is contingent on em-ployees' training their right- and left-hand people to do their jobs, so that people can be flexible and constantly prepared to move. "Everyone has a sheet with their 'A' and 'B' incum-bents. People like it because it shows promotability. We share the backup condition with people. It's not a mystery."

Sue DeNuccio, Target's vice-president of training and employee relations, thinks that retailing is the perfect industry for the job seeker who isn't sure what he or she wants to do. "Everyone's a shopper. They feel if they can shop, they can retail. Unlike other careers, you start supervising very early." She disputes retailing's reputation for competitiveness. "People use the term, but it's not more competitive than other industries. It's not ruthless. We're not in the global economy—like high technology; *that's* war. It's just that mistakes show up faster and your competitors are much more accessible. Just go to Wal-Mart," she explains, naming one of Target's rivals.

Target's training program for salespeople takes the new employee into the stores as soon as is decently possible: an hour and a half after arrival. "Adults don't want to sit in classrooms," DeNuccio states matter-of-factly. College graduates may enter the merchant training program, which lasts thirteen weeks, because that's the length of time of the average school quarter, "the time period students can think in." Still, these hires are in the stores on their fourth day, to see the customers. Target recruits at eleven universities: the Big Ten and the University of Chicago.

DeNuccio, who holds a master's in counseling and psychology from Purdue (Big Ten) and an MBA from the University of Denver, tries to disseminate Dayton Hudson's values during training. "You hear the word 'honest' a lot." Rules of conduct worth mentioning are "no deals from vendors, no drinking at lunch, and keeping your personal life discreet."

She joined Target in 1973. "Even then Target was where you wanted to end up. It was intense, go-go-go, and the excited commitment to the customer." Though she has two young children, Sue must maintain a travel schedule that usually means being out of town two nights a week to supervise the staffing of all new stores and distribution centers. "I try to visit any time strategic planning goes on. I don't go to a lot of new stores, but I visit markets that are having difficulty—if they lose sales or we haven't done our best job at pulling together the management team. Performance appraisals are for the employees, not the managers. I tell my people that if the developmental stuff is on review again, both of us have failed. It takes the pressure off them."

A housekeeper helps keep order at home, but Sue gives the majority of the credit to her husband, who works for 3M (see p. 390). "His support enabled me to be a success. You *do* discuss business at home. All the people on this floor [of corporate headquarters] have some sort of family obligations—even single mothers. Working in the stores can be flexible, but you must work long hours and weekends. You need a compatible spouse."

Larry Gilpin has suffered periodic bouts of homesickness. This Kentucky native joined IBM after graduating from the University of Kentucky, then was recruited to Minnetonka, Minnesota, for a high-level industrial job. He missed the South. After two years he was moved to Florida and noticed he was watching *Little House on the Prairie* with tears in his eyes. He's been with Target since 1977, and by all accounts he's not looking to move. Anyway, he ascribes his restlessness to "a youthful sense of adventure, when my kids were young and flexible. Part of it was a conscious 'get it out of the system,' " he says, as if he has to apologize. "My wife's career is now a lot more important to her and me. To move now would be hard." Two of his four children were in school in former hometowns, so he would always get a fix of the South.

Larry is Target's senior vice-president of personnel. "I deal with systemwide problems— oops—opportunities," he says, knowing the company line when he says it. "I try to create meaningful jobs and careers."

A full 30 percent of Target Store personnel are here for their career. "I want that commitment from people. And it's good for them, too." A store manager with a college degree can expect to run a whole store within six to eight years. That's talking about a profit center of approximately $20 million per year. However, if you aspire to corporate headquarters, be aware that 10 percent or fewer of those who move into those jobs started in the stores.

"We're very deliberate in communicating our relationship with Dayton Hudson. Its values help in how we're perceived, and our retention."

Jack Fontaine, Target's senior vice-president of property development, entered retailing the way many have: in a part-time position as a kid. Specifically, it was in a drugstore in Grand Forks, North Dakota, at the age of ten. Fontaine was one of Target's first employees when this operating division opened its second, third, and fourth stores simultaneously in September 1962. In the employees' lunchroom, he says, "Doug Dayton was the president of this new company called Target. I knew nothing about discount stores, and I wanted to be a department store buyer in the worst way. He interviewed me during the grand opening, which was gangbusters. I'd never seen anything like it. They were practically giving stuff away. If they had interviewed me before the opening, I would have said, 'Hell, no!' I had wanted Dayton's. It was the top of the line in retailing."

Fontaine moved around the country with the fast-growing company. He lived in St. Louis,

eighty-hour weeks. For me, balance is important. I'm not the kind of guy who wants money and no time to spend it. All the other things in life mean more to me." Besides, "I noticed a real difference between investment bankers and how they deal with people—caustically and arrogantly—and how I handle people."

He thinks recruiting is the toughest aspect of running an organization. "We probably look for the same things everyone else does. The essence of Dayton: positive attitude—can people work well and communicate with people? I've been able to see it in some people."

Corporate Accounting is a "busy department. We operate on the 'lean and mean' theory. We issue reports constantly. Lots of deadlines create pressure for us, especially during tax reform or if there's an acquisition or a divestiture." Nelson arrives at work between 7:00 and 7:30 A.M. He works a fifty- to sixty-hour week, which he calls "appropriate. That's what I'm paid for. I think it's reasonable. There's never too much work or pressure to be over your head. You get a bit of adrenaline; you know you *can* do it." (Nelson has since left the corporate staff to become the general accounting manager of the Dayton Hudson Department Store Company.) The intensity of his work does not interfere with Bruce's life outside of Dayton Hudson. "For the most part, I can forget about work at home. My wife and I share ideas and frustrations about work." On the side he's a musician, able to hold his own on the clarinet, saxophone, and flute. "A lot of days when I sort of pass out, I'd love to read more, play music. TV is so trashy, yet I'm burned out. I haven't picked up an instrument in a few years. It used to be a big part of my life."

Mike Wahlig is another member of the corporate staff, an attorney and legal services specialist. He started with Dayton Hudson sixteen years ago while earning his law degree at night at the William Mitchell College of Law in St. Paul, which, he points out, was ex–Chief Justice Warren Burger's alma mater. He wasn't sure he wanted to be a lawyer, but he thought law school would be interesting. He never worked in private practice.

"We sell our legal services to the operating companies, and they have the option of using us or not. We've got to be the best—we're always worried about the folks who pay the bills." As at a private firm, the legal department charges by the hour. Wahlig echoes Bruce Nelson's "lean and mean" strategy. "Part of the Dayton Hudson culture is to put the emphasis on where the money is made." Today there are eleven lawyers working full time in the department, with room for one more. "Each operating company has the option to have its own law department." Mervyn's and Target each have attorneys on their staffs (two and three, respectively). "Obviously, outside firms do litigation, and we use outside counsel in a lot of states. We're not here to supplant the work of outside law firms."

The structure of the Law (they never say "Legal") Department is rather flat: "We have all chosen specifically to use the title 'attorney.' There used to be a lot of titles." Naturally, there is a general counsel (a senior vice-president of the corporation), "who sets the tone for the department." Even here there is an emphasis on career development. "We spend time on it. Many lawyers are specialists. We hope our law staff culture is not different from the corporate staff culture. We have to work within the environment and not be snobs. My father was a retailer, and his feet hurt. My feet never hurt. We still act like lawyers, but we try to meld into the organization.

"I see myself as a lawyer first. I enjoy practicing law, but I enjoy practicing law for a retailer." The Law Department gets a taste of the gamut of Dayton Hudson business. "Yesterday I spent all day on Santabear," Mike says, referring to the runaway toy hit Dayton Hudson promotes each Christmas. "Today will be fur shortage. Some groups require a lot more leasing, advertising, attention. You see the breadth of the whole company. [Our] lawyers have gone on to become CEOs of the operating companies."

Nevertheless, the Law Department has enjoyed a stability that's notable even for Dayton

Hudson. "Maybe two people have left in eighteen years. My boss has been here eighteen, three guys have been here seventeen, and I have sixteen years. It never gets boring. There are a lot of fun things to do."

Ken Macke thinks his job is fun, too. He joined Dayton Hudson in 1961 as a merchandise trainee, straight from Duke University, and has been its chief executive officer since 1976. "I don't know if I ever have considered it my whole career," he says in his office, which is undergoing renovation, "but I can honestly say I've never worried about what my next job was going to be."

Macke interviewed widely for his first postcollegiate job. "I didn't accept the job [with what was then the Dayton Corporation] until Kenneth Dayton interviewed me. I told him I didn't think I could fit in because my name wasn't Dayton. How far could I go?" Although Macke's name is also Kenneth, up until his ascendancy, no one made it to the top office who was not a member of the immediate Dayton family. Dayton reassured Macke that joining the company made sense. There have been no moments of doubt since.

His favorite job was as the home furnishings buyer. "It's more immediate feedback, like a hot fudge sundae—more instant gratification. I could buy and see. The change I effect now, I can't always see right away. It could take four or five years." The pressure of the top job does not seem to have affected Macke adversely. "I can always sleep. The boy's been happy here," Macke says comfortably from his chair, his jacket off and his shirtsleeves rolled up. "My family's always said, 'We'll go where you go.' There's been no pressure to stay; no family ties in Minnesota."

On the subject of loyalty, Macke says this: "Loyalty is overdefined. I'm not sure why I'm loyal to Dayton Hudson. I could tell you why I'm happy and have stayed, but I don't know if you'd call it 'loyal.' The board reviews me every year, and then I see if I stay. I've been treated fairly by my bosses. It's a growth company. We promote from within." He agrees that his starting at Dayton Hudson as a trainee is "a good story. I created opportunities along the way."

Macke describes his assumption of the Dayton Hudson culture. "You're not taught it; you learn it," he draws the distinction. "I observed the Dayton Brothers' community involvement, but they were also successful and good, so I tried it. When I went to Target, we had a 25 percent increase in United Way giving every year for eight years. They saw me active and involved. And it trickled down. Now if Target opens a store in a new community, they are leaders in giving."

Of all the accolades Macke has received during his tenure, the ones of which he is most proud are " 'He's fair; he has integrity which would not be questioned; he has a sense for action.' I want people to *do*. People know I care. A behavioral guy said I saw myself as a soft old panda bear and my people see me as a tough old son of a bitch. I'm a part of the success, not the reason for it. I don't know of anything I've done myself. [A longtime, rather senior employee opines, "Macke denying responsibility for management is like God denying responsibility for flowers."] Maybe I was the catalyst. I think I'm good at my job. I must set an example. I go to the lake and mow the lawn and think. I think about the strategy of the company. I don't spend a lot of time thinking about how I want to behave. To be a great CEO, I'll be known for a lot of little things and a commitment to growth."

Macke takes a moment to consider the question of his management style; is it open? "Pat [his secretary] screens my calls, but I guess I would be considered open." He travels about two days out of each week, "and it's very rare that I'd visit a city and not visit the stores."

As CEO of one of Minnesota's largest, most important, and influential corporations, Macke's job includes being a visible public figure—a BMOC—with political overtones. He's been involved in tax reform. He's been a generous participant in boards of directors. "People who put me on boards as a figurehead are wrong. I'm on boards because I'm the CEO of Dayton Hudson, but I'm not a chairman of committees because I'm a chief executive officer." Among the boards on which he sits are Northwestern Bell and the Walker Art Center, and he's an alumnus trustee of Drake Unversity.

Cynthia Mayeda had a bunch of jobs before being recruited by Dayton Hudson's corporate staff. She includes branch manager for Kelly Services (temporary employment agency), talent manager, advertising salesperson, and fifteenth-floor receptionist at Dayton Hudson "twelve years ago for five months" among her former accomplishments. The manager of a local theater, she was recruited six years ago by the Dayton Hudson Foundation, and she is now its managing director.

As a former grant seeker, Cynthia had "always had a high regard for the foundation. I was not job hunting; it was the chance of a lifetime." Accepting a job with "them" was not an easy decision, though. "I loved working in my theater, every day—even the dark, gruesome days. Out of the difficult times came strong bonds." Her theater experience lasted two and a half years, a long stretch for her. "My whole career has been a surprise," she says, looking a bit corporate. "This is the longest I've ever been anywhere."

Cynthia's work requires her to interact on a weekly basis with about 10 people on the corporate staff, including lawyers, accounting, MIS, research, and public relations personnel. She reports on a high level, to the corporation's president. Approximately 40 percent of the foundation's grants go to the arts and 40 percent to social action, while 20 percent falls into a category called "miscellaneous." The foundation does not give this last percentage to "higher education, science, or health since everyone else does. Each operating company has its own [philanthropic] mechanism. I have the responsibility to sign the checks, but I don't decide myself."

Those who have the opportunity to give away serious money fall into traps, which Mayeda is careful to avoid. "The potential is toward arrogance and power. The temptation to think it's *your* money. Unlike private foundations, our primary goal is to make money." Even though she identifies strongly with the fact that she works for a retailer, Cynthia does not feel like a stepchild, removed as she is from the main business of Dayton Hudson. "I have no bad feelings about not being part of the money-making operations."

In 1987 the total for donations, including both the foundation and the corporation, was more than $19 million. Recipients included Minnesota Public Radio ($86,000), Independent Choreographers of Twin Cities ($26,500), Twin Cities Public Television ($140,000 for arts programming and $250,000 for capital support), Opportunity Industrialization Centers ($100,000), and the United Negro College Fund ($15,000).

Cynthia emphasizes that the gifts are not accompanied by a need to control. "We don't program our TV, theater, ballet, et cetera like other corporate philanthropists." Her offices are resplendent with part of the company's art collection, selected by the moonlighting curator at General Mills (see p. 373). Some of the work is too controversial, and thus gets rejected by the employees whose offices are decorated. "People go flippo; they return it to our offices." On the other hand, some pieces are coveted. The collection is heavily weighted toward local artists.

Bob Brummer is the vice-president, personnel planning and development for the Dayton Hudson Department Store Company, which means that all divisions of human resources— recruiting, hiring, training, and employee relations—report to him. As far as recruiting goes, "we're often looking for someone with retailing experience, but we're not looking for only the best retailers. We're looking for a broader perspective and the best people. We're strongly liberal arts–oriented. They're the best workers."

The process begins at the career fairs held in October, at which Dayton Hudson offers two distinct training programs to college seniors: Area Customer Service Manager or Associate Buyer. "Students are not sure which program suits them best. They want to be in the stores, with people." Students sign up for interviews that take place the following February. "We're good at seeing who's sincere. We look at body language." Training lasts twelve to thirteen weeks.

Michael Hyter, the Department Store Company's director of executive placement, planning, and recruitment, says of the organization, "It's an easy sell. We let the statistics speak for themselves. We have a ninety-two percent internal promotion rate. Community giving makes Dayton Hudson attractive to students—they're already aware of it." The Twin Cities are universally lauded for their exceptionally high quality of life. "The company doesn't feel midwestern to me, except for the prevailing work ethic," Mike says. He and his colleagues characterize the metropolitan area as "a melting pot, with active lifestyles, a strong sense of values—family, ethics, church, cleanliness—not an industrial city." A colleague uses "punk, interracial, fashionable" to describe the city. Others call it a city with "a New England–Eastern aura." "I have raccoons, quail, rabbits outside my door," Linda Novotney Kemp declares, "and I'm just nine miles away!" Admittedly, Minnesota has to live down its reputation for harsh winters. "It is really hard to get southerners up north, although in general the location is not an obstacle. The majority of our workers are midwestern."

In the recruiting biz—dealing with recent college graduates who have been in classrooms for at least the last sixteen years—one can provide comfort by means of a job that starts in the classroom.

Over and over again, managers here tout the training that is the foundation of a sound work environment and the cornerstone of a company that is widely hailed as an excellent place to work. Even if you are not a member of one of the two executive recruitment training programs, avoiding Dayton Hudson training is almost impossible. Even the trainers get training.

Employees admit that notwithstanding the respect they have for Dayton Hudson, "there are mercenary aspects to this business. If you're making forty thousand dollars and some other department store offers you a new title at eighty thousand, you leave." But money is not the object of everyone's desire. Though Dayton Hudson remunerates competitively—no, make that generously—according to some, it's the culture that stimulates dedication. "Ideas come from the bottom up, not down [from the top]. The avenues are technically open for anyone to make suggestions to people who can act on them." Still, this is one happy bunch. They wander through the store every day (and are good shoppers, with their employee discounts), their families are entitled to more than adequate benefit packages, and they actually use the word "love" when discussing their attitude toward their employer. But with the knowledge that the company has a financial agenda with which to comply, they do have to face the real world. "Uncertainty becomes certainty. With mergers, expansion, et cetera, companies can give no security. It's scary."

Did I mention that today is Linda Novotney Kemp's birthday? (Her husband gave her a Movado "museum watch" she selected from the jewelry counter of her favorite store.) She is the director of human resources development for the corporation, having started her thirteen-year career at Dayton Hudson at Hudson's in Detroit after two years as the training director for the Girl Scouts of Macomb County, Michigan. She was never a Girl Scout herself.

"It feels like a different company every few years. The changes come fast and often." To the rescue: Partners in Growth, a large-scale training program she developed in six weeks, which employees participate in at their own pace. The program includes videotapes, lectures, and exercises such as "The DHDSC Store Trivia Quiz," "Managing Personal Growth; Self-Awareness Inventory," and "Partners for Growth Crossword Puzzle."

Linda and Barbara Grigsby, now ex-director of public relations for DHDSC, who were classmates at Mary Grove College eighteen years ago, want to talk about the store's stellar promotions. At the top of the list is Santabear, a large, white plush bear in a muffler and stocking cap that sold over 2.5 million units from Christmas 1985 to Christmas 1987. (Buying Santabear outright cost $25, *or* just $10 with every purchase of $50 or more.) Retailing has been overwhelmed by the store bear phenomenon. "By this year," Grigsby sniffs, "everyone's going to do bears. Carson's [Carson Pirie Scott] has Chicago Bear, Woodies' [Woodward and Lothrop] is doing Kringle Bear, Lazarus is doing Lazzy Bear, and Liberty [in Hawaii] is doing Aloha Bear." Don't forget, Santabear had his own TV special on ABC, *Santabear's Christmas*, narrated by Kelly McGillis, now available on videocassette ($12.99), and in his own book and audiotape ($12.99 for the package).

The merchandise first started shipping in October, 1985 for the most spectacularly thorough promotion imaginable. American Express ran two double-truck—two-page—ads in *USA Today* advertising Santabear merchandise. "We're taking Santabear national with General Mills," Grigsby adds breathlessly. "He's already on four million boxes of Cinnamon Toast Crunch, with stickers in the packages."

Stephen Watson says forcefully, "This is my career." He's the chairman and chief executive officer of the Dayton Hudson Department Store Company and has been with the corporation for fifteen years, following Williams College (class of 1967), the Army ('71), and Harvard Business School ('73). With his academic credentials, Watson could have chosen any career. Why retailing? "My father was in the business all his life." During the summer between his first and second years of business school, he worked at Filene's, Boston's premiere department store and a member of the Federated Group, for which Steve's father worked. "My father was a major influence, without question. It's a business known for a lot of responsibility at an early age. It's marketing-related—one of the purest forms of marketing other than advertising. It's got a quick turnaround in decision making. You can just try it. I liked the people; I liked the horse-racing aspect of it. Every day. Other industries might only see quarterly returns. It's wonderful when it's good. And I haven't been disappointed."

Watson interviewed at several other important department stores around the country. "The reason I came here? I liked the people I met here better. Dayton's culture made the company seem attractive. The communication I got was that they cared for me. Also, I liked Minneapolis. Emotionally, it became what I wanted."

At forty-three he's a young CEO. (Indeed, he was made chairman and CEO when he was forty.) "Being CEO was a goal, somewhere. I liked the idea of being responsible. I was sure I could do it. This is the job I wanted at some company. I wanted to be able to strategize and set the culture with folks I worked with. I love it, but I certainly won't work all my life. I will retire in my early fifties. There's more to life than just this." There are not too many positions Watson could assume in the corporation that are senior to his. "Mervyn's and Target are bigger chains, so are they better? Who knows?"

He is both well liked and respected. Employees credit him with establishing a tone for the business. Watson says his legacy will be a "highly expansive, expanded company." He sees the organization's success as twofold: in financial performance and "as a company where people like to work. It's okay to be an entrepreneur, People work in partnership toward some goals. People care about you. People don't scream at you."

If you want to move around, let it be known. Cathy Agee's had eight moves in eleven years, which she said she initiated. [Author's note: We spoke before she made her ninth move: outside the company.] "But I felt confident I could. I felt the environment allowed me to pursue my aspirations." She's from a small town in Minnesota "like Lake Wobegon," where she worked in small specialty stores. "But Dayton's delivered." After graduation from the University of Minnesota, she spent a year as a VISTA volunteer, then returned home to earn her MBA at the university. "I sent a résumé to Dayton's. I was a consumer before and thought I understood the customer. I thought it had the best fit for me." She started as a financial analyst, which lasted two years, until she went on maternity leave. She returned after just over two months—relying on a full-time housekeeper—as a financial analyst for the department stores. From there she became "the liaison between merchandise and financials" until she found a spot in "seasonal planning. It was a once-in-a-lifetime opportunity with the head merchant." She stayed there a year because "I recognized the need to enter management to rise the way I wanted to." Her next job was in accounts payable, supervising 130 people. To further her goal of managing, "I lobbied for the general accounting manager—a payroll job—which I did for a year. Obviously, I've had a lot of support."

Agee became the director of financial planning, accounting, and payroll in 1982. "It was a major thing for me. I became a member of the KMG [Key Managing Group]. That was exciting. Other women had been in supervisory positions; I was not the first, but I was the first in these positions."

Cathy was offered something out of the blue the following year. "I was recruited to be the director of strategic planning at Mervyn's. It was a hard decision to make. I had never been divorced, and it felt like a divorce. I kept my daughter with me. My husband stayed here. He commuted [between Minneapolis and Hayward, California] three out of four weekends for two and a half years. I thought my husband would move, but he was given a great promotion at the same time. I never considered saying no to Mervyn's. I felt it was a once-in-a-lifetime opportunity. My husband felt I shouldn't say no." Cathy and her daughter lived in Palo Alto. In 1984 there was another change for Cathy. She went into buying for the first time, in bedspreads and comforters for Mervyn's, a $30-million-a-year business.

"I decided merchandising was not a good fit for me," she said in 1985. "Although I'm glad I did my year, and I learned a lot." Moreover, "It was important for me to keep my family together." She was the corporation's director of planning and analysis when we met. For how long? "I'll probably be content to stay here an extra year. As you move up, the pyramid narrows. One of the reasons I chose finance was because of its portability. But it's fun to be in retail. I don't know if I could get excited about widgets." Cathy would like to make a point about stereotypes. "The perception is that financial people are more disciplined; the accountant. It's hard to get rid of the image. It keeps hanging on. Merchants are creative. We like to emulate merchants."

Agee's track record didn't portend staying put. Yet, she said, "This is the only large company I would work for. It's a good group of people to work with. I love Ken Macke's influence. He *is* Dayton Hudson." She, too, evoked the famed integrity of Dayton Hudson. "I never felt I had to compromise my values to be a part of the company. There's a respect for people's privacy. They support family and a spiritual component. That's why I'm here."

Fast forward to Hayward, California, Mervyn's corporate headquarters. The place is vast and cavernous—a warehouse of walls, desks, and people. Chris Matthews, a chic blonde, is a divisional merchandise manager with years in the fashion business, in both the manufacturing and retailing sides. (After her graduation from the University of California at Davis, she entered the training program at Emporium Capwell, a California department store chain.)

She credits her own experiences but now says, "I think I'd feel at a disadvantage being in the fashion business outside Mervyn's." Having moved around a lot in the industry, Chris "had known many people at Mervyn's from my previous life. I chose it because the culture was people-oriented and because you get the feeling that, yes, you run your own business.

"I think you have to figure out what you're good at," she advises, "and you can't hate coming to work. I could have more free time; I could make more money. But I love the variety of tasks." She's changed jobs once, in her six years here. "I love seeing the results on the bottom line. After you work at a few places, you realize that no place is perfect. I'm not twenty-two, and I don't want to run the company. I don't want to be involved in politics. I love to be close to the merchandise." Matthews' own wardrobe is a bit pricier and trendier than the clothes she selects for the stores. That's not a problem. "I'm not a Mervyn's customer," she says, "but it's funny that you see a lot of our merchandise on people here." That's evidently their choice and not a directive from the chiefs.

"I can live with Mervyn's—even though it's getting bigger and more corporate—as long as I'm allowed to be creative and make mistakes."

Ron Johnson, a buyer of menswear, has lived out an interesting scenario. He graduated from Stanford University in 1980 with a degree in economics. For three years he was a consultant in the Minneapolis offices of Peat, Marwick, Mitchell. During the summer of 1983, he worked at Salomon Brothers, the New York investment firm. He was shopping for his first job in between his first and second years at the Harvard Business School. In a radical departure from the norm, "I decided to work in an operating company. I wanted to be with people, and I wanted to manage a business. I felt retailing was best for me since it was the most people-intensive." He's just across a bridge from the Silicon Valley; how did he resist that? "I've never been too excited about technology," he says.

He seems to be the only MBA here; certainly the only one with a Harvard pedigree. "We don't talk about it," he says from his spare office. "I downplay Harvard. My friends there thought I was crazy, but I realized this was a good fit." If there are other MBAs at Mervyn's, "they're on their own. There's no recruitment program." A native of Minnesota, Ron was very much a child of Dayton Hudson. "The values played a big part in getting me here. Decision making is moved down to the bottom. It's important to respect what senior management does, but at the same time it is important to challenge decisions. This is much less conformist than the other places I've worked. No one can believe there's only one way to do things.

"I don't think this is an intensely political company. You get promoted fairly. You get recognized adequately. I *feel,* more than understand, the culture. I know what I want. I expect to spend my whole career here. I'm just a real long-term player."

Walter Rossi, Mervyn's president and CEO, recalls, "when I became Mervynized, I felt I worked for a company whose values I could fit in with, but also aspire to." Rossi is proud that Mervyn's gave out 123 college scholarships to employees' children in 1987. "Knowing the company is involved in the community gives you a reason to be proud. At new store openings, we make donations to local charities. The community program was a Dayton Hudson program, and we got it from them."

Interview:

JUDY QUYE

*J*udy Quye is the first female store director of Mervyn's original San Lorenzo store, which is thirty-nine years old and has been remodeled sixteen times. When she received this promotion, at the age of twenty-six, she was also the youngest female store director ever named in the history of the company. She became affiliated with Dayton Hudson in 1978 at Hudson's in downtown Detroit. When her job as division sales manager was eliminated in 1982, she was offered an intercorporate transfer to Mervyn's, which required her family's support and acquiescence. "Since Mervyn's was in a growth phase and promised help and a good offer, we moved for this job. My husband had always wanted to live here in California. He's a journeyman electrician, and we had a three-month-old daughter."

The Quyes moved to Sacramento, where Judy was made an assistant store director. "Mervyn's seemed too good to be true. I was waiting for the catch. Once you realize they're not going to get you, you can relax and enjoy it. I fit into Mervyn's real well. I'm zany. My first day, everyone was in Western wear for Western Week. You can do blanket sale contests—it's perfect for me."

Although Mervyn's culture was not incompatible with the Dayton Hudson culture, and in fact by now the two are almost indistinguishable, Judy saw a disparity. "At Hudson's my supervisors said, 'Did you do this and this . . . ?' At Mervyn's they're more trusting in relationships. There's more room to skin your knee and learn from the experience. You could turn down jobs and not be penalized. The growth opportunities are phenomenal. The sky's the limit. You can see it happen." Quye positively gushes with excitement. "Each time I move, I work with a new group of people and forget past failures and bring with me my successes." She has moved nine times within the Mervyn's organization.

Judy is resolutely a Mervyn's person, although she admits her first impression was that the store was "very California. My challenge as a store director was to take the California style and enhance it. I feel I relate a lot to my customer. I *am* my customer." So is her sales force, 60 percent of whom are working mothers. "I relate to their needs, and they see they're working for someone they can relate to. Mervyn's is their family, and they don't all realize how important they are to us."

Judy's family now numbers four. A few years ago she had a Scottish nanny helping out at home. "I never knew such harmony . . . you just make the decision you can't do it all."

Mervyn's has expanded Judy's horizons. "Working here has very definitely made me more ambitious. I've told people I could be the first female vice-president, but I don't always believe in myself." Quye's manner is very caring and maternal. Walking around the store, her hands graze hangers and racks as if they were children. It is so refreshing to watch someone whose career is on an upward slope but who doesn't have the hard edges that often accompany professional desire.

"I can have an immediate impact. If business is bad, I can add new people. I run my business. People are always asking how I'm doing, and they want to help. And they mean it. Half of Mervyn's culture is knowing it's okay to ask for help. I have a district manager supervising me. I don't know that I feel he's watching over me; he's my partner. You can make mistakes and learn from your failures. You know you're not going to walk in and lose your job."

Judy's earnestness is the result of an abiding affection for the companies that have given her opportunities she never imagined. She inspires dedication in her staff, which numbers three hundred and fifty ordinarily but swells up to six hundred during the holidays. When she says,

"My store treats me well," she minimizes any sense of personal entitlement and instead feels privileged to work as hard as she does for a company that has heart.

Profile: *Santabear*

Date of Birth: Christmas 1985.

Place of Birth: Seoul, Korea.

Parents' Names: Steve Watson, John Pellegrene, and Paul Starkey.

Weight at Birth: Approximately three ounces.

Best Colors: "I'm a Winter." Santabear looks best in bright colors like red and green.

Hometown: Minneapolis, Minnesota.

Number of Cousins: 160 (at last count), including Santabear sleepshirts, Santabear scarves, Santabear mitts, Santabear aprons, Santabear red watch, Santabear anklets, mitten—Santabear, beret—Santabear, Santabear earmuffs, pajama Santabear, Santabear jog suit, earring trio Santabear, curly-Q hair Santabear, Santabear boxed undies, Santabear ice scraper, Santabear knit tie, Santabear paw pant, Santabear platter, Santabear cookie jar, and half-pint Santabear ice cream maker.

Favorite Experience: "Visiting the White House" during the 1987 holiday season. He was one of Nancy Reagan's featured guests at a party for the children of Washington's diplomats.

Management Style: "I like to think of myself as a people person. I like interfacing with everyone."

GENERAL MILLS

HISTORY & OPERATIONS

General Mills traces its origins to 1856, when "business genius" Cadwallader C. Washburn formed the Minneapolis Milling Company to lease power rights to mill operators. Ten years later, Washburn built a flour mill near a Minnesota waterfall. The locals dubbed the enterprise "Washburn's Folly," believing there was no real market for flour made from midwestern spring wheat. But Washburn, a natural innovator, proved them wrong. He replaced the mill's grinding stones with steel rollers, acquired a newfangled purifying machine, and was soon turning out a high-quality flour that rivaled that of other mills. The advances Washburn introduced brought Minneapolis to the forefront as the country's milling center.

As the Washburn Mills prospered, Washburn expanded his facilities. In 1877 he entered into partnership with John Crosby. The following year, a flour-dust explosion decimated the mills. The partners quickly rebuilt with updated equipment and ultimately established the first automatic roller mill in the world. They entered the first Miller's International Exhibition in 1880, and their flours swept the awards, winning, gold, silver, and bronze medals. In consequence, they named their top-grade flour Gold Medal.

In 1888 merchant miller James S. Bell, regarded by fellow millers as the "greatest merchandiser" of his time, assumed leadership of the Washburn Crosby Mills. Bell engineered an expansion program, constructing a new mill in Buffalo, New York, and hiring an advertising manager to promote the Gold Medal brand name. In the 1890s, small advertisements for the flour, which used the popular slogan "Eventually—Why not now?" began appearing in magazines. By the 1920s, Gold Medal had achieved a national market and the slogan was displayed on billboards all across the country. In 1921 the company created a commercial character to personalize its products to housewives. Betty Crocker was promoted as a "helpful friend," and in 1928 she hit the airwaves with the radio program *Betty Crocker Cooking School of the Air*.

Also during the 1920s, the Washburn Crosby Mills diversified into packaged foods with a line of products launched under the Gold Medal umbrella. The most popular and enduring of these was Wheaties—Breakfast of Champions, which was originally advertised by a group called "The Wheaties Quartet." (Later the company promoted Wheaties through the sponsorship of major league baseball radio broadcasts, and its popularity skyrocketed). In 1925 James Ford Bell, the son of James S. Bell, took over as president of the company, and in 1928 he merged the holdings of Washburn Crosby with those of several other midwestern millers and formed General Mills. The following year, when the company merged with the Sperry Flour Company, the largest miller on the Pacific Coast, General Mills became the largest flour producer in the world.

General Mills survived the Depression, and while it still focused primarily on flour, it continued to develop new products. In 1930 the company launched Bisquick, a flour-and-shortening mixture—discovered inadvertently by a company sales executive—which provided housewives with a shortcut to baking. Cheerios (advertised by the Lone Ranger) and Kix cereals were introduced in the early 1940s. In 1943 the company formed a chemical division to process soybeans for animal feed. Between 1945 and 1959, General Mills expanded rapidly, adding a number of new products to its line of packaged foods, including the first Betty Crocker cake mixes.

Beginning in 1960, the company shifted its focus away from milling. It closed over half of its flour mills and sold the chemical division, and in 1966 embarked on a program of growth through the acquisition of a number of different kinds of consumer goods companies.

By the beginning of the 1980s, General Mills was competing in five major industries and accordingly organized into five divisions: Consumer Foods, which encompassed flour, cereals, and mixes, in addition to products like Tom's snack foods, Gorton's frozen seafoods, Yoplait yogurts, and Saluto pizzas; Restaurants, which included the Red Lobster Inns, York Steak Houses, and Good Earth chains; Toys, with products including Parker Brother's Monopoly, Kenner's Star Wars toys, and Lionel trains; Fashion (including Izod/Lacoste Sportswear, Ship 'n' Shore blouses, Foot-Joy golf shoes, Lord Jeff sweaters, Monet and Ciani jewelry, and Lark Luggage; and Specialty Retailing and Furniture Group, with Talbots for women's wear, Eddie Bauer for outdoor wear, Wallpapers to Go, LeeWards which sold home crafts and kitchen utensils. The furniture business was made up of Kittinger, Pennsylvania House, and Williamsburg Furniture, but it was sold in 1986. By 1982 General Mills was a worldwide operation with annual revenues in excess of $4 billion and 66,000 employees.

In 1984 the company's toy and fashion divisions floundered, putting an end to twenty-two straight years of earnings increases. The following year, General Mills spun off both divisions into freestanding companies, Kenner-Parker Toys and Crystal Brands. The move was part of an overall restructuring—altogether, twenty-six individual companies or divisions were spun off or divested—through which General Mills shed most of its consumer businesses in order to narrow its focus primarily to packaged goods and restaurants. (Kenner-Parker Toys has since merged with Tonka Toys, and retains its own brand names and product lines.)

Today, under the leadership of H. Brewster "Bruce" Atwater, Jr., who joined the company in 1958 and rose through the marketing ranks to become president in 1977 and CEO in 1981, the company is once again performing strongly. Revenues for fiscal 1987 reached $5.19 billion, and earnings rose over 95 percent, from a low of $113.7 million in 1985 to $222 million. General Mills now employs approximately sixty-six thousand employees, the majority of whom work in the United States.

The company's operations are organized into three broad divisions. Consumer Foods, the largest, accounts for over two thirds of total sales and earnings and produces more than two hundred products, including Gold Medal flour (number one in its market with no close competitors), Cheerios, Wheaties, Total, Trix, Lucky Charms (the company is in second place behind Kellogg's in the fiercely competitive cereal market), Bisquick, Betty Crocker cake mixes, frosting mixes, and instant potato mixes, Hamburger, Chicken, and Tuna Helper, Nature Valley Granola bars and other granola snacks, Fruit Corners fruit snacks, Yoplait yogurts, Gorton's frozen fish, and a recently launched line of shelf-stable salads. (The International Foods Division, which is included in the Consumer Foods Division, sells General Mills products in several European countries, Latin America, Canada and Australia, and accounts for less than 10 percent of revenues). The Restaurant Division, whose chains are Red Lobster Inns, which was acquired as a chain of three restaurants in 1970 and has since grown to the country's largest full service dinner house chain, with 392 restaurants in thirty-five states, Japan and Canada; the Olive Garden, a chain of appproximately seventy Italian restaurants located in the Midwest and Southwest, started in 1985; and York's, a chain of 113 steak houses concentrated in the Midwest. (Leann Chin's, a handful of Chinese restaurants and carryout emporia in the Twin Cities, was acquired in 1985 and sold back to Mrs. Chin and other investors in 1988.) And Specialty Retailing, with Talbots, the country's largest retailer of "updated, classic women's apparel" (130 stores in addition to a substantial mail order business, including twenty-five new stores planned for fiscal 1988) and Eddie Bauer (fifty-four stores and a significant mail-order business with plans for between fifteen and twenty new stores in fiscal 1988). [Author's Note: As of May 1988, General Mills planned to sell off Talbots and Eddie Bauer, the last properties of its Specialty Retailing Division.]

Through a foundation established in 1954, General Mills contributes generously to a range of charities with donations of cash and food. The company encourages its employees to volunteer in programs that benefit their communities, and has a Community Action Team at its Minneapolis headquarters.

(Information provided by Terry Thompson, company spokesman.)

1987 *Fortune* 500 RANKING: Seventy-seventh among all companies, tenth among food companies.

REVENUES: $5.19 billion in fiscal 1987.

EARNINGS: $222 million in fiscal 1987.

INITIAL PUBLIC OFFERING: 1928.

NUMBER OF SHAREHOLDERS: Over 50,000.

NUMBER OF EMPLOYEES: Approximately 66,000, the majority in the continental United States. Although General Mills does have growing businesses in Europe and elsewhere, it is not a company with a huge international presence.

AVERAGE AGE OF EMPLOYEES: Information not available.

EMPLOYEE TURNOVER: Information not available.

RECRUITMENT: The company recruits at approximately twenty-six institutions across the country. It goes to the best business schools in the country, looking primarily for finance and marketing MBAs, though it hires for a broad range of disciplines. It also recruits widely at the undergraduate level, for people with backgrounds that vary from food scientists (for their six-hundred-person research and development laboratory) to engineers to accountants to information systems to personnel to manufacturing.

NUMBER OF NEW HIRES PER YEAR: Information not available. "It varies from year to year, and we're not willing to estimate."

RANGE OF STARTING SALARIES: MBAs: Approximately $38,000–$47,000; non-MBAs: "It would start lower and it would not go higher."

POLICY FOR RAISES: "Employees are reviewed yearly for salary purposes, and our raises are determined on the basis of performance."

TRAINING PROGRAMS: No formal programs for new employees. Lots of informal training programs for different disciplines. It's mostly on-the-job training, and there's a conscious effort to expose new employees to the broadest number of activities early in their careers.

BENEFITS: Life insurance (four types), business travel accident insurance, medical and dental insurance, sick leave, disability coverage (long- and short-term), retirement income plan (employees get 50 percent of final average earnings less Social Security after thirty years with the company; they can be vested after ten years of service), spouse's pension benefit (provides a lifetime income for the surviving spouse of an employee fifty-five years or older who has five or more years of service and dies while actively employed by the company), voluntary investment plan (permits employee contributions of 1–15 percent of pay on a before-tax and/or aftertax basis; company matches 50 percent of the total contributions up to the first 5 percent, and educational assistance (upon approval for work-related study).

VACATION: Ten days after one year, eleven days after two years, seventeen days after five years, twenty-two days after fourteen years, twenty-seven days after nineteen years, and thirty-two days after twenty-four years, in addition to twelve regular paid holidays per year.

ADDITIONAL PERKS: General Mills offers adoption assistance, which covers 80 percent of eligible expenses up to $1,000 for each adoption. The company's dependent care plan enables employees to deduct money (up to $5,000 per year) on a before-tax basis to be used to assist in caring for dependents (children under fifteen and those dependents physically or mentally incapable of caring for themselves). The company also has a service station on the grounds of its main office and a place where employees can get their cars repaired at competitive rates. The company has an employee cafeteria that often uses General Mills products. And employees are often among the first to sample new company products.

BONUSES: "Not available to employees at all levels, but based on an evaluation of job significance, contribution, and technical know-how. Furthermore, a couple of other factors intervene,

including the company's total performance, departmental performance, an individual performance." Bonuses are awarded annually.

ANNUAL PARTY: General Mills does not host regular annual parties. The company has had
picnics on the lawn to celebrate two very good years, but these were informal gatherings of
employees, without their spouses.

AVERAGE WORKDAY: At Minneapolis headquarters, 8:30 A.M. to 4:30 P.M., with half an hour
for lunch.

DRESS CODE: No stated dress code, but it's a relatively conservative style of dress. "Minneapolis
is a sophisticated community culturally, financially, socially, and governmentally, so these
things have an impact on how people dress. While it's conservative, it's not a dour style.
Upbeat, but tending toward conservative."

SOCIAL ATMOSPHERE: "Some people fraternize, some don't. There's no subtle pressure to be
part of an after-hours social circle. You don't have to commingle if you don't want to, but
there are plenty of opportunities to do that. No feeling of coercion or that you have to socialize
to stay in step. That's phony stuff, and it's rejected."

NUMBER OF CONSUMER FOODS PRODUCTS: More than two hundred.

NUMBER OF NEW PRODUCTS LAUNCHED PER YEAR: More than forty.

MOST POPULAR PRODUCT: Cheerios. (With its sibling, Honey Nut Cheerios, "they constitute
the leading franchise in the entire [huge] ready-to-eat cereals industry, in terms of dollars and
volume.")

HEADQUARTERS: Approximately two thousand people in the main building not far from the
Minneapolis/St. Paul Airport, including food, marketing and corporate staff, and six hundred
people in the technical center (research and development). Designed by Skidmore, Ourlys and
Merrill.

ART COLLECTION: Over 1,000 pieces by Picasso, Jasper Johns, Miro, Jim Dine, and Jennifer
Bartlett, among others. The General Mills collection is considered to be among the "more
adventurous" corporate art collections in that the works are "electric, provocative, contemporary, and thought-provoking." The company focuses to a large degree on living artists, on the
theory that "art should reflect the tempo of the times." The art is available to General Mills
employees for their offices.

CHARITABLE CONTRIBUTIONS: In 1987 the General Mills Foundation contributed $6.7 million
in the areas of social services and health, culture, civic affairs, and education. The corporation
donated another $1.3 million. In addition, the company donated over 3 million pounds of
food to food banks across the country. Altcare—a joint venture of General Mills and the
Wilder Foundation based in St. Paul—focuses on long-term care for the elderly, exploring
alternatives to nursing homes. In 1986 Altcare established a twenty-eight-unit development
in a Minneapolis suburb (which will serve as a prototype for replication) that allows residents
to own or rent their own apartments, offering twenty-four-hour nonmedical supervision and
access to a full range of health and social services, and costs 30 percent less than standard
nursing homes. In 1987 Altcare won two prestigious national awards for its services to the
elderly. In addition, the company encourages both active and retired employees to volunteer
their time in a wide range of community programs.

I asked her, "How do you get from here to there, and where is there?" She answered, "I have some sense of where 'there' is, and how to get General Mills to recognize that. We've got good skills in problem solving but a narrow road for financial people here. I feel that most people don't have a sense of other divisions. Yes, it's a problem, recognized by management. A rotation would be great. Eddie Bauer managers spend four days a year behind the counter, she points out longingly. Judy Mares's bottom line is "Nobody owes me anything. 'Owing' doesn't represent this relationship." (Her next "there" was to assistant treasurer, a promotion, in which she managed the corporate balance sheets. She left General Mills in the spring of 1988 to work for a bank.)

Susan Hausknecht was still new at General Mills when we talked. At Williams College she majored in economics, "a really neat major," and worked for two years before entering Stanford Business School, where she was in the class of 1985. "I was born in Cincinnati and loved the Midwest. California was not for me. I came out here on the coldest day of the year for my interview and loved it. General Mills was my first interview. I loved it. You know how you just click with people? It never happened elsewhere. Nowhere were they so articulate and fun. It was a riot. General Mills has an outstanding reputation at Stanford as the best consumer marketing company. There are six of us from Stanford, out of a class of thirty-five new assistant product managers." They socialize together at Happy Hours on Fridays.

"This company allows you to think strategically early on. You're promoted within your first twelve to fourteen months." Susan is armed with the facts as only an eager newcomer can be. (And in fact, by publication time, she was promoted to assistant product manager.) "Attrition usually occurs in the second year or later. I feel I could stay here awhile. That's my intention. I would be quite content to spend my career or life here. It's different from the others." She's lucky to be working in "Big G," the cereal division, specifically on presweetened cereal. Lucky because in a way, cereal is the corporation's signature product. It may be the best way to really learn the company.

"Big G has a unique climate to produce excellence," Susan declares. Keith Seick calls Big G " 'the Tiffany division.' Here in Minneapolis, the food division of General Mills is the preferred place to work. There's steady growth, and that's what General Mills is. It's two thirds of our business. Other divisions are in other places with other cultures."

Susan is working on the launch of a new children's cereal. Even though it will be announced in *Advertising Age* way before this book is printed, she is so protective she will not reveal the cereal's identity. "Confidentiality is something to be aware of," she explains. Barbara Jackson found the cloak-and-dagger aspect of the cereal business fun. "You get to assign code names to new products. S'mores became 'Project Campfire.' You do get off on that." The cereal business is a competitive one, and Susan is aware that part of her mission is to win the market share battle against Kellogg's, Post (General Foods), Ralston-Purina, and Quaker Oats (see p. 159).

Big G feels more clannish than other areas of General Mills. It's filled with business jocks, people who "work hard and play hard"—they actually say this—and admit to a macho attitude toward work. They celebrate their successes. The group seems in control. They are as conversant with the breakfast preferences of seven-year-old boys as they are with ski conditions. Hausknecht arrives at the office by 7:15 in the morning and leaves at 6:15 P.M. to take an aerobics class. It's hard to picture her not succeeding. In addition to socializing over drinks on Fridays, Susan plays darts on Tuesday nights and is a Big Sister in the community. "There's a real conscious effort to do community stuff."

Paul Parker praises the tradition of corporate citizenship nurtured by General Mills's management. "Executives fill out objective questionnaires every year, including 'How will you be a good citizen this year?' It's tied right to your bonus. Getting young people involved in corporate social responsibility is not unselfish. A person involved is less likely to go elsewhere when a job's offered."

Ivy Bernhardson is in the last trimester of her second pregnancy. A native Minneapolitan, she started working for the company during school summers as a tour guide. (General Mills no longer offers tours to the public.) "I needed a job, and I can't type." As a second-year law student at the University of Minnesota, she was hired as a law clerk here. After graduation, she became a staff attorney. The company paid for her bar review course. Ivy's professional universe has always been General Mills.

"I did not work eighty hours a week the first few years [as her classmates in private practice did], but I worked hard. They have no lives outside their jobs. You can only do that so long. I have friends in private practice who envy me. I have more experience, more travel, et cetera. General Mills is considered a good place to work."

The law staff is structured somewhat like a firm. The staff attorney category has three levels of seniority. First is associate counsel (which is tantamount to junior partner), then senior associate counsel, associate general counsel (there are two of these), and then one general counsel, who is not on the board of the corporation, which is unusual. The pressure to upgrade one's station is minor, if not nonexistent. Working as a lawyer for General Mills must be satisfying, because most of the professional staff stay a long time. "One lawyer was here for thirty years, and several have been here over twenty. You get to know the company and its history. It makes you valuable."

The department is broken up into specialties, most prominently Finance, Securities, Acquisitions, and Divestitures. "It clearly can all drop in a lawyer's lap. We have [outside] experts in other areas and can use their expertise. When General Mills is in contract negotiations, we get to be the bad guy. I have a code of professional behavior and ethics I personally take very seriously, and I never forget that I'm an officer of the state of Minnesota. I never forget who my employer is. But I hope I never forget that I'm a lawyer first."

Given the attorneys' dual role as corporate officials, the practice of law in this environment is "more preventive. We're trying to spot problems before they occur. We're trying to avoid litigation. It's sooo expensive," Bernhardson emphasizes. "We don't do our own litigation, and since General Mills is in every state, we could get sued [in product liability] in every state. We tend to be conservative. This society's so litigious; it's down to the lowest common denominator. We're perceived as having deep pockets, so we're sued." It may not be a threatening situation; a lawsuit could be instigated by a purchaser of a damaged box of Lucky Charms.

Six women work in the law department, of a staff totaling seventeen in corporate headquarters, and three more lawyers work with the restaurant group, based in Orlando, Florida. "I rarely leave my job at the end of the day," Ivy says, "and I would do the same if I were a waitress. It helps to have a baby." (Indeed, I would say that of all the people I met in the course of researching this book, the ones who had the happiest work lives were those who had families. A full life at home is the quickest way to erase the tension of the workday. It seems to put one's priorities in order.) Ivy took six weeks off when she had her first child and was preparing to do the same with her second. *"Not* because it's career-enhancing," she says of the short hiatus, "I was ready to work." She has the advantage of having her mother nearby, and she is able to stay with the kids during the day. "Child care is a nationwide crisis and concern. General Mills doesn't have day care facilities on the premises, but there is a dependent care plan" (see p. 376). Mothers who breast-feed their babies may express their milk in the medical department. Nursing isn't done.

Sometimes Bernhardson wonders whether she should have taken the MBA route. "I've been asked to take nonlegal [work] here, but I want to practice law. Maybe if I had, I'd become a vice-president sooner. But just when I think things are getting boring, something happens." One of the most challenging projects took all of 1985, when General Mills spun off its toy and clothing divisions. The amalgamation of Kenner and Parker Brothers toys, plus Lionel Trains, subsidiaries of the corporation, as well as the fashion businesses of Izod, Monet (costume jewelry), and Ship 'n' Shore, became two smaller companies, known as Kenner-Parker Toys and Crystal Brands, respectively. "These were instantly public autonomous businesses." In the summer 1985 edition of *Family,* General Mills's in-house magazine, Bruce Atwater explained the rationale behind the spin-offs:

"By 1982, we had changed from 95 percent consumer foods to 51 percent consumer foods, 16 percent restaurants and 33 percent non-foods . . . In our strategic evaluations of the company starting three years ago, we recognized that very few companies are able to compete in five different industries and still perform in the top quartile of American companies.

". . . Of the largest 1,000 companies in the United States, only nine companies besides General Mills have turned in top-notch results competing in five or more businesses. The companies with the very best results concentrate their resources and their management in a very limited number of businesses which they know well. Quite clearly our strategic conclusions for General Mills were that competing successfully in five businesses is a very hard thing to do. In addition, being in five businesses would effectively preclude the company from considering any so-called sixth area, if another attractive industry area should develop.

". . . There are also advantages for the General Mills investor who expects to have relatively steady growth to avoid the volatility of toys and fashion.

". . . Given the strategic decision to exit the toy and fashion businesses, the choice between a sale of those assets for cash or a spin-off to shareholders is made based on the relative value to shareholders. . . . All of us have a strong interest in seeing that these companies are very well received in the marketplace, and we are doing everything we can to enhance their prospects."

Atwater's hunch paid off. In 1987 General Mills reached a high on the New York Stock Exchange of $56.00 a share. Crystal Brands achieved 28⅝, and Kenner-Parker reached $51.50 before merging with Tonka Toys that year.

Stephen Sanger is one of those people who grew up in Cincinnati, aspiring always to work for local giant Procter & Gamble. "Three out of five Cincinnati families derive some employment from P and G," he says. After graduating from DePauw and receiving his MBA from the University of Michigan, he got his coveted job as product manager there. "I spent a good three years there, and enjoyed it. Then General Mills contacted me. I'd spent enough time in Cincinnati. Everything I liked about P and G I could find here, and things I didn't like I didn't have here. P and G is very serious; they took themselves seriously. This business is fun. Cereal marketing especially—there's a lot of goofy stuff. People here are willing to admit they've screwed up. They almost enjoy [their mistakes]."

Sanger's first job at General Mills, fourteen years ago, was as an assistant product manager on Wheaties. "A job change means a new language, learning just how to find things. My first day on the job, I didn't know what I'd do. I was scared." He was told to handle the NFL Rookie of the Year contest. It was won by Boobie Clark of the Cincinnati Bengals. "My first day I was told to customize his winning Dodge car. I think Boobie was pleased."

Steve is presently the president of Yoplait. When we talked, he was working on new business development in the Consumer Foods Division, "identifying major new food businesses that General Mills is not involved in; new products with no precedent. It's so undefined compared to being marketing director of cereals, for example." Sanger's mandate could lead him to recommend an acquisition or to sponsor an invention. His areas of investigation were concentrated in snack foods. "We're looking at ice cream novelties," he admitted. General Mills accepted his suggestion and bought Vroman Foods, makers of the Gold Rush bar, a premium chocolate-covered bar, in 1985.

The Vroman acquisition was a short process. "We identified the ice cream product area as early as 1983, and the actual decision to make the offer was in December 1984. They were a privately held company. There was no investment bank. We talked directly to the president-founder of this thirty-million-dollar company. We closed April 1985." As a property of General Mills, Vroman needs to be somewhat enculturated, but "we need to maintain separate identities. It's smaller and has less money for advertising."

Likening the new business group to a venture capital team, Sanger says he and his immediate colleagues "try to do things beyond the range of what General Mills does. Any new product may get extensive testing, but not test marketing. We get a lot of suggestions from consumers. We ask opinions. Anything that requires significant finances needs to be brought to top management. There are no solo operators; the team goes into play. It's fun to work with those guys."

Steve is a team player but, as we've seen, able to be flexible and think of his career apart from the corporation. "I thought of General Mills as a long-term thing, but not my whole career. I still don't. My ultimate goal is to open a hot dog stand on a San Diego beach."

John Machuzick was an enthusiastic manager of sales operations when we spoke. He's since been promoted to region manager in Southern California. One of three people in national sales, he took General Mills's more than two hundred products on the road for eight years, on a totally different path from the product managers. "Marketing people have been to Harvard and Yale and have MBAs, but they lack street sense. Supermarket people have to work their way up." It's not that he has anything against college graduates; he's one himself. He attended St. Joseph's University in Philadelphia, where he got a bachelor of science degree in—of all things—food marketing.

His path is clear; in sales, movement is purely vertical. He started at General Mills as a sales rep in Baltimore, moved up to territory manager in Reading, Pennsylvania, became a regional sales assistant in Valley Forge, relocated back to Baltimore to become the account manager for A&P, Food Fair, and Acme Stores, and then was the district manager for Washington, D.C. [Author's note: In case there was ever any doubt, the most Yoplait yogurt sold anywhere in his regions was in the "Social Safeway" on Wisconsin Avenue in Washington. You know the store—no one is admitted unless they're wearing cute running shorts with the name of their prep school, college, law school, or division of the Justice Department printed on one leg.]

"We didn't call on Mom-and-Pop stores, but stores with four or five cash registers—minimum. It's a fact that you must have Cheerios and Gold Medal flour in all grocers. It's kind of a slap in the face if there's more corn flakes [Kellogg's] than Cheerios." John knows a lot about the eating habits of Americans. For example, "Hamburger Helper sells better in the

South" than in any other region of the country. "Flour sales go up from September to February."

It's hard to imagine anyone more gung-ho or brand loyal than John. He says, "It's a thrill to see your products on the shelves." He refers to Lee Iacocca as his role model. "He got knocked down a few times but didn't give up."

And his evaluation of General Mills is fairly exalted. "The company's not afraid to give you challenges. It's not a strict structure. If you have ambition, we'll give you challenge. I will stick it out with the company. They've been good to me. I hope to be a region manager of one of our seventeen regions. I don't mind moving. [Author's note: Congratulations, John.]

"I think I'd make a heck of a lot more money elsewhere—we're not at the highest end of the pay scale for the industry—but I don't think I'd have the same caring environment."

The sales ladder is a better fit for John than the marketing side. "My boss is totally hands-off. He lets us run our own businesses. I don't have to beg. It's more intrapreneurial in sales. Most people in sales are not MBAs. MBAs are less loyal. The sales organization only promotes from within. We're associated with Betty Crocker. We *are* Cheerios. You're the things people eat. You have a bond with these products. You feel good about these products, feel great pride." His favorite product is Honey Nut Cheerios, but he experiences occasional cravings for nacho-flavored Bugles snacks. "I could shoot my wife every time she buys [Ralston's] Rice Chex."

Interview:
SALLY FRAME-KASAKS OF TALBOTS

Sally Frame-Kasaks (née Frame) is the president of Talbots (né The Talbots), the successful women's clothing chain founded in 1947 in Hingham, Massachusetts, a suburb of Boston. It was purchased by General Mills in 1973 and is a focal point of the corporation's Specialty Retailing Group. Long a bastion of conservatively tailored sportswear (see *The Official Preppy Handbook*, pp. 154–155. Well, other people use it as a reference; why not me?), the company grew through a long and successful history of mail order. In fiscal 1987 the company mailed out over 60 million copies of twenty-one different catalogues. Talbots is now focusing on opening new retail outlets. Frame-Kasaks is updating the Talbots look by applying the same savvy she demonstrated as president and CEO of Ann Taylor. Part of her housecleaning has been to drop the "The" preceding Talbots' name.

She moved to Boston in November 1986. "The first eight weeks were a blur. I really felt I started at the first of the year." It seems she was thrown into the fray with little time for adjustment. "I felt like saying, 'Cut me a break; I don't even know where the ladies' room is.' Fortunately, I have a way of acknowledging and saying 'I don't know.'"

She was born in Detroit but spent much of her childhood in Iran, where her father was a medical missionary. High school was in Forest Hills, New York, a gentrified neighborhood in Queens. A graduate of American University, where she majored in government and public administration, Sally's college career got off to an inauspicious start. "I got the worst case of mono. I was bedridden from Thanksgiving to February freshman year. I lost the year." She returned home to New York and attacked *The New York Times'* classified ads. She applied for, and got, a job selling junior sportswear at Arnold Constable, a now defunct department store.

To her interview she wore a navy suit, red shoes, a veil, and a hat and carried a handbag. It was 1962.

At the end of the summer, Frame was invited to enter Constable's training program, but she wanted to return to school. Besides, ironically enough, "I detested shopping. The stores were hot and humid—an unpleasant environment."

When she returned to Washington and academic life, she realized, "I immediately missed the independence of making my own money. I found it distasteful to ask my parents for money." She rearranged her schedule to be able to work part time in retailing. Every Thursday night and Saturday, she was in the handbag department of Lord & Taylor in Chevy Chase. "I loved service, and I worked harder at school. I made dean's list a lot. I was very organized. I had a work life, a school life, and I began to feel like a grown-up." Sally was able to finish school on schedule with her class, completing all her course work in three years.

By now Frame realized that she "loved selling. I loved the competition. I wanted to be a top seller. I felt it was a natural. I had thought of law school and urban planning" [she had said earlier that being in Washington during the Kennedy administration was exhilarating. "I got caught up by Kennedy's inaugural address. It truly struck a chord."] and even took the GREs, but I enjoyed retailing."

She stayed at Lord & Taylor. "I worked with individuals who made the industry great. I feel a direct link—the Magnins, Marcuses—I feel I'm a part of that tradition." She did well. As a department manager she took home a staggering $70 per week. Her rent was $110 a month. She was recruited by Garfinckel's, a top Washington area department store. "My boss refused my resignation." Nevertheless, she moved on and became first a buyer and then the fashion director. "I discovered that I could make a difference. My commitment made results. While I was the youngest department manager, I could manage people older than I. Adults trusted my judgment as a kid."

As Garfinckel's fashion director, with jurisdiction over all its stores, "I could give the organization a direction, a point of view. It was the first job where I couldn't do everything myself. It was frustrating, all the stuff I couldn't accomplish. I [learned how to achieve] success through other people." By 1975 Frame also decided it was time to go. "I wanted New York. I started to think, there's more to this for me. And I was tired of fighting retailing stereotypes."

At Saks Fifth Avenue, Garfinckel's New York cousin, Sally became the vice-president of merchandising sales for the New York store. She specialized in intimate apparel, "which was different from fashion. The pay was the same as I was making in D.C., which meant a pay cut [when having to survive in the pricier city]." Soon she was running a multistore operation, merchandising for thirty outlets.

Once again Frame knew it was time to find a new challenge. "I wanted specialty stores. Department stores were too impersonal, and my stamp was always to personalize, to motivate my division. I felt that over the long haul, within retail, there would be something bigger. My sense of it was that growth wasn't going to be in huge, conservative stores. (Twenty-five percent of our underwear sales happen in four weeks for Christmas.) I left Saks impulsively without a job. After a positive review with a raise. I'd learned there, but it was not a great fit.

"I'd always talked to headhunters," she continues. "You get great exposure to interesting, neat people. Salary never motivated me." Sally found two "very bright guys to talk to," executives of Abraham & Strauss, one of Federated Department Stores—Bloomingdale's, Lazarus, Filene's—eastern chains. "I took the job at A and S in April 1979 because of these two great merchandising guys, one of whom, Mickey Drexler, later headed up The Gap, and the other of whom, Mike Jeffries, started Alcott & Andrews." En route to Brooklyn, A&S's headquarters, Frame got a call from the head of Ann Taylor. It was when "Ann Taylor started to harness its momentum."

One month later, Frame became the vice-president and director of stores for Ann Taylor, then owned by Garfinckel's. (Today it's part of the Allied Stores—Jordan Marsh, Bon Marché, Maas Brothers—empire.) "We had thirty stores then, but no money, no field organization. I ended up learning how to run a store. It's twenty-four hours a day. I felt I reached my niche." After seventeen years of buying, merchandising, and selling experience, Sally hadn't had a taste of operations.

"We started the delicate task of increasing our market share as our customer was changing. We didn't want to lose our old customers." That meant striking a balance between the fashion-forward and the stylistically reticent.

Sally Frame-Kasaks sees many similarities between Ann Taylor and Talbots. For one thing, the concept of "private label," garments exclusively designed and manufactured under the store's label, was one of her great successes at Ann Taylor that's extremely compatible with the Talbots look. "Make a friend with a twenty-eight-dollar sweater. Our lady will buy three sweaters if she loves them. Our label will be the most important label we sell. We'll offer quality and fashion."

The first catalogues of the Frameified Talbots reveal a harmony of classic, tailored clothes with newer, more contemporary lines. (Not that different from some of the private label Ann Taylor merchandise.) Frame-Kasaks herself, a statuesque five feet ten inches, dark, and attractive, is wearing a composite look: a long dirndl-y skirt with a white blouse (high collar fastened with a bar pin) and shawl. It is impossible to contemplate any occasion, save for black tie, in which her ensemble would be inappropriate.

"It was only since I left that I realized how big Ann Taylor was. I was too busy to realize it. My mother was very proud. The fact that her friends shopped there meant I'd arrived. It worked. People noticed. I was made president in 1982. We had seventy-five stores by the time I left." One of the more difficult aspects of her departure was saying good-bye to New York.

"Leaving was very difficult, but this was so exciting! Even more than I had imagined. The actual 'courtship' only took three to four weeks. I saw my future here. I just knew it was right." Talbots' pretty corporate park in Hingham, a few miles away from the original store, is beautifully landscaped. Its forty-five acres boast a beautiful freshwater pond, stocked with the help of the Audubon Society. Really. It's a combination of old guard and high tech. The main building is multileveled and bright, filled with glossy colors and skylights and "the imprint of founders Rudy and Nancy Talbot is still here." The warehouse, a mammoth operation of machinery and thousands of pieces of clothes and accessories was recently moved to Lakeville, Massachusetts, leaving an enormous space. A space planning committee was formed to determine what to do with it. Separated from all this by giant panes of glass is a huge bank of telephone operators, armed with computers and the actual garments themselves, so that they can answer questions ("How long is the skirt? Does it have a deep hem? Is it royal or navy blue?" etc.) with the stuff in their hands.

Research is a key ingredient to the new Talbots. Again, Frame-Kasaks' charge is to retain the existing customers while expanding the target customer pool. Surveys reveal that the median age of Talbots' targeted customer is forty-eight, and that 85 percent of the customers are between thirty-five and sixty years of age.

For the first time in Frame-Kasaks' career, she is working for a huge corporation, whose primary business is not fashion. Approximately two months after her arrival, General Mills made her a vice-president of the corporation. "I don't feel I'm working for a corporation or anyone," she says. "I'm doing it for myself. That's exciting. I don't feel [General Mills's presence] except in the most positive, supportive sense that I'm part of something bigger. We're an investment, and we are acutely aware that we have a responsibility to our shareholders.

"There's something about being part of a large organization that's stimulating. I was a little apprehensive. There was a little distrust. But the numbers are working. We're doing our job and honoring our parameters." When she wanted to revise the graphic look of Talbots' printed matter and packaging, "I didn't have to show them [to the General Mills brass], but I did, and they 'got it.' "

Running Talbots is a different job from running Ann Taylor. "I'm learning to be presidential," Frame-Kasaks confides. "I lower my voice and hold my hands. Sometimes there's pain when the nails dig in. People learn your style from working with you. Once I suggested something in a meeting, and it got done. It was very sobering. I must be precise. I must elicit opinions and not be flip—people can take things the wrong way. There's an understanding here that I'm playing many roles until we get organized together. Sometimes I'll make a distinction and say, 'I'm saying this to you as a vice-president of merchandising.'

"My sense is that people want leadership and want a set of boundaries and perimeters. My first day I met two hundred people. We were sizing each other up. I drew some very strong conclusions that day, and since then time has confirmed my expectations. (I'd been watching the company from afar for a while.) Our women want to look good, but not be the first on their block to wear the new styles. People don't want to be noticed for what they're wearing. 'Classic' has great connotations."

Famed for its high-quality customer service—a necessity in the mail-order business, Talbots' "customer service doesn't just happen by [a mission statement] being posted on the wall. It's been our story. Our phone people are amazing. We're leaders in telemarketing." Interestingly, the land of palm trees and pastel leggings is a big market for Talbots' shop-by-mail service. "Californians can't shop for these clothes [locally]. If I moved to California, I would not become blonde, five feet two and a size two." The company's single most profitable area bears the zip code 10021, in Manhattan's "Silk Stocking District."

Sally Frame-Kasaks is confident but cautious. "Success can be your undoing. You can't get carried away. Personally, you shouldn't believe your own press. You shouldn't lose your edge. You should know your limits and define your values."

The company over which she presides had revenues of $300 million in 1987. When she arrived, Talbots had eighty-six stores. Within the year, they were opening sixteen more. One thousand and forty-four people work in the corporate headquarters in Hingham, another 500 work in the Lakeville Fulfillment Center about forty-five miles south of Hingham, and 2,228 work in the retail stores around the country.

MINNESOTA MINING AND MANUFACTURING (3M)

HISTORY & OPERATIONS

3M, which was ranked thirty-seventh among the 1987 *Fortune* 500, was founded in 1902 by five eager businessmen who thought they could exploit the discovery of corundum—the hardest pure mineral in the world next to diamonds—near their home town of Two Harbors, Minnesota. Each of the five contributed $1,000, and they established Minnesota Mining and Manufacturing (3M) to sell the mineral to eastern manufacturers of grinding wheels. Unfortunately, there were no buyers. (It eventually became apparent that 3M's corundum cache was of inferior quality and ultimately worthless as an abrasive). 3M slid deeply into debt, and in 1905 the founders agreed to sell 60 percent of their shares to anyone who could keep the company afloat. Edgar B. Ober, one of the original purchasers of 3M stock, teamed up with another investor and assumed the company's debts with the provision that 3M be converted into a maker of sandpaper and abrasive wheels. Ober was elected president, and three of the original founders retired from the board.

The company set up a plant and began manufacturing sandpaper. Using alternative abrasives and innovative sales methods, by 1914 the company was slowly becoming profitable.

About this time, 3M developed a coated abrasive that quickly earned the reputation of being the best for metalworking. Within two years gross sales doubled and in the last quarter of 1916 the board of directors made the first dividend payments to the company's 193 shareholders. (3M has paid quarterly dividends ever since.)

By 1919, 3M had reached $1 million in annual revenues. During the twenties the company diversified with the invention and production of two of their best-known products, Scotch brand masking tape and Scotch brand cellophane tape, both of which were immediate and huge successes. There had been no comparable adhesives before and certainly none since. During this time, 3M began exporting to foreign markets, as well as establishing some joint ventures overseas. Much of the credit for 3M's growth—both financially and geographically—goes to W. L. McKnight, who joined the company in 1907 as an assistant bookkeeper (at $11.55 per week) and became general manager in 1915 and president in 1929. McKnight became chairman in 1949 and retired from 3M in 1973. McKnight's name is still evoked as a champion of progressive personnel policies, research, and high standards of quality.

3M established a central research division in 1937. By this time, the company's products included sandpaper, tape, liquid adhesives and coatings, and granules for asphalt roofing shingles. After the war, the company continued to expand and to further diversify its product lines. In 1946, 3M went "big league," when it was listed for the first time on the New York Stock Exchange. Revenues at the time were $75 million, and 3M employed eight thousand people.

In 1948, 3M's annual sales exceeded $100 million for the first time, and the company was reorganized along divisional lines. During the late forties and fifties, 3M expanded its product line to include reflective sheeting, magnetic recording tape, copying machines, electrical products, an outdoor advertising business (which employed reflective signing materials manufactured by the company), printing products, protective chemicals (like Scotch-Guard for fabrics), and decorative ribbon products. Also during the fifties, 3M began to make investments overseas, setting up wholly owned foreign subsidiaries. The company also expanded domestically, establishing new plant sites throughout the United States. In 1954, 3M was cited as one of the five best-managed companies in the country by the American Institute of Management.

In 1965 the company had its first $1 billion sales year. 3M continued to expand and develop new products throughout the sixties and early seventies. (Among its more visible achievements during that time was the use of 3M products in the moon walk of 1969). The company acquired Riker Laboratories, Inc., in 1970, and in 1972, 3M formed its Health Care Group, whose products continue to contribute significantly to the company's revenues.

In 1979 Lew Lehr took over as 3M's chairman and chief executive officer. In order to consolidate the company's multidivisional structure, Lehr reorganized 3M's forty divisions into four market groups, which today include the Industrial and Electronic Sector; Information and Imaging Technologies Sector, Life Sciences Sector (which includes Health Care Products), and Commercial and Consumer Sector. International Operations carries on the business of these four sectors, which encompass about eighty-eight technologies in all around the world. Throughout the seventies and up to the present, 3M has continued to grow in terms of both its product lines and its profits. Revenues doubled between 1975 and 1980 (though growth has been slower since then). The company's products cut across virtually every industry: from videocassettes and optical discs (part of the highly competitive telecommunications market on which 3M has recently been focusing its energies—the company is the world's largest producer of magnetic media), to pharmaceuticals, surgical masks, and orthopedic casts, to theft detection systems for retail stores, to tooth-colored dental fillings, to photocopies and graphic preparation products, to electronic imaging systems for X rays, to absorbent materials to soak up oil spills, to Buf-Puf brand facial cleansing products, and to Scotch tape, still the company's best-known product. 3M products are sold in virtually every grocery, hardware, stationery, and department store in the country.

Today, under the leadership of Allen F. Jacobson, a chemical engineer who took over as chairman and CEO in 1986 after heading the company's domestic divisions, 3M markets over 45,000 products. Of the approximately 82,000 employees worldwide (10 percent of whom have technical degrees and of those, 1,600 have *advanced* technical degrees), about 48,000 are employed domestically, with the remainder working overseas. Revenues in 1987 were $9.4 billion, with approximately 60 percent generated by domestic sales and 40 percent generated by international sales. The company now maintains a presence—mostly wholly owned subsidiaries—in fifty countries.

3M is known for its proemployee policies and for nurturing innovation and creativity. The company is considered a mecca for inventors and is structured in such a way that employees are given every opportunity to test the commercial potential of new ideas and discoveries. (A 3M slogan, known as the "Eleventh Commandment," is "Thou shalt not kill a new product idea." Post-it Note Pads, one of the company's most important new products in recent years, were originated by a 3M scientist who wanted an efficient means of marking his place in a hymnbook). Turnover at 3M is low, and the company has a firm policy of promoting almost exclusively from within.

3M's St. Paul headquarters is a campuslike area situated on 425 acres, with twenty-two major buildings and close to twelve thousand employees engaged in research and administrative activities. The complex includes about seventeen employee cafeterias. The headquarters houses all but four of the company's approximately forty-three divisions, and employees are grouped by division or staff group. (In addition to the divisions, which are the company's operating units, there are companywide staff units such as data processing, finance and human resources.) Most of more than six hundred technical Ph.D.s at headquarters work with the teams responsible for marketing their products, although a group of scientists works independently in the corporate research laboratories, where they invent products for the future. 3M completed the first phase of construction of an additional headquarters facility in Austin, Texas, which opened in September 1988 and will house another research and administration center and will include the four company divisions not located in the Minnesota headquarters. (3M currently leases space in Austin for its administrative center.) The facilities will be expanded over a five- to ten-year period.

(Information provided by Don Fischer, company spokesman.)

1987 *Fortune* 500 RANKING: Thirty-seventh.

REVENUES: $9.4 billion in sales in 1987.

EARNINGS: $918 million in net income in 1987.

INITIAL PUBLIC OFFERING: 1902.

NUMBER OF SHAREHOLDERS: 106,600.

OFFICES: 114 sales offices in the United States and 274 abroad.

PLANTS: Ninety-four located in the United States and ninety-three abroad.

INTERNATIONAL PRESENCE: 3M has operations in fifty countries, thirty-nine with some manufacturing.

NUMBER OF EMPLOYEES: Approximately 82,000. Of these, about 48,000 are employed in the United States and roughly 34,000 abroad.

AVERAGE AGE OF EMPLOYEES: Information not available.

TURNOVER: The average length of service of a 3M employee is seven and a half to eight years. Some job functions (sales) have a higher turnover rate, while others (technical) have a much lower rate.

RECRUITMENT: The company recruits at more than fifty colleges and universities all over the country. Most of the graduates recruited come out of programs in engineering, science, finance (i.e., accounting), data processing, and sales.

NUMBER OF NEW HIRES PER YEAR: Varies so widely from year to year that company will not give out figures. "The number of new employees hired each year depends on business conditions which have an impact on 3M's needs."

RANGE OF STARTING SALARIES: Company will not disclose. "3M offers salaries that are competitive with those offered by similar companies of our size and type of business. We use some conference board salary analysis services and other surveys to make sure we are competitive. We feel that any specific figures might become obsolete."

POLICY FOR RAISES: Raises are awarded by performance reviews, the first of which takes place after an employee's first six months, and thereafter annually. In some cases an employee may be reviewed and awarded a raise within a shorter interval of time. Raises are awarded entirely on merit.

TRAINING PROGRAMS: There is a common orientation for all new employees, but no companywide training programs. Technical and Engineering have their own programs, and each division trains its sales and marketing people. For the most part, all other employees receive on-the-job training.

BENEFITS: Medical and dental and life insurance, pension plan, employee stock purchase plan, 401(k) savings plan (through which employees can defer taxes by setting aside anywhere from 1 percent to 19 percent of their income in a savings plan, which reduces the gross income on which they pay taxes; the company matches the first 6 percent employees save through this plan on a four-to-one basis, meaning that for every four dollars an employee saves, up to 6 percent of his or her earnings, the company contributes a dollar's worth of stock into the fund), and tuition reimbursement for classes that are directly applicable to an employee's career at 3M.

VACATION: Two weeks after one year, three weeks after eight years, four weeks after eleven years, and five weeks after twenty years.

ADDITIONAL PERKS: The 3M Club, which includes a camera club, a men's chorus, an orchestra, an aviation club for flight training, a snowmobile club, etc. (fifty different organized special interest groups). Various 3M divisions located in the United States and abroad have their own versions of this club. Members of the 3M club who work in the St. Paul area can also use the Tartan Park, an employee country club with a clubhouse, a golf course, softball fields, archery ranges and picnic grounds. Membership costs $10 per year. 3M has an employee store where selected company products are available at the company's selling cost.

BONUSES: No real bonuses except for some compensation programs for salespeople.

AVERAGE WORKDAY: Eight hours, with forty-five minutes for lunch. Employees involved in particular projects may work late evenings and on weekends.

ANNUAL PARTIES: At most 3M locations, there is an annual banquet to honor long-service employees. Individual units host their own Christmas parties. For the most part, all parties are determined by the individual divisions.

DRESS CODE: No published dress code, but people are expected to look "businesslike." Research Ph.D.s wear whatever they want for lab work, but everyone else dresses pretty much in corporate conservative garb.

SOCIAL ATMOSPHERE: "There is some common corporate culture that would be detectable in our operations all around the world. It's a culture of innovation, financial stability, and individual initiative that prevails at all 3M companies."

NUMBER OF PRODUCTS: More than 45,000.

MOST POPULAR PRODUCTS: Scotch brand tape and Post-it brand notes.

RESEARCH AND DEVELOPMENT OUTLAY: $624 million in 1987.

HEADQUARTERS: In St. Paul, twenty-two major buildings situated on 425 acres and housing close to 12,000 employees. The company is currently completing a second U.S. research and administration center in Austin, Texas, the first phase of which was scheduled for occupancy in late summer, 1988.

CHARITABLE CONTRIBUTIONS: In 1986, the last year for which figures are available, the company donated $17,566,562 in the following areas: education, 44.4 percent; health care, 16.3 percent; arts, media, and culture, 14.3 percent; civic and community, 9.5 percent; federated-programs, 6.9 percent; human services, 4.9 percent; government special projects and international, 3.6 percent.

INTERESTED APPLICANTS CAN SEND RÉSUMÉS TO:
Staffing Department
Building 224-1W-02, 3M Center
3M Company
St. Paul, Minnesota 55144-1000
(612) 733-1110

Even when you read serious publications like annual reports prepared for readers who don't work at 3M, you have to scrape around to verify that those Ms stand for Minnesota Mining and Manufacturing. This gargantuan manufacturer of everything from acetate slides to contact lenses, to Scotch tape, to Buf-Pufs, to Scotchcal brand drag reduction tape ("based on 3M's microreplication technology, simulates the tiny grooves in a shark's skin. It minimized turbulence around the yacht's [*Stars & Stripes*, winner of the America's Cup] hull, reducing friction drag and adding to its speed"), to building material, to Post-it notes, to the blue stuff dentists make you bite on to make impressions doesn't try to hide behind its long name. It's just 3M; a great company, and one that takes itself less seriously than you might imagine.

Based in St. Paul, 3M's headquarters look more like a university campus or a small city than the United States' thirty-seventh largest industrial corporation (according to the 1987 *Fortune* ranking). The twenty-two buildings are enormous and modern, and some are connected to one another by walkways. Close to twelve thousand of the company's total 82,000-person work force work here. (Remember that 3M is an international corporation, with facilities all over the country and the world.) At least a thousand of them have advanced degrees. "There are enough Ph.D.s to staff several universities." And few of them don't regard their jobs as a lifetime career.

With a sincerely implemented "promote from within" policy, it would be difficult not to look ahead and see your future here. Besides, the Midwest in general and the Twin Cities in particular seem to breed a certain stability in terms of jobs. Once settled, there is less impetus to move around or away. So many employees are sons and daughters of fathers who worked contentedly for the big industrial companies *their* entire lives, it is unlikely that the pattern will be broken.

The secret to a visit to 3M is to not allow yourself to feel overwhelmed. Everyone understands his or her place, and to try to comprehend how the behemoth works could be counterproductive in a short trip. The language of the administration of 82,000 employees is a bit impersonal and boggling. There are sectors, divisions, departments, groups, and stuff, but don't let that confuse you. According to 3M's 1987 Product Directory (206 pages of product names!), "3M product groups, divisions and other operating units are grouped into four major business sectors, called Industrial and Electronic, Information and Imaging Technologies, Life Sciences, and Commercial and Consumer.

Just allow everyone you meet to explain what he or she does, and the company seems more manageable.

That it is a human and humane company that espouses those values is unassailable. Retired Chairman of the Board and CEO Lewis Lehr, who still sits on the board of directors, wrote about the corporate goals and objectives before he stepped down. Perpetuating the philosophy he inherited, they primarily champion the individual, his quality of life, and his contribution to this enormous organization. " . . . the preservation of individual identity in an organizational structure which embraces widely diverse businesses and operates in different political and economic systems throughout the world. From this endeavor there has developed an identifiable 3M spirit and a sense of belonging to the 3M family.

" . . . 3M management believes that it is essential to provide an organizational structure and work climate which respects the dignity and worth of individuals, encourages initiative, challenges individual capacities, provides equal opportunity for development and equitably rewards effort and contribution. . . . It believes 3M employees are the Corporation's most valuable resource."

Clyde Hause, a large, affable man, earned his degree in chemical engineering at the University of Illinois. He's been with 3M a mere thirty-eight years. He explains, "You grow as it grows." He started with the company in Detroit. "The greatest thing about 3M is the tremendous freedom we have. And it's a fun place to work." Clyde seems like a person who would have fun no matter what he did or where he worked, but as a career-researcher-turned-research-manager, he's having a blast, plus feels he's engaged in worthwhile pursuits. He talks about the emphasis on quality that's been a trademark of the company.

"The first technical person ever hired was in Quality Control. An idea is like a new kid.

Your bottom line comes later." He cites the example of W. L. McKnight, who developed the philosophy that permeates 3M to this day. "He started in 1907 as an assistant bookkeeper and retired the chairman in 1966. Quality was his theme." The message is disseminated in part through a steady diet of continuing education. "Management practices change," Hause says, and "attempts at knowing our heritage" are part of the program. "Every supervisor goes." Performance reviews are part of the process. "Every year, everyone states their accomplishments."

In his supervisory role (department manager, New Products Department, Industrial and Electronic, Sector R&D), Hause tries to maximize the number of applications of the new inventions of the engineers and inventors of his team. He pulls out a sheaf of reusable paper, invented by Bob Arens. This stuff, which uses special markers, looks like something we've seen in a James Bond movie. The ink can disappear in moments, only to be revived with another marker. Or it can be reused altogether. All of it made by 3M. [Author's note: When I talk of the espionage possibilities to Mr. Hause, he's not even offended; he's amused.]

One of the reasons 3M is such a prolific and efficient source of new inventions is that the designers of new products begin to brainstorm with the marketing people almost immediately. "While one person might be able to do everything, you're better off spreading it around and getting support and expertise from others. When we come up with ideas, there may be five hundred applications. How do you know how to develop them? You're already hooked, because you're pursuing *your own* idea." An invention in hand, 3M's mission is twofold: "trying to satisfy the customers' requirements, and making money [for the company]."

The average development time of an invention is five years (till it reaches the marketplace). In addition to kicking ideas around within the company, lab people go out in the field and see customers. When Clyde was the technical director of tape, in one year he made 18,000 contacts with customers. "You as an employee get 15 percent free time" to engage in personal research. Which you are expected to pursue. In addition, the corporation gives out " 'Genesis Grants'—money to work things out." Hause mentions that "twenty-five percent of our products didn't exist five years ago."

There are fifty-five different labs at 3M in the United States, not counting those in twenty-one foreign countries, but if you are interested in finding a job as an inventor, you would probably interview at half a dozen. 3M has eighty-eight technologies—coating, ceramics, etc.—"which belong to the whole company." As an inventor, one joins a distinct career ladder. (Administrative is the other.) Plus, there is a third option, quite elite, called corporate scientist," who now number about thirty-five. The rewards for developing a successful product are not monetary. "When you invent something, you get a lot of recognition. And the freedom to go back and do it again."

Speaking of which, 3M likes to trot Art Fry out for visitors. My day at the company was no exception. He is actually the man responsible for the Post-it note—those sticky yellow notepads of the "What did we ever do before they made these?" caliber of inventions. (I feel a tad sorry for him since he gets dragged out of his lab so frequently.) My only hesitation about repeating his story is that it's already appeared in airline magazines (Post-it notes *are* eight years old), and I fear that you, the reader, may have seen it.

If you have, please bear with me. Art Fry steps into the visitor's area wearing a tattered brown cardigan, looking exactly like the veteran inventor. (Perhaps he wears something else in his private life.) With his beard, he looks like singer Roger Miller or a younger version of Henry Fonda in *On Golden Pond*. He wears two gold rings (one of them has diamonds), a tad incongruous with his outfit. One is his 3M twenty-five-year ring, and the other is his "Challenge '81" ring, which he compares [rightfully] to a humongous Super Bowl ring, "for the best product. Only five have ever been awarded." The others were for Scotchgard carpet protector, Stamark pavement marking film, Scotch VHS format videocassettes, and Scotch casting tape.

While an undergraduate at the University of Minnesota studying chemical engineering, Fry started working for 3M, an arrangement he calls, "an ad hoc internship." He joined the new product development group or sector or whatever, "straight from graduation, although they used to require a five-year incubation period before" you got into that highly desirable department. "They had faith in me, and I had new ideas right away. Retirement will be hard," he digresses, "because there are so many ideas."

While singing in the choir of the North Presbyterian Church in North St. Paul, Fry would get frustrated about losing his place in his hymnal. He'd use bookmarks, but when he and his book stood up, the slips of paper would fall onto the floor. "I'd heard of an adhesive during a golf game at Tartan Park (3M's employee country club—more on that later). Dr. Spencer Silver invented it, and it didn't do what he wanted it to do. He was looking for a high-tack, aggressive adhesive. I knew it existed. We had some of it in our group." Dr. Silver's "failed" adhesive "only held one item to another—it didn't have to be heavier—and it wouldn't ruin good paper. I didn't see Post-it notes as notes. I saw them as bookmarks. I made my first samples on Monday, the day after church. Then you discover other uses." Yellow was chosen because it's perceived as "clean and neither masculine or feminine, and copies as white on copiers." Fry himself uses the 1½-by-2-inch size as "flagging tabs."

He grew up on a farm in a town in Iowa with three hundred people and used to build toys and cars. "My mentors growing up were my uncles. I thought they were gods. They were nine and ten years older, and they were very warm to me. One was an electrical engineer." (So was Art's father.) "They were solid people, and what they did sounded like fun. I liked Rube Goldberg things and anything mechanical. I daydream about mechanical things, too. My early report cards said, 'Art is a terrible daydreamer.' I was always taking things apart. Now I know that's a good thing. I probably daydream more than most people. My sister says, 'Ask Art the time, and he'll tell you how to build a clock.'"

Nighttime is the most fecund time for his "daydreams." "I think about a problem at night: What needs to be solved in the morning? It just opens up like a computer screen. It's a very creative time. I've made things at home, tenuous things that I'm not sure of and don't want the scrutiny of making them here.

"When you don't have words for things yet, you've got to learn them through sensory ways and then give names to them. It often takes three or four or five prototypes for me to know what I want."

His personal style would belie his penchant for recognition. He claims he enjoys talking to reporters. "I think it's a good thing," Fry says, "that's tied down—the guy who invented Post-it notes. It's as close as you get to immortality. They have changed my visibility. My grandkids will use them." All inventions created here are owned by 3M. Inventors do not receive royalties. When I ask how he feels about 3M's making all that money on his product, Fry seems never to have thought about it (or cared to) before. That's not the point. "It's my job," he says simply. "My aim is really not to make a buck for the company; it's to improve our true value. I have exactly the same amount of time as my father and grandfather. If I can change a design to make something elegantly simple . . .

"In my lifetime I couldn't have done Post-its without 3M. I couldn't have raised the money. Even at a smaller company, there wouldn't have been the marketing, et cetera. Making a product or process is fun, it's hilarious, it's very simple. I'm awfully glad I invented Post-its." And he doesn't face the same risks an entrepreneur would. No, this is definitely the preferable route. Called a division scientist at this point, Fry does admit to one ambition: "I aspire to corporate scientist.

"I'm still a guy who walks around with a smock with primer and adhesive on it and tools in my pocket. Now people say, 'Hi, Art!' and I don't know them." He also cannot show visitors his office, as its contents—his work in progress—are considered classified. "When people [outside the company] ask me what I do, I say, 'I invent things.' 'Like what?' the dialogue continues. 'Post-it notes.' I used to carry them around me to explain." Obviously, he no longer needs to resort to show-and-tell. "The church takes a lot of pride," he's pleased to say. "The choir loft's books sprout yellow Post-it notes."

"There's a certain thing about 3M people," says Bob Backlund, the former executive director of human resources (presently the staff vice-president, administrative services, 3M Austin). "They're open, sharing, and willing to help other people. Even if you don't know them, they'll help." Backlund's looking at his thirty-fifth year with the company. In the last fifteen years he's had seven different jobs, including a stint as plant manager. "I can't fathom any significant advantages leaving here."

Recruits are flown to St. Paul for a full day or more of interviews. "By the end of the process, you know if these are the kinds of people you want to work with, and vice versa. It's not a mold, necessarily." Backlund adds that the group that enters 3M each year is also a product of self-selection, with applicants weeding themselves out during their day(s) of scrutiny.

"We try to figure out why people don't accept our offer." The company acknowledges that they are competing against oil companies for chemical engineers, against the aircraft industry for mechanical engineers, and against the semiconductor and computer businesses for electrical engineers. Minnesota is "only accountable for a small percentage" of rejections. (The state boasts an elevated quality of life, and the majority of job seekers are midwesterners, anyway.)

Each year, thirty to thirty-five thousand unsolicited applications are mailed to the St. Paul headquarters alone. Ph.Ds interested in working in a corporate research lab "are asked to give a seminar on what they're working on. Are they blowing smoke technically? Are they thinking on their feet?" Between recruits and unsolicited begging, hundreds of students are invited to 3M annually, depending on staffing needs.

If you are not a "techie," there may still be a place for you. "It's a technologically driven company, but there are good opportunities for nontechs. You'll have a harder time in the beginning of your career if you don't have that background, but you'll have good people working for you who do." Admittedly, most new college recruits do come in with engineering degrees. (Coincidentally, the University of Minnesota's chemical engineering department is ranked number one nationally.) But there's room for accounting and finance majors, as well as liberal arts students. "At the entry level, hiring compensation is based on education." 3M will even hire the sundry MBA. "We grow a lot of MBAs here." Say those magic words with me: "Tuition reimbursement."

Again and again, the virtuous pledge "promote from within" is chanted. But again, it is meant. "Very, very, very, *very* seldom is someone hired above a certain level, because they can work within and upward." Bob Backlund maintains that after a divisional orientation and then adjustment to its particular system, there is great freedom at 3M. "There are people who might not be comfortable with so little structure."

The culture of 3M seems so progressive that it is a bit surprising that this is the way it's been since W. L. McKnight. "The culture goes back in history. Young employees may not know who Mr. McKnight was, but they are aware of the culture nonetheless. The last few chairmen didn't create it, but they continued it. Our history fosters new products and new things." One "upfront philosophy" governs inventions. All patents for products invented by 3M employees (while they're employed by the company, obviously) are assigned to 3M.

Career planning—again—taken seriously, "is an automatic process each year." 3M likes to think of itself institutionally as "your [you, the employee] partner. But you are the major ingredient in your career planning. There's no fast track to get hired on. We want *you* to succeed in *your* job, so *you* can move, unless *you* don't want to. Your responsibility level is important, but we're not a company that gives out a lot of titles."

3M is run openly. "An employee could request an audience with Jake and get one." Jake? Oh, that's Allen Jacobson, the chairman and chief executive officer of Minnesota Mining and so on. "He's 'Mr. Jacobson' at your first meeting, and a little later he's 'Jake.' If you've worked together, you're not in awe of him; you *know* him."

Bill McLellan, the division vice-president, Orthopedic Products Division, has only worked for 3M for twenty-eight years. An English major at a local college, he came to 3M during the summer between his junior and senior years as a sales representative. He earned $350 a month and got a car to drive selling Scotch tape. "I thought I'd work here a couple of years, come up with a great idea, get rich, and move to Barbados." He did move, but instead of escaping to the Caribbean, he rose on the sales ladder, from Pittsburgh to Cleveland to Madison, Wisconsin, getting bigger territory and more responsibility with each new locale. He was selling tape and ribbon.

3M was getting started in the health care market in the early sixties. McLellan moved to Atlanta to work in it in 1969. As an emerging business, it was involved primarily in surgical tape and masks. It was a department then, not a division. Here's the distinction: "Fifteen to thirty million dollars a year is a division."

McLellan moved to Philadelphia, then London, Ontario, "and back to 'Mecca' in 1975, when Surgical Care split from Medical." Now they were both big enough to be divisions, and McLellan was Surgical Care's national sales manager. To give you an idea of 3M's rapid and massive growth, the "Orthopedics Project" begun in 1977 became a division in 1982, making hip and shoulder implants and surgical tools. Bill became a vice-president in 1984 (there are only thirteen vice presidents) and stayed there until 1985. To make a complicated story simple, McLellan calls himself "the mother hen" of Health Care Specialties, "five little businesses" under one umbrella, but together large enough to be a separate division.

As a nontechie, he's experienced bouts of "low self-esteem. You're sitting around with Ph.Ds, and they make you make a decision." But his extended team, made up of researchers, is naturally willing to help. So McLellan has never bemoaned his lack of technical training. (Besides, someone's got to sell.) Furthermore, "you can learn fairly rapidly, and your customers are happy to help you." As a sales representative, he used to "intern as an orderly in the hospital," and he became familiar with the arena for which his products were intended.

"It's hard to get bored," he says. "I haven't had a job long enough to get bored. But it's easy to be scared. Sometimes I get feelings of *déjà vu*—I've done this before. I know it's hard work, and I know I work hard. I've made some big mistakes, but I've gotten great support. People cover for you. The emotional rewards are enormous. You don't get that in an organization that's trying to establish itself." In the United States, approximately four hundred people report to McLellan, and he knows them all.

Gini Johnson, the market development and training manager in the Audio Visual Division, joined 3M when she was forty, originally on a consulting basis. "It wasn't a 'job' job. I gave myself a six-month window. It was terribly intimidating. It was *so big*. Now I see it differently. I know my own people [her universe touches three hundred training people and managers], but I don't know the other people on this floor. I enjoyed my consultant status and wanted to stay that way, but they wouldn't let me. It was the *best* decision," she admits emphatically. "In eleven years she has had five different jobs. "I am happy. I don't have the need to move."

Although 3M does have a woman on its board of directors, Gini works in a predominantly male environment (typical of technologically driven industries). "I was the first woman supervisor in this division, but now we have others. Things have changed significantly since I arrived. I think about being a woman here. This is a patriarchal, male-dominated company, with stellar attitudes toward women. I'd be seeing this very differently as a twenty-five-year-old. The X's and Y's won't come into balance in my lifetime."

The organization has demonstrated some concern about helping women achieve more senior positions. A group called the Women's Advisory Committee is made up of twenty-five women, not engaged in setting policy, but to make reports to the 3M Human Relations Advisory Committee. Gini resigned, because "there was not a single issue or grievance. It *is* an issue that there aren't more visible women, and *they* funded us."

Laurie Altman came to 3M in 1981 directly from school, with a master's degree in chemical engineering from Notre Dame. Now she's a supervisor in Chemical Processing Development. She's also a past president of a group at the company called "Visiting Women Scientists," which sends 120 female volunteers from the company to junior high schools in the Twin Cities "to encourage girls to take math and science for their careers." [Author's note: At the time of my visit, Minnesota's Board of Education required only that students take science and math through the ninth grade (although some districts have additional requirements).]

Laurie became a real boss at twenty-seven. Her team is made up of "five degree people and three technicians," or lab assistants. Most of them are older than she. "My manager is good at performance appraisal. He showed me the process. He enrolled me in Supervisory Development," a course offered at 3M. "Things are discussed with the employees. The people who work for me were watching me [at first]. They're accepting." As a supervisor, Laurie can't spend as much time as she'd like working actively in the lab. The trade-off for her promotion is that she's much more confined to an office.

But because her culture is a lab culture, "we don't expect things to happen too fast. We're used to waiting. We're more laid back. (This doesn't mean we're not results-oriented.) It feels like school. We're encouraged quite strongly to take courses here and at the university." Altman attended the University of Minnesota Business School at night, and 3M paid for her MBA.

"I'm surprised about the number of people who know me and what I'm doing. I've definitely made clear what my career objectives were. My management offers me the chance to state them. I'm doing much better than I thought I could do. I took on a lot. I see myself as being here for the long term. I'm very happy with my time here. The money doesn't hurt. Within the next five years I expect a new promotion. Not in research; my experience is limited. I want to go to a factory or a division. I want to know operations better; I want to know 3M better. Manufacturing, marketing, and research and development are all in the operations of divisions. The path I've chosen would indicate that I will probably not be the inventor. But I can envision facilitating."

An ardent believer in teamwork, Altman explains, "Some people don't work as well in teams. The people who work with me are good at it. It's a do-or-die situation. There's no way you can do a job yourself." With her group in mind, Laurie thinks ahead to having children. "I would try to confine my maternity leave to as short as possible—six weeks. Some planning will be involved. I would rather have things fairly well established so that things could run by themselves."

You've heard about it; now read about it. The Tartan Park, the 3M Club's official home, almost five hundred acres of leisure opportunities, is one more manifestation of 3M's corporate culture. This is one of management's gestures to its people. Only eight miles from the center of campus, the facility "tries to improve the quality of life after eight-to-five," according to Jim Urick, the club's administrator.

Jim had been working in the sales area for eight years before he defected to the park, "a dramatic decision." But sensing the tremendous corporate support for the club and extracurricular activities, he has not looked back. On the one hand, he says, "we don't make a lot of this club because of the non–St. Paul employees." On the other hand, the Tartan Park comes in handy as a recruiting tool for applicants considering a job in the area. (There are other 3M Clubs in other cities, "but nothing this elaborate. Some may not have facilities at all.") There are no happy hours here. Anyway, "after work, people may not want to raise hell in front of their bosses."

Every employee is automatically a member of the 3M Club. For thirty years membership cost a dollar per year. It was recently raised to ten dollars a year, deducted from payroll. Further funding of the 3M Club of St. Paul, Inc., as it's officially known, comes from the commissions collected from vending machines at headquarters. The organization is run by a board of volunteers, elected for three-year positions. Independent of the actual facilities, the club sponsors special interest activities to enrich the lives of employees. Currently there are about fifty-five activity clubs, including skiing, aviation, six language groups, and so on.

The clubhouse, which resembles a lodge at any private country club, was built in 1969. One can drive over for lunch or dinner daily, not to mention special events like the Mother's Day Buffet, St. Patrick's Week, Friday Fish Fries, etc. "We're booked solid every night of the week," Urick boasts, "and we do real well on wedding receptions."

The plant includes two golf courses, one eighteen-hole, and one nine-hole; twelve outdoor tennis courts, accommodating the four hundred players in the league. ("They're booked every night of week from five to nine" during the summer months.) 3M is a softball-loving company. *Twenty-two hundred* employees play here regularly.

SUPER VALU

HISTORY & OPERATIONS

Super Valu, which in 1987 was the single largest diversified service company in the country for the second consecutive year, did not become Super Valu as such until 1954. The company traces its origins to two pioneering Minneapolis wholesale grocery firms called B. S. Bull and Co. and the Newell and Harrison Co., both founded in the 1870s. Various mergers led to the formation in 1926 of the Winston and Newell Company, which was created to improve service to independent retail grocers, who were being crushed by the emergence in the 1920s of a new surge of retail grocery chains. This company, which ultimately became Super Valu, operated on the premise that if independent grocers banded together under the auspices of a leading wholesaler, they would be better able to compete against the unified chains. Over the years, Super Valu has proved that premise correct.

Though Super Valu is still essentially a wholesale grocer—more than 85 percent of its sales and earnings come from that side of the business—it prefers to call itself a "retail support company." In addition to supplying each of its 3,000 affiliated stores in thirty-two states with approximately seventy percent of both its food and nonfood groceries, the company helps its independent retailers run every single aspect of their supermarkets. Through the sophisticated research and marketing methods of its various divisions, Super Valu guides these independents through every step of the process, setting up entrepreneurs with investment money, finding sites for stores, designing stores, financing equipment, setting up shelves, training staff, planning promotions, writing advertising, handling money, and insuring the entire operation from products to personnel. In this way, Super Valu puts its retailers on equal footing with the established chains. And the better the independents fare, the more groceries they buy from Super Valu's nineteen warehouses (called "distribution centers") scattered across the country.

Super Valu has expanded into a $9.4 billion empire, and it continues to grow. Its major strategy for expansion entails buying up small wholesale food distributors, some of which have stores of their own (and all of which have customers—retail food stores of interest to Super Valu)—preferably in regions where the company hasn't yet established a presence—redesigning them from top to bottom, selling them to franchisees, and then expanding the chain. Though roughly 97 percent of its affiliated stores are either independents or franchises, the company does maintain corporately owned stores. Some of these serve as proving grounds for new experimental methods before eventually being sold to independents. Others, such as a grocery chain called Hornbacher's in North Dakota and a discount, nonfood general merchandise chain called ShopKo, remain permanently in the hands of the corporation. A chain of grocery stores called Cub Foods (forty-eight stores, thirty-one of them franchises) is perhaps Super Valu's most innovative success. The stores, which sell most products at a cheaper cost than standard grocery stores do, are enormous, warehouse-style establishments that sell an immense variety of standard and exotic foods (octopus, banana blossoms, cactus leaves) as well as nonfood products. Items are strategically placed to lure customers into buying more than they would normally buy—and the strategy works. Some customers travel as far as fifty miles to shop at a Cub store.

Super Valu's profits have increased steadily each year since 1959. Today, under the leadership of chairman and CEO Mike Wright (who joined Super Valu as senior vice-president for administration in 1977), the company employs approximately 35,000 people. In addition to supplying stores with goods, Super Valu produces its own goods, both food and nonfood, under several brand and generic labels. These labels account for approximately 12 percent of the groceries it supplies to its retailers and company-owned stores.

(Information provided by Rita Simmer, company spokesperson.)

REVENUES: $9.4 billion in fiscal 1988 (year ending February 27, 1988).

EARNINGS: $111.8 million in net earnings (or $1.50 per share). Both figures represent a 25 percent increase from fiscal year 1987.

INITIAL PUBLIC OFFERING: 1967.

NUMBER OF SHAREHOLDERS: 9,238.

AFFILIATED STORES: 3,000 in thirty-two states.

WAREHOUSES: Nineteen around the country.

NUMBER OF EMPLOYEES: 35,000. About 750 work in the home office.

AVERAGE AGE OF EMPLOYEES: Information not available. Employees' ages run the spectrum. Mike Wright is fifty.

TURNOVER: 12 percent for employees in salaried positions.

RECRUITMENT: The company has a pretty casual college recruitment program. It has established relationships with a number of schools, none of which it's willing to name.

NUMBER OF NEW HIRES PER YEAR: Super Valu hires an average of 140 new college graduates companywide per year. Following are the kinds of entry-level positions they fill: seventy-five management trainees, fifteen accountants, ten industrial engineers or production managers, five in finance, five in marketing or market research, ten in merchandizing/buying, five in advertising/communications, ten in information services (data processing), five in personnel/industrial relations. In 1987 Super Valu hired 5,000 new employees, all told. In a year of acquisitions, this number by no means represents the yearly average.

RANGE OF STARTING SALARIES: $17,500–$25,000 for salaried, just-out-of-college, entry-level positions.

POLICY FOR RAISES: Employees are reviewed annually, and raises are awarded on merit.

TRAINING PROGRAMS: Most entry-level employees are trained on the job rather than through formal programs. Retail counselors, who are in essence the company's field staff, go to Super Valu's headquarters for seven weeks of intensive training in supermarket operations. Though all have had retail experience, they learn basic hands-on skills such as baking, meat cutting, and deli preparation, in addition to supermarket financing and other more complex matters. When they get to a certain point in their training, they hold a sale, generally of bakery and deli products, for employees in the home office. In addition, the company offers other training programs, administered both internally and externally, to employees at various levels. Among those offered internally are "Targeted Selection" (training managers how to interview and choose prospective hires), "Career Management" (planning and directing your career), "Individual Development Planning Workshop" (how to create and develop plans), "Financial Decision Making," "Training Leadership and Effectiveness," and "Negotiating to Yes." Among those offered externally are: "Food Executive Program" (at Cornell University), "Leadership Development Program" (offered by Creative Institute on Leadership), and "Individualized Coaching for Effectiveness" (at Personnel Decisions, Inc., Minneapolis). Programs range in duration from half a day to several days.

BENEFITS: Major medical (with three HMO options available), dental, life insurance, salary continuation of up to one year for major illnesses or accidents, long-term disability insurance, a retirement plan, a 401K plan, and tuition reimbursement for employees of at least one year. "There are two plans available. One, 75 percent of tuition. Or two, 100 percent of tuition, books, and course fees if you and your supervisor have a written development plan of which the course is a part and advanced approval for the development plan and all courses has been obtained."

VACATION: One week of vacation after six months, two weeks after one year, three weeks after seven years, four weeks after fourteen years, five weeks after nineteen or more years, plus nine regular paid holidays.

BONUSES: Employees at the level of department manager and above are eligible.

ANNUAL PARTY: Depends on the division. Some divisions have Christmas parties, etc., throughout the year. "Each of the retail support divisions is fairly autonomous and operates pretty much as a separate company with its own personality."

AVERAGE WORKDAY: 8:00 A.M. to 4:30 P.M. for most employees. Warehouses are open twenty-four hours a day, and employees work in shifts. Some people work evenings and on the weekends, but it's up to the employee, his or her supervisor, and the workload.

DRESS CODE: Varies by division. At the home office men generally wear suits or jackets and dress shirts, and women are much more likely to wear dresses or skirts than pants. Dress tends to be more casual for those who work in the warehouses.

SOCIAL ATMOSPHERE: Again, depends on the division. "Some divisions have a family spirit, while others are less congenial."

HEADQUARTERS: The company maintains headquarters in a three-story building housing about 750 employees situated on the southwest shore of Bryant Lake. The 140-acre site boasts an eleven-acre pond; a ¾-mile walking path, and covered walkways from the parking lot to the building. The area is inhabited by "many forms of wildlife."

CHARITABLE CONTRIBUTIONS: Company will not disclose.

INTERESTED APPLICANTS CAN SEND RÉSUMÉS TO:
Super Valu Stores, Inc.
11840 Valley View Road
Eden Prairie, MN 55344
(612) 828-4000

S uper Valu is, simply, the largest grocery wholesaler in the entire United States of America. Now that we have your attention, we should mention that since groceries are not considered "sexy," do not feel bad if you've never heard of Super Valu before. While it is the second largest business, in sales, in the upper Midwest after Dayton Hudson (see p. 355), most Minnesotans haven't heard of the company either.

So don't be embarrassed. You've heard of Cub Foods, Pantry Pride, Food Giant, ShopKo, and Charley Brothers? These are some of Super Valu's acquisitions. These names are resolutely not being changed. "Our operating companies don't need to use our name." This is Mike Wright, Super Valu's president, chairman, and chief executive officer, speaking. "They know they're Super Valu, and the local communities know they're the largest local companies. To eliminate established names would be wrong. We want to foster local recognition."

Without further ado, let it be known that Super Valu, located in a nicely landscaped corporate park in Minneapolis, stocks chains of supermarkets, some owned by them and some not. "There is nothing glamorous about moving food from one location to another," an employee says. In place of glamor, there is the potential for making a lot of money, which, of course, could buy glamor, or at least a fleet of fancy cars, which is almost the same thing.

The food warehousing biz is traditionally male-dominated, and Super Valu is no exception. Zeke Goldman, Super Valu's senior vice-president in charge of food operations, explains that "this pattern permeates the industry: you become a bag boy in school and fall in love with the business. As you go through school, this is the business you want to enter. I could run down this floor," he says, gesturing through the open executive top floor, "and I could point to fifty men with the same experiences." It's a man's world. Even women at Super Valu tend to rely on sports metaphors when talking about what they do. This public company has one female director and no female employees above middle management. Which is not to say that this is an unpleasant environment for the working woman.

Kathy Krukemeyer has worked at Super Valu since 1973. She started the summer before her senior year of high school as a payroll file clerk and liked it so much she returned full-time after graduation. At night she took accounting courses, for which she was reimbursed 50 percent of her tuition. She is enthusiastic about Super Valu because she's been encouraged to be ambitious and seek out new challenges. She has been promoted up way beyond her expectations. "After five years I became a junior accountant, and then moved into internal audit for two years." Her next three years saw her in corporate tax, and then she was moved into financial services for another three. "Now I'm a cash management specialist. My function is to get projects funded, to work on loans and investments. I work with five banks, including investment banks, on a daily basis. This is the most challenging job I've had. An MBA is in my job description," she says bashfully, having never earned her bachelor's degree.

The management of Super Valu has repeatedly tried to get Kathy to earn her CPA degree, but she says, "I like my free time. I meet with a lot of bankers who want to know where *I* went to school. They assume I have a master's. There was no emphasis on degrees five years ago compared to now. I like my current job, but they've left more than a hint that I can't move up a lot without more school.

"You have a lot of in-house training" in order to move up the corporate ladder. "You can't get somewhere by pushing. You have to get along with your supervisor, and your supervisor has to be willing to move you. Not getting along with a boss is the worst fear I've had. If you say you're willing to try a bigger challenge and can't hack it, you can't move backwards. They've already filled your job, and you'd have to look outside."

One would think, with the time and interest invested in Kathy, that all women would get the bug for increased responsibility and involvement at Super Valu. Instead, Kathy echoes the reason for the paucity of females. "There are few women in management because the food business is traditionally male. Women who were aggressive and pushed turned people off." Besides, at Super Valu more men than women have college degrees. Women do populate the clerical and secretarial jobs. There are no male secretaries.

Secretarial turnover is low. So far the record for long-term employment as a secretary is forty-four years. "There's a tremendous loyalty among secretaries here," one says. "The people I work with are understanding, but it's so busy that there's no time to read or goof off."

Rather than complain that they're not prodded toward professional growth and upward mobility, the secretaries have a set of gripes about life away from their desks. "Day care's a problem," one says. "We bring it up during employees' lunches once a month, but they never approve it. We have a lot of single parents in this building, but senior management makes a lot of money, and many have wives who don't work." At least she presumes this is management's rationalization. Mike Wright is keenly aware that this situation provokes discontent but at this point is not prepared to alter his position. "My answer is that there is a Montessori day care program" nearby, and "it's not our problem."

Another exigency of being a working mom at Super Valu is "at other companies if your kid gets sick you get your own sick day off. Not here. We have to lie. I don't know a mother who could leave her kid alone."

That Super Valu is well run is beyond question. Its closest competition is not even half as large. But when it comes to being happy at work, employees give Super Valu a mixed report card. Let's call it a B minus. On the one hand, people enjoy working for the industry leader.

"I'm always amazed by how big and powerful we are." On the other, many people came here because they needed a job, not more. And that is all they expect. Those who landed at Super Valu more or less by accident may not say they feel they have found a career. They may call their stint a "job." It doesn't mean they seek escape, however.

One manager of almost twenty years' duration freely admits he chose Super Valu because "this was where I could get a job." But that's not why he stayed. "For me, the company's compatible with my nature. I don't lie awake at nights thinking about it. I like the customer service philosophy of the company. Everyone at Super Valu is a salesman. We're an event-driven company, and priorities can change within a day. We're always ready to jump on an opportunity. I'm sure there are five-year and ten-year plans, but the only plan I've heard is to make this a coast-to-coast company. Great! 'Let's go for it!' as Mike Wright says."

Even as the largest wholesaler in the country, Super Valu's influence currently extends over only thirty-two states. The total number of stores that that encompasses is 3,000. Today. Like the tote board at a telethon, that number could change dramatically overnight, as Super Valu aggressively buys up new chains of stores and builds wholesale distribution centers in new states.

Super Valu is involved in the proverbial Big Picture. While the management and movement of food, beverages, toiletries, and cleansing products from one location to another is a simplified view of its major endeavor, Super Valu has its hands in other specialized, but integrated, fields.

Planmark, a subsidiary of Super Valu, employs seventy employees who design stores as well as ventilation, heating, air-conditioning, and refrigeration systems for stores and warehouses. Located in Super Valu's main building, they're the people who, for example, deal with the problem of "overly freezing stores in the summer," a designer explains. "We get a lot of high marks for supermarket design at Planmark. Our competitors undercut our price, but they blow zone control [the coordination of interior space], which is the most critical component."

Planmark is prepared to deal with the boom market of the late eighties. It is just as aggressive as its parent company. "Planmark gave most every technical person a raise last year, but still the salaries are low. Headhunters tempt us with stories of five- to seven-thousand-dollar raises," one employee says. "I passed up several because I like the environment and didn't want to jeopardize my responsibility, but my eyes are open." Headhunters are good "tools to get raises. You can scream for a raise all you want, and it won't do anything until you get an offer. But by then your loyalty is eroded."

Nevertheless, he is resisting other job proposals. "This is a good place to work; it's very relaxed. At first, I thought it was real casual—I could wear jeans and flannel shirts. But management is looking for us to 'dress for success.' Now I wear a tie. If you don't conform, you do get comments. Everyone does. If you don't wear a tie, someone says, '*Nice* tie.' You can tell when someone gets held back because of appearance, or manner or something.

"Technical is an extension of art. It's creative. I expected some more loose, hip people," he says. No older than thirty, this fellow is staying. At least for the rest of the year.

As far as creative work goes, Super Valu provides advertising for stores "on a voluntary basis. We're more and more strategic, and try to help them be competitive. The food business is not mass market anymore." Some of the advertising is co-op, meaning the costs are shared by the manufacturer and the stores themselves, and some exclusively sell Super Valu—"This Week at Super Valu" being one of the more memorable campaigns. But the advertising department here in Minneapolis realizes that what will work in Pittsburgh may not be effective in Atlanta, and tries to plan for all markets. Companywide, in 1986 the combined expenditures for broadcast advertising were $4.5 million, and for print, about $10–$12 million dollars. (The company will not disclose more recent figures.)

Super Valu's advertising department is made up of several veterans of the advertising business, from both the client and agency sides. "Creative problem solving is what I enjoy," one of them says. But compared to his former life, "this is going straight. I can't have as much fun as I used to. I'm not around crazies anymore. Here, *we're* perceived as crazy." He has traded wackiness for security.

Insurance is another concern of Super Valu, and another wholly owned subsidiary, Risk Planners, takes care of "insurance for stores, for products, for product liability, and employees." One risk planner—there are fifty-six in this division—says he spends his whole day facing a computer screen. "I relieve the tedium by talking to other people here. I've been doing the same thing for four years. You could say I'm bored. Before vacation it was terrible; I didn't know how I got up every day." He is considering a return to school, but not because of antipathy toward Super Valu. "They give you a lot of latitude to keep your own personality. The benefits are good. I think the company as a whole is really good about grievances, complaints, but not Risk Planners. It's easier to look for jobs elsewhere, although Risk Planners pays a lot better than most insurance jobs. A lot of people have arrived in the last year, and no one is leaving."

Minnesotans enjoy and have learned to expect a higher quality of life than that in most other states. Employees of Super Valu probably assume their lives at work will match the standards of their lives away from work. Super Valu's in-house critics' mild discontent makes them passive. Perhaps they're waiting for the situation that frustrates them to be alleviated. And their physical plant indicates that management is trying to make their lives pleasant. Indeed, a weight room, sauna, a running trail, and highly acclaimed subsidized lunches in a glassed-in cafeteria overlooking a pond are perks of a job at Super Valu and its on-premises subsidiaries. And Super Valu makes sure potential employees are aware of them. An employee of Risk Planners recalls, "They showed me the facilities during my interview to convince me why I should work here."

One guy admits, "Lunch time is a big thing here." A woman says, "In years past, men and women used to be segretated at lunch. Now about half the tables are mixed. They're mostly middle management mixes. One girl initiated it. Some couples eat together."

Yes, there *is* dating at Super Valu. "This is where you meet people. There's even one couple living together who work in this building. It's watched. Departments are clique-y."

By and large, however, people praise Super Valu's hands-off attitude. "Your time is yours. Deadlines matter." But you can manage your time any way you want as long as your project is completed on time. "Some use the weight room for an hour in the middle of the day or take two-hour lunches. It breeds a certain laziness." Also a certain amount of busywork, which, in the final analysis, is preferable to no work.

A woman in the Communications Department gives Super Valu's corporate culture a name. "I'd call it 'shirtsleeves.' Strong, but relaxed. One of the first things some of the executives do in the morning is take off their [suit] jackets. It says, 'I'm open, I'm ready for you.' We're on a first-name basis. And they know our names.

"One of the reasons I stay is because it's a very ethical people company. Everyone does more than their share because we're known as a lean company." Sometimes a conversation about business could be mistaken for football talk. Lean. Mean. Winning. Let's not overlook the team. One woman says, "I've learned to use sports metaphors. I've never been a sports fan, but now I'm part of the team." Team spirit. Many men at Super Valu believe that a history of active team sports participation is the best preparation for a job here. This is a guy-ish competitive environment as rich with talk about the Vikings as with talk of winning at work. "I hope this is a team orientation," Wright says. "Who is a Super Valu person? We don't consciously look for fit. You should have a willingness to participate in decision making and be a good sport." So far, drug testing is not being done. (Except on truck drivers.)

Mike Wright is quoted constantly by his team, on every possible subject. One senior manager says, "I couldn't be comfortable with a smooth talker. He's a good businessman. He inherited the work ethic." A star football player at the University of Minnesota who went pro in Canada, Wright joined Super Valu in 1977 as the senior vice-president for administration, from the company's law firm. He had been offered a more junior position fifteen months earlier but turned it down, saying "it sounded too boring. I wanted responsibility for sales and market development." Wright became intrigued with the second offer, "as Super Valu was turning upwards." Moreover, I don't have the feeling of sameness here that I had in law." No wonder. In 1978 he was promoted to president and chief operating officer. In 1981 Wright was named CEO while retaining his president title, and in 1982 he added "chairman" to the rest.

He uses the language of the athlete to express himself. "The ball game can change overnight," he'll say, in his shirtsleeves the model employees emulate.

Right now the guys Super Valu may not be attracting have probably spent more time on the tennis courts than on basketball courts. "We need the training and skills of the MBA, but it's hard to get them here. The mainstream of the guts of the operation is alien to the MBA culture—hard, hands-on work, the standards of a warehouse." Zeke Goldman says, "It's a tough, grubby life. It doesn't give them the satisfaction of Bloomingdale's, but it pays better than Bloomie's." Besides other wooers in retailing, today's top MBA candidates are being lured to Wall Street and management consulting firms for big money. Mike Wright assumes that "kids don't want to wear aprons. They feel they're college graduates." It's problematic that the grocery support company can attract the best students, although, as Super Valu gets "bigger and better, it gets easier."

"Our people are turned on all the time," Goldman says. "We make independent businessmen. It's working. It's fun. We're dedicated to the American dream. With our decentralized management, people are allowed to do things, and we make people rich."

The lucky guys of which he speaks may not work in Super Valu's Minneapolis headquarters. In fact, it is much more likely that they are the associated grocers who purchase their goods from Super Valu. "Independent retailers are entrepreneurs." They can make serious money. (Upscale [urban] gourmet stores with two hundred kinds of vinegars and five hundred brands of mustard are perfect examples of the new grocer.) Additionally, Super Valu has seen a demand for "a lot of nonfood. Maybe three hundred million health and beauty aids and utensils. The shopping habits of our customers are changing so fast, we must increase by a billion dollars per year."

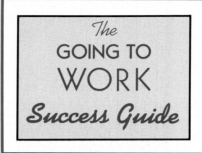

The
GOING TO
WORK
Success Guide

This little *Baedeker* will help direct you to the success that's destined to be yours. You (for the moment, alone) know that one day greatness is possible. It's just a matter of how and when. Therefore, in this, the self-help guide for self-starting achievers, you will acquire the jargon, accoutrements, accompaniments, and garnish to propel you and your licensees on that climb upward.

Going to Work

All successful people have offices. No matter what you read about Hef wearing his PJ's all day, he wears them in his office. You will need an office. Even if it's in your studio apartment. Create a professional surrounding, and you will be professional. I personally believe that daily bathing is a key to professional success. While I, like Hef, do not leave my hutch for days, I arise early and shower, to give the illusion of hygienic, officelike behavior. Discipline and vigilance, dear reader! (Which isn't to say you can't read *People* magazine during the day; just make sure you read it at a desk.)

Office Decor

YES	NO
Glass coffee table	Old college trunk as table
Original Impressionist painting	Poster of Impressionist painting (or posters of Paulina the model)
Desktop computer	Sticker that says "I ♡ Computers"
Photographs of the kids	The kids ("Mommy [or Daddy] is sick and can't watch them" is no excuse!)
Art deco ashtray	Old shells and beer cans
Fresh flowers (spell power)	Paper or wax flowers
Wet bar	Oyster bar

Important Success Tip: If you can't afford a secretary, take a typing course. Learn how to use all your fingers. (Your thumbs handle the space bar.)

Travel

Successful people travel for *business,* not for work. While this is a subtle distinction, it is an important one. It is far more impressive to travel lightly and efficiently than to show that all of your salary was invested in a set of smart canvas-with-leather-trim luggage. This is what belongs in your stunning overnight bag:

MAN	WOMAN
Clean underwear	Clean underwear
Spare shirt	Alternate silk blouse
Spare silk tie (just because it doesn't wrinkle is no reason to wear polyester)	Spare panty hose. The color of your legs. (Just because the color is suntan doesn't mean anyone will think you just returned from Hawaii.)
Dopp kit	Something to sleep in
Newest, trendiest management strategy book on the market	New copies of *Money, Fortune,* and *People*
Something—anything—you bought from The Sharper Image Catalogue	Calculator
	Running shoes and gear
	Health and beauty aids, including vitamins

Love

Since love puts that certain bounce in one's step, a successful love life is essential to the attainment of a successful corporate lifestyle. Please remember that no level of professional success is worth jeopardizing for a pleasant liaison. Be careful in your appraisal of members of the opposite sex who work where you do. They may look good to you at the company Christmas party, but remember, at last year's soiree you tried to kiss the water cooler. You will rationalize and tell yourself that the two of you have much in common. Don't forget that you also have quite a bit in common with Princess Margaret. If, finally, you can't deny the true stirrings of amour, ask yourself if you treasure your job. Perhaps it would be wiser if one of you looked for a new workplace. Where the walls don't have eyes and ears and very big mouths.

Art and Literature

As far back as the *Ant and Bee* books, we've been conditioned to aspire upward. We're entitled. This is the required reading list for our crowd, with appropriate comments. And it is so useful! In addition to building a good vocabulary and better reading comprehension, attempting this beguiling list will ensure that you will never fail at a favorite competitive sport: cocktail party conversation.

BOOKS YOU SHOULD HAVE READ AND WHAT TO SAY OR KNOW ABOUT THEM IF YOU HAVEN'T (YET)

Austen, Jane: *Pride and Prejudice*

Basis for inspirational film *How to Marry a Millionaire*. Also basis for film *Pride and Prejudice*. Teaches women who are tired of "having it all" that they can ditch the workaday treadmill and find a rich guy to marry instead. Encourages same to find husband who looks like the young Laurence Olivier.

Burnett, Frances Hodgson: *The Little Princess*

Makes the young readerette wish she'd been born in England when men were men and dolls had porcelain faces. The story of Sara goes from riches to rags to riches, teaching the importance of good manners. Great illustrations.

Collins, Jackie: *Hollywood Wives*

"Sociologically primitive, yet literarily insightful look at lunch at the Bistro Garden in Beverly Hills. (I once had a good poached salmon there for lunch.) Reveals the darker side of those who wear false eyelashes during *daytime* hours!"

Comfort, Alex: *The Joy of Sex*

To give and receive as novelty gift—before it goes out of print. (We know you knew that stuff already.)

Dunne, Dominick: *The Two Mrs. Grenvilles*

Yes, darling, a nouvelle classique. Remember that Mrs. Grenville was really Mrs. Woodward, and the narrator bears a more than passing resemblance to Truman Capote, enfant terrible of the Colony set. (It's okay if you don't know what the above means. It's got that certain *je ne sais quoi*.)

Eliot, George: *Silas Marner*

The first really important novel about surrogacy and single parenting. Is George a guy or a gal? I always forget. (Tell admissions director at Ashley's potential nursery school you were not among the majority of students who found book boring. Who'll ever know the difference?)

Harvard Student Agencies: *Let's Go!*

"Last book actually read. Travel guide we used that summer in Europe. I left my copy at Heathrow Airport. I figured another student—one on a budget—could use it." Updated annually by Harvard students.

Hemingway, Ernest: *A Moveable Feast*

Paris on no francs a day. "Wouldn't it be intense to just go and hang out in the cafés and, like, drink coffee and write? I swear, if I didn't have the mortgage and the baby, I'd be tempted to do just that!"

Jong, Erica: *Fear of Flying*

Considered a major symptom of the women's movement. Allowed women to talk about their orgasms (but not in the boardroom). Condoned adultery. Coined term "zipless f-word."

McInerny, Jay: *Bright Lights, Big City*
   Say, "I couldn't finish it; could you?"

Márquez, Gabriel García: *One Hundred Years of Solitude*
   The supernatural in South America, where winter falls during the summer. Cool book which, if placed just so on your coffee table, will make you seem smarter than you actually are. Small type.

Piper, Watty: *The Little Engine That Could*
   "It's a charming little book, but most of all, I learned a lot about myself."

Plath, Sylvia: *The Bell Jar*
   Recent addition to list because of lesbian psychiatrist lawsuit. Comment that if you ever considered therapy (not that you ever have), that you would never seek advice from a former asylum inmate. Talk about civil liberties for the artist! Talk about first amendment! Have a drink with a poet or a lawyer.

Saint-Exupéry Antoine de: *The Little Prince (Le Petit Prince)*
   More intellectually fulfilling if "read" in French (*en français*). A good indication of what life (*la vie*) would be like if there were no such things as food processors or VCRs: boring. Relate to the prince and learn to say, "It's a little book, but a charming one. Most of all, I learned a lot about myself."

Salinger, J. D.: *Franny and Zooey*
   Neurosis, Manhattan Style. (Less creamy than the old-fashioned New England kind. Made with tomatoes.) Written after *Catcher in the Rye*. (Toasted is nicer.)

Updike, John: *Too Far to Go*
   Short stories (your favorite literary form other than captions) about a marriage gone sour. Public Television series (send in your contribution today, dammit!). Starred Blythe Danner and Michael Moriarty. They looked good together; too bad they're not married. Depressing.

Art

Truly cultured people know a bit about fine arts, too. They have picked up this knowledge rather carelessly through osmosis. Don't feel badly, sport. Memorize the following, and you'll do just fine:

Van Gogh, Vincent. Post-Impressionist. Dutch. Pronounce his name "Van Go." Some people will unfortunately attempt the more Flemish "Van Hock," which is pretentious even in these circles. Say, "He was a tortured genius." Don McLean sang a song about him. Say, "Talk about painterly!"

Matisse, Henri. Post-Impressionist. French. Never say, "I've got sheets that look like that!" Never say, "Wouldn't those make great towels?" Liked jazz.

Monet, Claude. Impressionist. French. Reproductions are exhibited in hotel rooms all around the United States. Think, "Boy, he painted before they invented aerobics," but don't ever say it. Jewelry company named for him.

Degas, Edgar. Impressionist. French. Painted ballet dancers. "I never know, is it 'Day-gah' or 'Deh-gah.'" Inspired generations of mothers of little girls to send them to ballet lessons.

Nieman, LeRoy. Sporty. American. Mustachioed. Always there (Wimbledon, Olympics, Kentucky Derby) when you need him. Smokes small cigars.

van Rijn, Rembrandt. Early. Dutch. Designed the Dutch Masters cigar picture. Liked medical stuff. Very smart. "What a rich palette!" Known (like Cher, Charo, Sammy, Engelbert, the Incomparable Hildegarde, etc.) by first name only.

David, Jacques-Louis. Painted the labels for Courvoisier. A real Napoleon fanatic. Probably not tall.

Schnabel, Julian. Euroglitz. Poses a lot in *Vanity Fair* with wife. Uses old broken china in his paintings. Say, "I love it, but darling, is it Wedgwood?" Painting featured in movie *Wall Street* caused New York audience to heckle.

Film

A teeny compendium for your viewing pleasure.

The Big Chill. Yes, this is your movie. Rent it, buy it, see it a hundred times to receive validation. Watch it with your friends and play roles. Are you the JoBeth Williams character or more the Mary Kay Place type? Tells members of the postwar generation that just because you have modern appliances doesn't mean you have no values.

Citizen Kane. Journalists can make money *and* afford a house outside the city. Remember that Orson Welles was only twenty-six years old when he wrote, directed, and starred in film. Realize that you're never going to live up to his promise. Then again, be grateful you're not overweight.

Splash. Comedic portrayal of classic male achievers' fantasy: a sinewy, long-limbed blond beauty who doesn't speak and doesn't wear much in the way of clothing. Luckily for reality's sake, there *are* men who appreciate women in sensible shoes.

Desperately Seeking Susan. Yes, dear, this is punk. The movie that launched the meteoric career of the virgin chanteuse and ensured that future generations felt it was okay to wear one another's clothes without asking first.

Gandhi. Where toga parties come from.

Kramer versus Kramer. Meryl's first starring role. Shot on Upper East Side of Manhattan, near where you (once) live(d). Say, "It really blew the lid on advertising." Say, "My brother-in-law looks like Dustin Hoffman." Proves once and for all that the Burberry trench is the definitive executive raincoat.

Saturday Night Fever. Man versus discotheque. Disco wins.

The Women. Claire Boothe Luce oeuvre about women and why you should learn to do your own manicures. Examined friendship, betrayal, infidelity, and quickie Reno divorces. Starred Joan Crawford, Norma Shearer, Rosalind Russell, et al. Paved the way for TV movie *Lace.*

Jagged Edge. Ask yourself which former prosecutors you know who could afford to wear skintight designer suits in a court of law and also sleep with a guy who looks like Jeff Bridges. Call someone to find out whether your ten-year-old LSATs are still valid.

Tootsie. If that's what Dustin Hoffman looks like as a woman, how would I look? How would Jessica Lange look as a man? Would Sam Shepard still love her? Mikhail Baryshnikov? Why does she keep getting these great guys?

Blue Velvet. So you didn't understand it—big deal! Tell everyone Dennis Hopper was weird and remark on the bulk of Isabella Rossellini's body. That's why her ads are all head shots. Poor Ingrid.

Stand by Me. Early male bonding. Who wouldn't want to adopt those boys? (First get them off cigarettes.) Good scene with leeches.

Hannah and Her Sisters. Because you need to say something about Woody Allen. Why? Because. Talk about *Hannah* feeling like a home movie. Wonder why Woody and Mia named their son Satchel.

Nothing in Common. "Oh, my God! It's just like my agency!"

Wall Street. Who does Michael Douglas remind you of? Carl Icahn? (No.) Saul Steinberg? (No.) Asher Edelman? Think about similarities to *your* trading floor. Who does Charlie Sheen remind you of? Your friend from business school? (No.) Your younger brother? (No.) Judd Nelson? Which of Oliver Stone's jungles is more dangerous? Vietnam? Wall Street? The Motion Picture Academy?

Broadcast News. What TV must be like. What Washington is like: No one is married. Guys are good dressers, better than the women. Debate Jane's choice with your friends. Mention casually that you believe in love triangles. See if anyone laughs. Wonder why you're a chiropodist when you belong in a newsroom.

Job Titles of the 1980s

TITLE	EXEMPLAR
Pop Psychologist	Dr. Irene Kassorla
Porn King	Russ Meyer; Bob Guccione
Supermodel, also Model-Actress	Paulina Porizkova
Computer Whiz	Bill Gates
Superwife	Elizabeth Dole
Superagent	Irving "Swifty" Lazar
Management Guru	Kenneth Blanchard; John Naisbett
Writer-Director	James Brooks; Barry Levinson

Cable King	Michael Fuchs
Crime Buster	Rudolph Guiliani
Ex–Beauty Queen Former Miss America }	Bess Myerson; Phyllis George
Takeover Artist	Carl Icahn
Cookie Queen	Mrs. Fields
Cookie King	Famous Amos
Nutrition Entrepreneur	Dr. Robert Giller; Richard Simmons
Consumer Advocate	David Horowitz
Pop Sociologist	"Dr." Srully Blotnick
Celebrity Chef	Wolfgang Puck; Jill St. John
Talk Show Host (Free-lance)	Dick Cavett; Joan Rivers
Talk Show Guest (Free-lance)	Don King; Teri Garr; The Collins Sister Who Isn't on Dynasty
Celebrity Divorce Lawyer	Marvin Mitchelson; Raoul Felder
Bimbo, also Plastic Surgery Advocate	Jessica Hahn; Donna Rice; Birgitte Nielsen
Perennial Candidate	Gary Hart

Extinct Job Titles

Yuppie Arbitrageur

Televangelist

Farmer

Astronaut

ALMA MATERS OF CEOS, CHAIRMEN, MANAGING PARTNERS, OWNERS, THE CHAIRMEN OF MANAGEMENT COMMITTEES, NAME PARTNERS, EXECUTIVE PRODUCERS, ETC.

Apple Computer	John Sculley	Brown University
Arthur Andersen & Company	Duane Kullberg	University of Minnesota

Bain & Company	Bill Bain	Vanderbilt University
Bristol-Myers	Bruce Gelb	Yale University
The Chase Manhattan Bank	Willard Butcher	Brown University
Chiat/Day	Jay Chiat	Fordham University
Covington & Burling	John Ellicott (Chairman of five-person management committee)	Princeton University
Crain Communications	Mrs. Gertrude Crain	
Dayton Hudson	Kenneth Macke	Drake University
Delta Airlines	Ronald Allen	Georgia Institute of Technology
The Detroit Baseball Club	Tom Monaghan Jim Campbell	University of Michigan Ohio State University
Domino's Pizza	Tom Monaghan	University of Michigan
Drexel Burnham Lambert	Fred Joseph	Harvard University
Esprit de Corps	Doug Tompkins	
Ford	Donald Peterson	University of Idaho
Gannett Company	Allen Neuharth	University of North Dakota
General Mills	Brewster Atwater	Princeton University
Ginnie Johansen Designs	Gerry Johansen	Northwestern University
Hewlett-Packard	John Young	Oregon State University
Hill, Holliday, Connors, Cosmopulos	Jack Connors	Boston College
Kekst & Company	Gershon Kekst	University of Maryland
King & Spaulding	Bradley Hale	University of Alabama
Kohn Pedersen Fox Associates	Gene Kohn	University of Pennsylvania
Korn/Ferry International	Lester Korn	University of California at Los Angeles
Leo Burnett	Cap Adams	Williams College
Levi Strauss	Robert Haas, Jr.	University of California at Berkeley
The Levy Organization	Larry Levy	Northwestern University
Lorimar Telepictures	Merv Adelson	Menlo Park Junior College
Lotus Development	Jim Manzi	Colgate University

Marvin Glass & Associates	Jeffrey Breslow	University of Illinois
MCI	Bill McGowan	King's College (Pennsylvania)
3M	Allen F. Jacobsen	Iowa State University
Mitchell, Silberberg & Knupp	(five-member management committee, whose members are reelected and whose names have been protected)	
MTV	Tom Freston	Saint Michael's College
Plum Productions	Chuck Sloan	
Polaroid	William McCune	Massachusetts Institute of Technology
Prescriptives	Dan Brestle	Villanova University
Quaker Oats	Bill Smithburg	De Paul University
R/Greenberg Associates	Robert Greenberg	Parsons College (Iowa), Arizona State University, University of Chicago, Northwestern, no degree
	Richard Greenberg	University of Illinois
Rainier Bancorporation	John Mangels	University of Washington
Robert Stock Designs	Robert Stock	
Rosewood Hotels	Robert Zimmer	University of Southern California
Scali, McCabe, Sloves	Marvin Sloves	Brandeis University
Security Pacific Bank	Richard Flamson	Claremont Men's College
Southland Corporation	Jere W. Thompson	University of Texas
Staubach Company	Roger Staubach	U.S. Naval Academy
Super Valu	Mike Wright	University of Minnesota
The Tom Peters Group	Tom Peters	Cornell University
Wachtell, Lipton, Rosen & Katz	(No managing partner; heads of firm are the four name partners):	
	Herbert Wachtell	University of Pennsylvania
	Martin Lipton	New York University
	Leonard Rosen	City College (New York)
	George Katz	City College (New York)
Young & Rubicam	Alex Kroll	Rutgers University

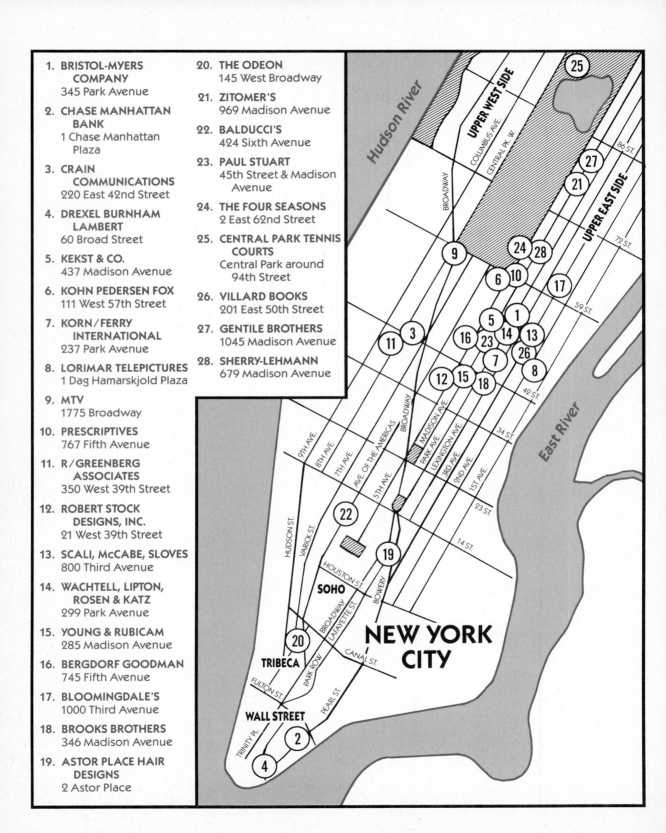

1. **BRISTOL-MYERS COMPANY**
   345 Park Avenue

2. **CHASE MANHATTAN BANK**
   1 Chase Manhattan Plaza

3. **CRAIN COMMUNICATIONS**
   220 East 42nd Street

4. **DREXEL BURNHAM LAMBERT**
   60 Broad Street

5. **KEKST & CO.**
   437 Madison Avenue

6. **KOHN PEDERSEN FOX**
   111 West 57th Street

7. **KORN/FERRY INTERNATIONAL**
   237 Park Avenue

8. **LORIMAR TELEPICTURES**
   1 Dag Hamarskjold Plaza

9. **MTV**
   1775 Broadway

10. **PRESCRIPTIVES**
    767 Fifth Avenue

11. **R/GREENBERG ASSOCIATES**
    350 West 39th Street

12. **ROBERT STOCK DESIGNS, INC.**
    21 West 39th Street

13. **SCALI, McCABE, SLOVES**
    800 Third Avenue

14. **WACHTELL, LIPTON, ROSEN & KATZ**
    299 Park Avenue

15. **YOUNG & RUBICAM**
    285 Madison Avenue

16. **BERGDORF GOODMAN**
    745 Fifth Avenue

17. **BLOOMINGDALE'S**
    1000 Third Avenue

18. **BROOKS BROTHERS**
    346 Madison Avenue

19. **ASTOR PLACE HAIR DESIGNS**
    2 Astor Place

20. **THE ODEON**
    145 West Broadway

21. **ZITOMER'S**
    969 Madison Avenue

22. **BALDUCCI'S**
    424 Sixth Avenue

23. **PAUL STUART**
    45th Street & Madison Avenue

24. **THE FOUR SEASONS**
    2 East 62nd Street

25. **CENTRAL PARK TENNIS COURTS**
    Central Park around 94th Street

26. **VILLARD BOOKS**
    201 East 50th Street

27. **GENTILE BROTHERS**
    1045 Madison Avenue

28. **SHERRY-LEHMANN**
    679 Madison Avenue

NEW YORK CITY

NEW
YORK
CITY

I t's not the most dangerous city in the world or even in the United States. It's maybe not even the noisiest or dirtiest. It probably is the costliest. (Unless you were considering working in Honolulu.) But New York City is the most exciting American city. Even those of you who've said for years "I wouldn't want to live there," have got to agree.

It is such a thankless, redundant task trying to reduce Gotham into a few chauvinistic paragraphs. Forgetting the tour guide tributes for a moment, let me just say that New York is eminently livable. If you have the patience, you will find an affordable domicile. (It may not be in Manhattan, and the patience required might be Jobian in scale, but you'll find it.) Eating and entertaining can be done stylishly on a modest budget. Almost anything sold retail can be purchased at a discount. (Even Cartier wristwatches, Limoges china, and theater tickets.) With a credit card. In a safe neighborhood.

Everyone should experience living in New York. Even for a month. When you live here, you don't have to do all the things tourists feel obliged to do. New Yorkers don't go out every night, they don't go to museums every weekend, they don't cram every minute with activity.

They eat pizza in front of their TV sets like normal people. (They probably do not watch *The Facts of Life* or *We've Got It Made,* however. They do watch *Jeopardy!* and an increasing number of them even tape it since they may be in their offices past 7:30 P.M., after "Final Jeopardy.")

New York's metabolism is fast. People do things with a sense of urgency. (In psychology class they'd attribute that to the "crowd mentality.") People work hard here. Everyone works. And they work late. A nine-to-five schedule job is rare, or rather, not a property of a high-powered job. People in New York have high-powered jobs. (Even those who work for themselves.) These are often attended, after work, with business dinners, making after-hours decompression a bit difficult. There is less hesitation about starting one's own business here than you might find elsewhere. New Yorkers are confident, and if it doesn't work out, they'll look for a job. Eventually. (They also tend to be less loyal to the organizations that hire them. They see less nobility in being able to boast, à la their friends in the Midwest, "I've had the same job for twenty-four years.")

Businesswomen shy away from undue frills. While they are beyond blue suits, white blouses, and foulard ties—look-at-me-I-look-like-him insecurity—many wouldn't dream of wearing makeup to work that's discernible to the human eye; that would make them appear to be frivolous, too concerned with nonbusiness matters. Which isn't to say they don't pamper themselves. They do. They shop. They get massages and private workouts and facials, but nothing that's too noticeable. Businessmen in New York no longer wear three-piece suits, a welcome relief. (And most have learned that brown is not the first-choice suit color.)

New Yorkers don't gawk at celebrities, unless they're Jackie Kennedy, her children, or the recent victor in a tender offer. Sylvester Stallone? Don't make me laugh. Eddie Murphy? Who cares? The new famous are the people who hire press agents just to announce increments in their wealth. It used to be not nice to announce one's wealth or even talk about money in Gotham. Now it's a way of life. (One unifying characteristic that brings New Yorkers together, like surviving a blackout, a transit strike, or a stock market crash: a collective loathing of Donald Trump. Many out-of-towners don't realize this.) Some New Yorkers may quietly vote Republican, but it's a city of Democrats. (Many New Yorkers are so insulated from the rest of the country that they still haven't figured out how Reagan got two trips to the White House.)

Young New Yorkers are discovering the pleasure of families. (Remember that most New Yorkers come from out of state. How can you tell? Native New Yorkers don't pay attention to car makes and models when walking down the street, and they have no teenage anecdotes to share about going "parking" or what happened to them at the drive-in.) They marry at a much later age than any other Americans (they almost don't understand a marriage of twenty-five-year-olds) and are late in seeing that children are the greatest joy on earth. (Having to write applications to nursery school while in labor seems but a small cross to bear.) Oh, hell. I've lived in New York my whole life. You should have asked someone else.

BEST NEIGHBORHOODS WITH DECENT PUBLIC SCHOOLS: Katonah (Westchester), Chappaqua (Westchester), Scarsdale (Westchester), Westport (Connecticut), Greenwich (Connecticut), Short Hills (New Jersey), Upper East Side (Manhattan—Sixty-eighth–Ninety-first Streets, between Lexington and Fifth Avenues)

NICEST NEIGHBORHOODS (BUT YOU'LL PROBABLY HAVE TO SEND YOUR KIDS TO PRIVATE SCHOOL): Parts of all five boroughs, especially Manhattan, Riverdale (the Bronx), Brooklyn Heights, Harrison (Westchester)

BEST PLACES TO LIVE IF YOU'RE AN ASPIRING ARTIST OR YOU WANT TO LIVE NEAR PEOPLE WHO WEAR ONLY BLACK: East Village, Tribeca, Soho (Manhattan), Hoboken (New Jersey)

BEST NEIGHBORHOOD WITH TAKE-OUT FOOD AND SINGLE PEOPLE WHO ARE ALSO REPUBLICANS: Upper East Side, especially east of Lexington Avenue

MOST OVERPRICED COMMUNITIES FOR SUMMER HOMES: West Hampton, Quogue, South Hampton, Water Mill, Wainscott, Sagaponack, Bridgehampton, East Hampton, Amagansett, Montauk, Sag Harbor, Shelter Island, Fire Island, Connecticut

BEST PUBLIC SCHOOLS: New York City: P.S. 6, Stuyvesant High School, Bronx High School of Science, Fiorello LaGuardia High School; Westport (Connecticut): Staples High School; Westchester: Scarsdale High School; New Jersey: Teaneck High School, Millburn High School

BEST PRIVATE SCHOOLS: Brearley (girls, all grades), Collegiate (boys, 1–12), The Town School (coed, K–8), Horace Mann School (coed, all grades), Riverdale Country School (coed, all grades), Ethical Culture—The Fieldston School (coed, all grades), Dalton (coed, all grades)

BEST ALTERNATIVE SCHOOLS: Elizabeth Seeger, Friends Seminary, Professional Children's School (for child stars, grades 4–12)

LIVING ARCHITECTS WHO HAVE MOST INFLUENCED THE CITY'S SKYLINE: Philip Johnson, John Burgee

DEAD ARCHITECT WHO HAS MOST INFLUENCED THE CITY'S SKYLINE: Stanford White

MOST POPULAR RESIDENTIAL ARCHITECTS: Richard Meier, Robert A. M. Stern (both coveted for their design of East Hampton homes)

SOCIALLY INCLINED REALTORS: Manhattan: Alice Mason, Edward Lee Cave; Hamptons: Mrs. Condie Lamb; Connecticut: William Pitt; southern Westchester: Julia B. Fee

DECORATORS WHO WOULD DECORATE HOMES PURCHASED THROUGH THOSE REALTORS: MAC II, Mario Buatta, Sister Parrish

DEALER IN THE FINEST, MOST VALUABLE ART: Wildenstein Gallery

TRENDY GALLERY FOR PEOPLE WHO WEAR ALL BLACK AND HAVE A LOT OF MONEY: Gracie Mansion

MOST EXCLUSIVE GOLF CLUBS: Piping Rock (Locust Valley, New York—restricted); Century Country Club (Purchase, New York—"Our Crowd")

BEST PUBLIC GOLF FACILITIES: Bethpage

MOST EXPENSIVE HEALTH CLUBS: Vertical Club, Sports Training Institute (one-on-one training)

BEST HEALTH CLUBS FOR MEETING POTENTIAL MATES: Vertical Club, New York Health and Racquet Club ("Ring by spring or your money back")

BEST HOTELS FOR BUSINESS TRIPS: Regency, Ritz-Carlton, The Pierre

BEST HOTELS FOR TRYSTS: Earl, Seville

RESTAURANTS KNOWN FOR BEST CUISINE: Lutèce, Le Bernardin, Quilted Giraffe, Le Cirque

BEST RESTAURANTS FOR PEOPLE WHO WEAR BLACK: Le Zinc, Odeon, Exterminator Chili, Indochine

BEST RESTAURANTS FOR AN INEXPENSIVE DATE: Il Vagabondo, Cafe Divino, Sugar Reef, Jose Sent Me, Chin Chin

NOISIEST RESTAURANTS (INTIMACY IMPOSSIBLE): America, Ernie's, Café Luxembourg, Memphis

BEST SPORTS BARS: Sports Bar, Runyon's

BEST DARK BARS: Oak Bar (Plaza Hotel), Bemelmans Bar (Hotel Carlyle)

BEST GIMMICKY BARS: Café International, Cadillac Bar

BEST BAR TO IMPRESS A CLIENT: The bar at The Four Seasons or at "21," or anywhere they know your name that isn't a Blarney Stone

MOST EXCLUSIVE CITY CLUBS: Century Association, The River Club, The New York Athletic Club, The Racquet Club

FANCIEST WINE STORE WHENCE CEOS PROBABLY STOCK THEIR OWN CELLARS: Sherry-Lehmann

GOURMET STORES GUARANTEED NOT TO RUN OUT OF GOAT CHEESE OR SUN-DRIED TOMATOES: Neuman & Bogdonoff, Word of Mouth, Balducci's, Zabar's, Dean & Deluca, Barefoot Contessa (East Hampton)

NICEST MOM-AND-POP GROCERY STORE: Gentile Brothers

LARGEST DRUGSTORE WITH MOST REMARKABLE SELECTION: Zitomer's

CORPORATE PARTY PLANNERS: Projects Plus

HIGH-SOCIETY PARTY PLANNERS: Karen Bacon, "Celebrations"

POWER BARBERS: Paul Molé, Pio

NEW WAVE HAIR STYLIST: Astor Place Hair Designers

JUNIOR LEAGUE BEAUTY PARLORS: Monsieur Marc, Kenneth's, Joseph Morrissey

PLACES WHERE LADIES WHO LUNCH ARE LIKELY TO HAVE TEA AFTER A HARD DAY OF SHOPPING, VOLUNTEER WORK, AND TENNIS: Mayfair Regent Hotel, Palace Hotel, Plaza Hotel

BEST STORES FOR EXECUTIVE WOMEN: Paul Stuart, Alcott & Andrews, Bergdorf Goodman

BEST STORES FOR EXECUTIVE MEN: Paul Stuart, Brooks Brothers, Barney's

BEST STORES FOR DRESS-UP CLOTHES: Bergdorf Goodman, Martha's (women only), Barney's

BEST SHOPPING RESOURCE FOR PEOPLE WHO ONLY WEAR BLACK CLOTHES: Charivari, Comme des Garcons, Parachute

DEBUTANTE BALL: Infirmary Ball

BUSIEST SOCIAL SEASON OF THE YEAR FOR THOSE WHO CARE ABOUT SUCH THINGS: Labor Day to Memorial Day

SOCIAL HIGHLIGHTS: Black tie openings of the Metropolitan Opera, the American Ballet Theatre, and the Costume Institute at the Metropolitan Museum (good chance of seeing Jacqueline Onassis and Diana Vreeland); for ages twenty-one to thirty-five, Junior Committee fundraisers for museums, especially the Whitney and the Guggenheim; for those really light-of-foot (age seventeen to twenty-one), there's always the Gold and Silver Ball (black tie, music by Lester Lanin), which will be good practice for later life

MOST RELIABLE FLORISTS: Rhinelander Florist, Irene Hayes Wadley & Smythe Lemoult

MOST EXOTIC FLORISTS: Salou, Mädderlake, Twigs

TOP JEWELER FOR RESETTING MOTHER'S EMERALDS: Harry Winston

MOST COMPLETE BRIDAL REGISTRIES: Bloomingdale's, Michael C. Fina

PROMINENT PHYSICIANS: Chiefs of departments at New York Hospital; Dr. Wayne Isom (cardiac surgeon), Dr. Jeremiah Barondess (internist), Dr. Jose Meller (cardiologist)

PROMINENT PLASTIC SURGEONS WITH EQUALLY PROMINENT CLIENTELE: Dr. V. Michael Hogan, Dr. Donald Baker

PROMINENT GYNECOLOGIST: Dr. E. Thomas Steadman

PROMINENT PSYCHIATRIST: Dr. Peter Neubauer

BEST SEAMSTRESS OR TAILOR FOR ALTERATIONS: Dova

BEST SEAMSTRESS OR TAILOR FOR CUSTOM TAILORING: Madame Mezei

POPULAR FACIAL SALONS: Georgette Klinger, Mario Badescu, Christine Valmy

POWER TOOLS

MEN'S POWER DRESSING

BROOKS BROTHERS
346 Madison Avenue
New York, NY 10017
(212) 682-8800

BEST-SELLING EXECUTIVE SUIT: Three-button, midweight, navy blue chalk stripe, 100 percent wool, $560

POWER SHIRT: Oxford cloth button-down, white, 100 percent cotton, $40

POWER TIE: Rep tie (striped)—red, white, and blue, 100 percent silk, $25

POWER LUNCHES

LE CIRQUE
58 East 65th Street
New York, NY 10021
(212) 794-9292

POPULAR EXECUTIVE LUNCH ITEMS:
Lobster salad, $21.75
Spaghetti primavera, appetizer $10.75, main course $18.75
Fettuccine with wild mushrooms, appetizer $10.75, main course $18.75
Crème Brulée, $6.00

PROMINENT CLIENTELE: Former President Nixon ("here all the time, two or three times a month at least"), Malcolm Forbes (and his sons), Ronald Perelman ("of course"), Martin Zimet (the owner of French & Co.—an antiques and art dealer), the Wildenstein family, Alfred Taubman (owner of Sotheby's and shopping mall magnate, and his son), Kirk Douglas, Michael Douglas, Burt Lancaster, Alan King, Beverly Sills, Barbara Walters ("always here"), Anthony Quinn ("always here"), Irwin Winkler (producer of "Rocky" films), David Brown (producer), Helen Gurley Brown (inveterate *Cosmopolitan* girl), Alice Mason (real estate), Jonathan Tisch, Saul Steinberg, Robin Leach, Ken Taylor (Canadian ambassador), John Guttfreund (chairman of the board of Salomon Brothers), Donald Trump, Ivana Trump, Calvin Klein, Valentino ("was a client of ours"), Missoni, "so many more."

THE FOUR SEASONS
99 East 52nd Street
New York, NY 10022
(212) 754-9494

APPETIZERS:
Blue point oysters, $11.50
Fettucine primavera, $14.50

MAIN COURSES:
Crisp shrimp with mustard fruit, $32.00
Dover sole meunière, $40.00

DESSERT:
Chocolate velvet (made without flour), $8.00

PROMINENT CLIENTELE: Philip Johnson, S. I. Newhouse (author's publisher), Pete Peterson, Mort Zuckerman (chairman of Boston Properties and *The Atlantic Monthly*), George Lois, Edgar Bronfman (Jr. and Sr.), John Loeb (Jr. and Sr.), Sandy Weill, Alexander Liberman (Condé Nast), George Whaling, Paul Gitlin, Alan Greenspan (Federal Reserve chairman), Charles Goldschmidt.

POWER ACCESSORIES

GUCCI
685 Fifth Avenue
New York, NY 10022
(212) 826-2600

MEN'S SHOES: Gucci loafer ("Required apparel item for financial people in New York at the country club, on the trading floor, even with tuxedos"), $195.00

EXECUTIVE MISCELLANY: Briefcases (men's and women's)—top of the line is their crocodile briefcase, which sells mostly to advertising people—"people who can get away with being more flashy." Most attaché cases and briefcases range from $300–$3,500; watches (men's and women's), $175–$450; belts (men's), $95–$250

POWER WATCHES

WEINSTOCK & YAEGER
23 West 47th Street
New York, NY 10036
(212) 398-0780, 819-0413

BEST SELLER AMONG EXECUTIVE MEN: Rolex High-Line Presidential, $10,500; an all-gold Rolex, day, date, and second hand, eighteen-carat solid gold.

BEST SELLER AMONG EXECUTIVE WOMEN: Cartier Panther, $8,000; square face, date, and second hand, eighteen-carat brick-laid bracelet. "Women are buying dressier watches. This model is so popular we can't even get enough of them. It's on back order."

The store has in excess of a hundred customers daily, most between the ages of thirty and forty. Half of its executive clientele buy watches for themselves and the other half buy for a companion. Most have at least two watches, one for day and one for evening.

"Watches are more of a prestige item now than ever. Rolexes are the best value because they have the highest resale value. Two years ago people were buying steel and gold watches, now they're buying solid gold."

Weinstock & Yaeger offers discounts on most makes of watch, from 25 to 50 percent.

POWER HAIR

PAUL MOLÉ
144 East 74th Street
New York, NY 10021
(212) 988-9176

Paul Molé is the barbershop to which young boys in Manhattan graduate after their last haircut on a horsie (usually courtesy of Michael's Barbershop, 1263 Madison Avenue). Conveniently located on the Upper East Side, Molé's customers usually stay on forever, making the transition from Mummy or Daddy paying for haircuts to having to figure out the tip themselves. With over sixty years of experience, Molé can cut the wiliest of executive heads. We talked to Adrian Wood, the barbershop's owner.

ON TRENDS IN EXECUTIVE HAIR: "On the whole, successful men are very conservative and they don't change their style. They want to be predictable and project an image of predictability. They always want to look the same so you know what you're going to get from them. They have certain power looks. You'll find a big executive will like a power look. Generally off the face, a more severe type haircut, like Donald Trump."

ON GRAY HAIR: "Adrian sees more requests for a very natural hair coloring. If it bothers the guy, if he's forty-five years of age and wants to stay looking forty-five, then I'll recommend coloring it. It depends on what kind of business he's in. A doctor might want to look gray; an advertising guy might want to stay looking forty-five."

ON PERMS: "No, definitely not for male executives. I've had them have the hair straightened. But usually they wouldn't go for a curly look, that's a softer look."

ON FACIAL HAIR: "Out. It depends on what business you're in. Doctors, psychiatrists—they'll wear facial hair, but usually the business executives won't."

ADVICE FOR THE EXECUTIVE WHO IS LOSING HIS HAIR: "I'm not in favor of hairpieces because the guy's too vulnerable in a hairpiece. The thing can fall off, and he can end up looking like an idiot. If a guy's successful, it doesn't matter if he's bald or not. The more successful guys don't care, they're too self-secure to care. Jerome Robbins, no hair, he'll get his beard and his hair cut very short and it will look the best it can." For those who insist on altering nature's course, Adrian will refer his customers to hair specialists.

ON MANICURES AND SHAVES: Only a quarter of Paul Molé's clientele request manicures, which is enough to keep manicurists on staff. As to shaves, "we don't do them and we don't recommend them. Since the health scare that's been going on in New York, we don't like to use a blade from one person to another, we only use sterile, replaceable blades and they don't give as good a shave so it's not worth it."

ON EXECUTIVE MANNERS: "They want service immediately. If they come in on a Saturday, it's different."

ON NETWORKING IN THE SHOP: It happens. "Everyone knows each other."

PROMINENT CLIENTS: Donald Trump, Dan Rather, Rupert Murdoch, Frank Lorenzo, Jerome Robbins, Mike Wallace, Joshua Logan, Jim Lurie, William F. Buckley, Jr., Art Carney. "I have so many big executives coming through, I don't even pay attention to what they do."

MOTTO: "We take care of tykes and tycoons." Adrian says, "We try and go for the father and the son. Most of these guys come in with their sons. Donald Trump comes in with his kid. It's more of a family thing. We're not a fancy place."

HOURS: 7:30 A.M. to 7:00 P.M. (first appointment 8:00 A.M., last appointment 6:30 P.M.), Monday to Saturday. ("We get more and more women first thing in the morning. We've had a lot of young lady brokers. They want to be one of the guys. We charge them the same price as the men.")

FEES:
Basic man's haircut, $15 without shampoo, $20 with
Son's haircut, $14 without shampoo, $18 with ("Most kids don't get shampoos until they're teenagers")
Manicure, $9
Coloring, $35
Body wave, $35

Beard styling, $15
Face massage, $15 ("We have a young lady who does that")
Shoeshine, $1.50
Hot towel, free

HOUSE OR OFFICE CALLS: Paul Molé prefers not to offer this service officially. "If one of our customers is sick, we'll go to his house, or if one of our customers is stuck, we'll go to his office, but we don't charge them. They pay us next time they're in the shop."

EXECUTIVE FITNESS

THE TRAINER'S EDGE
1568 Second Avenue, 2nd Floor
New York, NY 10028
(212) 517-4904

The Trainer's Edge provides clients with one-on-one fitness training either at home or in its spare but thoroughly appointed Upper East Side gym. It was founded in 1986 by Cheryl Jones (known to all as C.J.), twenty-seven, who graduated with a bachelor's degree in physical education from Central Connecticut State University, and Cara E. Sax, twenty-five, who graduated from Penn State University with a combined physical education and business degree. The women, who formerly worked for another New York City one-on-one fitness training facility, started their own gym with money borrowed from clients and friends.

The Trainer's Edge now has close to two hundred clients, 70 percent of whom are executives, most between the ages of twenty-five and thirty-five, with an even ratio of men and women. The gym employs eight trainers, and all training is done by private appointment. C.J. offered the following insights into her executive clientele:

WHY DO EXECUTIVES CHOOSE ONE-ON-ONE TRAINING?

"Part of their motivation and commitment is knowing that a trainer is waiting for them. It's just like everything else in their lives. Most corporate people—that's how they think. Everything has to be regimented throughout their day. They have an appointment for lunch, they have an appointment to work out." And "the corporate people are used to dealing with professionals. They deal with professionals all day. To maintain that consistency, they hire a professional to work with their body, just as they have a lawyer or accountant to work with their finances."

HOW DO EXECUTIVE CLIENTS DIFFER FROM OTHER CLIENTS?

"They're a little bit more goal-oriented. They have to have a number. 'How many repetitions?' Depending on what they do, they're a little more aggressive, a little more 'Let's get down to business.' And they have a lot of questions. 'Why am I doing this, what will it do?' Unless they're traveling a lot, they're real committed. They sign up, and they do it. They work out consistently. And if they're going to travel, most people will ask for a travel program and if there's a gym in their hotel, they'll try to exercise."

WHAT KIND OF SHAPE ARE THESE EXECUTIVES IN WHEN THEY COME TO THE TRAINER'S EDGE?

"Most of them are weekend athletes—tennis, skiing, fun stuff. Those people are already motivated. On the other hand, you have the people that are so stressed out from their jobs that they don't want to have to think about working out. They want a one-on-one trainer who will be there and tell them what to do."

DO THEY COME BECAUSE OF VANITY OR FOR HEALTH REASONS?

"The two go hand in hand. I think a lot of people want to stay looking good. So a certain part of it is vanity. No question. They want to fit into their suits. But a lot of it is that exercise decreases stress. People have to have that because they have high-pressure jobs and exercise physiologically decreases their stress and helps them cope.

HAVE YOU SEEN ANY MAJOR TRANSFORMATIONS?

"One guy who works for a major investment banking firm. Twenty-eight years old. He was an excellent athlete in college, always in good shape his whole life. Then he got into a corporation and was really stressed out. In the three years after finishing his MBA he didn't work out and got grossly overweight. He came to us in January, right after the holidays, and he started working out consistently. Now, eight months later, he's dropped sixty pounds and he did a triathlon last week. He came in third in our Trainer's Edge Fitness Challenge. He looks so good and he's so happy, he brought us about ten clients from his bank.

FEES:

45-minute workout at gym, $30.00 (sold in blocks of twenty session for $600)

45-minute workout at home, $50.00 (sold in blocks of ten sessions for $500)

8-session nutrition program, $375.00 (once a week for eight weeks)

The Trainer's Edge offers a specialized running program and a pregnancy program, either at home or in the gym, for the same prices as the regular training. It also offers special protocols for specific problems such as lower back pain, knee complications, shoulder dislocations, hypertension, diabetes, and exercises for specific sports. C.J. and Cara anticipate opening a midtown facility within the next two years.

MOM-AND-POP GROCER

GENTILE BROTHERS, INC.
1054 Madison Avenue
New York, NY 10021
(212) 879-2717

Gentile (pronounced Gentillee) Brothers, the consummate neighborhood grocery store, was founded in 1918 by native Italian Antonio Gentile, a cook during World War I, and his five brothers. Antonio started the original store on Manhattan's Upper East Side, on Eighty-fourth Street and Lexington Avenue. (The store has moved several times in the same neighborhood since, and has been at its current location, on Madison Avenue between Seventy-ninth and Eightieth Streets, since 1970.) With a viable business, Antonio envisioned expanding by having each of his brothers open his own store. But before World War II, three of the brothers went back to Italy, and the store was ultimately left in the hands of Antonio and his three sons. (Ironically, Patrick D'Agostino, Gentile Brothers' head clerk, later realized Antonio's vision when he founded D'Agostino Supermarkets, now a chain of twenty-one upscale grocery stores located primarily in New York City.)

Antonio retired in 1958 and his son Gennaro took over the store in 1960. Gennaro currently runs Gentile Brothers with his three sons, Tony, Sal, and Jimmy. (He also has three daughters who are not involved in the business.) The store offers an array of delectable foods—from the freshest fruits and vegetables to homemade salads and sandwiches, the finest meats and cheeses, gourmet foods like paté and imported olives to a variety of standard and gourmet packaged foods—as well as various and sundry items such as paper towels, dishwashing detergent, and cigarettes. These goods are displayed in one 1,000-square-foot shop that also contains a deli/ butcher counter.

The vast majority of Gentile Brothers' customers are well-heeled, Upper East Side families who can afford to pay for quality and convenience. Most of them have charge accounts with the store, and most—a full 95 percent—order their groceries over the phone for delivery. The phone rings constantly, and store employees bustle with the activity of packaging orders and waiting on those customers who do come in to shop. Although the space is cramped and people often bump into one another, no one seems to mind and a remarkably friendly atmosphere prevails.

We spoke to Tony, the eldest of the third generation of Gentile brothers, about the family business.

WERE YOU AND YOUR TWO BROTHERS EXPECTED TO GO INTO THE BUSINESS, OR DID YOU DECIDE TO DO SO ON YOUR OWN?

"Our father expected us to go into it. Jimmy wanted to, and so did I. Sal wanted to do something different, but he got pulled into it. He was supposed to become a lawyer. I went to SUNY [State University of New York] Buffalo and majored in psychology. Sal was a business major at SUNY Albany, and he went to graduate school in Pennsylvania in arbitration. Jimmy [the youngest] never went."

DO YOU HAVE ANY CHILDREN WHOM YOU PLAN TO BRING INTO THE BUSINESS?

"I have a little girl, Natasha, who's three years old. I don't want her to go into the business. I want her to learn accounting and do our books. I don't know what Sal and Jimmy plan on doing."

DO YOU HAVE MANY CORPORATE CLIENTS?

"There are some corporations with commissaries that buy food from us every day, but most of our clients are large families in New York. A few third-generation, a lot of second-generation. We try to stay away from really big accounts—they hold us up before paying, and they're a lot of work. Most people buy everything from us: toiletries, dry goods, vegetables, meats, cheeses. We're mostly a service store—a *reliable* service store. Eighty-five percent of our customers are regulars, and eighty-five percent of our business is charge."

WHERE DO YOU MAKE MOST OF YOUR MONEY?

"Fruits and vegetables. That's what we're known for."

AS PEOPLE HAVE BECOME MORE SOPHISTICATED EATERS, HOW HAS YOUR BUSINESS CHANGED?

"It's changed the products that we sell. Frozen things are on the decline. Canned goods are on the decline. We sell a lot more fresh vegetables and fruit, a lot more cheeses, and, as far as deli meats go, people are into leaner cuts of meat. Items like that. And then, of course, there are new products. A whole array of wild mushrooms—it's a whole new field. Fresh herbs—it used to be just parsley and dill—now we carry all sorts of fresh herbs. There are vinegars and olive oils and olives—many different things. People used to let Bird's Eye and Campbell's feed them, now they're doing it themselves."

WHAT ARE SOME OF YOUR MOST UNUSUAL REQUESTS FOR FOOD?

"We get people asking for things like eggplant squash and blue onions. I would say things like truffles, but that's all standard, not unusual anymore. Baby corn, baby zucchini—there's a whole different thing of small vegetables now—avocados that are an inch long with no pits, corn that's an inch and a half long. They sell. I mean, it takes time for people to become familiar with them, but they sell. Like once, before, no one ate parmesan cheese. Then they started putting it on their pasta, and now it's one of our big sellers. And sun-dried tomatoes —no one knew what that was . . . "

WHERE ARE SOME OF THE PLACES YOU GO FOR THE FOOD YOU SELL IN THE STORE?

"Some of the best places are on Arthur Avenue and 116th Street, for mozzarella, Italian bread, ricotta cheese. (Little Italy is a tourist trap.) In the summertime we deal exclusively with a local farmer. I have a little piece of their farm. We started that five or six years ago."

YOU SEEM TO HAVE CULTIVATED FRIENDSHIPS WITH THE MAJORITY OF YOUR CUSTOMERS.

"Yes, mostly all of them. We know literally ninety-nine percent of all our customers on a personal basis. It's our personalities—just our attitude, I guess. You're small, and people get to know you. You start knowing what they want, and they have a party and need a favor and you get on a first-name basis. That's how it takes place."

DO YOU HAVE ANY PLANS FOR EXPANSION?

"We do. It's just a matter of finding a place in the neighborhood. We need four more people and another thousand square feet of space. But it has to be within a three-block radius of where we are. You move more than that and it's like moving into a different neighborhood."

POWER PLAY: ELOISE LIPSCOMB, PERSONAL SHOPPER

F.A.O. SCHWARZ
767 Fifth Avenue
New York, NY 10022
(212) 644-9400

Eloise Lipscomb is greeted each morning by the sound of children's voices chiming, "Welcome to our world, welcome to our world, welcome to our world of toys." The singing emanates from a grinning clock face set in an enormous three-tiered birthday cake adorned with a bobbing jack-in-the-box, tapping red-sequined shoes, Humpty Dumpty perching precariously on a wall and a cheerful choo-choo train whirling around a track. Giraffes dance, tin soldiers march, and a monkey nods its head. The impact is enchanting. Eloise works at F.A.O. Schwarz.

F.A.O. Schwarz is probably the grandest toy store in the world. Celebrities and notables shop there for their children. So do ordinary parents and grandparents. And Eloise, as the store's personal shopper, guides whomever seeks her services through the overwhelming panoply of playthings. The operative word is guide, as Eloise isn't there (merely) to push customers to buy. She's there to help them choose. She can tell a dazed parent or grandparent which toys are age-appropriate for their children, which ones kids are guaranteed to like and which ones will withstand sustained rough play. "I'm not a real salesperson. I like the toys, and I like the people." But she admits to having a knack for the multiple sale (though she's never worked on commission and she didn't even get a decent raise for several years). "I'm a genius at add-on sales. It's not really a sales pitch. It's mostly because I like the stuff." The kids like it, too. Lots of it.

Eloise more or less lucked into her job, though some might call it fate. She grew up in St. Louis and came to New York after college as a semi-aspiring actress. She needed a job, and F.A.O. Schwarz appealed to her—it's where her toys came from when she was a kid. So she walked in off the street one day to make inquiries, and the first person she approached agreed to interview her. "I thought he was just some peon, so I was relaxed and funny." It turned out he was the store manager, and Eloise was hired. She'd gone in on a Friday, and she started work the following Monday as a salesperson.

F.A.O. Schwarz launched a personal shopping service for the holiday season, and Eloise was one of six people chosen for the job. As the others were mostly supervisors and didn't have enough time to devote to personal shopping, soon it was down to just Eloise. "I was the best man for the job." She took to it like a duck takes to water, and through three years (excluding a three-month stint in France and a slew of other F.A.O. Schwarz jobs during the nonholiday months) a change of store management, and the store's move to a new location, Eloise maintained her preeminence as F.A.O. Schwarz's number one personal shopper.

Included among Eloise's clientele though not necessarily given preferred status—she treats her customers equally—are Mick Jagger ("he really knows his kids"), Billy Joel and Christie Brinkley, Michael Jackson (who once actually came into the store wearing a surgical mask), Gary Coleman, Diana Ross, Betsey Bloomingdale, Richard Thomas, and Frank Perdue. The most lavish toys she's sold are a kid-sized Ferrari Testarosa and a Lamborghini ($12,500 each) which go up to thirty miles per hour but are not licensable for the road. Her average sale per customer is approximately $1,500, and her biggest sale to one customer for a single child was for about $15,000 (it was a guilt-ridden father in the middle of a divorce). Eloise sells on tours of the store, over the telephone, and out of one of two plushly appointed sitting rooms that serve as the store's Personal Shopping offices.

Recently Eloise decided to leave F.A.O. Schwarz to try working as a paralegal. She couldn't go any further as a personal shopper, and she didn't want to remain in retail. Her colleagues responded to the news of her departure with a mixture of surprise and regret. Said one veteran saleswoman, "But Eloise, you *are* F.A.O. Schwarz." Though Eloise will miss F.A.O. Schwarz, she doubts that the store will miss her and says with a certain resignation, "I believe F.A.O. Schwarz is indestructable. When you leave, it still goes on without you."

BRISTOL-MYERS COMPANY

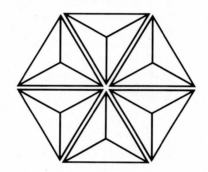

HISTORY & OPERATIONS

When William McLaren Bristol and John Ripley Myers bought the floundering Clinton Pharmaceutical Company for $5,000 in 1887, they knew next to nothing about either business or pharmaceuticals. Commented Bristol at a later date, "I have often wondered at our nerve." Bristol was looking for a means of supporting himself, while Myers, who came from a well-heeled family, was looking for a sound investment. The company was located in Bristol's rural hometown of Clinton, New York (population at the time 2,000), where both young men had attended Hamilton College, a small liberal arts school.

The Clinton Pharmaceutical Company was among the first companies in the country to manufacture over- and under-the-counter drugs. (Formerly, physicians rolled pills at their patients' bedsides.) A salesman who traveled the countryside in a horse and buggy sold the company's first products directly to doctors and dentists. Though the partners worked hard, it was tough going, and for years the company operated in the red. (In the early years, Myers often had to supplement the business from his own pocket, and Bristol often chose to go without his salary in order to meet their payroll.) By 1889 the company—which by then consisted of nine employees with a weekly payroll of $32—had been renamed Bristol, Myers Company and had moved its headquarters to Syracuse, New York. Myers contracted tuberculosis and died that year at the age of thirty-six.

Bristol-Myers—the comma was replaced by a hyphen soon after Myers' death—did not turn a profit until 1900, by which time it had started to produce consumer products in addition to pharmaceuticals. (The company has been profitable every year since 1900.) Between 1903 and 1905, sales skyrocketed due to the enormous success of two of these products: Sal Hepatica, a laxative mineral salt dubbed "the poor man's spa," and Ipana, a toothpaste made with a disinfectant to protect against bleeding gums. The immense demand for Sal Hepatica and Ipana spurred the company's growth from a regional into a national and ultimately an international corporation.

Bristol's son Henry, who was appointed general manager in 1915, determined that the company should abandon the manufacture of pharmaceuticals and devote itself entirely to consumer products. Bristol-Myers began to market its two biggest products directly to consumers through the now classic advertising campaign: "Ipana for the smile of beauty; Sal Hepatica for the smile of health." In 1919 the company established headquarters in New York City. In 1924 profits exceeded $1 million for the first time and the company's products were on sale in twenty-six countries. In 1929 the company went public, and it continued to prosper throughout the Depression.

During World War II, when penicillin was in great demand, Bristol-Myers resumed the production of pharmaceuticals to aid the war effort, and it continued to manufacture them along with consumer products after the war ended. With the introduction of television during the fifties, the company became a major network sponsor and large-scale advertiser.

In 1957, under the leadership of President and CEO Frederic N. Schwartz, Bristol-Myers adopted a corporate strategy of acquiring small, well-managed companies. The first major move in that direction was the purchase in 1959 of Clairol, a thriving family-owned company that produced hair-care products. By this time Bristol-Myers' annual revenues exceeded $100 million, and within the next three years the market price of its shares quadrupled. Within a dozen or so years after the acquisition of Clairol, the company purchased a number of other companies, including Drackett, Mead Johnson, Zimmer, and Westwood Pharmaceuticals.

Bristol-Myers' evolution into a truly international company was based primarily on its medications, along with nutrition and consumer products. Today, the company is the leading anticancer drug-producing company in the world, one of the top three makers of antibiotics worldwide, and a major manufacturer of central nervous system, dermatological, and cardiovascular drugs. Its line of nutrition products for babies is the broadest in the industry, and it is a world leader in orthopedic implants. Among its most familiar consumer products are: Bristol-Myers products: Excedrin, Bufferin, Ban, Nūprin, Comtrex, Vitalis; Clairol products: Nice 'n Easy, Loving Care, Ultress, Miss Clairol, Final Net, Sea Breeze, Clairol appliances; Drackett products: Windex, Endust, Drāno, Vanish, Renuzit, O-Cedar; Westwood Pharmaceuticals products: Keri Lotion, Alpha Keri, PreSun sunscreen products; and Zimmer products: The Total System (hip-replacement products).

Richard Gelb, the son of Clairol's founder, took over as CEO of Bristol-Myers in 1972 and became its chairman of the board in 1976. He created a massive $160 million research facility (the biggest capital investment in the company's history) in Wallingford, Connecticut, for the development of new products. Bristol-Myers has additional research facilities in Tokyo, Montreal, Paris and Montpellier, France, Syracuse, Buffalo, and Evansville, Indiana (home of Mead Johnson).

In 1987 Bristol-Myers collected $5.4 billion in revenues, $1.75 billion of which was generated from foreign sales, and $789.6 million in net earnings. The company now employs approximately 34,000 people in operating offices and manufacturing facilities located in more than 100 countries. Bristol-Myers is organized into the following divisions: The Consumer Products Group, which includes Bristol-Myers Products, Drackett, Clairol, Bristol-Myers Products Canada, and Monarch Crown (which markets many of the company's consumer products to military bases around the world); The Health Care Group, which makes and markets nonpharmaceutical health care products; The U.S. Pharmaceutical and Nutritional Group, which manufactures and markets pharmaceuticals and nutrition products; Bristol-Myers International Group, which markets pharmaceutical, nutrition and consumer products in more than a hundred countries; and The Science and Technology Group, which includes the Pharmaceutical Research and Development Division.

In 1986 Bristol-Myers acquired Seattle-based Genetic Systems and a share in its subsidiary, Oncogen—a purchase that will take the company into the new areas of biotechnology and genetic engineering.

One of the many products currently under development is Oncogen's vaccine against AIDS. The company filed an application with the U.S. Food and Drug Administration requesting its consent to begin testing the vaccine on humans. (It was approved in November 1987, and initial clinical studies are taking place at the University of Washington in Seattle.) Bristol-Myers means to "participate in the biomedical advances that are expected to dominate drug discovery and therapy during the early part of the next century." The company entered into partnership in 1987 with Westinghouse, owners of Group W, to produce several new television series. Thus far, it has sponsored several half-hour health specials—*Critical Minutes*, *The Fighting Edge*, *Ageless America*, and *The Hidden Addict*—which were syndicated to over 150 stations nationwide.

Bristol-Myers makes every effort to be an equal opportunity employer and has developed a number of programs to ensure that women, minorities, Vietnam veterans, and the handicapped are well represented throughout its ranks. Among the company's efforts in that direction are a specialized recruitment program for minority and women MBA candidates, a number of minority college programs, a pharmacy program that encourages minority students to choose careers in the pharmaceutical industry, a number of local programs to hire the disabled, active recruitment of Vietnam veterans by all divisions, internships for disadvantaged youths, employee training programs developed specifically for women and minorities, numerous scholarship programs, and a number of other initiatives. As of 1987, 11.8 percent of the company's work force was made up of minorities, and 30.5 percent was women.

(Information provided by Ralph Weaver, company spokesman.)

RANKING IN THE 1987 *FORTUNE* 500: Seventy-sixth.

REVENUES: $5.4 billion in sales in 1987.

EARNINGS: Net earnings of $789.6 million, or $2.47 per share, in 1987.

INITIAL PUBLIC OFFERING: 1929.

NUMBER OF SHAREHOLDERS: Approximately fifty thousand.

WORLDWIDE PRESENCE: Operating offices and manufacturing facilities in more than 100 countries. The company's products are sold in more than 100 countries around the world, most notably in Canada, France, Germany, Italy, Japan, Mexico, the Philippines, Taiwan, and the United Kingdom.

NUMBER OF EMPLOYEES: Approximately 34,000 worldwide, of which roughly 19,100 work in the United States.

AVERAGE AGE OF EMPLOYEES: Thirty-nine

TURNOVER: Information not available.

RECRUITMENT: "The company does some recruitment for specialized needs." Bristol-Myers actively recruits women, minorities, Vietnam veterans, and the handicapped through its separate divisions.

NUMBER OF NEW HIRES PER YEAR: "Currently, employment at Bristol-Myers is stable. Job opportunities for any given year depend on openings at corporate headquarters and divisions. Bristol-Myers emphasizes promotion from within to fill openings. Bristol-Myers recruits to replace individuals who leave, and to add specialized skills not already available in house."

RANGE OF STARTING SALARIES: Company will not disclose. "Starting salaries depend on the position, and the individual's experience and educational level."

POLICY FOR RAISES: "Bristol-Myers' divisions normally review salaries on an annual basis. Compensation is related to achievement, and is highly competitive."

BENEFITS: Group medical, life, and dental insurance, travel accident and survival income plans, pre- and after-tax savings programs (with a company matching provision), tuition aid, matching gifts program.

VACATION POLICY: Three weeks after one year, four weeks after fifteen years, five weeks after twenty years, and six weeks after twenty-five years, in addition to twelve regular paid holidays per year (for employees in corporate headquarters in New York—number may be different at other company locations), and one optional holiday that can be used for "a special religious, patriotic, or ethnic holiday, a day of personal significance, or in any other manner desired by the employee."

ADDITIONAL PERKS: The corporate headquarters and other locations have stores where employees can buy company products at discount prices. All divisions have employee cafeterias. Bristol-Myers has a travel club, for which all employees are eligible, which sponsors group vacations. Because of the company's support of the arts, all New York employees are entitled to free admission to the leading museums and receive discount tickets for the theater and cultural events. Perks vary by locale.

BONUSES: "The company awards bonuses generally to those people in middle management and above. Bonuses are determined solely on the basis of whether or not the company's profit objectives are realized. The company also provides cash service awards for those not in middle management. This is based on length of service with the company."

ANNUAL PARTIES: "In New York we host an annual holiday reception and Big Apple picnic. Elsewhere, activities vary by locale."

AVERAGE WORKDAY: Depends on the office.

DRESS CODE: No stated dress code, but dress is conservative and subdued.

SOCIAL ATMOSPHERE: "Recreational and specialized interest programs encourage after-hours socializing. Each year in New York, the company sponsors an all-sports dinner to thank employees who participated in the company's basketball, volleyball, softball, bowling, and running activities."

BRAND NAME PRODUCTS THAT LEAD THEIR MARKETS: Ban Quick Dry Anti-Perspirant Roll-On Deodorant (leading roll-on deodorant), Extra-Stength Bufferin Coated Tablets (leading buffered aspirin), Aspirin-Free Excedrin P.M. tablets (leading sleep aid analgesic combination), Vitalis Hair Care Products (leading men's hair preparation product), Clairol Nice 'n Easy (leading retail hair-coloring brand), Clairol Loving Care (leading semipermanent hair coloring), Sea Breeze (leading facial antiseptic), Vanish Bowl Cleaner (leading toilet bowl cleaner), Drāno (leading drain cleaner), O-Cedar Brooms (leading handle goods), Windex (leading glass cleaner), Clairol Style Setter heated rollers (leading heated hair rollers), Clairol Benders (leading heated flexible hair shapers), and Foot Fixer (leading foot care system).

RESEARCH AND DEVELOPMENT BUDGET: $342 million in 1987, or 6.3 percent of total sales.

HEADQUARTERS: The company occupies twelve floors of a high rise at 345 Park Avenue in New York City. The principal architect of the building was McMillen, Inc. "The pharmaceutical research center in Wallingford, Connecticut, located on a 177-acre site, serves as the world headquarters of pharmaceutical research at Bristol-Myers. Dermatological research is based in Buffalo, New York."

CHARITABLE CONTRIBUTIONS: Bristol-Myers contributes to the Bristol-Myers Fund, established in 1953, the Mead Johnson Foundation, and makes direct donations from the company and its divisions. "In 1987, donations totalled approximately $10 million. Medical research, health-related, and community service organizations received 51 percent of combined company and Fund contributions. Educational institutions and education-related programs received 28 percent, and cultural and civic activities received 21 percent." The company also has a matching gifts program through which it matches employee contributions.

INTERESTED APPLICANTS CAN SEND RÉSUMÉS TO:

Bristol-Myers Company
45 Park Avenue
New York, NY 10154
(212) 546-4000

Bristol-Myers International Group
345 Park Avenue
New York, NY 10154
(212) 546-4000

Bristol-Myers Products
345 Park Avenue
New York, NY 10154
(212) 546-4000

Bristol-Myers Pharmaceutical Group (includes Mead Johnson)
2404 Pennsylvania Street
Evansville, IN 47721-0001
(812) 429-5000

Clairol, Inc.
345 Park Avenue
New York, NY 10154
(212) 546-4000

Drackett Company
5020 Spring Grove Avenue
Cincinnati, OH 45232
(513) 632-1500

Genetic Systems Corp.
3005 First Avenue
Seattle, WA 98121
(206) 728-4900

Pharmaceutical Research and Development Division
345 Park Avenue
New York, NY 10154
(212) 546-4000

Zimmer USA, Inc.
Boggs Industrial Park
Box 708
Warsaw, IN 46580
(219) 267-6131

Westwood Pharmaceuticals
100 Forrest Avenue
Buffalo, NY 14213
(716) 887-3400

According to one of its employees, Bristol-Myers, the nation's third largest pharmaceuticals company, and number seventy-six in the latest *Fortune* 500, is appealing for its inherent class. Actually, that's not what he said. He said, "it's the bluest of the blue chips." After spending some time with employees at the corporation's Park Avenue headquarters, this is one of the themes that emerges when they describe the roots of their satisfaction.

Some have called Bristol-Myers conservative. It has maintained the same CEO, Richard Gelb, for the last seventeen years, a long tenure in the executive suite. The company has grown through acquisition, yet, in this age of the quick (and often hostile) takeover, Bristol has made methodical, friendly, and slow purchases, one taking nine years from start to finish. But everyone here speaks contentedly of working for a company they respect, and that is the key to their longevity.

Pam Kasa has been with the company since 1976. She's a lawyer and vice-president (officially, the corporate secretary and vice-president). Having been unhappy at another company for several years, she waited for this job, "the only one that looked like an improvement." During her previous jobs, she felt a lot of problems stemmed from "the lack of respect for women by their male colleagues." Then, during the interviews at Bristol, she met a fellow who filled her with confidence. "I could've had two heads and been green and it wouldn't have fazed him. I was amazed that these were people who just cared about getting the job done." Pam is allowed to be herself and do her work.

Being a member of the minority is not new to Kasa, who was always involved in the sciences. After graduating from a predominantly male science high school, she was in the first coed class at Rensselaer Polytechnic Institute, where she majored in chemical engineering. "I couldn't find a job as an engineer, so I accepted the fact that I had to start all over again." At law school she specialized in patents, a frequent home for nonpracticing engineers. She worked for the New York City government and three public corporations before joining Bristol-Myers' legal department, which has seventy-five members, forty-one of them based in New York.

Like most other public corporations, Bristol-Myers does not hire lawyers straight out of law school. Associates with three to five years' experience are considered, however, and working in house seems to appeal to a different breed of attorney than those who ache to make partner at a private firm. "You go to work for a corporation at the time when you'd make junior partner or partner. In law firms the emphasis is on litigation. Not here. A nice thing about being a lawyer at Bristol-Myers is that you're really involved in business. The defensive legal work is under control. You're doing pharmaceuticals, patent law, international law, and negligence, and moving into business is easy for lawyers. Each operating company has its own legal staff. A division's counsel becomes a vice-president of the division and part of the process. The pace is the same as the pace of the business. Our problems are a lot more short term than a law firm's."

Kasa says the legal department's identity and culture are different from those of the rest of the corporation. "We work at it. We have monthly lunches on a national level for associate counsels. Everyone shares their common legal problems. Things are considered very thoroughly here. Most people I work with have been doing this a long time. We don't expect too many surprises."

The blue chip aspect is not what keeps Pam at Bristol-Myers. Neither is it the company's long history of success. She respects her employer's ethics. "I wouldn't work for a company that wasn't ethical. If I could only do one thing," she fantasizes about a well-spent life, "I'd find the cure for cancer. But you know . . . I am . . . I am involved. Even when I worked for hair coloring. Even when I review press releases."

In fact, Bristol-Myers is the leading pharmaceutical spender in cancer research, a fact that makes employees—who may only get as close as Bufferin—proud. Wayne Davidson began his career with pharmaceutical leader Mead Johnson in 1958. A manufacturer of formulas for well and not-so-well babies, vitamins, vaccines to combat the pediatric diseases bacterial meningitis and epiglottitis, and other products, the company was acquired by Bristol-Myers in 1967. Davidson became president of the division, headquartered in Evansville, Indiana, in 1977, and moved to New York in January 1984. "Until I moved to New York, I thought of myself in the Mead Johnson context as much as the Bristol role." As an officer of Bristol-Myers, he now carries the title of president, U.S. Pharmaceutical and Nutritional Group, and, senior vice-president, Bristol-Myers Company.

"I think it's important that upper management of each division thinks more and more like the parent company," he says. "The objectives and ethics have to be consistent with Bristol corporately." Maintaining the Mead Johnson name is important, though. "The name has equity and a good reputation in the medical community. To do away with 'Mead Johnson' would be doing away with some of what Bristol-Myers bought. There are not great differences in the cultures of the two companies. The culture of Bristol-Myers is the composite of all its companies and subsidiaries," although there is more homogeneity in Evansville, which Davidson now visits approximately once a month.

Of Bristol-Myers' twenty current divisions, eleven have been acquired. George Peter Kooluris, the vice-president of corporate development, has been involved in many of these transactions over his nineteen-year career at the corporation. "This company is a melting pot. Three of the companies we purchased—Zimmer, Clairol, and Drackett—were privately held family companies. We're comfortable with new people coming in through acquisition. We're very disciplined in our acquisitions. We've passed over companies because their management styles were incompatible. They might be good business, but they had bad chemistry. We're a family business and must be careful. We're as careful that the other [hypothetically speaking, acquirable] company knows as much about us as we know about them. Investment bankers may say we move too slowly, but we make few mistakes. We can move pretty fast when we want to. Only one in fifty transactions has come from an investment banker."

Wayne Davidson cites the corporation's "evolving emphasis on research. Our medical side is the fastest-growing side of the company. We're hiring more scientists to accelerate the shift."

You may not be aware that Bristol-Myers is "the leading company in terms of sales of medication in chemotherapy. We did not do all the research, but we did the development. We're the largest people and budget involved in anticancer research." In keeping with this in-house trend, the corporation acquired Genetic Systems, in Seattle, for $300 million, simply for their research and development function. (Without a portfolio of products, Bristol-Myers is betting on Genetic Systems' long term, a return in the 1990s.)

While procuring the approval of the Food and Drug Administration is "frustrating and maddening," Davidson reports that "prelaunch trials are the same for all pharmaceutical companies." From concept to launch is approximately a seven-year process costing about $100 million. "The interpretation is what can vary. Companies vary in how they report their results." Bristol-Myers is again considered conservative in this category.

Each floor in the corporate headquarters has a different feel. The forty-fourth floor, filled with senior executives, is quiet, beige, and decorated with original John James Audubon prints. It is connected by an extremely imposing set of staircases to the forty-third floor,

CEO Land, creating in one area a two-story, Oriental-carpeted, hushed, portrait-laden lobby that looks like an exclusive men's club, not everyone's idea of an office. The Clairol offices are a little more contemporary-looking. Some of the other floors look just like the law firms that also populate this midtown building. And while there is a consistency to the culture—serious, subdued, no-nonsense—there is an autonomy that informs everyone's experience. The people in painkillers have a different work life from those in hot rollers, those on the corporate staff, and those in advertising.

Bristol-Myers is the nation's sixth largest advertiser. With a combined budget of $919 million spread over network, local, cable, and syndicated television and print (as well as promotion), they are unusual for purchasing their own broadcast time themselves and planning their print buys, functions ordinarily reserved for one's advertising agencies. Peggy Kelly is the director of media and program services with fifteen years at Bristol-Myers under her belt. She answers the obvious question, "Why do this in house?" with "We save money and exert more control. We can keep the venues in sync with our brands." With over 285 consumer brands sold in the United States, Bristol's advertising is shared by twenty-five agencies, including Grey Advertising and DDB/Needham.

Peggy says, "This function is autonomous. Few corporations have it. We have a great deal of connection with the different brand groups, more than people in other, say, manufacturing functions." Kelly works in a small office filled with the networks' upcoming programming schedules and lots of videocassettes. "We prescreen every show. We pulled out of twenty shows since the first of the year. They were not suitable carriers for our [class of] messages." The class and quality that are (becoming) synonymous with Bristol-Myers come from the "top down," which is why advertising will be pulled from shows that the media brass consider too violent or sexy. And everything is pretty much corporately determined. Air time is brand-directed. Sea Breeze, a popular astringent aimed at a young audience, sponsored, for example, the 1987 MTV Music College Tour. Clairol's top-of-the-line hair color, Ultress, as well as Nūprin, an analgesic, aired commercials on 1987's Oscar, Tony, and Emmy award presentation broadcasts. "We like to be in miniseries. We buy blocks of time without knowing which brand we'll sell. Each brand person lobbies for buys."

Again, the personality of this department may not remind you of other departments within the corporation. "This is a lean department. There's no room for people who can't make decisions. With sixty-seven people [in both media planning and buying] you have to play Solomon to some extent. People need room to make decisions and mistakes." Kelly admits there are different buying styles within the group, but overall, "we're tough negotiators, but not grinders. Not to the last penny. We're not like an agency that's going to lose an account. We're looking for a long-term relationship."

Having weathered several jobs before landing at Bristol-Myers—"Being a customer service rep. for the phone company was the worst job," she says—Peggy didn't regard this placement as a career at the outset. "After a few years it become clear it was a career. I was recognized. I got promoted. I didn't need pats on my back. I needed better jobs and compensation. I'm not bored."

You would never know that Elizabeth Means's hair has been colored. It's *that* subtle, that natural-looking. As the director of marketing of professional hair color at Clairol, Elizabeth felt she was a better salesperson as a user of her product. She arrived, taking a not untried route, via the advertising agency, DDB/Needham (né Doyle Dane Bernbach). A history of ideas major at Williams College, Elizabeth says she left the agency, "so that I'd never have to answer the MBA question again." In the late seventies and early eighties, there was such an emphasis on the graduate business degree at advertising agencies that mere college graduates were made to feel like stepchildren. Today advertising agencies would be lucky to get first-string MBAs at all; those folks go straight to financial services, without even passing Madison Avenue. "I was always on junior varsity," Means said wryly. "I wanted to play varsity. In advertising, I hated being erased from my work. I could only recommend, not decide. Here, I can be a decision maker."

Means called her world the "old girl system. It's a function of open doors. Who you market to is fun. We get ideas from consumers. We do focus groups." Moreover, there is more time to make those ideas stick, since this is not the quick-turnover business of fashion. "We're a wonderful hybrid: we're in between Elizabeth Arden and P and G. *Within* Bristol-Myers we're trendy. Punk rockers have done a lot for us."

There are approximately 3,060 people in the Clairol Products Division. For Means, that meant "Maybe five key people from ten different departments who were daily contacts, and two hundred infrequent contacts. In a day-to-day sense, I didn't *feel* Bristol-Myers. Hospital-related products didn't relate to me. I had no contact with some hospital business, and who cares? It's their structure. It's their profit." Betsy stayed at Clairol for two and a half years.

Being part of a large organization, or even part of a small one, necessitates a certain amount of competition for attention. "This company is very competitive. I don't think anyone knows what you've done if you don't tell them. One doesn't take personal credit. I believe that as a manager you get credit for sharing credit."

Gil Griffin is the vice-president of employee relations. This is his second tour of duty at Bristol-Myers. He oversees everything from minority college relations to labor relations, sexual harassment, and employee assistance programs. Why did he leave Bristol-Myers in the first place? "For better pay and a higher position." We'll accept that answer. Then why did he return? "Bristol-Myers has a better culture. Politics are diminished. We have a low-key, family image. We're not so Victorian that people can't interface socially."

Because the corporation is located right in the heart of New York, "you don't have to play golf," George Kooluris says. There might be groups of people who play tennis, and Bristol-Myers will pay the membership dues for [lunch] clubs for senior executives, "but there is no pressure on anyone to socialize outside the office. You can have privacy."

Frances Sica has only worked at Bristol-Myers since January 1986, yet she feels a strong allegiance to the company. With a degree from the Philadelphia College of Pharmacy and Science, she knew when she was very young that she wanted to be a pharmacist. She became one and then spent seven years with one of Bristol-Myers' competitors. She arrived here to work on Paraplatin (carboplatin), an anticancer product, in the international market. She travels on four or five major business trips per year, averaging three to four weeks apiece, sometimes with less than two days in each country. Frances speaks German, "a great plus," and some Spanish. She tells me that as the embodiment of Bristol-Myers to her customers, which include foreign hospitals, clinics, and physicians, she is the beneficiary of a positive perception of the company and its products. "When I was a pharmacist, Bristol-Myers always had credibility.

"I want to be part of anticancer health care. I like to feel our products make an impact. I could spend my career working here. (I wouldn't be as gratified selling Pearl Drops or Crest.) The company is ethical and stands behind their good products. They've made a commitment to anticancer. And it's a relationship; I feel confident they'd reward me. I'm happy because I feel good about what I do. The people and environment are important, but that's not necessarily why I stay. If I got a phone call that said, 'We've got a great job for you and your best friend is working in the office next door'—so what? The company and the product and the challenge are what matter."

Frances flies in economy or business class, she travels alone, and she works. Forget that it's Paris or Buenos Aires or Montreux. "On a personal trip I might camp out or spend some time outside cities, but I don't have time to sightsee, et cetera, on business trips. I feel it's Bristol sending me out to do a job. And I won't sightsee. If I sat on the forty-third floor [the senior executive offices] and carried the ultimate checkbook, I'd want the people who worked for me to be working for the benefit of the company."

John Stosko equated being recruited by Bristol-Myers with "being traded by the Chicago Cubs to the New York Yankees." When he first arrived at the company in 1974, he remembers feeling, "The carpet was so thick, I said, 'What am I doing here?'" Although his work is in finance, at Clairol, being part of this ethical and venerated health care company is one of his job perks. "You even feel you're doing good things in consumer goods." Stosko admitted that "Bristol-Myers is very conservative and cautious. It moves surely but wants a high batting average. It's risk-averse. Our risks are prudent. Every company it's acquired has been a successful building block. We pick companies in related fields, go slowly, and stick to our knitting. It's been a pretty good strategy. We're cash rich—in the neighborhood of $1.6 billion—and have no debt. We're too big to be a takeover target."

Clairol, Stosko's bailiwick and the world's first creator of hair mousse (Condition, 1985), is the division that gave Bristol-Myers Dick Gelb and his brother Bruce. Presiding over Clairol at the time of its acquisition, Dick Gelb was catapulted into the top executive slot at the parent company in 1972. (He was named chairman of the board in 1976. Bruce Gelb became vice-chairman in 1985.) "There's no favoritism towards Clairol," Stosko explained. If anything, "maybe we get scrutinized more. Dick Gelb is thought of as Bristol-Myers' CEO, not Clairol's." There is corporate concern as to who will be able to follow in Gelb's footsteps. Many say that the passing of the mantle will be Bristol-Myers' most important challenge in the coming years. "The Chairman of the Board sets the tone," a senior vice-president explains. "That should be a strong concern for the next fellow. The people planning the future won't be here in twelve years."

John Stosko characterized the hair care division as "a fast-moving, fashion-oriented beauty company that attracts young, impatient, creative, ambitious people. Most of our recruits are women." Very few of them have made it to the vice-presidential level or above. "Maybe it's just a time issue. Let's wait until they get there."

Life is far from hopeless for women at Bristol-Myers. The women who have penetrated the upper ranks are interesting, opinionated, and self-possessed. Margaret Maruschak is the director of issues management. "It's not a public relations job in that we're broadcasting 'good news.'" With a background in government and a few years at Clairol, Margaret was asked by Bristol-Myers to "describe a 'sky's the limit' version of the job that was needed here. We looked for long-term, highly emotional, often political and controversial issues that bedevilled Bristol."

Many of these fall under the category of ethical issues. South Africa, new medicines, and chemical hazards are just part of the territory. "Some issues start in the divisions, but they're bigger than the division. They affect the entire company and its reputation and threaten its survival. Once an issue is informally designated a 'corporate issue'—there are currently six of those and the list is growing—a team is organized with relevant output. It's job is to keep the Policy Committee of Bristol-Myers well informed."

Each issue has its own life span. South Africa, the site of two plants owned by Bristol-Myers' international operations, is no longer a "thumping issue," according to Maruschak, but certainly not a mordant one either and has been a subject of concern over the last decade. [Bristol-Myers adheres to the Sullivan Principles.] "During peaks, the team works hard; during valleys, they don't. The letters we receive these days on South Africa are very sophisticated" compared to earlier mail of the "Why are you there?" variety.

Margaret is grateful for her job. "This is an extraordinary fit, and I had the ideal background. Also, Catholic schools gave me a good insight into how issues are resolved. What does it mean to be a responsible corporation?", Maruschak muses. "I'm not making any money for the company; only helping them not lose. This kind of job didn't exist years ago." Today, while the department consists of only Margaret and her secretary, their input is met at a high level. "Today, society expects so much of companies. The people on their forty-third and forty-fourth floors are as sensitive and honorable as anyone in corporate life."

THE CHASE
MANHATTAN
CORPORATION

HISTORY & OPERATIONS

In early 1799, an epidemic of yellow fever hit New York City. It was believed that the disease was spreading from the water supply, and residents petitioned the city council to establish a municipally controlled water company. Meanwhile, a group of civic leaders, including political rivals Aaron Burr and Alexander Hamilton, argued that the city's water should be entrusted to a private company. They won, and in March the State Legislature approved a bill to establish The Manhattan Company, which was capitalized at $2 million and charged with keeping the water supply "pure and wholesome." Then Burr, a strident anti-Federalist, secretly lobbied for a clause that would allow the new company to make a range of financial transactions with monies not needed for the waterworks. His motive, which was eventually realized, was to set up a rival to The Bank of New York and the Bank of the United States, both run by Hamilton's Federalist allies. The provision was included in The Manhattan Company's charter, and in September 1799, The Bank of the Manhattan Company opened its doors. Hamilton was enraged by Burr's duplicity. A violent animosity between the two men ensued, culminating in 1804 when Burr challenged Hamilton to a duel. Hamilton was shot dead, and Burr, his political career snuffed, went into hiding. Such were the stormy origins of the Chase Manhattan Corporation, which keeps the pistols used in the duel in its historical collection.

The Bank of the Manhattan Company prospered. Founded when banking was still a new field, it evolved largely by trial and error. In 1808, when The Manhattan Company's water-works were floundering, the legislature permitted it to sell them to the city and devote its entire capital to banking.

Chase National—which eventually merged with The Bank of the Manhattan Company to form The Chase Manhattan Bank—was founded in 1877 by John Thompson, a former schoolteacher. Within several months of its opening, the bank's success had surpassed its founder's most optimistic expectations. Established in September with $3,000 in capital, the bank's deposits totaled $628,625 by December. By 1927, under the leadership of Albert Wiggin, one of the country's leading bankers, the bank had more than $1 billion in total resources, and by 1930 Chase was the country's leading lender to businesses. That year, the bank merged with Equitable Trust, the eighth largest bank in the country, which was owned by John D. Rockefeller, Jr., and run by his brother-in-law, Winthrop Aldrich. Wiggin became chairman of the new bank—which was then the largest in the world—but was forced to resign in disgrace when, in 1934, it was discovered that he and his associates had used bank funds to speculate in Chase stock.

Winthrop Aldrich, a national spokesman for the banking community, took over the leadership of Chase upon Wiggin's resignation. Aldrich was a leader in the movement to separate commercial and investment banking, which became law under the Glass-Steagall Act in 1932. Under Aldrich, Chase stepped up its overseas business, and after World War II, the bank was the first to open branches in Germany and Japan.

By 1951 Chase National had become a leading corporate, correspondent, and international bank. But with consumer branches only in Manhattan, it was weak in retail banking. In 1955, after four years of negotiations, Chase National, then the country's third largest bank, merged into The Bank of the Manhattan Company, by now the fifteenth largest, to form The Chase Manhattan Bank. (The reason Chase merged into The Bank of The Manhattan Company, rather than vice versa, was to circumvent The Bank of the Manhattan Company's original charter, which prohibited it from merging into another institution without unanimous stock-holder approval.) The combination of Chase's strengths added to The Bank of The Manhattan Company's strong retail banking network resulted in a well-rounded operation. The chairman of the new bank was John J. McCloy, an oil lawyer, former World Bank president, and U.S. high commissioner for occupied Germany.

Over the next three decades, Chase Manhattan Bank focused on expanding its overseas activities. In 1961 David Rockefeller—the youngest of John D. Rockefeller, Jr.'s five sons and the only one of them to go into his business—became Chase's co-chief executive officer with George Champion. (Under David Rockefeller, a power broker on an international scale, Chase became associated with U.S. foreign policy, a reputation which drew it into controversy. For example, in 1965 the bank decided to purchase a major share in the second largest bank in South Africa. That move triggered protests against Chase Manhattan, as did Rockefeller's decision to open a Chase branch in Saigon in 1966—David Rockefeller was a vocal supporter of the Vietnam War—built of granite and sandstone to withstand attacks.

In 1969 The Chase Manhattan Corporation was formed as a one-bank holding company. The move was made in order to allow Chase the flexibility to expand beyond traditional banking, into the financial services industry, which was restricted by the Glass-Steagall Act [Author's note: The bank has been in the forefront of efforts to repeal it as of this writing.] and a reaction against the Bank Holding Company Act, which had been passed about the same time and which limits the geographical expansion of banks. David Rockefeller took over as chairman of the newly formed corporation.

During the 1970s, Chase Manhattan was beset by problems. It lost hundreds of millions of dollars in bad loans and was placed on the Federal Reserve's list of "problem" banks—banks that needed to be monitored federally. Overseas, it lost ground to Citibank, which eventually surpassed it (as did Bank of America) in this country as well. Then, in 1982, Chase reported a quarterly loss of $16.1 million—the first time in recent history that one of the country's ten largest banks had reported a quarterly loss—as a result of its dealings with a small New York securities firm, Drysdale Government Securities, Inc., and an Oklahoma bank, Penn Square Bank of Oklahoma City, both of which collapsed. Despite these difficulties, the bank managed to regain ground and remains among the wealthiest and most powerful financial institutions in the world.

Today the bank is led by Willard C. Butcher, who joined Chase after his graduation from college in 1947, became CEO in 1980, and took over as chairman when David Rockefeller retired in 1981. (In keeping with the bylaws of the bank, Butcher will retire in October 1991, when he turns sixty-five.) In terms of assets, The Chase Manhattan Corporation is the second largest bank holding company in the country, after Citicorp—it recently surpassed Bank of America again—and approximately the thirty-seventh largest in the world. Chase, which has long focused on expanding its international business, currently maintains a presence in over fifty-five countries as well as almost every state in the United States. The corporation employs about 42,000 people, 30,000 of them in the United States and the remainder abroad.

The Chase Manhattan Bank is divided into three major units; the Global Bank, which provides corporate customers with a range of traditional and investment banking services; the Institutional Bank, which serves middle-market businesses with a range of services, including leasing, and is also responsible for real estate finance and relationships with correspondent banks; and the Individual Bank, which serves individual customers worldwide. The Individual Bank includes regional banks in New York, Florida, Ohio, Arizona, and Maryland, consumer finance and home mortgage offices nationwide, educational financing, and credit cards.

(Information provided by Ken Mills, Richard Colister, and Amy Sudol, bank spokespersons.)

ASSETS: Over $99 billion in assets as of December 31, 1987.

EARNINGS: Chase reported losses in 1987 "because of a $1.6 billion special addition to the reserve for possible credit losses in light of developments pertaining to refinancing countries. In the wake of the special addition, Chase reported a net loss for the year of $895 million."

SHAREHOLDERS: Approximately 50,000.

OFFICES: Chase has a presence in nearly every state and over fifty-five countries. The bank could not provide more specific information.

EMPLOYEES: More than 42,000, with 30,000 in the United States and the rest abroad.

AVERAGE AGE OF EMPLOYEES: Information not available.

TURNOVER: Information not available.

RECRUITMENT: College recruitment is broken into three areas. The first is called a "corporate relationship," where a senior person at the bank might be on the board of a school. The second is called a "corporate school," where the bank has a staff liaison with particular schools. The third is "component-specific," meaning that one area of the bank has relationships with schools that suit its particular needs. "We recruit at all levels nationwide. There are so many different levels that it's hard to be specific at what schools." Recruits hail from diverse educational backgrounds. "We're interested in recruits from every background."

NUMBER OF NEW HIRES PER YEAR: An average of 7,500 worldwide.

RANGE OF STARTING SALARIES: MBAs: $45,000–$55,000; non-MBAs: $23,000–$30,000. "For all new employees it depends on the market they work in and their function."

POLICY FOR RAISES: Employees are eligible on an annual basis. Raises are determined for each individual component on the basis of merit and performance.

TRAINING PROGRAMS: "Chase presents a wide variety of entry-level options for the early career professional or recent graduate. Opportunities range from broad 'integrator' roles, involving the pulling together of multiple Chase resources to meet a complex need, to specialized or technical roles, where state-of-the-art expertise is critical to our effectiveness. The skills required, like the opportunities themselves, span a broad range.

"Chase offers formal training programs for each of its business components. Courses of study and length of each program vary. One of the largest programs is the Global Bank Entry Professional Development Program. This program trains participants to become relationship managers who will serve the worldwide wholesale banking community with a line of financial products and services that is constantly changing. Other specific training programs range from the Metropolitan Community Bank Management Development Program, which prepares college graduates to assume management positions within Chase's extensive branch network, to the Corporate Operations and Systems Management Training Program, which trains new hires to use Chase's technology base to help meet the needs of Chase's customers worldwide.

"These programs are recognized as premiere programs in the financial services industry."

BENEFITS: Medical insurance, educational reimbursement for employment-related course work, matched savings plan, pension plan.

VACATION: Two weeks per year for people in training programs, four weeks per year for all officers—officers are those at assistant treasurer level and above—in addition to all bank holidays. The number of bank holidays differs among states—in New York, for instance, it's ten a year.

ADDITIONAL PERKS: "Perks vary throughout the corporation, depending on location. In New York, for example, Chase employees get free checking, a 2 percent annual discount rate on Visa and Mastercard, the annual fee for those credit cards waived. There is a fitness lab [an exercise center] for New York vice-presidents. In London, employees are eligible for reduced-rate mortgages."

BONUSES: "Chase does award bonuses. There are a number of bonus plans throughout the corporation which are based upon employees' performances within certain job categories. Chase's bonuses are competitive within the banking industry."

ANNUAL PARTY: "Throughout the bank, parties are held on an individual basis by department to entertain customers and for the benefit of all employees. One example: 1987's tenth annual Night at the Philharmonic to entertain customers at Lincoln Center."

AVERAGE WORKDAY: "There is no set average workday for employees at Chase Manhattan Bank, but officers generally begin workdays early in the morning, before 9:00, and work for nine hours or more each day."

SOCIAL ATMOSPHERE: "Typically members of the training program classes socialize with each other during training periods. After and in addition to the training periods, it is difficult to generalize about the social atmosphere of the corporation."

HIERARCHY: After being hired by Chase as a trainee, an employee can subsequently be promoted to assistant treasurer, second vice-president, vice-president, senior vice-president, executive vice-president, vice-chairman, president, and chairman.

HEADQUARTERS: Chase occupies forty-two floors of One Chase Manhattan Plaza in the Wall Street area of New York City and twenty-one other facilities in New York as well, not including branches.

CHARITABLE CONTRIBUTIONS: $9.7 million in 1987. Chase's primary areas of giving are culture and the arts, education, health and human services, housing and development, international public policy and economic education.

INTERESTED APPLICANTS CAN SEND RÉSUMÉS TO:
Professional Recruitment
The Chase Manhattan Bank
One Chase Manhattan Plaza
New York, NY 10081
(212) 552-2222

For many, being a banker is a dream of professional respectability come true. Those who get to call themselves "Chase bankers" believe that *that* title is the apotheosis of prestige in the commercial banking world. "There's something about being a 'Chase banker,' " a second vice-president in tassel loafers and red suspenders muses.

Is it that Chase Manhattan Bank is historically affiliated with both Aaron Burr and Alexander Hamilton? Could it be the Rockefeller connection? Certainly, Chase Manhattan has long held a franchise on the image of the purebred Ivy Leaguer who goes to the office with a squash racquet under his arm while his blond wife, Sally, stays home with the children. But as banking enters a period of intense marketing and probable further deregulation, neither Chase nor any other commercial banking institution can afford not to hire the best people, no matter who they or their parents might be.

Banking is the industry many liberal arts students find themselves (suddenly, mysteriously, unprecedentedly) attracted to as their senior year in college reaches job-seeking frenzy. To its credit, the field is greatly interested in snapping up these generalists—being an economics major is not a prerequisite. Christie Hanfman, a vice-president and the manager of professional recruitment, joined the bank immediately after graduating from Montclair State College in 1968, where she majored in English. "I can relate to grads coming out now and not knowing what they want to do," she says.

When she graduated from college, "there were women in business, not in management," but her father worked in the trust department of another bank, and she was the eldest child. If nothing else, at least banking was familiar. Hanfman enjoyed her interviews at Chase and was accepted there first. "It wasn't an insightful decision," she says, "but the money, people, et cetera" seemed right enough. "At the acceptance of the job, I assumed it would be for the long term."

Since she's looking at tomorrow's bankers, Christie thinks that "students are now more sophisticated. There's an emphasis on MBAs and several years' business experience." She likes "the average kid [who] will be a good team player with a good personality. Chase is increasingly interested in the team player. Banking's become more competitive." To assess an applicant's ability to work in a team, Christie et al. look at his or her extracurricular activities and summer jobs. "Any job in the bank is collaborative."

In 1987 the Global Bank (primarily wholesale business) hired twenty-four MBAs and forty-six others, including BAs. The noncredit segment (including the Individual Bank—Chase Manhattan's worldwide retail banking activities—the Service Products Sector, which includes cash management, trade, securities handling, and information businesses), and the functional areas of operations and systems, auditing, human resources, and the Corporate Controller.) hired eight MBAs and eighty-five BAs. The majority of the undergraduate hires come from campus recruiting visits, where Chase line managers are often swamped with interview requests. Students who make a positive impression will be invited back for a "full schedule—a full day of interviews with five or six line managers in areas that've expressed interest in you." Candidates get their verdicts within the week.

"You want people who want to get ahead, but not at the expense of others. They wouldn't succeed if they couldn't work together." One of the carrots commercial banks dangle in front of prospective recruits is the matter of "lifestyle." Since the younger siblings of many of those English and music majors who sought out commercial banking in the seventies are now aiming at management consulting and investment banking, the two most popular fields at this point, "we sell the lifestyle and time. There's not quite the same degree of giving up your life" as there would be in those desirable, travel-intensive, high-pressured, and—perhaps most important—high-paying careers. Starting salaries for college graduates in 1988 range between $23,000 for the Metropolitan Division and $30,000 for Credit. MBA starting salaries are more negotiable, averaging around $50,000.

A further attraction for the would-be banker is the company's rigorous training program, conducted in actual classrooms, which replicates college, the basic training needed for a job. (It even includes tests and grades.) If nothing else, recent graduates know they can survive in a classroom. Training provides trainees with a comfortable, collegial atmosphere filled with peers from similar backgrounds with whom to socialize after work. Chase Manhattan's training programs are considered among the best, if not the very best. (A niggling fear among the human resources people is that students might choose Chase for its wonderful and costly training and then ditch the bank when they finish.) In fact, Chase is in the process of investigating the most efficient and cost-effective training methods. In 1988 it reduced classroom time for MBAs to forty-one days (down from a year). BAs spend approximately fifty days in training. An additional component in accounting and tax is available to those who need it. Further training is offered on an as-needed or as-deserved basis.

Karen Keating, a vice-president, is the bank's charismatic entry professional development executive. She directs credit training, the core program that most BAs enter. It begins with a technical orientation, when trainees are given HP 12-C calculators. Then the emphasis is "line-driven." The class learns to analyze a balance sheet and becomes familiar with the bank's wide range of products. "We train up front. We send 'em to the line. We get 'em productive. Your investment stays lower, and they return to the institution."

Keating also supervises the new forty-one-day (and shrinking) MBA training program at the bank's training center. "It's like the real world, but they also go to classes. It's similar to the BA program, but more advanced. They analyze real cases. We can't give them experience. We can't teach them good negotiating. But at the end of the training process, they can be pretty decent bankers." Like your neighbors on your corridor freshman year of college, graduates of the training program share a special kinship with one another, and they network [Author's note: their word, not mine] on business problems and projects for years to come. And, call it a job perk if you like, the graduates of both training programs are also entitled to identify themselves as "Chase bankers."

It's time to talk about the new corporate culture at Chase Manhattan, the product of several years of concentrated work. "Nineteen eighty-four ended the blue bloods," a veteran of a decade declares. But it's much more than that. As an industry, banking is getting ready for the nineties. That means firing up the staff and getting them to accept the remarkably high birthrate of new products. "The bank is constantly inventing and spewing out new products, at a rate of two or three a day. They are very specific products aimed at specific needs."

Chase's management hired McKinsey & Company to get things cracking. Focusing especially on a "specific statement of strategies," the consultants also made presentations to the bank on staffing and ethics. "The new Chase is teamwork. People are more approachable. It used to be more punitive."

In case you thought banking was a service business, you're right, but the word "product" permeates the speech of every single employee at Chase so thoroughly you might think you were at the headquarters of a manufacturer or retailer. Loans are products, but so is financial consulting. "Banking is sales-driven. Loans are the backbone of the business. They help build relationships with customers. But you need to sell fee-based products. Loans aren't profitable enough." Besides actively selling its various products, Chase is promoting them aggressively, too—hardly a bankerly activity. Blending the best of service and manufacturing, people talk of "mentoring," "teamwork," and other buzzwords of management that reflect a heightened appreciation of employees. "Businesspeople will look to their bankers as advisers, like their accountants and attorneys." Or, put another way, Chase is trying to foster what it calls "the whole banker. The guy who can respond to all the needs of a customer and understand all the products available and use all of them." Another witness to the change says, "A banker is now a sales representative. People always sold, but they never thought of it as selling."

Karen Keating says, "Everything that an investment bank can do, we can do outside the United States. We can own a discount brokerage house. All we can't do is underwrite debt and equity. The investment banking image makes it sexier. The image is faster-paced."

Leslie Hollander, a vice-president, is one of the people in charge of Global Entry Professional Development. She helps develop and revise new training programs to change as the bank's culture changes. Her mandate is to be flexible.

"We report on a high level. We don't have to check first. We can *do*. It's not a matter of getting it right and that's it. The business is moving too quickly to leave clients to train for a week. Employees have the responsibility to do work on their own." The innovations are less clear than the fact that they are constant. In general, the language of change requires a certain vigilance in order to escape vagueness. One must probe in order to figure out what's so new.

It is said, "There's no difference from the way it was ten years ago, except for the mindset of driving forward."

Leslie, with her olive suede suite and long straight hair, doesn't look like a banker. She joined the bank in 1971. "I wanted to move to New York, and I didn't know what I wanted to do. Chase seemed interesting. I was originally hired to hire secretaries and tellers. We had a thousand openings a day." Hollander does not have an MBA. "I was not premeditative about my own career." Still, she believes "it [the degree] matters. Because it's a ticket of entry." Bankers who arrive at Chase sans MBA have several opportunities to earn them at the bank's expense, and many do.

Michael Brettell is an assistant treasurer in the Global Bank, Primary Industries Division. After graduating from Harvard in 1981, he spent a couple of years in Europe, working, studying, and traveling, mostly wondering what he should do with his life. His search took him to Penn's Wharton School. He was in the minority of students who interviewed at commercial banks in 1985.

"It was out of vogue," he says. "It still is. People think commercial banking leads to boring careers. It's not true. Investment banking is interesting, but the lifestyles are bad."

With a more livable regimen, Brettell still gets enormous exposure to a wide variety of companies and businesses. "The Global Bank's role is dealing daily with *Fortune* 500 companies. We try to link up all services. I have nine or ten accounts as primary or secondary contact. I deal with clients as high up as I can go—maybe treasurer. It *is* financial consulting."

Michael gets to sell Chase's investment banking services. It can be a tough sell, since they cannot be transacted in the United States. "IPOs [initial public offerings] have to be done in London. But they will be. Some clients will kick and scream as we take them by the hand to London. Sometimes they'll even get a financial advantage."

The hugeness of the bank and the volume of dollars (or pounds sterling) could prove intimidating to the young banker. "If I make a mistake, I could get fired," Brettell admits, "but I probably wouldn't. There are enough controls that someone would catch it first. I'm glad that there are people better than me at the bank."

The Credit Audit Division is a small, elite group, highly coveted for its extensive travel and collegiality. Susan Fritts had recently completed her rotation there when we talked. Having a father in the State Department, she lived in Japan for a few years as a kid. At Williams College, she majored in political science. Her junior advisor ended up at Chase Manhattan two years earlier, also in the Credit Audit Division.

Her training began in September 1983 and ended in May 1984. Fritts was one of the lucky few who was chosen to enter Credit Audit immediately. "It was a dream first job. You get to travel on someone else, and it's a terrific way to see the bank." You have to be prepared to put the rest of your life on hold, however. "You can't organize your life. You have to be ready to drop anything. Once you say you can't take a trip—most of which last two to six weeks or longer, you are taken off the 'A'—ready to travel—list." Those trips could be two weeks in Texas or a month in Paris. Susan speaks French, which didn't hurt. "I didn't need a strong financial background, but I sacrificed line experience, which could slow me down a bit later on." She stayed in Credit Audit for two years.

"After a year and a half you start thinking about your next job." She's now in Real Estate Finance, with the title of second vice-president, "the second promotion 4 years from your hire." Being ambitious will pay at Chase. Young bankers say there is a competitive atmosphere, but they say they like it that way. Nevertheless, one enters a rigid structure in which it is possible to predict—more or less—one's future. You know when you are entitled to a new title or promotion, and, moreover, you know exactly what the next level will be. Fritts knew, for example, when she was a month away from becoming a second vice-president.

"That's two years from the date of your assistant treasurer promotion. Mostly these things are not a mystery."

Fritts doesn't work in One Chase Manhattan Plaza, Chase Manhattan's giant building in the financial district, near Wall Street. (The edifice is so enormous it has its own subway entrance.) "Once you choose to go into real estate, it's a world unto itself. We're at Fortieth and Park, a midtown location. I only come downtown for lunch." She's working on a team of five, specifically on New Jersey accounts. "The logical next step is bigger and better accounts. There are about twenty officers in the New Jersey group. They might move us to New Jersey. It makes sense. You can blow the day in travel. The Boston and Washington, D.C., groups were moved. The Florida, Texas, and California groups are on site."

But the "they": who are they, how many of them are there, and can one person ever feel truly connected? [Author's note: With a work force of 42,000, Chase Manhattan is surely not the largest corporation I visited for this project. Yet there was something about it—perhaps the skyscraper some divisions occupy—that made it seem bigger and maybe less personal than it is.] Susan says, "Chase cares about you, depending on who you are or who you know. Everyone feels frustrated from time to time. We're given positive feedback. [Credit Audit has quarterly reports and postjob reports.]

"You can't be good at an industry without liking it. You must like people, because real estate is people-intensive." She has to deal with lawyers, insurance brokers, builders, etc. "I think of myself as a real estate lender." She's out of the office at least one day a week, but that means she's no further than New Jersey and can go home at night. "I can have a regular life now. I can plan weekends, take trips."

Susan's giving thought to possibly going to business school. "I still think about it. I wasn't an econ major. I'd do it at night. Chase will pay if you get Bs or higher each semester. I want [the degree], but I won't be hurt without it."

Richard Bochicchio, a second vice-president in the Metropolitan Community Bank (New York branches), attended the NYU Business School at night, courtesy of Chase. A native New Yorker who craved the prestige of being able to be a "Chase banker"—"I remember one business magazine, *Forbes* or *Business Week,* had an article on David Rockefeller and Chase, and I remember a forecast of $350 million that year was correct," he recollects dreamily—he's moved to four divisions in eight years, starting out in Operations. He was promised he'd get to move, and he considered his career at the bank long-term from the first day.

"I asked them—senior managers—how I should direct my career. I asked, 'How do I end up in the chairman's office?' " Bochicchio absolutely aspires to be chairman. He regards senior management as having almost heroic proportions. "Tom Lebreque," he mentions, citing the president and chief operating officer of the corporation, "took twenty years from entry. And he never issued a loan." He's memorized these facts.

"Most of the time, the name 'The Chase' will get you in the door. You do something with the Chase logo pinned to you." He's worked with *Fortune* 500 customers and now mines the *Inc.* magazine 100 (the 100 fastest-growing small public companies) to find new clients. "Companies in the fifty- to hundred-million-dollar range have lots of borrowing needs. They will need IPOs and private placements. In theory, Chase has the capacity to loan 750 million dollars. Depending on the size, loans need four to five signers."

Rich is proud of a deal he managed for a client in the printing industry at the beginning of 1987. "We did it very quickly. The client had outgrown smaller banks." The term loan was for $10 million. "We increased business for the client. It's the 'royal we,' " he adds a tad self-consciously. He's called a " 'relationship banker,' a term they came up with in 1983. A relationship manager is a conduit for questions in the area, sort of like the coxswain for the bank." His own conduits are made up of his classmates from his training session. "Rarely do

I not use the network." What's nice about listening to Bochicchio is that after eight years, he's as impressed with the machinery of Chase Manhattan as a hopeful job applicant. He seems freshly in awe of the vast resources of the bank around the world. "I have a phone contact in Brazil!"

Nancy Bridgman, an assistant treasurer in the Global Bank, Consumer Goods Component, did not grow up in New York, where the Chase name evokes a legacy of refinement and money. "I never realized the prestige [was a factor] until after I got here. I attended a Twyla Tharp concert with clients, about twenty people. We underwrite the troupe. Everyone went nuts when David Rockefeller showed up. The prestige and history of the bank come into play every so often."

Bridgman says working here is not daunting. "I never think of all forty-two thousand people. It's just part of working for a major player in the financial world. I work on six accounts for different vice-presidents in each one. There's one person in charge of all eighteen associates in our component." And the associates are assigned to a counselor, or adviser, for support. She maintains the bank is good to employees. "It monitors careers. I'm not overwhelmed; I'm challenged. The bank has an investment in training and keeping me, and in that way they've been good to me. I have new skills. If I go away, all that goes away, too.

"I feel loyal to my clients." The term "client" always assumes possessive pronouns. "You want to do what's best for your customers, but you never forget for a second who pays your bills. I never feel conflicted."

Nancy majored in accounting at Bucknell University, worked at Peat, Marwick, Mitchell for a couple of years, and passed her CPA exam. She says, "You will never make it through without accounting." But take heart, all you humanities students. "Maybe one or two" at most don't last through the training program.

"I take recruits out to lunch and say, 'I'm not an interviewer. I don't speak to the people in personnel. If you think you have questions too stupid to ask a vice-president, ask me.' " Was banking the correct choice for Bridgman? "Oh, yeah, I'm doing what I want to do right now. Accounting was so conservative. Banking has the reputation of being conservative, but it doesn't feel that way to me." I ask Nancy if she can be herself at the office. "There are several Nancy Bridgmans," she answers. "I think people are different at work from the way they are at night with their buddies or the way they act with their parents. I try to keep my private life private, but it was hard in the training program, because it was so intense and everyone's the same age."

I was introduced to Tighe Sullivan when he was an assistant treasurer in Trading and Securities. (He's now a money market salesman for Chase Investment Bank in London.) He interviewed at investment and commercial banks when he was a senior at Colgate University. "My general plan was to go to an investment bank as an analyst, get my MBA, and then return. But I like the people and the credit training program here. I wanted a formal, structured training program. And I didn't want to work a hundred hours a week."

After credit training, Sullivan lucked into the Credit Audit Division, for which he traveled to Thailand, Brazil, Argentina, Mexico, and Paris. As ideal as that may sound, he was chomping at the trading bit. "I waited to get this job. I just pushed and pushed. To anyone I knew in trading and securities." But this has never been the traditional career path for someone with only credit experience. "There are maybe only a handful of people worldwide from credit training who've gone to trading. It's a matter of interest," he says, suggesting that few would choose both disciplines. "I had no experience for trading. I just read and got on-the-job training.

"Credit people would say the trading floor people are crazy, maniacs, nuts, high-strung. You have to be a certain person," he says, "to want to work on the trading floor with all the ensuing pressure." Funny, he doesn't look stressed-out. "You're rarely sitting even. You're losing or gaining. There are maybe two hundred people in trading [in New York City]. It's a mixed crowd. There are not a lot of older guys on the trading floor. It's fast. People approach their work in their own way. Trading is an individual business. Yes, you're trying to make money for The Chase Manhattan Bank, and that's whose capital you're risking. But you're given your own P and L [profit and loss] statement every morning. [Author's note: It's called *The Wall Street Journal*.] It affects my year-end bonus."

Tighe arrived at work most mornings at seven, since most of his trading happened in London. Every morning at 8:00 there's a fifteen-minute strategy meeting, although "it changes every minute. Business quiets down in the afternoon. Dramatically. I never leave later than five P.M. People will talk to Tokyo and Singapore four times a night. From home." This means that Sullivan has less of a social life than the commercial retail bankers do. So much for the leisure hours of the Chase banker.

"No one knows what they're doing. I'm *serious*. If everyone knew, they'd be on a beach making a phone call. Some of the best traders are MBAs from Wharton or high school graduates from deep in Brooklyn. Trading's changed my life. I don't really see myself in banking. I didn't enjoy it. I'm not a corporate animal. I'm not marching to the beat of the Chairman, because I don't report to him. But there is more than one set of values [at Chase]. I have a better fit for trading, though I didn't know that [at first]. I'm interested in the mighty dollar. All of us are." Because investment banking at Chase is neither the bank's forte nor as lucrative to the individuals doing it as it would be at actual investment banks, turnover is high. "That's no secret. It's a business where you're concerned with yourself and your bottom line. People jump ship for offers. There's no reason to earn less than what you can," Sullivan says candidly.

Peter Walraven's decision to join the North American Corporate Finance Sector, né Chase Investment Bank Private Placements Division, was not because he couldn't get a job at a "real" investment bank. In between his first and second years at Duke's Fuqua School of Business, he worked for Karen Keating. "You spend the summer meeting with the top twenty to twenty-five officers of the bank. From Butcher [Willard C. Butcher, chairman and chief executive officer] on down." By the end of the summer program, Walraven was sure he'd want commercial banking, and "by the end of business shcool, I knew I'd be in the investment bank at Chase [now called the North American Corporate Finance Sector].

"I felt I'd be comfortable here. Maybe I wouldn't be a millionaire partner as at Goldman Sachs, but I was married and expected a kid. I didn't want to work eighty-plus hours a week. I don't have to beat discreet investment banks at their own game." Walraven is a young family man living in New Jersey, interested in succeeding in New York but not succumbing to it. He commutes by train and PATH [the Port Authority Trans-Hudson trains]. He leaves home at 7:00 A.M. and leaves the office between 7:00 and 8:00 P.M. The return trip takes an hour and a half. "My business school classmates are driving fancy cars and living in nicer houses. If I could wear jeans every day, I would, but a Brooks Brothers suit is good."

The North American Corporate Finance Sector has 300 employees in New York, plus there are an additional 450 corporate professionals worldwide. It's growing quickly. Members of it learn to reconcile their appetite for doing deals with the dominant Chase culture. Walraven feels that "every area of the bank has a different personality. I didn't realize how blue-blood Wall Street was until I got here. Anyone who goes corporate has to expect to be changed by the place. Some companies I avoided because of their characters. People here are known as 'characters' and haven't suffered for it."

Bob Mantilia has seen the bank from many vantage points in his fifteen-year tenure. He had always anticipated going into his family's business after graduation from St. Bonaventure

University in upstate New York, "but for the hell of it, I went on some interviews." Chase offered him a job in the branch system's management development program, at the time twenty-one months long. [Today it's been accelerated to twelve months.] The program prepares its students to become assistant branch managers. "I was planning to enter my father's business after training," Bob recalls. "I always thought I'd go back, but things went well and I enjoyed it here."

One of the reasons Mantilia keeps staying at Chase is because he gets to move around and consequently feels valued. "I've had over six jobs in fifteen years." He's had to uproot his family in the process, working in Manhattan, then Buffalo, then Brooklyn, then Queens, then Manhattan again. (His family only moved three times; Bob's spent a lot of time on trains.)

Climbing up the branch ladder, one of his favorite jobs was running "Chase Center 60," which marketed the bank's services and products to the over-sixty set. "It was fun, it fulfilled a social obligation for the company, and it made money." (Yet, the program is no longer in operation.) It was after Mantilia had been with Chase for ten years that he entered the credit training program. "It was obvious I needed lending. My pyramid was narrowing, and I had only done marketing and management.

"My deskmate was a twenty-three-year-old woman. I was married and settled." It was tough going back to the classroom after having been out in the field and estranged from the dynamics of school for so long. "All you had to do was worry about yourself for a year. I was 'Joe Trainee.' I wanted to do very well. There was satisfaction in beating Harvard MBAs."

Bob didn't lose his remuneration momentum. Although his classmates earned starting salaries, he "was paid commensurate with the ten-year salary and even got a raise. There were advantages in having taken the training program so late." His studies are more vivid memories than they would be for Bob's peers. He was probably the only member of his class to take his child on a vacation when the program ended. He still savors that trip to Disney World. "It was great; no one needed me."

It is apparent from Mantilia's comments that he feels taken care of by the bank. He feels he matters to the powers that be. "There are people who don't know me, but they know my performance. A good relationship with your manager means you're discussing your plans with your manager." The bank's bureaucracy doesn't daunt him. "You try to be a good, fair manager. You're honest and moral. There's a right way and a wrong way to do things."

Now Bob is a vice-president and individual and institutional bank professional development executive. [Author's note: As Chase's culture warms up, its titles seem to grow longer.] "I took the job because training is so important." He says, "Kids don't have to learn professional decorum. They already take life seriously. You want to look good, and your friend wants to look good, so you are even more serious about dealing with your pals."

Calling the training floor a "microcosm of the real world," Mantilia thinks trainees are treated well and carefully. "A lot of people remember what it was like when they were training and how they would have liked to have been treated." Beginning with a three-day orientation —a number of sessions are held annually—trainees are bombarded with an introduction to the financial services industry, regulations, and competition on day one, a breakdown of how "the Chase" works on day two, and, on day three, a breakdown of the organizational chart. "In the beginning of orientation, people say 'they' when they say Chase. By the end it's 'we.'" It doesn't hurt that every employee of the corporation is also a customer and stockholder.

DREXEL
BURNHAM
LAMBERT

Drexel Burnham Lambert

HISTORY & OPERATIONS

Drexel Burnham Lambert, now among the largest and certainly one of *the* most profitable investment banking firms on Wall Street, began in 1935—at the peak of the Depression—as Burnham and Company, a stock brokerage firm founded by I. W. "Tubby" Burnham II. Burnham, a graduate of the Wharton School of Finance at the University of Pennsylvania, started the firm with $100,000 in borrowed capital and a partner, Oscar Krieger. Having lived through the stock market collapse, when paper-rich men became paupers overnight, Burnham placed a high value on ready capital and engineered his firm's growth accordingly. He joined the New York Stock Exchange, cultivated a group of clients, and did a respectable amount of business in the firm's early years.

In 1942 Burnham enlisted in the Navy for active duty. The following year, while on leave, he dissolved his partnership with Krieger, naming his wife and David Minton as partners in his absence. Burnham returned after the war, and by 1946 Burnham and Company had grown to five partners. With business sluggish in the mid-1940s, Burnham determined to reduce the firm's dependence on the vicissitudes of the stock market by diversifying into other areas of finance. In 1946 the firm established an Investment Advisory Research Department—one of the first of its kind—and in 1948 it conducted its first underwriting when it helped take B. T. Babbitt, a manufacturer of household cleaners, public. In 1950 the firm established an international department and became one of the first securities firms to penetrate international markets. In the mid-fifties, it launched a Corporate Finance Department to handle underwriting efforts and mergers and acquisitions, and in 1959 it computerized to keep better track of its dealings.

During the sixties, Burnham and Company expanded its underwriting and retail and research operations, opening retail branches across the country and acquiring a couple of small out-of-state firms. By 1966 it had 660 employees and $18 million in capital. In 1971 the firm incorporated, and, with approximately $40 million in capital, it was poised to make some major acquisitions. In 1973 it acquired Drexel Firestone, Inc., a once prominent Philadelphia investment banking firm, to form Drexel, Burnham & Co., Incorporated. In 1976 it merged with the Lambert (pronounced "Lambear") Brussels Witter Group, the holding company for a top Wall Street research firm. By the end of that year, Drexel Burnham Lambert had over $67 million in capital, 1,800 employees, and thirty-two offices around the world.

The firm continued to diversify throughout the seventies, forming a Commodities Department and acquiring two retail houses and a government bond trading business. But it pushed hardest for growth in the area of investment banking. During the seventies, Drexel Burnham, which was still considered minor league by more established firms—it ranked nineteenth among underwriters of corporate securities in 1975—began trading in high-yield, low-rated securities, a market other reputable Wall Street firms shunned. [Author's note: Older, more "establishment" firms like Goldman Sachs (founded 1869) and Lehman Brothers (1850) looked down on the upstart Drexel Burnham.] "Junk bonds"—a term Drexel management tried to discourage in favor of "high-yield"—are bonds that the Moody's and Standard & Poor's rating services designate as being non-investment grade. Due to their status, they pay a significantly higher interest rate than do higher-rated bonds. Furthermore, since conventional ratings evaluate a company's financial history, they tend to neglect its future prospects. Michael Milken, a brilliant young trader who had studied low-rated securities, concluded—as had academic studies conducted years earlier—that over time, even with their greater frequency of default, the bonds' higher interest rates ultimately yielded greater profits than did investment-grade bonds. Frederick Joseph, then Drexel's senior executive vice-president, supported Milken's early junk bond trading activities.

The junk, or high-yield, bonds Drexel initially began trading in were most often bonds issued by formerly investment-grade-rated companies that had fallen on hard times. Drexel operated on the theory that few such companies go bankrupt and their fortunes can only rise. Then, in 1977, Joseph and Milken came up with the idea of floating original-issue "junk"— bonds issued by small-to-medium-sized companies not in a position to issue debt ranked as investment grade. Investors who were already trading in junk securities were ready to buy them. In 1978 Milken persuaded Drexel's management to let him move from Wall Street to Beverly Hills, where his operation thrived.

With its entrance into and cultivation of the high-yield securities market, Drexel Burnham Lambert expanded meteorically and permanently changed the face of financing. (Mike Milken has been called the most innovative and influential financier since J. P. Morgan.) In 1983 revenues reached $1 billion. By 1984 Drexel became famous for high-yield financed acquisitions. The firm employed over six thousand people and had become the second largest underwriter of corporate securities in the country. That year, companies issued an aggregate of $14 billion in high-yield securities, a full 70 percent of which was underwritten by Drexel. By then, other Wall Street firms were competing for a piece of the market that Drexel had virtually invented and clearly monopolized.

The growth of Drexel's junk bond operation helped spur the takeover boom of recent years. By the mid-1980s, Milken could pull institutional investors together with unprecedented speed to raise vast sums of money for a client's takeover attempt. Drexel had become known for its trademark letter—stating that the firm was "highly confident" it could raise the money for a given acquisition. And Milken/Drexel moved beyond merely advising clients to becoming minority participants in clients' deals. Milken had gradually put together a number of high-profile clients—including Armand Hammer, Saul P. Steinberg (see p. 554), Carl C. Icahn, Ronald Perelman, T. Boone Pickens, Irwin Jacobs, and Ted Turner—all of them aggressive, high-risk investors.

In 1986, a year in which Drexel earned $4 billion in revenues, approximately $500 million in profits, probably making it the most profitable firm on Wall Street, it was beset by scandal. In May, Dennis B. Levine, a managing director in Drexel's Corporate Finance Department, was indicted in the largest insider trading case in the history of the Securities and Exchange Commission. (Most of Levine's illegal activities preceded his arrival at Drexel.) Martin Siegel, another corporate finance managing director, fell next. Then, in November, Drexel Burnham Lambert as an entity and Michael Milken and other Drexel executives came under investigation for possible violation of securities laws as part of a criminal probe into the illegal insider trading activities stemming from the Ivan Boesky case that *surpassed* the Levine case as the largest and most sensational insider trading scandal in history. (Boesky was fined $100 million and sentenced to three years in jail.)

Although, as of this writing, the government has not pressed criminal charges and Drexel has consistently stood behind its practices and its people, firmly denying any wrongdoing, the investigation isn't over yet, and the firm's reputation has been tarnished. There's little doubt that Drexel will survive the investigations. Clients both old and new still flock to the firm. DBL weathered 1987's stock market crash in good shape. They had not added as many people as other Wall Street firms. While they are focusing on reducing expenses, there have been far fewer layoffs than in any other firm on the Street.

Under Frederick Joseph, who became CEO in 1985, Drexel now employs some 10,500 people. Despite its large size, Drexel takes pride in its nonbureaucratic structure, claiming it draws the kind of creative financiers for which the firm has become celebrated. It also admits that the atmosphere is attractive to the avaricious.

Drexel used the profits generated by its investment banking operations to continue diversifying into other areas of finance, including the creation of a mortgage-backed securities department and the expansion of its Municipal Finance and Corporate Finance divisions. Drexel Burnham ended 1987 with gross revenues of $3.2 billion. Since October 19, 1987— "Black Monday"—(until press time) Drexel has had 53.4 percent of the market share of all high-yield business in total dollar volume, or 54.8 percent of all deals.

(Information provided by the firm's Corporate Communications Department—special mention to Abby O'Neil.)

REVENUES: Gross revenues were $3.2 billion in 1987.

EARNINGS: The firm is privately held and will not disclose.

OFFICES: In forty-three offices in thirty-eight cities in the U.S. and in ten cities abroad. The firm's headquarters are in New York City, and additional offices are located in: Atlanta, GA;

Baton Rouge, LA; Beverly Hills, CA; Chicago, IL; Columbus, OH; Dallas, TX; Darien, CT; Denver, CO; Detroit, MI; Encino, CA; Fort Lauderdale, FL; Hartford, CT; Hato Rey, Puerto Rico; Houston, TX; Jenkintown, PA; Kansas City, MO; La Jolla, CA; Lauderhill, FL; Los Angeles, CA; Miami, FL; Miami Beach, FL; Minneapolis, MN; New Orleans, LA; Newport Beach, CA; Orlando, FL; Palo Alto, CA; Paramus, NJ; Philadelphia, PA; Phoenix, AZ; Providence, RI; Rossmoor, CA; San Francisco, CA; Seattle, WA; South Miami, FL; St. Louis, MO; Washington, DC; White Plains, NY; Amsterdam; Brussels; Geneva; Hong Kong; London; Paris; Singapore; Tokyo; Zurich; and São Paulo.

NUMBER OF EMPLOYEES: Approximately 10,500 worldwide as of year end, 1987.

AVERAGE AGE OF EMPLOYEES: Not available.

TURNOVER: "Drexel Burnham's turnover rate is one of the lowest in the industry."

RECRUITMENT: Drexel Burnham Lambert annually visits forty "top colleges" nationwide for the recruitment of graduating undergraduates. "Recent graduates are frequently hired in a variety of departments across the firm, including sales and trading, corporate finance and operations. The firm interviews graduates majoring in a range of academic areas from economics to literature. In addition, Drexel actively recruits from leading graduate business schools across the country for each of the firm's departments."

NUMBER OF NEW HIRES PER YEAR: The firm has doubled the number of employees since 1983.

TRAINING PROGRAMS: "Recent college graduates hired for the following areas participate in Drexel training programs: corporate finance, municipal finance, retail sales, mortgage-backed securities, and finance and accounting. Both the finance and accounting department and retail sales areas have formal training programs which last for eighteen months and are held at New York headquarters. In addition, a two-year analyst program is sponsored by the corporate finance, municipal finance and mortgage-backed securities departments."

RANGE OF STARTING SALARIES: "Drexel Burnham's compensation (salary plus bonus) is believed [to be] above industry averages."

POLICY FOR RAISES: "Employees are generally eligible for raises on an annual basis."

BENEFITS: "Employees of Drexel Burnham are eligible for a complete range of benefits, including medical and dental coverage, disability insurance, life insurance options, retirement benefits, profit-sharing and stock bonus plans, and tax-deferred savings plan. In addition, DBL provides college and graduate school tuition reimbursement and offers a college scholarship program for dependent children of employees. The tuition reimbursement program enables employees to study almost any subject in a degree or non-degree-related program. Drexel Burnham will reimburse employees providing grades are an "A," "B," or "pass."

VACATION: "The company's vacation policy is based on an employee's job category. Personal days and legal holidays are separate."

ADDITIONAL PERKS: There are exercise facilities at a number of the firm's offices. Employees get discounts on brokerage fees. "A confidential drug and alcohol program providing psychological consultation is available for employees and their immediate families."

BONUSES: "The firm has a long standing annual bonus plan in which each employee participates. Bonuses are distributed based on departmental productivity."

ANNUAL PARTY: "Each department has an annual year-end holiday party."

DRESS CODE: "No stated dress code policy," but people dress professionally.

AVERAGE WORKDAY: "If you are joining Drexel expect to work hard."

SOCIAL ATMOSPHERE: "Drexel Burnham prides itself on being an employee-oriented firm. The firm supports a variety of sports and social activities for its employees. Drexel is an industrious, creative, friendly place to work."

HEADQUARTERS: Headquarters are at 60 Broad Street in the Wall Street area of lower Manhattan. Over 4,000 Drexel employees are located in that building and adjacent office spaces.

CHARITABLE CONTRIBUTIONS: The firm would not disclose figures. "The Drexel Burnham Lambert Foundation makes grants in the areas of health and education. The firm is the largest corporate donor for AIDS research. Other important charities the firm sponsors include The Medical Genetics and Birth Defects Center at Cedars-Sinai Medical Center and Variety Clubs International. Numerous community charities throughout the country are supported by the firm's branch offices."

INTERESTED APPLICANTS CAN SEND RÉSUMÉS TO:
Gary Mass, Vice President
Campus Relations
2 Broadway, 16th Floor
New York, NY 10004
(212) 480-6000

S it back. You are about to learn about an organization that's in the news almost every day, and you will see that it is not at all what you expected, or at least what I expected. In the siege mentality that's stricken Wall Street in the past several years, only Drexel Burnham Lambert did not renege on its promise to open itself up for this book. If nothing else, Drexel's welcome is a substantial indication of its corporate culture.

And let's get this out of the way, shall we? This is not a story about Mike Milken, his fortunes, or the junk bond business. By the time this book is published, his investigation will, in all probability, be a thing of the past. This is the story of a hardworking underdog that has made incredible strides in the last decade.

Gutsy and happy, Drexel is one of the single most profitable securities firms in the country. A vice-president in the Beverly Hills office says it's "a place you're excited to be at at six A.M." The Corporate Finance Department, the subject of this chapter, is a remarkably collegial and cohesive bunch on both coasts who, after typically sixteen-hour-long days, red-eye flights, and high stress, choose to spend their free time with one another and their families. I liked them.

These are not the investment bankers of inheritance. Although almost everyone I met attended an Ivy League or top-tier college, and most of the MBAs did come from Harvard, they are a scrappier, more heterogeneous lot than one would find at other old-line securities firms, easily able to identify with their clients, who by and large are entrepreneurs who own and run midsized companies with revenues of $25–$250 million. Most of the Corporate Finance people here can say with assurance that they are self-made.

Fred Joseph is the chief executive officer of Drexel Burnham Lambert. But you already knew that. His Wall Street office is smallish by CEO standards, filled with perhaps thousands of Lucite-enclosed miniature prospecti and "tombstones," the trophies of the trade. (They are the notices of completed offerings that are announced in the press. A managing director says, "They are symbolic of reaching the finishing line because a lot of deals don't make it. They're a reminder.") "We still have the shabbiest offices of any investment bank," he says, maybe a bit proudly. Although even bicycle messengers in the financial industry probably would recognize Joseph on the street, he wears a photo ID badge clipped to his suit jacket. He is not tall, he has a bushy head of salt-and-pepper hair, a wide, toothy smile, and a vestigial Boston accent. He grew up there, the son of a cab driver.

He moved up the ranks in the Corporate Finance Department, Drexel Burnham's second (or first) largest division. He's been bombarded so regularly by reporters that by the time we meet, he anticipates most questions with a smile. (Actually, by the time of our appointment, he is in the midst of a moratorium on interviews. He made an exception for this book.) He graduated from Harvard College with a degree in English—"I was a defrocked physics major" —and matriculated to the business school. "I'd been heading toward marketing. The first time I heard about investment banking was in my second year. The only excuse for saying you knew about investment bankers was your father was one." In other words, the field was less than hot. In 1963 he got a job at E. F. Hutton after school. His initial salary was $7,500. In 1970 he moved to Shearson Hammill.

"I didn't even know I could get rich eventually. Money wasn't even a consideration. We worked hard and were winning and loving it." By thirty-two, Fred Joseph was Shearson's chief operating officer. He was recruited by Drexel, a relatively second-string firm, in 1974. "I believe people do not know anything about the company they join," he says. The real variable that should affect one's decision "is just people. Then it's our job to make them want never to leave. The outside view of the firm is that we're warriors. The inside is that we're family. I spend most of my time figuring out how to make it better for the guys. Everyone who meets us is surprised by how nice and honest our people are."

Several years ago, before he assumed the top job, Joseph was in charge of recruiting. The four things he looks for are "intelligence, motivation/energy, integrity, interpersonal skills. A good proxy for intelligence and motivation are grades from a top business school." For the rest, he applies more visceral criteria: "I call it the 'red-eye' test. Would you want to spend time with the applicant on a plane? Did I like that kid? I know in my gut."

"My job is very different now. I got this job at forty-eight." He lives in Short Hills, New Jersey, a sixty-minute ride to work when he commutes—early in the day, late at night. Three mornings a week, he has business breakfasts, which usually begin around seven, and if he doesn't have a business dinner (he ordinarily does), he stays at the office till 8:30 P.M. "I do 'twofers,' " as he calls them. "I take out my wife to dinner alone four nights a week, after an earlier client dinner." He eats lightly. The Josephs have been married twenty-eight years. They have five kids and one grandchild. His wife does not really have to play a "first lady" role. "She's outgoing, but not very involved."

Joseph must set an example for his people. "With over ten thousand employees, this isn't chopped liver," he says. "You lead by going over the hill, not by flying first class and letting them sit in coach. I sit in coach.

"Drexel is the best place for the best people. We're probably the most profitable private firm in the country and the most profitable securities firm. Last year Drexel saw $4 *trillion* in transactions." [Author's note: I didn't even know trillion was a real word, let alone a real amount. One trillion equals one million millions or a thousand billions, in case you were wondering. I asked Joseph about "zillion," but he just laughed and said there was no such thing.] Stockholders' equity was $1.5 billion, "seventy-five percent of which is owned by two thousand shareholders."

[Author's note: Let me add that since enduring negative press, Drexel has attracted even more deals than before. If clients were concerned about alleged wrongdoing, they certainly haven't shown it. Since Dennis Levine, Martin Siegel, and Ivan Boesky smeared Drexel's name by association, the firm's old clients have rallied and new ones are still banging on their doors. And certainly no one would accuse the firm of fostering insider trading. Not even the U.S. Attorney General's office.] Joseph not only addresses the firm's problems; he raises them himself. "The neat thing about our troubles is, the esprit de corps is better. There's more of a cause. It's taken away our pomposity. Now I know about criminal law," he laughs. Drexel has also captured a higher percentage of MBAs than ever before. Fifty-three percent of the students who were offered jobs here accepted them in 1987 as opposed to 51 percent in the boring, uncomplicated previous year. And if you subscribe to the "any publicity is good publicity" theory, Drexel's got it made. "We used to be an undifferentiated commodity." No more.

Fred Joseph seems expansive and relaxed. He gets tired by Friday night but works every Sunday afternoon. As a public figure, he sits on the boards of Channel 13 (New York's PBS station), the Legal Aid Society, the Cerebral Palsy Foundation, and the Harvard Business School Club of New York. He's a registered Democrat who sometimes votes Republican.

He mentions John Kissick's name frequently. The movie star-handsome Kissick runs the Los Angeles office of Drexel Burnham and is something of a protégé of Joseph's. His official titles are executive vice-president and director of West Coast corporate finance. They worked closely together in New York and still talk every day on the phone. (I think they love each other.) The Beverly Hills Corporate Finance Department does feel different from its New York counterpart. Maybe it's the sun blazing outside the window or the fact that they are separated from the financial center, but people appear less hurried; there's still time to schmooze. Certainly, since the group is approximately one third as large as New York's, it seems a more personal place.

Kissick grew up in Washington, D.C., the son of a Foreign Service officer. He spent his senior year of high school in Ankara, Turkey. He majored in economics at Yale, entered the Navy in San Diego, and received his MBA from Stanford in 1970. "Stanford was a long way away from Wall Street, and very few firms came to interview. We had no knowledge of investment banking. I started commuting to New York for interviews. I got a job which informally won the 'best job' vote at Stanford. It was with a little investment bank boutique. The market made a downturn in April 1970. I started my job on August first, and I was fired August fifth.

"My first thought was shock, et cetera, but my second was, 'Hell, I have no house, wife, boat'—I would return to California, but I wanted to prove I could make it in New York." He took a job with Blythe & Co. "It was not a job I would have taken out of Stanford. It was staid, old-line, unexciting." After a year and a half Kissick moved to Shearson and Fred Joseph. When Joseph left Shearson two years later, he called Kissick, who was now working in Shearson's Atlanta office. "He offered me the opportunity to open a Drexel office in California. It was an unsettling time for Shearson—they had just merged with Hayden, Stone. Drexel had no story in 1975, just Joseph. It was not a bad thing, though. I liked him; he liked me. He's a great leader. All he was offering was dreams, but he's not a bad guy to dream with.

"The stakes weren't *that* high. I didn't view it as much of a risk. I wasn't married. I opened this office in 1975. My dreams were that in five or ten years, there would be maybe five or ten corporate finance people here, and we would stay that way for years, as a toehold." When

Mike Milken moved to Beverly Hills with twelve professionals in 1978, there were two corporate finance people working at Drexel/Los Angeles. "From 1979 to 1981 we started catching on, getting visibility. Then we got clobbered by the recession of 1981–82. On January 3, 1983, we had three professionals in Corporate Finance." Now the office consists of seventy-five professionals and fifty support people.

"When the business started coming in very fast, even if I worked a hundred hours per week, we couldn't handle it. It's easier to hire someone you're not positive about with fifty people than it is with one. I wanted people to say, 'Those first hires are quality.' For us to grow from three to four to five to six was very hard. I had to talk very hard and convince people they wouldn't lose on their career paths, they would still be on the learning curve. The first few people came from the New York office. It was like leaving the womb for a branch office. What helped was Milken. Corporate Finance and Milken's department grew together."

John explains that aside from Drexel's powerhouse presence on the West Coast, "the number of investment bankers in L.A. hasn't grown appreciably. I didn't worry about being away from the home office because I trusted Fred Joseph. I felt comfortable, although I was three thousand miles away. We grew sixty to seventy percent a year. There's a faster delegation of responsibility. Our people don't get scared of being tossed in the water. We work in teams of two to four. The question is, 'How fast can you be the top people on a deal?' Some people can be on top of a mini pyramid after a short time, two to three years.

"We're helping small and medium-sized companies access capital. You don't have to have a lot of creativity for a General Motors underwriting, but for small companies you must analyze, use judgment—it's exciting. While it's not altruistic, we do flow capital more efficiently, which does good things for the companies, which does good things for the employees, which does good things for the American economy." In 1987, working in the Los Angeles office was not only *not* a hard sell, it was laughably easy. To be offered a job at Drexel and given the choice of L.A. or New York—"it's all equal. People choose for personal reasons. The sizzle and power don't keep people here. What keeps people here is the continuous new challenge."

Kissick continues, "I believe if you want to work for the best, you'll be on a fast learning curve. The best investment banker in 1980—if you put [him or her] in a time capsule until 1987 [he or she] wouldn't recognize the industry [when he or she was let out]. They couldn't function. The stock market changes by a hundred points or more in a single day. That used to be a whole year!"

We talk about the relentless pressure and the brutal schedule of the Corporate Finance Department (never begrudged by its denizens, so far as I could see). He says, "I work harder because of Mike Milken. I thought I was a workaholic until I met him. It's twenty-four hours a day [figuratively speaking]. He's put that into hundreds of people. Fred Joseph works as hard as anyone. Our partners haven't eased up. I imagine the average hours between associates and partners would be the same. The associates might say, 'Bullshit!' I'm usually the first guy in in the morning, between five and 5:30 A.M. Not because I want people to say, 'Kissick's here,' but because I don't stay as late." He usually leaves at around 7:00–7:30 P.M.

John tells people who arrive from other firms, "You gotta earn your spurs. You must work seventy to eighty hours per week. The single best thing not unique to Drexel but fairly unique to investment banking is the continuous challenge. Nothing gets boring. Sometimes I want the comfort of repetition, but ultimately, we're stimulated by new things. My wife says, 'Wouldn't you like to be under less stress?' Not after three weeks [of vacation—he gets restless]. My own view is, there's a lot of wasted time [in life]. Do you need forty hours a week of decompression? A lot of people in our office are in before a lot of people in New York." The time takes its toll, and the price is exhaustion.

"It's not a marriage breaker." (*Au contraire,* if anything, there seems to be pressure to get married. And raise a family. At the time of my visit to the Beverly Hills office, two members of the Corporate Finance Department were expecting their first children, and one's wife had just given birth.) Working here might be a marriage delayer, however, as John admits it was in his life. He married at forty. He's now forty-six and has a three-year-old son. "If you're working this hard, it's easier to be monogamous than fool around. (We're not making a judgment on lifestyle.)"

But asking one's people to stay late or go on an unexpected business trip has a side benefit of making them feel needed, important, and loyal. "Loyalty is the responsibility of the company. I'm never bothered by applicants who say, 'I want to try investment banking for a few years and then do something else.' My response is 'that's okay'; I was the same way. Give them exciting things to do. We haven't faced much leaving.

"They've worked hard. We get our money's worth. We pay a lot and get a lot. Very quickly. I'm amazed by the contributions of people who are here just three months."

John Kissick reports to Herb Bachelor. "I run Investment Banking," says Herb. "It's Fred's old job." He joined Drexel in 1978. From his New York office, Bachelor oversees the more than 350 professionals of Corporate Finance countrywide (including fifteen in Boston and ten or eleven in San Francisco) and the 100–110 professionals in Municipal Finance. "As we've grown, we've been concerned about management. You can't hire professional managers to run investment bankers." The group he calls the " 'purely administrative staff' are the compliance people. They don't have to be bankers. They manage word processing, internal accounting, et cetera. I really spend time talking to people. I coach and cheerlead. I try to catch problems early. I have to explain why we're moving into less profitable areas to grow new businesses."

Now that Bachelor has a large constituency, he says, "I hope there's a sense of fun. The environment is informal. I'm not fooling myself. Junior associates don't walk into senior partners' offices to talk, but the open approach is do-able. Teamwork is stressed." In evaluating his team-at-large, he puts a high priority on the following: "I watch to see if people are building a business. You see who's willing to work hard. Business isn't slow; you don't have to fake it." He observes the quality of social interaction. "Someone with problems with secretaries will probably have problems with clients. You must commit yourself to the time. I do think a personal life is important. I don't believe investment banking must be littered with broken marriages. You must learn to say no. In fact, the worst thing you can do is take on too much."

Bachelor was another wayward science student at Harvard. "I thought I'd be a biochemist. We're all frustrated scientists. I became an economics major. I went straight to Harvard Business School because I didn't know what to do. Investment banking was an accident. I never heard of it until business school. I was impressed with investment bankers during the interview process. I wanted to work on the same series of problems, the variety. I felt I could make an impression."

Art Bilger, the third arrival in the Corporate Finance Department in Beverly Hills, was on the fast track in investment banking almost from the time he was in high school on Long Island. "I was one of those people who, though caught up in the sixties, was intrigued by wheeling and dealing. No one wanted to go to Penn [specifically the Wharton School of Finance]. I applied early decision." He then went to business school at the University of Chicago. Fred Joseph, then the head of Corporate Finance, hired him in 1977. "He spent five hours with me during the interview process. More than anyone else. I was the twenty-third member of the department. We had no business. I had never heard of a guy named Milken.

"I liked the people. I liked the smallness." Bilger moved to the West Coast office in 1982. "When I worked in New York, I arrived at work at 7:30; here, it's six or 6:30, and I leave probably at seven or 7:30. In eleven years there hasn't been a day I've dreaded coming in." He's a managing director and spends time in administrative duties, one of which is "maintaining the culture. A high priority when interviewing is how [the applicant] will fit in.

"People are smart, hardworking, at ease with each other, and don't take themselves too seriously." Recruits spend time with professionals in social settings as well as in front of a desk. "The average person who joins us in September will probably have spent at least fifty hours face to face with us. We incorporate their wives and girlfriends. [Author's note: And husbands, and boyfriends.] We put people up at the Beverly Wilshire [directly across the street on South Rodeo Drive]. We had a few guys who liked to play tennis when they arrived, but no more. Anyone who asks about hours or time is probably not going to be hired. 'Workaholic' does characterize the place, but I don't characterize this as work. My goal is not to work fifteen hours a day, 350 days a year. We work harder than any of us would like to. Balancing time is the toughest part of the job. I've seen bright people held back because of their inability to juggle. We could lead more normal lives." But they don't want to.

[A small, intimate aside, apropos of the shared obsession these guys and gals have toward their work. When not long ago about thirty guys from Drexel convened for a bachelor party preceding a colleague's wedding, they stayed utterly in character. They talked business. Nonstop. The requisite strippers they hired were frustrated in their attempts to get the attention of the revelers. Finally, one of them announced a group activity. If the men would hide money (bills, not loose change) on their bodies, the women would retrieve it . . . somehow. Annoyed at the intrusion, one of the guests slapped a hundred-dollar bill on the table and said, "Save yourself the trouble." This story is almost definitely true. Alas, since I must protect my sources, you did not hear it from me.]

Art says, "No matter what level I've been at, I've always been one of the hardest workers. This is an investment banker's dream. We don't have to make calls." When Drexel was understaffed, "to make it less busy, we stopped answering the phone. Deals are everywhere you turn. No matter how this plays out in the end, this is one of the great business stories of the seventies and eighties."

Bilger inherited the job of assigning projects from Kissick. "Some people might be working on two; some on ten deals. Some are all-encompassing." Professionals turn in their schedules every Friday, showing how their time was divided by client. "My goal is to rotate," Art says. "To get as many different people exposed to different people. If I had my way, every junior would have the opportunity to work with every partner."

This would be an opportune moment to go into titles at Drexel. In fact, some of the older [Bilger is thirty-five] people here use the partnership titles.

Without an MBA, one can start as an analyst, normally a two-year position. MBAs start out as associates. Herein follows the route of the fastest track on Drexel's bullet train. After three and a half years, they become vice-presidents and two years later they're first vice-presidents [the equivalent of junior partners], and then managing directors [partners] two years later. Yet there is no lockstep. People are rewarded with titles and remuneration when they deserve it. Bonuses can be significant, to put it mildly.

"In a perfect world, at the end of every deal you sit down with every team and review. It generally doesn't work out that way. We have been pressed for time—I feel—on everything." First-year professionals are reviewed twice, in June and in December. Thereafter, once annually at year's end. Drexel's culture is not one of excessive hand holding or training. "You have to be self-reliant. You're always working over your head, in terms of experience and knowledge. Your feedback comes when people want you to work on new things [with them]. We all have our own radar to keep ourselves informed."

Bilger disputes the claim of most investment banks that they are entrepreneurial. "It's bullshit. But here some of it is true. You're out with your own client book and have the support and prestige of the company." Many times people I met exclaimed their surprise at the amount of trust the company invested in them before they felt they had proven themselves. "How much on your own you are depends on the deal, the client, the business, the person." Ordinarily, the smaller the deal, the more authority one will have. Art says "a two-and-a-half year guy handled a hundred-million-dollar deal for Circus Circus. I was the most senior guy on the deal, but the other guy was the day-to-day guy. Throughout the month, he dealt with me every day."

I wondered how it felt to be dealing in figures like $100 million, noticing that people at Drexel dismiss seven-digit figures like one week's allowance. "Initially, adjusting to all this money was strange. And deals are *much* larger today. It doesn't faze me that much. I went from paying $200 a month rent to the world of billions. I don't believe I've totally lost touch with reality. I do worry about some people here. I would do what I do the way I do it even if they didn't pay me this much. Do I spend what I make? Obviously not. Money is recognition."

The opulent spending associated with the high salaries and bonuses earned at Drexel is fiction more than fact. For the most part, people are prudent. They volunteer that Dennis Levine's spending habits, including a Ferrari—good for Manhattan driving—were yet another symptom of his bad fit at Drexel. In Los Angeles, Drexel people live pretty modestly, but they do drive premium cars. (Well that's L.A.) In New York, people own their own apartments or summer homes, or sometimes both. No one I met was profligate or too ostentatious. In fact, many boast of their frugalities, e.g., "I drive a Dodge." Remember that many people here come from middle-class homes and will be financially cautious. The younger ones may still have student loans to repay. And many support, in part, members of their families. This is a theme that permeates both offices.

Bruce Raben, another managing director at the Los Angeles office by way of New York, first contemplated being a capitalist while working as a sailmaker and sailboat racer in Connecticut. "It occurred to me while racing my client's sailboats—worth between $250,000 and $1,000,000—that I'd never get one of my own." So, the Vassar graduate went to Columbia Business School. "A lot of people went to grad school to figure out what to do." He applied to Drexel to be a summer associate after his first year at Columbia. "I got a phone call saying, 'You have an interview with Fred Joseph.' I said, 'Great! Who's Fred Joseph?'

"That summer, I was converted to Drexel and investment banking. The culture was heterogeneous—physically, educationally, temperamentally, sartorially—a ragged collection." He got his MBA and returned to a department that had grown substantially during his last year of business school. He moved to the Beverly Hills office in 1984, "after a two-year conversation with John Kissick, who wanted to grow the office." Bruce enumerates his reasons for moving.

"One, the office in New York had grown enormously and wasn't a small group with intimacy. Two, I got tired of the city—the Seventh Avenue IRT breaking down in the summer. Three, the high-yield department was here, and I wanted the chance to work closely with Milken. Four, to help grow a small shop. By definition, a six-person office is intimate. It's very much Drexel, but it's L.A. Drexel is legitimately a bicoastal firm. I consider not being surrounded by other investment bankers a plus. Being three thousand miles away helps you focus on business."

On the work itself: "Teams are formed around clients. From the day you and your client agree to a closing in a typical public financing transaction, it's a three- to four-month proposition because of [waiting for] the SEC. After the transaction, the team stays in place to service that client."

Associates will be responsible for more legwork and fewer clients than senior people, "who have to worry about fifty to sixty client accounts and twenty different transactions, but on a supervisory level."

Most new associates have MBAs. "For better or worse. Not every one of the senior people has them." Interviewing MBAs is difficult. "At this point they are so slick and so coached it often degenerates into a fencing match." In a recent policy change, Drexel offered associate-ships to two analysts who had only BA degrees. Raben says, "I don't know if [business] school is inherently useful to do this well, but it's a filtering device and is valuable for some technical training."

Recruitment turn-ons: "Independent, aggressive, and combative without being obnoxious about it. Tenacity. An ability to take the heat. People who've made something of their lives on their own." Recruitment turn-offs: "Arrogant, overly slick people who want investment banking for the mystique. Who can't wait to wear suspenders and smoke a cigar."

Bruce (like everyone else) says that turnover at the firm is low. "It's fun to work at the hot shop. We win a lot. We've made the play-offs every year for the last five years. People tend to have a good time." Is there a point at which one can say with assurance, "I can do this"? He answers, "Yes, there was a point, but God knows when. My whole time has been a blur. It's like jumping into a sports car going a hundred twenty miles per hour and hasn't stopped. There are periodic points when you say, 'I can do this stuff' and right after, you get hit from behind. If you don't reach a level of mastery, you do reach a level of competence and confidence." Considering the client brings Drexel's investment bankers back to earth. "The needs of the client are the needs of the firm. We're a service business. If we don't please our clients, they don't pay us."

The workday at Drexel never seems to end. "It's hard to leave the job. It does take over your life. You are constantly on call. Your life is not your own. Spouses can't be too dependent." Raben travels for business at least once a week. To tune it out, he works out twice a week with a trainer and goes to the beach when he can. Remember the sailboat that motivated Bruce in the first place? "Now I can afford it, but I haven't bought it since there's no time to race."

Alison Mass, a young managing director in the Mergers and Acquisitions Department in New York, can't believe her good fortune. "I'm making so much money," she says in a voice of unpretentious, conscious wonderment. "I bought my mom an apartment. I loaned my brother the money to buy a house. I helped my sister through grad school. I'm earning more than my parents did at this age."

Make no mistake. Money is not why she's here. She atttended Friends Seminary in New York City, a fairly upscale, bohemian private (Quaker) school, chosen because "there were fewer wealthy students than at other private schools in the city. It was eclectic. I was one of these motivated kids. At seventeen I thought I was incredibly sophisticated." She skipped the eleventh grade, went to NYU, where she was an accounting major, was offered a scholarship to graduate school, and got her MBA at twenty-two. "I wanted to work quickly." Alison was attracted to the prestige of the Big Eight public accounting firms. She won an award, something like "Most Likely to Succeed in a Big Eight Firm," and interviewed "everywhere. Accounting firms, computer firms, and at every commercial bank."

She was persuaded to apply to Drexel by a guy her mother dated who worked here. "I am convinced I got the job because I wasn't nervous. I got called in for a full day and got an offer. I was shocked by how easy it was. I still had no clue what investment banking was. I was offered a hundred and fifty percent of what I'd earn in public accounting."

Marla Thomas grew up primarily outside Washington, D.C., although, since her father is a government official (the former head of the Peace Corps in Sierra Leone, among other positions) she lived overseas as well. At Wellesley College, she studied economics and American studies and became student body president. She went straight to Morgan Stanley after graduation, entering their analyst's program in its second year. ("My father steered me to investment banking.")

"I didn't enjoy the culture at Morgan." She looked around and decided to go to business school, which she financed herself. "My parents paid for college entirely. I felt I should pay for grad school." Marla sent herself to Harvard, getting her MBA in 1982. Although Morgan was not a good fit, she was not averse to finding another job in investment banking. "Drexel Burnham Lambert was the most eclectic of all firms." Their message was " 'We don't care where you come from or who your parents are.' Being a black female, I didn't want to step into a mistake. [I saw] middle-class people with middle-class values, people who are ecstatic to be here and feel they're making more money than they deserve."

Marla, Alison, and I are eating in a private dining room upstairs, which is as elegant as any facility in any investment bank. [Author's note: Before they reneged on their agreements to participate in this book, the other investment banks I dealt with—who shall remain nameless —wooed me with breakfasts in their private dining rooms. So I am able to make comparisons.] We are given menus and attended by a waiter. These are nice, bright women, who clearly love what they do and where they do it. They can afford a good life, although that was not the only reason they chose this field.

"There was no honeymoon, no wining and dining" when they arrived at the firm. "They start you with a regular dose immediately. Being a woman in this business could be bad or good. There are only four women partners in the firm. There are no footprints in the sand to follow." When Mass made partner after just five and a half years, she was the youngest female partner in Drexel's history. Both she and Marla refer to her access as "legitimate power." Although they confess to devoting most of their time and emotional energy on their work, Thomas and Mass have been able to develop serious relationships outside the office. Alison lives with a guy and eventually wants to marry and have a child. Marla is engaged to be married, but she's not sure she wants to have children.

In the past, Marla and Alison and other Drexel friends have shared summer rentals in the Hamptons. They won't be doing it again this year, since everyone involved has become a homeowner. Marla bought a house in Bridgehampton. They say that even the intense lack of privacy has not fomented affairs. ("There's a remarkable lack of soap opera stuff here. It's rampant elsewhere," they think.)

They've been here too long and are far too introspective to be appreciative of their circumstances in a wide-eyed way, but Thomas and Mass have no trouble being enthusiastic about the business of Drexel. "When I started, I looked at VPs and said, 'I'll never know as much as Trevor.' Then, three years later, I'm a VP, but Trevor's a partner. It takes between one and three years to become proficient in the mechanics. Right before partnership, you're already the senior person on a deal." Do they ever get nervous about deals? Have these poised women ever experienced sheer panic? "Panic is a relative term. You never stop learning. The legal, tax, and legislative consequences are always changing. You can never know a hundred percent.

"We're a service business. Our clients have more needs than *Fortune* 500 companies. We compete by believing in a company before anyone else will. There are guys from the Midwest who all of a sudden are being loved. Generally, our clients don't go shopping, except for pricing. Some clients," they say in an aside, "social climb after making it through DBL. Deals have an average life of three months. You know it won't go on forever. Our goal is getting a deal done. We're in a hurry. We fly in, fly out, a.s.a.p. In between deals you take the client out, you celebrate his birthday."

Alison explains the practice of collecting the Lucite cubes preserving the documents of completed deals. "It's what we've accomplished. In most service businesses there's no beginning or end. Except the cube. There's a letdown when deals are over, postpartum depression. It's a tangible award and a way for people at Drexel to know what you're doing."

It took Managing Director John Sorte a relatively long time to get to Drexel. At Rice

University, he was in the five-year chemical engineering program (and cofounded the school's radio station). Like so many others here, he went to the Harvard Business School, whence he was recruited by Shearson's Fred Joseph. In those days 1972–80, "Shearson was a lot like Drexel is today." Naturally he was wooed to Drexel by old pals Joseph and Bachelor. "Coming here was a relatively easy decision," he says, "although it took two years. I kept getting on big deals at Shearson. The time wasn't right to leave." At Drexel, Sorte directs Corporate Finance's specialty in energy. "I was the forty-ninth professional hired in the [Corporate Finance] department. (Now there are 350.) My only regret is that I didn't come here sooner."

John's best friend was a fellow Shearsonite, Paul Higbee. "I was his best man. I promised Shearson I wouldn't recruit Paul. I didn't instigate it. He could see I loved it." You can guess how this anecdote ends. Higbee is now a managing director at Drexel.

How Sorte enjoys his life here! "My best friends are here, in various different levels." Some people think associates and seniors shouldn't socialize. Not he. His first marriage was a casualty of the hours and commitment he made to his career at Shearson. John's since been divorced, remarried, and become a father of three. "I met my current wife when I was a vice-president. Our whole relationship was with me as an investment banker. From day one she saw what could happen. I got called home from a ski trip once."

"At my level, my life is more predictable most of the time. I leave at seven P.M. I live in the city. [He has a weekend house in Connecticut.] It's not outrageous. I try to balance my time."

His biggest test came in 1986, at the christening of his twin daughters. "I was in the middle of a hostile takeover. The clients were in Texas. They were unhappy at first (that I couldn't skip the church ceremony), but we moved the meeting to New York. It's hard to know where to draw the line. Clients pay us a lot, and they believe we should be available twenty-four hours a day for what they pay us." Sorte agrees.

"Clients are people. I enjoy most of them. I want them to feel they can call me and I'm interested. We're doing this most of our waking hours. My wife knows how important our clients are to Drexel and me and thus to her."

Sorte appreciated his clients more than ever when they showed their loyalty to the firm during Drexel's dark days in the press. Within weeks of a major negative article in *The Wall Street Journal*, "Boone Pickens invited me to go hunting with him, and two weeks later Oscar Wyatt [CEO of Coastal Petroleum] invited me. These were their votes of confidence. We're fighting bad publicity. We know the *Journal* is wrong, and we'll correct the misunderstanding." What's most galling is the jubilation of Drexel's detractors. "It's like a toothache that doesn't go away. We've really created something here. From an also-ran to the most powerful investment bank."

You've read about how other professionals at the firm discuss the importance of maintaining their relationships with clients in between deals. "We don't play golf or anything," Sorte explains. The most important mechanism to stay in touch is through the annual three-and-a-half-day Institutional Research Conference, known familiarly as the Bond Conference, held every year in Beverly Hills. It is attended by three thousand clients from around the world, who are treated to speeches and presentations, not to mention big-ticket entertainment and stretch limos up the wazoo. The 1987 conference featured a Kenny Rogers concert, a "casino night" sponsored by client Bally Manufacturing, Inc., an evening at the studios of Lorimar Telepictures, another client (see p. 298), attended by some of its TV stars, and dinner at Chasen's restaurant, with entertainment by Ella Fitzgerald. And it's this lavish every year. In 1988 Diana Ross sang to the assemblage at the Century Plaza Hotel, in addition to "fashion night" and "movie night."

But that doesn't mean the Drexel partners live it up all year long. "I view Herb and myself as products of Fred. We've worked for him virtually all of our professional lives. Everyone knows Fred flies coach and takes the train and PATH to work. There are no limousines, high-society trappings, et cetera. Mike Milken [reputedly the highest earner in the country in the last year, with estimates for 1987 ranging from $40 million and up] lives in a nice house in Encino.

"Most of us, including me, didn't start to spend money until the last few years. Dennis Levine had the only Ferrari in the department. People buy a house or an apartment. After they get a place to live out of the way, they reinvest in partnerships and shares. No one's been making this kind of money for so many years that they can treat it cavalierly."

But Drexel is an enthusiastic host of celebrations for its people. There are summer outings, departmental parties, the works. The Corporate Finance Christmas party is held in New York every year, and members from other offices are flown in. In recent years, they've been held at Regine's, the Palladium, the Plaza Hotel, and in 1987 the Park Avenue Armory. First-year associates do skits. In 1982 the theme was "Let's Make a Deal." Steven Fischer, now a first vice-president, starred as "Monty Joseph." The 1986 Christmas party was a tribute to *Star Trek,* with—no surprise—Captain Fred Kirk.

Susan Humphreville met her husband, Jack, at Paine Webber, in whose New York office they both worked. "He moved to Drexel with the understanding he'd move to Beverly Hills." So Susan transferred to Paine Webber's Beverly Hills office. Sounds tidy. Unfortunately, it was "awful. There were only three people there. We did nothing." She says that most investment banks offices in California (or away from the main headquarters) are "just regional offices. Maintenance. I didn't want that.

"At that point there were fifteen people at Drexel in Corporate Finance. My husband suggested visiting. Drexel was the only firm in L.A. with a real New York–style investment banking experience. My husband loved it. I liked the people. I had known them socially. I approached John Kissick. I was aware they were growing. He didn't have a problem with our being married. Art Bilger was concerned that my marriage wouldn't work out—not that Drexel wouldn't work out. I got an offer I really couldn't turn down. I joined in 1984."

Susan's husband is now a managing director in Mergers and Acquisitions, across the hall. The Humphrevilles are not by a long shot the only close relatives working at Drexel. Both Fred Joseph's and Mike Milken's brothers work at the firm, in far from nominal courtesy jobs at that. A set of sisters works here. Leon Black, the head of Mergers and Acquisitions in New York, has two brothers-in-law in Corporate Finance in L.A. No one's bothered by it. "It's better to work for the same firm than to work for competitors," Susan feels. "You can talk about work at home, but it's hard to *not* talk about work." Furthermore, since Humphreville's life is circumscribed by Drexel, "it's hard to meet anyone outside this world. My husband's college roommate lives in Pasadena. We've met some people through them. You must make an effort.

"This is the first place I've worked where I've ever felt loyalty to the organization."

Susan had a baby in 1986. "I worked fourteen hours the day before she was born. I had a compulsion to get everything organized in a burst of energy." The baby was born in May, and Susan didn't return to work until after Labor Day. "I didn't keep up by phone. I wanted to immerse myself in motherhood. Coming back wasn't hard. I wasn't enjoying it enough to stay away. We have a Scottish live-in nanny. I don't really feel guilty now, but I wish I could spend more time with my daughter.

"This is a demanding job in terms of time and pressure to keep clients happy." Susan's lucky that most of her clients are based locally. "I work a twelve-hour day, 6:30 to 6:30, unless something unusual happens, which happens maybe twice a week. I try to bring work home on weekends and not come here. I try to be disciplined [to *not* work all the time]."

She tries to stay away. It requires effort. What makes working here so irresistible? "Part of it is Drexel, part of it is investment banking. Transaction fever. Some tasks are boring, but the basic business is a lot of fun. Our clients are more fun than others'. They're entrepreneurs or risk takers and usually own a substantial stake of their companies—twenty percent— whereas *Fortune* 500 CEOs own about point five percent," which affects their involvement considerably. "Compared to other people's clients, most deals are custom-made per situation. There's more creativity in an analytical sort of way. Our clients tend to be much less bureau- cratic. They have a big interest in getting rich, which we have as well. Our clients are as compulsive as we are.

"We don't waste time with someone who might do business in three years. We're in a hurry, but our deals are more complicated [than the average]. We try to maintain our relationships so that they'll give us their next business. We talk to clients every few weeks to keep up. We schmooze. The assumption when we decide to do a deal is that a company will do lots of business [with us] in the future." Which doesn't mean Drexel doesn't turn down deals. It does all the time. Nevertheless, "you ought to want to come here, because we can do it all—it's part of our pitch.

"We're still private. A lot of investment opportunities are made available to partners. To build wealth we buy stock in Drexel. It's voluntary."

Bennett Goodman, a former associate, worked at Arthur Andersen and Co. (see p. 103) for three years in its consulting group straight after graduation from Lafayette College. That seductress, Harvard Business School, beckoned, however. During the job-seeking phase, a guy named Fred Joseph, who was in charge of MBA recruitment at Drexel, spoke at Harvard. "I thought Drexel Burnham was a pharmaceuticals firm in Philadelphia. Twenty people showed up and ten of them mistakenly." Bennett liked Joseph's presentation and signed up. "He was the first person I met at that level I thought I'd want to work for. As a human being. I respected him." (He says that nowadays when Joseph appears at Harvard, he gets standing room only crowds. Not only that, but when Mike Milken appeared his SRO was enhanced by the presence of Harvard's entire business faculty and security guards. Steven Fischer, Harvard Business School '82, admits, "It does matter what HBS says and feels about DBL.")

"Other firms described Drexel as 'not real corporate finance,' like it was beneath them, gross." They referred to Drexel's track record as " 'junk finance' and thought it was all some guy named Mike, and smoke and mirrors." Today those other firms pay strict attention to the magic of Drexel.

Here's what Goodman liked about his company. "It's as close to a meritocracy as possible. Some associates make more than vice-presidents, and some vice-presidents make more than partners.

"We don't have to look for work. We don't have to court or beg. We have a unique product.

"I'm surprised by how little contention there was within our class." One reason may be that there's no lockstep. I have been continually amazed by how smart these people are."

He cited the Underwriting Assistance Committee, which meets every Monday morning. "They approve every deal we do. A guy like me walks them through the transactions. We have to show them the pros and cons. I've spent somewhere between six weeks and six months in depth, immersed. These guys read my memo—six to seven pages of text and exhibits. I am amazed by how well they assimilate the information. They give their answer on the spot!"

Bennett wouldn't disagree that the pressure could be brutal. But what Drexelites consider tough may be on a different plane from the average human being. "I don't travel that often," he said. In his case that meant, "at most one night a week. I take day trips to Milwaukee and Cleveland. That's like working in midtown for the day. Tonight I plan to be here till one A.M. The price gets more dear every year. It's the physical cost. I killed myself in two days;

let's see if I can do it again in one and a half years." Luckily, Goodman's married. There's no way, he thought, he could have pursued a single social life. "It's tough for single men. And if you're a single woman . . . "

Here's Richard Hochman's story. In brief. He's in a hurry to attend a charity dinner with his wife, and he manages to sneak glances at his Quotron while regaling me with it. "Harvard Business School 1969. Hired by John Shad at E. F. Hutton. Fred Joseph was there until May 1970. Stayed at Hutton. Had a good career there. Fred called me spring '81 for lunch. Shad left Hutton for D.C. in '81. That year Hutton was more profitable and had better perceived value than Drexel. Fred promised Shad he wouldn't recruit from Hutton until Shad left.

"I should've gone to Fred in '81. You get tremendous inertia. You do very well. Investment bankers have loyalty; who wants to start all over again? From a known to an unknown quantity? In 1983 I saw Drexel getting on the way. I called Fred. We got specific in terms of salary and bonus. Nineteen eighty-three was a bull market." [Author's note: Just a pause to point out that people in investment banking wax nostalgic about the stock market the way other people reminisce about legendary baseball seasons.] "I had lots of fees and high visibility. I came so close. I was such an asshole. I led Fred on. I now shiver at the thought of staying at Hutton.

"I sent a colleague here in 1983. I became a Drexel Moonie. In 1984 people started leaving Hutton for Drexel, and I'm trying to convince people to stay at Hutton.

"Fred said, 'Let's put Hutton out of its misery.' " By then Hochman had been at Hutton for fifteen years. Joseph told him, " 'If you're really serious and don't want to be seen, we'll go to Trader Vic's [a dark Polynesian restaurant in the basement of the Plaza Hotel]. If you just want a raise and want to be seen, we'll go to Christ Cella [a Midtown steakhouse popular with businessmen].'

"We went to Trader Vic's."

Hochman arrived as a managing director in New York. "Fred took me out to lunch my first week, visited my office once or twice, and that was it. I think I fit."

Jeffrey McDermott is a vice-president in the Beverly Hills office. He has the enthusiasm of a convert. "It was great that this office was in L.A.," the California native says. "But if it were in Saigon, I'd have joined it. I'm the kind of person who, if I wanted to be a waiter, I wouldn't be a busboy. I had confidence, and I always wanted influence over my tasks."

An undergraduate at the University of California at Berkeley, McDermott learned about Drexel during his second year as a graduate student at the UCLA Business School. "Once I made the decision [to want to work here], it was an immediate clicking. I never looked back. A large part of it is liking people. And more than clicking," he adds, "I felt I could fulfill a feeling of self-worth more effectively. I wouldn't choose a job for friends," he clarifies.

"Working here is like sticking your finger into a light socket for eight to ten hours a day. [Author's note: What about the other six to eight hours of the Drexel workday?] Otherwise, I'd be in competitive professional sports, to get a sense of self-worth. Everyone's best interest is to push you to a senior level as quickly as you can make it. In the beginning, I was asked to do things I didn't think I could do. The first three months were uncomfortable. The learning curve was steep. There was a tremendous possibility of screwing up. It was like juggling hand grenades; drop one, you blow up. Screwing up leaves major consequences. They lose trust in you. It sets you back. If," on the other hand, "you don't do it again, it's forgotten."

And Jeff points out that although you work in a team, you're definitely on your own. "No one says, 'Do this for eight hours.' My job is to make senior people look good. You're running deals that are a major corporate event.

"Why do I love this job? A company has $150 million in sales. I spend time with this guy [the CEO]. Quality time. It's exposure to the boardroom—you at twenty-eight who's been doing this for three years, and when the CEO looks at the partner for advice, it's based on your foundation—your advice and analysis. People are good about sharing credit. It helps keep people motivated. They're also critical. There are no taboos about it. 'I don't care that you had two hours' sleep,' " he quotes.

"People are driven. I'm never surprised by working this hard. The most important thing I've got is that I matter. I went to Catholic school. 'Wasted potential is one of God's greatest sins,' the nuns said.

"There's a commonality about the people here. They are not just successful investment bankers, they're successful people—nice and kind. They're not fat, lonely workaholics toiling into the night. If the building blew up, the superstars would go through the rubble and continue. Everybody wants to win and will sacrifice and pull hard." Jeff says vertical, nonhorizontal staffing alleviates internal competition. "My classmates and I have never worked on the same deal. There's no enmity, but everyone here wants to be the best. When a partner gets a difficult, high-profile deal, I want him to say, 'Jeff—do you have a minute?' "

McDermott participates in recruiting. "In recruiting, everyone likes to hire a mirror image of themselves. I favor a guy like me—very hungry, who cares." He warns applicants that it's hard to pursue a life outside. "I tell people, 'Let's say your work becomes your life for the first three to five years.' This job postpones the inevitable moments of truth—serious relationships. Senior people don't have to come in on weekends because people like me will be here. If I thought investment banking would take this much time, et cetera, in ten years as it does now, I wouldn't stay. Kissick says, 'People have different thresholds of pain.' I don't know of anyone who's more tenacious."

And—sorry to bring this down to the mundane—but there is the matter of money. "I know a twenty-nine-year-old who retired who's living off the interest off two million dollars." Jeff, the eldest of five children from a modest home, clearly wants to succeed financially. He speaks easily of "when," as in "when it happens," as opposed to "if." At Drexel he has been given to expect financial security. As simple as that. "For guys who make it, the money doesn't mean shit. People who just want a lot of money in the long term won't make it. My definition of a hero isn't Donald Trump. It's a postman, an honest guy who raises his family from a poor, broken home. It's important for me to look in a mirror and feel in a holistic sense I'm doing something good.

"Most people here know what matters in life. Honesty, hard work, family. I believe that."

Interview:

HERBERT A. ALLEN, JR.

*T*his is not a story about Allen & Company, Inc. the small, private investment banking firm. Rather, this is a collection of reflections by scion and majority shareholder Herbert A. Allen, Jr.—a sliver of one of his afternoons in his paneled office in the Coca-Cola building on Fifth Avenue, far from Wall Street, decorated with serious oil paintings (including a Childe Hassam). Allen is particularly antipathetic toward publicity. This is no coy pose; we are meeting today on the spur of the moment, strictly as a favor to a mutual friend. When I later suggest it might be appropriate to talk with his colleagues at Allen & Company, Inc., he makes it clear that he is not interested. In the first place, he barely recalls having spoken with me at all; in the second, having been in the news at the time for an attempted purchase of Ticketron from Control Data, he feels he's gotten much too much attention. A graduate of Williams College, he joined the company at twenty-two and was made president at twenty-six. As a college senior in 1962, he was asthmatic and branded 4-F by the Selective Service. "I had no plan, but I had the luxury of not having to plan."

He is now forty-eight years old. Does his work get repetitive? "Oh, yes. This is not a business where we sell a product. About fifteen people do deals. My interaction with fifteen people stays reasonably fresh."

Allen displays a biting sense of humor, much of it self-directed. "It doesn't suggest that my job isn't serious; I take life with a sense of humor. I was made president because I had the name and the family and no one took the division seriously. I was president of nothing. I knew I could do that. I got over that at an early age."

He says that at twenty-five, "there's youth and vitality. By thirty-five it's too boring. What if you're flying to L.A. and you get bored out of Newark—assuming you left from Newark?" He eschews one-company towns, like Hollywood and Washington, D.C. "Why are they dull? Because the job is everything. I don't say that from a throne on high; I am just the arbiter of my own taste."

So what does he think of all the businesspeople who repeatedly talk of the challenges presented them in the line of nine to five? "I don't understand 'challenges.' I'm not a mountain climber. A challenge should imply a threat. There's something self-congratulatory about dealing with challenges. It's like saying, 'I don't do it for the money.' "

As a member of the board of directors of Columbia Pictures (a situation that achieved an indecent amount of publicity—much more than Allen would have wanted—and that is a key reason he no longer talks to the press), Allen engineered the studio's acquisition by Coca-Cola. "It made me look like a genius. Two years before I'd been 'immoral.' One's standards rise as your wealth increases. Once you've achieved a certain wealth and status, you can afford to be moral," Allen adds derisively. "In America, if you make five hundred thousand dollars, you're an oracle. If you're a shopping center magnate, they ask you how you feel about President Aquino.

"Wealth is as debilitating as poverty. It's like cocaine. I tell my kids to pray that the people around them do cocaine. They'll have fewer competitors.

"What I admire in business leaders," Allen continues, "is the human touch. I assume they can do business. It requires understanding, time, power. Making profits is not enough. They should improve life for their employees. The success or failure of business doesn't mean someone's smart. Someone could fail here, and it doesn't mean they're dumb. I'll be darned if I can tell what a person is by way of business.

"I don't think I do things the way other people do, and vice versa." Rather than actually seeking credit for his good business decisions and management, Allen talks about life at Allen & Company, Inc., as if he were almost passive. "I like the people here. If they disappeared, I don't think I'd start again." He refers to his hiring practices as "totally haphazard and spur-of-the-moment. I hire when I'm in the mood to hire or when there's a vacancy. It's different from Wall Street—there are no specific slots to fill. We don't hire or fire very much. It's based on what I see in an individual. If someone here walks in and says, 'Where will the firm be in five years?' I say, 'Wherever you take us.' "

Investment bankers at Allen & Company, Inc. must put themselves on the line. "This is a very rough place to work," Allen says of the stately offices. "There are no salaries or guarantees. There's a terrific downside. People can go broke here. I'll ask them to put their own money in deals—if they don't believe in the deal, why should I? We're not a company of associates;

we're a company of principals." Of his small staff, he says, "They don't have final authority, but it's based on the respect I have for them. It's unlikely I wouldn't follow their recommendation. They have freedom to come and go as they please. We provide capital backing, but it's like their own company. You don't have to do the same thing every day."

Although he never got an MBA, Allen thinks business school offers "great training for traditional investment banking and great training for corporate life. MBAs want to know where they'll land; *we're* interested in takeoff. They don't make the best investments for us. For the most part, they don't help us."

On broader topics, "I think everyone worries about what people think [of them]. Everyone wants to be well liked. Once you have a couple of bad articles and wake up and see you haven't died, you get over it."

What is greatness? "Baseball. A kid who hits .385 one year."

He says "the best experiment—other than human compassion—is to try to sell. The first rule: Forget all rules."

A registered Democrat, Allen believes that "running for office in this country is demeaning." His opinion of Mr. Reagan? "I have no regard for him as president."

Listening to Herbert A. Allen, Jr., speak, you wonder how you can best package his aphorisms and maxims, which fly by with an unexpected velocity from his mild-mannered exterior.

"I would rather deal with the law than with morality" and "You better tell the truth at my age; you can't keep track of lies."

A final note: "To me, this is the system—a degree of socialism plus free enterprise." Then Allen's secretary buzzes him to announce his daughter has come for a visit. In a burst of down parka, hugs, and homemade brownies, she has surprised him on his birthday.

KEKST AND COMPANY

KEKST AND COMPANY

KEKST AND COMPANY

HISTORY & OPERATIONS

Kekst and Company, a corporate and financial public relations consulting firm, was founded in New York in 1970 by Gershon Kekst. Kekst, who had been employed by the high octane public relations firm Ruder & Finn since his graduation from college, was dissatisfied working for someone else and decided to move out on his own. He took office space on Third Avenue and started Kekst and Company with a secretary and a handful of clients.

According to Gershon Kekst, the firm went into corporate/financial public relations primarily in response to its first clients (rather than any desire on Kekst's part to specialize in the field). Anecdotal information about the firm's debut is scarce, largely because Kekst and Company remains consciously private. Unlike most public relations firms Kekst and Company keeps a low profile and stays very much behind the scenes. Firm policy precludes Kekst and Company from publicizing itself. The organization will not allow its name to be used in articles about its client companies, and it keeps the names of those companies in strict confidence.

Kekst and Company quickly gained a reputation for doing good work, and the firm grew —adding more professionals as needed and building up its roster of clients—on the basis of that reputation. As the firm expanded, it moved offices twice, first moving to Park Avenue and later to its current headquarters on Madison Avenue. Today, Kekst and Company employs a staff of fifty-six, twenty-five of whom are professionals.

When a new client company seeks the firm's services, Kekst and Company's first step is to thoroughly learn the client's business. (Ordinarily the client also maintains an in-house public relations staff.) Firm professionals work closely with management at every level of a client company in order to get a feel for the company and for how the company perceives itself. They then work with the client to determine the best communications strategies for conveying that perception to the public.

The following is just a sampling of the firm's services. Kekst and Company professionals might write a client company's annual reports, quarterlies, fact books, fact sheets, mission statements, scripts for industrial videos, or speeches for its chief executive officer. In short, Kekst and Company provides ample opportunity to feel creative, to research and to write. And write.

Another of its services is called issue advocacy, whereby it assists a chief executive in selecting a particular area or issue to champion. Issue advocacy covers anything from a specific issue endemic to a CEO's organization or industry, to a broader concept such as entrepreneurism or innovation, to a social cause. Kekst and Company helps the CEO become known for the particular issue by writing speeches, arranging speaking engagements, developing activities around the issue (such as fund-raisers), seeking legislative support (if the issue lends itself to a legislative solution), and writing testimony, advertisements, and "advertorials" (advertisements that express an editorial position or opinion).

Investor relations is another area of service. Kekst and Company maintains or generates contact with the investment community through shareholder meetings, corporate literature, publicity, and special events; by targeting industry analysts and arranging field trips for them; and by stimulating interest among new and existing shareholders. (Investor outreach is especially useful when a company is in play.)

The firm also provides public relations that enhance a client's marketing activities. Kekst and Company conducts—among a particular segment or segments of a client's market audience —special events, speaking engagements, and other forms of publicity, and might even work with a company's advertising agency to coordinate marketing strategies.

Kekst and Company engages in media relations, which entails talking to the press on behalf of a client company, placing stories, advising clients on how to conduct an interview (what kinds of things to discuss and what to avoid), working with reporters to develop stories on its client companies, and writing op ed pieces. The firm also helps plan special events, conferences, meetings, and symposia.

The area for which Kekst and Company is perhaps best known—and which contributes about a third of its total business activity—is what the firm calls "special situations" communications, which involves advising clients on how to handle general communications strategies and publicity during a merger or acquisition (for both hostile takeovers and friendly mergers, for both the acquirer and the acquired), and other corporate reorganizations.

Kekst and Company is loosely structured, and most of the firm's professionals are generalists. Typically, more than one professional works on each client company's account. Partners are assigned to an account with another partner and/or one or more associates. Though Kekst and Company is not divided into departments and most professionals do "a little bit of everything," some may have an area of expertise—in terms of the services it provides, not a particular industry—that the firm recognizes and utilizes.

Kekst and Company's professionals come from diverse backgrounds, and the great majority have had some prior work experience before joining the firm. The trend toward an eclectic staff is fairly recent—in former years Kekst hired mostly people with backgrounds in public relations. But as the firm's role broadened to more or less that of a public advocate, Kekst felt it was better to employ professionals with more general exposure to the world. Many are former academicians. Professionals are hired as associates, and historically it has taken about five years from associate to partner. The distinction between associates and partners is a matter of stock ownership rather than function.

Although some companies hire the firm for specific assignments such as special situations consulting, Kekst and Company has long-term arrangements with most of its client companies. The firm's client list of over 150 U.S. and foreign companies ranges from *Fortune* 500 companies to small start-up ventures and the people who run them. Clients cover the full spectrum of business and include both public and private firms. Kekst and Company is a privately held company controlled by founder Gershon Kekst.

(Information provided by Lissa Perlman, partner and company spokesman.)

REVENUES: Company is privately held and will not disclose.

EARNINGS: Company will not disclose.

OFFICES: One in New York City.

NUMBER OF EMPLOYEES: Fifty-six total, with thirteen partners, twelve associates, and thirty-one support staff.

AVERAGE AGE OF EMPLOYEES: Thirty-two.

TURNOVER: No specific figures. "Very low among both professionals and support staff."

RECRUITMENT: No college recruitment program. "The company is always interested in individuals whose experience demonstrates intellectual achievement combined with excellent communications skills."

NUMBER OF NEW HIRES PER YEAR: No average figures. "The company hires consistent with its needs."

SUMMER INTERNS: Kekst and Company hires a few summer interns—generally between two and four—each year. Interns are only qualified to do research work (though are not necessarily employed in the research department) and are not exposed to the full range of the firm's activity. They are paid.

RANGE OF STARTING SALARIES: Company will not disclose.

POLICY FOR RAISES: Employees are eligible for raises annually, based on performance.

TRAINING PROGRAMS: "New professionals are assigned to a group composed of several partners and associates. Although there is no formal training program, new associates are supervised and have access to information and guidance from fellow group members."

BENEFITS: Comprehensive medical insurance, life insurance, profit sharing, and pension plan. Partners become stock owners.

VACATION: Two weeks after one year, three weeks after five years, four weeks after ten years, plus eight regular paid holidays per year.

ADDITIONAL PERKS: Professionals are entitled to participate in a corporate membership at one of two New York City health clubs. These memberships are free, with certain minimum attendance requirements. If employees don't reach them, they pay their own fees.

BONUSES: All employees are eligible for biannual bonuses awarded on the basis of performance.

ANNUAL PARTY: Kekst and Company hosts a party for all employees in December. "Typically, the holiday party takes place at a restaurant or hotel facility and features dinner and dancing."

DRESS CODE: "Usual business attire."

AVERAGE WORKDAY: Support staff work from 9:15 A.M. to 5:30 P.M., although they're expected to work overtime (with compensation) with little notice. The hours for professionals are much longer. "Demands on your time are erratic and unpredictable." Professionals generally work from 8:45 A.M. to 6:30 P.M., and quite a bit more when their workload demands it. "Working evenings and weekends is totally to be expected."

SOCIAL ATMOSPHERE: "Very little socializing among employees after hours."

HEADQUARTERS: One full floor of approximately 10,000 square feet in a Madison Avenue building.

CHARITABLE CONTRIBUTIONS: Company will not disclose.

INTERESTED APPLICANTS CAN SEND RÉSUMÉS TO:
Andrew Baer
Kekst and Company
437 Madison Avenue
New York, NY 10022
(212) 593-2655

Meet the press agents of Kekst and Company. Anne, the head of research, was a classical music radio producer before she joined a Chicago bank's public affairs office. She's been here ten years. Lissa, a new partner with five years under her belt, is a lawyer and former press secretary for political campaigns in her native Connecticut. Roy, who has a Ph.D. from Princeton, is Archibald MacLeish's official biographer. An editor as well as writer (he collaborated on the third volume of Robert Frost's biography), he's been with Kekst for almost two years. Mary was the editor of her school paper, *The Dartmouth,* and came to Kekst three years ago from Arthur Andersen & Company. (See p. 103.) Richard, who has a Ph.D. in Italian history from Columbia, was the associate dean of the School of Education at St. John's University before arriving at Kekst three years ago. Fred earned his Ph.D. in Chinese history at Brown. He's been with Kekst since 1981. Jim, one of the original partners of Kekst and Company, was a sportswriter at *The New York Post* while earning his MBA from Adelphi at night. Just your typical flacks. Public relations never had it so good.

Kekst and Company is a quietly powerful public relations firm that really should find a new appellation. In fact, the business it is engaged in is promotion, protection, and investor relations, but in an industry with a somewhat (justifiably) shabby image—people begging for ink, pushing their way onto TV shows, and, worst of all, lying, Kekst is an anomaly. Kekst has carved out a particular specialty, corporate public relations, and behind the scenes these people help engineer many of the takeovers and mergers you've read about in the financial section of the newspaper. That's not all they do, and it is important not to let this "sexy" part of Kekst's practice overshadow its day-to-day endeavors. You'll never read the name "Kekst and Company" in the press, and unless you run a business in need of public relations consulting, you may not have heard of this company.

Gershon Kekst, a cigar-smoking, self-deprecating, fifty-three-year-old man, found work at Ruder & Finn, a well-established, well-thought-of PR firm, after graduating from the University of Maryland. Married, with children, he discovered he wasn't happy working for someone else and decided to go off on his own. He more or less allowed his first clients to determine what kind of public relations practice he would offer. "If a dress manufacturer had hired us, we might be in the fashion business." Possibly. While it may be happenstance that directed Kekst and Company into corporate and financial work, its growth in this area is not accidental. Kekst is substantially smaller than its competitors but is winning accounts from them with a vengeance.

Keeping a low profile contributes to a certain mystique, all the more vivid due to the nature of the business. "The mystique makes it appealing," one of the professionals says. "It's different, intriguing. I have no sense of what PR firms do, anyway. We're not organized, we have no titles, no teams, no 'structural efficiency.' Gershon says we're 'advocates.' Everyone here is a generalist, by industry and by function. There's no fixed body of knowledge. This is a judgment business."

One new hire without a background in PR admits he "didn't really know what we were getting into here. When I was hired, the deal was 'Work here and see what you think.' It wasn't a probation period; it was a chance for me to see what it was all about. I didn't come here committed to Kekst and Company or a career in public relations. I just wanted to see."

Keksties cherish that which makes them unique. "This is not a nine-to-five place. There are no 'warm fuzzies.' It saves time not to be surprised, since there's no training. When you arrive, it's sink or swim. People may or may not be helpful. You learn on the client." Those who survive are astonished at the responsibility and access they have right away. "Within my first six months, I was working one to one with the CEO and CFO of *Fortune* 500 companies." It's a pretty fair payoff.

The amount of responsibility is considered a perk, not a threat. "You won't be cast adrift with responsibility for gaining or losing an account. Gershon's remarkable talent is in gauging when people are ready. He'll give you as much responsibility as you can take."

Don't expect a coldhearted environment, however. Led by Gershon, there is a warmth, a collegiality, a *Yiddishkeit,* that is blind to seniority and conspicuous in its strictly businesslike setting. People kid around, have personal relationships with each other, and agree that it's a "nice place." But it is pointed out that "you don't join Kekst because of the people. A lot of our work is done on an individual basis."

Although formal structures are eschewed, the company is small enough that no one gets lost. Kekst himself is the primary assigner of work, and since the culture is based on the assumption that smart people know their limits and their abilities, no one need fear protesting or soliciting an assignment. The worst that could happen is that Gershon will say no. This is not a demeritocracy. Each professional in the firm has a primary client responsibility. "That person has to be the industry insider and know as much as possible."

One's contacts with the client could range from the in-house public relations office to the CEO. Usually connections are made on many levels. "Sometimes the client's PR people are resentful of us. You must convince them you're helping them, especially when they're not the ones who hired you." Kekst finds much of its new work through referrals, many of them from investment banks and lawyers. If a takeover is in the works, Kekst could be recommended by, say, Lazard Frères, the investment bank, or Wachtell, Lipton, Rosen & Katz, the law firm (see p. 577)—or vice versa. In other words, in that kind of transaction, the public relations function is perceived to be just as integral as the other two. It is not unthinkable that Gershon might be consulted *before* the lawyers are brought in. "Most of our work is not takeover, but that gets the biggest splash. It may be a small computer company with an initial public offering (IPO) that doesn't know how to tell its story to investors."

Gershon decides who and what the firm will handle, "although he may ask around. There's no policy committee." Conflicts of interest are worked out. Employees must sign confidentiality documents, since they are privy to information which could—especially these days—be irresistible to potential investors.

Kekst and Company is made up of thirteen partners, twelve associates, and thirty-one support staffers. Associates may be on long leashes, but a partner is always hovering in the background. Partners "get their names on the stationery, attend meetings, and have principal account responsibility. 'Making partner' takes approximately five years, which can be shortened. There is no winnowing process. The expectation is that anyone we hire will succeed. Yet, since Kekst and Company is controlled by Gershon Kekst, the partnership, strictly speaking, is not one of equals. Associates are eligible to purchase stock after one year at Kekst. Everyone has an equity position in the firm, a stake. No one is supposed to know how many shares anyone else owns. Getting shares "is supposed to be an incentive. It's Gershon's commitment to you, the option holder."

If the culture is at all competitive, it might be in vying for Gershon's attention and affection. "Everyone wants him to know how well they're doing." Some jockeying could occur in the attempt to work on pieces of business that Gershon himself directs. "If you value your weekends," apple polishers are cautioned, "sometimes it's better not to work with Gershon." In terms of distribution of rewards, "it's egalitarian. You won't do better sucking up to him." One's first performance review comes after six months, with an attendant salary increase. Afterwards, there are two bonuses handed out per year, at midyear and year end, with an annual raise given on January 1.

"The briefest possible discussion of your performance" precedes one's remuneration. Billable hours are taken into consideration, as is the difficulty or complexity of assignments. "Also, the frequent circulation of good work around the office, like the annual report you helped to write or a speech you wrote" keeps others informed. People at Kekst are loyal to their clients and even to their colleagues' clients. You'll hear things like, "I saw that shitty piece on your client" (if it were at all negative) or "Nice op ed piece!" People are pretty generous with praise for their peers.

In the midst of a crisis or short-term transaction, one can hardly tell Kekst professionals from the investment bankers or lawyers with whom they work. ("If there are negatives about working here, it's that our involvement can be perceived by clients and others as negligible, like a fad. They figure they need us for *something*. Lawyers sometimes encroach on us, yet we do certain things better. Sometimes lawyers and bankers write press releases. Sometimes our PR strategy makes a difference.") They look the same. Their education is often the same. Their hours are the same. Gershon says he could find out on three o'clock on a Friday afternoon that one of his clients has just been informed of a plan for a hostile takeover. Within moments, he could mobilize a staff to research the situation, poll shareholders, and write reports for the chairman that would be on his desk at 8:00 A.M. Monday. (Admittedly, this is not his favorite way to spend his weekends or execute an assignment, but if he is called on to do so, he can perform.)

Employees have griped about the hours. "During transactions, your life is unpredictable. It's exciting, and the chance to work under pressure is valuable. But the erraticism drives you crazy. It's hard to develop a life [outside the office]. You have to be able to say, 'Fine. I can do it,' whether that means a late night or a weekend. If something needs to be done, you do it. You don't question. If a client needs it, your personal life will suffer. That's the way it works. But if you had a wedding to go to, a partner would say, 'Let's see if I can get someone else.' They're pretty reasonable." Married employees complain less. They do not have to pursue a social life with the same vigor single people must. Perhaps the younger (single) associates, unsure how to manage with little structure, devote more time to work than they have to. It could be that they volunteer for overtime duty more than they realize. They claim they would never work late just to be observed working late.

"When you hear a giant groan (and we're all sensitized to each other's groans), you know something very big has come in. And you divide it up according to who has the best background in the company or in the industry."

Kekst's staffing policy allows for people to be hired year round to achieve a growth that's characterized as "bit by bit. We're always a few people behind what we need."

Jim Fingeroth will be pleased to read that he looks about half his age. (He's forty-five years old.) He wants you to know that he means to answer his own phone when he can and that "we return our calls as soon as possible. *Write that down.*" A joint major in business and journalism ("the perfect study combination for this") at NYU, class of '65, he had taken a few courses from David Finn, a founder of Ruder & Finn. After spending a couple of years covering sports for *The New York Post* and getting his MBA part time, he joined Finn's PR firm. "Those were its halcyon days." After four and a half years there, he "saw people like Gershon leaving. I wondered why. These people *were* making it. The principals didn't want to build long term. To grow in this business, you have to start your own. I felt Gershon Kekst was destined to succeed. He was head and shoulders above most people in the field." Fingeroth defected six to eight months after the creation of Kekst and Company. His risk was minimal, since the firm already had clients.

Jim agrees that "corporate PR" is not quite an adequate definition of their business. "Mostly our clients agree to retain us for twelve months. For special situations, M and A's [mergers and acquisitions], tender offers, and proxy fights, we work project to project. We work very hard to grow relationships. A number of our clients who hire us for transactional service and who do stay with us have us do stuff that has nothing to do with the reason they hired us. We're kidding ourselves if we think we're management consultants—it smudges into that, but I'd rather not refer to ourselves that way. Once we hired Harvard MBA's to do consulting, and they didn't want to get their hands dirty. That's bullshit. We deal with the press. First and foremost, we're communications professionals.

"Clients may have hired us because they heard that Gershon Kekst is the smartest man in the United States. But we've got a whole firm to back him up. Gershon explains how it works. It's the same as working with Joe Flom [a partner at Skadden, Arps, Slate, Meagher & Flom, he's considered to be one of the two best takeover lawyers in the country] [Author's note: Martin Lipton of Wachtell, Lipton—see p. 577—is the other.] but you're not always going to work with number one. We try not to have personality cults. He does stay involved in almost everything, to some degree."

Fingeroth emphasizes the lack of standardization in this emerging business. "We don't do long-term planning. We don't know what'll happen in five years. What's the corporate world going to be in five years? We're blazing new trails. Our approach is that we do not have a formularized approach." And there is an appreciation for maintaining Kekst and Company as a small company. There are no branch offices outside of the one in New York. (Which looks like a law firm or investment bank but *feels,* actually, more relaxed. Maybe it's that people can have their own styles. Gershon Kekst doesn't seem to tolerate too many clones.)

Some more notes on how business is conducted here. "We don't make young people do dumb stuff just because they're young. Every new person is attached to one or two partners, who act as the new person's rabbis, advocates. We are a service business, which must be understood from day one. In a lot of ways, we're where the bullshit stops. We don't tell our client what we think he wants to hear to keep the account. With press, there's a level of accountability." And moral responsibility. Accessible to the kind of information that has sent Wall Streeters to jail, employees of Kekst and Company may not trade on what they learn at work. "We cannot make any investment without Gershon's expressed approval."

Kekst and Company's tenets for maintaining long-term relationships with clients include establishing relationships with the in-house public relations professionals, not just the CEOs, so that they will be perceived as allies, not interlopers. "We spend a lot of time traveling to *their* offices. We know we're outsiders. We add that objectivity."

In Fingeroth's case, the blend between advising and doing is very satisfying. "I run to my door every morning to get *The Wall Street Journal* at six A.M. It's my report card. It's like seeing last night's reviews. We get feedback and are judged every day. I don't want to be carried out of here, but I can't imagine doing what we do in a more wonderful environment."

As you may recall, Fred is the ex-academic with a doctorate in Chinese history. "I never imagined I'd be doing this," he says in the conference room. "This is an accident. Now there's a pretty good chance I'll live out my career here. I don't know what else I'd do. The opportunities are extensive. We have a great client list. The pay is good."

Fred doesn't call himself "Doctor" or append his "Ph.D." to his name, but his background has definitely helped him in his work for Kekst. "One of my first assignments was to write a brochure for a pharmaceuticals company that acquired a biotechnology company. My skills in translation [Chinese to English] were useful in dealing with technical language. It's nice to hear from the press that we can discuss business fluently." The press values this service and consequently honors the professionals' desire to be referred to as "spokesmen for XYZ Company," rather than as members of Kekst and Company. Furthermore, "reporters recognize we're good sources for them and it makes them look like they've done their homework."

The thrill of learning and discovery, Fred's reward in academia, has been frustrated by the lack of time in the business world. Time is considered an unattainable luxury. But after half a lifetime in a respectable but financially impoverished state, the monetary compensation at Kekst and Company is a motivator. "This is a great opportunity for ex-academics," Fred says. "It's research and writing and advocacy." Ex-academics, used to working hard, still find the money a kick. "You're motivated by it but not obsessed by it, as an academic would be. Money can become an addiction. Handling big money also takes an adjustment." The people at Kekst get intimate with transactions of $10 million to $100 million and more, sometimes *much* more. Those amounts "are not fathomable." (He says that "titles can't possibly drive you.")

Anne Shillinglaw, who directs Kekst's research department with a decade at the firm to her credit, calls herself "a mother hen." She has strong opinions about the way business is conducted here. "Our business is our clients' business, not what's going on at Kekst. We're not about fancy brochures. (That would take time away from our clients.) Most new business is by referral. We don't have to beat the streets. I don't know of any instance where we have gone out and pitched business. If a company wants to come in and hear more about Kekst, fine. But we're not about to get on a plane and look for it. They might not be a good personality fit or really need us. They might only need a free-lance writer to do their annual report, and not Kekst."

As you might have guessed by now, there is a real pride at Kekst in being different from other public relations firms. "There are no flip charts, et cetera. That goes against everything we stand for." Today's research staff consists of Shillinglaw, two other professionals ("college graduates, not research professionals"), and a support person. Anne prefers young people who are "able to juggle, to switch gears at once, who are intelligent, curious by nature, and can write." They have to surmount the constant aggravation of never having enough time.

"To someone who does market research and regression studies, they'd blanch at what we do. We don't need the world's opinion, just a well-selected few. Our view is, if you talk to the right people, you can get a good sample. Most research we do is at the request of someone at Kekst, not the client, although the expenditure must be approved by the client. We don't do projects on spec." Most projects can be completed in five to six weeks. Others can be all-nighters. After being initiated to the fast pace, Kekst's researchers seem to prefer the quick turnover and its attendant results. "Our personalities wouldn't be able to research [for example] cancer for ten years. We'd get bored. We don't have that kind of tenacity."

Anne continues, "I think the greatest thing about my job is, once my project is done, it's done. My personality suits this job just fine. After school I had no idea what I wanted to do, but I thought I'd take the world by storm. It was a long process figuring out what I was meant to be and what I was good at. I always liked the flexibility that research offered me. When I got here, I knew nothing about PR and I couldn't balance my checkbook.

"I don't have as much client contact or public recognition as the client side, but I'd never want to be on the other side of the office. I don't feel like a second-class worker. Gershon puts a lot of emphasis on research, as do a lot of other people in the office. We make them look good." The research department hires between two and four summer interns. Their agendas, which Anne tries to vary, are *not* filled with photocopying and messengering. Companywide, she maintains, "we're looking for bizarre people. It helps to be Jewish." [She's referring to the fact that a subdialect of the Kekst culture is Yiddish. One of the ultimate compliments here is not that one has done a good job, but that one is a *mensch*. Also, people are not scared to react to each other and ideas. Emotions are welcome.] "It's Jewifying," the Gentile Anne says, proud of her enhanced vocabulary. "There are more non-Jews here, but on Good Friday there are no secretaries in the office, and on Yom Kippur there are no professionals," she exaggerates.

Jim Fingeroth inadvertently provides the best summation for this chapter. "We feel very strongly that what we've created here is very special. We'd be crazy to blow it."

KOHN PEDERSEN FOX ASSOCIATES PC

KOHN PEDERSEN FOX ASSOCIATES PC

HISTORY & OPERATIONS

Like another American success story, the architectural firm Kohn Pedersen Fox Associates (KPF) was started on July 4. The year was 1976. The three founding partners had all held key positions at the New York office of John Carl Warnecke & Associates, a large national firm with a reputation for conservative design. A. Eugene Kohn, KPF's original founder and its president, was the president of Warnecke/New York. William E. Pedersen, the firm's senior design partner, had been working for the firm of legendary architect I. M. Pei when he was recruited by Gene Kohn to become the vice-president of Warnecke. Sheldon Fox had become Warnecke's senior vice-president before joining KPF as its senior administrative partner. Patricia Conway—whose name is not included among the founding partners because her degree is in urban planning and the others are all registered architects—serves as the planning partner for KPF and the president of its interior design subsidiary, Kohn Pedersen Fox Conway Associates, Inc., which was spun off in 1984. (Conway had been Warnecke's associate director of planning when she left to cast her fortunes with Kohn, Pedersen, and Fox.)

Kohn had been dissatisfied with the limitations inherent in working for a large firm, particularly someone else's, so he left to start his own. Launched in the middle of a serious economic recession, without business or even the hope of business, the firm's initial success was remarkable. Though the founding partners had anticipated a lean first few years, they landed three assignments in three different states within three months of opening shop. These first commissions, like most of the firm's business in the years before it had any existing buildings to its credit, are largely attributed to the brilliant salesmanship of Gene Kohn, who has been called "perhaps the most persuasive salesman in the architecture business" and who is said to have an advantage over many architects in that he's comfortable in the business world and puts executives at ease. When Kohn founded the firm, he met with a number of business-people to ask them what they would look for in hiring a team of architects. The qualities most often mentioned—attention from partners, quality design, and respect for budgets—became KPF's primary operating rules.

In 1977 the firm was joined by two more former Warnecke architects, Arthur May and Robert L. Cioppa, both of whom became partners in 1978. And in 1979 Bill Louie, who had also worked at Warnecke, joined KPF. He became a partner in 1980.

The firm's first significant projects were an administrative building and television studio for ABC on Manhattan's Upper West Side (completed in 1978) and a medium-sized office tower in Lexington, Kentucky (completed in 1980). Then came an AT&T office complex located in Oakton, Virginia, near Washington, D.C. (completed in 1980). In 1979 the firm received an important job through Kohn's friend Henry Lambert (the founder of Pasta & Cheese and the senior vice-president of the Reliance Development Group), who hired KPF to design a thirty-six-story building for Amoco in Denver (completed in 1980). That commission put Kohn Pedersen Fox in the company of the small and elite group of architectural firms that build high rises (currently the mainstay of KPF's practice). Yet despite these early coups, the firm still had to scramble for commissions. During its first years, it did work for real estate development firms (as opposed to designing corporate headquarters or public use buildings), mainly feasibility studies. Most of the designs were never built, and most were the kinds of assignments a more established firm would have had the luxury of turning down.

Though KPF's early buildings are generally regarded as being superior to most commercial architecture, they are not considered to be as accomplished as the firm's more recent work. The first building that won KPF national critical acclaim was a riverfront skyscraper in Chicago, 333 Wacker Drive. Designed by Bill Pedersen and completed in 1983, the structure is a green glass tower on top of a granite-and-marble base. The side facing the Chicago River curves gracefully along its bank, while the side facing the city conforms to the city's more angular lines. The building, which instantly became a Chicago landmark and is pictured on countless local postcards and souvenirs, illustrates KPF's primary design philosophy, which is described as "contextual." KPF aims to design buildings that will exist in harmony with their surroundings in the belief that a building's context is essential to its form. Another of the firm's major critical successes is the Procter & Gamble world headquarters in Cincinnati, which was also designed by Pedersen and was completed in 1985. Dubbed "the Ivory Towers" by the local press (a play on Ivory Soap, one of P&G's most ubiquitous products) and considered by some critics to be the firm's best work to date, the building is a seven-story, L-shaped complex with two seventeen-story octagonal towers set on either side of the "L." Made of limestone to complement Procter & Gamble's existing structure and designed with features that allude to some of Cincinnati's most oustanding older buildings, the complex is another example of contextual design. Both 333 Wacker Drive and the Procter & Gamble world headquarters won the American Institute of Architects National Honor Award (in 1984 and 1987, respectively.)

Today, a little over a decade since it was founded, KPF employs more than 180 people—8 partners, 13 associate partners, 124 architects, and more than 35 support staff—and is ranked among the ten largest architectural firms in the country—(fifth or seventh, depending on the survey). To date, the firm has completed buildings in 60 cities in 27 states and 7 countries, most of them skyscrapers, though other projects have included hotels, residential buildings, a retail/office/church facility, and an addition to the Graduate School of Business at Stanford University. It now has 40 projects under development in 18 cities, including 12 in its hometown, New York City, 1 in Frankfurt, London, and Sydney, Australia. The style of the firm's buildings is most often categorized as postmodern—structures that blend features of both modern and classical architecture. Some of KPF's buildings have been praised by critics as being equal in stature to the work of world-class architects I. M. Pei, Philip Johnson and John Burgee, Kevin Roche, and Skidmore, Owings & Merrill. The firm has surpassed all other contemporary firms in producing postmodern work for the commercial marketplace on a large scale.

KPF's practice is organized around teams that generally consist of five design people, eight construction documents people, and three construction people and are normally administered by one managing partner and one design partner. The responsible team stays with a project from the design phase through the construction phase. (In this the firm differs from many others, which retain separate divisions for development and production.) Senior staff members work on between one and three teams; while less experienced people work on only one team at a time. Known as a firm in which junior- and middle-level architects receive an unusual amount of responsibility and autonomy, KPF created the title of "associate partner"—a position that pays a relatively high salary but doesn't include an ownership stake in the firm —for its outstanding young architects. Each architect is involved in up to four projects a year.

(Information provided by Carol McCutchen, firm spokesperson.)

REVENUES: $28 million in fees in 1987.

EARNINGS: $2 million in after-tax earnings in 1987.

NUMBER OF EMPLOYEES: More than 280 including the approximately 100 employees of Kohn Pederson Fox Conway Associates. Of that, 8 are partners, 13 are associate partners, 124 are architects, and the rest are support staff.

AVERAGE AGE OF EMPLOYEES: Mid-thirties.

TURNOVER: 5 percent.

RECRUITMENT: The firm has no formal college recruitment program, but its staff members lecture at different schools througout the country, enabling them to "identify professional employees." Staff members lecture at the University of California at Los Angeles, Columbia University, Cornell University, Harvard University, Parsons School of Design, University of Pennsylvania, Pennsylvania State University, Pratt Institute, Rice University, Syracuse University, Washington University, Washington State University, and Yale University. However, new architects are hired on the basis of their portfolios and résumés and can be graduates of any architectural school. "We do not lack for applicants."

NUMBER OF NEW HIRES PER YEAR: Ten.

RANGE OF STARTING SALARIES: $20,000–$25,000.

POLICY FOR RAISES: Raises are awarded once a year and determined solely by performance.

TRAINING PROGRAMS: None.

BENEFITS: Major medical insurance, profit-sharing plan, pension plan, disability plan, and sick leave.

VACATION: Ten to twenty days per year, depending on position and seniority. Eight paid holidays annually.

ADDITIONAL PERKS: Professional license fees and seminars are subsidized.

BONUSES: Two bonuses a year: One at Christmas, based on salary and number of years with the firm, and one at mid-summer, based on performance. All staff people are eligible for both bonuses.

ANNUAL PARTY: The firm hosts an annual Christmas party for employees and their spouses. The party is held at a different place each year and generally includes a live band, dinner, and dancing. Dress is informal, and everybody "mingles and has a good time."

AVERAGE WORKDAY: The workday is officially eight hours, though most architects spend ten to twelve hours in the office. The support staff basically works from 9:00 A.M. to 5:00 P.M.

DRESS CODE: No stated dress code. "For the most part, people are very conscientious about their dress, especially senior people in the firm." This means stylish, rather than conservative.

SOCIAL ATMOSPHERE: "Very compatible." Many people are friends who socialize outside of work.

REPEAT CLIENTS: Lincoln Properties Company, Reliance Development, JMB/Urban Investment, the American Broadcasting Companies, Olympia & York.

SOFTBALL TEAM: The KPF Fliers, members of the SLAM League (which is comprised of competing architectural firms). Gene Kohn pitches and Bill Pedersen plays short/center. In 1987, the team made it to the league championships—13 wins, 0 losses—only to lose in the last game against Gwathmey Siegel & Associates.

HEADQUARTERS: The firm leases three-and-a-half floors, at 111 West 57th Street in Midtown Manhattan. It occupies about 32,000 square feet of office space.

CHARITABLE CONTRIBUTIONS: $71,220 in 1987. Among the charities the firm contributed to were: the American Jewish Committee, the Lighthouse, the Boys Club of America, the Girls Club of America, the Chicago City Ballet, Multiple Sclerosis, the College of Fellows, the Metropolitan Museum of Art, the American Cancer Society, the Museum of Modern Art, the New York Building Congress, and the United Way.

INTERESTED APPLICANTS CAN SEND RÉSUMÉS TO:
Kohn Pedersen Fox Associates PC
111 West 57th Street
New York, NY 10019
Attention: Mr. Robert Cioppa
(212) 977-6500

In the real world, the practice of architecture may be the very best melding of art and commerce. Sure, there's art dealing and curating, but buildings are miltimillion-dollar businesses. New York's Kohn Pedersen Fox Associates have been hailed not only for the elegance of their designs but for the sureness with which they handle business and its practitioners.

Much of the credit for the firm's binary success has been given to president A. Eugene Kohn. A native Philadelphian, he has always (to this day, he concedes) harbored dreams of becoming a sportscaster. Today, in addition to spearheading the successful KPF softball team, Kohn presides over the more than 180-member firm in a manner that is—to the business community—refreshingly businesslike. (Partner Arthur May says, "We try to dress like bankers to suggest fiscal responsibility," and indeed, the partners—albeit with a keener eye toward color, cut, and texture than most bankers—could pass muster as bankers, lawyers, doctors, or CEOs.) Gene and cofounders Bill Pedersen and Shelly (Sheldon) Fox, all refugees from John Carl Warnecke's New York office, have wrought an organization that maintains an unimpeachably clear division of labor.

Kohn says, "I handpicked my partners. Bill is an outstanding designer. Shelly is a straight manager." He adds that his own strengths are in cheerleading, marketing, and design. "I thought about this from the first day: balance of skills, personality, and energy. Three partners, three skills. No one really interferes in any partner's job." The firm's growth has been steady and even. Kohn Pedersen Fox, started in Kohn's backyard on July 4, 1976, is now among the nation's largest architectural practices and is based solely in New York City.

"It's a democracy, although final decisions are up to the partners." In the rare event that partners disagree, Gene Kohn is the final arbiter. One rule that evolved and is sacrosanct is that "no design partners—there are now four—deal with another's designs." Just Gene. "It wasn't deliberate; probably no one else tried." Others in the firm refer to him as "the glue of the firm. He's like a bee carrying pollen. He always picks the partners to work on a project, according to timing, speed, style, chemistry, et cetera."

There has always been a conflict between artists and businesspeople, according to Kohn. "The generic struggle has been that if you put making money first, you will shortchange the design. We try to show businesspeople that good architecture is good business for them. KPF has a balance: We want to earn money and live nicely. We get along with corporations because we speak their language.

"Our first priority is the quality of design and its execution, to build our reputation. The majority of architectural firms are not capable of doing great work. The problem is that this is a service business." The reason it's a problem is that artists usually feel they have to pursue *their* ideas, ideals, and vision before accommodating those of a customer or patron. Participating in a service business means yielding one's ego to the demands of the client. "It requires talent, hard work, a team effort. Clients should participate. How do you build a team? Look at sports: The team knows the same plays, has good-looking uniforms, skill, good coaching, a game plan, and a commitment to performance.

"For me, it was taking the long view. We don't expect the impossible immediately. But our goal from the first was to achieve a place in history. Posterity. Ten years from now will be our most important time," Gene adds, just months after the tenth anniversary celebration.

As a scholarship student at the University of Pennsylvania, Gene was pressured by a dean to consider architecture. "I couldn't even spell it," the urbane, silver-haired Kohn jokes. "My first year was almost a disaster. I didn't take it seriously. I wasn't in love with it." After graduation in 1953, he joined the Navy via the OCS. In Morocco and Newfoundland, the Navy "taught me leadership. It taught me I loved being a leader. I didn't misuse my stripes; I learned to deal with people effectively. You could be nice *and* win." His college credentials suggested Kohn might be the guy to design and build an officer's club in northern Africa. "I used local materials and painted the paintings. It was the first thing I did on my own."

Upon his return to the States, Gene Kohn made a commitment to architecture by applying to graduate school. "I still wanted to be a sportscaster, but family pressures prevailed." He returned to Penn on a fellowship and with the aid of the G.I. Bill. "By far, Penn was the foremost architecture school at the time. Louis Kahn, my mentor, Paul Rudolph, Le Corbusier, Wright"—Kohn lists the world-famous architects who taught or lectured at Penn. "It rubbed off. It was an exciting time. The city was alive. There was a concentration of talent all working together—urban planning, landscape architecture." Kohn's allegiance to the university is still strong. In addition to his stints as a guest professor, KPF donates a scholarship to the School of the Arts at Penn, on whose board of overseers Gene sits.

"Two years after grad school, working in Philadelphia for an architect of commercial spaces, the light bulb went off, and I began to love it." Kohn, now married, had his first child in 1957, the year he earned his master's. In a few short years, he took and passed the test required of all architects to be registered and licensed, and designed a building for Westinghouse and a library for Lafayette University, which won national awards. "I got a lot of offers as a result. I was underpaid and always felt New York was the city where you could do best if you were good. As a Philadelphia hometown boy, I was shy." In preparing to move to New York, Gene says he discovered who he was. "People were receptive to me and my style."

It was 1963, and his first job, at Kahn & Jacobs, reunited Kohn with his college friend Shelly Fox. The process of establishing oneself as an architect traditionally takes two routes: working for a famous and influential star in the business for years, hoping to get more and more responsibility within while gaining a reputation (perhaps on the star's coattails) externally, or, for the more ambitious, moving around every few years, upgrading one's situation with each move. As an aside, someone explains the life expectancy of the typical architect. "At I. M. Pei you could be the best designer and not even make partner. A partner would have to die first."

Kohn moved to Warnecke's office in 1967. By the time he became president in 1972, construction and affiliated businesses were experiencing a sharp decline. The last thing corporations were doing was commissioning monuments. The financial frustrations were compounded by a general stylistic inhibition on the part of the people who did go ahead with new buildings. It was time to move on.

KPF opened its doors in this negative ambience. "I couldn't believe some of the early clients chose us." The founders had not a single prospect in their pockets when they went off on their own. "We just persuaded them." Kohn characterizes the firm's first work as "simple forms." The first building was a studio (where *One Life to Live* is produced) for ABC on Manhattan's West Side. From the start, Kohn Pedersen Fox was concerned with "contextualism"—how the building would merge with its surrounding neighborhood, buildings, and skyline. Designs, materials, and decorations had to be compatible and comfortable. "You, a nonarchitect, are much more sensitive than you know. You're more comfortable in front of the Empire State Building than you are in front of the World Trade Towers." Not just because the Empire State Building is lower; it rises in gradations. Your eye moves up the facade in steps; you don't have to take the entire building in at once as you do the World Trade Towers, which are sheer, uninterrupted stretches into the sky, thoroughly intimidating.

Spending time with architects is a treat for the uninitiated; their language is filled with emotion, historic references, artistic gambols, and reverie. There is time to meditate and philosophize. [Author's note: Much as being around someone afflicted with laryngitis unconsciously forces you to whisper with them, hanging around KPF seduces you into reviving the vocabulary you gleaned in art history courses years back and taking it for a spin.]

The offices of Kohn Pedersen Fox occupy three-and-a-half floors of a prewar office building at 111 West Fifty-seventh Street. Kohn Pedersen Fox Conway, the firm's interior design branch, is located in another midtown site. The design message is communicated as you step off the elevator. Gray and white are the colors of the offices, with rosewood and brushed stainless-steel picture frames—designed by Bill Pedersen—displaying photographs of the firm's work. The partner's offices are small—tiny, actually, compared to any other partnership I visited—and none of them has a door. Pedersen designed tables for the partners, elegant marble, rosewood, and brushed stainless steel, with inlays of mother of pearl, accents that repeat the *moderne* look of the picture frames. What they lack in space they make up for in the volume of architectural drawings, models, in varying stages of sophistication, and samples of materials—cubes of marble, granite, and limestone.

This is a story that Gene tells about KPF's modus operandi: "A young developer from Houston contacted us to go after the Third National Bank in Nashville. They [the developers] had very little high-rise experience. We knew we were up against heavy hitters. We sent Mark Strauss, an architectural historian, to Nashville for three days to do research. We wanted to persuade the bank to go for the New York–Houston team instead of people closer to home.

"We were able to link New York to Nashville to Houston—historically. The Allen family of Nashville had a daughter who married (Texan) Sam Houston, who became the governor of Tennessee. When Andrew Jackson (himself a former governor of Tennessee) became president, he sent Houston to Texas to fight the battle of the Alamo, which he eventually won. At the time, the city of Houston was called 'Buffalo.' The Allens renamed the city 'Houston' after their now ex-son-in-law. And Houston was the capital of Texas for one year.

"Strickland, the most revered architect in Nashville, was from Pennsylvania (as was I), Kohn relates. "He designed the Capitol.

"It turned out the [current] chairman of the bank had visited a building designed by another Penn graduate. After the slide show [that accompanied my presentation], he said, 'We're all one big family. You're hired.'

"Going into the South as 'slick New Yorkers' couldn't help. We weren't going to do a New York building in Nashville, but we had the benefit of our New York experience." Kohn says that, in fact, the New York image must be "overcome" to win some out-of-state clients. "We do it with humor, by being soft-spoken, and doing research. I still get excited about jobs. I still get blue when we lose."

New jobs usually begin with a slide show. Often but not always led by Kohn, they are really distilled histories of architecture and the growth of American cities from a sociological point of view. I attended one that was presented by associate partners Lee Polisano (who has since been made a partner), and Gary Handel.

For most of the firm's first ten years, there were six partners at the top of the heap. In 1985 the firm instituted a level called "associate partner," which was made up of nine architects who more or less started at the firm together as a class in 1978–79. When KPF restructured in 1988, two of the associate partners, Lee Polisano and Bob Evans, were named as full partners, and six junior architects were promoted to the associate partner ranks, for a total of eight partners and thirteen associate partners. The associate level is a cohesive group—all men and for the most part [although surely coincidentally] not as tall as the partners. With their increased responsibility and reputation, they take the lead on projects when partners are traveling or involved in other ventures, although every job has a managing partner (à la Shelly Fox), a design partner (à la Bill Pedersen), and an associate partner assigned to it. "We're not as autonomous as law partners," one associate says. "We're team-oriented—by choice—and most projects are brought in by Gene. It's not like one person brings in his own business and then runs it." As a matter of fact, Gene Kohn—and no one else—really bears the brunt of soliciting new business. Kohn says, "hiring an architect is like buying futures in someone's talent. We promise young people growth."

Shelly Fox maintains, "we deliberately did not impose strong layering. It's a loose structure, yet not freewheeling. We avoided associate partners for a long time, because [we thought that] people would get caught up in titles. I know all the associate partners will not stay with us. Others, we'll rethink. Still others will stay and become partners. We intend to make other associate partners."

Lee Polisano takes us through the work cycle. He says there are "between thirty-five and forty active projects in the office, anywhere from a bid to the final stages of construction. People work on more than one job at a time." The first several stages are literally all lodged on the drawing board. Clients pay a fee, "which barely covers our work," and plans are conceived and reconceived. "The first level of work is called a feasibility study. Master planning follows, then the schematic design comes next. The first thing we do is a one-to-one-hundred scale including all buildings" next to the one being designed. Here the architects sometimes start by working with clay. The schematic stage usually lasts between two and three months, during which several options are designed, "but we quickly arrive at one direction and define problems, estimate the budget," etc. Four or five people will be involved in this process. Design development lasts three to four months, during which the "massing" or shape of the building is figured out. Now it's time to work on the lobby, the building materials, etc., and to start working with the developers. The KPF team has now grown to eight. Paper models are commissioned "to test pieces in 3-D. As a firm, we concentrate more of our time and our fee on these stages. The results are better buildings and better value per dollar for our clients. Also, since we get paid a lump sum per project, we tend to lose money" for the extra attention at these early preconstruction phases.

The period of drawing up construction documents, which could last up to eight months for a large project, is when working drawings are made. These are hundreds of drawings of every detail of the building—the walls between elevators, the doorways to the fire escapes, the lobby concession stand, the window ledges, and so forth. About twelve or thirteen people are engaged then. Lee says, "This is the detail stage. Models are made for the client. When a client spends that kind of money, you don't want to give him surprises." The team that is assigned to the project at the beginning will remain with it until completion. (This means a managing partner, a design partner, a project manager—usually an associate partner, a project designer, and a job captain.) When more people are needed, the team grows around them. Once the ground is broken, during construction administration, the staff shrinks back to two full-time architects.

Polisano talks about "my hours," making it clear that they are of his own devising. "I frequently work seven days a week. It's not peer pressure; it's self-inflicted." Monday through Friday he works twelve-hour days; weekends he's in the office only six hours per day. "I work when I'm here. And I have that much work to do. It's my choice."

But work is never done for these [or, from what I'm told, any] architects. "I go to a movie and spend time looking at buildings. In the movie, I look at the buildings and clothes, and when I leave the theater, I look at buildings. I've gotten into two car accidents looking at buildings, once in Denver and once in Miami." (There were no casualties.) "I spend lunch hours at {fashion designer} Norma Kamali's store since she's so creative." This is more than a full-time obsession. Polisano, who is married, mentions in passing "a rumor that architects have a high divorce rate." Interestingly, for vacation, Lee has enjoyed going to Utah. "There are open spaces and no buildings."

"When I arrived at KPF, the excitement was incredible. There were thirty people, and I said, 'This is amazing—Gene, Bill, and Shelly are sitting in open stalls.' The energy was high, but the work was unusual. There were urban concerns, contextual concerns; it was experimental." Nevertheless, Polisano confesses, "I never thought I'd stay more than two years." He'd previously worked at another, more conventionally run firm, the kind where junior members are the underpaid and unthanked. Prior to becoming a partner, he said, "I don't have a problem with credit or lack of credit. I'm getting more responsibility than I would at any other firm. Associates will begin to hire and fire more. If it were any more structured, I'd have left years ago. I would never leave here to go work for another firm. We have an incredibly talented group here. We get the best people from the best schools."

One of the things that keeps motivating architects-as-artists is posterity. "I think every single architect thinks about the body of work that will be remembered by future generations, and at one time or another thinks about the book that'll be written about them." Since the division of labor that starts at the top of KPF permeates the entire firm, younger members begin to be directed toward management or design, and some of those who are gradually rerouted from the design function have naturally been disappointed. "It is very difficult to make people rising on the management side not feel like second-class citizens," a partner says. Polisano is a managing partner, which suits him well. He is the only designer who moved himself to administration. He is organized and deals well with clients.

Bob Cioppa, one of the eight partners, is a manager and also the de facto director of human resources for KPF. He praises the division of labor. "The partnership was set up to allow the original three partners to do what they do best and not have to practice the whole complement of architectural skills. It's based on a real respect on the partners' parts for each others' roles. There's little interference." The firm's goals have always been clearly articulated: "To be one of the most respected and outstanding firms in America that could be passed down after the founders retire."

Cioppa attributes the first winning ten years to the following: "One, Gene's skills in marketing set KPF apart from the beginning. Another senior architect has said that Gene is the single best architectural marketer of the decade, if not the century. Two, great chemistry. There *must* be chemistry; you have to get along well. It's such a goddamn struggle just to *graduate* from architecture school. The attrition rate is high."

Cioppa was an English major at Boston College, "but I felt more excited by the buildings of Boston than I was by English." By the mid-seventies, he was working at Warnecke's, when the economic climate soured. "In 1974–75, you simply waited to be fired. For your turn." He was laid off in 1976. Bob joined KPF in January 1977, just six months after the firm opened its doors. He was hired for a one-year stint, specifically to work on the ABC studio project. "KPF was full of confidence, and I decided a year of active work would help me decide whether I should stay in architecture. Many {of his colleagues and acquaintances from other firms} didn't.

"ABC was fun to work with. It was glamorous. Then KPF asked me if I wanted to stay. I hadn't thought about it. I just said yes." He liked the chemistry that filtered down, "although it was not far to go; there were only fifteen people here. I was asked to become a partner in seventy-nine or eighty. I was terrified of the potential egos, backbiting, and politics, but in fact the public image and the private image are the same: fun and congenial."

Bob prefers the process of making buildings to the design process. He assists Gene in the matching of architects and projects. He's in charge of "raises, salaries, geography—moving people about, hiring and firing, and evaluation." His jurisdiction now extends to more than 180 people. "The employee who joins KPF today doesn't know or remember when we were a rip-roaring company of 20. There's relatively little time I can show a new person the ropes.

"The place is getting too big for me to handle this the way I'd like. I used to sit with each employee at the end of their project work, to see what they wanted to do next. Large percentages of staff have to be reallocated. It requires a sensitivity to clients." On the plus side, "someone in their late twenties or early thirties will have responsibilities for part of a thirty- to one-hundred-million-dollar project."

As you may know, many architectural assignments are the result of competitions. Just having an interesting and substantial body of work is not enough. In wooing a client, there's the matter of negotiating personal style, budgets, local politics (getting the approval of zoning boards and the like), and more. Like so many other businesses, getting a building made may have nothing to do with the virtues of the structure itself. Cioppa says, "Partners have tremendous optimism. They say, 'Every job will work; every building will be made.' You can't project growth on the basis of optimism. I have to figure the realistic. We started our job numbers at 100. Today it's up to 664, but we only have 36 buildings fully built. I'm on 8 projects myself now. There are 27 others I know nothing about. I need the truth, unadulterated by optimism or pessimism."

According to Cioppa, the KPF culture is a reflection of Kohn and Pedersen. "They'll fly on the red-eye from Los Angeles to make a KPF softball game. The firm is a direct reflection of them. (I've heard the 'allergic reaction to Warnecke.' theory" which suggests that K, P, and F set out to create a culture that would be the polar opposite of that which spawned them. "But though they won't admit it," Cioppa continues, "there's a lot of similarity to Warnecke.) The difference is that KPF cares about its employees."

Since the atmosphere is an intimate one (for the first few years architects work in "bullpens" —open areas with drawing boards) there is very little privacy. A bad fit would have a more profound negative impact than it might in a conventional office setting. Obviously, KPF gets to flex its cultural muscle in the hiring process. "Hiring an architect is a peculiar thing to do. You have to separate stylistic preference from talent." Verbal skills are as important as graphic skills. But there's the possibility of "someone who could be trouble; you just don't feel right.

"I feel the majority of people who walk in here are decent, hardworking people who will be willing to do work either because of architecture or because of money." The money is not what you'd think. Walking around the various offices, you see well-dressed, chic people who seem comfortable with themselves. What is surprising is how little architects are paid. Historically the occupation of the rich dilettante, "the path used to be someone from the upper middle class and an Ivy League school would work for a name architect and build houses for his parents, his uncles, and himself. You can't get rich in architecture." Starting salaries are in the secretarial range—about $20,000 to $25,000.

Bob Evans, design partner (the fourth), won the prestigious Prix de Rome the year after he graduated from Rice University's architecture program. He's pleased he made the design cut at the firm. "For the most part, people would like to design." Design at KPF follows two separate schools: that of Bill Pedersen and that of Arthur May. "Arthur and Bill are stylistically similar—'high modern'—with similar backgrounds—I. M. Pei and Warnecke. They have made strong efforts to create individual stylistic preferences—different stones, scale. They were mushed before. Arthur had been abstract and is now more classical. Bill's now more decorative. It's sort of an atelier system where Arthur and Bill tend to work mainly with one {associate partner} or another. Staffing comes from the top."

Bob's working on three projects now. He says he's learned to juggle his time and keep track of his hours. "Learning to delegate requires good relationships with your team. Obviously, someone has to do bathroom detail. Not everyone can do the lobby." Yet he, too, credits the division of labor with freeing him from "lots of stuff I'm not interested in. And it's great I don't have to be. Like contracts and stuff.

"No matter how hard you work, you never know how a building will work out. You have a good idea. But clients don't. They can't imagine scale shifts, color changes . . . When a building is completed it's interesting, but it's an old idea. You're onto new things. I'm lucky. For the most part I've been on jobs that are real jobs. That's Bill. Some people wouldn't mind paper {i.e., unrealized} jobs. I do. It's okay if it's a month. If it's a year, it's a blow."

Generalizing does seem safe in the area of "the certain generic qualities of architects. An interest," Evans enumerates, "in how things are put together." He points to a history of working with Lincoln Logs, Lego blocks, and other primitive forms of building material. "A curiosity about how tangible objects are composed. Also [enjoying] making pretty things that work." Bob agrees that architects are obsessive people who think architecture twenty-four hours a day. When he takes vacations, he plans his travels around buildings he wants to see. "Architects love to buy Victorian houses and fix up the kitchen and say, 'This is all I could do.' We don't want to commit." Because the work can always be improved upon. It's either fixing the kitchen and throwing up your hands, or completely rebuilding the house. Several times.

B ill Pedersen actually designed his own apartment, which is cool and elegant. Another past winner of the Prix de Rome, he grew up in Minnesota. His father and grandfather were in architectural engineering and construction. "Architecture seemed inevitable. My initial success as a student was diminished by my hockey career at the University of Minnesota."

After Italy, he worked for I. M. Pei before joining the Warnecke office presided over by Gene Kohn. He refers to the beginning of Kohn Pedersen Fox as a quest for survival. "In New York City in 1976, there was almost eighty percent unemployment in architecture. Gene left to start his own firm, and I didn't intend to join forces. It was a debate. I almost moved back to Minnesota to open a small office." A large office seemed unreasonable to him for the enormous responsibility it conferred. A small office seemed more appealing.

"Gene asked me to join him {on a study for a major developer}, and I realized that decision would take us into a path of larger work." Bill was faced with "the dilemma of all serious architects: to do smaller, more personal residences versus larger {less personal} buildings. In trying to come to grip with things, we would never have begun a large practice if we had taken our own advice.

"There was no long-term goal at first. We were still not aiming for a big practice. We didn't know we'd be successful. We did know the three of us had a good balance of personalities and abilites. We're always willing to share responsibility and *credit* for work produced. We have respect for each other's domains. Ego is much less an issue here than at other firms." We won't name names, but architecture is well known for breeding a certain flamboyant prima donna personality type. "We try not to get involved in that sort of thing. Gene's the one who focuses credit on me and Arthur."

No one at Kohn Pedersen Fox ever mentions it, but one must wonder whether there is a certain competition between Pedersen and May and their ateliers. The designers in the trenches merely raise their eyebrows and smile in response. "We're all competitive with one another," Pedersen says. "It's very important to artistic growth here. That kind of competition could destroy an office. Gene's personality is the controlling force. We talk to each other through Gene.

"It would've been possible in the beginning for me to decide I wanted to control all design. After one year I asked Arthur May to join us as a partner. I've been stretched in a way. I'm trying to adjust now. I want the luxury of more intimate responsibility as I had five and six years ago. In an ideal situation, I like to think of myself working totally independently. I feel my imprint on every single piece [I design]."

Perhaps KPF's most celebrated building is the stunning general use office building Pedersen designed for 333 Wacker Drive in Chicago. Other than Gene Kohn's brilliant marketing skills, 333 Wacker is probably most responsible for getting KPF new work. (Unfortunately, though, when some clients said they wanted "another 333 Wacker Drive," they meant *it* literally. They wanted the exact same building. "We couldn't do it," Kohn says, "it was the wrong context." Besides, what artist wants to repeat his work, line for line?)

Pedersen says, "When I see a building—Wacker Drive—it's like someone else did it. Like I was six years ago. You can never be satisfied. I believe intensely in the buildings we produce, but you must compare them to the history of architecture. I don't think anyone can *aim* for history," Pedersen says, being pragmatic. "One doesn't set out to do a beautiful building. You solve a problem, work within certain boundaries, and break some new ground. I look back on ten years' work, and I'm not sure what it is, except that it's paid the bills."

He does see the organization he's helped forge as a source of satisfaction. "There's no encouragement for personal growth at big firms. We're distinguished by how quickly we bring some young people up. The associate partners are remarkable people. All of them are now capable of carrying out independent work. There might have been a time when they needed me. Now, no longer.

"The sense of family here keeps me here. People feel strongly about each other. You can't take that lightly."

Arthur May agrees that competition does exist at KPF, even at the partner level. Another Prix de Rome winner and alumnus of Warnecke, he says the competition is fueled by the number of buildings that, for a variety of reasons, never get built. This sense of frustration is endemic to the very nature of the architecture business. "It's very disappointing when a building doesn't happen. You could work for two or three years, and it's like a show closing out of town. It's especially frustrating for young people who only work on one project.

"Only one third of the projects we study go through. If we go through schematics, the odds are fifty percent, and so forth. We're very product-oriented and want it to work for the client. It's important to get work built. That's how you get new work. We don't work for awards. Building models isn't enough.

"I personally enjoy competitions and getting up for them. It's like a race. You can go out on a limb creatively." But as far as the neophyte architect is concerned, May warns, "Working for buildings so big that they move slowly is not a good first job. A good first job is at a smaller firm with smaller projects that can move faster. Here you can get lost doing door detail for three months. On a huge building. It's better to do a house. And in terms of design, a house is as complicated." May also cautions the loner against getting involved in such a massively collaborative organization.

"It's not a good place for the monk who'll sit and draw. We need outgoing people who can take criticism well and not feel offended. It's not personal. You need a strong sense of self and assurance. And it's hard to sense that in an interview."

That being said, May considers himself "rather shy. Not entrepreneurial. I don't enjoy getting out there and the cold calls." Consequently, he praises the division of labor and calls KPF a "democratic firm with a participatory attitude." Still, this design partner says, "One of my problems is that I have no name identity. It's a problem since our clients don't carry all our names in their memory." May is the designer of One Logan Square in Philadelphia, the Hercules Inc. headquarters in Wilmington, Delaware, and 180 East Seventieth Street in Manhattan, an apartment building *New York Times* architecture critic Paul Goldberger called "among the finest postwar apartment buildings on the Upper East Side."

But Arthur May's great pleasure is drawing and painting. In architecture "you never get the feeling the job is done. In oil paintings, the paint stays wet. You can fix things."

Craig Nealy used to want to be a painter. His parents wanted him to be a doctor. "Architecture seemed like a compromise." He moved to New York after graduating from Cornell. At twenty-eight, Craig won a Fullbright Scholarship and designed furniture in Rome. He joined KPF in 1982. His title is now senior designer. "I've been at this twelve years," he tells me. "I'm really an architect.

"Everyone's smart. My staff all attended Columbia and Princeton and have graduate degrees. These people don't want to be told what to do. One thing that's astonishing is that we're free of internal politics. It's not competitive. How good a building is governs all decisions.

"I must like what I do; I don't get paid hourly." [Author's note: Don't say you weren't warned; as already indicated architecture is the least remunerative profession.] "I absolutely feel a part of the process. My job is fitting pieces together. If I didn't feel a personal sense of involvement, I wouldn't stay.

"I'm attracted by the paradox: on the one hand, you have to be a dreamer. On the other hand, you must know how the screw fits in the hole."

Alex Ward, an associate design partner, was one of those fourth-graders (they had them in every school) who knew he wanted to be an architect. "I started sketching buildings then, even plans. It was the idea of building buildings that excited me." He studied art history at Princeton and attended the Harvard Graduate School of Design (a common breeding ground for future employees of Kohn Pedersen Fox) before coming to the firm in 1979.

"The thrill of living in New York was palpable. There was something heady working for a hot new company full of optimism and positive aggression, and the thrill, after being a student for almost twenty years, of being a professional."

Ward took a sabbatical from KPF during academic year 1984–85 to teach part-time, first at the Rhode Island School of Design and then at Washington University in St. Louis and to pursue his own work. "I needed a break. I had spent three years flat out on P and G [Procter and Gamble's headquarters in Cincinnati] and before that Wacker Drive. I needed time to reflect and speculate. I turned down an associate partnership because I had already accepted the teaching job, and I wasn't sure I'd come back. Getting out of New York City was important. The pace of the Midwest was slower. I felt I could face KPF again." He received his promotion to associate partner, upon his return.

"My ultimate objective is to be on my own. The year away made me feel what I was able and unable to do on my own. I had no idea I could get jobs on my own, and I did some free-lance projects." Interestingly, despite the six- and seven-day work weeks, many architects at KPF, notably some on the associate partner level, have moonlighted on other projects—some on private residences, others on paintings, furniture design, and tableware. "Freelance isn't encouraged," Ward explains, "but no one raises a fuss if it's not a conflict. Working with a different [read: smaller] scale is healthy. Most people end up doing a job for friends or friends of friends. A big project wouldn't be possible because of time." If nothing else, these extra-curricular activities supply a sense of control and completion to architects who are otherwise engaged in a piece of a bigger project that could take a long time and possibly never see fruition.

"Getting a building built is a thrill—visiting the site and seeing it happen. Free-lance work is *so* important; a building can take two years. And it's hard to accept compliments. It's such a team effort."

As Kohn Pedersen Fox grows, Alex sees dramatic change. "The firm gets fragmented. There used to be nothing made by the office that I didn't like. Now there is. Projects are more formula than before. They end up being corporate, and that bothers me. We're trying to be a corporate firm that's also trend-setting. Few firms get this close. I still get excited about what I do. Or I wouldn't do it."

Ward's comments reflect the tension implicit in the situation of working for others while having personal ambitions that can't be abandoned or pursued individually. Having achieved associate partner status is a double-edge sword for some. It says you're ready to handle serious responsibility on your own, but you're still subordinate. And this at a firm which is loose, has a flat hierarchy, and tries more than most in the industry to give juniors a break. Alex relies on red wine and travel to decompress. "I no longer try to please just Bill [Pedersen]," he avers. "Now, if anything, I try to please myself, the client, and Gene, since he has to sell everything. I like to keep everyone happy."

Architecture students can get a taste of the real world through apprenticeships, or "preceptorships," as they're called at Rice University, one of the leading architecture schools at the undergraduate level. Steve Hamilton got to live in New York and work for Kohn Pedersen Fox during the academic year 1986–87. At Rice, architect students are not treated like mere liberal arts students. After the first four years and a portfolio of work, one must apply for two more years, one of which is spent on a work project. In Hamilton's class, the attrition rate was about average: It started with thirty, and by year six it had dwindled to thirteen students.

"There's a list of firms that accept Rice students. You apply to three and Rice matches you up." Hamilton moved to New York in August 1986. Somehow he and four classmates found that elusive "incredible, big apartment with manageable rent" that is unavailable to actual full-time New Yorkers. In this quasi-student, quasi-grown-up setting, he experienced his first taste of professional architecting.

"It would be pretty hard to screw up," Steve said. "At first we check shop drawings [the work of the construction people] and compare them to the architects' drawings." Then he started building models. "What's great about the firm is that people were willing to put their work down and spend time with me, talk about the firm, New York, etc."

Even Steve spent an average of sixty hours per week at work here. He got paid by the hour, so overtime was not too onerous. "It's incredible how much time people here spend in details and picky things. We're struggling over the height of rails in an elevator. I mean, who cares?" Since his apartment mates were preceptors at other architectural firms in the city, "you sometimes feel you work for those other firms. Some get to do more design, but they may be working too hard." He said his experience at KPF compared favorably to his friends' preceptorships.

"KPF has a more horizontal structure. I feel that I know Bill Pedersen—sort of—and he knows me by my first name. We're treated more equal. You can ask me to do something, but you can't tell me." Bob Cioppa was in charge of Steve and the three other students at KPF. Hamilton said they didn't have too much contact with Cioppa, but he did get steady feedback from his various bosses on his various projects.

"Preceptors sign a commitment to return [to Rice]." He said, "I'm dreading going back to school. It'll seem like a step back." If Hamilton decides after graduation that he wants to work for Kohn Pedersen Fox, he will have to reapply. "A woman two years ahead of me [at school] now works here. It's like a carrot dangling over me." Are these the people with whom he wants to surround himself in his first real job? Although Hamilton and his fellow students are going through an extended orientation, the rest of KPF are in the middle of more advanced stages of life. "It was frustrating at first because people didn't want to go to nightclubs at night, they wanted to go home to their families." Steve tried to go to the Museum of Modern Art every Thursday night and has made friends through a mysterious "underworld of architects in New York."

His final impression of the firm? "Everybody wears black here. I even bought black clothes," he says, *en noir*.

"This is a good fit for me. I'm not the lonely artist." So says Genevieve Gormley, whom I met just three months after she joined KPF. "It calls upon more than just your creative impulses and desires. You have to be in the real world, yet you can draw all day." After graduating from Barnard College in 1979 with a degree in anthropology, Genevieve seemed to try anything to avoid architecture. "My sister is an architect, and I felt I shouldn't be like her." Giving in, she sent a portfolio of etchings, freestyle drawings, and architectural drawings done during a postgraduate year taking "junior studio" at Columbia to Harvard's Graduate School of Design. (She also had to take calculus and physics, prerequisites for admission.)

After graduation in June 1986, Genevieve showed up at KPF when the firm was engaged in a competition. She was hired as a free-lance temp to do some drawings. "I did a good job. The guy I worked for spoke up for me. It was like a three-week-long interview. I didn't do the basic interview process. I had looked in the Yellow Pages, where there are zillions of architecture firms, but when you try to imagine yourself working for them, the list is small." The buzz at Harvard on KPF was good, and Gormley thought a firm this big would be "better for me." (As a newcomer, her decision to work here reflected a desire to work for a large firm. It's a good indicator of how fast KPF has grown.)

Her first real job is that of "junior designer, but I'm not sure of the title. Names depend on what you get paid. It's cloudy, but titles help when talking with clients and contractors." When she's off the premises these days, Genevieve tells people who ask what she does for a living, "I'm an architect. I would mention Kohn Pedersen Fox. People are familiar with the firm from *The New York Times* [where the firm gets a lot of ink]. I used to be hesitant about saying I was an architect since I'm not registered. [Author's note: She took the exams in June, 1988.] I used to qualify it by saying, 'I work as an architect,' but it's nice to say it."

While we're on the subject, it is necessary to be certified by the American Institute of Architects, the field's official professional society. Further, each state requires that architects, except those singularly involved in individual private residences, be registered and licensed, which means memorizing a lot of statutory codes. The whole process requires a master's degree [at Harvard, for example, a three-and-a-half-year proposition], an apprenticeship—three years at an AIA-certified firm—and a large batch of tests called the Architecture Licensing Exams, held every June. Approximately 30 percent of the test takers pass it the first time around. Those who fail must wait a year to take it again.

Is graduate school a good indicator of what life as an architect is like? "In school you don't realize how much money matters. KPF is a good firm because they can work with reduced budgets and still do good design. It's not the theoretical world of great design only. They're good at regrouping and fixing things. They make good decisions quickly. You get to see a collaboration. In school, the most important work is done by yourself, not by teams."

Gormley continues, "It is collegial. The people are wonderful and sharp. Deadlines are real. You're given work to do. You've got to get it done. You've got to do it well. You want to be sure people know you care. If your spirits are flagging, it helps to have people around. It's like playing tennis with someone who's better than you. I heard this place is competitive, but I haven't experienced it." It's not just a job, though. After work, Genevieve says, "I find myself thinking about work and the people around me, who they are, and how I fit in."

Given the loose nature of management at KPF, I ask Genevieve what it is like to be a new person on the team. Calling yourself an architect is one thing, but what does a junior architect actually *do* every day? "I didn't know where I'd start. It's not what I expected. I expected to be a total lackey, and that's not how I feel. I basically do know what I'm supposed to be doing every morning. It may be the same thing as what I'm doing in the afternoon. A phone call from Seattle [where she was involved in a thirty-story office building] may change things. I can do stuff right away. It says good things about my supervisor.

"I draw as soon as I arrive. Every drawing represents a change until it's too late. Maybe because a detail hasn't been drawn yet, or because the building needs to be seen from another view. Everyone has imput."

Loretta Ost arrived at Brandeis University as a premed, but after taking architectural history and loving it, she switched to fine arts. "Architecture was a compromise between wanting to do something creative but not having the guts to live the life of an artist," she says. Parental pressure was another factor. "Architecture I could sell to my parents. It seemed respectable and professional." So she went directly to Harvard's Graduate School of Design. "I was so directed, I went from high school to college to Harvard and never allowed myself a crisis or to find out if I were right or wrong. Working my tail off first year, I started questioning." Loretta began to consider the alternative of set design after her second year.

The following summer, she got a job working in a set design workshop which was involved in TV commercials. "It was totally different. I returned to Harvard thinking I'd do that, but I felt the tug of the old direction. Plus there was the fear of the unknown. I'm still unsure about the film world and if I could do set design. I know I can do architecture," she says softly.

Kohn Pedersen Fox felt right. "I had a sense that people were very well educated and professional. I thought they did good work and cared about quality." We met during Loretta's first month at the firm.

"There haven't been many surprises, except that the atmosphere is very schoollike: the dialogue that goes on, the way people express themselves verbally. People are very interested in ideas. At other places, architects resign themselves to not being able to do what they want. Here, you assume you can do anything."

Though a relatively free environment, KPF does impose a formal probation period on new employees, lasting three months. Loretta says "I don't feel secure yet; I'm on trial. People at my level are usually laid off [from most firms when competitions are lost or a big project is concluded]. I'll feel better after probation. I know I'm not indispensable. I try to maintain a sense of the whole process. If I weren't here, a few other people would work a few extra hours doing stuff they wouldn't want to do. I do a lot of junky work—technical modification, manual labor, shading. It's critical, but not fun. It's very meticulous, and you need concentration. A lot of my peers feel above it. They feel they shouldn't have to do 'shit work.' Especially because our peers are making $65,000 a year as lawyers.

"Now I try to leave at six P.M. And when I leave, I'm leaving a full office." [Author's note: Ost passed probation and now leaves the office at 7 P.M.]

Will KPF accept just any assignment? Bill Louie, the third design partner, says, "I would suggest a big money job that didn't contribute to our reputation, we'd turn down." Another truant from Warnecke's office, he's proud of all his buildings. "They're like children." But Louie et al. make up only one side of the family tree. Clients make up the other branches. "For a lot of them, this may be the only building they'll ever build."

Letting go of ownership is sometimes a tough thing to do. It's like sending your kids away to camp or school for the very first time. "Buildings are totally derived from one person, and then the collaboration begins." Within the office, and with the client, contractor, and builder. "Compromises are needed. How much can we push esthetics and meet economic needs?" Louie and his colleagues say over again that Kohn Pedersen Fox's clients are a braver lot than most. It is thought that a conservative patron who wants a straitlaced building wouldn't approach KPF in the first place. One of the phrases one hears around the offices is, "We've gotten the client to love it."

Shelly Fox concedes, "We've been able to do a lot of interesting work. We've been allowed to build and have our clients' appreciation." And the firm has grown beyond his wildest dreams. "We said, 'Gee, when we grow to seventy-five people we'll be big!' We were seventy-five in five years. We used to have annual picnics at my house in Connecticut, but when we reached a hundred people, we had to stop. We've grown every year, but without a quota or a conscious goal.

"We're talking about opening other offices elsewhere [maybe London, maybe Los Angeles], to compete in new marketplaces and to allow the entrepreneur [within] to shine. But how do you control your design?" Furthermore, as it is, projects have been undertaken despite occasional objections or dissent among the partners. Fox describes them as "philosophical differences—is it the right building for the place?" And since KPF's reputation is definitely tops for office buildings, the work can sometimes get repetitive. It is the collective dream of the partnership to get a commission for a museum (the embodiment of architecture as historic object), as well as more special use buildings—airports, schools, theaters, hospitals, etc.

Shelly thinks the reasons for KPF's success stem from "good commissions; people like us" and the well-defined checks and balances. He is rarely a designer, but rather the master administrator. "I'm managing partner in terms of money, contracts, and general administration, and I also have eight projects. Unless you're a design partner, you can't design that much if you're a principal. I think I'm able to not be an architect. Yet I personally visualize in 3-D. Even in my dreams."

Although Fox got his first New York job through his wife—she was the dental hygienist of Mrs. Louis Kahn, and he found work at Kahn & Jacobs—the unending commitment to architecture can be quite a burden to the spouse of an architect. "I didn't design our house; I found one. It saved our marriage," Shelly says wryly.

Nonarchitects can also find work at Kohn Pedersen Fox, primarily as accountants (five full time at KPF), and in marketing. Carol McCutchen, the director of new business development, says a background in design is not a prerequisite for marketing and promotion, but it can't hurt. (She and Gail LaCava in marketing are blessed with the appropriate backgrounds.) "Writing and communicating skills help, too." The secretarial and support staff numbers 160 people.

A few final notes. Although there's some disagreement as to whether the KPF culture is a competitive one there's no question that the young architect gets a broader opportunity to test his or her talents here than might be true at other top firms. Will Kohn Pedersen Fox get a museum? Will it open new offices in other cities? Will it create a deeper internal structure? Will it win next year's Architect League softball championship? Stay tuned. The next decade will be critical for the firm as it loses its new-kid-on-the-block status and becomes deeply entrenched in the heavy hitter league.

KORN/FERRY
INTERNATIONAL

HISTORY & OPERATIONS

Korn/Ferry International, the world's largest executive search firm—whose practitioners are familiarly known as "headhunters"—was started in 1969 in Los Angeles by two young partners from Big Eight accounting firm Peat, Marwick, Mitchell & Co. Lester Korn, a California native, attended UCLA, where he earned a BS with honors in 1959 and an MBA in 1960. In 1961, after an aborted stint of working toward a Ph.D. at Harvard Business School, Korn returned to Los Angeles, joined Peat, Marwick as a management consultant, and went on to run the firm's new West Coast executive search division. Dick Ferry grew up in Ohio, received an accounting degree with honors from Kent State University in 1959, and went to work as a staff accountant for Big Eight firm Haskens & Sells. He moved to Phoenix a year later to work as a controller for a real estate developer and left in 1965 to start a management consulting firm with several partners. Unhappy with the arrangement, he left shortly thereafter and was recruited to work for Peat, Marwick in Los Angeles. Ferry started out as a consultant, moved to the firm's search division for a year, and eventually took over as its manager when Korn assumed wider responsibilities.

Korn and Ferry, who'd met some years earlier in Phoenix, became good friends at Peat, Marwick. Both were smart and extremely driven, and both made partner within five years of joining the firm. (Korn, at thirty, was the youngest partner in the firm's history, and Ferry, at thirty-two, was also exceptionally young for that designation.) Together they built up Peat, Marwick's executive search division to the point where it was the largest single headhunting practice in Los Angeles, with twenty consultants and approximately $2 million in revenues. Despite their success, they were not content to work within the bureaucratic confines of a large firm, and in 1969 they put up $5,000 apiece and left to form a private practice.

Though Korn/Ferry Enterprises (soon changed to Korn/Ferry International) was originally conceived to offer a range of personnel consulting services, the partners quickly narrowed their focus to headhunting, the area they knew best. Their success was immediate, remarkable, and sustained. They worked long hours, landed some assignments for major corporations, and within five months of opening, they'd pulled in close to $300,000 in billings.

In the firm's early days, several key executive search consultants left Peat, Marwick to join Korn/Ferry, weakening Peat, Marwick's L.A. division and thus lessening Korn/Ferry's competition. The partners soon extended their reach beyond the West Coast, and within three years they employed forty-two professionals in New York, San Marino (California), Houston, Atlanta, Chicago, and San Francisco. In 1972 annual billings reached $1.8 million, and in the firm's first three years of operation, its earnings just about doubled each year.

In 1972 the partners took the firm public—a move unprecedented in the industry—selling a little more than a quarter of the practice to outsiders. In the same year, they expanded their practice abroad by merging with the London headhunting firm G. K. Dickenson Ltd. In 1974, with the firm's stock prices falling (although revenues and earnings had continued to increase), the (then twenty-three) partners bought back their shares and took the firm private again. Meanwhile, they continued to open more offices, both in the United States and overseas. By 1979, only ten years after opening its doors, Korn/Ferry International had become the biggest executive search firm in the world.

From the organization's outset, the aggressively ambitious partners—who hired professionals from diverse ethnic and educational backgrounds—were resented as interlopers in a field formerly dominated by restrained East Coast WASPs, most of whom were retired or fired executives. (In the mid-seventies, Korn/Ferry was denied membership in the industry's trade association, the Association of Executive Recruiting Consultants.) Nonetheless, its impact on the staid field was tangible. Korn/Ferry introduced a number of innovations that facilitated its growth and virtually transformed the headhunting industry. First, it created specialized areas of expertise, which focus on recruiting in particular industries and are generally headed by professionals formerly employed in those industries. Second, it developed a computerized data base that enables its professionals all over the world to obtain information on potential search candidates quickly and easily. And finally, it built a global network that encompasses the major financial centers in the world and has far surpassed its competitors' reach. Also, following Korn's lead, the firm has marketed itself assiduously. From its early days, Korn/Ferry employed public relations firms to build its image and keep its name in the press. As part of that effort, it publishes numerous surveys on various aspects of executive demographics, including its *National Index of Executive Vacancies,* a regularly published survey that the firm claims is a general indicator of the economic climate. As a result of the firm's high profile, when companies need to hire a headhunting firm, often the first name they think of—much to its competitors' consternation—is Korn/Ferry.

Another factor contributing to Korn/Ferry's success—mostly orchestrated by Ferry—is that, unlike other executive search firms, which are generally loosely run organizations, this practice is structured like a formal business, requiring consultants to fill out detailed time sheets and establishing an efficient and clearly delineated hierarchy: researchers, research directors, associates, senior associates, managing associates, vice-presidents, revenue center vice-presidents, specialty practice managers, office managers, managing directors, and senior officers. (Everyone who has reached the level of vice-president is a partner, though they're not all equal partners.) The research staff keeps track of the candidate and client files and feeds information to the associates at the next level. Associates contact potential candidates, conduct preliminary interviews, and narrow the search to several final cadidates. The top-level managers—the ones who generate business and the only ones who have contact with the client companies—interview all final candidates before presenting them to a client. The firm, which generally won't conduct a search for a position that pays less than $75,000, collects fees equal to roughly a third of a candidate's first-year salary. The majority of the search positions pay $100,000 and up.

Today Korn/Ferry employs a staff of more than three hundred professionals in thirty-seven offices located in sixteen countries. Billings, which have increased at an average annual rate of 30 percent since the firm was founded, reached $66.1 million in 1987, approximately one third of which was generated abroad. The firm's client list now numbers 1,250 companies, and 70 percent of Korn/Ferry's business each year comes from clients for whom they have completed searches in the past. The firm's practice includes the following specialty divisions: Financial Services (the largest), High Technology, Energy, Fashion/Retail, Real Estate, Hospitality/Leisure, Entertainment, Health Care, Government/Not-for-Profit/Education, and Board Services.

In July 1987 Lester Korn was recruited away from Korn/Ferry by the Reagan White House for the temporary position of U.S. representative to the Economic and Social Council of the United Nations. (He's taken a leave of absence for the position.) The council coordinates social, economic, and cultural activities, and Korn's role there is to bring the United Nations' spending more into line with U.S. policy goals. The new job pays Korn about one tenth of his most recent salary and bonus, which he reported at $799,751 for the fiscal year ending in April 1987. After learning that he had been picked from five or six final candidates, Korn remarked, "It was a classic search."

(Information provided by Stephanie Rosenfeld and Lucie Adam, company spokespersons.)

REVENUES: $66.1 million in fiscal 1987.

OFFICES: Thirty-seven offices worldwide in sixteen U.S. cities: New York, Los Angeles (two offices), Atlanta, Boston, Chicago, Cleveland, Dallas, Denver, Houston, Minneapolis, Newport Beach (California), Palo Alto (California), San Francisco, Seattle, Stamford (Connecticut), and Washington, D.C.; and twenty foreign cities: Amsterdam, Brussels, Caracas, Frankfurt, Geneva, Guadalajara, Hong Kong, Kuala Lumpur, London, Madrid, Melbourne, Mexico City, Monterrey (Mexico), Paris, São Paulo, Singapore, Sydney, Tokyo, Toronto, and Zurich.

NUMBER OF EMPLOYEES: 509 worldwide: 308 domestic, and 201 international. Partners—112 total (72 domestic and 40 international), associates—111 total (76 domestic and 35 international), researchers—57 total (23 domestic and 34 international), support staff—201 total (116 domestic and 85 international), corporate professionals (data processors and corporate communications people)—28 total (21 domestic and 7 international).

AVERAGE AGE OF EMPLOYEES: Forty-two.

TURNOVER: Information not available.

RECRUITMENT: None.

NUMBER OF NEW HIRES PER YEAR: Forty.

RANGE OF STARTING SALARIES: For professionals, $25,000–$35,000.

POLICY FOR RAISES: Employees are reviewed annually, and raises are on the basis of "quantitative and qualitative performance measures."

TRAINING PROGRAMS: The firm has a formal two-day orientation program, conducted at corporate headquarters, for all new professional employees. Korn/Ferry also offers training seminars for professionals at later points in their careers.

BENEFITS: Life, medical, and dental insurance, long-term disability insurance, travel accident insurance, a retirement plan, and a 401(k) plan.

VACATION: "Ten to fifteen days of vacation, depending on your position," plus nine regular paid holidays per year.

ADDITIONAL PERKS: "Can't think of any."

BONUSES: All professionals are eligible, on the basis of "quantitative and qualitative performance measures."

ANNUAL PARTY: Each office is separate, but most have a Christmas party. In New York, the Christmas party is generally held at a private club. It includes drinks, dinner, and dancing for employees and their spouses or guests. The party is dressy, but not black-tie. Small party favors are generally handed out to all in attendance.

AVERAGE WORKDAY: The average workday for professionals is ten hours, which includes breakfasts and dinners with clients. For support staff and corporate professionals, the workday is seven and a half hours.

DRESS CODE: "Business dress, basically."

SOCIAL ATMOSPHERE: "I think that we spend such long hours that sometimes our business spills over into the social, but I don't know that people socialize all that much. It's hard to describe. When they're socializing, it's more like business. The hours are long, and people might eat dinner together, but I suspect that after that people want to go home. We spend a lot of time together working."

HEADQUARTERS: "We really have two coporate headquarters." Corporate and administrative offices are located on two floors in one building in Century City in Los Angeles, and executive offices are located on one floor in one building in midtown Manhattan.

CHARITABLE CONTRIBUTIONS: The firm will not disclose specific amounts of donations. It is "very involved" with the United Way on both the corporate and employee contribution basis. The bulk of Korn/Ferry's charitable donations go to health and medical organizations, and to higher education. To a lesser degree, the company is also involved in community cultural organizations.

INTERESTED APPLICANTS CAN SEND RÉSUMÉS TO:
Korn/Ferry International
Executive Office
237 Park Avenue

New York, NY 10017
(212) 687-1834

OR

Korn/Ferry International
Corporate Offices
1800 Century Park East
Los Angeles, CA 90067
(213) 879-1834

Korn/Ferry International is the country's largest executive recruiting firm. It is also the youngest major player in the industry and has consequently provoked ire and jealousy in the field. (Companies with long histories in the search business talk about the white shoe old boy network. While Korn/Ferry has its share of pedigreed Ivy Leaguers, it is made up of scrappier, more heterogeneous stock, which to some of its rivals constitutes a flagrant disrespect for the WASPy search culture.) Started in Los Angeles in 1969 by Lester Korn and Dick Ferry, the two youngest full partners at Big Eight accounting firm Peat, Marwick, Mitchell & Co., talk of Korn/Ferry still shockingly hovers around Korn's Jewishness, as if that were an affront to the field he has pursued so aggressively. [Author's note: You've never read or heard so many Faginesque or Shylockesque adjectives in your life as when competitors and even certain segments of the press talk about Korn and his empire.]

Search is a service business whose commodity is people. Its practitioners must learn about their clients—corporations, not-for-profit institutions, boards of directors—and their cultures before embarking on their matchmaking efforts. When asked to describe the culture of Korn/Ferry in its thirty-seven offices around the world, professionals find it easier to discuss the cultures of their clients. They identify so closely with them that they have generally become specialists.

There is a definite personality here, though it's a bit hard to pinpoint, since there is not a single "Korn/Ferry way" to do a job or a single point of view that is shared by all. Yet all meetings begin with a ritual handing out of business cards, an action both polite and businesslike. "We're very aggressive. Very mixed. Everyone doesn't look like everyone else. People come from all walks of life." Put another way, "We've got people who graduated from colleges we've never heard of. We're more a bunch of street fighters here."

Search is not a first job, and many professionals first encountered Korn/Ferry when they were objects of searches themselves. The work force here thus reflects who they were before they joined the firm, an identity they don't have to shed.

A specialist in banking looks and thinks like a banker. He used to be a banker. A retailing expert looks like a retailer—because he once was one. He has stacks of *Women's Wear Daily* on his desk. Similarly, the entertainment department could easily blend into a talent agency or studio. With signed pictures of celebrities on the walls and copies of *Variety* and *The Hollywood Reporter* lying around; only the outside corridor is the tip-off that the rest of the company will feel different.

The client is the company in need of a new executive, not the person looking for work. (Besides, the company, not the job seeker, pays Korn/Ferry's fees.) The search process begins with visits to the client's headquarters and meetings with the prospective employer. "I'm getting a tone about the place," Ann Kern explains. "Do people address each other as 'Mr. and 'Mrs.'? Is it relaxed? Buttoned-down? Are desks compatible with mine?" Not every search will require extensive sniffing around, since Korn/Ferry has a lot of repeat business. Most searches—regardless of familiarity with the institution—last about three months.

"People like people like themselves," Ann Kern, a partner, says. Often that's all a professional has to go on, especially in a start-up company that hasn't yet figured out its culture. A former fund-raiser at NYU, she is Korn/Ferry's primary source for not-for-profit clients on the East Coast. A "preliminary grapevine check" precedes an in-person meeting. Next, a phone conversation will determine "how bright someone seems. Is he articulate? Is he warm or cold? We want to know a lot about a person before they come in."

Nevertheless, candidates can be and are dismissed for "strange reasons." David Smith, one of Korn/Ferry's thirteen senior officers, recalls the case of the "clicking teeth. A finalist for an executive position's teeth clicked. The client was put off." Furthermore, if the client is, say, a bank in a small town, the candidate's wife must be prepared to participate in the search process" as she is married to a man who would be a public figure.

It should be pointed out that most candidates for a position are not shopping around for new jobs, at least not openly. They get a call out of the blue from a headhunter, and most of them are surprisingly receptive. Dave Smith says, "The majority of executives have some degree of unhappiness and think it'll be better elsewhere. They're not recognized where they are, et cetera. It's not the money. So when somebody like me calls them, they listen. Recruiters have to be dazzling over the phone, create interest over the phone." This sounds much easier than it is, since the recruiter may *not* reveal the identity of his client.

But back to the idea that "it's not the money." "We will not conduct a search for compensation of under $75,000 a year," a professional says. "We say you should get at least thirty percent compensation upgrade. The guts of the business is middle management and up, about $100,000." In exchange, Korn/Ferry takes one third of the cash compensation of the new executive's first-year salary. Salaries tend to be higher in New York ("where life is tough") and Los Angeles, where life is expensive. "The career opportunity will sell the job more than the dollar."

Searches are increasingly hard to accomplish since the advent of the two-career couple. "Today it's a family decision. Even the five-year-old gets a vote. People don't want to move." [Author's note: It should be pointed out that not all searches entail a geographical move.] Everyone at Korn/Ferry concurs. Kern maintains the hardest party to persuade is the parent of a teenager. (Between the trauma of adolescence and the need for a steady high school record and recommendations for the college-bound, the likelihood of a geographical move by a family with high school students is small.) Perhaps there is consolation in that at senior levels (candidates likely to have children that age), "there are very few working spouses."

Lester Korn called Bob Rollo in as a candidate for a search. Rolla had worked his way up in a "hotshot regional" bank on the lending side and then as president of a small business computer company, he was hired by Korn as a partner for one of the two Los Angeles offices. A native of southern California, Rollo earned his MBA at USC and spent four years in the Navy. After seven years at Korn/Ferry, he declares, "Our business looks a lot more exciting or romantic from the outside." In reality, "this is a very disciplined kind of business. You make a lot of calls during the day, and a lot of them are nonproductive. An outstanding candidate won't make a change. Or a candidate with a great reputation doesn't have it. The best people are not necessarily the best candidates. 'Fit' is the key."

Professionals at Korn/Ferry frequently lament the (irrational) idealism of their clients. "Clients don't know how to ask for what they want," one says. "They're defining Superman. We get four- and five-page descriptions" detailing the virtues they seek. "It's like matrimony."

A standard search will start with eighty possible candidates, who are quickly winnowed down to ten, then two or three. "What I admire," says Ann Kern, "is a CEO who knows himself but is effective and warm and conveys an interest—whether it's real or not—in the person they're talking to." Rollo continues, "Our best partners are the ones who present the candidates objectively and put their minds in the clients' position." Even if a headhunter has strong opinions about the best person with the best fit, he or she should not indicate a preference, although the client will often say, " 'But who do *you* like best?' You can make recommendations [as opposed to making a real choice]. Often the person who's selected was the person I thought." It's a quiet satisfaction.

"The thrill of the hunt motivates me in this business," Rollo explains. "Not the kill. I'm a fisherman. I throw back into the water. Some guys pop champagne open after a search; I'm filled with remorse. I get very disappointed when that level of intensity is over."

At forty-one, Rollo's title is managing director. He evaluates his career so far: "I'm the youngest senior partner by a ways. Most are fifty or older. They've had another career. Most of them should say this is the best thing to happen to them. Maybe I should, too. This is a great business, pays well, and I've met great people. But I'm forty-one. Anyone who's good in business shouldn't eliminate themselves."

Another fisherman, Lee Van Leeuwen, has draped a wall of his Century City (Los Angeles) office with a huge sailfish—his wife didn't want it at home—as well as a bust of John Wayne. Born in Amarillo, Texas, and with a bachelor's degree in psychology from UCLA, Van Leeuwen says, "I never took a single business course in my life. I'm proud of that." While participating in a search in 1967, Lee got drafted into the search business. "That's how we get ninety percent of our people. An executive of any consequence will send his résumé to Korn/Ferry, and we're capturing them. I'm surprised that in the last three or four years people are actively looking for executive search positions. It never used to be that way. The sizzle is the lure. The sizzle from the outside is, we know who's vulnerable, we know who's on the outs, who's on the way up. We're corporate gynecologists." Before, search was traditionally a last job, one that relied on the expertise of industry veterans or, in Van Leeuwen's words, "the place for elephants to die."

Van Leeuwen joined Korn/Ferry six months after its doors were opened. It was 1970, and Korn, Ferry, five consultants, and two secretaries were cramped into one office. "I remember my first day. I showed up at 7:15 to impress people. I'd been given a key. I heard typewriters going. I walked in, and everyone else was already there. I said to myself, 'Holy shit!' I saw what I was getting into."

Van Leeuwen's experience was in real estate, still his area of focus. A managing vice-president, he runs the National Real Estate Division. (In fact, Lee left Korn/Ferry in 1973 to open his own real estate company with another partner from the firm. "I was thirty-three years old, cocky and naive. We thought the real estate clients were ours, not Korn's and Ferry's. We walked right into the real estate recession of 1974–75 and spent *everything*. I had to go to the bank every first and fifteenth of the month to deduct our payroll from my savings account. It was painful. I was down to my car and house." The two returned to Korn/Ferry in 1975.)

"Korn/Ferry was a fast start-up company in an industry that was going nowhere. Lester Korn did the unheard-of—he retained public relations counsel [Gershon Kekst, see p. 479] [Author's note: Korn/Ferry confirmed this information. It is unlikely that Kekst and Company —with its concern for client confidentiality would have revealed this.] which shocked people. By 1973 our name was recognized by *The Wall Street Journal* and *Business Week*. No search firm has been in these waters. We couldn't look at how another firm behaved when they did sixty million dollars of business.

"It's sinful how we've monopolized Los Angeles." Five years later, Korn/Ferry "cracked

New York." One secret of its success is the firm's choice of location. "We were only located in the right buildings with the right clients. Take this building, for example"—a standard-issue office building, though set in Century City (adjacent to Beverly Hills), a prestigious business neighborhood. "We have O'Melvenney [& Myers, a top law firm] and Goldman Sachs here." Even before Korn/Ferry was the biggest firm in its industry, "we mimicked being biggest. Les had us get involved in community and philanthropic activities." Now that the organization has grown to 509 people, "the company is run the same way. Les arrives early each day to see who called whom on the phone message lists."

Van Leeuwen happily points to "Les Korn's original genius: He spotted the potential for the industry, he utilized public relations, and he and Ferry were CPAs and businessmen. We had financial strength, which allowed us to expand when others contracted." As far as his troops are concerned, "like anything else, it's just hard work. You see Korn getting angrier and angrier at people who leave early."

The key to the firm's growth is finding new clients. "We say we donate our management time here. Our business is to bring in business. [Indeed, Korn/Ferry has instituted an incentive called a 'Contact and Development Credit,' a reward for bringing in new clients. Needless to say, one's credits are carefully tallied, especially at bonus time.] Our primary mission is to find out if someone's qualified *and* interested. We have to make fifty calls to find one [candidate]. We have to assess the chemistry. That's an art, not a science. The magic is in listening. It's so seductive to get a call from a Korn/Ferry headhunter. You can't help it. We've got to force both parties to deal with reality."

Even after the search has been conducted and the candidate has started work, Korn/Ferry's challenge may not be over. If the first six months don't prove comfortable, the firm must engage in a new search without fee. "You have to be honest; these vaccinations have to take. It's part of our ongoing involvement."

Vice-President Virgil Baldi has always worked in search. After graduating from the University of Pennsylvania Law School, he went to Europe, where he met his American-born wife, and he became the head of personnel for industrial companies in Spain and Liberia. He has been with Korn/Ferry for six years. Having worked in industries as diverse as semiconductors and cosmetics, he says, "I have no specialty, but they've recently made me the focal point for the board of directors practice." He may have about a dozen searches to direct simultaneously, but "I divide my time according to who's breathing down my back the hottest. I'm easily satisfied. I don't try to get more accounts—as I should." Everyone's contribution to profit is recorded. "Numbers are published here. You know who's doing well and who isn't. There is competition here, but I have compensation and security.

"I'm fairly independent," he says languidly, "and I don't feel imposed upon here. I feel provided for. I enjoy the business. I would enjoy it anywhere if I were left alone." Despite his stated preference for solitude, Baldi has selected a "people-intensive business." [Author's note: Forgive this terminology. I'm trying to compensate for not having gone to business school.] He offers, "Each arc in the process is delightful; knowing a little bit about all businesses, not in a lot of depth. If you put someone into a company, you have a stake in the company as long as they're there."

You can see Bob Nesbitt's allegiance to the industry that spawned him, retailing. A veteran of Genesco and Levi Strauss (see p. 624, and a former instructor at the NYU Graduate School of Business, he's been with Korn/Ferry for nine years.

"I finally came to the realization I wasn't a merchant prince," Nesbitt, perhaps the most stylishly attired Partner—reflecting the industry to which he ministers—says. "I loved the field, but not like Joe Brooks [CEO of Lord & Taylor] or Marvin Traub [CEO of Bloomingdale's]. I'm not a captain of industry. I got tired of corporate hockey. It wasn't in my blood.

But I felt the field had an aspect I could be great in. Search was a natural. I had done something like it, but unofficially." Now a managing vice-president, Nesbitt remembers hearing things like, "Bob, you know everybody, who should we get?"

His arrival at Korn/Ferry was notable, since "today we're still the only top-tier firm to do retailing." At business schools, retailing is still treated like a poor relative to big business. "Korn/Ferry is a great organization. I'm not just saying that because I work here. The guys at the top are good leaders. They're very entrepreneurial, and so are we. We understand the industry. I'm usually looking for someone I once was."

This chapter is perhaps a bit misleading, since it features partners with industry specialties. In fact, most of Korn/Ferry's professionals are generalists and feel it's very important to stress that point. What gets a tad confusing is how one protects his or her territory from poachers. As a rule, clients prefer dealing with one principal to a confederation of headhunters. John Sullivan, a partner in the downtown Los Angeles office, explains. "For a business development call I fill out a form that says I called on *X* at *Y*." This information is entered into a computer, printouts of which are distributed corporatewide. Professionals are urged to consult with one another to defray potential conflicts. It usually works. "I don't think of search as a team sport. We'll hear that it is, but I've never been able to buy that intellectually. Each partner has to be able to define his practice." As to the turf conflicts, "it's not verbalized. My most effective competitors are within the firm. We call them partners, but really they're competitors." No one seems too concerned with external competition. Dave Smith in New York states, "We're probably forty percent larger than number two and twice as large as number three. Bob Rollo says, "Our competition are clients who don't do searches. Other firms compete against *us*."

Sullivan adds that in another maverick move, Korn/Ferry hired McKinsey & Company to consult. "Just the fact that managment called them in! We're run more like a business. We adopted their recommendations." One of them was for each managing vice-president to project the annual output for his or her office or specialty.

John, a Georgia native, is a vice-president and Managing Director in the downtown L.A. office. After winning a Navy ROTC scholarship to Duke and serving three years after graduation, he got a job at the company of his dreams, IBM. He was warned against accepting a job there, but "it was the only big company I'd wanted to get into, and it was a hard job to get. I respected my peers, and that made me work better. IBM was almost a religion to me." After twelve years he recognized that "I had a job I always wanted but didn't have freedom to do anything. Decision making was rising to the top. The bureaucracy was getting bigger. Like most men my age, I had wanted to become the president of IBM." Leaving his corporate home was traumatic. Over breakfast Sullivan confesses, "The last time I cried was when I left IBM."

His specialty is still in high technology. He continues to read the trade press, anticipating the arrival of his copy of *Electronic News* every Monday, but whereas "I used to have to know bits and bytes and nanoseconds, et cetera, which was sometimes drudgery, now my satisfaction comes from people."

Christine Houston's field is a little different from most search professionals at Korn/Ferry. While living in Tokyo for six years (initially to accommodate her banker husband's career), she established a small search business there "because it was hard for foreign women to find work in Japan." It grew by referrals until she reached the point where "I had achieved all I could there. Korn/Ferry called me in Tokyo and wanted to hire me there." She demurred, as she was in the process of getting divorced, but later joined the firm's New York office to conduct searches for Japanese businesses located in this country. She finds being a woman an advantage in her practice.

Her work cuts across all disciplines. According to Houston, "Search is about as close to owning your own business," without taking those kinds of start-up risks. "This is entrepreneurial. If you don't produce, you're out. We each keep our own counsel and go after our own business. My area overlaps with everyone but has an expertise others don't have. I never go into existing accounts.

"This job requires you to juggle a lot at once. I can be working on as many as nine searches at once, although it's usually four or five. It makes me more efficient. There's not a lot of paperwork." But there is never any time when Christine is "off." "I'm like a real estate agent," she says with a laugh. She compares the inadvertent meeting of a new prospect with a broker's noticing a new property: " 'Nice house! Interested in selling?' I've worked in other jobs where all you had to do was breathe; not here. No other job appeals to me as much as what I do here. Very few people get to create what they do."

With her undergraduate degree in economics (plus a smattering of Asian studies) from Hofstra University, she chose retailing, specifically at Bloomingdale's, rather than following her advisers' insistence that she go into banking or insurance ("Boring"). Promoted to manager of the gourmet foods department, she gained forty pounds. "I didn't know what I wanted to do until I reached my late twenties, early thirties." Today she is a slim vice-president.

Dave Smith talks of the emerging respectability of search. "We've come of age. The image has changed from personnel. We're considered professionals now." As a bonus, he offers this advice to potential job seekers. "If you want to look good, stay at your job for two years, so you have a good reason to leave. Don't be a job jumper.

MTV:
MUSIC
TELEVISION

HISTORY & OPERATIONS

MTV started out as an innovative programming idea that Warner Amex Satellite Entertainment Company—the joint venture formed by Warner Brothers and American Express to develop cable television services—began researching in December 1980. [They had already launched the Movie Channel, the first twenty-four-hour all-movie network in 1979.] Cable systems, which promised a forum for new kinds of programming not available on the networks, had begun to spring up all over the country. The way for a new nonsubscription channel to obtain representation on a system as well as advertiser support was to develop programming targeted at an audience group advertisers wanted to reach. MTV's originators designed their network to appeal to the generation of twelve-to-thirty-four-year-olds who had been weaned on television and rock 'n' roll. Conceived as a twenty-four-hour channel hosted by VJs—"video jockeys," the video counterparts of DJs—broadcast in stereo and programmed with short rock video clips, MTV was also relatively cheap and easy to produce. Many rock groups were already making promotional videos, and MTV could exploit the existing material, which it got gratis, while providing exposure for the bands.

MTV was more or less a group idea, though must of the credit goes to John A. Schneider, the company's president and CEO, who supported the concept from the beginning, and Robert Pittman (see p. 527), an award-winning radio and television programmer in his late twenties, who designed the channel's glitzy, fast-paced, youth-oriented look. Despite the retrospective soundness of the concept, MTV initially proved difficult to sell. Warner Amex's board of directors remained skeptical about its actual appeal, and record company executives, from whom Pittman sought a commitment to supply the channel with free clips, were reluctant to provide expensive videos that hadn't yet been proven to be record sellers. Once these objections had been surmounted, the key cable systems of New York and Los Angeles refused to carry the channel.

MTV was nonetheless launched on August 1, 1981, at 12:01 A.M. (Eastern Time) to 2.5 million homes. With an initial strong showing in cities such as Tulsa and Des Moines, a Manhattan cable system offered to carry the network for several hours a day. But MTV executives, who felt that the key to the channel's success was its around-the-clock availability, took an all-or-nothing stance. In 1982 the channel designed a series of commercials featuring rock stars such as Mick Jagger and Pete Townshend, who urged viewers to "demand their MTV." The campaign worked. Cable operators were inundated with calls from young viewers, and by the end of the year, MTV was adding an average of 750,000 new homes to its viewership each month.

Record company executives began to realize the value of MTV as a promotional vehicle when sales of particular records skyrocketed in areas of the country where they hadn't even received radio play. When it was revealed that MTV had been airing videos of the songs, the record companies responded by producing more and better videos. Products such as Levi's, Atari, and Pepsi-Cola began marketing to the channel's built-in teenage audience, which had previously been difficult for them to isolate. Some began to design advertisements exclusively for MTV which incorporated the channel's style.

By mid-1983, MTV had a projected audience of 13.4 million, 83 percent of them between the ages of twelve and thirty-four. A Nielsen poll of twelve- to thirty-four-year-olds found that the majority claimed their record purchases had been influenced by the channel and that 88 percent said they received their first exposure to new music via MTV. Events bore out the poll's findings. Previously unknown groups and performers—including Duran Duran, Cyndi Lauper, Bon Jovi, and Madonna—became stars after their videos appeared on MTV.

MTV changed the way record labels market performers, not to mention the way performers market themselves. As they tried to outdo one another in visual sophistication, the quality of the videos improved. When top Hollywood directors, including John Landis and Brian De Palma, tried their hand at making them, videos were elevated to the stature of an art form. (And the price of producing videos climbed, from an average of $25,000 to $45,000 in 1983, to between $50,000 and $250,000 today). MTV's style also infused the popular culture, spawning movies (e.g., *Flashdance*), television programs (e.g., *Miami Vice,* whose original concept was *MTV Cops*), and fashion trends (e.g., Madonna's "virginal" look).

In 1985 a group of MTV executives including Robert Pittman failed in its attempt to take the channel private in a leveraged buyout. That year, Viacom International, an owner of television and radio stations and a distributor of television programming, bought MTV. In 1986, with ratings falling and the excitement of the network waning, Pittman, who had been appointed president and CEO in 1985, resigned to start his own media company. In 1987, Sumner H. Redstone, the chairman of National Amusements Inc., bought Viacom and became the new owner of the MTV networks, which included MTV: Music Television; VH-1/Video Hits One, another twenty-four-hour-a-day video service with a softer sound, aimed at an older audience; Nickelodeon and Nick-at-Nite, programming for children and preteens.

MTV formed the first of its foreign ventures in 1984 with Japanese television, which now licenses fourteen hours of MTV programming per week. In April 1987 the company launched MTV Australia, which airs twelve hours a week on Network 9. And on August 1, 1987, it launched MTV Europe, a twenty-four-hour cable service that emanates from London and reaches thirteen European countries. The programming for foreign countries is done in the MTV style and is made up of a mix of American videos and those of particular interest in the countries that receive the service. MTV is currently exploring additional foreign ventures, including one in South America with a projected launch date of late 1988 or early 1989.

Today, under the leadership of Tom Freston, who became president upon Pittman's departure, MTV employs approximately 650 people and reaches more than forty million cable homes. Though revenues have continued to rise (from a reported $71 million in 1984 to $111 million in 1986) [Author's note: The company will neither comfirm nor update these figures, which were gleaned from *Time* magazine (June 29, 1987).] the ratings haven't picked up much since they slipped in 1985. (MTV executives dispute the Nielson ratings, claiming that the sample underrepresents males between the ages of twelve and twenty-four, a significant portion of the channel's audience.) Nonetheless, MTV still has a strong impact on the music industry.

In an attempt to enliven MTV's format—critics claim that the great majority of videos have become repetitive and old hat—and boost ratings, the channel's programming has been diversified to include guest VJs (celebrities with a hip appeal), more live concerts, more special presentations and location events, reruns of sitcoms (such as *The Monkees*) and comedy programs (i.e., *Monty Python's Flying Circus*) a weekly rock and fashion news program, interviews with performers, rock documentaries, a game show called *Remote Control* (in which college-aged contestants win prizes based on their knowledge of pop culture trivia), the annual MTV Music Video Awards, and increasingly lavish promotional events. Two of the more sensational MTV contests were: MTV/Madonna's Make My Video Contest, in which viewers were asked to produce the "official American video" for Madonna's single "True Blue." The winners received a $25,000 director's fee from Madonna, and their video was put into rotation on MTV. (They were subsequently offered a $25,000 contract with Geffen Records to produce videos. This was not part of the contest.) And the more recent (September–October 1987) "Ask Michael Anything" contest, in which viewers were to send in three original questions for Michael Jackson, ten semifinalists were chosen, and they were given screen tests. Jackson himself picked the three "grand prize winners" who appeared as hosts on *Motown on Showtime,* which starred Michael. Then the winners, each with a guest, took a private tour of Michael's mansion and flew to Australia to see Jackson in concert there. The trip included $3,000 in spending money, round-trip airfare, luxury hotel accommodations, and limousine transportation. One grand prize winner, Troy Council, then a junior at Florida State University, asked Michael, "Musically, what impact do you hope to make on the world?" Another was Cathy Burke, a twenty-nine-year-old innkeeper at an Irish pub in Atlantic City, who won with her "What was the happiest moment in your life?" query.

MTV slated the biggest promotion in its history from March 1988 to the end of the year. Called MTV's Museum of UnNatural History, the promotion was a traveling exhibition featuring live dramatic corporate-sponsored displays integrating music, style, fashion, and technology. Apple's (see p. 642) booth promoted the Macintosh. Its booth had two exhibits. One featured a number of computers hooked into keyboards which demonstrated the Macintosh's musical abilities. Participants could access a particular instrument within a musical composition, and control it. The second featured a world map, which, when a city was punched up, would offer tourist information for that location. Polaroid (see p. 78) had a booth dedicated to its new instant camera. In exchange for a refundable cash or credit card deposit, visitors could borrow a camera and keep the pictures they took for free. They could also be photographed in settings suggesting they were rock stars. Clairol used its booth to advance its Pazazz temporary hair color product. Clairol provided makeup and hair experts to give participants a new {free} look. Each exhibit area was hosted by a "Vid-head," a life-size mannequin with a video monitor head displaying footage of MTV VJs talking about specific sponsor displays. The exhibit traveled to twenty-seven shopping malls across the country.

(Information provided by Barry Kluger and Andrea Smith, company spokespersons.)

REVENUES: Company is privately held and will not disclose.

EARNINGS: Company will not disclose.

INITIAL PUBLIC OFFERING: MTV went public in 1984 and then went private again in 1985, when Viacom acquired it. MTV and Viacom are now subsidiaries of National Amusements, Inc.

OFFICES: MTV has headquarters in New York City and additional offices in five American cities (Detroit, Chicago, Atlanta, Los Angeles, and San Francisco), and one in London.

NUMBER OF EMPLOYEES: Approximately 650 all in the United States. (The London office has a different payroll.)

AVERAGE AGE OF EMPLOYEES: Twenty-eight.

TURNOVER: 2.5 people per month.

RECRUITMENT: MTV has no strict recruitment program. However, it has an internship program and works with television and production departments at such schools as Emerson, Syracuse University, and Hofstra University.

NUMBER OF NEW HIRES PER YEAR: Sixty.

RANGE OF STARTING SALARIES: $14,000–$20,000.

POLICY FOR RAISES: Employees are reviewed annually, and raises are awarded on the basis of merit.

TRAINING PROGRAMS: MTV has a two-day formal orientation program for all new employees, as well as ongoing skills programs on management supervision, negotiation classes, and management workshops.

BENEFITS: Medical and dental insurance, pension plan, group life insurance, long-term disability insurance, and tuition reimbursement for courses that benefit an employee's career at MTV.

VACATION: Two weeks after one year and three weeks after five years, in addition to three personal days each year and a number of regular paid holidays.

ADDITIONAL PERKS: An employee assistance plan, through which employees can take out loans at a discount rate and receive psychotherapy, marital and family counseling, and substance abuse counseling. Contrary to popular belief, employees do not get free tickets to rock concerts and like events. But they do get to buy chotchkes imprinted with the MTV logo at a lower cost.

BONUSES: Bonuses are awarded at the management level and are determined on the basis of merit and company performance.

ANNUAL PARTY: MTV has an annual Christmas party and a company picnic. The Christmas party "is usually something that fits in with the MTV philosophy—it's wild." The party is for employees only and is held outside the office. (In 1986 and 1987 it took place at the Cadillac Bar, and before that it was at the World Trade Center.) Festivities include live music, dinner, and dancing, and employees wear anything from suits to rock 'n' roll attire. In addition, Viacom holds a company-wide employee picnic every summer to which MTV people are invited. The picnic takes place at New Jersey recreational area and includes music, softball, swimming, and "general merriment." MTV often hosts an annual New Year's rock 'n' roll ball, broadcast live over the network, for employees and industry people. The party, which has a different theme every year (in 1986 it was "Roman"—"there were lots of columns all over the place") takes place in a "very large venue." Employees, who dress in "rock 'n' roll black tie," eat and dance on national television to the music of famous performers. In 1987 the network did not program a live party for New Year's Eve. It offered a pretaped party instead. "We wouldn't be MTV if we kept doing the same thing."

DRESS CODE: No stated dress code. Executives, for the most part, wear suits and ties—women executives wear comparable dress—and everyone else is casual. Some people wear jeans.

AVERAGE WORKDAY: Close to ten hours a day, on average. A lot of people are in at 8:30 A.M. and a lot are still working at 7:00 P.M.

SOCIAL ATMOSPHERE: "Incredibly social. Everyone is here because of the nature of the business, and we tend to also mesh well with personal interests." Many people are friends outside of work.

HEADQUARTERS: MTV occupies four floors of a New York City high-rise building, encompassing 110,000 square feet. Its studio is located several blocks away.

CHARITABLE CONTRIBUTIONS: The company will not disclose the amount of its donations. A few of the organizations it supports are AMC (cancer research), Students Against Multiple Sclerosis, and the Urban League.

INTERESTED APPLICANTS CAN SEND RÉSUMÉS TO:
Human Resources
MTV Networks
1775 Broadway
New York, NY 10019
(212) 713-6400

As time goes by, it becomes trickier to write about MTV, the world's first all-music video network. When the concept was invented and introduced in August 1981, it was as avant-garde as could be. Finally, rock aficionados could see the stories and images behind their favorite songs. (Who could have predicted that the subtext of so many tunes would be a woman in a camisole or teddy and spike heels applying her makeup?) Not to quibble. The ethos and esthetics of rock 'n' roll were finally available to kids outside the hip time zones, and grown-ups no longer able to attend live concerts with the same comfort and gusto were able to stay in touch.

MTV has reached its postadolescence. No longer a novelty, it must now insist on being INNOVATIVE and FUN, and for its confirmed audience, it can still provide a good time. MTV has evolved beyond a new form of entertainment; it is without doubt a hugely successful marketing effort that is able to put together phenomenally cohesive joint promotions aimed at its target group. Its challenge, now that it's in its fourth incarnation, is to enter the nineties with its audience and freshness intact.

MTV's offices, on Broadway in midtown New York (appropriately, just across the street from the Hard Rock Café), are appropriately rock 'n' roll-y. Stippled walls with shiny black and red pillars tell you that you are entering the land of Cool. Eight TV monitors set to MTV remind you of your whereabouts. As the work force enters early on a spring Monday morning, the ratio is approximately seven to one jeans to suits. (To be fair, more suits work upstairs. MTV occupies four floors in all.) Overnight bags accessorize most outfits, as employees seem to have returned from their beach houses this morning. (Some will be off to Winston-Salem, North Carolina, at noon to conduct a bunch of focus groups.) You couldn't even mistake MTV's people for the creatives in an advertising agency, they look *that much* like music people: Women in loose-fitting long dresses with cowboy boots, lots of sunglasses, leggings, and as much leather as the weather (ninety degrees Fahrenheit this muggy day) will tolerate. (In all fairness, that means boots and low-slung belts. No one could be that impervious to the heat. This isn't L.A., after all.)

Every office has a sophisticated sound system, television, and VCR. While it's almost quiet at nine o'clock, most TVs are on, although the sound is muted. By noon, MTV's corridors are noisy places. Music of all kinds drifts out of every room, and the environment allows for people to call out of and into each other's offices. No whispering or phone calls if you're within shouting distance.

Bob Friedman's office looks like the fantasy of every college man minus the waterbed: gold and platinum records compete for wall space with examples of some of MTV's fab promotional art. A silver lamé hightop sneaker decorated with MTV's logo is placed on his desk as a pencil holder, and there's all that video and sound equipment. Bob wears a suit and a conservative red silk club tie. At thirty-two, he's a bona fide old-timer (in every sense of the word) at MTV, having spent eight years in marketing. He has an MBA from Columbia and came to what was then called Warner Amex (a joint venture of Warner Communications and American Express) Cable Communications in 1981 after eighteen months in account work at Grey Advertising, where he worked the Procter & Gamble account. "Warner was on the front pages because of its new technology," he explains of his then dramatic decision to enlist. At the time, Warner Amex was on the air with its Nickelodeon/The Movie Channel [the latter introduced in 1979] services. "Working in advertising, I couldn't avoid hearing about these people. Everyone wanted to be here. The buzz was for real. This place turned out to be an eclectic group." Nevertheless, people with Bob's credentials weren't heading here with the same vigor as were diehard entertainment people. His colleagues at Grey and his friends from business school thought he was nuts.

His first position was with Warner Amex Satellite Entertainment, "with the promise of a twenty-four-hour music channel in a month." He was the Marketing Manager for the Northeast for all services. After a series of jobs in marketing, Friedman developed the Marketing and Promotional Development Department, which he runs as its senior vice-president. Besides dreaming up new ways to promote MTV (adding new sponsors to its roster of about 225 advertisers), Bob also guards the MTV logo against overuse. "The logo has a lot of value in itself. We protect it. The number of licensing agreements can be counted on two hands. And sponsors are willing to pay for that association.

"The rock 'n' roll attitude is what we're trying to capture and deliver to twelve- to thirty-four-year-olds. MTV is more than just video; it's a lifestyle vehicle for this demo[graphic]." Some of the promotions of which he is proudest include The Lost Weekend with Van Halen, sponsored by Honda, Paramount Pictures, and Atari, which, though won by a guy, proved to be as decadent as promised. MTV's Body-Snatching Contest (1987) was sponsored by 20th Century-Fox's *Revenge of the Nerds* and Stridex medicated pads. An on-the-air announcement of a contest can generate more than one million entries. To advertisers, that's considered serious proof that their target audience is paying attention. The hardest part of Friedman's job is "pleasing advertisers *and* kids. We have to convince both constituencies about our attitude."

His suit and degree notwithstanding, Bob loves the music. (Obviously, since he deals primarily with outsiders, he can deal more effectively if he is attired as they are.) "You could do this without loving rock, but it would be hard. This environment is lots of young people who love music and entertainment. It gets in your blood. After eight years, it's still a hell of a lot of fun." He *has* to go to concerts. He *has* to go to parties. He *has* to listen to music, watch TV, and attend movies. Movie promotions are becoming a bigger part of MTV, with premieres and parties now a staple of its programming. As MTV moves into the international market (Japan and Australia love their MTV, although it's only broadcast fourteen and twelve hours per week, respectively, and Europe enjoys twenty-four-hours-a-day programming), it is looking for new ways to exploit its "demo" in the States. A coventure with Vestron Home Video is distributing a series of tapes, MTV's Closet Classics. There is talk of producing an MTV movie. Friedman sees about fifty projects and proposals a day. "Planning's tough. The music's always changing."

Furthermore, since 1981, MTV has undergone four corporate transitions. Warner Communications spun off two thirds of MTV (including Nickelodeon, and VH-1/Video Hits One), taking it public in 1984. Viacom (which owns Showtime, syndicates shows like *The Mary Tyler Moore Show* and *Perry Mason* and owns *The Cosby Show,* and *Matlock,* among other properties), bought MTV, Nickelodeon, and VH-1 in late 1985 in a friendly takeover. (As of 1983 The Movie Channel, Warner Amex's first on-air venture, merged with Viacom to form Showtime/The Movie Channel Inc. In 1985 Warner Amex sold its interest to Viacom.) On June 9, 1987, all of Viacom was purchased by Sumner Redstone, the owner of National Amusements, Inc., in Boston. Bob Pittman, the visionary credited with the design of MTV (see p. 527), left the company after failing to buy it from Viacom. Friedman says, "Our owners have pretty much left us alone. We've welcomed them and their capital."

Cheerfully, Doug Herzog apologizes for keeping his sunglasses on today because of a "hideous" eye surgery aftermath. (We ask; he won't divulge more.) "The fun moves very quickly. It's a creative atmosphere. It rarely feels like a job." Doug's a kid, albeit a married one. At twenty-nine he's MTV's vice-president of news and long form production, with experience garnered at CNN and *Entertainment Tonight.* "I was hired as the news director [at twenty-five] just when they decided to beef up news in terms of budget and staff." Today, what was known as *Music News* has grown into *MTV News*—it's more than items about rock stars, their tours, and their opinions. "It's celebrity and lifestyle stuff." Long Form Production means such specials as the 1986 Amnesty International Concert, Spring Break—(then-VJ Alan Hunter in Florida offering on-site interviews and concerts), the *Top 20* show, aired weekly, and a ten-part series on groupies. Doug's in charge. Doug refers to MTV as "another misunderstood network." In fact, he so embodies the attitude of MTV that if the network had not existed, someone would have had to invent it so he could work there.

"News is a daily thing," he says from his large office. " 'Emergencies'—a group breaking up, accidents, people having babies, like Mick and Jerry [Jagger and Hall]—we think people should hear it first on MTV." The network's taping schedule—Monday tapes Tuesday; Tuesday tapes Wednesday and Thursday; Wednesday tapes Friday; Thursday tapes Saturday and Sunday; Friday tapes Monday—allows for late-breaking news to be aired fairly quickly. A serious emergency could be inserted within hours, if the tape were brought out to the transmission center on Long Island.

"I've got the perfect job for me," Herzog says with a smile. "It's a cool job. I've always been a big music fan and collector." Working here has changed his musical tastes. Now "I have an appreciation of heavy metal—the fun of it. People say, 'Wow! You work at MTV; that must be fun!' I'm having like the greatest time of my life."

Sam Kaiser likes his job, too. He was in touch with Donna Rice, Jessica Hahn, and Fawn Hall to gauge their interest in being guest VJs. (The retiring, nonopportunistic Miss Rice considered the offer.) Kaiser is a new boy here, having spent only two years as MTV's vice-president of programming, after ten happy years at Atlantic Records. Before his plane takes off for the South, Kaiser volunteers his thoughts. He's wearing white jeans, sneakers, and an oversized polo shirt embroidered with a band's logo. After being a teen DJ in his native Missouri, Kaiser dropped out of junior college with three credits (one class). He knew he wanted to work in the music business. "I always loved the radio. I always loved music."

He became an area rep and promoter for Atlantic in Missouri and Illinois. At Atlantic, involved in artists' relations, Kaiser "handled video promotion. So most faces here were familiar to me when I came over. I had an idea of what the channel was like; I had *no* idea what to expect. I know my way around a record label, a concert hall, a recording studio—I didn't know what television was like. It's fast." Sam is thirty-four in a company with an average age of twenty-seven or twenty-eight. It was difficult for him to leave a company where he was content and join a younger organization during a period of change. "The first three months were difficult. But there were a lot of new people, and we all learned together. Now I feel I belong here." He was a seller then; he's a buyer now.

After an entire career in rock 'n' roll, Sam thinks that "business and rock are inseparable. We take it very seriously. Other TV people think of us as lowbrow," he says, sneaking yet another look at his television screen. When talking to the management of MTV, you sometimes must inure yourself to talking to someone whose eyes are constantly in motion, checking out their videos. (You imagine that as kids their parents were constantly rebuking them for watching too much TV.) "You never feel finished—there's no beginning or end. This music is very emotional. I love rock 'n' roll, and I always will. I blew out an amp last weekend, playing Judas Priest. I guess I'm obsessive about it."

One thing Kaiser et al. take quite seriously is their mandate "to think like a sixteen- or seventeen-year-old. I sometimes forget what it's like to be a teenager." That's why MTV relies on focus groups. And that's why their advertising is perceived to be successful; sponsors customarily design specific campaigns exclusively for the network. "We have a responsibility toward kids. You're programming to eighteen-year-olds, but twelve-year-olds watch, too." This is why MTV will run public service announcements about the use of condoms but not advertisements for condoms or a program about teenage pregnancy. "We're an entertainment medium." Besides the notorious trio of Jessica, Donna, and Fawn, Kaiser has dream guest VJs: Madonna, Bruce Willis (mentioned here only because we didn't want the book to be deprived of his name); and the three surviving Beatles—"the ultimate rock freak's fantasy." His eyes really do light up.

"Bob Pittman brought me in. I was nervous about arriving after his exit." Looking down the road, Kaiser envisions approximately five years with the channel. "I want to work for myself one day. Maybe own a management company."

Perhaps you are interested in MTV's famous "M." The logo, so prized and protected, was developed even as the programming was being determined. Judy McGrath, the creative director and a senior vice-president of MTV, is in charge of the M. Formerly a copywriter for several Condé Nast magazines, Judy got a call in 1981 from a friend who said, "You love rock 'n' roll—you should go there." Although not unhappy where she was (and still collecting royalty checks for a teenage health and beauty book called *Pretty Girl*), she interviewed at MTV. "I was asked who my favorite band was. I said, 'Bruce Springsteen,' and I was told I was *wrong*." Hired anyway, she says, "I was a basic liberal arts student. Nothing prepared me for this job. I had no TV experience. TV is the quick turnaround, not like three-month deadlines.

"I set up an editorial department. I hired writers from *Rolling Stone*. We did promos in teams, an art director and a copywriter." At this point you notice her office would make an art director's look like a high school principal's. A large pet iguana in a tank—a gift— primordial and grotesquely scary, dominates the window sill, sitting next to a take-out salad (his diet). A bust of Michael Jackson in his Sergeant Pepper jacket (before his last few operations) is a desk lamp, with a bulb and lamp shade sticking out of Michael's Afro. It's also a gift.

"I think I have the best job in television and the best job here. I work with a lot of people who don't work in video." McGrath's department creates the constant stream of humorous, decorous, *moderne,* dramatic, beautiful, and always memorable promotions, both for contests and for the logo. "I do animation, graphics, and on-air promotion. I do it here because I don't think there's any place to do it with such abandon." She explains the genesis of the original MTV logo, first seen on a flag stuck into the surface of the moon. "First of all, that black-and-white footage is free from NASA. But the man on the moon [Neil Armstrong, July 20, 1969] was the first big event we all remembered watching on TV. So we made the U.S. flag the MTV flag. Now we shoot our own stuff. The M says it all. We didn't want a corporate-looking logo. We wanted rock 'n' roll. The Manhattan Design Company came up with the M for us. It was designed to fill in." (In fact, what makes the M so distinctive is its various animated colorings.) "Lots of people hated it. The MTV rocket launch music was composed in-house."

Although she's essentially been doing the same thing, albeit with more authority, since 1981, McGrath says, "It doesn't feel repetitive. The staff is eager. It's people in their twenties who sit around their offices watching reruns of *The Brady Bunch* on TV. We almost can't even do all the things we think of. There are so few rules. The logo is our only rule. We usually spend about two to three thousand dollars per promo." A pittance. "We still manage to get by on 'We're young.' Rock people like our staff because they're not slick. Illustrators like to work for us because they can do the stuff they can't do for others. Peter Max came in. We've worked with Jean Michel Basquiat." McGrath calls her position "an irresistible combination. I can be an executive here and know the difference between 'speed metal' [e.g., Megadeth] and 'thrash metal' [e.g., Motley Crüe]." This is a woman who is dressed for success. Only her stockings, embroidered with seashells, might be remarked upon in banking. "My friends at the magazines think I'm Cyndi Lauper. . . ."

Having established that Bob Pittman was a tough act to follow, meet the man who now occupies his office: Tom Freston is the new president and CEO of MTV Video Networks. His office, upstairs on the suit floor, has just been repainted with its own new textured paint—with occasional squiggles. A former advertising executive who bailed out of big-time agency life to start his own import business, Freston "always had an affinity for music and the music business." In his approximately eight years at MTV since 1980 he's had eight different jobs. He was one of the first MBAs hired, even before the launch of MTV, to run marketing for Nickelodeon and The Movie Channel.

"I still believe in what we're doing," he says. "Rock 'n' roll is enjoyed by two generations. We offer an audience without a lot of waste. Advertisers don't advertise on us for ratings; we're part of a different agenda." The A. C. Nielsen Company is the traditional measurer of TV viewers. For the record, although considered somewhat controversial for its findings, MTV's Nielsen ratings are low. MTV isn't bothered by them, citing a skewed sample that doesn't take into account teenage boys, a large segment of the rock channel's audience. "More people are watching MTV every day. It's growing at a rate of fifteen thousand a week. We do our own research. We've become an institution. People aren't talking about *Time* magazine every day either."

Freston is a distinguished forty-two years old, he thinks that makes him the third oldest person in the company. "I love rock 'n' roll. I love the energy of the music and how it makes people feel inside. I'm not out at clubs every night, though." His age is not a handicap. In fact, the average age of MTV's viewers is probably higher than most people think: a healthy, self-supporting twenty-four. As president and CEO, his responsibilities include talking to suppliers, artists, managers, publicists, cable distributors, and the media. On four continents Freston travels about 50 percent of his time. "The best part is dealing with programming. It's the immature bent in me."

In response to the standard carping aimed at the videos, Freston says, "A good video is irresistible. Some are repetitive. It's a creative problem. Record labels ask for our creative input, and we don't give it. If we say what we like, we've tainted the creative pool." As to the network's imitators, Freston isn't worried. "Our biggest asset is that we're broadcasting twenty-four hours a day."

He has confidence in MTV as a "marketing success. I don't want to seem overly mercenary, but we're filling a void. I walk a fine line between rock and business. I'd never wear a suit at a rock concert, but I don't want to look like a hippie to a cable operator." Tom's favorite performers include David Bowie, Peter Gabriel, Los Lobos, Suzanne Vega, World Party, and Tom Petty. "I was right on stage during the entire Live Aid concert. It was the high point of my career."

Interview:
VJ CAROLYNE HELDMAN

*T*his is the story of Carolyne Heldman, a member of the second generation of MTV VJs, one of their four permanent video jockeys. (Besides Carolyne there are Kevin Seal, Adam Curry, and Julie Brown.) A native of Aspen, Colorado, she moved to New York in order to work at MTV. "New York itself was the hardest part," she says, adjusting a skintight denim outfit she'll be wearing on the air in a few minutes, "being surrounded by humanity and separated from nature."

After graduating from the University of California at Santa Barbara in 1984 with a degree in film production, Carolyne returned to Aspen to work at radio station KSPN, with an AOR (album-oriented rock) playlist. She was hired immediately as a full-time DJ. "My love wasn't radio. I thought it would be fun, a lark. It was music. I was always into music." And acting, although in college, she "lost faith in myself as a performer."

Heldman's story of winning this job sounds like a modern-day fairy tale: "In June 1986, when I was at the station, I picked up a trade magazine, *Radio and Records,* which I never read. *Never.* I was glancing in the help wanted section, and there was an ad for a national VJ search at MTV. The ad was really intimidating. I remember some of it: 'Could you make conversation with a brick wall? Would a picture of you today look good on the cover of *Rolling Stone*?' It said, 'Rush a tape to MTV.'" Although happy with her job, she figured it was worth a "what the hell" effort. "They didn't say what to do on tape, but a friend helped me make one. I just told my résumé, which I edited to my favorite music: English Beat, Bob Marley, the Del Fuegos, and the Beet Farmers. It took two days to make the tape, which lasted three minutes."

Although she's wearing a high-style outfit, Carolyne has on knee socks rolled down to the ankles and no shoes or makeup. She's naturally charming and sits on her feet remembering every detail of her attempts to penetrate MTV. "I Federal Expressed the tape on a Tuesday and got a call Thursday morning at eleven. They said they loved the tape, but their machine ate it up and they needed another. I Federal Expressed another that day." She was *dying.* "I *still* can't believe it."

"Then I just waited and waited. It was a long cat-and-mouse game, as far as I was concerned. All summer long I watched MTV all the time. I didn't want to tell anybody about my application because I never thought it would happen. I wasn't going to jeopardize my job. Meanwhile, at KSPN, I was just promoted to music director." At twenty-four, she was probably the youngest female music director of any FM station in the country. "I started to see a big future [at the radio station], which I didn't want because of that teeny little crack in the door at MTV." Having not heard a word all summer, except vague assurances that she was still in the running, Carolyne did the virtually unthinkable: she quit her job in Aspen and moved to New York. "I thought if I didn't get the job at MTV, I'd try to get a job with a record company. I'd made a lot of contacts in my week as music director."

The fairy tale continues. She left Colorado on September 19, visited her grandma in Ohio on the twentieth, and arrived in New York on the twenty-first. Her accommodations were on the floor of a friend's apartment. Carolyne called MTV upon arrival and was told, "Oh, we would have flown you in sooner or later." Unfortunately, they didn't reimburse her for her plane ticket, but Heldman shot tape the first day she visited the people at MTV. "They asked me my schedule, and I said, 'I'm pretty free.' I'm sure I was terrible." The result? She was asked to return every day that week, to fill in for an absent VJ. "I actually auditioned on the air. They didn't pay me that first week. Then they said, 'Come back next week, and we'll pay you.'" This arrangement lasted four weeks, until Heldman was offered a real contract. Meanwhile, her boyfriend moved to New York, too, Carolyne found an entertainment lawyer she trusted—not only was she her friend's upstairs neighbor, but she had previously been MTV's attorney—and the lawyer helped Heldman find an affordable and decent apartment in the West Village *right away.* Stories like this are not common in New York. Out-of-towners, take note.

Today, with a three-year contract, Carolyne feels secure in her job. "This is better than radio. I would never go back. It's a good break into performance. I must admit, I miss being close to the music. I miss playing it and talking about it. I still try to react to it, though. But the camera allows you to communicate in many more ways." Heldman would never just announce the menu of music, as some VJs have interpreted their jobs. "I wouldn't be just a cheerleader. You should know the videos you're about to show and screen them, so you can talk about them. I am a person who's naturally interested in people. That comes through. I'm friendly, and that helps. But it's weird; it's not acting, for the most part. You can't improve on being yourself. It *is* difficult," she confesses, "to get excited about music you don't like."

Heldman's work schedule is not too taxing. She works typically five-hour days, five days a week, unless she's traveling, which she does about twice a month. She never feels like a celebrity except away from New York, when she gets recognized a lot and people treat her like a star. "I couldn't believe it. In Lexington, Kentucky, they rolled out the red carpets. People asked me for my autograph!" She seems so surprised. Yet since the inception of MTV, none of the on-air personalities has become a star. They don't appear on talk shows, and they are not the subject of gossip or much ink at all, for that matter, in the press. "I think the management now wants us to be more famous. Earlier, they wanted the VJs to be more normal Joes." (The relationship between management and the on-air people is friendly, but not cozy. The VJs rarely hang out at the corporate headquarters, and vice versa.)

Unlike most working people, Heldman is ministered to by a fashion coordinator, who shops for or with her. "I can't wear repeats, and mostly we get to keep the stuff." With her constant tugging and stretching of this stone-washed ensemble, one gets the impression she doesn't wear much of this rock 'n' roll regalia when she's off the air. "They don't so much dictate our images as enhance them. Shopping is part of the job. They get my hair cut, but I do my own hair and makeup." If it weren't for Heldman's passionate asides about music, you'd never know she was a performer in the music business. You'd guess, in her slouchy position, that she was a student. Or maybe worked in a shop.

She is conscientious. "Every night I read the next day's scripts, I prepare for interviews, and I look at videos." Of Heldman's dialogue, she estimates 60 percent is ad-libbed, the rest scripted. Although her channel has coined the new phrase, "doing video," Carolyne swears she's never "done it" herself.

She refers to the on-air director as "my boss. We review my tapes together once a week. I feel I'm in a low period right now. In the beginning, it seemed perfect. I felt I was born to do it. Now the honeymoon's over." It's back to work. Carolyne gets ready to do the Top Twenty show with comedian Rich Hall as her cohost. Perhaps her life sounds charmed. But, as evidenced, she has made her own good luck. With another tug on her rock 'n' roll outfit, she extends her hand and is off, to be transformed into a star.

Interview:
BOB PITTMAN

*B*ob Pittman's résumé is probably ten pages long. He's almost thirty-five years old. The son of a Methodist minister in Mississippi, Bob was one of the creators of MTV (the one who gets the lion's share of the credit, anyway), and is now the CEO of MCA-financed Quantum Entertainment. NTB. (Not Too Bad, initially.) "I had the highest ACT scores in my high school class," he says, continuing the theme. We are talking in his Rockefeller Center offices, which are filled with expensive audio/video equipment and art, the exact duplicate of his MTV office. "I just put the furniture back in its slots." Bob is wearing an Italian-cut suit.

But he didn't go to college like the rest of his classmates. At fifteen he got his first job as a disc jockey. He zoomed through the airwaves of Mississippi, Wisconsin (stopping briefly for some college), Detroit, and Pittsburgh, ending up at WMAQ-AM in Chicago, "the Number One most listened to country station in the U.S." Known as "The Mississippi Hippie," Pittman was twenty. "By then I made more money than my dad ever did. At the time radio was considered 'art' and programmers were considered wise."

In his move to WKQX-FM, Bob left country music for a more sophisticated AOR (album-oriented rock—more avant-garde than a Top Forty format) playlist. His power look consisted of shoulder-length hair and a full beard. Swiftly, he was lured to New York, where at twenty-three he was the youngest program director ever of WNBC and possibly of any station in the top five markets. "I fired [Don] Imus and Cousin Brucie," he says of two of the most popular New York radio personalities of all time.

Television was the logical next step. NBC asked Pittman to host and produce a contemporary rock show for their owned and operated stations. "[Programming head] Herb Schlosser loved me," he says. "He put me under contract and gave me more money than I'd ever heard of. Then Schlosser left, and Fred Silverman arrived. It took me six months to persuade him I was not an idiot."

In December 1979 Showtime pay cable started The Movie Channel, the first twenty-four-hour movie service. "They gave me the chance to do a fourth network," he says nonchalantly. At about the same time, Pittman realized there was already an emerging rock video business. "There were a hundred and fifty clips out there already. I figured more could be made. I made a pitch to Steve Ross [chairman of Warner Communications] and Jim Robinson [chairman of American Express]. I said, 'How much can we lose? Eleven million dollars?' We lost forty million dollars, but we made much more."

Originally called the Warner Amex Music Channel, Pittman became its chief financial officer in 1983. It now included MTV and Nickelodeon, the pay cable service for kids, which has the highest number of families that subscribe to basic cable.

Pittman became the CEO of MTV. And, of course, the service flourished, becoming a part of our vocabulary and creating a new esthetic. MTV became self-referential as rock groups created product especially for it. The network made stars out of telegenic musicians who might not have burst out of the second string otherwise. The annual MTV Video Awards were the music fans' version of Oscar nights. Still, the service was not as profitable as its original projections. Warner Amex put it up on the selling block. Then Pittman resigned.

"I was probably one of the most successful programmers in the country—in all formats. My friends asked, 'How can you leave this?'" Bob explains. "I'm motivated by starting things. I'm a nontraditional thinker. I tend to think if I approach things in a new way, I'd do better, and I'm noticed because of my huge, visible success."

Furthermore, he believes one does better by not staying anywhere too long. It helps him separate himself from MTV today. "My job does not become my identity. That only would happen if you stay in a job too long. I can't always be 'Bob Pittman, MTV.'" When Warner Amex announced their intention to sell MTV, he tried to buy it with the help of venture capital firm Forstmann Little & Co. He lost out to Viacom, but he made a bundle in the process. "If it had happened [the buyout], I'd still be there. When Viacom bought it, I realized I'd just be an employee. I didn't want the dullness of power, I wanted scrappiness, pressure."

Bob thinks his tremendous success is derived, in part, from his being able to exist in both the creative and business worlds. "I'm absolutely a creative person who's now a businessperson. Very few creative people enjoy business. I do. Now I manage creative people. Having a financial success behind me gives me a credibility for the people who require it. I would agree that I'm neurotic and very driven, and that if I were well adjusted, I'd be a farmer. I'm not hooked on work; I like the lifestyle and the challenge. I have to support my lifestyle."

Pittman is not risking his high-octane lifestyle with this start-up. His co-op in Manhattan and his farm in Connecticut have both been photographed as the subjects of articles on home design. "Having another home is another reality."

Quantum Entertainment is not starting small. Pittman is attempting to launch a record label, a television division, movie development, and home video all at once. Quantum's first release, an instantly produced home video of the Marvin Hagler–Sugar Ray Leonard fight, sold an astounding sixty thousand-plus units, making it the best-selling sports video of 1987. He's signed singers Jimmy Davis and Ella Brooks, whom he compares to Whitney Houston and Tina Turner, as well as comedian Gilbert Gottfried to recording contracts. He has an on-air series commitment for thirteen half-hour episodes with CBS. He produces the notoriously incendiary *Morton Downey, Jr., Show*. And he's searching for companies to buy. (Pittman et al. were one of J. Walter Thompson's suitors.)

"The purpose of the company is to understand the consumer," he declares. Quantum is financed entirely by MCA, the parent company of Universal Pictures and G. P. Putnam. "They finance a hundred percent and own half," he says with a smile. "Today it seems that our mission is to have a high overhead and low revenues." There are presently eight executives at Quantum besides Pittman, three of whom came from MTV, two of whom have MBAs from Harvard, and two of whom are based in Los Angeles. "We're living well and treating ourselves well—we're now rationalizing the virtues of coach airfare," he says in a confidential voice. "A lot of friends can't give up those trappings.

"I'm doing fine in this world without the background." One minute he says, "I wish I'd spent more time in school," and the next he says, "In a way, I'm glad I don't have more education. No one's told me how to think." After a minute he adds, "Something's gonna work out of all this, and we'll get it right."

PRESCRIPTIVES

PRESCRIPTIVES

HISTORY & OPERATIONS

Prescriptives, an upscale line of makeup and skin treatment products aimed at young professional women, is a wholly owned subsidiary of Estée Lauder, Inc. In 1979, the company originally launched the products in response to the then new market of women professionals. The line was not an immediate success, and in fact Estée Lauder decided to withdraw and entirely reformulate it at a considerable financial loss (though the company is privately held and will not give out figures, the cost was estimated at around $40 million). Although the strategy worked and the new Prescriptives finally caught on, the line did not become profitable until June 1987, nine years after its original introduction.

Prescriptives, like Estée Lauder's three other independent subsidiary lines, Estée Lauder, Clinique, and Aramis, is a separate entity with its own marketing and sales department, its own accounts, and its own research scientists. The line, like all of Estée Lauder, Inc.'s lines, is sold only in "better" department stores (Prescriptives now has sales counters at approximately 390 such stores across the country, as opposed to three thousand "doors" carrying the other Lauder lines). Prescriptives is sold by the team of 750 "analysts" (not "salespeople").

The company hires the analysts and puts them through three one-day training sessions to familiarize them with the products and sales methods. The company's corporate staff numbers only twenty-four—seven men, the remainder women—all located in the New York City headquarters.

The way a new product—and even the original full line itself—is launched is this: Corporate staff people come up with an idea for a new product and pass it on to the scientists, who fomulate in their laboratory. Then it's packaged, marketed, and the department store analysts introduce it to their customers. Each year Prescriptives launches several new products as well as a whole new color range for their makeup products. Color '89 is called Visions. At last count the line included thirty-four lipsticks, eleven lip-coloring pencils, thirteen blushers, thirteen eye shadows in single packs, eight eye shadow trios (three colors in one compact), fifteen glossing sticks, twenty eye-coloring pencils, eight shadow pencils, seven mascaras, sixty foundations, sixteen finishing powders, and two concealers. They also make custom-blend foundation (which matches a customer's complexion exactly and sells for $45 an ounce), which is now sold in twelve cities with imminent plans for expansion.

In cosmetics, the Prescriptives philosophy is called "Exact Color." All of the makeup falls into one of four color groups geared to complement four different skin tones—yellow/orange, red/orange, red, and blue/red. All analysts are trained to analyze the skin tones of any customer. They will "colorprint" her by applying a stripe of foundation in each of the four basic groups to her cheek. The foundation that is "accepted into the skin" indicates the customer's color type. The analyst then uses a color wheel to show her the products most flattering to her. That's if the customer wants a "natural" look. If she wants to buy makeup to match a particular outfit, the analyst will use the color wheel to show her a whole different range of colors.

Prescriptives manufactures twenty treatment products for skin, body, and sun care. Line Preventor, originally developed in 1985 and touted by the company as "the first preventive skin care," was designed to neutralize "free radicals," the molecules that ostensibly cause visible signs of aging. Line Preventor—according to Prescriptives' claims—keeps facial skin looking and feeling younger and softer and prevents new lines from forming. Although it was far and away Prescriptives' best-selling product, in December 1987 the company elected to remove existing stock from stores to make way for an improved version that was developed by Dr. Walter Smith, the vice-president/director of research and development for all of Estée Lauder.

Flight Cream, available in tube or jar, was designed to protect the skin from the excessive dryness caused by frequent airplane trips. When Prescriptives originally offered a sun care line, the products ranged from those that offered minimal protection to those that completely blocked out the sun. Now, concerned about preventing unsafe exposure to ultraviolet rays, their eight sun products begin with SPF 15 and go up to SPF 23. In late 1987 Prescriptives launched Body Conscious, an overall body cream developed to firm the skin, prevent stretch marks, and reduce the visibility of existing marks. The company's most exciting new product, Extra Firm, actually strengthens facial skin in the delicate, wrinkle-prone areas.

(Information provided by Anne Slowey and Joh Siff, company spokespersons.)

REVENUES: The company is privately held and will not disclose. Prescriptives became profitable for the first time in June 1987.

FOREIGN MARKETS: Austria, Canada, Italy, Germany, and the United Kingdom.

NUMBER OF EMPLOYEES: Twenty-four corporate staff people in New York headquarters; seven hundred and fifty "analysts" hired by Prescriptives to sell the products in department stores across the country.

AVERAGE AGE OF EMPLOYEES: Thirty-one.

TURNOVER: In the New York office "there have been only two executive changes in two-and-a-half years." At the counters, the rate has been 80 percent since inception.

RECRUITMENT: Prescriptives' facility in Melville (Long Island) has a formal college recuiting program for production people (people interested in manufacturing and packaging). The New York corporate office occasionally recruits but has no formal program.

NUMBER OF NEW HIRES PER YEAR: One or two, depending on need, are hired into the New York office.

RANGE OF STARTING SALARIES: "Starting salaries are competitive." The company would not disclose figures.

POLICY FOR RAISES: Employees are reviewed annually for salary increases. Employees get an automatic yearly increase, the amount of which is also based on merit.

TRAINING PROGRAMS: Three one-day programs geared primarily for analysts though also attended by new corporate staff people: Basic Training School, which explains the background of Prescriptives, how to color print, the breakdown of products, and how to function at the sales counters; a course developed specifically to introduce employees to the new color line launched each year; and an advanced business school (for analysts only), which focuses on selling skills. All new analysts work their first week at the counter under the guidance of a senior team member.

BENEFITS: Medical, dental, and life insurance, pension, tuition reimbursement (for courses which directly benefit an employee's career at Prescriptives), and an employee thrift plan under which employees have the option of investing a portion of their salary in a mutual fund. After three years with the company, Prescriptives will match the employee's investment up to 6 percent.

VACATION: One week after an employee's first six months and an additional week after the second six months. Then two weeks per year until five years, after which they get three weeks. On average there are ten paid holidays per year.

ADDITIONAL PERKS: Corporate employees get free admission to major New York City museums. All employees get a 50 percent discount on Estée Lauder products. Employees are also entitled to a certain (unrevealed) amount of free Prescriptives merchandise.

BONUSES: The company awards Christmas bonuses to its employees "reflecting their outstanding contribution to the success of Estée Lauder, Inc." Everyone gets one, and the amount is loosely based on seniority.

ANNUAL PARTIES: Several private Prescriptive parties plus a corporate Christmas party for all of Estée Lauder, Inc.

AVERAGE WORKDAY: 9:00 A.M. to 6:00 P.M. for corporate staff.

DRESS CODE: No dress code, but "Prescriptives gives its team an eye to the contemporary." Employees would not wear jeans, but almost anything else is okay.

SOCIAL ATMOSPHERE: Congenial; employees do socialize with one another after work.

DOMINANT COLOR GROUP AMONG FEMALE EMPLOYEES AT PRESCRIPTIVES: Yellow/orange, though for *all* women the dominant group is blue/red. No, Prescriptives does not have a hiring bias for orange/yellows.

CITIES WHERE CUSTOM-BLEND FOUNDATION IS AVAILABLE: Boston, Chicago, Dallas, Los Angeles, New York City, San Francisco, and Washington, D.C.

CHARITABLE CONTRIBUTIONS: This is a corporate function of Estée Lauder, Inc. Prescriptives does not donate to charity on its own.

HEADQUARTERS: Prescriptives occupies part of the thirty-ninth floor—5,000 square feet of office space—at 767 Fifth Avenue, The General Motors Building, in midtown Manhattan. "The design and overall aesthetic is pared-down and sophisticated lines—modern and forward-thinking. "Estée Lauder, Inc., occupies five floors in total.

INTERESTED APPLICANTS CAN SEND RÉSUMÉS TO:
Estée Lauder, Inc.
767 Fifth Avenue
New York, NY 10153
Attention: Human Resources
(212) 572-4200

OR (FOR THOSE INTERESTED IN WORKING AT THE COMPANY'S RESEARCH AND DEVELOPMENT PLANT):
Estée Lauder, Inc.
350 South Service Road
Melville, NY 11747
(516) 454-7000

While the language of makeup is often so vague as to be unintelligible, people in the cosmetics industry are straightforward and businesslike, and, if forced to look for contrasts between them and us, we'd have to settle on the fact that they look more polished, more pampered, and maybe just a little better than the rest of us. (Rumors abound that they are genetically preselected for this field. It makes sense since even their hair is perfect.)

"Exfoliant," "hydrating lotion," "emollient," "superrich," "toner," "with collagen": these are the handiwork of their laboratories and copywriters. In fact, makeup people do make sense, and they can even make sense of this gobbledygoo—or make that plain goo. When they lecture on the virtues of their products, they can make the freshest-faced lovely with the smoothest of skins pay a small fortune so that small lines won't form around her sweet little eyes.

Prescriptives is the youngest and most upscale line of the Estée Lauder empire. Created in 1979, its mission focused on marketing, not on its products. Bob Nielsen, Prescriptives' first (and former) president, says, "I think Prescriptives was probably the only line developed with a specific consumer in mind. It was developed with the understanding that the baby boomer would be with us."

As readers of every major newsmagazine can attest, when boomers consider their purchases, they require good design, healthy ingredients, results, and the opportunity to spend a lot of money. They need to know where to find products with these attributes, although they stubbornly refuse to be "brand loyal," compared to other wedges of the demographic pie.

The twenty-four people who make up Prescriptives' small corporate staff have a definite sense of their customers' identities. Indeed, they've targeted the customer who doesn't even know she is fated to use Prescriptives products. Her age is somewhere between twenty-seven (when skin begins its inevitable demise) and forty. She is likely to be a college graduate. If she's a housewife, she's a "juggler." She's "career-involved, not just a working woman." She'd better be. Prescriptives' stuff doesn't come cheap. She's more likely to buy designer clothes than postyuppette attire, but she's busy enough that she wants simple products requiring few beauty procedures. (Fewer than five steps.) She's very today. If she is unenlightened about Prescriptives, don't blame her; in these early years of the company, Prescriptives is just now indulging in advertising. There is no question, however, that this woman—the Prescriptive woman—will get excited about this line when she discovers the products and their innovative properties.

Prescriptives is mining a definite snob appeal. The packaging is handsome; the products are considered (by their progenitors) to be "feel good" goods. The colors and preparations are sensible and useful. (Sun products with a minimum SPF of 15. A moisturizer for frequent flyers intended to counterbalance the dryness of a plane's cabin. A soap that almost any skin type can use. A body lotion that will prevent the formation of stretch marks or dramatically minimize the appearance of existing stretch marks.)

Like many other industries, cosmetics is populated by its prototypical customer. This usually means women, although many cosmetic and fragrance—and ladies' apparel, for that matter—companies are run by men. Women are often drawn to the makeup business simply because they *like* makeup—wearing it, experimenting with it, and being around it and the worlds it circumscribes: beauty and fashion. The first lipstick and compact have always signified an important rite of passage for young women. Often these women are introduced to the business of selling makeup through summer jobs at department stores, and the field just feels right.

Since Estée Lauder owns four brands—Estée Lauder, Clinique, Prescriptives, and Aramis (for men)—there is a sort of matchmaker magic that goes on during the interview process. [It should be noted here that the international aspects of each line are organized together as a fifth division, "International," since the needs of the world market are more similar to one another than they are to the domestic ones.] The personnel function is a corporate one, and while it is certainly appropriate to express a preference for a particular division, part of being sized up is spent finding out which brand you "are." (Chances are, you are what you wear. People do have a pretty good feel for that.) While there is certainly a good deal of overlap, especially in the public perception of target customers, Clinique is technically for the youngest makeup wearer (although it's the company's most successful line), Estée Lauder for her mother, and Prescriptives for her successful older have-it-all sister (somewhere between *Thirtysomething* and *L.A. Law*).

A Prescriptives vice-president who has worked elsewhere in the corporation claims, "In the elevator when you see people, you can tell which division they work for. Clinique people have a feeling of blondness, a very WASP thing, pale and clean. Very consistent. Estée Lauder is more elaborate, and Prescriptives is a bit more dramatic and more diverse, maybe the trendiest."

And not surprisingly, each company has a distinct look and feel that is immediately evident on a tour through Lauder's corporate offices in the General Motors building on Fifth Avenue (also home to Revlon). Estée Lauder: decorated in the brand's signature colors of blue and white, some flowery upholstery, very ladylike and grown-up. Clinique: white-tiled, white-washed, very clean, spare. Aramis: browns and earth tones, and men at work. All benefit from an extensive and significant corporate graphics collection.

As the newest company, nestled somewhat autonomously within Estée Lauder's bosom, Prescriptives' offices look like a cross between a trendy marketing company and a political campaign office. There's something tentative about the modernistic setup, as if these people are waiting until their time comes. That time is soon. Perhaps they'll even get bigger headquarters.

Continung the campaign motif, there is a slight sense of urgency informing the moves of the staff, as if late-breaking news were imminent. While they don't monitor the cash registers at all the stores where Prescriptives is sold—department stores only, and only the crème de la crème; don't bother looking for this brand in even the toniest pharmacy; it'll never be there—on a daily basis, everyone's mission is to beat last year's sales figures. This is felt by the analysts (*never* "salespeople") at the stores right up to Dan Brestle, Prescriptives' executive vice-president and general manager, and probably Mrs. Estée Lauder herself. But there is such a happy elfin quality to the daily life of the Prescriptives people that the bottom line seems strangely irrelevant, cold, and incongruous.

Prescriptives rewards team efforts. Employees refer to themselves as "Team Prescriptives": "A dedicated group of professionals working together to help other people look and feel better about themselves." A newsletter written with the bouncy enthusiasm of a letter home at Christmas thanks the analysts who have made the biggest sales and congratulates members of the team who have invented new sales strategies and angles. [In the lead article position is a love letter to T.P. from Bob Nielsen, the father of the company before he departed from Prescriptives.] " . . . I'm so pleased you're with Prescriptives. I hope you're enthusiastic about selling Prescriptives. Be proud of the quality in *your* Prescriptives products. Be proud to be a member of Team Prescriptives. We're so very proud to be working with you! I hope to see you real soon."

Estée Lauder, Inc., is very profitable and very private. Run by personages referred to in their offices as "Mrs. Estée," "Mr. Leonard," and "Mrs. Evelyn" (Mr. Leonard's wife), these top officers actually do make all major decisions. In 1979, when Prescriptives was conceived, "Mr. Ronald" was heavily involved. He's Mrs. Estée's younger son and was recently the U.S. ambassador to Austria. (He is currently seeking Representative George Hockbrueckner's eastern Suffolk County congressional seat.) Those employees handpicked by the Lauders to start the Prescriptives division naturally felt honored. As one of them recalls, "How many people get to introduce fabulous products to the world? I felt so strongly about our brand."

The catch was, "We failed. If anyone says otherwise, they're kidding. Prescriptives was a system. It was positioned as the Erno Laszlo of Estée Lauder, and it didn't live up to our expectations." Intended originally as a skin care line, the makeup "was just a service for customers. It was, however, the best launch in the history of the company. We had the best publicity, style, support, everything. The products didn't work." Well, actually they worked, but they were interdependent. They just didn't work too well alone. Prescriptives was hailed immediately for its attractive design. The packaging was gunmetal gray, beige, and high-tech-y, and appealed to customers who were too young to afford it.

So they went back to the lab and concocted a new brand. "It just shows you how great this company is." No one was penalized for the mistake, and since the resources provided by the Lauders were so vast, relatively little pain was felt. There was never any doubt that the problem could be corrected. "Our color was fantastic." A fact. So they decided to bide their time and build a color business until the rest of the line was reconceived. Prescriptives is advantaged in being entitled to use the laboratories and manufacturing plants that are part of the Lauder coffers. Although (scientist) Dr. Walter Smith, vice-president/director of research and development, "belongs" to all of Lauder, Prescriptives has a singular relationship with him. Team Prescriptives feels the pride of ownership that entrepreneurs feel, without any of the usual stomach-jiggling jeopardy.

Jim Gager is the senior vice-president/creative director of Prescriptives, a member of the team since 1980. Since 1983 he has enjoyed his own design department, which oversees everything. "Otherwise everything would be too fragmented." He orchestrates the design of the bottles, jars, tubes, brushes, lipsticks, and compacts, the packaging, the in-store displays, the promotional designs, the ads, you name it. "Now I know everything. I've done layout. I've done mechanicals." Having studied industrial design and packaging as an undergraduate and graduate student, he feels his job is the "culmination of all aspects of my training."

When Prescriptives began the customarily long process of launching its first fragrance, Calyx, Jim remembers with pride that the company asked for his opinions and took them seriously. "I got to talk about my feelings for it." Jim was asked to smell the fragrance during all its phases of development, and he was solicited for suggestions for its name. (By the way, "calyx" means the green cone-shaped underside of a flower's bud. Apparently, even school-children in England are familiar with the word.) Gager says, "The passion here comes from latitude. I wouldn't feel that way if after I designed a bottle, they had someone else design the display.

"Prescriptives people rely on each other," he says. "No one's terribly afraid of giving opinions. There's not a lot of politics." The degree of design freedom, at least, is substantially more than what's available at the other divisions of Estée Lauder, which share a corporate design staff. (All advertising is coordinated by AC&R, an outside agency with expertise in the fashion and beauty areas.)

People at Prescriptives do have something else with which to compare their experiences here. In many cases, that means a job at another Lauder division (which means they can be drafted *out* of Prescriptives into another division, again). Patti Walton, Prescriptives' former training director (now working as a skin-care consultant to the line), was a recruit from Clinique. Although she had the comfort of being selected by Leonard Lauder and staying within the company at large, she did hesitate at first.

"Clinique was a well-oiled machine. People there really see it as a religion, an established culture. Leaving there was like leaving my family." The excitement of joining something new was attractive, though, to this ex-English teacher. "I could have stayed at Clinique, but because of my faith in the Lauder corporation, I didn't see it [moving to Prescriptives] as a risk." She spent three years in the maverick division, a decision that delighted her. "The best part is to feel our credibility. We used to have just color authority, now we have that in treatment. We're at the cutting edge."

Walton's job was to communicate Prescriptives' culture throughout the system, by training the trainers. [Today Julie Bell has the job of executive director of training and education.] "It's very important to make the analysts feel a part of Prescriptives. Their major source of pride is in their job, and their climate is such that they do have to punch a clock, which is not always pleasant." Each analyst who comes on board receives a letter of welcome personally signed by Julie Bell. Perhaps this contributes to the analysts (currently 750 in number) feeling they actually know senior executives of the company and refer to them by their first names. Walton established an incentive program, "The Prescriptives Achievers," for all analysts who colorprint one thousand faces. It is still in place.

"Colorprinting" is Prescriptives' signature service, a system in which every customer's skin undertone is found in one of four color groups: yellow/orange, red/orange, red, or red/blue. The *Analyst Guidebook* describes the procedure. "Focus lamp on customer at high intensity. Cleanse the cheek area above the jawline with Skin Balancer [a light toner]. Apply a stripe of each foundation with your finger. Gradually pat off excess while observing. Three families will remain apparent while the correct family will be accepted into the skin. . . . Explain the process to your customer as you work and point out which color family has been accepted on her skin . . ." Analysts offer this service to anyone who comes to the counter and record the results on a card for the files. Then it's time for the color wheel, which explains which colors complement and highlight one's skin tone. So far there are sixty shades of foundation from which to choose, and blushers, shadows, lipsticks and liners are coordinated for each of the four groups. Every member of Team Prescriptives is naturally aware of her color group. Since identifying with the products is extremely important, she wears Prescriptives' products exclusively and wouldn't think of doing anything else. (She gets a certain amount of them for free.)

Analysts can feel less like salespeople and more like counselors working at the Prescriptives counter. And they are urged to stay in touch with their customers, via phone or postcard, to maintain communication and loyalty. Analysts do have a sense of propriety toward their customers, and it's reciprocal. There's nothing like touching a customer's face to make her feel cared for.

After a few years in venture capital and institutional trading, Mary Van Lawrence decided to pursue her interest in makeup professionally. She studied the industry and wrote an "aggressive, 'you must hire me' letter" to Dan Brestle, then Prescriptives' national sales manager (now the executive vice-president and general manager). "I was a customer and a fan." While he was receptive, there were no openings. So Mary took a job in management consulting in Boston. Eventually a position did open up. It was located in the front cosmetic salon at Bergdorf Goodman, and it was as the custom blender. (Prescriptives actually has a top-of-the-line foundation only available initially at two of America's most elite stores: Bergdorf's in New York City and the main branch of Neiman-Marcus in Dallas. (It has since been added to ten other cities. It is custom-made usually by appointment after a colorprinting. The mixture is recorded for posterity, and the result, in a glass bottle containing one fluid ounce, costs $45.)

So that's what Mary did, even though "it was hard to leave my professional job with a secretary, et cetera, for a counter job." (For stargazing, the custom blend job is no slouch. In New York Christie Brinkley, Bernadette Peters, Julianne [Mrs. Bruce] Springsteen, Annie Lennox of the Eurythmics, Candice Bergen, Cher, and Jane Pauley have all gotten blended.) Van Lawrence had some misgivings at first. "I always thought I should have an office job. But I thought, if I don't do this, would I spend the rest of my life wondering? I got discouraged. My friends thought I was bananas, but you have to love what you do, and I love working here. They know it. I have the enthusiasm of a zealot." After a year of hard work and glowing reviews, she was promoted to product manager of Custom Blend, opening more of these counters around the country. She has since been promoted to Prescriptives' San Francisco account executive.

In a company as small as Prescriptives, every employee feels she or he makes a difference. Everyone is encouraged to use products-in-progress and report on their opinions. Prescriptives

International (now four people) feels frustration, sometimes, at being sequestered on Lauder's international floor, away from the rest of the team. So in between trips to Paris, there's a lot of elevator travel. "You want to be a part of the creative process and brainstorm." And on business trips especially, looking perfect (their words, not mine) is a must.

When people inside corporate Prescriptives talk about their mission, you'd swear you were listening to entrepreneurs talking about their very own companies. No one seems bound by old rules and traditions, and everyone is eager to create new ones. Unity of purpose prevails. Susanne Kirtland, the director of creative communications, writes all Prescriptives copy and directs the crucial effort to name products. "There is a lot of satisfaction in the work itself. There's that great sense of being able to say to yourself, 'I think I've solved this problem.' It doesn't require an audience."

I talked to Jane Hertzmark when she was new. She said then, "So one is really confined to their titles. My title is marketing manager, but I'm really in operations. My ultimate responsibility is to see that Flight Cream gets to the shelves. But in my first month, I was asked to come up with a three-year marketing plan. On my first day, I was included in meetings right away; I didn't know where or when I'd eat lunch." [Today Jane is the director of marketing, responsible for coordinating "all product introductions, marketing strategies, and marketing calendar." She also works with production and shipping, staying involved in operations.] If you're right for Prescriptives, they encourage you to be an intimate right away. In exchange for the passion of the employees, they offer their instant trust. "You're involved in-it all," Hertzmark enthuses. "There's not a piece of it you miss. You work very hard because everyone wants it to be a success. We're like *The Little Engine That Could.*"

Susanne echoes the "I think I can" mentality of people poised at the edge of stardom. "I love this because we can wing it in the halls. It's like those old Mickey Rooney movies—'Let's do a show in the barn!'"

Let's do a great makeup company!

Interview:

LEONARD LAUDER

*L*eonard Lauder, president and chief executive officer of the company bearing his mother's name, is preparing to tour the offices belonging to Estée Lauder, Inc., high above Central Park. First there's a refreshment, a mixture of orange juice and Perrier served in a crystal glass, in a bright corner office decorated with a large Morris Louis canvas, a Claes Oldenburg sculpture of a typewriter eraser drooped on a pedestal, two Christo drawings of the wrapped Pont Neuf, a Kenneth Noland, two boxes of Joseph Cornell (one in need of repair), family photographs, a serious marble inkwell, and a handful of other tokens of his artistic appreciation. He stops to say hello to the corporate vice-president—his wife, Mrs. Evelyn Lauder, down the hall—and then it's off. In between saying hi to some of the hundreds of employees filling the five art-filled floors who straighten their posture and smile a big smile at his entrance, he asks quick questions about their progress and projects and makes observations about his career and his concerns.

Working in a family environment is "both exhilarating and frustrating. It's twenty-four hours. You discuss business on weekends, in the car, you can't escape it. You're never off duty, although you might be skiing, sailing, traveling. At a dinner party, I check to see the lipstick a guest is taking out of her purse, and if it's ours, I smile, and if not, I chastise her. I sneak away and look into medicine cabinets, not with evil intent." He's not looking for Valium or the personal hygiene secrets of his hosts; he's checking out the cache of Estée Lauder, Clinique, Aramis, and Prescriptives. "When your name is on every product . . ."

Aside from the bathrooms of the Social Register, Leonard Lauder has his hands in every pot. Literally. He decides the name of every major product. "I didn't create the name 'Beautiful,' but it was my decision," he explains of Estée Lauder's successful fragrance, introduced in 1986. "Mrs. Lauder"—this is how he refers to his mother—"was against the name. She wanted 'Fleur 2000.' Why is it the number one hit for Estée Lauder? Because it's a world-class fragrance."

Obviously, Lauder cannot attend to absolutely everything within all five operating divisions (International is run separately), so he turns his attention selectively as he thinks it is needed. "I'm more of a catalyst than a day-to-day manager. I burst into a room, even if I'm down. I'll take steps two at a time, even if there's an elevator, and keep people revved up. It's contagious.

"My attentions are a mixed blessing. I make people move faster than they're prepared to do. I can be a little overbearing." Why is he turned on and on duty all the time? Lauder feels that "success if my narcotic. I wish I could stop growing. I'm a prisoner of my position. People say to me, 'Do you want to be the richest man in the graveyard?' "

Although his interests are wide-ranging: art, history—"I dragged my poor wife to Verdun and the Maginot Line. Battlefields aren't her thing!"—movies—"*Hannah and Her Sisters* is the perfect movie"—he could never contemplate working in another business than cosmetics. "I'm so wrapped up in what I do now. What you're dealing in here is a passion, a single-mindedness of purpose." On reflection he admits, "I wish my parents had spent more time broadening themselves. Their lives were bound by New York, Palm Beach, and the south of France. I read; they didn't read."

Leonard Lauder is the elder son of Estée and the late Joseph Lauder, who created the business in 1946. A member of the Wharton School class of 1954, he joined his family's company in 1958 after studying at Columbia Business School and a tour in the Navy. The huge success of the private company as it has approached the $1.95 billion mark is generally attributed to him. "You have to rely on your instinct, your gut," he says. "It's not like Mrs. Lauder says, 'We need a new moisturizer.' Ideas flow up. My job is to teach people with ideas. Here the product is king. You'll find product on every desk." And an executive, regularly, behind a counter. "Everyone in the company has to work behind the counter. That's how my poor wife got phlebitis. That's what this business is all about."

And, undeniably, that's how the business was started. Before Estée Lauder became "Estée Lauder," she sold her creams, lotions, and cosmetics herself and made women up whenever she had the chance. Obviously, Leonard Lauder is filled with respect and admiration for his parents and the empire they wrought with moisturizers and perfumes. Mrs. Lauder pioneered the Gift with Purchase—giving samples to ensure a future sales—which has become an industry practice. "I brought my own thing to the company," Leonard says. "Completely different from what she and Dad did. I was the one who wanted to do International. It was time." That was 1960, and today the Estée Lauder lines are the most popular in the world.

Leonard's trademark is also felt in hiring. "You have to like women to do well. All male Harvard MBAs are failures here," he says. "I'd eventually like to see my sons come in." William, aged twenty-seven, is the eastern field sales manager of Prescriptives U.S.A. Gary, twenty-five, is a venture capitalist with E. S. Jacobs & Company. But is there a chance that the Lauders would ever go public or sell some or all of the company? "It's out of the question. We're still growing. We'd never have the luxury of failing if we had to answer to anyone else. And look at the successes our early failures turned out to be?"

SAVING FACE: A PERSONAL CAREER UPDATE

When you're a young girl growing up in Manhattan, its lure is as powerful and potent as any elixir. Without even planning, you indulge—guiltily at first, then with more zest and appetite, until you are almost spent. And then ashamed. Soon your imaginary calendar repeats itself weekend after weekend: you've spent the last three years wandering through the makeup aisles on the main floor of Bloomingdale's.

Thus it was with the unbridled joy of a lottery winner that I accepted the invitation of Leonard Lauder, CEO of Estée Lauder, Inc., with the benediction of Bob Nielsen, then president of Prescriptives, Lauder's top-of-the-line line, to sell Prescriptives for a week at Bloomingdale's flagship store on Lexington Avenue in New York City.

This was not as easy as it may sound, as it required extensive training. Not to mention learning to blend.

Let me be candid: I am not a makeup wearer. Oh, I've tried, but invariably, when I feel I've done an artistic job on myself, someone will say, "Lisa, what did you do to your face?" in a tone that is more concerned than complimentary. I thought I was wearing enough when I arrived at my training. Executives poked their heads in, and I heard them tsking me, their voices rife with pity, a look of yearning on their sad faces. To them, I was a pitiful, underused canvas.

To add to the complications, my week, June 9, 1986, was very special. It was to be the last GWP ever. A GWP is a Gift with Purchase (as opposed to a PWP—Purchase with Purchase, wherein you buy a body lotion you don't want for the privilege of buying a plastic makeup case you could sort of use). A GWP, announced via postcard to all Prescriptives customers, meant more traffic and more sales.

I learned to demonstrate Line Preventor. "Have you tried our Line Preventor? It's our most exciting breakthrough product." I learned to be a part of the team. "Team Prescriptives" as it's known, is "a dedicated group of professionals who make women look and feel better about themselves." Unlike at other companies, here the word "team" is sincere and serious.

People start lining up outside Bloomingdale's about twenty minutes to ten, when the doors open, as if you have to suffer to do it right. By 10:03 A.M. the street is clear, and while the earlybirds might have secured their first purchase of the day, the store is still relatively empty.

It seems that people who have nothing to do, do it until lunchtime at Bloomingdale's. They feel the first floor is a good place for that. I began to see faces on day one that I would see every day thereafter.

Prescriptives has an excellent location. It's near an exit and has its own stockroom. Which is rare. Boasting the best uniform from Adrien Arpel to Yves St. Laurent, I couldn't wait to take my place beside my six team members on Monday.

By Monday lunch, two hours after I started, not only was I loyal, I hated those stupid girls from an unnamed company sashaying by like thin, weak does in their dumb red hats.

I froze when my first customer wanted me to make her up. Steven and Kenneth, our makeup artist, were busy, and frankly, I was hungry for a big sale. I had a quota to meet, after all. I willed my eye to understand my customer's undertone and palette. I tried, with a trembly hand, to blend. I was nervous. There was more color on my hand than on her face. I didn't touch her chin enough. But it wasn't terrible.

An attractive woman in her late thirties came in for a refill of our moisture-protective makeup. She had the faintest accent: maybe born in Germany, I thought, educated here. In fact, her surname was the same as a famed German philosopher. I had it written on my customer card before she spelled the second syllable, and she was amazed that I could get it right. She expected so little of a saleswoman.

I made my quota on Monday, thanks to my friend Debbie, who bought a bottle of Anti-Bac (blemish zapper) at $17.50. ("I swear it's good. Let me buy it for you.") It put me over the top.

I was trying to be one of the team; no special favors. It's hard when you don't know where anything is and when you panic and forget prices. I have to say, it never occurred to me that my colleagues would be made uneasy by my presence; I was such an obvious novice. I should have realized that a writer on board meant a spy with a pen (and an audience). But no one ever asked me what I did when I wasn't at the counter, what I'd done previously. In the years between the publication of *The Official Preppy Handbook* and this selling experience, it was the first time I had been around a group of strangers for more than a few minutes who didn't ask me something about it. Perhaps my colleagues didn't know I had written a book before. Only two ever expressed any curiosity about me whatsoever. When photographer Henry Grossman arrived to take my picture, they accepted it as just another aberration in the week. And when talk show hostess Sally Jessy Raphael came in for sun block, the fact that her salesgirl had appeared on her TV program was just another one of those things.

On Wednesday a customer approached, saying, "I bet you went to my college." I asked her her alma mater. Wheaton. Wheaton is the alma mater of my agent, Esther Newberg. I began to say, "My ag . . . " when I realized that no cosmetic analyst *has* an agent. "I didn't go there; a friend did," I said. "I went to Brown," I added, and began to blush. (I didn't know of anyone at Brown who sold; in fact I didn't know of anyone at Brown who wasn't a lawyer. I hated this feeling.) Talking about college is still a favorite topic, and we engaged in a lengthy chat about eastern universities. My customer's sons had attended the same school as one of my brothers, and I attributed my familiarity with the subject—when asked—to the fact that my brother had just graduated from college. I wasn't lying, I was just trying to stay incognito. Finally, discussion over, I was blending foundation on her jawline when she said, "I know who you are. [Pause]. Lisa, what do you think of Middlebury?" I became wildly nervous. Should I explain what I was doing here? I didn't want my colleagues to overhear and think I was embarrassed to be among them. Would she believe me? More important, would she still buy the bottle of foundation?

She bought the story and the makeup. Herewith are more general observations. The people behind the counter take their work seriously. They must. It's hard. It can be tedious. This is not a summer or occasional job. This is what they do. They also identify strongly with their products and probably couldn't sell or be motivated to beat last year's record if they didn't.

The worst thing in the world, when standing upright all day, is being idle. With a customer in hand, there was no fatigue. In between, standing in the aisle hawking the GWP, straightening up the counter, refilling trays of cotton balls and swabs, cleaning the glass shelves, totaling the figures, it is hard to suppress a yawn and forget about your feet. On Friday afternoon, a friend told me I should have been wearing the saleswoman's secret weapon: support hose. I wish I'd known.

It was the hawking that really got to me. How many times did I cavalierly pass by a salesperson offering a flyer at a department store? Trying to spritz me with a fragrance? Each day I spent a couple of hours in front of the counter myself, trying to find original ways of saying "Prescriptives has a gift for you today." And I was hurt when people just brushed past me. I knew not to take it personally, but it felt like performing for an uninterested audience.

Before my week at Bloomingdale's, I was worried I would love the work so much, I'd be tempted to abandon my life as a writer in favor of getting made up each day for a collegial sales experience. (I had even calculated how much Line Preventor I'd have to sell to pay back my publisher.) By the end of the first day, I was so disappointed: I was so much less able than my colleagues, and too tried to read or remember the commonest of names and facts. By midweek it was pointed out to me that compared to what I usually do, this was ego-denying. (The last time I had perched near a counter at Bloomingdale's was to sign copies of one of my books.) Being one of a group, in this case, was not as satisfying as working for myself. I fantasized about the team disappearing and my having to work alone on a busy afternoon.

While almost everyone was quite pleasant to me, I suppose I was basically a nuisance—someone in constant need of assistance. I was not trained or authorized to use the cash register, so I had to engage the help of another analyst, who might be busy, too. Moreover, not until my last day, when it was disclosed to absolutely everyone that I was not being paid salary or commission [I thought they all knew], did I gain acceptance. They still didn't know much about me and hardly revealed much about themselves, but our mutual ignorance had become friendly. I was even told, "If the writing doesn't work out, you could always come back."

R/GREENBERG ASSOCIATES, INC.

R / G R E E N B E R G
A S S O C I A T E S

HISTORY & OPERATIONS

R/Greenberg Associates, Inc., the most technically sophisticated film production house on the East Coast, was founded by the brothers R. Greenberg—Richard and Robert—who grew up in Chicago. Richard (the elder), the company's creative director, started out in architecture at the University of Illinois and later switched to graphic design. Unable to find the kind of work he wanted in Chicago, Richard moved to Los Angeles, hated it, and relocated to New York, where he wound up designing the letter sequences for *Sesame Street*. Robert, R/Greenberg's executive producer, was a liberal arts student in college. His first real job was working for an uncle who owned a mirrored tile business which was bought out by Royal Crown Cola. Bob eventually ran the subsidiary's Canadian division. In 1977, with $15,000 in savings, the brothers decided to merge their talents in their own production/design company. They started R/Greenberg Associates with animation director Ken Stytzer in a cramped New York City brownstone where the Greenbergs lived, worked, and housed their equipment.

R/Greenberg's first assignments came from advertising agency Batten, Barton, Durstine & Osborn (BBD&O) to produce television commercials for IBM and Black & Decker. Their strong visual effects impressed Frankfurt Communications head Steve Frankfurt (the former president of Young and Rubicam) (see p. 588), who hired them to produce the teaser [teasers can be up to eighty-two seconds long and require no actual film footage], trailer [two-and-a-half minutes long, always with footage], and television commercials for the movie *Superman*. They went on to create the film's stunning titles—bright blue letters streaking into place like comets, pausing, and then evaporating into deep space—which won them acclaim and wide recognition in the movie industry. At the New York opening of *Superman*, the audience actually burst into applause after the title sequence.

Within less than two years, R/Greenberg had grown enough to acquire sophisticated computer graphics equipment and to move its headquarters to Madison Avenue. Early on, the brothers' strategy was to diversify their business so as not to become pigeonholed in any one specialized area. They became known as generalists who could create strong visual effects in virtually any medium. In a short time they had as much work as they could handle.

In addition to producing advertisements, movie trailers, and industrial and designing titles and logos, R/Greenberg Associates gained a reputation as "film surgeons" able to repair other people's defective work. As their technical know-how increased, the company became legendary for creating striking and seemingly impossible special effects, such as a baby flying effortlessly through the air in the title sequence of *The World According to Garp* (1982) and the startlingly realistic effects in Woody Allen's *Zelig* (1985), in which they superimposed Woody Allen's live action image into stock film footage. (Since 1982's *A Midsummer Night's Sex Comedy*, R/Greenberg has worked on all of Woody Allen's films except for *Broadway Danny Rose* and *Hannah and Her Sisters*, which had no opticals or special effects.) With the addition of a feature promotion division in 1982—headed by Richard's wife, Paula Silver, the former vice-president and associate creative director of Frankfurt Communications—the company began to create complete advertising campaigns for feature films (including print materials), acting as a de facto agency minus the media planning and buying.

In 1984, when the rent on its Madison Avenue headquarters became unwieldy, R/Greenberg purchased an unused truck terminal on West Thirty-ninth Street—in a neighborhood known as Hell's Kitchen—and transformed it into a film studio that is reputedly the most technologically advanced in the world. (The reported total cost of the move, completed in June 1985, was approximately $5.5 million.) Today the company employs a full-time staff of seventy, making it the largest production employer on the East Coast. Though six of those employees belong to the unions, the company worked out a unique arrangement with the unions that allows workers to move from one type of equipment to another (union workers are generally restricted to a single function). As a result of this flexibility, the company can have creative people on its technical staff rather than strict technicians.

As its reputation for technological expertise grew, more and more of R/Greenberg's assignments were for visual effects that were considered difficult, if not nearly impossible. Some of their most notable work includes: Television commercials: Renault *Bulge* (1985), Smith Barney *Gulliver* (1985), Timex *Technicians* (1985), Coronet *Spokesangels* (1986), Pillsbury Doughboy (1986–87), and IBM *Fractuals* (1987); Trailers: *All That Jazz* (1979), *Alien* (1979), *Superman —The Movie* (1979), *Tron* (1982), *Tootsie* (1982), *Ghostbusters* (1984), *Body Double* (1984), *Back to the Future* (1985), *Armed and Dangerous* (1986), and *Predator* (1987) (Academy Award nominee); Feature opening title sequences: *All That Jazz* (1979), *Superman—The Movie* (1979), *The World According to Garp* (1981), *The Dead Zone* (1983), *Ladyhawke* (1984), *Body Double* (1984), *Lethal Weapon* (1987), and *The Untouchables* (1987).

R/Greenberg is organized into the following departments: Administration, Live Action Production, Design, Editorial, Animation, Opticals, Computer-Generated Imagery, Motion Control, and the Model Building Shop. [In April 1988 Paula Silver left R/GA, disbanding

Stuart Robertson works in Opticals. "What we do is basically trick photography; we manipulate stuff that's already been shot. We do to live action what people do to animation." A native of Kentucky, Stuart earned his MFA in painting at the Chicago Art Institute. When he's not working at R/Greenberg, he's home in New Jersey, painting. He explains his talents by saying, "I'm a complete moron in math, but I'm very good at spatial relations." He doesn't feel his creative juices are spent after workdays that are typically fourteen hours long. "My painting doesn't get touched by what I do here." Furthermore, his commute through industrial towns is his "salvation." Those towns also show up in his paintings.

A committed coffee drinker, Stuart is able to function on less sleep than most people. "I would like to see my family more often. I've made a point of going home early one night a week, so that my family [which includes two youngsters] can rely on seeing me three nights a week. I could work around the clock and would prefer working seventy-two straight hours to nine to five, five days a week." His discipline and conscientiousness are not products of working at R/Greenberg. "I always worked this hard in previous jobs. Most people here are very responsible. I've had to tell other poeple to go home. People get caught up in the rhythm of their projects." Robertson says his work load averages three projects simultaneously, "one major, two minor. Most projects last one to two months. The last three to four weeks are the most intense." His pleasure in seeing his work on television or on a movie screen is real.

He seems to revel in having a job that most people outside his company cannot comprehend. "People here have specific, weird talents, and we're irreplaceable, except by other weird people who'd be harder to live with than us. There is not one particular department that totally drives or dominates this place; there's a lot of feeding back and forth." As the company has grown from fewer than twenty when Robertson joined it to about seventy, he confesses that it feels less personal, more company than family, which is a concern of the Greenberg brothers as well.

Paul Johnson works for Stuart. He's a designer/animator and graduated from Cooper Union in 1979. His first job was at a smaller firm, and he thinks that was ultimately a smart decision. "I was lucky to go to a small company to start, because I could learn and excel, so that I could become somebody, and not just a cog in a wheel. Being in a larger company, you can learn from the people around you, and the pressure from deadlines gets greater and greater. Sometimes at five A.M., when things are going wrong, I wonder why I'm doing it. But the quality of work here is excellent, and that sustains you. Bob Greenberg sets the tone of this place."

Paul feels that working for the Greenbergs has improved his design and presentation skills. When it comes to pitching his ideas, he echoes Liz Beloff's opinion that "you always want yours picked, unless you feel that someone else's are better." Johnson warns, "If a person's too giving, it could be hard—they could be taken advantage of—but everything—even commercials—is collaborative." He vacillates between wondering whether the company is too big for him and appreciating the advantages of working in a larger group. "People here are good. Sometimes they're not too happy, but then they remember about their benefits. We're working on good projects and we have some influence, and we will get attention. There's also a supply of coffee and sodas, and if you work late, you get paid overtime, get dinner, and a cab home."

All the while that Lisa Fisher was an undergraduate English major at Princeton, she dreamed of attending the Yale School of Drama to study theater management. A native of New Haven, Yale was her logical choice. During graduate school there she interned at R/Greenberg, having met Richard and his wife Paula Silver through a professor. Neither Paula nor the Greenbergs were enamored of the idea of hiring interns since they had little time to teach. Incredibly, Yale didn't live up to Lisa's expectations, but it was hard to give up her illusions. "I complained to Paula about Yale. So Paula said, 'Just stay here.' They hadn't expected anything positive to come from me as an intern, and when it did, they were very responsive."

The transition from intern to full-time employee took a while. "I hadn't had too much exposure or interaction with other people here, because Feature Promotion was a tiny little island. But people were glad to have an extra person around, since Paula was always off everywhere." Lisa is now a producer of commercials as well as film trailers, and she is well respected in the white building.

Working in film had never been an interest. "Coming here was as much a function of hating drama school and sensing a career and needing a decent living. Now I really feel like a producer, but what's funny is that I don't think of myself as a 'film person.' In the course of working here I find all kinds of work which are appealing to the generalist: creative, managerial, writing, working with people, et cetera. Not to mention psychology: There are seventy people at R/GA, and each has three personalities. You have to figure out which wavelength people are on."

As "we're expanding into a 'real' business," Fisher compares her experience to the "straighter" work lives of some of her college friends. R/Greenberg's early employees feel a sense of ownership that newcomers can't feel. As the business grows, some of the former feel nostalgic about the family qualities that are difficult to preserve. Simply put, they miss the good old days. "I arrived during the Middle Ages of Greenberg Associates. It was five or six years old. When I got here there were forty employees. I still don't have to fight through layers of people to work with people like Richard. My opinions are taken seriously.

"I hear big corporations are better at keeping people than small ones, but I like the informality here. Perhaps more human relations [efforts] are needed, but I don't particularly want to live in a large, structured, corporate environment. When you want to increase your responsibilities, you have to spot holes and ask for them. There are things I'd like to change, but I don't own the company. The physical space is terrific. I would like to work in a company where everyone is happy and doing good, creative work." She shrugs, "I guess that's an impossible ideal. But I get to work on neat, exciting projects. There are very bright, sensitive, creative, articulate, diverse, likable, interesting people working here."

Bob Greenberg looks surprised as he says, "It's funny. We now have a history in this business. We're straightforward Midwestern people who take our work seriously." R/ G R E E N B E R G is so successful, there is a temptation to maintain the business exactly as it is today, or, in the parlance of many up-to-date managers, to "stick to our knitting." "I'm not a person who gambles," Bob says. "I went to Las Vegas and didn't gamble." Nevertheless, "we opened up a development department and added different directors. We're going to open a West Coast office. We'll be even more unique . . . a ministudio."

Bob's done a lot of reading about management. "I do think about my style of management, but you can't apply corporate management to this—not to these people. Managing that high a number of creative people makes it difficult. How would *you* like to run a company with high overhead, huge payroll, et cetera, and not know what you'll be doing in three weeks?"

There is something about the advertising business—a significant portion of R/Greenberg's work—that breeds relief in simply *existing* professionally, let alone thriving. "No one feels secure in advertising now. There are five hundred professionals out on the streets," Greenberg points out, due to the nervous merger mentality of 1987. The Greenbergs persist in their caution, whether they originate their own feature films, raise money through a public offering, or invent new techniques for computer-aided design. Bob says, "Our biggest achievement is we've been in business for eleven years." Richard adds, "We never bargained for this success. We thought, "Wouldn't it be nice to be recognized in this world?" "

GOING TO WORK

March 25, 1987. 7:30 P.M. This evening Richard Greenberg is directing the opening title and closing credit sequences of Columbia Pictures' megabuck release *Ishtar*. There are maybe a hundred crew members here, on a semibarricaded corner by Radio City Music Hall. It is Richard's fifteenth wedding anniversary, but his wife, Paula Silver, has given him dispensation to celebrate the next day. (In case you did not see the movie—as most people didn't—you probably know enough about it to obviate the need for an explanation of the characters.) But in this shot, Dustin Hoffman and Warren Beatty, playing Chuck Clarke and Lyle Rogers, respectively, admire their record album, *Rogers & Clarke In Concert*, in the center of Sam Goody's record store window. (The neon Radio City sign is reflected, too.) This is the last scene of the movie, providing a happy symmetry to the first scene, in which they look longingly into a display touting Simon and Garfunkel, the Talking Heads, etc., reassuring themselves that they'll make it in show business.

Dustin Hoffman arrives first, looking through the viewfinder and conferring with Richard and *Ishtar*'s director, Elaine May. Some crew members are drinking coffee, some are cleaning Sam Goody's window, and two are arranging the mock-ups of the Rogers & Clarke album covers in the window. Greenberg seems unfazed by the complications of the evening. There is the steady rumble of activity from many passersby. In this case, a majority are apparently guests at the New York Hilton, pleased at the payoff of visiting New York and actually seeing something you don't see every day at home. Richard actually seems amused.

8:27. Warren Beatty arrives, adding a secondary agenda to those watching the movie making. His circuit, circumscribed by the females hovering within the stanchions, is the subject of equal curiosity. [Author's note: Yes. He did approach me. I swear to God.] [Author's note II: I didn't take it personally.] Paparazzi seem to appear out of nowhere, and Hoffman, Beatty, and May are the subjects of many candid snapshots. Crew guys are now eating chicken soup and sandwiches. It's time to rehearse the extras. A balmy evening for early spring, the extras are overdressed for this scene, which takes place in winter. Huddled under the awning of a Duane Reade drugstore, it is difficult not to feel sorry for them as their walks past the record store are choreographed. No stars will be discovered tonight.

8:45. Greenberg, May, and the production manager are in discussion. The cameraman, using a trunk as a worktable, is meticulously scratching the edge of a glass slide with a Swiss army knife. Elaine May reluctantly leaves her place near the camera to pose officially with Beatty and Hoffman in front of Sam Goody's. She first hides her head in Beatty's jacket, then covers her head with her fringed scarf. In our elementary school yearbooks, they'd have called her "camera shy."

9:10. Traffic on West Fifty-first Street is stopped for the first time by a phalanx of production assistants and cops.

9:30. It appears that something cinematic is happening. Richard Greenberg is working.

10:00. Dinner break. One hour. Of the principals, only Elaine May and Richard Greenberg do not evacuate and instead quietly wait within the record store. It is now rather windy, and the temperature outside has dropped by at least ten degrees. A few people wonder where Warren Beatty is, and with whom. [Okay. I was wondering.] Richard Greenberg explains why he and his company have been engaged for this endeavor. The shot, you see, is more complex than just a shot of two guys in the street, because of the glare from the window and because the movie's producers wanted "a visual representation of the plot ending." Peter Frankfurt, a young man enjoying an extended paid leave from his most recent job and a former (and beloved) employee of R/ G R E E N B E R G, arrives at the shoot to watch his friends and schmooze.

11:15. The extras return. The Sam Goody window is being restored to its initial design. All those dressed for spring are now uncomfortably chilled, and the extras seem to be in great shape for the late-night climate.

11:20. Warren Beatty, Dustin Hoffman, and his wife, Lisa, return, the actors now dressed in their seedier, styleless outfits for the first record store scene. [Author's note: There is something reassuring about seeing Beatty in a stocking cap.] Elaine May discusses this scene with them. Richard Greenberg looks like he's cold and yields to his first cup of coffee of the night.

11:50. Out of nowhere, again like the paparazzi, a sudden big rain falls. Chairs—yes, including canvas director's chairs with the stars' names on them—are hauled under Radio City's formidable overhang. Instantly, those who can't fit under it are given little plastic pouches, the size of panty hose wrappers, containing Weather-Rite Ponchos, style number 1690: "Heavy gauge Waterproof poncho . . . with . . . No-Rust side snaps . . . Poncho can also be used as a ground cloth." It's kind of cozy here, everyone scrunched together. Dustin Hoffman admires a PA's neon-orange jumpsuit and inquires where it was purchased. Actor Danny Aiello has also arrived. We're told that since the rain was not backlit it will not "read" (on film). Elaine May decides she wants to light the rain. Crewmen in their Weather-Rites go about their jobs, lighting the rain. By the time they've completed their chores, the rain has stopped.

12:10 a.m. The window has been redressed. The lights have been readjusted. There is no rain. It is cold. It's time for the second shot. Elaine May calls action. Hoffman and Beatty are acting.

12:30. Your reporter checks out.

2:30. The shoot is wrapped.

May 7, 1987. 7:00 P.M. First large-audience screening of *Ishtar* at the Ziegfeld Theatre, New York City. Guests include Eddie Murphy, Peter Allen, Peter Boyle, Kevin Kline, John Cleese, Bill Murray, Carly Simon, Twyla Tharp, Milos Forman, Robert Altman, film critics, members of the New York film community. Richard Greenberg is not among them. The two shots Richard Greenberg supervised last a total of three and a half minutes.

Interview:

SAUL STEINBERG

S aul P. Steinberg is not like the rest of us. He seems, forgive me, happier. A smile informs his wide, animated face, whether he's speaking or listening. Photographs of his family crowd some of the important artwork in his large, comfortable office at the Reliance Group Holdings, Inc., headquarters off Park Avenue in New York.

Long feared for his financial fearlessless, Steinberg became a multimillionaire in his twenties.

Being rich is now easy. It's been part of his identity for two decades. His mammoth wealth has transformed him into a public figure. Being recognized is, however, a double-edged sword for him. He is unable to be inconspicuous, at least in this country. His wife, Gayfryd, has grabbed the limelight as well, has appeared on magazine covers, and seems to generate great interest on her own. Steinberg's philanthropy is so public that he can't give money to the Metropolitan Museum or to PEN or to the ballet or the UJA or to his alma mater, the University of Pennsylvania's Wharton School of Finance, without it making the papers. (The Steinbergs can't even redecorate their thirty-four-room Park Avenue triplex—which used to belong to John D. Rockefeller, Jr.—without its gaining media attention.) Still he smiles.

Don't let me forget to describe our surroundings. First, there's the reception area, dominated by a framed thirteen-star ship's pennant from the U.S.S. *North Carolina,* replete with gunholes dating from 1852–1855. Steinberg often poses beneath it. The floors are slate, and peoples' footsteps resonate loudly as they walk around the triplex area. A bowl of apples at the three-person reception desk looks inviting but intimidating. If allowed to linger, you could easily wonder whether someone might record that you took an apple. This is enough to squelch the desire.

Steinberg and I are meeting in his office on a muggy summer afternoon. Although he has repeatedly turned down requests for interviews by *Lifestyles of the Rich and Famous,* he has agreed to talk to me as a favor to a mutual friend. He says, "I hear I will enjoy our chat." Uh-oh. How can I tell him I'd like to start with a complete inventory of all the stuff in his office? In lieu of this, we start out with his childhood.

Saul Steinberg was born in Brooklyn in 1939. His father had a factory that made drainboards, the first nonslip bathmats, and other household products he characterizes as "less expensive Rubbermaid stuff, seconds." He spent summers working there. "I knew what I wanted to do when I was ten or eleven. I called it 'finance.' I didn't know what really went on." At about the same time, the Steinbergs moved on to Long Island's Five Towns, a collection of upwardly mobile, predominantly Jewish suburbs. Saul still attended school in Brooklyn until the tenth grade.

An unregenerate capitalist, in high school "my hero was Howard Hughes. He was mysterious and a ladies' man." Steinberg's interest in money led him to Wharton, about which he offers no memories. Then again, maybe I forgot to ask. It's hard to concentrate when you're talking to a famous multimillionaire whose art objects make you salivate. "I was unemployable after college. So I started my own company." He moved back home in 1959 and married a girl ("poor") from the Five Towns. "We had no aspirations except to have more. I gave her an IOU that said in three years I'd buy her a little house."

Steinberg started Leasco "on a hunch. I started the whole computer leasing industry. I thought this must be a brilliant idea. To get the idea, I actually read the consent decree for IBM and the Justice Department." The eldest child in his family, Steinberg says his father "was particularly supportive. He discussed his business with me as an equal. He felt anything I cared to do, I could do. My mother was still fearful.

"I was turned down by forty banks." Every bank he approached. Until one bank agreed to loan him half a million dollars with no capital. Leasco's first full year of operation was 1960–61. The company made $50,000. By 1966 its revenues were $2.5 million, the next year they doubled, and so on. Steinberg and his wife moved from Forest Hills (Queens) to Hewlett Bay Park—the most expensive and prettiest area in the Five Towns—to New York City, each move as symbolic as that of any of Thomas Hardy's heroes.

In 1967 he started a management consulting firm with $100,000. Today it "generates sixty million dollars in revenues." He acquired Reliance in a hostile takeover in 1968. "I was twenty-eight years old, and everyone thought it couldn't be done." To the naked eye, Steinberg has a golden touch—excuse the cliché. His insurance company, part of Reliance Group Holdings, Inc., is the twenty-fifth largest insurance company in the country, with revenues of $3.5 billion in 1987; and earnings of $25 million. The insurance division (there's also real estate and an investment group) employs 9,500 people. It's on an upswing. He bought Yankelovich, Skelly & White, the public interest firm, and sold it—at a profit—to the Saatchis. Telemundo, the country's largest Spanish-language television network, is one of his pet holdings. Steinberg talks about his properties as one might discuss one's garden, or a prize rosebush, or a litter of pedigree puppies.

"We've invested in Symbol Technologies. They make the laser gun for bar coding. This little company has been great fun for me. The guy who heads it up has grown a lot. He has five hundred employees and knows them all. I love that!" He compares Symbol Tech's growth to that of Leasco. "It [the former] went from eight million to forty-five million dollars. I never miss a meeting." Indeed, when Steinberg or Reliance invests heavily in any company, he ordinarily joins its board. "I like the hands-on, tactile. It gives me great pleasure to see or make people get rich."

By some estimates Steinberg is worth $650 million. That doesn't make him unhappy, but he does complain about the attention it brings. "The press has turned businessmen into supercelebrities. I can't go anywhere without being recognized. You can't study people; you go to restaurants, and people recognize you." When he does go out to dinner, he goes to the "few restaurants where people are sensitive to my sensitivities. I don't need adoration, and it gets in the way. I want to enjoy my life for another thirty years.

"I took a boat for a Colorado raft trip. I hadn't talked to regular folks in years." He met a San Francisco fireman and an emergency room nurse.

The irony is, of course, that ten years ago, while Steinberg was a figure of mystery à la his childhood idol, Howard Hughes, he was reviled for being a bad boy engineering hostile takeovers for his own personal gain. "I've only attempted three hostile takeovers in my life: Reliance, Disney, and Chemical Bank," he defends himself. Who knew raiding would become so chic? "I made a big leap in my public perception in the late seventies. Suddenly, establishment types wanted to be in business with us. We're part of—ah—America. Based on accomplishment, not money."

Now that his money looks good to the types who prevented Steinberg from joining their clubs, they're courting him to finance these clubs. Steinberg is on the short A list at the Metropolitan Museum of Art, by all accounts a social charity. "My first dealings with the Met were to create a guide to the museum." He bounds over to his bookshelves to show me the book he commissioned and financed. "I pay for all in-house exhibitions. I paid for the Frank Lloyd Wright room." In exchange for his generosity, protocol was broken for Steinberg, whose daughter Laura was married on April 18, 1988 to Jonathan Tisch, the son of Loewe's magnate Preston "Bob" Tisch, a friendly billionaire. Their wedding reception was held in the main hall of the museum. (Laura had several years earlier celebrated her twenty-first birthday in the Temple of Dendur. As a policy, the museum no longer accommodates private parties.) *Life* magazine requested to cover the event. Although he says he was flattered, he nixed the idea.

Other beneficiaries of Steinberg's goodwill include the Long Island Jewish Hospital—"I gave the main building in honor of my father"—and a chair in psychiatry at the Cornell Medical Center of New York Hospital.

"I'm devoted to democratic capitalism. We should teach capitalism as a dogma. You can't have it and have a closed society.

"What differentiates world-class capitalism from businessmen is, in a downturn, there's an opportunity. I'm an optimist. I'm smart. I listen well. I'm very disciplined. I have very high standards of ethics."

Steinberg says his family is the most important thing in his life. He has five children, three still living at home. "I exercise and have breakfast at home. I walk home and walk to work most days. Every night we're home at six o'clock to have dinner with the children. If I miss four nights a year [with them] in New York, I'd be surprised." (Which doesn't mean he doesn't step out into his high-powered social whirl after his kids' dessert.)

"I'm not tense at work. I can't wait to come to work, but I'm not compulsive anymore."

Oh yes. The art. The office features a Barlac, a Giacometti sculpture, and a Picasso oil. "In the country"—Quogue, a beach community in the Hamptons—"I have the greatest Francis Bacon triptych!" and an extensive contemporary art collection. The Park Avenue apartment is filled with old masters. "I have a great Rubens, a great Rembrandt, a great Titian, a great Brueghel, and a great Hals." But it's 5:45. He has to walk home.

ROBERT STOCK DESIGNS, INC.

HISTORY & OPERATIONS

Men's fashion designer Robert Stock started his career as a teenager, working first as a stock boy and later as a salesman for New York City–based clothing companies. After serving two years as an apprentice trouser designer for Paul Ressler, Ltd., Stock started his own business—Country Britches—to design men's dress slacks and jeans. By the time he was twenty-one, the company's sales had reached $1 million. in 1973, Stock sold Country Britches in order to partner with famed designer Ralph Lauren on his critically acclaimed "Chaps" collection. (Stock owned 20 percent of the company.) Later, Stock and Lauren parted by mutual consent and Stock sold his share of Chaps to Lauren. Creighton Shirtmakers approached Robert to design his own line of casual men's sportswear, and produced "Country Roads" by Robert Stock, a collection that ultimately won Stock the Coty Award, the most coveted award in the fashion industry, in 1978.

Stock formed his design studio, Robert Stock Designs, Inc., in 1981. In 1979, Stock entered into his first licensing agreements with the Japanese, making him something of a pioneer among American designers. In 1982 he negotiated a broad-based licensing agreement with manufacturer Oxford Industries. Beginning with two employees—himself and another designer—Stock established his own label for a line of men's tailored clothing and sportswear. When this venture proved successful, Stock added dress shirts, men's ties and accessories, and outerwear for fall and winter. In 1985, under the terms of another licensing agreement with a company called Lord West, he launched a collection of men's formal wear and formal accessories. The same year, he introduced a small collection of couture menswear called Finery, which he produced through his own company rather than with an outside manufacturer. Though the collection was a critical success, the market for high-priced luxury menswear wasn't big enough for him to sustain a full line, and after three seasons he limited the collection to a custom design basis. In 1986 Stock won the Cutty Sark award, the most prestigious award in men's fashion, in the category of best American designer.

Today, Robert Stock Designs has licensing agreements with five manufacturers in the United States and Canada, as well as agreements with trading companies in Japan, where trading companies sublicense everything to manufacturers. Atlanta-based Oxford Industries, which represents the bulk of Stock's American business, manufactures Robert Stock Dress Shirts and Robert Stock Tailored Clothing. Stock has additional U.S. licensing agreements with Renauld International to make sunglasses (which first hit stores in spring 1987) and with Lord West for a line of formal wear and formal accessories, the items of which are sold or rented nationally through specialty formal wear stores. Robert Stock is involved in a joint venture with Nantucket, Inc., to manufacture and distribute Robert Stock Sportswear (formerly part of the Oxford agreement). In Canada, which has a market about 75 percent smaller than the U.S. market for Robert Stock clothing, the company has a licensing agreement with Ballin, which produces Robert Stock Sportswear, Tailored Clothing, Outerwear, neckwear, belts, and dress shirts. The Canadian clothing is basically the same as the American lines, with some additions and subtle variations in color and design.

The items sold in Japan include the Sportswear, Tailored Clothing, and Outerwear lines, in addition to neckwear, small leather goods, belts, men's jewelry, socks, sunglasses, dress shirts, custom shirts, handkerchiefs, luggage, towels, and robes. Manufacturing takes place all over the world, with the bulk done in the southern United States and the Orient. The manufacturing companies with which Stock has licensing agreements assume all of the manufacturing, distribution, advertising, and related costs for the lines, while Robert Stock Designs, Inc., which picks up the design costs, earns royalties on sales.

The "Robert Stock man," around whom Stock designs all of his lines, can be described as an athletic, rugged, outdoorsy, quintessentially all-American male. Some items—in particular sweaters, which make up roughly 30 percent of the design studio's output—incorporate sporting motifs (baseball, football, hockey, etc.), and the newly created Robert Stock logo, dubbed "the jaunty sportsman," embodies the overall image. The clothing is launched in four separate seasons: holiday (cruisewear), spring/summer, fall 1, and fall 2 (winter)—and the lines are designed approximately one year in advance of each launch.

Today, Robert Stock Designs employs six people full time, including Stock himself (who has final approval on all designs generated within the studio), a vice-president of design, a designer, a vice-president of sales and merchandising, an office manager, and an accessories' designer—Robert's wife Nancy. The studio employs about six semiregular free-lancers as the need arises, as well as the occasional fashion student intern.

Stock recently started what he refers to as a "fashion think tank." This new division, a joint venture with Leisure Concepts, Inc., is called Robert Stock Enterprises, Ltd. It will be a design/marketing entity and will create all new product, including the production of catalogs according to "concept designing"—the design of clothing around particular ideas and themes. Stock will come up with the designs and Leisure Concepts will seek out manufacturers to market and distribute the clothing.

Robert Stock is now partnered with Ascot Chang, the "world's premier shirtmaker," in a joint venture to reintroduce the Finery line, which Stock describes as a "Savile Row-quality" couture collection updated for the eighties, but with a slight sense of humor. The labels in the both off-the-rack and custom-made formal wear, pants, shirts, suits, sportcoats, and neckwear, available exclusively at the Ascot Chang shop on West Fifty-seventh Street in New York reads, "Finery by Robert Stock for Ascot Chang." They are manufactured in Hong Kong.

Possible future plans for Robert Stock Designs include opening free-standing Robert Stock stores in accordance with a new trend called "creative conceptual retailing," which entails creating a distinct and encompassing image for both clothing and the environments in which it is sold. Stock is also considering designing a small women's line of clothing—many women already wear Stock shirts and sweaters—and he is attempting to penetrate the French, Italian, and British markets either through representation by existing stores or by establishing his own stores. Robert Stock Designs, Inc., is wholly owned by Robert Stock.

(Information provided by Robert Stock.)

REVENUES: Company is privately held and will not disclose.

EARNINGS: Company will not disclose.

NUMBER OF EMPLOYEES: Six full-time in the design studio, about half a dozen regular free-lancers, and some consultants.

AVERAGE AGE OF EMPLOYEES: Thirty.

TURNOVER: "We usually get rid of somebody every three to five years."

RECRUITMENT: Robert Stock Designs doesn't have a college recruitment program, although it does have an internship program with FIT (Fashion Institute of Technology) and Parsons School of Design in New York City. Each year the company typically hires one or two interns, who work three months for the studio and receive a small stipend.

NUMBER OF NEW HIRES PER YEAR: Generally one.

RANGE OF STARTING SALARIES: "Competitive with industry standards."

POLICY FOR RAISES: Employees receive raises once a year after a review with Robert. The amount is based on merit, an employee's work load, and how well the company is doing.

TRAINING PROGRAMS: No formal programs. Most Robert Stock employees have a background in design and receive further training on the job.

BENEFITS: Major medical and dental insurance and tuition reimbursement for courses that directly benefit an employee's career at the design studio.

VACATION: One week for each year an employee has worked for the company (no vacation until after a full year's work) with a ceiling of four weeks.

ADDITIONAL PERKS: A discount on company products that is "comparable to industry standards." Also, everybody except the office manager gets to travel to Europe and the Orient on business.

BONUSES: Bonuses are given out on an informal basis, and everyone is eligible. The amount is based partially on merit and partially on the profit margin of the company. If the profit margin in a given year doesn't allow for bonuses, the company gives employees extra vacation days.

ANNUAL PARTY: The company hosts an annual holiday party for employees only, held every year at a "nice" restaurant. "It's wild. It's like a toga party." [Author's note: This was said somewhat facetiously.] In 1986 it was held at Amsterdam's in Soho. In 1987 it was at the Odeon in Tribeca. Employees dress up. "It's a party of designers. Everybody does their own schtick."

AVERAGE WORKDAY: Official hours are 10:00 A.M. to 6:00 P.M. "We work a lot at nights and on weekends due to seasonal pressures."

DRESS CODE: Employees can wear pretty much anything they want, except in meetings and presentations, when professional attire is required (which simply means "looking your best"). Male employees are not required to wear Robert Stock clothing.

SOCIAL ATMOSPHERE: "It's like a party here all day long. People work hard, but it's very congenial and quite informal."

HEADQUARTERS: Robert Stock Designs is headquartered in a postmodern loftlike space of three thousand square feet with traditional details. The offices are divided into four showrooms, four design studios, and three executive offices. Stock's headquarters are located in a brownstone in the garment district.

NUMBER OF PIECES SOLD PER YEAR: Close to one million.

CHARITABLE CONTRIBUTIONS: Company will not disclose amounts. It donates money to the National Conference of Christians and Jews, the American Cancer Society, and a number of AIDS charities.

INTERESTED APPLICANTS CAN SEND RÉSUMÉS TO:
Robert Stock Designs, Inc.
21 West Thirty-ninth Street
New York, NY 10018
(212) 391-7373

When Americans wake up to Bryant Gumbel in the morning, they may unconsciously take in a subtle fashion message. Uncredited, designer Robert Stock dresses him. He dresses Dick Clark. He designed a lot of the clothes in Oliver Stone's movie *Wall Street*. His work has been hailed for its all-American, masculine good looks. A former Coty Award winner, Stock won the 1986 Cutty Sark menswear fashion award for best American designer. (Since the last Coty Awards were presented in 1984, the Cutty Sark has become the highest award bestowed in the fashion community.) And yet, in his sporadic ad campaigns he never flaunts his own image, unlike his better-known counterparts for whom the clothes themselves often seem secondary. (Have you ever really gotten a good look at the clothes in a Calvin Klein or Ralph Lauren ad? Well?) Stock intentionally maintains a low profile and is probably better known in the Midwest than on Fifty-seventh Street in New York, a few blocks from his home.

As a kid in the Bronx, Robert, the son of a gas station owner, became enamored of beautiful clothes and fabrics while a stock boy in a local specialty store, Alvin Murray, on the Grand Concourse, next to the Paradise movie theater. He'd open boxes and see the new, fresh merchandise. With his discount he'd buy clothes, and with his savings he'd pay to have them dry-cleaned. His first trip to Brooks Brothers during high school revealed a fantasy world of elegance, style, and money. "I became infatuated with the heavy wooden store," he says. "It was clean and masculine. It seemed like everyone had money; everything was expensive. Some of the suits were not even hanging—they were folded on tables. They made those incredible heavy, baggy shirts. I felt if I dressed that way, people would think I had a little money." His first purchase was "probably a shirt. I was always a conservative dresser. I wore mostly khaki pants and white button-down shirts." (These days, Stock generally confines his attire to khaki pants and denim shirts, unless he has important meetings or social occasions.)

A sales rep for a neckwear line who sold to Alvin Murray, a fellow Bronxite named Ralph Lauren, recommended Stock to Paul Ressler, an early manufacturer of flare-legged pants. "It was right after the mod revolution," Robert remembers. "Ressler developed classic-looking flared trousers, then wide-legged ones in tweeds, printed corduroys—interesting fabrics." It was 1969, and Stock was now a salesman. With a hungry territory consisting of Manhattan, the Bronx, Staten Island, and New Jersey, he drove the samples around in his yellow Volkswagen. He'd try them on for his customers. He sold to stores with names like Limbo, Conspiracy, The Naked Grape, The Different Drummer [Author's note: Whence the author's first pair of bellbottoms came], and Revelation. He made a lot of money for an eighteen-year-old kid.

Stock often made design suggestions to Ressler. One day his boss asked him, " 'Would you like to design?' I asked, 'How much does it pay?' He said, 'Not as much as selling.' I said, 'Why should I?' He said, 'We're going to cut your territory anyway.' " Robert's territory was too profitable to remain intact, so he decided to try designing for real. He had never taken so much as one class in design.

"I had good taste and good fabric and color sense. I was never a technician. I worked with pattern makers, et cetera. I couldn't sketch. I guess I was really more a stylist or an orchestrator. I was good at putting things together." Robert no longer remembers his first design that made it to production. He laughs when asked whether he saved his early work.

In 1972 Stock and a partner from Ressler's company met with a guy who would finance their own company. They called it Country Britches. Its concept was to adapt the classic jean in sophisticated, unusual fabrics. They used khaki, corduroy, velveteen, seersucker, patchwork madras. It was successful. A fan of Country Britches, Ralph Lauren, approached Robert in 1973 about designing a less expensive Polo-like line. "I thought it was a good idea and it would further my career." The line was christened Chaps. For the first time Stock was no longer confined to designing trousers and was now creating sportcoats, suits, then shirts and sweaters. He sold his interest a couple of years later and took jobs with large companies, like Manhattan Industries and Eagle Shirtmakers.

He thinks it was in 1976 that Creighton Shirtmakers talked to him about designing a full sportswear collection. They called it Country Roads. "It was really the forerunner of the rugged, updated L. L. Bean type clothing, with a more fashion look. It was functional but styled for gentlemen, not farmers."

After two years that included his Coty award win in 1978, Robert decided to go off on his own and license his own name. It was a risk. "Even though I got credit for the Chaps and Country Roads lines, I never had my name on the label. It never said 'Robert Stock for Country Roads.' [Although his name was mentioned in the ads.] It never said 'Chaps—designed by Robert Stock.' Since I'd never tried licensing before, I made a few mistakes by licensing to too many people." Stock was being pulled in too many directions. The company that licensed his sweaters was different from the one that did his shirts, which was different from the one that did his ties. He struck a deal with Yagitsuscho, a manufacturer in Japan. He was spread too thin.

1981 was the year it all changed. He signed a licensing agreement with Oxford Industries to make all sportswear and tailored clothing. He maintained his relationship with Yagitsuscho. He could consolidate under fewer roofs. That year he also established Robert Stock Designs.

Today he runs a design studio in Midtown in the garment center. He has five employees (plus himself), most of whom are designers. Robert Stock Designs, Inc. is a private company owned by Stock. He estimates that about a million pieces bearing his name are sold each year. "It's a very mercenary, very tough business—worse than ever. Lots of stores knock off designs themselves." In the last few years Robert has become involved in consulting to large retailers, offering conceptual advice. A new division called Robert Stock Enterprises Ltd. "is like a design think tank," aimed at coordinating merchandise and the catalogues that sell it and to present a unified look. Future plans may include retail stores for Robert or a women's line.

David "the Rave" McTague was a vice-president of the concern. He joined Robert in August 1985 after graduating from Virginia Commonwealth University. During his senior year, he worked at the Richmond branch of Britches of Georgetown, an upscale classic clothing store, where he again works. "I had always been clothes conscious, and my mother is an interior designer, so I was always exposed to creativity through expression in fabrication and color."

Robert, Dave's brother-in-law, used Dave to sell his new couture line, Finery. It was a small line, doing about $250,000 to $300,000 a year. It gave McTague the opportunity to learn every aspect of the business: placing orders for piece goods [raw materials], finding manufacturers, selling. Most of the line was made in the Northeast, and Dave hand-packed each order, hand-wrote each invoice, and shipped everything out. Finery was a critical smash. Stock won glowing reviews from the fashion press, who adored the luxurious details and the consistency of vision. For customers, the line was expensive, and many pieces were perhaps a bit too advanced for the average fellow. Finery was disbanded after three seasons, but David had done a good job and he earned a promotion.

According to McTague, "I was promoted purely as a result of my achievements, not because of nepotism." If anything, to this reporter, McTague appeared to have worked harder as overcompensation for his coincidental kinship. He spent half his time working with lawyers and pursued a self-styled tutorial in business and legal studies. Dave also took courses at Parsons School of Design, not because he wanted to design but because "I want to know everything there is to know about this business. Period."

Constantine Kouros is Robert Stock's vice-president of design. Born in Athens, Kouros waged a long struggle with his father, who always pressured him to be a lawyer. By the end of high school, Constantine knew he wanted to do something in fashion. After doing poorly his first semester in law at Athens University, he went off to complete his two years' mandatory service in the Greek army. He then became a purser for Olympic Airlines and traveled the world.

In 1976, against his father's wishes, Kouros enrolled in New York's Fashion Institute of Technology. He says, "I knew at that point it was really fashion design." He graduated in

1978, specializing in women's wear and winning the Gold Medal for best student designer of the year. Between 1978 and 1985, Constantine designed women's clothes for Simon Ellis, Lloyd Williams, and Gant for Women. Robert Stock discovered him at Gant and asked him to join him as design director.

"I picked up men's design after a few months, and now I think it's the best thing that ever happened to me. I love the working environment here, and I respect Robert's approach to menswear." Constantine doesn't particularly project the image he designs, integrating classic items from the collection with some hipper basics. He feels comfortable now as a designer of both menswear and women's wear. "I design myself, but Robert approves everything and guides us." Kouros does have final say on all the designs for Ballin, Robert Stock Design, Inc.'s Canadian licenser, along with Robert. "It's my responsibility to make sure that it's correct for the Canadian man. He's influenced by Europe, and it's slightly more sophisticated but still representative of the Robert Stock man."

The work cycle is as follows: Design takes between two and three months for each collection. Another fourteen months will go by before it hits the stores, during which time the designers travel to Italy and the Orient to select fabrics. Robert and his team try not to succumb to industry trends, although they are certainly aware of them. The 1988 collections are "Bar Harbor"—bright, primary colors for winter—and "Bayou Tones"—more muted shades for spring. "It takes a long time to zero in." Constantine spends a lot of time walking around looking at the "Robert Stock man," looking for inspiration. "Robert treats us well."

Ali Taghavi may be the only knitwear designer in the world who is allergic to wool. He was offered a job by Robert when he showed up at his studio wearing one of his designs. (It was made of cotton.) However, Ali says he doesn't much like wearing sweaters at all. Born in Iran, he was raised in England and earned his degree in textiles from the Brighton Polytechnic in 1983. He moved to the States in 1985.

Robert Stock Designs has earned high marks for its sweaters, which make up 30 percent of each line. Ali says he designs the lion's share of them. Dark and bearded, he is not the typical "Robert Stock man" and hence does not wear his own work. "My concept of the RSM is very all-American. We use American motifs like baseball, football, and hockey. [And 1986's Statue of Liberty sweater, one of the best sellers of the year.] The image is athletic, which doesn't mean anything to me." At first, adhering to the image was "a stretch, but it comes easily now. At first, a lot of times I would pick color schemes which were too intricate, too outrageous, and too difficult to make in the Orient. A lot ended up being too expensive to produce. Now I know the limitations and the mentality of what Robert wants, and Robert approves nine out of ten designs." Out of a possible eighty designs, thirty will actually get produced.

"I don't get bored. I'm happy, I still like the environment, I have a lot of responsibility, and I've grown. Many companies are stiff, and at Robert Stock I've had the rare opportunity of designing right out of school."

SCALI,
McCABE,
SLOVES, INC.

SCALI, M^cCABE, SLOVES

HISTORY & OPERATIONS

Scali, McCabe, Sloves, Inc. (SMS), was founded in 1967 by five talented ad men, all in their thirties, who were discontented with working for other people's agencies and wanted to set up shop for themselves. Four of the original five founders, listed with their original titles, were Marvin Sloves, president; Sam Scali, vice-president and art director; Alan Pesky, vice-president and director of account services; and J. Leonard Hultgren, vice-president and director of agency services. All four had worked for the New York agency Papert, Koenig & Lois, while the fifth, Ed McCabe, vice-president and copy director, came from Carl Ally, another New York agency. All of them had reached the level of vice-president at their former agencies, and each of them specialized in a different aspect of full service advertising. As tough, aggressive, young men from a variety of ethnic and educational backgrounds, the five represented new blood in an industry previously dominated by Eastern establishment Ivy Leaguers. The partners outlined clear goals for the new agency—"We wanted to make a lot of money; we wanted to be large and employ lots of people; we wanted to leave an important imprint on the advertising community"—and shared high standards for what they believed should be "humane, relevant, intelligent advertising."

SMS rented office space in a two-room suite at New York's Gotham Hotel and went to work with one secretary/receptionist/typist, no clients, and enough money to operate for a year with zero billings. They provided their first work free to Citizens for a Quieter City, a grass roots anti–noise pollution organization. Then, two weeks after they opened, Volvo, which had formerly been with Carl Ally (though Ed McCabe was not the copywriter on their account), brought its business to SMS.

Volvo meant $10 million in annual billings, and the agency's highly successful advertising campaign for the carmaker earned it the beginnings of a reputation for creative advertising with aggressive selling power. Other accounts followed, and SMS grew rapidly. Within two months after opening, the agency moved to a Madison Avenue address, and two years later it moved again to Park Avenue.

SMS continued to grow during the seventies, a decade during which many advertising agencies suffered or went out of business entirely. The partners were the pioneers of the dog-eat-dog selling style that came to characterize the era, which entailed selling a given product by going after the jugular of rival products. An example of this strategy was SMS's campaign for Seneca apple juice, which showed triplet toddlers, one drinking Hawaiian Punch, one drinking Hi-C, and the third drinking Seneca, with voice-over copy that read: "Hi-C has 10 percent real fruit juice, and kids love it. Hawaiian Punch has 11 percent real fruit juice, and kids love it. Seneca has 100 percent real fruit juice, and kids love it. Which one would you rather have your kids guzzle down?" SMS's most visible success during this period was its campaign for Perdue chickens, which made an instant celebrity of Frank Perdue and made chicken, which people had formerly bought without regard to the packager, a brand name product. SMS took on the Perdue account in 1971, and within four years Perdue's sales increased 125 percent. By 1973 SMS had a staff of seventy-five and annual billings of $25 million.

In 1974 Ed McCabe was the youngest person ever elected to the New York Copy Club Copywriter's Hall of Fame. The agency, which was by then known as one of the hottest shops in town, moved to permanent headquarters on Third Avenue that same year. In 1975 *Advertising Age* picked SMS as its Agency of the Year. With $28 million in billings at the time, it was the smallest agency ever to win the honor. In 1977 Ogilvy & Mather, a large public agency, bought SMS for nearly $15 million as a wholly owned subsidiary. The founders became millionaires, and Ogilvy & Mather guaranteed it would never interfere with SMS's business and that the two agencies would remain competitors.

During the late seventies and eighties SMS expanded dramatically—both in the United States and abroad—by acquiring existing agencies and founding new ones. In 1977 it opened branch offices in Canada and Australia (SMS/Toronto, SMS/Montreal, and SMS in Melbourne). In 1979 it acquired a minority interest in Abbot, Mead, Vickers, a London agency with a strong creative reputation; in 1981 it bought the Mexico City agency Hart Associates (now SMS de Mexico); and in 1982 it acquired the Dusseldorf agency Hildmann, Simon, Rempen & Schmitz/SMS. In 1985 the agency added the French agency Audour, Soum, Larue/Scali, McCabe Sloves, and two U.S. agencies, Scali, Macabe, Sloves/West (in Los Angeles) and Scali, McCabe, Sloves/South (in Atlanta). In 1986, SMS further enlarged its U.S. presence by acquiring the majority interest in two American agencies with reputations as "hot shops." The first, Fallen, McElligott, is a Minneapolis agency that was founded in 1980 and picked as Agency of the Year by *Advertising Age* only three years later (besting SMS's own record as the smallest agency ever to be thus honored). Fallon, which turned down offers from many other agencies before agreeing to sell an 80 percent interest in itself to SMS, has a client list that includes *The Wall Street Journal*, Federal Express Zap Mail, Armour frozen foods, and *Rolling Stone* magazine. The second hot shop, the Martin Agency, Inc., is a medium-sized agency based in Richmond, Virginia, with a client list that includes Coty, Inc., Pet, Inc., and General Motors Corporation. In 1986 Scali McCabe also purchased a minority interest in Stevens & Buchsbaum and opened SMS/Brazil. Since then, it has added offices in Vancouver, Calgary, and Madrid.

Leonard Hultgren resigned from the agency at the end of 1981, Ed McCabe left in 1986, and Alan Pesky departed at the end of 1987. Marvin Sloves, chairman and CEO, and Sam Scali, president and worldwide creative director, remain at the helm. Today, Scali McCabe Sloves employs approximately 1,200 people—382 in its New York office—and has three U.S. offices and twelve abroad. Its 1987 worldwide billings reached $653 million—$507 million of which were domestic—ranking it as the eighteenth largest agency in the country. Among the clients on its roster are: Volvo, Perdue, Hertz Corporation, Chase Manhattan Bank, Sharp Electronics, Equitable Life Insurance of the United States, Ralston Purina, A. H. Robbins, Toys 'R' Us, Kids R Us, Schering Corporation, and Maxell Corporation of America.

In 1987, SMS negotiated to buy 20 percent of itself back from Ogilvy & Mather, with the option to reacquire 10 percent more. It plans to exercise that option by buying another 5 percent in 1988 and the remaining 5 percent in 1989. In the beginning of 1988, the agency restructured, eliminating its Los Angeles and Atlanta offices, and announced its strategy for further growth. In the words of Chairman Marvin Sloves: "There are very few businesses with changes so radical on a constant basis as the advertising industry. Scali, McCabe, Sloves is no different than any other agency. It's only different in how it approaches changing problems. For example, in 1988, we decided to close our Los Angeles and Atlanta offices. We decided that the Scali, McCabe, Sloves Confederation should acquire agencies that are already established, creative and entrepreneurial. There is no virtue in having your name on every door, no matter what it costs you."

(Information provided by Marvin Sloves, chairman, and Louise Carlson, company spokesperson.)

RANKING: Eighteenth among U.S. agencies in terms of worldwide gross billings in 1987.

BILLINGS: $653 million worldwide in 1987, $507 million of which were domestic.

EARNINGS: The agency will not disclose.

OFFICES: The agency has headquarters in New York and fourteen additional offices in Minneapolis, Richmond, Calgary, Dusseldorf, London, Madrid, Melbourne, Mexico City, Montreal, Paris, São Paulo, Rio de Janeiro, Toronto, and Vancouver.

NUMBER OF EMPLOYEES: 1,200, with 382 working in the United States—New York headquarters is the agency's only U.S. office in which employees are considered to be working for SMS rather than an affiliated agency—and the rest working abroad.

AVERAGE AGE OF EMPLOYEES: 33.7.

TURNOVER: Agency will not disclose.

RECRUITMENT: None.

NUMBER OF NEW HIRES PER YEAR: No average figures, SMS hired 240 new employees in 1987.

RANGE OF STARTING SALARIES: $11,000—$18,000 for nonexempt employees (people entitled to overtime); $18,000–$24,000 for entry-level (exempt) account coordinators, traffic people, media people, etc.

POLICY FOR RAISES: Employees are eligible annually, and raises are based on merit.

TRAINING PROGRAMS: No formal programs.

BENEFITS: Medical, dental, and life insurance. Officers receive additional benefits that the agency won't disclose.

VACATION: Two weeks up to the fifth year, three weeks from the fifth through tenth years, and four weeks over ten years, in addition to ten regular paid holidays per year.

ADDITIONAL PERKS: "Those are negotiated based upon your level."

BONUSES: "Bonuses are based on company and individual performance. Officer level is eligible, which is not to say that someone else couldn't get one, but most of the time they're awarded on a high executive level. The better [the agency] does, the better everyone else does."

ANNUAL PARTIES: The agency hosts an annual Christmas party—for employees, no spouses—at a different place each year, with music, dancing, drinking, and food. SMS celebrated its twentieth anniversary in May 1987 with a big party at the Four Seasons restaurant, for vice-presidents and above, to which the press was invited, as well as clients and competitors. There was also an all-staff anniversary party. Each staffer received twenty one-dollar bills to commemorate the occasion. Scali McCabe also holds an annual officers' luncheon at the Four Seasons—generally on the day of the Christmas party—for vice-presidents and above. In 1986, the agency instituted an annual international conference—usually in June—where all of the "heads of state" from Scali's affiliated agencies meet and catch up. In 1986, the conference was held in the south of France, and in 1987 it was in Venice.

AVERAGE WORKDAY: Official hours are 9:30 A.M. to 5:30 P.M. "Sometimes people work around the clock. Sometimes people work weekends getting ready for a particular project. That's everybody, including the mail room, and it happens often. It's a hard-working place and people come here to work knowing that they may often be expected to work long hours." During the summer, the agency closes at 1:00 P.M. on Fridays.

DRESS CODE: Dress code is rather dependent on where you work. Creative is the most relaxed and casual, and noncreative staff people dress fairly conservatively. "There are a lot of suspenders around here. Writers and art directors dress very casually; however, the secretaries in the Creative Department have to maintain certain standards, which include no sneakers, no jeans, no shorts. On summer Fridays, when we close early, people tend to dress much more casually. But aside from that, everyone is pretty much well dressed."

SOCIAL ATMOSPHERE: "A lot of the creatives spend so much time together on a particular assignment that they often take breaks for dinner and then come back and work late into the night. A lot of personal relationships do develop among people who work together and work well together."

HEADQUARTERS: The agency leases nine full floors and part of two additional floors in a building in midtown Manhattan. It has 85,000 square feet of office space, with "white walls and gray carpeting, a sparse, modern look."

CHARITABLE CONTRIBUTIONS: The agency will not disclose.

INTERESTED APPLICANTS CAN SEND RÉSUMÉS TO:
Scali, McCabe, Sloves
Personnel Department
800 Third Avenue
New York, NY 10022
(212) 735-8000

A visit to Scali, McCabe, Sloves is rewarding in that it looks like what you think an advertising agency should look like—whatever that means. The offices and its inhabitants look prosperous and properly trendy, the account side appropriately buttoned-up, and the creative side appropriately unconventional. Well thought of for its creative contributions to the field, the agency is entering a new phase, and it is possible even for an outsider to feel the changes under way.

They all started when Ed McCabe announced he would be leaving Scali, McCabe, Sloves. Aas a self-styled *enfant terrible* and the first copywriter on board, he was the creative force who brought an audaciousness to the agency and in turn new clients, who wanted to share in their creative risk taking. At the time of his resignation, he was also a president. His departure paved the way for a serious regrouping and the development of a new imprint.

Sam Scali, creative director, cut his teeth at Doyle, Dane, Bernbach, for years universally hailed as the most innovative agency. "Without DDB there would never have been an SMS," he says from his sunny office overlooking Third Avenue in New York. "I hadn't really known anything about advertising. I always liked to draw, and I went to an art high school. I thought I'd want to be an illustrator, but for me the fun was in conceiving more than in drawing." By a process of elimination, Scali decided to pursue advertising. By 1967, as an art director at Papert, Koenig, Lois, Scali and his friends Marvin Sloves and Allen Pesky recognized that "agencies were broken up, specializing in different things. It was an à la carte business. The five of us [Hultgren and McCabe] represented different disciplines—two creative, two marketing, one research. We were structured like a big agency."

Planning for the new agency took six months. Then, on May 1, 1967, Scali, McCabe, Sloves opened its doors to a tiny two-room office in a hotel. "We got a phone call from Volvo on June first," Scali recalls, a piece of advertising history as familiar and mythologized as the day the Revolutionary War was won, "and we got the account on June fifteenth." Winning a client so quickly—without an organizational track record—is practically unheard of. "In retrospect, we were stupid enough to think it would be easy." Today, twenty-one years later, SMS still has the Volvo account, which, is one of the agency's largest pieces of business. "In 1967 Volvo was an inexpensive European car. Now its image is luxury. That's gratifying."

"When it came to creative, Ed and I ran it; Marvin ran the agency, and he still does." It was important to the partners, as defectors from other agencies, that they run their office as openly as possible. "I usually leave my door open, and people know they can approach me. Everyone knows who makes decisions, but I don't want people scared of me." It is difficult to imagine that this soft-spoken man—who still lives in the Queens neighborhood where he grew up—could be intimidating, but advertising, with its toxic degree of insecurity, seems to choreograph a lot of scared running around.

"People who come to work here love the business and work hard. Yes, there's high pressure.

For creative people, if the pressure isn't there, we create it. Competition I don't try to foster. I try for people to not settle. I don't like people to say, 'I finished. What's next?' "

SMS is now a big agency, to the surprise of those who joined it as and because it was a small one. The first big growth spurt came in 1971–72, a year that was hard on the rest of the industry, and the second spurt followed the agency's winning *Advertising Age*'s Agency of the Year award in 1975. SMS was the youngest and smallest agency ever to win the coveted honor. "It gets harder to run the agency as it gets bigger. I know we're a big agency, but we run it like a small one."

If there are so many virtues to being to a small organization, why expand this one? "There's no such thing as a great middle-sized or small agency. You go to sleep and get bored, disgruntled." Growth, to the partners, is an imperative. "Who wants to be an agency that's not going anywhere? If you're good, you've got to grow.

"We haven't tripled in one year. We've had manageable growth. It's hard to turn down good business. It's not hard to find good people." And an offer from Scali, McCabe is hard to turn down.

In 1987, the agency was involved in approximately thirty pitches for new business. "To me, when you produce a campaign and see it to life, that's the most exciting," Scali feels. When SMS wins a new account, he believes "the client is mostly buying the way we think, not the pitched campaign."

One reason for corporate bullishness is Scali, McCabe's posture on acquisitions. Having themselves been acquired by the giant Ogilvy & Mather in 1977, albeit with the promise of autonomy, SMS itself has purchased some of the newer hot agencies, the Scali, McCabes of today and tomorrow, in fact. "In acquisitions, we buy agencies with which we have a lot in common. We're a confederation of agencies with one thing in common: excellent work. We want the best in the area." Indeed, while New York is effectively the center of advertising, one no longer has to live and work here to be taken seriously. You don't even have to pay your dues in New York. "The business has changed," says Scali. "I think more people are going to leave New York to work." Fallon, McElligott, Rice, a boutique in Minneapolis, was 1983's Agency of the Year, breaking Scali's record as the smallest agency ever to win. SMS bought Fallon, McElligott (Rice had left by then) in 1986 and also bought the controlling interest in The Martin Agency in Richmond, Virgina, perhaps the Southeast's "hottest" agency. "We're acquiring people, not businesses. We believe the same things about advertising as our acquisitions. So culture's not a problem. There are no conflicts. We don't have to give up accounts."

Earl Cavanah is considered one of the stars in the creative department. An executive vice-president and associate creative director, he comes from El Centro, California, a small town near the Mexican border. He arrived at Scali sixteen years ago. "In those days you had to get your New York experience," he says resignedly. Earl lives outside the city in Westchester County and after all these years still hasn't grown fond of New York. Why does he stay? "I have too much stuff to move." No, Earl, be serious. "I can't think of a better job right now. I think I have the kind of job people in New York want. I'd be a summer camp counselor, but that wouldn't pay enough money." He does have a cool office, one must admit, filled with carousels of Magic Markers and his art director awards. "You can wear jeans and look creative. If you're doing a good job, you should be able to wear a three-piece suit." While not bowing totally to the pressure to be hip, Earl is wearing a thin tie, gray jacket and jeans.

His title implies administrative obligations. "We manage accounts, not people. It's a disorganized system, like a pickup football game. You get to float around. You don't stay on one account too long. It's a difficult system to administer. I have to rely on people to tell me what they're doing. I don't go looking for them. It's a good system to hide out in." However, "clients like continuity. That's where we fit in." There is one person—let's call her "Sandra Sims"—who keeps track of which of the thirty-eight creatives are working on what. When a team is free—a creative usually marries a partner, as it were—it gets the next assignment. Supervisors are in the pool, too.

"We do know that some teams work better than others. You are always doing something new. You can turn jobs down. There are no cigarette accounts here, because the whole agency turned them down. We did have *Playboy*." Cavanah remembers that SMS did good work for the magazine. "Women would have been able to turn it down [without jeopardizing their standing at the agency] but none did."

Satisfaction is derived from the ability to do good work for a client. It's even better when you respect that client. "Volvo's a very good client. They actually buy our good ideas. What makes a *good* client? Someone perceptive enough to recognize a good idea or come up with a good idea." In exchange for living up to these requirements, the people at Scali who work for you will be loyal to you. "I drive a Volvo," Earl concedes. "I even *own* one." If it came down to a tug-of-war between the agency and the client, however, "I represent the agency. I've witnessed Volvo wanting one thing and the agency wanting something else." Those disagreements can happen all the time, with clients who are "good," "bad," or indifferent. Conflicts usually arise between the creative idea and the client's goals. Sometimes they can be resolved between the two parties. Sometimes the account people have to step in. Since the client pays for the advertising, though, it's usually the winner.

In a creatively driven agency such as Scali, McCabe, Sloves, keeping the creatives happy is not a low priority. "The agency has always been respectful of the creative staff. (Also of our marketing.) The creative person is in control," Cavanah says. "You can think up a little joke and put it on national TV. Commercials have the personality of the team that created them." Earl works with Larry Cadman. We're known as a humor team. We do some sarcastic work."

No matter how long someone's been working in advertising, he or she still enjoys seeing the fruits of his or her labor on television. They are susceptible to good advertising. "Advertising people are the best consumers. We know if it's claimed on TV it's probably true. We know how hard it is to get stuff across." For Earl, car advertising is the most fun. It's also expensive advertising, and one where trends can change quickly. "We were one of the first companies to use a black car. (They had been considered mysterious and Darth Vader-like.) They were never used before because they get too hot in sunny weather and look like hearses. Now everyone shows black cars."

Larry Cadman has worked at Scali for fourteen years, "pretty unusual for an agency this size." (He's thinking back to the days when Scali was small.) As another executive vice-president and associate creative director and Cavanah's partner, he says his longevity is due to "pure money motivation combined with camaraderie and the corporate culture." Cadman asked himself is he could be comfortable at SMS before he moved there.

"Because this place is newer and more pioneering, there's less politics than at bigger agencies." After a few years at other agencies, "I learned to trust myself. I had solved 'fit' problems by leaving other agencies. I'd brood a lot. I'd say things like 'They're doing it to me.' I was spending too much time not feeling good." Not that there isn't adequate reason to feel insecurity. "Especially in creative. There are some emotional characters. There is competition to do good work, to get good assignments. A lot of it is unspoken."

Cadman made the transition from worker to supervisor painlessly. "One day you realize you're no longer one of the guys sitting around complaining about your boss. You're one of the ones *they're* complaining about." Being one of "them" instead of one of "us," Larry nevertheless prefers to leave the job of reviewing other people's work to Earl. A writer, Cadman has, like most, wondered what he would ever do if he left the agency. Perhaps it's a function of former advertising personnel making it big in other areas. Most creatives everywhere have a "plan B." "If I won the lottery, would I leave tommorrow? No. I think I would do a screenplay with Earl. I'd take acting lessons. Maybe it's just talk." What's keeping him at SMS? "I didn't fit in so well at big agencies, where you have to be visible and tied in to the 'right' people. Scali is small. It's run by one highly motivated, smart, ass-kicking guy. The quality of the work has always been good. There's freedom. Most of our work sees fruition." And, to the untrained eye, there are at least three Clio (the Academy Award of advertising) statuettes displayed in his office.

Yet, this vote of confidence doesn't imply he'll stick around for another fourteen years. If or when he leaves, Larry stresses it won't be because the the small agency he selected has become a big one. "There's nothing I would like to see more than for this place to grow. If I left, it wouldn't be due to dissatisfaction; just to follow a personal agenda. In retrospect, people look back on the 'good old days,' " he says, "but there was stuff that was just okay then. I'm one of the few people here who'd say our standards are as high now as they were before [the agency grew]."

He is a premeditator. An English major, class of 1964 at the University of Michigan, Cadman is another small-town native. "So I wanted the biggest, most frightening city I could imagine: New York!" His intention was to write the great American novel. His wife was a secretary at J. Walter Thompson and suggested that while he was waiting for the muse he try to write advertising copy. After three years, "I looked at my life and knew it would never happen again, so my wife and I spent six months in Europe." They returned on schedule.

"Someday, I'd like to have my own company. You reach a level—recognition, money, awards—what's next? There aren't many companies that are better than this one."

Jeff Johnson, a relative newcomer, earned his Ph.D. in psychology and found jobs doing reseach "in as many different places as would pay me." These included studies for *Psychology Today, Money* magazine, and work on Gail Sheehy's book *Pathfinders*. He wanted to work in the private sector and says now, "I knew nothing about business at the time. My father had managed an A and P store. I was young. It wasn't a love of advertising. It was pure circumstance." After interviewing "everywhere" from banks to AT&T, he got a job offer from another agency. "A lot of places won't talk to Ph.D.'s." He enjoyed his work and even went so far as to say that "People were smart . . . comparatively speaking. I didn't know that that was specific to advertising."

At Scali, McCabe, Sloves, to which he was recruited, Johnson's mission is strategic planning as it's senior vice-president. "I've been able to create this job that's good for me. It just evolved. This is the least structured place I've ever worked." However, "the management style varies a lot from account to account. It bothered me a lot at first. It's harder here for young people. Although they do hire young people, I wouldn't send someone brand new here. Older people can handle less structure." Johnson adds, "I've been working on Marvin [Sloves, chairman] to start a training program."

Johnson corroborates that SMS is creatively driven. A noncreative (technically), he says, "It's the most comfortable place I've ever worked in terms of relationships with creatives." But "it's transitional. Now they want to be more marketing and strategic driven. I wouldn't call this place high-pressure at all. Clearly, some weeks you have to stay late and can't go out to dinner . . ." He uses the expression "leanly staffed," explaining that "Marvin will fire people for incompetence. You've got to be pretty bad to get fired, and you will. Marvin's very, very loyal to people, though."

It is interesting that the employees who identify with the account or business side describe their SMS experiences as reflections of Marvin Sloves, and that those who are in the creative department talk about McCabe or simply about their own work. Perhaps there are really two Scali, McCabe, Sloveses. Perhaps there are even more.

"One of the bad things about this place is, there's no annual evaluation. People at a junior level have no idea how they're doing. I think it's because Marvin still thinks there are only twenty-two people working here." Annual raises are calibrated to one's anniversary of employment. "Even if Marvin doesn't know who you are, the executive vice-president of your group knows, and that's close enough to him. You're not here too long before Marvin and Sam know who you are. It makes a difference."

Jeff would not use the word "competitive" to describe the personality(ies) of the agency, but he admits, "It is natural to compare yourself to people at your level. You have to keep an eye out toward other people. This is a business, not a social club." However, he adds, "I need to work in a friendly environment where people like me."

For some, advertising is an ambition that started with an early devotion to Darren Stephens, the frantic, constantly threatened, worrywart of an adman played by Dick York (and later Dick Sargent) on the Elizabeth Montgomery sitcom *Bewitched* (1964–72). Myron Goble, child of the television generation, left Atlanta for New York in order to work for an old boss who moved up to Scali. "I always thought Darren Stephens had a good job," he says in a slight southern accent. "That may sound stupid. I even told the real estate broker I wanted an apartment like Ann Marie {the character portrayed by Marlo Thomas in the 1966–71 sitcom *That Girl*} had. And she found me one."

There was something a tad dewy-eyed about Myron, just eight months after his arrival to the land of make-believe. For one thing, he found an affordable apartment half a block from his office. For another, the man he followed to SMS he characterizes as "my mentor and my best friend." Lest you think his breaks are too lucky to be true, Goble admits, "I've been buried here in this office. It's taken me awhile to acclimate myself. It's much more demanding here. It requires a new discipline." He's in marketing, a smaller division, now as a vice-president and managing supervisor. "Most account people consider themselves frustrated creative people. The goal of the agency is to get the best creative productions out there."

Given the tension that can exist between the agency and the client, Myron says, "I work for Scali. I love my client. I want the agency to win. I want to win, too." On his bulletin board there is a color snapshot of Myron's recent birthday celebration, filled with (new) friends. These are the people he cares about in his new home. "Edna {my boss} lets me know how I do, and if I feel neglected or down or kicked-on, I pop the question. {'How am I doing?'} She gives me a thoughtful answer. There are no formal mechanisms that give you feedback."

Titles are not important here, Goble says. As proof, everyone from Marvin down is on a first-name basis. "VIPs are common. Money is not *that* important a motivator. Everyone wants in because of the glamour. Glamour draws you into advertising, and you redefine glamour as you go on." Glamour? Working with a celebrity on a commercial shoot will be fun at first, but essentially you know you're in for just another long day on the job.

Barbara Titus, a tall, elegant woman, looks right at home in her large elegant office. As director of research for SMS, she reports to Marvin Sloves but is partisan to neither creative services nor account services. She says the agency's image was more a reflection of McCabe than it was of Sloves, but feels the identity as a small (family) agency is the most pervasive. She's been at SMS for twelve years, and her job is to be an advocate for the consumer.

"We become the client's market researchers, if, like Perdue, they don't have that department. We plan and keep the needs of the consumer in mind when developing a campaign. The question I keep asking is not, 'What's in it for us?' but 'What's in it for the consumer?' " Barbara is the person who commissions and/or executes studies to help size up her clients' consumers. "We take the out-of-pocket costs and bill them to the client. Sometimes we bill seventeen percent. Our time and service are part of the full service commission. We're not a profit center and were never meant to be. We do most postresearch analysis ourselves. We understand our client better and can bring our insight to it."

The research department has thirteen members. "We're probably top-heavy," Titus says. "There are more senior-level people here." Each person is responsible for two to three accounts (except for Perdue, which is research intensive), accounting for half a million dollars of business per year. "You get excited about your business when you see the social aspects of the studies —finding out how many single men buy Perdue Done-it [precooked] chickens. Our orientation is not math. I like to understand what's *under* the numbers. There's a lot of reward in getting serious about all of this."

Barbara is happy at Scali, her third agency, because "we get respect from creative." Furthermore, because Sam Scali believes that research should be "spread into creative," her department is located on a "creative floor. And this is an agency that believes in listening to the consumer." She was hired by one of the original partners, Len Hultgren, who was a researcher. "He hired me with the understanding that within six months it'd be my department. And it was. He was great." As a hirer, Barbara looks for people "with advertising agency experience who understand my philosophy. Although I'm prejudiced toward the liberal arts, that background is not important. One of the last things I want is someone who studied market research." She's interested in "curiosity about motivations, an insight into what people say versus what they mean. We're not technicians." Titus knows when she's met an applicant with the right fit. "You can see it when you talk to them. I can tell you within fifteen minutes if they'll work out."

Barbara is married without children. "It was a conscious decision. I admire women who can do it all, but I had to recognize I couldn't."

Depending on with whom you speak, Keith Green in SMS's single most controversial employee. Brought in by Marvin Sloves from Atlanta [he is Myron Goble's mentor, previously mentioned], he ran what he calls the "fastest-growing agency in Atlanta" from 1979 to 1983. When he was diverted by other interests and his agency suffered, "I met Marvin Sloves, who said he'd try to save the agency, and if he couldn't, he'd own me." That's how he got to New York four years ago. Keith speaks of Sloves alternately as his boss and as his friend. More precisely, he says, "Marvin's my best friend. No matter what they pay, it's not worth coming to work [for the money]. I like these people."

Green says his title is "ad hoc assistant to the chairman," sort of. "My job is to do what I'm told," he says at first. Then, on a serious note, he adds, "I try to articulate the strategy for us and our clients. I'm consciously trying to facilitate people working together." Green provokes dissent because people aren't exactly sure what it all means. Does believing in his mission force people to take sides? It seems to. He's shaking things up, and no one's sure of the consequences. "Getting to know me involves certain risks," he claims obliquely. "It's my cross to bear." [Nevertheless, Keith has since been dubbed executive vice-president, director of marketing services.]

Part of Green's charter is "to be better. We don't want to be better than Ted Bates [a huge agency, now part of the Saatchi empire], we want to be better at being Scali. I'm describing Marvin or Scali: dignity, style, class, love. We're purging Ed [McCabe] from today's Scali. He rejected us." Anyway, the creative force "wasn't *just* Ed. It was Ed and Sam. Ed was sharkier. Sam's a better leader. He's a more mature player." Green arrived at SMS as McCabe was leaving. (It was a gradual process.) "I don't think he's relevant to the Scali story today, except that he exists and he made a huge contribution to the industry."

And now, ladies and gentlemen: Marvin Sloves, Scali's longtime chairman. A liberal arts graduate of Brandeis, he is the son of Johnny Murray, a featherweight boxing champion known as the "Bronx Bonecrusher." After college, Marvin studied Chinese language and culture at the University of Chicago, thinking he'd teach or find work with the State Department. "I had no idea what to do. Someone said if you have no idea and are glib, try advertising or public relations." His first advertising job was as a "research flunky" at Leo Burnett [see p. 123]. Eventually, Sloves became research director there. It was only in 1963, when he was hired to do account work, that he began to feel comfortable in the industry. "From then on, it's been great."

The beginnings of Scali, McCabe, Sloves demonstrated the partners' collective convictions: "I believed we'd be unique. All our traditions are based on great creative. We were honest, wouldn't accept cigarette accounts, our work would speak for us, and we took pride in our work." Sloves', Sam Scali's, and Allen Pesky's departures "were the death knell of Papert, Koenig, Lois. We did say to ourselves, 'Let's not make the same mistakes as they.' "

Besides the Volvo account, Marvin didn't really believe his fledgling agency was a long-term proposition until "we leased space in a still incomplete building and saw a huge banner announcing us as tenants." That was in 1970, when SMS had billings of $7.1 million. That was also one building ago. Today's headquarters have Marvin's name on more than nine floors of prime office space. At twenty-one, SMS can still pick the top advertising candidates. Which doesn't mean the company is populated with Harvard MBAs. "I do not covet MBAs. It doesn't mean that people have the proper intelligence [for this work]. I don't have an MBA, and I have no idea where our top people went to school. You can't teach people how to read an ad, how to talk to people." Sloves addresses the issue of glamour, one that, however ill-conceived by outsiders, still appears to help in the recruitment of novices. "That notion started with media people's expense accounts. We've always entertained well. But," he adds, smiling, "what's glamorous now is investment banking."

As the agency confronts the challenge of growth, Marvin says, "I don't miss the days of being small. I miss the days of being young. There's no virtue in being small. I say to Sam and others, 'Always keep asking questions.' I'm constantly surprised by this. I didn't know I could change." Sloves does admit the agency has some stress, brought on by what some perceive as politics; others cite the expansion. "We're accused of not letting people do work. By people who don't want to do work. Morale is down. It's depressing to hear it, but I don't give a shit. Morale is not my job. Morale is not a corporate function; it's personal. The truth is that every agency in New York is firing people, so morale is low. Ed's [McCabe] screaming meant someone cared. Now that we're a seven-hundred-million-dollar company, you can't scream. The best thing about *running* a seven-hundred-million-dollar company is *building* a seven-hundred-million-dollar company."

In lieu of screaming, Sloves talks daily with his other agencies, building "a polyglot of people with common denominators." He tries to deemphasize all the money, and to remember, as he stays in the finest hotels, that he used to have to hitchhike.

John Malecki, vice-president and copywriter, is an interesting bridge between the old and the new. He looks like the prototypical creative: cowboy boots, an earring, long hair. His office is filled with toys, chotchkes that telegraph his wit—a fortune cookie fortune taped to his desk that says, "When time permits, your personal life will be exciting"—and photographs chosen for their yuks potential. He calls himself "an oddball." He came to Scali in January 1985 for the opportunity to work with Ed McCabe, who was phasing himself out. Malecki worked in an agency in Albany before moving downstate.

"This was my first stop, and I didn't have to go any farther. My first instincts were [like ads] done by people here. It was great; like coming home. I came here to be beat over the head by Ed McCabe. I wanted to learn from him. I had heard that he ran the place. He had to approve everything that went out." His introduction to McCabe was on an ad that never ran. "Which was unusual. He had mellowed. He wasn't the guy I'd heard he'd be."

What sets SMS apart from most agencies, John thinks, is, "unless a person is at the point of physical or mental exhaustion, they don't want to do just do-able work. They'll pound their heads to the wall to do the most spectacular. Because they're driven, and because of McCabe and the legacy of creative here. I'm never satisfied with what I've done after it's finished. It's annoying. Most people who are trying to do something terrific are like that. I don't know if that defines someone who's good, but it gives you a better shot. Being here makes you try to be good. Most advertising runs from mediocre to totally awful. It presupposes a lack of intelligence and a low caliber of human being as audience."

At thirty-three, Malecki was more or less handed the reins of the prized Perdue account, by all accounts a major coup for someone so young. "I still don't understand the series of events that led to the assignment, but I'll accept them. Ed hired me. He gave me a chance. He let me work on the hardest and worst assignments. I did coupon ads for paper towels. I did ads for Hertz: 'Our rates are cheap in Florida.' But they weren't the cheapest. On a small budget, I thought I did it all very uneventfully. After five months, Ed gave me a Perdue assigment. My partner and I did piles and piles of ads which he rejected. I must have spent three solid weeks on an eight-sentence body copy [the text below the headline].

"There might have been one or two people who thought they were in line for this account. Other great writers couldn't necessarily write Perdue. It calls for a certain kind of discipline I never had to have before. Ed created the whole personality of Perdue. I saw him come up with the ending to some copy that was both brilliant and hysterically funny. I walked away and thought, 'God, I'll never be that brilliant.' Ed turned the supervision of Perdue over to Sam and gave me and my partner the account. While Sam would help, you're on your own."

Malecki realizes that his opportunity was unusual. He revels in working for the "tough man who makes a tender chicken." "Frank Perdue and I have screamed and sworn at each other. He's obsessive about quality, too, and it's a hard act to follow after McCabe." The Perdue people "have a bullshit screen a mile high. It's extremely rare to find a client who understands the works and needs. Frank is a grown-up egg and chicken farmer. The man's been around enough shit to know how it smells. He knows he's a lot like the people he deals with." John is so proud of handling the Perdue work that he says, "They can call me 'janitor,' but if I have to have someone write coupon copy for Perdue, it's got to be good. To have that kind of power. . . . As far as I'm concerned, it's the best account group in the agency, good research people. It's possibly the account that was most like what Scali, McCabe was supposed to stand for. It's a creatively driven group with a clear idea of right and wrong.

"Stories are legendary about Ed going through writers. He would beat people up. He wasn't being an egomaniac; his standards were really higher. There's a secret society of writers—an art director won't watch words as you will. I am on my own, with just my partner to rely on. The biggest lesson I got from Ed was that you can't expect someone else to be watching over you to make sure it'll be as good as you want it to be."

Old Scali, according to Malecki, "was easier to keep a shared philosophical focus. As it grew, people didn't come for the ideology; they came for money and prestige." Now he sees a subspecies he calls the "suspender people. They are more business. Suspenders represent certain modes of thought that nonsuspenders wearers don't agree with. I don't think Marvin's main concern is money, but he's a businessman. People who come from the account side know it's a creatively driven agency.

"I look around, and I don't know where else I'd go. It's corny, but accurate. It's like a family, the way people get along with each other. Some you cannot stand; some you love. There are days when my partner and I eat all three meals together. We can spend more time together than with the girlfriends we sleep with every night. It's like a marriage." And so, as dusk falls over Manhattan, Malecki and his partner, Wolper, prepare to study antibiotics. "We have an hour meeting on Friday on antibiotics. Chicken antibiotics."

WACHTELL, LIPTON, ROSEN & KATZ

WACHTELL, LIPTON, ROSEN & KATZ

HISTORY & OPERATIONS

The New York City law firm Wachtell, Lipton, Rosen & Katz was founded by the four name partners—who knew one another at New York University Law School—in 1965. George Katz, Martin Lipton, Leonard Rosen, and Herbert Wachtell, all in their early thirties when they started the firm, built an early reputation based on their ability to provide highly specialized advice with exceptional speed. The firm grew at a regulated pace and made a name for itself in the mid-1970s as a specialist in corporate takeover law. The case that first drew Wachtell, Lipton notice for this prowess took place in 1974, when the firm represented the Loews Corporation in its fiercely contested attempt to acquire the Chicago-based CNA Financial Corporation. The case dragged on for nine months in the midst of a nasty political and publicity campaign waged by CNA's management. Loews ultimately acquired CNA in what came to be perceived as the classic corporate takeover battle.

Wachtell, Lipton grew from the four founding partners and three associates in 1965 to fifty lawyers, twenty-three of them partners, in 1979. By that time, with the manifold increase in hostile takeover disputes and complicated corporate mergers, the firm was involved in almost every major transaction of that kind, representing either one of the corporations concerned or its investment bankers. Its only real rival as the leading firm in this area was (and is) Skadden, Arps, Slate, Meagher & Flom, which often represents the opposing side. Although Wachtell, Lipton is still best known for its corporate practice, the firm has developed expertise in other areas to reduce its dependency on that one. And though it is still relatively young and modest in size—today the firm employs eighty-four lawyers, forty-six of them partners—its practice is as prominent, vital, and lucrative as that of most larger New York City corporate law firms.

Wachtell, Lipton is one of the most loosely structured firms in the city, operating by consensus of the partners rather than by formal votes. Day-to-day operations are overseen by an informally selected administrative committee. Partnership meetings take place only once a year, and all of the partners participate in the decision to admit new associates into the partnership. Throughout its history, Wachtell, Lipton has had an overall one-to-one ratio of partners to associates—in fact, there are now more partners than associates—which is highly unusual among major corporate law partnerships.

Today, Wachtell, Lipton's practice is structured in the following departments: Corporate, with twenty-eight lawyers (eleven partners and seventeen associates); Litigation, with thirty lawyers (nineteen partners and eleven associates); Bankruptcy, with fourteen lawyers (nine partners including one of counsel and five associates); Tax/Trust/Estates, with six lawyers (four partners and two associates); Antitrust Litigation, with three lawyers (two partners and one associate); and Real Estate, with three lawyers (two partners and one associate). The firm represents corporations listed on the American and New York stock exchanges, major investment banking firms, major commercial banks, and other financial institutions. The firm's key clients have included Allied Corporation, Avon Corporation, Bell & Howell Company, Dart & Kraft, Inc., E. M. Warburg, Pincus & Co., Goldman, Sachs & Co., John Hancock Life Insurance Company, Levi Strauss (see p. 624), Loews Corporation, R. H. Macy & Company, Manufacturers Hanover Trust Company, McGraw-Hill, Inc., Norton Simon, Inc., Orion Pictures Corporation, Salomon Brothers, Inc., United Technologies Corporation, U.S. Industries, and Western Union Telegraph Company.

In order to retain its informal, nonbureaucratic structure, Wachtell, Lipton has carefully moderated its growth over the years. The firm hires an average of only six to eight new associates each year, the number varying from year to year with no minimum quota. (For each of the past three years, the firm has hired an average of six new associates.) Wachtell, Lipton recruits the top-performing students—"preferably with law review, journal, or other significant writing experience"—at a handful of top law schools around the country. All associates are hired under the assumption that they'll be qualified to make partner, and the firm offers associates considerably better partnership prospects than many other major firms. Associates, who are paid as well as those at larger firms, select a department when they join the firm and work for a number of different partners within it. Most remain in that particular area of practice. Each associate's performance is reviewed at the annual partnership meeting, and a partner is designated to discuss performance and compensation matters with each associate. An associate generally makes partner after six years (unlike at most other major firms, where it generally takes eight to ten years). The fact that most Wachtell, Lipton associates will make partner and that each associate is judged purely by individual merit, added to the fact that the four founding partners are still firmly ensconced on the top rung of the firm, makes for less competition and political jockeying than at many other major law firms.

Wachtell, Lipton encourages its lawyers to participate in pro bono activities. The firm has represented a number of groups on a pro bono basis, including the Brooklyn Jewish Hospital and Medical Center, Phoenix House Foundation, *The Columbia Daily Spectator* (the Columbia University student newspaper), New York University, the First All-Children's Theater, the

American Friends of Hebrew University, the Federation of Jewish Banks, and Freedom National Bank, the only black-owned and operated commercial bank in New York, which Wachtell, Lipton defended from a hostile takeover. Approximately 1–3 percent of all the firm's work is done on a pro bono basis.

(Information provided by Michael Schwartz, partner.)

REVENUES: Firm will not disclose.

EARNINGS: Firm will not disclose.

OFFICES: One, on Park Avenue in New York City.

NUMBER OF EMPLOYEES: 84 lawyers—46 partners, 37 associates, 1 of counsel—and 228 support staff.

NUMBER OF WOMEN LAWYERS: 2 partners and 8 associates.

NUMBER OF MINORITY LAWYERS: 1 Hispanic associate.

AVERAGE AGE OF EMPLOYEES: Information not available. "We tend to be a younger firm. Most senior people are in their mid-fifties, and a raw guess at the average age would be around thirty."

TURNOVER: No specific figures. "The turnover rate has historically been extremely low because we're so careful when we hire. Only a very small number of people leave."

RECRUITMENT: The firm recruits at a handful of top law schools, Boalt Hall (University of California at Berkeley), University of Chicago, Columbia University, Fordham University, Harvard University, University of Michigan, New York University, University of Pennsylvania, Stanford University, and Yale University. "We hire people at the top of their classes."

NUMBER OF NEW HIRES PER YEAR: An average of six associates each year for the past three years.

RANGE OF STARTING SALARIES: For new associates in 1988, $71,000 per year; for secretaries, $600–$625 per week.

POLICY FOR RAISES: Raises are determined annually by the partners, and everybody in the same class receives the same base compensation.

SUMMER ASSOCIATE PROGRAM AND NEW ASSOCIATE TRAINING: Summer associates, the majority of whom have completed their second year of law school, worked an average of ten weeks in 1987 at a salary of $1,250 per week. The firm hired twenty-four summer associates that year (as opposed to only ten in 1986). The percentage of summer associates who join the firm on a permanent basis is not carved in stone. (In 1986 only 40 percent joined, whereas in 1984 80 percent joined.) Summer associates and new associates learn on the job. "We are well known as a place that tries to give young lawyers a lot of responsibility early in their careers. First because we are hiring people with superior educational backgrounds, and also because we consciously keep our size small. People have to be able to carry their own weight very early, which is something that is important to the firm as well as to our young lawyers. The best training you can have is to equip somebody and then give them the chance to do it right or wrong."

BENEFITS: Family hospitalization insurance, family major medical insurance, long-term disability insurance, pension plan, savings plan, travel/accident insurance, life insurance, and an educational supplement.

VACATION: Three weeks for the first three years, four weeks after three years, plus two personal days per year and a number of regular paid holidays.

ADDITIONAL PERKS: The firm pays associates for taking the bar review, and also pays for the review course. If someone in the firm has a legal problem, he or she is entitled to legal services at a reduced rate. The firm has a "perfect attendance bonus" for nonlegal staff, awarding $750 to employees who don't take any sick days in a whole year. For maternity leave, Wachtell, Lipton offers a leave of absence of up to one year to associates (with four months paid) and a leave of up to six months (two months paid) to nonlegal personnel who have been with the firm for at least one and a half years. (Those who have been at the firm for less than that are entitled to a six-month leave of absence—unpaid.) For women partners, maternity leave is determined on a case-by-case basis.

BONUSES: Part of the compensation for salaried associates comes in the form of significant bonuses, which are awarded on the basis of seniority, the firm's performance, and merit. (Partners' compensation is a share of the firm's net earnings.) Members of the support staff receive bonuses based on merit and seniority.

ANNUAL PARTIES: The firm has an annual party in the spring for lawyers, their spouses, and friends of the firm, which is held at different "exotic" locations. One year it was at the Water Club, another year it was at Wave Hill (an estate in Riverdale), and in 1987 it took place at the Museum of American Crafts. The party is fairly informal (one year it was black tie at Maxim's, and nobody liked it), and the lawyers dine and dance—"It's a big do." At Christmastime there's another big party for lawyers and support staff (no spouses). The firm typically takes a few rooms at the Waldorf or another New York hotel, and employees drink, dine, and dance. Wachtell, Lipton also hosts three or four cocktail parties and other types of entertainment for its summer associates. The firm stresses socializing by summer associates so that they can become acquainted with the lawyers in the firm and the lawyers can get to know them.

DRESS CODE: "Professional attire."

AVERAGE WORKDAY: Official hours are 9:30–5:30, but most people come in earlier and work later.

SOCIAL ATMOSPHERE: "It's a very intimate atmosphere in the sense that we're a very closely knit firm. We're all in one building, all on floors that are contiguous by staircase or elevator. Everybody keeps their doors open and talks to everybody else all the time. There's a lot of talking. It sometimes feels more like a law review office than a law firm. It's a very unstructured environment, and lawyers are encouraged to say what they think. Some people fraternize, some don't. There was at least one instance in the last year or so where one associate married another associate." (Although one of them left the firm, marriages between lawyers in the firm are discouraged.)

HEADQUARTERS: Wachtell, Lipton has office space on four floors of a midtown Park Avenue building. The firm occupies all of two floors and about half of the other two. The firm is about to expand into more space on those four floors. They are decorated with contemporary art and lavish flower arrangements in the reception areas.

CHARITABLE CONTRIBUTIONS: The firm donated $4,128,320 in 1987 to the following organizations: legal pro bono organizations, human rights organizations, law schools, universities, UJA/Federation, cultural and civic associations, and health-related charities. The Wachtell, Lipton Foundation donated an additional $2,716,485.

INTERESTED APPLICANTS CAN SEND RÉSUMÉS TO:
Ruth Ivey
Wachtell, Lipton, Rosen & Katz
299 Park Avenue
New York, NY 10016
(212) 371-9200

"Someone like us" is how the partners of New York's Wachtell, Lipton, Rosen & Katz describe their ideal recruit. After meeting with some of them, even I knew what they meant, although I'm afraid I may not be able to articulate it. Contrary to what you may expect in a firm that reached prominence as a specialist in hostile takeovers (tender offers), it is not filled with workaholic barracudas looking for their next kill, and it is not only in the business of takeovers.

Founded on January 1, 1965, by four NYU law school graduates, Wachtell "still does not today have a written partnership agreement." For a firm with as strong an office culture as one could find east of Disneyland, the founders do not particularly seem to care that it is codified or explicitly handed down to the associates. "We're loose, less formal; we communicate without paper." They know who will fit in, and they make few mistakes in the hiring process.

"We're looking for people who'll understand us. And we hope everyone who joins the firm will make partner." This is a unique posture among major New York corporate firms. "If you run the course with us, you will become a partner, regardless of what department you're in. There are no quotas." The partnership track here is six to seven years, up from five. To put Wachtell's bullishness into perspective, most New York firms have an apprenticeship of eight to ten years. And departments ordinarily try to control the limited numbers of partnerships, creating internal power struggles. The ratio of associates to partners at Wachtell is almost one to one (not by department, but overall). "The theory is that associates are like partners in a way. The people who work here are part of the firm, part of the governance." This attitude allows associates to focus on their work and not worry endlessly about their futures. No one has to fail in order for someone else to succeed. Several lawyers compare the associates' tenure to premarital cohabitation. "They're partners-in-training."

Compensation is another area usually potentially rife with backbiting. The four name partners earn the same salary as one another, and so on down the line. Wachtell, Lipton uses the lockstep system, in which each attorney is paid the same, according to the year he or she graduated from law school. "It could present problems with a nonproductive goof-off," one partner rationalizes, "but we have not had to face that." Bringing in new clients garners no residual bonus.

In 1965, when Wall Street standard-bearer Cravath, Swain, Moore—traditionally the highest-paying law firm in the country—announced it would pay starting associates a whopping $15,000 a year, "double the going rate, the upstart firm of Wachtell, Lipton announced we'd match them or better. We got attention," name partner George Katz says. "We were young. Aggressive. We had to find very confident graduates of ability. It was difficult. We said responsibility would come early. 'You can shape your own destiny.' " From the start its reputation was one of "doing quality deal work and litigation." Insurance companies and lending institutions (blue chip industries by any standard) were among its early clients, "not for corporate housekeeping, but for more complicated transactions."

Partner Michael Schwartz had taught law for four years at NYU. He recalls, "I knew I didn't want to make it my life. It was now five years after I graduated from [Harvard] law school. I was an 'old man.' " It was the fall of 1973, and Wachtell, Lipton had twenty-two or twenty-three lawyers at the time. "I'd never heard of the firm," he continues, "but it had a good reputation at the bar."

Katz picks up the story. "We were hustling, sure. It was preadvertising and pre–*American Lawyer* [the preeminent trade journal of the profession] days. Our quality work was gaining notice and attracting the young lawyer with a gleam in his eye." Schwartz: "It was a full-court press in every arena."

Everyone describes the firm as a collegial group of people who like the law and like each other. People make an effort to walk around its four floors and schmooze. It's okay to be yourself here, and probably impossible to be anyone else. Frequently during my visits, I witnessed lawyers agreeing to cover for each other when one had a family obligation or just not enough time. "I remember once flying to Texas and taking a deposition the next day on a deal I wasn't working on." Katz explains that "business getting is important, but not the be-all or end-all. A new client is *our* client," he stresses, "not an individual's client. Regardless of who brought them in, the best person does the work." Team spiritedness is encouraged by the organization of the physical office space. Lawyers are not placed according to department, but in a cross-fertilizing mix. "We want everyone to know what's going on. When we close a deal or win in litigation, we throw a party. We're always looking for an excuse to throw a party."

Perhaps the most unusual fact about Wachtell, Lipton, Rosen & Katz is its size. There are currently eighty-four lawyers on board, lilliputian for an organization that does business of its importance and volume. Unlike other firms that regard themselves as businesses first, no one here is interested in growth for growth's sake. That wouldn't enhance the firm's significance. Indeed, because the culture is so deliberately a product of personalities and not structure, wanton growth would be counterproductive. Besides, Wachtell, Lipton, Rosen & Katz is not hungry for new work. "We turn work down regularly. We don't need just to keep the beast fed. We don't pretend to do everything. We're not a full service firm. We're lawyers' lawyers. I don't know what the perfect size is," Katz says. "I guess we're practicing reasonably controlled growth—whatever that means."

One of his partners says, "Managing growth is very hard for the founding partners as Depression children." Wachtell, Lipton was already a seriously profitable partnership when the founding partners were still cautious about their success. (George Katz said he stopped worrying about paying his bills in 1974.)

"We're not going to hire bodies. We hire about six associates a year. If there's a doubt about someone, we won't hire them. Sometimes we take a chance. We don't want to hire twenty to get a good five. Clinkers are felt." Moreover, the partners are not golfers or tennis players with JD degrees. They're at work at nights and on weekends almost as often as the associates. Sometimes more. But if they were unable to attend to a particular matter, they would entrust it to whoever could. Which could mean an associate. "We want to be able to sleep nights." The partners are *that* confident in their associates.

Most hires come straight from law school. "Only once was a partner hired from the outside —Peter Canellos—and it was one of the best decisions we ever made. He had been passed over at another firm for a quota in their tax department." One of the nice surprises about life at Wachtell, Lipton is that when a lawyer is referred to, it's always by name, none of the "I think we once hired a fellow . . ." sort of thing. This is a very intimate place, with, for the moment, no branch office.

"We have time to train six new people a year. We still see the same sense of the firm at eighty-four lawyers as we did at twenty." A revelation about the new kids: "My God! They're all like me." Back to that. "Like me" could mean smart, funny, conscientious, easy-going, driven, down-to-earth, family-minded, has the same taste in books, plays harmonica, paints, collects rare books, art, or coins, married his/her high school sweetheart, Jewish, Gentile, Democratic, Republican, happy, gemütlich. (The founders are clearly, openly Jewish. At the time they began their careers it was harder for Jews to find work at non-Jewish firms. But they make "no attempt to hire a particular race, color, creed, et cetera" and end up with a heterogeneous "like us." Let me emphasize: Although I met lawyers at Wachtell who come from various backgrounds, are members of different generations, colleges, and law schools, and represent both sexes and several creeds, *everyone* offered this same sentiment, sometimes verbatim. *Everyone.*

"We're pleased we've created a culture that caught on," Katz says. "The next generation is enthusiastic about perpetuating it. They especially appreciate it when comparing notes with their contemporaries at other law firms. The internal life here is far more satisfying."

Richard Katcher went the traditional corporate route after graduating from NYU Law School in 1966. He interviewed at Wachtell, which he'd "never heard of. I came home and told my wife, 'I just met the greatest guys!' But I took a job at Simpson, Thatcher & Bartlett." He's not complaining about his experience there. One day, one of his neighbors, a partner at Wachtell, said to Katcher, " 'We just hired a friend of yours. When are we going to hire you?' I said, 'Interview me, Bernie.' 'Can you come up Friday?' 'For what, Bernie?' 'For your interview.' " He showed up and met George Katz.

"George Katz said, 'Where's your résumé?' I didn't have one. He said, 'Why not?' 'I'm not looking for a job.' 'Okay, we'll fly blind.' " That day, Katcher met "Lipton, Kantor, Nussbaum," he remembers. "I didn't meet Wachtell, but I knew Fogelson. I liked the firm. The people were extremely bright and nice." By the end of the day, he was offered a job. He accepted the job, "without knowing my new salary. I just did. It seemed irrelevant. I was told I wouldn't be disadvantaged by coming here. I thought, 'This could be fun.' I was twenty-seven years old. I wondered, 'Are these guys going to be in business in a few years?' I figured I could always get another job." It was June 1968 and "I thought I was doing well at Simpson, Thatcher. George Katz told me if I were good, I'd get to argue [litigate] et cetera, sooner than I'd expect. I could play lawyer.

"Two or three weeks after I arrived, there was the annual summer party—that year at Katz's house in King's Point. My wife said, 'Oh, this is like a fraternity party!' The oldest person there was thirty-five. Everybody knew everybody else well, and everyone's wife, the names of their kids, and who was sick."

While Katcher subscribes to the "like us" opinion, he makes the distinction "Not everyone is the same. These are very, very smart, nice people who are willing to work very hard when necessary and get pleasure out of the accomplishment." There may be less alchemy to the brew in his mind then in mine. "There are many lawyers elsewhere who could fit in here," he says. His own office reflects his own brand of "like me." It is decorated in the most modern of contemporary art, including a Keith Haring and a Richard Katcher. He collects (often at East Village galleries), and that interest has drawn him to paints and canvas himself.

The thing is, no one complains about working hard. "People by and large are excited when it's hectic. The high visibility and pressure are fun. They're like the finals of the U.S. Open or the Super Bowl. You are doing what you do and winning." Is it competitive? "Yeah, but not with each other. People are willing to pitch in on a deal, even if it's not theirs. At the highest level, everyone wants to do everyone else's job: [on a deal that means] investment banker, public relations, as well as law." Richard laughs as he repeats, "I told my client last Saturday night, 'Don't screw up my deal!' "

These deals are heavy duty. In 1971 "an eight-million-dollar all-cash deal for a portion of Lehigh Industries was the largest all-cash deal we had." Since then, the firm in general and Katcher in particular have worked on the Beatrice leveraged buyout, which was $6 billion—so far, among the richest. No one can be too cavalier about this much money. "Our decisions affect people's lives. You can get nervous and lose sleep. But people here have a sense of 'We can do this.' It doesn't mean you can use the same strategies. You can't do everything the way you did it before."

Katcher disputes the preconception that to succeed at Wachtell, Lipton you must surrender the rest of your life. For some young associates, the long hours are proof of a kind of professional machismo, which disappears after enough all-nighters. "One can have a regular life working here, but you can also have theater plans which are precluded because of an emergency. I'm quite senior, and I was stuck here last weekend. There's no sense of 'This is your problem, not mine.' It's more like 'We've got to solve it.' "

Dan Neff says he is a typical first child. "I always seemed to be in a hurry. I don't know why." After his sophomore year at Brown, he decided to go to law school, "not necessarily to be a lawyer. I didn't know the process." Neff volunteers that his GPA was 3.5, but he did not get into the Harvard or Yale law school due to low law boards. He went to Columbia. "I did exceedingly well. Better than I'd done at Brown. I got in off the wait list and arrived pissed, but I made Law Review."

His best friend at Columbia was a summer associate at Wachtell, Lipton and told Neff, "This place would be perfect for you!" Why? There were only thirty-seven lawyers here, "ambitious, aggressive, nonpolitical." Meanwhile, Dan was a summer intern at a big, prestigious firm he does not name. "A big firm is a pipeline clogged with people. There was no privacy. Everyone knew which fourth-year associate did the first closing on his own. The partners took two-hour lunches, left at 5:30, and weren't geniuses. You got made partner if your department needed one and the department had clout that year. My sense was, it never got better. My boss was forty-eight and scared. The pot of gold did not look like much.

"I also had a businessman's view: If you go to a mature institution, you take a risk. They don't really need new people. I didn't want the fate of my family to depend on the organization, determined by some people who didn't know my work.

"I was looking for a take-off opportunity and a fair shake."

Dan offers this advice. "You have to prioritize your hierarchy of values. This place didn't have Happy Hour at 5:30 on Fridays, and it's not the smoothest group of guys." [Author's note: Only if compared to the unrumpled shirtfronts of more staid firms.] I don't socialize with the people here. I like them a lot, but enough's enough.

"I know I'm a competitive person, though not obviously so. I worked like an absolute crazy person. Everyone knew me. I got a lot of responsibility. I worked and haven't stopped." He was made partner in 1983. He calls Wachtell's partnership policy "demystified. People aren't scared to come into my office. It saves a lot of time. We talk about our work a lot. People solicit each other's opinions." He pauses. "I realize it's not the broadest approach to life."

In looking for the next generation of lawyers, Dan sometimes gets confused. "I don't know if I'm supposed to interview people or sell them. There's always a tension. Everyone's looking for people in their own image. I like people who are clearly ambitious and understand what they're getting themselves into. I don't like résumés with just grades. I like to know that somebody, sometime, made a commitment to something. This place is about commitment. Our ethos is that you've got to know the law better than anyone else and draft better than anyone else."

Who turns him off? "I don't like anyone who's got to go sailing every Friday. I don't like glib sorts, political sorts. I want someone who can carry a conversation. We don't want guys here for a two-year tour of duty who cash it in with a friendly client. I don't want greasy guys; I don't like smoothies, bullshitters. I don't care if you're wearing a Hermes tie as long as you do good work."

Neff defines the organization: "A decidedly no-bullshit place. Extraordinarily hardworking. It's an honest system; 'Spare me the bullshit and just do the work.' The fact that you get a fair shake permeates the place."

He claims that each department has its own personality. When departmental issues such as possible new clients arise, "we can give fast answers." His department, corporate, has a "mergers and acquisitions emphasis." He quotes, "The corporate lawyer is the general who has to employ specialists." He takes pride in the fact that although Corporate has approximately the same number of lawyers as Litigation, it has "a lot fewer partners."

The corporate department has achieved fame in the person of name partner Martin Lipton —Wachtell, Lipton's best-known lawyer—and certainly the attorney considered to be one of the two best M&A (Mergers and Acquisitions) specialists in the country (alongside rival Joseph Flom of Skadden, Arps, Slate, Meagher & Flom). Neff says, "Here it's very clear who the leaders are. The founders are here. The clarity is incredibly useful. There aren't jurisdictional battles."

But if Lipton is the superstar, the rest of the Corporate Department (and the rest of the firm) are far more than just the chorus. They are supporting players with solos and soliloquies. "It's certainly a star's business, and we benefit from that. People want a star to represent them. The show's different from fifteen years ago. Lawyers' names are now well known." Dan adds that most transactions are conducted "in the glare of the spotlight," so you don't have to be Lipton to get attention. On the other hand, he says, "we still view ourselves as upstarts. At least I do."

How has partnership changed Neff's life? "My hours haven't improved in five years of partnership. What's changed is, I have more responsibility. As you get more senior, it's harder to forget you're a lawyer. Partners work incredibly hard, which is one reason we do so well.

"There's only one thing worse than too much work," he adds. "That's too little."

Steve Barna, a partner in the Litigation Department, is a graduate of Rutgers and Rutgers Law School, class of 1968. ("I chose law school to avoid the draft and because it sounded more attractive than being a graduate student in history, which I considered.") He joined Wachtell, Lipton in the fall of 1969, after spending one year clerking for a federal judge on the Third Circuit Court of Appeals in Philadelphia.

He interviewed at several firms as his clerkship drew to a close. "I was very unsophisticated," he says. "I didn't really know I wanted to be a lawyer, even then. I wasn't looking for a particular thing. I just wanted to try a law firm."

Wachtell was recommended to him by a placement counselor at Rutgers. All Barna knew about the place was that there were approximately fifteen lawyers working there, and, "with a couple of exceptions, it was 'an NYU firm.'

"I was struck, at my interviews, by the people. The firm had achieved a certain degree of success, and everyone was youthful. I met all the senior partners that day. They were all in their mid- to late thirties. There was a sense of enthusiasm and that the firm was going somewhere. Keep in mind," he warns, "I wasn't excited about being a lawyer. I do remember thinking—with concern—'What if I don't like this; what'll I do?' "

Steve wasn't sure he'd made the right decision the first year, when he was in the Corporate Department, the wrong fit. He didn't give in, though, obviously, and switched to Litigation. "There wasn't much else at the time. I stayed because of the people. They were good friends.

"I began to enjoy practicing litigation right away, especially the way it's done here. We try harder. We put on the best effort all the time." Barna became a partner in his fifth year.

The road to trial and the trial itself "are the most exciting time in the litigating life cycle. A trial is the ultimate experience for a litigator. It's still thrilling, but I haven't already tried three thousand cases. Most don't reach the trial stage. The uncertainty makes life more exciting and dramatic. Most cases are hard to predict. Usually you have mixed emotions when a case gets settled, particularly if you have a competitive nature and a solid case."

Ironically, although the departmental change removed all Steve's doubts both about being a lawyer and about being a lawyer at Wachtell, Lipton, he says, " 'Department' is a misnomer. There's so little formal structure here. People work so closely together." His office is on the twenty-eighth floor, the last floor to become Wachtellified. He calls it " 'the new frontier.' The twenty-eighth floor happens to be Litigation. It was not intended that way. There are more litigators proportionally than at most firms. There was no master plan to separate us. The lawyers have grown by six times since I arrived, and the staff has grown geometrically.

"There's no basic change in the character of the firm, which is surprising because of its size. You don't know everyone as well as you used to. It's impossible. It used to be very easy to say, 'I know everyone,' but close relationships haven't disintegrated. I don't consider everyone my friend, but there are not many I don't like."

Barna is dismayed by the undue attention given to the wealth of the firm's practice. Many students who know of Wachtell, Lipton are attracted to the organization because it is rumored that partners here make more money per capita than at any other partnership in the country. "I would prefer not to recruit on the basis of our profitability." How do you prevent the money from selling the firm? "It's hard. People know about the money. They don't have to hear it from you." It's generally not difficult to ferret out the financially motivated students, but "to try to gauge a person's basic character in twenty minutes? Good luck. If we see arrogance in interviews, I suspect we'd screen away."

When asked, finally, to describe the values of the firm, Barna says, "We take pride in the best work we do. I hate to sound like a recording."

I met Patricia Vlahakis when she was still an associate. While at Columbia Law School, she recalled, she was looking for "a small firm with a national reputation. I had heard virtually nothing of the firm at school. Wachtell was not considered an 'in' firm at Columbia. I don't know why. It's still not. (We're very in at Harvard this year," she slips in.) "[Wachtell] had a reputation of being very hardworking and tough to get a job at, similar to Bryn Mawr [my undergraduate college]. The competitiveness about getting in made it very appealing to me."

Pat was further intrigued by the fact that the summer intern program was known to be relatively tougher than programs elsewhere, which devote a lot of the summer to showing off New York's cultural and gustatory landmarks to their interns in an attempt to lure them back as associates when they graduate from law school. [Author's note: only to be surprised by what it means to do law.] She says, "The program is not so aggressively social. It mostly involves getting to know the partners."

George Katz says that Wachtell, Lipton's summer associate program "is designed for them to look at us and vice versa. We don't coddle them or give them easy jobs. We treat them as first-year associates so that they won't be misled. We still show them New York and entertain them, but that's a side focus. The system works best if you can rely on summer associates. We both have the option to say, 'Sorry.' It's not an automatic offer."

Vlahakis got married after graduation from law school and arrived at Wachtell "very ready to work. I was sick of being a student. My first week here I pulled an all-nighter, and I never did that in college *or* in law school." Her reaction to the hard work came in stages: "The first stage was being excited about being needed, the second was feeling imposed upon, and the third was signing on. This is what you want to do.

"If you enjoy what you're doing, you don't complain. People only complain when something's boring. The work is very dramatic. You get an adrenaline high from working on deals. When you work on something that's in the paper the next day, a high results from that." She makes a distinction between the attitudes implicit in the terms "driven," which is frequently used to describe the tenor of the firm, and "committed," to her a more appropriate description. "People don't feel pushed. It's as relaxed as it can be, although people do carry this home with them."

As a new person here, the perks of working on high-octane deals can be head-spinning. "After a year and a half, I was flying on the Concorde to London. It was exciting. (I was four months pregnant.) But the thrill of flying in a corporate jet and meeting heads of investment banks does wear off. We have the 'coming here for the wrong reason' concern. I tell students if the money is the reason they want to work here, to forget it. After a month there will be no time to shop and spend it."

You will not impress your seniors at Wachtell by simply staying late at the office. Summer associates who are seen jockeying politically will harm their chances at careers here. The team is king. As she approached the end of her apprenticeship, Pat made no coy references to "what-ifs." "It's nice to know you can continue to enjoy what you do," she says. The mother of a toddler, she and her husband consciously planned her pregnancy. "I wanted to wait until people knew me, until I was a known quantity. There's a written policy that you can take off a year and not lose stature." Vlahakis employs a woman to care for her child during the day and gets extra help from her mother, her mother-in-law, and her husband.

If anything, despite the fact that the verdict was ahead of her, Pat seemed totally calm and unassuming. "I'm a corporate lawyer, and I'll always be a corporate lawyer." Pat was made partner effective January 1, 1988.

George Katz sums up his firm: "We all love the law. The firm can be a collegial environment and do well economically." In an age when lawyers are known to be fiercely discontented (especially when they see their investment banker counterparts making more money than they on the same deals), Wachtell, Lipton isn't losing lawyers. These attorneys never seem to complain about being inhibited by their roles as advisors. Katz thinks the law is losing good people because "structured firms give associates arcane research projects whose piece isn't comprehended in the whole. There's a failure of not bringing [associates] into the team and exposing them to the transactions." Not here.

"The firm is number one. If you are recognized by enhancing the team, it's a vehicle from which your ego can be vaulted further. The way a case is handled shouldn't differ according to who does the work. The discrepancy between the best and worst is small. We have the smartest, straightest lawyers. No politics. Virtue will out. God will take care of you."

YOUNG & RUBICAM, INC.

Y&R

HISTORY & OPERATIONS

Young & Rubicam, Inc., the largest independent advertising agency in the country and the second largest in the world, was founded in Philadelphia in 1923 by John Orr Young and Raymond Rubicam. Rubicam, the brilliant and multitalented ad man who orchestrated the agency's outstanding success, was born the youngest of eight children in Philadelphia in 1892. His father died when he was a child, and Rubicam moved among the homes of his older brothers and sisters, dropping out of school in the eighth grade to clerk full time in a grocery store. With ambitions to become a writer, Rubicam took a job as a junior reporter on a Philadelphia newspaper. When he wanted to marry, he decided to pursue a career as an advertising copywriter, figuring he could fulfill some part of his literary aspirations, in a more secure profession.

Rubicam broke into advertising in 1915 through sheer perseverence and wrote copy for Philadelphia agencies F. Wallis Armstrong and N. W. Ayer. Though his talents shone—among his most enduring slogans in his early years was one for Steinway Pianos, "The Instrument of the Immortals," which increased company sales and remained Steinway's slogan for decades—as a creative, he had virtually no chance of being elected into an agency's partnership ranks. (Agencies were then run almost exclusively by men on the account side of the business.) Thus in 1923, at the age of thirty-one, he joined with his colleague and friend John Orr Young, an account and new business man, to form a new agency.

Rubicam and Young launched Young & Rubicam, Inc. with no business and little cash. Their first client was the group of companies that later became General Foods. Young approached the management and urged them to test the agency's abilities on the company's most difficult product, which turned out to be Postum, a noncaffeinated drink with sinking sales. Rubicam's resulting campaign, which touted Postum as a sleep inducer, revived the product's sales, won a Harvard Bok prize, and established Y&R as a real agency. General Foods gave Y&R its prosperous Grape Nuts account and promised more business if the partners would relocate in New York City. In 1926 Young and Rubicam complied.

With its early success, the agency expanded quickly. The partners hired an eclectic group of talent—the majority of whom were not college graduates—and cultivated a dynamic and informal creative atmosphere. Rubicam originated the credo "Our job is to resist the ordinary" and pushed the creative department to come up with fresh and daring solutions to campaigns. Departing with industry tradition, he gave creative control to copywriters and artists rather than to administrators and account executives, rewarding his best art and copy people with a partnership stake and stock. Rubicam also put great faith in research, and in 1932 he hired pollster George Gallup to work full time for the agency, gathering information on consumer preferences. With the addition of Gallup, Y&R was uniquely positioned in the industry as an agency that designed sharp, creative campaigns backed up by quantifiable consumer research.

In 1934, with the consensus among the partners that he wasn't pulling his weight, Young was pressured to resign from the agency. (While Rubicam was a workaholic, Young tended to work short hours and take long vacations.) Y&R continued to thrive, reaching $22 million in billings in 1937 (up from $6 million in 1927 and $12 million in 1935). In addition to General Foods, the agency's client list by that time included top tier companies in the fields of insurance (Travelers), oil (Gulf), prestige cars (Packard), whisky (Four Roses), and pharmaceutical drugs (Bristol-Myers). By the time Rubicam retired in 1944, at the age of fifty-two, the agency had come from nowhere to rank as the country's second largest—behind J. Walter Thompson—with $51 million in annual billings.

After Rubicam's retirement, Y&R remained among the largest agencies in the country. It expanded gradually, opening new offices around the country and overseas, and by 1970 it had twenty-five offices around the world. However, by 1970—a year in which billings actually declined—Y&R was fat and floundering, with no clear direction for the future. Many of its campaigns were off target due to a lack of solid research, clients were taking their business elsewhere, and staffers were quitting the agency in numbers. That year, Edward Ney, who had joined Y&R in 1951, took over as the agency's president and chief executive officer. After his first year of leadership, he fired approximately one third of the agency's staff and announced that Y&R intended to become the best agency on Madison Avenue.

Ney led the agency on a course of acquisitions designed to expand its geographic presence and, more importantly, to broaden its expertise to encompass a whole range of specialty advertising fields as well as diverse communications services. Ney's strategy was to offer clients the "whole egg," replacing the many communications suppliers used by a company with one source—Y&R. In 1973 the agency acquired Sudler & Hennessey, a health care specialty agency, and nine months later it bought Wunderman, Ricotta and Kline, a prominent direct marketing firm. In 1976, it purchased Cato Johnson Associates, a sales promotion specialist, and in 1978 it acquired Stone & Adler, another direct marketing agency. Y&R also added more than a dozen general consumer agencies around the country and overseas, including small regional agencies that specialized in marketing to farmers and industrial companies. Y&R's last major purchase occurred in 1979 with the acquisition of Marsteller International, then the twentieth largest advertising agency in the country, and Burson-Marsteller, with what became the world's largest public relations practice (by 1983). These purchases allowed Y&R to grow from the third largest agency in the country to surpass J. Walter Thompson as the first.

Between 1972, when Ney announced his game plan, and 1980, when the Burson purchase was concluded, Y&R's worldwide billings quadrupled. In 1972 the agency employed 3,400 people; by 1982, it had 6,300 employees. At the end of 1982, Y&R had one hundred twenty-six offices around the world.

Y&R also instituted programs to improve its overall creative output and research sophistication in the mid-1970s. Alex Kroll, who was then the worldwide creative director, wrote a handbook—distributed to the entire worldwide creative staff—that outlined consistent strategies for incorporating solid research into creative campaigns. Teams of creative directors traveled to Y&R offices all over the world offering month-long intensive creative workshops. These efforts paid off, and in 1979 Y&R was one of two agencies (N. W. Ayer was the other) designated as *Advertising Age*'s Agency of the Year.

At the end of 1982 Ney appointed Alex Kroll as Y&R's president and CEO, retaining the title of chairman for himself and remaining active in the agency. In 1984 Y&R surpassed Japan's Dentsu (with which it formed a joint venture in 1981) as the largest agency in the world. (As of mid-1987, Dentsu had again surpassed Y&R as the world's largest agency.) In 1986 Kroll initiated a major restructuring of the agency's various divisions in order to more fully integrate all of Y&R's disparate services. He appointed Peter Georgescu president of Y&R Advertising, in charge of all Y&R's worldwide advertising offices and specialty advertising subsidiaries, and personally retained control over Burson-Marsteller and two joint venture agencies.

Today Y&R is structured into two primary operating divisions: Young & Rubicam Advertising, which includes its subsidiaries Wunderman Worldwide; Stone & Adler; Chapman, Stone & Adler; and the USA specialty companies Sudler & Hennessey; Cato Johnson/Y&R, and CYB; and Burson-Marsteller, which has fourteen offices in the United States and Canada, including its subsidiary Rogers Merchandising Inc., a marketing and promotion firm with offices in New York and Chicago, and a second public relations network, Cohn & Wolfe, with offices in Atlanta and New York. Additionally, Y&R has two joint ventures: HDM (Havas, Dentsu, Marsteller), the recently combined venture of two existing joint ventures DYR, formed between Dentsu, and Y&R, and HCM, formed between Eurocom and Y&R, and Paine Webber/Young & Rubicam Ventures, Inc. (founded in 1986), which provides clients with consumer marketing—oriented investment banking services.

The agency employs 10,844 people—roughly half in the United States and half abroad—in 212 offices in 39 countries. Y&R's client list of over two thousand companies includes The agency employs 10,844 people—roughly half in the United States and half abroad—in 212 offices in 39 countries. Y&R's client list of over two thousand companies includes Adidas, Colgate-Palmolive, Walt Disney, Dr. Pepper, Ford Motor [see p. 257], General Foods (a client for over sixty years), Johnson & Johnson (a client for over sixty years), Metropolitan Life Insurance (a client for over fifty years), Pillsbury, R. J. Reynolds, Trans World Airlines, the U.S. Army, the U.S. Postal Service, and Warner-Lambert.

has managed to sustain a reputation for creative excellence. The agency, which spends considerable resources on the recruitment and training of its staff, has an exceptionally low turnover rate and promotes primarily from within. Staffers work on accounts in product groups made up of account management people, creative people, account support people, and, after a campaign has been conceptualized, production people.

(Information provided by Aviva Ebstein, agency spokesperson.)

RANKING: Y&R is the largest independent agency in the country (and has been for nine consecutive years) and the second largest in the world.

WORLDWIDE BILLINGS: $4,905,710,000 in 1987.

GROSS INCOME: $735.49 million worldwide, of which $385.76 million is derived from the United States, in 1987.

NET INCOME: The agency is privately held and will not disclose.

OFFICES: 212 in 38 countries plus the United States: Argentina, Australia, Austria, Belgium, Brazil, Canada, Chile, Colombia, Denmark, Dominican Republic, Finland, France, West Germany, Greece, Hong Kong, India, Italy, Japan, Malaysia, Mexico, the Netherlands, New Zealand, Norway, Panama, People's Republic of China, the Philippines, Portugal, Singapore, South Africa, Spain, Sweden, Switzerland, Thailand, United Kingdom, Uruguay, Venezuela, Zambia, and Zimbabwe.

NUMBER OF EMPLOYEES: 10,844 at the beginning of 1988, with roughly half working in the United States and the other half abroad.

AVERAGE AGE OF EMPLOYEES: Information not available.

TURNOVER: Information not available, but comparable to industry norms.

RECRUITMENT: Y&R recruits in two areas—account management and creative. Account management, which looks primarily for MBAs, goes to Columbia University, Harvard University, Northwestern University, and the Wharton School of Finance. Recruitment for creative positions operates somewhat less formally. Y&R looks for copywriters at both liberal arts colleges and state universities. Most copywriters have degrees in English or communications/journalism with a specialization in advertising (although they do come from a variety of backgrounds). The agency recruits fewer than ten new copywriters each year, in order to spend time developing each year's group. Past copywriting target schools were Amherst College, University of Illinois, Northwestern University, University of North Carolina, and University of Texas. For art directors, the agency looks mostly in the New York market, with many new recruits coming from the School of Visual Arts, but they also often find talented recruits at the Art Center College of Design in Pasadena, California.

NUMBER OF NEW HIRES PER YEAR: The agency hires about nine hundred new employees at a professional level each year, for all of Y&R, Inc. worldwide.

RANGE OF STARTING SALARIES: "It's hard to pinpoint a range, given that there are so many different departments. Salaries are competitive with industry norms."

POLICY FOR RAISES: Employees are reviewed annually and raises are awarded on merit.

TRAINING PROGRAMS: All new employees go through an orientation session, which takes about half a day. Then individual departments provide training for new hires as needed, most of which is on the job rather than administered through formal programs. In addition, the agency offers numerous workshops in all areas for people at various points in their careers, most of which are conducted on a worldwide basis. The Advertising Skills Workshop, held in New York since 1978 in an annual four-and-a-half-week session, is a sort of graduate program to which employees worldwide are invited.

BENEFITS: Medical and dental insurance, savings plan, life insurance, educational incentive plan (a college fund for children of employees), career compensation plan (a pension plan), and long-term disability insurance. Y&R offers about 10 percent of its professional employees the option to buy stock in the company.

VACATION: Ten days from six months to three years, fifteen days after three years, and twenty days after ten years, in addition to three floating holidays each year (which employees can take at their discretion) and twelve regular paid holidays per year.

ADDITIONAL PERKS: The agency has a recreation club which offers employees discounts on tickets to cultural events. It also has a matching fund through which it will match employees' contributions to college alumni organizations. Y&R New York gives each of its employees gifts several times each year for different holidays or seasons. Sometimes in spring, sometimes for July Fourth, some years at Thanksgiving—(in 1987 employees received a cake plate for Christmas)—and all birthdays.

BONUSES: At Y&R New York, all employees are eligible for two bonuses. Everyone receives a regular annual bonus, which amounts to a fixed percentage of salary. The agency also awards merit bonuses, determined by managers, to outstanding employees.

ANNUAL PARTIES: All Y&R units host annual parties that are left up to the discretion of the individual offices. Y&R New York holds an annual meeting in December, generally in a hotel, for all employees. Employees get dresssed up. There are speeches early in the evening, after which the meeting turns into a big party with dinner and dancing.

DRESS CODE: No stated dress code. "Clothes seem to reflect the entire fashion spectrum. There are really corporate people, and some dress casually. Account management people tend to be more corporate, and the creative department tends to be more casual—but that varies, too. It's pretty much left up to individual discretion."

AVERAGE WORKDAY: 9:00 A.M. to 5:00 P.M., though a lot of people come in earlier and stay later.

SOCIAL ATMOSPHERE: "Y&R has always prided itself on its wide reputation for being very people-oriented, so you'll find that it's relaxed and informal. Which is not to say that there isn't pressure. People work long hours sometimes, and there are tense moments, but I find that it's pretty much a team spirit and people pull together." People do tend to fraternize with one another after working hours. "I know I've made some very good friends here, and I assume I'm not unique."

HEADQUARTERS: Located in Y&R's New York building on Madison Avenue, which the agency owns and solely occupies. The building consists of 24 floors that house about 200 corporate employees and about 1,450 Y&R New York employees. There are 211 other offices worldwide.

CHARITABLE CONTRIBUTIONS: In 1987 the agency gave about half a million dollars in cash donations and another half million in public service advertising. Approximately two hundred organizations received cash contributions, among them Covenant House, National Corporate Fund for Dance, Hospital for Special Surgery, Salvation Army, Phoenix House, United Way, WNET (New York Public Television), Metropolitan Museum of Art, Museum of Modern Art, United Negro College Fund, Boy Scouts of America, Girl Scouts of America, Boys Club of New York, Museum of Broadcasting, Asia Society, YWCA, and the YMCA Harlem Branch. The agency conducted public service advertising for the American Cancer Society, Big Brothers/Big Sisters, Coalition for the Homeless, Covenant House/Under 21/New York City, Drop-

Out Prevention Fund, Foreign Policy Association, Greater New York Blood Drive, Literacy
Volunteers of America, National Urban League, New York University Medical Center, Summer Jobs for Youth, and the United Negro College Fund.

INTERESTED APPLICANTS CAN SEND RÉSUMÉS TO:
Young & Rubicam, Inc.
Personnel Department
285 Madison Avenue
New York, NY 10017-6486
(212) 210-3000

As advertising agencies merge and take over and spin off and consolidate, there's really
been only one clear winner. It's not the client, and it's certainly not the agency
employees. The winner is . . . Young & Rubicam. The large Madison Avenue-based agency
has garnered many of the accounts that were lost in conflict-of-interest tugs-of-war that
emerged in mergers. For a time it seemed that any account that left an agency in protest or
any account that was dropped because rival products were already on the roster of the newly
configured postmerger company (are you following me?) sought out Y&R. According to the
July 28, 1987, *Advertising Age,* the agency had grown by $415 million worth of new business,
much of it due to other agencies' shakedowns. This includes Colgate-Palmolive (which was
already a client for some of its products), Eastman Kodak, TWA, Nabisco, and Warner-
Lambert.

The agency had long been the biggest independent agency in the business. With almost
eleven thousand employees worldwide (about nine hundred new people hired *each year*), and
approximately two thousand clients, its size often dwarfed the reputations of individual departments. Rather than focus on its strengths, outsiders often assumed it was just a big, decent
place. In reality, it's a generalist in the best sense of the word. Creative is strong; client
services are strong. Young & Rubicam believes in being "the whole egg." They've alighted
upon this image of purity, naturalness, and simplicity as their metaphor for a total persuasion
corporation. They own Burson-Marsteller, the largest public relations firm in the world. The
attitude at Y&R is that between advertising, PR, and direct marketing, surely they are able
to sell the pants off their competitors.

A visit to Y&R's building is like entering a world unto itself. Just before nine in the
morning, there is a governing principle at work that organizes the potential chaos. Everyone
swarming inside works here or has work with the agency. They feed themselves into the proper
elevator banks with an air of belonging that seems, somehow, enviable.

Peter Georgescu is president of Y&R Advertising. He's also the number two man in the
entire organization. He left his native Romania thirty-four years ago and joined the agency in
1963 straight from Stanford Business School. He had been thinking of working for an oil
company, since that was his father's business. When few students showed up for appointments
with the Y&R recruiter, one of the placement officers at Stanford begged Peter to meet him,
so that Y&R wouldn't cross Stanford off its list. "It was a game. The guy produced a ticket on
the spot," Georgescu says. "And twenty-five years later, here I am."

He started out in research. "This was a company that really cared about the customer. We
did great advertising from knowing the consumer." Time passed. "I was here. I was in my
mid-thirties. I didn't think about fit," he says as if that were the most remote notion in the

seventies. "The guys [his superiors] wanted me to go run something overseas. I always refused offers to go to Europe. I didn't want to be on the frontier without a cavalry at my back door.

"My wife helped. I really wanted to sign on to the business. Not just the industry; it was Y and R. I wanted to sign on," he repeats. "Y and R was my career. It wasn't a career in advertising, marketing, or communication. Ideas are our business. We have a broad canvas. Nothing is as exciting as giving birth to ideas.

"I wanted to run something. I wanted a new challenge, and I needed to get pushed." In 1974 the Georgescus moved to Amsterdam for two and a half years. "By the time I left, I knew I could do it." Peter makes an important point: One must have confidence in one's own abilities, since the industry is so volatile. You can rely only on yourself. You can only hope to reach a point at which *you* know you can handle the generic and specific challenges that affect your work. Then, you're indispensable. "I can never say to my wife, 'Hi, honey, we're *there.*' We'll hopefully try to raise it to the next level. We'll never get there. We're Sisyphuses and enjoy pushing the rock."

Although some of the most recent growth came knocking on Young & Rubicam's door, Georgescu believes that growth is a necessity. "Y and R had first to be a superb small agency, then a superb midsized agency. We've got to continue. It's not just financial. We have a very clear vision of what we do: To achieve tremendous business success with style and humanity. People count and must be part of the total equation. Every decision is matched against that statement. We need a clear vision.

"I think the leader needs to be the vision. Not just say it; *be* it. People look to see you, not to hear you. To the extent that our people see me, I must roll up my sleeves, get dirty, take risks. There can't be any doubt what I stand for. You must ask anyone." Calling Y&R "a changing idea," Peter Georgescu says that in its execution of Y&Rism, there should be no conflicts between what is right for the client and what is right for the agency. "The best interest of the agency must be the best interest of the client. There is no difference.

"My job is for key managers to understand that. I don't intend to be just a cheerleader—many presidents can do that."

Remember, we're still talking about advertising. "It requires enough innate intelligence. We're not geniuses. We must develop the ability to take an idea and demonstrate we can do something with it. It's the difference between intelligence and willingness to do something. I yearn to allow people to do something, and feel good about themselves. You can be a superstar, but the best results are team efforts."

Considering his matriculation in advertising was something of an accident, Georgescu has overcompensated by reflecting intensely on what he does. He's thought about his life apart from Y&R. "I do envision life after Y and R. I don't have a timetable. I never predicted my next job correctly in twenty-five years. Which has made me infinitely happier. Time goes very quickly. When I stop driving myself, I hope I have the wisdom to turn around and have a cadre of teammates who'll carry the ball. The magic is to continue."

John McGarry, the chairman of Y&R New York and the chairman of Client Services Worldwide, says, "Peter's like my brother." At one time John was Peter's traffic person on the Bristol-Myers account. "Top management's very close." It is October, and the World Series is on TV. From time to time emeritus chairman Ed Ney and others come in to watch on John's television set or keep score. McGarry is so energized, so excited, he speaks almost breathlessly. "I was the first one in the family to go to college." He attended Villanova. "It was very heavy for me and for my family. Working for an oil refinery was assumed." He lives in a posh Westchester suburb, and his children go to private schools. In his yellow "power tie" and well-tailored suit, one would never know he wasn't born into this white collar service business. "I come from the wrong side of the tracks. Ed Ney is style, such class. The way he dresses, he's fit—you'll notice we're all fit—the way he comports himself, the way he speaks . . ."

John's future wife had worked at Y&R in casting before they married. "It helps to have the understanding of a wife who worked in the business. It's a high-pressure business, and she's very interested and supportive. There is no hesitation about attending three client dinners per week. The kids see you get excited about your work. There's something magical about film. When the kids watch TV, they see Dad's work." They don't see Dad as often, unfortunately. He's got business obligations several nights a week as noted, and stays in an apartment he keeps in the city when it's too late to come home. "The kids know I may not see them every day of the week, but it's special when I do."

Winning the Kentucky Fried Chicken account was one of McGarry's choicest coups. "It was a battle. I can remember it as if it were yesterday." It happened in the fall of 1978. "My wife placed a photo of me on the refrigerator door and said, 'Kids, this is your father. Lest you forget.' The pitch took six months from beginning to end. Maybe it didn't take every weekend, but it took a hell of a lot of them. Kentucky Fried Chicken started with twenty agencies, and then it came down to us and Ted Bates. We pitched one campaign. Bates switched between two campaigns. I said to my teammates, 'Gentlemen, we just won.' " [Author's note: I believe he is quoting verbatim.]

"My parents and wife and kids jumped up and down, crying, 'You won! Daddy, you won!' Tell me that's not exciting. My kids sat on the colonel's lap before he died. You can't trade that moment for a lot of things.

"Now they're billing hundreds of millions of dollars. And I have similar stories about other campaigns."

The younger folks in the agency may not bring the same degree of passion to the office. "I don't kid myself," John says. "The generation coming up is different. I grew up with a breed of guys who had to push their way up. Nobody handed anybody anything. I'm sure the new guys want it [success], but I'm not sure they're like us. It'll be interesting to see if the team a decade from now will be a team. We've been together a long time. We've won a lot of 'Super Bowl victories' together."

McGarry works about twelve hours a day, he says. "But you love it. It goes very quickly." It also takes a lot out of you; it has to. "We're all workaholics. It's a totality kind of thing. I can remember doing two new business pitches in one day. A win is everyone's win. A loss is a personal responsibility for me. Sometimes there's luck, but I think you make your own luck."

The key to John's enthusiasm, he says, is "the thing that influences the personality of the agency. Creativity. It's a battery. Account executives have to feel they're creative. Research people have to feel they're creative. A memorable campaign that could run a long time helps." Feeling his soul was sparked during the creative process, at one time he considered moving over to the creative side. "I felt that it was such a part of me, which was unique for a management type person. But I was told I sold well and pure, that I could stimulate a client and sell him brilliant stuff."

McGarry puts great store in loyalty. To encourage others to feel the same, he is big on rewards and celebrations. "For any announced promotion, everyone gets a personal letter from me," for starters. "Last night we had an anniversary party for Y and R Entertainment. We took the creatives to see a new foreign film at the Cinema III. Plus, every year we give out six gifts to everyone." Two annual gift occasions are the first day of spring and Labor Day. The presents could be as modest as Y and R beach towels for July 4, or as fancy as crystal Finlandia pitchers for Christmas, luggage for Valentine's Day, or a Tiffany silver bowl for each employee's birthday. "These are over and above the regular bonuses. On the executive level—for senior VPs and above, we give a Y and R Lett's [British leather-bound] calendar for Christmas.

I mean," he clarifies, "I'm not a gift-giving fool. There's a side of me that wants people to enjoy life. I'm probably more serious than perceived in interviews."

Sometimes McGarry is shocked by his good fortune. Young & Rubicam has allowed him to have a life he never even dreamed of. "I can't believe I am what I am. The first time I saw Venice, I thought my heart stopped. I never saw anything so beautiful. I never thought I'd live to see it. I came right back with my kids. I couldn't stand their not having seen it with me the first time."

At forty-one, Tim Pollak has been named the president and chief executive officer of HDM, Y&R's joint venture with Japan's Dentsu, the largest independent agency in the world, and Eurocom, the largest agency in Europe. A graduate of Dartmouth (1967) and Columbia Business School (1969), he entered the business when "it wasn't cool to go to business." He pauses. "Well, it was better than Vietnam." He went straight to Doyle, Dane, Bernbach. "I think I was the second MBA at Doyle, Dane. I left advertising in '72 to do political writing and consulting in Delaware" (his home state). After six months in the Delaware State Senate, Pollak moved back to New York in 1974 to work with Dave Garth, the famed Democratic political media consultant.

Three years later, Tim thought that "working there was limiting at the end. I felt I could always go back to politics. I was thirty-one years old. I decided to try consumer advertising. Y and R was hot. They were very much in the news. They were having a winning streak. I wanted to stay with the best.

"Y and R took a very enlightened view to my [advertising] background, which was beer [at Doyle, Dane]. They had just gotten the Pabst account. They said, 'Give us a year on beer and we'll give you package goods' [the ultimate goal of nuts-and-bolts advertising]. Y and R was a place to hold your head high." So Tim was the account executive on Pabst in 1978. "They kept their promise. Within eleven months I got package goods." In 1980 Pollak became the account supervisor on Jell-O, a product of General Foods. [Author's note: You would probably like to know that cherry is the most popular flavor.] The following year, he was made a vice-president.

Pollak's account of his career is made without a trace of bravado. This is simply the chronology of his years at Young & Rubicam. In the early eighties, he worked on new business and spent a couple of years working on the Kentucky Fried Chicken international account. As the director of marketing and a senior vice-president—"no coronation"—in 1984, "I got asked to pick up the Colgate business, which was rocky." In other words, Tim was now the worldwide account director on Colgate, "the world's largest toothpaste producer, with thirty-eight percent of the market." (Here are the places Colgate is sold: Argentina, Australia, Austria, Brazil, Canada, China, Denmark, England, Fiji, Finland, France, Germany, Holland, Hong Kong, India, Malaysia, Mexico, New Guinea, New Zealand, Norway, the Philippines, South Africa, Spain, Sweden, Switzerland, Thailand, the United States, Venezuela, Zambia, and Zimbabwe. This is what we call "penetrating the international market.")

Pollak says there are similarities between Y&R/Colgate here and there(s). However, "account executives in India are women wearing saris."

By now he had been working for Y&R the better part of a decade. "I didn't know whether this would be a long-term place. In this business there's a lot of temptation to leave. I happen to believe there's a *right place* for everyone. For me, this is the right place. You're treated like an adult and a professional. Like you have a business to run. You're asked for solutions." (He admits, "It is very daunting to think of the big money.") Are the managers tough? "Yeah, of course. They're critical and demanding. How else can you be good? The people who rise have the mettle to stand up for what they believe."

Young & Rubicam's size notwithstanding, Tim dismisses the notion of employees' needing to promote themselves. "It's more a meritocracy than a matter of politics. It's the job of managers to make sure their people get the credit they deserve. We do not do a lot of gushing or patting ourselves and each other on the back. If your psyche needs constant reaffirmation or applause, this may not be the place for you. But yes, we are appreciative in terms of raises and promotions. There's no way everyone on the sixth {senior executive} floor can know everyone. Names start appearing on the same short list. Once a new person becomes dependable, you use him. You'll hear, 'Get him.' And then they fall off. When I travel, I'm less visible and less called on."

Titles are important. "There are a lot of vice-presidents. If you haven't earned it, you wonder why. Your title becomes the recognition of your performance and your stature in the organization. Occasionally you'll see something and say, 'Hmm . . .' But by and large the best people end up in the biggest jobs. You can only fake it so long."

He continues, "I think there is security in this place, but it shouldn't be a sinecure. We don't fire people to make up for lost income." The agency that Pollak (and Georgescu and McGarry) describe sounds like a more humane and cerebral place than the way most agencies are usually portrayed. "This is not an agency that gets by on the Madison Avenue stereotype. It's a smart agency. We're all serious professionals. We're not flashy or frivolous. If you're good at Y and R, you could be good anywhere. Not vice versa. Most people stay. When they leave it's because the training they get here holds big cachet. I *can't* imagine leaving here today. It's very much home."

Is there stress? Yes. "Always." Especially when people have more than one boss. And for some reason, advertising stress is more visible than say, manufacturing stress—it's a service business—and much more colorful. "When I offer an outrageous piece of advertising to the client, my job's on the line." Pollak will say that he "can't turn it off. Ever. You can't call the Far East until nine P.M." The job requires socializing with the client. He rarely lunches more than twice a week with clients, but those meals are "intensively business-focused. A good client will motivate his business despite his personal likes and dislikes. He must reach a housewife when *he's* a fifty-year-old executive."

If you think these guys sound driven, wait till you meet John Ferrell, one of Young & Rubicam's three creative directors. [Author's note: Y&R was restructured after my visit into three groups to better manage the size. When Ferrell and I met, he was the sole creative director.] Small, wiry, bow-tied—his sartorial trademark—he takes up very little space in an office that's filled with four Victorian chairs, three telephones, two typewriters, and at least eight of his twenty-five or so Clio award statuettes. When Ferrell started at Y&R, he was famous for arriving at work between 4:30 and 5:00 in the morning. "I've gone at it pretty hard since then," he says, although he has limited his days to about 12 hours—7:00 or 8:00 A.M. to 7:00 P.M.

He's a little sensitive about his reputation. "I think I've taken every day of vacation I've been entitled to. I don't think I'm the workaholic I've been depicted as. Marriage helped. I've discovered it's important to have a life outside. People spending *all* of their time on their careers don't spend the time well."

As a boy in smalltown Illinois, Ferrell said he "always knew advertising was what I was going to do. I always liked commercials and felt they were the most interesting part of TV." At the University of Illinois, he majored in journalism and communications. He found a job at Leo Burnett (see p. 123) after graduation. "The business was centered in New York. Sooner or later I thought I'd have to move here if I were serious about the business. Y and R spoke to me. It was the only place that was large *and* creative. Someone who was fairly junior had the chance to work on the biggest, best, most prestigious accounts in the agency. The best people in the business were all here at the time." That was about twenty-one years ago, approximately the time Y&R creative gave the world "Should a gentleman offer a lady a Tiparillo?" and "Number one in the sun" (Eastern Airlines). Ferrell says, "I knew it was right from almost the moment I arrived."

He loves advertising still. He is not one of the well-paid disgruntled who's plotting his big escape. "A lot of people regard advertising as the thing itself, not just a way station," he defends, identifying himself with this group. "I'm not on my way to being a Hollywood screenwriter." [Author's note: this seems to be a common cry among advertising interviewees in this book. One wonders where all the screenwriters *are* coming from.] There are about 175 writers and art directors in New York who make about 840 television commercials a year, not to mention 6,650 print ads, 538 radio spots, and numerous billboards. "I don't see every ad that comes out of here, but you've got to care and encourage the creative staff.

"There will always be a place for the big creative agency," he says, prepared to describe the people who might fit into his department. "I'd respond to eagerness, energy, drive. People who drive themselves to do something different in a different way. People who regard any threat to their idea as an intrusion should get out. Particularly in commercials. Print and radio are more solitary. When I first came into this business, the writer was king. The team idea happened in the late sixties at Doyle, Dane.

"Frito Lay's 'No one can eat just one,' " he rhapsodizes. "That's what can put one agency above the others." Ferrell often quotes Y&R lines. "A mind is a terrible thing to waste"—the United Negro College Fund. "Brush your teeth with Dentyne." "Make Jell-O and make some fun." Ferrell asks himself, "Do you have to love advertising to do good advertising? It helps. You won't lose interest or get frustrated. I have not gotten tired of it. You're looking at an old product in a new way, e.g., Jell-O. It has a most interesting set of attributes: wiggle, wobble, transparency. We're capturing the soul of a product. Every product is new."

A few days later we meet again, this time to view the agency's current reel together. John can barely contain himself, editorializing, evaluating, and appreciating the latest crop of tiny movies to come out of his shop. I feel I am attending a special tutorial, Creative Advertising 101. We start with the stunning new campaign for Diet Dr Pepper, a mock video personal ad. There are three of them on the tape, each of a different sexy person, two women and one man. The sets are cool and urban. To jazzy accompaniment, the tag line is "Throw your diet a curve." Ferrell, with mounting excitement: "There's always one of these around the corner. I don't think anyone tires of coming up with solutions. I mean, six months ago, this wasn't invented! Instead of a group of people and a big production number [typical of soft drink commercials], there's one person. Sometimes we even amaze ourselves!"

A group of Lincoln-Mercury spots show cars driving, with no visible drivers, through different terrains and locations. Rod Stewart—for *real,* no cheap imitation—serenades the autos with successively "You're in My Heart," "Tonight's the Night," and "Do You Think I'm Sexy?" Ferrell: "Any car commercial is expensive. But they're working and making billions of dollars for Ford, and we keep making them. We are trying not to be part of a crowd. We're trying to reach out and stretch."

Other masterpieces on the VCR include the Palmolive dishwashing liquid commercial with the breaking of the dirty dishes, pianist Phyllis Grandy playing a Chopin polonaise for Anacin's Arthritis Pain Formula; and Bill Cosby trying to rustle up a posse of prepubescent cowboys with a promise of Jell-O Pudding. Y&R has worked with Cosby for thirteen years, his earliest pitch work.

"It's a ball to see your work on TV." A (co-) creative director, Ferrell says, "I have the most creative job of all—just because I don't sit down by the typewriter twice a week. I get to touch about a billion dollars' worth of advertising. The creative director has control over the people and the environment. It's the best job in the business, and I'm not done with my agenda yet.

"You've got to make it fun. That's why I took 325 people on a boat ride, give theater tickets away every month for the best commercial, print ads, radio spots. We celebrate great work." One of his missions is to be conscientious about reviewing his people. "We're getting better at it. We're becoming more frank. I really can't hide what I feel."

Susan Gianinno is the marketing director of Y&R New York. Her office is serene, large, and light, and she is dressed to match. (Although she is slim.) She says working here is rewarding, because "we have a very high regard for the consumer. It's at the top of our minds always. We are a genuinely consumer-driven company. For a combination of reasons: the development of a talented research department who are first and foremost consumer advocates; a new leader in Peter Georgescu (who has high regard for research since it was where he got his start in advertising); we've seen that it works, if you can capture the moment of union between you and the customer; the market pushes us in this area. Product proliferation has driven our products towards commodities."

She regards her department's charter as "reducing the distance" between advertising personnel isolated on Madison Avenue—not to mention the clients removed from shoppers in their corporate headquarters—and the consumers themselves. "I encourage people to go out on the field and observe a product-consumer encounter [read: someone buying something] because New York advertising people have little contact with the products and their consumers. It's a personal accomplishment if creatives feel close to the end user."

To prove its sincerity in this area, Y&R has assembled a large Consumer Insights department —sixty professionals in the New York office alone. "Research used to be a training ground for account management. Not at Y and R. Most people come in as professionals, not as advertising people." Working here (or at any agency, for that matter) was hardly part of Susan's original plan. She was working toward her doctorate in behavioral psychology at the University of Chicago. One of her professors left school to become the research director of Needham, Harper's Chicago branch. He then went on a recruiting binge, raiding his former department, including Susan and her husband. "I never thought I'd leave academics," Gianinni says. "My whole family was doctors. I never knew anyone in business. It was very serendipitous. I liked it a lot. I had always enjoyed people research." Gianinni never got her Ph.D. "It doesn't quite fit my image of myself, not finishing school." When her husband was offered a research position at Yale, it was time to move East. She joined Young & Rubicam in January 1982.

"Our job is not to do the best research in the world, it's to leverage the consumer's point of view. If you were just going to do research studies, you could train anyone. We're trying to do good advertising, too." Presently her staff includes art history, English, political science, and computer science majors, as well as some MBAs. "I'm looking for anthropologists, psychologists, sociologists—people to go in with a vigorous sense of inquiry. It's a real liberal arts department. People here are integrated into the business of the agency. They are totally involved. A researcher should know much more than just whether the consumer likes Kraft mayonnaise." She adds that he or she should understand how the creative expression communicates the essence of mayonnaise. "We design a lot of projects. It's a match between skills and the situation." The department will be working on many projects simultaneously. A cohesive unit, it has its own review board and its own parties.

As in the rest of advertising, Consumer Insights has to sell its ideas. "If the client isn't prepared to buy the right strategy, we must be prepared to know it. It's a business of rejection. Being genuinely consumer-driven helps. Consumer acceptance is more important than client acceptance. Much time is spent negotiating or bemoaning with clients." Much of Susan's time is also devoted to being the mother of a teenage girl and commuting to work from Connecticut. "I have taken a strong stand in the department to allow part-time work if business circumstances allow it. I want to keep talented people in the work force. Research is substantive, not contact-driven."

Missourian Jane Brite started her career as a reporter in Springfield, Missouri. It was a bold move in the days when "career counseling was not geared toward women. They wanted you to teach. I had in mind living in New York. I wasn't sure I could get a job as a reporter in New York. I set my mind on Y and R. I don't even know why." In retrospect she guesses advertising seemed to embrace "how people tick—working with a variety of disciplines, people—other options seemed a little narrow. But I was uninformed.

"I figured I'd end up as a copywriter, but I liked the idea of managing. I wanted to run something." (Jane profited by Y&R's recent restructuring, going from group director on approximately thirteen accounts to a group general manager with approximately one third of Y&R New York reporting to her.) "I was real happy right away. Within the first six months I felt I was doing well and learning. In those days we had interviews with five vice-presidents every six months. They'd promote five people out of sixty. I don't remember being scared. There's not any one person—there are several people—who, after you've been here a while, you should know. They do more serious promotions." Interestingly, she adds, "When you're evaluated, you're assessed in terms of your ability to train others."

Jane's seventeen years here don't make her unusual. "An incredible number of top managers are lifers. They were people who would never walk out." She considers herself ambitious. "I never arrived thinking I'd be CEO. I only started looking at the next job after mine. Success makes you more evaluative. But today's graduate students are not willing to give so much to the companies without a return.

"The industry must come to terms with this—there's more loyalty to oneself. You're not going to get rich in advertising, but you can earn a good living if you stay in. Those who are mainly interested in money don't usually stay long. They have to work too long and hard." She thinks the best question to ask of recruits is, "Can you contribute to this industry in the next ten years? We're another smart head to bounce ideas."

Brite is looking for "intelligence and flexibility and curiosity about things and people. You should be outward-directed and analytical. You have to care about the consumer."

Of Young & Rubicam itself, she says, "Y and R hasn't had to be flashy since we got prestige so early. It's straightforward. I'm put off by hypersale, by bullshit. People here aren't flashy. Even the way they dress.

"I know Y and R is bureaucratized, but it doesn't feel that way to me. I imagine that agency people just know how to get things done. You don't just report vertically. You don't allow the structure to get in the way. Now that I'm higher up and responsible for creating bureaucracy, I try not to create too much.

"We must be careful because of all the money. Billions get deployed. It doesn't change your life when you're running accounts. It's the same as it always was. I like to think Y and R's values are the values of the real world. The pressure of making money makes it hard to remember the value of the consumer. Y and R tries to keep them, but it's not always easy."

When Art Klein was finishing up at Columbia Business School in 1962, commercial banking was all the rage. "For the hell of it I signed up for an interview {at Y&R}. Advertising had a glamour banking didn't have. I was called back again, and two weeks later I was offered a job by mail. My father thought I was crazy {to accept}."

Klein is proud to say, "I've never worked anywhere else. All of us could have left many times. The bottom line was, we didn't. Aside from the compensation, this is a nice place, a great agency, and if we're not the best, we're close. If there's a theme here, that's it." The president of Y&R New York and the president and chief operating officer of the Y&R Direct Marketing Group, he also talks about the collegiality of the most senior managers at the agency. "We've grown up together, we're a good team together. Yes, we're friends. We have to be. We've watched our kids grow up. {He even married a former Y&R-er.} It's been twenty-six years. We've lost very few people that we really wanted to keep. Our people work hard. I've been told the younger kids don't have the same loyalty.

"Y and R always is able to hire at entry levels because applicants know they'll get good training. We offer people a *career* in advertising, direct sales, public relations, et cetera." Klein says the culture of the agency is the product of people who intend to stay there for the duration of their careers from the very beginning, not people who just want jobs. And "many jobs pay more money, so the remuneration wouldn't be an adequate reason to show up for a job interview on Madison Avenue."

He doesn't interview much any longer, and the applicants he does meet have already been screened and recommended by others, but Klein says he can recognize good fit when he sees it, using the scientific "gut feeling." It takes about a year, according to him, to be utterly comfortable with "the Y&R way." Again, this means no flash, respect—if not out-and-out love—for the consumer, and a familiarity with the way the agency is organized.

He emphasizes the competitiveness of the organization. [Author's note: Many people point out during my visits to Y&R that Alex Kroll, the chairman of Y&R, Inc., was a professional football player (for the New York Titans, the forerunners of the Jets) before his advertising career. Some say the need to win stems from him.] In the advertising industry, one must vie for new accounts all the time, trying to beat other agencies to the punch. This yearning is exacerbated by the fact that "many of our blue chip clients use more than one agency." If that's the case, part of your job might be to look better than the other company. [Author's note: Didn't Susan Gianinni call it "a business of rejection?"] Not to mention what happens inside the offices. "The atmosphere that we like," claims Klein, "is to do better than the guy down the hall. I guess," he adds, "it is possible to get complacent or lazy here, but it is not easy."

He says Y&R started two trends that are now mainstays of advertising: Integration—combining advertising, public relations, direct marketing, and sales marketing; "We started acquiring in the early seventies and bought the best in those fields"—and globalization—"most blue chip clients want global coverage, consolidation." Clients should not expect their Y&R teams to be pushovers, simply following orders. "We don't give clients what they want. If that's all they want, they don't need Y and R. We fight pretty hard for our point of view. We want to build our clients' businesses. If you have a good relationship, you have a chance."

In the final analysis, Art Klein says, "As long as I want to stay in advertising, I want to stay here. Now I know I am capable and can handle problems that can turn up both personally and professionally. Sometimes I leave at the end of the day feeling like I've run a marathon. I've made my mark here. I've contributed a lot to Y and R. From 1962 to whenever I leave, the company's changed and grown, and I've contributed to that. It makes me feel good."

Last, but not least, Nick Rudd, the senior vice-president of Management Services. A native of Manhattan, he attended Columbia College and Business School. He's been with Y&R since 1968. What got him here in the first place? "Number one, I didn't want to sell toilet paper for P and G. Number two, I couldn't raise 1.4 million dollars for an entrepreneurial idea. Number three, I was intrigued with Y and R as a good advertising agency. I thought any place that was so creative as to win awards could pay the bills."

Rudd's particularly attuned to global thinking (which actually predated the agency's own). "Because as an MBA trainee, I was asked to start three months early to rewrite the Personnel Policy Manual. I was asked to think of the impact of the company from every office's point of view. Even though I grew up in this office, I think of the more than two hundred profit centers around the world."

When he joined the agency, there were perhaps thirty-five or forty offices outside New

York. "Ed Ney built up international in the fifties and sixties. We sent out monks from the mother church and set up clones of ourselves. We didn't have global clients, though. We didn't buy existing places. We had to find new business on our own. Our New York monks brought the New York culture with them. We were determined that each office should do fifty percent local and fifty percent international business."

Nick is responsible for the Advertising Skills Workshop, which is a sort of a concentrated program in how to best work within Y&R, while simultaneously reinforcing that which is Y&R. In its creation he "compressed a lot of material into a learning experience of four and a half weeks that would simulate seven years. We get people all pumped up, and they return to Paris, San Francisco, Tokyo, Oslo, et cetera, involved with our culture and values. They get it in context." The sessions are conducted in a classroom within the building. About sixty people at a time attend. A typical issue might be "What are the ethics of recommending a subsidiary of ours to a client if their work isn't that good?"

In its ten years of existence, the Advertising Skills Workshop has graduated more than 550 people. Attendees have generally had four to five years of experience at the agency; most have reached the rank of supervisor or above. The program engenders a high degree of loyalty on the part of its participants. "More than three hundred are still with the company," Rudd boasts. "It's like a glue. If I can inculcate people into learning how to build their business, that ensures more of what we want. The graduates of early Advertising Skills Workshops now run offices." Giving employees a sense of ownership is more productive than telling them how to do their jobs. "In essence, *you* make up your own mind. *You* reach your own conclusions, *you* decide. And then, you do *your* best. There's real value here in ideas.

"This is not so much a company as much as an idea made concrete. It began as an idea in Ray Rubicam's head: Creative people ought to be as important as business people." Nick dismisses the term "advertising" as being the best way to define this big idea. He favors "responsible commercial persuasion."

After spending "a dozen years running accounts, I have become a fairly competent manager," he says. "Now I'm helping managers manage change. Starting the ASW was just another assignment to me. From time to time I thought about missing the momentum of account management," but he keeps turning down new assignments.

"I make my life what it is. I've kept assuming new responsibilities. I've told the board, 'We're not in the business of making money, but money will help measure our business.' I care a lot about making this place work right. The people in this place could solve any problem. I want to ensure their preparedness. It's so good already. That's why I feel appreciated and understood.

"It's not easy to find motivation and meaning in life and in the world. Human beings need meaning and seek it in organizations, which have to provide purposes, and they have to be bigger than ourselves."

Interview:

LEONARD STERN

*L*eonard Stern is relaxing at home after a workday. With Perrier in hand and crudités on an art- and bibelot-topped coffee table, he has been home (a magnificent mansion on Fifth Avenue) since before 6:00 P.M., standard operating procedure.

Stern is the chairman of Hartz, the company that was started by his father, Max, who, as a young refugee from the Hartz Mountain region of Germany, brought a supply of singing canaries to this country and began what has become the largest pet supply company in the world. Stern *fils* expanded Hartz, first in real estate, investing in uninteresting swampy land in New Jersey now known as the Meadowlands, and in 1985 buying *The Village Voice,* New York's weekly newspaper, outright from Rupert Murdoch, to list his best-known acquisitions. (A new Manhattan weekly, more "uptown" in its appeal, called *7 Days,* was launched on March 24, 1988.)

His motivation to spread out into these myriad directions? "Primarily, not to be bored. I could not dream of doing one business. Three years after joining the pet supply business, I entered real estate."

Now Leonard Stern's reputation is that of a deal maker. The exact industries in which he's involved are secondary to the deal. He talks about the basic skills needed to engage in big-ticket transactions. "At some point it requires reason, intellect, and balance, punctuated at moments by intuitive judgment, to know whether to move forward or retreat. You can always do all the research on a deal, but the buck stops with instinct. I knew at age fifteen I could do it.

"I don't think of myself as a risk taker," he says. "I don't make more than one, two, or three *critical* decisions a year. I don't risk what I need for what I don't need. I never risked ten percent of what I had." As a rule, he tries "never to do a deal that will cause me to lose a night's sleep." There is a moment before Stern makes his final decision when he experiences "thirty seconds of utter peace. It's the absolute quiet before the storm. Everything else goes blank in my mind. It's almost euphoric—a very beautiful, peaceful, serene, harmonious feeling. You cannot create a decision if there's manic behavior or manic thoughts."

Stern hails the management he has installed at Hartz as "good people. The best I've known. High ethics. Well adjusted emotionally. There are no dramatics or workaholics. I'd sacrifice opportunities of hiring brilliant neurotics—I'm not willing to pay that cost." He employs no mysterious techniques to find his staff. "You interview, check references, hire. What else can you do? There's no way to test. There's always a twenty-five percent chance of error—even in choosing a lover. You never know until they work for you. All major divisions are autonomous. Each reflects the personality of the division leader. We allow no feudal kingdoms," he says flatly. The thought that he might be imitated by his employees doesn't offend him. He assumes the responsibility willingly. "If I start smoking a cigar, other people start smoking a cigar. If I start to wear brown suits, so will they. Being a leader is interesting.

"Being the sole owner of the entire enterprise, if tomorrow I had to work for someone else, I'm sure I would behave exactly the way my key employees do. If I had to crawl and beg for food and shelter, I would, but with difficulty."

One of the lessons he's learned in his more than twenty-five years in business is that "the least able people are the owners of private business. I'm fifty years old, and I've bought maybe thirty companies in my day. I have one rule when I buy a family company: They leave with the check. They're not as interesting as bureaucrats, teachers. With their one to ten million dollars, they pontificate on everything from external affairs to civil rights. They're assholes, and I don't make apologies for them.

"You're not going to find brilliance in the fields that count monetary awards," he rails. "Take a hundred Rhodes, Fulbright, and Watson fellows and see how many want to go into business. Instead of rewarding the teacher, scientist, or bureaucrat, we reward movie stars and business-men," he says with a sneer.

"Power is corrupting in itself. Those of us who have the power must understand. Everyone kisses our ass and asks our advice about things we know nothing of. People come over to me. I don't have to *walk* anymore."

His sarcasm belies his pleasure. "No matter how you deride it, it's a thrill. It changes you. *Fortune* ran an article in 1974, 'The New Rich of the 70's.' I was the youngest and richest of all. They said, 'whiz kid without peer.'

"I was very proud. I knew it was transitory and I couldn't live up to it. I knew it wasn't true, and I knew I wasn't worth seven hundred million dollars, but I knew I would be." Stern's holdings are so vast, his wealth so immense, it is easy to anthropomorphize it. His money is like a companion sitting on the leather chair near him. It is never not there, whether it takes the shape of the pre-Columbian head in the drawing room, the Van Gogh in the living room, the staff in the kitchen, or just because he can discuss it so matter-of-factly. Stern doesn't dress flashily; his brown suit may be custom-tailored, but then again, it might not be. His (second) wife, Allison, who comes into the room to listen, is wearing a gray sweatshirt and shorts— nothing fancy. But it's there. Or maybe *he's* there. Stern says he has learned to make distinctions between friends and acquaintances. And he can recognize the telltale signs of sycophancy.

He has no individual role model, with the possible exception of his father, because "I've met very few successful people who are contented. Working people are content people. The laborer or handyman achieves success when his boss has none. I learned that because I made so much money so young. I remember when I made my first fifty million dollars. I was in my twenties. I remember thinking, 'I'm worth fifty million dollars and I'm not happy?' I knew I had to take inventory. I felt poor inside. I entered analysis."

He is happy today. He says every ten years is a new life, and since falling in love with Allison, Leonard has entered a contented cycle. "I love my work." He corrects himself. "It's my passion. But I don't work at night. My friends know not to call at night." Allison charts his renewed serenity by what she calls "PGD and AGD," pre-and after trips to the Golden Door spa in Escondido, California. Stern agrees. There the couple meditated. He realized, "Here I was, in love. With all the material success a grown man should or could want and a grown family. I felt there was nothing wrong with my life."

Although Stern is still enlarging the Hartz empire, he is looking ahead to the time when his major activity will be philanthropy. He has already taken up the cause of the homeless and has built three shelters in and around New York City. The latest, on Staten Island, has 1,800 beds. His son Manny works for his father's homeless program full time. At his alma mater, NYU, the Leonard Stern Hall was open for business in 1986. He donates generously to Jewish charities.

"I don't believe in large, inherited wealth. The greatest gift a man can have is a passion. People are entitled to the comforts they can buy and have grown accustomed to. I want my three children to be provided for and to show my love for them, but how do you give power to someone who hasn't earned it? Most of what I have, I will give away in my lifetime. I could live on a fraction. I just hired a full-time foundation director.

"My late father did it. He actually dissipated his capital. He provided my stepmother every luxury she'd had, and everything else went to the foundation. He planned his foundation for six years.

"I didn't surmise this was my father's plan; he articulated it to me. The Jewish people feel a responsibility to their communities. My vision is a broader one than the parochial, Orthodox Jewish community. I can't imagine a happier old age—which in our society could be twenty years—donating as creatively as you amassed it. I expect never to retire, but I expect to spend more of my time giving it away."

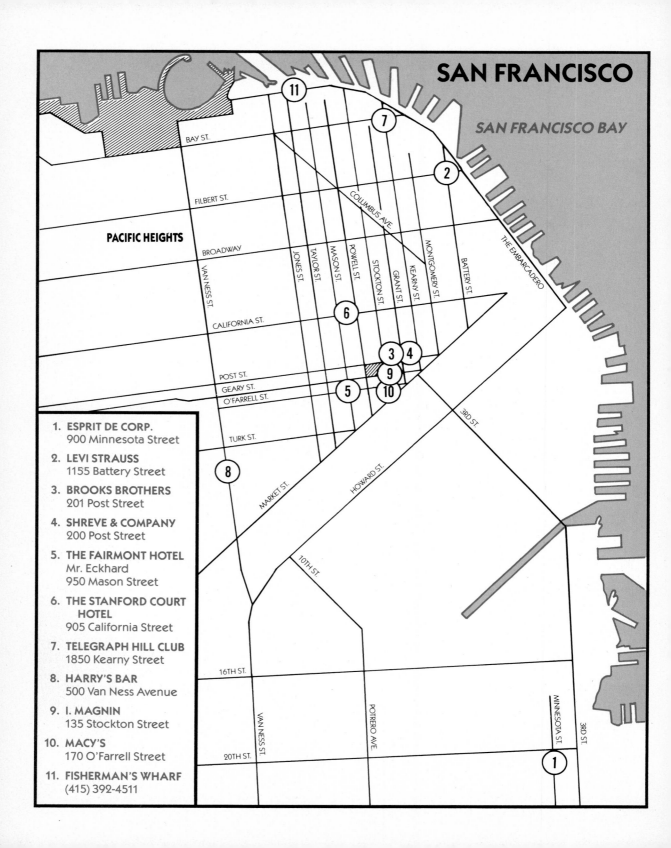

SAN FRANCISCO

SAN FRANCISCO BAY

PACIFIC HEIGHTS

BAY ST.

FILBERT ST.

BROADWAY

CALIFORNIA ST.

POST ST.

GEARY ST.

O'FARRELL ST.

TURK ST.

MARKET ST.

HOWARD ST.

16TH ST.

20TH ST.

COLUMBUS AVE.

THE EMBARCADERO

VAN NESS ST.

JONES ST.

TAYLOR ST.

MASON ST.

POWELL ST.

STOCKTON ST.

GRANT ST.

KEARNY ST.

MONTGOMERY ST.

BATTERY ST.

3RD ST.

10TH ST.

VAN NESS ST.

POTRERO AVE.

MINNESOTA ST.

3RD ST.

1. **ESPRIT DE CORP.**
   900 Minnesota Street

2. **LEVI STRAUSS**
   1155 Battery Street

3. **BROOKS BROTHERS**
   201 Post Street

4. **SHREVE & COMPANY**
   200 Post Street

5. **THE FAIRMONT HOTEL**
   Mr. Eckhard
   950 Mason Street

6. **THE STANFORD COURT HOTEL**
   905 California Street

7. **TELEGRAPH HILL CLUB**
   1850 Kearny Street

8. **HARRY'S BAR**
   500 Van Ness Avenue

9. **I. MAGNIN**
   135 Stockton Street

10. **MACY'S**
    170 O'Farrell Street

11. **FISHERMAN'S WHARF**
    (415) 392-4511

SAN FRANCISCO

SAN FRANCISCO

I t is the most cosmopolitan, lovely, stylish, and romantic of small cities, especially if you do not insist on driving everywhere. Metropolitan San Francisco, with a population of 700,000, is a jewel filled with some of the greatest sights, walks, and food in the whole country. According to the most recent census, San Francisco is considered the fourth largest city in the United States, but that's because they folded in the whole Bay area—Oakland, the Silicon Valley, Berkeley, and Marin County—total pop. 5,809,300.

In reality, the city feels so intimate that if you're a member of the 'A' social set—it really exists, people know who's in it, and it *matters*—you cannot wear the same outfit twice. (This small group could be accused of snobbery. *Tant pis.*)

It's the most liberal of big cities in terms of social programs. And when it comes to aiding those afflicted with AIDS, San Francisco is head, shoulders, and torso above the next most concerned city. (Obviously, San Francisco has been hardest hit by the tragic epidemic, but they're not waiting for the federal government to do something about it.)

It is also a serious corporate city. And the companies that call San Francisco home are among the most humane when it comes to thinking about the quality of life for their employees. Levi Strauss and Esprit de Corp., included here, provide beautiful surroundings for their employees to work in. And it doesn't stop there. They almost create surrogate families in their concern for their workers. Business people in this city are as no-nonsense as their counterparts anywhere. They may be closet liberals, but at the office they are simply professionals. For years San Francisco was the financial capital of the West Coast. Bank of America, which was until recently the largest bank in the country, is based here. (I visited it for this book when it was beset by a long string of woes, so I omitted it, but the people there were remarkably supportive of their leadership and hopeful that their situation would be straightened out.)

Young professionals here are unusually intent on continuing education. They will form reading groups, wine-tasting groups, or foreign language conversation groups *because they want to*. Naturally, they're conscientious about working out and staying fit. They're more likely to see the latest Czechoslovakian film than to rush to see Disney's latest production. That's just the way they are. They can order sushi in Japanese or prepare it themselves. (They took courses in exotic cuisines.) Author's personal recommendation: Diet before your next trip to San Francisco so you can eat big meals without fear.

San Francisco is a city of readers and culture mavens. It's a city of Democrats and dressing-up. (Ever since people saw pictures of themselves in the Haight-Ashbury days, they've made a commitment to meticulous personal hygiene.)

It is a city of diverse therapies. What does this mean to the average business traveler? Chances are your cab driver may be a therapist of some type or at least studying some form of Rolfing, psychotherapy, or crystal healing. If not your cab driver, it could be your waiter or bellperson. (It's too progressive a city to say "bellman.") So it's wise to bring along reading material if you are not receptive to self-improvement.

BEST NEIGHBORHOODS WITH DECENT PUBLIC SCHOOLS: Piedmont, Ross

NICEST NEIGHBORHOODS (BUT YOU'LL PROBABLY HAVE TO SEND YOUR KIDS TO PRIVATE SCHOOL): Presidio Heights, Pacific Heights, Seacliff

BEST PLACE TO LIVE IF YOU'RE AN ASPIRING ARTIST OR YOU WANT TO LIVE NEAR PEOPLE WHO WEAR ONLY BLACK: SOMA (South of Market) near Folsom Street

BEST NEIGHBORHOOD WITH TAKE-OUT FOOD AND SINGLE PEOPLE WHO ARE ALSO REPUBLICANS: There are no Republicans in San Francisco

MOST OVERPRICED COMMUNITIES FOR SUMMER HOMES: Carmel, Woodside, Nappa

BEST PUBLIC SCHOOLS: Lowell (high school), Ross School (high school), Redwood High School, Piedmont High School

BEST PRIVATE SCHOOLS: Hamlin School, Marin County Day, University, Mt. Tamalpais School (K-8), Katherine Branson

BEST ALTERNATIVE SCHOOL: Waldorf School

ARCHITECTS WHO HAVE MOST INFLUENCED THE CITY'S SKYLINE: William Pereira & Associates (designed Transamerica Pyramid); Skidmore, Owings & Merrill

MOST POPULAR RESIDENTIAL ARCHITECTS: Sandy Walker, Bernard Maybeck—dead, but his homes are still the most popular ones

SOCIALLY INCLINED REALTORS: Florian Moore, Vincent Friia (socially inclined and overreaching)

DECORATOR WHO WOULD DECORATE HOMES PURCHASED THROUGH THAT REALTOR: Michael Taylor Interior Designs

DEALER IN THE FINEST, MOST VALUABLE ART: John Berggruen

TRENDY GALLERIES FOR PEOPLE WHO WEAR ALL BLACK AND HAVE A LOT OF MONEY: Artspace, New Langton, Mincher/Wilcox

MOST EXCLUSIVE GOLF CLUBS: Olympic Club, Silverado, Pebble Beach

BEST PUBLIC GOLF FACILITY: Harding Golf Course

MOST EXPENSIVE HEALTH CLUBS: Bay Club, Physis

BEST HEALTH CLUBS FOR MEETING POTENTIAL MATES: Telegraph Hill Club, Bay Club

BEST HOTELS FOR BUSINESS TRIPS: Mandarin, Portman, Clift, Fairmont, Stanford Court, Donatello, Vintage Court (inexpensive)

BEST HOTELS FOR TRYSTS: Mansion, Hyatt Regency, Vintage Court

RESTAURANTS KNOWN FOR BEST CUISINE: Chez Panisse, Stars, Donatello, Masa's, Fleur de Lys

BEST RESTAURANTS FOR PEOPLE WHO WEAR BLACK: Taxi, Billboard Café, Rings, Rosalie's, RAF, Eddie Jack's, Tutto Bene

BEST RESTAURANTS FOR AN INEXPENSIVE DATE: E'Angelo, I Frattelli, Yank Sing (lunch), Little Italy, Stoyanoff's

NOISIEST RESTAURANTS (INTIMACY IMPOSSIBLE): Cadillac, MacArthur Park, Hamburger Mary's, Hunan

BEST SPORTS BARS: Pat O'Shea's, or any Irish bar on Geary

BEST DARK BARS: Caspian, Nightbreak, Gino's

BEST GIMMICKY BARS: There are none in San Francisco

MOST SAN FRANCISCAN BAR: Harry's

BEST BARS TO IMPRESS A CLIENT: Stars, L'Etoile, Carnellian Room (a view), Compass Rose

MOST EXCLUSIVE CITY CLUBS: Pacific Union Club, Bohemian Club

FANCIEST WINE STORE WHENCE CEOS PROBABLY STOCK THEIR OWN CELLARS: Draper & Esquin, John Walker's

GOURMET STORES GUARANTEED NOT TO RUN OUT OF GOAT CHEESE OR SUN-DRIED TOMATOES: Curds & Whey, The Oakville Grocery (Nappa), Bon Appetit, Oppenheimer's, Judith Ets/Hokins Culinary Company, Vivande

NICEST MOM-AND-POP GROCERY STORES: Le Beau (Nob Hill); you can also go to the Marina Safeway—they're nice there, too.

LARGEST DRUGSTORE WITH MOST REMARKABLE SELECTION: Walgreen's (Lombard Street)

CORPORATE PARTY PLANNERS: Horn, McClotchy & Coblentz; Irene Alltucker; Truffles & Flourishes

HIGH-SOCIETY PARTY PLANNER: There's only one—Charlotte "Tex" Maillard

POWER BARBER: Mr. Eckhard at the Fairmont Hotel

NEW WAVE HAIR STYLISTS: Lori D'Ambrosio, Anne Marie Colavito (A A Concepts), Roy Oliver

JUNIOR LEAGUE BEAUTY PARLOR: Mr. Lee's

PLACES WHERE LADIES WHO LUNCH ARE LIKELY TO HAVE TEA AFTER A HARD DAY OF SHOPPING, VOLUNTEER WORK, AND TENNIS: Neiman-Marcus; Narsai's Café (I. Magnin), Clift

BEST STORES FOR EXECUTIVE WOMEN: Neiman-Marcus, Alcott & Andrews, Saks Fifth Avenue, Wilkes Bashford, Nordstrom

BEST STORES FOR EXECUTIVE MEN: Wilkes Bashford, Nordstrom, J. Briggs, Brooks Brothers

BEST STORES FOR DRESS-UP CLOTHES: Gianni Versace, Wilkes Bashford, Hermes, Neiman-Marcus

BEST SHOPPING RESOURCES FOR PEOPLE WHO WEAR ONLY BLACK CLOTHES: M.A.C., California!, Carnivale

DEBUTANTE BALL: The Cotillion

BUSIEST SOCIAL SEASONS OF THE YEAR FOR THOSE WHO CARE ABOUT SUCH THINGS: Opera/symphony openings, Christmas

PARTICULAR SOCIAL HIGHLIGHTS: Halloween, especially the Exotic Erotic Ball; opera opening; Black & White Ball, Golden Gate Bridge celebration every fifty years (the next one is in 2037)

MOST RELIABLE FLORIST: Podesta Baldocchi

MOST EXOTIC FLORIST: Bloomers

TOP JEWELER FOR RESETTING MOTHER'S EMERALDS: Klaus Murer

MOST COMPLETE BRIDAL REGISTRIES: Gump's, Neiman-Marcus

PROMINENT PHYSICIANS: Dr. Art White, Dr. Robert Gamburd

PROMINENT PLASTIC SURGEON WITH EQUALLY PROMINENT CLIENTELE: Dr. Robert Brink

PSYCHIATRIST MOST OFTEN QUOTED IN THE LOCAL PRESS: Psychics are quoted, but not psychiatrists

DERMATOLOGIST WHOSE PICTURE APPEARS MOST OFTEN IN THE LOCAL PRESS: Allyn Beth Landau

BEST SEAMSTRESS OR TAILOR FOR ALTERATIONS: Hiromi

POPULAR FACIAL SALONS: Lena & Sula's, Elizabeth Arden, Georgina Acosta

POWER TOOLS

MEN'S POWER DRESSING

BROOKS BROTHERS
201 Post Street
San Francisco, CA 94109
(415) 397-4500

BEST-SELLING EXECUTIVE SUIT: Three-piece, regular weight, gray herringbone, 100 percent wool, $520.

POWER SHIRT: Pinpoint button-down, blue or white, 100 percent cotton, $46.

POWER TIE: Rep tie (striped), blue and maroon, 100 percent silk, $25.

POWER WATCHES

SHREVE & COMPANY
200 Post Street
San Francisco, CA 94108
(415) 421-2600

BEST SELLER AMONG EXECUTIVE MEN: Rolex Date-Just, $2,950; two-tone steel-and-gold bracelet watch with date.

BEST SELLER AMONG EXECUTIVE WOMEN: Rolex Date-Just, $2,425; two-tone steel-and-gold bracelet watch with date.

About half of the [executive] men buy watches for themselves, and the other half receive them as gifts. Approximately seventy-five percent of the women receive watches as gifts, and the remaining twenty-five percent buy them for themselves.

"Most men coming in to get the Rolex generally already have a watch. After they get the Rolex, they get a Patek-Philippe with a gold band or leather strap. [$6,000–$15,000]. Most women have one dressy watch, and they buy the Rolex as a sporty watch. For their dressy watches, most women buy a Patek-Philippe or Audemars-Piguet [$7,000–$15,000]."

POWER HAIR

MR. ECKHARD
The Fairmont Hotel
950 Mason Street
San Francisco, CA 94106
(415) 982-6600

Mr. Eckhard caters primarily to male clients, who make up 70 percent of his customers. "We are the only salon to offer private rooms. We have six private cutting rooms, a private facial room and facialist full time, and a full-time masseur combining shiatsu and Swedish massage. We always use private rooms for perms, rinses, streaks, conditioning services, and manicures and pedicures for men. We also offer phone hook-ups to each chair, which is very important to our executives. We also serve lunch from the hotel."

Eckhard reports that overall men's interests in grooming have increased over the last several years. Now 50 percent get manicures and 15 percent get pedicures, compared to two years ago, when "male indulgence was only five percent in these areas. We even do eyebrow waxing for men." Mr. Eckhard has a staff of six male hairdressers, eleven female hairdressers, five manicurists, one facialist, and one masseuse.

ONE TRENDS IN EXECUTIVE HAIR: "Executives want conservative, elegant hairstyles, yet always something young-looking."

ON COLORING: "We like to keep a ratio of twenty to twenty-five percent gray hair to the rest of the head of hair. Hair shading is fifteen to twenty percent of our business. We find the right pigmentation to complement the gray. Pigmentations from different colors are used to make up a natural look."

ON BALDING: "We find Minoxidil to be highly successful for clients who are beginning to have hair loss. We recommend implants also for bald spots, so long as there is some surrounding hair and there is a front hair line. Otherwise, you can see all of the plugs and it's not very attractive. If someone is really losing a lot of hair and it seems to be an irreversible situation, I like to suggest a mustache, which gives the illusion of hair—maybe not on the head, but it transfers the gaze to the facial hair, as opposed to the balding head of hair. Many clients have also had their eyelids lifted to make for a more youthful appearance when undergoing baldness. It takes away from that droopy look."

ON FACIAL HAIR: "A smaller percentage of executives now have facial hair. However, you do see a large percentage of bearded and mustached executive men from the artistic fields of business—designers, artists, et cetera. They do not prefer quite as manicured a look as the normal business executive."

ON EXECUTIVE MANNERS: "Executives are definitely under time pressure, but once you establish a pattern with them for appointments—for instance, manicures, hair shadings, et cetera —they seem to fit it all into their schedules."

ON NETWORKING IN THE SALON: "It's very important. Men and women both love to meet and chat in the salon. You may overhear them saying they'll call someone on this or that. We have phone hook-ups to every chair, and the women executives are generally much more discreet on the phone. Sometimes you can tell when a client is working on an important decision."

FEES:
Basic cut (including shampoo & conditioner), $20
Manicure, $11
Pedicure, $25
Facials, $25 for half an hour, $40 for an hour

INTERIOR DESIGN

MICHAEL TAYLOR ASSOCIATES
3352 Sacramento Street
San Francisco, CA 94118
(415) 931-3352

Michael Taylor Associates is a leading interior design firm in San Francisco. We spoke to Tom Marks about the firm's executive clientele.

IS THERE ANY PARTICULAR STYLE OF INTERIOR DESIGN YOUR EXECUTIVE CLIENTS SEEM TO PREFER?

"It varies according to the client and what they already own, for example, antiques and artwork."

WHAT'S THE SIZE OF THE AVERAGE SAN FRANCISCO EXECUTIVE HOME?

"Seven thousand square feet."

DO EXECUTIVES GENERALLY WANT MORE OR LESS INPUT INTO THEIR INTERIOR DESIGN THAN NONEXECUTIVE CLIENTS?

"Definitely more input. They are very involved in the whole process. As we are known as a custom interior design firm and we can design everything in the home, the possibilities are wide open. The more input we have for the client, the better for us to service his or her needs."

DO EXECUTIVE CLIENTS HAVE THE FIRM'S DESIGNERS CHOOSE THEIR ARTWORKS?

"Many clients have their own existing art collection, but for those who don't, we most certainly are willing, able, and do assist them in purchasing works of art."

WHAT KIND OF DESIGN IS YOUR FIRM KNOWN FOR?

"Mr. Taylor was specifically known for creating the 'California Style' ten year ago. This constitutes light, neutral, and pastel tones, overstuffed upholstered furniture (which he designed himself), as well as wicker furniture. We have also designed wooden tables, for example, with marble tops, et cetera."

DO EXECUTIVE CLIENTS SEEM OUT TO IMPRESS WHEN CHOOSING THE DECOR FOR THEIR HOMES?

"No. They are not so conspicuous here. They of course want quality, but comfort is also an important factor in their lives."

ESPRIT
DE CORP.

ESPRIT

HISTORY & OPERATIONS

Esprit de Corp., the San Francisco-based fashion company with the instantly identifiable graphic image, got its start in 1968. That year, Susie Tompkins founded The Plain Jane Dress Company, a line of California-style casual wear, in partnership with her friend Jane Tise. The new company's budget was initially so tight that Susie delivered orders in her own car, with her two young daughters in the back seat. Her husband, Doug Tompkins, had started the mountaineering apparel firm the Northface in 1965 with $5,000 from the sale of his 1953 MG convertible, and sold it in 1969 for $50,000, when he joined his wife's company. Plain Jane expanded. Within ten years, it consisted of four separate labels—Plain Jane, Jasmine Teas, Rose Hips, and Sweet Baby Jane—loosely unified under the umbrella company Esprit de Corp. Starting in 1978, Doug and Susie Tompkins—Jane Tise had by then left the company—made dramatic changes that ultimately propelled Esprit's growth into a worldwide empire.

Before 1978, the company had specialized in "knock-offs," quick copies of trendy styles, and had no recognizable style of its own. The Tompkinses changed that when they designed an original line of women's sportswear. As part of the effort to break from anonymity, they united the separate labels under the Esprit name, hiring graphic designer John Casado to create a consistent and distinctive corporate image, and fashion photographer Oliviero Toscani to refine and integrate the look. With the design of a streamlined logo, the consolidation of a breezily off-beat style, and the implementation of astute and prolific marketing strategies, the new Esprit was born. Sales tripled in 1979 and continued to increase as the company expanded and penetrated new markets.

In 1979, the new Esprit launched an aggressive promotional compaign with a glossy, outsized mail order catalogue sent to retailers across the country to acquaint them with the company's look and name. The following year, 850,000 catalogues went into upper-income homes across the country, where they produced an order response three times greater than the average response to mail order catalogues. The books featured mid-priced, mix-and-match separates in bright colors and prints. The clothing was loose fitting and designed for both comfort and chic. In a departure from the standard fashion industry practice of using unnaturally glamorous models, Esprit employed cosmetic restraint, and in kicky, unconstrained poses, emanated fresh-faced originality rather than calculated sex appeal. The "Esprit woman" —a consistently maintained image that has been widely adopted by fashion labels aimed at the same market—defined herself by what she could do in the world more than by what she could do for a man. The image sold and the Tompkinses extended it to multiple venues.

Esprit expanded to two separate lines of women's clothing. Esprit and Esprit Sport, and Esprit Kids, a children's line, was launched in 1982. The Esprit Sport collection caters to young, sporty women (target group: fifteen to twenty-five years old), while the Esprit collection—on which the company is currently focusing its promotional efforts—is for an older, upscale, more sophisticated consumer (target group: twenty-five to thirty-five years old). Each line is updated eleven times a year, enabling Esprit to keep abreast of the latest whims in fashion and to cut short its losses on any slow-selling items from a previous shipment. (Returned merchandise—generally about a season old—is sold from Esprit's San Francisco outlet store at a 30 to 40 percent discount.)

Esprit also makes shoes and accessories and has licensing agreements with Optyl for a line of sunglasses, and with Westpoint Pepperel for a line of bed and bath linens, both of which appeared in stores in fall 1987. (Esprit Bath & Bed has since expanded to include a children's line.) In addition, the company has a new denim line, Esprit Jeans, launched in winter 1987, and a brand-new menswear line, being produced in Italy.

In 1984, Esprit discontinued its direct mail-order business (although it continues to produce catalogues, which currently go out to 1.5 million customers). That year marked Esprit's push into retail—making it one of the few American fashion manufacturers to enter that aspect of the business—with the grand opening of a free-standing store in Los Angeles. (The company had opened the San Francisco outlet store in 1981, and had opened a test store with new merchandise in Hong Kong in 1983. The Hong Kong store is still used as a proving ground for Esprit retail concepts.) The Los Angeles store, designed by Joe D'Urso to reflect Esprit's "fashion-forward" image, took fifteen months and an estimated $10 to $15 million to complete. The 30,000-square-foot structure, originally built as a bowling alley and later converted into a disco skating rink, has 18,000 square feet of selling space. The merchandise is attractively and sparingly presented, with large areas of "negative space"—space without merchandise—intended to make shopping a more soothing and hence gratifying experience. Separates are shown with complementary pieces and accessories, encouraging customers to shop for full outfits. Rock music sets the mood and salespeople are schooled in soft-sell tactics such as striking up a conversation with a customer rather than asking "Can I help you?" Sales boomed immediately at the Los Angeles store, and Esprit has since opened fourteen similar company-owned stores in the United States and at least fifteen more abroad. The company launched a franchise program in 1986 and currently has thirty-eight U.S. franchise stores, with more on the way.

Esprit now has 2,200 accounts with department stores, down from a high of 4,000 in 1985. Eighty of these accounts are so-called shop-in-shops, an Esprit retail strategy implemented in 1984 on the premise that "Esprit clothes don't say much when bunched in with other clothes." The shop-in-shops are essentially Esprit boutiques, modeled after the free-standing stores, located within department stores. Esprit architects design them, and though they are staffed with department store employees—something the company would like to change—Esprit point-of-sales teams visit the shop-in-shops regularly to ensure that they accurately reflect the company image. Esprit has been steadily decreasing the number of its department store accounts with the goal of eventually converting all of its retail venues into either separate stores or shop-in-shops.

Esprit's astounding success can be largely attributed to the Tompkinses' almost fanatic attention to detail in every aspect of creating and maintaining a consistent corporate image. The company advertises heavily to convey that image to the public. Esprit received a flurry of attention—both positive and negative—when it launched a print campaign in 1984 that featured photographs of its own employees, clad in Esprit clothing, with a short quote from each one revealing something quirky and personal about herself. The following year, the employees were replaced by Esprit customers, who are still featured in the advertisements today.

Esprit clothing is either produced, designed, or distributed in twenty-five foreign countries. Foreign sales account for approximately 60 percent of the company's revenues, and Esprit is one of only a handful of American fashion manufacturers to so successfully saturate foreign markets. The company manufactures one line for America, designed in San Francisco, and a second line, designed out of Dusseldorf by Europeans, for overseas markets. The lines are very similar, although the European clothing is made of heavier materials—geared for a colder climate—and is designed with a "European flair." Esprit decided to make the European line available to its American customers, and introduced it in the fall of 1988 at all of the company's free-standing U.S. stores.

Under the leadership of Doug Tompkins, co-founder and CEO, and Susie Tompkins, co-founder and design director, Esprit now employs four thousand people, approximately half in the United States and the other half abroad. Rumors that the glory days of Esprit-U.S. may be waning do abound, but the company is privately owned by the Tompkinses, who will not disclose financial information. (The last time they were announced, in 1985, annual sales were estimated at more than $825 million.)

(Information provided by Lisa Ross and Stuart Adamson, company spokespersons.)

REVENUES: The company is privately held, and revenues are unpublished.

EARNINGS: Company is privately held and won't disclose.

NUMBER OF EMPLOYEES: Approximately 4,000 worldwide—half domestic and half international.

AVERAGE AGE OF EMPLOYEES: Twenty-five.

NUMBER OF COMPANY-OWNED STORES: Fifteen company-owned, free-standing stores in San Francisco, CA, Los Angeles, CA, Corte Madera, CA, Aspen, CO, San Jose, CA (4 stores), Dallas, TX, Orange County, CA (4 stores), Boulder, CO, and Georgetown, Washington, D.C.

NUMBER OF FRANCHISES: Forty-four open as of April 1988. Currently located in Puerto Rico, U.S. Virgin Isands, Washington, D.C., Maryland, New York, New Jersey, Hawaii, New Hampshire, Massachusetts, Connecticut, Ohio, Tennessee, North Carolina, Nevada, Florida, Louisiana, and New Mexico. Another twenty-five will be open by December 1988.

NUMBER OF SHOP-IN-SHOPS: Eighty as of January 1988, with many more on the way.

NUMBER OF DEPARTMENT STORE ACCOUNTS: 2,200 as of January 1988.

INTERNATIONAL BUSINESS: Twenty-five countries have design, production, wholesale, and/or retail operations: Australia, Austria, Belgium, Brazil, Canada, Chile, Colombia, Denmark, France, Hong Kong, Italy, Japan, Luxembourg, Mexico, the Netherlands, New Zealand, Norway, Panama, Peru, Singapore, Sweden, Switzerland, Taiwan, United Kingdom, and West Germany. Sixty percent of Esprit's sales are foreign.

TURNOVER: Not available.

RECRUITMENT: Esprit does not visit campuses. "However, twice yearly the company places items on the job boards of the following colleges and universities: U.C. Berkeley, San Francisco State University, S.F. University, Stanford, Brown, F.I.T., Wesleyan, and Yale."

NUMBER OF NEW HIRES PER YEAR: 75 to 100 in San Francisco, at headquarters and the outlet store.

RANGE OF STARTING SALARIES: $16,000–$22,000 for entry-level administrative positions.

POLICY FOR RAISES: Salaries are up for review twice a year and raises are awarded on the basis of performance.

BENEFITS: Standard medical and dental. The company subsidizes continuing education only if an employee's supervisor feels that a given course or program will benefit that employee's career at Esprit.

VACATION: Two weeks for the first three years, three weeks after three years, and four weeks after five years, in addition to twelve regular paid holidays per year.

ADDITIONAL PERKS: All employees are entitled to attend free morning and evening aerobics courses at company headquarters, which also boasts an outdoor par course and a lawn tennis court. Employees are automatic members of Esprit's "culture club," which gives 50 percent rebates on up to two tickets to all cultural events. Esprit has a subsidized café at its headquarters for employees, and another café, located next to its San Francisco Factory Outlet store, which is open to the public and where Esprit employees receive a 10 percent discount. All full-time employees get a 40 percent discount on all merchandise in all stores. Doug Tompkins considers Espirit's campuslike headquarters to be a perk in itself.

BONUSES: Bonuses were discontinued in December 1986. They were formerly awarded four times per year to employees at all levels for "performance above and beyond the call of duty."

AVERAGE WORKDAY: 9:00 to 5:30.

DRESS CODE: Relaxed. People wear anything they want, but dress leans toward working hip. High heels are discouraged.

SOCIAL ATMOSPHERE: Very congenial. Employees socialize both during and after work.

HEADQUARTERS: Esprit's headquarters are located on a 10-acre site in the warehouse district south of downtown San Francisco. Originally a winery built in the 1880s, the building is three stories with a brick façade. The renovated interior is subdivided by walls of glass and wood, creating large rooms and wide hallways, with exposed wooden posts and beams; 535 employees work there.

CHARITABLE CONTRIBUTIONS: Esprit does not make cash donations, but gives clothing to the "very very needy," through local San Francisco organizations. Among the thirty-five charities to which Esprit donated clothing in 1987 were the United Way, Big Brothers/Big Sisters, and the Child Abuse Prevention Center.

INTERESTED APPLICANTS CAN SEND RÉSUMÉS TO:
Esprit de Corp.
Personnel Department
900 Minnesota Street
San Francisco, CA 94107
(415) 648-6900

Enter the Esprit de Corp. environment, and you are assaulted by Esprit culture. It is what you expected: Everyone looks like those zowie Esprit advertisements photographed by Toscani, and many of them were; everyone looks young (because they are young; average age is twenty-five) and has asymmetric hair. You will see interesting outfits on Esprit's four thousand employees. At Esprit, "Dress for success" means looking like Esprit. It can mean leggings and sneakers. Stripes with paisley. It *does* mean wearing flat-soled shoes. If you arrive wearing high heels or any kind of footgear determined by the receptionist to be capable of pedicellate violence, you will be given a pair of Esprit huaraches to wear to soften the blow of your footsteps on the soft pine floors. This would be the only similarity between Esprit's neato headquarters and a bowling alley.

Esprit is an apparel manufacturer. But none of the employees ever talks about being in the fashion or garment biz. Don't forget, they are 3,084 miles from Seventh Avenue. A brochure prepared for job applicants says, "We sell a lifestyle product to a certain segment of the market —youthful, intelligent, fitness and fashion oriented, quality conscious types of people, of all ages." You don't hear too much about cotton and rayon in these ultra-California headquarters. (In fact, you hear more about packaging.) The lifestyle talk, with little encouragement, becomes rhapsodic.

Doug Tompkins is Esprit's co-founder and CEO. (Perhaps you've seen his picture in the Esprit ads also featuring Susie Tompkins, his wife, co-founder and design director.) Everyone credits Doug with developing the ethos of Esprit, of coining the patterns of thought and forms of expression used by one and all. "There's a lot of discussion of Esprit's philosophy internally," he says, sipping a giant hot chocolate in Esprit's on-campus café. "Especially by young people who haven't thought all this stuff out yet. We're in the lifestyle marketing business. We try to hire people we market to. In clothing, we don't know exactly what we want. We sell products with an aura around them."

Moreover, Esprit has minted its own esthetic. The company is devoted to its consistent look and communicating it in every way possible. (Esprit's eminently talented art director, by the way, speaks little English. He was recruited from a design studio in Japan.) The commitment to designing distinctive and exciting shoeboxes is as important as that of designing distinctive and exciting shoes. Of course, the ads are a big part of the semiology. And so are the (redesigned) business cards.

Esprit first exploded on the trendy fashion scene as a mail order catalogue. From tiny but eye-catching ads that ran in the back of *Glamour, Seventeen,* et al., to an increasing number of items included in editorial layouts, the name, in its familiar logo, became associated with well-priced sportswear. The catalogues were like a test market in which the look and its expression were honed. Surprisingly, by 1984, when the first Esprit shop opened (in Los Angeles, in what was formerly a roller-skating disco), and the first in-store boutiques were opening in department stores around the country, the catalogue was becoming a money loser. As it was being eased into oblivion, the big signature ads began to appear. The look, while still evolving, was secure.

When Esprit's message had been successfully absorbed by members of the appropriate lifestyle, the company embarked on a college recruitment campaign. The personnel people tested Esprit's on-campus appeal at career days around the country and were practically embarrassed by the crowds that flocked to their new-wave booths (especially when compared to the smaller groups at other recruiters' kiosks).

Barbara, Esprit's personnel director (well, she *was,* although titles here are eschewed), asked applicants why they wanted to work at Esprit, and the answer often was "It sounds like fun." That's okay with Esprit. It wants its employees to think they're having fun on the job. "For a lot of positions we take a risk," she said. "They may not have experience or education, but they have a fit." In other words, they look right and love the product.

Here's a look at some of the recruitment material:

ESPRIT CHECKLIST

If you don't have a sense of style, imagination, initiative, and a good sense of humor—forget ESPRIT!! You better try Wall Street or a chemical company.

ESPRIT is style, fashion, fun, and design; by and for women and men who are whimsical, intelligent, international, attractive, liberated, sporty, and fit.

Would you like to work with a great team? We are not just a clothing company, but a complex team of youthful people working in great environments dedicated to tough challenging jobs, a sense of accomplishment and above all . . . excellence.

If you are not *all* of the following, then ESPRIT is not the right place for you.

Health Conscious	Enthusiastic
Style Conscious	Positive Thinking
Design Conscious	Open Minded
Intelligent	Strong Minded
Tough Working	Driven
Whimsical	Organized
Into Fashion	Flexible
Team Player	Quality Minded
Tolerant	Self-Confident

Independent
International
Youthful

Spirited
People Oriented

Let's talk about great environments. Esprit people love where they work, whether it be the redwood-and-pine tree house–like corporate headquarters at 900 Minnesota Street, the high-tech showroom directly across the street, or the open, bright, and colorful warehouse-like retail and outlet stores. The young men and women (by far mostly women) become so attached to the niceness of where they work that after a year or more at Esprit they begin to harbor negative thoughts (a no-no) about what they imagine the outside corporate world to be. For them, college grads or not, Esprit is their haven: they're scared to leave—even for substantial raises—because it'll be icky *out there.*

The real world of their nightmares won't have a pretty campus with a park, a huge collection of Amish quilts [Esprit published a guide to the corporate quilts, organized by Esprit's in-house quilt curator. Really.], daily exercise classes, optional morning Italian and Japanese language lessons [Discontinued 1987] (because Doug admires both cultures, and guess what? So does everyone who works at Esprit. Those not of Italian or Japanese descent say they aspire to travel to or live in those countries), a subsidized café with really good food [Author's note: I ate there. It's fine.], or subsidized rafting trips every summer. [Discontinued 1986] (Doug is an outdoorsman. Guess what? So is everyone who works at Esprit.)

Personnel says, "We don't redo people. We don't want to. We want people who are comfortable." Well, at the time of my visits everyone got her hair cut short at Panache. It must be coincidence. Anyway, long hair is in again. Please don't misunderstand. There are originals here. One absolutely doesn't get the feeling that Doug Tompkins engages in brainwashing or proselytizing. It's just that when a successful, interesting, and attractive forty-five-year-old man runs a company comprised of impressionable young women . . . it's crush time. As a matter of fact, while Esprit is small and cozy enough to foster an intimate ambience, Doug is less like a daddy than a dashing, sometimes absentee uncle—with a penchant for adventure and danger. Doug often goes on climbing, rafting, and just plain treks to exotic places where they don't have telephones. A trip to Africa resulted in an exhibit of his photographs, "Faces of Bhutan" in a corridor gallery. Many of Esprit's women regard him with a touch of awe. He may naturally be the stuff of their dreamland fantasies. Don't forget that for many of the employees, Esprit is their first real job. They are grateful to be working here. By the way, a minor but real job perk for many people is the positive reaction they receive from strangers when they mention their employer. Not to underestimate this, Esprit's cachet among the young, trendy, and marketing-savvy is high.

Susie Tompkins is less of a palpable presence on Minnesota Street. She and her design staff are often away, overseeing the manufacture of the lifestyle products in the Far East.

Esprit's employees work hard. Many talk of their multiple jobs and responsibilities. They work hard for love, not for money. An undercurrent of dissatisfaction with the wage structure is somewhat subdued, but its fugue follows the aforementioned rhapsody. When complaints reach Doug's ears, he points out that the perks (environment, café, exercise classes, etc.) are equivalent to about 35 percent of one's salary. Esprit's offices, by the way, are located in a warehouse district near the Embarcadero, not in a convenient neighborhood for going out to lunch with friends from within or without. There is something very sequestered about Esprit. You arrive in the morning, stay through lunch, and leave after exercise class in the evening.

Your best friends in San Francisco are likely to be other Esprit people, especially if you're not a native. It would seem to be fairly difficult to meet anyone else.

Inside the tree house—my term, not theirs—work spaces are open, with individual offices reserved for the most senior department heads. Accounting embraces fifty-five employees who work together in two large rooms. As open and airy as the physical space is, what is surprising is how quiet the facilities remain throughout the day. That the tree house encompasses what looks like several newsrooms is misleading. There is no shrieking and little huddling, unlike in a newsroom.

Employees who have been approached by other companies use the term "scary" when considering leaving Esprit, substantial salary inducements be hanged. Many consider these other options so lethargically that the recruiters impatiently look elsewhere. No decisions have actively been made; Esprit-ers abdicate and let the recruiters make these decisions for them.

Esprit's famous advertising campaign-blitzkrieg did a great deal for personnel morale—not that it was flagging. Its original stars were Esprit's employees. "It got the whole company involved," says a young missy who worked on the campaign. No one got paid to appear in the ads, and no one got to keep the outfit she wore. (Employees do get a 40 percent discount. Interestingly, they wear a lot of Esprit, but not as much as you would imagine.) What captured the public's attention was not so much the clothes as the miniautobiographies that accompanied each model:

". . . I'll try anything once, but I especially like food, boys, and scooter riding . . . I'm planning to go back to Tokyo to do some more modeling."

". . . For breakfast my boyfriend and I make Belgian waffles, or I have a soft boiled egg that's been cooked exactly 2 minutes and 45 seconds so that it's still runny. I have a bunny named Bumper who chews on electrical cords after she's pulled the plug from the wall."

". . . I guess I'm a typical Gemini—half of me is very old fashioned and likes to wear lace camisoles and bloomers to bed, the other half is very avant and likes Japanese designers."

The image is boy, food and clothes crazy, although that too is changing. The new ad campaign features customers, often young mothers with their new wave offspring, and guys, too. An Esprit ad is not unlike a Dewar's profile set to rock music. Customers at Esprit's own stores (Los Angeles, San Francisco, Corte Madera, Aspen, San Jose, Dallas, Orange County, Boulder, and Georgetown, with more on the way) could get tapped for ads by Esprit's shooting teams. (Customers in Dallas, Hawaii [franchise store], and Amsterdam have recently been photographed.) "There's a common thread of youth, zaniness, and a sense of energy," says a young woman who works in Esprit's in-house advertising agency, of the employee ad series. "They were not supposed to be serious. Each model was interviewed by Beth, a twenty-two-year-old copywriter. She asked each one the same fifteen questions."

Esprit is private, owned by Doug and Susie. It is an extremely attractive company, the subject of inquiries by anxious suitors. Doug will not be tempted, he says, to go public. He does not wish to answer to a board of directors or shareholders. His agenda is long; his plate is full. Yet, at some point in the future, it is likely that he, the veteran of many false starts and successful careers, will find something else to do.

As the company founded in 1968 comes of age, new businesses are on the horizon. Sunglasses and a line of bed and bath items are already in stores, with menswear scheduled for the end of 1988. In 1986 Esprit opened one in-store boutique *a day* somewhere in the United States. It is enjoying success in twenty-five other countries as well. These operations are run by licensing agreements. Strict licensing agreements. They cover everything from finances to placement of dressing room mirrors, and they are vigilantly maintained.

LEVI STRAUSS & CO.

HISTORY & OPERATIONS

Levi Strauss & Co., the biggest blue jeans manufacturer in the world, was started in the mid-nineteenth century by an immigrant Jewish peddler from Bavaria. In 1847, at the age of seventeen, Levi Strauss came to New York City, where his brothers had established an import business. From there he traveled to remote areas of the country, selling his brothers' goods from a backpack. In 1853 news of the Gold Rush drew him to San Francisco, where he peddled his wares to miners. When the men complained about their need for and lack of durable pants, Strauss took his surplus tent canvas to a tailor, who used it to fashion the first predecessors of today's Levi's 501 (button fly front) jeans.

Strauss established a thriving dry goods business in San Francisco that was supplied by his brothers in the East. By 1872, Strauss was a millionaire and Levi Strauss & Co. consisted of five partners, all related by blood or marriage. That year an immigrant tailor in Reno, Nevada, offered to let the company in on his invention of work pants strengthened with copper rivets. The riveted pants, made in white duck cloth and blue denim, were patented in 1873 and advertised to "farmers, mechanics, miners and working men in general." Demand quickly outstripped supply and the company set up a factory operation in the East comprised of sixty women with sewing machines.

Levi Strauss & Co. incorporated toward the end of the century. In 1902, Strauss died, and as he'd never married or produced children, he bequeathed the company to his nephews. Though the pants and some additional items of riveted work clothing were profitable by then, they still comprised only a small part of the dry goods business. The company floundered for years in the aftermath of the 1906 San Francisco earthquake (which destroyed its headquarters) and the Wall Street panic of 1907. It then revived for a bit. In 1929, just before the stock market crashed, annual revenues were $4.2 million, 70 percent of which was generated by sales of riveted clothing. During the Depression, revenues slipped by half and the company continued producing primarily to keep its workers employed. Though it managed to survive —thanks to severe pay cuts and the family's independent fortunes—annual sales did not reach 1929 levels again until 1941.

During the 1930s, Levi's 501 jeans, which were still essentially a workingman's garment, gained broader exposure from cowboy movies and the new stream of Easterners vacationing at dude ranches in the West. The company broadened the line to include decorated work shirts and leather coats and jackets. During World War II, 501s were declared an essential industry, and only people directly connected to the war effort were allowed to wear them. After the war, demand for the jeans was astronomical, and in 1948 the company abandoned dry goods wholesaling—which still made up 75 percent of its business but only 19 percent of its profits —to devote itself entirely to the manufacturing of clothing.

By its centennial in 1950, the company was selling $22 million worth of goods annually and had obtained national distribution. It expanded its line to include sportswear, and revenues subsequently increased. In the mid-fifties, when James Dean and Marlon Brando wore Levi's 501s in their movies and thus popularized the jeans as a romantic symbol of youthful rebellion, kids across the country started buying them in droves. By 1956 sales had topped $34 million and the company employed 2,500 workers in nine facilities. By the end of the decade, with the firm in the hands of the third generation of the founding family, sales had reached $40 million.

In the early sixties, with sales and profits skyrocketing, Levi Strauss further diversified its clothing line and gradually expanded into Canada and Europe. During the late sixties, Levi's zipper-fly bellbottoms became the uniform of disenfranchised American youth and later of the denim-mad population around the world. In 1966 sales approached $200 million, ranking the company among the six largest apparel makers in the country. By 1971 the company was expanding so quickly that it needed outside financing; that year, the family took it public. By the following year, Levi Strauss employed 22,000 workers in fifty facilities around the world, and in 1975 sales exceeded $1 billion for the first time.

As the jeans market started to level out in the late seventies, the company sought to stimulate growth by further diversification of its clothing lines. Starting in 1979, Levi Strauss entered into a number of apparel ventures outside of basic jeans, including licensing agreements with high-fashion designers Perry Ellis, Alexander Julian, and Andrew Fezza. During the early to mid-1980s, sales went into decline. As profits slipped, Levi Strauss was forced to close down twenty-three plants and let go of 6,500 workers. In 1984 net income fell to its lowest level since 1974. In 1985, under the leadership of Robert Haas, the great-great-grandnephew of Levi Strauss, the company went private again in a $2 billion leveraged buyout —(at the time) the largest apparel industry LBO in history—by the founding family. Since then, Levi Strauss has been divesting itself of most of its subsidiary clothing lines in order to refocus on jeans and activewear. [In 1986 the company transferred its Perry Ellis agreement to Manhattan Industries, and dissolved the agreement with Andrew Fezza as well.]

An immensely successful advertising campaign for Levi's 501s ("The 501 Blues"), which was launched in 1984 and has thus far cost the company over $100 million, has significantly boosted jeans sales.

Today, the company employs approximately 32,000 people around the world and is organized into the following four operating divisions: The Jeans Company, which manufactures and markets mens' and boys' jeans and jeans-related products (such as jean jackets); Levi Strauss Sportswear, which encompasses menswear (sold under different brand names, such as Dockers, a maker of men's sport pants), Levi's Action Family (which makes suit separates and other men's leisure wear, generally in polyester, and also includes the David Hunter line, which is more stylish), women's wear (a full line of women's jeans and sportswear, including the couture sportswear line designed by Alexander Julian, the only designer with which the company is now affiliated), and the Men's Shirts Division (which makes a wide range of shirts from those meant to be worn with jeans to some with button-down collars); Levi Strauss International, which manufactures and markets jeans and jeans-related products throughout the world (manufactured in about thirty countries and sold in about seventy); and Britannia Sportswear, Ltd. (a newly acquired company which manufactures jeans and sportswear for men and women under the Britannia label). Each division introduces new products four times a year for the new selling seasons.

From its beginnings, Levi Strauss & Co. has been known for its generous and humane corporate policies. Since its earliest days, the company has always made an effort to provide good working environments and fair compensation to its workers. It kept employees working during the Depression (at a loss to the company), while also distributing stock to workers at all levels of the company, and during the fifties, long before civil rights laws were enacted, the company was among the first to integrate its plants in the South, while making a conscious effort to buy goods from minority-owned firms. In 1972 the company established Community Involvement Teams (CITs), through which employees take an active role in programs that benefit the communities in which the company maintains a presence. There are now seventy-two CITs around the world. Levi Strauss was one of the first companies to educate its employees about AIDS and to provide comprehensive medical coverage to employees stricken with the disease. Through a foundation established in 1941, the company distributes about $6 million annually to a wide range of progressive charities.

Since 1982 Levi Strauss & Company has been headquartered on an attractive campus often referred to by outsiders as "Levi Strauss University." The complex, which is situated on the waterfront near San Francisco's Telegraph Hill, is built on 8.2 meticulously landscaped acres that contain a plaza with a fountain and a grassy park. The campus is made up of three contemporary buildings—all of red brick and tiered to complement the terracing of Telegraph Hill—and two refurbished landmark buildings. The largest is only seven stories high, and each floor has a patio. Within headquarters employees are grouped by division.

(Information provided by Joyce Bustinduy, company spokesperson.)

REVENUES: $2.87 billion in 1987.

EARNINGS: The company is privately held and will not disclose. However, the company would say that 1987 was the highest year ever in earnings from operations.

WORLDWIDE FACILITIES: Seventy-seven production and distribution facilities worldwide. In the United States, forty-one production facilities—thirty-six manufacturing plants, and five distribution centers—in twelve states. Internationally, fifteen manufacturing plants and twenty-one distribution centers in twenty countries.

NUMBER OF EMPLOYEES: More than 32,000 (most of whom work in manufacturing facilities), with 7,700 working abroad and the rest in the United States.

AVERAGE AGE OF EMPLOYEES: Information not available.

TURNOVER: Information not available.

RECRUITMENT: None at present. A minority recruitment program is planned for the future.

NUMBER OF NEW HIRES PER YEAR: Information not available.

TRAINING PROGRAMS: New hires employed in production facilities undergo extensive training for their function. In the corporate office, there are a number of development programs for new employees, depending on the requirements of their specific jobs. Not all employees go through training.

RANGE OF STARTING SALARIES: Company will not disclose. "Our pay is above average relative to all other employers in the San Francisco Bay area, both in terms of salaries and benefits and in terms of capital accumulation programs such as employee savings plan, pension program, profit sharing, and 401K plan."

POLICY FOR RAISES: Levi Strauss's home office operates on a pay-for-merit system. Employees are reviewed once a year and ranked by their supervisors. Raises, which are not automatic, are based strictly on performance.

BENEFITS: Medical care (a choice of two plans), dental care, orthodontia, life insurance, travel insurance, accident insurance, tuition reimbursement (for 100 percent of costs, after one year of service and upon manager's approval for job- or career-related courses at an accredited school), pension plan, profit-sharing plan, employee savings plan, 401K plan, long- and short-term disability leaves, unemployment compensation, lifetime membership in the Employee Credit Union, homeowner's, renter's, and auto insurance programs. In addition, the company provides child-care assistance through a program called "Dependent Care." All employees in the home office are eligible, and can pay for up to $5,000 in child care with pretax dollars. Also, Levi Strauss provides videotapes and other materials that educate employees on how to find proper day care. Child care leave is available to mothers and fathers for up to five months, unpaid.

VACATION: In the home office, employees get two weeks after one year, three weeks after five years, and four weeks after fifteen years, plus eleven regular paid holidays per year.

ADDITIONAL PERKS: The home office has a fitness center available to all employees, with toning equipment, exercise rooms, showers, and classes for a nominal fee.

At least four times a year, Levi Strauss publishes a catalogue for employees, offering them company clothing discounted to roughly wholesale. The company also periodically distributes sales catalogues from which employees can purchase clothing items at less than wholesale prices. Employees can wear jeans to work (see below).

BONUSES: Senior-level managers are eligible for bonuses, which are awarded on performance, based on how well their divisions do. The company also has a number of recognition award programs—all of them cash awards—for employees at all levels except senior management. In addition to particular awards programs in each division, all employees are eligible for the

Koshland Award "for achievements that reflect the commitment to excellence and the human-itarian values for which Daniel E. Koshland {an early Levi Strauss CEO and a member of the founding family] will always be remembered."

AVERAGE WORKDAY: 8:00 A.M. to 4:45 or 5:00 P.M. In a crunch, they'll work longer hours or on weekends. "It's not extremely prevalent to work on weekends, though some people do." There is some job sharing.

ANNUAL PARTIES: The only major party is an annual Christmas party, which has been held since 1983. The party is hosted on a weekend day for employees and their families and includes clowns, jugglers, face painters, and other activities for kids (such as toy making). Other parties include "seasonal cookies-and-punch type of things" held on holidays like Halloween and St. Patrick's Day. All of the above are given by the home office. Divisions outside of the home office host their own parties.

DRESS CODE: Very informal. "We don't think that dress has anything to do with work productivity." The company used to have a rule that Levi's could be worn every Friday, but in December 1986 it was announced that that would be expanded to every day. If employees are meeting with people outside the company whom they know would be uncomfortable meeting them in their jeans, they'll dress up. If not, they wear anything they want. Even top manage-ment wears Levi's. "Bob Haas [the company's CEO] wears his with snappy red suspenders."

SOCIAL ATMOSPHERE: "People get along." The company has a softball team, intramural sports, CITs, and other company programs that engender a team spirit among employees. "We tend to be a friendly group of people willing to help each other out."

CHARITABLE CONTRIBUTIONS: The Levi Strauss Foundation (which was established in 1941 as the Yerba Buena Foundation and reincorporated as the Levi Strauss Foundation in 1952) distributed about $6 million in cash contributions in 1987. The foundation's two major funding programs are the Special Emphasis grants program and the Community Involvement Team grants program. Through the Special Emphasis program, grants are awarded to organi-zations that "enhance the economic options of economically disadvantaged population groups, including the working poor, and others at risk of slipping into poverty," in particular, programs that address the economic barriers faced by women, minorities, and teens. Grants made through Community Involvement Teams—employee volunteer groups that "review local community needs, then develop and implement projects to meet those needs"—range from $1,000 to $15,000 and go to a broad range of local civic, cultural, social, health, and educational activities. There are seventy-two CITs located around the world in almost every community in which the company maintains a facility. Levi Strauss has been very generous in AIDS-related philanthropy. [See below.]

HEADQUARTERS: Three buildings situated around a plaza in north waterfront area of San Francisco, across the street from the Bay. Of the 763,000 square feet of available office space, Levi Strauss occupies about half.

ART COLLECTION: Comprising more than three hundred pieces, all by contemporary American artists, including Robert Rauschenberg, Josef Albers, Sol Lewitt, Joel Shapiro, and Donald Judd.

OTHER: Walter Haas, Levi Strauss & Co.'s honorary chairman of the board, is the owner of the Oakland A's baseball team.

MOST COMMON SIZE OF LEVI'S 501 SHRINK-TO-FITS: From 30 to 36 inches for both waist and inseam.

BEST-SELLING NONBLUE JEANS ITEM: Jean jackets.

LEVI'S HOTLINE: (800) 227-5600 (a toll-free number people can call to find where a particular Levi's product is sold in their hometown).

INTERESTED APPLICANTS CAN SEND RÉSUMÉS TO:
Levi Strauss & Co.
Employment Department
P.O. Box 7215
San Francisco, CA 94120
(415) 544-6000

LEVI STRAUSS AND AIDS

Levi Strauss & Co. is considered a leader among companies dealing actively with the problem of AIDS, specifically with AIDS in the workplace. Between 1981 and 1987, the company and foundation donations to AIDS organizations totaled $386,000. Aside from grants made to already existing programs, such as The San Francisco AIDS Foundation, the Shanti Project, The Home Care Hospice, and matching gifts from employees, Levi Strauss is also considered a pioneer in creating its own AIDS service and information programs. Employees afflicted with the disease are urged to stay at work as long as they can, with flexible work schedules or part-time jobs made available where possible. They are provided with complete medical coverage, which includes offering home health care and hospice care for the terminally ill, as well as regular hospital coverage. And although the company encourages openness, employee confidentiality is very protected. Through a venue called "Speakeasy," employees can ask questions about AIDS (and other personal questions) anonymously. Levi Strauss also provides extensive employee education programs to combat fears and prejudices.

Part of the pleasure of working for Levi Strauss & Company is that its name and products are so well known and well liked. Other bonuses lie in the company's terrific headquarters, nicknamed "Levi Strauss University," overlooking the bay of San Francisco, and the management's famed humanism. Working here allows one to pursue two goals: working for a serious corporation and having a cool job. The fact that the company's signature product is blue jeans does not mean there's a casual approach to business. Founded in 1873, the company has moved from a private, family-owned organization to a publicly held corporation with shares traded on the New York Stock Exchange (1971) to a private company, by means of a leveraged buyout in 1985 by the Haas family, descendants of Mr. Levi Strauss himself.

A day at Levi Strauss's campus is a day spent with people who like what they do but take special pride in the legacy and leadership of their company. They may not realize it, but life at Levi's seems more relaxed than the life at other companies the same size. [Author's note: At the time of my visit, every Friday was "Levi's Apparel Day" and employees were encouraged to wear jeans to work, unless they had an outside meeting where jeans would have been inappropriate. Since then, *every* day is Levi's Apparel Day, with the same reservation. Imagine —being encouraged to wear jeans to the office!]

Unlike a fashion trend marketer, people at Levi Strauss look like people for whom comfort transcends style; these are not people balanced on the edge of the avant-garde. You don't see too many dramatic outfits or makeup around here. Levi Strauss does not talk about its contribution to the fashion business as much as providing a product which lends itself to many ways of life. You don't even hear people talking about *lifestyles* here, so basic a fact of life are jeans.

The offices are decorated with an extensive collection of contemporary American art which, if nothing else, creates a distraction from weightier issues.

In terms of numbers of applicants alone, Levi Strauss is a very desirable place at which to work. Jesse Warr is one of four personnel recruiters. Fifty to 60 percent of his constituency is made up of insiders looking toward lateral or upward moves, and the rest are outsiders. "In a fast-moving year, I must place a hundred twenty people," he says. "In slow years, we have sophisticated out-placement to help layoffs get new jobs." The former teacher sees mostly humanities and arts backgrounds among the work force. "We're known for promotion from within. In so many jobs a degree is *not* the credential." Jesse and his colleagues consider much of what they're looking for to be "intangible. People need flair and creativity. It can't be taught, and it can't be measured."

New job openings (with the exception of senior executive and part-time secretarial positions) are published in house every Wednesday. They are distributed nationally "to give Levi's people the jump on competition." Some promotions happen without job posting. And almost all secretaries are hired from the outside. ("A lot of them move to lower and mid-management.") Compensation is determined on a grade level.

Warr's advice for anyone at Levi Strauss who thinks he or she is at a professional dead end: "One, go to night school and get tuition reimbursement. It's always an option. Two, cross-train. Contact other people here whose skills you'd like to have. Shadow them. Three, move to another job via the JOL—job openings list. It's very competitive. Moving within the company is as hard as getting into the company." In his opinion, Levi Strauss's good reputation as an employer (he mentions that both *Savvy* and *Mother Jones* magazines have named the company among the ten best places for women to work) is predicated on the well-known practice of corporate philanthropy.

The Haas family is "a politically liberal family who did civic uplift before the term 'corporate philanthropy' was coined." The Levi Strauss Foundation not only donates money generously to a group of beneficiaries, it "teaches people to be involved in their own community." Community Involvement Teams are Levi Strauss-sponsored extracurricular activities that focus on help for the aging, families, community development, naturalization of Hispanics, and equity programs for women. The Foundation usually kicks off a CIT with a grant ranging from $1,000–$15,000. There are seventy-two of them in operation around the world.

Furthermore, Levi Strauss & Co. has been a model for corporations in dealing with AIDS.

The company's policy, echoing that of the city of San Francisco, is "no discrimination against anyone afflicted with the disease."

Kathy Hester became the executive aide to Robert Haas, Levi Strauss & Co.'s president and CEO, in August 1981. She started at the company earlier that year as a temp in the legal department. [She's still at Levi Strauss, but working in Personnel.] As Haas's assistant, she says her job required "attention to detail, tact, discretion, and quick decision making when he was gone; knowing his style and putting myself in his place," which she had literally just done. This interview was conducted in his office, since he was out of town. Haas has three signed Ansel Adams photographs on his walls and two large terraces outside two corners of his comfortable, neutral-colored office. Every Monday Kathy and Bob Haas would discuss the forthcoming week. "A lot he doesn't want to hear, but needs to hear. He never asks where the information comes from. But there's not too much he doesn't know." Hester said, unbeknownst to most employees, "I think most decisions that affect the daily operations of the company come from the middle. Yet we were the bad guy."

She's referring to the Haas decision to take the company private, not perceived as popular by many at the time (1985), since employees held 9 percent of the outstanding shares of Levi Strauss & Co. stock. "There was a lot of concern," she said five months after the transaction was consummated. "People wanted to know, 'Will my job be eliminated?' He communicated with employees all the way. He held our hands. Overall, employees didn't panic and were happy."

At age thirty-eight, Kathy has been strongly influenced by Bob Haas and his style of management. "All Haases answer their own phones," she says admiringly. "It blows people away. They believe in treating employees with respect and dignity. I [used to] block off a few days before the holidays so he could go from building to building [to greet employees with seasonal greetings]." She's learned about MBWA—Managing By Wandering Around—in her years with the president and CEO. "Sometimes when he didn't have an appointment, he'd say, 'I'm going to roam.' He did it more and more. He didn't plan where he'd go."

"My job changed . . . as Bob's jobs changed. His style has changed. I liked working for him—even if he wasn't president. I was always challenged." She seemed right at home in this executive splendor. "When we started here, it was *so* beautiful, big, and spacious. Now it's just an office. You don't think about it. It's the environment you need to get the job done." Her days began at 8:00 A.M. and ran till 4:45 or 5:00 P.M. "I've never been expected to stay later."

Hester considers Levi Strauss's Fitness Center to be the greatest of all perks. She uses it two to three times per week. "Bob uses it, too."

"I heard stories," Donna Tewert recalls, "when Levi Strauss was [first] private, that Walter [Jr.] and Peter [Haas—the chairman of the board and honorary chairman of the board, respectively] knew everyone by name. But the company was much smaller." Even if only as anecdotes, these are the stuff of employee loyalty. Donna is the human resources manager. "They're real," Donna says of the Haases and the allegiance they stimulate. When she talks about Levi Strauss's values, she refers to the way people are treated. "We encourage managers to meet with employees on an ongoing basis. At least once a year there's a documented session that coincides with salary consideration. Most managers need some training in dealing with people—how to be supportive in praise and criticism." [Author's note: This is an area in which most corporations feel inadequate.] "Employees need help in how to receive their appraisals and how to respond to them.

"Little perks you might not get elsewhere" is how she describes the fitness center, child care leave (not just for mothers, and even for adoptive parents), job sharing, and the employee purchase plan, which allows employees to buy the company's merchandise at a significant discount. "If 501s [Levi's oldest and most popular jeans, shrink to fit, with button flies] sell in the high twenties, they're fifteen dollars. There are also sample sales."

"A pair of jeans will last a thirty-five-year-old a hell of a lot longer than it would a teenager." John Wyeck is the company's director of strategic research, and his mission is to understand Levi Strauss's consumers and plan for trends of the future. "What will life be in the 1990s? Will people wear jeans? There will be ten million fewer teenagers by the end of the generation." Wyeck explains that strategic research is market research *times* tactical thinking. It sounds more social science–based than merely relying on numbers. What makes John's job tough is that the organization's business is so strongly affected by factors beyond its control. Needless to say, *Rebel Without a Cause* and other movies depicting the alienated youth of the fifties affected dungaree sales to an unprecedented extent. When *Urban Cowboy* was released in 1977, it was held responsible for popularizing the Western look and creating the attendant demand for bootleg jeans.

"Basic jeans are like bags of sugar or rice. Consumers are not measuring stitches by the inch or seams." In truth, a basic pair of jeans, say, the 501s, are really a commodity. Although Levi Strauss manufactures a wide range of apparel from casual leisure wear—some in polyester —to women's couture sportswear, Colours for Women by Alexander Julian (through a licensing agreement with Alexander Julian), "the massive volume of the basic jeans business is what pays our lighting bills." Think about it: the 501 has been the best-selling garment in this country for 150 years.

Nancy McCready was the director of consumer marketing. She said there's a nine-month lead required in advance of the introduction of a new style, which makes being a fashion company a bit tricky. (And since Levi Strauss doesn't invent new trends but rather responds to them, it must be cautious.) Her efforts were concentrated in women's jeans, and she had proofs of Ladies' 501 advertisements in her office. On her wall was a framed still from her best-known commercial, a takeoff on the 1956 film *Giant*, showing a woman in a cowboy hat in jeans slung in the back seat of a convertible. Unlike that particular commercial, known as "Travis"—the most memorable word of dialogue in it—"most of the advertising now is urban. The new test spots have an L.A. look and are very feminine." High heels are in evidence. "We get lots of mail, like our ads are Rorschach tests—everyone sees something else in them." For the time being, all Levi's advertising is handled by the San Francisco office of Foote, Cone & Belding, which has had the account—with one small exception about seven years ago—since 1927.

You may be interested to know that despite Levi Strauss's artless dependability, they are very much aware of Guess!, Girbaud, and other trend-setting denim manufacturers. "They've obviously met a need," Nancy said. "We're mainstream America." Which isn't to say when stirrup pants were hot (for almost a year) that Levi Strauss didn't manufacture them. They did. "In women's fashion you *have* to stay in style. We're too big to stay on the leading edge of fashion." Predicting what'll be new in Milan is one thing (and Levi Strauss does need to keep abreast of high fashion), but this is a company that also makes clothes for the older, untrendy consumer. Their Bendover line is 100 percent polyester and very popular, especially in the Midwest. Without emphasizing the Bendover line in the media—only "two promotions in one and a half years"—it's grown by over 50 percent.

McCready found her job through a classified ad in 1982. She liked "working with products I feel good about." She said the typical executive here works about fifty hours a week. Nancy tried to confine her work to the weekdays, "keeping weekends for myself."

Janet Liszewski calls her fit at Levi Strauss "a perfect match. One of my best friends worked here," recalls the Boston native, a self-proclaimed "flower child" who moved to the Bay area in 1968. "I met other people through her, and I liked them and what they said about the company."

She joined the company in 1972. Her first job was as the secretary to the national sales manager of the Panatella Division, "one of the first non-jeans ventures," in what is known today as the menswear division. "It was really a challenge. The division got cut up, put back . . . so I never got bored or tired. I never felt threatened. Eight years went by without my realizing it or wanting a new job." Somehow, though, Janet had become the national sales administrator.

"After eight years in menswear, people teased me: 'Aren't you going to try for another job?' " At the 1980 shareholders meeting, Liszewski had an epiphany. Upon hearing the five-year plan for women's wear, she knew that's where she wanted to go next. She used to say to her friends, "I'm tired of being in men's pants." Using the job-posting mechanism, she applied for a management position in women's wear, in charge of selling remaindered products. "A 'bene'[fit} was, I could identify with the business." She worked closely with stores in marketing, "and then I thought about production, to learn about merchandising."

Janet moved to the plants, spending most of her time in the Southeast and Texas. "I missed the aggressiveness and flash of sales and marketing." Now she's back in San Francisco as the company's manager of sales administration. "I'm happy to be back here. I'm replacing someone who did the same job for sixteen years. I hope I can do the same."

Her enthusiasm is infectious. Janet says the biggest change to affect the employees was not the leveraged buyout, but the company's move from its former quarters on Battery Street, a thirty-four-story skyscraper, to the campus in the Telegraph Hill section of town, just eight years after commissioning the skyscraper in 1974. By all accounts the Battery Street facility was too big, too corporate, too impersonal—not at all the real Levi Strauss. "Everyone's much happier here." The only issue that concerns Janet and her friends in the LBO was "now we don't have a stock purchase plan. But they'll match you fifty cents on the dollar if you invest in Levi's investment portfolio. Overall, everyone seems positive. There's a lot to be gained. The Haases seem more positive about being taken out of the headlines, out of the microscope."

Over the ultimate grazer's lunch at the popular Fog City Diner nearby, Assistant General Counsel Seth Jaffe and Public Affairs Director Nancy Peterson talk about the essential values of Levi Strauss. "The bottom line is, we make a quality product, a 'user-friendly' product (we used the phrase before it became popular). We're a nonpolluting company. Our personal standards are high—we are socially responsible. In this community, when you say you work at Levi's, people's mouths drop. Being a 'good company' and the substance behind it—what management stands for—is what brings you to work."

And the fun. The company stages musical reviews in the plaza in the center of "LSU." Senior managers have performed in *Levi Mania,* and *Alice in Levi Land.* "Bob Haas has sung in front of all the employees."

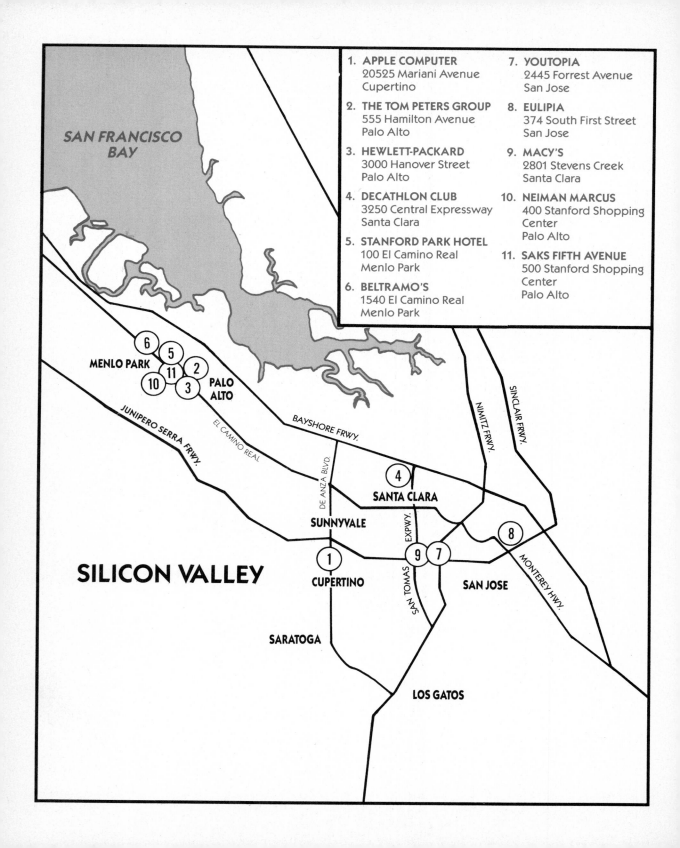

1. **APPLE COMPUTER**
   20525 Mariani Avenue
   Cupertino

2. **THE TOM PETERS GROUP**
   555 Hamilton Avenue
   Palo Alto

3. **HEWLETT-PACKARD**
   3000 Hanover Street
   Palo Alto

4. **DECATHLON CLUB**
   3250 Central Expressway
   Santa Clara

5. **STANFORD PARK HOTEL**
   100 El Camino Real
   Menlo Park

6. **BELTRAMO'S**
   1540 El Camino Real
   Menlo Park

7. **YOUTOPIA**
   2445 Forrest Avenue
   San Jose

8. **EULIPIA**
   374 South First Street
   San Jose

9. **MACY'S**
   2801 Stevens Creek
   Santa Clara

10. **NEIMAN MARCUS**
    400 Stanford Shopping
    Center
    Palo Alto

11. **SAKS FIFTH AVENUE**
    500 Stanford Shopping
    Center
    Palo Alto

SAN FRANCISCO BAY

MENLO PARK

PALO ALTO

JUNIPERO SERRA FRWY.

EL CAMINO REAL

BAYSHORE FRWY.

NIMITZ FRWY.

SINCLAIR FRWY.

DE ANZA BLVD.

SANTA CLARA

SUNNYVALE

SILICON VALLEY

CUPERTINO

SAN TOMAS EXPWY.

SAN JOSE

MONTEREY HWY.

SARATOGA

LOS GATOS

SILICON VALLEY

SILICON VALLEY

The Silicon Valley is considered a separate city for the purposes of *Going to Work* for several reasons: While it's a confederation of communities with a population of about 1.4 million, it has a culture so distinct from that of San Francisco it would be inappropriate to lump them together; that culture is a deliberate one and hence valid; and, finally, eleven cities didn't have the curved, balanced, and symmetrical ring of twelve.

I remember when I first heard the expression "Silicon Valley" in the early seventies, I pictured little transistor chips growing in dusty, sunburnt fields. To my great surprise, the Silicon Valley is as green as any area filled with corporate parks and, due to the humanist efforts of many of its denizens, probably greener and healthier.

Certainly there is a higher premium placed on ecology, "wellness," and the self here than in most other places of work. The region is home to many mavericks gone straight. The *folks* (a Silicon Valley locution) still find jeans and Birkenstocks perfectly suitable for all occasions. They are perhaps passively pursuing their riches, aggressively pursuing their riches, or passively aggressively pursuing a financially secure future. (The BMW, a symbol of upward mobility, is one of the most popular and visible automobiles on the highway.)

The fallout from the information revolution of the mid-eighties put some high technocrats through the wringer. Japan and IBM threw wrenches into their big plans. Changes in lifestyle have happened with unprecedented velocity.

As the high-technology fields come of age, the concerns of its progenitors have changed. Now they are learning there's more to life than work and are seeing that their colleagues with families have endured volatile times with the smallest amount of psychic damage. To the strains of New Age music emerges the chorus: Children! The next frontier!

The Silicon Valley is more or less a brainchild of Stanford University. So Palo Alto is more or less the unofficial capital of the valley. (San Jose is the official center. It's the biggest city, with a population of roughly 719,000, and the locus of the area's airport.) Both William Hewlett and David Packard graduated from that fine school, and the corporation they founded is still the benchmark to which other high-technology companies are compared. With its Hoover Institute (a feeder to the Reagan White House), Stanford is not alone in its Republican sympathies. A growing number of the newly minted bedungareed capitalists are voting their enriched pocketbooks/knapsacks.

Sometimes the correctness of the populace is startlingly humorless. Just try smoking a cigarette around here, and you'll see the tolerance of the wellness tribe. (Of course, they're right; you knew that before the speech.)

Valspeak here bears no relation to the surftalk of the other well-known California valley to the south. It's filled with bits, bytes, and nanoseconds and increasingly reveals a fascination with artificial intelligence (AI).

The wily Monterey Jack cheese finds its way as a topper on all styles of cuisine here. It is not a joke when a waitperson inquires whether you'd like sprouts on your plate.

The following list represents the services and resources used by those people on the way up the corporate ladder, by their nonworking spouses, and by those who've already made it. The information has been gathered from sources close to the author, all of whom are valued for their good taste. The word "yuppie" will not appear elsewhere in this book, and this list does not just represent that small (though acquisitive) segment of the population. Wherever possible, we have tried to narrow down specific members of the customer base, i.e., "Nicest Neighborhoods (But You'll Probably Have to Send Your Kids to Private School)" or, "Best Health Club for Meeting Potential Mates." Sometimes the category will simply be headed with the word "best." This means a group of discerning individuals has been unanimous in its praise. These lists are an attempt to reflect the way people live in a particular city, although the categories were ours, not theirs.

BEST NEIGHBORHOODS WITH DECENT PUBLIC SCHOOLS: Willow Glen (San Jose), anywhere in Los Gatos or Saratoga

NICEST NEIGHBORHOODS (BUT YOU'LL PROBABLY HAVE TO SEND YOUR KIDS TO PRIVATE SCHOOL): Rosegarden (San Jose)

BEST PLACES TO LIVE IF YOU'RE AN ASPIRING ARTIST OR YOU WANT TO LIVE NEAR PEOPLE WHO ONLY WEAR BLACK: Between South First Street and South Eighth Street in downtown San Jose

BEST NEIGHBORHOOD WITH TAKEOUT FOOD AND SINGLE PEOPLE WHO ARE ALSO REPUBLICANS: Sunnyvale

MOST OVERPRICED COMMUNITY FOR SUMMER HOMES: Aptos

BEST PRIVATE SCHOOLS: Bellarmine College Preparatory (all-boys high school in San Jose), Castelleja High School (all girls, junior high through high school)

DEALER OF THE FINEST, MOST VALUABLE ART: J. J. Brookings & Co. (San Jose)

TRENDY GALLERY FOR PEOPLE WHO WEAR ALL BLACK AND HAVE A LOT OF MONEY: Allegra Gallery

MOST EXCLUSIVE GOLF CLUBS: Almaden Golf & Country Club, Saratoga Country Club

BEST PUBLIC GOLF FACILITIES: Fairway Glen Golf Course, Shoreline Golf Course

MOST EXPENSIVE HEALTH CLUB: The Decathlon Club

BEST HEALTH CLUB FOR MEETING POTENTIAL MATES: The Decathlon Club

BEST HOTELS FOR BUSINESS TRIPS: Doubletree Hotel (Santa Clara), Stanford Park Hotel (Menlo Park)

BEST HOTEL FOR TRYSTS: Madison Street Inn (Santa Clara)

RESTAURANTS KNOWN FOR BEST CUISINE: Emile's (San Jose), Paolo's (San Jose)

BEST RESTAURANT FOR PEOPLE WHO WEAR BLACK: Eulipia (San Jose)

BEST RESTAURANTS FOR AN INEXPENSIVE DATE: Hong Sing Tea House (San Jose), El Matador (Santa Clara), Fionillo's Pizza (Los Gatos)

NOISIEST RESTAURANTS: El Dorado Café (Palo Alto), any Chili's Restaurant

BEST DARK BAR: J. J.'s Lounge (San Jose)

BEST GIMMICKY BAR: Baritz (Cupertino)

BEST BAR TO IMPRESS A CLIENT: Upstairs at Eulipia (San Jose)

FANCIEST WINE STORES WHENCE CEOS PROBABLY STOCK THEIR OWN CELLARS: Beltramo's (Menlo Park), Ernie's (Los Gatos)

GOURMET STORE GUARANTEED NOT TO RUN OUT OF GOAT CHEESE OR SUN-DRIED TOMATOES: Cosentino's (San Jose)

NICEST MOM-AND-POP GROCERY STORE: ("Really none. Everything is chains and big.")

LARGEST DRUGSTORE WITH MOST REMARKABLE SELECTION: Long's

CORPORATE PARTY PLANNER: Amazing Events Unlimited (Palo Alto)

HIGH SOCIETY PARTY PLANNER: "There is no 'high society' in Silicon Valley."

POWER BARBER: Joseph's Hairstyling at the Red Lion Inn (San Jose)

NEW-WAVE HAIR STYLIST: Yosh (Palo Alto, San Jose)

JR. LEAGUE BEAUTY PARLOR: Youtopia (San Jose)

PLACE WHERE LADIES WHO LUNCH ARE LIKELY TO HAVE TEA AFTER A HARD DAY OF SHOPPING, VOLUNTEER WORK, AND TENNIS: Victoria Emmons (Menlo Park)

BEST STORES FOR EXECUTIVE WOMEN: Easton & Rowe, Alcott & Andrews

BEST STORES FOR EXECUTIVE MEN: Eli Thomas, The Boardroom

BEST STORES FOR DRESS-UP CLOTHES: Trudy's, Saks Fifth Avenue (Palo Alto), Neiman-Marcus

BEST SHOPPING RESOURCE FOR PEOPLE WHO ONLY WEAR BLACK CLOTHES: Galleria

BEST PLACE TO BUY BIRKENSTOCKS: Footloose Birkenstock Store (San Mateo)

BUSIEST SOCIAL SEASON OF THE YEAR FOR THOSE WHO CARE ABOUT SUCH THINGS: Spring

PARTICULAR SOCIAL HIGHLIGHT: Silicon Valley Charity Ball, Santa Clara University Golden Circle Theatre Party

MOST RELIABLE FLORIST: Citti's

MOST EXOTIC FLORIST: Marlowe's Flowers & Gifts

BEST SEAMSTRESS OR TAILOR FOR ALTERATIONS: Hector's (San Jose)

BEST SEAMSTRESS OR TAILOR FOR CUSTOM TAILORING: Hector's (San Jose)

POPULAR FACIAL SALONS: Renata's (Palo Alto), From Head to Toe (Saratoga)

POWER TOOLS

WINE MERCHANT

BELTRAMO'S
1540 El Camino Real
Menlo Park, CA 94025
(415) 325-2806

Beltramo's was founded in 1882 by the family bearing its name. It has operated continuously in this location since the repeal of Prohibition in 1935. (A second location, at 325 Sharon Park Drive, Menlo Park, is newer.)

Although Beltramo's sells hard liquors and spirits, Greg St. Clair estimates that 70 percent of the store's business is in wines. "There are three coefficients of wine buyers: income, education, and travel. Our clientele represents all three. Those who travel are more willing to try new wines." Beltramo's sells more California wines than imported ones and "a lot more white than red."

"The corporate folks don't have as much time and haven't read as much as the ultimate buffs," who may come to browse here "as readers might in a bookstore," and may not be afraid to spend real money on wines. Beltramo's regulars are so well versed in oenology that a good 40 percent are self-reliant when it comes to choosing their own vintages. For the other 60 percent (which includes a big tourist trade), "we have six people here with multiple years in the wine industry. Among them every wine will be covered."

To maintain an educated constituency, Beltramo's offers a weekly tasting bar, from 3:30 P.M. to 7:30 P.M. Fridays and Saturdays. Tasters, who pay 10 percent of the bottle cost per glass (i.e., a bottle that costs $12.50 will cost $1.25 per glass), number in the low hundreds every weekend. "We have a devoted clientele in the tasting room," St. Clair says, "though not necessarily for buying." Seminars and a newsletter round out the educational services.

Beltramo's is preparing for the future. With a nod toward the increased traffic and congestion of the Silicon Valley, St. Clair believes more customers will order by phone in the future. "You wouldn't want to drive all day to buy your wine for dinner . . . "

POWER DRIVE

STANFORD BMW
3045 Park Boulevard
Palo Alto, CA 94306
(415) 324-4488

Yes, the Bavarian driving machine appears to be the overwhelming choice of the new rich in the Silicon Valley. "Executives buy BMW because of its great luxury and sports performance," sales manager Peter Sovczynski says. "Dealers take care of buyers with convenience and service."

What makes the BMW so special? "The cars are the ultimate in computer technology. They speak to you. If the car needs to be serviced the problem appears on the dashboard. If more than one thing is wrong, the computer analyzes the gravity of the problems and lists them in order of importance. The computer has thirty-five different features. It even has a memory bank for mirror positions as you change seat positions."

Let's get down to business. The 735-600 series is the most popular here. At $55,000, the 735 four-door is the ultimate automobile, while the two-door (635 series) comes in at $50,000. Young executives buy the 535i. "It's sportier." In 1988 approximately 55 percent of Stanford BMW's clients ordered car phones.

The newest, most fashionable, up-and-coming model: the 750il. Its features include a V-12 engine, 300 horsepower, four doors, a roomy back seat, twenty cubic feet of trunk space, a large-capacity gas tank (24½ gallons), and a built-in phone. The tab: $70,000.

APPLE COMPUTER, INC.

HISTORY & OPERATIONS

Apple Computer, Inc., which is credited with ushering in the era of personal computers, was founded in 1976 by two college dropout whiz kids. Steve Wozniak and Steve Jobs, friends since high school, used to tinker with electronics in the garage of Jobs's parents' home in Los Altos, California. (Among their early joint ventures was the manufacturing and selling of "blue boxes," which were used to break into long distance telephone lines and make free calls to anywhere in the world. Naturally, they were illegal.) Wozniak, a stellar engineer, dropped out of Berkeley after his junior year and went to work for Hewlett-Packard. Jobs left Reed College after his freshman year, worked briefly for Atari, toured India for a while in search of enlightenment, and then returned to Atari. The friends continued to tinker in the garage at night. It was mostly Wozniak who in 1975 designed and built the original Apple I computer circuit board—which had no keyboard, case, or graphics—strictly for his own use, from parts that he and Jobs took from their workplaces. But it was Jobs—who has been referred to as "the Henry Ford of the computer age"—who foresaw the commercial potential in their creation.

Wozniak and Jobs formed the Apple Computer Company on April Fool's Day in 1976. Jobs had chosen the name for the new company as a symbol of purity and simplicity. Wozniak was twenty-six at the time, and Jobs was twenty-one. At Jobs's urging, he and Wozniak offered low-cost Apple I kits to their acquaintances in the Homebrew Computer Club, based in Palo Alto. In order to raise enough money ($1,350) to fill the subsequent requests, Jobs sold his Volkswagen and Wozniak sold his Hewlett-Packard calculator. Jobs then secured an order from The Byte Shop, a local computer store, for fifty Apple I boards. He managed to buy parts on credit to fill the order, and he and Wozniak built the machines in his parents' garage. In July, the Apple I board was released for sale at the price of $666.66.

Wozniak made improvements on the Apple I, which ultimately resulted in the Apple II— the first personal computer that could generate color graphics—which came with a keyboard, a power supply, and a case. Jobs made deals with suppliers, manufacturers, dealers, and top public relations and advertising people, and eventually with venture capitalists who advanced the money to start a business. Chief among the company's early financial backers was A. C. "Mike" Markkula, Jr., then thirty-eight, a veteran of Fairchild Semiconductor and Intel, who was then a retired millionaire. Markkula, who saw the computer's promise, put up his own money and raised other money, coming out of retirement to work full time for Apple. In January 1977, Apple Computer, Inc., was incorporated with Markkula as its chairman, and the company moved from the garage to a building in Cupertino.

Apple grew remarkably in its first few years of operation, and sales of the Apple II, which became available in June 1977, virtually spawned the brand-new field of personal computers. (Though there were other companies manufacturing personal computers at the time, none had anywhere near the impact of Apple.) In its first full year, revenues totaled $800,000. By 1978 annual sales jumped to $17.5 million, and Apple increased its payroll to 150 employees. In 1979, sales mushroomed again to $75 million, and the number of employees grew to four hundred.

In December 1980, Apple went public. Every share was bought within minutes of the offering, making it the largest public offering since Ford [see p. 257] went public in 1956. Jobs, Wozniak, and Markkula, in addition to many of the other original investors and employees—the two Steves were generous with equity—became multimillionaires overnight. Inspired by the success of the Apple II in the home, educational, and small to medium-sized business markets, Apple designed the Apple III, a more powerful machine, in order to penetrate the bigger business market. Launched in 1980, the Apple III was an immediate disaster. Fourteen thousand defective machines had to be recalled, and the computer never gained momentum. Then IBM entered the personal computer market with its first PC, which outsold the Apple III almost immediately. Despite an estimated $100 million spent on the project, the failure of Apple III did not seriously damage Apple's prospects. Apple IIs were still the best-known personal computers in the world, and Apple's annual revenues continued to increase ($139 million in 1980 to $583 million in 1982).

In 1983 Jobs persuaded John Sculley, then president of Pepsi-Cola USA, to become president of Apple. (Sculley allegedly received a $1 million sign-up bonus, a $1 million annual salary, $1 million in guaranteed severance pay should things not work out, options on 350,000 shares of Apple stock, and help in buying a $2 million house.) Sculley managed to streamline the company's unwieldy structure by consolidating its nine operating divisions into just three. That year, Apple launched two new products: the Apple IIe, an improved version of its popular predecessor which gained immediate market acceptance, and the Lisa, a three-year, $50 million project that introduced the "mouse"—a handheld device which, used to point at "icons" or symbols on the screen, truly made the computer user-friendly. Yet the Lisa was a flop. While it won critical acclaim for its advanced technology and ease of use, Lisa's high price tag ($10,000) was prohibitive. Business still preferred IBM PCs, and none of the Apples were IBM-compatible, so the Lisa faded into obsolescence. Nonetheless, Apple's 1983 revenues reached $983 million.

In January 1984 Apple introduced the Macintosh (amid unprecedented fanfare), which, though less expensive than the Lisa, had many of the same advanced capabilities. It had the mouse. Though it took some time for the new computer to catch on, and though it didn't make the inroads into the business market Apple had hoped it would, the Macintosh managed to survive the competitive marketplace. The Apple II line earned a record performance in 1984 (the IIc, a portable version of the IIe, had been introduced), and Apple's revenues jumped to $1.5 billion, although earnings that year slipped below the previous year's earnings.

Despite predictions to the contrary, the personal computer revolution did not affect every household in America, and in 1985 Apple's sales began to decline, largely due to the general slump that was affecting sales throughout the industry. That year, both of the original founders left the company due to increasingly stressful internal politics.

Jobs, who had been in charge of the Macintosh group—which had been secluded in its own building and enjoyed special privileges not awarded to the rest of Apple's employees— engendered a rivalry between it and the Apple II group. Wozniak, who was one of the main engineers in the Apple II group, left in February, disgruntled. Then Sculley, who was under pressure from Apple's board of directors, restructured the company to leave no operating position for Jobs, who had been chairman of the board since 1981. After several months with nothing to do and a failed attempt to wrest power from Sculley, Jobs resigned his post in September, taking five key Apple employees with him to start a new computer company called neXt. Apple subsequently filed a suit against Jobs, charging him with misappropriating Apple secrets and breaching his fiduciary responsibility while still acting as chairman of the board. The suit was later settled out of court, and Jobs was barred from marketing his new computer until late 1987.

In order to pare operating costs, Sculley laid off one fifth of Apple's six thousand employees and closed down three of six factories. (The total costs of reorganizing the company were almost $40 million.) Then Apple focused its efforts on introducing new additions to its existing product lines. The Macintosh Plus, a faster and more powerful version of the Macintosh, was launched in 1986. That year, the Macintosh took over the Apple II line as the company's biggest seller. Later that year, Apple introduced the IIgs, a computer that combined some of the best features of both the model II series and the Macintosh. In 1987 Apple introduced the Macintosh SE and the Macintosh II, Apple's most advanced computer yet. All of its new computers, which are "open" in design—as opposed to the original Macintosh, which Jobs deliberately designed to discourage add-ons—have the capacity for increased power and IBM compatibility, and the two new Macintoshes were specifically designed to compete with IBMs in the business market.

The corporation, which was in rocky financial shape in 1985—though '85 revenues increased to $1.9 billion, Apple reported its first quarterly loss in its history—has managed to revive. (Apple, which has never been in debt and has substantial cash reserves, has never been so seriously periled that folding was a consideration.) In the first quarter of 1986, Apple's earnings were the highest in its history, and annual revenues that year reached $1.902 billion. In 1987, net sales were $2.66 billion. Today, Apple employs approximately 7,000 people, more than a quarter of whom work overseas. Foreign sales account for one third of revenues, and Apple products are now sold in eighty countries worldwide. Its primary foreign markets are Canada, Australia, and France.

One of the keys to Apple's continued success has been the wide variety of software packages available for its computers, the vast majority of which were designed by outside companies.

In 1986 sales of software for Apple computers accounted for 25 percent of all software sales worldwide. In 1987 the company announced the formation of a new software venture, called Claris, which it eventually plans to spin off into a freestanding company. Claris, which is headed by Apple's former executive vice-president of sales and marketing, produces and markets software that Apple already makes for its own machines, acquires products from outside developers, and develops new programs on its own. None of the products uses the Apple name.

From its inception, Jobs and Wozniak modeled many of Apple's philosophies after those of Hewlett-Packard (see p. 657), long known for its humanistic values and for fostering an environment conducive to creativity. Apple has clearly articulated business ethics, and its charitable activities and generous employee benefits are among its most notable achievements. In 1983 Apple launched a program called "Kids Can't Wait" through which it donated a complete Apple IIes personal computer system to each of nearly 10,000 schools throughout California. In 1987, the company donated more than $4 million in equipment and cash to a range of social service and arts groups, primarily to nonprofit organizations "which will do creative things with technology."

(Information provided by Carleen Levasseur and Kate Paisley, company spokespersons.)

1987 FORTUNE 500 RANKING: 152.

REVENUES: $2.66 billion in 1987.

EARNINGS: $217 million in net income in 1987.

INITIAL PUBLIC OFFERING: December 12, 1980.

NUMBER OF SHAREHOLDERS: 124,385,360.

WORLDWIDE PRESENCE: Headquarters in Cupertino, California, and spread around the Silicon Valley; wholly-owned subsidiaries in fifteen countries: Australia, Austria, Belgium, Canada, France, West Germany, Hong Kong, Ireland, Italy, Japan, the Netherlands, Norway, Spain, Sweden, and the United Kingdom. The company's main foreign markets are Australia, Canada, and France, and products are on sale in over eighty countries around the world.

NUMBER OF EMPLOYEES: Approximately 7,000, with roughly 1,750 working overseas and the rest in the United States.

AVERAGE AGE OF EMPLOYEES: Twenty-nine.

TURNOVER: Information not available, though the company claims turnover is low compared to industry standards.

RECRUITMENT: Apple recruits from all over the country, and target schools change from year to year as the company's needs change. In 1987 the company hired primarily technical students; however, in another year it might focus more on marketing and finance.

NUMBER OF NEW HIRES PER YEAR: The company will not disclose.

RANGE OF STARTING SALARIES: Company will not disclose, as salaries vary too much by position and experience to specify a range. "We offer very competitive salaries."

POLICY FOR RAISES: "We review compensation and performance every six months. And we are on a true merit system where raises are based on performance."

TRAINING PROGRAMS: Training programs are provided through Apple University, described as "a university without walls; a resource to help you become great." Apple offers classes, on-the-job training, workshops, seminars, forum discussions, programs for family members, and an extensive collection of books, articles, tapes, and other learning aids to employees at every level of the company, from secretaries to top management.

INTERNSHIP PROGRAMS: Apple has internships programs for both undergraduates and graduates. In 1986, it hired 50 interns, in 1987 there were 70, and the company hired about 120 interns in 1988. Most of those hired in 1988 were in computer science and electrical engineering.

BENEFITS: Apple is one of only a few companies in the country that offers flexible benefits. Depending on an employee's salary, the company allots a certain percentage of additional monies which can be used to buy additional insurance in areas not included in the standard benefits package. In this way, employees can tailor their benefits to their particular needs (e.g., a single woman might want different benefits than a father of five). Standard benefits include a choice of six medical plans, a dental plan, a vision plan, life insurance, accidental death and dismemberment insurance, a profit-sharing plan, a stock purchase plan, a savings and investment plan, a number of educational programs (including Apple University), and tuition assistance for courses that will enhance an employee's job at the company, including MBA degrees.

VACATION: Twelve days per year in the first three years (for employees working a forty-hour week) and fifteen days after three years, plus six national holidays, the Friday after Thanksgiving, and the whole week between Christmas and New Year's.

ADDITIONAL PERKS: Apple gives a "baby bonus" of $500 to every employee who has a child, and it offers up to $3,000 in assistance to employees who adopt children. The company has a program whereby employees "loan to own" an Apple computer. "We believe that every employee should own an Apple." Employees borrow the computer of their choice (at no cost) and a year later, it's theirs to keep. Employees can get massages in their offices (at a cost to their department) upon their supervisor's approval. Apple has recently made arrangements for an off-site day care center to provide employees with day care at a nominal cost. In the "Re Start Program," after five years of service, Apple gives employees a six-week paid sabbatical with full benefits (which can be extended by adding on accumulated vacation time). The company creates T-shirts commemorating special occasions and new products, which are given away free and which many employees wear. Apple has a health and recreation club called the Fitness Center, which is used by approximately 60 percent of employees at headquarters. The company also has a store that offers a wide array of products with the Apple logo.

BONUSES: "We have a variety of bonus programs, which the majority of employees are eligible for. That's the only statement I can make on it. Each one is its own case." Managers have funds whereby they can reward special efforts throughout the year.

ANNUAL PARTIES: Apple is a company that loves to celebrate its successes. It hosts an annual Christmas party for employees and their spouses, which is black tie and "done in the Apple style." The party generally features a live band (in 1985 it was the Pointer Sisters; another year they had Robin Williams). In 1986, in place of a Christmas party, the company celebrated its tenth anniversary by hosting a formal party with a "Wizard of Oz" theme. Huey Lewis and the News performed in 1987. There were tables of hot and cold food, and employees and their spouses or guests dined and danced. The company hosts an annual employee picnic each summer, in addition to Friday beer busts ("for morale"), special events parties for events like the launch of a new product, and quarterly "employee communications programs," at which CEO John Sculley talks about what's important to the company. Apple also holds an annual sales meeting for the entire sales staff, which consists of a week of intensive seminars held in one central spot (in 1987 the meeting took place in Hawaii).

AVERAGE WORKDAY: Apple works on flextime, which allows people the freedom to come in pretty much when they choose, as long as they work an eight-hour day. Many people work considerably longer days, as well as weekends, depending upon their particular work load. (The Macintosh team became legendary for working days on end without stop.)

DRESS CODE: "There is no dress code. Everyone has their own style. It depends on the group that you work with and how much interface you have with the general public. You use your own judgment. The dress code really does range from blue jeans to blue suits."

SOCIAL ATMOSPHERE: "It's very much of a team atmosphere. A lot of teamwork, a lot of camaraderie, a lot of very, very intelligent, interesting, innovative, creative people. We really do have a unique group of people who work here." Many people do socialize with one another outside of the office.

HEADQUARTERS: Apple is headquartered in Cupertino, but its buildings are spread out around the Silicon Valley. "We do not publicize the number of buildings we have on our campus. For one thing, it changes often, and it's very difficult to pin down. Apple leases more than one million square feet of research and development and office space in the Cupertino area. We're organized by groups. For instance, all of Creative Services is in one building, all of Distribution is in one building, all of Human Resources is in another."

CHARITABLE CONTRIBUTIONS: Close to $4 million in 1987, mainly through donations of computer systems to nonprofit organizations, social services and art groups, and special projects in schools from kindergarten through twelfth grade. Small cash grants were made to similar organizations in the areas in which Apple employees live and work.

INTERESTED APPLICANTS CAN SEND RÉSUMÉS TO:
Staffing
Apple Computer, Inc.
Mail Stop 9C
20525 Mariani Avenue
Cupertino, CA 95014
(408) 996-1010

If it's corporate culture you want, corporate culture you'll get at Apple Computer. The personal computer pioneer, founded by Steve Jobs and Steve Wozniak in 1976, wears a mantle of iconographic interest, and it is happy to oblige the curious. Cupertino, California, smack in the middle of the Silicon Valley, is the mecca to which techie pilgrims flock, and at the Apple headquarters there is a tiny museum exhibiting the still-brief history of the machine that has changed so many people's lives. A visit to Apple is gratifying because it lives up beautifully to a visitor's expectations, no matter how naive and idealistic they may be.

"People tend to want to come here because they think they can change the world," Steve Scheier says. "That's why I got here." [Important note: Not everyone at Apple is named Steve. Being called Steve will not help you get employed at the company.] He's the manager of creative services at Apple, a vague but cool-sounding title, and within six years at the company he's had six different jobs. "I wanted a private sector experience in an exciting company." After working in the California State Legislature, his first responsibility at Apple was working on the "Kids Can't Wait" project, a program which introduced the computer to the California public school system by distributing them gratis around the state.

Now Steve heads up a department of 120 people, 54 of them part-timers. Creative Services is the group that "maintains Apple's image. It originally came under Steve Jobs's tutelage. We do events, trade shows, work on design—standards even IBM tries to emulate.

"We're still not heavily bureaucratized. People go nuts at the very hint of bureaucracy. We find people via the 'Marlin Perkins Method'—find someone, shoot him down, and tag him. Our culture's in transition, and I don't think we know how it'll end up. People want to do what's right and make a difference. What are we going to be? I felt the decade of the twenties [when Steve and his peers were in their twenties] was service, the thirties are cash, and the forties will be service again. People want to make money here, but you can't work ninety hours a week to do that. People who leave Apple don't do it because the money's better elsewhere. They leave because of philosophical differences, or they're too tired, or they want to do other things. I'm here to see if the culture will evolve."

When very bright people form an organization in order to pursue intellectual properties, one attribute of their work lives is a certain self-consciousness. The constant self-examination is not so belabored that it interferes in the accomplishment of work, but it is very absorbing. "I think about my job a lot," Scheier says. "My wife could certainly discuss that. She'd say I'm self-absorbed. That's a problem. I want balance in my life, but I'm not willing to do it. Steve Jobs got you to understand that being good isn't good enough. They press you to keep doing better work. A lot of the culture today is still part of his influence. Not even our finance people are 'normal.' People do things because of relationships. We're so consensual—we make everyone buy into the pie, i.e., 'Let's see, does the janitor have an opinion?' Even to this day, I'm much more interested in people than in computers."

While Steve is an example of someone who wanted in because of the company's reputation, others were indeed driven by being part of the high-technology revolution. Not to mention those who actually helped make that revolution happen.

Chris Espinosa and Randy Wiggenton were original members of the Homebrew Computer Club in 1973. It was one of the many clubs that sprung up for hackers and hobbyists that are now romanticized since their early participants, once ridiculed for their obsessiveness, became millionaires. Since Chris was only fifteen, he used to get rides to and from the club with Steve Wozniak. One day, "Woz" asked Chris, "What are you doing Christmas vacation? How'd you like to spend your vacation in an unheated garage?" This is the stuff of history. The Apple I was born in that garage, which belonged to Jobs's parents. (If there were a shrine in the Silicon Valley, candles would be lit in this garage.) Chris then graduated from high school and eventually commuted to college, the University of California at Berkeley, where he majored in English while working full time for the fledgling company.

Bill Fernandez, who introduced Woz to Jobs, was another member of the garage team, while working full time at Hewlett-Packard with Woz on hand-held calculators. After Apple was incorporated, he was its first employee. With Jobs ousted from the company he cofounded and Wozniak having exiled himself to "consultant" status, Bill, Chris, and Randy are the best tour guides to the old Apple. They have prospered beyond their wildest dreams; financially speaking, they probably do not have to work. Yet here they are, looking like graduate students in jeans, T-shirts, and windbreakers. Actually, they look like they're still undergraduates.

Bill writes, "In the early days there was magic in the air. We were excited about the possibilities of our little start-up company, of starting from scratch and making a go of it." Chris adds, "Doing things excellently is the only way." It is agreed. "Apple puts trust in people who haven't done this stuff before. It gives people big jobs. Apple only rewards those who perform. We're a product development company—that's how we get our jollies."

Our trio traces the beginning of the "new Apple" to 1980, during the development of the Lisa computer [Author's note: no relation.] when the company became divisionalized: "The most important event was when Lisa was moved to its own building—amidst major security. Ordinary Apple employees couldn't even get in." The same thing happened in 1982, when Macintosh was in development. "The Macintosh group was the smallest and most renegade after Jobs was thrown off Lisa. He stole people from all around. He was extremely excellent at hiring." They characterize the staffing process as "picky. We're hiring a friend. Can you be a member of our family? Will you wear Vans"—a highly decorated slip-on sneaker that is impossibly conspicuous—"as a symbol of whimsy?" The rumors of Macintosh favoritism are legion—Jobs procured lavish kitchens for his teams filled with exotic bottled waters and the juices of fruits which cannot even be grown in North America or its allies, as well as massages for his overworked crew. These privileges were not available to other Apple employees. All of this is true and definitely contributed to Jobs's demise.

"It is a necessity to be outrageous and different, to almost fly in the face of standard operating procedure. When there is flexibility, we take advantage of it. Sometimes it has its drawbacks. Working at Apple means constantly being inundated with people who want to work here. We often feel Apple has a hundred thousand people, although only seven thousand work here now. And businesses don't always take us seriously."

The pluses far outweigh the minuses. "The production cycle here starts with inspiration, then labor, then fulfillment." The guys estimate that fulfillment actually occurs 80 to 90 percent of the time. "There's always something to do. I've never felt bored or uninterested. Which makes it hard to take vacations." It is difficult to decompress from the intensity and the deadlines (or the intensity of the deadlines). "I live two miles down the road, but I have the mental discipline to turn it off," one says. Bill Fernandez actually left the company for two years to teach the Bahai faith in Japan. Somehow that doesn't seem surprising.

Jim Schmidt is the director of human resources. Although he wears the short hair and button-down shirt of an executive, his photo ID badge, taken more than seven years ago, shows a guy with long hair. His more conventional appearance notwithstanding, that photograph reveals the Apple of our fantasies. He is asked what he looks for in an interview that alerts him to Apple material in a job applicant. "We're not perfect at spotting it, otherwise recruiting would be easier. But the person has to have passion. They have to get excited about changing the world. We're looking for the individual who's excited about what they can do here. We try to screen for it by doing a ton of interviews. People are mostly asked the same questions. The technical evaluation is less important. People are looking for a spark and a good fit. What makes it a problem is that people come in with a lot of knowledge about Apple. Fortunately, it usually works out."

Apple aggressively hires on campus, because college kids "are not tainted by what life was like at Company X. The transition's easy; it's a lot like college." Apple's campus (referred to, in fact, as the "campus") is spread out over many buildings. The typical outfit for many employees is jeans and a T-shirt, often commemorating a special day—the launching of Macintosh or a companywide party—or the logos of Apple Computer. Like school, there is an orientation program and several cafeterias offering salad bars with a pay-per-ounce pricing system in addition to the usual cafeteria fare. "People who came from other companies can be a bit jaded. If they came from companies with a good humanistic culture—à la Hewlett-Packard, they can't always figure us out, because they see it as the 'HP way.' If people come from companies without a strong value system, it's easier to make the transition." Yes, there are beer busts, as widely rumored, but no, they are no longer integral to the enculturation of new people or to the perpetuation of the old days.

A pple is one of the rare companies where the word "values" issues lightly forth from most people's mouths. It's not a concept that is taken lightly, however, although it's shorthand for the presumed ontology. You work at Apple, therefore you share the values, ergo you are a good person. But, as simplistic as that may sound, it's pretty much true. Apple marriages make sense and, according to people at the company, are far from rare. "The values are similar." Or spouses come to Apple after their partner gives the organization high marks. It all comes down to shared values.

John Sculley, Apple's chairman of the board and chief executive officer, signed the introduction to the smashingly well designed booklet entitled, "The way we do business. A guide to Apple's business ethics." He writes, "At Apple Computer we are justifiably proud of the values that spur our innovation and success. They are values that promote individuality, self-management, accountability, and ownership. But our adherence to principles isn't limited to our internal culture. Rather, we want to shape an environment that fosters, as well, the highest standards in business ethics and professional integrity. Ethics that reflect the same commitment to excellence found in Apple products and Apple values. Ethics that maintain an allegiance to the primacy of fairness. Ethics that strike a note for integrity and honesty."

John Schmidt says that "Apple-izing" the new employee does begin more or less at once. "The values are inherited after arrival. People want to be part of something important. No matter what else happens to them—like Woodstock—they'll have been here. You can make a difference and still be cool, too."

With Jobs out and Sculley, an MBA from the Wharton School of Finance and the ex-president of Pepsi-Cola USA, holding the reins Apple seems more businesslike that it had. There are more people wearing jackets and ties. (Or jackets and pearls, as the case may be.) There are more MBAs. There are also two—almost three—generations of college students who have graduated since the company was founded, most of them familiar with the organization and many of them users of its products. (And not only because college students can buy Apples at significant discounts.) There are now thousands of students who enter college and graduate school, in other words, with the intention of applying for a job at Apple, a concept that would have been implausible to the early folks. "We can't be young mavericks forever,"

Schmidt explains. "Whether it's good or bad, people are trying to incorporate traditions. People are receptive to change here. We're not selling out. What were valuable values and what was bastardized? We weren't antibusiness; we were different. Our informality makes sense. It helps foster the team. Then, though, it became like, if you weren't wearing Levi's, you weren't a member of the club. Now we've changed our image. Informality can mean wearing a tie."

"Ne dites pas à ma mère que je suis chez APPLE. Elle me croit ingénieur chez IBM."

"Don't tell my mother that I'm at APPLE. She thinks I'm an engineer at IBM."

When the sign above-left appeared in ads in France, it created a sensation. Now it hangs in the office of Jean-Louis Gassée, Apple's vice-president of research and development. A product of Catholic boarding schools, Gassée says, "I was in love with computers since I was fourteen. I'm a mathematician by trade. You talk to one hundred people here, and eighty-five of them have the same behavioral patterns. We're tinkerers." He began his career in 1968 at Hewlett-Packard, moved to Data General, and then to Exxon Office Systems before joining Apple in early 1981, when he launched Apple France. Gassée says that Jobs and Wozniak were as well known in France as they were in *les Etats-Unis*. "I was very responsible for the culture. As a representative of a California company, I felt what the French wanted was French, but *not* French. When you need to import a culture, it's got to be blended. It just happened." He moved to the States in 1985. "If you're Moslem, it's good to live in Mecca. When you're French, you understand the Silicon Valley better than the natives. Everyone gets in bed with everyone, and contrary to genetics, it works out beautifully.

"I'm where I want to be. The French don't consider me very French anyway, since I've worked at American companies." *Une autre pensée:* "When you move from the parish to the Vatican, you're not the one structuring your time. I try never to explain who I am. I have to be more cautious about leveling criticism. I'm not paternalistic—I don't want to impose my values. I can influence by *example*." He adds, self-mockingly, "Modesty has never been an Apple value." Gassée felt "I'd reached my apex of bliss at Apple France for four years. I could do no wrong. What a feeling! I felt good because I assembled the group. Instead of being King of France, I'm [tied for] third or fourth or fifth in the organization."

His imprint is on his hires. "I look for people who can wallow in complex technical details. I love people who think in layers. I try to recruit people who will say no. You can make more money by saying no than by saying yes. I tend to pick people who are more literate than the average guy." Gassée's written a book in the last few years, *The Third Apple*. "Why not? At Apple it is possible to show the poetry of technology. We are the kind of company that attracts those people. I came here to learn, not to do things I'd already done. I keep a list in my head of my past mistakes. They keep me watchful."

Jean-Louis is "living a dream," having finally nested in the Silicon Valley. "I would never have had this job if our dear departed cofounder hadn't left. Desire is very interesting. It drives you in ways you don't even know." Now ensconced at the top of the technological heap, Gassée is watchful of what Apple will become. "The counterculture made the product attractive. But now we must be who we are. Apple is making the transition from adolescent to adult. We must keep the dream with the reality and accept the consequences of what we do. We are selling an experience, not a dream, and we deliver." Apple is in the process of becoming an interesting adult.

Apple Computer International looks a bit more business-y than its domestic counterparts. For the most part the staff in the United States has selected to work in International because their backgrounds have been in foreign languages and international relations. There is relatively little movement between domestic and International. Stefan Winsnes was International's director of human resources at the time of my visit. He has been with the company for seven years [now as the director of Apple University]. He says, "The challenge [of International] is to merge Apple with the country in which we operate. Unlike other multinationals, we hire local people, not Americans, in key leadership positions. Out of 1,500 employees worldwide [internationally], only eight or ten are Americans living abroad. I feel the people I work with overseas are my friends, even though we haven't met. Sculley says that whenever he goes into an Apple office, he feels Apple." John Sculley visits Apple facilities around the world two or three times a year, though not every site. It's "very important. We lost our marketing impulse for a while, and Sculley reminded everyone." More than the CEO, however, "our hero is Mike Spindler," the senior vice-president of International. "He has never told us what to do. We've exceeded what *we* said we'd do."

International business is kept separate because of its inherent complications, such as twenty-two different keyboard versions, including two just in English. Apple operates in eighty countries around the world. The division is relatively small and decentralized. "We have two people for training and two for events, as opposed to forty in the United States. We're open, and there's very little internal politics." The cost of starting up in a new country is about $100,000 (in 1987 precrash dollars) per country. The first foreign language computer was launched in 1982, and now France, Australia, and Canada are the three strongest markets for Apple. "Apple is 190 in the *Fortune* 500," I am reminded at the time. Using that figure, International alone would be 470. [Author's note: In *Fortune*'s newer ranking, Apple is 152. change International accordingly. Math was never my subject.] As International becomes more significant, we want to raise domestic's awareness of us. We're not homogeneous. We have less resources.

"In a way, we are a bit more pure Apple there than here. Because we spend so much time figuring it out," said Winsnes, after having spent time in the Paris office. "Foreigners are interested in their countries. It's very strong in Europe, and what is regarded as pretty normal here is sensational there. Apple people overseas are more risk takers than non-Apple foreigners. If you buy an Apple, it says something about you. It says 'individualism.' " Because Apple's presence overseas is still new enough to have an ad hoc feel to it, joining the company is not always an easy decision for an International employee to make. "It starts with a handful of people with enthusiasm. The common denominators of these people are independence, a search for personal satisfaction, balanced lives outside their work, and (for some reason) most played one musical instrument. Lots of pianists."

A project called "A Day in the Life of Apple" illustrated some of the more unusual uses for the computers. In Australia, "MacStud" was a program devised by a cattle breeder, and monks in Tibet have used Apples with their congregations.

No matter which part of the company you visit, you will find a reinforcement of the Apple culture you seek. It might be in the person of a hiring manager who says she's looking for a candidate who is "happy, creative, flexible (to fit into our flexible environment), with love for the industry, belief in our products, and care for the customers." [This is startlingly different from the usual "bright, hardworking, and motivated's" one usually hears.} It could be in a brand-new MBA from Northwestern—Cammie Marsden—who, resisting the prevailing trend to go into high finance, says, "The impact of the individual here is greater than elsewhere." She's wearing a suit (albeit pastel) but still enjoys "the definite mystique about working for Apple. People in business school think the glitz is in wearing three-piece suits and power lunches. They're all workaholics now." A paid sabbatical program called "Re Start," in its third year, is yet another way Apple shows its concern for its people. Employees are entitled to take six weeks off every five years. On sabbatical, you are encouraged to rest, so that you will return refreshed and energized. "For women, the sabbatical can be attached to the maternity leave," which, in California, is another four months. In 1987 one thousand people took advantage of the program. Including Del Yocum, who was promoted to executive vice-president and chief operating officer and learned of his promotion while on sabbatical. {He wasn't totally shocked.}

With life settling down after the shakeout on top in the winter of 1985, morale at Apple is back up. Despite having to endure months of being asked "Is the company financially stable?" and "What's it like without Steve Jobs?" people are excited about the new products and the fact that they can succeed at Apple without the presence of its founding visionary. The company has celebrated its first decade with some flash, hiring the Pointer Sisters and Kenny Loggins to entertain at a Christmas party, hiring the Jefferson Starship for a sales conference.

C all it "Apple values" or call it "Apple sense," or anything else you like, employees speak widely about the trust that exists internally. (As opposed to the secrecy which must be imposed externally in the Silicon Valley, where sabotage is not always a stranger.) Furthermore, it is something of a mystery how work is conducted efficiently around here. When asked to describe the typical day at Apple, people in all divisions respond with a game plan that sounds just one step short of corporate anarchy. It's not that people don't do their work; it's just that there are few structures. "You know damn well what you have to do when you get in in the morning. And you have to be open to incorporate new advances." People may be working solitarily, but they are part of teams, and those teams may be part of other teams, and one must learn how to move in and out of different groups while still accomplishing his or her quota of work. One piece of advice: "You must be careful you're working here for the right reasons, not just latching on. Pride can turn to elitism."

Although reassured that the company is firmly forward-directed and profiting from more consistent management, it is possible to hear such statements as "I hope Apple will be here in five years. I want to pay off my mortgage." It is gallows humor. Certainly, anyone fearing the worst would probably not express it so glibly to a reporter. During the period of layoffs in 1986, "We weren't worried; they kept us apprised." Anyway, "everyone is prepared. We've got our résumés in our Laser Writers {Apple's most powerful printer/typesetter}."

Back to the confusion. Job descriptions are fairly well defined, though no one feels limited by them. "You have to arrange stuff yourself. But you have an incredible network." A programmer volunteers, "It's not my business to approve or pay attention to TV commercials, but if I saw {an Apple} one that I hated or loved, I'd call someone. So would everyone else." It is almost impossible to emphasize the personal stakes employees feel for their Apple, defined differently by everyone as is their wont. "If I weren't paid to do this and I didn't have to worry about money, I'd do this."

If you work hard, good person, you will be rewarded. Not just spiritually, but materially as well. There are bonuses—ranging from dinner for two in a good restaurant to $10,000 cash —for an especially good contribution. Working at Apple can provide a conscientious worker with a quicker fix than a shot on *Wheel of Fortune*. "I gave my employee five hundred dollars last week. People are generous. If you do a good job, your manager can send you on a trip to Hawaii or a shopping spree at Neiman-Marcus." Apple people love to regale visitors with stories of bonuses, making them sound less like New Agers than like fans of *Lifestyles of the Rich and Famous*. It's funny, because Neiman-Marcus sounds so incongruous to the hordes of the T-shirted. You'd think they'd prefer getting a bag o'circuits, or a new pair of Birkenstocks. (This might be a good time to mention that the parking lots have seen a fair share of serious imports. You know the kinds.) "Apple is a lot like school, except instead of grades, you get money," a longtime employee says.

"Often people are working two and three jobs at once. You don't get a bonus for doing your job; you get one for doing an *incredible* job." Sometimes it is necessary to be a self-promoter. With all the tumult, "you could do a great job here and not be visible." Long hours are not the key; since the environment is so informal, it might be just a matter of chatting with a colleague in the corridors. It's collegial self-monitoring. Consequently, "a perfect nonfit is someone who needs to know where they'll be. Apple is a perfect mirror of the Silicon Valley."

Barbara Krause is Apple's manager of public relations. Her background—in politics—included five years as a speechwriter and a position as chief of staff to the first woman mayor of San Jose. She aspired to working for Apple because "it seemed history was being made in my city by Apple. I really wanted to be here. I knew that high technology was really going to change the world and history was being made here, now." Armed with a frontier spirit though lacking in a technological background, Barbara felt "I could understand the staff at Apple. When there were no jobs here, I took a job at Atari. I was very aggressive about getting here. I was persistent. Now that I've been in this position, I try to remember what it was like [trying to get in the door]. But now I need to hire people with technological backgrounds.

"Apple does live up to everything I thought it would. At Apple I feel the whole world is watching." The intensity of the commitment of Apple's people is something Krause relishes. "It would be a mistake to push [achieving balanced lives]. You'd lose what's great about Apple. You'd lose those kinds of people. I keep picturing the company as a big basketball game. We have a lot of faith in our co-workers. We can get so much accomplished, so quickly. Nothing is ever final here. We don't take no for an answer. Yet we have an overall sense of what we're doing as a company. Is it anarchy?" she ponders. "Yes, though it's more disciplined under John Sculley." The drama that accompanied 1985's power struggle was "exciting. I really did not know how Apple would turn out. I felt I was watching a demise in history. That's why this victory is so sweet." (Incidentally, Barbara mentions that the massages, symbol of Apple's managerial problems, are now available to all employees of the company, at their supervisors' discretion and their department's cost.)

Life Under Sculley is best explained by Apple's support people, for the most part nontechies who also wanted to be pioneers. "There's less workaholism now than before," a secretary volunteers. "Before [the introduction of] the Mac, I worked eighty-hour weeks and loved it. And—oh gosh—I only work a sixty-hour week now and worry that I'm not enjoying it enough. If I left between five and 5:30 P.M., I'd feel guilty. I'd leave with my head down." A user support person adds, "I don't think I'd be valuable to Apple without a satisfying personal life. I work better when I don't have to work weekends." Of the four sitting in the conference room (named, as all conference rooms in this building, after soap operas—this one is "Days of Our Lives"), none had a high-tech background. (A random sampling of other meeting rooms reveals "Matisse," "The Price Is Right," "Dynasty," "Wall Street," "Zinfandel," "The Queen Mary," and "I Hear You; No Problem.") Amy, John Sculley's secretary, remembers her first day. "I was really scared, thinking 'How can they expect me to do something on a computer?' They asked me to type something. A big tear welled up. And then I typed and printed it up. And I jumped up!"

The "typical day" is practically a meaningless phrase at Apple. "Some people will be spoiled with attention, and others will be neglected. Most days the company feels small." Buzzwords such as "good management" mean very little to the people behind the people behind the headlines. "It means nothing; it's like 'eat right.' " As always, it is simply a matter of doing good work. "Politics exist," someone in the group states flatly, "but they don't negatively affect us. It's more on the VP or senior VP level. There's not a lot of negative gossipy stuff. It's a good place for women to work, and one of the best places for working mothers." It is agreed that "people get emotional about the products. We all feel like we're a part of them."

Leslie Andrews is a good person to meet. During her previous four years at Hewlett-Packard (which seems, according to whom you meet, to be a proving ground for future Apples), she was a satisfied member of the human relations staff. Now, as Apple's manager of benefits and relocation, she's not looking back. "It was really hard to leave HP. It took a year to be glad to be here." Her mission is to try to say yes to as many requests as possible. Given Apple's generous benefit plans, she seems to have succeeded. "The most difficult thing here is telling people 'No, it can't be done.' What's hard to communicate is that the pot of money for benefits isn't endless. We spend *a lot* of time trying to work things out. Apple must be considered a 'good guy.' " That's the point. It is far easier to work for the good guys. For Leslie, there was an epiphany: "I really knew I really really liked it here when I started to recruit my close friends to come and work here."

You might consider Apple's Fitness Center to be a perk. In addition to offering classes in aerobics at one dollar per class for drop-ins, yoga, weight training, etc., the center also functions as the recreation center for nonphysical activities such as courses in oil painting, dog training, and ballroom dancing. "We put together travel packages," a Fitness Center staffer says. "It's neat working for Apple. They spend time on employees." Here's an example of the good guys who like to live it up: The day of Apple's tenth anniversary party, the Fitness Center was converted into a beauty parlor, providing hairdressers, manicurists, and makeup artists to transform the female employees before the big night. While the facilities are for the exclusive use of employees, spouses can take advantage of the travel and discount plans. Smoking cessation and stress and weight management programs are offered (cost: $50–$100), and if you attend 80 percent of the classes, your tuition will be reimbursed. More than a thousand Apple people have had fitness evaluations in the four years since the Fitness Center opened. "We probably affect 60 percent of all employees." To simply work out alone does not cost a dime. The Fitness Center's peak hours are 6:30–8:00 A.M. Registration begins with a computer. "I'm not into computers personally," a former director of the Center admitted. Six professionals work here full time with two interns and two part-time people.

Dorothy Largay used to be one of the directors of Apple University. Founded in January 1982, it is *not* a training and development organization, but rather a group of people who design a collection of "great events to empower people to be the best they can be. We reaccess their sense of mission and purpose. We're business partners." What does this mean? Apple University works with a coalition of colleges that have been Apple-ized in an effort to exploit further the variegated uses of the different computers. AU tries to make Apple's universe smaller by connecting scholars and researchers around the world. (T-shirts are available.) Largay left the company for two years "to build a house and to build a relationship. One thing I've failed at is leaving Apple." [Now she's the manager of senior management development.]

Oh Lisa, you're whining—I can hear you! *What about the nerds? Doesn't Apple have any?* The Software Engineering Group is proud that it upholds the nerd standards for which computer people are known. Three of them are loading up on carbs this afternoon at lunch, but none is wearing a "pocket pal." Scott, then a veteran of six years at Apple, admits, "I would call myself a nerd, and I'd call Dan [Dan is sitting next to him] a nerd, but not Kyle [also present and accounted for]. My products are used by nerds," he says with a mixture of pride and indignation. His nerd quotient is enhanced with "I used to think it was great working for a company where the two visionaries dropped out of college."

Even the nerds admit you don't have to love computers to love working at Apple or at least to love the work itself. "Computer science is not a prerequisite. Mostly we need people with zeal and fervor to communicate with outsiders." They admit that the frontline group, which deals with the outside world, are almost "evangelists, in order to make outsiders make software for us." Of all the programs that work with Apple's computers, eight are "internal private label, and tens of thousands are made by outsiders." The Software Engineering people are as impassioned as any employees here. "Everyone here has an opinion about what we're doing. We all use the computer. If you believe in something strongly enough, it's amazing how far you can go and how much access you will get. It's not a major deal to get someone who can make a decision to see it. The individual is important at Apple."

Finally, dear friends, if you have learned nothing else about Apple, please note that by midafternoon the scent of popcorn wafts through the halls. Someone might add a touch of dill for a healthy taste. People care about doing good works while earning a competitive living. They have fun, often working ridiculously long hours, learning to juggle different jobs and their personal lives. Smokers would be uncomfortable. And it's okay to believe in the old Apple. You won't be alone.

HEWLETT-PACKARD COMPANY

HISTORY & OPERATIONS

Hewlett-Packard Company (HP), a major manufacturer of electronic instruments and computers that ranked forty-ninth among the *Fortune* 500 in 1987, was started in 1938 in a one-car garage in Palo Alto, California. Bill Hewlett and Dave Packard, close friends and fellow engineering graduates of Stanford University, used the garage to make a new improved type of audio oscillator—an electronic instrument used to test sound equipment—which had been the subject of Hewlett's master's thesis. Among the initial orders for the new product was one from Walt Disney Studios requesting them to design a different version of the oscillator to aid in the studio's creation of a sophisticated new sound system. The partners complied, and Disney purchased eight of the oscillators for use in the movie *Fantasia*.

With the first success, Hewlett and Packard formally organized their partnership in 1939. In 1942, HP constructed its own building to house its headquarters.

HP expanded as the partners designed and added more employees and designed new measuring instruments to their product line. During World War II, Hewlett served in the army and Packard remained in Palo Alto to run the business.

By 1950, Hewlett-Packard had two hundred employees, seventy products, and $2 million in annual sales. The 1950s marked the beginning of a period of sustained and substantial growth as the company diversified its product line and expanded its entries into the microwave business. In 1956, HP built a new engineering/manufacturing complex in Stanford Industrial Park, which also became its headquarters. The company went public in 1957.

In 1959—when it was twenty years old—Hewlett-Packard began to establish a presence abroad by creating a European marketing organization in Geneva, and establishing its first overseas plant in West Germany. During the early sixties, it acquired several companies with the goal of expanding its product line. The company's two most significant purchases were: the Sanborn Company of Waltham, Massachusetts, a pioneer in electrocardiography and a major supplier of other recording instrumentation, and the F&M Scientific Corporation of Avondale, Pennsylvania, a manufacturer of gas chromatographs. These two acquisitions enabled Hewlett-Packard to extend its electronics technology to the fields of medicine and analytical chemistry. By 1960, HP had grown and changed so much that the partners needed to restructure. They did so by establishing small (generally no more than two thousand employees), semiautonomous divisions formed along product lines, which essentially functioned as independent entrepreneurial companies. The partners wanted to stimulate growth while retaining the feeling of a small company. By 1964, Hewlett-Packard had 7,500 employees on its payroll.

In 1966, HP introduced its first computer, which was designed specifically to work with HP instruments. In 1968, the company announced its development of a powerful desktop calculator, and in 1972, it introduced the world's first hand-held scientific calculator, the HP-35. Introduced at $395, the HP-35 had 17 functions, weighed 9 ounces and measured 5.8 inches by 3.2 inches. (By comparison, the company's newest calculator, the HP-28S introduced in January 1988 costs $235, has 1,500 functions, weighs 8 ounces with a battery, measures 7.5 inches by 6.3 inches by ½ inch when unfolded, and has a full alphabetic keyboard that enables the user to punch in formulas and write a limited amount of text and a memory of 128K.) Hewlett-Packard sold 300,000 HP-35s during the new product's first three years.

These products were the first in a long and increasingly sophisticated line of computers and calculators, which now represent a little more than half of Hewlett-Packard's revenues. Known more for its technical and business computers than for personal computers for home use, the bulk of the company's computer line is comprised of mini computers designed for business, manufacturing, and engineering applications.

In a bold move beginning in the mid-1980s, Hewlett-Packard has been gradually converting its entire line of computers to the company's version of a new technology called Risc (Reduced Instruction Set Computing). Risc-based computers—which run considerably faster than conventional computers and can be made and sold more cheaply—though promising are as yet unproven in the marketplace. Skeptics dispute that they can match conventional computers in overall performance, and there is also concern that even newer technology will soon render them obsolete. Hewlett-Packard has reportedly spent hundreds of millions of dollars on its transition to the new line. The first Risc-based machines were shipped in November 1986, and the conversion of the full line will take place over the next twelve to fifteen years. Although HP reports that it is pleased so far with the sales of the new computers, it will be several years before the ultimate success or failure of the strategy can be assessed.

Since its inception, Hewlett-Packard, which has been referred to as "perhaps the most egalitarian of the world's major corporations," has been known as a great place to work. The partners built the company on the belief that "men and women want to do a good job, a creative job, and that if they are provided the proper environment, they will do so." As part of that overall philosophy, HP has a policy of open door management (and what the company calls "Management By Wandering Around"), a time-tested policy of no layoffs (twice during hard times, rather than firing anyone, HP asked its employees to take two days off per month without pay), and generous plans through which the company shares profits and distributes stock to employees. In 1979, HP hired an outside firm to interview its employees and get their feedback on various company practices, and the results were overwhelmingly positive. In 1984, HP was ranked third overall in a *Fortune* survey of the most admired corporations in America and first in the category of "ability to attract, develop, and keep talented people." The average tenure of HP employees is about eight years.

At the beginning of 1987, at the age of seventy-three, William Hewlett stepped down as vice-chairman of the company and he now sits on the board as director emeritus. Dave Packard still acts as chairman of the board, and John Young, who joined HP in 1958, is president and CEO. Today HP employs approximately 82,000 people worldwide. About half of the company's revenues are generated from foreign sales. John Young made new structural changes in 1984 to reflect changes in the marketplace, and the company is now organized into the five following broad divisions: Marketing and International, Measurement Systems, Systems Technology, Technical Systems, and Business Systems.

What binds it all together is the "HP/Way," a unifying principle and *modus operandi*—encompassing the company's "business practices," "people practices," and "management practices"—which employees believe in and admire.

(Information provided by Kevin O'Connor, company spokesman.)

1987 FORTUNE 500 RANKING: Forty-ninth.

REVENUES: $8.1 billion in 1987.

EARNINGS: $644 million in net earnings in 1987.

INITIAL PUBLIC OFFERING: 1957.

NUMBER OF SHAREHOLDERS: Approximately seventy thousand.

PLANTS: About fifty manufacturing entities in twenty-four U.S. cities, as well as operations in about seventeen foreign countries.

OFFICES: Sales offices in 149 U.S. cities and 334 sales support and distributorships in 77 foreign countries.

FOREIGN OPERATIONS: Company sells products in about seventy-seven countries, and roughly 50 percent of its revenues are generated outside of the United States.

NUMBER OF EMPLOYEES: Approximately 82,000 worldwide, with 53,000 employed in the United States and 29,000 abroad.

AVERAGE AGE OF EMPLOYEES: Information not available.

TURNOVER: Approximately 5 percent per year—which is very low.

RECRUITMENT: HP recruits at about one hundred schools nationally, for positions in all company divisions. In addition, the company recruits at sixty to eighty local schools for openings in local divisions. Between 75 and 80 percent of the graduates HP recruits are people with technical majors. The rest are people with general business backgrounds, a significant portion of whom are marketing majors with some technical background or MBAs with undergraduate technical degrees.

NUMBER OF NEW HIRES PER YEAR: Typically, between 2,000 and 5,000 per year. In the near future, the numbers will be on the lower end of the range as the company will focus on retraining and relocating people in the current work force. The company receives roughly one hundred applications for every opening, but for positions in certain technical areas (such as computer science), they do not get enough applications for open positions from qualified people.

RANGE OF STARTING SALARIES: Company will not disclose. Pay at HP "ranks among other leading companies" and is subject to changes within the marketplace.

POLICY FOR RAISES: Based entirely on performance. First performance review takes place after six months on the job, and thereafter it's done on an annual basis. Managers assess an employee's performance based on a personal development plan plus HP evaluation criteria, and then compare the evaluation with those of other employees in similar jobs. The technique is intended not only to establish pay level, but to help employees develop and achieve professional goals. HP promotes almost entirely from within.

TRAINING PROGRAMS: All new employees go through an orientation, which takes a few hours. Then, after about six weeks, they take a two-day program called "Working at HP," which gives them a general overview of the entire company. After about six months on the job, employees go through another program, the intent of which is to familiarize them with specific policies to give them an idea of why the company does things the way it does, "the HP Way." This third program is adminsitered at a time when an employee is comfortable in his or her job and is starting to have questions about how the rest of the company operates. After several years, employees can take courses designed for potential managers.

BENEFITS: Medical and dental insurance, comprehensive retirement plans, profit sharing (in a range of 4 to 7 percent of pay and paid twice a year), a stock purchase plan that enables employees to invest a portion of their pay in the company's stock (HP pays one dollar for every three dollars an employee invests), and a tax-deferred savings plan to which the company contributes on a one-for-three basis. HP also offers tuition reimbursement for courses that are directly job related, or enhance an employee's skills, and in many cases it offers reimbursement for advanced degrees.

ADDITIONAL PERKS: Most HP offices have some kind of exercise facilities, the type and scope of which vary greatly from location to location. The company also has nine vacation facilities, five of them in the United States, which employees can reserve for a period of time. Some of the more exotic spots are in the Scottish Highlands, the German Alps, and a Chinese junk in Hong Kong Harbor. HP also owns property in Ontario and the Pocono Mountains. Most of the vacation facilities have camping and picnic areas, and one or two have cabins. Some HP divisions throw annual parties for employees and their families at these sites. In addition, employees are entitled to a 40 percent discount (roughly, depending on the product) on HP products.

VACATION: In addition to regular paid holidays, employees who have been with the company for at least six months are entitled to fifteen flexible days off per year, which can be used as sick time or vacation time at the discretion of the employee. Employees can use the flexible time off in increments of as little as one hour for doctors' or dentists' appointments.

BONUSES: The only bonus is cash profit sharing (see Benefits), which is awarded to all employees who have worked at the company for at least six months.

ANNUAL PARTIES: Determined by individual divisions as the company is much too large to host all-company parties. Most divisions host parties for employees and their families at HP campsites. Many divisions throw some kind of party every few weeks. HP also has a companywide practice of holding twice-daily ten-minute coffee breaks (company supplies beverages and snacks) to give employees an opportunity for informal chat.

AVERAGE WORKDAY: Depends on the position. Some employees, such as assembly-line workers, have to work a standard schedule. But many people work on flextime—arriving any time between 6 A.M. and 9 A.M. and leaving eight hours later.

DRESS CODE: With the exception of safety rules governing dress at HP plants, most divisions determine their own dress codes. The more customer traffic through a given division, the more formally employees in that division tend to dress. Three fourths of the company dress fairly informally, with men wearing open collars and women wearing pants or skirts. Most of the company still follows a tradition of dressing down on Fridays, which, in the company's early history, were the days when products were shipped.

SOCIAL ATMOSPHERE: "There is a definite emphasis on teamwork within this company. We feel that people who know each other and like each other and enjoy working together make better team players. It's easier to work with someone when you know them personally as well as professionally, which is the idea behind HP parties and coffee breaks. HP is not a company where superstars and people with huge egos do real well, because the focus in on small groups of people working on projects and working on common goals, rather than individuals going off on their own and expecting a lot of attention and gratification."

RESEARCH AND DEVELOPMENT: Approximately $901 million spent in 1987. HP typically allots about 10 to 12 percent of annual earnings to R&D.

NUMBER OF PRODUCTS: HP manufactures and markets more than 10,000 products.

MOST POPULAR PRODUCT: The HP LaserJet Printer Series—the company can't say for certain which printer is most popular. They range in price from $2495 to $3995.

HEADQUARTERS: Corporate headquarters is on twenty-six acres in the Santa Cruz foothills. The four-story building that encompasses 487,000 square feet of office space is set into a slight hill so that the four floors are not equal in size. The approximately two thousand employees who work there have access to a basketball court, a par course for runners, locker and shower facilities, and an employee cafeteria.

CHARITABLE CONTRIBUTIONS: Total grants of $5.5 million in 1987, the bulk of which was in the form of equipment gifts to colleges and universities.

INTERESTED APPLICANTS CAN SEND RÉSUMÉS TO:
Corporate Staffing Administration
Hewlett-Packard Company
3000 Hanover Street
Palo Alto, CA 94304
(415) 857-1501

Hewlett-Packard isn't just a major corporation, an early leader in the computer industry that has maintained its prominence over the years; it's an ambition, an aspiration, a place to work for one's entire career—if you get the chance.

Finding employment here is like getting into Stanford or MIT as a freshman, but with lifelong tenure as a researcher and professor. *One of Hewlett-Packard's signature policies is guaranteed employment; no layoffs.* One senior manager remarks that going from Stanford to HP is "like marrying the girl next door." Leslie Itano, a Stanford alumna (undergraduate and graduate degrees in electrical engineering), manager, Circuit Technology Department, Hewlett-Packard's Stanford Park Division, readily agrees. "Certainly every Stanford EE graduate would want to work for HP." She seems almost surprised at the obviousness of the question. "HP has broad-based appeal: a comfortable environment, challenging work, and stability—especially now. People have broad ranges of needs, and HP tries to suit them." It is a company that actually considers its employees first, and how their work lives can be improved upon. It is a company that contemplates its values and its role as a value maker. In return, employees try to be worthy of the organization, as their comments reflect. "I give a lot of thought to my job outside the office," many say.

And it is a company where "teamwork" is not only *not* a cliché; it is a heartfelt way of life.

When asked about their successes, employees talk of their pleasure in the team, not their individual accomplishments. "Your goals are the team's goals. Once you're on a project, you don't spend much energy on thinking about your personal promotion. When someone doesn't do a great job, you try to console them. 'Teamsmanship' is explicitly pointed out during your review." A salesperson adds, "Even with individual sales quotas, 'teamsmanship' may be rated higher." People coach one another. There is no feeling that your colleague's win will nullify your chances at success. Success is to be shared. "Every group tries to get the resources they need. You fight for them—not in the sense of preventing others from getting them." A vigilantly upheld open door policy furthers team thinking, since everyone—including John Young, HP's president and CEO (and even director emeritus Hewlett and chairman of the board Packard themselves (who are called "Bill" and "Dave" and who still spend time here), is visible and approachable. Senior management works in glassed-in environments. Their offices have no doors, just permanent open entryways.

The interaction's virtue is that it's a method of ensuring that "top people know you're doing good work. It's a lot of responsibility or freedom," says someone who hasn't quite decided which just yet. Yet, for those who prefer to work by themselves, "there are loners here, too."

Hewlett-Packard's offices and labs do look like offices and labs. Despite the presence of cubicles and, in some facilities, little private space—in other words, what appears to be an impersonal environment—employees have only kudos for the warm and personal sensibility that defines management. "Open cubicle, cluttered desk," Tim Vachon said. "I like it." Some areas look like mazes, yet, at regular intervals, there are snack areas filled with herbal teas, coffee, fresh fruit, etc., that encourage conversation and a chance to relax in the middle of the day. HP discontinued its practice of supplying free doughnuts, so often someone will bring in cookies, muffins, or bagels to share with his or her colleagues. Fluorescent lighting notwithstanding, this is a convivial place. (The dispensers offering eyeglass cleaning wipes on the walls of some hallways is another friendly gesture.)

While some of the "techies" will be wearing jeans and most of the sales or marketing people will be dressed in ties and jackets or dresses, this is an informal place. Women who wear dresses do it because they want to, not because it will propel them toward success. (Besides, they have more important things to think about.) A software programmer volunteers, "In R and D, away from customers, dress is casual, jeans and cords. I wear a tie once a week or so, so I don't forget how to tie one." A supervisor of engineers admits he's been sartorially manipulated since arriving here. "They made me wear shoes. I used to wear flip-flops." One manager describes the dress code as " 'no dress code.' People who frown on other people's dress are frowned on."

HP is both serious and fun-loving. Everyone takes his or her job seriously, but they cultivate life outside of their company and are able to laugh with one another. [Author's note: Maybe the pronounced dearth of laughter at many corporations should qualify this as a perk. Any thoughts? Write in.]

Imbued with the awareness that Hewlett-Packard is home to the top graduates in their fields (engineers and computer scientists, by and large), there is a sense of well-being and respect for one's fellow HP-ers. Employees assume that co-workers (even those unknown to them) are competent, bright, and loyal. "You get a sense of the overwhelming HP brain-power," an engineer says. "People are just happy to be here."

The will to work hard is actually self-imposed. "HP will give you as much responsibility as you can take," an electrical engineer says. "The downside is, you tend to work too hard. Since it's so open-ended, you take on too much—you don't know if it's enough, too much, et cetera, and you can waste yourself." Tim Vachon (now a former test engineering manager) continued, "A lot of people put in lots of hours. The company lore is against it. Bill and Dave says, 'Go home to your family. You work too hard.' "

Since many are hired directly from school, they arrive with a ready-made peer group, bringing with them a set of compatible interests. (It is not unusual for two or three people working in the same lab to share living quarters, especially those who are new to the Bay area.) There is literally no palpable feeling of competitiveness in the halls of the various HP campuses in the Silicon Valley. Not even focused outward at other companies. ("They may regard *us* as competition . . .") As a senior manager says, "There's a high level of profession-alism and respect. People here will say 'IBM [HP's head-on competition for business clients] is a great company.' "

These qualities—call them collectively the "culture" of the company—certainly provide an incentive to do good work. Retha Caldwell, an R&D section manager in Stanford Park, started with HP over thirty-three years ago, shortly after her husband joined the company. "I started in the stockroom," she said with a smile. "Seeing things come about is satisfying. Making improvements in the process is satisfying." Her reason for working at HP is that "I've felt I've made a contribution after all these years. I've expanded my responsibilities. My rewards came by merit." Tim Vachon spoke for all when he said, "I've had the feeling that what I do affects the whole company. It matters." Retha's background was in business administration, although she never earned a college degree. "Obviously, I'd need more qualifications to step into this job today."

One thing that's not exactly a prerequisite: a love of high technology. It helps. It probably makes working at HP more fun, but for positions in personnel, law, finance, and public relations, for example, computer literacy is not mandatory (though it will most certainly follow).

Employees at every level tout HP's flexibility. After spending just a little time here, it's one of the words that reappears most frequently in their evaluations. "One of the company's strengths is flexibility," says Bryon Look, R&D manager, for the Personal Computer Group. "Our management style tends to accommodate all kinds." Then train your ear to hear "oppor-tunities," a word filled with the promise of never staying put for too long. Leslie Itano explains standard operating precedure: "Staffing is flexible. When feasibility is determined, more and more people are added on." People are encouraged to move around, even to take time off if they think a break will make them more productive.

Craig White, HP's general manager of finance and remarketing (part of the Corporate Treasury) comments on the importance of education to the organization. "HP is very high on education. Consistently." It doesn't mean scouting for impressive advanced degrees, necessarily. "It's going on for seminars afterward." Employees take a short orientation course upon arrival. Technical training for most functions is offered in house, including "one like 'HP 101.' But everything changes so fast, there's very little formal training. Everyone feels free and takes advantage of proposing new methods." A process engineer not out of school too long says, "It's a lot less pressured than school. There are no exams." Darlene Yaplee, who is a marketing manager in the logistics and retail vertical markets of the commercial systems division, "People are very well educated here. You forget it until you leave."

The advancement of HP values is a tacit part of the recruitment process. "I do college recruiting at HP because it worked for me," a sixth-year employee says. The team players of Hewlett-Packard begin interviewing "not too long after you get here." One engineer from the East, now in his ninth year, says, "I took the interview to get a free trip to California. The day was filled with the people I'd be working with. I liked them. I decided I wanted to work here."

During a candidate's visit, he or she will learn about the "HP way." The way has three components: "Business Related, People Related, and Management By Wandering Around and Open Door Policy." In a brochure entitled, "There's something special about this place," two HP-ers from Boise, Idaho—Dick Hackborn and Don Harris—are credited with the most concise definitions of the HP way:

BUSINESS PRACTICES

PAY AS WE GO. NO LONG-TERM BORROWING.
* Helps us maintain a stable financial environment during depressed business periods.
* Serves as an excellent self-regulating mechanism for HP managers.

MARKET EXPANSION AND LEADERSHIP BASED ON NEW-PRODUCT CONTRIBUTIONS.
* Engineering excellence determines market recognition for our new products.
* Novel new-product ideas and implementations serve as the basis for expansion of existing markets or diversification into new markets.

CUSTOMER SATISFACTION SECOND TO NONE.
* We sell only what has been thoroughly designed, tested and specified.
* Our products have lasting value—they are highly reliable (quality) and our customers discover additional benefits while using them.
* Offer best after-sales service and support in the industry.

HONESTY AND INTEGRITY IN ALL MATTERS.
* Dishonest dealings with vendors or customers (such as bribes and kickbacks) are not tolerated.
* Open and honest communication with employees and stockholders alike. Conservative financial reporting.

PEOPLE PRACTICES

BELIEF IN OUR PEOPLE.
* Confidence in, and respect for, HP people as opposed to dependence on extensive rules, procedures, etc.
* Trust people to do their jobs right (individual freedom) without constant directives.

- Opportunity for meaningful participation (job dignity).
- Emphasis on working together and sharing rewards (teamwork and partnership).
- Share responsibilities; help each other; learn from each other; learn from mistakes.
- Recognition based on contribution to results—sense of achievement and self-esteem.
- Profit sharing, stock purchase plan, retirement program, etc. aimed at employees and company sharing in each other's success.
- Company financial management emphasis on protecting employment security.

A SUPERIOR WORKING ENVIRONMENT.
- Informality. Open and honest communications, no artificial distinctions between employees (first-name basis), management by wandering around and open-door communication policy.
- Develop and promote from within. Lifetime training, education and career counseling give employees maximum opportunities to grow and develop within the company.
- Decentralization. Emphasis on keeping work groups as small as possible for maximum employee identification with our business and customers.
- Management by objective (MBO). Provides a sound basis for measuring performance of employees as well as managers; is objective, not political.

MANAGEMENT PRACTICES

A fundamental strength of the company has been the effectiveness of communication upward and downward. Two key ingredients for making this happen are:

MANAGEMENT BY WANDERING AROUND.
- To have a well-managed operation, managers and supervisors must be aware of what happens in their areas—at several levels above and below their immediate level.
- Since people are our most important resource, managers have direct responsibility for employee training, performance and general well-being. To do this, managers must move around to find out how people feel about their jobs—what they think will make their work more productive and meaningful.

OPEN DOOR POLICY.
- Managers and supervisors are expected to foster a work environment in which employees feel free and comfortable to seek individual counsel and express general concerns.
- Employees have the right to discuss their concerns with higher-level managers. Any effort, through intimidation or other means, to prevent an employee from going "up the line" is absolutely contrary to company policy—and will be dealt with accordingly.
- Use of the open-door policy must not in any way influence evaluations of employees or produce any other adverse consequences.
- Employees have open-door responsibilities, too. They should keep their discussions with upper-level managers to the point and focused on concerns of significance.

The "way" is so clearly articulated that any employees who find themselves incompatible with it should probably excuse themselves form working here. "A lot of people say there isn't enough structure," a five-year employee admits. "There are probably some who won't be comfortable with the openness. They would prefer little offices and privacy. But [the system allows for] making decisions and doing real stuff immediately." Furthermore, "as you tend to get good at something, you get more of those tasks." Another employee explains, "The HP way can vary from manager to manager, but one guy can spoil it." With experience, one gains confidence in understanding and furthering the organization's ethos, so that "when a new boss isn't strong, you can't always rely on him" or blame yourself for his new interpretations. Shirley Gilbert, the Cupertino site communications manager, believes that people who fail at HP have "personalities which can't get things done through other people. They don't listen. They're insecure. It's not a technical background or lack of it that could penalize it."

MBWA—Managing By Wandering Around—validates the kind of learning one gets in hallways and elevators. "It is critical that you talk to people a lot." HP-ers say that compared to IBM, "nothing is written down. Some days you say, 'I talked all day.' That's work." Consequently, eloquence is prized. "Of all the engineers I knew in school," one says, "the ones with the best communication skills gravitated toward HP. It's a priority here. Anyone might deal with a customer." The "way" encourages "intrapreneurialism" as well as driving decision making to its lowest possible level. "There's a heroic confidence that you can trust your people. Especially if it's your entrepreneurial baby."

Nancy Anderson, the general manager of the Commercial Systems Division, at the Cupertino campus, had worked in sales for a competitor of HP's "and kept losing competitions to HP. It was the only company I felt nervous about in competitive situations." An interview with Hewlett-Packard was irresistible. "I thought I'd be coming in for a one-hour interview," she recalls, "but it was a grueling day. People kept saying the same thing all day, sincerely. I had read the books. The culture is true. If I didn't work here, I'd think it was all exaggerated."

As one of the most senior women in the entire corporation, Anderson says, "This is as equitable a place for women to work. Ten years ago women blamed their situation on being women. But there is no way that being women is an issue any longer." Maternity leaves are not the stuff of nightmares and waiting until you "show" to tell. "I've never seen anyone who has a problem leaving to have a baby. You get a three-month pregnancy leave with your same job back."

Anderson especially appreciates her employer, having had another with which to compare. She almost seems to envy those who come here straight from college. "They come so young and grow up with the company. They can only compare it to perfect." One of her colleagues says, "Recent college graduates take to the 'baptism by fire' approach right away. Also, they don't have preconceived notions of what you're 'supposed' to do."

Craig White, the general manager of the finance and remarketing division, praises the flextime, which, with twenty-four-hour clearance, allows most people to work eight consecutive hours as long as they arrive between 6 A.M. and 9 A.M. "Time is on the honor system. People come in very early to beat the commuter traffic. If you work a weekend day, you get a day off." He sums up: "You have to regard HP as the company where you'll spend the rest of your life." If this all sounds too wonderful to be true, take comfort in knowing, as one software development engineer puts it, that "after a few weeks, the HP awe goes away."

Before HP's growth rate had reached a booming twenty-five hundred new hires per year, "you could walk across the hall and find the guy who knew the answer. Now there's more bureaucracy. It doesn't seem better or worse, but now there are so many uninformed players. I used to feel I knew what was going on." A substantial amount of reorganization has transformed HP from "an instruments company to a marketing-driven company. You might wake up one day and find out your job title's different, redefined, et cetera, but you still have a job. And the company has the same soul."

Hewlett-Packard's structure does elicit a widespread comparison to "family." (That's another official term.) A transplant from the East Coast says, "This has replaced my family in

Vermont. I don't care for the Silicon Valley at all. I'm only here because of HP—I wouldn't want to work elsewhere in the valley." Social hanging-out happens easily and often. It could be tennis at lunchtime at one of HP's courts, aerobics or ski conditioning classes at HP's recreation facility, the "Pizza Club," a weekly pizza-and-beer event for one of the labs, or the El Torito on Friday nights. It is clear that fraternizing goes on during off-times, if only for the number of celebrations that occur during the workday. [Author's note: In one day, I glimpsed at least three parties wedged into cubicles, all featuring cakes and some with decorations, honoring birthdays, retirements, babies, etc.] HP marriages are not uncommon, but couples are discouraged from working together too closely.

O ne gets the feeling that in lieu of bowling leagues, the average HP-er might get involved in a wine tasting or reading group, common in the valley. "Singles are dependent on their work groups," one of the unmarried says. It is said that meeting new people in the Silicon Valley is expensive and difficult. A (mostly unspoken) rule of the valley is to be discreet when talking business at a local "watering hole." Believe it or not, industry eavesdropping is so widespread that guidelines (HP calls theirs "Be Aware Before You Share") actually exist prohibiting employees at the high-tech companies in the area from discussing their work too technologically or loudly. HP's attitude toward this seems rather—excuse the expression—mellow, but it might prevent some intercorporate coupling. According to the San Jose Chamber of Commerce, forty people move to the Silicon Valley each day, making prices in Palo Alto, Cupertino, etc., skyrocket. Few single people are able to afford one-bedroom apartments by themselves. "That's status."

Job security: It's here. Development engineer Chris Christenson says, "Projects and divisions may come and go, but I will have a job. This assurance comes from a division disbanding that I went through." The company that Bill and Dave created has been gratified by the enormous reciprocal loyalty of their people. Bob Parrish, a site personnel and facilities manager, claims "I don't return calls from headhunters." Whether or not employees have had the opportunity to get to know Hewlett or Packard, they hold tight to the tenets of these two men, proud of the legacy of good deeds they initiated. [A legendary Bill and Dave story surrounds a military contract they refused years ago, when they needed the business. It was not a moral call against the Department of Defense; it would have meant having to fire members of their staff.] Craig White remembers a pivotal conversation early on in his career at Hewlett-Packard. While it was not with Bill or Dave, it epitomizes the HP way of thinking. "I had the CFO [Ed Band Bronkhurst, now retired] look at me and say, 'Craig, you're not going to get rich here, but it's a rich environment.' I'll never forget it."

THE TOM PETERS GROUP

The Tom Peters Group

NOTE: Tom Peters read the earliest draft of *Going to Work,* whereupon he generously offered to write the foreword to this book. He did not solicit any changes in this chapter.

HISTORY & OPERATIONS

Tom Peters, the self-proclaimed "Dr. Feelgood of Management," formed The Tom Peters Group in Palo Alto, California, in 1983. Peters, a former management consultant with McKinsey & Co.—who holds two degrees in engineering from Cornell and two in business from Stanford Business School—had recently co-authored *In Search of Excellence: Lessons from America's Best-Run Companies* with a McKinsey colleague, Robert Waterman. The book grew out of a research project the two had conducted, entitled the "McKinsey Excellent Company Survey," which examined the attributes shared by companies with first-rate management records. In *In Search of Excellence,* the authors distilled the management techniques of forty-three successful companies into eight succinct philosophies they claimed had the potential to improve the overall performance of any company that adopted them. (Included among the forty-three "best-run" companies were Boeing, 3M [see page 390], Hewlett-Packard [see page 657], Delta [see page 10], Maytag, Wang Laboratories, Procter & Gamble, Frito-Lay, Mary Kay Cosmetics, and Tupperware.) Published during the recession of 1982, when unemployment had reached 10 percent and the sense that Japanese management techniques were superior to ours was the rage, the book struck a nerve and shot to the top of best-seller lists. It became the second fastest selling nonfiction book in publishing history—*Roots* was the fastest—and the best selling management book in history (it topped *The New York Times* best-seller list for 50 of the 130 weeks it remained on the list).

Ultimately translated into fifteen languages, *In Search of Excellence* made Peters into a world-famous management authority. Waterman remained at McKinsey & Co.; Peters had left seven months before the book was published to set up a private consultancy practice. (One story says he resigned, while another, promoted by Peters himself, says he was fired for eccentric misbehavior—such as wearing shorts to work.) When *In Search of Excellence* became the "bible" of the business world, Peters became one of the hottest speakers on the lecture circuit, making four or five impassioned speeches a week—his style has been likened to Elmer Gantry's—and commanding upwards of $15,000 per speech (now more than $20,000), though he has always conducted roughly a third of his talks at no cost. He found that his message lent itself to a number of other media—eventually including video- and audiotapes, computer software, a newsletter, a short-lived column in *U.S. News & World Report,* a syndicated newspaper column, radio spots, magazine features, public television specials, management seminars, executive development films, a television film of *In Search of Excellence,* and a second and third book—and The Tom Peters Group became the umbrella organization for all of his various enterprises.

Peters coauthored his second book, *A Passion for Excellence: The Leadership Difference,* with Nancy Austin, a former Hewlett-Packard manager who was then in charge of The Tom Peters Group's publishing arm (Austin has since left). The book presented anecdotal information about forceful managers who had pioneered the management practices set forth in *In Search of Excellence.* (Among them: Steve Jobs, the founder and former chairman of Apple Computer [see p. 642], Debbi Fields, the founder of Mrs. Fields Cookies, General Bill Creech of the Air Force's Tactical Air Command, Don Vlcek, vice-president of Domino's Pizza, Inc. [see p. 247], and Frank Perdue, chairman of Perdue Farms, Inc.) Published in 1985, *A Passion for Excellence* hit the top of the best-seller lists in its first week and remained on *The New York Times* best-seller list for forty-one weeks.

Peters's message is, by intention, relatively simple. Unlike traditional management theories, which emphasize the bottom line, Peters's philosophy is people-oriented. Peters stresses that service to the customer should be a top priority for every company. In essence, he claims that by ensuring that goods and services are unfailingly of first-rate quality, by introducing frequent innovations in accordance with customer feedback, and by engendering company pride in employees as well as giving them the freedom and encouragement to become "champions," managers can make their businesses flourish. Though some deride his theories as being overly simplistic, many are drawn to them as the kind of commonsense, back-to-basics principles that have been lacking in American business management for too long.

In October 1987 Peters's third book, written alone, was published to the now usual clamor. In *Thriving on Chaos,* Tom rethinks his philosophy of excellence and urges managers to brace themselves for change. Appearing within what seemed like hours of "Black Monday," it too reached the best-seller list with no difficulty and as of April 1988, it was in its eleventh printing with 410,000 copies in print.

Peters runs The Tom Peters Group, which now includes twenty employees. Made up of five main enterprises, each headed by a "partner"—though Peters himself holds the majority stake in each of the companies—the divisions are managed as separate entrepreneurial ventures. The Tom Peters Group's four main businesses are *TPG/Learning Systems,* which provides training programs and packages based on the "Excellence" principles including Skunk Camp®; *Palo Alto Consulting Center,* which provides management consulting services; *The Skunkworks, Inc.,* which sponsors Tom Peters's custom speaking engagements (Peters averages well over two hundred speeches per year); and *TPG Communications,* a research and publishing group that produces and licenses audio, video, and software products and creates print materials, including books, magazine and newspaper articles, and a subscription newsletter. TPG's subsidiary division is *TPG Europe,* the international arm of *The Tom Peters Group,* based in Stockholm.

The staff at The Tom Peters Group includes: five consultants, two coordinators for the consultants, a full-time general counsel, three events managers; a Skunk Camp coordinator, an editor who edits Tom's work as well as the company newsletter, a chief financial officer and two others in accounting, a researcher for all communications projects, one person who administers all European activities from the Stockholm office, the head of TPG/Learning Systems (who coordinates training programs), and four clerical people.

Employees, most of whom do not hold fast to real titles, dress casually and are encouraged to "have fun" while taking on a maximum of responsibility. The staff occupies a floor of offices surrounding an open area that contains a large table and two desks, and Peters, a staunch proponent of the Hewlett-Packard school of "Management By Wandering Around," works either in the open area or in one of the offices of his support staff.

Products now available from The Tom Peters Group include: Speeches: More than two hundred per year, which generate an average of $1.5 million in fees ($20,000 for a two-hour speech, $30,000 for a day-long presentation); Books: *In Search of Excellence: Lessons from America's Best-Run Companies* ($19.95 hardcover, $10.95 paperback, more than 5 million sold), *A Passion for Excellence: The Leadership Difference* ($19.95 hardcover, $10.95 paperback, more than 508,000 sold), *Thriving on Chaos: Handbook for a Management Revolution,* by Tom Peters (available in bookstores in October 1987 and in its eleventh printing six months later, $19.95 hardcover); video: *A Passion for Excellence* ($795), *In Search of Excellence, The Film* ($375 video, $1,300 film), *In Search of Excellence: Management Action Program* (three videocassettes, $300), *A Passion for Customers* ($795), *A World Turned Upside Down* ($695), *What Have You Changed Lately? Managing for Innovation in Health Services* ($385)—almost all the videos are accompanied by printed discussion guides; audio: *The New Masters of Excellence* (six cassettes, $54.95), *Beyond a Passion for Excellence* (one cassette, $7.95), *The Excellence Challenge* (six cassettes, $52.50), *Excellence in the Organization* with Robert Townsend (six cassettes, $52.50); multimedia: *Toward Excellence* ™ (multimedia management development program, approximately $10,000 licensing fee plus $150 per participant for written materials); seminars, consulting: "Skunk Camp: A Top Management Seminar" (four-day retreat, $3,800); one-, two- and three-day "customized" consulting programs (price varies); other writing: *Tom Peters: On Achieving Excellence* ® (newsletter; subscription $197 per year); newspaper column (syndicated to approximately fifty-five daily papers); free-lance articles (in journals and magazines); and *Occasional Papers by Tom Peters* (collected in a set of eight paperback books, $24.95 for the set).

(Information provided by Kathy Dalle-Molle, company spokesperson.)

REVENUES: "Greater than $5 million." Company will not disclose exact figures.

EARNINGS: Company will not disclose.

OFFICES: Three. Palo Alto—eighteen employees plus Peters's; Stockholm—one employee; Los Angeles—one employee.

NUMBER OF EMPLOYEES: Twenty-one including Tom.

AVERAGE AGE OF EMPLOYEES: Company will not disclose.

TURNOVER: Company will not disclose.

RECRUITMENT: None.

NUMBER OF NEW HIRES PER YEAR: No average number. "We're such a small company that it's hard to say."

RANGE OF STARTING SALARIES: Company will not disclose.

POLICY FOR RAISES: Employees are reviewed annually, and raises are determined by merit.

TRAINING PROGRAMS: None.

BENEFITS: Health and dental insurance, pension plan, and profit sharing.

VACATION: Two weeks per year plus seven regular paid holidays each year.

ADDITIONAL PERKS: "The only thing really is that the office does grocery shopping for the staff once a week. We have a fully stocked refrigerator full of food—anything from health food stuff like tofu to Oreo cookies and crackers. Whatever employees want to put on the list."

BONUSES: All employees are eligible for bonuses, and the company has three different levels of bonuses: executive, principals, and junior and clerical staff. Junior staff receives bonuses four times per year, and the more senior levels get them twice per year. All bonuses are determined on the basis of company performance and merit.

ANNUAL PARTY: The company hosts an annual party at Christmas, which varies from year to year. In 1987 it was an informal, catered buffet dinner held at Tom Peters' house. Employees and their spouses or guests as well as the regular Federal Express delivery person, the stationery delivery person, Tom Peters' typist, and others were invited. The company also celebrates its successes as well as milestones in the lives of its people.

DRESS CODE: No dress code. Employees basically wear anything they want, including jeans. If people are going to have contact with clients, they'll dress up more.

SOCIAL ATMOSPHERE: "Groups of people go out after work. One time this past winter a big group went out to dinner and then a play. Things like that. Or, if somebody has a holiday party, they'll invite everybody from the office. Nobody is ever excluded from anything. There seem to be a lot of friendships within the office."

HEADQUARTERS: The Tom Peters Group occupies the third floor of a three-story building. Everybody has an office, none of them enclosed. "You can hear what's going on in the whole building."

CHARITABLE CONTRIBUTIONS: Company will not disclose.

Tom Peters does not wish to provide an address to which people can send résumés.

I t confirms your expectations. The Tom Peters Group, occupying a postmodern aerie above Palo Alto (the only place in America where you can get a really good Monterey Jack burger), is filled with nurturing, casually attired women who seemingly have no last names ("Hello, The Tom Peters Group, this is Kathleen) and care passionately about the businesses of the faceless people who call them, looking for the guru over the phone. Excitement foments when Tom Peters himself is on the premises, rare appearances due to his brutal travel schedule. It is then that the office goes into overdrive, the floor filled with whoops of laughter and hyperactivity.

As you know, Peters is the McKinsey & Co. dropout who co-wrote, with Bob Waterman, *In Search of Excellence.* Now a buzzword (and perhaps a cliché) of businesses that want to demonstrate their good intentions, "excellence" is the term synonymous with Peters, more so since the publication of his second book, *A Passion for Excellence,* written with Nancy Austin.

The Tom Peters Group embraces five separate corporations: TPG/Learning Systems, which produces seminars and products; Palo Alto Consulting Center, a management consulting firm; The Skunkworks, Inc., which schedules Peters's speeches and public appearances; TPG Communications, which is Peters's publishing and licensing company, and TPG Europe. Approximately twenty people work here in varying capacities, sometimes moving back and forth among the companies.

Mara, one of the earliest employees (though as of publication a former one), said, "Tom is our core; we are the satellites. My roommate was Tom's office manager in 1982, when it was just Tom, Bob LeDuc {a former principal in TPG}, and some secretaries." Mara, a former singing telegram chanteuse, became the office manager in her roommate's place. "Tom was in and out of the office, and one day he said to me, 'You seem to be a nice person. What do you do here?' I told him, 'I organize your life.' " Mara's title, shared with Melissa, was "events manager; I made it up myself."

Mara's new cubicle {TPG had just moved in the previous week}, was filled with flowers, tiny framed photographs of the staff she considered "family," skunkabilia, and posters touting "Excellence." "I'm a good diplomat, communicator, and caring person. This philosophy of being good to your employees and caring about your customers is a way of life to me. It's been a huge motivator to me. I came in thinking that the people at the top of business would be assholes. And delightedly, I can tell you I've shifted my beliefs."

Mara has a history of entrepreneurialism. One of her more successful past ventures was Mara's Quiche Express. ("We could only bake four quiches at a time. More equipment would have meant another level of commitment and too much capital.") Fancying herself in between start-ups when she joined the organization, she thought, "In the beginning, I figured I'd get a good sense of business. After one dog year I thought, 'I don't want to be in business by myself. I like a team.' Even as a singer, I preferred duets to solos. Harmony excited me."

Simply *being* at The Tom Peters Group does force employees to think about what works for them. You can't advise businesspeople without taking your own business life into consideration. Whether dressed in jeans, jumpsuits, dresses, or jackets and ties (there are a few men here), people at The Tom Peters Group do not take a casual approach to the SOSs that flood their office.

Melissa Manson had no idea she'd get excited about business until her serendipitous arrival in 1984. At the time she taught aerobics both in Fresno where she had her own small business and in Santa Cruz, where she taught at the Cabrillo Courthouse. Nancy Austin was one of her students. "She asked me if I wanted to be the on-site coordinator for a business seminar she was planning. It was the first Skunk Camp. I'm so glad I didn't know who'd be there," she recalls. Don Burr (People Express), Stew Leonard (of Stew Leonard's, the now legendary—to readers of the excellence literature—supermarket in Connecticut), and Frank Perdue were among the participants. "It was a very high-powered group of guys. They were going to play volleyball with me? It turned out they showed up for *every* activity. They were wonderful."

Melissa stayed around for the seminars and discussions. "I sat in the back of the room with my mouth hanging open. Those four days probably changed my whole view of American business. They changed the way I ran my little business, the way I ran my life. I became totally dedicated. I was totally enthralled with everything that was going on. People cared about their people. One guy cried. It was intense. I never really had a concept that I as an employee *mattered*."

The following year, she was invited to plan a reunion of the first camp group, "which came to be known as the 'Black Jacket Skunk Camp' because they had special one-time-only black jackets made up for them. During the planning, they made it clear they'd make a full-time position for me at TPG." Manson is now the chief information officer and one of three events managers.

Some of her responsibilities include handling all activities involving Tom's personal appearances, which are now booked over two years in advance (by Christmastime 1987, the 1990 calendar had to be cracked open): contracts, client liaison, press, and travel and lodging arrangements. She logs all his mail and phone calls, distributing photocopies of all lists throughout the office ("there are no secrets") so that others can take over when Peters is away. She prepares Tom's weekly agendas. "Sometimes he has two or three events a day. There are weeks where the agendas are fifty to sixty pages long." Since Peters rarely talks with the clients he will address before he zips into town, Melissa's in charge of getting all relevant materials to Tom so he can review them en route. "He has no canned speech. He collects information from the client for his presentation." Although the middle-of-the-night phone call from Tom ("I just arrived in Chicago and the hotel doesn't have my reservation") happens less and less, Melissa and her associates in "Survival," as it is called, are on twenty-four-hour call. If Peters is on the road and Manson knows she'll be out for the evening, she leaves numbers where she can be reached. And "he's got my home phone numbers memorized."

She is well liked throughout the organization and respected for her conscientiousness. "They trained me on the job. They paid me well. I never did any of this stuff before. I never completed my education," she stresses, showing the trust TPG placed in her. "When I was twenty I said I really wanted to do something that'll change the world. Having been both an employee and an entrepreneur, I realize how much Tom's message is needed. I know he's sincere; I'm close to him.

"*This* is more valuable than what I was getting in school. *This* is my education."

I t's almost as if TPG's offices were a halfway house for conscientious objectors, um, managers. Here you get a friendly voice, support, and people who will not think you are crazy. Want to rent some videotapes over the weekend, but don't have a VCR? Borrow one from the office. Have no place to park your kids for the afternoon? Bring 'em in to work. Need to stay at home for a few days? Work from home. (Do keep your phone line open to receive your calls, however.) If nothing else, The Tom Peters Group is informal.

The workplace itself has a sense of fun and wackiness. Candid photographs of employees and Tom, framed book covers, awards, and tear sheets as well as clients' tributes clutter the entry. A huge stuffed skunk, a gumball machine, and doodads remind visitors that this is supposed to be *fun,* that running a business can be *fun,* and that taking oneself seriously is not important. Taking the mission seriously is another matter altogether.

"In the beginning, I was hearing these incredible things [from customers] daily. It felt so wonderful." At this point in the conversation, Tom has called in sick, asking Mara to cancel an appointment. "I've looked at Tom," she says after hanging up, "and he has benes [benefits] and perks, but he's paid the price. His weekends are his own. His rule is not to get called. Only occasionally do I respect that, but I want to give to him so he can do it. It's valuable. He's given people this validity."

Malka worked on the "Skunk Camps"—the series of intensive four-day working seminars The Tom Peters Group offers to civilians, which reinforce managers' searches for excellence. (At $3,800 per camp, all-inclusive, with five sessions per year, TPG is looking at bookings that approach one year in advance.) [More on this later.]

A refugee from New York, Malka says her arrival at the company was similar to that of other employees. "I had a bit of a personal connection with someone who worked here. There's quite a bit of that. Many senior-level people come from referrals, and there are a lot of best friends. People handle it much better than I would have expected. It's not incestuous." Since her arrival (and departure), the company has expanded in all directions. "It feels like a growing family. It feels like we're adding uncles and aunts and adopting new kids." She says the new office is tantamount to a new home, and the culture, its decor.

"Excellence is what binds some people here. Others respect it and do good jobs. People who are newer or part time may just be doing their job, but it's our culture that keeps people here. Happiness with one's job is as important as the money you earn. And there's not a whole lot of discussion of salary here. This place is flexible enough so that my responsibilities in life and my responsibilities on the job can work out. There's a lot of work to do here. I could take it home. The expectation is that the job gets done. Where you spend your time is irrelevant. If we're all working toward a deadline, that takes priority."

"With the loss of an office manager, we've lost some internal structure," an employee says. So "if the phone is ringing, you pick it up." There are few "supposed-to's." When you're working with a "revolutionary" (in the words of an employee), you don't need the rules of the masses.

As Peters has stressed in his books, speeches, and audio- and videocassette programs, success is worth celebrating. And he is extremely generous in sharing his wealth from good works with his staff. When the millionth copy of *In Search of Excellence* was published, he hired stretch limos to take staff and guests to a restaurant in San Francisco. "It was a big deal," one employee says. "I'd never been in a stretch limo before!"

As members of the force describe the work environment of The Tom Peters Group, a unified culture falls into place. Everyone is on a first-name basis. People are allowed to be themselves here. Interoffice socializing, though not an official mandate, just happens, and at any given time, one might find three sets of roommates among staff members. (Privacy may be a slightly rare commodity.) As a non-high-tech company in the Silicon Valley, several employees came from neighboring pioneers in technocracy, and there is an openness to new ideas and an attendant flexibility.

Jayne, a writer who chucked her life in New York and a position at *Forbes* for the unknown at TPG Communications, is editing and writing a newsletter, *Tom Peters: On Achieving Excellence,* with Peters. As a new person in the group, she was still sorting out her preconceived notions from the reality of life in Palo Alto. "I don't think people realize it's a segmented business," she said, still awaiting the shipment of her stuff from New York. "They think he's a speaker and a writer."

For all the fun and looseness, these are real businesses with the same exigencies as any other profit-making organization. True, Peters could simply give lectures (at his standard fee of $20,000–$30,000 a pop, although he will make adjustments depending on the group), write books, and hoard his fortune. He believes he can be a positive influence, although he feels that "if it hadn't been me, it would've been someone else.

"My avocation is the history of ideas. Within that is another more specialized field called the history of discovery. There is a term, 'doubles and triples,' which means that great inventions were invented three times within a two-year period—even Newton, Copernicus, Pasteur, Curie—the reality was, the world was moving in roughly this direction, and someone's name gets associated with the invention, but that's pure happenstance. It was in the wind. Linus Pauling discovered DNA's double helix two weeks after Thomas J. Watson, who won the Nobel for it with James Crick. Human beings don't think impersonally. We talk about 'Newtonian' physics. We don't talk about 'earth around the sun' physics. One feels more comfortable with the idea that a living, breathing person came up with it as opposed to an alien planet."

Don't start thinking that Peters is a guy with a huge ego who compares himself to Sir Isaac Newton and considers the excellence lessons to be in the same league as the law of gravity. He doesn't. Honest to God, if Peters has a favorite word it might be "bullshit"—a term with which he curses himself as well as others. (He will, after all, dress up in an extra-large skunk suit, voluntarily.)

"The fame would be scary if you took yourself seriously," he says in Key Biscayne, Florida, after a hugely well-received speech that could make Jerry Falwell sweat. "The time is right for the message we have, but unless you're a total egomaniac, you can't look at yourself as a 'fixer.' Two percent of the people listen, and two percent of that actually do anything about it, and that's terrific and I'm delighted by it. You get all this stuff about, 'You changed my life when I started reading your books,' and that's pure bullshit. Basically it means that somebody believed it to begin with, and you gave them something to sign up for."

Jayne says, "You can't take Peters's appeal for granted." Another employee talks of the value added by the mere mention of his name. "When we use Tom's name, we're basically putting out his philosophy. We're earning based on his ideas and the simplicity of his ideas."

No one recognizes more than Tom that his ideas have been assailed as the emperor's new clothes. And with each article, column, speech, and book, he hears the same criticism that he's repeating himself. His critics repeat themselves. He is as frustrated as his audience. "You say it over and over again, and then you get beat up for not saying anything new. We said there is nothing new. And we meant it."

SKUNK LIKE ME

It's the eighties version of Woodstock; instead of hitchhiking or coming by van or motorcycle, forty of us were coming, mostly by plane and then limousine, to Monterey, California, for Skunk Camp—"Implementing In Search of Excellence"—Tom Peters' specialized four-day sleep-away camp for managers who want to be better managers (or just want to be near Tom Peters).

Our journey began on January 27, 1986, a Monday. I learned that Skunk Camp, offered five times a year, ordinarily begins on Sundays, but due to Super Bowl XX was delayed a day to accommodate the sports fans who'd signed up. As a guest of The Tom Peters Group, getting my money's worth was not a concern. Just the limo ride from San Francisco, shared with the Rolscreen Company's Steve Bragg, was worth the price.

It was as romantic as only conferences can be; set in a pretty condo colony called Pajaro Dunes near the country's foremost Brussels sprouts farms, our rustic apartments were right on the beach, facing the water. We had plumbing, heating, buffets, telephones, and freebies. Upon arrival, one is given a Skunk Camp sweatshirt, tote bag, flashlight, mug, nametag, pens decreeing such maxims as "Nurturing Champions . . . Creating Heroes" and "Bone-Deep Beliefs," and heavy loose-leaf notebooks filled with various readings and exercises.

Although we had filled out brief questionnaires identifying ourselves by our nicknames, employers, and hobbies, I was very curious about whom I would meet and, most important, with whom I would bond.

Small talk was the first order of business, sitting around card tables with campers wearing nametags. Although this particular session would boast the highest number of women (six) who'd ever come to camp, I was the first woman in the lounge. As someone who travels for a living and chooses to dine alone courtesy of room service, I was uncomfortable being among middle-aged men. I was afraid someone would say "bottom line" and I'd retreat back to my room. This wasn't my crowd at all. Later Peters would say, "We tend to get reasonably weird people at our Skunk Camps."

Everyone was congenial, polite, and eager to meet him and for the thing to start, which it did over cocktails. By now everyone was skunked up—wearing their nametags, sweatshirts, relaxed. The TPG has a rule that prohibits companies' sending more than three people at once to a single session (where there is a preferred maximum of forty campers), in an attempt to allow for more intermingling. Everyone made an effort.

As at so many parties, we started with a game. Everyone was given the name of another camper whom he or she had to meet, interview, and then introduce to the assemblage. My partner was Lennart Arvedsen, who runs the European operation of The Tom Peters Group in Stockholm. His English was good, his daughter's boyfriend went to Brown, and I had once visited Sweden, so we had quite a bit in common. The icebreaker was effective.

Days start early—breakfast at seven, first seminar at eight. The utterly gung-ho (or those with jet lag) could take an aerobics class at six, run by TPG staffers Melissa Manson and Erin Fleming. All present made an effort to move around and get to know their fellow campers. No cliques had yet formed, although there was already a visible buddyship between apartment-mates. Everyone took this experience seriously. Discussions were long. When a participant rustled a newspaper she was reading instead of paying attention, she was reprimanded. We were a tad embarrassed for her.

My campmates included representatives of Stew Leonard's (the lavish supermarkets in Connecticut featured in *In Search of Excellence*), AmeriFirst Mortgage Corporation, Rolscreen (makers of fine windows and glass doors), Casual Corner, Bell Atlantic, Davgar (a major franchise holder of Burger King restaurants), 3M, Dominos Pizza Distribution, BancOne of Columbus (Ohio), Ford, and two representatives of the archdiocese of Chicago.

We wore our nametags everywhere.

Our head counselor, Tom Peters, started off each day with an impassioned talk, often accompanied by slides. Day one's program celebrated the Customer with a capital "C" while elucidating our Thirty-Day Action Agendas. People pay to come here to get results. (They have to justify their four-day absence from their offices and the $3,800 fee, after all.) From

Tuesday's notes: "An understanding of the unique and crucial role of top management in the competence-building process. . . . Listening doesn't mean 'sorta' or 'kinda.' If you're not out there sniffing your customer, you're out of touch. Worst sin . . .'I think it's an understatement to say that our international skills suck.' The reason Coca-Cola is so successful in Japan is because they were there for twelve years without making a profit. With the exception of Classic Coke, all products are tailored for the market. Pizza Hut in Japan—put squid on it. In Mexico City they have jalapeño. 'There's no magic to any of this stuff. It's the most boring stuff in the world.' "

Like campers, we were divided into small groups for various exercises. Our counselors made an effort to jiggle the mix for each group project, so that we would all get to know one another. At the conclusion of each project, the group elected a spokesperson to present its work. Everyone was comfortable with the tools of the trade—easels—and had obviously substantial experience at making presentations. The funny thing was, although the sessions were clearly informal, there wasn't anything funny going on. People smiled and seemed ready to enjoy themselves, but in the context of work. Only Tom joked around.

Day two was devoted to what the assembled managers could do to foster a climate of innovation and push that creativity down the ranks. By now the note taking had reached a frenzy. "If you think the people who work for you are turkeys, it's not working. Don't treat them as kindergarteners. They have the same stake and interest in the product. When you park your car next to the executive elevator, you don't meet a hell of a lot of people."

There was more student participation, more bonding, and much more ongoing snacking throughout. (A refreshment table in the back of the room was always stocked with beverages and healthy snacks.) Smokers used breaks to fill the sand-filled ashtray vats with cigarette stubs—they began to resemble planters with tiny, noxious buds.

In team tasks, roles began to form: the reticent, the leaders, the team players, and the individuals with personal needs. Most brought experiences that were general enough to be of value to the assemblage. In a couple of unpopular cases, some skunks were more determined to find solutions appropriate to their own companies, instead of throwing themselves into group projects. (Although little gossiping occurred during the first two days, by the final evening everyone knew who these skunks were, and had there been less maturity and a longer camp session, they might have been censured.) Campers felt they were part of something so special that they did try to focus on their missions at all times. Recesses were filled with "What did you think of this morning's program? Is Tom what you expected? Had you met him before? Is this just like his books?" There was little chat about sports or extracurricular matters. A niggling, "Did you call your office?" was whispered here and there, but there was little opportunity to do so, and even less encouragement.

Skunk Camp requires almost total immersion. (This way you have no opportunity to feel self-conscious in your sweatshirt.) The only exception to this rule is the third afternoon, which is free time. This is the one real chance to be a civilian—you don't even have to keep your nametag on—while counting the payoff for all one's networking efforts. (I spent my afternoon with Tom's staff in Carmel eating as much as we possibly could.) There were trips to the aquarium in Monterey and probably long calls to the office and home. An embarrassed couple of skunks (a male and a female, not representing the same company) had run into two of his acquaintances from his small hometown. Nothing untoward was afoot (and these two were wearing nametags, thus identified as conventioneers), but it did create some excitement.

O ther nuggets: "Listening does not equal talking. It's *listening*. Abbott Northwestern Hospital does little things. The executives greet day patients and walk them to their rooms. They provide valet parking for patients and their families. Doctors forego preferred parking. Anesthesiologists give Sony Walkmen to patients awaiting surgery.

"There's no such thing as a product. A product is a service and a product. There's no excellent manufacturer. There are excellent service companies that also make things."

O ur final group project was introduced with the proviso that it could take all night. Still, there was the Petersian sense of fun in the project's title: "Hey, Wait a Minute! Are We Really Serious About This Stuff?"

"In preparing to report on your work, each work team should: 1) make the strongest possible case *in support of* the statement they have been assigned, 2) make the strongest possible case *against* the statement they have been assigned, and 3) outline the group's consensus opinion on how these two opposing positions should be most appropriately resolved. Each of the three parts of the assignment should be outlined on one sheet of flip-chart paper."

My team's statement: "Constant tries are the simple watchwords of innovating and most of those tries will fail. Simply put, top management must tolerate (even encourage) failure, if it wants the organization to be an innovative one."

Our group consisted of a community college teacher–consultant–public speaker, a vice-president and regional manager of a bank, a communications manager of a regional Bell Telephone company, a regional managing officer of a fast food restaurant chain, the executive director of a public television network, the associate pastor of a parish in the Chicago Arch-diocese, and the director of fresh products (primarily meat and fish) of Stew Leonard's. Needless to say, the teacher, TV director, pastor (and I) were firmly pro failure, while the rest of the group was wildly pro bottom line. (In all fairness, the Bell executive, a former news and documentary producer, was torn. Being a woman, she veered toward the reasonable.) Although polite at first, we experienced a severe breakdown when, several hours into our debate, we discovered we were the last group still at work and that an unofficial campwide poker game [Skunk Camp's first] was in session in another bunkhouse.

We screwed up. With visions of poker chips dancing in their [it wasn't me, I swear] heads, Group Four hastened toward a conclusion, one that was neither fully thought out nor reason-able. For the self-employed worker, the process of reaching consensus was fascinating. It necessitates a kind of compromise with which I was (naïvely) not familiar. Factored into the experience was the context: Did the decision matter for real? In the case of this last work night of Skunk Camp, it finally became clear that this was an elective seminar and that our decision would bear no consequences save a bit of public humiliation when it was presented in public the next morning. Had real dollars been involved in a real business, chances are a poker game could not have threatened our mandate.

In planning Skunk Camps, The Tom Peters Group actually prepares a banquet and awards ceremony for the final night. The food is fancier than usual, and there's even a cocktail hour. [Author's choice: guacamole.] Each skunk gets a personalized certificate of accomplishment—"You did great and we are glad you were here"—individuals are encouraged to create and present their own awards to one another, and prizes and speeches are made. When Tom appears in a special costume (he also distributes personally autographed hardbound copies of his books), mayhem ensues, and although forty campers and a handful of staff have just spent only about seventy-four hours together (counting sleep), the evening verges on the sentimental. There is a final morning program to follow, but it is optional, and many campers leave the Pajaro Dunes to catch flights and make meetings, so this is the last time we are all together. Although still ensconced in skunkabilia, many campers make special grooming efforts for this gala evening.

(Incidentally, months later, the network is still intact. Skunks from our session are still in touch, still feeling the effects of the force of our seminar. One manager actually burned his company's manual to shake up the old ways of doing business. Others sent more representatives of their companies to learn the message firsthand. As for me, the weekend after camp I excoriated—in public and not quietly—a rude and sullen hostess in a restaurant, to my family's horror. And I've written dozens of letters of praise to people I've encountered in business who did more than was asked of them.)

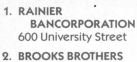

1. **RAINIER BANCORPORATION**
   600 University Street

2. **BROOKS BROTHERS**
   1401 Fourth Avenue

3. **THE SEATTLE CLUB**
   At Pike Place Market
   2020 Western Avenue

4. **FOUR SEASONS OLYMPIC**
   411 University Street

5. **SEATTLE GOLF CLUB**
   210 Northwest 145th
   Street

6. **GENE JUAREZ**
   At Nordstrom
   1501 Fifth Avenue

7. **NORDSTROM**
   1501 Fifth Avenue

8. **PIKE PLACE MARKET**

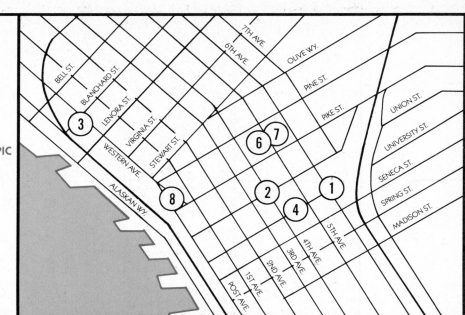

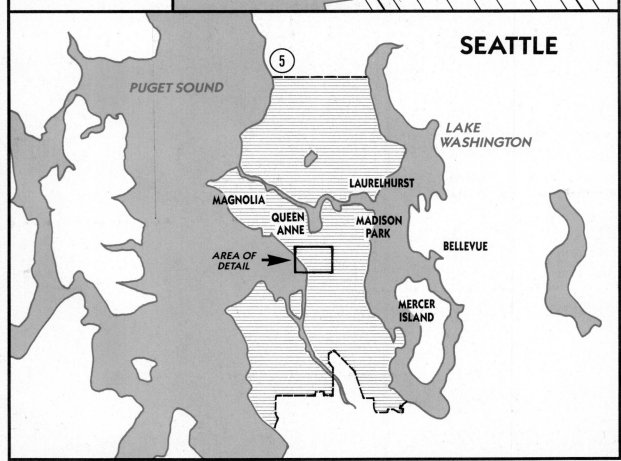

SEATTLE

SEATTLE

SEATTLE

Loving Seattle has, unfortunately, become a fad, like naming babies Samantha or Joshua. It's even trendier when these proclamations are made by those who've never been to the capital of the Northwest. (Not to be confused with the capital of Washington, which is Olympia.)

Why Seattle is lovable: It's beautiful. With extraordinary views including Lake Washington, Lake Union, Puget Sound, Mount Rainier, and Mount St. Helen's. There are lots of islands in the bay, and lots of pretty ferry rides that even natives enjoy. (They also take picnics and go for hikes.) Seattle is sophisticated. With salmon the unofficial favorite state food, even kids seem to prefer seafood to fast food. It's a city of film connoisseurs. And not because of the rain, either. Movie studios often test their productions here in advance of their release dates because Seattle audiences are open-minded, interested, and appreciative. Their reactions color what the rest of the country views, since post-Seattle editing is not a rarity.

And the people are nice. Just what does that mean? Well, it means people are patient and tolerant and go the extra distance for you, even if they don't know you well. They seem more trusting than the ordinary American. Their hospitality is sincere. Their intentions seem honorable. They'll even humor visitors by taking them to the top of the Space Needle, a relic of the 1962 World's Fair, to dine in the revolving restaurant. (And as they and you know, revolving restaurants don't spin because they're prized for their fine cuisine.)

Most Seattlites live in houses. There are a lot of cozy-looking Victorian homes with nice porches painted in pastel colors. The city is known as one of the most livable in the country. Traffic seems modest, prices are not astronomical, and salmon is plentiful.

Re: the Rain. They say it rains all the time. And while I've seen clouds, most of the times I've visited Seattle the sun has shone, and I've never been there during the summer. I mean *blazing* sunshine, the kind that requires sunglasses indoors, if your hotel room is near the water. I exaggerate not. Winters are pretty gray, I'll grant them that, but the excessive rain may be part of a myth perpetrated by Washingtonians who do not want to fall the way of so many Heathers and Jasons. If they hype the rain, maybe the rest of us will stay away.

Boeing is the city's major employer. Regrettably, they turned down *Going to Work,* so that's all I'll say about them. Seattle is becoming a force in dealings with the Pacific Rim—it's a great port, after all, and local businesses are demonstrating increased awareness, efforts, and expertise in dealing with the challenges of generating joint enterprises with capitalists from the Orient. (This also means there are terrific Oriental restaurants here. Just taste what they can do with salmon.)

BEST NEIGHBORHOOD WITH DECENT PUBLIC SCHOOLS: Laurelhurst

NICEST NEIGHBORHOODS (BUT YOU'LL PROBABLY HAVE TO SEND YOUR KIDS TO PRIVATE SCHOOL): Queen Anne, Magnolia, Washington Park

BEST PLACE TO LIVE IF YOU'RE AN ASPIRING ARTIST OR YOU WANT TO LIVE NEAR PEOPLE WHO WEAR ONLY BLACK: Belltown

BEST NEIGHBORHOOD WITH TAKE-OUT FOOD AND SINGLE PEOPLE WHO ARE ALSO REPUBLICANS: Madison Park

MOST OVERPRICED COMMUNITIES FOR SUMMER HOMES: Decatur Island, Bainbridge Island

BEST PUBLIC SCHOOLS: Mercer Island, Bellevue

BEST PRIVATE SCHOOLS: Lakeside School, Bush School, Forest Ridge School

DEVELOPER WHO HAS MOST INFLUENCED THE CITY'S SKYLINE: Martin Selig

MOST POPULAR RESIDENTIAL ARCHITECTS: Ed Weinstein & Associates, Repass & Fulton

SOCIALLY INCLINED REALTORS: M. Randell (Randell & Associates), J. Brian Losh (Ewing & Clark), Ron Metcalf (Era Metcalf)

DECORATORS WHO WOULD DECORATE HOMES PURCHASED THROUGH THOSE REALTORS: David Weatherford, Sandra Lindsay

DEALERS IN THE FINEST, MOST VALUABLE ART: Foster/White Gallery, Woodside Braseth Gallery

TRENDY GALLERY FOR PEOPLE WHO WEAR ALL BLACK AND HAVE A LOT OF MONEY: Linda Farris Gallery

MOST EXCLUSIVE GOLF CLUB: Seattle Golf Club

BEST PUBLIC GOLF FACILITIES: West Seattle

MOST EXPENSIVE HEALTH CLUB: Washington Athletic Club

BEST HEALTH CLUB FOR MEETING POTENTIAL MATES: Seattle Club (Pike Place Market)

BEST HOTELS FOR BUSINESS TRIPS: Four Seasons Olympic, Westin

BEST HOTELS FOR TRYSTS: Sorrento, Alexis

RESTAURANTS KNOWN FOR BEST CUISINE: Saleh al Lago, Fuller's, Le Gourmand, Cafe Sport, Chez Shea

BEST RESTAURANTS FOR PEOPLE WHO WEAR BLACK: Pink Door, Raison d'Etre

BEST RESTAURANTS FOR AN INEXPENSIVE DATE: Cutter's Bayhouse, Trattoria Michell, Santa Fe Café

NOISIEST RESTAURANTS: F. X. McRory's, Jake O'Shaughnessy's, McCormick's

BEST SPORTS BARS: F. X. McRory's, Jake O'Shaughnessy's, Sneakers

BEST DARK BARS: Sorrento Hotel, Il Bistro, Labuznik

BEST GIMMICKY BARS: Tlaquepaque, Library Bar (Alexis Hotel)

BEST BARS TO IMPRESS A CLIENT: Garden Court (Four Seasons Olympic Hotel), Ray's Boathouse (Shilshole Bay), Columbia Tower Club, Mirabeau

MOST EXCLUSIVE CITY CLUBS: Seattle Tennis Club, Seattle Golf Club

FANCIEST WINE STORES WHENCE CEOS PROBABLY STOCK THEIR OWN CELLARS: Dike & Western, McCarthy & Schiering, De Laurenti, La Cantina

GOURMET STORES GUARANTEED NOT TO RUN OUT OF GOAT CHEESE OR SUN-DRIED TOMATOES: Queen Anne Thriftway, Larry's Market

NICEST MOM-AND-POP GROCERY STORES: Leschi Market, Medina Market

CORPORATE PARTY PLANNER: Gretchen's of Course

HIGH-SOCIETY PARTY PLANNER: Market Place Catering

POWER BARBER: Gene Juarez

NEW WAVE HAIRSTYLISTS: Akio's, Rosalie Cantrell

JUNIOR LEAGUE BEAUTY PARLOR: Gene Juarez, Gary Bocz

PLACE WHERE LADIES WHO LUNCH ARE LIKELY TO HAVE TEA AFTER A HARD DAY OF SHOPPING, VOLUNTEER WORK, AND TENNIS: Four Seasons Olympic Hotel

BEST STORE FOR EXECUTIVE WOMEN: Nordstrom

BEST STORE FOR EXECUTIVE MEN: Nordstrom

BEST STORES FOR DRESS-UP CLOTHES: Helen's of Course, Butch Blum

BEST SHOPPING RESOURCES FOR PEOPLE WHO WEAR ONLY BLACK CLOTHES: Mario's, Zebra Club

DEBUTANTE BALL: Christmas Ball

BUSIEST SOCIAL SEASON OF THE YEAR FOR THOSE WHO CARE ABOUT SUCH THINGS: Spring

SOCIAL HIGHLIGHTS: Poncho Auction, opening day of boating season

MOST RELIABLE FLORISTS: R. David Adams, Robert Hutchison, 45th Street Florist

MOST EXOTIC FLORIST: Pickity Patch

TOP JEWELER FOR RESETTING MOTHER'S EMERALDS: Fox's Gem Shop

MOST COMPLETE BRIDAL REGISTRY: Frederick & Nelson

PROMINENT PHYSICIANS: Dr. Lester Sauvage, Dr. Lawrence Donohue, Dr. Jack Lamey, Dr. Abraham Bergman, Dr. David Karges, Dr. St. Elmo Newton III, Dr. Hugh Toomey, Dr. Ivar Birkland, Dr. Steven Bramwell, Dr. Robert Winquist, Dr. Tate Mason

PROMINENT PLASTIC SURGEONS WITH EQUALLY PROMINENT CLIENTELE: Dr. Alfred Blue, Dr. William Champion

GYNECOLOGIST MOST OFTEN QUOTED IN THE LOCAL PRESS: Dr. Richard Soderstrom

BEST SEAMSTRESS OR TAILOR FOR ALTERATIONS: Nordstrom

POPULAR FACIAL SALON: Gene Juarez

POWER TOOLS

MEN'S POWER DRESSING

BROOKS BROTHERS
1401 Fourth Avenue
Seattle, WA 98101
(206) 624-4400

BEST-SELLING EXECUTIVE SUIT: Three-button, tropical weight, navy, 100 percent wool, $520

POWER SHIRT: Pinpoint button-down, white, 100 percent cotton, $46

POWER TIE: Rep Tie (striped), navy, red, and white, 100 percent silk, $25

POWER WATCHES

WEISFIELD'S
800 South Michigan Street
Seattle, WA 98108
(206) 767-5011

BEST SELLERS AMONG EXECUTIVE MEN: Heuer, $425; two-tone, black with yellow accents, bracelet made of plated stainless steel in black and gold, with day and date.

Longines 1000, $595; yellow gold-plated heavy link bracelet with a rectangular dial, gilt face, "very delicate looking," no day, no date—simple two-hand dial.

BEST SELLERS AMONG EXECUTIVE WOMEN: Michel Herbelin, $195; gold-plated bangle watch, cushion-shaped case with a white Roman numeral dial, bangle of heavy wire, "very elegant, different-looking watch."

Lady's Seiko, $275; very thin yellow gold-plated baguette style with smooth bracelet and faceted edge, gilt-stick dial. "It's been the best-selling lady's Seiko for a considerable period of time, and it stays that way."

"More [executive] men are buying watches for themselves these days, and women, too. Even if they're getting one for a gift, they're involved in the selection process. Especially with men, there's a very high proportion of self-purchase."

"In almost every case, the men are buying a second, third, or fourth watch. The same thing applies to women for slightly different reasons. A woman may want to have a more sophisticated watch for the office or one with diamonds for the evening and also one she can wear for sports. Watch manufacturers are trying to give you a reason to buy another watch and designing different models for various kinds of activities. And they're doing a good job of it —customers are responding."

EXECUTIVE FITNESS

SEATTLE CLUB
2020 Western Avenue
Seattle, WA 98121
(206) 443-1111

The Seattle Club, with arguably among the most comprehensive facilities in the country, offers personal training, aerobics, Nautilus, free weights, a swimming pool, basketball, fencing, karate, a running track, a ski group, seven racquetball and squash courts, softball, a triathalon club, massages, children's programs, physical therapy, two restaurants, conference rooms, laundry service, and a child care center, all for reasonable membership rates. Fees are $500 to join (one-time initiation cost) and $67 per month thereafter. The club, located in downtown Seattle, is "basically a business club," and its executive clientele is comprised of roughly 60 percent men and 40 percent women. We talked to Jacqueline de Jong, who works in marketing at the club.

GIVEN YOUR PREDOMINANTLY EXECUTIVE CLIENTELE, IS NETWORKING ENCOURAGED OR DISCOURAGED?

"It's not discouraged. Although there's no formal networking at the club, a lot of business contacts are made."

HAVE YOU OBSERVED AN INCREASE IN THE NUMBER OF EXECUTIVES WORKING OUT?

"Yes. It makes them much more productive. Before and after work hours are our busiest times."

DO YOUR EXECUTIVE CLIENTS SEEM TO GRAVITATE TOWARD ANY PARTICULAR SERVICES OR ACTIVITIES THE CLUB OFFERS?

"They like convenience and service, which is all-inclusive for no additional fees. But there isn't any particular specialty they enjoy in terms of their workout—they vary."

WHY DO EXECUTIVES CHOOSE YOUR CLUB OVER OTHERS IN TOWN?

"No other club in the Seattle area compares in terms of the personal service and convenience we offer our clients. All snobbishness aside."

BUYING THE EXECUTIVE HOME

ERA METCALF
200 Queen Anne Avenue North
Seattle, WA 98109
(206) 282-0040

We spoke to realtor Kit Richardson.

WHERE DO SEATTLE EXECUTIVES CHOOSE TO LIVE?

"Probably sixty percent of all executives live in the 'burbs, and forty percent in the city. Seattle is an extremely residential city, with the more exclusive, older, and more gracious homes in the Colonial and Tudor styles in the city proper."

WHAT KINDS OF HOMES DO THEY SELECT?

"We find a fairly mixed variety of desired home types. However, there is probably a much greater leaning toward an older, more traditional home. I can sell a Colonial in fifteen minutes, whereas modern homes just don't sell as fast."

ON AVERAGE, HOW MUCH DO EXECUTIVES SPEND FOR THEIR HOMES?

"It depends on where they decide to live." The average prices for brand-new construction are: South Seattle proper, $120,000; mid-level executive homes, $150,000; Bellevue (upper level executives), $300,000. But "prices are definitely going up."

WHAT ARE THEIR PRIORITIES?

"The young executive couple is definitely knowledgeable about what they want. It's what we call a bungalow. It's usually built before 1912, has a front porch, built-in hutches in the dining room, a big kitchen, two bedrooms, one bath, and hardwood floors, on a fifty- by one-hundred-foot lot selling for around $120,000. They are definitely willing to work on a home that may be in less than perfect condition. The older executive is much less willing to move into a less-than-mint-condition home. They want good kitchens and good master baths.

"Executives go for area first and schools second, as they can always (and usually do) send their children to private schools.

"On the whole, the executives want good, consistent, traditional homes. They prefer, for example, traditional and original baths and fittings as opposed to a marble bathroom with sunken jacuzzi tubs. They know what they want and what they don't want. One thing that is very important out here is the emphasis on family things, like skiing (which is one hour away), hiking, and boating and windsurfing on the Puget Sound and lakes Union and Washington."

WHAT ABOUT EXTRA FEATURES LIKE SWIMMING POOLS AND TENNIS COURTS?

"Swimming pools are a definite disadvantage in the Seattle area. We just don't have that much regular solar activity out here. People may say, if there is a pool on the grounds, 'Oh, so that comes with it, too?!' There really aren't many tennis courts, because, again, the weather, and also there's not that much land in the city on which to put one up."

RAINIER
BANCORPORATION

RAINIERBANK®

HISTORY & OPERATIONS

Rainier Bancorporation, the holding company for what used to be the largest independent bank in the state of Washington (until Security Pacific Corporation acquired it in 1987) [see p. 331], was founded in Seattle by Robert Spencer in 1889. Spencer, an ambitious Iowa City banker who was looking for opportunities on the West Coast, researched locations thoroughly before settling on Seattle, which was then undergoing a rapid transformation from a frontier settlement to a thriving world port. Spencer raised $72,500 in Iowa City and returned to Seattle to launch his bank.

Founded in April as the Bank of Commerce of Seattle—a year later it changed to a national charter and became the National Bank of Commerce of Seattle—the bank's first headquarters were in the corner room of a bookstore on Front Street. Though business was off to a favorable start, less than three months after it opened the office was destroyed in the Seattle fire of 1889. The bank's losses were minimal, and two days after the fire, Spencer reopened in a tiny office in a grocery store. Several days later, the bank moved to cramped quarters in a larger building, where it quickly prospered. On the day of the fire, deposits totaled some $60,000; three weeks later, they'd grown to $104,000. In November 1889, seven months after the bank opened, Washington became the country's forty-second state.

Between 1888 and 1892, the number of banks in Seattle tripled. Within the following decade, National Bank of Commerce felt an economic pinch. Deposits shrank, and loans failed. By 1898 the economy was recovering and, by the end of the century, the bank's deposits had grown to $1 million. Not all banks were so prosperous. In the panic of 1903, many of them went out of business.

In 1906 the National Bank of Commerce merged with Washington National Bank. Founded by Manson F. Backus, the son of a New York State banker, only a few weeks after Spencer opened his bank, Washington National was profitable from the outset (although it, too, lost money in the panic of 1903). When the banks merged, Washington National had amassed $5 million in deposits and the National Bank of Commerce had $4 million. Though the merger benefited both banks, Washington National had been forced to vacate its head-quarters and needed to relocate immediately. In his eagerness to finalize the deal, Backus consented to Spencer's stipulation that the bank retain the name National Bank of Commerce. Leadership of the new bank was distributed evenly, with a Commerce executive appointed as honorary chairman, Backus as president, and Spencer and another Commerce executive as co-vice-presidents.

Upon the merger, the National Bank of Commerce became the largest bank in terms of deposits in the Northwest. Though the bank suffered another setback in the panic of 1907, by 1909 deposits had reached a new high of more than $13 million. After the First World War, the bank's growth peaked.

In 1928 an aging Backus sold the bank to financier Andrew Price (Spencer had by then died). Price, the son of an investment banker, began his career in his father's Seattle firm. In 1919 father and son started Marine National Bank, which quickly thrived. But their ambitions for expansion were limited by Washington State's ban on bank branching. In 1923 the Prices founded the Marine National Company as a securities firm and eventually molded it into a holding company for the acquisition of more banks. By 1927 the Marine National Company owned three profitable Seattle institutions. That year, the Prices established the Marine Bancorporation as a larger, public bank holding company with enough capital to make further acquisitions. The National Bank of Commerce, which in 1928 was among the largest banks in the city, was Marine Bancorporation's largest purchase.

Andrew Price expanded his banking concerns on the principle that banks, most of which had built their capital on corporate or wealthy depositors, could cater to the average man with a weekly paycheck and still turn a profit. A vocal advocate of branch banking, he continued to acquire small banks, some of which he merged into the National Bank of Commerce. His strategy, called group banking, was a less efficient precursor of branch banking. By 1930 the Marine Bancorporation was the sixteenth largest banking group in the country. In 1933, when Congress passed the Branch Banking Act as one of the measures to revive the Depression economy, Price converted all of his holding company's units into branches of the National Bank of Commerce and continued to acquire banks in other parts of the state as additional branches. Over the next fifteen years, Price broadened the Marine Bancorporation's activities by launching a consumer loans department, a residential mortgages department, and a trust department.

In 1948 Price, who had been weakened by a severe stroke, resigned as president of the bank and assumed the position of chairman. Maxwell Carlson, who suceeded him as president, carried out the expansion plans Price had put into place. Over the next twenty years, the National Bank of Commerce opened more than seventy new branches, increasing its total number of branches to almost one hundred. Deposits grew from $344 million in 1949 to more than $1 billion in 1969. Carlson also set out to develop foreign business and launched an international department. The bank's most significant foreign dealings were in the Far East, and by 1969 it had a wholly owned subsidiary in Hong Kong with five offices, a full-service bank in London, an office in Tokyo, and an international office in New York. Though still relatively modest in size and stature (it was dwarfed by Seattle's First National Bank, then the largest in Washington), it was one of the most solid and well-managed banks in the state.

In 1973, G. Robert Truex, an executive vice-president of California's Bank of America, was recruited as the chief executive officer of the Marine Bancorporation. Starting in 1974, Truex made dramatic changes. His first move that year, made to give the National Bank of Commerce a more distinct and unified image, was to rename both the bank and its holding company Rainier—after Mt. Rainier, a 14,410-foot-high dormant volcano that towers over Seattle. Truex then replaced many of the bank's top executives. He transformed the bank's by-then obsolete branch management system, replacing the administrative hierarchies at each branch with centralized offices that handle most of the bank's administrative needs. He inaugurated a program of personalized service, assigning a "personal banker" to every several hundred customers. He substantially increased the bank's corporate activities, encouraging staffers to hit the streets and attract midsized companies as customers. And Truex renewed emphasis on foreign expansion, primarily in the prosperous Far East.

By the mid-1980s, Rainier was the fourth largest American bank operating in Asia. With steadily increasing assets and profits, a network of 140 branches in Washington and Oregon, and business relationships with more than half the households in Washington—the second largest banking state west of Texas—Rainier had become the largest bank in Washington and one of the foremost financial institutions in the Pacific Northwest. By the end of 1986, its assets had grown to $9.2 billion, as compared to $2.7 billion when Truex took over.

In 1986 earnings reached $70 million, and the bank had six thousand employees. Its holdings included "three commercial banks, a state savings bank, and a mortgage company in 234 locations in 8 Western States, as well as 20 international offices in 9 countries concentrated around in the Pacific Rim."

In February 1987, in one of the biggest mergers in banking history, Los Angeles-based Security Pacific Corporation, the sixth largest bank holding company in the country, announced that it had agreed to acquire Rainier Bancorporation for $1.15 billion. In July of the same year, Robert Truex stepped down as chairman and CEO of Rainier Bancorporation, relinquishing the post to John D. Mangels, who joined the bank in 1950 and had risen through the ranks to become the corporation's president. (Truex, at sixty-four, remains chairman of Rainier's executive committee and became a member of Security Pacific's board of directors.) The merger with Security Pacific was finalized on August 31. Though Rainier's assets were added to Security Pacific's, the bank's name, identity, and board of directors remain in place.

After the merger with Security Pacific, Rainier Bancorporation determined that it could serve both its international customers and those outside of Washington State as efficiently, if not better, through Security Pacific offices. Accordingly, it sold or consolidated many of its operations in Asia and the western states in order to refocus its resources on the Pacific Northwest. At present, Rainier National Bank, the holding company's largest subsidiary, is Washington State's second largest commercial bank, with 141 offices throughout the state. Its other principal subsidiaries include Oregon Bank, based in Portland, with 56 offices in the western part of the state; United Bank, based in Tacoma, Washington, with 16 offices in Tacoma and Pierce County; Rainier Bank Alaska, N.A., with 5 offices in Anchorage; and Rainier Brokerage Services, a Seattle-based discount brokerage company licensed in Washington, Oregon, and Alaska. Rainier and its subsidiaries have approximately 5,100 employees, with 4,800 employed by Rainier and 300 employed by its other subsidiary companies.

(Information provided by David Jepsen, bank spokesperson.)

ASSETS: $9.2 billion as of December 31, 1987.

EARNINGS: $55.3 million in 1987.

INITIAL PUBLIC OFFERING: The bank has been public since 1927.

NUMBER OF SHAREHOLDERS: 6,676 as of June 30, 1987 (before the finalization of its merger with Security Pacific). Since the merger, Security Pacific is the sole shareholder.

OFFICES: 219 total. Rainier National Bank has 141 offices, Oregon Bank has 56 offices, United Bank has 16 offices, Rainier Bank Alaska, N.A., has 5, and Rainier Brokerage Services has 1 office.

NUMBER OF EMPLOYEES: Approximately 5,100, with 4,800 employed by Rainier Bancorporation and its subsidiary Rainier Bank, and 300 employed by the holding company's other subsidiaries.

AVERAGE AGE OF EMPLOYEES: Thirty-six.

TURNOVER: 22.4 percent per year.

RECRUITMENT: No formal program. "Educational backgrounds differ with each position. The most attractive job applicants have relevant work experience, coupled with an applicable educational background."

NUMBER OF NEW HIRES PER YEAR: About 700.

RANGE OF STARTING SALARIES: $5–$9 per hour.

POLICY FOR RAISES: "The rate of pay of all employees is examined annually to determine whether an adjustment is necessary. Every employee's salary is reviewed eleven months from the last salary action, with any adjustment being made in the following month. Salary adjustments are initiated after considering employee performance; salary budget; salaries of other employees in comparable positions; minimum starting salary for the pay range; employee's position in the pay range; salary growth for the employee; and reason for the change, such as promotion or lateral transfer. Certain positions at Rainier are incentive-eligible, based on market pay practices. Being included in an incentive plan is not a guarantee an employee will receive an incentive award. It simply allows an employee an opportunity to earn one. Incentive plans are designed at the division level as another way to meet division business goals. A plan may be based on individual, department, or division performance."

TRAINING PROGRAMS: One formal program, called the Credit Training Program. It lasts sixteen to eighteen months and "provides selected employees with the technical expertise necessary for transaction of personal loans, loans to small and medium businesses, domestic and international loans."

BENEFITS: "Rainier provides a comprehensive package of benefits for its employees. For most plans, Rainier pays the full cost of employee coverage. The package contains medical, dental, life insurance, long-term disability insurance, personal accident insurance, business travel accident insurance, pension plan and a 401k thrift plan."

VACATION: "Vacation length is determined by the vacation policy in effect when the employee was hired or by the present vacation policy, whichever is more advantageous to the employee. All full-time and part-time fixed employees scheduled to work at least twenty hours per week are eligible for vacation pay. Eligible employees begin to accrue vacation time when hired, but vacation is not actually earned until twelve months of continuous employment are completed. Vacation scheduling is done through supervisors. One float day is allowed each year to full-time and part-time employees scheduled to work twenty or more hours per week. The purpose is to accommodate personal and religious needs of employees. The company recognizes ten holidays per year, with minor variations based on locally recognized holidays."

ADDITIONAL PERKS: "Rainier supports participation in the American Institute of Banking (AIB) and other well-known banking schools and executive development programs. A tuition reimbursement program helps employees reach their goals for higher education."

BONUSES: "Rainier offers bonuses, as well as incentive plans and commissions based on measurable operations by a variety of people in a multitude of positions. Bonuses are based on a variety of ingredients. The most heavily weighted is performance."

ANNUAL PARTY: "Many divisions and offices host annual parties at various times throughout the year."

AVERAGE WORKDAY: "Most of us full-time staff people work from 8:00 A.M. to 5:00 P.M. However, exempt personnel—those who are not paid hourly—are expected to get their job done. If it can't be done between 8:00 and 5:00, people will work longer hours. If you come in at around 7:00 in the morning or 6:00 at night, you'll find people around. But not much before or after that."

DRESS CODE: "Dress varies between divisions and offices, but is generally semiformal to formal corporate attire."

SOCIAL ATMOSPHERE: "Rainier Bank has been characterized by other writers as 'Nepotism City.' Many employees and their spouses work at Rainier Bank. There is an informal, family atmosphere at most offices. Most senior officers, for example, prefer to be called by their first names. These working relationships extend after working hours, in many cases. However, the days of heavy drinking in local watering holes after work disappeared with today's increased concern for drinking and driving, and with the competitive pressures of a deregulated environment."

HEADQUARTERS: "Rainier Bancorporation is headquartered principally in Rainier Bank Tower designed by Minoru Yamasaki. Other locations housing Rainier staff functions include One Union Square building, Second and Spring building, and the Logan Building. Last year, Rainier added an East Side headquarters, Rainier Bank Plaza, in downtown Bellevue, Washington.

"All domestic facilities of Rainier and company-owned vehicles became smoke-free on October 1, 1986. The company is committed to a healthful and comfortable environment for all employees. The smoking policy has been developed because research identifies the negative health effects of tobacco smoke and the growing concern of employees regarding smoke in the workplace."

CHARITABLE CONTRIBUTIONS: $1,808,000 in 1987. $510,000 went to education, $435,000 went to United Way, $433,000 went to the arts, $256,000 went to civic groups, $133,000 to human services, and $41,000 to special projects. Furthermore, "Rainier encourages financial contributions to charitable organizations and educational institutions by matching employee gifts of $25 to $100."

INTERESTED APPLICANTS CAN SEND RÉSUMÉS TO:
Rainier Bank
P.O. Box 3966, NO5-4
Seattle, WA 98124
(206) 621-4111

Seattle is a friendly city, and Rainier Bancorporation is a friendly company. As simple as that. The bank prizes what it calls "relationship banking," which means exactly what you might think, and its customers around the state appear to have close ties to the institution. Bruce Emry, vice-president and manager of corporate communications, says, "Washingtonians' perception of the bank is that it's socially involved and a good corporate citizen." He adds, "That's part of our corporate culture. Our health is derived from the health of our community." The payoff—sorry to be so crude—is that "we have at least one relationship with fifty percent of the families in the state."

Oak Kaarma, a native of South Korea, moved to Seattle when her husband was transferred here for his work in the Department of Defense. "I read about Rainier in 1977 in a nice article in *The Wall Street Journal,* and I applied. About twelve years ago they opened a management training position for women and minorities; that's how I got in. I do not have an MBA." Petite and soft-spoken, Kaarma is a vice-president in the International Marketing Group.

"It seems people really cared about people. I cannot think of any boss who didn't. I went beyond my work and was very appreciated. I think that's what motivates me, too—being appreciated." Which is manifested in Oak's raises and being sent off to seminars. She feels she counts. She says the caring comes from the top down. "People look up to the leader. Very much."

In case she has any doubts about her progress, Oak is reviewed every year around the anniversary of her start date. "It's not scary. I'm looking forward to it. My boss is open. I haven't managed anyone, so I don't review people. Thank God," she says with a laugh.

She's tired today because one of her two children has been ill with pneumonia and seizures. Luckily, her mother-in-law lives with the Kaarmas and cares for her kids. ("We get stress from her, but the benefit is greater. She's always right.) If I were more powerful, I'd arrange for day care." Just talking about being powerful is an indication of how profoundly Oak's life has changed in the last two decades. In Korea, she studied pharmacy and chemistry. "I never imagined myself as an executive; I didn't like Korea's way of treating women. The chauvinism makes me boil. My feelings are stronger than even the average American woman." She joined the Seattle Women's Network, which has a lot of banker members. "We try to help each other."

Oak has a new identity. "I take pride in working here. In a way, I'm a big American banker," she says wryly. She must travel to the Pacific Rim for her work. It reminds her of how far she's come, from a culture in which she was supposed to be subservient. "Asian stewardesses treat Asian women so badly. It's the worst thing about travel." Plus, "You fight with credit people, etc. It's hard work. You must be physically strong to travel overseas." One thing Kaarma has noticed is that titles matter outside the bank more than they do within Rainier. "Especially with Asians. They're very impressed with titles. They'd rather deal with people they perceive as powerful."

Her life is one of "lots of coping. My boss comes in at 7:30 and leaves at 7:30, and takes work home. I arrive at 8:30 and leave at 6:30. I take work home and don't touch it. In the last few years I've tried to turn it off [at the end of the day]. I get home at seven o'clock and teach my son piano lessons every evening. My family demands me. My work demands me." Oak's resolution: "This is a lifetime career. I would like to see myself retiring from Rainier."

Joe Zavaglia is a senior vice-president and deputy group manager, headquartered in suburban Bellevue—"more lower buildings and more sprawl than Seattle, less pedestrian traffic, more corporate parks, lots of start-up businesses." He's a comer. He was thirty-seven when we met—the kind of thirty-seven that's really a grown-up. In order to make Rainier the bank of first choice among the community's entrepreneurs, he inaugurated the Business Networking Breakfasts, held every month since October 1985 at the Bellevue Red Lion. "I saw people here were excited," he says. "My people came up with ideas, and I made it okay with our superiors. There was little financial risk, so I got approval. Customers said this market is growing so fast, it's hard to keep track of it. We've expanded our contacts."

The breakfast was Joe's baby. [Note: As of February 1987, however, a local business journal assumed responsibility for the get-togethers.] He offered the typical breakfast agenda. "People arrive at six-thirty A.M. From seven to seven-forty, people set up displays and network. At seven-forty-five they enter the eating area. People go around tables of ten and introduce themselves. They eat for twenty minutes. Then we introduce the businessperson of the month —a small businessman, local customer. Then a guest speaker. It's over by nine A.M." Some of the speakers Joe had been able to attract—there's no fee—were a Seattle Seahawk, the president of Evergreen College, a former CEO of a local company, and a vice-president of Rainier Bank.

The popularity of the breakfasts was accomplished through word of mouth. Rainier charged $12.50 admission, which allowed them to break even. The attendees were "the affluent yuppie —thirty-five to forty-five, the next generation of movers and shakers. We got direct, measurable results. People say, 'Thank you, Rainier.' "

Zavaglia had been the director of training and public relations for a not-for-profit educational institution in the western part of the state. He finished graduate school in June 1973. "I decided to get married, but I couldn't support a wife and family on my salary. I interviewed at Rainier."

In August 1975 he became a career development trainee in the bank's one-year branch manager training program, which concentrates on operational functions. "Being a banker scared the hell out of me. I had to wear a suit. It was very structured and formal. Banking used to attract number crunchers. What scared me the most was, it did not seem an innovative environment." Since he finished his training two months early, he floated around for a while before being assigned, in September 1976, to Aurora Village, as an assistant operations supervisor. "The bank has a policy that you have to have a job for eighteen months (if you're exempt [nonhourly]) in order to move on to the next. To show staying power. After eleven months, they made me supervisor."

In June 1979, Zavaglia applied for a job as a personnel administrator for branch banking. "When I did, everyone said I never had a prayer. Generally, an employee must provide initiative in order to change. Otherwise, people will keep the same job for years, as long as they're performing. Rainier seems people-oriented and pays people for performance. So if you do a good job, you'll be rewarded." The next step for Joe after personnel administrator was as assistant district manager, traveling three out of every five days to his twenty-six branches. In March 1983 he was promoted to manager of the Mercer Island district—a high-priced neighborhood where many of Rainier's senior people live. "The per capita income is $60,000 plus," Joe says.

"Seafirst [Seattle's biggest bank] was our prime competitor there, but we overturned them. We grew by a million dollars a month in deposits." Joe knew people including the pastor on Mercer Island. It was comfortable for him. He had an open house called "Customer Appreciation Day." The climax was a raffle to win $500 or the bank manager for the day. "I ended up cooking an Italian dinner for an older couple—a customer and his wife. I made fettucini, homemade meatballs, we had wine, et cetera, in the branch kitchen.

"We created an image. Plus we advertised in the newspaper. We wanted to have fun and be professional."

The eighteen-month promotion rule always seemed to be bent for Joe. He got his next job fifteen months later, and the next [the job he had when we met] four months after that. "People have always been good to me, waiving the time in job requirement. My father's advice was, 'Make the person you work for look good. He will make you look good.' I'm a pretty competitive person, but I have never been treated so well by people I work with. There's a high degree of loyalty. Being opportunistic, I saw opportunities to do things."

When Zavaglia received his ten-year pin, he felt "it was a real honor for me. I've never felt more appreciated. People want to take care of me to make sure I'm happy."

Talking to Joe makes you realize that banking these days means peddling products. An aggressive salesman, he says, "The eighties and I were made for each other. 'What do I have to do to get your business?' " is the question he notices himself asking strangers most often. "In January 1986 I got the largest account from the largest law firm on the East Side [where the affluent live and work]. They perceived themselves as the most successful, and they perceived us as a moving force.

"If we have to work till midnight, we'll do it. We gave them a better rate. The services we can offer are the same as other banks. It's the people who make the difference. If you know me and have a problem, I'll do whatever I can to do something. It's service. It's trust."

It must be evident by now that Zavaglia is a zealous adherent. The son of a lifelong employee of Boeing, he places a great deal of value in being of value to a major organization himself. "My wildest fantasy? Being division manager. It's not a frightening thought. It's at least three to five years down the road." He was the student government president in high school. "I keep looking at the quality-of-life issue. I have five kids. Financial resources I never worry about. I don't focus on the money we've got. I appreciate it." He rises every day at five for "alone time. I read, eat, and get my head together." He returns home at 7:00 P.M., spends thirty to forty-five minutes with his children, then spends time with his wife. "I make time. On days when I feel I can't take it, I leave, I flush my brain. I work at home, I visit customers —do something different. I used to have guilt feelings—I'd screwed the bank out of two hours—but I'm more effective afterward."

It seems that everyone at Rainier is grateful to the bank for treating them well. "They've been good to me" is the attitude of Joe Scott, a personal banking officer at the Kent branch. A Nutmegger (he's from Connecticut), Joe fell in love with Washington while on vacation, when he was working at Connecticut Bank & Trust. "I talked to people and heard good things about Rainier. I decided this was where I wanted to work. I interviewed and heard 'yes' two months later." We met when he'd been out here only a year and a half. Due to the cultural differences between the Northeast and the Pacific Northwest, not knowing too many people here before he arrived, and, as a black man, being in a much more stark minority, Scott still considered himself "new."

"Being new is tough. East is faster, more aggressive. It's slower and more laid back here. Customers say, 'Slow down!' I went back East, and I knew it wasn't right. The sky wasn't as blue, and there were no mountains. I really do enjoy it. It's not the pay, it's the people. (And it's just a little cheaper to live out here.)" Okay, if Joe has to have any misgivings about moving across the country, it's because "I do miss the U.S. Open."

His favorite part of the job is soliciting new customers. "Every Wednesday I stop in the office in the morning and then hit the streets. I knock on doors of businesses. I like cold calls —no appointments. I say, 'Hi, I'm Joseph Scott from Rainier.' For every ten calls, I really get thirty percent. I try to develop a rapport over sports." He calls knowing how to read potential customers " 'banking sense.' You don't want to pester them. I'll take 'em out to lunch if it's near a closing. We have budget restrictions.

"I don't compete; I create. I don't take accounts from other branches. Or branch officers. A highlight of my day is to open an account on *another bank's* checks." Joe reinforces the service culture explained by Joe Zavaglia. "We're not giving out toasters or cars. People want access to their banker."

Scott spends a lot of time thinking about his existing customers, too. "Roughly eighty percent of our deposits come from twenty percent of our customers. They don't come in every day. They're not worriers. I contact them more than they contact me. I keep the date they came in, their account number, and their birthdays on file."

A lot of Joe's time is spent in making—"booking"—loans. "I like to loan money. The first loan I ever booked went bad—but you learn something from it. Bankers take risks. Any bozo can book a good loan. You try not to be sympathetic one way or the other. This isn't the 'Scott Bank & Trust,' it's Rainier Bank & Trust. It doesn't hurt to say no."

By all accounts, Joe Scott is doing very well at Rainier. "I could never do the things I've done without the support of the tellers and staff. But my customers pay my salary; I'm there when they need me."

Dinner tonight is at the Mercer Island home of John and Joan Christofferson. He is the heir apparent to the reins of Rainier Bancorporation, serving as the vice-chairman. (Soon after my visit, he was made president. He was forty-five years old.) Their house is decorated with art collected on various job tours of duty around the world, especially from the Orient. Don and Linda Summers are here, too. He is the senior vice-president and manager of personnel administration for the corporation.

"The best way to differentiate between Rainier and other banks is through values," they say. "Our top managers have communicated values, better than most companies'. How people are treated sends out a clear message. This is a fine group of people—successful and well meaning." Both John and Don credit G. Robert Truex, Jr., with creating this message and concretizing the value system. [He stepped down as CEO on July 16, 1987 after fourteen years in that position, but he is still the chairman of Rainier's Executive Committee.] "Truex is sincerely interested in the people who work here. He does things that are gracious. There's loyalty to Rainier because of what he represents. He puts himself out so you put yourself out. The only leadership style worth following is example."

n his large and memento-studded office, Bob Truex serves coffee before his interview. During the three or four days I was in Seattle with Rainier before our meeting, everyone wanted to know whether I would be introduced to their CEO. When I answered affirmatively, everyone said, "You'll love him; he's great!" He certainly was easy to talk to, with a self-deprecating sense of humor. A native New Jerseyan and Rutgers graduate, he firmly feels Seattle is his home. Before coming to the Northwest he was in the number two slot at Bank of America and before that at Irving Trust in New York City.

"I'm unconvinced I have a management style," he laughs. "I had someone poll everyone to find out what that is. I don't consciously employ one. I don't take myself too terribly seriously. I don't want people to bow down. I make my own phone calls. I believe in the Golden Rule.

"As a young man in banking, at Irving Trust, I was terrified of the CEO. I'm not going to let that happen to me. I overuse consensus," he volunteers, "to the point where I could be called indecisive. Sometimes I don't make decisions because it's not time for them. Occasionally you feel against the wall and it's up to you, but not a lot." Truex prizes employees he considers smarter than himself, and he gives them credit for their ideas and work. "Bright people adapt quickly. They can conceptualize."

Like Truex himself, many bankers at Rainier are the products of other institutions. "We don't have a corporate culture because people come from everywhere. Almost all senior people came from elsewhere." New employees joining at "a fairly high level" get evaluated by a psychologist who spends two days a month at headquarters. "Most of the people on this floor" —and an opulent executive floor it is—"score higher than I do."

He may deny he's left a strong imprint, but Truex allows tidbits to trickle out that sound to me like a management style or corporate culture—call it what you want. "Everyone wants to be remembered, but it's not my goal to make my mark. I'm not striving to be the biggest, just the best. I know it sounds trite. We try to be among the top statistical performers. We try to do better each year. There're no three, five-, ten-year plans; just year to year. 'Strategic plans' are gobbledygook in a leather binder that no one will read. Things happen too fast to abide by long-range plans." His proudest achievement is the bank's growth since his arrival. "Twelve years ago Rainier Bank's total worth was fifty million dollars. Today it's up to seven hundred million." [At press time, the bank's total worth is $932 million.] "I believe there's no essential conflict between the bottom line and people. If you do the right thing, it'll be reflected in earnings. I believe with all my heart that if you do that for stockholders, you're doing right. I believe corporations are pieces of paper chartered to do business. And the public can technically withdraw our charter. I don't know; I'm no different from any other CEO. You pray all month that your P and L statement will be good."

The bank Truex moved to Seattle to run was called the National Bank of Commerce. In a *New York Times* article (August 22, 1976), he was quoted as saying, " 'I wasn't keen on the name . . .' It didn't have the pizzazz, the marketability that a modern bank needed. Also, eighteen other banks carried similar names, and 'people who wanted to buy our stock were confused.' " Truex hired a corporate identity consultant who helped him select Rainier after the volcano outside Seattle.

With Truex at the helm, Rainier also became a first-name operation internally. "It used to be a real stuffed-shirt place. The former CEO—he still calls me 'Mr. Truex.' I've been criticized about our generosity toward fires. Outside the ground rules of personnel, I've paid people for up to two years after they were let go. I try not to be a zealot or a preacher. I think the word 'values' is a turn-off."

Once again I will dispute Truex's self-proclaimed passivity and cite his introduction of the Social Policy Committee. His influence has made Rainier a philanthropic corporation. "We do what we reasonably can. We hope others will follow our example, and we hope it works."

Rainier gives generously to education, to the United Way, to the arts, and to other charities. "It's unselfish, but selfish. We can't just give away stockholders' money without some benefit."

We discussed the subject of takeovers. He seemed only mildly interested. "Most bank takeovers are of bad, unhealthy banks." In other words, he was not interested in buying another bank himself. "We don't want to buy used cars." As a takeover target his view was, "The best protective device to ward off takeovers is to become expensive to buy. We have people—domestic and foreign—who play footsie with us. Our price would be one billion dollars. That's a big bite."

Indeed, on July 14, 1987, the shareholders of Rainier Bank voted to accept Security Pacific Corporation's merger offer (see p. 331). And, in fact, the deal was for $1.150 billion. Months after the merger went into effect, Joe Zavaglia said the outright signs of change were minimal. "The main difference for the average employee working for Rainier—and that could be upper management or middle management or a teller—is a feeling that you have a real supporter there in Los Angeles. There's a sense of excitement at the bank right now and an eagerness to prove to Security Pacific that they made a good decision in buying us."

On a day-to-day basis, "most employees do not feel the Security Pacific presence. Management decisions for Rainier are still being made in Seattle, not in Los Angeles." And the only differences noticed by customers are in the increased number of products now available to them.

How about this unsolicited encomium? "When people compare pre-Truex Rainier Bank to post-Truex Rainier Bank, it's a 360-degree change. It used to be a 'bank.' It's almost like two different institutions. There's a momentum going already. Too many people feel good about it. At the managers' meeting in '83 or '84, they gave Truex a fifteen-minute standing ovation. He never took credit himself for leadership. He's almost like Gandhi in India. Truex issues magic. The leaders he has put in place have pulled the organization together. He has a huge impact. The image he projects in the community is one of a maverick, not fitting in with the status quo. I like that; I relate to it. Most bankers would drive a Cadillac. He drives a Jaguar. Truex is a wool man with wild ties. He's phenomenal with names." This from Wally Webster.

Webster adds, "In 1977, I never thought I'd work in a bank in 1978!" Lured away from Boeing, Washington's single largest private sector employer, he was hired to be the director of Rainier's equal opportunity program. "Attracting minorities to Rainier was difficult. No doubt about it. Because of the industry, especially." Not to mention that the black population of Seattle hovers between 9 and 11 percent. At first he felt "affirmative action was like a body extremity at Rainier: not necessary. (I decided after our goals were achieved I'd like to be part of the heart or lungs.) Once we got a person here, it was not difficult to keep them here. I could convince them to stay with Rainier, even if it was raining." He once recruited an assistant vice-president from Chase Manhattan [see p. 447], a coup in his eyes. "We don't try to compare Seattle to New York. We emphasize Seattle and the outdoors, the recreational aspects. It's a good environment to raise children in.

"I experienced an excellent attitude toward affirmative action and minorities. It was the attitude of senior management. I used to meet with [then president, now CEO] John Mangels every two weeks as scheduled, and often *more*.

"I enjoyed Boeing. Leaving it was tough." He was introduced to Rainier through a headhunter. "I agreed to interview as a courtesy. I was going from a broad responsibility at Boeing to a narrow responsibility here." After two years in equal opportunity, however, Webster "went on the fast track program to become a retail branch manager for a couple of years, and then to a commercial branch." When we met, he was a group administrative officer for the Metropolitan Group with a jurisdiction over 76–79 branches in the greater Seattle area, spanning 100 miles from Tacoma to Marysville.

After ten years at Rainier, Wally characterizes the corporation as "a risk taker, self-confident. An organization that rewards. The culture of the organization allows you to make a mistake—with prudence. It's not fatal. It's reinforced by your peers. I can be creative in this organization. Since this organization isn't that big, you can feel the CEO's personality. It truly permeates. I feel it. Even low down, you can hear the unique footsteps of Bob Truex."

Webster's dream is "the ability to influence, and the power that goes along with that. Being involved in decision making. I do have a big ego, but it's under control. That's what brought me to Rainier Bank, and that's what could take me away. Pride of ownership would take me away.

"Staying here the next ten to twenty years is certainly my plan at the present time." Wally is now a vice-president and manager, Employee Loan Center. "Rainier Bank is a very fair organization. Rainier Bank has been very good to me." If you think he's a one-man guy, listen to this. "John Mangels has impressed me the most. He's the most humane person of any at the top. He puts human values above money."

Frances Evans has spent her entire real world time at Rainier. "I've been here sixteen years, straight from college." She was an anthropology major, and recognized "in the seventies having a business degree or MBA became pretty important. The culture changed. We went from being a bank to being a financial institution. Truex came in." She enrolled in a nighttime MBA program "to give me an edge in image—it's a problem for women. I wanted the credential. I wanted to feel, for myself, more legitimate. If *I* see two people equally right in terms of personality traits and one has a business background, that's the person I'll hire. I found that myself in competing with my peers."

On the other hand, she says, "I think we think of performance, not male, female, et cetera. What really counts is how much you can contribute to the bank, increasingly. The best thing is to ignore [gender] and do a good job. The few people who focus on it, people want to avoid. They're making too big a deal. We don't have too many women in senior management, but they don't have enough years' experience.

"I only stayed at the bank because it *has* changed," she says, whereas "I only came here because I got a job here." Frances took a career aptitude test and found she was well suited to the industry.

"I hadn't really selected a job; I'd chosen a senior management. I had a future here if senior management made the right decisions. I identify with the senior management of this company. I believe we have integrity. A corporation is a tough place to be—you must have a return for your stockholders. And yet, we have a value system here. As long as I can continue to grow, I'll stay here. I don't know—the allure of doing my own thing is very strong."

The challenge Evans faces now as a vice-president and manager of investment portfolio is managing an investment portfolio of $887 million. She says the securities side of Rainier is fun and "really separate from the bank. I think I love the business first and the bank second. Our time is coming."

At work, Frances has noticed "I'm really a very competitive person by nature." And ambitious. But her elementary school–aged daughter is the primary source of her pleasure. "She comes first. My family is the most important thing. If you're happy at home, you can conquer the world. My husband is supportive and proud of me." Evans's husband, the president of a manufacturing company, "gets our daughter ready in the morning. He can do pigtails and braids, he does all the shopping and cooking. I have to be at work at six A.M. I really want to make my own contribution in how I raise my child. What happens is that you don't have time for yourself. Big deal. That won't last forever. I couldn't commit to making my career a bigger part of my life for the next few years, because of our daughter.

"You have to know your limitations. Saying 'no' takes finesse. No company can afford to lose a good employee. The worst I could do would be to take on too much and fail. I don't want to fail. I like this company."

1. **COVINGTON & BURLING**
   1201 Pennsylvania
   Avenue, N.W.

2. **GANNETT CO.**
   1100 Wilson Boulevard
   Arlington

3. **MCI COMMUNICATIONS
   CORPORATION**
   1133 19th Street, N.W.

4. **BROOKS BROTHERS**
   1840 L Street, N.W.

5. **URI & ASSOCIATES**
   3109 M Street, N.W.

6. **MAISON BLANCHE**
   1725 F Street, N.W.

7. **THE WATERGATE HOTEL**
   2650 Virginia Avenue, N.W.

8. **THE JOCKEY CLUB**
   2100 Massachusetts
   Avenue, N.W.

9. **THE CAPITOL**

10. **THE WHITE HOUSE**

WASHINGTON, D.C.

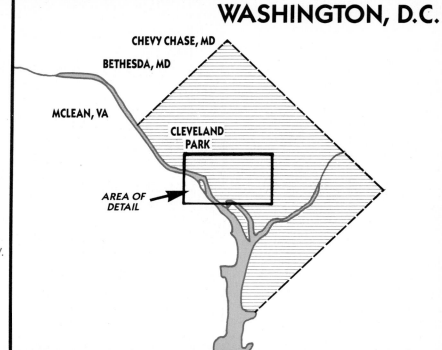

CHEVY CHASE, MD

BETHESDA, MD

MCLEAN, VA

CLEVELAND PARK

AREA OF DETAIL

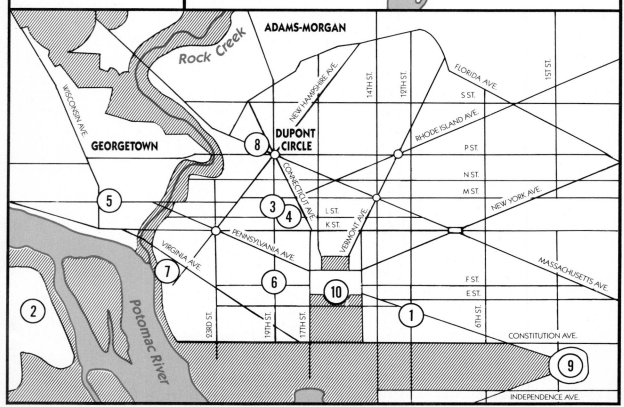

Rock Creek

ADAMS-MORGAN

NEW HAMPSHIRE AVE.

14TH ST.

12TH ST.

FLORIDA AVE.

1ST ST.

S ST.

RHODE ISLAND AVE.

P ST.

WISCONSIN AVE.

GEORGETOWN

DUPONT CIRCLE

CONNECTICUT AVE.

N ST.

M ST.

NEW YORK AVE.

L ST.

K ST.

VERMONT AVE.

PENNSYLVANIA AVE.

VIRGINIA AVE.

MASSACHUSETTS AVE.

F ST.

E ST.

Potomac River

23RD ST.

19TH ST.

17TH ST.

6TH ST.

CONSTITUTION AVE.

INDEPENDENCE AVE.

WASHINGTON, D.C.

WASHINGTON, D.C.

Washington cannot be considered a corporate city unless you think of the federal government as one huge, bureaucratic organization. With zillions of students on internships throughout the year, D.C. also is a gigantic university campus. Either you're a lawyer or a poli. sci. major, or you're in a service business catering to the same. Okay; you're not a lawyer. But you did take your LSATs. Or you're studying for them. Look, you knew this would be biased.

If you are indeed an attorney, there are tons of options for you: law firms (Washington's largest, Covington & Burling, is just pages away), any federal agency, congressman's staff, or law school faculty. For the rest of you who just want to live near limestone buildings, the Potomac, or Larry King, two of the capital's leading civilian businessess are included in this chapter: Gannett and MCI. (Marriott is also based here.) True, most major (*Fortune* 500) corporations maintain representatives here who lobby Capitol Hill, but life in D.C. and its suburbs is about the news of the day. And with the exception of MCI chief Bill McGowan's recovery from a serious heart attack and *USA Today*'s ascent to profitability, corporate news rarely gets national coverage.

There are enough Washingtons to satisfy several consituencies. Georgetown is charming, seriously expensive, and trendy beyond belief. Try that new pesto gelato? Got enough cotton sweaters? Satisfy yourself in Georgetown. Need groceries? You better dress up. If it's warm, put on your school crest—adorned running shorts or T-shirt and wander the aisles of the "Social Safeway" on Wisconsin Avenue and see who you can meet. In inclement weather, go in your business clothes but comb your hair first. Every night is singles night! Find a soulmate and then walk hand in hand along the avenue, as all the other couples who look like you are doing. Can't afford G'town? Try Dupont Circle. But hurry! Prices are getting steep. If you've already won the social sweepstakes (it's said that there are six women in the metropolitan area for every man) and found a mate, then you're probably ready to move to the suburbs. Bethesda and Chevy Chase are the wealthiest in Maryland; McLean and Old Towne Alexandria in Virginia are nice. (Old Towne has its own Safeway—less active than Georgetown's, but worth a visit.)

As any city filled to the brim with recent college grads, D.C. cultural hotspots are in heavy use. People go to museums and national monuments with a vengeance, even if they've already lived here a year. They drink in the culture in earnest and score a notch for every event or exhibit they've witnessed. They've got to hurry; many move here knowing it won't be for long.

If you are at all affiliated with politics, the average length of residency in Washington is brief—unless you were raised here or have a visible media job. People feel like old-timers after two or three years and like dinosaurs after the current administration ends. It is truly a city of transients with rapid personality changes determined by each successive head vagrant, the President of the United States.

BEST NEIGHBORHOODS WITH DECENT PUBLIC SCHOOLS: Bethesda, (Maryland), McLean, (Virginia)

NICEST NEIGHBORHOODS (BUT YOU'LL PROBABLY HAVE TO SEND YOUR KIDS TO PRIVATE SCHOOL): Georgetown, Cleveland Park

BEST PLACES TO LIVE IF YOU'RE AN ASPIRING ARTIST OR YOU WANT TO LIVE NEAR PEOPLE WHO WEAR ONLY BLACK: Adams-Morgan, Dupont Circle

BEST NEIGHBORHOOD WITH TAKE-OUT FOOD AND SINGLE PEOPLE WHO ARE ALSO REPUBLICANS: Georgetown

MOST OVERPRICED COMMUNITIES FOR SUMMER HOMES: Locally: Middleburg (Virginia) and the Eastern Shore (Maryland); but most "in" Washingtonians still head for Martha's Vineyard

BEST PUBLIC SCHOOLS: Walt Whitman High School (Maryland), Langley High School (Virginia)

BEST PRIVATE SCHOOLS: Landon, St. Albans (for boys), Cathedral (for girls), Sidwell Friends (for Quakers and Jews)

BEST ALTERNATIVE SCHOOLS: Georgetown Day, Edmond Burke

LIVING ARCHITECT WHO HAS MOST INFLUENCED THE CITY'S SKYLINE: I. M. Pei (e.g., east wing of the National Gallery)

DEAD ARCHITECT WHO HAS MOST INFLUENCED THE CITY'S SKYLINE: Pierre L'Enfant ("He was the architect of the U.S. Capitol—what could be more important?")

MOST POPULAR RESIDENTIAL ARCHITECTS: Dunn & Brady

SOCIALLY INCLINED REALTOR: Michael Sullivan

DECORATOR WHO WOULD DECORATE HOMES PURCHASED THROUGH THAT REALTOR: Diane Doswell

DEALER IN THE FINEST, MOST VALUABLE ART: Lacy Neuhaus

TRENDY GALLERIES FOR PEOPLE WHO WEAR ALL BLACK AND HAVE A LOT OF MONEY: Neuhaus Collection, Wallace-Wentworth

MOST EXCLUSIVE GOLF CLUBS: Burning Tree Country Club, Congressional Country Club

BEST PUBLIC GOLF FACILITIES: "D.C. is the worst place in the country for public golf facilities"

MOST EXPENSIVE HEALTH CLUB: McLean Racquet and Health Club

BEST HEALTH CLUB FOR MEETING POTENTIAL MATES: The new YMCA to meet men; Somebodies to meet women

BEST HOTEL FOR BUSINESS TRIPS: Four Seasons

BEST HOTELS FOR TRYSTS: Watergate, Grand

RESTAURANTS KNOWN FOR BEST CUISINE: Germaine's, L'Auberge Chez François

BEST RESTAURANTS FOR PEOPLE WHO WEAR BLACK: Au Pieds de Cochon, the Tasty Diners

BEST RESTAURANTS FOR AN INEXPENSIVE DATE: The Hard Times Café

POWER LUNCH: Maison Blanche

NOISIEST RESTAURANT: Perry's Sushi

BEST SPORTS BAR: Champions

BEST DARK BARS: F Street Club, the 9:30 Club

BEST GIMMICKY BARS: Tune Inn, Cities—a bar that's redecorated each month to resemble a different city, complete with appropriate food

BEST BARS TO IMPRESS A CLIENT: Hay Adams, Four Seasons, Willard Room

MOST EXCLUSIVE CITY CLUBS: Cosmos Club, Georgetown Club

FANCIEST WINE STORES WHENCE CEOS PROBABLY STOCK THEIR OWN CELLARS: Watergate Liquor, MacArthur Liquor

GOURMET STORE GUARANTEED NOT TO RUN OUT OF GOAT CHEESE OR SUN-DRIED TOMATOES: Sutton Place Gourmet

NICEST MOM-AND-POP GROCERY STORE: Neam's Market

LARGEST DRUGSTORE WITH MOST REMARKABLE SELECTIONS: People's Drug Store (a chain)

CORPORATE PARTY PLANNER: Muffie Brandon (former social secretary to Nancy Reagan) at Rogers & Cowan

HIGH-SOCIETY PARTY PLANNER: Ridgewells (caterers as well)

POWER BARBER: Uri & Associates

NEW WAVE HAIRSTYLIST: Uri & Associates

JUNIOR LEAGUE BEAUTY PARLOR: Uri & Associates

PLACE WHERE LADIES WHO LUNCH ARE LIKELY TO HAVE TEA AFTER A HARD DAY OF SHOPPING, VOLUNTEER WORK, AND TENNIS: Four Seasons

BEST STORES FOR EXECUTIVE WOMEN: Saks Fifth Avenue, Garfinckel's

BEST STORES FOR EXECUTIVE MEN: Arthur Adler, Britches, Brooks Brothers

BEST STORES FOR DRESS-UP CLOTHES: Saks Fifth Avenue, Claire Dratch

BEST SHOPPING RESOURCE FOR PEOPLE WHO WEAR ONLY BLACK CLOTHES: New York City

DEBUTANTE BALLS: The Holly Ball, Magnolia, and Thanksgiving

BUSIEST SOCIAL SEASON OF THE YEAR FOR THOSE WHO CARE ABOUT SUCH THINGS: for the city: Christmas; for the horsey set: hunt season, in both fall and spring

SOCIAL HIGHLIGHT: White House Christmas Party (held on two nights; famous people are equally distributed so guests don't feel that one night is more significant than the other; somewhere around five hundred people attend each night)

MOST RELIABLE FLORISTS: Johnson's, Caruso

MOST EXOTIC FLORIST: Ultraviolets

TOP JEWELERS FOR RESETTING MOTHER'S EMERALDS: Black, Starr & Frost; Tiny Jewel Box

MOST COMPLETE BRIDAL REGISTRIES: Bloomingdale's, Martin's

PROMINENT PHYSICIANS: Dr. James Kane, Dr. Sandra Read (dermatologist), Dr. Ann Minehart (dentist)

PROMINENT PLASTIC SURGEONS WITH EQUALLY PROMINENT CLIENTELE: Washingtonians must go to Los Angeles or New York for plastic surgery

GYNECOLOGIST MOST OFTEN QUOTED IN THE LOCAL PRESS: Dr. Gundrund Augustine-Reuchert

PSYCHIATRIST MOST OFTEN QUOTED IN THE LOCAL PRESS: Dr. Dorothy Starr

BEST SEAMSTRESS OR TAILOR FOR ALTERATIONS: European Master Tailor

BEST SEAMSTRESS OR TAILOR FOR CUSTOM TAILORING: DeSantis Custom Tailoring

POPULAR FACIAL SALONS: Somebodies, Elizabeth Arden

POWER TOOLS

MEN'S POWER DRESSING

BROOKS BROTHERS
1840 L Street, N.W.
Washington, DC 20036
(202) 659-4650

BEST-SELLING EXECUTIVE SUIT: Three-button, tropical weight, charcoal gray, 100 percent wool, $465

POWER SHIRT: Oxford cloth button-down, blue or white, 100 percent cotton, $40

POWER TIE: Rep stripe tie, navy and burgundy, 100 percent silk, $25

POWER HAIR

Uri & Associates
3109 M Street, N.W.
Suite 300
Washington, DC 20007
(202) 342-0944

Local sources mentioned Uri & Associates to *Going to Work* as *the* place in Washington where the powerful go to get groomed. The shop's staff consists of sixteen hairdressers, two manicurists, one facialist, one makeup artist, and one masseuse. Men, most of them executives, account for approximately 25 percent of the shop's clientele, and women executives make up a significant portion of the remaining 75 percent. We spoke to Uri Emsalem, the proprietor, who says of his executive clients: "It is very important for them to present themselves in the most presentable way possible. Appearance is important. It makes you feel better about yourself and makes people look at you with a better eye."

ON TRENDS IN EXECUTIVE HAIR: "Most are interested in keeping the same hairstyle. Their hairstyle has brought them to where they are now, and they don't want to change it. If there is any variation, it is very small."

"For men, it is very short. For women, it's medium length with lots of layers. This allows for lots of variation—they can blow-dry and be on the run, and in the evening they can put it up. when hair is cut in layers, the feeling is very comfortable. A lot of my clients attend White House parties and other key Washington parties, so they have to be able to put their hair up in a classy way. They don't want to be too different; they want to be acceptable."

ON PERMANENTS: "Body waves are more popular. Most of the executive women are getting body waves—it gives them an extra dimension. Root perms are even better. They give the hair a lift, look very good on any cut, any style, and save the client time, too. Root perms are subtle. Women don't want anything too curly. They need more maintenance but look good all the time. A root perm will last about six to eight weeks on average."

ON COLORING: "Some gray looks great on people. But then, some people have skin tones that don't work with gray hair at all. It makes them look sallow or washed out. This is not good.

I suggest they either cover it up or highlight it. Whichever you choose will depend on your hair color and skin tones."

ON BALDING: (Uri laughed at this.) "Honestly, I don't see that many people who are balding. Most of my clients are beautiful people. If it was up to me, I would recommend weaving. But I never come across people with this problem."

ON FACIAL HAIR: "The clean look is more acceptable here. The *GQ* look is pretty much what we do—neat, well cut, and balanced for the client."

ON EXECUTIVE MANNERS: "Everyone is equally demanding. Everyone wants to look good. The only demand for executives is time. If we are late for them, they get upset. Time is very important."

ON NETWORKING IN THE SALON: "Not a lot. Yes, they will start talking about business. But they will be private about it and won't say anything secretive (they don't want hairdressers to know about secrets). But yes, they will engage in conversation about business."

PROMINENT CLIENTS: "Senator Barkus (Montana) and his wife (she's a wonderful artist), Mrs. David Pryor, Mrs. Jack Kemp, Mrs. Gephardt, Sally Quinn, Jennifer Harrisburg . . ." (Jennifer Harrisburg got on the phone at this point to say, "Uri is a great hairdresser, this is the best salon in town, and it is very beautifully decorated.")

URI'S MOTTO: If I had a motto, it would be this: 'Personal service based on knowing our clients.' "

HOURS: Monday to Saturday, 8:15 A.M. to 7:00 P.M.

FEES:
Haircut, $55–$60 from Uri, $45–$50 from the other hairdressers (includes blow-dry)
Perms, $65–$70 (Uri doesn't do this)
Coloring (one-process color), $35
Highlights, $100
Manicure, $15
Facial, $47 for deep cleansing, $40 for regular
Massage, $45

POWER WATCHES

BLACK, STARR, AND FROST
Tyson's Corner Center
McLean, VA 22102
(703) 790-8850

BEST SELLERS AMONG EXECUTIVE MEN: Rolex Presidential, $9,750; solid eighteen-karat gold, bracelet, day and date on the face.

Second most popular, Rolex two-tone, $2,950; eighteen-karat gold and stainless steel, two-tone bracelet, yellow gold in middle and stainless steel links on either side of the gold, with date (no day).

BEST SELLER AMONG EXECUTIVE WOMEN: Baume & Mercier, $1,500–$2,000; fourteen-karat gold bracelet with a thin case, usually without a date or second hand, just a plain dial (the price of the model depends on the weight of the gold and the type of bracelet it has).

"Most people, both men and women, buy watches for themselves. Also, some corporations come in to buy a Rolex for a gift or to use as sales incentives. Quite a few of the executive men own three or four watches. Women usually have only one watch."

POWER LUNCHES

MAISON BLANCHE
1725 F Street, N.W.
Washington, DC 20006
(202) 842-0070

EXECUTIVE FAVORITES:
Dover sole, $24.00
Medallion of veal with cream sauce and wild mushrooms, $24.50
Cold seafood salad (jumbo shrimp, Maryland crabmeat, Alaska shrimps, sea scallops), $16.50
Fresh fruits (dessert), $6.25

POWER ART

NEUHAUS COLLECTION
1649 35th Street, N.W.
Washington, DC 20007
(202) 342-7595

Lacey Neuhaus became a Georgetown art dealer after the oil business in her hometown of Houston became less solvent. Frequently romantically linked with some of Washington's most eminent bachelors, she was an art history major at the now defunct women's college Briarcliff, north of New York City. After graduation she married, moved to Manhattan, "acted, sang, and danced." Most notably, Neuhaus had bit parts in two movies about the world with which she was most familiar, Director Robert Young's *Rich Kids* and Sidney Lumet's *Just Tell Me What You Want*. She also had the female lead (opposite pre–Sonny Crocker Don Johnson) in a television season of *From Here to Eternity,* which required her to live in Los Angeles. But show business is brutal to those who do not quite make it, and Neuhaus's practical side decided selling would be a better career. "I preferred selling something other than myself."

Returning to Houston after Hollywood and a divorce gave her access to the titans of energy, many of whom were from the Middle East. She sold art to these clients, who were building and decorating new homes.

She moved to Washington in 1981, worked as a private dealer, and opened the Neuhaus Collection in March, 1986. Fully half of its customers come from the corporate sector, a group that grew in both numbers and value of acquisitions during the stock market's bullish days.

"Henry Kravis [of the leveraged buyout firm Kohlberg, Kravis & Roberts] gets credit for creating the educated collector," she says over the phone while on a holiday in the Southwest. In the early 1980s Lacey saw a lot of new big money investors looking for names and prestige, art being a most visible way to show one's wealth and "taste" without too much knowledge or a developed appreciation for the artists they were collecting. "It was an epidemic. They were buying signatures." That's changed. "Guys began to study their own collections. They've hired curators who do research for them." These buyers are hunting down "art at the highest level: Old Masters, Impressionists, American Impressionists."

Occasionally "wives will still say, 'Carolyne Roehm [Mrs. Henry Kravis] has this in her dining room. Can you get one for me?' " Consequently, "a certain bracket of paintings comes back to the market every three or four years. It's easy to understand. They have outgrown them." These are second-string works by big-name artists. As their owners learn more about art, their sensibilities and collections become more refined.

Neuhaus prefers working with the educated collector, although "it's great to get carte blanche from a client."

Surprisingly, although the gallery's works start at $500 (but easily stretch into seven figures), there are off-the-street sales. "People can walk in and fool you. They can be wearing old khakis and torn shoes and walk out with two Jamie Wyeths!" (Wyeth, son of Andrew is one of the few living artists whose work Lacey represents. She sells his canvases for an average of $20,000 to $100,000.

HOURS: Tuesday to Saturday, noon to 6:00 P.M.

COVINGTON & BURLING

HISTORY & OPERATIONS

Covington & Burling, the largest law firm in Washington, D.C., was founded in 1918 by Chief Justice of the Supreme Court of the District of Columbia J. Harry Covington, who had decided to return to private practice. At the beginning of 1919, Covington was joined by Edward B. Burling, who had left a private practice in Chicago to serve as counsel for the Shipping Board during World War I. When Covington and Burling joined forces, both were forty-nine years old.

In 1921, by which time the firm had added an associate and a law clerk and moved to the Union Trust Building, George Rublee, the man who had introduced Burling to Covington in 1917, joined Covington & Burling as a partner. In consequence, the firm's name was changed to Covington, Burling & Rublee. Expansion continued at a gradual rate. In 1926, after two associates left to form their own firm, the partners promoted four associates to partner. Over the next ten years, no additional partners were added to the existing seven, and until 1941, the number of partners exceeded that of associates.

Though the firm developed a thriving local general practice in its early years, the majority of its work involved representing out-of-town clients in government-related cases. In addition, it cultivated a practice in tax and tax-related matters, a specialty that had been virtually unknown before the war and that contributed 60 percent of the firm's fees between 1923 and 1932.

Between 1933 and 1949, the firm more than quadrupled in size, increasing from seven partners and five associates to twenty partners and thirty-six associates, more than twice the size of the second largest firm in Washington, D.C. In 1933, to honor two of its more outstanding partners, the firm's name was elongated to Covington, Burling, Rublee, Acheson (as in Dean) & Shorb. Covington died in 1942 and Rublee retired in 1944. Business blossomed after the war, and annual fees increased by 80 percent between 1945 and 1948. During the postwar years, when continued growth appeared inevitable, the firm was one of the first in the country to institute a systematic approach to the regular recruiting of new associates. It was also one of the first, during this time, to launch a program for summer clerks. In 1951 the firm permanently changed its name back to Covington & Burling.

Growth continued during the fifties, and the firm substantially broadened its base of clients. By 1960 Covington & Burling employed one hundred lawyers. Burling, who was still somewhat active in the practice, died in 1966. The seventies saw yet another growth spurt, and by 1981 the firm had outgrown its office space and relocated its headquarters to 1201 Pennsylvania Avenue. Today the firm's staff of 641 consists of 93 partners [87 men; 6 women], 8 senior counsel, 2 counsel, 136 associates, 48 paralegals, and 354 support staff.

Judge Covington and Edward Burling came from opposite ends of the political spectrum— Covington was a liberal Democrat and Burling was a Staunch Republican—and from its beginnings, the firm has made it a priority to hire lawyers from a variety of backgrounds and points of view. This regard for diversity also applies to its practice, which encompasses virtually every major area of the law. Most lawyers work in more than one area (although some specialize), and in order to retain its flexibility, the firm has deliberately avoided decentralizing into separate departments. Rather than acting as "general counsel" to a fixed number of clients, Covington & Burling is most often called upon to act as counsel to specific cases, both by clients with whom it has ongoing relationships and by new clients who seek its expertise on a particular matter. The firm represents corporations, countries, organizations, and individuals. Areas covered in its practice include: antitrust and other trade regulation; banking; bankruptcy, creditors' rights and reorganization; communications; corporate and securities; employment; energy and resources development; environment; food and drug; government contracts; international; litigation; pro bono; real estate; sports law; state government/human services; taxation, trusts and estates; trade associations; transportation; and miscellaneous (which includes trademark and copyright work, press-related matters such as defamation and privacy, and work for the Department of Agriculture, among other types of legal services).

Covington & Burling has a long record of public service. Many of its lawyers have served in government positions, taking leaves from the firm in order to do so, in these capacities: U.S. senator; under secretary of the Treasury; adviser to the president for National Capital Affairs; special counsel to the president; assistant secretary of defense; assistant attorney general; U.S. attorney; assistant staff director of the U.S. commission on civil rights, secretary of state [Dean Acheson] and many more.

Further, the firm employs a full-time public service coordinator, who matches public interest organizations with the Covington & Burling lawyers who can best serve their needs. The coordinator interviews all new associates to determine their interest in pro bono work, and the firm takes on hundreds of pro bono cases each year.

Since the early years, when partners outnumbered associates, Covington & Burling has tried to downplay distinctions of hierarchy. Associates work directly with partners, meeting with clients and sharing major responsibilities on cases. New associates generally work in at least two different areas of the practice, with several different partners. Partners annually review the associates with whom they've worked and discuss with them their strengths and weaknesses. The track from first-year associate to partner takes eight years, but after their fifth year with the firm, and each year thereafter, associates are informed of their partnership prospects.

(Information provided by Bobby Burchfield, partner.)

REVENUES: Firm is private and will not disclose.

EARNINGS: Firm will not disclose.

OFFICES: Headquarters in Washington, D.C., and a small office in nearby Tyson's Corner, Virginia.

NUMBER OF EMPLOYEES: Approximately 641: 239 lawyers, 48 paralegals, and about 354 support staff.

NUMBER OF FEMALE LAWYERS: Six partners, one of counsel, and forty-one associates as of January 1, 1988.

AVERAGE AGE OF EMPLOYEES: "The average age of associates is probably around thirty.

TURNOVER: Information not available.

RECRUITMENT: The firm recruits at about fifteen law schools throughout the country, including University of California at Berkeley, University of Chicago, Columbia University, Duke University, Georgetown University, George Washington University, Harvard University, Howard University, University of Michigan, New York University, University of Pennsylvania, Stanford University, University of Texas, University of Virginia, and Yale University.

NEW HIRES PER YEAR: The firm hires twenty-five to thirty new lawyers each year as full-time associates, a significant proportion of whom have served as clerks to federal and state judges. Covington & Burling also hires a number of paralegals each year (for nonlegal research), most of whom have recently graduated from college and most of whom leave the firm after approximately two years to attend either graduate or law school.

RANGE OF STARTING SALARIES: Starting salaries for associates beginning in fall 1987, were $55,000 plus a guaranteed year-end bonus of a minimum of 5 percent base salary.

POLICY FOR RAISES: "Virtually all employees are eligible for raises each year. Nonlawyer raises are based upon seniority and performance. Associate raises generally follow a uniform stairstep pattern for the first seven years. Associates are generally considered for partnership in the eighth year after their graduation from law school."

SUMMER ASSOCIATE PROGRAM: "The firm hires twenty-five to thirty second-year law students (or graduates interested in employment prior to taking a judicial clerkship) for a period during the summer. Virtually all of those who spend a summer with the firm eventually come back for full-time employment as associates after finishing law school or after clerking for one or more judges." Of 1987's thirty summer associates, twenty-eight were offered permanent positions. In 1987, summer associates were paid $900 a week.

BENEFITS: "Choice of group medical insurance or health maintenance organization plans, various life insurance plans, accidental death insurance, and automobile liability insurance for travel in the course of employment. The firm's pension plan applies to all employees after they have completed three years of service. New associates receive reimbursement for certain expenses in connection with admission to the D.C. Bar, and associates may be eligible for reimbursement for certain moving expenses."

VACATION: "The firm's vacation policy provides every employee with twenty working days of vacation each year, except that employees with thirty years of service or more get twenty-five working days of leave a year. The firm observes the federal national holidays."

ADDITIONAL PERKS: Unlimited sick days. Ten weeks' maternity leave, treated as sick leave. Two weeks of paternity leave to new fathers immediately following the birth of a child.

BONUSES: "In general, the only bonus awarded is a seniority bonus to each nonlegal employee based upon the number of years with the firm."

ANNUAL PARTIES: The firm hosts a Christmas party for all employees at a neighboring hotel, a picnic for employees and their families each September, a July Fourth event on the roof of the office building to observe the fireworks on the Mall, periodic wine-and-cheese parties for all employees (or various categories of them), informal late Friday afternoon beer parties for lawyers and/or paralegals, an occasional firmwide art show or talent show, occasional lunches for various firm personnel, and a periodic retreat for lawyers and spouses.

AVERAGE WORKDAY: "There are probably 239 different answers to that." The firm's regular office hours are 9:00 A.M. to 5:30 P.M., though many lawyers come in earlier and many leave later. Covington & Burling used to have Saturday hours from 9:00 A.M. to 1:00 P.M., but not anymore. However, it's not unusual for lawyers to put in time on the weekends.

DRESS CODE: "There is no formally established dress code; normal good taste is expected to prevail at all levels. Male lawyers invariably wear suits, as do many (but not all) female lawyers."

SOCIAL ATMOSPHERE: "It is difficult to describe any generally prevailing social atmosphere at the firm. Many employees indeed fraternize with one another after working hours, although it is also assumed that a number do not, depending on their personal circumstances, etc."

HEADQUARTERS: "Except for about two to five employees in the Tyson's Corner office, all employees are located on six floors of an office building at 1201 Pennsylvania Avenue, N.W."

CHARITABLE CONTRIBUTIONS: "We do not release information concerning the firm's total charitable contributions. We have had a longstanding policy of making contributions to law schools around the country keyed to personal contributions of individual lawyers. In addition, the firm contributes to various legal charitable organizations in the Washington, D.C. area. More directly related to our legal practice is the work of the firm lawyers on a wide variety of public interest or pro bono matters, for which the firm is not reimbursed by the clients. Traditionally, this public interest work constitutes about 9 percent or 10 percent of the total hours worked by firm lawyers."

INTERESTED APPLICANTS CAN SEND RÉSUMÉS TO:
For attorney, summer associate, law clerk, and paralegal positions:
Ms. Lorraine Brown
Covington & Burling
1201 Pennsylvania Avenue, N.W.
P.O. Box 7566
Washington, DC 20044
(202) 662-2000

For other positions:
Mr. Charles Faddis
Covington & Burling
1201 Pennsylvania Avenue, N.W.
P.O. Box 7566
Washington, DC 20044
(202) 662-6000

Welcome to the hushed, serious, and high-powered world of Covington & Burling. The largest—by far—law firm in Washington, D.C., it is known for its representation of governments—states and countries—as well as multinational corporations. Covington & Burling's list of past and present clients is impressive, if not downright intimidating: IBM, Exxon, DuPont, Procter & Gamble, Upjohn, Penn Central, Textron, the National Football League, the State of Connecticut, the Secretary of the Interior, and the United States of America.

Occupying the top six floors of a building on Pennsylvania Avenue, not far from the White House, Covington & Burling wields so much influence that when it relocated to this then-underdeveloped business neighborhood, it was immediately dubbed "the new legal neighborhood" and other firms moved here. The library, with fifty-five thousand books and five hundred periodicals in its stacks, is the largest law library in a private firm in the city. "Tasteful" is the key word in describing the offices' decor; occasional antiques punctuate the hallways, as well as a collection of paintings and prints.

Of the day-to-day life of the firm, partner Edward Dunkelberger says, "There's no decentralization here. We keep our identity as a firm, instead of departments. We say, 'This is a 239-man law firm.' " Naturally, however, the attorneys develop expertise in the areas in which they have most experience.

Those interviewed claim their work is interesting and not repetitive. "It remains intellectually satisfying." Covington & Burling does have a reputation for working its people hard, but "we certainly try to avoid being a sweatshop. If someone comes in with real heavy hours, we tell them to take it easy. It could mean they have trouble meeting deadlines."

Regulatory work, product liability, antitrust, copyright, corporate law, pro bono work, international issues—the practice is diverse, the client base national and international. Many of the firm's corporate clients already have an in-house counsel staff of up to a hundred lawyers. They'll consult with Covington & Burling "when they're looking for a new form of expertise. Our lawyers will be hired by their lawyers. For most of our clients, we're not the only firm they use."

It is maintained that "a lawyer could turn down a case if he didn't believe in it." One of Covington & Burling's clients is the Tobacco Institute. A strong believer in pro bono law since the thirties, "nine to ten percent of all hours go to pro bono work," Dunkelberger says. "One lawyer is the full-time pro bono coordinator. In the Neighborhood Legal Services Program, we have three lawyers and a staff of about six rotating [for six months] in storefronts to help the poor with Social Security and leases and to work with inmates, Planned Parenthood, civil liberties, environmental law. The American Civil Liberties Union refers a lot of cases to us. Three Covington lawyers are on the ACLU screening committee."

About twenty-five to thirty new lawyers are hired each year. Between thirty and forty percent of them come form Harvard Law School. "You are hired based on your law school [the competitiveness of the school, as well as your record there], not on your LSATs." Dunkelberger has noticed that each year's new group has a successively older median age. "More of our applicants had earlier careers. We have ex-doctors, teachers, ministers, and mothers."

A further statement about the "C&B kind of person": "Someone for whom the dollar is not the first consideration; someone who is loyal. You enjoy being involved in national matters, even if you are on the 'wrong side.' "

For an associate, joining the firm means a serious dose of prestige and respectability, in terms both of social stature and professional credibility. One of them talks about "expectations versus reality. People think that everyone here is really smart. How much smarter than us are they? I never felt mentally overwhelmed." Going in, one is told that partnership is based on an eight-year track (relatively long for a lawyer in any city). It's nonnegotiable. (Associates with several years' previous experience elsewhere, say as clerks, in industry, or at other firms must work at C&B at least five years to be considered for partner.) Partnership decisions are made in the fall following the eighth anniversary of graduation from law school. It is not assumed that everyone hired will make it that far; indeed, it seems that most associates presume they won't. "Anyone who comes here with the idea of making partner is making a big mistake. Will they like it? Will they like Washington?" Those are not secondary matters. Annual reviews are conducted carefully, with both printed forms and personal interviews.

Only 20 to 25 percent of an entering class will make partner. Partnership is more than an achievement; the quest for that caliber of security is the grail that whets the competitive appetites of many of the country's top law school graduates. Therefore undue attention is paid to one's progress at the firm, a journey that can be difficult and unassured. (By the way, associates say that "partners continue to stay very involved and busy. They're not golfers.")

"Most people who come here think they'll give it a shot. It's like the lottery. They have no idea how they'll compete here. A lot leave on their own." Partnership nitty-gritty begins in the fifth year. That's when associates embark on their close relationships with C&B's evaluation committee. "By the fifth year, the percentage of associates who will get elevated is up to fifty percent."

Associates are rotated around the firm, orchestrated by the managing partner for personnel, "the mother hen," according to a partner. "There are long- and short-term assignments. The people are bright, young, and attractive. You sort of care about them."

Covington & Burling is politically rather nonpartisan. "Some consider it Democratic because of [former partner turned secretary of state under Presidents Roosevelt and Truman] Dean Acheson." Others would say the firm could correctly be called "conservative"—"Some younger partners are active in the Republican Party, but we almost never take a government person as a partner. Others do that a lot." Perhaps "staid" is more apt. This is not to say narrow-minded. Almost fifty women work as lawyers here. "By now I believe we interview sex-blind," a partner says. "There's no significance attached to gender anymore." There is one point at issue, however. "Motherhood is a problem. It's their problem, but we try to help them out. Part-time work will not take you out of the partnership rotation, but you will still need your five years here. You still need exposure to partners in different areas."

When we met, Bobby Burchfield was an associate whose future at Covington seemed assured. [He has since made partner.] Although our conversation dwelt on the partnership question [Author's note: I may have been partially to blame], he claimed, "You don't get involved in institutional stuff; you just work hard." Rather than worrying about making partner, he says of his years here, "I think I've become a better attorney." A graduate of Wake Forest University and George Washington University Law School, he said, "I always wanted to be a litigator." New associates in litigation start with two cases. Seventy-five percent of all cases get settled out of court. Going to trial "makes the dull days worthwhile. It's worse than cramming for exams; it's real." He divulges "the cardinal rule of cross-examination: Never ask a question for which you don't know the answer."

Burchfield estimated he billed 2,300 to 2,400 hours a year (which translates into an average work week of just over forty hours). Not the unreasonable back-breaking stuff of legend. That included 200 hours of pro bono work. The average associate bills between 1,800 and 1,850 hours per year, which is *not* based on a quota. Travel time is billable if one travels during work hours and works en route, not if one travels nights or weekends. Are Covington's offices jam-packed during off-peak hours? "Our offices are designed for privacy," he answers. "You never know if others are here."

He believes in the protocol set forth by his elders. "Everyone's almost on a first-name basis," he explains. "Until they expressly say, 'Call me by my first name,' I won't. Three out of two hundred thirty-nine isn't bad." He looks the part of a young lawyer. "I always wear a suit and tie. You should be reasonably well groomed. The use of deodorant is encouraged," he jokes. "Women lawyers wouldn't wear pants, but secretaries can." Bobby relaxes his dress code when traveling, when he wears a blue blazer and gray flannel trousers, "depending on the client."

As a seventh-year associate, one's future in or apart from Covington & Burling's partnership should be evident. Those who ignore the signs to the contrary and stay the full length of the apprenticeship only to be turned down for partner can occasionally become permanent associates. "It's also for people who don't want to be partner. It's not formalized, but we'll probably increase the number. Eight years creates an attachment."

In the interest of fairness, a partner admits that "a problem of the big firm is creating morale and friendliness." This is clearly on the minds of those who affect the culture of Covington & Burling. One antidote to the potential indifference of a firm the size of C&B is the Homestead Weekend. It is held every two or three years at the Homestead Hotel in Hot Springs, Virginia. Every lawyer and his or her spouse is invited. "The unmarried used to be a big issue; not now." Single lawyers may now bring their companion of choice. "It's very important to feel 'family.' Some go with apprehension; some don't go."

In hiring, nepotism is contrary to policy, although one couple was hired together a few years ago. "There is a fair amount of intrafirm dating, though."

A Christmas party for all 641 employees (sans spouses and friends) is an annual social highlight of the firm. "For the last ten or twelve years, every Monday an outside speaker has come to speak at lunch. Partners and selected associates are invited. There's also a summer picnic for whole families." When the weather permits, sometimes wine-and-cheese parties develop on the building's terrace. And "every now and then" the partners can look forward to a black tie dinner.

Covington & Burling likes the way it works. "We will continue to do topflight law for topflight clients." Being good does not mean relying on state-of-the-art, newfangled methods of getting the work done. The firm did not jump on the computer bandwagon early, for example. "There's not a hell of a lot of ways to write a brief. We don't want to be stodgy, but you don't make changes just to make changes."

In a stunning bow toward modernity, Covington & Burling has opened a four-or-five-lawyer office in Tyson's Corner, Virginia, "the new Silicon Valley." [Author's note: Writing the *College Book,* I noticed one of the most relentless clichés of academia was when an institution called itself "the Harvard of . . ." Likewise, industry keeps looking for "the new Silicon Valley." Every neighborhood's got one.] Xerox and Honeywell have established bases in Tyson's Corner, as have two other "old white shoe" law firms. "Now it's the thing to do," says a partner who won't sacrifice quality for fashion.

GANNETT CO., INC.

GANNETT
A WORLD OF DIFFERENT VOICES
WHERE FREEDOM SPEAKS

HISTORY & OPERATIONS

The Gannett Co., Inc., now the largest newspaper group in the United States, was started in 1906, when a group of investors led by Frank Gannett bought a half interest in *The Elmira* (New York) *Gazette* for $20,000. The funds came from $3,000 in savings, $7,000 in loans, and $10,000 in notes. Gannett's holdings expanded gradually, first with another Elmira newpaper that was merged with the original to become the *Star-Gazette* and later with *The Ithaca Journal*, located in nearby Ithaca.

In 1918 Gannett and his associates moved to Rochester, New York, where they created *The Rochester Times-Union* out of two existing publications. In 1923 Frank Gannett bought out his associates' interests and formed the Gannett Company, Inc., then made up of six newspapers in four upstate New York cities. During the next twenty-five years, the company continued to expand by buying newspapers and later radio stations located throughout the Northeast. The corporate strategy was to make purchases in places where there was little or no competition. By 1947 Gannett operated twenty-one local newspapers and six local radio stations.

In 1957 Paul Miller was elected president and CEO of the Gannett Company which then owned twenty-eight papers in five states. Frank Gannett died shortly thereafter, leaving no heirs associated with his company. Miller, who was president of the Associated Press before joining Gannett, is credited with masterminding the company's modern expansion efforts. During the 1960s, Gannett made a number of acquisitions that propelled its growth from a regional group of small papers to a company with a solid national base. By 1966, according to figures compiled by the Audit Bureau of Circulations, the company's daily newspapers had a readership of 1,156,861, and its weeklies a readership of 505,835. Its television audience was composed of 539,600 viewers, and it had a radio audience of 439,240 listeners. In 1967 the company went public, and by the end of the decade its holdings included thirty-three newspapers, twelve weeklies, six radio stations, and two television stations. Since going public, Gannett's earnings have increased for eighty-one consecutive quarters.

Allen Neuharth, like Frank Gannett a country boy, pursued his career in journalism as a reporter and editor and joined Gannett in 1963. He rose rapidly through the ranks to become president and COO in 1970, CEO in 1973, and chairman in 1979. Under Neuharth's leadership, Gannett has undergone the most aggressive period of expansion and diversification in its history, ultimately becoming the biggest newspaper group in the country. In 1979 the company created the largest communications merger in history when Gannett purchased Combined Communications Corporation and thus acquired two large newspapers (*The Cincinnati Enquirer* and *The Oakland Tribune*), television stations (KUSA-TV, Denver; WUSA-TV, Washington, D.C.; WTLV-TV, Jacksonville; WXIA-TV, Atlanta; WLVI-TV, Boston; KARE-TV, Minneapolis-St. Paul; WFMY-TV, Greensboro, NC; KOCO-TV, Oklahoma City; KVUE-TV, Austin; and KPNX-TV, Phoenix), thirteen radio stations, and an outdoor billboard advertising empire. By 1980 Gannett's holdings were eighty-one daily newspapers and twenty nondaily newspapers with a total circulation of 3.56 million, seven television stations, thirteen radio stations, and the billboard business.

In 1982 Neuharth established *USA Today,* a national daily four-color newspaper intended to be a second paper for avid news readers of the television generation. *USA Today* was launched in street dispensers designed to resemble television sets. Though it has met with a measure of scorn from the journalistic community, in mid-1986 it unseated *The Wall Street Journal* as the most widely read daily paper in the country and *The New York Daily News* as the most widely read general interest daily newspaper in the country. Gannett also launched an international version of *USA Today,* which reaches more than fifty countries throughout Asia, Europe, North Africa, and the Middle East. Despite a reputation for unprecedented brevity, *USA Today* has won praise for its innovative use of statistics, and splashy color graphics, which other papers across the country have since tried to imitate. Although Gannett was still based in Rochester, *USA Today* was headquartered in Washington, D.C. In 1985 the company relocated altogether to be near its flagship publication. *USA Today* which reportedly had operating losses of $457 million at the end of 1986, had its first profitable quarter at the end of 1987.

Under Neuharth's tenure, Gannett continues to make substantial acquisitions each year. Today the company employs more than 36,000 people in the following operations: ninety daily newspapers (with a daily paid circulation in excess of 6.1 million—*USA Today* alone now has a daily paid circulation of more than 1.6 million and a daily readership of 5.5 million); thirty-five nondaily newspapers (including *USA Weekend,* a weekly magazine with a 14.6 million circulation that appears in 294 Gannett and non-Gannett newspapers); 10 local, independent television stations, all affiliated with different networks (which reach 10 million households and give Gannett an 11.2 percent share of the national television market); sixteen radio stations; the largest outdoor billboard advertising group in North America, which operates in seventeen major markets in the United States and twenty-seven in Canada; Gannett

News Service, which was established in 1942 and provides Gannett newspapers, television stations, and radio stations with news stories from its headquarters in Washington and bureaus scattered across the country; GTG Entertainment [see p. 729], a television production company in partnership with Grant Tinker; Louis Harris & Associates, an international research company; Gannett National Newspaper Sales; and *USA Today Update*, an electronic information service.

In addition to the company's holdings, Gannett operates a foundation, the Gannett Foundation, established by Frank Gannett in 1935, which in 1987 donated $28 million to community and educational projects. The company is noted for having the most progressive hiring and promotion program for women and minorities of any news operation in the country, and in the latest year for which figures are available, 20 percent of its staff were minorities and 39 percent were women. There are now twenty-three women publishers at Gannett newspapers.

In 1986 Allen stepped down as CEO and handed the job to John J. Curley, who had been president and COO since 1984. Though Neuharth retains the title of chairman and is still very active in the company's operations, Curley will take over as chairman when Neuharth reaches retirement age in 1989.

(Information provided by Celeste James and Sheila Gibbons, company spokespersons.)

1987 FORTUNE 500 RANKING: 141st.

REVENUES: $3.08 billion in operating revenue in 1987 (up 10 percent from 1986).

EARNINGS: $319.4 million in net income in 1987, up 20 percent from the previous year.

INITIAL PUBLIC OFFERING: 1967.

NUMBER OF SHAREHOLDERS: Approximately 11,000.

NUMBER OF EMPLOYEES: More than 36,000.

OFFICES: The company has headquarters in Rosslyn (part of Arlington, Virginia) and additional operations in forty states, Guam, the Virgin Islands, Canada, Great Britain, Hong Kong, Singapore, and Switzerland.

NEWSPAPERS: Ninety daily papers (including *USA Today*), with a daily paid circulation in excess of 6.1 million, and thirty-five nondaily newspapers, for which company does not keep circulation figures.

BROADCASTING: Ten independent television stations and sixteen radio stations scattered across the country.

AVERAGE AGE OF EMPLOYEES: Thirty-eight.

NUMBER OF NEW HIRES PER YEAR: 5,161 in 1986, and 5,169 in 1987.

TURNOVER: Information not available.

RECRUITMENT: Individual operating units recruit at a number of colleges and universities located all over the country, primarily for undergraduate students in journalism, business, and broadcast programs.

RANGE OF STARTING SALARIES: There are too many different kinds of jobs within the company in too many different locations for Gannett to publish a realistic entry-level salary range. "A reporter starting out at a small paper might make as little as $10,000, while someone starting out at *USA Today* might make as much as $30,000. Same goes for TV and radio."

POLICY FOR RAISES: Raises are determined annually by performance review. The amount of a raise is based entirely on merit.

TRAINING PROGRAMS: No companywide program for all new employees, but Gannett does have programs for certain specialized areas. Sales and Circulation offers a program that is administered by individual Gannett operating divisions. The company also has a supervisory training program which, like the Sales and Circulation program, is run by individual Gannett units. Gannett also offers a number of workshops for managers in topics that include "Setting Performance Standards," "Equal Opportunity in Employment," and "Employment Appraisal."

BENEFITS: The benefits package varies slightly from one Gannett property to the next. The corporate package includes major medical and dental insurance, vision care, tuition reimbursement for academic study that's clearly related to an employee's career at Gannett, and maternity leave. Those who have reached managerial level are entitled to life insurance and stock incentive plans.

VACATION: On a sliding scale tied to an employee's tenure with the company: two weeks after one year, three weeks after five years, up to five weeks after thirty years. There are six paid holidays per year and two floating days.

BONUSES: Employees at the managerial level are eligible for bonuses, which are awarded strictly on merit. The amount is based on the performance of the individual, the performance of his or her operating unit, and the performance of the company as a whole.

ANNUAL PARTY: Parties are left up to the individual Gannett operation, and practices vary throughout the organization. However, Gannett corporate throws an annual Christmas party (called a "holiday season" party), and *USA Today* celebrates its birthday each year at a party that includes the corporate staff.

AVERAGE WORKDAY: People are paid for a seven-and-a-half-hour workday, and hourly employees receive overtime for anything beyond that. Most people work more than seven and a half hours each day—how much more depends on the level of responsibility and amount of work —and no one works less.

DRESS CODE: There is no stated dress code and what people wear depends largely on where they work. "Corporate people don't wear jeans, but they dress more casually than, say, people who work in a law firm." At the newspapers people often wear jeans. Al Neuharth dresses exclusively in black, white, and gray, but that's a matter of personal style.

SOCIAL ATMOSPHERE: "It's a very friendly place. There's a lot of teamwork at the company and very much a 'can-do' spirit here at corporate headquarters."

HEADQUARTERS: Gannett leases eleven floors in a 210,000-square-foot, thirty-one-story building in Rosslyn (a section of Arlington, Virginia). (Gannett variously calls its home Arlington and Rosslyn.) A conference/training center is on the twenty-first floor, and executive suites are on the thirty-first floor.

CHARITABLE CONTRIBUTIONS: The company makes educational, civic, and charitable contributions through the Gannett Foundation (a separate legal entity from the Gannett Company), which was established by Frank Gannett in 1935. The Foundation makes contributions to local communities in which Gannett has holdings, through the recommendations of the staff of those holdings. In 1987, the Foundation made total donations of approximately $28 million.

COMPANY SLOGAN: "A World of Different Voices Where Freedom Speaks."

PEOPLE INTERESTED IN WORKING FOR ONE OF GANNETT'S OPERATIONS SHOULD CONTACT THE PARTICULAR PROPERTY DIRECTLY. THOSE INTERESTED IN A CORPORATE POSITION CAN SEND RÉSUMÉS TO:

Gannett Co., Inc.
Personnel
1100 Wilson Boulevard
Arlington, VA 22209
(703) 284-6000

The Gannett building rises like a cliff over the crowded shores of the Potomac in suburban Rosslyn (part of Arlington), Virginia. Big, brassy, new, it reflects the sensibility of the fast-growing media empire within. What was once a modest newspaper company in Rochester, New York, moved in 1985 to America's news center. Terraced gardens—showy stuff—greet you in the multilevel lobby, which also includes a small shopping arcade.

Both Gannett and its britches have gotten awfully big in the last eighteen years, since Allen Neuharth was named president. As is the case of any company run by a strong-willed charismatic leader, his personality informs the corporation, more than 36,000 strong. Neuharth is as much the decor of his headquarters as he is *USA Today*, even though he is not known personally by many of his employees.

Those who have been lured here by Neuharth praise him extravagantly. "He wants to make Gannett into the best, best company," says a recruit. "It's a fun and exciting place to work, probably because of him," a corporate vice-president thinks. "I can't imagine working elsewhere." People at Gannett arrive for work early in the morning and leave sometime in the evening. Everyone has a lot to do and seems to enjoy having a great deal of work, but there appears to be a certain peer pressure that requires a visibly extended attendance record. If all your colleagues stay till 7:30 P.M., chances are you will, too. This is a feisty place, fueled by a feisty chairman and his feisty generals. And although successful publications (and TV stations) can't work without a team sensibility, this is a competitive place. One doesn't get the feeling that the troops are being monitored, but to fit in means to want to win.

USA Today is Gannett's flagship publication and certainly the one that has brought the most attention to the company. (It is surely the only publication that has procured the services of a former elected official—ex–Chicago Mayor Jane Byrne—to sing its jingle on national television.) In 1982, "when *USA Today* was launched, it made other [non–*USA Today* Gannett] staffers nervous about being forgotten," a female executive remembers. Indeed, it drew attention away from Gannett's then 119 newspapers. And Gannett has a policy of "loaners"—the company will loan staff from one location or publication to another in times of need. This happens especially during a start-up. The stepchild syndrome was exacerbated by *USA Today*'s establishment in Washington, when the rest of corporate Gannett was still located in Rochester, New York.

The announcement of the corporation's move to Washington was made in July 1984. "There was an uproar, but no one was too surprised," a pension executive says. "People had to give up Rochester. We paid for people to go on two or more house-hunting trips with a spouse, and we arranged our relocation policy with Merrill, Lynch. You could get two appraisals for your home and sell it for the average or wait sixty days to get a better deal. We paid closing costs, legal bills, six points toward the mortgage, and all moving arrangements. We agreed to pay duplicate mortgages on the house not lived in. We paid the cost of living increase." There were 150 people on the corporate staff in Rochester. Eighty-three of them moved, including a mailroom supervisor.

Working for Gannett was not necessarily the ambition of many of those who now work there. In a majority of cases, Gannett purchased a newspaper, TV station, or radio station, and the staff was retained.

Henry Freeman has been associated with Gannett since 1977–78, when Gannett acquired the publication for which he worked, *The Wilmington* (Delaware) *News-Journal* (where he met his wife). His career since then has been fairly typical of a Gannett journalist who's been put on the fast track by the big boys. He was transferred to Oakland, California, in 1979 to start *East Bay Today,* "a morning alternative to the *San Francisco Chronicle,*" because "John Quinn [then president of Gannett newspapers, now the editor of *USA Today*] took an immediate active interest in me and in keeping me at Gannett." Freeman, a soft-spoken man of forty-one "only had sixty days to find staff and develop the paper." Today, he is the managing editor of *USA Today*'s sports department. "In ten years I've lived in three cities. I've had many jobs. I have ten years of accrued benefits. There are places to grow without leaving the company."

Freeman was a member of the think tank that put *USA Today* together, after the blueprints were drawn. "In 1981 I made twenty-four trips cross-country to help plan *USA Today.*" They wanted him to handle sports, a beat he had left behind years before. "I never intended to get into sports and stay in it. *USA Today* was the only opportunity to return to sports that I would take. It's a good place to learn a little of everything. It's a different sports section. In a local daily, your reputation is built on local team coverage. We've got to be different. We can write about nonlocal events better. We sent fifty people altogether to the Olympics."

The sports section, running an average of twelve pages daily, is run like a separate newspaper. All sections are. Long stories in one section are continued within that section. Decisions that can be made within a section are.

And that's the thing about Gannett. The most satisfied workers there claim they feel they are working for themselves. There's a pride of ownership here that allows them to work long hours and be conscientious.

John Garvey has the title of vice-president/production, *USA Weekend.* He's been there since 1987. His six preceding years at *USA Today* followed twenty-two years with the corporation. He wakes up at 6:00 A.M. on workdays and does exercises for his bad back. Breakfast is usually coffee and a corn muffin, and he arrives before 7:30, "the first one here." Garvey tries to leave each evening at 7:30, but he is basically on twenty-four-hour alert, should there be an emergency. "If I had a night I could sleep through, it would be a miracle." He also works a half day on Saturday and Sunday.

The job is "stressful. Everything's multiplied by thirty." Since *USA Today* is printed in thirty locations around the country (and two abroad), the Rosslyn plant must transmit each page to each plant at precise five-minute intervals. Each color page requires four transmissions, so they're sent before black-and-white pages. It takes three shifts to print the entire newspaper. The first printing starts at midnight; the last one ends at 5:30 A.M. "You have to anticipate when things could go wrong. If you think something could go wrong in an ad, you call the engraver or the ad agency. We have six days to correct ads. We go out with salespeople to the agencies and discuss problems and what we can do."

When the paper was introduced "it was locked into forty-page formats. Now we're up to [a maximum of] fifty-six pages with double the color capacity." Garvey was part of the aforementioned task force that developed *USA Today*. One of the critical early endeavors was figuring out the feasability and credibility of a newspaper that depended on four-color printing. "They asked us if we could get magazine quality on newsprint," he remembers. "You don't say 'maybe' to a chairman.

"I remember the day he [Neuharth] announced *USA Today* in the Capitol Hilton. Loyalty comes from the top down." Garvey semijokingly refers to Chairman Neuharth as " 'Uncle Al.' We have the best goddamn editors in the business, and they see the warm side of Al." Garvey wears his gold ring carved with the *USA Today* logo, given to all "founders," on the ring finger of his left hand. "I'm married to it," is his not surprising rationale.

Roz Hooke is one of the most senior women at Gannett, a company that has been widely praised for its unbiased and generous attitudes toward women and minorities. She is the advertising vice-president of the Newspaper Division, which encompasses 125 newspapers (excluding *USA Today*). A native Briton, she defies the conventional American corporate female look and wears, instead, stylish dresses and flamboyant accessories. "I've always been myself," she says in her large office. "I am not a typical broad, as you Americans put it. I am opinionated. If you have balls, you have freedom."

With a position that requires extensive travel—75 to 80 percent of her time is spent away from Washington—being herself is especially key, as is her notion of preserving fun. "This is a funny place to work. I get funny notes all the time. You've got to make it fun." Just the same, the work can be grueling, and Hooke has paid a high price to stay on top. "I could not do this job if I were married." Period. She makes no apologies, seems to spend no time wrestling with the issues of motherhood, family, and career that plague so many women in the office today. "I've made a commitment to my career." On the other hand, she allows that "being single makes the job more difficult." Because she has to rely on cleaning ladies, etc. No angst of a more profound nature; she has made her peace.

For Hooke, as for everyone here, there is pressure to succeed. "The levels of excellence keep increasing. What you did last year is this year's standard. If you once walked on water, you're now expected to [be able to do that at will]."

Hooke revels in her job, which she admits is "particularly visible. The female visibility at Gannett is because of Neuharth. He's not particularly a feminist, but he wants especially fair representation of women and minorities."

After seven years with the company, the ebullient Roz Hooke says, "I can't imagine working elsewhere. I don't want to trade known pain for unknown pain."

What can you say about an employee who knows exactly how many days he's been on Gannett's payroll? That he loves his job, hates his job, is calculating his profit share, or just likes numbers? The last option applies to Mark Morneau, interviewed on the thirteenth day of the second month of his third year at Gannett. With an MBA from the University of Minnesota, he was tapped by a headhunter to work in the Division of Systems and Programming. Do not be misled by his fancy for figures; his take on life at Gannett reflects a keen facility with words and a fascination with the culture he shares.

"Gannett is a decentralized company, and each division has its own system. We're a service organization within the company. We're at others' beck and call," he says of the group that buys, commissions, and develops its own software. "People work hard here. They're constantly pushing decision making down [the ranks]." As far as sheer brute motivation, Morneau views the collective drive as stemming from Neuharth. "Otherwise, the responsibility is yours. You set a tone for the achievers you hire." There are 124 people in the computer department (75 in the Rosslyn Information Center), and he finds that strong inducements are not needed to secure new employees. "Gannett mostly sells itself. When someone comes in for an interview, I say, 'We've got exciting work, tedious work, and long hours.'"

"There's a peer pressure here that you can't believe. You feel guilty leaving at six P.M. We're a results-oriented company. There are heroes and dogs. You can be a hero one day and a dog the next day." Dog-hero-dog does not mean dog-eat-dog. Morneau, now the director of systems and programming, makes it clear there's no sabotage. "We're competitive without blacklisting. It's like saying, 'Your end of the boat is sinking.'"

Gannetters are compelled to work so that they can prove they care. "Management doesn't walk around to see who's here and who's not." People manifest a need to show they can work as hard as the next person, and "Gannett will load, load, load the work until you can take it no longer. We need achievers. Maybe you can't achieve a feeling of joy, but there is a sense of satisfaction. We all want busy days. We all want a lot to do. We all want control of our jobs.

"Gannett will let you consume yourself, and no one will say anything." It is fascinating that some employees seem to ache for work. They could probably survive here by applying more lenient standards to themselves. One hears a frequently quoted Neuharthism: "'You can go to Little League games, but not a lot.' Gannett learned a lot about managing through *USA Today*. Formerly, they managed by fear." Employees seem to be saying that your conscience is your supervisor. "You can structure your own job here," another noneditorial employee says, "but punishments and rewards exist. Journalists award themselves," he says, referring to attention and controversy-provoking stories, as well as such institutionalized prizes as those given by the Pulitzer committee. "My satisfaction comes from the fact that I feel like I'm working for myself. I control my own destiny, since they've allowed me to. I don't like to fail."

On the other hand, he doesn't feel he's working for himself when he takes a rare break. "You have to leave your number when you go away for vacation. (The last time) they called me every day. And Gannett holds a lot of weekend meetings." Still, out of respect for his job and his employer, this fellow finds himself "scheduling my business travel on nights or weekends"—his personal time—"for convenience." He could fly during his paid workday, but he's chosen against that.

"I admire Neuharth's guts and vision. When you're exhausted and finished and want to say 'screw it,' he's still screaming."

Chairman Allen Neuharth, referred to (in his absence) by his employees simply as "Neuharth," presides over three enormous, dramatically decorated offices (in Rosslyn, New York City, and Cocoa Beach, Florida). Gray and brass predominate, a mirror image of what he himself wears: black, white, and gray only, with touches of heavy gold, masculine jewelry. He is in his New York office today, talking on the phone with [then-Chief Justice] Warren Burger. He doesn't mind if we listen in; they're talking about celebrating the Bicentennial of the Constitution.

This office is decorated in Gannettabilia: six neatly fanned copies of *USA Today* and its weekend correlate *USA Weekend* (which appears in 294 Sunday newspapers), along with today's *New York Post, New York Daily News, New York Times, Washington Post,* and *The Wall Street Journal.* A glass *USA Today* blotter, a brass paperweight in the shape of the map of the United States with the *USA Today* logo, a wooden memo pad with Gannett's logo, and a glass Tiffany cube emblazoned with *USA Today* replace the personal photographs and mementos one sees in most offices. A *USA Today* coffee cup sits neatly on a *USA Today* paper napkin. A large console is fitted with three television sets, all of them on and soundless. One is tuned to CNN, one to BusinessNet, and on the third, tuned to CBS, Bob Barker is silently naming the correct retail price of a living room suite on *The Price Is Right.* Behind Neuharth, on a polished wooden perch to his left, sits a manual Royal typewriter. It appears to be an honored icon, a reminder of his roots. The persistent hum of the small built-in refrigerator under an elegant bar creates the only unwanted ambient sound.

Neuharth grew up in Sioux Falls, South Dakota. His journalism career began with a paper route when he was eleven. At the University of South Dakota (of which he is a valued alumnus and a member of the Board of Governors) he studied journalism and thought of law school. After two years as a reporter for the Associated Press in Sioux Falls, an attempt to publish his own paper failed, and at the age of twenty-nine, he "fled" to Florida, to escape his (imagined) ignominy.

It was 1953. Florida was attractive because of its climate and the fact that it was not far from home. Starting anew, Neuharth became a reporter for *The Miami Herald,* owned by the Knight family newspaper dynasty. Seven years later, as the assistant managing editor of the *Herald,* he was transferred to *The Detroit Free Press,* another Knight property. "I still consider myself a reporter," he says. "I have a reporter's eyes and ears. A reporter needs to be good at fact finding and decision making. I don't think you ever lose it." In 1963 he started his career with Gannett and was named president in 1970. "I could not write a better job description. I delegate a great deal but never assume anything I delegate won't get done. I monitor. I demand a lot of myself and the people who work with me. I like my employees to do their thing in their way."

Certainly Neuharth does his thing in his way. He has long been regarded an iconoclast by his peers. He is considered aggressive and perhaps more of a businessman than an editor. Indeed, his personal style is more flashy than the tweedy Ivy League look cultivated by members of the editorial fraternity. "I thrive on being different. I'm me. The leadership of a media company should be at variance with the norm."

Needless to say, stories about Neuharth abound, but all carry the caveat that they might be apocryphal. [Author's note: Okay, they say the one about the Last Supper is true.] In response to the apparently endless questions about who he is and why he is that way, Neuharth has printed up his favorite quotation on a heavy card, suitable for framing. He rummages around his desk drawer and finds it, mounted with a photograph of a street sign, an arrow pointing in two opposite directions. As he tosses it across the desk, he recites the three lines printed beneath the arrow, from "The Road Not Taken," the Robert Frost poem.

> "Two roads diverged in the woods, and I—
> I took the one less traveled by,
> And that has made all the difference."

Allen Neuharth owns homes in Middleburg, Virginia, Lake Tahoe (Nevada), Cocoa Beach, Florida, and rents an apartment in New York City. "I guess I'm a gypsy." He's been divorced twice. He is given credit for inventing *USA Today.* Whether people read it or mock it, *USA Today* rewrote the conventions of newspaper editing. "Part of our audience were nonreaders and the TV generation. In the beginning the paper was distributed in 113,000 vending machines, designed to look like television sets." Neuharth was twenty years old when television began to be manufactured on a mass scale.

"We don't want people to feel they've found their ideological home. The general public wants to be informed but is far less appreciative of getting newspapers' opinions rammed down their throats. They want more information and less dictation. Politically, we're aggressively independent. We try not to align ourselves. We do express opinions every day. We take strong stands on issues," but in the form of a printed debate. "We're not interested in making presidents."

This directed impartiality is evidently effective, as are the color photographs, short articles, charts, and graphs. Business exceeded Gannett's original plans. The newspaper is now in the black. Neuharth works himself as hard as he works his people, and, after a stiff diet of news, barely has time to read books. "I start them. I read Iacocca's book and *In Search of Excellence*. I finished *Lucky*," he offers. "I read *Time, Newsweek, U.S. News and World Report, Sports Illustrated*, and *People* regularly and look at *Forbes, Business Week, Fortune, Inc.*, and *Self*. The most effective corporate people are themselves while being in touch with what policy makers try to do."

GTG ENTERTAINMENT

It's the most elegant antebellum sight you'll ever see in Culver City, California. The white clapboard mansion outfitted with dark green shutters and set on fourteen acres, once David O. Selznick's studio, is known as Culver Studios, the new home of GTG Entertainment.

GTG is the marriage between television executive wizard Grant Tinker, formerly chairman of NBC, and the Gannett Co., Inc. Currently a production facility containing twelve soundstages, the facilities are being upgraded and expanded. Before their own TV shows were ready for the camera, GTG was leasing space and equipment to other productions.

Tinker, a Dartmouth graduate, worked in advertising in New York after college. Eventually he and his then wife, Mary Tyler Moore, started MTM, the television production company responsible for *The Mary Tyler Moore Show*, its spinoffs, *Rhoda, Phyllis*, and *Lou Grant, The Bob Newhart Show, WKRP, Hill Street Blues, St. Elsewhere*, and *Remington Steele*, among others. But you already knew that.

A dashing figure, he was credited with fostering NBC's emergence as the leading broadcast network. The announcement of his leaving was met with horror by employees, independent contractors, and shareholders. He was courted, as they say, by everyone in the business and surprised many industry observers when he joined up with Al Neuharth's Gannett.

"There was a mystique about me after NBC which I trafficked in shamelessly," he admits, in temporary, as-yet undecorated offices. He is wearing a green golf jacket, khaki trousers, yellow socks, and penny loafers, an ensemble that bears a close resemblance to that of Stu Erwin, Jr., his executive vice-president and ex-head of dramatic programming at MTM. While Stu wears a Polo cotton knitted vest in lieu of the jacket, the lemon yellow socks tucked into loafers give away L.A.'s new power look (in contrast to New York's and Boston's yellow ties). [Author's note: I was asked to ignore the socks, but unfortunately felt it was too delicious a detail. John T. Malloy, take note!]

"Gannett sought me out and emerged out of the pack interested. They were attractive to me because, one, they didn't know much about our business, and two, they're in Washington." It's hard to tell whether Tinker is really joking. In fact, he praises Gannett's management in a way that reflects a knowledge of the company's organizational chart and the personalities behind that matrix. "We like them, and we welcome their visits." According to Erwin and Tinker, Gannett's visits are just that, and not big brother looking over their shoulders. And GTG management is happy to cooperate when asked to make speeches or simply appear at Gannett functions. If they're not too busy.

The most publicized production to be developed by GTG is its nightly syndicated interpretation of *USA Today,* bearing the same name as the newspaper, produced by Steve Friedman, the former producer of NBC's *Today* show. (As Tinker was to NBC so was Friedman to *Today.* He was the swami responsible for *Today*'s beating the other networks in the breakfast business.) *USA Today* (the TV show) is produced out of the newspaper's Rosslyn headquarters, with bureaus in New York, Washington, D.C., Los Angeles, and Chicago. As of March 1, 1988, the program was presold to 104 markets nationwide. In an unprecedented move in the expensive world of television, Friedman et al. were given two months in which to rehearse the show prior to its September 12 debut.

For the time being, Tinker and Erwin are in the stages of expanding their company through the development of TV series, to create the same kind of energizing enivironment that spawned the classic shows of MTM. One difference between then and now is "with MTM, the thought was, 'let's start a show.' With GTG the thought is, 'Let's start a company.' This is more fun." By February 1988, eighteen writers and producers had made "overall deals" with the company —arrangements in which they give GTG the first look at shows they create in exchange for weekly stipends, offices, and additional support.

While they don't want to steal from the creative coffers of MTM, T & E are looking for the same quality as associated with that company. "The temptation is to move too quickly and hire B + 's. We want an A crowd with established writers." They are also looking for new writers who may never have written for television before. In this vein, sounding more corporate than other production executives, Erwin talks about "mentoring," pairing an experienced writer-producer with a novice, or at least installing a system of advising.

In preparation for the fall 1988 season, GTG had commitments for two new series. One, executive produced by Donald Todd, is called *The Van Dyke Show,* and stars Dick Van Dyke as a Broadway star coming to the rescue of his estranged son (played by real-life son Barry Van Dyke) who runs a struggling theater in Pennsylvania. It is a half-hour comedy for CBS.

Why on Earth is a one-hour "light drama" GTG will produce for ABC. About a group of observers on earth from another planet, it's being created, written, and produced by Gordon Dawson, with Michael Kozoll, a creator of *Hillstreet Blues* signed as "executive consultant." Three pilots have been commissioned, *TV 101*—executive produced by Karl Schaefer and Scott Brazil; *The Johnsons Are Home,* executive produced by Sam Bobrick and Louie Anderson; and *My Life Story,* written by Jane Anderson, executive produced by Deborah Aal, and consulted by Michael Kozoll.

Why would a creative team choose one household over another? In the case of GTG one gets the chance to work with experienced, highly thought-of executives known as champions of creative talent and the creative process. It doesn't hurt that they have a "humongous deal" at CBS. In other words, one's chances of realizing production are greater. Furthermore, "We're selling beyond the thrill of working together with us. We're offering a more benevolent deal in the back that should make people want to work here. And the old-fashioned notion that it should be fun to go to work."

MCI
COMMUNICATIONS
CORPORATION

HISTORY & OPERATIONS

MCI Communications traces its unlikely genesis to Joliet, Illinois, in the early 1960s. A group of two-way radio dealers, led by a man named Jack Goeken, devised a plan to increase sales. They would build a relatively inexpensive system of microwave towers between Chicago and St. Louis and thereby extend the range of communication for potential two-way radio customers. Later it occurred to Goeken and his colleagues that the same system could virtually duplicate the local telephone system and could be used to offer a variety of small-scale telecommunications services. In 1963 Goeken applied to the Federal Communications Commission for a license to build the towers. AT&T, unwilling to allow even a small-timer to infringe on its telecommunications monopoly, fought the application with an intensity disproportionate to the scope of Goeken's scheme.

With indefatigable determination and the aid of a communications lawyer and several financial backers who were intrigued by the prospect of a small businessman taking on the largest corporation in the world, Goeken struggled for four years to push his application through the FCC. Finally, in 1967, the FCC overrode AT&T's claims that Goeken's system was not viable and was redundant. On August 8, 1968, MCI (Microwave Communications, Inc.) was incorporated. The following year, the FCC issued Goeken a license. Meanwhile, Goeken had been introduced to Bill McGowan, a Harvard MBA with years of experience as a management consultant, and a genius for raising venture capital. McGowan was looking for a fresh challenge and wanted a piece of the new company. Goeken, reluctantly conceding his own inadequacy as a financial manager, agreed to split the business fifty-fifty with him.

McGowan, who had higher sights than Goeken, immediately proceeded to pave the way for a number of identical microwave tower systems in other regions of the country. By 1971, when the FCC voted that any newcomer could enter the long distance telephone market without hearings or red tape, he already had plans to create an alternative telephone system that would span the entire country. With nothing to offer except his ambitious plan, McGowan made a public offering of Micom (the name he used for the regional microwave systems) stock and raised $3.3 million. He then hired a team of engineers and construction workers who began erecting microwave towers at an unheard-of rate.

Flouting the FCC ruling, AT&T obstructed MCI from obtaining vital interconnections to its existing local telephone systems. MCI was completely stalled, losing money quickly, and in imminent danger of going under. Backed against the wall, McGowan decided to sue AT&T. It was 1974.

That year, Goeken resigned from the company; McGowan had virtually taken over.

MCI operated in the red and borrowed more and more money from banks as its suit dragged on against AT&T. McGowan continued to build microwave towers, despite the distinct possibility that the company would never be able to use them. He established headquarters in Washington, D.C., and hired V. Orville Wright—who had a strong background in management at IBM, RCA, and Xerox—to run the daily operations of the company as president and chief operating officer. Finally, in 1978, the FCC ruled that AT&T had to promptly provide all interconnections to MCI. With that decision, the company was free to grow.

Between 1979 and 1983, MCI expanded at an explosive rate, and all the early investors got rich. Though customers had to dial a long string of numbers to connect to the system and the voice quality wasn't as good as AT&T's, MCI offered long-distance rates that, in some places, were a much as 50 percent lower than AT&T's. In 1980 the company launched an aggressive television and print advertising campaign that had customers signing up in droves. That same year, MCI won its private suit against AT&T when a jury found AT&T guilty of violating antitrust laws and awarded MCI $1.8 billion in damages. Though AT&T appealed and the amount was ultimately reduced to $113.3 million it was a clear victory for MCI.

By 1981 MCI's long distance telephone service was on solid financial ground and McGowan was ready to break into new services. The company began investigating international expansion and in 1983 launched an innovative new service called "MCI Mail," which enables personal computer users all across the country to send messages back and forth to one another. (Though MCI Mail offers are an array of sophisticated services—among them a "four-hour" letter that is printed on company stationery with the sender's signature—it had yet to turn a profit when the company changed its classification from a service to a product in 1986.)

By the end of 1983, MCI had topped $1 billion in annual revenues, and both McGowan and the company were perceived as unstoppable. In the meantime, the Justice Department ordered AT&T to divest itself of all of its local telephone companies over a two-year period beginning in 1984. With the divestiture, all long distance phone companies—there were a number in addition to MCI by this time—would have equal access to the local telephone companies' interconnections and could thus offer service equal in ease of use and quality to AT&T's. Customers had the option of choosing whichever company they wanted.

With divestiture interconnections became much more expensive, and competition grew more fierce. Since then, MCI has had to continually lower its rates, thus cutting into its profits, just to stay in the contest against AT&T and its other rivals. Though it is the second largest long distance company in the country (with U.S. Sprint running a close third for several years), it has only about 10 percent of the market (by MCI's own estimate), compared with AT&T's approximately 80 percent. In addition, MCI's rates are now only marginally lower than AT&T's—depending on the length of the call, the time of day, and the calling destination, they are anywhere between 26 percent and 1 percent lower—and MCI will have to continue to struggle to maintain even that edge.

In 1986, though the company collected $3.5 billion in revenues, it ultimately lost $448.4 million due to shrinking profit margins and old debts. At the end of that year, MCI laid off approximately 15 percent of its work force. In 1987, MCI and Lotus Development Corporation [see p. 69] announced that they would jointly sell computer software that would make MCI Mail more versatile and easier to use. Their product is called Lotus Express for MCI Mail.

Today MCI is lead by McGowan and V. Orville Wright. (In April 1987, Bill McGowan had a heart transplant. Wright acted as CEO until McGowan's return, and now the two men share the office and duties of the chief executive office. McGowan is also chairman of the board.) MCI employs approximately fourteen thousand people in one hundred fifty offices across the country. Revenues rose to $3.94 billion in 1987, and the company was profitable, with $88 million in net earnings, despite another rough year.

(Information provided by Gary Tobin and John Houser, company spokespersons.)

REVENUES: $3.94 billion in 1987.

EARNINGS: $88 million in net income in 1987.

INITIAL PUBLIC OFFERING: 1975.

NUMBER OF SHAREHOLDERS: 69,000 shareholders.

OFFICES: 7 main regional offices, an international office in Rye, New York, and headquarters in Washington, D.C. In all, MCI has 150 offices all across the country and another 45 around the world.

NUMBER OF EMPLOYEES: Approximately 14,000.

AVERAGE AGE OF EMPLOYEES: Thirty-two companywide, and in some divisions the average age is in the twenties.

TURNOVER: 10 to 15 percent. The company is fast-paced, and it encourages employees who are not happy there to leave. They also encourage people who have left to come back. Employees don't lose accumulated benefits if they leave and return.

RECRUITMENT: MCI has no centralized recruitment program. Operating divisions recruit for their own needs. MCI looks specifically at schools with telecommunications programs, such as Capitol Institute of Technology, in Laurel, Maryland, University of Colorado, University of California at Davis, Pennsylvania State University (Wilkes-Barre), and Virginia Polytechnic University. The company also awards college scholarships to promising telecommunications students in hopes that they will join MCI after graduation. Thus far, it's worked.

NUMBER OF NEW HIRES PER YEAR: On the average, the company hires in excess of one thousand people each year.

RANGE OF STARTING SALARIES: MCI takes regional cost of living into account. The average range for entry-level positions is $10,800–$25,000, though some positions (like engineer or lawyer) pay more.

POLICY FOR RAISES: New employees are reviewed after six months, and from then on, they're reviewed annually. If an employee receives a promotion, the next review is six months later. Raises and promotions are awarded entirely on merit.

TRAINING PROGRAMS: All new employees go through orientation. There are formal training programs in some areas such as Operations, Engineering, Transmission Systems, and National Account Selling, but other divisions have no formal programs.

BENEFITS: Standard medical, dental, and life insurance, employee stock ownership plan, pension plan, and moving and relocation expenses. The company pays tuition reimbursement for both job-related courses and degree programs. Reimbursement is based on grades, and the company pays 100 percent for As and Bs, 50 percent for Cs, and nothing for anything lower than a C.

VACATION: Two weeks after one year, three weeks after five years, four week after ten years, and five weeks after twenty years. In addition to eleven regular paid holidays, employees are entitled to two personal days, called "floating days," per year.

ADDITIONAL PERKS: The company considers its open door policy—under which any employee can have access to any senior executive for any reason—a perk. Also, all employees get $25 per month credit on their long distance phone bills.

BONUSES: MCI awards bonuses at the director level and above, in the form of an incremental percentage of salary that senior managers earn based on their own performance and the company's performance. At manager level to director level, there are sometimes cash bonuses or stock shares awarded for performance. All nonmanagerial employees are eligible for a program called "Excellence in Service," under which each division nominates candidates, and winners and a companion of their choice are flown somewhere (it's a different city each year) to meet with all the senior executives in the company in a social setting. No business is conducted on these trips, which include tours, parties, and dinners. All senior executives are required to attend. The sales division has a similar program for its people. Individual divisions have individual contests.

ANNUAL PARTY: Divisions host annual parties for their employees, but none are given at the corporate level.

AVERAGE WORKDAY: "We're a hard-working company, and people work as long as they need to get things done. It's not unusual for people to work evenings and on weekends, but nobody forces them to."

DRESS CODE: No official dress code. "Employees are required to wear appropriate attire for the work they're doing." Suit and tie in the office and comparable dress for women.

SOCIAL ATMOSPHERE: "It's hard to say if there's a social atmosphere at the company. Because we're a young company and younger people tend to be more single, there's probably a lot of socializing after work, but that's more a product of the age of the employees than the style of the company. Now, you might argue that the style of the company is what attracts younger people."

HEADQUARTERS: MCI is the sole occupant of its own twelve-story building in downtown Washington, D.C. The headquarters, on 19th Street between L and M streets, is "within a block of the FCC."

CHARITABLE CONTRIBUTIONS: Over $1 million each year, a lot of which goes to colleges and universities that have telecommunications programs.

INTERESTED APPLICANTS CAN SEND RÉSUMÉS TO THEIR LOCAL MCI OFFICE OR:
MCI Communications Corporation
1133 19th Street, N.W.
Washington, D.C. 20036
(202) 872-1600

If you expect your corporate environment to be a surrogate home including counseling sessions, birthday parties, and weekend retreats, you will not find it at MCI, formerly formally known as Microwave Communications, Inc. [MCI uses only its initials now.] The twenty-year-old company, best known as the David that took on the Goliath AT&T and *won*, is a fast-paced no-frills company and doesn't want to replace the comforts of home. William McGowan, MCI's charismatic chairman and co-CEO, says, "We have no credit union, no [corporate] Christmas party. I want people at the edge of the cliff. Enough people like it. Lots are restless. Occasionally they'll jump off the cliff. Some will move on." But it is an exciting and satisfying place to work for people who enjoy being part of a notorious start-up.

People change jobs at MCI with surprising frequency. It is not unusual for a hard-working employee to have to move to new offices three times within one year. (Of the first eleven people questioned on this subject, nine had been promoted. On the fast side, one received his first after three months, while another employee had to wait almost two years. The rate appears insignificant to all involved, however, in light of the fact that as the company grows and changes, job descriptions get altered almost organically.) These moves are generally accompanied by raises in salary and are made with the minimum of trauma and a maximum of efficiency through the furniture maintenance department, which boxes everyone's belongings, orders plants, makes keys, hangs artworks, and keeps the furniture in good shape.

MCI's personality is ambitious, tempered with caution. No one is bound by traditional job descriptions, or, as one senior manager chides, "Haven't you heard? There *are* no job descriptions at MCI." Many employees were attracted to the company for its iconoclasm, for its bucking the system in a big way. However, once inside the sleek Washington, D.C., headquarters, it appears corporate, and not the funky home of black sheep. People dress conservatively, there are more men than women in the higher ranks, and work spaces are well appointed if rather impersonal. (Some employees call their office space their "home away from home" since they decorate them with personal items and artwork. One first-year employee refers to offices as "company status symbols," since most people work in "cubes.")

"MCI's work force is very proud of working at a maverick [one hears this word a lot] that's a little outside the corporate norm," one satisfied manager says. But there is absolutely no sense that once having learned McGowan's management's entrepreneurial lessons, that employees will use them for their own benefit elsewhere. These are people who are content to be part of the fantasy without having extracurricular fantasies of their own. They are not about to jump ship. They think they will stay put. "There is nowhere else I'd rather work," says an otherwise cynical three-year pro. "This is a career move," is heard often in response to this question.

And still, there is a palpable sense that this is a job and not more. One senior female says, "I don't consider myself particularly ambitious. I don't feel dominated by my job. I don't dream of being at a certain level at a certain point." She's been with MCI four years, "a long time for MCI." Some of the most senior personnel are in their thirties.

MCI had to weather eleven years of legal battles to get where it is today, the nation's second largest communications carrier. (As of this writing, it's a distant second with about 10 percent of the market to AT&T's lead of roughly 80 percent.) Imagine the psychic costs of working for a corporation that has been in the courts almost its entire lifetime. Imagine giving your all to an entity that has not been legally validated. McGowan understood the odds ahead of him and his company, but "I couldn't tell anyone here what we were facing. It wasn't fair to them. We had two missions: winning court battles and surviving."

That was, in part, the picture of MCI's work force until December 27, 1985, when the last of the antitrust court battles ended and MCI was in the position, for the first time, to funnel all energies and monies into expansion, rather than supporting myriad legal staffs. The final settlements belonged to the regional operations, and at 4:00 P.M. Eastern Standard Time, the veil was formally lifted.

In a conference room in the Virginia offices of the midatlantic region, across the river from MCI's downtown D.C. headquarters, Brian Thompson, then the region's president, called everyone on his floor to make the announcement. Thirty or thirty-five people slowly made their way inside, somewhat distractedly, unsure why they had to interrupt their busy afternoon. Their reactions were sober, to say the least. No balloons, no screams, hugs, or popped champagne corks. Even smiling was subdued. Could this have been a reaction to the reporter standing in a corner? Or was it an exhausted anticlimax?

Have you gotten the feeling that this is a no-nonsense company? MCI does have a sense of humor, which was reflected in its advertising debut with Joan Rivers as one of its spokespersons. (That campaign and its progenitors, the agency Ally & Cargano, have been terminated.) But MCI's employees don't seem to have time to talk at length about their jobs; they just want to work.

An employee reveals, "MCI works on the self-motivator principle. They give you almost no guidance. You are expected to do your work and then report to your immediate supervisor, who reports to his, et cetera; to the top director or vice-president in your department." If this 3 sounds at all like a complaint, let us point out that this is from another satisfied person who glowingly reports that initiating a project of one's own and seeing it through to completion makes her job rewarding.

One division president said, "Two things struck me when I joined the company: Everyone had come here at some tremendous pay cut, and it was something other than money that made it meaningful." MCI is among the top five employers in Washington, after the government. And Washington is certainly a city of passions. It's city of commitment to a party, a platform, an ideology. Perhaps the MCI-ers have adopted this attitude to be in sync with their city.

"No one comes here to get rich. McGowan likes to maintain downtown offices because people are 'hungry and mean' when they get to work." Quoting McGowan is a favorite pastime (as long as it doesn't take too much time away from official duties). He is the formidable leader, who, with the Horatio Algeresque humble beginnings that often fuel ambition, was able to envision a system that would soon be integrated into our way of doing things, if not our vocabulary. Born in Wilkes-Barre, Pennsylvania, he worked in the railroad yards from 11:00 P.M. to 7:00 A.M. while in college (the local King's College) in order to pay his bills. Is it any wonder this man is famous for such bite-the-bullet aphorisms, as "I don't pay you to exercise"?

McGowan eventually found himself at—yes—the Harvard Business School. Although he was proud of his wrong-side-of-the-tracks—hell, the tracks themselves—background, he loved it. (He is still quite devoted to Harvard and cosponsors an entrepreneurial research program there as well as a management research program at MIT's Sloan School of Management.) With his MBA degree, he found himself in the business of consulting. He says he'd visit businesses "and I arrived with gimmicks. No matter what they said their problems were, I'd say, 'That's my specialty,' and they'd be relieved. Whatever they did, I did the opposite. If they were automated, I'd manualize. I'd shake the place up." After three years of embarking on four or five "missions, I said, 'Hell, I'll start my own company.'

"There are four kinds of people in the world," he states in his comfortable office suite, decorated with a Grid, an Apple, a Hewlett-Packard, and an IBM computer, in addition to a Rubik's Cube. "Ten percent are high risk tolerant, forty percent are low risk tolerant, forty percent are risk averse, and ten percent are phobic." Identifying with the first quadrant, he admits to having endured "maybe five to ten sleepless nights in my life only. I was willing to take risks, but AT&T wasn't, really."

People at MCI are attracted by thier co-chairman's survival. [Even more so, since his recovery from cardiac surgery.] They see themselves as survivors, too. One senior officer remarks on the "Darwinian philosophy" that prevails. "If people don't work here, they'd work for a small company or not work." Indeed, as another confirms, "There are no trappings, no corporate bullshit." Since we can correctly assume the personality trickles down from Mc-Gowan himself, MCI in some ways reflects the best of him. "He's secure. He doesn't get angry, so people don't get penalized for making a mistake." Put it another way: "The biggest mistake is to do nothing. Your tush is not on the line."

In creating his cool/permissive corporate culture, McGowan doesn't expect people to stay at MCI forever. "It shouldn't be a profession. I have no administrative assistants, and my secretaries leave me [by prearrangement] after a year and a half. There are no internships unless students can talk someone into it."

What? No internship program? "We're very frustrating for people who want structure. What are we? We're feisty, irreverent street fighters." So what if the speaker, Brian Thompson, is another Harvard MBA? You get the feeling he had to undergo a lot of ribbing from his Wall Street classmates when he took this job. By choosing MCI in lieu of, say, an investment bank, you get the feeling he voluntarily traded in his silk club ties for polyester. (But that's far from the case for Thompson, now MCI's executive vice-president of marketing.)

A woman executive adds, "You do co-opt into the job philosophy, which is not particularly a problem." So she doesn't go out to lunch much. She couldn't care less. "There are no distractions. We're here to do work."

Those, like her, who will succeed at MCI, should identify with the risk-tolerant group. Although most people claim they work from 8:00 A.M. until 6:00 P.M. five days a week, they say the offices are full when they leave in the evening.

The trappings of power, often magnified in this city, seem meaningless when you've got work to do. One woman, in response to a query about her brand of briefcase, watch, pen, computer, date book, and car, said: "Leather. Don't wear one. A pen is a pen. Company issue (Wang). Date book is the current year. I have a gray car."

The only common complaints about life at the maverick concerned ridding the company of some "driftwood in middle management." Praise goes to the company's leadership, although junior employees wish they could see more of them more often.

One question kept bothering me. In these times of takeovers and mergers, why hasn't anyone tried to raid or buy MCI? "Because people think we're crazy. Seriously."

Interview:

WADE ALLEN

One of the most enthusiastic employees at MCI is Wade Allen, a six-year veteran of the maintenance department. He takes his responsibilities seriously but joyfully. "I have to analyze people's needs: for example, will they have a personal computer in their offices, etc. I enjoy my job because I give people pleasure. People move so much they sometimes get frustrated. We say, 'Hey, we'll take care of everything.' I'll come by and babysit."

In recognition of Wade's exemplary work and attitude, he was awarded with the "Excellence in Service" award, given every year to approximately one hundred and fifty people representing all departments. It is extremely competitive. "I was finishing invoices when I first found out [that I won]," he recalls. "I didn't believe it. I got a free trip to Boston and $250 spending money. They rented the whole Aquarium for the night, and you got to converse with all the senior guys. They always treat you like one of them, and not like workers. They speak to you, pat you on the back. They're working on million-dollar deals, and you don't want them worrying about small, tedious things."

For Wade, who has exposure to all offices and all levels of personnel, MCI is a friendly, supportive place. It has taught him to believe in himself, as he has developed more and more responsibility. Wade is grateful to have been encouraged to take classes in management writing and computing. "I believe it's the challenge that makes it special, the thrill of advancing, becoming productive and growing. One day," he dreams, "I'd like to wear a suit and tie."

Wade keeps photocopies of his favorite inspirational poem in his desk. It's called "Don't Quit."

> When things go wrong as they sometimes will,
> When the road you're trudging seems all up hill,
> When the funds are low and the debts are high
> And you want to smile, but you have to sigh,
> When care is pressing you down a bit,
> Rest, if you must, but don't you quit.
> Life is queer with its twists and turns,
> As everyone of us sometimes learns,
> And many a failure turns about
> When he might have won had he stuck it out:
> Don't give up though the pace seems slow—

You may succeed with another blow.
Success is failure turned inside out—
The silver tint of the clouds of doubt,
And you never can tell how close you are,
It may be near when it seems so far;
So stick to the fight when you're hardest hit—
It's when things seem worst, that you must not quit.

MCI
COMMUNICATIONS
CORPORATION

739

THE BESTS, MOSTS, AND OTHER EXTREMES

COOLEST BUSINESS CARD: Esprit de Corp.

FUNKIEST CORPORATE CAFETERIA: Esprit de Corp.

BEST ALL-AROUND FOOD: The Levy Organization

COOLEST EXISTING HEADQUARTERS: R/Greenberg & Associates

FUNKIEST HEADQUARTERS: Chiat/Day Los Angeles. Building, to be opened in 1990, will include a Claes Oldenberg–designed binoculars as entry foyer to Frank Gehry design on Venice Beach

MOST HEARTFELT OPEN DOOR POLICY: Hewlett-Packard and Bain & Company

T-SHIRTS FOR EVERY OCCASION: Apple Computer and The Tom Peters Group

MOST FUN DRESS POLICY: Levi Strauss & Company: jeans at work

BEST COMPANY STORE FOR NONCOMPANY ITEMS: Apple Computer, "The Apple Collection." (Honda Helix Scooter with Apple license plate frame, $2,598; Braun Wall Clock, $42; F2 America 360 Sailboard with giant Apple logo on five-square-meter sail, $1,100; the Apple Tiffany Collection: Desk Clock, $325; Crystal Decanter, $40; Sterling Silver Elsa Peretti Key Ring with Apple Logo, $72.)

BEST CORPORATE STORE OR CORPORATE ITEMS: 3M

NICEST PERKS: Covington & Burling: Two weeks paternity leave following the birth of a child; Rosewood Hotels: Forty free nights in the hotel per year for employees with three years' seniority

BEST PERK: Ford Motor Company—senior executives are leased two new cars each year at a significant discount and get to borrow non-Ford cars; Apple Computer—the Loan to Own Program: All employees get to select the computer of their choice to work with at home. After a year, it's theirs to keep

OLDEST CEO: Mrs. Gertrude Crain, Crain Communications (77; date of birth: March 9, 1911)

YOUNGEST CEO: Jim Manzi, Lotus Development Corporation (36)

HIGHEST PAID CEO: Jim Manzi, Lotus Development Corporation, 1987 total compensation: $26,297,000. (No one else even comes close.)

MOST EMPLOYEES: Ford Motor Company, 350,100

FEWEST EMPLOYEES: Plum Productions (five full time, two part time); Robert Stock Designs, six full-time employees

BEST CORPORATE TRAVEL POLICY: Leo Burnett, everyone flies first class

LONGEST HOURS: Drexel Burnham Lambert; Bain & Company; Wachtell, Lipton, Rosen & Katz

MOST TRAVELED: Drexel Burnham Lambert and Bain & Company

BEST DRESSED (CONSERVATIVE): Drexel Burnham Lambert and Bain & Company

BEST DRESSED (FASHIONABLE): Prescriptives (women), Kohn Pederson Fox Associates (men)

BEST DRESSED (FUNKY): Esprit de Corp.; honorable mention: MTV

BEST GROOMED: Ginnie Johansen Designs

CEO WITH MOST PRONOUNCED STYLE: Allen Neuharth, Gannett, who wears only black, white, and gray

MOST ASTOUNDING CORPORATE SUCCESS STORY: Tom Monaghan, Domino's Pizza, and owner of the Detroit Tigers

CHAIRMAN WHO RESIGNED POST UNDER MOST DURESS: Steve Jobs, Apple Computer

CHAIRMAN WHO RESIGNED POST UNDER LEAST DURESS: Mitch Kapor, founder of Lotus, who left on his own to return to research

WEALTHIEST COMPANY OWNER: Rosewood Hotels' Caroline Rose Hunt, number 138 in the *Forbes* 400, worth $875 million

GREATEST PERSONAL ART COLLECTION: Saul P. Steinberg; honorable mention: Leonard Lauder, Leonard Stern

MOST CHARITABLE: Dayton Hudson Corporation. Levi Strauss & Co.; Polaroid Corporation. And in terms of philanthropies earmarked for AIDS, no one beats Drexel Burnham Lambert

MOST CHRISTIAN WORK ENVIRONMENT: The Staubach Company; honorable mention: Ginnie Johansen Designs, Domino's Pizza, Inc.

BEST CORPORATE COUNTRY CLUB: 3M—Tartan Park

MOST EXTENSIVE TRAINING FACILITY: Arthur Andersen & Co's Professional Education Center

MOST RIGOROUS TRAINING PROGRAM: Bain & Company's "Boot Camp" for associate consultants

BEST KNOWN TRAINING PROGRAM: Chase Manhattan Bank's entry-level Credit Training Program

BEST DAY CARE: Hill, Holliday, Connors, Cosmopulos; Apple; Polaroid (offers vouchers that discount parents' choice of day care)

LEAST LIKELY TO PROVIDE DAY CARE IN FORESEEABLE FUTURE: Super Valu

BEST SHOPPING IN CORPORATE HEADQUARTERS: Bain & Company, Copley Place (Rizzoli Bookstore, Louis Vuitton, Charles Jourdan, Laura Ashley)

MOST GENEROUS VACATION POLICY: Covington & Burling: four weeks for starters, plus unlimited sick days. Plum Productions: a loose plan translates to about four weeks per employee. Runner-up: Bristol-Myers: three weeks after first year

BEST COMPANY SLOGAN: Gannett: "A World of Different Voices Where Freedom Speaks"

MOST EQUITABLE TO WOMEN AND MINORITIES: Gannett

MOST SELF-DEPRECATING CEO: Gershon Kekst

MR. CONGENIALITY AWARD: Larry Levy, CEO of The Levy Organization; runner-up: G. Robert Truex of Rainier Bancorporation (now ex-CEO, current chairman of the executive committee)

BEST CORPORATE PARTY: Leo Burnett's birthday party; Drexel Burnham Lambert's bond conference (they hate when you call it a party, though)

BEST-LOOKING PARTNERSHIP: Kohn Pederson Fox Associates

BEST EMPLOYEE ASSISTANCE PROGRAM: Levi Strauss, Security Pacific, and Lotus (resources listed on floppy diskette)

CORPORATION MOST WILLING TO ALLOW EMPLOYEES TO PLAY WITH TOYS DURING OFFICE HOURS: Marvin Glass & Associates

CORPORATION MOST WILLING TO SEND EMPLOYEES TO ROCK CONCERTS: MTV

CORPORATION LEAST LIKELY TO ENCOURAGE ATTENDANCE AT ROCK CONCERTS: Arthur Andersen & Company

BROTHERS CLUB: Larry and Mark Levy, The Levy Organization; Rance and Keith Crain, Crain Communications; Richard and Robert Greenberg, R/Greenberg & Associates; Dick and Bruce Gelb, Bristol-Myers; Walter and Peter Haas, Levi Straus; Fred and Stephen Joseph, Drexel Burnham Lambert; honorable mention, brother-in-law: Robert Stock and David McTague, Robert Stock Designs